D1171705

McDougal Littell

THE LANGUAGE OF
LITERATURE

BRITISH LITERATURE

THOMAS HARDY

ANDREW MARVELL

WILLIAM BUTLER YEATS

MARY WOLLSTONECRAFT

JAMES JOYCE

W. H. AUDEN

DORIS LESSING

ROBERT BROWNING

GERARD MANLEY HOPKINS

SAMUEL JOHNSON

EDMUND SPENSER

PERCY BYSSHE SHELLEY

WILLIAM BLAKE

JOHN KEATS

D. H. LAWRENCE

JONATHAN SWIFT

ALEXANDER POPE

ELIZABETH BOWEN

GEOFFREY CHAUCER

LORD BYRON

SEAMUS HEANEY

VIRGINIA WOOLF

T. S. ELIOT

CHARLOTTE BRONTË

KATHERINE MANSFIELD

SAMUEL TAYLOR COLERIDGE

WILLIAM SHAKESPEARE

JOHN DONNE

JOHN MILTON

SAMUEL PEPYS

WILLIAM WORDSWORTH

McDougal Littell

THE LANGUAGE OF
LITERATURE

BRITISH LITERATURE

Arthur N. Applebee

Andrea B. Bermúdez

Sheridan Blau

Rebekah Caplan

Peter Elbow

Susan Hynds

Judith A. Langer

James Marshall

McDougal Littell
A HOUGHTON MIFFLIN COMPANY
Evanston, Illinois • Boston • Dallas

CUR
63
ML
12
2006

Acknowledgments

Reading Model

    A. P. Watt Ltd.: "The Ant and the Grasshopper" by W. Somerset Maugham, from *The Collected Stories of W. Somerset Maugham.* Reprinted by permission of A. P. Watt Limited on behalf of the Royal Literary Fund.

Unit One

    Dutton Signet: Excerpts from *Beowulf,* translated by Burton Raffel. Translation Copyright © 1963 by Burton Raffel, Afterword © 1963 by New American Library. "Fifth Day, Ninth Story" retitled "Federigo's Falcon," from *The Decameron* by Giovanni Boccaccio, translated by Mark Musa and Peter Bondanella, Translation copyright © 1982 by Mark Musa and Peter Bondanella. From *Le Morte D'Arthur* by Sir Thomas Malory, translated by Keith Baines. Translation copyright © 1962 by Keith Baines, renewed © 1990 by Francesca Evans. Introduction © 1962 by Robert Graves, renewed © 1990 by Beryl Graves. Used by permission of Dutton Signet, a division of Penguin Putnam Inc.

    The New York Times: "A Collaboration Across 1,200 Years" by D. J. R. Bruckner, from *The New York Times,* July 22, 1997. Copyright © 1997 by *The New York Times.* Reprinted by permission.

Continued on page 1525

iv

Senior Consultants

The senior consultants guided the conceptual development for *The Language of Literature* series. They participated actively in shaping prototype materials for major components, and they reviewed completed prototypes and/or completed units to ensure consistency with current research and the philosophy of the series.

Arthur N. Applebee Professor of Education, State University of New York at Albany; Director, Center for the Learning and Teaching of Literature; Senior Fellow, Center for Writing and Literacy

Andrea B. Bermúdez Professor of Studies in Language and Culture; Director, Research Center for Language and Culture; Chair, Foundations and Professional Studies, University of Houston-Clear Lake

Sheridan Blau Senior Lecturer in English and Education and former Director of Composition, University of California at Santa Barbara; Director, South Coast Writing Project; Director, Literature Institute for Teachers; Former President, National Council of Teachers of English

Rebekah Caplan Senior Associate for Language Arts for middle school and high school literacy, National Center on Education and the Economy, Washington, D.C.; served on the California State English Assessment Development Team for Language Arts; former co-director of the Bay Area Writing Project, University of California at Berkeley

Peter Elbow Emeritus Professor of English, University of Massachusetts at Amherst; Fellow, Bard Center for Writing and Thinking

Susan Hynds Professor and Director of English Education, Syracuse University, Syracuse, New York

Judith A. Langer Professor of Education, State University of New York at Albany; Co-director, Center for the Learning and Teaching of Literature; Senior Fellow, Center for Writing and Literacy

James Marshall Professor of English and English Education; Chair, Division of Curriculum and Instruction, University of Iowa, Iowa City

Contributing Consultants

Linda Diamond Executive Vice-President, Consortium on Reading Excellence (CORE); co-author of *Building a Powerful Reading Program*

Lucila A. Garza ESL Consultant, Austin, Texas

Jeffrey N. Golub Assistant Professor of English Education, University of South Florida, Tampa

William L. McBride, Ph.D. Reading and Curriculum Specialist; former middle and high school English instructor

Sharon Sicinski-Skeans, Ph.D. Assistant Professor of Reading, University of Houston-Clear Lake; primary consultant on *The InterActive Reader*

Multicultural Advisory Board

The multicultural advisors reviewed literature selections for appropriate content and made suggestions for teaching lessons in a multicultural classroom.

Julie A. Anderson, English Department Chairperson, Dayton High School, Dayton, Oregon

Vikki Pepper Ascuena, Meridian High School, Meridian, Idaho

Dr. Joyce M. Bell, Chairperson, English Department, Townview Magnet Center, Dallas, Texas

Linda F. Bellmore, Livermore High School, Livermore, California

Dr. Eugenia W. Collier, Author; lecturer; Chairperson, Department of English and Language Arts; Teacher of Creative Writing and American Literature, Morgan State University, Maryland

Dr. Bill Compagnone, English Department Chairperson, Lawrence High School, Lawrence, Massachusetts

Kathleen S. Fowler, President, Palm Beach County Council of Teachers of English, Boca Raton Middle School, Boca Raton, Florida

Jan Graham, Cobb Middle School, Tallahassee, Florida

Barbara J. Kuhns, Camino Real Middle School, Las Cruces, New Mexico

Patricia J. Richards, Prior Lake, Minnesota

Continued on page 1509

Teacher Review Panels

The following educators provided ongoing review during the development of the tables of contents, lesson design, and key components of the program.

CALIFORNIA
Steve Bass, 8th Grade Team Leader, Meadowbrook Middle School, Ponway Unified School District

Cynthia Brickey, 8th Grade Academic Block Teacher, Kastner Intermediate School, Clovis Unified School District

Continued on page 1509

Manuscript Reviewers

The following educators reviewed prototype lessons and tables of contents during the development of *The Language of Literature* program.

David Adcox, Trinity High School, Euless, Texas

Carol Alves, English Department Chairperson, Apopka High School, Apopka, Florida

Continued on page 1510

Student Board

The student board members read and evaluated selections to assess their appeal for 12th-grade students.

Daniel Birdsall, Muhlenberg High School, Reading, Pennsylvania

Shane M. Cummins, Loudoun County High School, Leesburg, Virginia

Carrie Mitchell, Butler Traditional High School, Shively, Kentucky

Jennifer Schwab, MacArthur High School, San Antonio, Texas

Sarah Marie Slezak, Union High School, Grand Rapids, Michigan

Staci Talis Smith, Ramsay Alternative High School, Birmingham, Alabama

Eve E. Tanner, Justin F. Kimball High School, Dallas, Texas

The Language of Literature
Overview

Table of Contents

Student Resource Bank

Literature Connections

Each of the books in the *Literature Connections* series combines a novel or play with related readings—poems, stories, plays, personal essays, articles—that add new perspectives on the theme or subject matter of the longer work.

Listed below are some of the most popular choices to accompany the Grade 12 anthology:

Hamlet by William Shakespeare

Pride and Prejudice by Jane Austen

Jane Eyre by Charlotte Brontë

Tess of the d'Urbervilles by Thomas Hardy

Pygmalion by George Bernard Shaw

Great Expectations by Charles Dickens

A Tale of Two Cities by Charles Dickens

Beowulf

The Canterbury Tales by Geoffrey Chaucer

1984 by George Orwell

Things Fall Apart by Chinua Achebe

Nervous Conditions by Tsitsi Dangarembga

When Rain Clouds Gather by Bessie Head

THE LANGUAGE OF LITERATURE

Reading Strategies

UNIT ONE

The *Anglo-Saxon* and *Medieval Periods* 449–1485

Part 2 Reflections of Everyday Life

UNIT TWO The *English Renaissance* 1 4 8 5 – 1 6 6 0

Part 2 A Passion for Power 313

UNIT THREE

The *Restoration* and *Enlightenment*
1660–1798

514

UNIT FOUR The *Flowering* of *Romanticism*

1798–1832

UNIT FIVE

The *Victorians*
1832–1901

UNIT SIX

Emerging Modernism

1901–1950

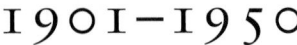

UNIT SEVEN

Contemporary Voices

1950–Present

Student *Resource Bank*

Selections by Genre

Poetry

Drama

Electronic Library

The *Electronic Library* is a CD-ROM that contains additional fiction, nonfiction, poetry, and drama for each unit in *The Language of Literature*. Here is a sampling from the 47 titles included in Grade 12.

The Nun's Priest's Tale
Geoffrey Chaucer

Everyman
Anonymous

My True Love Hath My Heart
Sir Philip Sidney

Easter-Wings
George Herbert

Sonnet 73
William Shakespeare

L'Allegro
John Milton

To a Mouse
Robert Burns

London, 1802
William Wordsworth

A Dissertation upon Roast Pig
Charles Lamb

Ode to a Nightingale
John Keats

The Blessed Damozel
Dante Gabriel Rossetti

The Darkling Thrush
Thomas Hardy

Terence, This Is Stupid Stuff
A. E. Housman

Professions for Women
Virginia Woolf

The Horse Dealer's Daughter
D. H. Lawrence

The Wild Swans at Coole
William Butler Yeats

The Boarding House
James Joyce

The Shield of Achilles
W. H. Auden

Miss Brill
Katherine Mansfield

A Voyage to Cythera
Margaret Drabble

Special Features in This Book

Author Study

Learning the Language of Literature

Comparing Literature of the World

Related Readings

Milestones in British Literature

Writing Workshops

Communication Workshops

Building Vocabulary

Sentence Crafting

Assessment Pages

THE Language OF LITERATURE

Timeless Stories

What do Beowulf, Star Wars, *and* Frankenstein *have in common? Each tells a powerful story that for generations has held readers or moviegoers spellbound. And each contains characters, themes, and conflicts similar to those in hundreds of other stories. Read the following comments about these classic tales:*

"One of the most frequent questions asked by students is 'Why do we study this stuff, especially *Beowulf,* an epic story of Vikings and monsters? What place does it hold in today's society?' My response is, 'If it is so out of date, why do so many blockbuster films of today resemble the plot and the characteristics portrayed in *Beowulf?*'"

Richard L. Cameron III
Teacher

"*Star Wars* has always struck a chord with people. There are issues of loyalty, of friendship, of good and evil. . . . The themes came from stories and ideas that have been around for thousands of years. . . ."

George Lucas
Movie Director

"Mary Shelley, whose 200th birthday is this year, completed her novel *Frankenstein* 180 years ago. The book has never been out of print.... Cinematic attempts to piece together a family for Frankenstein have spawned a bride (1935), a son (1957), and a daughter who, in the rebellious '60s, joined up with Jesse James."

Lee Neville, Journalist

- Why do some stories survive through the centuries?
- How do people living in today's technology-filled world find ways to connect to classic tales about monsters and heroic quests?
- How can YOU find relevance in literature from centuries ago?

The answers lie on the next few pages.

Get Involved with the Literature

Think of any activity you enjoy—sports, music, traveling, painting. How did you really learn to understand and appreciate it? By watching others, or by participating yourself? Just about any activity is richer, more interesting, and more exciting when you are actively involved. The same is true with literature. You can't simply sit back and absorb the words on a page. You have to jump into the stories and participate.

Your Reader's Notebook

Almost any kind of notebook can be used to help you interact with literature. Use your Reader's Notebook to keep track of what's going on inside your mind as you read. Here are three ways to interact.

❶ Record Your Thoughts

In your 📖 **READER'S NOTEBOOK**, jot down ideas, responses, connections, and questions before, while, and after you read a selection. (See "Strategies for Reading," page 7.) Summarize important passages, and include sketches and charts, too, if they will help. If you wish, compare your ideas with those of a classmate.

READING MODEL

Alongside "The Ant and the Grasshopper" are comments made by two 12th-grade students, Christopher Domm and Marcy Ellis, while they were reading the story. Their comments provide a glimpse into the minds of readers actively engaged in the process of reading. You'll notice that Chris and Marcy quite naturally used the Strategies for Reading that were introduced on page 5. You'll also note that these readers responded differently to the story—no two readers think about or relate to a literary work in exactly the same way.

To benefit from this model of active reading, read the story first, jotting down your responses in your reading log. Then read Chris's and Marcy's comments and compare theirs with your own. The more you actively engage in reading and sharing ideas, the more you'll learn about yourself and others.

The

Ant

and

the Grasshopper

W. SOMERSET MAUGHAM

STRATEGIES FOR READING

The Brothers Bernheim-Jeune, Art Dealers and Publishers (early 20th century), Pierre Bonnard, Musée d'Orsay, Paris, France, Erich Lessing/Art Resource, New York.

"The Ant and the Grasshopper"
by W. Somerset Maugham

(page 9) The narrator says, "in an imperfect world industry is rewarded and giddiness punished." Why does he say "in an imperfect world"?

Important Idea
This story really got me thinking about myself. I remember when I first learned the fable "The Ant and The Grasshopper." The moral was quite clear to me: those who play may seem to be getting the most out of life, but in the end those who work will be rewarded while those who play will suffer for their irresponsibility.

Complete the specific 📖 READER'S NOTEBOOK
activity on the first page of each literature lesson.
This activity will help you apply an important skill
as you read the selection.

"The Ant and the Grasshopper"
by W. Somerset Maugham

Writing Idea
- I could also write a modern-day story based on a fable.
- My uncle is a lot like the character Tom. I could write
  a fable about him.

When I was a very small boy I was made to learn by heart certain of
the fables of La Fontaine, and the moral of each was carefully explained
to me. Among those I learnt was *The Ant and The Grasshopper*,
which is devised to bring home to the young the useful lesson that in
an imperfect world industry is rewarded and giddiness punished. In
this admirable fable (I apologize for telling something which everyone
is politely, but inexactly, supposed to know) the ant spends a laborious
summer gathering its winter store, while the grasshopper sits on a
blade of grass singing to the sun. Winter comes and the ant is comfortably provided for, but the grasshopper has an empty larder: he goes
to the ant and begs for a little food. Then the ant gives him her
classic answer:

"What were you doing in the summer time?"
"Saving your presence, I sang, I sang all day, all night."
"You sang. Why, then go and dance."

I do not ascribe it to perversity on my part, but rather to the inconsequence of childhood, which is deficient in moral sense, that I could
never quite reconcile myself to the lesson. My sympathies were with
the grasshopper and for some time I never saw an ant without putting
my foot on it. In this summary (and as I have discovered since, entirely
human) fashion I sought to express my disapproval of prudence and
common sense.

I could not help thinking of this fable when the other day I saw George
Ramsay lunching by himself in a restaurant. I never saw anyone wear
an expression of such deep gloom. He was staring into space. He looked
as though the burden of the whole world sat on his shoulders. I was
sorry for him: I suspected at once that his unfortunate brother had
been causing trouble again. I went up to him and held out my hand.

"How are you?" I asked.
"I'm not in hilarious spirits," he answered.
"Is it Tom again?"
He sighed.
"Yes, it's Tom again."

"Why don't you chuck him? You've done everything in the world
for him. You must know by now that he's quite hopeless."

I suppose every family has a black sheep. Tom had been a sore trial
to his for twenty years. He had begun life decently enough: he went
into business, married, and had two children. The Ramsays were perfectly
respectable people and there was every reason to suppose that Tom
Ramsay would have a useful and honorable career. But one day, without warning, he announced that he didn't like work and that he wasn't
suited for marriage. He wanted to enjoy himself. He would listen to
no expostulations. He left his wife and his office. He had a little money
and he spent two happy years in the various capitals of Europe. Rumors
of his doings reached his relations from time to time and they were

Chris: I like this line right here—I
think people can relate that to their
own lives.
EVALUATING

Chris: I can imagine the ant with a
stern look on her face and the
grasshopper being all happy-go-
lucky.
VISUALIZING

Marcy: Wow! I always looked down on
the grasshopper. It surprises me that
the narrator looks down on the ant.
CONNECTING/CLARIFYING

Marcy: I don't know what the
connection is going to be between the
fable and whatever this story is about.
I'll need to keep the fable in mind as I
read on.
MONITORING

Chris: "Why don't you chuck him?" I
don't really understand what he means.
QUESTIONING

Marcy: "Chuck him"? That's weird
language!
QUESTIONING/EVALUATING

Marcy: I'm seeing the parallel between
the brother and the grasshopper. He'll
probably be like him and fail.
CLARIFYING/PREDICTING

THE ANT AND THE GRASSHOPPER   9

❸ **Collect Ideas for Writing**

Be aware of intriguing themes, passages, and
thoughts of your own as you read or complete
follow-up activities. In a special section of your
📖 READER'S NOTEBOOK, jot down anything that
may later be a springboard to your own writing.

Your Working Portfolio

Artists and writers keep portfolios in which
they store works in progress or the works
they are most proud of. Your portfolio can
be a folder, a box, or a notebook—the form
doesn't matter. Just make sure to keep
adding to it—with drafts of your writing
experiments, summaries of your projects,
and your own goals and accomplishments as
a reader and writer. Later in this book, on
the Reflect and Assess pages, you will choose
your best or favorite work to place in a
Presentation Portfolio.

Become an Active Reader

The strategies you need to become an active reader are already within your grasp. In fact, you use them every day to make sense of the images and the events in your world. And you really exercise them when you are watching a television program or a movie!

Take a look at this shot from a film version of *Gulliver's Travels.* The four strategies shown here—Question, Predict, Clarify, and Connect—are among those you can use to understand and interpret the situation. These and the other reading strategies listed on the next page can help you interact with literature as well.

Question *What in the world is happening here? Where are these people? And WHO are they?*

Clarify *It looks like the little people have tied the big guy up and are questioning him.*

Predict *I bet he'll pop the ropes and scare off the little people.*

Connect *I remember situations where I've felt as out of place as this guy looks.*

Strategies for Reading

Following are specific reading strategies that are introduced and applied throughout this book. Use them when you read and interact with the various literature selections. Occasionally **monitor** how well the strategies are working for you and, if desired, modify them to suit your needs.

PREDICT Try to figure out what will happen next and how the selection might end. Then read on to see how accurate your guesses were.

VISUALIZE Visualize characters, events, and setting to help you understand what's happening. When you read nonfiction, pay attention to the images that form in your mind as you read.

CONNECT Connect personally with what you're reading. Think of similarities between the descriptions in the selection and what you have personally experienced, heard about, and read about.

QUESTION Question what happens while you read. Searching for reasons behind events and characters' feelings can help you feel closer to what you are reading.

CLARIFY Stop occasionally to review what you understand, and expect to have your understanding change and develop as you read on. Reread and use resources to help you clarify your understanding. Also watch for answers to questions you had earlier.

EVALUATE Form opinions about what you read, both while you're reading and after you've finished. Develop your own ideas about characters and events.

On the next page, you will see how two readers applied these strategies to the story "The Ant and the Grasshopper."

Go Beyond the Text If you really become an active reader, your involvement doesn't stop with the last line of the text. Decide what else you'd like to know. Discuss your ideas with others, do some research, or jump on the Internet.

 More Online
www.mcdougallittell.com

Alongside "The Ant and the Grasshopper" are comments made by two 12th-grade students, Christopher Domm and Marcy Ellis, while they were reading the story. Their comments provide a glimpse into the minds of readers actively engaged in the process of reading. You'll notice that Chris and Marcy quite naturally used the Strategies for Reading that were introduced on page 5. You'll also note that these readers responded differently to the story—no two readers think about or relate to a literary work in exactly the same way.

To benefit from this model of active reading, read the story first, jotting down your responses in your reading log. Then read Chris's and Marcy's comments and compare theirs with your own. The more you actively engage in reading and sharing ideas, the more you'll learn about yourself and others.

The Ant and the Grasshopper

W. SOMERSET MAUGHAM

The Brothers Bernheim-Jeune, Art Dealers and Publishers (early 20th century), Pierre Bonnard, Musée d'Orsay, Paris, France, Erich Lessing/Art Resource, New York.

When I was a very small boy I was made to learn by heart certain of the fables of La Fontaine, and the moral of each was carefully explained to me. Among those I learnt was *The Ant and The Grasshopper*, which is devised to bring home to the young the useful lesson that in an imperfect world industry is rewarded and giddiness punished. In this admirable fable (I apologize for telling something which everyone is politely, but inexactly, supposed to know) the ant spends a laborious summer gathering its winter store, while the grasshopper sits on a blade of grass singing to the sun. Winter comes and the ant is comfortably provided for, but the grasshopper has an empty larder: he goes to the ant and begs for a little food. Then the ant gives him her classic answer:

"What were you doing in the summer time?"

"Saving your presence, I sang, I sang all day, all night."

"You sang. Why, then go and dance."

I do not ascribe it to perversity on my part, but rather to the inconsequence of childhood, which is deficient in moral sense, that I could never quite reconcile myself to the lesson. My sympathies were with the grasshopper and for some time I never saw an ant without putting my foot on it. In this summary (and as I have discovered since, entirely human) fashion I sought to express my disapproval of prudence and common sense.

I could not help thinking of this fable when the other day I saw George Ramsay lunching by himself in a restaurant. I never saw anyone wear an expression of such deep gloom. He was staring into space. He looked as though the burden of the whole world sat on his shoulders. I was sorry for him: I suspected at once that his unfortunate brother had been causing trouble again. I went up to him and held out my hand.

"How are you?" I asked.

"I'm not in hilarious spirits," he answered.

"Is it Tom again?"

He sighed.

"Yes, it's Tom again."

"Why don't you chuck him? You've done everything in the world for him. You must know by now that he's quite hopeless."

I suppose every family has a black sheep. Tom had been a sore trial to his for twenty years. He had begun life decently enough: he went into business, married, and had two children. The Ramsays were perfectly respectable people and there was every reason to suppose that Tom Ramsay would have a useful and honorable career. But one day, without warning, he announced that he didn't like work and that he wasn't suited for marriage. He wanted to enjoy himself. He would listen to no expostulations. He left his wife and his office. He had a little money and he spent two happy years in the various capitals of Europe. Rumors of his doings reached his relations from time to time and they were

---

Chris: *I like this line right here—I think people can relate that to their own lives.*
EVALUATING

Chris: *I can imagine the ant with a stern look on her face and the grasshopper being all happy-go-lucky.*
VISUALIZING

Marcy: *Wow! I always looked down on the grasshopper. It surprises me that the narrator looks down on the ant.*
CONNECTING/CLARIFYING

Marcy: *I don't know what the connection is going to be between the fable and whatever this story is about. I'll need to keep the fable in mind as I read on.*
MONITORING

Chris: *"Why don't you chuck him?" I don't really understand what he means.*
QUESTIONING

Marcy: *"Chuck him"? That's weird language!*
QUESTIONING/EVALUATING

Marcy: *I'm seeing the parallel between the brother and the grasshopper. He'll probably be like him and fail.*
CLARIFYING/PREDICTING

profoundly shocked. He certainly had a very good time. They shook their heads and asked what would happen when his money was spent. They soon found out: he borrowed. He was charming and unscrupulous. I have never met anyone to whom it was more difficult to refuse a loan. He made a steady income from his friends and he made friends easily. But he always said that the money you spent on necessities was boring; the money that was amusing to spend was the money you spent on luxuries. For this he depended on his brother George. He did not waste his charm on him. George was a serious man and insensible to such enticements. George was respectable. Once or twice he fell to Tom's promises of amendment and gave him considerable sums in order that he might make a fresh start. On these Tom bought a motorcar and some very nice jewelry. But when circumstances forced George to realize that his brother would never settle down and he washed his hands of him, Tom, without a qualm, began to blackmail him. It was not very nice for a respectable lawyer to find his brother shaking cocktails behind the bar of his favorite restaurant or to see him waiting on the box seat of a taxi outside his club. Tom said that to serve in a bar or to drive a taxi was a perfectly decent occupation, but if George could oblige him with a couple of hundred pounds he didn't mind for the honor of the family giving it up. George paid.

Once Tom nearly went to prison. George was terribly upset. He went into the whole discreditable affair. Really Tom had gone too far. He had been wild, thoughtless, and selfish, but he had never before done anything dishonest, by which George meant illegal; and if he were prosecuted he would assuredly be convicted. But you cannot allow your only brother to go to jail. The man Tom had cheated, a man called Cronshaw, was vindictive. He was determined to take the matter into court; he said Tom was a scoundrel and should be punished. It cost George an infinite deal of trouble and five hundred pounds to settle the affair. I have never seen him in such a rage as when he heard that Tom and Cronshaw had gone off together to Monte Carlo the moment they cashed the check. They spent a happy month there.

For twenty years Tom raced and gambled, philandered with the prettiest girls, danced, ate in the most expensive restaurants, and dressed beautifully. He always looked as if he had just stepped out of a bandbox. Though he was forty-six you would never have taken him for more than thirty-five. He was a most amusing companion and though you knew he was perfectly worthless you could not but enjoy his society. He had high spirits, an unfailing gaiety, and incredible charm. I never grudged the contributions he regularly levied on me for the necessities of his existence. I never lent him fifty pounds without feeling that I was in his debt. Tom Ramsay knew everyone and everyone knew Tom Ramsay. You could not approve of him, but you could not help liking him.

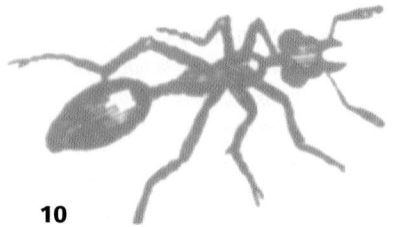

Poor George, only a year older than his scapegrace brother, looked sixty. He had never taken more than a fortnight's holiday in the year for a quarter of a century. He was in his office every morning at nine-thirty and never left it till six. He was honest, industrious, and worthy. He had a good wife, to whom he had never been unfaithful even in thought, and four daughters to whom he was the best of fathers. He made a point of saving a third of his income and his plan was to retire at fifty-five to a little house in the country where he proposed to cultivate his garden and play golf. His life was blameless. He was glad that he was growing old because Tom was growing old too. He rubbed his hands and said:

"It was all very well when Tom was young and good-looking, but he's only a year younger than I am. In four years he'll be fifty. He won't find life so easy then. I shall have thirty thousand pounds by the time I'm fifty. For twenty-five years I've said that Tom would end in the gutter. And we shall see how he likes that. We shall see if it really pays best to work or be idle."

Poor George! I sympathized with him. I wondered now as I sat down beside him what infamous thing Tom had done. George was evidently very much upset.

"Do you know what's happened now?" he asked me.

I was prepared for the worst. I wondered if Tom had got into the hands of the police at last. George could hardly bring himself to speak.

"You're not going to deny that all my life I've been hardworking, decent, respectable, and straightforward. After a life of industry and thrift I can look forward to retiring on a small income in gilt-edged securities. I've always done my duty in that state of life in which it has pleased Providence to place me."

"True."

"And you can't deny that Tom has been an idle, worthless, dissolute, and dishonorable rogue. If there were any justice he'd be in the workhouse."

"True."

George grew red in the face.

"A few weeks ago he became engaged to a woman old enough to be his mother. And now she's died and left him everything she had. Half a million pounds, a yacht, a house in London, and a house in the country."

George Ramsay beat his clenched fist on the table.

"It's not fair, I tell you, it's not fair. Damn it, it's not fair."

I could not help it. I burst into a shout of laughter as I looked at George's wrathful face, I rolled in my chair, I very nearly fell on the floor. George never forgave me. But Tom often asks me to excellent dinners in his charming house in Mayfair, and if he occasionally borrows a trifle from me, that is merely from force of habit. It is never more than a sovereign.

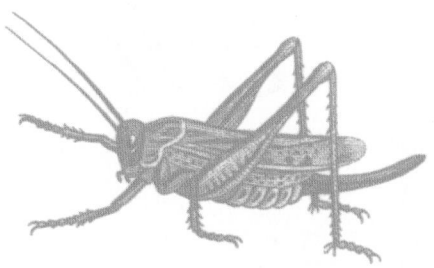

Chris: *I think George is jealous of Tom's life.*
EVALUATING

Chris: *I think this is funny right here. Tom's brother was so reserved and watched everything he did. Tom, on the other hand, took a chance in life. He didn't worry about the future; he just enjoyed life.*
EVALUATING/CLARIFYING

Chris: *Usually the fable holds true to life, but this time it didn't.*
CLARIFYING

Marcy: *It's not fair! I'd be upset. Of course George will still have his money—his retirement—but that's not much. Maybe Tom will share with George, but I don't think so. I doubt if he'll even pay back the money George gave him.*
CLARIFYING/EVALUATING/PREDICTING

Literary Map of
The British Isles

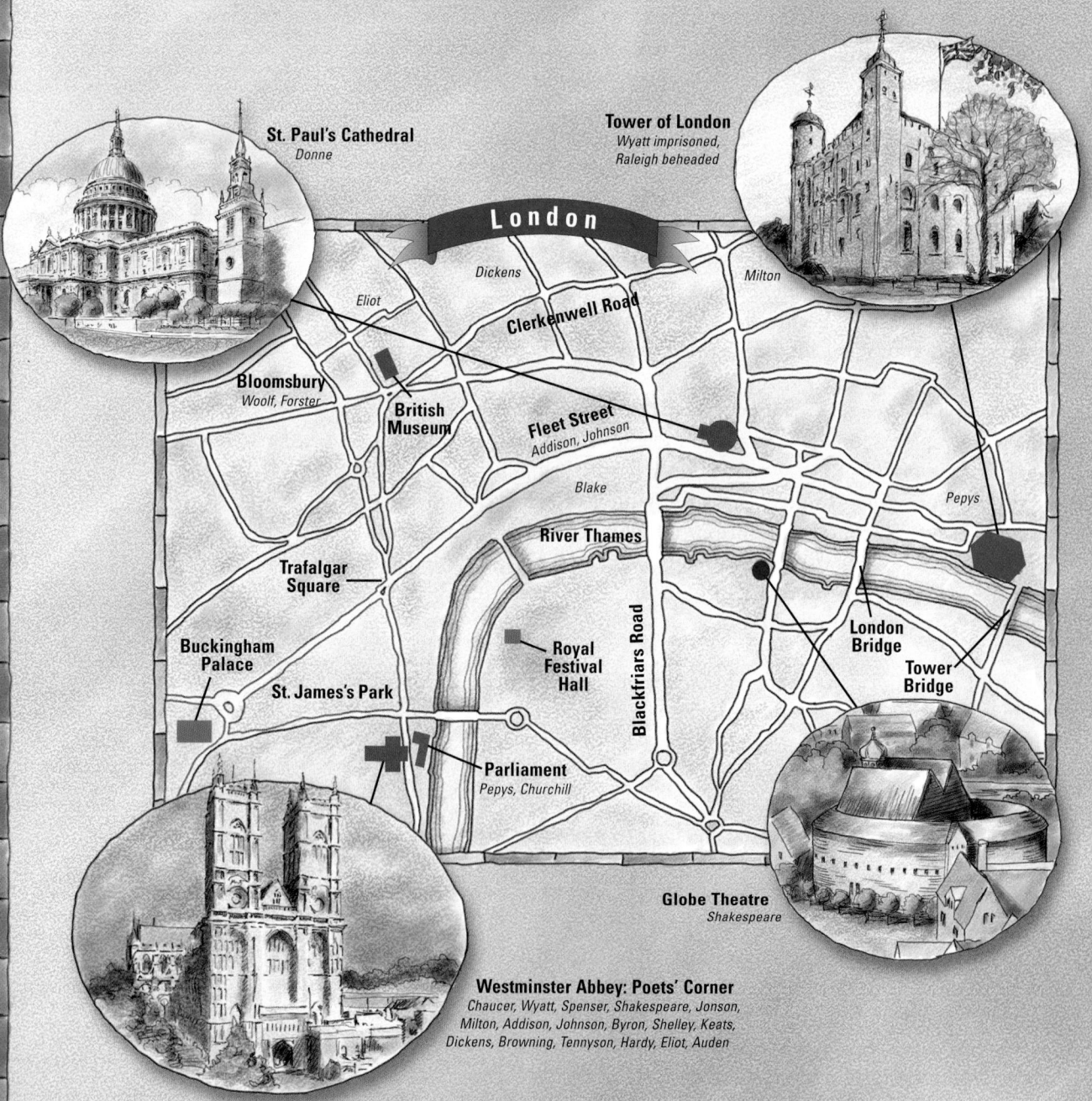

St. Paul's Cathedral
Donne

Tower of London
*Wyatt imprisoned,
Raleigh beheaded*

London

Dickens

Milton

Eliot

Clerkenwell Road

Bloomsbury
Woolf, Forster

**British
Museum**

Fleet Street
Addison, Johnson

Pepys

Blake

River Thames

**Trafalgar
Square**

**Buckingham
Palace**

St. James's Park

**Royal
Festival
Hall**

Blackfriars Road

**London
Bridge**

**Tower
Bridge**

Parliament
Pepys, Churchill

Globe Theatre
Shakespeare

Westminster Abbey: Poets' Corner
*Chaucer, Wyatt, Spenser, Shakespeare, Jonson,
Milton, Addison, Johnson, Byron, Shelley, Keats,
Dickens, Browning, Tennyson, Hardy, Eliot, Auden*

John o'Groats

Inverness

Macbeth at Dunsinane,
Shakespeare

Dunsinane •
**Birnam
Woods**

Glasgow • **Edinburgh**
Boswell, Spark

SCOTLAND

Jarrow
Bede

N. IRELAND

Grasmere

Belfast •
Heaney

ENGLAND

York
Auden

Sligo

Haworth

Yorkshire moors, where
the Brontës lived

IRELAND

Manchester
Gaskell

Somersby
Tennyson

Galway

Dublin •
*Swift, Yeats,
Lady Gregory,
Joyce, Bowen*

St. Asaph
Hopkins

Dove Cottage,
home of the
Wordsworths

Newstead Abbey
• *Byron*

Norwich
Pastons

Cambridge
*Spenser, Marlowe, Bacon, Milton,
Pepys, Gray, Wordsworth,
Coleridge, Tennyson,
Brooke, Sassoon, Hughes*

Doneraile
Spenser

Wexford •

**Stratford-
upon-Avon**
Shakespeare

County Cork
Trevor

WALES

Hampstead
*Keats, Mansfield,
Lawrence, Orwell*

Sutton Hoo
ship burial,
Beowulf

Swansea
Dylan Thomas

Tintern

Oxford
*Raleigh, Donne,
Lovelace, Addison,
Johnson, Arnold,
Hopkins, Housman,
Brittain, Huxley,
Auden, Lively*

⭐**LONDON**

Twickenham
Pope

Canterbury

Nether Stowey
Coleridge

Chawton
Austen

Dorchester
• *Hardy*

Dean Prior
Herrick

Land's End

Ruins of Tintern Abbey,
inspiration for Wordsworth

St. Thomas à Becket,
from stained glass window in
Canterbury Cathedral,
Chaucer

Outer Hebrides

**Inner
Hebrides**

UNIT ONE

THE ANGLO-SAXON AND

The Bayeux tapestry (late 11th century–early 12th century). Musée de la Tapisserie, Bayeux, France, Giraudon/Art Resource New York.

449-1485

MEDIEVAL PERIODS

In reading great literature, I become a thousand men
and yet remain myself.

C.S. Lewis
NOVELIST AND ESSAYIST

THE ANGLO-SAXON AND MEDIEVAL PERIODS

EVENTS IN BRITISH LITERATURE

400 | 600 | 800

c. 750 Surviving version of *Beowulf* probably composed

c. 975 Anglo-Saxon verse collected in Exeter Book

EVENTS IN BRITAIN

400 | 600 | 800

449 Traditional date of Anglo-Saxon invasion

597 Christian missionaries land in Kent; Christianity begins to spread among Anglo-Saxons

793 Vikings begin first of many raids on Anglo-Saxon kingdom ➤

871 Alfred the Great becomes king of Wessex (to 899)

EVENTS IN THE WORLD

400 | 600 | 800

500 Mathematician in India calculates value of pi

527 Justinian I becomes Byzantine emperor

630 Prophet Muhammad conquers Mecca, which becomes holiest city of Islam

800 Charlemagne, who unites much of Europe, crowned emperor of Holy Roman Empire

c. 800 Chinese invent gunpowder

c. 880 Mayan culture begins decline

Hadrian's Wall, built by Romans (A.D. 122–128)

PERIOD PIECES

Roman sandals

Medieval candlestick

Sundial for telling time

1000   **1200**   **1400**

c. 1000 Surviving version of *Beowulf* written out by monks

The Prioress

c. 1375 *Sir Gawain and the Green Knight* composed

c. 1387 Chaucer begins *The Canterbury Tales*

c. 1420 Earliest surviving Paston letter written

1485 William Caxton prints Sir Thomas Malory's *Le Morte d'Arthur*

1000   **1200**   **1400**

1016 Canute, a Dane, becomes king of England (to 1035)

1066 Norman Conquest—William the Conqueror defeats Harold at Hastings and becomes king of England

1166 Henry II institutes judge-and-jury system throughout England

1170 Thomas à Becket murdered

1171 Henry II declares himself lord of Ireland, beginning centuries of English-Irish conflict

1215 King John signs Magna Carta

1282 England conquers Wales

1295 Model Parliament assembled under Edward I

1301 Edward II becomes first Prince of Wales, a title thereafter given to male heirs of British throne

1337 Hundred Years' War with France begins (to 1453) ➤

c. 1430 Modern English develops from Middle English

c. 1476 Caxton establishes first printing press in Britain; prints first dated book in English language (1477)

1000   **1200**   **1400**

1054 Christian Church divides into east and west branches

1095 First of "holy wars" called Crusades begins (to 1272)

1192 Japanese emperor takes title of shogun

1206 Genghis Khan begins Mongol conquest of much of Asia (to 1227)

1235 West African kingdom of Mali emerges

1275 Marco Polo arrives in China

c. 1300 Renaissance begins in northern Italy

1325 Aztecs establish Tenochtitlan, site of present Mexico City

1347 Bubonic plague reaches Europe, soon killing millions

1431 Joan of Arc burned at stake

1453 Ottomans conquer Constantinople

c. 1455 Gutenberg Bible produced on printing press

THE ANGLO-SAXON AND MEDIEVAL PERIODS

449-1485

The British Isles, just off the west coast of continental Europe, enter recorded history in the writings of the Roman general Julius Caesar. In 55 B.C., fresh from his conquest of Celtic peoples known as Gauls, Caesar sailed from what is now France to Britain, largest of the British Isles, to assert Rome's authority over it. There he encountered a Celtic people called the Britons, from whom the island takes its name. Also living on Britain were Picts, remnants of a pre-Celtic civilization, and farther west, on Ireland (the next-largest British island) was another group of Celtic speakers, the Gaels.

The Britons had a thriving culture by most standards of the day. They were skilled in agriculture and metalwork, traded with their Celtic neighbors overseas, and had an oral tradition of literature and learning preserved by a priestly class known as druids.

Detail of a Celtic container

They were, however, no match for the Romans. About a century after Caesar's visit, Roman armies returned to Britain to make good his claim. Despite resistance, they rapidly conquered the Britons and drove the war-

A.D.
449
Germanic tribes invade Britain.

55 B.C.
Julius Caesar lays claim to Britain.

Scotland

Gaels

Picts

IRELAND

BRITAIN

Wales

Britons

FRANCE

like Picts northward to what is now Scotland. Britain became a province of the great Roman Empire, and the Romans introduced cities, fine stone roads, written scholarship, and eventually Christianity to the island. As they adapted to a more urban way of life, the "Romanized" Britons came to depend on the Roman military for protection; but early in the fifth century, with much of their empire being overrun by invaders, the Roman armies abandoned Britain to defend the city of Rome. It was not long before Britain too became the target of invasion.

Above: Celtic cross

The Anglo-Saxon Period
449–1066

In an invasion traditionally assigned to the year A.D. 449 but actually taking place over several decades, Angles, Saxons, and other Germanic peoples (such as Jutes and Frisians) left their northern European homelands and began settling on Britain's eastern and southern shores. The Britons—perhaps led by a Christian commander named Arthur—fought a series of legendary battles in an effort to stop the invasion. Eventually, however, they were driven to seek refuge in Cornwall and Wales on the western fringes of the island; in the northern area now called Scotland, where Gaels from Ireland were also settling; and in an area on the west coast of continental Europe that would come to be known as Britanny. In southern and central Britain, Celtic culture all but disappeared. The Germanic tribes eventually organized themselves into a confederation

Development of the English Language

Just as Britain's fifth-century invaders eventually united into a nation called England, their closely related Germanic dialects evolved over time into a distinct language called English—today usually called Old English to distinguish it from later forms of the language. Old English was very different from the English we speak today. Harsher in sound, it was written phonetically, with no silent letters. Grammatically, it was more complex than modern English, with words changing form to indicate different functions, so that word order was more flexible than it is now. The most valuable characteristic of the language, however, was its ability to change and grow, adopting new words as the need arose.

LITERARY HISTORY

Although the early Anglo-Saxons did have a writing system, called the runic alphabet, they used it mainly for inscriptions on coins, monuments, and the like. Their literature was composed and transmitted orally rather than in writing. In the mead halls of kings and nobles, where the Anglo-Saxons gathered to eat, drink, and socialize, oral poets called scops celebrated the deeds of heroic warriors in long **epic poems.** They also sang shorter, **lyric poems.** In some of these, deaths or other losses are mourned in the mood of bleak fatalism characteristic of early Anglo-Saxon times. Many of the lyrics composed after the advent of Christianity express religious faith or offer moral instruction. Others reflect a more playful nature: the brief Anglo-Saxon **riddles,** for example, describe familiar objects, like a ship or a bird, in ways that force the audience to guess their identity.

of seven kingdoms called the Heptarchy. In the southeast was Kent, kingdom of the Jutes. Further west were the Saxon kingdoms of Sussex, Essex, and Wessex. To the north were the kingdoms of the Angles—East Anglia, Mercia, and Northumbria. Perhaps because the Angles were dominant in the early history of the Heptarchy, the area of Germanic settlement became known as Angle-land, or England, and its people came to be called the English. Modern scholars, however, usually employ the term *Anglo-Saxon* to refer to the people and culture of this period of English history.

Like all cultures, that of the Anglo-Saxons changed over time. The early invaders were seafaring wanderers whose lives were bleak, violent, and short. With them, they brought their pagan religion—marked by a strong belief in *wyrd*, or fate—and their admiration for heroic warriors whose *wyrd* it was to prevail in battle. As they settled into their new land, however, the Anglo-Saxons became an agricultural people—less violent, more secure, more civilized. One of the most important civilizing forces was the Christianity they began accepting late in the sixth century.

THE GROWTH OF CHRISTIANITY

Despite the collapse of Roman power there, Christianity had never completely died out in the British Isles. Early in the fifth century a Romanized Briton named Patrick had converted Ireland's Gaels to Christianity. When the Gaels began colonizing Scotland, they brought Christianity in their wake. From the isle of Iona off the Scottish coast, missionaries spread the faith among the Picts and Angles in the north. Later, in 597, a Roman missionary named Augustine arrived in the kingdom of Kent, where he established a monastery at Canterbury. From there, Christianity spread so rapidly that by 690 all of Britain was at least nominally Christian.

On Lindisfarne, a tiny island off the Northumbrian coast, monks produced the beautiful Bible manuscript known as the Lindisfarne Gospels.

After the fall of the Roman Empire, monasteries became centers of intellectual, literary, artistic, and social activity. The Book of Kells is an illuminated gospel book begun in an Irish monastery in the late eighth century.

THE DANISH INVASIONS

In the 790s, a new group of northern European invaders—the Danes, also known as the Vikings—began to devastate Northumbria's flourishing culture. Coming at first to loot monasteries, the Danes in time gained control of much of northern and eastern England. They were less successful in the south, where their advance was halted by a powerful king of Wessex, Alfred the Great. After inflicting defeats on the Danes in 878 and 886, Alfred forced them to agree to a truce and to accept Christianity.

Although Alfred's reign was a high point in Anglo-Saxon civilization, the tug-of-war with the Danes resumed after his death. In 1016 a Dane named Canute even managed to become king of all England; he proved a successful ruler and won the support of many Anglo-Saxon noblemen. Less successful was the deeply religious Edward the Confessor, who came to the throne in 1042. Edward, who had no children, had once sworn an oath making William, duke of Normandy, his heir—or so William claimed. Later, Edward was persuaded to name Harold, earl of Wessex, as his heir. When Edward died in 1066, the English witan (an advisory council of nobles and church officials) supported Harold's claim. Incensed, William led his Normans in what was to be the last successful invasion of the island of Britain: the Norman Conquest. Harold was killed at the Battle of Hastings, and on Christmas Day of 1066, a triumphant William—who would go down in history as William the Conqueror—was crowned king of England.

Ornamental pin commissioned by Alfred the Great

LITERARY HISTORY

The spread of Christianity in Britain was accompanied by a spread of literacy and by the introduction of the Roman alphabet in place of the runic alphabet. Though poetry remained primarily an oral art, poems were now more likely to get written down. In this age before printing, however, the only books were manuscripts that scribes copied by hand. Thus, only a fraction of Anglo-Saxon poetry has survived, in manuscripts produced centuries after the poems were composed. The most famous survivor is the epic *Beowulf,* about a legendary hero of the northern European past. A manuscript known as the Exeter Book contains many of the surviving Anglo-Saxon lyrics, including "The Seafarer," "The Wife's Lament," and over 90 riddles.

Most Old English poems are anonymous. One of the few poets known by name is a monk called Caedmon,  described by the Venerable Bede in his famous eighth-century history of England. Like most scholars of his day, Bede wrote in Latin, the language of the church. It was not until the reign of Alfred the Great that writing in English began to be widespread. In 891, Alfred initiated the compiling of the *Anglo-Saxon Chronicle,* a historic record in poetry and prose that was added to, on and off, until early Norman times. He also encouraged English translations of portions of the Bible and other Latin works.

Inset above: Detail from an illuminated Bible

The Medieval Period
1066-1485

Like the Danes of Britain, the Normans (whose name means "north men") had originally been Viking raiders from northern Europe. However, after settling in the region that became known as Normandy, just northeast of Britanny on the coast of France, the Normans had adopted French ways. Now William introduced these practices to England, beginning the medieval (or middle) period in English history.

Probably the most significant of William's introductions was feudalism, a political and economic system in which the hierarchy of power was based on the premise that the king owned all the land in the kingdom. Keeping a fourth for himself and granting a fourth to the church, William parceled out the rest of England to loyal nobles—mostly Norman barons—who, in return, either paid him or supplied him with warriors called knights. The barons swore allegiance to the king, the knights to their barons, and so on down the social ladder. At the bottom of the ladder were the conquered Anglo-Saxons, many of whom were serfs—peasants bound to land they could not own. To protect Norman interests, barons were encouraged to build strong castles from which they could dominate the countryside and defend the realm from attack; at the same time, great cathedrals and abbeys were erected on the new church lands.

Because William's successors were less strong and organized than he, power struggles among the barons

Hoping to influence the church, Henry II appointed his friend Thomas à Becket archbishop of Canterbury. When the archbishop began favoring church interests over those of the crown, Henry's sharp criticisms prompted four loyal knights to murder Becket. Henry quickly proclaimed his innocence and reconciled with the church; Becket was declared a saint, his shrine at Canterbury becoming a popular destination for Christian pilgrims.

Canterbury Cathedral, begun in the 11th century, reflects the influence of Norman architecture.

were common in the decades after his death. When William's son Henry I died in 1135, the barons took sides in a violent struggle for power between Henry's daughter Matilda and his nephew Stephen. The near anarchy ended in 1154, when Matilda's son Henry Plantagenet took the throne as Henry II. One of medieval England's most memorable rulers, Henry reformed the judicial system, instituting royal courts throughout the country, establishing a system of juries, and initiating the formation of English common law out of a patchwork of centuries-old practices.

At least as colorful as Henry II was his wife, Eleanor of Aquitaine, a former French queen who had brought as her dowry vast landholdings in France. From French court circles she also brought the ideals of chivalry, a code of honor intended to govern knightly behavior. The code encouraged knights to honor and protect ladies and to go on holy quests—like the Crusades, the military expeditions in which European Christians attempted to wrest the holy city of Jerusalem from Moslem control.

Henry's son Richard I, called Richard the Lion-Hearted, spent much of his ten-year reign fighting in the Crusades and in France, where English possessions were threatened. During his absence, his treacherous brother John—the villain of many Robin Hood legends—plotted against him. When Richard died and John became king, he found that the royal

Jousting knights

Development of the English Language

The Norman Conquest led to great changes in the English language. Despite their Viking origins, by 1066 the Normans spoke a dialect of Old French, which they brought to England with them. Norman French became the language of the English court, of government business, of the new nobility, and of the scholars, cooks, and craftspeople that the Norman barons brought with them to serve their more "refined" needs. The use of English became confined to the conquered, mostly peasant population. Ever adaptable, however, English soon incorporated thousands of words and many grammatical conventions from Norman French. These changes led to the development of Middle English, a form much closer than Old English to the language we speak today.

LITERARY HISTORY

As English became the language of a mostly illiterate peasantry, the common folk again relied on the oral tradition to tell their stories and express their feelings. Many of their compositions were folk ballads, brief narrative poems sung to musical accompaniment. The later Middle Ages saw the flowering of **mystery** and **miracle plays,** which dramatized episodes from the Bible and from saints' lives, and **morality plays,** which taught moral lessons. From these simple plays, intended to convey religious truths to an audience only partly literate, arose the great tradition of English drama.

Right: Flexible body armor called mail was made from iron links.

treasury had been bankrupted by overseas warfare. In 1215 he was forced to sign the Magna Carta ("Great Charter"), which limited royal authority by granting more power to the barons and thus was an early step on the road to democracy. During the reign of John's son Henry III, an advisory council of barons—now called a parliament—began to meet regularly. Under his successor, Edward I, the Model Parliament of 1295 established the inclusion of commoners (eventually to become the House of Commons) as well as barons (the "House of Lords") in the council.

THE DECLINE OF FEUDALISM

The growth of the commoners' power went hand in hand with the growth of medieval towns, a result of an increase in trade that was stimulated in part by the Crusades. In the towns, merchants and craftspeople formed organizations called guilds to control the flow and price of goods and to set up rules for advancing from apprentice to master craftsman. The

King Philip II of France *(above),* along with Richard the Lion-Hearted and Frederick I of Germany, was a leader of the forces attempting to recapture Jerusalem in the Third Crusade (1189–1192).

Right: Magna Carta, 1215

Wool, an important product in medieval commerce, was shipped from sheep farms to market towns, where merchants exchanged money for goods.

The spread of ideas was greatly assisted by a landmark innovation in 15th-century Europe—the printing press.

growth of towns meant the decline of feudalism, since wealth was no longer based exclusively on land ownership. On the other hand, the crowding of townspeople in conditions of poor sanitation ensured that diseases like plague could spread rapidly.

As towns were becoming centers of commerce, universities were becoming England's chief centers of learning. At Oxford University, 13th-century scholars like Roger Bacon advanced the study of science and mathematics. A century later, an Oxford scholar named John Wycliffe led an effort to end widespread church corruption. Though his followers, the Lollards, were suppressed, his ideas spread to John Huss in central Europe and through him influenced the later religious reformer Martin Luther.

THE HUNDRED YEARS' WAR

Wycliffe's reform efforts took place during the Hundred Years' War, a long struggle between England and France that had begun in 1337 during the reign of Edward III. As the war continued on and off for more than a century, England also had to weather several domestic crises, including a great epidemic of plague known as the Black Death, which killed a third of England's popu-

Religious faith was a vital element of medieval English life and literature. One of the most distinctive products of the age is the long poem known as Piers Plowman, a dream vision that explores Christianity's spiritual mysteries. Religious devotion is also the key concern of *The Book of Margery Kempe,* an autobiography in which Kempe focuses on her spiritual growth. In contrast, far more worldly attitudes are expressed in the surviving correspondence of the Paston family. These remarkable letters, written from about 1420 to 1500 and discovered centuries later by one of the Pastons' descendants, provide fascinating glimpses of life in later medieval times.

Especially popular in the Middle Ages were **romances**—tales of chivalric knights, many of which feature King Arthur and the members of his court. For centuries the oral poets of the Britons in Wales had celebrated their legendary hero Arthur just as Anglo-Saxon scops had celebrated Beowulf. Then, about 1135, the monk Geoffrey of Monmouth produced a Latin "history" based on the old Welsh legends. Geoffrey's book caught the fancy of French, German, and English writers, who soon produced their own versions of the legends, updating them to reflect then-current notions of chivalry. In about 1375, an anonymous English poet produced *Sir Gawain and the Green Knight,* recounting the marvelous adventures of a knight of Arthur's court. A century later, in *Le Morte d'Arthur,* Sir Thomas Malory retold a number of the French Arthurian tales in Middle English.

Development of the English Language

As warfare with France dragged on, English not only survived but triumphed. Among England's upper class it came to seem unpatriotic to use the language of the nation's number one enemy, especially since the Anglo-Norman variety of French was ridiculed by the "real" French speakers across the English Channel. By the end of the Hundred Years' War, English had once again become the first language of most of the English nobility.

LITERARY HISTORY

In the rebirth of English as a language of literature, no writer was more important than the 14th-century poet Geoffrey Chaucer, the towering figure of Middle English letters. Chaucer's masterpiece, *The Canterbury Tales,* is a collection of tales supposedly narrated by a group of pilgrims traveling from London to Canterbury to visit the shrine of Thomas à Becket. The pilgrims, who come from all walks of medieval life—the castle, the farm, the church, the town—are introduced in the famous "Prologue," where Chaucer weaves a vivid and charming tapestry of English life in the later Middle Ages.

lation; the Peasants' Revolt of 1381; and Richard II's forced abdication in 1399, which brought Henry IV to the English throne. The war itself had many famous episodes—like Henry V's great victory over the French at Agincourt and the French army's lifting of the siege of Orléans under the inspired leadership of the young peasant woman Joan of Arc. When the war finally ended in 1453, England had lost nearly all of its French possessions. It was also on the verge of a conflict in which two rival families claimed the throne—the house of York, whose symbol was a white rose, and the house of Lancaster, whose symbol was a red rose. The fighting, known as the Wars of the Roses, ended in 1485, when the Lancastrian Henry Tudor killed the Yorkist king Richard III at Bosworth Field and took the throne as Henry VII. This event is usually taken as marking the end of the Middle Ages in England.

In medieval art, the Black Death was often portrayed as a skeleton.

During the Hundred Years' War, the use of the longbow helped the English to inflict heavy casualties on the French, who were armed with the less efficient crossbow.

The Anglo-Saxon and medieval periods were ones of turmoil and change—times when people's courage was frequently put to the test. Amid this turmoil, the tests of courage often took the form of physical challenges, such as confronting a dreaded foe or battling to survive on the high seas. Other tests of courage involved spiritual or emotional challenges, such as standing up for one's religious beliefs or enduring the absence of a loved one. As you read about tests of courage in this part of Unit One, try to place yourself in the distant past and imagine how you would respond to similar challenges.

LEARNING *the Language of* *Literature*

The Epic

Oral Heroic Narrative— An Epic Task

Imagine that you're performing with an improvisational theater group. First, you are asked to pretend that you're an Automated Teller Machine (ATM) that intentionally tries people's patience. Easy, you think. Next, you must play a butcher who can't stand the sight of meat. No problem. Then a scholarly-looking man asks you to recite a long narrative poem about the heroic struggles of a legendary figure who uses strength, cunning, and help from the gods to survive perilous trials—and you have to use elevated, solemn language throughout. You're speechless, uncomprehending, until it hits you—the man wants an epic.

What Is an Epic?

An **epic** is a long narrative poem that celebrates a hero's deeds. The earliest epic tales survived for centuries as oral traditions before they were finally written down. They came into existence as spoken words and were retold by poet after poet from one generation to the next. Most orally composed epics date back to preliterate periods—before the cultures that produced them had developed written forms of their languages.

Many epics are based in historical fact, so that their public performance by poets (known in different cultures by such names as *scops* or *bards)* provided both entertainment and education for the audience. Oral poets had to be master improvisers, able to compose verse in their heads while simultaneously singing or chanting it. These poets didn't make up their stories from scratch, however; they drew on existing songs and legends, which they could embellish or combine with original material.

One characteristic feature of oral poetry is the repetition of certain words, phrases, or even lines. Two of the most notable examples of repeated elements are stock epithets and kennings.

Stock epithets are adjectives that point out special traits of particular persons or things. In Homer, stock epithets are often compound adjectives, such as the "swift-footed" used to describe Achilles.

Kennings are poetic synonyms found in Germanic poems, such as the Anglo-Saxon epic *Beowulf.* Rather than being an adjective, like an epithet, a kenning is a descriptive phrase or compound word that substitutes for a noun. For example, in *Beowulf* "the Almighty's enemy" and "sin-stained demon" are two kennings that are used in place of Grendel's name.

Stock epithets and kennings were building blocks that a poet could recite while turning his attention to the next line or stanza. Epithets had an added advantage—they were designed to fit metrically into specific parts of the lines of verse. In skillful hands, these "formulas" helped to establish tone and reinforce essentials of character and setting.

Characteristics of an Epic

Epics from different languages and time periods do not always have the same characteristics. Kennings, for example, are not found in Homer's epics. However, the following characteristics are shared by most epics, whether they were composed orally or in

writing, in the Middle Ages or last year, in Old English or in Slovak:

- The hero, generally a male, is of noble birth or high position, and often of great historical or legendary importance.
- The hero's character traits reflect important ideals of his society.
- The hero performs courageous—sometimes even superhuman—deeds that reflect the values of the era.
- The actions of the hero often determine the fate of a nation or group of people.
- The setting is vast in scope, often involving more than one nation.
- The poet uses formal diction and a serious tone.
- Major characters often deliver long, formal speeches.
- The plot is complicated by supernatural beings or events and may involve a long and dangerous journey through foreign lands.
- The poem reflects timeless values, such as courage and honor.
- The poem treats universal themes, such as good and evil or life and death.

The *Epic* Across *Cultures*

The epic is not a dead form. Although epics were sung by Sumerians as far back as the third millennium B.C., new oral epics continue to be created and recited in places like the Balkans and Southeast Asia. Many poets around the world still write poems in the epic tradition, and the epic spirit animates many prose works, such as J. R. R. Tolkien's *The Lord of the Rings,* a popular fantasy novel. Many contemporary films are also cast in an epic mold, including such Hollywood hits as the *Star Wars* trilogy, which features an intergalactic struggle between the forces of good and evil.

YOUR TURN What evidence of epic features might you expect to find in the *Star Wars* trilogy?

Strategies for Reading: The Epic

1. Notice which characteristics of epics appear in the poem you are reading.
2. Decide what virtues the hero embodies.
3. Decide if the epic's values are still held today.
4. Determine the hero's role in bringing about any changes in fortune for the characters.
5. Use a list or diagram to keep track of the characters.
6. If a passage confuses you, go back and summarize the main idea of the passage.

7. When reading *Beowulf* (page 32) or the *Iliad* (page 67), use the accompanying Guide for Reading to help you clarify the language and form your own interpretation.
8. **Monitor** your reading strategies and modify them when your understanding breaks down. Remember to use your Strategies for Active Reading: **predict, visualize, connect, question, clarify,** and **evaluate.**

PREPARING to *Read*

from Beowulf

Epic Poetry by the BEOWULF POET
Translated by BURTON RAFFEL

Comparing Literature of the World

Beowulf and the *Iliad*

This lesson and the one that follows present an opportunity for comparing the epic heroes in *Beowulf* and the *Iliad.* Specific points of comparison in the *Iliad* lesson will help you contrast Beowulf's heroism with that of characters in Homer's epic poem.

Connect to Your Life

Brave Heart According to *The American Heritage Dictionary of the English Language,* a traditional hero is someone "endowed with great courage and strength" and "celebrated for his bold exploits." Are courage, strength, and boldness qualities you look for in a modern hero? Would you say that a hero's deeds have to be celebrated, or at least widely known? Think about people in today's world that you consider heroic. Then, in a cluster diagram like the one shown, jot down the qualities that make these people heroes in your eyes. Use your ideas to help you formulate your own definition of *hero.*

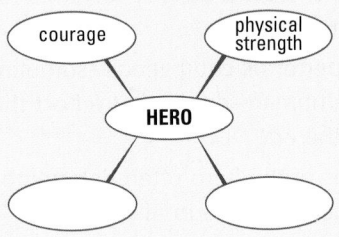

WORDS TO KNOW
Vocabulary Preview

- affliction
- cowering
- fetter
- gorge
- infamous
- lament
- livid
- loathsome
- murky
- pilgrimage
- purge
- relish
- talon
- taut
- writhing

Focus Your Reading

LITERARY ANALYSIS **ALLITERATION** **Alliteration** is the repetition of consonant sounds at the beginning of words. Poets frequently use alliteration to emphasize particular words or images, heighten moods, or create musical effects. In works of the oral tradition, alliteration was also used to aid memorization. In his translation of *Beowulf,* Burton Raffel has used alliteration to suggest the sound and style of the Old English poem.

> *The ancient blade broke, bit into*
> *The monster's skin, drew blood . . .*

Look for other examples of alliteration as you read the excerpts from *Beowulf.*

ACTIVE READING **MAKING JUDGMENTS** On pages 28–29, you were introduced to the characteristics shared by many **epics.** Look for evidence of these characteristics in *Beowulf,* and, on the basis of the evidence you find, **make judgments** about the ways in which the poem resembles and differs from other epics.

READER'S NOTEBOOK Use the information provided on pages 28–29 to create a chart in which you list common characteristics of epics. Then, as you read the excerpts from *Beowulf,* record evidence of the presence or absence of those characteristics in the poem. In your judgment, is *Beowulf* a typical epic?

Build Background

The Birth of the *Beowulf* Epic After the fall of the Western Roman Empire to Germanic tribes in the fifth century A.D., Europe entered a chaotic period of political unrest and economic and cultural decline. Among the Germanic-speaking tribes of northern Europe, life was dominated by frequent bloody warfare, which drove some of them to abandon their homes for foreign shores. These tribes included groups of Angles, Saxons, and Jutes who settled on the island of Britain, where they established what is now called Anglo-Saxon civilization. Their famous tale of the great hero Beowulf, however, takes place on the European mainland, among two related tribes, the Danes of what is now Denmark and the Geats (gēts or gā-əts) of what is now Sweden.

Beowulf is a Geat warrior who crosses the sea to aid the Danes and later returns to Sweden to succeed his uncle Hygelac (the Higlac of this translation) as king of the Geats. While we cannot be sure whether Beowulf ever really lived, we do know that Hygelac was a historical figure who led a military raid some time around the year 525. The action of *Beowulf* is presumably set not long afterward.

At that time, the northern Germanic societies had not yet adopted Christianity. Their warrior culture celebrated loyalty and deeds of great strength and courage. For entertainment the people gathered in mead halls, large wooden buildings where they feasted, drank mead (an alcoholic beverage), and listened to tales of heroic achievements. Such tales were presented both in the form of long epic poems and in the form of shorter verse narratives. Poet-singers— called scops (shōps) in Anglo-Saxon society— recited the poems in a chanting voice, usually accompanying themselves on a harp.

Old English Text *Beowulf* is the most famous of the early Germanic heroic poems that survive. The form of the poem that has come down to us dates from sometime between the eighth

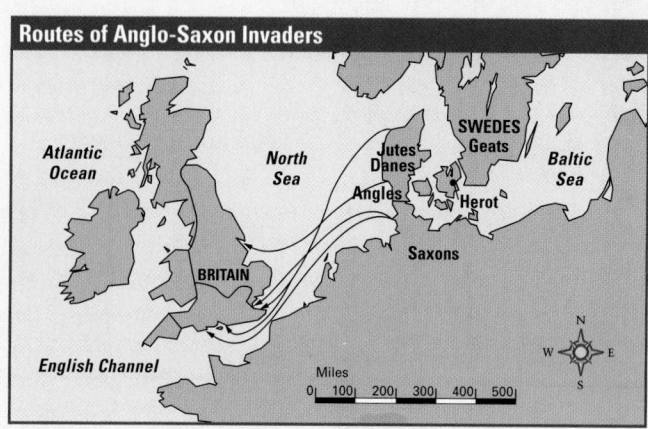

Routes of Anglo-Saxon Invaders

and tenth centuries—after the Anglo-Saxons' conversion to Christianity. It is written in Old English, the language spoken in Britain in the Anglo-Saxon period. As the lines shown below illustrate, Old English neither looks nor sounds like Modern English, and it must therefore be translated for most modern readers.

Old English poetry has a strong rhythm, with each line divided into two parts by a pause, called a **caesura** (sĭ-zhŏŏr'ə). In the Old English text printed here, the caesuras are indicated by extra space in the lines. In his translation, Burton Raffel has often used punctuation to reproduce the effect of the caesuras.

Lines from *Beowulf* in Old English

Ða com of more   under misthleoþum
grendel gongan—   godes yrre bær;
mynte se manscaða   manna cynnes
sumne besyrwan   in sele þam hean.

Modern English translation by Burton Raffel

*Out from the marsh, from the foot of misty
Hills and bogs, bearing God's hatred,
Grendel came, hoping to kill
Anyone he could trap on this trip to high Herot.*

from B EO

WULF

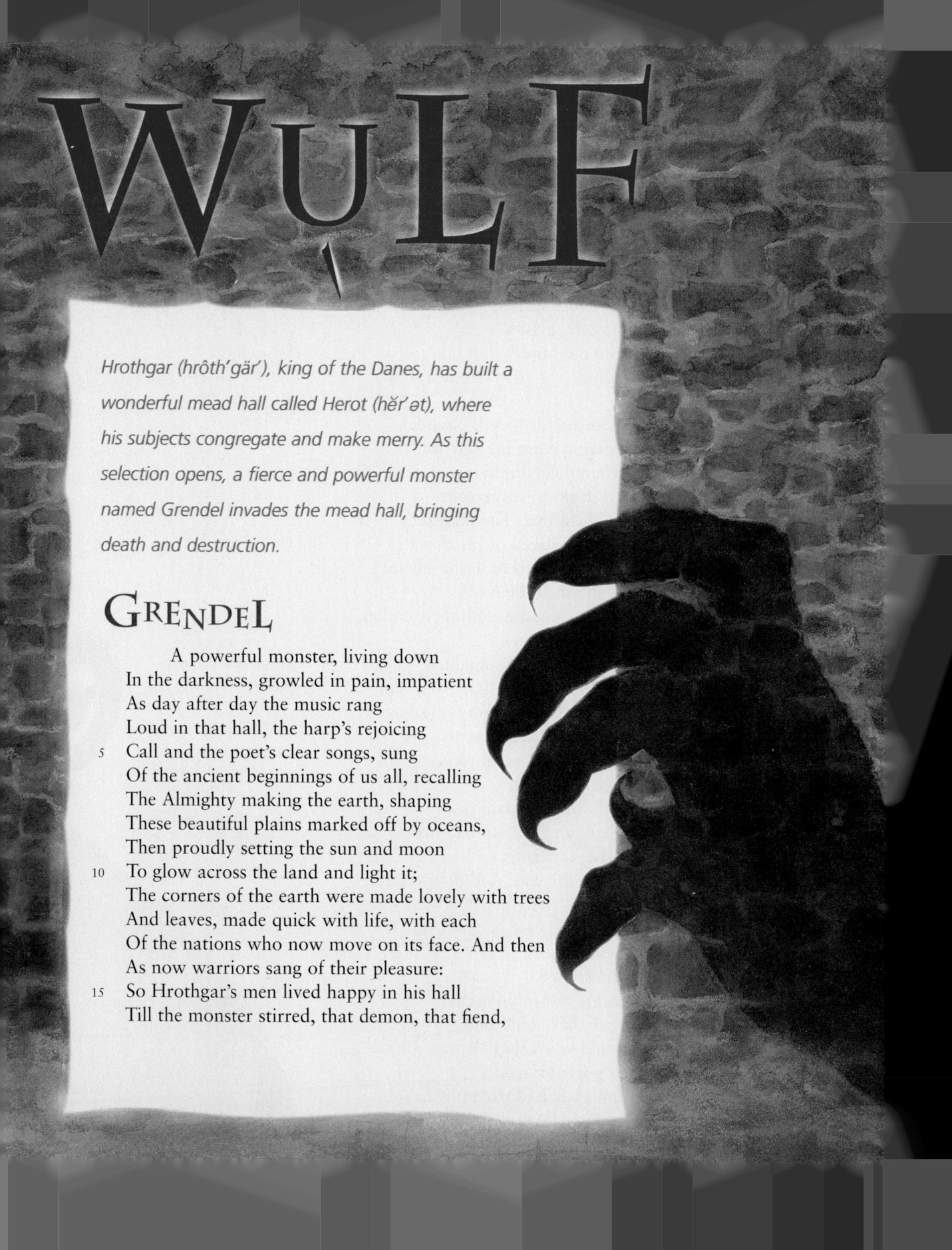

Hrothgar (hrôth´gär´), king of the Danes, has built a wonderful mead hall called Herot (hĕr´ət), where his subjects congregate and make merry. As this selection opens, a fierce and powerful monster named Grendel invades the mead hall, bringing death and destruction.

GRENDEL

     A powerful monster, living down
In the darkness, growled in pain, impatient
As day after day the music rang
Loud in that hall, the harp's rejoicing
5   Call and the poet's clear songs, sung
Of the ancient beginnings of us all, recalling
The Almighty making the earth, shaping
These beautiful plains marked off by oceans,
Then proudly setting the sun and moon
10 To glow across the land and light it;
The corners of the earth were made lovely with trees
And leaves, made quick with life, with each
Of the nations who now move on its face. And then
As now warriors sang of their pleasure:
15 So Hrothgar's men lived happy in his hall
Till the monster stirred, that demon, that fiend,

Grendel, who haunted the moors, the wild
Marshes, and made his home in a hell
Not hell but earth. He was spawned in that slime,
20 Conceived by a pair of those monsters born
Of Cain, murderous creatures banished
By God, punished forever for the crime
Of Abel's death. The Almighty drove
Those demons out, and their exile was bitter,
25 Shut away from men; they split
Into a thousand forms of evil—spirits
And fiends, goblins, monsters, giants,
A brood forever opposing the Lord's
Will, and again and again defeated.

30   Then, when darkness had dropped, Grendel
Went up to Herot, wondering what the warriors
Would do in that hall when their drinking was done.
He found them sprawled in sleep, suspecting
Nothing, their dreams undisturbed. The monster's
35 Thoughts were as quick as his greed or his claws:
He slipped through the door and there in the silence
Snatched up thirty men, smashed them
Unknowing in their beds and ran out with their bodies,
The blood dripping behind him, back
40 To his lair, delighted with his night's slaughter.
     At daybreak, with the sun's first light, they saw
How well he had worked, and in that gray morning
Broke their long feast with tears and <u>laments</u>
For the dead. Hrothgar, their lord, sat joyless
45 In Herot, a mighty prince mourning
The fate of his lost friends and companions,
Knowing by its tracks that some demon had torn
His followers apart. He wept, fearing
The beginning might not be the end. And that night
50 Grendel came again, so set
On murder that no crime could ever be enough,
No savage assault quench his lust
For evil. Then each warrior tried
To escape him, searched for rest in different
55 Beds, as far from Herot as they could find,
Seeing how Grendel hunted when they slept.
Distance was safety; the only survivors
Were those who fled him. Hate had triumphed.
     So Grendel ruled, fought with the righteous,

GUIDE FOR READING

17 moors (mŏŏrz): broad, open regions with patches of bog.

19 spawned: born.

21 Cain: the eldest son of Adam and Eve. According to the Bible (Genesis 4), he murdered his younger brother Abel.

19–29 Who were Grendel's earliest ancestors? How did he come to exist?

40 lair: the den of a wild animal.

49 What is meant by "The beginning might not be the end"?

58 In what way has hate triumphed?

Prow of ninth-century Oseberg ship

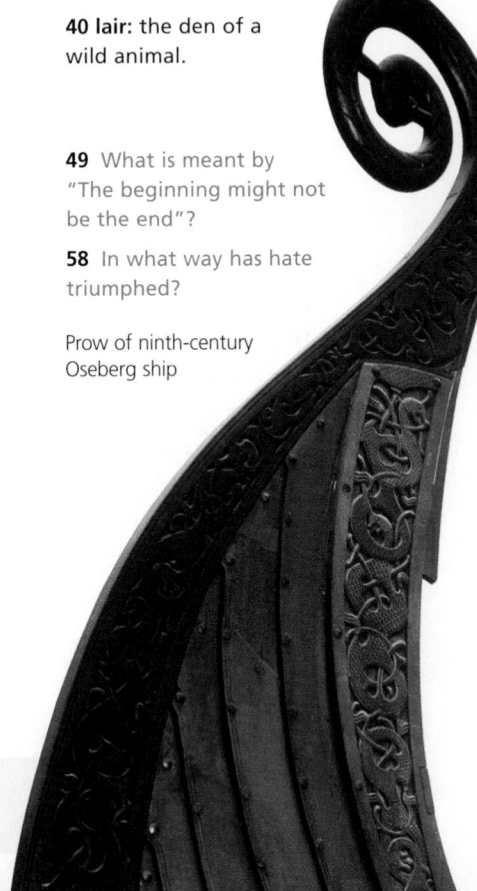

WORDS
TO
KNOW
   lament (lə-mĕnt') *n.* an audible expression of grief; wail

60　One against many, and won; so Herot
　　Stood empty, and stayed deserted for years,
　　Twelve winters of grief for Hrothgar, king
　　Of the Danes, sorrow heaped at his door
　　By hell-forged hands. His misery leaped
65　The seas, was told and sung in all
　　Men's ears: how Grendel's hatred began,
　　How the monster relished his savage war
　　On the Danes, keeping the bloody feud
　　Alive, seeking no peace, offering
70　No truce, accepting no settlement, no price
　　In gold or land, and paying the living
　　For one crime only with another. No one
　　Waited for reparation from his plundering claws:
　　That shadow of death hunted in the darkness,
75　Stalked Hrothgar's warriors, old
　　And young, lying in waiting, hidden
　　In mist, invisibly following them from the edge
　　Of the marsh, always there, unseen.
　　　　So mankind's enemy continued his crimes,
80　Killing as often as he could, coming
　　Alone, bloodthirsty and horrible. Though he lived
　　In Herot, when the night hid him, he never
　　Dared to touch king Hrothgar's glorious
　　Throne, protected by God—God,
85　Whose love Grendel could not know. But Hrothgar's
　　Heart was bent. The best and most noble
　　Of his council debated remedies, sat
　　In secret sessions, talking of terror
　　And wondering what the bravest of warriors could do.
90　And sometimes they sacrificed to the old stone gods,
　　Made heathen vows, hoping for Hell's
　　Support, the Devil's guidance in driving
　　Their affliction off. That was their way,
　　And the heathen's only hope, Hell
95　Always in their hearts, knowing neither God
　　Nor His passing as He walks through our world, the Lord
　　Of Heaven and earth; their ears could not hear
　　His praise nor know His glory. Let them
　　Beware, those who are thrust into danger,
100　Clutched at by trouble, yet can carry no solace
　　In their hearts, cannot hope to be better! Hail
　　To those who will rise to God, drop off
　　Their dead bodies and seek our Father's peace!

64 What does the phrase "hell-forged hands" suggest about Grendel?

73 reparation: something done to make amends for loss or suffering. In Germanic society, someone who killed another person was generally expected to make a payment to the victim's family as a way of restoring peace.

84 The reference to God shows the influence of Christianity on the Beowulf Poet. What does Grendel's inability to know God's love suggest about him?

91 heathen (hē′thən): pagan; non-Christian. Though the Beowulf Poet was a Christian, he recognized that the characters in the poem lived before the Germanic tribes were converted to Christianity, when they still worshiped "the old stone gods."

WORDS
TO
KNOW

relish (rĕl′ĭsh) v. to enjoy keenly
affliction (ə-flĭk′shən) n. a cause of pain or distress

Beowulf

So the living sorrow of Healfdane's son

105   Simmered, bitter and fresh, and no wisdom
Or strength could break it: that agony hung
On king and people alike, harsh
And unending, violent and cruel, and evil.
    In his far-off home Beowulf, Higlac's

110   Follower and the strongest of the Geats—greater
And stronger than anyone anywhere in this world—
Heard how Grendel filled nights with horror
And quickly commanded a boat fitted out,
Proclaiming that he'd go to that famous king,

115   Would sail across the sea to Hrothgar,
Now when help was needed. None
Of the wise ones regretted his going, much
As he was loved by the Geats: the omens were good,
And they urged the adventure on. So Beowulf

120   Chose the mightiest men he could find,
The bravest and best of the Geats, fourteen
In all, and led them down to their boat;
He knew the sea, would point the prow
Straight to that distant Danish shore.

Beowulf and his men sail over the sea to the land of the Danes to offer help to Hrothgar. They are escorted by a Danish guard to Herot, where Wulfgar, one of Hrothgar's soldiers, tells the king of their arrival. Hrothgar knows of Beowulf and is ready to welcome the young prince and his men.

125   Then Wulfgar went to the door and addressed
The waiting seafarers with soldier's words:
    "My lord, the great king of the Danes, commands me
To tell you that he knows of your noble birth
And that having come to him from over the open

130   Sea you have come bravely and are welcome.
Now go to him as you are, in your armor and helmets,
But leave your battle-shields here, and your spears,
Let them lie waiting for the promises your words
May make."
        Beowulf arose, with his men

135   Around him, ordering a few to remain
With their weapons, leading the others quickly

104 Healfdane's son: Hrothgar.

109–110 Higlac's follower: warrior loyal to Higlac (hǐg'lăk'), king of the Geats (and Beowulf's uncle).

Along under Herot's steep roof into Hrothgar's
Presence. Standing on that prince's own hearth,
Helmeted, the silvery metal of his mail shirt
140 Gleaming with a smith's high art, he greeted
The Danes' great lord:

　　　　　　　"Hail, Hrothgar!
Higlac is my cousin and my king; the days
Of my youth have been filled with glory. Now Grendel's
Name has echoed in our land: sailors
145 Have brought us stories of Herot, the best
Of all mead-halls, deserted and useless when the moon
Hangs in skies the sun had lit,
Light and life fleeing together.
My people have said, the wisest, most knowing
150 And best of them, that my duty was to go to the Danes'
Great king. They have seen my strength for themselves,

139 mail shirt: flexible body armor made of metal links or overlapping metal scales.

140 smith's high art: the skilled craft of a blacksmith (a person who fashions objects from iron).

142 cousin: here, a general term for a relative. Beowulf is actually Higlac's nephew.

Front view of a wooden Viking house in Trelleborg, Denmark, that serves today as an outdoor museum. Such houses had a main door at each end and contained a huge central room where a great fire burned.

Have watched me rise from the darkness of war,
Dripping with my enemies' blood. I drove
Five great giants into chains, chased
155 All of that race from the earth. I swam
In the blackness of night, hunting monsters
Out of the ocean, and killing them one
By one; death was my errand and the fate
They had earned. Now Grendel and I are called
160 Together, and I've come. Grant me, then,
Lord and protector of this noble place,
A single request! I have come so far,
Oh shelterer of warriors and your people's loved friend,
That this one favor you should not refuse me—
165 That I, alone and with the help of my men,
May purge all evil from this hall. I have heard,
Too, that the monster's scorn of men
Is so great that he needs no weapons and fears none.
Nor will I. My lord Higlac
170 Might think less of me if I let my sword
Go where my feet were afraid to, if I hid
Behind some broad linden shield: my hands
Alone shall fight for me, struggle for life
Against the monster. God must decide
175 Who will be given to death's cold grip.
Grendel's plan, I think, will be
What it has been before, to invade this hall
And gorge his belly with our bodies. If he can,
If he can. And I think, if my time will have come,
180 There'll be nothing to mourn over, no corpse to prepare
For its grave: Grendel will carry our bloody
Flesh to the moors, crunch on our bones
And smear torn scraps of our skin on the walls
Of his den. No, I expect no Danes
185 Will fret about sewing our shrouds, if he wins.
And if death does take me, send the hammered
Mail of my armor to Higlac, return
The inheritance I had from Hrethel, and he
From Wayland. Fate will unwind as it must!"

190   Hrothgar replied, protector of the Danes:
"Beowulf, you've come to us in friendship,
and because

172 linden shield: shield made from the wood of a linden tree.

172–174 Beowulf insists on fighting Grendel without weapons. Why do you think this is so important to him?

185 shrouds: cloths in which dead bodies are wrapped.

188 Hrethel (hrĕ*th*′əl): a former king of the Geats—Higlac's father and Beowulf's grandfather.

189 Wayland: a famous blacksmith and magician.

WORDS
TO
KNOW

purge (pûrj) *v.* to cleanse or purify
gorge (gôrj) *v.* to stuff with food

Of the reception your father found at our court.
Edgetho had begun a bitter feud,
Killing Hathlaf, a Wulfing warrior:
195 Your father's countrymen were afraid of war,
If he returned to his home, and they turned him away.
Then he traveled across the curving waves
To the land of the Danes. I was new to the throne,
Then, a young man ruling this wide
200 Kingdom and its golden city: Hergar,
My older brother, a far better man
Than I, had died and dying made me,
Second among Healfdane's sons, first
In this nation. I bought the end of Edgetho's
205 Quarrel, sent ancient treasures through the ocean's
Furrows to the Wulfings; your father swore
He'd keep that peace. My tongue grows heavy,
And my heart, when I try to tell you what Grendel
Has brought us, the damage he's done, here
210 In this hall. You see for yourself how much smaller
Our ranks have become, and can guess what we've lost
To his terror. Surely the Lord Almighty
Could stop his madness, smother his lust!
How many times have my men, glowing
215 With courage drawn from too many cups
Of ale, sworn to stay after dark
And stem that horror with a sweep of their swords.
And then, in the morning, this mead-hall glittering
With new light would be drenched with blood, the benches
220 Stained red, the floors, all wet from that fiend's
Savage assault—and my soldiers would be fewer
Still, death taking more and more.
But to table, Beowulf, a banquet in your honor:
Let us toast your victories, and talk of the future."
225   Then Hrothgar's men gave places to the Geats,
Yielded benches to the brave visitors
And led them to the feast. The keeper of the mead
Came carrying out the carved flasks,
And poured that bright sweetness. A poet
230 Sang, from time to time, in a clear
Pure voice. Danes and visiting Geats
Celebrated as one, drank and rejoiced.

193 Edgetho (ĕj'thō): Beowulf's father.

194 Wulfing: a member of another Germanic tribe.

191–206 What service did Hrothgar perform for Beowulf's father?

Reconstruction of helmet
from Sutton Hoo ship burial

After the banquet, Hrothgar and his
followers leave Herot, and Beowulf and
his warriors remain to spend the night.
Beowulf reiterates his intent to fight Grendel
without a sword and, while his followers sleep, lies
waiting, eager for Grendel to appear.

The Battle with Grendel

Out from the marsh, from the foot of misty
Hills and bogs, bearing God's hatred,
235 Grendel came, hoping to kill
Anyone he could trap on this trip to high Herot.
He moved quickly through the cloudy night,
Up from his swampland, sliding silently
Toward that gold-shining hall. He had visited Hrothgar's
240 Home before, knew the way—
But never, before nor after that night,
Found Herot defended so firmly, his reception

233–235 The translator uses punctuation to convey the effect of the midline pauses in the original Old English verses. How does the rhythm created by the midline punctuation reinforce the account of the action here?

So harsh. He journeyed, forever joyless,
Straight to the door, then snapped it open,
245   Tore its iron fasteners with a touch
And rushed angrily over the threshold.
He strode quickly across the inlaid
Floor, snarling and fierce: his eyes
Gleamed in the darkness, burned with a gruesome
250   Light. Then he stopped, seeing the hall
Crowded with sleeping warriors, stuffed
With rows of young soldiers resting together.
And his heart laughed, he relished the sight,
Intended to tear the life from those bodies
255   By morning; the monster's mind was hot
With the thought of food and the feasting his belly
Would soon know. But fate, that night, intended
Grendel to gnaw the broken bones
Of his last human supper. Human
260   Eyes were watching his evil steps,
Waiting to see his swift hard claws.
Grendel snatched at the first Geat
He came to, ripped him apart, cut
His body to bits with powerful jaws,
265   Drank the blood from his veins and bolted
Him down, hands and feet; death
And Grendel's great teeth came together,
Snapping life shut. Then he stepped to another
Still body, clutched at Beowulf with his claws,
270   Grasped at a strong-hearted wakeful sleeper
—And was instantly seized himself, claws
Bent back as Beowulf leaned up on one arm.
          That shepherd of evil, guardian of crime,
Knew at once that nowhere on earth
275   Had he met a man whose hands were harder;
His mind was flooded with fear—but nothing
Could take his talons and himself from that tight
Hard grip. Grendel's one thought was to run
From Beowulf, flee back to his marsh and hide there:
280   This was a different Herot than the hall he had emptied.
But Higlac's follower remembered his final
Boast and, standing erect, stopped
The monster's flight, fastened those claws
In his fists till they cracked, clutched Grendel
285   Closer. The infamous killer fought

246 threshold: the strip of wood or stone at the bottom of a doorway.

WORDS
TO
KNOW

talon (tăl′ən) *n.* a claw
infamous (ĭn′fə-məs) *adj.* having a bad reputation; notorious

41

For his freedom, wanting no flesh but retreat,
Desiring nothing but escape; his claws
Had been caught, he was trapped. That trip to Herot
Was a miserable journey for the <u>writhing</u> monster!

290   The high hall rang, its roof boards swayed,
And Danes shook with terror. Down
The aisles the battle swept, angry
And wild. Herot trembled, wonderfully
Built to withstand the blows, the struggling
295 Great bodies beating at its beautiful walls;
Shaped and fastened with iron, inside
And out, artfully worked, the building
Stood firm. Its benches rattled, fell
To the floor, gold-covered boards grating
300 As Grendel and Beowulf battled across them.
Hrothgar's wise men had fashioned Herot
To stand forever; only fire,
They had planned, could shatter what such skill had put
Together, swallow in hot flames such splendor
305 Of ivory and iron and wood. Suddenly
The sounds changed, the Danes started
In new terror, <u>cowering</u> in their beds as the terrible
Screams of the Almighty's enemy sang
In the darkness, the horrible shrieks of pain
310 And defeat, the tears torn out of Grendel's
<u>Taut</u> throat, hell's captive caught in the arms
Of him who of all the men on earth
Was the strongest.

         That mighty protector of men
Meant to hold the monster till its life
315 Leaped out, knowing the fiend was no use
To anyone in Denmark. All of Beowulf's
Band had jumped from their beds, ancestral
Swords raised and ready, determined
To protect their prince if they could. Their courage
320 Was great but all wasted: they could hack at Grendel
From every side, trying to open
A path for his evil soul, but their points
Could not hurt him, the sharpest and hardest iron
Could not scratch at his skin, for that sin-stained demon
325 Had bewitched all men's weapons, laid spells
That blunted every mortal man's blade.

278–289 Up to this point Grendel has killed his human victims easily. Why might he be trying to run away from Beowulf?

322–326 Why do you think no weapons can hurt Grendel?

W O R D S	**writhing** (rī′thĭng) *adj.* twisting and turning in pain **writhe** *v.*
T O	**cowering** (kou′ə-rĭng) *adj.* cringing in fear **cower** *v.*
K N O W	**taut** (tôt) *adj.* pulled tight

And yet his time had come, his days
Were over, his death near; down
To hell he would go, swept groaning and helpless
330 To the waiting hands of still worse fiends.
Now he discovered—once the afflictor
Of men, tormentor of their days—what it meant
To feud with Almighty God: Grendel
Saw that his strength was deserting him, his claws
335 Bound fast, Higlac's brave follower tearing at
His hands. The monster's hatred rose higher,
But his power had gone. He twisted in pain,
And the bleeding sinews deep in his shoulder
Snapped, muscle and bone split

338 sinews (sǐn'yōōz): the tendons that connect muscles to bones.

340 And broke. The battle was over, Beowulf
Had been granted new glory: Grendel escaped,
But wounded as he was could flee to his den,
His miserable hole at the bottom of the marsh,
Only to die, to wait for the end
345 Of all his days. And after that bloody
Combat the Danes laughed with delight.
He who had come to them from across the sea,
Bold and strong-minded, had driven affliction
Off, purged Herot clean. He was happy,
350 Now, with that night's fierce work; the Danes
Had been served as he'd boasted he'd serve them; Beowulf,
A prince of the Geats, had killed Grendel,
Ended the grief, the sorrow, the suffering
Forced on Hrothgar's helpless people
355 By a bloodthirsty fiend. No Dane doubted
The victory, for the proof, hanging high
From the rafters where Beowulf had hung it, was the monster's
Arm, claw and shoulder and all.

355–358 Why do you think Beowulf hangs Grendel's arm from the rafters?

　　　And then, in the morning, crowds surrounded
360 Herot, warriors coming to that hall
From faraway lands, princes and leaders
Of men hurrying to behold the monster's
Great staggering tracks. They gaped with no sense
Of sorrow, felt no regret for his suffering,
365 Went tracing his bloody footprints, his beaten
And lonely flight, to the edge of the lake
Where he'd dragged his corpselike way, doomed
And already weary of his vanishing life.

The water was bloody, steaming and boiling
370 In horrible pounding waves, heat
Sucked from his magic veins; but the swirling
Surf had covered his death, hidden
Deep in <u>murky</u> darkness his miserable
End, as hell opened to receive him.
375   Then old and young rejoiced, turned back
From that happy <u>pilgrimage</u>, mounted their hard-hooved
Horses, high-spirited stallions, and rode them
Slowly toward Herot again, retelling
Beowulf's bravery as they jogged along.
380 And over and over they swore that nowhere
On earth or under the spreading sky
Or between the seas, neither south nor north,
Was there a warrior worthier to rule over men.
(But no one meant Beowulf's praise to belittle
385 Hrothgar, their kind and gracious king!)
        And sometimes, when the path ran straight and clear,
They would let their horses race, red
And brown and pale yellow backs streaming
Down the road. And sometimes a proud old soldier
390 Who had heard songs of the ancient heroes
And could sing them all through, story after story,
Would weave a net of words for Beowulf's
Victory, tying the knot of his verses
Smoothly, swiftly, into place with a poet's
395 Quick skill, singing his new song aloud
While he shaped it, and the old songs as well. . . .

389–396 What role do poets seem to play in Beowulf's society?

Thinking Through the Literature

1. **Comprehension Check** What characteristics does Grendel have that make him particularly terrifying to the Danes?

2. What impressions of Beowulf do you have after reading this part of the poem?

3. What do you think causes Grendel to attack human beings?

THINK ABOUT
{
• his relatives and ancestors
• his actions and attitudes
• the Danish warriors' reactions to him
}

4. Why do you think Beowulf offers to help a tribe other than his own, in spite of the danger?

WORDS TO KNOW

murky (mur′kē) *adj.* cloudy; gloomy
pilgrimage (pĭl′grə-mĭj) *n.* a journey to a sacred place or with a lofty purpose

Although one monster has died,

another still lives. From her lair in a cold and

murky lake, where she has been brooding over her

loss, Grendel's mother emerges, bent on revenge.

GRENDEL'S MOTHER

So she reached Herot,
Where the Danes slept as though already dead;
Her visit ended their good fortune, reversed
400 The bright vane of their luck. No female, no matter
How fierce, could have come with a man's strength,
Fought with the power and courage men fight with,
Smashing their shining swords, their bloody,
Hammer-forged blades onto boar-headed helmets,
405 Slashing and stabbing with the sharpest of points.
The soldiers raised their shields and drew
Those gleaming swords, swung them above
The piled-up benches, leaving their mail shirts
And their helmets where they'd lain when the terror took
hold of them.
410 To save her life she moved still faster,
Took a single victim and fled from the hall,
Running to the moors, discovered, but her supper
Assured, sheltered in her dripping claws.
She'd taken Hrothgar's closest friend,
415 The man he most loved of all men on earth;
She'd killed a glorious soldier, cut
A noble life short. No Geat could have stopped her:
Beowulf and his band had been given better
Beds; sleep had come to them in a different
420 Hall. Then all Herot burst into shouts:
She had carried off Grendel's claw. Sorrow
Had returned to Denmark. They'd traded deaths,
Danes and monsters, and no one had won,
Both had lost!

400 vane: a device that turns to show the direction the wind is blowing—here associated metaphorically with luck, which is as changeable as the wind.

404 boar-headed helmets: Germanic warriors often wore helmets bearing the images of wild pigs or other fierce creatures in the hope that the images would increase their ferocity and protect them against their enemies.

421 Why do you think Grendel's mother takes his claw?

Devastated by the loss of his friend, Hrothgar sends for Beowulf and recounts what Grendel's mother has done. Then Hrothgar describes the dark lake where Grendel's mother has dwelt with her son.

425 "They live in secret places, windy
　　　Cliffs, wolf-dens where water pours
　　　From the rocks, then runs underground, where mist
　　　Steams like black clouds, and the groves of trees
　　　Growing out over their lake are all covered
430　With frozen spray, and wind down snakelike
　　　Roots that reach as far as the water
　　　And help keep it dark. At night that lake
　　　Burns like a torch. No one knows its bottom,
　　　No wisdom reaches such depths. A deer,
435　Hunted through the woods by packs of hounds,
　　　A stag with great horns, though driven through the forest
　　　From faraway places, prefers to die
　　　On those shores, refuses to save its life
　　　In that water. It isn't far, nor is it
440　A pleasant spot! When the wind stirs
　　　And storms, waves splash toward the sky,
　　　As dark as the air, as black as the rain
　　　That the heavens weep. Our only help,
　　　Again, lies with you. Grendel's mother
445　Is hidden in her terrible home, in a place
　　　You've not seen. Seek it, if you dare! Save us,
　　　Once more, and again twisted gold,
　　　Heaped-up ancient treasure, will reward you
　　　For the battle you win!"

425–432 What sort of place is the underwater lair of Grendel's mother? How does the translator's use of alliteration make this description more effective?

447–449 Germanic warriors placed great importance on amassing treasure as a way of acquiring fame and temporarily defeating fate.

Bronze matrix for pressed foil, cast with carved details. Björnhovda,
Torslunda, Öland. 7th century A.D.

*Beowulf accepts Hrothgar's challenge,
and the king and his men accompany
the hero to the dreadful lair of
Grendel's mother. Fearlessly, Beowulf
prepares to battle the terrible creature.*

THE BATTLE WITH GRENDEL'S MOTHER

450   He leaped into the lake, would not wait for anyone's
Answer; the heaving water covered him
Over. For hours he sank through the waves;
At last he saw the mud of the bottom.
And all at once the greedy she-wolf

455 Who'd ruled those waters for half a hundred
Years discovered him, saw that a creature
From above had come to explore the bottom
Of her wet world. She welcomed him in her claws,
Clutched at him savagely but could not harm him,

460 Tried to work her fingers through the tight
Ring-woven mail on his breast, but tore
And scratched in vain. Then she carried him, armor
And sword and all, to her home; he struggled
To free his weapon, and failed. The fight

465 Brought other monsters swimming to see
Her catch, a host of sea beasts who beat at
His mail shirt, stabbing with tusks and teeth
As they followed along. Then he realized, suddenly,
That she'd brought him into someone's battle-hall,

470 And there the water's heat could not hurt him,
Nor anything in the lake attack him through

The building's high-arching roof. A brilliant
Light burned all around him, the lake
Itself like a fiery flame.

                    Then he saw
475 The mighty water witch, and swung his sword,
His ring-marked blade, straight at her head;
The iron sang its fierce song,
Sang Beowulf's strength. But her guest
Discovered that no sword could slice her evil
480 Skin, that Hrunting could not hurt her, was useless
Now when he needed it. They wrestled, she ripped
And tore and clawed at him, bit holes in his helmet,
And that too failed him; for the first time in years
Of being worn to war it would earn no glory;
485 It was the last time anyone would wear it. But Beowulf
Longed only for fame, leaped back
Into battle. He tossed his sword aside,
Angry; the steel-edged blade lay where
He'd dropped it. If weapons were useless he'd use
490 His hands, the strength in his fingers. So fame
Comes to the men who mean to win it
And care about nothing else! He raised
His arms and seized her by the shoulder; anger
Doubled his strength, he threw her to the floor.
495 She fell, Grendel's fierce mother, and the Geats'
Proud prince was ready to leap on her. But she rose
At once and repaid him with her clutching claws,
Wildly tearing at him. He was weary, that best
And strongest of soldiers; his feet stumbled
500 And in an instant she had him down, held helpless.
Squatting with her weight on his stomach, she drew
A dagger, brown with dried blood, and prepared
To avenge her only son. But he was stretched
On his back, and her stabbing blade was blunted
505 By the woven mail shirt he wore on his chest.
The hammered links held; the point
Could not touch him. He'd have traveled to the bottom of the earth,
Edgetho's son, and died there, if that shining
Woven metal had not helped—and Holy
510 God, who sent him victory, gave judgment
For truth and right, Ruler of the Heavens,
Once Beowulf was back on his feet and fighting.

476 his ring-marked blade: For the battle with Grendel's mother, Beowulf has been given an heirloom sword with an intricately etched blade.

480 Hrunting (hrŭn'tĭng): the name of Beowulf's sword. (Germanic warriors' swords were possessions of such value that they were often given names.)

490–492 How important is fame to Beowulf?

Then he saw, hanging on the wall, a heavy
Sword, hammered by giants, strong

515 And blessed with their magic, the best of all weapons
But so massive that no ordinary man could lift
Its carved and decorated length. He drew it
From its scabbard, broke the chain on its hilt,
And then, savage, now, angry

520 And desperate, lifted it high over his head
And struck with all the strength he had left,
Caught her in the neck and cut it through,
Broke bones and all. Her body fell
To the floor, lifeless, the sword was wet

525 With her blood, and Beowulf rejoiced at the sight.
The brilliant light shone, suddenly,
As though burning in that hall, and as bright as Heaven's
Own candle, lit in the sky. He looked
At her home, then following along the wall

530 Went walking, his hands tight on the sword,
His heart still angry. He was hunting another
Dead monster, and took his weapon with him
For final revenge against Grendel's vicious
Attacks, his nighttime raids, over

535 And over, coming to Herot when Hrothgar's
Men slept, killing them in their beds,
Eating some on the spot, fifteen
Or more, and running to his loathsome moor
With another such sickening meal waiting

540 In his pouch. But Beowulf repaid him for those visits,
Found him lying dead in his corner,
Armless, exactly as that fierce fighter
Had sent him out from Herot, then struck off
His head with a single swift blow. The body

545 Jerked for the last time, then lay still.
The wise old warriors who surrounded Hrothgar,
Like him staring into the monsters' lake,
Saw the waves surging and blood
Spurting through. They spoke about Beowulf,

550 All the graybeards, whispered together
And said that hope was gone, that the hero
Had lost fame and his life at once, and would never
Return to the living, come back as triumphant
As he had left; almost all agreed that Grendel's

555 Mighty mother, the she-wolf, had killed him.

Viking sword

550 graybeards: old men.

49

Gold torque (a collar or necklace) from Snettisham in Norfolk in eastern England, made sometime in the middle of the first century B.C.

The sun slid over past noon, went further
Down. The Danes gave up, left
The lake and went home, Hrothgar with them.
The Geats stayed, sat sadly, watching,
560   Imagining they saw their lord but not believing
They would ever see him again.
                     —Then the sword
Melted, blood-soaked, dripping down
Like water, disappearing like ice when the world's
Eternal Lord loosens invisible
565   <u>Fetters</u> and unwinds icicles and frost
As only He can, He who rules
Time and seasons, He who is truly
God. The monsters' hall was full of
Rich treasures, but all that Beowulf took
570   Was Grendel's head and the hilt of the giants'
Jeweled sword; the rest of that ring-marked
Blade had dissolved in Grendel's steaming
Blood, boiling even after his death.
And then the battle's only survivor
575   Swam up and away from those silent corpses;
The water was calm and clean, the whole
Huge lake peaceful once the demons who'd lived in it
Were dead.
            Then that noble protector of all seamen
Swam to land, rejoicing in the heavy
580   Burdens he was bringing with him. He

578 that noble protector of all seamen: Beowulf, who will be buried in a tower that will serve as a navigational aid to sailors.

WORDS
TO   **fetter** (fĕt′ər) *n.* a shackle or chain; restraint
KNOW

50

And all his glorious band of Geats
Thanked God that their leader had come back unharmed;
They left the lake together. The Geats
Carried Beowulf's helmet, and his mail shirt.
585 Behind them the water slowly thickened
As the monsters' blood came seeping up.
They walked quickly, happily, across
Roads all of them remembered, left
The lake and the cliffs alongside it, brave men
590 Staggering under the weight of Grendel's skull,
Too heavy for fewer than four of them to handle—
Two on each side of the spear jammed through it—
Yet proud of their ugly load and determined
That the Danes, seated in Herot, should see it.
595 Soon, fourteen Geats arrived
At the hall, bold and warlike, and with Beowulf,
Their lord and leader, they walked on the mead-hall
Green. Then the Geats' brave prince entered
Herot, covered with glory for the daring
600 Battles he had fought; he sought Hrothgar
To salute him and show Grendel's head.
He carried that terrible trophy by the hair,
Brought it straight to where the Danes sat,
Drinking, the queen among them. It was a weird
605 And wonderful sight, and the warriors stared.

593–594 Why do you think the Geats want the Danes to see the monster's skull?

604 queen: Welthow, wife of Hrothgar.

Thinking Through the Literature

1. **Comprehension Check** What heroic action does Beowulf perform in this part of the poem?

2. Do you think you would have enjoyed living among the Danes of Beowulf's day? Why or why not?

3. What qualities does Beowulf display in this second battle?

THINK ABOUT
{
- the description of Grendel's mother and her actions
- the details describing her lair
- Beowulf's motives and actions

4. Are Beowulf's words and deeds those of a traditional **epic hero?** Support your opinion with evidence from the poem.

5. Does the behavior of Grendel's mother seem as wicked or unreasonable as Grendel's behavior? Explain your answer.

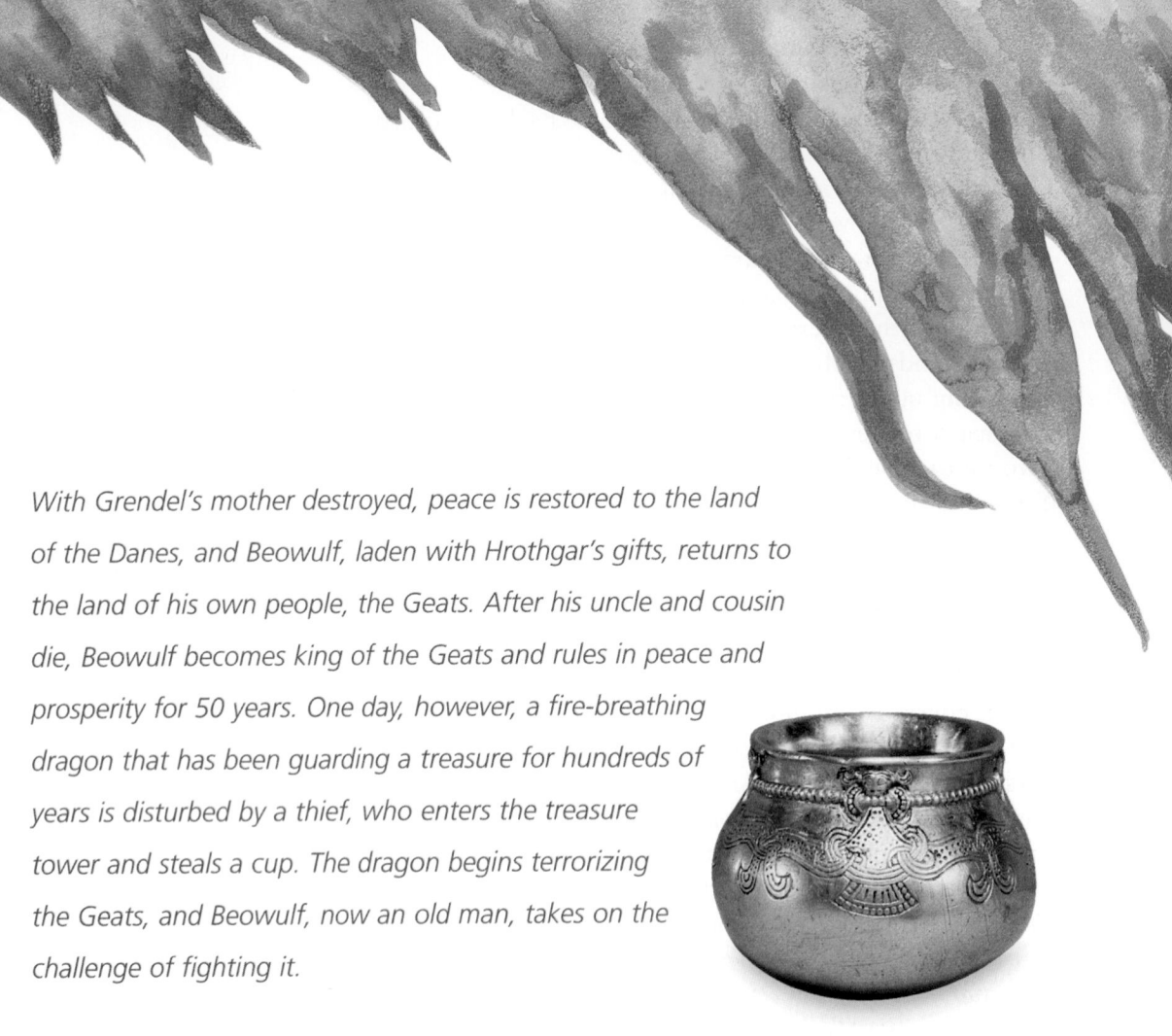

With Grendel's mother destroyed, peace is restored to the land of the Danes, and Beowulf, laden with Hrothgar's gifts, returns to the land of his own people, the Geats. After his uncle and cousin die, Beowulf becomes king of the Geats and rules in peace and prosperity for 50 years. One day, however, a fire-breathing dragon that has been guarding a treasure for hundreds of years is disturbed by a thief, who enters the treasure tower and steals a cup. The dragon begins terrorizing the Geats, and Beowulf, now an old man, takes on the challenge of fighting it.

Viking cup, silver and gilt

BEOWULF'S LAST BATTLE

And Beowulf uttered his final boast:
"I've never known fear, as a youth I fought
In endless battles. I am old, now,
But I will fight again, seek fame still,
610 If the dragon hiding in his tower dares
To face me."
           Then he said farewell to his followers,
Each in his turn, for the last time:
"I'd use no sword, no weapon, if this beast
Could be killed without it, crushed to death
615 Like Grendel, gripped in my hands and torn
Limb from limb. But his breath will be burning
Hot, poison will pour from his tongue.
I feel no shame, with shield and sword
And armor, against this monster: when he comes to me

620 I mean to stand, not run from his shooting
Flames, stand till fate decides
Which of us wins. My heart is firm,
My hands calm: I need no hot
Words. Wait for me close by, my friends.

625 We shall see, soon, who will survive
This bloody battle, stand when the fighting
Is done. No one else could do
What I mean to, here, no man but me
Could hope to defeat this monster. No one

630 Could try. And this dragon's treasure, his gold
And everything hidden in that tower, will be mine
Or war will sweep me to a bitter death!"
      Then Beowulf rose, still brave, still strong,
And with his shield at his side, and a mail shirt on his breast,

635 Strode calmly, confidently, toward the tower, under
The rocky cliffs: no coward could have walked there!
And then he who'd endured dozens of desperate
Battles, who'd stood boldly while swords and shields
Clashed, the best of kings, saw

640 Huge stone arches and felt the heat
Of the dragon's breath, flooding down
Through the hidden entrance, too hot for anyone
To stand, a streaming current of fire
And smoke that blocked all passage. And the Geats'

645 Lord and leader, angry, lowered
His sword and roared out a battle cry,
A call so loud and clear that it reached through
The hoary rock, hung in the dragon's
Ear. The beast rose, angry,

650 Knowing a man had come—and then nothing
But war could have followed. Its breath came first,
A steaming cloud pouring from the stone,
Then the earth itself shook. Beowulf
Swung his shield into place, held it

655 In front of him, facing the entrance. The dragon
Coiled and uncoiled, its heart urging it
Into battle. Beowulf's ancient sword
Was waiting, unsheathed, his sharp and gleaming
Blade. The beast came closer; both of them

660 Were ready, each set on slaughter. The Geats'
Great prince stood firm, unmoving, prepared

648 hoary (hôr′ē): gray with age.

Behind his high shield, waiting in his shining
Armor. The monster came quickly toward him,
Pouring out fire and smoke, hurrying
665 To its fate. Flames beat at the iron
Shield, and for a time it held, protected
Beowulf as he'd planned; then it began to melt,
And for the first time in his life that famous prince
Fought with fate against him, with glory
670 Denied him. He knew it, but he raised his sword
And struck at the dragon's scaly hide.
The ancient blade broke, bit into
The monster's skin, drew blood, but cracked
And failed him before it went deep enough, helped him
675 Less than he needed. The dragon leaped
With pain, thrashed and beat at him, spouting
Murderous flames, spreading them everywhere.
And the Geats' ring-giver did not boast of glorious
Victories in other wars: his weapon
680 Had failed him, deserted him, now when he needed it
Most, that excellent sword. Edgetho's
Famous son stared at death,
Unwilling to leave this world, to exchange it
For a dwelling in some distant place—a journey
685 Into darkness that all men must make, as death
Ends their few brief hours on earth.
        Quickly, the dragon came at him, encouraged
As Beowulf fell back; its breath flared,
And he suffered, wrapped around in swirling
690 Flames—a king, before, but now
A beaten warrior. None of his comrades
Came to him, helped him, his brave and noble
Followers; they ran for their lives, fled
Deep in a wood. And only one of them
695 Remained, stood there, miserable, remembering,
As a good man must, what kinship should mean.

        His name was Wiglaf, he was Wexstan's son
And a good soldier; his family had been Swedish,
Once. Watching Beowulf, he could see
700 How his king was suffering, burning. Remembering
Everything his lord and cousin had given him,
Armor and gold and the great estates
Wexstan's family enjoyed, Wiglaf's

670–671 Why do you think Beowulf keeps fighting?

678 ring-giver: king; lord. When a man swore allegiance to a Germanic lord in return for his protection, the lord typically bestowed a ring on his follower to symbolize the bond.

Mind was made up; he raised his yellow
705 Shield and drew his sword. . . .
        And Wiglaf, his heart heavy, uttered
The kind of words his comrades deserved:
        "I remember how we sat in the mead-hall, drinking
And boasting of how brave we'd be when Beowulf
710 Needed us, he who gave us these swords
And armor: all of us swore to repay him,
When the time came, kindness for kindness
—With our lives, if he needed them. He allowed us to join him,
Chose us from all his great army, thinking
715 Our boasting words had some weight, believing
Our promises, trusting our swords. He took us
For soldiers, for men. He meant to kill
This monster himself, our mighty king,
Fight this battle alone and unaided,
720 As in the days when his strength and daring dazzled
Men's eyes. But those days are over and gone
And now our lord must lean on younger
Arms. And we must go to him, while angry
Flames burn at his flesh, help
725 Our glorious king! By almighty God,
I'd rather burn myself than see
Flames swirling around my lord.
And who are we to carry home
Our shields before we've slain his enemy
730 And ours, to run back to our homes with Beowulf
So hard-pressed here? I swear that nothing
He ever did deserved an end
Like this, dying miserably and alone,
Butchered by this savage beast: we swore
735 That these swords and armor were each for us all!"

694–705 How is Wiglaf unlike Beowulf's other subjects?

717–723 What does Wiglaf suggest is the reason Beowulf has failed to defeat the dragon?

Wiglaf joins Beowulf, who again attacks the dragon single-handed; but the remnant of his sword shatters, and the monster wounds him in the neck. Wiglaf then strikes the dragon, and he and Beowulf together finally succeed in killing the beast. Their triumph is short-lived, however, because Beowulf's wound proves to be mortal.

THE DEATH OF BEOWULF

Beowulf spoke, in spite of the swollen,
<u>Livid</u> wound, knowing he'd unwound
His string of days on earth, seen
As much as God would grant him; all worldly
740 Pleasure was gone, as life would go,
Soon:

"I'd leave my armor to my son,
Now, if God had given me an heir,
A child born of my body, his life
Created from mine. I've worn this crown
745 For fifty winters: no neighboring people
Have tried to threaten the Geats, sent soldiers
Against us or talked of terror. My days
Have gone by as fate willed, waiting
For its word to be spoken, ruling as well
750 As I knew how, swearing no unholy oaths,
Seeking no lying wars. I can leave
This life happy; I can die, here,
Knowing the Lord of all life has never
Watched me wash my sword in blood
755 Born of my own family. Belovèd
Wiglaf, go, quickly, find
The dragon's treasure: we've taken its life,
But its gold is ours, too. Hurry,
Bring me ancient silver, precious
760 Jewels, shining armor and gems,
Before I die. Death will be softer,
Leaving life and this people I've ruled
So long, if I look at this last of all prizes."

737–738 What view of fate does the image of the unwinding string convey?

741–763 What values are reflected in Beowulf's speech?

Viking purse clip of gold, garnet, and glass, from Sutton Hoo ship burial

WORDS
TO
KNOW

livid (lĭv′ĭd) *adj.* discolored; black and blue

56

Gold buckle from Sutton Hoo
ship burial, showing animals,
snakes, and birds

Then Wexstan's son went in, as quickly
765 As he could, did as the dying Beowulf
Asked, entered the inner darkness
Of the tower, went with his mail shirt and his sword.
Flushed with victory he groped his way,
A brave young warrior, and suddenly saw
770 Piles of gleaming gold, precious
Gems, scattered on the floor, cups
And bracelets, rusty old helmets, beautifully
Made but rotting with no hands to rub
And polish them. They lay where the dragon left them;
775 It had flown in the darkness, once, before fighting
Its final battle. (So gold can easily
Triumph, defeat the strongest of men,
No matter how deep it is hidden!) And he saw,
Hanging high above, a golden
780 Banner, woven by the best of weavers
And beautiful. And over everything he saw
A strange light, shining everywhere,
On walls and floor and treasure. Nothing
Moved, no other monsters appeared;
785 He took what he wanted, all the treasures
That pleased his eye, heavy plates
And golden cups and the glorious banner,
Loaded his arms with all they could hold.
Beowulf's dagger, his iron blade,
790 Had finished the fire-spitting terror
That once protected tower and treasures
Alike; the gray-bearded lord of the Geats
Had ended those flying, burning raids
Forever.

Then Wiglaf went back, anxious
795 To return while Beowulf was alive, to bring him
Treasure they'd won together. He ran,
Hoping his wounded king, weak
And dying, had not left the world too soon.
Then he brought their treasure to Beowulf, and found
800 His famous king bloody, gasping
For breath. But Wiglaf sprinkled water
Over his lord, until the words
Deep in his breast broke through and were heard.
Beholding the treasure he spoke, haltingly:
805   "For this, this gold, these jewels, I thank
Our Father in Heaven, Ruler of the Earth—
For all of this, that His grace has given me,
Allowed me to bring to my people while breath
Still came to my lips. I sold my life
810 For this treasure, and I sold it well. Take
What I leave, Wiglaf, lead my people,
Help them; my time is gone. Have
The brave Geats build me a tomb,
When the funeral flames have burned me, and build it
815 Here, at the water's edge, high
On this spit of land, so sailors can see
This tower, and remember my name, and call it
Beowulf's tower, and boats in the darkness
And mist, crossing the sea, will know it."
820   Then that brave king gave the golden
Necklace from around his throat to Wiglaf,
Gave him his gold-covered helmet, and his rings,
And his mail shirt, and ordered him to use them well:
     "You're the last of all our far-flung family.
825 Fate has swept our race away,
Taken warriors in their strength and led them
To the death that was waiting. And now I follow them."
     The old man's mouth was silent, spoke
No more, had said as much as it could;
830 He would sleep in the fire, soon. His soul
Left his flesh, flew to glory. . . .
     And when the battle was over Beowulf's followers
Came out of the wood, cowards and traitors,
Knowing the dragon was dead. Afraid,
835 While it spit its fires, to fight in their lord's

816 spit: a narrow point of land extending into a body of water.

805–819 How will Beowulf continue to aid his people after his death?

833 In what sense are Beowulf's followers traitors? Whom or what have they betrayed?

Defense, to throw their javelins and spears,
They came like shamefaced jackals, their shields
In their hands, to the place where the prince lay dead,
And waited for Wiglaf to speak. He was sitting
840 Near Beowulf's body, wearily sprinkling
Water in the dead man's face, trying
To stir him. He could not. No one could have kept
Life in their lord's body, or turned
Aside the Lord's will: world
845 And men and all move as He orders,
And always have, and always will.
        Then Wiglaf turned and angrily told them
What men without courage must hear.
Wexstan's brave son stared at the traitors,
850 His heart sorrowful, and said what he had to:
        "I say what anyone who speaks the truth
Must say. . . .
Too few of his warriors remembered
To come, when our lord faced death, alone.
855 And now the giving of swords, of golden
Rings and rich estates, is over,
Ended for you and everyone who shares
Your blood: when the brave Geats hear
How you bolted and ran none of your race
860 Will have anything left but their lives. And death
Would be better for them all, and for you, than the kind
Of life you can lead, branded with disgrace!". . .
        Then the warriors rose,
Walked slowly down from the cliff, stared
865 At those wonderful sights, stood weeping as they saw
Beowulf dead on the sand, their bold
Ring-giver resting in his last bed;
He'd reached the end of his days, their mighty
War-king, the great lord of the Geats,
870 Gone to a glorious death. . . .

836 javelins (jăv'lĭnz): light spears used as weapons.

837 jackals (jăk'əlz): doglike animals that sometimes feed on the flesh of dead beasts.

859 bolted: ran away; fled.

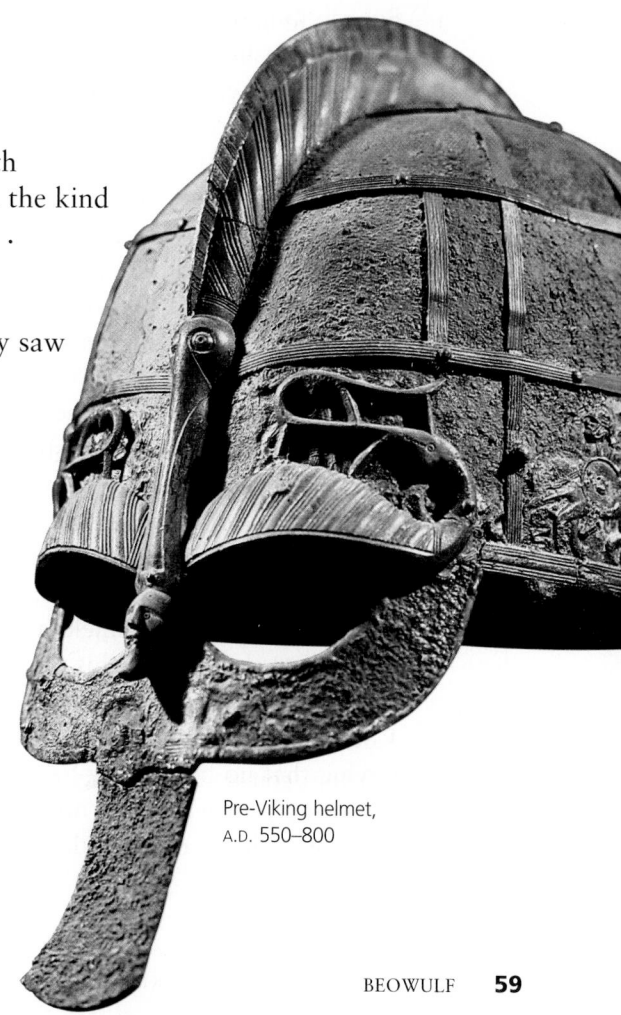

Pre-Viking helmet,
A.D. 550–800

MOURNING BEOWULF

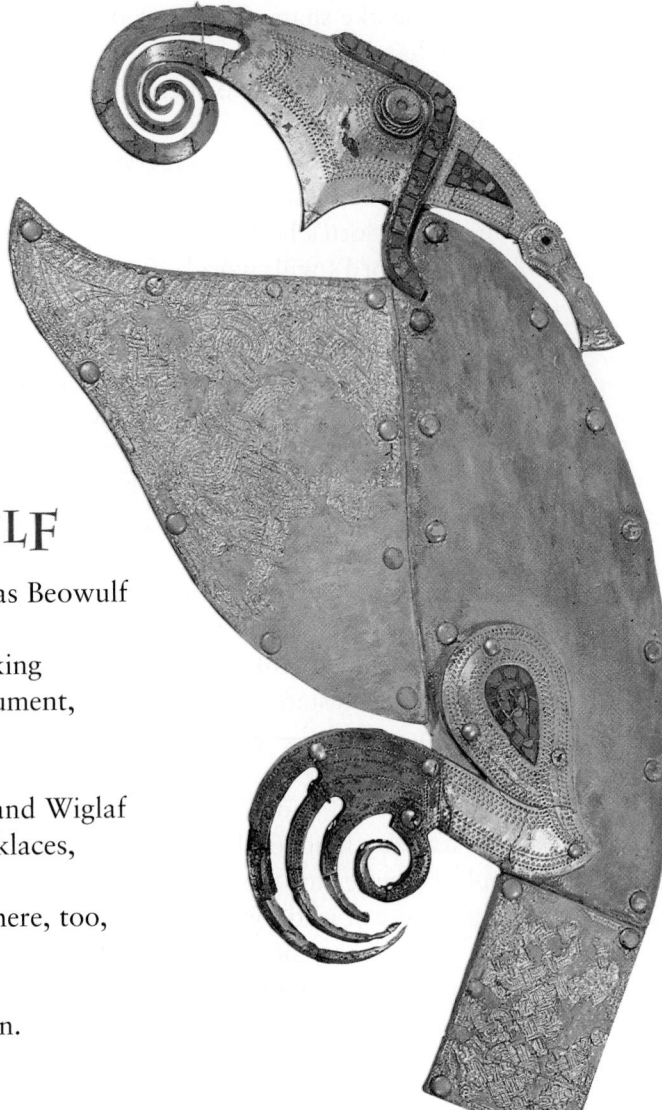

Then the Geats built the tower, as Beowulf
Had asked, strong and tall, so sailors
Could find it from far and wide; working
For ten long days they made his monument,
875 Sealed his ashes in walls as straight
And high as wise and willing hands
Could raise them. And the riches he and Wiglaf
Had won from the dragon, rings, necklaces,
Ancient, hammered armor—all
880 The treasures they'd taken were left there, too,
Silver and jewels buried in the sandy
Ground, back in the earth, again
And forever hidden and useless to men.
And then twelve of the bravest Geats
885 Rode their horses around the tower,
Telling their sorrow, telling stories
Of their dead king and his greatness, his glory,
Praising him for heroic deeds, for a life
As noble as his name. So should all men
890 Raise up words for their lords, warm
With love, when their shield and protector leaves
His body behind, sends his soul
On high. And so Beowulf's followers
Rode, mourning their belovéd leader,
895 Crying that no better king had ever
Lived, no prince so mild, no man
So open to his people, so deserving of praise.

Ornamental bird used as
decoration on a shield, from
the Sutton Hoo ship burial

896 mild: gentle or kindly. Do you
agree that Beowulf was a mild
ruler? Why or why not?

A COLLABORATION ACROSS 1,200 YEARS

Review by D. J. R. Bruckner

A Modern Scop *Listening to the story of Beowulf sung by a scop playing a harp is no longer an experience confined to the past. American musician and medieval scholar Benjamin Bagby has begun performing Beowulf in the original Anglo-Saxon to enthusiastic audiences. Bagby likens Beowulf to a "campfire ghost story" and compares his performances to rap and jazz, both of which involve improvisation and spontaneity. The following review, written in 1997, captures the excitement of Bagby's Beowulf.*

European noblemen of a thousand years ago had much more exciting and intelligent entertainment than anything to be found now. Anyone who doubts that need only look in on Benjamin Bagby's astonishing performance of the first quarter of the epic poem *Beowulf*—in Anglo-Saxon, no less—tonight at the Stanley H. Kaplan Penthouse at Lincoln Center. It will be the last of his three appearances in the Lincoln Center Festival.

From the moment he strode on stage on Sunday for the opening night, silencing the audience with that famous first word, "Hwaet!" ("Pay attention!"), until hell swallowed the "pagan soul" of the monster's maw, there were bursts of laughter, mutters and sighs, and when Mr. Bagby's voice stopped at the end, as abruptly as it had begun, there

was an audible rippling gasp before a thunderclap of applause from cheering people who called him back again and again, unwilling to let him go.

Mr. Bagby—a Midwesterner who fell in love with *Beowulf* at 12 and who now is co-director of a medieval music ensemble, Sequentia, in Cologne, Germany—accompanies himself on a six-string lyre modeled on one found in a seventh-century tomb near Stuttgart. This surprisingly facile instrument underscores the meter of the epic verses and is counterpoint to Mr. Bagby's voice as he recites, chants and occasionally sings the lines.

On the whole, this is a restrained presentation. The performer captures listeners at once simply by letting us feel his conviction that he has a tale to tell that is more captivating than

any other story in the world. He avoids histrionic gestures, letting the majestic rhythms of the epic seize our emotions and guide them through the action. Gradually the many voices that fill the great poem emerge and the listener always knows who is speaking: a warrior, a watchman, a king, a sarcastic drunk. A translation is handed out to the audience, but after a while one notices people are following it less and just letting the sound of this strange and beautiful language wash over them. Perhaps not so strange, after all—enough phrases begin to penetrate the understanding that one finally knows deep down that, yes, this is where English came from.

How authentic is all this? Well, we know from many historical sources that in the first millennium at royal or noble houses a performer called a scop would present epics. Mr. Bagby has lived with this epic for many years, as well as with ancient music, and his performance is his argument that *Beowulf* was meant to be heard, not read, and that this is the way we ought to hear it. It is a powerful argument, indeed. The test of it is that when he has finished, you leave with the overwhelming impression that you know the anonymous poet who created *Beowulf* more than a dozen centuries ago, that you have felt the man's personality touch you. That is a much too rare experience in theater.

Thinking through the LITERATURE

Connect to the Literature

1. What Do You Think?
How do you think you would have reacted to Beowulf's death if you had been one of his subjects?

Comprehension Check
- Who is the only person to help Beowulf battle the dragon?
- What happens to Beowulf as a result of the battle?
- What happens to the dragon and its treasure?

Think Critically

2. How would you describe Wiglaf's **character traits?**

3. Beowulf is able to defeat evil in the form of Grendel and Grendel's mother, yet he loses his life. What **theme** does this suggest about the struggle between good and evil?

4. In your opinion, what view of youth and old age does *Beowulf* convey? In answering, consider not only the details in the last part of the poem but also the earlier portrayals of Beowulf and Hrothgar.

5. On the basis of your reading of *Beowulf*, what qualities or values do you think the Anglo-Saxons admired?

THINK ABOUT
- Beowulf's reputation, position, and wealth
- Beowulf's behavior before and during his battles
- the behavior of other characters

6. **ACTIVE READING** **MAKING JUDGMENTS** According to the evidence that you recorded in the chart in your **READER'S NOTEBOOK**, how well does *Beowulf* conform to the characteristics of a typical **epic?**

Extend Interpretations

7. Critic's Corner In his famous essay "Beowulf: The Monsters and the Critics," the author and scholar J.R.R. Tolkien wrote, "*Beowulf* is in fact so interesting as poetry, in places so powerful, that this quite overshadows the historical content, and is largely independent even of the most important facts . . . that research has discovered." Do you think Burton Raffel's verse translation captures that poetic power, or do you think this selection's greatest value is in its depiction of early Germanic tribal life? Explain your opinion.

8. Connect to Life In today's society we have our own kinds of "monsters" that threaten our safety or way of life. Who or what are today's monsters, and what threats do they pose?

Literary Analysis

ALLITERATION Old English poetry is often called alliterative verse because of the poets' extensive use of **alliteration**—the repetition of consonant sounds at the beginning of words. In modern poetry, alliteration may be used to emphasize certain words or images, heighten moods, or create musical effects. In Old English poetry, it was an integral part of the structure of the verse itself, like rhyme in much later European poetry.

Even if you can't understand these Old English lines from *Beowulf*, you can tell that the repeated sound is *w* in the first line, *g* in the second, and *f* in the third:

> *Wod under wolcnum   to þæs he winreced,*
> *goldsele gumena,   gearwost wisse,*
> *fættum fahne. . . .*

In translating *Beowulf*, Burton Raffel could not reproduce the original alliteration, but he did use alliteration whenever possible. In this translation of the Old English lines above, notice how Raffel uses repeated *k* and *s* sounds to reinforce the image of Grendel's movement:

> *He moved quickly through the cloudy night,*
> *Up from his swampland, sliding silently*
> *Toward that gold-shining hall. . . .*

Paired Activity Work with a partner to identify more examples of alliteration in Raffel's translation of *Beowulf*. Then explain what image, mood, or idea the alliteration helps to emphasize in each case.

Writing Options

1. A Warrior's Letter Imagine that you are one of Hrothgar's warriors. Write a letter to a comrade, in which you describe Grendel, his nightly visits, and your fears about what might happen.

2. Director's Notes Imagine that you are a movie director about to shoot scenes involving the three monsters that Beowulf fights: Grendel, his mother, and the fire-breathing dragon. To help you direct the scenes, make notes about each monster's motives, actions, strengths, and weaknesses and about the outcome of the monster's battle with Beowulf.

3. Anglo-Saxon News Story Write a news story describing one of Beowulf's three battles. Include details from the selection and statements from imaginary witnesses to the event.

4. Comparison Essay In an essay, compare and contrast Beowulf with a hero from popular culture, such as Indiana Jones, Batman, or Luke Skywalker. What makes each character heroic? You might organize your ideas in a Venn diagram like the one shown here. Place the essay in your **Working Portfolio**.

Writing Handbook
See page 1367: Compare and Contrast.

Activities & Explorations

1. Cartoon Hero Choose one of Beowulf's three battles and turn it into a comic strip in which the action is largely or entirely conveyed by means of the illustrations that you draw. (If you prefer, you can use a pad of paper to create a flipbook version of the battle, so that the characters will appear to move.) ~ **ART**

2. Beowulf Aloud Divide up the selection with a small group of classmates so that each of you is responsible for a different portion. Then, imagining that you are scops of old, present *Beowulf* in a series of oral recitations, in which the reciter or another member of the group strums a harp, a guitar, or another stringed instrument as musical accompaniment. ~ **SPEAKING AND LISTENING**

3. A Video Scop View the video of a storyteller telling the legendary tale of Beowulf's battle with the monster Grendel. What did you like most about this interpretation? Least? How did it affect your understanding of the character of Beowulf? Choose a passage from the epic and develop your own storytelling version of it. ~ **VIEWING AND REPRESENTING**

 VIDEO Literature in Performance

Inquiry & Research

1. Religious Beliefs Find out more about the religious beliefs of the Germanic peoples in Beowulf's day and of the Anglo-Saxons after they adopted Christianity. Who were the pre-Christian Germanic gods? What role did fate play in pre-Christian Germanic beliefs? When were the various Germanic peoples converted to Christianity? What role did Christianity play in the Anglo-Saxons' daily life? Present your findings in a written report.

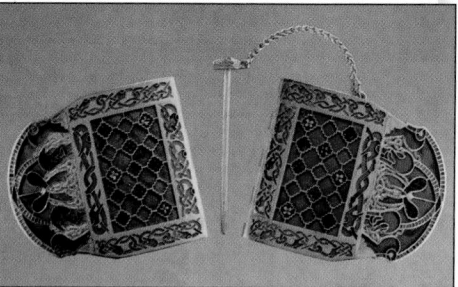
Shoulder clasps from the Sutton Hoo burial

2. Sutton Who? Investigate the discovery of the ship burial at Sutton Hoo in Suffolk, England. Who was buried there, and when was he most likely buried? Why was he buried in a ship? What have the artifacts found at the site revealed about Anglo-Saxon culture? Share your research with the rest of the class.

More Online: Research Starter
www.mcdougallittell.com

Vocabulary in Action

EXERCISE A: CONTEXT CLUES On your paper, write the vocabulary word that best completes each sentence.

1. With each razor-sharp _____, Grendel tore his victim's flesh.
2. Grendel loved evil and seemed to _____ his nightly visits to Herot.
3. After the battle, Grendel was left _____ in agony on the floor.
4. The Danes rejoiced when Beowulf was finally able to _____ Herot of Grendel.
5. Grendel and his mother lived in the _____ depths of a dark lake.
6. Many people went on the _____ to see the lake where Grendel had died.
7. Beowulf was not one of the warriors _____ in fear of the monsters.

EXERCISE B: WORD MEANING On your paper, write *T* for each true statement and *F* for each false statement.

1. Grendel's visits were an **affliction** for the Danish people.
2. Grendel liked to **gorge** on Danish people, not pastry.
3. During their battle, Grendel tore flesh out of Beowulf's **taut** throat.
4. Grendel lost his claw because Beowulf locked it in tight **fetters**.
5. Grendel's mother was another **loathsome** monster.
6. Beowulf's fight with the dragon left him with a swollen, **livid** wound that would prove fatal.
7. To the Geats, Beowulf was an **infamous** king.
8. Not one **lament** was sung at Beowulf's funeral.

WORDS TO KNOW				
affliction	gorge	livid	pilgrimage	talon
cowering	infamous	loathsome	purge	taut
fetter	lament	murky	relish	writhing

Building Vocabulary
For an in-depth study of context clues, see page 938.

The Beowulf Poet
About 750?

An Anonymous Author Nothing is known about the author of *Beowulf* except what can be inferred from the poem itself. Clearly the author was an educated person familiar with Christianity and the Bible; details in the poem also suggest that he knew something of ancient epics, such as Virgil's *Aeneid*. From their study of the poem's language and ideas, some scholars have concluded that the poet lived in northern England in the eighth century A.D. Others, however, dispute that conclusion, maintaining that he probably lived in southwestern England two centuries later. Whenever he lived, he drew on an oral tradition of poems celebrating the hero Beowulf.

A Famous Manuscript Only one copy of *Beowulf* has survived from Anglo-Saxon times. Dating from about the year 1000, it is the work of Christian monks who preserved the literature of the past by copying manuscripts. After escaping destruction several times, the *Beowulf* manuscript is now safely housed in the British Library in London.

The Electronic Beowulf Today, the most up-to-date technology is being used to preserve the fragile manuscript. The Electronic Beowulf Project is creating detailed digital images of every page so that scholars can study them on computers, without handling the actual manuscript.

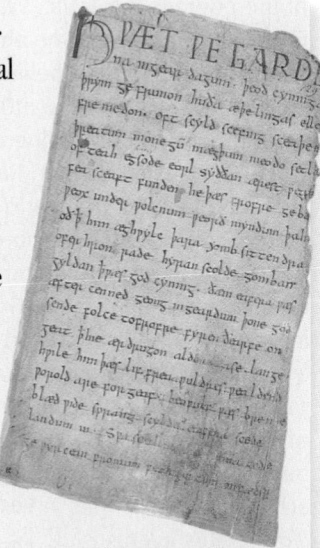

First page of the Beowulf manuscript, showing fire damage

from the Iliad

Epic Poetry by HOMER
Translated by ROBERT FITZGERALD

Comparing Literature of the World

The Epic Hero Across Cultures

Comparing *Beowulf* and the *Iliad* The *Iliad* was written centuries before *Beowulf.* Nonetheless, there are many similarities between the two poems.

Points of Comparison

As you read the following excerpt from the *Iliad,* compare the heroes Hector and Achilles with Beowulf. Consider the following characteristics of an epic hero as you make your comparisons:
- heroic actions that determine the fate of nations or groups of people
- heroic deeds and actions that reflect the values of the age
- the hero's interaction with supernatural beings and events

Yugoslavia
Bulgaria
Macedonia
Albania
Greece
Turkey
Ionian Sea

Build Background

When Greeks and Trojans War The *Iliad* is an epic poem believed to be the work of a Greek poet named Homer in the eighth century B.C. The setting of the poem is the Trojan War, a conflict between Greeks and Trojans at the ancient city of Troy in Asia Minor. Most historians believe that some type of conflict involving Greeks and Trojans did in fact occur around 1200 B.C. According to Homer's poem, the Trojan War resulted when Paris, a prince of Troy, kidnapped Helen, the world's most beautiful woman, from her Greek home. This action naturally offended her husband, King Menelaus (mĕn'ə-lā'əs), who gathered an army of Greeks and set out to invade Troy and bring Helen home. Under the leadership of his brother Agamemnon (ăg'ə-mĕm'nŏn'), the Greeks laid siege to the walled city of Troy for ten years before finally achieving victory. The *Iliad* relates events that took place in the final year of that siege. The excerpts in the following selection show the grim results of clashing loyalties.

WORDS TO KNOW
Vocabulary Preview

abstain	flouting
clamor	havoc
defile	ponderous
destitute	quell
elude	scourge
evade	vulnerable
evocation	whetted
exult	

Focus Your Reading

LITERARY ANALYSIS SIMILE AND EPIC SIMILE

A simile is a figure of speech that uses *like* or *as* to make a comparison between two things. For example, when the poet says, "Now like a lion at one bound Achilles left the room," he uses a simile to compare the Greek warrior to a lion in his speed and strength. An **epic simile** is a long figurative comparison in an epic poem that often continues for a number of lines. An example can be found in lines 89–92 of the *Iliad.* As you read this selection from the *Iliad,* look for other examples of similes and epic similes.

ACTIVE READING CLASSIFYING CHARACTERS

The *Iliad* is a complex story involving many characters—both human and divine. In order to understand what is happening in the epic, it is important to keep track of these various characters.

READER'S NOTEBOOK Create a list of the following characters: Achilles, Hector, Thetis, Zeus, Patroclus, Pallas Athena, Apollo, Hermes, and Priam. As you read, use the notes that accompany the text to help you classify each character as a Greek, a Trojan, or a god. For each god, indicate whether he or she is helping the Greeks or the Trojans. Jot down the important actions and characteristics of each character.

from THE ILIAD

HOMER

While the Greeks are laying siege to Troy, a quarrel breaks out between Agamemnon and his greatest warrior Achilles (ə-kĭl'ēz). As a result, the angry Achilles decides to remain in his tent and let the Greeks fight without him. With Achilles off the battlefield, the Trojans, under the leadership of Hector, are able to drive the Greeks back to the sea. During the battle, Hector kills Achilles' best friend, Patroclus (pə-trō'kləs). While grieving for his friend, Achilles is visited by his mother, Thetis (thē'tĭs), a goddess of the sea.

Death of Hector, sixth-century B.C. Corinthian bowl painting

from Book 18
THE IMMORTAL SHIELD

Bending near
her groaning son, the gentle goddess wailed
and took his head between her hands in pity,
saying softly:

"Child, why are you weeping?
5   What great sorrow came to you? Speak out,

do not conceal it. Zeus
did all you asked: Achaean troops,
for want of you, were all forced back again
upon the ship sterns, taking heavy losses
10 none of them could wish."

                                    The great runner
groaned and answered:

                                        "Mother, yes, the master
of high Olympus brought it all about,
but how have I benefited? My greatest friend
is gone: Patroclus, comrade in arms, whom I
15 held dear above all others—dear as myself—
now gone, lost; Hector cut him down, despoiled him
of my own arms, massive and fine, a wonder
in all men's eyes. The gods gave them to Peleus
that day they put you in a mortal's bed—
20 how I wish the immortals of the sea
had been your only consorts! How I wish
Peleus had taken a mortal queen! Sorrow
immeasurable is in store for you as well,
when your own child is lost: never again
25 on his homecoming day will you embrace him!
I must reject this life, my heart tells me,
reject the world of men,
if Hector does not feel my battering spear
tear the life out of him, making him pay
30 in his own blood for the slaughter of Patroclus!"

Letting a tear fall, Thetis said:

                                        "You'll be
swift to meet your end, child, as you say:
your doom comes close on the heels of Hector's own."

Achilles the great runner ground his teeth
35 and said:

                                        "May it come quickly. As things were,
I could not help my friend in his extremity.
Far from his home he died; he needed me
to shield him or to parry the death stroke.
For me there's no return to my own country.

6–7 Previously Achilles asked Thetis to persuade Zeus (zōōs), ruler of the gods, to turn the tide of battle against the Greeks so that they would see how much they needed him.

7 Achaean (ə-kē′ən): Greek.

12 Olympus (ə-lĭm′pəs): the highest mountain in Greece, on whose peak the Greek gods and goddesses were thought to dwell.

16–17 Patroclus wore Achilles' armor to frighten the Trojans. "Despoiled him of my own arms" refers to Hector's taking the armor from Patroclus' corpse.

18 Peleus (pē′lē-əs): Achilles' human father.

38 parry: to turn aside the thrust of a sword.

40　Not the slightest gleam of hope did I
　　afford Patroclus or the other men
　　whom Hector overpowered. Here I sat,
　　my weight a useless burden to the earth,
　　and I am one who has no peer in war
45　among Achaean captains—

　　　　　　　　　　　　　　　　　though in council
　　there are wiser. Ai! let strife and rancor
　　perish from the lives of gods and men,
　　with anger that envenoms even the wise
　　and is far sweeter than slow-dripping honey,
50　clouding the hearts of men like smoke: just so
　　the marshal of the army, Agamemnon,
　　moved me to anger. But we'll let that go,
　　though I'm still sore at heart; it is all past,
　　and I have <u>quelled</u> my passion as I must.

55　Now I must go to look for the destroyer
　　of my great friend. I shall confront the dark
　　drear spirit of death at any hour Zeus
　　and the other gods may wish to make an end.
　　Not even Heracles escaped that terror
60　though cherished by the Lord Zeus. Destiny
　　and Hera's bitter anger mastered him.
　　Likewise with me, if destiny like his
　　awaits me, I shall rest when I have fallen!
　　Now, though, may I win my perfect glory
65　and make some wife of Troy break down,
　　or some deep-breasted Dardan woman sob
　　and wipe tears from her soft cheeks. They'll know then
　　how long they had been spared the deaths of men,
　　while I <u>abstained</u> from war!
70　Do not attempt to keep me from the fight,
　　though you love me; you cannot make me listen."

46 rancor (răng′kər): bitter, long-lasting ill will.

48 envenoms (ĕn-vĕn′əmz): fills with poison.

59–61 Heracles (hĕr′ə-klēz′): the greatest legendary hero of ancient Greece, son of Zeus and a mortal woman named Alcmena (ălk-mē′nə). Zeus' wife, the goddess Hera (hîr′ə), hated and persecuted Heracles until his death.

62–63 How has Achilles' loyalty to Patroclus affected his attitude toward his own life?

66 Dardan (där′dn): Trojan.

Achilles seeks to avenge Patroclus by slaughtering Trojans. Apollo, a god who protects Troy, opens the gates of the city so that the Trojans can rush to safety inside the walls. Only Hector is left outside. Achilles chases him around the walls of Troy three times. Finally the goddess Pallas Athena (păl′əs ə-thē′nə), **disguised as Hector's brother Deiphobus** (dē-ĭf′ə-bəs), **appears to Hector and persuades him to fight Achilles**.

WORDS
TO
KNOW
quell (kwĕl) *v.* to quiet; suppress
abstain (ăb-stān′) *v.* to hold oneself back deliberately

from Book 22

DESOLATION BEFORE TROY

And when at last the two men faced each other,
Hector was the first to speak. He said:

"I will no longer fear you as before,
75 son of Peleus, though I ran from you
round Priam's town three times and could not face you.
Now my soul would have me stand and fight,
whether I kill you or am killed. So come,
we'll summon gods here as our witnesses,
80 none higher, arbiters of a pact: I swear
that, terrible as you are,
I'll not insult your corpse should Zeus allow me
victory in the end, your life as prize.
Once I have your gear, I'll give your body
85 back to Achaeans. Grant me, too, this grace."

But swift Achilles frowned at him and said:

"Hector, I'll have no talk of pacts with you,
forever unforgiven as you are.
As between men and lions there are none,
90 no concord between wolves and sheep, but all
hold one another hateful through and through,
so there can be no courtesy between us,
no sworn truce, till one of us is down
and glutting with his blood the wargod Ares.
95 Summon up what skills you have. By god,
you'd better be a spearman and a fighter!
Now there is no way out. Pallas Athena
will have the upper hand of you. The weapon
belongs to me. You'll pay the reckoning
100 in full for all the pain my men have borne,
who met death by your spear."

He twirled and cast
his shaft with its long shadow. Splendid Hector,
keeping his eye upon the point, <u>eluded</u> it
by ducking at the instant of the cast,

76 Priam (prī′əm): the king of Troy.

80 arbiters (är′bĭ-tərz): judges; referees.

84–85 The Greeks and Trojans generally returned the bodies of the slain to their commanders or companions.

90 concord (kŏn′kôrd′): peace or harmony.

94 glutting with his blood the wargod Ares (âr′ēz): satisfying Ares, the god of war, by bleeding to death.

97–98 Pallas Athena, the goddess of wisdom, favors the Greeks.

WORDS
TO   **elude** (ĭ-lōōd′) *v.* to avoid or escape
KNOW

70

105　so shaft and bronze shank passed him overhead
　　and punched into the earth. But unperceived
　　by Hector, Pallas Athena plucked it out
　　and gave it back to Achilles. Hector said:

　　"A clean miss. Godlike as you are,
110　you have not yet known doom for me from Zeus.
　　You thought you had, by heaven. Then you turned
　　into a word-thrower, hoping to make me lose
　　my fighting heart and head in fear of you.
　　You cannot plant your spear between my shoulders
115　while I am running. If you have the gift,
　　just put it through my chest as I come forward.
　　Now it's for you to dodge my own. Would god
　　you'd give the whole shaft lodging in your body!
　　War for the Trojans would be eased
120　if you were blotted out, bane that you are."

　　With this he twirled his long spearshaft and cast it,
　　hitting his enemy mid-shield, but off
　　and away the spear rebounded. Furious
　　that he had lost it, made his throw for nothing,
125　Hector stood bemused. He had no other.
　　Then he gave a great shout to Deiphobus
　　to ask for a long spear. But there was no one
　　near him, not a soul. Now in his heart
　　the Trojan realized the truth and said:

130　"This is the end. The gods are calling deathward.
　　I had thought
　　a good soldier, Deiphobus, was with me.
　　He is inside the walls. Athena tricked me.
　　Death is near, and black, not at a distance,
135　not to be <u>evaded</u>. Long ago
　　this hour must have been to Zeus's liking
　　and to the liking of his archer son.
　　They have been well disposed before, but now
　　the appointed time's upon me. Still, I would not
140　die without delivering a stroke,
　　or die ingloriously, but in some action
　　memorable to men in days to come."

Achilles dragging the body of Hector around the walls of Troy (about 520 B.C.), attributed to the Antiope Group. Attic black figure hydria, courtesy of the Museum of Fine Arts, Boston, William Francis Warden Fund.

120 bane: a cause of distress, death, or ruin.
125 bemused (bĭ-myōōzd′): dazed; confused.

135–139 Zeus' "archer son" is Apollo, god of the sun, whose arrows may represent the sun's rays. Until now, Zeus and Apollo have assisted the Trojans.

With this he drew the whetted blade that hung
upon his left flank, ponderous and long,
145 collecting all his might the way an eagle
narrows himself to dive through shady cloud
and strike a lamb or cowering hare: so Hector
lanced ahead and swung his whetted blade.
Achilles with wild fury in his heart
150 pulled in upon his chest his beautiful shield—
his helmet with four burnished metal ridges
nodding above it, and the golden crest
Hephaestus locked there tossing in the wind.
Conspicuous as the evening star that comes,
155 amid the first in heaven, at fall of night,
and stands most lovely in the west, so shone
in sunlight the fine-pointed spear
Achilles poised in his right hand, with deadly
aim at Hector, at the skin where most
160 it lay exposed. But nearly all was covered
by the bronze gear he took from slain Patroclus,
showing only, where his collarbones
divided neck and shoulders, the bare throat
where the destruction of a life is quickest.
165 Here, then, as the Trojan charged, Achilles
drove his point straight through the tender neck,
but did not cut the windpipe, leaving Hector
able to speak and to respond. He fell
aside into the dust. And Prince Achilles
170 now exulted:

                "Hector, had you thought
that you could kill Patroclus and be safe?
Nothing to dread from me; I was not there.
All childishness. Though distant then, Patroclus'
comrade in arms was greater far than he—
175 and it is I who had been left behind
that day beside the deepsea ships who now
have made your knees give way. The dogs and kites
will rip your body. His will lie in honor
when the Achaeans give him funeral."

180 Hector, barely whispering, replied:

153 Hephaestus (hĭ-fĕs'təs): the god of fire and blacksmith of the gods, who made Achilles' new armor.

160–161 Hector is wearing the armor of Achilles that he took from Patroclus' body.

177 kites: hawklike birds of prey.
178 "His [body]" refers to that of Patroclus.

WORDS   **whetted** (hwĕt'ĭd) *adj.* sharpened **whet** *v.*
TO   **ponderous** (pŏn'dər-əs) *adj.* very heavy
KNOW   **exult** (ĭg-zŭlt') *v.* to feel great joy, especially in conquest or triumph

"I beg you by your soul and by your parents,
do not let the dogs feed on me
in your encampment by the ships. Accept
the bronze and gold my father will provide
185 as gifts, my father and her ladyship
my mother. Let them have my body back,
so that our men and women may accord me
decency of fire when I am dead."

Achilles the great runner scowled and said:

190 "Beg me no beggary by soul or parents,
whining dog! Would god my passion drove me
to slaughter you and eat you raw, you've caused
such agony to me! No man exists
who could defend you from the carrion pack—
195 not if they spread for me ten times your ransom,
twenty times, and promise more as well;
aye, not if Priam, son of Dardanus,
tells them to buy you for your weight in gold!
You'll have no bed of death, nor will you be
200 laid out and mourned by her who gave you birth.
Dogs and birds will have you, every scrap."

Then at the point of death Lord Hector said:

"I see you now for what you are. No chance
to win you over. Iron in your breast
205 your heart is. Think a bit, though: this may be
a thing the gods in anger hold against you
on that day when Paris and Apollo
destroy you at the Gates, great as you are."

Even as he spoke, the end came, and death hid him;
210 spirit from body fluttered to undergloom,
bewailing fate that made him leave his youth
and manhood in the world. And as he died
Achilles spoke again. He said:

"Die, make an end. I shall accept my own
215 whenever Zeus and the other gods desire."

At this he pulled his spearhead from the body,
laying it aside, and stripped

185–186 Hector's father is Priam, and his mother is Hecuba (hĕk′yə-bə).

188 Burning the bodies of the dead was customary. Truces were often arranged for this purpose.

194 carrion (kăr′ē-ən) **pack:** the wild animals that feed on dead flesh.

197 Dardanus (där′dn-əs): the founder of the line of Trojan kings. Here "son" means "descendant."

205–208 Although Achilles is still alive as the *Iliad* ends, other tales of the Trojan War tell how he is eventually killed by Hector's brother Paris, with the aid of Apollo.

Replica of Trojan Horse

the bloodstained shield and cuirass from his shoulders.
Other Achaeans hastened round to see

220 Hector's fine body and his comely face,
and no one came who did not stab the body.
Glancing at one another they would say:

"Now Hector has turned <u>vulnerable</u>, softer
than when he put the torches to the ships!"

225 And he who said this would inflict a wound.
When the great master of pursuit, Achilles,
had the body stripped, he stood among them,
saying swiftly:

"Friends, my lords and captains
of Argives, now that the gods at last have let me

230 bring to earth this man who wrought
<u>havoc</u> among us—more than all the rest—
come, we'll offer battle around the city,
to learn the intentions of the Trojans now.
Will they give up their strongpoint at this loss?

235 Can they fight on, though Hector's dead?

But wait:
why do I ponder, why take up these questions?
Down by the ships Patroclus' body lies
unwept, unburied. I shall not forget him
while I can keep my feet among the living.

240 If in the dead world they forget the dead,
I say there, too, I shall remember him,
my friend. Men of Achaea, lift a song!
Down to the ships we go, and take this body,
our glory. We have beaten Hector down,

245 to whom as to a god the Trojans prayed."

Indeed, he had in mind for Hector's body
outrage and shame. Behind both feet he pierced
the tendons, heel to ankle. Rawhide cords
he drew through both and lashed them to his chariot,

250 letting the man's head trail. Stepping aboard,
bearing the great trophy of the arms,
he shook the reins, and whipped the team ahead

218 cuirass (kwĭ-răs′): an armored breastplate.

224 Hector's torching of the ships occurred when the Trojans forced the Greeks (fighting without Achilles) back to the sea.

228–229 captains of Argives (är′jīvz′): Greek officers.

240 The "dead world" is the house of Hades, or the underworld, where the Greeks believed the shades of the dead to reside.

WORDS
TO
KNOW

vulnerable (vŭl′nər-ə-bəl) *adj.* open to attack; easily hurt
havoc (hăv′ək) *n.* widespread destruction

74

into a willing run. A dustcloud rose
above the furrowing body; the dark tresses
255 flowed behind, and the head so princely once
lay back in dust. Zeus gave him to his enemies
to be <u>defiled</u> in his own fatherland.
So his whole head was blackened. Looking down,
his mother tore her braids, threw off her veil,
260 and wailed, heartbroken to behold her son.
Piteously his father groaned, and round him
lamentation spread throughout the town,
most like the <u>clamor</u> to be heard if Ilion's
towers, top to bottom, seethed in flames.
265 They barely stayed the old man, mad with grief,
from passing through the gates. Then in the mire
he rolled, and begged them all, each man by name:

"Relent, friends. It is hard; but let me go
out of the city to the Achaean ships.
270 I'll make my plea to that demonic heart.
He may feel shame before his peers, or pity
my old age. His father, too, is old.
Peleus, who brought him up to be a <u>scourge</u>
to Trojans, cruel to all, but most to me,
275 so many of my sons in flower of youth
he cut away. And, though I grieve, I cannot
mourn them all as much as I do one,
for whom my grief will take me to the grave—
and that is Hector. Why could he not have died
280 where I might hold him? In our weeping, then,
his mother, now so <u>destitute</u>, and I
might have had surfeit and relief of tears."

263 Ilion (ĭl′ē-ən): another name for Troy.

268–270 Think about Priam's decision to approach Achilles. What does this reveal about his sense of honor and loyalty?

282 surfeit (sûr′fĭt): more than enough for satisfaction.

Achilles and his warriors return to their camp and carry out the burial rites for Patroclus. Three times, Achilles drags Hector's body behind his chariot around Patroclus' grave. Afterwards, the gods cleanse and restore the body, and Zeus asks Thetis to tell Achilles to return the body to the Trojans. Priam sets out for the Greek camp, accompanied only by an old servant, to ask Achilles to return the body. He is not aware that the god Hermes (hûr′mēz) **helps him by putting the sentries to sleep and opening the gates. Hermes leads Priam to Achilles' tent and then vanishes.**

WORDS
TO
KNOW

defile (dĭ-fīl′) *v.* to make filthy; violate the honor of
clamor (klăm′ər) *n.* a loud, confused noise or outcry
scourge (skûrj) *n.* a source of great suffering or destruction
destitute (dĕs′tĭ-tōōt′) *adj.* lacking in resources; bereft

from Book 24
A GRACE GIVEN IN SORROW

Priam,

the great king of Troy, passed by the others,
285 knelt down, took in his arms Achilles' knees,
and kissed the hands of wrath that killed his sons.

When, taken with mad Folly in his own land,
a man does murder and in exile finds
refuge in some rich house, then all who see him
290 stand in awe.
So these men stood.

Achilles

gazed in wonder at the splendid king,
and his companions marveled too, all silent,
with glances to and fro. Now Priam prayed
295 to the man before him:

"Remember your own father,

Achilles, in your godlike youth: his years
like mine are many, and he stands upon
the fearful doorstep of old age. He, too,
is hard pressed, it may be, by those around him,
300 there being no one able to defend him
from bane of war and ruin. Ah, but he
may nonetheless hear news of you alive,
and so with glad heart hope through all his days
for sight of his dear son, come back from Troy,
305 while I have deathly fortune.

Noble sons

I fathered here, but scarce one man is left me.
Fifty I had when the Achaeans came,
nineteen out of a single belly, others
born of attendant women. Most are gone.
310 Raging Ares cut their knees from under them.
And he who stood alone among them all,
their champion, and Troy's, ten days ago
you killed him, fighting for his land, my prince,
Hector.

It is for him that I have come

315 among these ships, to beg him back from you,
and I bring ransom without stint.

316 stint: limitation.

Achilles,
be reverent toward the great gods! And take
pity on me, remember your own father.
Think me more pitiful by far, since I
320 have brought myself to do what no man else
has done before—to lift to my lips the hand
of one who killed my son."

Now in Achilles
the evocation of his father stirred
new longing, and an ache of grief. He lifted
325 the old man's hand and gently put him by.
Then both were overborne as they remembered:
the old king huddled at Achilles' feet
wept, and wept for Hector, killer of men,
while great Achilles wept for his own father
330 as for Patroclus once again; and sobbing
filled the room.

But when Achilles' heart
had known the luxury of tears, and pain
within his breast and bones had passed away,
he stood then, raised the old king up, in pity
335 for his grey head and greybeard cheek, and spoke
in a warm rush of words:

"Ah, sad and old!
Trouble and pain you've borne, and bear, aplenty.
Only a great will could have brought you here
among the Achaean ships, and here alone
340 before the eyes of one who stripped your sons,
your many sons, in battle. Iron must be
the heart within you. Come, then, and sit down.
We'll probe our wounds no more but let them rest,
though grief lies heavy on us. Tears heal nothing,
345 drying so stiff and cold. This is the way
the gods ordained the destiny of men,
to bear such burdens in our lives, while they
feel no affliction. At the door of Zeus
are those two urns of good and evil gifts
350 that he may choose for us; and one for whom
the lightning's joyous king dips in both urns
will have by turns bad luck and good. But one

326 overborne: overcome; overwhelmed.

Ajax and Achilles playing dice, Greek vase painting

336–348 Compare the impression of Achilles you got from lines 87–94 with the impression you get from these lines.

WORDS
TO   **evocation** (ĕv′ə-kā′shən) *n.* a bringing to mind
KNOW

77

to whom he sends all evil—that man goes
contemptible by the will of Zeus; ravenous
355   hunger drives him over the wondrous earth,
unresting, without honor from gods or men.
Mixed fortune came to Peleus. Shining gifts
at the gods' hands he had from birth: felicity,
wealth overflowing, rule of the Myrmidons,
360   a bride immortal at his mortal side.
But then Zeus gave afflictions too—no family
of powerful sons grew up for him at home,
but one child, of all seasons and of none.
Can I stand by him in his age? Far from my country
365   I sit at Troy to grieve you and your children.
You, too, sir, in time past were fortunate,
we hear men say. From Macar's isle of Lesbos
northward, and south of Phrygia and the Straits,
no one had wealth like yours, or sons like yours.
370   Then gods out of the sky sent you this bitterness:
the years of siege, the battles and the losses.
Endure it, then. And do not mourn forever
for your dead son. There is no remedy.
You will not make him stand again. Rather
375   await some new misfortune to be suffered."

The old king in his majesty replied:

"Never give me a chair, my lord, while Hector
lies in your camp uncared for. Yield him to me
now. Allow me sight of him. Accept
380   the many gifts I bring. May they reward you,
and may you see your home again.
You spared my life at once and let me live."

Achilles, the great runner, frowned and eyed him
under his brows:

                    "Do not vex me, sir," he said.
385   "I have intended, in my own good time,
to yield up Hector to you. She who bore me,
the daughter of the Ancient of the sea,
has come with word to me from Zeus. I know
in your case, too—though you say nothing, Priam—
390   that some god guided you to the shipways here.

358 felicity (fĭ-lĭs′ĭ-tē): happiness; good fortune.

359 Myrmidons (mûr′mə-dŏnz′): a people of Thessaly in Greece, subjects of Achilles' father, Peleus.

363 "Of all seasons and of none" suggests that Achilles expects an early death for himself.

367–368 Lesbos (lĕz′bŏs) . . . **Phrygia** (frĭj′ē-ə) . . . **the Straits:** Lesbos is an island off the western coast of Asia Minor; Phrygia was an ancient kingdom in western Asia Minor; the Straits are the Dardanelles.

387 "The Ancient of the sea" is the sea god Nereus (nîr′ē-əs), father of Thetis.

No strong man in his best days could make entry
into this camp. How could he pass the guard,
or force our gateway?

Therefore, let me be.

Sting my sore heart again, and even here,
395   under my own roof, suppliant though you are,
I may not spare you, sir, but trample on
the express command of Zeus!"

When he heard this,

the old man feared him and obeyed with silence.
Now like a lion at one bound Achilles
400   left the room. Close at his back the officers
Automedon and Alcimus went out—
comrades in arms whom he esteemed the most
after the dead Patroclus. They unharnessed
mules and horses, led the old king's crier
405   to a low bench and sat him down.
Then from the polished wagon
they took the piled-up price of Hector's body.
One chiton and two capes they left aside
as dress and shrouding for the homeward journey.
410   Then, calling to the women slaves, Achilles
ordered the body bathed and rubbed with oil—
but lifted, too, and placed apart, where Priam
could not see his son—for seeing Hector
he might in his great pain give way to rage,
415   and fury then might rise up in Achilles
to slay the old king, <u>flouting</u> Zeus's word.
So after bathing and anointing Hector
they drew the shirt and beautiful shrouding over him.
Then with his own hands lifting him, Achilles
420   laid him upon a couch, and with his two
companions aiding, placed him in the wagon.
Now a bitter groan burst from Achilles,
who stood and prayed to his own dead friend:

"Patroclus,

do not be angry with me, if somehow
425   even in the world of Death you learn of this—
that I released Prince Hector to his father.
The gifts he gave were not unworthy. Aye,
and you shall have your share, this time as well."

395 suppliant (sŭp′lē-ənt): one who begs or pleads earnestly.

401 Automedon (ô-tŏm′ə-dn) . . . **Alcimus** (ăl′sə-məs).

408 chiton (kīt′n): a shirtlike garment; tunic.

The Prince Achilles turned back to his quarters.
430 He took again the splendid chair that stood
against the farther wall, then looked at Priam
and made his declaration:

                                        "As you wished, sir,
the body of your son is now set free.
He lies in state. At the first sight of Dawn
435 you shall take charge of him yourself and see him.
Now let us think of supper. We are told
that even Niobe in her extremity
took thought for bread—though all her brood had perished,
her six young girls and six tall sons. Apollo,
440 making his silver longbow whip and sing,
shot the lads down, and Artemis with raining
arrows killed the daughters—all this after
Niobe had compared herself with Leto,
the smooth-cheeked goddess.

                                        She has borne two children,
445 Niobe said, How many have I borne!
But soon those two destroyed the twelve.

                                        Besides,
nine days the dead lay stark, no one could bury them,
for Zeus had turned all folk of theirs to stone.
The gods made graves for them on the tenth day,
450 and then at last, being weak and spent with weeping,
Niobe thought of food. Among the rocks
of Sipylus' lonely mountainside, where nymphs
who race Achelous river go to rest,
she, too, long turned to stone, somewhere broods on
455 the gall immortal gods gave her to drink.

Like her we'll think of supper, noble sir.
Weep for your son again when you have borne him
back to Troy; there he'll be mourned indeed."

**Priam and Achilles agree to an 11-day truce. During that
time, the Trojans will mourn Hector's body before its burial.**

436–455 The mortal woman Niobe (nī′ə-bē) claimed that having so many children made her superior to the goddess Leto (lē′tō), who had only two. Leto's son and daughter, Apollo and Artemis (är′tə-mĭs), punished Niobe by killing all her children. After many days of grieving, Niobe asked the gods to relieve her by turning her to stone.

452 Sipylus (sĭp′ə-ləs): a mountain in west central Asia Minor.

453 Achelous (ăk′ə-lō′əs): a river near Mount Sipylus.

455 gall: bitterness; bile.

Connect to the Literature

1. **What Do You Think?** What is your impression of Achilles? Share your thoughts with a classmate.

Comprehension Check
• What does Achilles refuse to promise the dying Hector?
• What does Achilles do with Hector after he kills him?
• Identify the character who pleads for the return of Hector's body.

Think Critically

2. In your opinion, does Achilles' loyalty to his friend Patroclus justify the way he treats Hector? Explain your answer.

3. How would you describe the relationship between Achilles and Priam?

 THINK ABOUT
• Achilles' killing of Hector
• the dialogue between the two men
• why Achilles gives Hector's body to Priam

4. To what extent do Achilles and Hector correspond to your idea of a **hero**?

 THINK ABOUT
• the kind of warrior each man is
• Hector's speech that begins "This is the end. . . ." (line 130, page 71)
• Achilles' treatment of Hector's body
• Achilles' response to Priam

5. How might your impression of Achilles be different if he refused to give Hector's body to Priam?

6. **ACTIVE READING** **CLASSIFYING CHARACTERS** Look back at the list you made in your **READER'S NOTEBOOK** and compare Achilles, Hector, and Priam. In your opinion, which **character** is the most courageous? Why?

Extend Interpretations

7. **Connect to Life** Achilles and Hector fight one-on-one. Do you think leaders of rival nations, tribes, or groups should settle differences between themselves without involving their followers? Is it possible or practical to settle conflicts this way? Support your responses.

8. **Points of Comparison** Compare and contrast Achilles and Beowulf. Consider their actions and the reasons for those actions. Think about how they are alike and how they are different. Who behaves more like a true **epic hero**?

Literary Analysis

SIMILE AND EPIC SIMILE A **simile** is a figure of speech that makes a comparison between two things that are actually unlike yet have something in common. The comparison is expressed by means of the word *like* or *as*. "Silent as death" and "John went down like a stone" are examples of similes. **Epic similes** are long comparisons that often continue for a number of lines. The epic simile in lines 145–148 of this selection compares Hector to an eagle. (In a translation, the word *like* or *as* may not appear; in the lines cited, *as* could be substituted for "the way.") What does the simile suggest about Hector's character?

Paired Activity Now analyze the simile in lines 154–158. What two things are being compared in the simile? How do the epic similes in lines 145–148 and lines 154–158 contribute to the telling of the story? With a classmate, make a list of all the similes that you can find in the poem.

REVIEW **EPIC** As you may recall, an **epic** is a long narrative poem on a serious subject, presented in an elevated or formal style. It usually traces the adventures of a great hero. Both *Beowulf* and the *Iliad* are epics. What similarities and differences do you see between the two poems?

Writing Options

1. Letter of Commendation As either a Greek or a Trojan general, write a letter of commendation for Achilles or Hector. Explain why you are awarding him your army's highest medal. Place the letter in your **Working Portfolio.**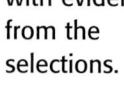

2. Character Sketch Think again about the relationship between Achilles and Priam. Then write a character sketch of Priam from Achilles' point of view.

3. Alternative Outline Imagine events as they might have occurred without the gods and goddesses. Write an outline for a version of the poem in which the human characters determine their own fate.

4. **Points of Comparison**
Compare and contrast in an essay the attitudes toward fame and ambition in *Beowulf* and the *Iliad.* Support your comparisons with evidence from the selections.

Writing Handbook
See page 1367: Compare and Contrast.

Activities & Explorations

1. Dramatic Reading With a classmate, give a dramatic reading of the encounter between Achilles and Priam. Use your voices and facial expressions to convey emotions such as sorrow, anger, desperation, compassion, and fear. ~ **SPEAKING AND LISTENING**

2. Dance Interpretation Create a dance interpretation of the battle between Hector and Achilles. Choose appropriate music to accompany it, and perform your dance for the class.
~ **DANCE / MUSIC**

3. Heroic Mural With a group of classmates, using large sheets of paper, sketch or paint a series of scenes from the *Iliad* and put them together to form a mural for your classroom. ~ **ART**

4. Homeric Epithets In line 10, the reference to Achilles as "the great runner" is an example of an **epithet,** a brief phrase that refers to a characteristic of a particular person or thing. Other examples are the references to Hector as "killer of men" and Priam as "great king of Troy." With a group of classmates, have one member of the group call out the names of current sports figures or other celebrities and then have the other members call out possible epithets for that person.
~ **SPEAKING AND LISTENING**

Inquiry & Research

1. Digging Up Troy Find out more about the real city of Troy. Where was it located? What have archaeologists discovered about the city? Present your findings to the class in an outline for a television documentary about Troy.

 More Online: Research Starter
www.mcdougallittell.com

2. Translations of Homer There have been many translations of Homer into English. The 18th-century poet Alexander Pope, for example, translated both the *Iliad* and the *Odyssey.* With classmates, find three modern translations of the *Iliad* in addition to the one you just read. Choose a brief passage and compare its treatment in the three versions. Then in class read the three translations of the passage aloud. Discuss the differences with your classmates.

Vocabulary in Action

EXERCISE: RELATED WORDS Write the letter of the word that is not related in meaning to the other words in each set.

1. (a) face, (b) meet, (c) evade, (d) confront
2. (a) ponderous, (b) swift, (c) weighty, (d) hefty
3. (a) clamor, (b) peacefulness, (c) silence, (d) calmness
4. (a) dirty, (b) cleanse, (c) defile, (d) corrupt
5. (a) strong, (b) vulnerable, (c) weak, (d) defenseless
6. (a) dodge, (b) capture, (c) elude, (d) escape
7. (a) destruction, (b) disaster, (c) havoc, (d) protection
8. (a) whetted, (b) dull, (c) blunt, (d) rounded
9. (a) disobey, (b) flout, (c) punish, (d) disregard
10. (a) promise, (b) exult, (c) rejoice, (d) celebrate
11. (a) defender, (b) guardian, (c) protector, (d) scourge
12. (a) act, (b) abstain, (c) proceed, (d) perform
13. (a) remembrance, (b) calendar, (c) reminder, (d) evocation
14. (a) soothe, (b) quell, (c) scold, (d) hush
15. (a) destitute, (b) needy, (c) deprived, (d) injured

WORDS TO KNOW					
abstain	destitute	evocation	havoc	scourge	
clamor	elude	exult	ponderous	vulnerable	
defile	evade	flouting	quell	whetted	

Building Vocabulary
For an in-depth lesson on how to expand your vocabulary, see page 1182.

Homer
c. 850 B.C.

Who Was Homer? Little is known about the Greek poet Homer. In fact, for centuries scholars have debated whether such a man ever really existed. Today, most agree that the author of two equally famous epics, the *Iliad* and the *Odyssey*, was indeed a man named Homer, who lived sometime between 800 and 600 B.C. Evidence of his life and authorship has been gathered indirectly from other writings of ancient Greece, from historical references, and from his poems. It seems likely that the mysterious poet was born either in western Asia Minor or on one of the nearby Aegean islands.

The Blind Bard According to legend, Homer was blind; however, some scholars believe that this legend is not likely to be literally true. They point out that the typical ancient Greek portrayal of a sage or philosopher was of a blind man with exceptional inner vision. Ancient Greeks viewed the *Iliad* and the *Odyssey* as works that revealed all-important truths about human beings and their place in the universe. Often, Greek children were required to memorize portions of the epics and to model their behavior on the heroic code set forth by their author. With the possible exception of Shakespeare, no other poet in the Western world has been quoted more often than Homer.

Oral Poetry Homer's poems probably had a long oral history before they were written down. It is believed that they were composed in verse partly because the meter made them easier to memorize. According to modern scholars, Homer was probably illiterate, living as he did at a time when writing was just being introduced among the Greeks. In his old age, the poet may have recited his epics for someone else to record.

PREPARING to *Read*

The Seafarer / The Wanderer / The Wife's Lament

Poetry from the EXETER BOOK

Connect to Your Life

Lonely Times Remember a time when you felt lonely or isolated. Perhaps you were separated from your friends or family as a result of a move or a vacation, or maybe you simply felt alone. How did you react to the situation—with anger or with sadness? What helped you cope with the situation? With a partner, discuss your personal definition of loneliness.

Build Background

Leaving Loved Ones Behind Life in Anglo-Saxon times was filled with hardships that separated people from their loved ones for long periods—or permanently. Outbreaks of disease, attacks by wild animals, and natural disasters such as storms and floods killed many before their time. Frequent warfare wreaked havoc on small communities, bringing untimely death to some and scattering others, who might be forced into permanent exile if their communities' protectors had been slain in the fighting.

Also facing the hardship of separation were the men who left behind their families and communities to travel the sea. Sailing the ocean in primitive boats and in all kinds of weather, these seafarers had to face both physical danger and intense loneliness. The women and children they left behind endured months and even years without knowing whether their husbands and fathers would ever return.

The three Old English poems you are about to read reflect the uncertainty of life in Anglo-Saxon times, as well as the Anglo-Saxons' human needs and desires. Each deals, in one way or another, with the effects of separation.

Focus Your Reading

LITERARY ANALYSIS **KENNING** A prominent characteristic of Old English poetry is the use of **kennings**—descriptive compound words and phrases—in place of simple nouns. Common kennings include *ring-giver* for a king or lord and *helmet bearer* for a warrior. Kennings are often metaphorical, like *heaven's candle* for the sun. The following lines from "The Wife's Lament" contain a kenning for the sea:

> *First my lord went out away from his people over the __wave-tumult__.*

Look for other examples of kennings as you read the three poems.

ACTIVE READING **INTERPRETING DETAILS** These poems from the Exeter Book are filled with **details** that can help you **visualize** the scenes, objects, and people being described. Interpreting these details will help you decide what ideas, **moods,** and attitudes the poems convey. For example, "lonely dawns" and "frozen waves" in "The Wanderer" suggest emptiness and desolation.

READER'S NOTEBOOK As you read each poem, create a cluster diagram like the one below to help you organize the **descriptive details** in the poem. Jot down the ideas, moods, or attitudes that the details seem to convey.

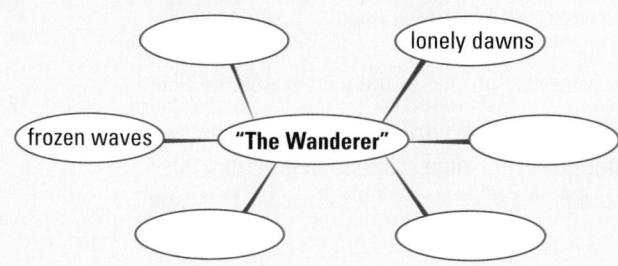

from The Seafarer

This tale is true, and mine. It tells
How the sea took me, swept me back
And forth in sorrow and fear and pain,
Showed me suffering in a hundred ships,
5   In a thousand ports, and in me. It tells
Of smashing surf when I sweated in the cold
Of an anxious watch, perched in the bow
As it dashed under cliffs. My feet were cast
In icy bands, bound with frost,
10   With frozen chains, and hardship groaned
Around my heart. Hunger tore
At my sea-weary soul. No man sheltered
On the quiet fairness of earth can feel
How wretched I was, drifting through winter
15   On an ice-cold sea, whirled in sorrow,
Alone in a world blown clear of love,
Hung with icicles. The hailstorms flew.
The only sound was the roaring sea,
The freezing waves. The song of the swan
20   Might serve for pleasure, the cry of the sea-fowl,
The death-noise of birds instead of laughter,

2–3 Did the sea literally sweep the speaker back and forth? If not, what might he mean?

The mewing of gulls instead of mead.
Storms beat on the rocky cliffs and were echoed
By icy-feathered terns and the eagle's screams;
25 No kinsman could offer comfort there,
To a soul left drowning in desolation.
   And who could believe, knowing but
The passion of cities, swelled proud with wine
And no taste of misfortune, how often, how wearily,
30 I put myself back on the paths of the sea.
Night would blacken; it would snow from the north;
Frost bound the earth and hail would fall,
The coldest seeds. And how my heart
Would begin to beat, knowing once more
35 The salt waves tossing and the towering sea!
The time for journeys would come and my soul
Called me eagerly out, sent me over
The horizon, seeking foreigners' homes.
   But there isn't a man on earth so proud,
40 So born to greatness, so bold with his youth,
Grown so brave, or so graced by God,
That he feels no fear as the sails unfurl,
Wondering what Fate has willed and will do.
No harps ring in his heart, no rewards,
45 No passion for women, no worldly pleasures,
Nothing, only the ocean's heave;
But longing wraps itself around him.
Orchards blossom, the towns bloom,
Fields grow lovely as the world springs fresh,
50 And all these admonish that willing mind
Leaping to journeys, always set
In thoughts travelling on a quickening tide.
So summer's sentinel, the cuckoo, sings
In his murmuring voice, and our hearts mourn
55 As he urges. Who could understand,
In ignorant ease, what we others suffer
As the paths of exile stretch endlessly on?
   And yet my heart wanders away,
My soul roams with the sea, the whales'
60 Home, wandering to the widest corners
Of the world, returning ravenous with desire,
Flying solitary, screaming, exciting me
To the open ocean, breaking oaths
On the curve of a wave.

22 mead: an alcoholic beverage made from fermented honey, frequently drunk in Anglo-Saxon gatherings. In contrasting mead with "the mewing of gulls," what is the speaker stressing?

24 terns: sea birds similar to gulls.

28 The "cities" of the seafarer's day were far smaller than modern cities—more like villages and encampments.

50 admonish (ăd-mŏn'ĭsh): criticize or caution.

53 sentinel (sĕn'tə-nəl): guard; watchman.

Thus the joys of God

65 Are fervent with life, where life itself
    Fades quickly into the earth. The wealth
    Of the world neither reaches to Heaven nor remains.
    No man has ever faced the dawn
    Certain which of Fate's three threats
70 Would fall: illness, or age, or an enemy's
    Sword, snatching the life from his soul.
    The praise the living pour on the dead
    Flowers from reputation: plant
    An earthly life of profit reaped
75 Even from hatred and rancor, of bravery
    Flung in the devil's face, and death
    Can only bring you earthly praise
    And a song to celebrate a place
    With the angels, life eternally blessed
80 In the hosts of Heaven.

The days are gone

    When the kingdoms of earth flourished in glory;
    Now there are no rulers, no emperors,
    No givers of gold, as once there were,
    When wonderful things were worked among them
85 And they lived in lordly magnificence.
    Those powers have vanished, those pleasures are dead,
    The weakest survives and the world continues,
    Kept spinning by toil. All glory is tarnished,
    The world's honor ages and shrinks,
90 Bent like the men who mold it. Their faces
    Blanch as time advances, their beards
    Wither and they mourn the memory of friends,
    The sons of princes, sown in the dust.
    The soul stripped of its flesh knows nothing
95 Of sweetness or sour, feels no pain,
    Bends neither its hand nor its brain. A brother
    Opens his palms and pours down gold
    On his kinsman's grave, strewing his coffin
    With treasures intended for Heaven, but nothing
100 Golden shakes the wrath of God
    For a soul overflowing with sin, and nothing
    Hidden on earth rises to Heaven.
      We all fear God. He turns the earth,
    He set it swinging firmly in space,
105 Gave life to the world and light to the sky.
    Death leaps at the fools who forget their God.
    He who lives humbly has angels from Heaven

75 rancor (răng′kər): bitter, long-lasting ill will.

80 hosts of Heaven: bands of angels.

80–85 To what glorious era might the speaker be referring?

91 blanch: turn white.

The Whale. MS. Ashmole
1511, f. 86v, The Bodleian
Library, Oxford, Great Britain.

To carry him courage and strength and belief.
A man must conquer pride, not kill it,
110 Be firm with his fellows, chaste for himself,
Treat all the world as the world deserves,
With love or with hate but never with harm,
Though an enemy seek to scorch him in hell,
Or set the flames of a funeral pyre
115 Under his lord. Fate is stronger
And God mightier than any man's mind.
Our thoughts should turn to where our home is,
Consider the ways of coming there,
Then strive for sure permission for us
120 To rise to that eternal joy,
That life born in the love of God
And the hope of Heaven. Praise the Holy
Grace of He who honored us,
Eternal, unchanging creator of earth. Amen.

Translated by Burton Raffel

110 chaste (chāst): pure in thought and deed.

114 funeral pyre (pīr): a bonfire for burning a corpse.

Thinking Through the Literature

1. **Comprehension Check** What conflicting emotions does the seafarer feel when he sets off on a sea voyage?

2. What **images** remain with you after reading this poem? Describe the images, or draw a sketch of them.

3. Why do you think the seafarer chose a life at sea in spite of its hardships?

THINK ABOUT
- the feelings he expresses in lines 58–64
- the problems recounted in lines 81–102
- the view of fate expressed in the final lines

4. Why do you think the seafarer tells about his life and its hardships? Cite details from the poem to support your opinion.

The Wanderer

This lonely traveler longs for grace,
For the mercy of God; grief hangs on
His heart and follows the frost-cold foam
He cuts in the sea, sailing endlessly,
5   Aimlessly, in exile. Fate has opened
A single port: memory. He sees
His kinsmen slaughtered again, and cries:
     "I've drunk too many lonely dawns,
Grey with mourning. Once there were men
10 To whom my heart could hurry, hot
With open longing. They're long since dead.
My heart has closed on itself, quietly
Learning that silence is noble and sorrow
Nothing that speech can cure. Sadness
15 Has never driven sadness off;
Fate blows hardest on a bleeding heart.
So those who thirst for glory smother
Secret weakness and longing, neither
Weep nor sigh nor listen to the sickness
20 In their souls. So I, lost and homeless,
Forced to flee the darkness that fell
On the earth and my lord.

GUIDE FOR READING

5–7 What has happened to the wanderer's kinsmen? How might his memory be like a port? How has fate limited him to a "single port"?

Leaving everything,

Weary with winter I wandered out
On the frozen waves, hoping to find
25 A place, a people, a lord to replace
My lost ones. No one knew me, now,
No one offered comfort, allowed
Me feasting or joy. How cruel a journey
I've travelled, sharing my bread with sorrow
30 Alone, an exile in every land,
Could only be told by telling my footsteps.

31 telling: counting.

For who can hear: "friendless and poor,"
And know what I've known since the long cheerful nights
When, young and yearning, with my lord I yet feasted
35 Most welcome of all. That warmth is dead.
He only knows who needs his lord
As I do, eager for long-missing aid;
He only knows who never sleeps
Without the deepest dreams of longing.
40 Sometimes it seems I see my lord,
Kiss and embrace him, bend my hands
And head to his knee, kneeling as though
He still sat enthroned, ruling his thanes.

43 thanes: followers of a lord.

And I open my eyes, embracing the air,
45 And see the brown sea-billows heave,
See the sea-birds bathe, spreading

45 What are the "brown sea-billows"?

Their white-feathered wings, watch the frost
And the hail and the snow. And heavy in heart
I long for my lord, alone and unloved.
50 Sometimes it seems I see my kin
And greet them gladly, give them welcome,
The best of friends. They fade away,
Swimming soundlessly out of sight,
Leaving nothing.
How loathsome become

55 The frozen waves to a weary heart.
    In this brief world I cannot wonder
That my mind is set on melancholy,
Because I never forget the fate
Of men, robbed of their riches, suddenly
60 Looted by death—the doom of earth,
Sent to us all by every rising
Sun. Wisdom is slow, and comes

60 looted: robbed by force. What was taken from the men who were "looted by death"?

But late. He who has it is patient;
He cannot be hasty to hate or speak,
65 He must be bold and yet not blind,
Nor ever too craven, complacent, or covetous,
Nor ready to gloat before he wins glory.
The man's a fool who flings his boasts
Hotly to the heavens, heeding his spleen
70 And not the better boldness of knowledge.
What knowing man knows not the ghostly,
Waste-like end of worldly wealth:
See, already the wreckage is there,
The wind-swept walls stand far and wide,
75 The storm-beaten blocks besmeared with frost,
The mead-halls crumbled, the monarchs thrown down
And stripped of their pleasures. The proudest of warriors
Now lie by the wall: some of them war
Destroyed; some the monstrous sea-bird
80 Bore over the ocean; to some the old wolf
Dealt out death; and for some dejected
Followers fashioned an earth-cave coffin.
Thus the Maker of men lays waste
This earth, crushing our callow mirth.
85 And the work of old giants stands withered and still."

He who these ruins rightly sees,
And deeply considers this dark twisted life,
Who sagely remembers the endless slaughters
Of a bloody past, is bound to proclaim:
90 "Where is the war-steed? Where is the warrior? Where is
his war-lord?
Where now the feasting-places? Where now the mead-hall
pleasures?
Alas, bright cup! Alas, brave knight!
Alas, you glorious princes! All gone,
Lost in the night, as you never had lived.
95 And all that survives you a serpentine wall,
Wondrously high, worked in strange ways.
Mighty spears have slain these men,
Greedy weapons have framed their fate.
These rocky slopes are beaten by storms,
100 This earth pinned down by driving snow,
By the horror of winter, smothering warmth
In the shadows of night. And the north angrily

66 craven (krā'vən): cowardly; **complacent** (kəm-plā'sənt): self-satisfied; **covetous** (kŭv'ĭ-təs): greedy.

69 spleen: bad temper. (The spleen is a body organ that was formerly thought to be the seat of strong emotions.)

77–82 In what different ways have the warriors met their fate?

84 callow mirth: childish joy.

95 serpentine: winding or twisting, like a snake.

Hurls its hailstorms at our helpless heads.
Everything earthly is evilly born,
105 Firmly clutched by a fickle Fate.
Fortune vanishes, friendship vanishes,
Man is fleeting, woman is fleeting,
And all this earth rolls into emptiness."
    So says the sage in his heart, sitting alone with
      His thought.
110 It's good to guard your faith, nor let your grief come forth
Until it cannot call for help, nor help but heed
The path you've placed before it. It's good to find your
    grace
In God, the heavenly rock where rests our every hope.

Translated by Burton Raffel

Thinking Through the Literature

1. **Comprehension Check** What happened to cause the poem's title **character** to become a wanderer?

2. What emotion does this poem chiefly evoke in you? Share your reaction with classmates.

3. How would you describe the wanderer's present life and his feelings about it?

THINK ABOUT
- the experiences he describes in lines 8–22
- the life he led before he became a wanderer
- his remarks in lines 90–108

4. Do you agree with the attitude toward grief expressed in lines 12–16? Why or why not?

The Wife's Lament

Poverty carrying a sack of wheat to the mill reaches a dangerous bridge (about 1450–1475). Rene I d'Anjou, King of Naples. From *Le Mortifiement de vaine plaisance*, M.705, f. 38v.

I make this song   about me full sadly
my own wayfaring.   I a woman tell
what griefs I had   since I grew up
new or old   never more than now.
5   Ever I know   the dark of my exile.

First my lord went out   away from his people
over the wave-tumult.   I grieved each dawn
wondered where my lord   my first on earth might be.
Then I went forth   a friendless exile
10   to seek service   in my sorrow's need.
My man's kinsmen   began to plot
by darkened thought   to divide us two
so we most widely   in the world's kingdom
lived wretchedly   and I suffered longing.

15   My lord commanded me   to move my dwelling here.
I had few loved ones   in this land
or faithful friends.   For this my heart grieves:
that I should find the man   well matched to me
hard of fortune   mournful of mind
20   hiding his mood   thinking of murder.

GUIDE FOR READING

1 To show the rhythmic structure of Old English poetry, this translator has divided each line into two units with a break called a caesura (sĭ-zhŏŏr'ə). The caesuras signal places where the scop, or poet-singer, probably paused for breath while reciting the poem.

2 wayfaring: journeying.

6 my lord: the speaker's husband.

7 wave-tumult: the sea. Why might the poet have used this kenning?

19 hard . . . mind: having a hard life and feeling sad.

Blithe was our bearing   often we vowed
that but death alone   would part us two
naught else.   But this is turned round
now . . .   as if it never were
25 our friendship.   I must far and near
bear the anger   of my beloved.
The man sent me out   to live in the woods
under an oak tree   in this den in the earth.
Ancient this earth hall.   I am all longing.

29 "Earth hall" refers to the speaker's living quarters. What kind of place do you think it is?

30 The valleys are dark   the hills high
the yard overgrown   bitter with briars
a joyless dwelling.   Full oft the lack of my lord
seizes me cruelly here.   Friends there are on earth
living beloved   lying in bed
35 while I at dawn   am walking alone
under the oak tree   through these earth halls.
There I may sit   the summerlong day
there I can weep   over my exile
my many hardships.   Hence I may not rest
40 from this care of heart   which belongs to me ever
nor all this longing   that has caught me in this life.

May that young man   be sad-minded always
hard his heart's thought   while he must wear
a blithe bearing   with care in the breast
45 a crowd of sorrows.   May on himself depend
all his world's joy.   Be he outlawed far
in a strange folk-land—   that my beloved sits
under a rocky cliff   rimed with frost
a lord dreary in spirit   drenched with water
50 in a ruined hall.   My lord endures
much care of mind.   He remembers too often
a happier dwelling.   Woe be to them
that for a loved one   must wait in longing.

42–50 In these lines, the speaker seems to wish for her husband the same sad, lonely life that he has forced her to endure.

Translated by Ann Stanford

Thinking through the LITERATURE

Connect to the Literature

1. **What Do You Think?**
   What is your reaction to the story told in "The Wife's Lament"?

   Comprehension Check
   • What happened after the wife's husband went to sea?
   • Why do the husband and the wife live apart?
   • What does the wife wish her husband to feel?

Think Critically

2. Evaluate the kind of life the wife has led. Support your evaluation with details from the poem.

3. How would you describe the wife's opinion of her husband's behavior?

   THINK ABOUT
   {
   • the influence of her husband's kinsmen
   • the vow that the husband and the wife made to each other
   • the wife's thoughts in lines 42–50

4. In your opinion, how might the husband respond to his wife's accusations?

5. **ACTIVE READING** **INTERPRETING DETAILS** Get together with a partner and discuss the cluster diagrams of **descriptive details** you created in your **READER'S NOTEBOOK**. What **moods** do the details help convey?

Extend Interpretations

6. **What If?** Suppose that the husband of the speaker in "The Wife's Lament" returned to her. Describe their reunion.

7. **Comparing Texts** Compare the plights of the three poems' title characters. Who do you think faces the most difficult hardships? What makes you think this way? Defend your opinion.

8. **Connect to Life** In the modern world, many refugees leave their countries to escape dangers, not knowing when or if they will ever return to the homelands and people they love. How do you think the loneliness and other hardships they face compare with those endured in Anglo-Saxon times? Cite evidence from the poems to support your opinion.

Literary Analysis

KENNING Anglo-Saxon poets made frequent use of **kennings,** descriptive terms and phrases substituted for simple nouns. In a translation of Old English poetry, a kenning may appear as a compound word, like *wave-tumult,* used for the sea in "The Wife's Lament." A kenning may also appear as a group of two or more words, like *swan road,* another common kenning for the sea. The name *Beowulf* itself can be interpreted as "bee-wolf," a kenning for a bear (because bears like honey and so are often found around beehives).

Cooperative Learning Activity
Identify two more kennings in the poems and explain what they mean. Then copy the chart below and try creating your own kennings for the words in the first column. Discuss your ideas and complete the chart with a small group of classmates.

Term	Kenning
city	
journey	
ship	
tree	
war	

REVIEW **ALLITERATION** Besides rhythm, the most important element of sound in Old English poetry is **alliteration,** the repetition of initial consonant sounds. Look for examples in all three poems.

Choices & CHALLENGES

Writing Options

1. Diary Entry Imagine that you are the title character of one of the poems. Write a diary entry describing a typical day in your life—for "The Seafarer," for example, you might describe a typical day at sea. Place the entry in your **Working Portfolio.**

2. Exploration Write a paragraph in which you explore the inner conflict of the title character in one of the poems. State the conflict that you perceive, and then support your statement with details from the poem.

Writing Handbook
See page 1359: Paragraphs.

Activities & Explorations

1. Weather Map Research the weather patterns over the waters surrounding Britain. Then draw a map showing the places where an Anglo-Saxon sailor may have encountered weather-related dangers and the types of dangers he may have faced. **~ SCIENCE**

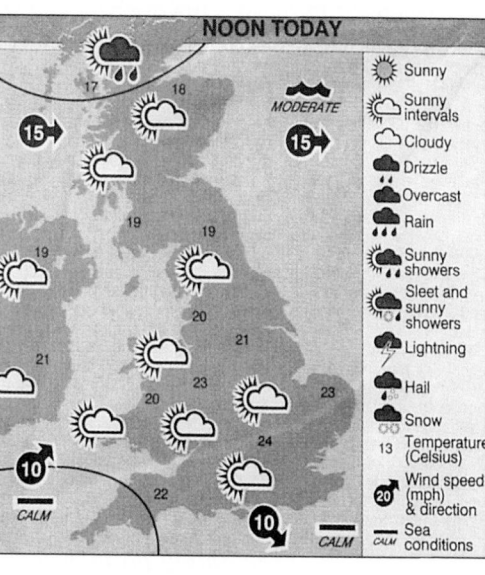

2. TV Interview With a group of classmates, stage a TV talk show in which a host interviews the title characters of the poems. The host should encourage the guests to discuss their hopes and plans for the future as well as their past experiences.
~ SPEAKING AND LISTENING

Inquiry & Research

Everyday Anglo-Saxons Use history books and other reliable sources to find out more about the Anglo-Saxons. Go beyond the accounts of historic events to investigate the lifestyles of the various classes of Anglo-Saxon society—women and farmers as well as kings and warriors. Prepare a written report on your findings.

Stained glass window depicting a farmer sowing seeds by hand

The Authors

Surviving Anonymity Nothing is known about the authors of "The Seafarer," "The Wanderer," and "The Wife's Lament." All three poems survive in the Exeter Book, a manuscript produced by scribes around A.D. 950. Leofric, the first bishop of Exeter in England, had this collection of Anglo-Saxon poems in his personal library. After he donated it to the Exeter Cathedral library sometime between 1050 and 1072, the Exeter Book was neglected and abused for centuries because few people were able to read the Old English language in which it was written. The original binding and an unknown number of pages were lost. Other pages were badly stained or scorched. Today the Exeter Book is handled with great care and treasured as one of the few surviving poetic manuscripts from the Anglo-Saxon period.

PREPARING to *Read*

from A History of the English Church and People

Historical Writing by THE VENERABLE BEDE

(**Connect to Your Life**)

Accepting Challenges, Making Changes Think about a time when you were challenged to make a major change in your life and you took on that challenge. How did the change affect the way you think or live? Share your experience with a group of classmates.

Build Background

The Christian Challenge The Venerable Bede, regarded as the father of English history, lived and worked in a monastery in northern Britain during the late seventh and early eighth centuries. His most famous work, *A History of the English Church and People,* is a major source of information about life in Britain from the first successful Roman invasion, about A.D. 46, to A.D. 731. Bede was a careful and thorough historian for his time. He sought out original documents and reliable eyewitness accounts on which to base his writing.

Bede's *History* is filled with stories about the spread of Christianity among the English between A.D. 597 and 731. Christianity had been introduced into Britain during the Roman occupation and had flourished for a time. The Anglo-Saxon tribes who began invading around A.D. 450, however, were pagans and brought their religion with them. By the late sixth century, Christianity had been abandoned in many areas. In A.D. 597, missionaries from Rome began arriving in Britain to persuade the Anglo-Saxons to reject their pagan beliefs and accept the challenge of the Christian faith.

WORDS TO KNOW
Vocabulary Preview

aspire   prudent
desecrate   render
devout   renounce
effectual   secular
profess   zealous

Focus Your Reading

LITERARY ANALYSIS   HISTORICAL WRITING   **Historical writing** is a systematic account, often in narrative form, of the past of a nation or a group of people. Historical writing generally has the following characteristics: (1) it is concerned with real events, (2) the events are treated in chronological order, and (3) it is usually an objective retelling of facts rather than a personal interpretation. Which of these characteristics are evident in this passage from Bede's *History?*

> *Then, full of joy at his knowledge of the worship of the true God, he told his companions to set fire to the temple and its enclosures and destroy them. The site where these idols once stood is still shown . . . and is known as Goodmanham.*

As you read the selection from Bede's chronicle, consider whether it displays the characteristics of historical writing.

ACTIVE READING   ANALYZING AN AUTHOR'S PURPOSE
An author may write to **inform,** to **describe,** to **narrate,** to **entertain,** or to **persuade.** Frequently an author writes to accomplish two or more of these purposes. To help you identify the Venerable Bede's purpose for composing his *History,* notice the following as you read:

- incidents the author recounts
- people the author describes
- descriptions that convey the author's stance or position
- the author's **tone** throughout the selection

📖 READER'S NOTEBOOK   Jot down details that suggest the author's purpose.

The Venerable BEDE

King Edwin was a powerful ruler of Northumbria — a kingdom in northern Britain — during the early seventh century. Although a pagan, Edwin married a Christian, Ethelberga of Kent, and allowed her to practice her Christian faith. Ethelberga's chaplain, Paulinus, challenged her new husband to convert to Christianity.

Portrait of the scribe Eadwine

When Paulinus had spoken, the king answered that he was both willing and obliged to accept the Faith which he taught, but said that he must discuss the matter with his principal advisers and friends, so that if they were in agreement, they might all be cleansed together in Christ the Fount of Life. Paulinus agreed, and the king kept his promise. He summoned a council of the wise men, and asked each in turn his opinion of this new faith and new God being proclaimed.

Coifi, the High Priest, replied without hesitation: "Your Majesty, let us give careful consideration to this new teaching, for I frankly admit that, in my experience, the religion that we have hither-to professed seems valueless and powerless. None of your subjects has been more devoted to the service of the gods than myself, yet there are many to whom you show greater favor, who receive greater honors, and who are more successful in all their undertakings. Now, if the

WORDS
TO
KNOW

profess (prə-fĕs′) v. to claim belief in or allegiance to

99

gods had any power, they would surely have favored myself, who have been more <u>zealous</u> in their service. Therefore, if on examination these new teachings are found to be better and more <u>effectual</u>, let us not hesitate to accept them."

Another of the king's chief men signified his agreement with this <u>prudent</u> argument, and went on to say: "Your Majesty, when we compare the present life of man with that time of which we have no knowledge, it seems to me like the swift flight of a lone sparrow through the banqueting-hall where you sit in the winter months to dine with your thanes[1] and counselors. Inside there is a comforting fire to warm the room; outside, the wintry storms of snow and rain are raging. This sparrow flies swiftly in through one door of the hall, and out through another. While he is inside, he is safe from the winter storms; but after a few moments of comfort, he vanishes from sight into the darkness whence he came. Similarly, man appears on earth for a little while, but we know nothing of what went before this life, and what follows. Therefore if this new teaching can reveal any more certain knowledge, it seems only right that we should follow it." The other elders and counselors of the king, under God's guidance, gave the same advice.

Coifi then added that he wished to hear Paulinus' teaching about God in greater detail; and when, at the king's bidding, this had been given, the High Priest said: "I have long realized that there is nothing in what we worshiped, for the more diligently I sought after truth in our religion, the less I found. I now publicly confess that this teaching clearly reveals truths that will afford us the blessings of life, salvation, and eternal happiness. Therefore, Your Majesty, I submit that the temples and altars that we have dedicated to no advantage be immediately <u>desecrated</u> and burned." In short, the king granted blessed Paulinus full permission to preach, <u>renounced</u> idolatry, and professed his acceptance of the Faith of Christ. And when he asked the High Priest who should be the first to profane[2] the altars and shrines of the idols, together with the enclosures that surrounded them, Coifi replied: "I will do this myself, for now that the true God has granted me knowledge, who more suitably than I can set a public example, and destroy the idols that I worshiped in ignorance?" So he formally renounced his empty superstitions, and asked the king to give him arms and a stallion—for hitherto it had not been lawful for the High Priest to carry arms, or to ride anything but a mare—and, thus equipped, he set out to destroy the idols. Girded with a sword and with a spear in his hand, he mounted the king's stallion and rode up to the idols. When the crowd saw him, they thought he had gone mad, but without hesitation, as soon as he reached the temple, he cast a spear into it and profaned it. Then, full of joy at his knowledge of the worship of the true God, he told his companions to set fire to the temple and its enclosures and destroy them. The site where these idols once stood is still shown, not far east of York, beyond the river Derwent, and is known as Goodmanham. Here it was that the High Priest, inspired by the true God, desecrated and destroyed the altars that he had himself dedicated.

---

1. **thanes:** freemen attached to the household of an Anglo-Saxon lord, serving as his personal band of warriors.

2. **profane:** desecrate.

WORDS TO KNOW

zealous (zĕl′əs) *adj.* filled with enthusiasm; eager
effectual (ĭ-fĕk′chōō-əl) *adj.* able to produce a desired effect
prudent (prōōd′nt) *adj.* showing wisdom or good judgment
desecrate (dĕs′ĭ-krāt′) *v.* to violate the sacredness of
renounce (rĭ-nouns′) *v.* to give up or reject

A page from the Venerable Bede's *History of the English Church and People*.
The Granger Collection, New York.

Caedmon (kăd′mən) is the earliest English poet known to us by name. According to Bede, Caedmon composed many poems; however, only his first poem, a hymn to God the Creator, has survived. In the following account, Bede describes how Caedmon, who was an illiterate cowherd, became an accomplished poet.

Friars singing in choir, miniature from the Psalter of Henry VI (detail). Cotton Domitian A. XVII, f. 122v, by permission of The British Library.

In this monastery of Whitby there lived a brother[3] whom God's grace made remarkable. So skillful was he in composing religious and devotional songs, that he could quickly turn whatever passages of Scripture were explained to him into delightful and moving poetry in his own English tongue. These verses of his stirred the hearts of many folk to despise the world and <u>aspire</u> to heavenly things. Others after him tried to compose religious poems in English, but none could compare with him, for he received this gift of poetry as a gift from God and did not acquire it through any human teacher. For this reason he could never compose any frivolous or profane verses, but only such as had a religious theme fell fittingly from his <u>devout</u> lips. And although he followed a <u>secular</u> occupation until well advanced in years, he had never learned anything about poetry: indeed, whenever all those present at a feast took it in turns to sing and

---

3. **brother:** a man who lives in or works for a religious community but is not a priest or monk.

WORDS
TO
KNOW

aspire (ə-spīr′) *v.* to strive to attain
devout (dĭ-vout′) *adj.* showing religious devotion and piety
secular (sĕk′yə-lər) *adj.* unrelated to religion

entertain the company, he would get up from table and go home directly he saw the harp[4] approaching him.

On one such occasion he had left the house in which the entertainment was being held and went out to the stable, where it was his duty to look after the beasts that night. He lay down there at the appointed time and fell asleep, and in a dream he saw a man standing beside him who called him by name. "Caedmon," he said, "sing me a song." "I don't know how to sing," he replied. "It is because I cannot sing that I left the feast and came here." The man who addressed him then said: "But you shall sing to me." "What should I sing about?" he replied. "Sing about the Creation of all things," the other answered. And Caedmon immediately began to sing verses in praise of God the Creator that he had never heard before, and their theme ran thus: "Let us praise the Maker of the kingdom of heaven, the power and purpose of our Creator, and the acts of the Father of glory. Let us sing how the eternal God, the Author of all marvels, first created the heavens for the sons of men as a roof to cover them, and how their almighty Protector gave them the earth for their dwelling place." This is the general sense, but not the actual words that Caedmon sang in his dream; for however excellent the verses, it is impossible to translate them from one language into another[5] without losing much of their beauty and dignity. When Caedmon awoke, he remembered everything that he had sung in his dream, and soon added more verses in the same style to the glory of God.

Early in the morning he went to his superior the reeve,[6] and told him about this gift that he had received. The reeve took him before the abbess,[7] who ordered him to give an account of his dream and repeat the verses in the presence of many learned men, so that they might decide their quality and origin. All of them agreed that Caedmon's gift had been given him by our Lord, and when they had explained to him a passage of scriptural history or doctrine, they asked him to render it into verse if he could. He promised to do this, and returned next morning with excellent verses as they had ordered him. The abbess was delighted that God had given such grace to the man, and advised him to abandon secular life and adopt the monastic state. And when she had admitted him into the Community as a brother, she ordered him to be instructed in the events of sacred history.[8] So Caedmon stored up in his memory all that he learned, and like an animal chewing the cud, turned it into such melodious verse that his delightful renderings turned his instructors into his audience. He sang of the creation of the world, the origin of the human race, and the whole story of Genesis. He sang of Israel's departure from Egypt, their entry into the land of promise, and many other events of scriptural history. He sang of the Lord's Incarnation, Passion, Resurrection, and Ascension into heaven, the coming of the Holy Spirit, and the teaching of the Apostles. He also made many poems on the terrors of the Last Judgment, the horrible pains of Hell, and the joys of the kingdom of heaven. In addition to these, he composed several others on the blessings and judgments of God, by which he sought to turn his hearers from delight in wickedness, and to inspire them to love and do good. For Caedmon was a deeply religious man, who humbly submitted to regular discipline,[9] and firmly resisted all who tried to do evil, thus winning a happy death. ❖

---

4. **harp:** In Anglo-Saxon times, poetry was often recited to the accompaniment of a small harp.

5. **translate . . . another:** Caedmon's verses were composed in Old English, but Bede wrote in Latin.

6. **reeve:** the officer who oversaw the monastery's farms.

7. **abbess** (ăb′ĭs): a woman in charge of a convent or monastery. The abbess of Whitby at this time was named Hilda.

8. **sacred history:** the narratives in the Bible.

9. **regular discipline:** the rules of monastic life.

Thinking through the LITERATURE

Connect to the Literature

1. What Do You Think?
What is your reaction to the type of events Bede describes? Explain.

> **Comprehension Check**
> • Why was Coifi willing to consider the faith professed by Paulinus?
> • Why did the abbess advise Caedmon to abandon secular life and adopt the monastic state?

Think Critically

2. Why do you think the king seeks the advice of his counselors before responding to the challenge to accept Christianity?

3. In your opinion, does Coifi's destruction of the temples show great courage?

THINK ABOUT
{
• Coifi's position as high priest
• his role as adviser to the king
• the crowd's reaction at the temple

4. **ACTIVE READING** | **ANALYZING AN AUTHOR'S PURPOSE** | Use the details you wrote in your 📖 **READER'S NOTEBOOK** to determine the Venerable Bede's **purpose.** How does his purpose affect the credibility of the events he relates?

Extend Interpretations

5. What If? What do you think life would have been like for Caedmon if, after having his dream, he had chosen not to compose poetry?

6. Critic's Corner In the introduction to his translation of Bede's *History,* Leo Sherley-Price writes, "Such is the interest of the subject matter and the vividness of Bede's characteristic style that the scenes and folk of long ago live again." Comment on whether the excerpts you have read support this view of Bede's subject matter and **style.**

7. Comparing Texts Contrast the portrayals of life in Bede's *History* and in *Beowulf.* What aspects of Anglo-Saxon culture are emphasized in each work? What might account for the differences between the two portrayals?

8. Connect to Life The decisions and actions of King Edwin and Coifi hastened the spread of Christianity throughout England in a relatively short time, producing a major shift in the entire society. Think of another time in history when a political decision or some significant event or development has had a great effect on a whole nation or culture. How did people respond to the challenges to their way of life?

Literary Analysis

HISTORICAL WRITING
The characteristics of **historical writing** include a concern with real events and a chronological and objective narration of the events. Of these three characteristics, objectivity is the hardest to achieve. In Bede's account, some of his statements and choice of details may reflect his feelings and opinions. For example, Coifi's assertion that "I have long realized that there is nothing in what we worshiped" could be a reflection of the author's own opinion rather than an objective retelling of an event.

Paired Activity Choose three passages from the selection. With a partner, create a bar graph like the one shown and rate the objectivity of each passage on a scale of 1 to 10, with 1 being the least objective and 10 being the most.

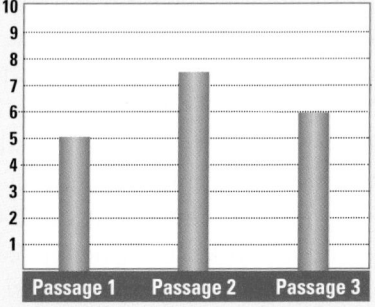

ACTIVE READING | **USING TEXT ORGANIZERS** | This **historical narrative** by the Venerable Bede uses text organizers, such as different type sizes, colors, and styles, to help clarify and structure ideas. Go back to the beginning of the selection and note the use of different treatments of type, especially in the paragraphs set off on pages 99 and 102. Identify the text organizers and note the purposes they serve in clarifying ideas.

Choices & CHALLENGES

Writing Options

Simile for Life One of the king's advisers uses a simile, comparing human life to the flight of a sparrow. Write your own simile for life and explain your comparison.

Activities & Explorations

Sketch of a Dream Recall Caedmon's dream. Then create a sketch or painting of the man who appeared to Caedmon and inspired him to write poetry. ~ **ART**

Inquiry & Research

Routes to Rome Research travel between Rome and Britain during the time of Bede. Find a map showing Europe as it was in the seventh and eighth centuries. Trace the probable routes from Rome to Britain. What means of travel were used? How long would a trip from Rome to Britain have taken? What dangers would travelers have faced? Record your findings and share them in an oral report.

Vocabulary in Action

EXERCISE: ASSESSMENT PRACTICE

Decide whether the words in each of the following pairs are more nearly synonyms or antonyms. On your paper, write *S* for *Synonyms* or *A* for *Antonyms*.

1. zealous—enthusiastic
2. renounce—abandon
3. prudent—unwise
4. effectual—effective
5. devout—pious
6. desecrate—honor
7. aspire—desire
8. secular—religious
9. render—interpret
10. profess—deny

The Venerable Bede
673?–735

Other Works
History of the Abbots
On the Reckoning of Time

Leaving Home At the age of seven, Bede was taken by his parents to a monastery at Wearmouth, on the northeast coast of Britain, where he was left in the care of the abbot, Benedict Biscop (bĭsh'əp). It is not known why the boy's parents left him or whether he ever saw them again. When he was nine years old, Bede was moved a short distance to a new monastery at Jarrow, where he was to spend the rest of his life.

A Devout Child Bede seems to have been a naturally devout and studious child. He read widely in the monastery libraries, studied Latin and perhaps a little Greek, and participated fully in the religious life of the monastery. He was exposed to the art and learning of Europe through the paintings, books, and religious objects brought from Rome by Abbot Benedict. Bede became a deacon of the church at the age of 19, 6 years earlier than normal, and was ordained to the priesthood when he was 30.

A Gifted Scholar Bede was a brilliant scholar and a gifted writer and teacher. He wrote about 40 books, including works on spelling, grammar, science, history, and religion. In addition, he popularized the dating of events from the birth of Christ, the system still in use today.

Lasting Reputation Bede's reputation as a scholar and a devout monk spread throughout Europe during his lifetime and in the centuries following. (The title "Venerable" was probably first applied to him during the century after his death.) Although Bede was influenced by the outlook of his time—as is evident in the miracle stories he included in his *History*—his carefulness and integrity are still respected and valued by scholars today, almost 1,300 years later.

W hat was life like for people in the Middle Ages? What made them laugh or cry? How did they carry out the business of living from day to day? In this part of Unit One, you will read selections that give insights into the nature of people's lives in the 14th and 15th centuries. The era will come alive for you as characters reveal their strengths and weaknesses, hopes and fears, joys and sorrows. Despite the hundreds of years that separate us from these interesting personalities, our similarities are quite astonishing.

Author Study
Geoffrey Chaucer

"There was never a man who was more of a Maker than Chaucer. . . . He came very near to making a nation."

—*G. K. Chesterton*

England's First Great Writer

Geoffrey Chaucer made an enormous mark on the language and literature of England. Writing in an age when French was widely spoken in educated circles, Chaucer was among the first writers to show that English could be a respectable literary language. Today, his work is considered a cornerstone of English literature.

1340?–1400

The facts that are known about Chaucer's life paint a portrait of a man as colorful as any of the characters he created. Explore the life and times of this groundbreaking English author.

BEFRIENDED BY ROYALS Chaucer was born sometime between 1340 and 1343, probably in London, in an era when expanding commerce was helping to bring the Middle Ages to a close. His family, though not noble, was fairly well off, having made money in the wine and leather trades (the name *Chaucer* itself comes from the French word for a shoemaker). Chaucer's parents were able to place him in the household of the wife of Prince Lionel, a son of King Edward III, where he

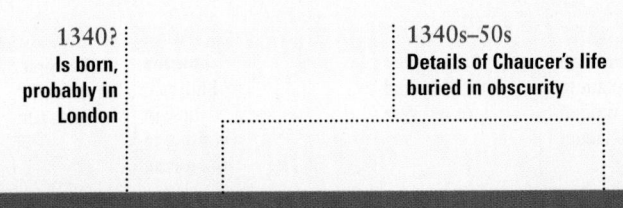

HIS LIFE
HIS TIMES

1340? Is born, probably in London		1340s–50s Details of Chaucer's life buried in obscurity
1340	**1345**	**1350**
1337 Hundred Years' War with France begins.		1349–50 Bubonic plague ravages England.

served as an attendant. Such a position was a vital means of advancement, teaching the young Chaucer the customs of upper-class life and bringing him into contact with influential people. It may have been during this period that Chaucer met Lionel's younger brother John of Gaunt, who would become Chaucer's lifelong patron and a leading political figure of the day.

While still a teenager, Chaucer joined the king's army to fight against the French in what we now call the Hundred Years' War. He was captured by the French during the siege of Rheims, and the king himself contributed to his ransom. Chaucer later served as a royal messenger, and he would be given more important diplomatic missions in years to come. His royal contacts also led to his marriage to Philippa, a lady in waiting to the queen, and his appointment as comptroller of customs for London in 1374.

EARLY INSPIRATIONS

Chaucer's diplomatic travels to the European mainland exposed him to the latest in French and Italian literature—

works that would stimulate his own writing. In Italy, for example, he discovered the works of Dante, Petrarch, and Boccaccio. Chaucer's earliest major writing effort

Chaucer's home above Aldgate in London from 1374–1385

was probably an English translation of part of *The Romance of the Rose,* a famous medieval French verse romance. Not long afterward, he produced his first important original work, *The Book of the Duchess,* a long narrative poem paying tribute to Blanche, John of Gaunt's first wife, who died of plague in 1369. It was followed a few years later by *The House of Fame,* a humorous narrative about the instability of renown.

TURBULENT TIMES

Despite his writing successes, Chaucer's primary career remained one of politics and diplomacy. Unlike many other courtiers of the era, Chaucer continued to enjoy royal favor throughout the turbulent reign of Richard II, who was still only a boy when he became England's king in 1377. Chaucer's next major work, *The Parliament of Fowls,* was probably written to commemorate Richard's

1357 **Becomes an attendant to the wife of Prince Lionel**	1359–60 **Captured in the Hundred Years' War**	1365? **Marries Philippa, lady in waiting to the queen**	1366 **Makes first diplomatic mission**	1369? **Writes *The Book of the Duchess***	1372 **Visits Italy; discovers Boccaccio's work**

Boccaccio

1355   **1360**   **1365**   **1370**   **1375**

	1362? **William Langland writes the first version of *Piers Plowman*.**	1364 **King John II of France dies in the Tower of London.**		1377 **Edward III dies; Richard II becomes king.**

marriage to Anne of Bohemia in 1382. Four years later, Chaucer was appointed a knight of the shire and became a member of Parliament. In the 1390s he continued to enjoy various royal appointments, including those of clerk of the king's works and subforester of a royal park.

Meanwhile, Richard II's reign was marked by conflict at home and abroad, including a peasants' revolt led by Wat Tyler and heightened agitation by the Lollards, a group of church reformers led by John Wycliffe. Finally, while Richard was off attempting to quell a rebellion in Ireland in 1399, his popular cousin Henry Bolingbroke wrested the throne from his control and was crowned as King Henry IV. The change of monarch did not affect Chaucer's political fortunes, since Henry was the son of Chaucer's longtime patron John of Gaunt. However, the writer had little time to enjoy the favor of the new monarch, for he died only a year after Henry came to the throne.

FRUITFUL YEARS The last two decades of Chaucer's life saw his finest literary achievements—the brilliant verse romance *Troilus and Criseyde* and his masterpiece, *The Canterbury Tales*, a collection of verse and prose tales of many different kinds. To join the stories together, Chaucer decided to pretend they are told by members of a group of travelers journeying from London to Canterbury. Though he may have written some of the stories earlier, most scholars think that he began organizing *The Canterbury Tales* about 1387. The work

Considered the greatest English writer before Shakespeare, Chaucer was praised in his lifetime and widely imitated after his death, when a group of 15th-century poets adopted his writing style. Later in the 15th century, when the printing press was introduced into England, *The Canterbury Tales* was among the first works to be printed.

Longer Poetic Works Chaucer is best known for his verse narratives. These include the following:

- *The Book of the Duchess*
- *The House of Fame*
- *The Parliament of Fowls*
- *Troilus and Criseyde*
- *The Legend of Good Women*
- *The Canterbury Tales*

Short Poems Chaucer also wrote several shorter poems, including these:

- "Complaint to His Empty Purse"
- "Words, to Adam, His Own Scrivener"
- "Truth"
- "Fortune"
- "Gentilesse [Nobility]"
- "Envoy [Message] to Scogan"
- "Envoy [Message] to Bukton"

Prose As outgrowths of his scholarly interests, Chaucer produced these prose works:

- *The Consolation of Philosophy* (translated from the Latin of Boethius)
- *Treatise on the Astrolabe*

		1386	1387	1389		1400
		Becomes a member of Parliament	**Begins to plan *The Canterbury Tales***	**Appointed clerk of the king's works**		**Dies and is buried in Westminster Abbey**

1380	**1385**	**1390**	**1395**	**1400**

1381	1382	1388	1395	1399
Peasants' Revolt breaks out.	**Richard II marries Anne of Bohemia.**	**Opponents of Richard II execute eight of his friends.**	**Lollards petition for church reform.**	**Richard II is deposed; Henry IV becomes king.**

Chaucer's London

Originally a walled town built by the Romans, London had become a bustling commercial city by Chaucer's day. Its walls enclosed a semicircular area of roughly a square mile, extending along the Thames River from the Tower of London to the Fleet River. On this small patch of land lived about 35,000 people, plus rats and other vermin, crowded together in noisy, unsanitary conditions. A marsh outside the city's north wall, although little more than an open sewer, nevertheless afforded excellent diversion when frozen over in winter.

was still unfinished at the time of his death; Chaucer had penned nearly 20,000 lines, but many more tales were planned.

UNCOMMON HONOR When he died in 1400, Chaucer was accorded an honor rare for a commoner—burial in London's Westminster Abbey. In 1566 an admirer erected an elaborate marble tomb for his remains. This was the beginning of Westminster Abbey's famous Poets' Corner, where many other great English writers have since been buried.

Chaucer's attitude toward his great

subsequent renown would probably be one of humility and amusement. In *The Canterbury Tales,* he portrayed himself as a short, plump, slightly foolish pilgrim who commands no great respect. Yet from the mind of this gentle poet came a host of memorable characters and some of the finest poetry ever created in the English language.

 More Online: Author Link
www.mcdougallittell.com

The Shrine of Canterbury

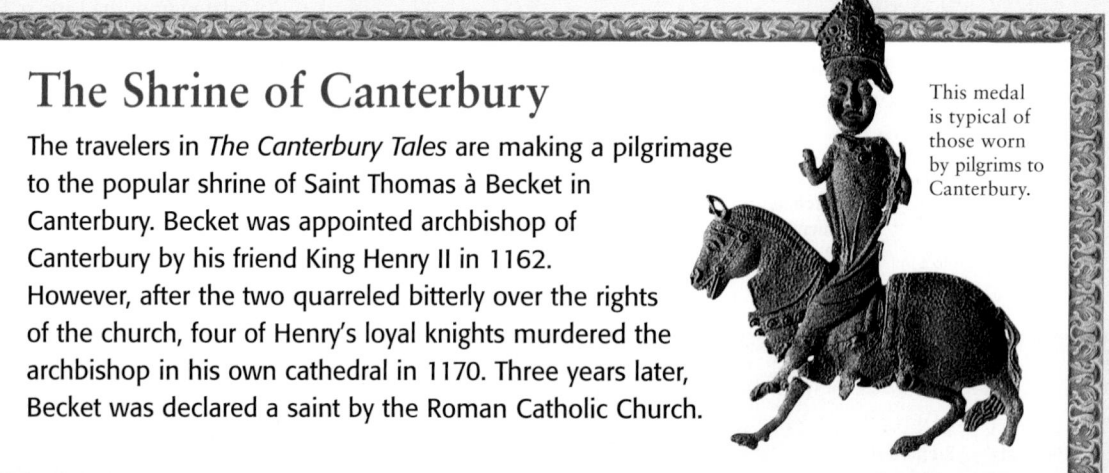

The travelers in *The Canterbury Tales* are making a pilgrimage to the popular shrine of Saint Thomas à Becket in Canterbury. Becket was appointed archbishop of Canterbury by his friend King Henry II in 1162. However, after the two quarreled bitterly over the rights of the church, four of Henry's loyal knights murdered the archbishop in his own cathedral in 1170. Three years later, Becket was declared a saint by the Roman Catholic Church.

This medal is typical of those worn by pilgrims to Canterbury.

The Prologue
from The Canterbury Tales

Poetry by GEOFFREY CHAUCER
Translated by NEVILL COGHILL

Comparing Literature of the World

The Canterbury Tales and The Decameron

If you wish to compare the storytelling tradition across cultures, you might read "Federigo's Falcon," the excerpt from *The Decameron* that follows the three excerpts from *The Canterbury Tales.* Points of Comparison between Chaucer's and Boccaccio's tales include the narrative structure of the frame story and the authors' focus on stories with love themes.

Connect to Your Life

Story Time Recall a time when you and some friends told funny stories about growing up. What situations inspire people to tell stories? What role does an audience play in making the telling of a story more interesting? Share your thoughts in a class discussion.

Build Background

Medieval Story Time In the "Prologue," or introduction, from *The Canterbury Tales,* a group of travelers from various walks of life gather in an inn outside London to make a pilgrimage to the shrine of Saint Thomas à Becket in the city of Canterbury. At the suggestion of the innkeeper (the Host), the group decides to hold a storytelling competition to pass the time as they travel. The portion of *The Canterbury Tales* that follows the "Prologue" consists mainly of the stories that various pilgrims tell.

WORDS TO KNOW **Vocabulary Preview**

accrue	disdain	mode
agility	dispatch	personable
courtliness	eminent	repine
defer	frugal	sedately
diligent	malady	wield

Focus Your Reading

LITERARY ANALYSIS **TONE** The **tone** of a literary work expresses the writer's attitude toward the work's subject or characters. A tone, for example, may be formal or informal, amused or impatient. In the "Prologue" the narrator uses a detached, **ironic** tone, often understating his criticisms or saying the opposite of what he really thinks. For example, in the following lines Chaucer reveals his attitude toward a Friar who dispenses God's forgiveness ("absolution") freely, as long as he receives a donation—an attitude he probably expects the reader to share.

> *Sweetly he heard his penitents at shrift*
> *With pleasant absolution, for a gift.*

ACTIVE READING **ANALYZING CHARACTERIZATION**

Characterization is the means by which a writer develops a **character**'s personality. A writer can use a number of techniques:

- description of the character's physical appearance
- presentation of the character's speech, thoughts, feelings, and actions
- presentation of other characters' speech, thoughts, feelings, and actions as they relate to the character

READER'S NOTEBOOK As you read the "Prologue," jot down words or phrases that convey the personalities of some of the characters the **narrator** describes, as well as the narrator himself. Be sure to include the Pardoner and the Wife of Bath.

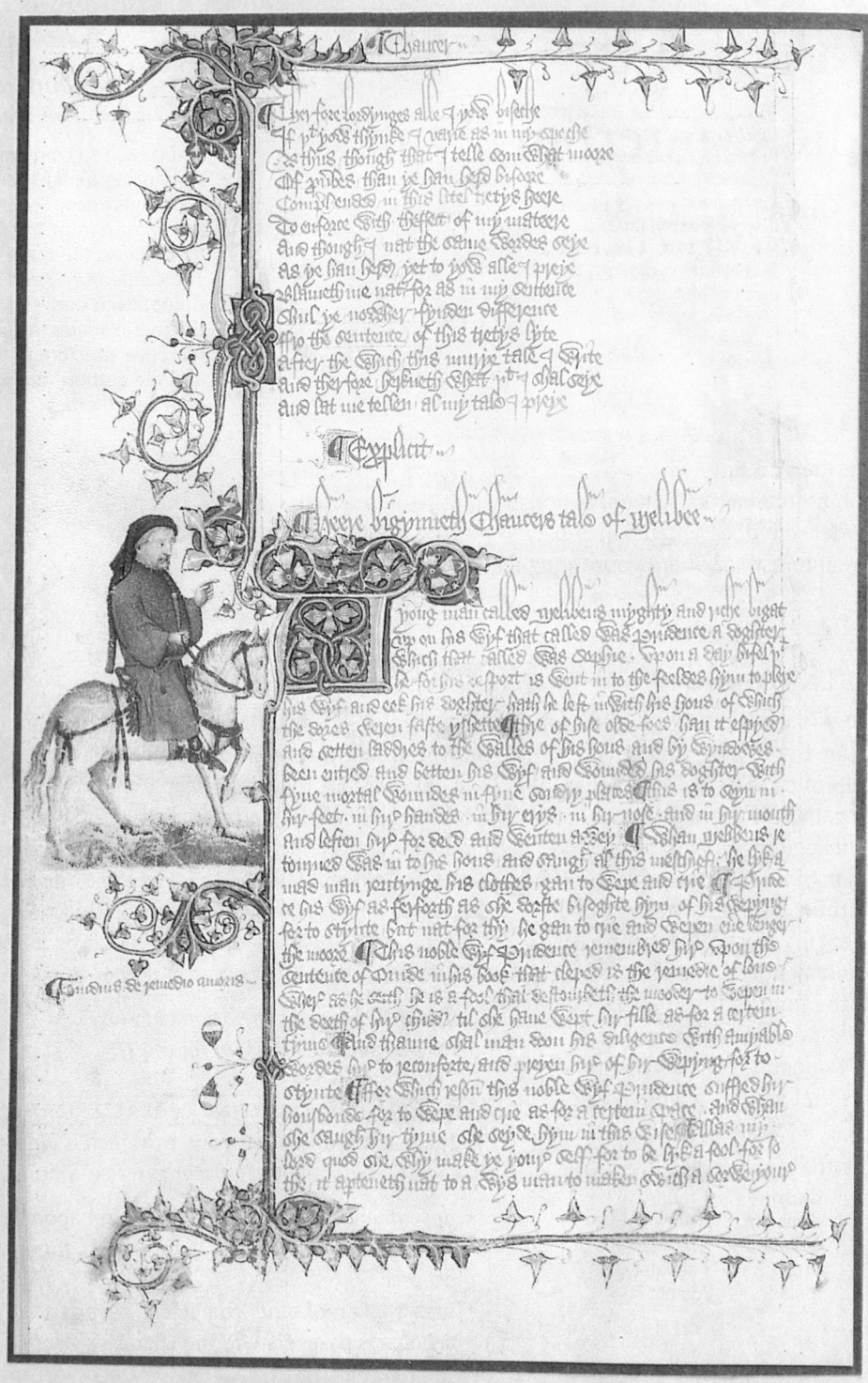

Chaucer on horseback. From the Ellesmere manuscript, EL 26 c. 9, fol. 153v, The Huntington Library, San Marino, California.

from

The Canterbury Tales

Geoffrey Chaucer

The Prologue

When in April the sweet showers fall
And pierce the drought of March to the root, and all
The veins are bathed in liquor of such power
As brings about the engendering of the flower,
5   When also Zephyrus with his sweet breath
Exhales an air in every grove and heath
Upon the tender shoots, and the young sun
His half-course in the sign of the *Ram* has run,
And the small fowl are making melody
10   That sleep away the night with open eye
(So nature pricks them and their heart engages)
Then people long to go on pilgrimages
And palmers long to seek the stranger strands
Of far-off saints, hallowed in sundry lands,
15   And specially, from every shire's end
Of England, down to Canterbury they wend
To seek the holy blissful martyr, quick
To give his help to them when they were sick.

It happened in that season that one day
20   In Southwark, at *The Tabard,* as I lay
Ready to go on pilgrimage and start
For Canterbury, most devout at heart,
At night there came into that hostelry
Some nine and twenty in a company
25   Of sundry folk happening then to fall
In fellowship, and they were pilgrims all
That towards Canterbury meant to ride.

The rooms and stables of the inn were wide;
They made us easy, all was of the best.
30 And, briefly, when the sun had gone to rest,
I'd spoken to them all upon the trip
And was soon one with them in fellowship,
Pledged to rise early and to take the way
To Canterbury, as you heard me say.

35 But none the less, while I have time and space,
Before my story takes a further pace,
It seems a reasonable thing to say
What their condition was, the full array
Of each of them, as it appeared to me,
40 According to profession and degree,
And what apparel they were riding in;
And at a Knight I therefore will begin.
There was a *Knight,* a most distinguished man,
Who from the day on which he first began
45 To ride abroad had followed chivalry,
Truth, honor, generousness and courtesy.
He had done nobly in his sovereign's war
And ridden into battle, no man more,
As well in Christian as in heathen places,
50 And ever honored for his noble graces.

When we took Alexandria, he was there.
He often sat at table in the chair
Of honor, above all nations, when in Prussia.
In Lithuania he had ridden, and Russia,
55 No Christian man so often, of his rank.
When, in Granada, Algeciras sank
Under assault, he had been there, and in
North Africa, raiding Benamarin;
In Anatolia he had been as well
60 And fought when Ayas and Attalia fell,
For all along the Mediterranean coast
He had embarked with many a noble host.
In fifteen mortal battles he had been
And jousted for our faith at Tramissene
65 Thrice in the lists, and always killed his man.
This same distinguished knight had led the van
Once with the Bey of Balat, doing work

35–41 What is the narrator going to take time and space to do? What is he interrupting?

45 chivalry (shĭv′əl-rē): the code of behavior of medieval knights, which stressed the values listed in line 46.

51 Alexandria: a city in Egypt, captured by European Christians in 1365. All the places named in lines 51–64 were scenes of conflicts in which medieval Christians battled Muslims and other non-Christian peoples.

64 jousted: fought with a lance in an arranged battle against another knight.

65 thrice: three times; **lists:** fenced areas for jousting.

66 van: vanguard—the troops foremost in an attack.

67 Bey of Balat: a Turkish ruler.

For him against another heathen Turk;
He was of sovereign value in all eyes.
70 And though so much distinguished, he was wise
And in his bearing modest as a maid.
He never yet a boorish thing had said
In all his life to any, come what might;
He was a true, a perfect gentle-knight.

Speaking of his equipment, he possessed
75 Fine horses, but he was not gaily dressed.
He wore a fustian tunic stained and dark
With smudges where his armor had left mark;
Just home from service, he had joined our ranks
80 To do his pilgrimage and render thanks.

He had his son with him, a fine young *Squire,*
A lover and cadet, a lad of fire
With locks as curly as if they had been pressed.
He was some twenty years of age, I guessed.
85 In stature he was of a moderate length,
With wonderful <u>agility</u> and strength.
He'd seen some service with the cavalry
In Flanders and Artois and Picardy
And had done valiantly in little space
90 Of time, in hope to win his lady's grace.
He was embroidered like a meadow bright
And full of freshest flowers, red and white.
Singing he was, or fluting all the day;
He was as fresh as is the month of May.
95 Short was his gown, the sleeves were long and wide;
He knew the way to sit a horse and ride.
He could make songs and poems and recite,
Knew how to joust and dance, to draw and write.
He loved so hotly that till dawn grew pale
100 He slept as little as a nightingale.
Courteous he was, lowly and serviceable,
And carved to serve his father at the table.

There was a *Yeoman* with him at his side,
No other servant; so he chose to ride.

77 fustian (fŭs´chən): a strong cloth made of linen and cotton.

81 Squire: a young man attending on and receiving training from a knight.

82 cadet: soldier in training.

88 Flanders and Artois (är-twä´) **and Picardy** (pĭk´ər-dē): areas in what is now Belgium and northern France.

The Squire, from the Ellesmere manuscript

103 Yeoman (yō´mən): an attendant in a noble household; **him:** the Knight.

105   This Yeoman wore a coat and hood of green,
     And peacock-feathered arrows, bright and keen
     And neatly sheathed, hung at his belt the while
     —For he could dress his gear in yeoman style,
     His arrows never drooped their feathers low—
110   And in his hand he bore a mighty bow.
     His head was like a nut, his face was brown.
     He knew the whole of woodcraft up and down.
     A saucy brace was on his arm to ward
     It from the bow-string, and a shield and sword
115   Hung at one side, and at the other slipped
     A jaunty dirk, spear-sharp and well-equipped.
     A medal of St. Christopher he wore
     Of shining silver on his breast, and bore
     A hunting-horn, well slung and burnished clean,
120   That dangled from a baldrick of bright green.
     He was a proper forester, I guess.

     There also was a *Nun,* a Prioress,
     Her way of smiling very simple and coy.
     Her greatest oath was only "By St. Loy!"
125   And she was known as Madam Eglantyne.
     And well she sang a service, with a fine
     Intoning through her nose, as was most seemly,
     And she spoke daintily in French, extremely,
     After the school of Stratford-atte-Bowe;
130   French in the Paris style she did not know.
     At meat her manners were well taught withal;
     No morsel from her lips did she let fall,
     Nor dipped her fingers in the sauce too deep;
     But she could carry a morsel up and keep
135   The smallest drop from falling on her breast.
     For <u>courtliness</u> she had a special zest,
     And she would wipe her upper lip so clean
     That not a trace of grease was to be seen
     Upon the cup when she had drunk; to eat,
140   She reached a hand <u>sedately</u> for the meat.
     She certainly was very entertaining,
     Pleasant and friendly in her ways, and straining
     To counterfeit a courtly kind of grace,
     A stately bearing fitting to her place,

113 saucy: jaunty; stylish; **brace:** a leather arm-guard worn by archers.

116 dirk: small dagger.

117 St. Christopher: the patron saint of foresters and travelers.

120 baldrick: shoulder strap.

122 Prioress: a nun ranking just below the abbess (head) of a convent.

124 St. Loy: St. Eligius (known as St. Eloi in France).

129 Stratford-atte-Bowe: a town (now part of London) near the Prioress's convent. How do you think the French spoken there differed from that spoken in Paris?

131 at meat: when dining; **withal:** moreover.

The Prioress

WORDS TO KNOW	**courtliness** (kôrt′lē-nĭs) *n.* refined behavior; elegance **sedately** (sĭ-dāt′lē) *adv.* in a composed, dignified manner; calmly

116

145 And to seem dignified in all her dealings.
As for her sympathies and tender feelings,
She was so charitably solicitous
She used to weep if she but saw a mouse
Caught in a trap, if it were dead or bleeding.
150 And she had little dogs she would be feeding
With roasted flesh, or milk, or fine white bread.
And bitterly she wept if one were dead
Or someone took a stick and made it smart;
She was all sentiment and tender heart.
155 Her veil was gathered in a seemly way,
Her nose was elegant, her eyes glass-grey;
Her mouth was very small, but soft and red,
Her forehead, certainly, was fair of spread,
Almost a span across the brows, I own;
160 She was indeed by no means undergrown.
Her cloak, I noticed, had a graceful charm.
She wore a coral trinket on her arm,
A set of beads, the gaudies tricked in green,
Whence hung a golden brooch of brightest sheen
165 On which there first was graven a crowned A,
And lower, *Amor vincit omnia*.

Another *Nun*, the secretary at her cell,
Was riding with her, and *three Priests* as well.

A *Monk* there was, one of the finest sort
170 Who rode the country; hunting was his sport.
A manly man, to be an Abbot able;
Many a dainty horse he had in stable.
His bridle, when he rode, a man might hear
Jingling in a whistling wind as clear,
175 Aye, and as loud as does the chapel bell
Where my lord Monk was Prior of the cell.
The Rule of good St. Benet or St. Maur
As old and strict he tended to ignore;
He let go by the things of yesterday
180 And took the modern world's more spacious way.
He did not rate that text at a plucked hen
Which says that hunters are not holy men
And that a monk uncloistered is a mere
Fish out of water, flapping on the pier,

The Monk

159 span: a unit of length equal to nine inches. A broad forehead was considered a sign of beauty in Chaucer's day.

163 gaudies: the larger beads in a set of prayer beads.

166 *Amor vincit omnia* (ä'môr wĭn'kĭt ôm'nē-ə): Latin for "Love conquers all things."

171 Abbot: the head of a monastery.

172 dainty: excellent.

176 Prior of the cell: head of a subsidiary group of monks.

177 St. Benet . . . St. Maur: St. Benedict, who established a strict set of rules for monks' behavior, and his follower St. Maurus, who introduced those rules into France.

180 What does the narrator mean by "the modern world's more spacious way"?

185 That is to say a monk out of his cloister.
That was a text he held not worth an oyster;
And I agreed and said his views were sound;
Was he to study till his head went round
Poring over books in cloisters? Must he toil
190 As Austin bade and till the very soil?
Was he to leave the world upon the shelf?
Let Austin have his labor to himself.

This Monk was therefore a good man to horse;
Greyhounds he had, as swift as birds, to course.
195 Hunting a hare or riding at a fence
Was all his fun, he spared for no expense.
I saw his sleeves were garnished at the hand
With fine grey fur, the finest in the land,
And on his hood, to fasten it at his chin
200 He had a wrought-gold cunningly fashioned pin;
Into a lover's knot it seemed to pass.
His head was bald and shone like looking-glass;
So did his face, as if it had been greased.
He was a fat and <u>personable</u> priest;
205 His prominent eyeballs never seemed to settle.
They glittered like the flames beneath a kettle;
Supple his boots, his horse in fine condition.
He was a prelate fit for exhibition,
He was not pale like a tormented soul.
210 He liked a fat swan best, and roasted whole.
His palfrey was as brown as is a berry.

There was a *Friar*, a wanton one and merry,
A Limiter, a very festive fellow.
In all Four Orders there was none so mellow,
215 So glib with gallant phrase and well-turned speech.
He'd fixed up many a marriage, giving each
Of his young women what he could afford her.
He was a noble pillar to his Order.
Highly beloved and intimate was he
220 With County folk within his boundary,
And city dames of honor and possessions;
For he was qualified to hear confessions,
Or so he said, with more than priestly scope;

190 Austin: St. Augustine of Hippo, who recommended that monks engage in hard agricultural labor.

194 to course: for hunting.

208 prelate (prĕl'ĭt): high-ranking member of the clergy.

211 palfrey (pôl'frē): saddle horse.

212 Friar: a member of a religious group sworn to poverty and living on charitable donations; **wanton** (wŏn'tən): playful; jolly.

213 Limiter: a friar licensed to beg for donations in a limited area.

214 Four Orders: the four groups of friars—Dominican, Franciscan, Carmelite, and Augustinian.

222 confessions: church rites in which penitents (people seeking absolution, or formal forgiveness, for their sins) confess their sins to members of the clergy, who usually require the penitents to perform certain tasks, called penances, as a condition of the forgiveness. Only certain friars were licensed to hear confessions.

WORDS
TO
KNOW   **personable** (pûr'sə-nə-bəl) *adj.* pleasing in behavior and appearance

He had a special license from the Pope.
225 Sweetly he heard his penitents at shrift
With pleasant absolution, for a gift.
He was an easy man in penance-giving
Where he could hope to make a decent living;
It's a sure sign whenever gifts are given
230 To a poor Order that a man's well shriven,
And should he give enough he knew in verity
The penitent repented in sincerity.
For many a fellow is so hard of heart
He cannot weep, for all his inward smart.
235 Therefore instead of weeping and of prayer
One should give silver for a poor Friar's care.
He kept his tippet stuffed with pins for curls,
And pocket-knives, to give to pretty girls.
And certainly his voice was gay and sturdy,
240 For he sang well and played the hurdy-gurdy.
At sing-songs he was champion of the hour.
His neck was whiter than a lily-flower
But strong enough to butt a bruiser down.
He knew the taverns well in every town
245 And every innkeeper and barmaid too
Better than lepers, beggars and that crew,
For in so eminent a man as he
It was not fitting with the dignity
Of his position, dealing with a scum
250 Of wretched lepers; nothing good can come
Of commerce with such slum-and-gutter dwellers,
But only with the rich and victual-sellers.
But anywhere a profit might accrue
Courteous he was and lowly of service too.
255 Natural gifts like his were hard to match.
He was the finest beggar of his batch,
And, for his begging-district, paid a rent;
His brethren did no poaching where he went.
For though a widow mightn't have a shoe,
260 So pleasant was his holy how-d'ye-do
He got his farthing from her just the same
Before he left, and so his income came
To more than he laid out. And how he romped,
Just like a puppy! He was ever prompt

225 shrift: confession.

230 well shriven: completely forgiven through the rite of confession. What role does money seem to play in the confessions that the Friar hears?

231 verity: truth.

237 tippet: an extension of a hood or sleeve, used as a pocket.

240 hurdy-gurdy: a stringed musical instrument, similar to a lute, played by turning a crank while pressing down keys.

The Friar

252 victual (vĭt′l): food.

261 farthing: a coin of small value used in England until recent times.

| WORDS TO KNOW | **eminent** (ĕm′ə-nənt) *adj.* standing out above others; high-ranking; prominent
accrue (ə-krōō′) *v.* to come as gain; accumulate |

265   To arbitrate disputes on settling days
    (For a small fee) in many helpful ways,
    Not then appearing as your cloistered scholar
    With threadbare habit hardly worth a dollar,
    But much more like a Doctor or a Pope.
270   Of double-worsted was the semi-cope
    Upon his shoulders, and the swelling fold
    About him, like a bell about its mold
    When it is casting, rounded out his dress.
    He lisped a little out of wantonness
275   To make his English sweet upon his tongue.
    When he had played his harp, or having sung,
    His eyes would twinkle in his head as bright
    As any star upon a frosty night.
    This worthy's name was Hubert, it appeared.

280   There was a *Merchant* with a forking beard
    And motley dress; high on his horse he sat,
    Upon his head a Flemish beaver hat
    And on his feet daintily buckled boots.
    He told of his opinions and pursuits
285   In solemn tones, he harped on his increase
    Of capital; there should be sea-police
    (He thought) upon the Harwich-Holland ranges;
    He was expert at dabbling in exchanges.
    This estimable Merchant so had set
290   His wits to work, none knew he was in debt,
    He was so stately in administration,
    In loans and bargains and negotiation.
    He was an excellent fellow all the same;
    To tell the truth I do not know his name.

295   An *Oxford Cleric*, still a student though,
    One who had taken logic long ago,
    Was there; his horse was thinner than a rake,
    And he was not too fat, I undertake,
    But had a hollow look, a sober stare;
300   The thread upon his overcoat was bare.
    He had found no preferment in the church
    And he was too unworldly to make search
    For secular employment. By his bed
    He preferred having twenty books in red

265 settling days: days on which disputes were settled out of court. Friars often acted as arbiters in the disputes and charged for their services, though forbidden by the church to do so.

270 double-worsted (wŏŏs'tĭd): a strong, fairly costly fabric made from tightly twisted yarn; **semi-cope:** a short cloak.

281 motley: multicolored.

282 Flemish: from Flanders, an area in what is now Belgium and northern France.

287 Harwich-Holland ranges: shipping routes between Harwich (hăr' ĭj), a port on England's east coast, and the country of Holland.

288 exchanges: selling foreign currency at a profit. From his dabbling in this practice, which was illegal in Chaucer's day, what can you conclude about the Merchant?

295 Cleric: a clergyman—here, a student preparing for the priesthood.

301 preferment: advancement; promotion.

303 secular (sĕk'yə-lər): outside the church.

305 And black, of Aristotle's philosophy,
Than costly clothes, fiddle or psaltery.
Though a philosopher, as I have told,
He had not found the stone for making gold.
Whatever money from his friends he took
310 He spent on learning or another book
And prayed for them most earnestly, returning
Thanks to them thus for paying for his learning.
His only care was study, and indeed
He never spoke a word more than was need,
315 Formal at that, respectful in the extreme,
Short, to the point, and lofty in his theme.
A tone of moral virtue filled his speech
And gladly would he learn, and gladly teach.

A *Sergeant at the Law* who paid his calls,
320 Wary and wise, for clients at St. Paul's
There also was, of noted excellence.
Discreet he was, a man to reverence,
Or so he seemed, his sayings were so wise.
He often had been Justice of Assize
325 By letters patent, and in full commission.
His fame and learning and his high position
Had won him many a robe and many a fee.
There was no such conveyancer as he;
All was fee-simple to his strong digestion,
330 Not one conveyance could be called in question.
Though there was nowhere one so busy as he,
He was less busy than he seemed to be.
He knew of every judgement, case and crime
Ever recorded since King William's time.
335 He could dictate defenses or draft deeds;
No one could pinch a comma from his screeds
And he knew every statute off by rote.
He wore a homely parti-colored coat,
Girt with a silken belt of pin-stripe stuff;
340 Of his appearance I have said enough.

305 Aristotle's philosophy: the writings of Aristotle, a famous Greek philosopher of the fourth century B.C.

306 psaltery (sôl′tə-rē): a stringed instrument.

307–308 Though a philosopher . . . stone for making gold: Practitioners of the false science of alchemy often sought the "philosopher's stone," supposedly capable of turning common metals into gold. What does the narrator mean by this statement?

319 Sergeant at the Law: a lawyer appointed by the monarch to serve as a judge.

320 St. Paul's: the cathedral of London, outside which lawyers met clients when the courts were closed.

324 Justice of Assize: a judge who traveled about the country to hear cases.

325 letters patent: royal documents commissioning a judge.

328 conveyancer: lawyer specializing in conveyances (deeds) and property disputes.

329 fee-simple: property owned without restrictions.

331–332 Explain the apparent contradiction here. How would you sum up the skill and work habits of the Sergeant at the Law?

334 King William's time: the reign of William the Conqueror.

336 screeds: documents.

The Franklin

There was a *Franklin* with him, it appeared;
White as a daisy-petal was his beard.
A sanguine man, high-colored and benign,
He loved a morning sop of cake in wine.
345 He lived for pleasure and had always done,
For he was Epicurus' very son,
In whose opinion sensual delight
Was the one true felicity in sight.
As noted as St. Julian was for bounty
350 He made his household free to all the County.
His bread, his ale were finest of the fine
And no one had a better stock of wine.
His house was never short of bake-meat pies,
Of fish and flesh, and these in such supplies
355 It positively snowed with meat and drink
And all the dainties that a man could think.
According to the seasons of the year
Changes of dish were ordered to appear.
He kept fat partridges in coops, beyond,
360 Many a bream and pike were in his pond.
Woe to the cook unless the sauce was hot
And sharp, or if he wasn't on the spot!
And in his hall a table stood arrayed
And ready all day long, with places laid.
365 As Justice at the Sessions none stood higher;
He often had been Member for the Shire.
A dagger and a little purse of silk
Hung at his girdle, white as morning milk.
As Sheriff he checked audit, every entry.
370 He was a model among landed gentry.

341 Franklin: a wealthy landowner.

343 sanguine (săng′gwĭn): In medieval science, the human body was thought to contain four "humors" (blood, phlegm, yellow bile, and black bile), the relative proportions of which determined a person's temperament. A sanguine person (one in whom blood was thought to predominate) was cheerful and good-natured.

346 Epicurus' very son: someone who pursues pleasure as the chief goal in life, as the ancient Greek philosopher Epicurus was supposed to have recommended.

349 St. Julian: the patron saint of hospitality; **bounty:** generosity.

365 Sessions: local court proceedings.

366 Member for the Shire: his county's representative in Parliament.

368 girdle: belt.

369 Sheriff: a royal tax collector.

370 landed gentry (jĕn′trē): well-born, wealthy landowners.

A *Haberdasher*, a *Dyer*, a *Carpenter*,
A *Weaver* and a *Carpet-maker* were
Among our ranks, all in the livery
Of one impressive guild-fraternity.
375 They were so trim and fresh their gear would pass
For new. Their knives were not tricked out with brass
But wrought with purest silver, which avouches
A like display on girdles and on pouches.
Each seemed a worthy burgess, fit to grace
380 A guild-hall with a seat upon the dais.
Their wisdom would have justified a plan
To make each one of them an alderman;
They had the capital and revenue,
Besides their wives declared it was their due.
385 And if they did not think so, then they ought;
To be called *"Madam"* is a glorious thought,
And so is going to church and being seen
Having your mantle carried, like a queen.

They had a *Cook* with them who stood alone
390 For boiling chicken with a marrow-bone,
Sharp flavoring-powder and a spice for savor.
He could distinguish London ale by flavor,
And he could roast and seethe and broil and fry,
Make good thick soup and bake a tasty pie.
395 But what a pity—so it seemed to me,
That he should have an ulcer on his knee.
As for blancmange, he made it with the best.

The Cook

There was a *Skipper* hailing from far west;
He came from Dartmouth, so I understood.
400 He rode a farmer's horse as best he could,
In a woolen gown that reached his knee.
A dagger on a lanyard falling free
Hung from his neck under his arm and down.
The summer heat had tanned his color brown,
405 And certainly he was an excellent fellow.
Many a draft of vintage, red and yellow,
He'd drawn at Bordeaux, while the trader snored.
The nicer rules of conscience he ignored.
If, when he fought, the enemy vessel sank,
410 He sent his prisoners home; they walked the plank.

371 Haberdasher: a seller of hats and other clothing accessories.

373–374 livery . . . guild-fraternity: uniform of a social or religious organization.

379 burgess (bûr′jǐs): citizen of a town.

382 alderman: town councilor.

388 mantle: cloak.

397 blancmange (blə-mänj′): in Chaucer's day, a thick chicken stew with almonds.

399 Dartmouth (därt′məth): a port in southwestern England.

402 lanyard (lăn′yərd): a cord worn as a necklace.

405 What might the narrator mean by calling the Skipper "an excellent fellow"?

406 vintage: wine.

407 Bordeaux (bôr-dō′): a region of France famous for its wine.

As for his skill in reckoning his tides,
Currents and many another risk besides,
Moons, harbors, pilots, he had such <u>dispatch</u>
That none from Hull to Carthage was his match.
415 Hardy he was, prudent in undertaking;
His beard in many a tempest had its shaking,
And he knew all the havens as they were
From Gottland to the Cape of Finisterre,
And every creek in Brittany and Spain;
420 The barge he owned was called *The Maudelayne*.

A *Doctor* too emerged as we proceeded;
No one alive could talk as well as he did
On points of medicine and of surgery,
For, being grounded in astronomy,
425 He watched his patient closely for the hours
When, by his horoscope, he knew the powers
Of favorable planets, then ascendent,
Worked on the images for his dependant.
The cause of every <u>malady</u> you'd got
430 He knew, and whether dry, cold, moist or hot;
He knew their seat, their humor and condition.
He was a perfect practicing physician.
These causes being known for what they were,
He gave the man his medicine then and there.
435 All his apothecaries in a tribe
Were ready with the drugs he would prescribe
And each made money from the other's guile;
They had been friendly for a goodish while.
He was well-versed in Aesculapius too
440 And what Hippocrates and Rufus knew
And Dioscorides, now dead and gone,
Galen and Rhazes, Hali, Serapion,
Averroes, Avicenna, Constantine,
Scotch Bernard, John of Gaddesden, Gilbertine.
445 In his own diet he observed some measure;
There were no superfluities for pleasure,
Only digestives, nutritives and such.
He did not read the Bible very much.
In blood-red garments, slashed with bluish grey
450 And lined with taffeta, he rode his way;

414 Hull . . . Carthage: ports in England and in Spain. The places named in lines 414–419 show that the Skipper is familiar with all the western coast of Europe.

416 tempest: violent storm.

424 astronomy: astrology.

430 dry, cold, moist . . . hot: in medieval science, the four basic qualities that were thought to combine in various ways to form both the four elements of the world (fire, air, water, and earth) and the four humors of the human body (see the note at line 343). An excess of any of these qualities in a person could lead to illness.

435 apothecaries (ə-pŏth′ĭ-kěr′ēz): druggists.

439–444 Aesculapius (ĕs′kyə-lā′pē-əs) **. . . Gilbertine:** famous ancient and medieval medical experts.

446 superfluities (sōō′pər-flōō′ĭ-tēz): excesses.

450 taffeta (tăf′ĭ-tə): a stiff, smooth fabric.

Yet he was rather close as to expenses
And kept the gold he won in pestilences.
Gold stimulates the heart, or so we're told.
He therefore had a special love of gold.

455   A worthy *woman* from beside *Bath* city
Was with us, somewhat deaf, which was a pity.
In making cloth she showed so great a bent
She bettered those of Ypres and of Ghent.
In all the parish not a dame dared stir
460 Towards the altar steps in front of her,
And if indeed they did, so wrath was she
As to be quite put out of charity.
Her kerchiefs were of finely woven ground;
I dared have sworn they weighed a good ten pound,
465 The ones she wore on Sunday, on her head.
Her hose were of the finest scarlet red
And gartered tight; her shoes were soft and new.
Bold was her face, handsome, and red in hue.
A worthy woman all her life, what's more
470 She'd had five husbands, all at the church door,
Apart from other company in youth;
No need just now to speak of that, forsooth.
And she had thrice been to Jerusalem,
Seen many strange rivers and passed over them;
475 She'd been to Rome and also to Boulogne,
St. James of Compostella and Cologne,
And she was skilled in wandering by the way.
She had gap-teeth, set widely, truth to say.
Easily on an ambling horse she sat
480 Well wimpled up, and on her head a hat
As broad as is a buckler or a shield;
She had a flowing mantle that concealed
Large hips, her heels spurred sharply under that.
In company she liked to laugh and chat
485 And knew the remedies for love's mischances,
An art in which she knew the oldest dances.

A holy-minded man of good renown
There was, and poor, the *Parson* to a town,
Yet he was rich in holy thought and work.

452 pestilences: plagues.

455 Bath: a city in southwestern England.

458 Ypres (ē'prə) . . . **Ghent** (gĕnt): Flemish cities famous in the Middle Ages for manufacturing fine wool fabrics.

461 wrath (răth): angry.

463 ground: a textured fabric.

466 hose: stockings.

470 all at the church door: In medieval times, a marriage was performed outside or just within the doors of a church; afterwards, the marriage party went inside for mass. Why might the narrator feel it necessary to mention that all five weddings were church weddings?

472 forsooth: in truth; indeed.

473–476 Jerusalem . . . Rome . . . Boulogne (bōō-lōn'), **St. James of Compostella and Cologne** (kə-lōn'): popular goals of religious pilgrimages in the Middle Ages.

480 wimpled: with her hair and neck covered by a cloth headdress.

481 buckler: small round shield.

490	He also was a learned man, a clerk,	**490 clerk:** scholar.
	Who truly knew Christ's gospel and would preach it	
	Devoutly to parishioners, and teach it.	
	Benign and wonderfully <u>diligent</u>,	
	And patient when adversity was sent	
495	(For so he proved in much adversity)	
	He hated cursing to extort a fee,	
	Nay rather he preferred beyond a doubt	
	Giving to poor parishioners round about	
	Both from church offerings and his property;	
500	He could in little find sufficiency.	**500 sufficiency:** enough to get by on.
	Wide was his parish, with houses far asunder,	
	Yet he neglected not in rain or thunder,	**501 asunder:** apart.
	In sickness or in grief, to pay a call	
	On the remotest, whether great or small,	
505	Upon his feet, and in his hand a stave.	**505 stave:** staff.
	This noble example to his sheep he gave	
	That first he wrought, and afterwards he taught;	**507 wrought** (rôt): worked.
	And it was from the Gospel he had caught	
	Those words, and he would add this figure too,	**509 figure:** figure of speech. What does the figure of speech in line 510 mean?
510	That if gold rust, what then will iron do?	
	For if a priest be foul in whom we trust	
	No wonder that a common man should rust;	
	And shame it is to see—let priests take stock—	
	A shitten shepherd and a snowy flock.	
515	The true example that a priest should give	
	Is one of cleanness, how the sheep should live.	
	He did not set his benefice to hire	**517 set his benefice** (bĕn'ə-fĭs) **to hire:** pay someone to perform his parish duties for him.
	And leave his sheep encumbered in the mire	
	Or run to London to earn easy bread	
520	By singing masses for the wealthy dead,	
	Or find some Brotherhood and get enrolled.	
	He stayed at home and watched over his fold	
	So that no wolf should make the sheep miscarry.	
	He was a shepherd and no mercenary.	
525	Holy and virtuous he was, but then	
	Never contemptuous of sinful men,	
	Never disdainful, never too proud or fine,	
	But was discreet in teaching and benign.	
	His business was to show a fair behavior	
530	And draw men thus to Heaven and their Savior,	
	Unless indeed a man were obstinate;	

WORDS
TO
KNOW
diligent (dĭl'ə-jənt) *adj.* painstaking; hard-working

And such, whether of high or low estate,
He put to sharp rebuke, to say the least.
I think there never was a better priest.
535 He sought no pomp or glory in his dealings,
No scrupulosity had spiced his feelings.
Christ and His Twelve Apostles and their lore
He taught, but followed it himself before.

There was a *Plowman* with him there, his brother;
540 Many a load of dung one time or other
He must have carted through the morning dew.
He was an honest worker, good and true,
Living in peace and perfect charity,
And, as the gospel bade him, so did he,
545 Loving God best with all his heart and mind
And then his neighbor as himself, <u>repined</u>
At no misfortune, slacked for no content,
For steadily about his work he went
To thrash his corn, to dig or to manure
550 Or make a ditch; and he would help the poor
For love of Christ and never take a penny
If he could help it, and, as prompt as any,
He paid his tithes in full when they were due
On what he owned, and on his earnings too.
555 He wore a tabard smock and rode a mare.

There was a *Reeve*, also a *Miller*, there,
A College *Manciple* from the Inns of Court,
A papal *Pardoner* and, in close consort,
A Church-Court *Summoner*, riding at a trot,
560 And finally myself—that was the lot.

The *Miller* was a chap of sixteen stone,
A great stout fellow big in brawn and bone.
He did well out of them, for he could go
And win the ram at any wrestling show.
565 Broad, knotty and short-shouldered, he would boast
He could heave any door off hinge and post,
Or take a run and break it with his head.
His beard, like any sow or fox, was red

536 scrupulosity (skrōō′pyə-lŏs′ĭ-tē): excessive concern with fine points of behavior. How would a lack of scrupulosity add to the Parson's effectiveness?

553 tithes (tīthz): payments to the church, traditionally one-tenth of one's annual income.

555 tabard smock: a short loose jacket made of a heavy material.

556 Reeve: an estate manager.

557 Manciple: a servant in charge of purchasing food; **Inns of Court:** London institutions for training law students.

558–559 Pardoner: a church official authorized to sell people pardons for their sins; **Summoner:** a layman with the job of summoning sinners to church courts. Why might the Pardoner and the Summoner be riding together as friends?

561 stone: a unit of weight equal to 14 pounds.

And broad as well, as though it were a spade;
570 And, at its very tip, his nose displayed
A wart on which there stood a tuft of hair
Red as the bristles in an old sow's ear.
His nostrils were as black as they were wide.
He had a sword and buckler at his side,
575 His mighty mouth was like a furnace door.
A wrangler and buffoon, he had a store
Of tavern stories, filthy in the main.
His was a master-hand at stealing grain.
He felt it with his thumb and thus he knew
580 Its quality and took three times his due—
A thumb of gold, by God, to gauge an oat!
He wore a hood of blue and a white coat.
He liked to play his bagpipes up and down
And that was how he brought us out of town.

585   The *Manciple* came from the Inner Temple;
All caterers might follow his example
In buying victuals; he was never rash
Whether he bought on credit or paid cash.
He used to watch the market most precisely
590 And got in first, and so he did quite nicely.
Now isn't it a marvel of God's grace
That an illiterate fellow can outpace
The wisdom of a heap of learned men?
His masters—he had more than thirty then—
595 All versed in the abstrusest legal knowledge,
Could have produced a dozen from their College
Fit to be stewards in land and rents and game
To any Peer in England you could name,
And show him how to live on what he had
600 Debt-free (unless of course the Peer were mad)
Or be as <u>frugal</u> as he might desire,
And make them fit to help about the Shire
In any legal case there was to try;
And yet this Manciple could wipe their eye.

605   The *Reeve* was old and choleric and thin;
His beard was shaven closely to the skin,
His shorn hair came abruptly to a stop

576 wrangler (răng′glər): a loud, argumentative person; **buffoon** (bə-foon′): a fool.

577 in the main: for the most part.

581 thumb of gold: a reference to a proverb, "An honest miller has a golden thumb"—perhaps meaning that there is no such thing as an honest miller.

585 Inner Temple: one of the Inns of Court.

594 his masters: the lawyers that the Manciple feeds.

595 abstrusest: most scholarly and difficult to understand.

597–598 stewards . . . Peer: estate managers for any nobleman.

604 wipe their eye: outdo them.

605 choleric (kŏl′ə-rĭk): having a temperament in which yellow bile predominates (see the note at line 343), and therefore prone to outbursts of anger.

WORDS
TO   **frugal** (froo′gəl) *adj.* careful with money; thrifty
KNOW

The Reeve

Above his ears, and he was docked on top
Just like a priest in front; his legs were lean,
610 Like sticks they were, no calf was to be seen.
He kept his bins and garners very trim;
No auditor could gain a point on him.
And he could judge by watching drought and rain
The yield he might expect from seed and grain.
615 His master's sheep, his animals and hens,
Pigs, horses, dairies, stores and cattle-pens
Were wholly trusted to his government.
He had been under contract to present
The accounts, right from his master's earliest years.
620 No one had ever caught him in arrears.
No bailiff, serf or herdsman dared to kick,
He knew their dodges, knew their every trick;
Feared like the plague he was, by those beneath.
He had a lovely dwelling on a heath,
625 Shadowed in green by trees above the sward.
A better hand at bargains than his lord,
He had grown rich and had a store of treasure
Well tucked away, yet out it came to pleasure
His lord with subtle loans or gifts of goods,
630 To earn his thanks and even coats and hoods.
When young he'd learnt a useful trade and still
He was a carpenter of first-rate skill.
The stallion-cob he rode at a slow trot
Was dapple-grey and bore the name of Scot.
635 He wore an overcoat of bluish shade
And rather long; he had a rusty blade
Slung at his side. He came, as I heard tell,
From Norfolk, near a place called Baldeswell.
His coat was tucked under his belt and splayed.
640 He rode the hindmost of our cavalcade.

608 docked: clipped short.

611 garners: buildings for storing grain.

617 government: authority. What opinion of the Reeve does his employer seem to hold? How might the Reeve take advantage of his position?

620 in arrears: with unpaid debts.

621 bailiff: farm manager; **serf:** farm laborer.

625 sward: grassy plot.

633 stallion-cob: a thickset, short-legged male horse.

638 Norfolk (nôr′fək): a county in eastern England.

The Summoner

There was a *Summoner* with us at that Inn,
His face on fire, like a cherubin,
For he had carbuncles. His eyes were narrow,
He was as hot and lecherous as a sparrow.
645 Black scabby brows he had, and a thin beard.
Children were afraid when he appeared.
No quicksilver, lead ointment, tartar creams,
No brimstone, no boracic, so it seems,
Could make a salve that had the power to bite,
650 Clean up or cure his whelks of knobby white
Or purge the pimples sitting on his cheeks.
Garlic he loved, and onions too, and leeks,
And drinking strong red wine till all was hazy.
Then he would shout and jabber as if crazy,
655 And wouldn't speak a word except in Latin
When he was drunk, such tags as he was pat in;
He only had a few, say two or three,
That he had mugged up out of some decree;
No wonder, for he heard them every day.
660 And, as you know, a man can teach a jay
To call out "Walter" better than the Pope.
But had you tried to test his wits and grope
For more, you'd have found nothing in the bag.
Then "*Questio quid juris*" was his tag.
665 He was a noble varlet and a kind one,
You'd meet none better if you went to find one.
Why, he'd allow—just for a quart of wine—
Any good lad to keep a concubine

642 cherubin (chĕr′ə-bĭn′): a type of angel—in the Middle Ages often depicted with a fiery red face.

643 carbuncles (kär′bŭng′kəlz): big pimples, considered a sign of drunkenness and lechery in the Middle Ages.

647–648 quicksilver . . . boracic (bə-răs′ĭk): substances used as skin medicines in medieval times.

650 whelks (hwĕlks): swellings.

656 tags: brief quotations.

658 mugged up: memorized.

660 jay: a bird that can be taught to mimic human speech without understanding it. What does the narrator's statement in lines 660–661 imply about the Summoner?

664 *Questio quid juris* (kwĕs′tē-ō kwĭd yŏŏr′ĭs): Latin for "The question is, What part of the law (is applicable)?"—a statement often heard in medieval courts.

A twelvemonth and dispense him altogether!
670   And he had finches of his own to feather:
And if he found some rascal with a maid
He would instruct him not to be afraid
In such a case of the Archdeacon's curse
(Unless the rascal's soul were in his purse)
675   For in his purse the punishment should be.
"Purse is the good Archdeacon's Hell," said he.
But well I know he lied in what he said;
A curse should put a guilty man in dread,
For curses kill, as shriving brings, salvation.
680   We should beware of excommunication.
Thus, as he pleased, the man could bring duress
On any young fellow in the diocese.
He knew their secrets, they did what he said.
He wore a garland set upon his head
685   Large as the holly-bush upon a stake
Outside an ale-house, and he had a cake,
A round one, which it was his joke to <u>wield</u>
As if it were intended for a shield.

He and a gentle *Pardoner* rode together,
690   A bird from Charing Cross of the same feather,
Just back from visiting the Court of Rome.
He loudly sang, *"Come hither, love, come home!"*
The Summoner sang deep seconds to this song,
No trumpet ever sounded half so strong.
695   This Pardoner had hair as yellow as wax,
Hanging down smoothly like a hank of flax.
In driblets fell his locks behind his head
Down to his shoulders which they overspread;
Thinly they fell, like rat-tails, one by one.
700   He wore no hood upon his head, for fun;
The hood inside his wallet had been stowed,
He aimed at riding in the latest <u>mode</u>;
But for a little cap his head was bare
And he had bulging eye-balls, like a hare.
705   He'd sewed a holy relic on his cap;
His wallet lay before him on his lap,
Brimful of pardons come from Rome, all hot.
He had the same small voice a goat has got.

673 Archdeacon's curse: excommunication—an official exclusion of a person from participating in the rites of the church. (An archdeacon is a high church official.)

675 How could a sinner's punishment be "in his purse"?

681 duress (dŏŏ-rĕs'): compulsion by means of threats.

682 diocese (dī'ə-sĭs): the district under a bishop's supervision.

685–686 the holly-bush . . . ale-house: Since few people could read in the Middle Ages, many businesses identified themselves with symbols. Outside many taverns could be found wreaths of holly on stakes.

690 Charing Cross: a section of London.

696 flax: a pale grayish yellow fiber used for making linen cloth.

701 wallet: knapsack.

705 holy relic: an object revered because of its association with a holy person.

WORDS TO KNOW	**wield** (wēld) *v.* to handle skillfully **mode** (mōd) *n.* a current fashion or style

131

His chin no beard had harbored, nor would harbor,
710 Smoother than ever chin was left by barber.
I judge he was a gelding, or a mare.
As to his trade, from Berwick down to Ware
There was no pardoner of equal grace,
For in his trunk he had a pillow-case
715 Which he asserted was Our Lady's veil.
He said he had a gobbet of the sail
Saint Peter had the time when he made bold
To walk the waves, till Jesu Christ took hold.
He had a cross of metal set with stones
720 And, in a glass, a rubble of pigs' bones.
And with these relics, any time he found
Some poor up-country parson to astound,
In one short day, in money down, he drew
More than the parson in a month or two,
725 And by his flatteries and prevarication
Made monkeys of the priest and congregation.
But still to do him justice first and last
In church he was a noble ecclesiast.
How well he read a lesson or told a story!
730 But best of all he sang an Offertory,
For well he knew that when that song was sung
He'd have to preach and tune his honey-tongue
And (well he could) win silver from the crowd.
That's why he sang so merrily and loud.

735   Now I have told you shortly, in a clause,
The rank, the array, the number and the cause
Of our assembly in this company
In Southwark, at that high-class hostelry
Known as *The Tabard*, close beside *The Bell*.
740 And now the time has come for me to tell
How we behaved that evening; I'll begin
After we had alighted at the Inn,
Then I'll report our journey, stage by stage,
All the remainder of our pilgrimage.
745 But first I beg of you, in courtesy,
Not to condemn me as unmannerly
If I speak plainly and with no concealings
And give account of all their words and dealings,
Using their very phrases as they fell.

711 gelding (gĕl′dĭng): a castrated horse—here, a eunuch.

712 Berwick (bĕr′ĭk) . . . **Ware:** towns in the north and the south of England.

715 Our Lady's veil: the kerchief of the Virgin Mary.

716 gobbet: piece.

717–718 when he . . . took hold: a reference to an incident in which Jesus extended a helping hand to Peter as he tried to walk on water (Matthew 14:29–31).

725 prevarication (prĭ-văr′ĭ-kā′shən): lying.

728 ecclesiast (ĭ-klē′zē-ăst′): clergyman.

730 Offertory: a chant accompanying the ceremonial offering of bread and wine to God in a mass.

739 The Bell: another inn.

Pilgrims leaving Canterbury (about 1400). English manuscript illumination, The Granger Collection, New York.

750 For certainly, as you all know so well,
He who repeats a tale after a man
Is bound to say, as nearly as he can,
Each single word, if he remembers it,
However rudely spoken or unfit,
755 Or else the tale he tells will be untrue,
The things pretended and the phrases new.
He may not flinch although it were his brother,
He may as well say one word as another.
And Christ Himself spoke broad in Holy Writ,
760 Yet there is no scurrility in it,
And Plato says, for those with power to read,

745–756 The narrator apologizes in advance for using the exact words of his companions. Why might he make such an apology?

759 broad: bluntly; plainly.

760 scurrility (skə-rĭl′ĭ-tē): vulgarity; coarseness.

761 Plato (plā′tō): a famous philosopher of ancient Greece.

"The word should be as cousin to the deed."
Further I beg you to forgive it me
If I neglect the order and degree
765 And what is due to rank in what I've planned.
I'm short of wit as you will understand.

Our *Host* gave us great welcome; everyone
Was given a place and supper was begun.
He served the finest victuals you could think,
770 The wine was strong and we were glad to drink.
A very striking man our Host withal,
And fit to be a marshal in a hall.
His eyes were bright, his girth a little wide;
There is no finer burgess in Cheapside.
775 Bold in his speech, yet wise and full of tact,
There was no manly attribute he lacked,
What's more he was a merry-hearted man.
After our meal he jokingly began
To talk of sport, and, among other things
780 After we'd settled up our reckonings,
He said as follows: "Truly, gentlemen,
You're very welcome and I can't think when
—Upon my word I'm telling you no lie—
I've seen a gathering here that looked so spry,
785 No, not this year, as in this tavern now.
I'd think you up some fun if I knew how.
And, as it happens, a thought has just occurred
To please you, costing nothing, on my word.
You're off to Canterbury—well, God speed!
790 Blessed St. Thomas answer to your need!
And I don't doubt, before the journey's done
You mean to while the time in tales and fun.
Indeed, there's little pleasure for your bones
Riding along and all as dumb as stones.
795 So let me then propose for your enjoyment,
Just as I said, a suitable employment.
And if my notion suits and you agree
And promise to submit yourselves to me
Playing your parts exactly as I say
800 Tomorrow as you ride along the way,
Then by my father's soul (and he is dead)
If you don't like it you can have my head!
Hold up your hands, and not another word."

767 Host: the innkeeper of the Tabard.

772 marshal in a hall: an official in charge of arranging a nobleman's banquet.

774 Cheapside: the main business district of London in Chaucer's day.

780 settled up our reckonings: paid our bills.

790 St. Thomas: St. Thomas à Becket, to whose shrine the pilgrims are traveling.

794 dumb: silent.

Well, our opinion was not long <u>deferred</u>,
805 It seemed not worth a serious debate;
We all agreed to it at any rate
And bade him issue what commands he would.
"My lords," he said, "now listen for your good,
And please don't treat my notion with <u>disdain</u>.
810 This is the point. I'll make it short and plain.
Each one of you shall help to make things slip
By telling two stories on the outward trip
To Canterbury, that's what I intend,
And, on the homeward way to journey's end
815 Another two, tales from the days of old;
And then the man whose story is best told,
That is to say who gives the fullest measure
Of good morality and general pleasure,
He shall be given a supper, paid by all,
820 Here in this tavern, in this very hall,
When we come back again from Canterbury.
And in the hope to keep you bright and merry
I'll go along with you myself and ride
All at my own expense and serve as guide.
825 I'll be the judge, and those who won't obey
Shall pay for what we spend upon the way.
Now if you all agree to what you've heard
Tell me at once without another word,
And I will make arrangements early for it."

830 Of course we all agreed, in fact we swore it
Delightedly, and made entreaty too
That he should act as he proposed to do,
Become our Governor in short, and be
Judge of our tales and general referee,
835 And set the supper at a certain price.
We promised to be ruled by his advice
Come high, come low; unanimously thus
We set him up in judgement over us.
More wine was fetched, the business being done;
840 We drank it off and up went everyone
To bed without a moment of delay.

807 bade him: asked him to. Why do you think the pilgrims are so quick to agree to the innkeeper's proposal?

831 made entreaty: begged.

Early next morning at the spring of day
Up rose our Host and roused us like a cock,
Gathering us together in a flock,
845 And off we rode at slightly faster pace
Than walking to St. Thomas' watering-place;
And there our Host drew up, began to ease
His horse, and said, "Now, listen if you please,
My lords! Remember what you promised me.
850 If evensong and matins will agree
Let's see who shall be first to tell a tale.
And as I hope to drink good wine and ale
I'll be your judge. The rebel who disobeys,
However much the journey costs, he pays.
855 Now draw for cut and then we can depart;
The man who draws the shortest cut shall start."

843 cock: rooster (whose cry rouses people from sleep).

846 St. Thomas' watering-place: a brook about two miles from London.

850 if evensong and matins (măt'nz) **will agree:** if what you said last night is what you will do this morning. (Evensong and matins are evening and morning prayer services.)

855 draw for cut: draw lots.

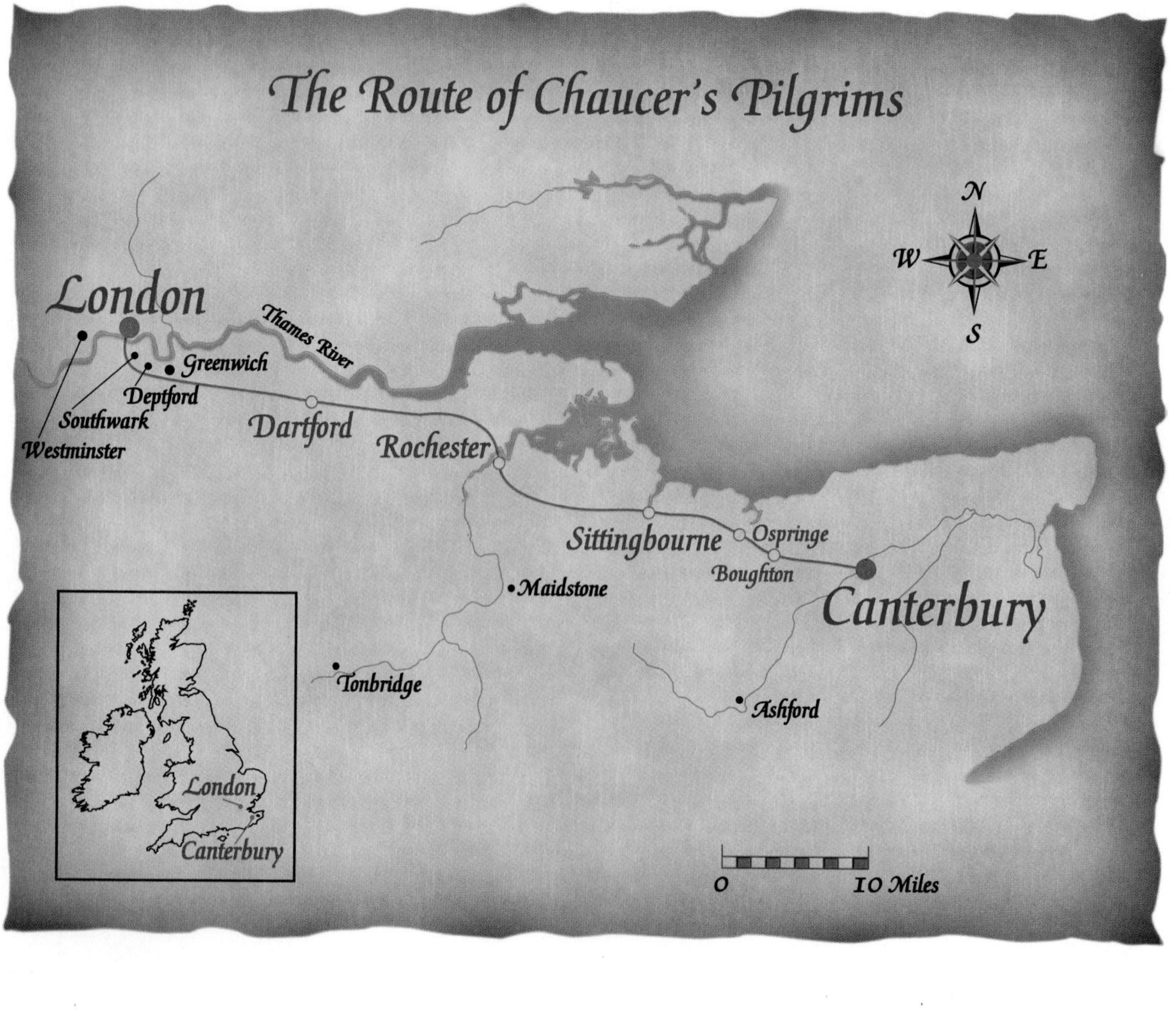

The Route of Chaucer's Pilgrims

London
Thames River
Greenwich
Deptford
Southwark
Westminster
Dartford
Rochester
Sittingbourne
Ospringe
Boughton
Maidstone
Canterbury
Tonbridge
Ashford

N
W   E
S

London
Canterbury

0   10 Miles

Connect to the Literature

1. **What Do You Think?** Would you like traveling with this group of people? Why or why not?

Comprehension Check
- In what month is the group making its pilgrimage?
- With what high-ranking person does the narrator open his descriptions?
- Who will judge the storytelling contest, and what will the prize be?

Think Critically

2. Consider the opening details about the season. Why would spring make people "long to go on pilgrimages"?

3. **ACTIVE READING ANALYZING CHARACTERIZATION**
As you read, study the cluster diagrams you created in your  **READER'S NOTEBOOK.** According to the information you gathered, which of the pilgrims does the narrator admire most? Which does he admire least?

4. How would you describe the **narrator**'s values?

THINK ABOUT
- his varied view of medieval life
- the characters he admires and those he criticizes
- his descriptions of himself

5. What impression does the narrator give of the church in his day? Cite details from his portrayals of religious figures to support your answer.

6. Why do you think the Host proposes the storytelling contest?

Extend Interpretations

7. **Critic's Corner** In 1700, John Dryden made a famous observation about Chaucer's characterization: "All his pilgrims are severally [individually] distinguished from each other; and not only in their inclinations, but in their very physiognomies [faces] and persons." Do you agree that Chaucer was able to create a number of distinctive characters? Explain.

8. **Connect to Life** Think of modern professions for some of the characters in the "Prologue." What might be the modern equivalent of the Knight? the Squire? the Pardoner? Explain your choices.

Literary Analysis

TONE In the "Prologue," much of the humor springs from the narrator's **tone,** which is detached and **ironic.** Instead of openly criticizing the scoundrels of his age for their greed and hypocrisy, he understates his opinions about them or says the opposite of what he really thinks. His seemingly impersonal attitude forces readers to draw their own conclusions.

In lines 208–211, for example, the narrator describes the Monk:

He was a prelate fit for exhibition,
He was not pale like a tormented soul.
He liked a fat swan best, and roasted whole.
His palfrey was as brown as is a berry.

The narrator's tone reinforces the discrepancies between the Monk's life and the ideal monastic life of humility and self-sacrifice.

Paired Activity Working with a partner, identify passages that reveal the narrator's tone. Look for evidence in the form of particular words and phrases. Organize your ideas in a chart like this one.

Character	What Narrator Says	What Narrator Means
Friar	Natural gifts like his were hard to match. (line 255)	He was a greedy flatterer.

Writing Options

1. Character Analysis Write a short analysis of one of the characters in the "Prologue." Consider his or her appearance, personality, and motives. Support your general statements about the character with specific details from the "Prologue." You might organize your ideas in an outline like this:

Character: _____

   I. General quality or motive
     A. Supporting detail
     B. Supporting detail

  II. General quality or motive
     A. Supporting detail
     B. Supporting detail

Writing Handbook
See page 1369: Analysis.

2. Sketch of a New Pilgrim Imagine how Chaucer would describe a modern-day person. Write a character sketch of that person, identifying his or her social role or profession. Use prose instead of rhymed lines of poetry if you prefer. Place your sketch in your **Working Portfolio.**

Activities & Explorations

1. Pilgrimage Poster Design a poster advertising a pilgrimage to Canterbury. If you like, you can use a computer drawing program. ~ **ART**

2. Pilgrim Predictions With a group, make predictions about the characters introduced in the "Prologue." Which ones will get along? Which will not? Which will tell the best stories? Record your predictions to share with the class. ~ **SPEAKING AND LISTENING**

Inquiry & Research

Medieval Inns Find out more about English medieval inns by consulting books about the history of society and travel. What role did inns play in Chaucer's day? Alternatively, explore the signs used to identify the inns, many of which featured symbols rather than words. Present your findings in a written report.

Vocabulary in Action

EXERCISE A: CONTEXT CLUES On your paper, answer the following questions, giving a reason for each answer. Your reason should show an understanding of the meaning of the boldfaced word.

1. Could bad weather **defer** the pilgrims' journey?
2. Would a fashionable pilgrim dress according to the **mode?**
3. Might the Knight **wield** a sword in battle?
4. Does the Parson show **disdain** for his rural parish by treating the parishioners well?
5. Were Chaucer's pilgrims all **eminent** figures of the day?
6. Would others call the pleasant Prioress a **malady?**
7. Was the Summoner, who was feared by children, a **personable** individual?

EXERCISE B: ASSESSMENT PRACTICE On your paper, indicate whether the words in each pair are synonyms or antonyms.

1. agility—clumsiness
2. dispatch—inefficiency
3. sedately—frantically
4. frugal—thrifty
5. repine—praise
6. accrue—accumulate
7. diligent—lazy
8. courtliness—elegance

WORDS TO KNOW	accrue	defer	dispatch	malady	repine
	agility	diligent	eminent	mode	sedately
	courtliness	disdain	frugal	personable	wield

Building Vocabulary
Most of the Words to Know in this lesson come from Latin. For an in-depth study of word origins, see page 206.

Build Background

John Gardner was a popular novelist as well as a medieval scholar. Among the best-known of his works of fiction is the novel *Grendel,* which tells the story of Beowulf's battle in Herot from the monster's point of view. *The Life and Times of Chaucer* is a lively nonfiction account of Chaucer and his age. The passage on these pages provides a horrifying glimpse into the administration of justice—and injustice—in London during the Middle Ages.

from

The Life and Times of CHAUCER

Nonfiction by JOHN GARDNER

IT HARDLY NEEDS SAYING THAT THE WORLD INTO WHICH GEOFFREY CHAUCER WAS BORN WAS NOT LIKE OURS. After careful thought, if we were given the choice of living then or now, we might well decide to scrap our modern world; but on first transportation to Chaucer's time, we would probably have hated it—its opinions and customs, its superstitions, its cruelty, its hobbled intellect, in some respects its downright madness. One need not talk of such blood-curdling horrors as public hangings, beheadings, burnings-at-the-stake, drawing-and-quarterings,[1] public whippings, blindings, . . . or of imprisonments in chains and darkness without hope of deliverance; or of trials by combat,[2] or of torturings . . . —all these were common,

---

1. **drawing-and-quarterings:** executions in which the criminals' arms and legs were tied to four horses, which were then driven in different directions.

2. **trials by combat:** procedures in which disputants (or people selected by them) would fight to the death in order to determine who was in the right.

the unavoidable experience of any man who had eyes to see or ears not deaf to the victims' shrieks; and if far less common in England than in France or, worse yet, Italy, where the family of Malatesta ("Badhead") filled a deep well with the severed heads of victims, the difference would strike a modern visitor as trifling. England's great poet of gentleness and compassion walked every day in a city where the fly-bitten, bird-scarred corpses of hanged criminals—men and women, even children— draped their shadows across the crowded public square. If the crime was political, the corpse was tarred to prevent its decaying before the achievement of the full measure of its shame. As Chaucer strolled across London Bridge, making up intricate ballades[3] in his head, counting beats on his fingers, he could see, if he looked up, the staked heads of wrongdoers hurried away by earnest Christians to their presumed eternal torment. With our modern sensibilities we would certainly object and perhaps interfere—as Chaucer never did—and for the attempt to undermine the king's peace, not to mention God's, our severed heads would go up on the stakes beside those others.

---

3. **ballades** (bə-lädz′): poems usually consisting of three 7-, 8-, or 10-line stanzas (with the same rhymes in each) along with an envoy, or closing stanza. Several of Chaucer's ballades have survived, and he probably composed a number of others.

Thinking Through the Literature

1. In the light of the information Gardner presents, what adjectives would you use to describe the world into which Chaucer was born?

2. **Comparing Texts** Compare and contrast the world that Chaucer presents in the "Prologue" with the world that Gardner describes. Would you say that Chaucer entirely ignores the negative side of medieval life? Cite evidence to support your evaluation.

3. What are some of the brutalities or injustices to which people in the modern world often close their eyes? What do you think Chaucer might have disliked if he had been transported forward in time to our world?

from The Pardoner's Tale
from The Canterbury Tales

Poetry by GEOFFREY CHAUCER
Translated by NEVILL COGHILL

Connect to Your Life

Roots of Evil "The love of money is the root of all evil," the Bible tells us. In a group discussion, share thoughts about the desire for money and the ways in which it influences human behavior. In what situations is the desire for money evil or harmful? When does the desire seem normal or legitimate to you?

Build Background

Begging Pardon Among the more memorable of the Canterbury pilgrims is the Pardoner, described in lines 689–734 of the "Prologue" (pages 131–132). Licensed by the church to grant indulgences (documents forgiving peoples' sins), pardoners were in theory supposed to grant them only to people who showed great charity. In practice, however, many pardoners simply sold their pardons to make money for the church or for themselves. To spur sales, unethical pardoners often threatened reluctant buyers with eternal doom. Chaucer's Pardoner encourages buyers with a story that illustrates the dangers of the love of money.

WORDS TO KNOW
Vocabulary Preview

adversary	parley
avarice	saunter
castigate	transcend
covetousness	vermin
pallor	wary

Focus Your Reading

LITERARY ANALYSIS **MORAL TALE** A **moral tale** teaches a lesson about what is right and wrong in human behavior. In a moral tale, good characters usually triumph and evil characters come to a bad end. These outcomes send a message, or **moral** (which is often stated explicitly in the tale). In "The Pardoner's Tale," the moral is the biblical observation that "the love of money is the root of all evil." The Pardoner states this moral in Latin, the language of the medieval Roman Catholic Church:

Radix malorum est cupiditas.

As you read this tale, pay close attention to the actions of the characters, as well as those of the Pardoner, the teller of the tale.

ACTIVE READING **PREDICTING** To make reasonable **predictions** about what will happen next and what will happen in the end, take the following into account:

- the characters, settings, and events presented in the story
- **foreshadowing,** or hints about what is going to happen
- your own knowledge of human behavior and experiences
- what you know of other literary works with similar characters, settings, or events

My Prediction	Lines It's Based On	Actual Outcome

READER'S NOTEBOOK As you read, jot down your predictions in a chart like this one. Continue reading to see if the events match your predictions.

from The Pardoner's Prologue

"My lords," he said, "in churches where I preach
I cultivate a haughty kind of speech
And ring it out as roundly as a bell;
I've got it all by heart, the tale I tell.
5   I have a text, it always is the same
And always has been, since I learnt the game,
Old as the hills and fresher than the grass,
Radix malorum est cupiditas.

I preach, as you have heard me say before,
10   And tell a hundred lying mockeries more.
I take great pains, and stretching out my neck
To east and west I crane about and peck
Just like a pigeon sitting on a barn.
My hands and tongue together spin the yarn
15   And all my antics are a joy to see.
The curse of <u>avarice</u> and cupidity
Is all my sermon, for it frees the pelf.
Out come the pence, and specially for myself,
For my exclusive purpose is to win
20   And not at all to <u>castigate</u> their sin.
Once dead what matter how their souls may fare?
They can go blackberrying, for all I care!

The Pardoner

GUIDE FOR READING

8 *Radix malorum est cupiditas* (rä′dĭks mä-lôr′əm ĕst′ kōō-pĭd′ĭ-täs′): Latin for "The love of money is the root of all evil"—a quotation from the Bible (1 Timothy 6:10).

10 mockeries: false tales.

16 cupidity (kyōō-pĭd′ĭ-tē): excessive desire for something, especially for money.

17 pelf: riches, especially those that are acquired dishonestly.

18 pence: pennies.

19–22 What is the Pardoner's attitude toward those who listen to him preach?

WORDS
TO
KNOW

avarice (ăv′ə-rĭs) *n.* an excessive desire for wealth; greed
castigate (kăs′tĭ-gāt′) *v.* to criticize harshly

142

And thus I preach against the very vice
I make my living out of—avarice.
25 And yet however guilty of that sin
Myself, with others I have power to win
Them from it, I can bring them to repent;
But that is not my principal intent.
<u>Covetousness</u> is both the root and stuff
30 Of all I preach. That ought to be enough.

"Well, then I give examples thick and fast
From bygone times, old stories from the past.
A yokel mind loves stories from of old,
Being the kind it can repeat and hold.
35 What! Do you think, as long as I can preach
And get their silver for the things I teach,
That I will live in poverty, from choice?
That's not the counsel of my inner voice!
No! Let me preach and beg from kirk to kirk   **39 kirk:** church.
40 And never do an honest job of work,
No, nor make baskets, like St. Paul, to gain
A livelihood. I do not preach in vain.
There's no apostle I would counterfeit;
I mean to have money, wool and cheese and wheat
45 Though it were given me by the poorest lad
Or poorest village widow, though she had
A string of starving children, all agape.
No, let me drink the liquor of the grape
And keep a jolly wench in every town!

50 "But listen, gentlemen; to bring things down
To a conclusion, would you like a tale?
Now as I've drunk a draft of corn-ripe ale,
By God it stands to reason I can strike
On some good story that you all will like.
55 For though I am a wholly vicious man
Don't think I can't tell moral tales. I can!
Here's one I often preach when out for winning. . . ."

WORDS
TO   **covetousness** (kŭv'ĭ-təs-nĭs) *n.* an excessive desire for wealth or possessions
KNOW

143

from The Pardoner's Tale

It's of three rioters I have to tell
Who, long before the morning service bell,
60 Were sitting in a tavern for a drink.
And as they sat, they heard the hand-bell clink
Before a coffin going to the grave;
One of them called the little tavern-knave
And said "Go and find out at once—look spry!—
65 Whose corpse is in that coffin passing by;
And see you get the name correctly too."
"Sir," said the boy, "no need, I promise you;
Two hours before you came here I was told.
He was a friend of yours in days of old,
70 And suddenly, last night, the man was slain,
Upon his bench, face up, dead drunk again.
There came a privy thief, they call him Death,
Who kills us all round here, and in a breath
He speared him through the heart, he never stirred.
75 And then Death went his way without a word.
He's killed a thousand in the present plague,
And, sir, it doesn't do to be too vague
If you should meet him; you had best be <u>wary</u>.
Be on your guard with such an <u>adversary</u>,
80 Be primed to meet him everywhere you go,
That's what my mother said. It's all I know."

58 rioters: rowdy people; revelers.

61–62 hand-bell . . . grave: In Chaucer's time, a bell was carried beside the coffin in a funeral procession.

63 tavern-knave (nāv): a serving boy in an inn.

72 privy (prĭv'ē): hidden; secretive.

72–81 Death is personified as a thief in the night, who slays his victims and then flees. Bubonic plague killed at least a quarter of the population of Europe in the mid-14th century.

144

The publican joined in with, "By St. Mary,
What the child says is right; you'd best be wary,
This very year he killed, in a large village
85 A mile away, man, woman, serf at tillage,
Page in the household, children—all there were.
Yes, I imagine that he lives round there.
It's well to be prepared in these alarms,
He might do you dishonor." "Huh, God's arms!"
90 The rioter said, "Is he so fierce to meet?
I'll search for him, by Jesus, street by street.
God's blessed bones! I'll register a vow!
Here, chaps! The three of us together now,
Hold up your hands, like me, and we'll be brothers
95 In this affair, and each defend the others,
And we will kill this traitor Death, I say!
Away with him as he has made away
With all our friends. God's dignity! Tonight!"

They made their bargain, swore with appetite,
100 These three, to live and die for one another
As brother-born might swear to his born brother.
And up they started in their drunken rage
And made towards this village which the page
And publican had spoken of before.
105 Many and grisly were the oaths they swore,
Tearing Christ's blessed body to a shred;
"If we can only catch him, Death is dead!"

When they had gone not fully half a mile,
Just as they were about to cross a stile,
110 They came upon a very poor old man
Who humbly greeted them and thus began,
"God look to you, my lords, and give you quiet!"
To which the proudest of these men of riot
Gave back the answer, "What, old fool? Give place!
115 Why are you all wrapped up except your face?
Why live so long? Isn't it time to die?"

The old, old fellow looked him in the eye
And said, "Because I never yet have found,
Though I have walked to India, searching round

82 publican: innkeeper; tavern owner.

86 page: boy servant.

99–107 How might the rioters' drinking be affecting their judgment and behavior?

109 stile: a stairway used to climb over a fence or wall.

120 Village and city on my pilgrimage,
One who would change his youth to have my age.
And so my age is mine and must be still
Upon me, for such time as God may will.

"Not even Death, alas, will take my life;
125 So, like a wretched prisoner at strife
Within himself, I walk alone and wait
About the earth, which is my mother's gate,
Knock-knocking with my staff from night to noon
And crying, 'Mother, open to me soon!
130 Look at me, mother, won't you let me in?
See how I wither, flesh and blood and skin!
Alas! When will these bones be laid to rest?
Mother, I would exchange—for that were best—
The wardrobe in my chamber, standing there
135 So long, for yours! Aye, for a shirt of hair
To wrap me in!' She has refused her grace,
Whence comes the <u>pallor</u> of my withered face.

"But it dishonored you when you began
To speak so roughly, sir, to an old man,
140 Unless he had injured you in word or deed.
It says in holy writ, as you may read,
'Thou shalt rise up before the hoary head
And honor it.' And therefore be it said
'Do no more harm to an old man than you,
145 Being now young, would have another do
When you are old'—if you should live till then.
And so may God be with you, gentlemen,
For I must go whither I have to go."

"By God," the gambler said, "you shan't do so,
150 You don't get off so easy, by St. John!
I heard you mention, just a moment gone,
A certain traitor Death who singles out
And kills the fine young fellows hereabout.
And you're his spy, by God! You wait a bit.
155 Say where he is or you shall pay for it,
By God and by the Holy Sacrament!

129 The old man addresses the earth as his mother (compare the familiar expressions "Mother Earth" and "Mother Nature").

135 **shirt of hair:** a rough shirt made of animal hair, worn to punish oneself for one's sins.

142 **hoary:** gray or white with age.

WORDS TO KNOW

pallor (păl′ər) *n.* a lack of color; extreme paleness

I say you've joined together by consent
To kill us younger folk, you thieving swine!"

"Well, sirs," he said, "if it be your design
160 To find out Death, turn up this crooked way
Towards that grove, I left him there today
Under a tree, and there you'll find him waiting.
He isn't one to hide for all your prating.
You see that oak? He won't be far to find.
165 And God protect you that redeemed mankind,
Aye, and amend you!" Thus that ancient man.

At once the three young rioters began
To run, and reached the tree, and there they found
A pile of golden florins on the ground,
170 New-coined, eight bushels of them as they thought.
No longer was it Death those fellows sought,
For they were all so thrilled to see the sight,
The florins were so beautiful and bright,
That down they sat beside the precious pile.
175 The wickedest spoke first after a while.
"Brothers," he said, "you listen to what I say.
I'm pretty sharp although I joke away.
It's clear that Fortune has bestowed this treasure
To let us live in jollity and pleasure.
180 Light come, light go! We'll spend it as we ought.
God's precious dignity! Who would have thought
This morning was to be our lucky day?

"If one could only get the gold away,
Back to my house, or else to yours, perhaps—
185 For as you know, the gold is ours, chaps—
We'd all be at the top of fortune, hey?
But certainly it can't be done by day.
People would call us robbers—a strong gang,
So our own property would make us hang.
190 No, we must bring this treasure back by night
Some prudent way, and keep it out of sight.
And so as a solution I propose
We draw for lots and see the way it goes;
The one who draws the longest, lucky man,
195 Shall run to town as quickly as he can

154–158 What accusations against the old man does the young man make?

169 florins: coins.

178 "Fortune" here means "fate." Do you think the young men will be blessed by Fortune?

The Three Living, from the *Psalter and Prayer Book of Bonne of Luxembourg, Duchess of Normandy.*

To fetch us bread and wine—but keep things dark—
While two remain in hiding here to mark
Our heap of treasure. If there's no delay,
When night comes down we'll carry it away,
200   All three of us, wherever we have planned."

196 keep things dark: act in secret, without giving away what has happened.

He gathered lots and hid them in his hand
Bidding them draw for where the luck should fall.
It fell upon the youngest of them all,
And off he ran at once towards the town.

205   As soon as he had gone the first sat down
And thus began a parley with the other:
"You know that you can trust me as a brother;
Now let me tell you where your profit lies;
You know our friend has gone to get supplies
210   And here's a lot of gold that is to be
Divided equally amongst us three.
Nevertheless, if I could shape things thus
So that we shared it out—the two of us—
Wouldn't you take it as a friendly act?"

215   "But how?" the other said. "He knows the fact
That all the gold was left with me and you;
What can we tell him? What are we to do?"

"Is it a bargain," said the first, "or no?
For I can tell you in a word or so
220   What's to be done to bring the thing about."
"Trust me," the other said, "you needn't doubt
My word. I won't betray you, I'll be true."

"Well," said his friend, "you see that we are two,
And two are twice as powerful as one.
225   Now look; when he comes back, get up in fun
To have a wrestle; then, as you attack,
I'll up and put my dagger through his back
While you and he are struggling, as in game;
Then draw your dagger too and do the same.
230   Then all this money will be ours to spend,

225–229 What does the young man's plan suggest about human nature and the desire for money?

WORDS
TO
KNOW   **parley** (pär′lē) *n.* a discussion or conference

148

Divided equally of course, dear friend.
Then we can gratify our lusts and fill
The day with dicing at our own sweet will."
Thus these two miscreants agreed to slay
235 The third and youngest, as you heard me say.

233 dicing: gambling with dice.
234 miscreants (mĭsʹkrē-ənts): evildoers; villains.

The youngest, as he ran towards the town,
Kept turning over, rolling up and down
Within his heart the beauty of those bright
New florins, saying, "Lord, to think I might
240 Have all that treasure to myself alone!
Could there be anyone beneath the throne
Of God so happy as I then should be?"

And so the Fiend, our common enemy,
Was given power to put it in his thought
245 That there was always poison to be bought,
And that with poison he could kill his friends.
To men in such a state the Devil sends
Thoughts of this kind, and has a full permission
To lure them on to sorrow and perdition;
250 For this young man was utterly content
To kill them both and never to repent.

243 Fiend: the Devil; Satan.

249 perdition: damnation; hell.

243–251 Why does the Devil have influence over the young man?

And on he ran, he had no thought to tarry,
Came to the town, found an apothecary
And said, "Sell me some poison if you will,
255 I have a lot of rats I want to kill
And there's a polecat too about my yard
That takes my chickens and it hits me hard;
But I'll get even, as is only right,
With <u>vermin</u> that destroy a man by night."

The chemist answered, "I've a preparation
260 Which you shall have, and by my soul's salvation
If any living creature eat or drink
A mouthful, ere he has the time to think,
Though he took less than makes a grain of wheat,
You'll see him fall down dying at your feet;
265 Yes, die he must, and in so short a while

WORDS
TO
KNOW
vermin (vûrʹmĭn) *n.* small animals that are destructive or carriers of disease

You'd hardly have the time to walk a mile,
The poison is so strong, you understand."

This cursed fellow grabbed into his hand
270 The box of poison and away he ran
Into a neighboring street, and found a man
Who lent him three large bottles. He withdrew
And deftly poured the poison into two.
He kept the third one clean, as well he might,
275 For his own drink, meaning to work all night
Stacking the gold and carrying it away.
And when this rioter, this devil's clay,
Had filled his bottles up with wine, all three,
Back to rejoin his comrades saunter he.

280 Why make a sermon of it? Why waste breath?
Exactly in the way they'd planned his death
They fell on him and slew him, two to one.
Then said the first of them when this was done,
"Now for a drink. Sit down and let's be merry,
285 For later on there'll be the corpse to bury."
And, as it happened, reaching for a sup,
He took a bottle full of poison up
And drank; and his companion, nothing loth,
Drank from it also, and they perished both.

290 There is, in Avicenna's long relation
Concerning poison and its operation,
Trust me, no ghastlier section to transcend
What these two wretches suffered at their end.
Thus these two murderers received their due,
295 So did the treacherous young poisoner too.

O cursed sin! O blackguardly excess!
O treacherous homicide! O wickedness!
O gluttony that lusted on and diced!

The Three Dead, from the *Psalter and Prayer Book of Bonne of Luxembourg, Duchess of Normandy* (14th century), fol.322r. Grisaille, color, gilt, and brown ink on vellum (4 15/16" x 3 9/16"). French, Paris. The Metropolitan Museum of Art, New York. The Cloisters Collection

288 nothing loth: not at all unwilling.

290 Avicenna's (ăv´ĭ-sĕn´əz) **long relation:** a medical text written by an 11th-century Islamic physician; it includes descriptions of various poisons and their effects.

294 Why does the Pardoner say that the young men "received their due"?

296 blackguardly: worthy of a scoundrel; villainous.

Dearly beloved, God forgive your sin
300 And keep you from the vice of avarice!

299 The Pardoner is now addressing his fellow pilgrims.

My holy pardon frees you all of this,
Provided that you make the right approaches,
That is with sterling, rings, or silver brooches.
Bow down your heads under this holy bull!

305 Come on, you women, offer up your wool!
I'll write your name into my ledger; so!
Into the bliss of Heaven you shall go.
For I'll absolve you by my holy power,
You that make offering, clean as at the hour

310 When you were born. . . . That, sirs, is how I preach.
And Jesu Christ, soul's healer, aye, the leech
Of every soul, grant pardon and relieve you
Of sin, for that is best, I won't deceive you.

One thing I should have mentioned in my tale,

315 Dear people. I've some relics in my bale
And pardons too, as full and fine, I hope,
As any in England, given me by the Pope.
If there be one among you that is willing
To have my absolution for a shilling

320 Devoutly given, come! and do not harden
Your hearts but kneel in humbleness for pardon;
Or else, receive my pardon as we go.
You can renew it every town or so
Always provided that you still renew

325 Each time, and in good money, what is due.
It is an honor to you to have found
A pardoner with his credentials sound
Who can absolve you as you ply the spur
In any accident that may occur.

330 For instance—we are all at Fortune's beck—
Your horse may throw you down and break your neck.
What a security it is to all
To have me here among you and at call
With pardon for the lowly and the great

335 When soul leaves body for the future state!
And I advise our Host here to begin,
The most enveloped of you all in sin.
Come forward, Host, you shall be the first to pay,
And kiss my holy relics right away.

340 Only a groat. Come on, unbuckle your purse!"

304 bull: an official document from the pope.

311 leech: physician.

319 shilling: a coin worth twelve pence.

330–331 The Pardoner reminds the other pilgrims that death may come to them at any time. Why does he emphasize this point?

340 groat: a silver coin worth four pence.

Connect to the Literature

1. **What Do You Think?** Discuss with a partner your reaction to the ending of this tale.

> **Comprehension Check**
> - Why are the three rioters looking for Death?
> - What do they expect to find under the tree, and what do they actually find?
> - What happens to the rioters?

Think Critically

2. **ACTIVE READING** **PREDICTING** Look back at the predictions you made in your  **READER'S NOTEBOOK**. Were you surprised by the tale's ending? If not, explain what details led you to **predict** the ending. If you were surprised, explain what details led you to predict a different ending.

3. Why do you think the rioters set out to kill Death?

   THINK ABOUT
   - what they learn from the boy and the innkeeper
   - their view of themselves
   - other factors that may influence their judgment

4. In what sense is the old man's statement that the rioters can find Death under the oak tree true?

5. Why do you think the **character** of the old man is included in the tale?

   THINK ABOUT
   - the story of his life
   - his views about Death
   - his directions for finding Death

6. In the light of the Pardoner's true **motives**, as revealed in the "Prologue," why is the moral of this tale **ironic**?

Extend Interpretations

7. **What If?** If the Pardoner hadn't revealed so much information about his practices, how might the other pilgrims have responded to his tale?

8. **Connect to Life** Do you think this story could serve as an effective warning against greed to people today? Why or why not?

Literary Analysis

MORAL TALE "The Pardoner's Tale" is a **moral tale,** a story that teaches a lesson about good and evil or about what is right and wrong in human behavior. In it, the Pardoner teaches that "the love of money is the root of all evil" by showing how characters who suffer from the sin of avarice, or love of money, destroy themselves in the end.

Paired Activity Working with a partner, analyze how the story's elements work together to teach the moral. Among the elements to consider are the events of the plot, the personalities and motives of the characters, and the details of the setting. You might organize the elements in a chart like this one.

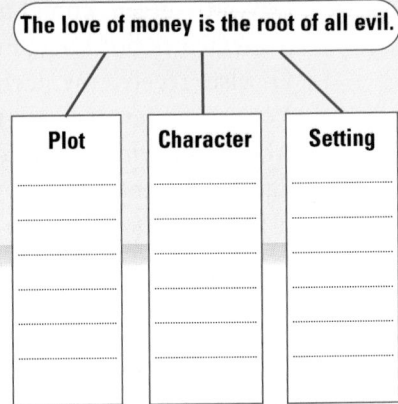

The love of money is the root of all evil.		
Plot	**Character**	**Setting**

Writing Options

1. Ye Olde News Write a news article about the discovery of the rioters' bodies and the events that led up to it. Include interviews with characters.

2. Personification Paragraph Write a paragraph explaining the personification of death in "The Pardoner's Tale." First explain the reasons why the Pardoner may have decided to personify death (turn death into a figure with human qualities). Then explain the effects you think this device has on readers. You might organize your ideas in a cause-and-effect diagram like this one.

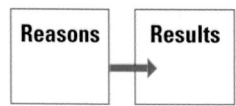

Writing Handbook
See page 1368: Cause and Effect.

3. Moral Tale Think of other proverbs or quotations about good and evil or right and wrong human behavior—for example, "Cheaters never prosper" or "What goes around, comes around." Then write a brief moral tale with that as its moral. You might state the moral at the start or the end of the tale.

Activities & Explorations

1. Oral Retelling Simplify the language and details of the tale to suit an audience of younger children. Arrange to tell the tale at a library or an elementary school. ~ **SPEAKING AND LISTENING**

2. Video Adaptation View the performance of "The Pardoner's Tale." Focus on the portrayals of the characters, particularly that of the old man. Then, in a class discussion, compare the portrayals with Chaucer's descriptions. ~ **VIEWING AND REPRESENTING**

 Literature in Performance

3. Ballad Version Turn "The Pardoner's Tale" into a ballad set to music. The music can be original or borrowed from an existing song. Perform the ballad live or audiotape it. ~ **MUSIC**

Inquiry & Research

Plague Write a brief research paper on the outbreak of plague in mid-14th-century Europe. Include information about its origins and its effects on European life and culture. Be sure to document your sources.

Vocabulary in Action

EXERCISE A: CONTEXT CLUES On your paper, fill in each blank with the vocabulary word that best completes the sentence.

1. Filled with distrust, the rioters were _____ of one another.
2. Did the rioter _____, or did he walk swiftly?
3. Death brought a _____ to her once-rosy face.
4. Does the Pardoner tell the tale to _____ sinners?
5. It is hard to _____ our sinful impulses, but we should try to move beyond them.

EXERCISE B: MEANING CLUES On your paper, indicate whether each statement is true or false. Give a reason for your choice.

1. Guests at the inn most likely ordered **vermin** for dinner.
2. Someone who counts his or her money all the time may be guilty of **avarice**.
3. Giving money away is a sign of **covetousness**.
4. You should expect an **adversary** to agree with you.
5. A **parley** might lead to peace between warring factions.

WORDS TO KNOW			
	adversary	pallor	vermin
	avarice	parley	wary
	castigate	saunter	
	covetousness	transcend	

Building Vocabulary
Several Words to Know in this lesson contain prefixes and suffixes. For an in-depth study of word parts, see page 1104.

The Wife of Bath's Tale
from The Canterbury Tales

Poetry by GEOFFREY CHAUCER
Translated by NEVILL COGHILL

Connect to Your Life

Love and Marriage You are probably familiar with the phrase "the battle of the sexes." This expression suggests that romantic relationships have an aspect of conflict, in which one party attempts to gain the upper hand. What are your own opinions on the subject? Would you say that a good marriage is basically an equal partnership, or do you think that one person needs to be the decision maker? Explain your opinions in a class discussion.

Build Background

Romance and Chivalry "The Wife of Bath's Tale" belongs to the so-called Marriage Group of *The Canterbury Tales,* in which different pilgrims offer stories that express their philosophies of love and marriage. Set in the days of Britain's legendary King Arthur, the story qualifies as a medieval **romance**—an adventure tale of knights and chivalry, in which the code of ideal knightly behavior (loyalty, faith, honor, and courtesy, especially to women) is stressed. In this story, however, a knight breaks the rules of chivalry and, as punishment, must undertake a quest.

WORDS TO KNOW
Vocabulary Preview

abominably	implore
bequeath	maim
concede	prowess
contemptuous	rebuke
cosset	statute
crone	temporal
dejected	tribulation
ecstasy	

Focus Your Reading

LITERARY ANALYSIS **NARRATOR** Whether a story is told in prose or verse, the **narrator** is the person or voice that tells the story. In *The Canterbury Tales,* the narrator of the "Prologue" introduces the characters who will serve as narrators of the tales that follow. Reread lines 455–486 of the "Prologue" (page 125), which introduce the Wife of Bath. Then try to predict the view of love and marriage that she might present in her tale.

ACTIVE READING **ANALYZING STRUCTURE** **Structure** is the way in which the parts of a literary work are put together. A **frame story** is a story that serves as a narrative setting or frame for one or more other stories. *The Canterbury Tales* as a whole has a frame structure, in which the story of the pilgrims serves as a frame within which the pilgrims tell their stories. The structure of "The Wife of Bath's Tale" features a main **plot** with several interruptions. For example, in the opening lines the Wife of Bath interrupts the main plot with a passage in which she criticizes friars. This particular interruption stems from the Wife's ongoing quarrel with the Friar as they travel to Canterbury.

READER'S NOTEBOOK As you read "The Wife of Bath's Tale," use a chart similar to the one shown to keep track of the interruptions to the main story.

Interruption	Reason
criticism of friars	Wife of Bath's quarrel with Friar in frame story

from The Wife of Bath's Prologue

The Pardoner started up, and thereupon
"Madam," he said, "by God and by St. John,
That's noble preaching no one could surpass!
I was about to take a wife; alas!
5   Am I to buy it on my flesh so dear?
There'll be no marrying for me this year!"

    "You wait," she said, "my story's not begun.
You'll taste another brew before I've done;
You'll find it doesn't taste as good as ale;
10 And when I've finished telling you my tale
Of <u>tribulation</u> in the married life
In which I've been an expert as a wife,
That is to say, myself have been the whip.
So please yourself whether you want to sip
15 At that same cask of marriage I shall broach.
Be cautious before making the approach,
For I'll give instances, and more than ten.
And those who won't be warned by other men,
By other men shall suffer their correction,
20 So Ptolemy has said, in this connection.
You read his *Almagest*; you'll find it there."

    "Madam, I put it to you as a prayer,"
The Pardoner said, "go on as you began!
Tell us your tale, spare not for any man.
25 Instruct us younger men in your technique."
"Gladly," she said, "if you will let me speak,
But still I hope the company won't reprove me
Though I should speak as fantasy may move me,
And please don't be offended at my views;
30 They're really only offered to amuse. . . ."

The Wife of Bath

3 noble preaching: In the passage preceding this excerpt, the Wife of Bath has spoken at length about her view of marriage.

15 cask: barrel; **broach:** tap into.

20 Ptolemy (tŏl'ə-mē): a famous astronomer of the second century A.D. The *Almagest,* his most famous work, does not, however, contain the proverb cited in lines 18–19.

WORDS
TO
KNOW

tribulation (trĭb'yə-lā'shən) *n.* suffering; great distress

155

The Wife of Bath's Tale

When good King Arthur ruled in ancient days
(A king that every Briton loves to praise)
This was a land brim-full of fairy folk.
The Elf-Queen and her courtiers joined and broke
35 Their elfin dance on many a green mead,
Or so was the opinion once, I read,
Hundreds of years ago, in days of yore.
But no one now sees fairies any more.
For now the saintly charity and prayer
40 Of holy friars seem to have purged the air;
They search the countryside through field and stream
As thick as motes that speckle a sun-beam,
Blessing the halls, the chambers, kitchens, bowers,
Cities and boroughs, castles, courts and towers,
45 Thorpes, barns and stables, outhouses and dairies,
And that's the reason why there are no fairies.
Wherever there was wont to walk an elf
To-day there walks the holy friar himself
As evening falls or when the daylight springs,
50 Saying his matins and his holy things,
Walking his limit round from town to town.
Women can now go safely up and down
By every bush or under every tree;
There is no other incubus but he,
55 So there is really no one else to hurt you
And he will do no more than take your virtue.

Now it so happened, I began to say,
Long, long ago in good King Arthur's day,
There was a knight who was a lusty liver.
60 One day as he came riding from the river
He saw a maiden walking all forlorn
Ahead of him, alone as she was born.
And of that maiden, spite of all she said,
By very force he took her maidenhead.

65 This act of violence made such a stir,
So much petitioning to the king for her,
That he condemned the knight to lose his head
By course of law. He was as good as dead

35 mead: meadow.

42 motes: specks of dust.

43 bowers: bedrooms.

45 thorpes: villages; **outhouses:** sheds.

47 wherever . . . elf: wherever an elf was accustomed to walk.

51 limit: the area to which a friar was restricted in his begging for donations.

54 incubus (ĭn′kyə-bəs): an evil spirit believed to descend on women while they sleep.

39–56 What seems to be the Wife of Bath's attitude toward friars?

61 forlorn: sad and lonely.

63–64 of that maiden . . . maidenhead: in spite of the maiden's protests, he robbed her of her virtue.

(It seems that then the <u>statutes</u> took that view)
70   But that the queen, and other ladies too,
Implored the king to exercise his grace

71 grace: mercy; clemency.

So ceaselessly, he gave the queen the case
And granted her his life, and she could choose
Whether to show him mercy or refuse.

65–74 What punishment do the king and the law demand? To whom does the king grant the final judgment?

75   The queen returned him thanks with all her might,
And then she sent a summons to the knight
At her convenience, and expressed her will:
"You stand, for such is the position still,
In no way certain of your life," said she,
80   "Yet you shall live if you can answer me:
What is the thing that women most desire?
Beware the axe and say as I require.

        "If you can't answer on the moment, though,
I will <u>concede</u> you this: you are to go
85   A twelvemonth and a day to seek and learn
Sufficient answer, then you shall return.
I shall take gages from you to extort
Surrender of your body to the court."

87 gages: pledges.

        Sad was the knight and sorrowfully sighed,
90   But there! All other choices were denied,
And in the end he chose to go away
And to return after a year and day
Armed with such answer as there might be sent
To him by God. He took his leave and went.

95   He knocked at every house, searched every place,
Yes, anywhere that offered hope of grace.
What could it be that women wanted most?
But all the same he never touched a coast,
Country or town in which there seemed to be
100 Any two people willing to agree.

        Some said that women wanted wealth and treasure,
"Honor," said some, some "Jollity and pleasure,"

WORDS   **statute** (stăch′ o͞ot) *n.* a law
TO   **implore** (ĭm-plôr′) *v.* to plead; beg
KNOW   **concede** (kən-sēd′) *v.* to grant or acknowledge, often unwillingly

Some "Gorgeous clothes" and others "Fun in bed,"
"To be oft widowed and remarried," said
105 Others again, and some that what most mattered
Was that we should be <u>cosseted</u> and flattered.
That's very near the truth, it seems to me;
A man can win us best with flattery.
To dance attendance on us, make a fuss,
110 Ensnares us all, the best and worst of us.

Some say the things we most desire are these:
Freedom to do exactly as we please,
With no one to reprove our faults and lies,
Rather to have one call us good and wise.
115 Truly there's not a woman in ten score
Who has a fault, and someone rubs the sore,
But she will kick if what he says is true;
You try it out and you will find so too.
However vicious we may be within
120 We like to be thought wise and void of sin.
Others assert we women find it sweet
When we are thought dependable, discreet
And secret, firm of purpose and controlled,
Never betraying things that we are told.
125 But that's not worth the handle of a rake;
Women conceal a thing? For Heaven's sake!
Remember Midas? Will you hear the tale?

Among some other little things, now stale,
Ovid relates that under his long hair
130 The unhappy Midas grew a splendid pair
Of ass's ears; as subtly as he might,
He kept his foul deformity from sight;
Save for his wife, there was not one that knew.
He loved her best, and trusted in her too.
135 He begged her not to tell a living creature
That he possessed so horrible a feature.
And she—she swore, were all the world to win,
She would not do such villainy and sin
As saddle her husband with so foul a name;
140 Besides to speak would be to share the shame.
Nevertheless she thought she would have died
Keeping this secret bottled up inside;

115 ten score: 200.

117 but she will: who will not.

120 void of sin: sinless.

127 Midas: a legendary king of Phrygia in Asia Minor.

129 Ovid (ŏv'ĭd): an ancient Roman poet whose *Metamorphoses* is a storehouse of Greek and Roman legends. According to Ovid, it was a barber, not Midas's wife, who told the secret of his donkey's ears.

133 save: except.

WORDS
TO   **cosset** (kŏs'ĭt) *v.* to treat like a pet; pamper
KNOW

It seemed to swell her heart and she, no doubt,
Thought it was on the point of bursting out.

145   Fearing to speak of it to woman or man,
Down to a reedy marsh she quickly ran
And reached the sedge. Her heart was all on fire
And, as a bittern bumbles in the mire,
She whispered to the water, near the ground,
150 "Betray me not, O water, with thy sound!
To thee alone I tell it: it appears
My husband has a pair of ass's ears!
Ah! My heart's well again, the secret's out!
I could no longer keep it, not a doubt."
155 And so you see, although we may hold fast
A little while, it must come out at last,
We can't keep secrets; as for Midas, well,
Read Ovid for his story; he will tell.

       This knight that I am telling you about
160 Perceived at last he never would find out
What it could be that women loved the best.
Faint was the soul within his sorrowful breast,
As home he went, he dared no longer stay;
His year was up and now it was the day.

165   As he rode home in a <u>dejected</u> mood
Suddenly, at the margin of a wood,
He saw a dance upon the leafy floor
Of four and twenty ladies, nay, and more.
Eagerly he approached, in hope to learn
170 Some words of wisdom ere he should return;
But lo! Before he came to where they were,
Dancers and dance all vanished into air!
There wasn't a living creature to be seen
Save one old woman crouched upon the green.
175 A fouler-looking creature I suppose
Could scarcely be imagined. She arose
And said, "Sir knight, there's no way on from here.
Tell me what you are looking for, my dear,
For peradventure that were best for you;
180 We old, old women know a thing or two."

147 sedge: marsh grasses.

148 bumbles in the mire: booms in the swamp. (The bittern, a wading bird, is famous for its loud call.)
What does this comparison suggest about the queen's whisper?

Sir Gawain, from an illuminated manuscript

179 peradventure: perhaps.

WORDS TO KNOW   **dejected** (dĭ-jĕk′tĭd) *adj.* sad; depressed

"Dear Mother," said the knight, "alack the day!
I am as good as dead if I can't say
What thing it is that women most desire;
If you could tell me I would pay your hire."
185 "Give me your hand," she said, "and swear to do
Whatever I shall next require of you
—If so to do should lie within your might—
And you shall know the answer before night."
"Upon my honor," he answered, "I agree."
190 "Then," said the crone, "I dare to guarantee
Your life is safe; I shall make good my claim.
Upon my life the queen will say the same.
Show me the very proudest of them all
In costly coverchief or jewelled caul
195 That dare say no to what I have to teach.
Let us go forward without further speech."
And then she crooned her gospel in his ear
And told him to be glad and not to fear.

They came to court. This knight, in full array,
200 Stood forth and said, "O Queen, I've kept my day
And kept my word and have my answer ready."

There sat the noble matrons and the heady
Young girls, and widows too, that have the grace
Of wisdom, all assembled in that place,
205 And there the queen herself was throned to hear
And judge his answer. Then the knight drew near
And silence was commanded through the hall.

The queen gave order he should tell them all
What thing it was that women wanted most.
210 He stood not silent like a beast or post,
But gave his answer with the ringing word
Of a man's voice and the assembly heard:

"My liege and lady, in general," said he,
"A woman wants the self-same sovereignty
215 Over her husband as over her lover,
And master him; he must not be above her."

---

181 alack the day: an exclamation of sorrow, roughly equivalent to "Woe is me!"

The Knight and the Old Lady

194 coverchief: kerchief; **caul** (kaul): an ornamental hair-net.

197 gospel: message.

199 in full array: in all his finery.

202 heady: giddy; impetuous.

203 grace: gift.

213 liege (lēj): lord.

214 sovereignty (sŏv′ər-ĭn-tē): rule; power.

214–215 How might a woman's power over a lover differ from her power over a husband?

WORDS
TO
KNOW   **crone** (krōn) *n.* an ugly old woman; hag

That is your greatest wish, whether you kill
Or spare me; please yourself. I wait your will."

    In all the court not one that shook her head
220 Or contradicted what the knight had said;
Maid, wife and widow cried, "He's saved his life!"

    And on the word up started the old wife,
The one the knight saw sitting on the green,
And cried, "Your mercy, sovereign lady queen!
225 Before the court disperses, do me right!
'Twas I who taught this answer to the knight,
For which he swore, and pledged his honor to it,
That the first thing I asked of him he'd do it,
So far as it should lie within his might.
230 Before this court I ask you then, sir knight,
To keep your word and take me for your wife;
For well you know that I have saved your life.
If this be false, deny it on your sword!"

    "Alas!" he said, "Old lady, by the Lord
235 I know indeed that such was my behest,
But for God's love think of a new request,
Take all my goods, but leave my body free."
"A curse on us," she said, "if I agree!
I may be foul, I may be poor and old,
240 Yet will not choose to be, for all the gold
That's bedded in the earth or lies above,
Less than your wife, nay, than your very love!"

235 behest (bĭ-hĕst′): promise.

    "My love?" said he. "By heaven, my damnation!
Alas that any of my race and station
245 Should ever make so foul a misalliance!"
Yet in the end his pleading and defiance
All went for nothing, he was forced to wed.
He takes his ancient wife and goes to bed.

244 race and station: family and rank.

245 misalliance (mĭs′ə-lī′əns): an unsuitable marriage.

    Now peradventure some may well suspect
250 A lack of care in me since I neglect
To tell of the rejoicing and display
Made at the feast upon their wedding-day.
I have but a short answer to let fall;
I say there was no joy or feast at all,

255   Nothing but heaviness of heart and sorrow.
He married her in private on the morrow
And all day long stayed hidden like an owl,
It was such torture that his wife looked foul.

Great was the anguish churning in his head
260   When he and she were piloted to bed;
He wallowed back and forth in desperate style.
His ancient wife lay smiling all the while;
At last she said, "Bless us! Is this, my dear,
How knights and wives get on together here?
265   Are these the laws of good King Arthur's house?
Are knights of his all so <u>contemptuous</u>?
I am your own beloved and your wife,
And I am she, indeed, that saved your life;
And certainly I never did you wrong.
270   Then why, this first of nights, so sad a song?
You're carrying on as if you were half-witted.
Say, for God's love, what sin have I committed?
I'll put things right if you will tell me how."

"Put right?" he cried. "That never can be now!
275   Nothing can ever be put right again!
You're old, and so <u>abominably</u> plain,
So poor to start with, so low-bred to follow;
It's little wonder if I twist and wallow!
God, that my heart would burst within my breast!"

280   "Is that," said she, "the cause of your unrest?"

"Yes, certainly," he said, "and can you wonder?"

"I could set right what you suppose a blunder,
That's if I cared to, in a day or two,
If I were shown more courtesy by you.
285   Just now," she said, "you spoke of gentle birth,
Such as descends from ancient wealth and worth.
If that's the claim you make for gentlemen
Such arrogance is hardly worth a hen.
Whoever loves to work for virtuous ends,

256 the morrow: the next day.

260 piloted: led. (In the Middle Ages, it was customary for the wedding party to escort the bride and groom to their bedchamber.)

261 wallowed (wŏl′ōd): rolled around; thrashed about.

Dante and his Poem,
Domenico di Michelino

WORDS TO KNOW

contemptuous (kən-tĕmp′chōō-əs) *adj.* scornful; openly disrespectful
abominably (ə-bŏm′ə-nə-blē) *adv.* unpleasantly; terribly

290 Public and private, and who most intends
To do what deeds of gentleness he can,
Take him to be the greatest gentleman.
Christ wills we take our gentleness from Him,
Not from a wealth of ancestry long dim,
295 Though they bequeath their whole establishment
By which we claim to be of high descent.
Our fathers cannot make us a bequest
Of all those virtues that became them best
And earned for them the name of gentlemen,
300 But bade us follow them as best we can.

"Thus the wise poet of the Florentines,
Dante by name, has written in these lines,
For such is the opinion Dante launches:
'Seldom arises by these slender branches
305 Prowess of men, for it is God, no less,
Wills us to claim of Him our gentleness.'
For of our parents nothing can we claim
Save temporal things, and these may hurt and maim.

"But everyone knows this as well as I;
310 For if gentility were implanted by
The natural course of lineage down the line,
Public or private, could it cease to shine
In doing the fair work of gentle deed?
No vice or villainy could then bear seed.

315 "Take fire and carry it to the darkest house
Between this kingdom and the Caucasus,
And shut the doors on it and leave it there,
It will burn on, and it will burn as fair
As if ten thousand men were there to see,
320 For fire will keep its nature and degree,
I can assure you, sir, until it dies.

"But gentleness, as you will recognize,
Is not annexed in nature to possessions.
Men fail in living up to their professions;
325 But fire never ceases to be fire.

285–292 What does the old woman think is the chief qualification of a gentleman? How would you define "gentle birth" and "gentleness" as used in this passage?

301 Florentines: the people of Florence, Italy.

302 Dante (dän'tā): a famous medieval Italian poet. The quotation in lines 304–306 is a paraphrase of a passage in Dante's most famous work, *The Divine Comedy,* which he completed in 1321.

310 gentility (jĕn-tĭl'ĭ-tē): the quality possessed by a gentle, or noble, person.

316 Caucasus (kô'kə-səs): a region of western Asia, between the Black and Caspian seas.

324 professions: beliefs; ideals.

WORDS
TO
KNOW

bequeath (bĭ-kwēth') *v.* to leave in a will; give as an inheritance
prowess (prou'ĭs) *n.* superior skill; great ability
temporal (tĕm'pər-əl) *adj.* of the material world; not eternal
maim (mām) *v.* to disable or permanently wound

God knows you'll often find, if you enquire,
Some lording full of villainy and shame.
If you would be esteemed for the mere name
Of having been by birth a gentleman
330　And stemming from some virtuous, noble clan,
And do not live yourself by gentle deed
Or take your father's noble code and creed,
You are no gentleman, though duke or earl.
Vice and bad manners are what make a churl.

335　　"Gentility is only the renown
For bounty that your fathers handed down,
Quite foreign to your person, not your own;
Gentility must come from God alone.
That we are gentle comes to us by grace
340　And by no means is it bequeathed with place.

　　"Reflect how noble (says Valerius)
Was Tullius surnamed Hostilius,
Who rose from poverty to nobleness.
And read Boethius, Seneca no less,
345　Thus they express themselves and are agreed:
'Gentle is he that does a gentle deed.'
And therefore, my dear husband, I conclude
That even if my ancestors were rude,
Yet God on high—and so I hope He will—
350　Can grant me grace to live in virtue still,
A gentlewoman only when beginning
To live in virtue and to shrink from sinning.

　　"As for my poverty which you reprove,
Almighty God Himself in whom we move,
355　Believe and have our being, chose a life
Of poverty, and every man or wife,
Nay, every child can see our Heavenly King
Would never stoop to choose a shameful thing.
No shame in poverty if the heart is gay,
360　As Seneca and all the learned say.
He who accepts his poverty unhurt
I'd say is rich although he lacked a shirt.
But truly poor are they who whine and fret
And covet what they cannot hope to get.
365　And he that, having nothing, covets not,

327 lording: lord; nobleman.

334 churl (chûrl): low-class person; boor. Why might the sentiment expressed in this line have been viewed as fairly radical in the Wife of Bath's day?

341 Valerius (və-lîr′ē-əs): Valerius Maximus, a Roman writer of the first century A.D. who compiled a collection of historical anecdotes.

342 Tullius (tŭl′ē-əs) **surnamed Hostilius** (hŏ-stĭl′ē-əs): Tullus Hostilius—in Roman legend, the third king of the Romans.

344 Boethius (bō-ē′thē-əs): a Christian philosopher of the Dark Ages; **Seneca** (sĕn′ĭ-kə): an ancient Roman philosopher, writer, teacher, and politician.

Is rich, though you may think he is a sot.

"True poverty can find a song to sing.
Juvenal says a pleasant little thing:
'The poor can dance and sing in the relief
370 Of having nothing that will tempt a thief.'
Though it be hateful, poverty is good,
A great incentive to a livelihood,
And a great help to our capacity
For wisdom, if accepted patiently.
375 Poverty is, though wanting in estate,
A kind of wealth that none calumniate.
Poverty often, when the heart is lowly,
Brings one to God and teaches what is holy,
Gives knowledge of oneself and even lends
380 A glass by which to see one's truest friends.
And since it's no offense, let me be plain;
Do not rebuke my poverty again.

"Lastly you taxed me, sir, with being old.
Yet even if you never had been told
385 By ancient books, you gentlemen engage,
Yourselves in honor to respect old age.
To call an old man 'father' shows good breeding,
And this could be supported from my reading.

"You say I'm old and fouler than a fen.
390 You need not fear to be a cuckold, then.
Filth and old age, I'm sure you will agree,
Are powerful wardens over chastity.
Nevertheless, well knowing your delights,
I shall fulfil your worldly appetites.

395 "You have two choices; which one will you try?
To have me old and ugly till I die,
But still a loyal, true, and humble wife
That never will displease you all her life,
Or would you rather I were young and pretty
400 And chance your arm what happens in a city
Where friends will visit you because of me,
Yes, and in other places too, maybe.

366 sot: fool.

368 Juvenal (jōō'və-nəl): an ancient Roman satirist.

375 wanting in estate: lacking in grandeur.

376 calumniate (kə-lŭm'nē-āt'): criticize with false statements; slander.

389 fen: marsh.

390 cuckold (kŭk'əld): a husband whose wife is unfaithful.

400 chance your arm: take your chance on.

WORDS
TO   **rebuke** (rĭ-byōōk') v. to criticize
KNOW

Which would you have? The choice is all your own."

The knight thought long, and with a piteous groan
405 At last he said, with all the care in life,
"My lady and my love, my dearest wife,
I leave the matter to your wise decision.
You make the choice yourself, for the provision
Of what may be agreeable and rich
410 In honor to us both, I don't care which;
Whatever pleases you suffices me."

"And have I won the mastery?" said she,
"Since I'm to choose and rule as I think fit?"
"Certainly, wife," he answered her, "that's it."
415 "Kiss me," she cried. "No quarrels! On my oath
And word of honor, you shall find me both,
That is, both fair and faithful as a wife;
May I go howling mad and take my life
Unless I prove to be as good and true
420 As ever wife was since the world was new!
And if to-morrow when the sun's above
I seem less fair than any lady-love,
Than any queen or empress east or west,
Do with my life and death as you think best.
425 Cast up the curtain, husband. Look at me!"

And when indeed the knight had looked to see,
Lo, she was young and lovely, rich in charms.
In ecstasy he caught her in his arms,
His heart went bathing in a bath of blisses
430 And melted in a hundred thousand kisses,
And she responded in the fullest measure
With all that could delight or give him pleasure.

So they lived ever after to the end
In perfect bliss; and may Christ Jesus send
435 Us husbands meek and young and fresh in bed,
And grace to overbid them when we wed.
And—Jesu hear my prayer!—cut short the lives
Of those who won't be governed by their wives;
And all old, angry niggards of their pence,
440 God send them soon a very pestilence!

404 piteous (pĭt'ē-əs): pitiable; pathetic.

411 suffices (sə-fī'səz): satisfies.
How does the knight's statement relate to what he has learned about "the thing that women most desire"?

The Lover and the Lady, from an illuminated manuscript

439 niggards: misers.

WORDS TO KNOW   **ecstasy** (ĕk'stə-sē) *n.* intense joy or delight; bliss

166

Connect to the Literature

1. **What Do You Think?** Were you surprised by the outcome of the knight's quest? Why or why not?

> **Comprehension Check**
> - What change does the queen make in the knight's sentence?
> - What information does the old woman give the knight?
> - What happens to the old woman after the knight agrees to abide by her decision?

Think Critically

2. In what way is the question that the queen poses to the knight related to the crime that he has committed?

3. What **theme,** or message, about marriage would you say the tale conveys? Do you agree with the message? Why or why not?

4. **ACTIVE READING ANALYZING STRUCTURE** Look over your chart in your **READER'S NOTEBOOK** and review the reasons you inferred. What do the interruptions tell you about what matters to the Wife of Bath?

5. Consider the **narrator** of the "Prologue." How would you describe his values?

THINK ABOUT
- his characterizations of people like the Summoner, the Pardoner, and the Wife of Bath
- his opinions of their actions
- his description of himself as "short of wit" in line 766 of the "Prologue" (page 134)

Extend Interpretations

6. **Comparing Texts** Which part of *The Canterbury Tales*—the "Prologue" or the two tales—did you find the most enjoyable or interesting? Give reasons for your choice.

7. **Critic's Corner** One critic has described Chaucer as "a modern writer," one whose work can be appreciated by every generation of readers. Do you agree with this observation? Cite specific passages of *The Canterbury Tales* to back up your opinion.

8. **Connect to Life** Do you see any similarities between the attitudes of the Wife of Bath and the old woman in "The Wife of Bath's Tale" and the attitudes of modern American women? Cite details to support your answer.

Literary Analysis

NARRATOR The teller of a story in prose or verse is known as the story's **narrator.** The narrator may be a character in the story or a voice outside the action. In the "Prologue" from *The Canterbury Tales,* a narrator (whom Chaucer identifies as himself) introduces several characters, who then narrate the various tales.

Cooperative Learning Activity In a small-group discussion, consider how the portrait of the Wife of Bath in lines 455–486 of the "Prologue" (page 125) relates to the tale that she tells. Then work with the group to create a chart in which you list as many details about the Wife of Bath as you can. Include details about her appearance, skills, social position, personality, attitudes, and motives.

Detail	Evidence
worthy	"Prologue," lines 455 and 469
somewhat deaf	"Prologue," line 456

THE AUTHOR'S STYLE
Chaucer's Realism as Entertainment

Chaucer's enduring appeal as a poet stems in part from the humor and realism of his characterizations. Chaucer had no illusions about humanity, yet he showed a genuine fondness for human beings—warts and all. His combination of detachment and sympathy distinguishes his writing style.

Key Aspects of Chaucer's Style

- a gentle irony that exposes characters' faults while emphasizing their essential humanity
- a use of vivid but spare imagery and figurative language in describing characters' physical appearance
- a clear differentiation between characters
- a stylistic appropriateness of the tales to their narrators (Each character has a particular "voice.")

Analysis of Style

On the right are five excerpts from *The Canterbury Tales.* Study the chart above and read the excerpts carefully. Then,

- find examples of the listed aspects of Chaucer's style
- explain what, if anything, is amusing about each excerpt and identify which aspects of style contribute to this effect
- go back through the selections from *The Canterbury Tales* and find other examples of these key aspects of Chaucer's style

Applications

1. Speaking and Listening With a partner, study the description of either the Pardoner or the Wife of Bath in the "Prologue." Then read aloud selected passages from the character's tale in the way that the character might have told it. Have your partner critique your oral interpretation and suggest improvements.

2. Illustrating Style Choose one of Chaucer's pilgrims whose physical appearance is vividly described. Then draw a picture of the character, based on Chaucer's description.

3. Imitating Style In poetry or prose, create a character (preferably from a modern profession) and describe him or her with the mixture of detachment and sympathy that Chaucer used to such advantage.

---

from the Prologue

About the Prioress:
For courtliness she had a special zest,
And she would wipe her upper lip so clean
That not a trace of grease was to be seen
Upon the cup when she had drunk; to eat,
She reached a hand sedately for the meat.

About the Doctor:
Yet he was rather close as to expenses
And kept the gold he won in pestilences.
Gold stimulates the heart, or so we're told.
He therefore had a special love of gold.

About the Summoner:
There was a Summoner with us at that Inn,
His face on fire, like a cherubin,
For he had carbuncles. His eyes were narrow,
He was as hot and lecherous as a sparrow.
Black scabby brows he had, and a thin beard.
Children were afraid when he appeared.

from The Pardoner's Tale

There is, in Avicenna's long relation
Concerning poison and its operation,
Trust me, no ghastlier section to transcend
What these two wretches suffered at their end.
Thus these two murderers received their due,
So did the treacherous young poisoner too.

from The Wife of Bath's Tale

Others assert we women find it sweet
When we are thought dependable, discreet
And secret, firm of purpose and controlled,
Never betraying things that we are told.
But that's not worth the handle of a rake;
Women conceal a thing? For Heaven's sake!

Choices & CHALLENGES

Writing Options

1. Pilgrim Dialogue How might the other pilgrims have reacted to the "The Wife of Bath's Tale"? Write a dialogue in which at least two pilgrims, as well as the Wife of Bath herself, comment on the story and its message about men's and women's roles. Try to keep the comments true to the personalities and attitudes of the pilgrims as conveyed in the "Prologue."

2. Comparing Knights The Knight on the Canterbury pilgrimage, described in lines 43–80 of the "Prologue" (pages 114–115) is usually considered a model of chivalry. Write a short compare-and-contrast essay in which you compare the Knight with the knight in "The Wife of Bath's Tale." You might organize your ideas in a Venn diagram. Put your essay in your **Working Portfolio.**

Writing Handbook
See page 1367: Compare and Contrast.

Activities & Explorations

1. Gender Debate Conduct a debate about the key ingredients in healthy relationships. Your debate might focus on the differing expectations and responsibilities of men and women in life and in relationships.
~ SPEAKING AND LISTENING

2. Medieval Manuscript Create your own manuscript page of a passage from "The Wife of Bath's Tale" or another tale by Chaucer. Include the text of the passage, an appropriate illustration, and a decorative border for the page. **~ ART**

3. Costume Drawings Imagine a live performance of one of the tales. Find or draw pictures that show how the characters might be dressed. **~ ART**

4. Woman's Roles Find out more about the roles of women in Chaucer's day. Was the Wife of Bath representative of her sex? Did widows like her have more independence than married or single women? What was life like for noble women? for women affiliated with the church? Answer these questions in an oral report. **~ HISTORY**

5. Medieval Justice The justice meted out in "The Wife of Bath's Tale" may seem unusual by modern standards. Find out more about justice in medieval England. What influence did the monarch have over the courts of justice? What role did the church play in justice? What exactly is English common law? What were trial by combat and trial by ordeal, and when did they cease to be used? How did the jury system evolve? How were lawyers trained? Research the answer to one of these questions or a related question, then share your findings in a written report. **~ HISTORY**

Inquiry & Research

Bath The city of Bath in England (pictured below) has a history that dates back to Roman times. Research this city, the home of the Wife of Bath. Present your findings in an illustrated time line entitled "Bath Yesterday and Today."

Scene from Bath today

Choices & CHALLENGES

Vocabulary in Action

EXERCISE A: SYNONYMS On your paper, write the word that is closest in meaning to the boldfaced word.

1. **concede:** follow, grant, start, end
2. **statute:** regulation, remark, area, sculpture
3. **prowess:** stress, talent, front, back
4. **cosset:** release, urge, indulge, intrude
5. **implore:** beget, beseech, believe, belittle
6. **crone:** murmur, wizard, hag, scream
7. **abominably:** awfully, feebly, unwisely, easily

EXERCISE B: ANTONYMS On your paper, write the word whose meaning is most nearly opposite the meaning of the boldfaced word.

1. **tribulation:** criticism, sorrow, peace, anger
2. **bequeath:** gain, argue, doubt, inherit
3. **rebuke:** praise, predict, question, answer
4. **dejected:** depressed, elated, inserted, wise
5. **temporal:** harsh, timely, worldly, spiritual
6. **ecstasy:** misery, fury, confusion, bliss
7. **contemptuous:** proud, kind, new, respectful
8. **maim:** scar, scorn, infect, heal

WORDS TO KNOW		
abominably	crone	prowess
bequeath	dejected	rebuke
concede	ecstasy	statute
contemptuous	implore	temporal
cosset	maim	tribulation

Building Vocabulary

Several Words to Know in this lesson derive from Old or Middle English. For an in-depth study of word origins, see page 206.

Chaucer's World

Author Study Project

MOCK INTERVIEWS

Research and present a series of mock interviews with English men and women of Chaucer's day. Begin by brainstorming a list of possible interviewees with the entire class. Consider the characters in the "Prologue" of *The Canterbury Tales* and the professions mentioned in the biographical information about Chaucer. Then get together with a partner and research one of the medieval people or lifestyles. Use your findings to prepare questions and discussion points for a mock interview in which one member of your pair takes on the role of interviewer and the other portrays a medieval person.

Primary Print Sources Consider reading letters and diaries from the era, as well as more of *The Canterbury Tales*. A brief general survey of English literature, such as one found in an encyclopedia, might help you locate appropriate medieval sources.

Secondary Print Sources Social histories, which focus on people's daily lives, may prove to be valuable sources. Biographies of Chaucer and other people of his day should also be useful. Consider books that combine biography and social history, such as John Gardner's *The Life and Times of Chaucer*.

Web Sites Search for the Web sites of Chaucer and Middle English societies, medieval museums, and British castles. Also use the Web to locate medieval studies departments at British and American universities.

 More Online: Research Starter
www.mcdougallittell.com

Federigo's Falcon

from The Decameron

Tale by GIOVANNI BOCCACCIO (jō-vä′nē bō-kä′chē-ō′)

Comparing Literature of the World

The Storytelling Tradition Across Cultures

The Canterbury Tales **and** *The Decameron* The 14th-century Italian collection of tales known as *The Decameron,* by Giovanni Boccaccio, greatly influenced Chaucer's writing of *The Canterbury Tales.*

Points of Comparison As you read one of Boccaccio's famous tales, compare it with Chaucer's work in terms of **narrative structure** and **themes** relating to love and human nature.

Build Background

Plagued by Love Boccaccio lived during the Italian Renaissance—a time of great achievements in art, music, and literature. Like Chaucer's *Canterbury Tales, The Decameron* is a collection of tales set within a frame story. The frame, or outer story, is about ten characters who flee to the country to escape a plague that is ravaging Florence, Italy. For ten days they amuse themselves by telling stories, each day selecting a "king" or "queen" who presides over the storytelling. Their 100 tales make up the bulk of *The Decameron.* As this selection begins, the queen of the day decides that it is time to tell her own story.

"Federigo's Falcon" is a tale of courtly love. In medieval times, marriages were often arranged. As a result, couples sometimes looked outside marriage for romantic attachments. This practice was not considered scandalous as long as the love remained idealized. Federigo is devoted to a married woman, Monna Giovanna (mō′nä jō′vä′nä), and will sacrifice anything to gain her love.

WORDS TO KNOW	**Vocabulary Preview**			
anguish	compel	discretion	meagerly	presumption
commend	deign	legitimate	oblige	reproach

Focus Your Reading

LITERARY ANALYSIS **PLOT** The **plot** of a literary work consists of all the actions and events in the work. A plot moves forward because of a **conflict**—a struggle between opposing forces. As you read the story, notice how the plot develops around the main conflict.

ACTIVE READING **ANALYZING CAUSE AND EFFECT**
In a well-crafted story, a single event often has an effect that becomes the cause of still another effect and so on. To identify true cause-and-effect relationships in "Federigo's Falcon," make sure the relationship between events is causal by connecting them with the word *because.* If the sentence makes sense, the relationship is causal.

READER'S NOTEBOOK As you read this story about love and its sacrifices, try to keep track of the relationships between events by making a cause-and-effect diagram like the one started here.

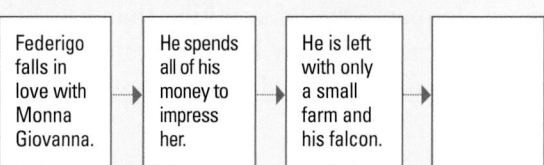

Federigo's FALCON

GIOVANNI BOCCACCIO

*F*ilomena had already finished speaking, and when the Queen saw there was no one left to speak except for Dioneo,[1] who was exempted because of his special privilege, she herself with a cheerful face said:

It is now my turn to tell a story and, dearest ladies, I shall do so most willingly with a tale similar in some respects to the preceding one, its purpose being not only to show you how much power your beauty has over the gentle heart, but also so that you yourselves may learn, whenever it is fitting, to be the donors of your favors instead of always leaving this act to the whim of Fortune,[2] who, as it happens, on most occasions bestows such favors with more abundance than discretion.

You should know, then, that Coppo di Borghese Domenichi,[3] who once lived in our city and perhaps still does, a man of great and respected authority in our times, one most illustrious and worthy of eternal fame both for his way of life and his ability much more than for the nobility of his blood, often took delight, when he was an old man, in discussing things from the past with his neighbors and with others. He knew how to do this well, for he was more logical and had a better memory and a more eloquent style of speaking than any other man. Among the many beautiful tales he told, there was one he would often tell about a young man who once lived in Florence named Federigo, the son of Messer Filippo Alberighi,[4] renowned above all other men in Tuscany for his prowess in arms and for his courtliness.

As often happens to most men of gentle breeding, he fell in love, with a noble lady named Monna Giovanna, in her day considered to be one of the most beautiful and most charming ladies that ever there was in Florence; and in order to win her love, he participated in jousts and tournaments, organized and gave banquets, spending his money without restraint; but she, no less virtuous than beautiful, cared little for these things he did on her behalf, nor did she care for the one who did them. Now, as Federigo was spending far beyond his means and getting nowhere, as can easily happen, he lost his wealth and was reduced to poverty, and was left with nothing to his name but his little farm (from whose revenues he lived very meagerly) and one falcon, which was among the finest of its kind in the world.

More in love than ever, but knowing that he would never be able to live the way he wished to in the city, he went to live at Campi, where his farm was. There he passed his time hawking whenever he could, imposing on no one, and enduring his poverty patiently. Now one day, during the time that Federigo was reduced to these extremes, it happened that the husband of Monna Giovanna fell ill, and realizing death was near, he made his last will: he was very rich, and he left everything to his son, who was just

---

1. **Dioneo** (dē′ô-nā′ō).
2. **Fortune:** a personification of the power that supposedly distributes good and bad luck to people.
3. **Coppo di Borghese Domenichi** (kôp′pō dē bōr-gā′zĕ dō-mĕ′nē-kē).
4. **Messer Filippo Alberighi** (mās′sĕr fē-lēp′pō äl′bĕ-rē′gē).

WORDS TO KNOW

discretion (dǐ-skrĕsh′ən) *n.* a sense of carefulness and restraint in one's actions or words

meagerly (mē′gər-lē) *adv.* poorly; scantily

La Pia de Tolommei (1868–1880), Dante Gabriel Rossetti. Oil on canvas, Spencer Museum of Art, University of Kansas.

growing up, and since he had also loved Monna Giovanna very much, he made her his heir should his son die without any <u>legitimate</u> children; and then he died.

Monna Giovanna was now a widow, and every summer, as our women usually do, she would go to the country with her son to one of their estates very close by to Federigo's farm. Now this young boy of hers happened to become more and more friendly with Federigo and he began to enjoy birds and dogs; and after seeing

Federigo's falcon fly many times, it made him so happy that he very much wished it were his own, but he did not dare to ask for it, for he could see how precious it was to Federigo. During this time, it happened that the young boy took ill, and his mother was much grieved, for he was her only child and she loved him dearly; she would spend the entire day by his side, never ceasing to comfort him, asking him time and again if there was anything he wished, begging him to tell her what it might be, for if it was possible to obtain

WORDS
TO
KNOW
legitimate (lə-jĭt′ə-mĭt) *adj.* born of parents who are legally married
to each other

173

She knew that Federigo had been in love with her for some time now.

it, she would certainly do everything in her power to get it. After the young boy had heard her make this offer many times, he said:

"Mother, if you can arrange for me to have Federigo's falcon, I think I would get well quickly."

When the lady heard this, she was taken aback for a moment, and then she began thinking what she could do about it. She knew that Federigo had been in love with her for some time now, but she had never deigned to give him a second look; so, she said to herself:

"How can I go to him, or even send someone, and ask for this falcon of his, which is, as I have heard tell, the finest that ever flew, and furthermore, his only means of support? And how can I be so insensitive as to wish to take away from this nobleman the only pleasure which is left to him?"

And involved in these thoughts, knowing that she was certain to have the bird if she asked for it, but not knowing what to say to her son, she stood there without answering him. Finally the love she bore her son persuaded her that she should make him happy, and no matter what the consequences might be, she would not send for the bird, but rather go herself to fetch it and bring it back to him; so she answered her son:

"My son, cheer up and think only of getting well, for I promise you that first thing tomorrow morning I shall go and fetch it for you."

The child was so happy that he showed some improvement that very day. The following morning, the lady, accompanied by another woman, as if they were out for a stroll, went to Federigo's modest little house and asked for him. Since the weather for the past few days had not

been right for hawking, Federigo happened to be in his orchard attending to certain tasks, and when he heard that Monna Giovanna was asking for him at the door, he was so surprised and happy that he rushed there; as she saw him coming, she rose to greet him with womanly grace, and once Federigo had welcomed her most courteously, she said:

"How do you do, Federigo?" Then she continued, "I have come to make amends for the harm you have suffered on my account by loving me more than you should have, and in token of this, I intend to have a simple meal with you and this companion of mine this very day."

To this Federigo humbly replied: "Madonna,[5] I have no recollection of ever suffering any harm because of you; on the contrary: so much good have I received from you that if ever I was worth anything, it was because of your worth and the love I bore for you; and your generous visit is certainly so very dear to me that I would spend all over again all that I spent in the past, but you have come to a poor host."

And having said this, he humbly led her through the house and into his garden, and because he had no one there to keep her company, he said:

"My lady, since there is no one else, this good woman, who is the wife of the farmer here, will keep you company while I see to the table."

Though he was very poor, Federigo until now had never realized to what extent he had wasted his wealth; but this morning, the fact that he had nothing in the house with which he could honor the lady for the love of whom he had in the past entertained countless people, gave him cause to reflect: in great anguish, he cursed himself and his fortune, and like someone out of his senses he started running here and there throughout the house, but unable to find either money or anything he might be able to pawn, and since it

---

5. **Madonna:** Italian for "my lady," a polite form of address used in speaking to a married woman. "Monna" is a contraction of this term.

was getting late and he was still very much set on serving this noble lady some sort of meal, but unwilling to turn for help to even his own farmer (not to mention anyone else), he set his eyes upon his good falcon, which was sitting on its perch in a small room, and since he had nowhere else to turn, he took the bird, and finding it plump, he decided that it would be a worthy food for such a lady. So, without giving the matter a second thought, he wrung its neck and quickly gave it to his servant girl to pluck, prepare, and place on a spit to be roasted with care; and when he had set the table with the whitest of tablecloths (a few of which he still had left), he returned, with a cheerful face, to the lady in his garden and announced that the meal, such as he was able to prepare, was ready.

The lady and her companion rose and went to the table together with Federigo, who waited upon them with the greatest devotion, and they ate the good falcon without knowing what it was they were eating. Then, having left the table and spent some time in pleasant conversation, the lady thought it time now to say what she had come to say, and so she spoke these kind words to Federigo:

"Federigo, if you recall your former way of life and my virtue, which you perhaps mistook for harshness and cruelty, I have no doubt at all that you will be amazed by my <u>presumption</u> when you hear what my main reason for coming here is; but if you had children, through whom you might have experienced the power of parental love, I feel certain that you would, at least in part, forgive me. But, just as you have no child, I do have one, and I cannot escape the laws common to all mothers; the force of such laws <u>compels</u> me to follow them, against my own will and against good manners and duty, and to ask of you a gift which I know is most precious to you; and it is naturally so, since your extreme condition has left you no other delight,

Peregrine Falcon. Raja Serfogee of Tanjore Collection, by permission of The British Library.

no other pleasure, no other consolation; and this gift is your falcon, which my son is so taken by that if I do not bring it to him, I fear his sickness will grow so much worse that I may lose him. And therefore I beg you, not because of the love that you bear for me, which does not <u>oblige</u> you in the least, but because of your own nobleness, which you have shown to be greater than that of all others in practicing courtliness, that you be pleased to give it to me, so that I may say that I have saved the life of my son by means of this

---

WORDS
TO
KNOW

presumption (prĭ-zŭmp′shən) *n.* bold or outrageous behavior
compel (kəm-pĕl′) *v.* to urge irresistibly; constrain
oblige (ə-blīj′) *v.* to make it one's duty to act

gift, and because of it I have placed him in your debt forever."

When he heard what the lady requested and knew that he could not oblige her because he had given her the falcon to eat, Federigo began to weep in her presence, for he could not utter a word in reply. The lady at first thought his tears were caused more by the sorrow of having to part with the good falcon than by anything else, and she was on the verge of telling him she no longer wished it, but she held back and waited for Federigo's reply once he stopped weeping. And he said:

"My lady, ever since it pleased God for me to place my love in you, I have felt that Fortune has been hostile to me in many ways, and I have complained of her, but all this is nothing compared to what she has just done to me, and I shall never be at peace with her again, when I think how you have come here to my poor home, where, when it was rich, you never deigned to come, and how you requested but a small gift, and Fortune worked to make it impossible for me to give it to you; and why this is so I shall tell you in a few words. When I heard that you, out of your kindness, wished to dine with me, I considered it only fitting and proper, taking into account your excellence and your worthiness, that I should honor you, according to my possibilities, with a more precious food than that which I usually serve to other people. So I thought of the falcon for which you have just asked me and of its value and I judged it a food worthy of you, and this very day I had it roasted and served to you as best I could. But seeing now that you desired it another way, my sorrow in not being able to serve you is so great that never shall I be able to console myself again."

And after he had said this, he laid the feathers, the feet, and the beak of the bird before her as proof. When the lady heard and saw this, she first <u>reproached</u> him for having killed a falcon such as this to serve as a meal to a woman. But

then to herself she <u>commended</u> the greatness of his spirit, which no poverty was able, or would be able, to diminish; then, having lost all hope of getting the falcon and thus, perhaps, of improving the health of her son, she thanked Federigo both for the honor paid to her and for his good intentions, and then left in grief to return to her son. To his mother's extreme sorrow, whether in disappointment in not having the falcon or because his illness inevitably led to it, the boy passed from this life only a few days later.

After the period of her mourning and her bitterness had passed, the lady was repeatedly urged by her brothers to remarry, since she was very rich and still young; and although she did not wish to do so, they became so insistent that remembering the worthiness of Federigo and his last act of generosity—that is, to have killed such a falcon to do her honor—she said to her brothers:

"I would prefer to remain a widow, if only that would be pleasing to you, but since you wish me to take a husband, you may be sure that I shall take no man other than Federigo degli Alberighi."

In answer to this, her brothers, making fun of her, replied:

"You foolish woman, what are you saying? How can you want him? He hasn't a penny to his name."

To this she replied: "My brothers, I am well aware of what you say, but I would much rather have a man who lacks money than money that lacks a man."

Her brothers, seeing that she was determined and knowing Federigo to be of noble birth, no matter how poor he was, accepted her wishes and gave her with all her riches in marriage to him; when he found himself the husband of such a great lady, whom he had loved so much and who was so wealthy besides, he managed his financial affairs with more prudence than in the past and lived with her happily the rest of his days. ❖

Translated by Mark Musa
and Peter Bondanella

WORDS
TO
KNOW

reproach (rĭ-prōch') v. to express disapproval of or disappointment in
commend (kə-mĕnd') v. to express approval of; praise

Connect to the Literature

1. **What Do You Think?** What is your reaction to the events in this story?

Comprehension Check
- How does Federigo lose his fortune?
- What happens during Monna Giovanna's visit to Federigo's house?

Think Critically

2. **ACTIVE READING** **ANALYZING CAUSE AND EFFECT** Get together with a classmate and compare your cause-and-effect diagrams in your 📖 **READER'S NOTEBOOK**. What does the story's chain of events suggest about the relationship between Federigo and Monna Giovanna?

3. Do you think Federigo acts nobly or foolishly? Use evidence to support your answer.

4. What is your opinion of Monna Giovanna?

THINK ABOUT
- her response to Federigo's love for her
- her visit to Federigo's house
- her response when Federigo tells her of the bird's fate
- her reason for taking Federigo as her husband

5. What do you think is the most important **theme,** or message about human nature, conveyed by this story?

Extend Interpretations

6. **What If?** Imagine that Monna Giovanna had explained the purpose for her visit as soon as she arrived at Federigo's house. What impact, if any, would this earlier disclosure have had on Monna Giovanna's son? on Federigo? on Monna Giovanna's decision to remarry?

7. **Connect to Life** In Boccaccio's time, women of Monna Giovanna's social class were expected to be married. Do women today feel the same pressure to marry? Are women and men under equal pressure to marry? Support your opinions with examples.

8. **Points of Comparison** Money plays an important role in both "Federigo's Falcon" and Chaucer's "The Pardoner's Tale." Compare Federigo's response to money with that of the "three rioters" in Chaucer's tale. What do the characters' reactions reveal about their personalities?

Literary Analysis

PLOT A narrative's **plot** can often be traced by identifying the following four basic elements:

- **exposition,** in which the characters are introduced, the setting is established, and the major conflict is identified
- **rising action,** in which suspense builds as the conflict intensifies and complications arise
- **a climax,** or turning point, which often occurs when a main character makes an important discovery or decision
- **falling action,** which shows the results of the climax and ties up loose ends

The events that make up the plot are driven by **conflict.** In "Federigo's Falcon," the main conflict is that between Federigo and Monna Giovanna. Federigo's attempts to make Monna Giovanna fall in love with him and her indifference to him are at the heart of each element of the plot.

Cooperative Learning Activity Use the cause-and-effect diagram you made on page 171 to help you decide which events make up the exposition, the rising action, the climax, and the falling action of "Federigo's Falcon." Discuss your decisions with a group of your classmates. Then label and briefly describe the story's plot elements on a diagram like the one below.

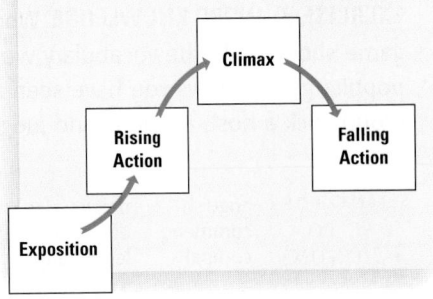

Choices & CHALLENGES

Writing Options

1. Monna Giovanna's Diary
Imagine Monna Giovanna's feelings when she discovers that she has dined on the falcon. Write a diary entry that she might compose to express her thoughts and feelings about the incident.

2. Frame Story Develop an idea for your own frame story. Using *The Decameron* as a model, determine the characters and setting of your frame, a reason for the characters to tell stories, and the duration of their storytelling. Share your ideas with other students.

3. Points of Comparison In a draft of an essay, compare and contrast Monna Giovanna's views about love and marriage with those portrayed in Chaucer's "The Wife of Bath's Tale." Include specific examples from both stories.

Writing Handbook
See page 1367: Compare and Contrast.

Activities & Explorations

1. Wedding Gift Think of the perfect wedding gift from Federigo to Monna Giovanna or from Monna Giovanna to Federigo. Then create the gift itself, or make a model or illustration of it. Keep in mind the giver's personality and financial status.
~ ART

2. Pantomime Presentation With a classmate, create a pantomime depicting Monna Giovanna's visit to Federigo's home. Make sure that your facial expressions and gestures reflect emotions appropriate to the actions.
~ PERFORMING

Inquiry & Research

1. The Art of Falconry Find out more about falcons and falconry. How does a falcon go after its prey? How is a falcon trapped and trained for sport?

 More Online:
Research Starter
www.mcdougallittell.com

2. Long Ago Love Traditions Prepare an oral report on the traditions of courtly love during the Middle Ages and the Italian Renaissance. Include information on what men did to woo their ladies and how the ladies were expected to respond. You might even suggest other things Federigo might have done to win Monna Giovanna's love.

Vocabulary in Action

EXERCISE A: SYNONYMS AND ANTONYMS Classify the words in each of the following pairs as synonyms or antonyms.

1. legitimate—lawful
2. commend—blame
3. compel—force
4. reproach—compliment
5. discretion—recklessness

6. presumption—impudence
7. oblige—release
8. anguish—sorrow
9. meagerly—abundantly
10. deign—refuse

EXERCISE B: WORD KNOWLEDGE Work with a small group of classmates to devise a game show, using the vocabulary words as either clues or answers. Think about popular game shows you have seen to help you decide on a format. From your group, pick a host, a helper, and judges, and then play your game with the class.

WORDS TO KNOW	anguish	deign	meagerly	presumption
	commend	discretion	oblige	reproach
	compel	legitimate		

Building Vocabulary
For an in-depth lesson on how to expand your vocabulary, see page 1182.

Giovanni Boccaccio

1313–1375

Other Works
"Elegy for Fiammetta"
"Treatise in Praise of Dante"

An Overbearing Father Although Giovanni Boccaccio began writing poetry as a child, his early talent was not rewarded. Instead, his merchant father demanded that his son forget about writing and learn business. While still a teenager, he was sent from his home in Tuscany to Naples, where he was apprenticed to a banker. When he failed at banking, his father arranged for him to study religious law. Boccaccio was unsuccessful at law too, and after about 12 years in Naples, he returned home to seek other employment. None of his jobs were very satisfactory, however, and he often lived on the brink of poverty.

A Source of Inspiration Fortunately, Boccaccio had continued to write in spite of his father's objections, and even during his unsuccessful venture in Naples, he produced an abundance of prose and poetry. It was also in Naples that he may have met his beloved "Fiammetta," a young woman who became the subject of much of his early writing and whose name he used for the narrator of "Federigo's Falcon" in *The Decameron.* The real identity of this woman has never been discovered.

An Influential Poet Boccaccio complained that because his father "strove to bend" his talent, he was unable to become "a distinguished poet." Eventually, of course, he did achieve distinction as a great poet, storyteller, and scholar. Along with his friend Petrarch, an Italian poet whose writings you will encounter in Unit Two, Boccaccio helped to set new directions for Italian literature and for the study of the classical poets of ancient Rome. With the publication of *The Decameron,* he became an international celebrity. In addition to his contemporary, Chaucer, many later poets writing in English—including Shakespeare, Dryden, Keats, Longfellow, and Tennyson—have been influenced by his work.

Author Activity

Love Story Read another story about love from Boccaccio's *The Decameron.* What does the story demonstrate about love or human nature? How is the theme similar to or different from the theme of "Federigo's Falcon"?

from The Paston Letters

by the PASTON FAMILY

(Connect to Your Life)

Person to Person Make a list of the various methods you use to communicate with other people. Also list the kinds of information you exchange by each of the methods. Which method do you use most often? Might one form of communication be better than the others in a particular instance? Share your thoughts with classmates.

Focus Your Reading

LITERARY ANALYSIS | **CONFLICT** | **Conflict** is a struggle between opposing forces that moves a narrative forward. Conflict may be **external,** with a character being pitted against some outside force, or it may be **internal,** occurring within a character. In the following excerpt from a letter by Margaret to her husband, notice how she and her husband seem to be involved in a deadly dispute with enemies:

> *I beg you with all my heart, for reverence of God, beware of Lord Moleyns and his men, however pleasantly they speak to you, and do not eat or drink with them; for they are so false that they cannot be trusted.*

As you read these letters, be aware of the various conflicts the writers experience, both in their dealings with the world as well as in their own feelings about people and events.

ACTIVE READING | **CREDIBILITY OF SOURCES** | Primary sources such as letters provide valuable insights into the thinking of people directly involved in the events they describe. As you read, you must take the writers' motives and objectivity into account when evaluating the credibility, or believability, of primary sources such as the Paston letters. Here are a couple of things to keep in mind.

- **Writer's Motives** Most of these letters deal with marriage and property. All of the people involved had different interests, both inside and outside the family. How might their interests have affected their interpretations and descriptions of people and events? For example, think about how the Pastons' views on marriage and property might influence the letters about the marriage of Margery to Richard Calle.
- **Objectivity** Is the information presented in the letters fact, opinion, or a mix of both? In reading about the disagreements between parents and child about a suitable marriage partner, for example, you must decide which statements are fact and which are opinion. Further, you must decide what motives a writer might have for holding a particular opinion.

READER'S NOTEBOOK As you read these letters, write down examples of ways in which each writer's motives might have influenced his or her description of people and events. Think about how the writer's level of objectivity might have influenced his or her interpretation of the facts.

Build Background

Landowners and Letters The 15th century in England was a period of great unrest and lawlessness. Landowners often attacked their neighbors' estates and betrayed their political allies. The Wars of the Roses, a conflict between two royal families for control of the kingdom, ravaged England between 1455 and 1485. In addition, several outbreaks of the plague devastated many English families during the century.

A firsthand record of this turbulent era survives in the more than 1,000 surviving documents and letters of the Pastons, an English landowning family. During the early 1400s, William Paston, a lawyer, began accumulating property in Norfolk, a county of eastern England, both through purchases and through his acquisition of estates inherited by his wife, Agnes Berry. William's extensive landholdings and growing prosperity, however, made him a number of

enemies. Some even challenged his claim to certain properties and brought grief to William's descendants for many years.

Business Matters In their letters, the Pastons exchanged information about their legal disputes and other problems in considerable detail. Although writing letters had become an important means of communication by the 15th century, sending the letters was not easy. They had to be delivered by hand, often by a servant or even a total stranger. Weeks might pass before a letter reached its destination, and many never arrived. Consequently, the matters discussed in letters were seldom frivolous, usually being confined to important business or family news. Despite these limitations, the Pastons wrote hundreds of letters over the course of 90 years, leaving an invaluable source of information about the social and political conditions of the times.

Family Tree A family tree traces genealogy—that is, the relationships of birth and descent in a family. The family tree on this page shows three generations of the Paston family. Before you read the letters, take some time to study these relationships. The names in red are those of the writers and recipients of the letters you will read.

Notice that William Paston and Agnes Berry had five children. The oldest, John I, inherited much of the family property when his father died in 1444, and his marriage to Margaret Mautby led to the acquisition of even more property from his wife's family. Like his father, John I was a lawyer, possessed of skills that were much needed in his constant legal battles over claims to various properties. His many legal disputes required John I to stay in London for long periods of time, leaving Margaret to

manage the Paston estates. Notice also that John and Margaret's large family included two sons named John. After the death of John I, his oldest son, John II, became responsible for much of the family business, even though Margaret was still living.

As you read the letters, refer often to the Paston family tree. Doing so may help you keep in mind that the people who communicated through these letters were real human beings who had many of the same needs, hopes, and fears that people have today.

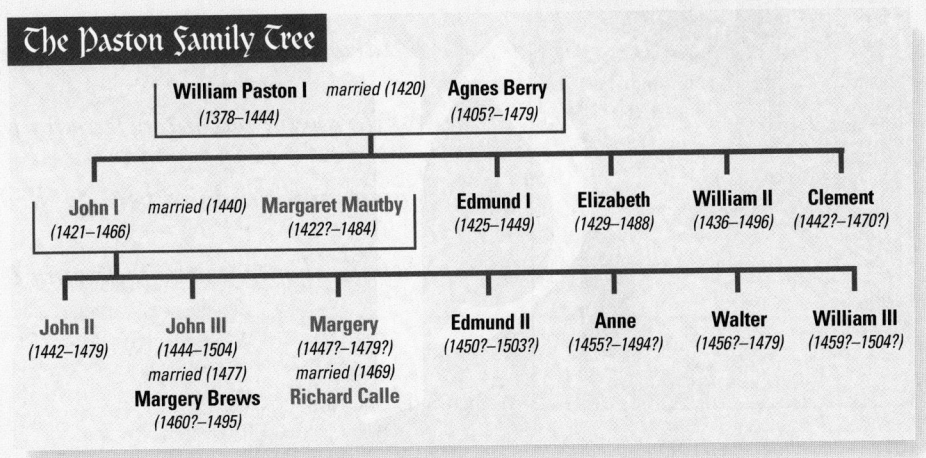

The Paston Family Tree

William Paston I (1378–1444) married (1420) Agnes Berry (1405?–1479)

- John I (1421–1466) married (1440) Margaret Mautby (1422?–1484)
- Edmund I (1425–1449)
- Elizabeth (1429–1488)
- William II (1436–1496)
- Clement (1442?–1470?)

- John II (1442–1479)
- John III (1444–1504) married (1477) Margery Brews (1460?–1495)
- Margery (1447?–1479?) married (1469) Richard Calle
- Edmund II (1450?–1503?)
- Anne (1455?–1494?)
- Walter (1456?–1479)
- William III (1459?–1504?)

from THE PASTON LETTERS

Women defending castle

$\mathcal{M}$argaret Paston, in the absence of her husband, John I, was able to deal equally well with small housekeeping problems and with family disasters, including attacks against the Paston manors. While she was living at the Paston estate of Gresham, it was attacked by a Lord Moleyns, who claimed rights to the property and ejected Margaret from her home. Margaret first escaped to a friend's house about a mile away; but later, fearing that Moleyns's band of men might kidnap her, she fled to the city of Norwich, where she wrote the following letter to her husband.

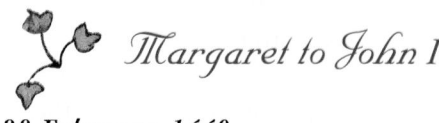

Margaret to John I

28 February 1449

Right worshipful husband, I commend myself
to you, wishing with all my heart to hear that
you are well, and begging that you will not be
angry at my leaving the place where you left me.
On my word, such news was brought to me by
various people who are sympathetic to you and
me that I did not dare stay there any longer. I
will tell you who the people were when you
come home. They let me know that various of
Lord Moleyns' men said that if they could get
their hands on me they would carry me off and
keep me in the castle. They wanted you to get
me out again, and said that it would not cause
you much heart-ache. After I heard this news, I
could not rest easy until I was here, and I did not
dare go out of the place where I was until I was
ready to ride away. Nobody in the place knew
that I was leaving except the lady of the house,
until an hour before I went. And I told her that I
would come here to have clothes made for
myself and the children, which I wanted made,
and said I thought I would be here a fortnight[1]
or three weeks. Please keep the reason for my
departure a secret until I talk to you, for those
who warned me do not on any account want it
known.

I spoke to your mother as I came this way,
and she offered to let me stay in this town, if you
agree. She would very much like us to stay at her
place, and will send me such things as she can
spare so that I can set up house until you can get
a place and things of your own to set up a
household. Please let me know by the man who
brings this what you would like me to do. I
would be very unhappy to live so close to
Gresham as I was until this matter is completely
settled between you and Lord Moleyns.

Barow[2] told me that there was no better
evidence in England than that Lord Moleyns
has for [his title to] the manor of Gresham. I
told him that I supposed the evidence was of
the kind that William Hasard said yours was,
and that the seals were not yet cold.[3] That, I
said, was what I expected his lord's evidence to
be like. I said I knew that your evidence was
such that no one could have better evidence,
and the seals on it were two hundred years
older than he was. Then Barow said to me that
if he came to London while you were there he
would have a drink with you, to quell any
anger there was between you. He said that he
only acted as a servant, and as he was ordered
to do. Purry[4] will tell you about the
conversation between Barow and me when I
came from Walsingham. I beg you with all my
heart, for reverence of God, beware of Lord
Moleyns and his men, however pleasantly they
speak to you, and do not eat or drink with
them; for they are so false that they cannot be
trusted. And please take care when you eat or
drink in any other men's company, for no one
can be trusted.

I beg you with all my heart that you will be
kind enough to send me word how you are,
and how your affairs are going, by the man
who brings this. I am very surprised that you
do not send me more news than you have
done. . . .

---

1. **fortnight:** two weeks.
2. **Barow:** one of Lord Moleyns's men.
3. **seals . . . cold:** A seal, often made by impressing a family
   emblem on hot wax, was placed on a document to show
   its authenticity. Margaret is suggesting that Lord
   Moleyns's documents are recent forgeries.
4. **Purry:** perhaps a servant or tenant of the Pastons.

In 1465, in still another property dispute, the Paston estate of Hellesdon was attacked by the duke of Suffolk, who had gained the support of several local officials. Although Margaret and John were not living at Hellesdon at the time, many of their servants and tenants suffered from the extensive damage. In the following two letters, Margaret tells her husband about the devastation.

 *Margaret to John I*

17 October 1465

. . . On Tuesday morning John Botillere, also John Palmer, Darcy Arnald your cook and William Malthouse of Aylsham were seized at Hellesdon by the bailiff[5] of Eye, called Bottisforth, and taken to Costessey,[6] and they are being kept there still without any warrant or authority from a justice of the peace; and they say they will carry them off to Eye prison and as many others of your men and tenants as they can get who are friendly towards you or have supported you, and they threaten to kill or imprison them.

The duke came to Norwich at 10 o'clock on Tuesday with five hundred men and he sent for the mayor, aldermen and sheriffs, asking them in the king's name that they should enquire of the constables of every ward within the city which men had been on your side or had helped or supported your men at the time of any of these gatherings and if they could find any they should take them and arrest them and punish them; which the mayor did, and will do anything he can for him and his men. At this the mayor has arrested a man who was with me, called Robert Lovegold, a brazier,[7] and threatened him that he shall be hanged by the neck. So I would be glad if you could get a writ sent down for his release, if you think it can be done. He was only with me when Harlesdon[8] and others attacked me at Lammas.[9] He is very true and faithful to you, so I would like him to be helped. I have no one attending me who dares to be known, except Little John. William Naunton is here with me, but he dares not be known because he is much threatened. I am told that the old lady and the duke have been frequently set against us by what Harlesdon, the bailiff of Costessey, Andrews and Doget the bailiff's son and other false villains have told them, who want this affair pursued for their own pleasure; there are evil rumors about it in this part of the world and other places.

As for Sir John Heveningham, Sir John Wyndefeld and other respectable men, they have been made into their catspaws,[10] which will not do their reputation any good after this, I think. . . .

The lodge and remainder of your place was demolished on Tuesday and Wednesday, and the duke rode on Wednesday to Drayton and then to Costessey while the lodge at Hellesdon was being demolished. Last night at midnight Thomas Slyford, Green, Porter and John Bottisforth the bailiff of Eye and others got a cart and took away the featherbeds and all the stuff of ours that was left at the parson's and Thomas Water's house for safe-keeping. I will send you lists later, as accurately as I can, of the things we have lost. Please let me know what you want me to do, whether you want me to stay at Caister[11] or come to you in London.

I have no time to write any more. God have you in his keeping. Written at Norwich on St. Luke's eve.[12]

M.P.

---

5. **bailiff:** the manager of an estate.
6. **Costessey:** an estate owned by the duke of Suffolk.
7. **brazier** (brā′zhər): person who makes articles of brass.
8. **Harlesdon:** one of the duke of Suffolk's men.
9. **Lammas:** a religious feast that was celebrated on August 1.
10. **catspaws:** people who are deceived and used as tools by others.
11. **Caister:** one of the Paston estates.
12. **St. Luke's eve:** the eve of St. Luke's Day, a religious feast. Writers often dated letters in this way instead of using days and months.

Margaret to John I

27 October 1465

. . . I was at Hellesdon last Thursday and saw the place there, and indeed no one can imagine what a horrible mess it is unless they see it. Many people come out each day, both from Norwich and elsewhere, to look at it, and they talk of it as a great shame. The duke would have done better to lose £1000 than to have caused this to be done, and you have all the more goodwill from people because it has been done so foully. And they made your tenants at Hellesdon and Drayton, and others, help them to break down the walls of both the house and the lodge: God knows, it was against their will, but they did not dare do otherwise for fear. I have spoken with your tenants both at Hellesdon and Drayton, and encouraged them as best I can.

The duke's men ransacked the church, and carried off all the goods that were left there, both ours and the tenants, and left little behind; they stood on the high altar and ransacked the images, and took away everything they could find. They shut the parson out of the church until they had finished, and ransacked everyone's house in the town five or six times. The ringleaders in the thefts were the bailiff of Eye and the bailiff of Stradbroke, Thomas Slyford. And Slyford was the leader in robbing the church and, after the bailiff of Eye, it is he who has most of the proceeds of the robbery. As for the lead, brass, pewter, iron, doors, gates, and other household stuff, men from Costessey and Cawston have got it, and what they could not carry they hacked up in the most spiteful fashion. If possible, I would like some reputable men to be sent for from the king, to see how things are both there and at the lodge, before any snows come, so that they can report the truth, because otherwise it will not be so plain as it is now. For reverence of God, finish your business now, for the expense and trouble we have each day is horrible, and it will be like this until you have finished; and your men dare not go around collecting your rents, while we keep here every day more than twenty people to save ourselves and the place; for indeed, if the place had not been strongly defended, the duke would have come here. . . .

For the reverence of God, if any respectable and profitable method can be used to settle your business, do not neglect it, so that we can get out of these troubles and the great costs and expenses we have and may have in future. It is thought here that if my lord of Norfolk would act on your behalf, and got a commission to enquire into the riots and robberies committed on you and others in this part of the world, then the whole county will wait on him and do as you wish, for people love and respect him more than any other lord, except the king and my lord of Warwick. . . .

Please do let me know quickly how you are and how your affairs are going, and let me know how your sons are. I came home late last night, and will be here until I hear from you again. Wykes came home on Saturday, but he did not meet your sons.

God have you in his keeping and send us good news from you. Written in haste on the eve of St. Simon and St. Jude.

By yours, M.P.

During the fifteenth century, most marriages among the upper classes were arranged by families, usually to strengthen economic or political ties. The Paston family was greatly alarmed, therefore, when they learned that Margery, a daughter of Margaret and John I, had secretly become engaged to the Paston bailiff Richard Calle. Eventually, the two were married in spite of bitter opposition from Margery's family. In the following letter to Margery—the only piece of their correspondence to survive—Richard expresses his feelings about their predicament. The next letter is the response of Margery's mother, Margaret, to the situation, written to her son, John II.

Richard Calle to Margery Paston

Spring-Summer 1469

My own lady and mistress, and indeed my true wife before God,[13] I commend myself to you with a very sad heart as a man who cannot be cheerful and will not be until things stand otherwise with us than they do now. This life that we lead now pleases neither God nor the world, considering the great bond of matrimony that is made between us, and also the great love that has been, and I trust still is, between us, and which for my part was never greater. So I pray that Almighty God will comfort us as soon as it pleases him, for we who ought by rights to be most together are most apart; it seems a thousand years since I last spoke to you. I would rather be with you than all the wealth in the world. Alas, also, good lady, those who keep us apart like this, scarcely realize what they are doing: those who hinder matrimony are cursed in church four times a year. It makes many men think that they can stretch a point of conscience in other matters as well as this one. But whatever happens, lady, bear it as you have done and be as cheerful as you can, for be sure, lady, that God in the long run will of his righteousness help his servants who mean to be true and want to live according to his laws.

I realize, lady, that you have had as much sorrow on my account as any gentlewoman has ever had in this world; I wish to God that all the sorrow you have had had fallen on me, so that you were freed of it; for indeed, lady, it kills me to hear that you are being treated otherwise than you should be. This is a painful life we lead; I cannot imagine that we live like this without God being displeased by it.

You will want to know that I sent you a letter from London by my lad, and he told me he could not speak to you, because so great a watch was kept on both you and him. He told me that John Thresher came to him in your name, and said that you had sent him to my lad for a letter or token which you thought I had sent you; but he did not trust him and would not deliver anything to him. After that he brought a ring, saying that you sent it to him, commanding him to deliver the letter or token to him, which I gather since then from my lad was not sent by you, but was a plot of my mistress [i.e., Margaret Paston] and James Gloys.[14] Alas, what do they intend? I suppose they think we are not engaged; and if this is the case I am very surprised, for they are not being sensible, remembering how plainly I told my mistress about everything at the beginning, and I think you have told her so too, if you have done as you should. And if you have denied it, as I have been told you have done, it was done neither with a good conscience nor to the pleasure of God, unless you did it for fear and to please those who were with you at the time. If this was the reason you did it, it was justified, considering how insistently you were

---

13. **my true wife before God:** In the 1400's, the spoken vow of a man and woman, even without a witness, was regarded as an official marriage.

14. **James Gloys:** the Paston family chaplain.

called on to deny it; and you were told many untrue stories about me, which, God knows, I was never guilty of.

My lad told me that your mother asked him if he had brought any letter to you, and she accused him falsely of many other things; among other things, she said to him in the end that I would not tell her about it at the beginning, but she expected that I would at the ending. As for that, God knows that she knew about it first from me and no one else. I do not know what my mistress means, for in truth there is no other gentlewoman alive who I respect more than her and whom I would be more sorry to displease, saving only yourself who by right I ought to cherish and love best, for I am bound to do so by God's law and will do so while I live, whatever may come of it. I expect that if you tell them the sober truth, they will not damn their souls for our sake. Even if I tell them the truth they will not believe me as much as they would you. And so, good lady, for reverence of God be plain with them and tell the truth, and if they will not agree, let it be between them, God and the devil; and as for the peril we should be in, I pray God it may lie on them and not on us. I am very sad and sorry when I think of their attitude. God guide them and send them rest and peace.

I am very surprised that they are as concerned about this affair as I gather that they are, in view of the fact that nothing can be done about it, and that I deserve better; from any point of view there should be no obstacles to it. Also their honor does not depend on your marriage, but in their own marriage [i.e., John II's]; I pray God send them a marriage which will be to their honor, to God's pleasure and to their heart's ease, for otherwise it would be a great pity.

Mistress, I am frightened of writing to you, for I understand that you have showed the letters that I have sent you before to others, but I beg you, let no one see this letter. As soon as you have read it, burn it, for I would not want anyone to see it. You have had nothing in writing from me for two years, and I will not send you any more: so I leave everything to your wisdom.

Letter from Richard Calle to Margery Paston, 1469

Almighty Jesu preserve, keep and give you your heart's desire, which I am sure will please God. This letter was written with as great difficulty as I ever wrote anything in my life, for I have been very ill, and am not yet really recovered, may God amend it.

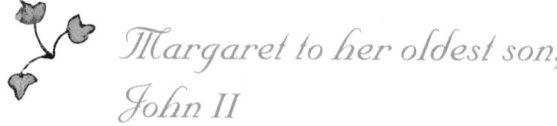

Margaret to her oldest son, John II

10 September 1469

. . . When I heard how she [Margery] had behaved, I ordered my servants that she was not to be allowed in my house. I had warned her, and she might have taken heed if she had been well-disposed. I sent messages to one or two others that they should not let her in if she came. She was brought back to my house to be let in, and James Gloys told those who brought her that I had ordered them all that she should not be allowed in. So my lord of Norwich has lodged her at Roger Best's, to stay there until the day in question; God knows it is much against his will and his wife's, but they dare not do otherwise. I am sorry that they are burdened with her, but I am better off with her there than somewhere else, because he and his wife are sober and well-disposed to us, and she will not be allowed to play the good-for-nothing there.

Please do not take all this too hard, because I know that it is a matter close to your heart, as it is to mine and other people's; but remember, as I do, that we have only lost a good-for-nothing in her, and take it less to heart: if she had been any good, whatever might have happened, things would not have been as they are, for even if he[15] were dead now, she would never be as close to me as she was. . . . You can be sure that she will regret her foolishness afterwards, and I pray to God that she does. Please, for my sake, be cheerful about all this. I trust that God will help us; may he do so in all our affairs. . . .

---

15. **he:** Richard Calle.

Women defending a castle with bow and crossbow (about 1326–1327). Manuscript illumination from *De nobilitatibus, sapientiis, et prudentiis regum* by Walter de Milemete (MS. CH. 92 F. 4r). By permission of the Governing Body of Christ Church, Oxford, England.

Although the Pastons were considered wealthy, they faced continual struggles. They even experienced occasional financial difficulties, particularly after the death of John I in 1466. John II, though frequently in London to deal with family legal matters, seems at times to have paid more attention to his own interests. The Pastons were also affected by the ravages of warfare and disease. The following three letters deal with some of their hardships.

 ## Margaret to John II

28 October 1470

. . . Unless you pay more attention to your expenses, you will bring great shame on yourself and your friends, and impoverish them so that none of us will be able to help each other, to the great encouragement of our enemies.

Those who claim to be your friends in this part of the world realize in what great danger and need you stand, both from various of your friends and from your enemies. It is rumored that I have parted with so much to you that I cannot help either you or any of my friends, which is no honor to us and causes people to esteem us less. At the moment it means that I must disperse my household and lodge somewhere, which I would be very loath to do if I were free to choose. It has caused a great deal of talk in this town and I would not have needed to do it if I had held back when I could. So for God's sake pay attention and be careful from now on, for I have handed over to you both my own property and your father's, and have held nothing back, either for myself or for his sake. . . .

 ## John II to Margaret

April 1471

Mother, I commend myself to you and let you know, blessed be God, my brother John is alive and well, and in no danger of dying. Nevertheless he is badly hurt by an arrow in his right arm below the elbow, and I have sent a surgeon to him, who has dressed the wound; and he tells me that he hopes he will be healed within a very short time. John Mylsent is dead. God have mercy on his soul; William Mylsent is alive and all his other servants seem to have escaped. . . .

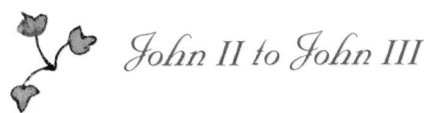 ## John II to John III

15 September 1471

. . . Please send me word if any of our friends or well-wishers are dead, for I fear that there is great mortality in Norwich and in other boroughs and towns in Norfolk: I assure you that it is the most widespread plague I ever knew of in England, for by my faith I cannot hear of pilgrims going through the country nor of any other man who rides or goes anywhere, that any town or borough in England is free from the sickness. May God put an end to it, when it please him. So, for God's sake, get my mother to take care of my younger brothers and see that they are not anywhere where the sickness is prevalent, and that they do not amuse themselves with other young people who go where the sickness is. If anyone has died of the sickness, or is infected with it, in Norwich, for God's sake let her send them to some friend of hers in the country; I would advise you to do the same. I would rather my mother moved her household into the country. . . . ❖

Connect to the Literature

1. **What Do You Think?**
   What is your impression of the events described in the Paston family letters?

   ....
   Comprehension Check
   - What did the duke of Suffolk do when he arrived at the Paston estate of Hellesdon?
   - Why did Margery Paston's family oppose her marriage to Richard Calle?
   ....

Think Critically

2. How would you describe Margaret Paston?

   THINK ABOUT
   - the **tone** she communicates in her letters
   - the nature of her responsibilities
   - how she deals with problems
   - her relationships with her husband and her children

3. What advice might you give Richard Calle and Margery Paston for dealing with their predicament?

4. **ACTIVE READING CREDIBILITY OF SOURCES** Look back at the examples you wrote in your **READER'S NOTEBOOK.** On the basis of your reading of these letters, how reliable do you think the Pastons' accounts are? Give reasons for your answer that address issues of **motive** and **objectivity.**

Extend Interpretations

5. **Critic's Corner** Virginia Woolf wrote of the Paston letters that "in all this there is no writing for writing's sake; no use of the pen to convey pleasure or amusement." What does this observation suggest about the lives of the people who wrote these letters?

6. **Connect to Life** Margaret Paston was forced to take care of family business while her husband was away. How do you think a contemporary businesswoman would view Margaret's handling of these matters?

Literary Analysis

CONFLICT Because of the turbulent times in which the Pastons lived, their letters present a number of **conflicts,** or struggles between opposing forces. In fiction, a conflict usually reaches a point of resolution; in a series of real letters, however, many of the conflicts described may necessarily remain unresolved.

In both fiction and nonfiction, the term **external conflict** is used to describe a situation in which a person is pitted against an outside force (such as another person, a physical obstacle, nature, or society). The term **internal conflict** refers to a struggle that takes place within a person.

Cooperative Learning Activity
With a group of classmates, go through the letters, creating a list of the various conflicts that are described by each writer. Decide whether each conflict is external or internal. Then choose one conflict and write an imaginative description of how it might have been resolved. Share your group's work with the rest of the class.

REVIEW TONE **Tone** is the expression of a writer's attitude toward his or her subject. Analyze the general tone of these letters. Think about the writers' purposes, the language used, the details included, and the recipients of the letters. Then try to come up with a one-word description of their tone.

Writing Options

1. Margery Paston's Diary Imagine that you are Margery Paston. Write a diary entry in which you express your thoughts about your mother's reaction to your marriage plans.

2. Opinion Paragraph In a paragraph, tell which of the persons mentioned in the Paston letters you would judge as the most interesting and which the least interesting. Explain your choices. Place the paragraph in your **Working Portfolio.**

Activities & Explorations

1. Map Mileage Scale On the map shown, locate the estate at Paston. Then use the mileage scale to estimate the distances between Paston and three other estates or towns mentioned in the letters you have read.
~ GEOGRAPHY

2. Illustrated Fashions Research the fashions of 15th-century England. Then make an illustration showing clothing that would have been appropriate for a man or woman of the Paston family.
~ ART

3. Dramatic Presentation With several other students, give a short dramatic presentation of one of the letters.
~ SPEAKING AND LISTENING

4. Panel Discussion Think about the limitations of communicating only through letters. If faster or easier methods of communication had been available to the Pastons, how might their lives have been different? With classmates, conduct a panel discussion in which you explore this question. **~ SPEAKING AND LISTENING**

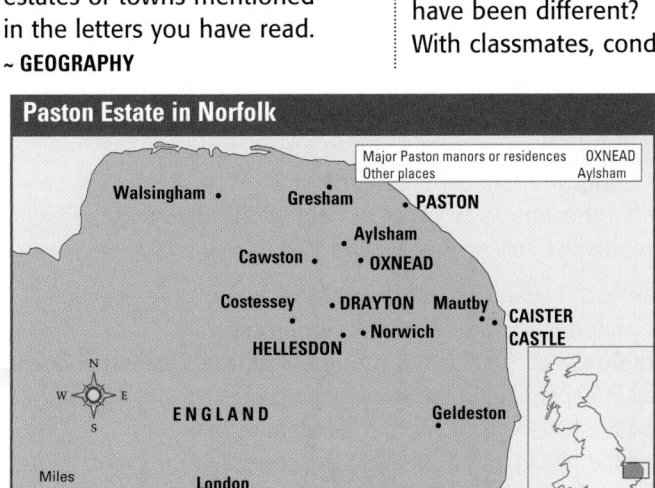

Inquiry & Research

1. Life Spans Using dates from the Paston family tree on page 181, calculate the life span of each person shown in the diagram. For this activity, assume that all approximate dates are exact. What was the average life span of the men? of the women?

2. 15th-Century History With three classmates, investigate one of these topics related to the 15th century: the Wars of the Roses, courtship and marriage, education, religion, medicine and life expectancy, the role of women, art and music, or life on a medieval manor. Present your findings to the class.

More Online:
Research Starter
www.mcdougallittell.com

Paston Estate in Norfolk

Major Paston manors or residences   OXNEAD
Other places   Aylsham

Walsingham
Gresham
PASTON
Aylsham
Cawston
OXNEAD
Costessey
DRAYTON Mautby
CAISTER CASTLE
Norwich
HELLESDON

N
W E
S

ENGLAND
Geldeston

Miles
0 5 10 15
London
Eye **Stradbroke**

PREPARING to *Read*

Barbara Allan / Sir Patrick Spens / Get Up and Bar the Door

Anonymous Ballads

Build Background

Songs That Tell a Story Throughout history, many of life's tragedies and comedies, real or fictional, have been depicted in song. Narrative songs called **ballads** were popular in England and Scotland during the medieval period, particularly among the common people, many of whom could not read or write. Minstrels traveled about, singing these narratives to entertain their listeners with dramatic stories about ordinary people. The best of the early ballads were passed on orally from one generation to the next and sometimes from country to country. Stories often changed in the retelling, sometimes resulting in dozens of versions of the same ballad. Most composers of these popular, or folk, ballads remained anonymous, and the songs themselves were not written down before the 18th century.

Focus Your Reading

LITERARY ANALYSIS **BALLADS** The early popular **ballads** share certain characteristics common to oral traditions. The typical ballad focuses on a single incident, beginning in the middle of a crisis and proceeding directly to the resolution, with only the most sketchy background information, character development, and descriptive detail. Popular subjects of these early ballads include tragic love, domestic conflict, crime, war, and shipwreck. As you read the three ballads in this lesson, note which treat tragic subjects and which treat comic matters.

ACTIVE READING **STRATEGIES FOR READING BALLADS** In the ballads you are about to read, certain words of Scottish **dialect** appear—*rase* and *guid,* for example. In order to help you understand the ballads, including dialect, follow these steps.

- Read each ballad through once, using the notes to help you decipher dialect and other difficult passages.
- **Paraphrase** each stanza as you read to make sure you understand what is happening in the story.
- Read the ballad again without referring to the notes.
- Read the ballad aloud, allowing the sounds of the words to help you appreciate the texture and flavor of the poems.

READER'S NOTEBOOK As you read, jot down notes about which strategies and steps you find most useful in helping you to understand the ballads.

Strategies

Paraphrasing
rereading

Barbara Allan

It was in and about the Martinmas time,
    When the green leaves were a-fallin';
That Sir John Graeme in the West Country
    Fell in love with Barbara Allan.

5 He sent his man down through the town
    To the place where she was dwellin':
"O haste and come to my master dear,
    Gin ye be Barbara Allan."

O slowly, slowly rase she up,
10   To the place where he was lyin',
And when she drew the curtain by:
    "Young man, I think you're dyin'."

"O it's I'm sick, and very, very sick,
    And 'tis a' for Barbara Allan."
15 "O the better for me ye sal never be,
    Though your heart's blood were a-spillin'.

"O dinna ye mind, young man," said she,
    "When ye the cups were fillin',
That ye made the healths gae round and round,
20   And slighted Barbara Allan?"

He turned his face unto the wall,
    And death with him was dealin':
"Adieu, adieu, my dear friends all,
    And be kind to Barbara Allan."

25 And slowly, slowly, rase she up,
    And slowly, slowly left him;
And sighing said she could not stay,
    Since death of life had reft him.

She had not gane a mile but twa,
30   When she heard the dead-bell knellin',
And every jow that the dead-bell ga'ed
    It cried, "Woe to Barbara Allan!"

"O mother, mother, make my bed,
    O make it soft and narrow:
35 Since my love died for me today,
    I'll die for him tomorrow."

1 Martinmas: November 11 (St. Martin's Day).

8 gin (gĭn): if.

9 rase (rāz): rose.

15 sal: shall.

17 dinna ye mind: don't you remember.

19 healths: toasts; **gae** (gā): go.

28 reft: deprived.

29 gane (gān): gone; **twa:** two.

30 dead-bell: a church bell rung to announce a person's death.

31 jow (jou): stroke; **ga'ed:** gave.

Sir Patrick Spens

The king sits in Dumferline town,
    Drinking the blude-reid wine:
"O whar will I get a guid sailor
    To sail this ship of mine?"

5 Up and spak an eldern knicht,
    Sat at the king's richt knee:
"Sir Patrick Spens is the best sailor
    That sails upon the sea."

1 Dumferline: the town of Dumferline in Scotland, site of a favorite residence of Scottish kings.
2 blude-reid (blŏŏd'rēd'): blood-red.
3 guid (güd): good.
5 eldern knicht (knĭкнt): elderly knight.
6 richt (rĭкнt): right.

The king has written a braid letter
        And signed it wi' his hand,
And sent it to Sir Patrick Spens,
        Was walking on the sand.

The first line that Sir Patrick read,
        A loud lauch lauched he;
The next line that Sir Patrick read,
        The tear blinded his ee.

"O wha is this has done this deed,
        This ill deed done to me,
To send me out this time o' the year,
        To sail upon the sea?

"Make haste, make haste, my mirry men all,
        Our guid ship sails the morn."
"O say na sae, my master dear,
        For I fear a deadly storm.

"Late late yestre'en I saw the new moon
        Wi' the auld moon in her arm,
And I fear, I fear, my dear master,
        That we will come to harm."

O our Scots nobles were richt laith
        To weet their cork-heeled shoon,
But lang owre a' the play were played
        Their hats they swam aboon.

O lang, lang may their ladies sit,
        Wi' their fans into their hand,
Or e'er they see Sir Patrick Spens
        Come sailing to the land.

O lang, lang may the ladies stand,
        Wi' their gold kembs in their hair,
Waiting for their ain dear lords,
        For they'll see thame na mair.

Half o'er, half o'er to Aberdour
        It's fifty fadom deep,
And there lies guid Sir Patrick Spens,
        Wi' the Scots lords at his feet.

10
15
20
25
30
35
40

9 braid (brād): broad; emphatic.

14 lauch (louкн): laugh.

16 ee: eye.

17 wha: who.

23 na sae (nä sā): not so.

25 yestre'en (yĕ-strēn'): yesterday evening.
25–26 the new moon . . . arm: a thin crescent moon with the rest of the moon's disk faintly illuminated by light reflected from the earth.
26 auld (ould): old.
29 laith (lāth): loath; unwilling.
30 weet: wet; **shoon:** shoes.
31 lang owre a' (läng our ä): long before all.
32 aboon (ə-bōōn'): above (them).

35 or e'er (ôr îr): before ever.

38 kembs: combs.
39 ain (ān): own.
40 na mair (nä mâr): no more.

41 half o'er: halfway over; **Aberdour:** a small town on the Scottish coast.
42 fadom (fä'dəm): fathoms.

Get *Up* and *B*ar the *D*oor

*I*t fell about the Martinmas time,
 And a gay time it was then,
When our goodwife got puddings to make,
 And she's boild them in the pan.

5 The wind sae cauld blew south and north,
 And blew into the floor;
Quoth our goodman to our goodwife,
 "Gae out and bar the door."

The Peasant Couple Dancing (1514), Albrecht Dürer. Engraving,
The Metropolitan Museum of Art, New York, Fletcher Fund,
1919 (19.73.102).

"My hand is in my hussyfskap,
    Goodman, as ye may see;
An it shoud nae be barrd this hundred year,
    It's no be barrd for me."

They made a paction tween them twa,
    They made it firm and sure,
That the first word whae'er shoud speak,
    Shoud rise and bar the door.

Then by there came two gentlemen,
    At twelve o'clock at night,
And they could neither see house nor hall,
    Nor coal nor candle-light.

"Now whether is this a rich man's house,
    Or whether is it a poor?"
But ne'er a word wad ane o' them speak,
    For barring of the door.

And first they ate the white puddings,
    And then they ate the black;
Tho muckle thought the goodwife to hersel,
    Yet ne'er a word she spake.

Then said the one unto the other,
    "Here, man, tak ye my knife;
Do ye tak aff the auld man's beard,
    And I'll kiss the goodwife."

"But there's nae water in the house,
    And what shall we do than?"
"What ails ye at the pudding-broo,
    That boils into the pan?"

O up then started our goodman,
    An angry man was he:
"Will ye kiss my wife before my een,
    And scad me wi' pudding-bree?"

Then up and started our goodwife,
    Gied three skips on the floor:
"Goodman, you've spoken the foremost word,
    Get up and bar the door."

10

15

20

25

30

35

40

9 **hussyfskap:** household chores.

13 **paction:** agreement.

15 **whae'er:** whoever.

27 **muckle:** a great deal.

35–36 **What . . . pan?:** What's wrong with using the broth the puddings are boiling in?

40 **scad:** scald; **bree:** broth.

Connect to the Literature

1. What Do You Think?
Which ballad would you say told the most interesting story? Share your thoughts with a classmate.

> **Comprehension Check**
> • Why does Barbara Allan want to die?
> • Why does Sir Patrick Spens shed a tear when he reads the king's letter?
> • What reason does the woman give for not barring the door?

Think Critically

2. What is your opinion of the relationship between Barbara Allan and Sir John Graeme?

 THINK ABOUT
• his request to see her
• the reason for his illness
• her statement "I'll die for him tomorrow" (line 36)

3. Why do you think Sir Patrick Spens chooses to sail the ship in spite of the risk?

 THINK ABOUT
• the elderly knight's opinion of him (lines 7–8)
• his reaction to the king's letter (lines 13–22)
• the warning from one of his men (lines 23–28)

4. How does the **tone** of "Get Up and Bar the Door" differ from that of the other two ballads?

5. In your opinion, which of the two tragic ballads tells the sadder story? Explain your opinion.

6. **ACTIVE READING** **STRATEGIES FOR READING BALLADS**
Consult the notes in your 📖 **READER'S NOTEBOOK.** Which strategy did you find most useful in helping you to understand the ballad?

Extend Interpretations

7. Comparing Texts Both Sir Patrick Spens and the **speaker** of "The Seafarer" (pages 85–89) go off to sea despite anticipated danger. Compare and contrast their motives and attitudes.

8. Connect to Life Recall your responses to the words *tragedy* and *comedy* in Connect to Your Life on page 192. What types of **tragedies** and **comedies** might you expect to find described in ballads written today?

Literary Analysis

BALLADS Typically, a **ballad** consists of four-line stanzas, or **quatrains,** with the second and fourth lines of each stanza rhyming. Each stanza has a strong rhythmic pattern, usually with four stressed syllables in the first and third lines and three stressed syllables in the second and fourth lines. Most ballads also contain **dialogue** and repetitions of sounds, words, and phrases for emphasis. Notice the patterns of **rhyme, rhythm,** and **repetition** in the following stanza from "Barbara Allan."

Ŏ slówly, slówly răse shĕ úp,
Tŏ thĕ pláce whĕre hĕ wăs lýin',
Ănd whĕn shĕ dréw thĕ cúrtaĭn bý:
"Yŏung mán, Ĭ thínk yŏu're dýin'."

Cooperative Learning Activity
Select a stanza from "Sir Patrick Spens" or "Get Up and Bar the Door" and determine whether its patterns of **rhyme** and **rhythm** are the same as those in the stanza from "Barbara Allan." Then look for examples of **dialogue** and **repetition** in the three ballads. What effects are created by the use of these four elements? Share your findings with the class.

Barbara | Spens | Door

Writing Options

1. Story of Barbara Allan Draft a short story in which you give a more detailed account of the relationship between Barbara Allan and Sir John Graeme. You might, for example, present events that may have occurred earlier in their relationship.

2. In Memoriam Create appropriate epitaphs for Barbara Allan and Sir Patrick Spens—brief statements, in prose or verse, that might be placed on their tombstones to memorialize their deaths.

3. Contemporary Ballad Try to write your own ballad on a contemporary subject. Focus on events leading up to the climax of a comic or tragic situation.

4. Descriptive Paragraph Think of an event you have heard or read about that you would call a tragedy—an accident resulting in death, for example, or a relationship ending in separation. Write a paragraph describing this event. Would this event be a good subject for a modern-day ballad?

Writing Handbook
See page 1363: Descriptive Writing.

Activities & Explorations

1. Illustrated Tragedy Imagine the exact circumstances of Sir Patrick Spens's death. Then create a drawing or painting of the incident. ~ **ART**

2. Dance Interpretation Choreograph a dance that portrays the action of one of these ballads. Perform your dance for the class. ~ **VIEWING AND REPRESENTING**

3. Ballad Role Play In most medieval ballads, the speaker has no personal involvement in the story. How might each of these ballads be different if it were told from the point of view of someone affected by the events—for example, the mother of Barbara Allan, or one of the two gentlemen who disturb the peace of the goodman and goodwife? Assume the point of view of someone other than the main characters in one of these ballads and then tell the story to the class from that point of view. ~ **SPEAKING AND LISTENING**

Inquiry & Research

1. Blues Music Research contemporary blues music and find examples of songs that combine characteristics of ballads with traditional tragic themes. Play recordings of these blues songs for your classmates.

Buddy Guy performing at the Chicago Blues Festival

More Online:
Research Starter
www.mcdougallittell.com

2. The Popularity of Tragedy Tragedy is still a common theme in contemporary forms of entertainment, such as plays, television dramas, soap operas, and documentaries. Discuss possible reasons for the popularity of tragic and comic subjects throughout human history.

3. History or Legend? The ballad of "Sir Patrick Spens" may have a basis in historical fact. Do some research to find out whether or not such a person existed and what historical voyage the ballad may indirectly commemorate.

Writing Workshop

Describing a Fascinating Person . . .

From Reading to Writing Good descriptive writing takes the reader inside the writer's world. Chaucer's remarkable character portraits in *The Canterbury Tales,* for example, transport the modern reader to the Middle Ages. Through carefully chosen details, Chaucer creates living personalities on the page—fascinating as individuals and for their universal human qualities. The same techniques are also applied to writing a **personality profile,** a common feature in newspapers and magazines. A personality profile combines compelling information and vivid language to describe a person.

For Your Portfolio

WRITING PROMPT Write a personality profile of a person of your choice.

> **Purpose:** To make readers feel like they know the person
> **Audience:** Your peers, family, or general readers

Basics in a Box

Personality Profile at a Glance

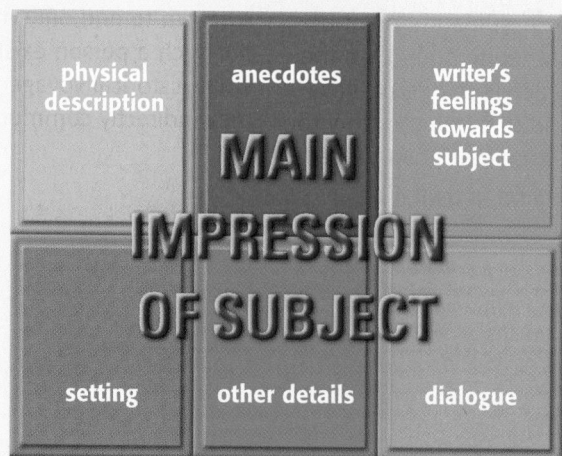

physical description

anecdotes

writer's feelings towards subject

MAIN IMPRESSION OF SUBJECT

setting

other details

dialogue

RUBRIC Standards for Writing

A successful personality profile should

- use lively descriptions, details, anecdotes, and/or dialogue to create a vivid impression of the person
- put the person in a context that helps reveal the subject's personality
- convey why the person is important to the writer
- paint a word portrait that shows the person's character
- create a unified tone and impression
- capture the reader's interest at the beginning and give a sense of completeness at the end

Analyzing a Student Model

Jenny Yu
Niskayuna High School

Her Three-Inch Feet

<u>She is different. Not just different, her presence in this big city seems anachronistic, misplaced.</u> She has a benign grandmotherly smile; skin like a piece of crumbled lined-paper flattened out with lines revealing her age; a petite, almost childlike, body; and tiny bound feet* only three inches long.

It is difficult to get a close look at her feet since she likes to move about constantly. She can never and will never stay in one place long enough. For most of her life, Great-Aunt Yeung worked diligently—first for her parents, then her husband, and later her children. In the seventy-six years she has lived, her life has been burdened by responsibility. And because of the challenges life has presented her, Great-Aunt Yeung possesses vigor that exceeds a teenager's.

However, if you have seen her feet, you will never forget them. They are small and pale. <u>They are like two pieces of sponge cake that have been accidentally mushed and tortured.</u> They are painful to look at, for one thinks how excruciating it must be to walk on them; yet, they are fascinating. They represent the ancient world of the East, a place of a thousand emperors and fabled dragons.

It is always a treat for me to visit Great-Aunt Yeung, though it means a three-hour drive to New York City. She lives on Mott Street, only three blocks from the heart of Chinatown. Her apartment isn't very big, and appears somewhat cluttered if compared to the typical Niskayuna four-bedroom colonial. It only has one bedroom, one bath, and a small space that one might call a living room. There isn't much to see in the living room, just a chair, a few pieces of furniture which she might have gotten from garage sales (since they don't quite match), a 13-inch TV, and a table.

But it's not just a table: it's the table of Chinese gods. The burning incense on it perfumes the whole apartment. The twice-daily ritual of worship consists of kneeling, lighting the incense, then bowing to the gods while holding up the incense with both hands above the head. It is quite a lovely scene. I like to watch her and pretend to be lost in the world of yin and yang, Confucius, and fortune cookies. <u>But deep down, I know I can never be a part of that inscrutable world.</u>

That is how I feel about my Great-Aunt Yeung. The combination of her and New York City is <u>as odd as eating rice topped with rocky road ice cream.</u> She prefers bamboo mats over soft mattresses, medicinal tea over creamy cappuccino, and cooked vegetables over raw salads. Great-Aunt Yeung will always have her own ways. The East and the West will always remain apart, and the best proof of that is seeing Great-Aunt Yeung plod the streets of New York in her size-one black-cloth shoes.

* Refers to the defunct Chinese custom of foot-binding, which produced small, deformed feet in women.

❶ The writer immediately establishes interest and tone with intriguing language and lively description details

Other Options:
· Start with a revealing anecdote.
· Describe the setting.

❷ The writer focuses on various concrete details and uses figurative language to create a word portrait.

Other Options:
· Show the person interacting with others.
· Use dialogue.

❸ Puts the person in a context

❹ Reveals the writer's own feelings

❺ Uses lively figurative language to fill out the picture

❻ Ends with an image that reinforces the main tone and impression

IDEABank

1. Your Working Portfolio
Look for ideas in the Writing Options you completed earlier in this unit:

- **Comparing Knights,** p. 169

- **Opinion Paragraph,** p. 191

2. Brainstorm
Discuss with classmates the kinds of people you admire and the traits of these people that stand out to you.

3. Match People and Categories
Think of qualities you admire, and then try to think of people to match those categories; for example, "The bravest person I can think of is _____."

Writing a Personality Profile

❶ Prewriting

Choose a person you want to write about. Try **making a list** of people you consider your heroes or admire in some way. They don't have to be famous. In fact, you may feel more comfortable writing about someone that you know well:

- a favorite relative
- a neighbor
- a teacher
- a coach

What comes to mind when you think about these people? Write a few words or phrases to describe each one. You also might try **writing a simile** to summarize each person. ("Listening to this person is like drinking sunshine.") See the **Idea Bank** in the margin for more suggestions. After you select a person you want to write about, follow the steps below.

Planning Your Personality Profile

▶ 1. **Explore your attitude toward the subject.** How do you feel about the person? Why is the person important to you? What details or incidents can you describe that show the importance of the subject to you?

▶ 2. **Picture your subject in a typical setting.** Try visualizing your subject in his or her usual surroundings. What stands out about your subject? You might make a chart like this one to record details.

Personality Characteristics			
Physical	What Person Says	How Person Acts	How Others React

▶ 3. **Research or interview to gather information.** You can research a historical or famous figure using library resources or the Internet. For a profile of a lesser-known person, interviewing is the best method of getting information. Interviewing the subject and other people who know the subject well may give you information that is not available anywhere else.

▶ 4. **Set your goal for writing.** What impression of the subject do you want to leave in the minds of your readers? Analyze your subject to find an angle—a dominant impression or theme that captures the essence of the person. Then look for special details that help a reader picture the person.

❷ Drafting

Make visible what, without you, might never have been seen.
Robert Bresson

Start drafting by simply getting your ideas down on paper. Keep your overall goal in mind as you try to get into the flow of your writing. Set down everything you want to say. Later you can cut what you don't need and add what you forgot.

Organizing Your Draft

Once you've gotten it all down, look for a way to organize what you want to say. As you rework your draft you are beginning your revision process. Here are some ways a personality profile might be organized.

- **In Chronological Order.** Narrate incidents in the time sequence in which they occurred. You might even focus on a day in your subject's life.
- **By Category.** Analyze different aspects of your subject's personality—such as characteristics, actions, and traits—one at a time.
- **By Setting.** Show your subject interacting in various settings or situations.
- **In Order of Importance.** Begin the essay with the most important incident or detail.

Choose one of these ways or any other way of developing your profile that works for you. Be sure to tie the incidents and descriptions you relate together with appropriate transitions.

Beginnings and Endings

Begin with something that will capture the reader's interest—a remarkable detail about the person or setting, some dialogue, or a good anecdote. You might end with a memorable detail or your personal reflections on the subject. Your ending should give a sense of completeness.

Elaborating on Ideas

Work to create a profile of your subject as a whole person, not just a one-dimensional figure. Lace your descriptions with details, specific scenes, and quotations or dialogue that indicate how the person you portray interacts with others. It should also be clear from your writing what things are important to the person you are profiling.

As you draft and refine your essay, be sure to consider the **purpose, audience,** and **occasion.** For example, if you are describing a situation in your school, include background information that a reader would need to know.

Have a Question?

See the **Writing Handbook**
Introductions, p.1358
Descriptive Writing, pp. 1363–1364

Ask Your Peer Reader

- What dominant impression did you get of my subject?
- How would you describe my attitude toward the person?
- What details are particularly vivid or memorable?
- What details, if any, distracted from the picture I was trying to present?
- What more would you like to know about my subject?

Need revising help?

Review the **Rubric,**
p. 200.

Consider **peer reader**
comments.

Check **Revision
Guidelines,** p. 1355.

❸ Revising

TARGET SKILL ▶ ADDING DETAIL In descriptive writing, concrete details and examples help the reader envision the scene. They *show* the subject's personality traits in action rather than just naming them. Remember, however, to add details selectively so that they build a coherent impression.

> But it's not just a table: it's the table of Chinese gods. The
> burning incense on it ~~fills~~ perfumes the whole apartment. ~~Twice a day~~
> ~~she kneels and lights~~ the incense. It is quite a lovely scene.
> , and then bowing to the gods
> while holding up the incense with
> both hands above the head.
> The twice-daily ritual
> of worship consists of
> kneeling, lighting

Confused by comma splices?

See the **Grammar Handbook,**
pp. 1396–1429.

❹ Editing and Proofreading

TARGET SKILL ▶ COMMA SPLICES With elaboration, you often have to link together several strings of ideas into more complex phrases and sentences. Commas, used carefully, add clarity to sentences and enable the reader to grasp how the parts relate. However, used incorrectly they can be distracting or confusing. One common error is the comma splice (or comma fault), in which the writer separates two sentences with a comma instead of the correct end mark.

> Great Aunt Yeung will always have her own ways; the east and
> the west will always remain apart. The best proof of that is see-
> ing Great Aunt Yeung plod the streets of New York in her size
> one black cloth shoes.

Publishing IDEAS

- Collect the class profiles in a booklet to distribute in your school, to local libraries, or to senior citizen centers in your community.
- Submit your profile to a student-writing Web site.

**More Online:
Publishing Options**
www.mcdougallittell.com

❺ Reflecting

FOR YOUR WORKING PORTFOLIO What did you discover about your subject while completing the personality profile? What did you learn about yourself or about life from this experience? Attach your answers to these questions to your finished personality profile. Save your personality profile in your **Working Portfolio.**

Read this opening from the first draft of a personality profile. The underlined sections include the following kinds of errors:

- **unsupported ideas**
- **incorrect possessives**
- **run-on sentences**
- **punctuation errors**

For each underlined phrase or sentence, choose the revision that most improves the writing.

<u>Her nickname is 'Mique, don't believe it.</u> Chamique Holdsclaw is anything
(1)
but meek. She's a powerhouse. <u>She has been called "the greatest women's

basketball player of all time," yet she always strives to be better.</u>
(2)

   <u>Holdsclaws'</u> intensity helps to motivate her teammates. "Once I get it up, it
   (3)
filters through the <u>team" she</u> says. <u>Her team is the Tennessee Lady Volunteers</u>
          (4)   (5)
<u>the team won three consecutive championships.</u> Holdsclaw is definitely the heart

and fire of the team. <u>Her determination helps her live up to her favorite saying.</u>
                    (6)

---

1. A. Her nickname is 'Mique don't believe it.

   B. Just because her nickname is 'Mique don't believe it.

   C. Her nickname is 'Mique, but don't believe it.

   D. Correct as is.

2. A. She has been called "the greatest women's basketball player of all time." Yet she always strives to be better.

   B. She has been called "the greatest women's basketball player of all time," or she always strives to be better.

   C. Although she has been called "the greatest women's basketball player of all time," yet she always strives to be better.

   D. Correct as is.

3. A. Holdsclaw's

   B. Holdsclaws

   C. Holdsclaws's

   D. Correct as is.

4. A. team, "she

   B. team." She

   C. team," she

   D. team". She

5. A. Because Holdsclaw plays for the Tennessee Lady Volunteers, the team won three consecutive championships.

   B. Her team is the Tennessee Lady Volunteers and the team won three consecutive championships.

   C. Her team is the Tennessee Lady Volunteers, winner of three consecutive championships.

   D. Correct as is.

6. A. Her determination helped her live up to her favorite saying.

   B. Her determination helps her live up to her favorite saying, which she follows every day.

   C. Her determination helps her live up to her favorite saying: "Don't Dream it. Be it."

   D. Correct as is.

Need extra help?

See the **Grammar Handbook**

Run-on sentences, p. 1409

Punctuation, pp. 1413–1414

Possessives, pp. 1392–1393

The Origins of English Words

The English language is growing and changing constantly. Notice the differences between this passage from *The Canterbury Tales* in Middle English and a modern English translation of the same lines.

> **And smale foweles maken melodÿe**
> **That slepen al the nyght with open ÿe**
> —Chaucer, *The Canterbury Tales*
>
> **And the small fowl are making melody**
> **That sleep away the night with open eye**
> —*The Canterbury Tales*,
> translated by Nevill Coghill

Modern English evolved from Middle English, which evolved from Old English. Along the way, words from other languages, including Latin and Greek, were added to English. One way to build your vocabulary is to explore the **etymology**, or history and origins, of words.

Etymology Information in Dictionaries Learning about how Modern English words came to be can help you understand their meanings. You can find information about the etymology of a word like *prologue* in most kinds of dictionaries. Examine the following dictionary entry to see how this word developed from words in other languages.

pro•logue (prō′lôg′) *n.* the preface or introduction to a story or play. [Middle English *prolog*, from Old French *prologue*, from Latin *prologus* preface to a play, from Greek *prologos*, part of a Greek play preceding the entry of the chorus, from *pro-* before + *logos* speech]	**Modern English** *prologue* **Middle English** *prolog* **Old French** *prologue* **Latin** *prologus* **Greek** *prologos* *pro-* + *logos* (before) + (speech)

Strategies for Building Vocabulary

❶ **Word Parts** Now that you have studied the word *prologue,* you know that the meaning of the word part *logue* involves speech. Suppose you later come across the word *epilogue.* You can assume that this word also has something to do with speech because it contains *logue.* If you also know that the prefix *epi-* can mean "after," then you can predict that the meaning of *epilogue* is somehow related to "after speech."

epi-   +   logue   =   epilogue
(after)   (speech)   (concluding section in a literary work)

❷ **Word Families** Groups of words that contain the same word parts are called **word families.** Knowing the meaning of one word in a family can help you predict the meanings of related words. The table in the next column shows a family of words that contain *logue* and are derived from the Greek word *logos.* Notice how the meanings of the words are related.

English Words Derived from Greek *logos*	
English Word	**Meaning**
prologue	the preface or introduction to a story or play
monologue	the speech of a character who is alone on stage, voicing his or her thoughts
dialogue	a conversation between two or more characters
epilogue	a concluding section in a literary work, often dealing with the future of the characters

❸ **Spelling** Learning the etymology of *prologue* can help you remember how to spell it and words related to it. For example, once you realize that *monologue, dialogue,* and *epilogue* all contain the word part *logue,* you may find it easier to remember the unusual spelling of the last syllable.

EXERCISE Use a dictionary to trace the etymology of these words from *The Canterbury Tales.*

companion	haughty	pain	technique
diversion	melody	solution	traitor
entertain	mischief		

Grammar from Literature

Writers vary sentence structure in both prose and poetry for a variety of reasons.

- To add interest.
- To shift the emphasis in a sentence.
- To achieve a poetic effect.

One way to vary sentence structure is by inverting, or reversing, the order of the subject and the verb.

> Subject first
>
>   subject   verb
>
> **Those two urns of good and evil gifts are at the door of Zeus.**
>
> Inverted
>
>   verb   subject
>
> **At the door of Zeus are those two urns of good and evil gifts.**
>
>   —Homer, the *Iliad*

The subject can also come after other sentence parts.

> adverb subject   verb
>
> **Eagerly he approached, in hope to learn.**
>
>   —*The Canterbury Tales*
>
> prepositional phrases   subject verb
>
> **At daybreak, with the sun's first light, they saw How well he had worked.**
>
>   —*Beowulf*
>
> direct object   subject verb
>
> **A medal of St. Christopher he wore.**
>
>   —*The Canterbury Tales*

As you look at your own writing, ask yourself these questions to see if you should consider using inverted word order:

- Are my sentences too similar in structure or length?
- Do I want to emphasize certain words or ideas?
- Would changing the order of some of the words create an interesting rhythm?

Usage Tip When you place a verb before a subject, make sure you choose the correct verb form to match the subject. Plural subjects need plural verbs; singular subjects need singular verbs.

> INCORRECT
>
>   verb   subject
>
> **Near the smoldering wreck stands the dazed victims.**
>
> CORRECT
>
>   verb   subject
>
> **Near the smoldering wreck stand the dazed victims.**

Punctuation Tip When you invert word order by moving a sequence of prepositional phrases from the end of a sentence to the beginning of a sentence, remember to put a comma after the last prepositional phrase in the sequence.

> **In the hall of Hrothgar, Grendel murdered many men.**
>
> **On the road to Canterbury, the people told tales.**

WRITING EXERCISE Change the structure of each of the following sentences by moving the underlined words to a different position within the sentence. Remember to punctuate correctly.

1. Grendel's mother goes to Herot to seek revenge <u>the night after Beowulf defeats Grendel</u>.
2. Beowulf fights <u>bravely</u> as the monster claws at him.
3. The pilgrims set off on a journey <u>from Southwark</u>.
4. <u>The seafarer</u> drifted <u>through winter</u> on an ice-cold sea.
5. Barbara Allan <u>is a cruel woman</u>.

PROOFREADING EXERCISE Rewrite the sentences below, correcting any errors in punctuation and usage.

1. Into Canterbury rides the 29 travelers and the innkeeper.
2. To Caedmon's account of his amazing dream listens the abbess and the reeve.
3. In the tale of Beowulf we learn about the heroism of a Geatish warrior.
4. Before the terrible monster lies the bodies of those who fell.
5. Outside the walls of Troy Achilles and Hector fight to the death.

Like the people of any age, those of the medieval period lived in an imperfect world. Nevertheless, they dreamed of what their lives could be. Some people looked to religion to teach them how to live virtuously. Others sought an idealized world in literature. Tales of chivalry, popular in this era, recount the adventures of heroic knights who live by a strict code of behavior. In this part of Unit One, you will read about characters who strive for—but don't quite attain—perfection. As you read, consider how your attitude toward them would be different if they were perfect.

from **Sir Gawain and the Green Knight**

Romance by THE GAWAIN POET
Translated by JOHN GARDNER

Connect to Your Life

A Person of Honor Suppose that you hear someone say, "The student-council president should be a person of honor." What qualities or ideals come to mind? Create a word web like the one shown, jotting down words or phrases that you think describe an honorable person.

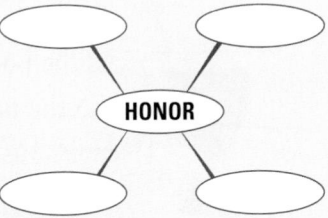

Build Background

An Ideal World Medieval aristocrats relished tales of adventure, especially stories of brave and gallant knights. Although real knights were far from perfect, the knights of legend strove continually to obey a code of chivalry, a set of rules for gentlemanly and heroic behavior. Their code represented a combination of Christian and military ideals, including faith, modesty, loyalty, courtesy, bravery, and honor. The ideal knight respected and vigorously defended his church, his king, his country, and victims of injustice.

Especially popular during the medieval period were legends of King Arthur and his heroic knights of the Round Table. The popularity of these tales was due in part to the idealized world in which they were set. It was a world of castles, heroes, courtly love, and magical spells—a world quite unlike the real medieval England, with its plagues, political battles, and civil unrest. Although Launcelot was often presented as the greatest and most distinguished of Arthur's knights, in early tales that role was given to Arthur's nephew Gawain (gə-wān'), who was famous for his courage and for his unfailing chivalry.

> WORDS TO KNOW
> **Vocabulary Preview**
>
> | | |
> |---|---|
> | aghast | pivot |
> | amended | renown |
> | chagrin | reproof |
> | daunt | respite |
> | efficacious | uncanny |
> | flinch | unwieldy |
> | heft | wince |
> | ingeniously | |

Focus Your Reading

LITERARY ANALYSIS **ROMANCE** The **romance** has been a popular narrative form since the Middle Ages. Generally, the term *romance* refers to any imaginative adventure concerned with noble heroes, gallant love, a chivalric code of honor, and daring deeds. Romances usually have faraway settings, depict events unlike those of ordinary life, and idealize their heroes as well as the eras in which the heroes lived. Medieval romances are also often lighthearted in tone and involve fantasy. Be aware of the characteristics of romance as you read the excerpt from *Sir Gawain and the Green Knight*.

ACTIVE READING **READING A NARRATIVE POEM** Like all narrative poems, *Sir Gawain and the Green Knight* contains the same elements as a short story—**setting, characters,** and **plot.** These elements combine to develop one or more **themes.** With any narrative poem, it is important to identify details of setting, character, and plot as you read.

📖 **READER'S NOTEBOOK** Keep track of the plot by writing brief notes about the actions of each character. Note the ways in which honor plays a role in the course of events.

from SIR GAWAIN and the

As the poem begins, Arthur and his knights are gathered to celebrate Christmas and the new year with feasting and revelry. In the midst of their festivities, an enormous man—who is entirely green—bounds through the door.

Splendid that knight errant stood in a splay of green,
And green, too, was the mane of his mighty destrier;
Fair fanning tresses enveloped the fighting man's shoulders,
And over his breast hung a beard as big as a bush;
5 The beard and the huge mane burgeoning forth from his head
Were clipped off clean in a straight line over his elbows,
And the upper half of each arm was hidden underneath
As if covered by a king's chaperon, closed round the neck.
The mane of the marvelous horse was much the same,
10 Well crisped and combed and carefully pranked with knots,
Threads of gold interwoven with the glorious green,
Now a thread of hair, now another thread of gold;
The tail of the horse and the forelock were tricked the same way,
And both were bound up with a band of brilliant green
15 Adorned with glittering jewels the length of the dock,
Then caught up tight with a thong in a criss-cross knot
Where many a bell tinkled brightly, all burnished gold.
So monstrous a mount, so mighty a man in the saddle
Was never once encountered on all this earth
20   till then;
           His eyes, like lightning, flashed,
           And it seemed to many a man,
           That any man who clashed
           With him would not long stand.

GUIDE FOR READING

1 knight errant (ĕr′ənt): a knight who wanders about, searching for adventure in order to prove his chivalry; **splay:** display.

2 destrier (dĕs′trē-ər): war horse.

5 burgeoning (bûr′jə-nĭng): growing.

8 chaperon (shăp′ə-rōn′): hood.

10 pranked with knots: decorated with bows.

13 forelock: the part of a horse's mane that falls forward between the ears.

15 dock: the fleshy part of an animal's tail.

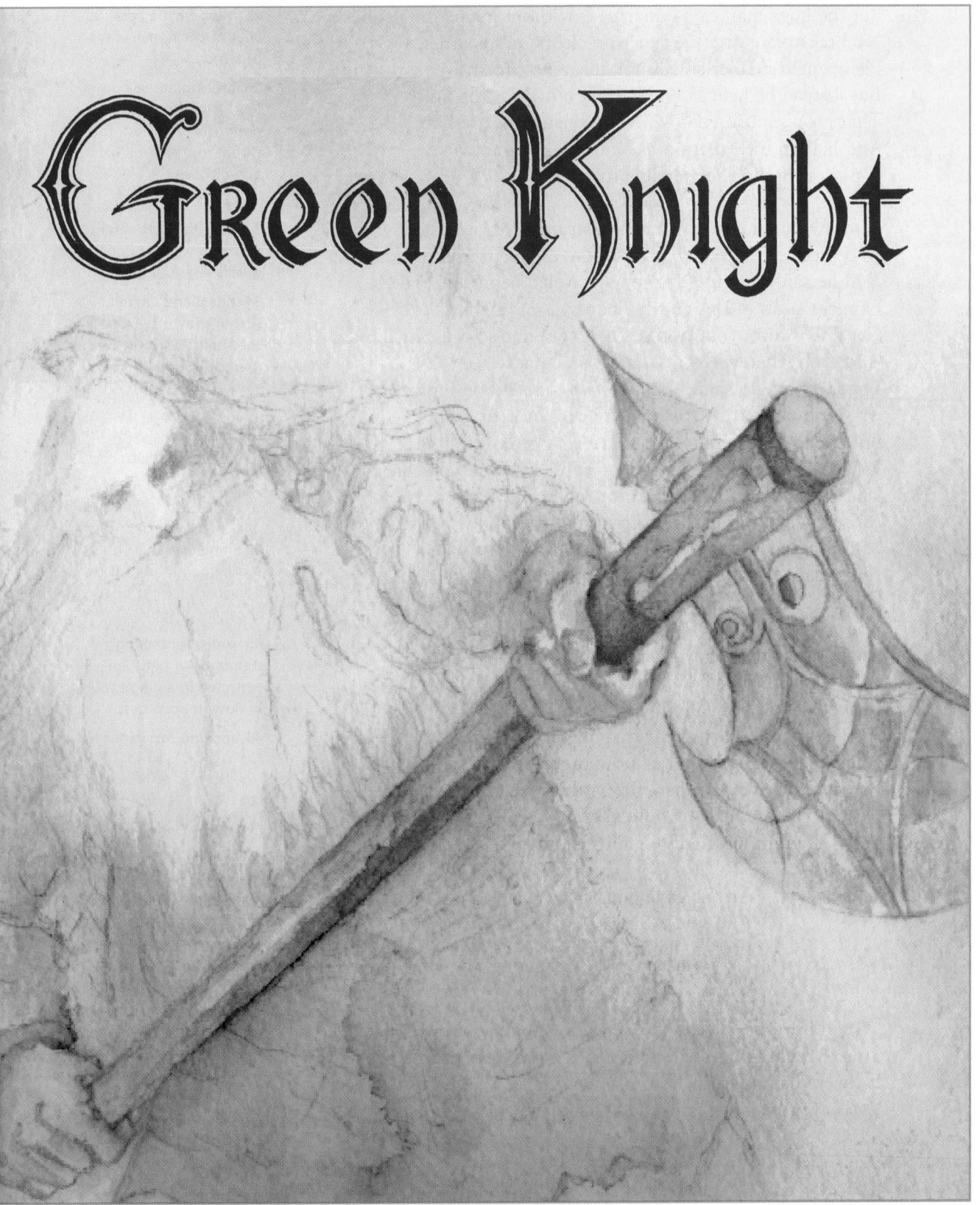

Green Knight

25 But the huge man came unarmed, without helmet or hauberk,
   No breastplate or gorget or iron cleats on his arms;
   He brought neither shield nor spearshaft to shove or to smite,
   But instead he held in one hand a bough of the holly
   That grows most green when all the groves are bare
30 And held in the other an ax, immense and unwieldy,
   A pitiless battleblade terrible to tell of.

King Arthur stared down at the stranger before the high dais
And greeted him nobly, for nothing on earth frightened him.
And he said to him, "Sir, you are welcome in this place;
35 I am the head of this court. They call me Arthur.
   Get down from your horse, I beg you, and join us for dinner,
   And then whatever you seek we will gladly see to."
   But the stranger said, "No, so help me God on high,
   My errand is hardly to sit at my ease in your castle!
40 But friend, since your praises are sung so far and wide,
   Your castle the best ever built, people say, and your barons
   The stoutest men in steel armor that ever rode steeds,
   Most mighty and most worthy of all mortal men
   And tough devils to toy with in tournament games,
45 And since courtesy is in flower in this court, they say,
   All these tales, in truth, have drawn me to you at this time.
   You may be assured by this holly branch I bear
   That I come to you in peace, not spoiling for battle.
   If I'd wanted to come in finery, fixed up for fighting,
50 I have back at home both a helmet and a hauberk,
   A shield and a sharp spear that shines like fire,
   And other weapons that I know pretty well how to use.
   But since I don't come here for battle, my clothes are mere cloth.
   Now if you are truly as bold as the people all say,
55 You will grant me gladly the little game that I ask
                                    as my right."
                    Arthur gave him answer
                    And said, "Sir noble knight,
                    If it's a duel you're after,
60   We'll furnish you your fight."

"Good heavens, I want no such thing! I assure you, Sire,
You've nothing but beardless babes about this bench!
If I were hasped in my armor and high on my horse,
You haven't a man that could match me, your might is so feeble.

25 **hauberk** (hô′bərk): a coat of chain mail (a type of armor).

26 **breastplate or gorget** (gôr′jĭt) **or iron cleats:** armor for the chest, the throat, or the shoulders and elbows.

32 **dais** (dā′ĭs): a raised platform where honored guests are seated.

34 **this place:** Camelot, Arthur's favorite castle and the site of his court of the Round Table.

44 In medieval tournaments, knights on horseback fought one another for sport.

45 **courtesy:** the high standards of behavior expected in a king's court; **in flower:** at its best.

48 **spoiling for:** eager for.

63 **hasped:** fastened.

61–64 What is the Green Knight's tone as he addresses King Arthur?

WORDS
TO
KNOW

unwieldy (ŭn-wēl′dē) *adj.* so large, heavy, or oddly shaped as to be difficult to hold or use

65   And so all I ask of this court is a Christmas game,
      For the Yule is here, and New Year's, and here sit young men;
      If any man holds himself, here in this house, so hardy,
      So bold in his blood—and so brainless in his head—
      That he dares to stoutly exchange one stroke for another,
70   I shall let him have as my present this lovely gisarme,
      This ax, as heavy as he'll need, to handle as he likes,
      And I will abide the first blow, bare-necked as I sit.
      If anyone here has the daring to try what I've offered,
      Leap to me lightly, lad; lift up this weapon;
75   I give you the thing forever—you may think it your own;
      And I will stand still for your stroke, steady on the floor,
      Provided you honor my right, when my inning comes,
                                        to repay.
                  But let the respite be
80   A twelvemonth and a day;
                  Come now, my boys, let's see
                  What any here can say."

      If they were like stone before, they were stiller now,
      Every last lord in the hall, both the high and the low;
85   The stranger on his destrier stirred in the saddle
      And ferociously his red eyes rolled around;
      He lowered his grisly eyebrows, glistening green,
      And waved his beard and waited for someone to rise;
      When no one answered, he coughed, as if embarrassed,
90   And drew himself up straight and spoke again:
      "What! Can this be King Arthur's court?" said the stranger,
      "Whose renown runs through many a realm, flung far and wide?
      What has become of your chivalry and your conquest,
      Your greatness-of-heart and your grimness and grand words?
95   Behold the radiance and renown of the mighty Round Table
      Overwhelmed by a word out of one man's mouth!
      You shiver and blanch before a blow's been shown!"
      And with that he laughed so loud that the lord was distressed;
      In chagrin, his blood shot up in his face and limbs
100   so fair;
                  More angry he was than the wind,
                  And likewise each man there;
                  And Arthur, bravest of men,
                  Decided now to draw near.

70 gisarme (gĭ-zärm′): a battle-ax with a long shaft and a two-edged head.

67–82 What challenge does the Green Knight offer?

97 blanch: turn white.

99–101 Why is King Arthur so angry?

WORDS
TO
KNOW
respite (rĕs′pĭt) *n.* a period of rest or delay
renown (rĭ-noun′) *n.* fame
chagrin (shə-grĭn′) *n.* a feeling of embarrassment caused by humiliation or failure

105　And he said, "By heaven, sir, your request is strange;
　　　But since you have come here for folly, you may as well find it.
　　　I know no one here who's <u>aghast</u> of your great words.
　　　Give me your gisarme, then, for the love of God,
　　　And gladly I'll grant you the gift you have asked to be given."
110　Lightly the King leaped down and clutched it in his hand;
　　　Then quickly that other lord alighted on his feet.
　　　Arthur lay hold of the ax, he gripped it by the handle,
　　　And he swung it up over him sternly, as if to strike.
　　　The stranger stood before him, in stature higher
115　By a head or more than any man here in the house;
　　　Sober and thoughtful he stood there and stroked his beard,
　　　And with patience like a priest's he pulled down his collar,
　　　No more unmanned or dismayed by Arthur's might
　　　Than he'd be if some baron on the bench had brought him a glass
120　　　　　　　　　　　　　　　　　of wine.
　　　　　　　　　　Then Gawain, at Guinevere's side,
　　　　　　　　　　Made to the King a sign:
　　　　　　　　　　"I beseech you, Sire," he said,
　　　　　　　　　　"Let this game be mine.

125　"Now if you, my worthy lord," said Gawain to the King,
　　　"Would command me to step from the dais and stand with you there,
　　　That I might without bad manners move down from my place
　　　(Though I couldn't, of course, if my liege lady disliked it)
　　　I'd be deeply honored to advise you before all the court;
130　For I think it unseemly, if I understand the matter,
　　　That challenges such as this churl has chosen to offer
　　　Be met by Your Majesty—much as it may amuse you—
　　　When so many bold-hearted barons sit about the bench:
　　　No men under Heaven, I am sure, are more hardy in will
135　Or better in body on the fields where battles are fought;
　　　I myself am the weakest, of course, and in wit the most feeble;
　　　My life would be least missed, if we let out the truth.
　　　Only as you are my uncle have I any honor,
　　　For excepting your blood, I bear in my body slight virtue.
140　And since this affair that's befallen us here is so foolish,
　　　And since I have asked for it first, let it fall to me.
　　　If I've reasoned incorrectly, let all the court say,
　　　　　　　　　　　　　　　　without blame."
　　　　　　　　　　The nobles gather round
145　　　　　　　　　And all advise the same:
　　　　　　　　　　"Let the King step down
　　　　　　　　　　And give Sir Gawain the game!"

106 folly: dangerous and foolish activity.

118 unmanned: deprived of manly courage.

121 Guinevere: King Arthur's wife.

128 liege (lēj) **lady:** a lady to whom one owes loyalty and service; here used by Gawain to refer to Queen Guinevere.

131 churl: rude, uncouth person.

136–139 How does Gawain's description of himself reflect a knight's code of chivalry?

WORDS
TO
KNOW
aghast (ə-găst') *adj.* struck with terror or amazement; shocked

214

Arthur grants Gawain's request to take on the Green Knight's challenge. The Green Knight asks Gawain to identify himself, and the two agree on their pact. Gawain then prepares to strike his blow against the Green Knight.

On the ground, the Green Knight got himself into position,
His head bent forward a little, the bare flesh showing,
150 His long and lovely locks laid over his crown
So that any man there might note the naked neck.
Sir Gawain laid hold of the ax and he hefted it high,
His pivot foot thrown forward before him on the floor,
And then, swiftly, he slashed at the naked neck;
155 The sharp of the battleblade shattered asunder the bones
And sank through the shining fat and slit it in two,
And the bit of the bright steel buried itself in the ground.
The fair head fell from the neck to the floor of the hall
And the people all kicked it away as it came near their feet.
160 The blood splashed up from the body and glistened on the green,
But he never faltered or fell for all of that,
But swiftly he started forth upon stout shanks

162 **shanks:** legs.

And rushed to reach out, where the King's retainers stood,

163 **retainers:** servants or attendants.

Caught hold of the lovely head, and lifted it up,
165 And leaped to his steed and snatched up the reins of the bridle,
Stepped into stirrups of steel and, striding aloft,
He held his head by the hair, high, in his hand;
And the stranger sat there as steadily in his saddle
As a man entirely unharmed, although he was headless
170   on his steed.
        He turned his trunk about,
        That baleful body that bled,

172 **baleful:** threatening evil; sinister.

        And many were faint with fright
        When all his say was said.

175 He held his head in his hand up high before him,
Addressing the face to the dearest of all on the dais;
And the eyelids lifted wide, and the eyes looked out,
And the mouth said just this much, as you may now hear:
"Look that you go, Sir Gawain, as good as your word,
180 And seek till you find me, as loyally, my friend,
As you've sworn in this hall to do, in the hearing of the knights.
Come to the Green Chapel, I charge you, and take
A stroke the same as you've given, for well you deserve
To be readily requited on New Year's morn.

184 **requited:** paid back. For what does Gawain deserve to be requited? How do you expect this will be done?

WORDS
TO
KNOW

heft (hĕft) *v.* to lift up; hoist
pivot (pĭv′ət) *adj.* acting as a center around which something turns

215

185 Many men know me, the Knight of the Green Chapel;
Therefore if you seek to find me, you shall not fail.
Come or be counted a coward, as is fitting."
Then with a rough jerk he turned the reins
And haled away through the hall-door, his head in his hand,
190 And fire of the flint flew out from the hooves of the foal.
To what kingdom he was carried no man there knew,
No more than they knew what country it was he came from.
What then?
The King and Gawain there
195 Laugh at the thing and grin;
And yet, it was an affair
Most marvelous to men.

As the end of the year approaches, Gawain leaves on his quest to find the Green Chapel and fulfill his pledge. After riding through wild country and encountering many dangers, he comes upon a splendid castle. The lord of the castle welcomes Gawain and invites him to stay with him and his lady for a few days.

The lord proposes that he will go out to hunt each day while Gawain stays at the castle. At the end of the day, they will exchange what they have won. While the lord is out hunting, the lady attempts to seduce Gawain. Gawain resists her, however, and on the first two days accepts only kisses, which he gives to the lord at the end of each day in exchange for what the lord has gained in the hunt. On the third day Gawain continues to resist the lady, but she presses him to accept another gift.

She held toward him a ring of the yellowest gold
And, standing aloft on the band, a stone like a star
200 From which flew splendid beams like the light of the sun;
And mark you well, it was worth a rich king's ransom.
But right away he refused it, replying in haste,
"My lady gay, I can hardly take gifts at the moment;
Having nothing to give, I'd be wrong to take gifts in turn."
205 She implored him again, still more earnestly, but again
He refused it and swore on his knighthood that he could take nothing.
Grieved that he still would not take it, she told him then:
"If taking my ring would be wrong on account of its worth,
And being so much in my debt would be bothersome to you,
210 I'll give you merely this sash that's of slighter value."
She swiftly unfastened the sash that encircled her waist,
Tied around her fair tunic, inside her bright mantle;
It was made of green silk and was marked of gleaming gold

205 implored: begged.

212 tunic: a shirtlike garment worn by both men and women; **mantle:** a sleeveless cloak worn over the tunic.

Embroidered along the edges, <u>ingeniously</u> stitched.
215 This too she held out to the knight, and she earnestly begged him
To take it, trifling as it was, to remember her by.

216 trifling: of little value.

But again he said no, there was nothing at all he could take,
Neither treasure nor token, until such time as the Lord
Had granted him some end to his adventure.
220 "And therefore, I pray you, do not be displeased,
But give up, for I cannot grant it, however fair
                              or right.
              I know your worth and price,
              And my debt's by no means slight;
225   I swear through fire and ice
              To be your humble knight."

"Do you lay aside this silk," said the lady then,
"Because it seems unworthy—as well it may?
Listen. Little as it is, it seems less in value,
230 But he who knew what charms are woven within it
Might place a better price on it, perchance.
For the man who goes to battle in this green lace,
As long as he keeps it looped around him,
No man under Heaven can hurt him, whoever may try,
235 For nothing on earth, however <u>uncanny</u>, can kill him."
The knight cast about in distress, and it came to his heart
This might be a treasure indeed when the time came to take
The blow he had bargained to suffer beside the Green Chapel.
If the gift meant remaining alive, it might well be worth it;
240 So he listened in silence and suffered the lady to speak,
And she pressed the sash upon him and begged him to take it,
And Gawain did, and she gave him the gift with great pleasure
And begged him, for her sake, to say not a word,
And to keep it hidden from her lord. And he said he would,
245 That except for themselves, this business would never be known
                              to a man.
              He thanked her earnestly,
              And boldly his heart now ran;
              And now a third time she
250   Leaned down and kissed her man.

242 Why do you think Gawain finally accepts the green sash?

When the lord returns at the end of the third day, Gawain gives him a kiss but does not reveal the gift of the sash.

WORDS
TO
KNOW

ingeniously (ĭn-jēn′yəs-lē) *adv.* in a way marked by skill and imagination; cleverly

uncanny (ŭn-kăn′ē) *adj.* frighteningly unnatural or supernatural; mysterious

On New Year's Day Gawain must go to meet the Green Knight. Wearing the green sash, he sets out before dawn. Gawain arrives at a wild, rugged place, where he sees no chapel but hears the sound of a blade being sharpened. Gawain calls out, and the Green Knight appears with a huge ax. The Green Knight greets Gawain, who, with pounding heart, bows his head to take his blow.

Quickly then the man in the green made ready,
Grabbed up his keen-ground ax to strike Sir Gawain;
With all the might in his body he bore it aloft
And sharply brought it down as if to slay him;
255   Had he made it fall with the force he first intended
He would have stretched out the strongest man on earth.
But Sir Gawain cast a side glance at the ax
As it glided down to give him his Kingdom Come,
And his shoulders jerked away from the iron a little,
260   And the Green Knight caught the handle, holding it back,
And mocked the prince with many a proud reproof:
"*You* can't be Gawain," he said, "who's thought so good,
A man who's never been daunted on hill or dale!
For look how you flinch for fear before anything's felt!
265   I never heard tell that Sir Gawain was ever a coward!
I never moved a muscle when *you* came down;
In Arthur's hall I never so much as winced.
My head fell off at my feet, yet I never flickered;
But you! You tremble at heart before you're touched!
270   I'm bound to be called a better man than you, then,
                     my lord."
            Said Gawain, "I shied once:
            No more. You have my word.
            But if my head falls to the stones
275   It cannot be restored.

"But be brisk, man, by your faith, and come to the point!
Deal out my doom if you can, and do it at once,
For I'll stand for one good stroke, and I'll start no more
Until your ax has hit—and that I swear."
280   "Here goes, then," said the other, and heaves it aloft
And stands there waiting, scowling like a madman;
He swings down sharp, then suddenly stops again,
Holds back the ax with his hand before it can hurt,
And Gawain stands there stirring not even a nerve;

258 his Kingdom Come: his death and entry into the afterlife; a reference to the sentence "Thy kingdom come" in the Lord's Prayer.

274–275 The Green Knight has proclaimed himself a better man than Gawain. How does Gawain dispute that idea in these lines?

WORDS TO KNOW

reproof (rĭ-pro͞of′) *n.* an expression of disapproval; criticism
daunt (dônt) *v.* to destroy the courage of; dismay
flinch (flĭnch) *v.* to pull back from something unpleasant or surprising
wince (wĭns) *v.* to spring back involuntarily, as in pain

285   He stood there still as a stone or the stock of a tree
        That's wedged in rocky ground by a hundred roots.
        O, merrily then he spoke, the man in green:
        "Good! You've got your heart back! Now I can hit you.
        May all that glory the good King Arthur gave you
290   Prove efficacious now—if it ever can—
        And save your neck." In rage Sir Gawain shouted,
        "*Hit* me, hero! I'm right up to here with your threats!
        Is it *you* that's the cringing coward after all?"
        "Whoo!" said the man in green, "he's wrathful, too!
295   No pauses, then; I'll pay up my pledge at once,
                         I vow!"

                 He takes his stride to strike
                 And lifts his lip and brow;
                 It's not a thing Gawain can like,
300   For nothing can save him now!

        He raises that ax up lightly and flashes it down,
        And that blinding bit bites in at the knight's bare neck—
        But hard as he hammered it down, it hurt him no more
        Than to nick the nape of his neck, so it split the skin;
305   The sharp blade slit to the flesh through the shiny hide,
        And red blood shot to his shoulders and spattered the ground.
        And when Gawain saw his blood where it blinked in the snow
        He sprang from the man with a leap to the length of a spear;
        He snatched up his helmet swiftly and slapped it on,
310   Shifted his shield into place with a jerk of his shoulders,
        And snapped his sword out faster than sight; said boldly—
        And, mortal born of his mother that he was,
        There was never on earth a man so happy by half—
        "No more strokes, my friend; you've had your swing!
315   I've stood one swipe of your ax without resistance;
        If you offer me any more, I'll repay you at once
        With all the force and fire I've got—as you
                         will see.

                 I take one stroke, that's all,
320   For that was the compact we
                 Arranged in Arthur's hall;
                 But now, no more for me!"

        The Green Knight remained where he stood, relaxing on his ax—
        Settled the shaft on the rocks and leaned on the sharp end—
325   And studied the young man standing there, shoulders hunched,

314–322 At this moment, how do you think Gawain would explain the fact that he has received only a slight cut from the Green Knight's ax?

WORDS TO KNOW   **efficacious** (ĕf'ĭ-kā'shəs) *adj.* effective

And considered that staunch and doughty stance he took,
Undaunted yet, and in his heart he liked it;
And then he said merrily, with a mighty voice—
With a roar like rushing wind he reproved the knight—
330 "Here, don't be such an ogre on your ground!
Nobody here has behaved with bad manners toward you
Or done a thing except as the contract said.
I owed you a stroke, and I've struck; consider yourself
Well paid. And now I release you from all further duties.
335 If I'd cared to hustle, it may be, perchance, that I might
Have hit somewhat harder, and then you might well be cross!
The first time I lifted my ax it was lighthearted sport,
I merely feinted and made no mark, as was right,
For you kept our pact of the first night with honor
340 And abided by your word and held yourself true to me,
Giving me all you owed as a good man should.
I feinted a second time, friend, for the morning
You kissed my pretty wife twice and returned me the kisses;
And so for the first two days, mere feints, nothing more
345   severe.
          A man who's true to his word,
          There's nothing he needs to fear;
          You failed me, though, on the third
          Exchange, so I've tapped you here.

350 "That sash you wear by your scabbard belongs to me;
My own wife gave it to you, as I ought to know.
I know, too, of your kisses and all your words
And my wife's advances, for I myself arranged them.
It was I who sent her to test you. I'm convinced
355 You're the finest man that ever walked this earth.
As a pearl is of greater price than dry white peas,
So Gawain indeed stands out above all other knights.
But you lacked a little, sir; you were less than loyal;
But since it was not for the sash itself or for lust
360 But because you loved your life, I blame you less."
Sir Gawain stood in a study a long, long while,
So miserable with disgrace that he wept within,
And all the blood of his chest went up to his face
And he shrank away in shame from the man's gentle words.
365 The first words Gawain could find to say were these:
"Cursed be cowardice and covetousness both,
Villainy and vice that destroy all virtue!"
He caught at the knots of the girdle and loosened them
And fiercely flung the sash at the Green Knight.

326 staunch: firm;
doughty (dou'tē): brave.

338 feinted (fān'tĭd):
pretended to attack.

337–343 What does the
Green Knight reveal about
himself?

350 scabbard (skăb'ərd): a
sheath for a dagger or
sword.

354 What was the Green
Knight's test?

368 girdle: sash.

370 "There, there's my fault! The foul fiend vex it!
Foolish cowardice taught me, from fear of your stroke,
To bargain, covetous, and abandon my kind,
The selflessness and loyalty suitable in knights;
Here I stand, faulty and false, much as I've feared them,
375 Both of them, untruth and treachery; may they see sorrow
and care!
I can't deny my guilt;
My works shine none too fair!
Give me your good will
380 And henceforth I'll beware."

At that, the Green Knight laughed, saying graciously,
"Whatever harm I've had, I hold it <u>amended</u>
Since now you're confessed so clean, acknowledging sins
And bearing the plain penance of my point;
385 I consider you polished as white and as perfectly clean
As if you had never fallen since first you were born.
And I give you, sir, this gold-embroidered girdle,
For the cloth is as green as my gown. Sir Gawain, think
On this when you go forth among great princes;
390 Remember our struggle here; recall to your mind
This rich token. Remember the Green Chapel.
And now, come on, let's both go back to my castle
And finish the New Year's revels with feasting and joy,
not strife,
395 I beg you," said the lord,
And said, "As for my wife,
She'll be your friend, no more
A threat against your life."

"No, sir," said the knight, and seized his helmet
400 And quickly removed it, thanking the Green Knight,
"I've reveled too well already; but fortune be with you;
May He who gives all honors honor you well."

And so they embraced and kissed and commended each other
To the Prince of Paradise, and parted then
405 in the cold;
Sir Gawain turned again
To Camelot and his lord;
And as for the man in green,
He went wherever he would.

370 **vex:** harass; torment.

371–372 What does
Gawain mean when he
says, "Foolish cowardice
taught me . . . to bargain
. . . and abandon my kind"?

384 **penance:** punishment
accepted by a person to
show sorrow for wrong-
doing; **point:** blade.

382–386 The Green Knight
is saying that Gawain has
paid for his fault by admitting it and offering his
head to the ax.

387–388 Why do you think
the Green Knight gives
Gawain the sash?

WORDS
TO
KNOW

amended (ə-mĕn′dĭd) *adj.* corrected **amend** *v.*

221

Connect to the Literature

1. What Do You Think?
What is your reaction to this romance?

Comprehension Check
- What challenge does the Green Knight present to Arthur and his knights?
- Why does the Green Knight raise his ax three times over Gawain's neck?

Think Critically

2. **ACTIVE READING** **READING A NARRATIVE POEM** Review the notes you took in your **READER'S NOTEBOOK** about the actions of Sir Gawain and the Green Knight. What do these actions reveal about each character's sense of honor?

3. Why do you think Gawain requests to take up the Green Knight's challenge?

THINK ABOUT
{
- the Green Knight's behavior
- the response of the other knights
- the code of chivalry

4. In your opinion, how well does Gawain fulfill the Green Knight's challenge? Use details from the poem to support your opinion.

5. Think about the way in which the Green Knight tests Gawain's virtues at the castle. Do you think the test is fair? Why or why not?

6. Look again at the word web you created for Connect to Your Life on page 209. Compare and contrast your own concept of honor with that of Gawain.

Extend Interpretations

7. What If? What might have happened if Gawain had refused to accept the sash? Explain your answer.

8. Comparing Texts Compare and contrast Gawain and Beowulf. In your opinion, who is the more honorable **character?**

9. Connect to Life King Arthur and his knights were judged by their conduct, specifically by how well they followed the code of chivalry. Do you think today's leaders are judged by a specific code of conduct? If so, what is it?

Literary Analysis

ROMANCE Set in a faraway time and place, a **romance** involves noble heroes who perform daring deeds according to a strict code of honor. In *Sir Gawain and the Green Knight*, for example, the noble Gawain accepts the Green Knight's deadly challenge to uphold the honor of Arthur's court. Like other medieval romances, the story is filled with extraordinary events and fantastic scenes, including this description of the Green Knight just before he addresses Sir Gawain:

He held his head by the hair, high,
in his hand;
And the stranger sat there as
steadily in his saddle
As a man entirely unharmed,
although he was headless. . . .

Although Gawain berates himself for not fully measuring up to his own ideals, his struggle for perfection is typical of the **hero** of romance.

Cooperative Learning Activity Get together in a group and discuss how a modern story or event could be retold as a romance. You might consider retelling a current news story or the plot of a realistic film. Use as many elements of romance as you can as you develop your story's setting, characters, and plot.

REVIEW **CONFLICT** A **conflict** is a struggle between opposing forces that moves a plot forward. What would you say are the key conflicts in *Sir Gawain and the Green Knight*? Note whether they are **external** or **internal.**

Writing Options

1. Questions for the Green Knight
Prepare a list of questions that you would ask the Green Knight in an interview for your school paper.

Questions for the Green Knight

1 _____

2 _____

3 _____

2. New Story Ending
Suppose that Gawain failed to meet the Green Knight in 12 months and a day. In prose, write a new story ending to show what you think might happen.

3. Essay on Romance
You have read that *Sir Gawain and the Green Knight* is a medieval romance. In a short essay, explain why you think the romance remains a popular narrative form.

4. Television News Report
Write a television news story in which you report the Green Knight's intrusion into Arthur's court. You might interview one of the knights at the Round Table for his eyewitness account of the strange event.

5. Speech Honoring Gawain
Imagine that you are King Arthur presiding over the Round Table. Write the speech that you would make upon Gawain's safe return to Camelot.

Activities & Explorations

1. Computer Game Challenge
Devise a computer game based on the Green Knight's challenge. Make one or more drawings to illustrate the way the game would be played. ~ **TECHNOLOGY**

2. Dramatic Presentation
With a small group of classmates, prepare a dramatic interpretation of a scene from the poem. After deciding on roles, lines, and actions, rehearse your performance before presenting it to the class. ~ **VIEWING AND REPRESENTING**

3. Special Effects Diagram
Investigate the techniques used to create special effects in movies. Then draw a diagram that illustrates the technique you would use to film the beheading of the Green Knight. ~ **ART**

4. A Set for a Play
Imagine that you are producing a play based on this selection. Choose a scene and design a miniature set for it, depicting the scenery, the props, and the characters. ~ **ART/DRAMA**

5. Storyboard Scene
Create a storyboard, or sequence of sketches, depicting the Green Knight's appearance and speech before Arthur and his knights. Write a brief caption or explanatory note for each sketch. ~ **ART**

Inquiry & Research

1. Weapons of War
Find out more about the armor and weaponry used in medieval England. How did real-life warriors typically prepare for battle? What were their weapons? If you have access to a CD-ROM encyclopedia or an on-line encyclopedia, you might use a computer to start your research.

More Online: Research Starter
www.mcdougallittell.com

2. Honorable Pursuits
Research the activities of real knights. How were they appointed? Who were they expected to defend? What, if anything, did they have to do to prove their bravery and strength?

Choices & CHALLENGES

Vocabulary in Action

EXERCISE: ANALOGIES Write the letter of the pair of terms that express the relationship closest to that of the capitalized pair.

1. RENOWN : FAME :: (a) greed : cowardice, (b) courtesy : politeness, (c) friendship : conflict

2. DAUNT : ENCOURAGE :: (a) notify : warn, (b) neglect : leave, (c) rejoice : mourn

3. WEIGHT LIFTER : HEFT :: (a) pianist : piano, (b) artist : draw, (c) actor : applaud

4. ERROR : AMENDED :: (a) accident : avoided, (b) storm : predicted, (c) crack : repaired

5. PAINFUL : WINCE :: (a) proud : succeed, (b) satisfied : eat, (c) funny : laugh

6. RESPITE : WEEKEND :: (a) exercise : jogging, (b) failure : victory, (c) problem : food

7. AGHAST : SHOCKED :: (a) angry : jealous, (b) surprised : shy, (c) cautious : careful

8. GHOST : UNCANNY :: (a) comedian : serious, (b) scholar : intelligent, (c) volunteer : numerous

9. EFFICACIOUS : USELESS :: (a) loyal : unfaithful, (b) honest : wise, (c) important : significant

10. FLINCH : UNSHAKABLE :: (a) perspire : cold, (b) gamble : daring, (c) smile : friendly

11. MANAGEABLE : UNWIELDY :: (a) wide : deep, (b) lost : crumpled, (c) light : heavy

12. INGENIOUSLY : CLEVERLY :: (a) slowly : speedily, (b) joyfully : nicely, (c) carelessly : recklessly

13. PIVOT : TURNING :: (a) vehicle : moving, (b) axis : rotating, (c) crosswalk : stopping

14. CHAGRIN : UNPLEASANT :: (a) regret : amused, (b) bliss : joyful, (c) impatience : calm

15. REPROOF : APPROVE :: (a) hatred : oppose, (b) assistance : encourage, (c) recognition : ignore

WORDS TO KNOW	aghast amended chagrin	daunt efficacious flinch	heft ingeniously pivot	renown reproof respite	uncanny unwieldy wince

Building Vocabulary
For an in-depth lesson on analogies, see page 1317.

The Gawain Poet

Mystery Man The identity of the author of *Sir Gawain and the Green Knight* is unknown. The only surviving early manuscript of the poem, produced by an anonymous copyist around 1400, contains three other poems—*Pearl, Purity,* and *Patience*—that are believed to be the work of the same man. (Since *Pearl* is the most technically brilliant of the four poems, their author is also known as the Pearl Poet.) The Gawain Poet's descriptions and language suggest that he wrote in the second half of the 14th century and was therefore a contemporary of Chaucer. His dialect, however, indicates that he was not a Londoner like Chaucer but lived somewhere in the northwestern part of England.

Man for All Seasons The Gawain Poet's works reveal that he was widely read in French and Latin and had some knowledge of law and theology. Although he was familiar with many details of medieval aristocratic life, his descriptions and metaphors also show a love of the countryside and rural life. Because of his rich imagination, sophisticated technique, and wide knowledge, he is considered one of the greatest of medieval English poets.

Author Activity

Locate a translation of *Pearl* and read excerpts from it. Then compare its themes and characteristics with those in *Sir Gawain and the Green Knight.* Share your findings with your classmates.

from Le Morte d'Arthur

Romance by SIR THOMAS MALORY
Retold by KEITH BAINES

Comparing Literature of the World

Le Morte d'Arthur and the Ramayana

This lesson and the one that follows present an opportunity for comparing legendary deeds in *Le Morte d'Arthur* and the *Ramayana*. Specific points of comparison in the *Ramayana* lesson will help you contrast characters and scenes in *Le Morte d'Arthur* with those in Valmiki's epic.

Connect to Your Life

A Second Chance Have you ever done or said something that you later regretted? If so, why did you regret it? Given a second chance, how would you have behaved differently? Share your thoughts with your classmates.

Build Background

Arthurian Legends The legend of King Arthur is one of the most popular and enduring legends in Western culture. Some historians believe that the fictional Arthur was modeled on a real fifth- or sixth-century Celtic military leader whose cavalry defended Britain against the invading Anglo-Saxons. However, the historical Arthur was undoubtedly very different from the king of later legend, who ruled an idealized world of romance, chivalry, and magic.

Since the sixth century, there have been many variations of the stories celebrating King Arthur. Most English-speaking readers have been introduced to the Arthurian legends through Thomas Malory's *Le Morte d'Arthur* or one of its many adaptations. Malory's work consists of a number of interwoven tales that chronicle the rise and fall of the Arthurian world. These tales are based on earlier English and French stories about Arthur's court and are populated by such famous characters as Merlin the magician, Queen Gwynevere (also spelled Guinevere), and a host of knights, including Sir Launcelot, Sir Gawain—whom you encountered in the previous selection—Sir Tristram, and Sir Galahad. Although the title *Le Morte d'Arthur* ("The Death of Arthur") perhaps applies best to the last section of Malory's work, it is by this title that the entire work has come to be known.

WORDS TO KNOW **Vocabulary Preview**

acquiesce	ensue	ravage
assail	entreaty	redress
depredation	forbearance	reeling
dissuade	guile	succor
dwindle	incumbent	usurp

Focus Your Reading

LITERARY ANALYSIS **CHARACTERIZATION**

Characterization is the way in which writers guide readers' impressions of characters. Malory combines details of appearance, speech, thoughts, and actions with comments on the characters to establish the essential nature of his characters.

> *During the absence of King Arthur from Britain, Sir Modred, already vested with sovereign powers, had decided to usurp the throne. Accordingly, he had false letters written—announcing the death of King Arthur in battle—and delivered to himself.*

As you read this story, be aware of details of appearance, behavior, and action that contribute to characterization.

ACTIVE READING **UNDERSTANDING CHARACTERIZATION**

In describing Malory's **characterizations,** one critic has said that Launcelot always seems noble in spite of his faults. As you read the selection, note Launcelot's words and actions and those of other characters in response to him. Think about whether these details of characterization support the view of Launcelot as flawed but noble.

READER'S NOTEBOOK Use a cluster diagram to record examples of Launcelot's speech and behavior, as well as the words and acts of others, that contribute to Malory's characterization of him.

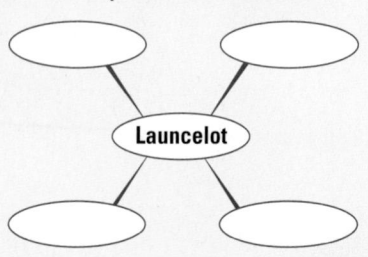

KING ARTHUR'S FAVORITE KNIGHT, SIR LAUNCELOT, HAS FALLEN IN LOVE WITH THE KING'S WIFE, GWYNEVERE. THE SECRET LOVE AFFAIR IS EXPOSED BY SIR MODRED, ARTHUR'S SON BY ANOTHER WOMAN, AND GWYNEVERE IS SENTENCED TO BURN AT THE STAKE. WHILE RESCUING THE IMPRISONED GWYNEVERE, LAUNCELOT SLAYS TWO KNIGHTS WHO, UNKNOWN TO HIM AT THE TIME, ARE THE BROTHERS OF SIR GAWAIN, A FAVORITE NEPHEW OF ARTHUR'S. AFTER A RECONCILIA-TION, LAUNCELOT RETURNS GWYNEVERE TO ARTHUR TO BE REINSTATED AS QUEEN. AT THE URGING OF SIR GAWAIN, WHO STILL WANTS REVENGE ON LAUNCELOT, THE KING BANISHES LAUNCELOT TO FRANCE, WHERE THE FOLLOWING EXCERPT BEGINS.

from
LE MORTE D'ARTHUR

The siege of Benwick

When Sir Launcelot had established dominion over France, he garrisoned the towns and settled with his army in the fortified city of Benwick, where his father King Ban had held court.

King Arthur, after appointing Sir Modred ruler in his absence, and instructing Queen Gwynevere to obey him, sailed to France with an army of sixty thousand men, and, on the advice of Sir Gawain, started laying waste[1] all before him.

News of the invasion reached Sir Launcelot, and his counselors advised him. Sir Bors spoke first:

"My lord Sir Launcelot, is it wise to allow King Arthur to lay your lands waste when sooner or later he will oblige you to offer him battle?"

Sir Lyonel spoke next: "My lord, I would recommend that we remain within the walls of our city until the invaders are weakened by cold and hunger, and then let us sally forth[2] and destroy them."

Next, King Bagdemagus: "Sir Launcelot, I understand that it is out of courtesy that you permit the king to ravage your lands, but where will this courtesy end? If you remain within the city, soon everything will be destroyed."

Then Sir Galyhud: "Sir, you command knights of royal blood; you cannot expect them to remain meekly within the city walls. I pray you, let us encounter the enemy on the open field, and they will soon repent of their expedition."

And to this the seven knights of West Britain all muttered their assent. Then Sir Launcelot spoke:

"My lords, I am reluctant to shed Christian blood in a war against my own liege;[3] and yet I do know that these lands have already suffered depredation in the wars between King Claudas and my father and uncle, King Ban and King Bors. Therefore I will next send a messenger to King Arthur and sue[4] for peace, for peace is always preferable to war."

---

1. **laying waste:** destroying.
2. **sally forth:** rush out suddenly in an attack.
3. **liege** (lēj): a lord or ruler to whom one owes loyalty and service.
4. **sue:** appeal; beg.

WORDS TO KNOW

ravage (răv′ĭj) v. to cause great damage to; devastate
depredation (dĕp′rĭ-dā′shən) n. destruction caused by robbery or looting

Accordingly a young noblewoman accompanied by a dwarf was sent to King Arthur. They were received by the gentle knight Sir Lucas the Butler.

"My lady, you bring a message from Sir Launcelot?" he asked.

"My lord, I do. It is for the king."

"Alas! King Arthur would readily be reconciled to Sir Launcelot, but Sir Gawain forbids it; and it is a shame, because Sir Launcelot is certainly the greatest knight living."

The young noblewoman was brought before the king, and when he had heard Sir Launcelot's entreaties for peace he wept, and would readily have accepted them had not Sir Gawain spoken up:

"My liege, if we retreat now we will become a laughingstock, in this land and in our own. Surely our honor demands that we pursue this war to its proper conclusion."

"Sir Gawain, I will do as you advise, although reluctantly, for Sir Launcelot's terms are generous and he is still dear to me. I beg you make a reply to him on my behalf."

Sir Gawain addressed the young noblewoman:

"Tell Sir Launcelot that we will not bandy words with him, and it is too late now to sue for peace. Further that I, Sir Gawain, shall not cease to strive against him until one of us is killed."

The young noblewoman was escorted back to Sir Launcelot, and when she had delivered Sir Gawain's message they both wept. Then Sir Bors spoke:

"My lord, we beseech you, do not look so dismayed! You have many trustworthy knights behind you; lead us onto the field and we will put an end to this quarrel."

"My lords, I do not doubt you, but I pray you, be ruled by me: I will not lead you against our liege until we ourselves are endangered; only then can we honorably sally forth and defeat him."

Sir Launcelot's nobles submitted; but the next day it was seen that King Arthur had laid siege to the city of Benwick. Then Sir Gawain rode before the city walls and shouted a challenge:

"My lord Sir Launcelot: have you no knight who will dare to ride forth and break spears with me? It is I, Sir Gawain."

Sir Bors accepted the challenge. He rode out of the castle gate, they encountered, and he was wounded and flung from his horse. His comrades helped him back to the castle, and then Sir Lyonel offered to joust. He too was overthrown and helped back to the castle.

Thereafter, every day for six months Sir Gawain rode before the city and overthrew whoever accepted his challenge. Meanwhile, as a result of skirmishes, numbers on both sides were beginning to dwindle. Then one day Sir Gawain challenged Sir Launcelot:

"My lord Sir Launcelot: traitor to the king and to me, come forth if you dare and meet your mortal foe, instead of lurking like a coward in your castle!"

Sir Launcelot heard the challenge, and one of his kinsmen spoke to him:

"My lord, you must accept the challenge, or be shamed forever."

"Alas, that I should have to fight Sir Gawain!" said Sir Launcelot. "But now I am obliged to."

Sir Launcelot gave orders for his most powerful courser[5] to be harnessed, and when he had armed, rode to the tower and addressed King Arthur:

"My lord King Arthur, it is with a heavy heart that I set forth to do battle with one of your own blood; but now it is incumbent upon my honor to do so. For six months I have suffered your majesty to lay my lands waste and to besiege me in my own city. My courtesy is repaid with insults, so deadly and shameful that now I must by force of arms seek redress."

"Have done, Sir Launcelot, and let us to battle!" shouted Sir Gawain.

---

5. **courser:** a horse trained for battle.

WORDS TO KNOW

entreaty (ĕn-trē′tē) *n.* an earnest request; plea
dwindle (dwĭn′dl) *v.* to become steadily less
incumbent (ĭn-kŭm′bənt) *adj.* required as a duty or obligation
redress (rĭ-drĕs′) *n.* repayment for a wrong or injury

Sir Launcelot rode from the city at the head of his entire army. King Arthur was astonished at his strength and realized that Sir Launcelot had not been boasting when he claimed to have acted with <u>forbearance</u>. "Alas, that I should ever have come to war with him!" he said to himself.

It was agreed that the two combatants should fight to the death, with interference from none. Sir Launcelot and Sir Gawain then drew apart and galloped furiously together, and so great was their strength that their horses crashed to the ground and both riders were overthrown.

A terrible sword fight commenced, and each felt the might of the other as fresh

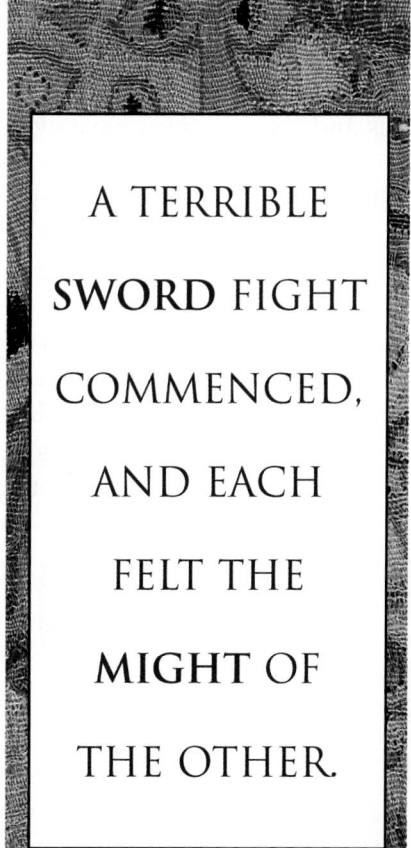

A TERRIBLE SWORD FIGHT COMMENCED, AND EACH FELT THE MIGHT OF THE OTHER.

wounds were inflicted with every blow. For three hours they fought with scarcely a pause, and the blood seeped out from their armor and trickled to the ground. Sir Launcelot found to his dismay that Sir Gawain, instead of weakening, seemed to increase in strength as they proceeded, and he began to fear that he was battling not with a knight but with a fiend incarnate.[6] He decided to fight defensively and to conserve his strength.

It was a secret known only to King Arthur and to Sir Gawain himself that his strength increased for three hours in the morning, reaching its zenith[7] at noon, and waning again. This was due to an enchantment that had been cast over him by a hermit[8] when he was still a youth. Often in the past, as now, he had taken advantage of this.

Thus when the hour of noon had passed, Sir Launcelot felt Sir Gawain's strength return to normal, and knew that he could defeat him.

"Sir Gawain, I have endured many hard blows from you these last three hours, but now beware, for I see that you have weakened, and it is I who am the stronger."

Thereupon Sir Launcelot redoubled his blows, and with one, catching Sir Gawain side-long on the helmet, sent him <u>reeling</u> to the ground. Then he courteously stood back.

"Sir Launcelot, I still defy you!" said Sir Gawain from the ground. "Why do you not kill me now? for I warn you that if ever I recover I shall challenge you again."

"Sir Gawain, by the grace of God I shall endure you again," Sir Launcelot replied, and then turned to the king:

"My liege, your expedition can find no honorable conclusion at these walls, so I pray you withdraw and spare your noble knights. Remember me with kindness and be guided, as ever, by the love of God."

"Alas!" said the king, "Sir Launcelot scruples[9] to fight against me or those of my blood, and once more I am beholden to him."

Sir Launcelot withdrew to the city and Sir Gawain was taken to his pavilion, where his wounds were dressed. King Arthur was doubly grieved, by his quarrel with Sir Launcelot and by the seriousness of Sir Gawain's wounds.

For three weeks, while Sir Gawain was recovering, the siege was relaxed and both sides skirmished only halfheartedly. But once recovered,

---

6. **fiend incarnate:** devil in human form.

7. **zenith:** highest point; peak.

8. **hermit:** a person living in solitude for religious reasons.

9. **scruples:** hesitates for reasons of principle.

WORDS TO KNOW **forbearance** (fôr-bâr′əns) *n.* self-control; patient restraint
reeling (rē′lĭng) *adj.* falling back **reel** *v.*

Sir Gawain rode up to the castle walls and challenged Sir Launcelot again:

"Sir Launcelot, traitor! Come forth, it is Sir Gawain who challenges you."

"Sir Gawain, why these insults? I have the measure of your strength and you can do me but little harm."

"Come forth, traitor, and this time I shall make good my revenge!" Sir Gawain shouted.

"Sir Gawain, I have once spared your life; should you not beware of meddling with me again?"

Sir Launcelot armed and rode out to meet him. They jousted and Sir Gawain broke his spear and was flung from his horse. He leaped up immediately, and putting his shield before him, called on Sir Launcelot to fight on foot.

"The issue[10] of a mare has failed me; but I am the issue of a king and a queen and I shall not fail!" he exclaimed.

As before, Sir Launcelot felt Sir Gawain's strength increase until noon, during which period he defended himself, and then weaken again.

"Sir Gawain, you are a proved knight, and with the increase of your strength until noon you must have overcome many of your opponents, but now your strength has gone, and once more you are at my mercy."

Sir Launcelot struck out lustily and by chance reopened the wound he had made before. Sir Gawain fell to the ground in a faint, but when he came to he said weakly:

"Sir Launcelot, I still defy you. Make an end of me, or I shall fight you again!"

"Sir Gawain, while you stand on your two feet I will not gainsay[11] you; but I will never strike a knight who has fallen. God defend me from such dishonor!"

Sir Launcelot walked away and Sir Gawain continued to call after him: "Traitor! Until one of us is dead I shall never give in!"

For a month Sir Gawain lay recovering from his wounds, and the siege remained; but then, as Sir Gawain was preparing to fight Sir Launcelot once more, King Arthur received news which caused him to strike camp and lead his army on a forced march to the coast, and thence to embark for Britain.

---

10. **issue:** offspring.

11. **gainsay:** deny.

The Day of Destiny

During the absence of King Arthur from Britain, Sir Modred, already vested with sovereign powers,[12] had decided to usurp the throne. Accordingly, he had false letters written—announcing the death of King Arthur in battle—and delivered to himself. Then, calling a parliament, he ordered the letters to be read and persuaded the nobility to elect him king. The coronation took place at Canterbury and was celebrated with a fifteen-day feast.

Sir Modred then settled in Camelot and made overtures to Queen Gwynevere to marry him. The queen seemingly acquiesced, but as soon as she had won his confidence, begged leave to make a journey to London in order to prepare her trousseau.[13] Sir Modred consented, and the queen rode straight to the Tower which, with the aid of her loyal nobles, she manned and provisioned for her defense.

Sir Modred, outraged, at once marched against her, and laid siege to the Tower, but despite his large army, siege engines, and guns, was unable to effect a breach. He then tried to entice the queen from the Tower, first by guile and then by threats, but she would listen to neither. Finally the Archbishop of Canterbury came forward to protest:

"Sir Modred, do you not fear God's displeasure? First you have falsely made yourself king; now you, who were begotten by King Arthur on his aunt, try to marry your father's wife! If you do not revoke your evil deeds I shall curse you with bell, book, and candle."[14]

"Fie on you! Do your worst!" Sir Modred replied.

"Sir Modred, I warn you take heed! or the wrath of the Lord will descend upon you."

"Away, false priest, or I shall behead you!"

The Archbishop withdrew, and after excommunicating Sir Modred, abandoned his office and fled to Glastonbury. There he took up his abode as a simple hermit, and by fasting and prayer sought divine intercession[15] in the troubled affairs of his country.

Sir Modred tried to assassinate the Archbishop, but was too late. He continued to assail the queen with entreaties and threats, both of which failed, and then the news reached him that King Arthur was returning with his army from France in order to seek revenge.

Sir Modred now appealed to the barony to support him, and it has to be told that they came forward in large numbers to do so. Why? it will be asked. Was not King Arthur, the noblest sovereign Christendom had seen, now leading his armies in a righteous cause? The answer lies in the people of Britain, who, then as now, were fickle. Those who so readily transferred their allegiance to Sir Modred did so with the excuse that whereas King Arthur's reign had led them into war and strife, Sir Modred promised them peace and festivity.

Hence it was with an army of a hundred thousand that Sir Modred marched to Dover to battle against his own father, and to withhold from him his rightful crown.

As King Arthur with his fleet drew into the harbor, Sir Modred and his army launched forth

---

12. **vested with sovereign powers:** given the authority of a king.

13. **trousseau** (trōō′sō): clothes and linens that a bride brings to her marriage.

14. **I shall curse you with bell, book, and candle:** The archbishop is threatening to excommunicate Modred—that is, to deny him participation in the rites of the church. In the medieval ritual of excommunication, a bell was rung, a book was shut, and a candle was extinguished.

15. **divine intercession:** assistance from God.

WORDS TO KNOW	**usurp** (yōō-sûrp′) v. to seize unlawfully by force
	acquiesce (ăk′wē-ĕs′) v. to agree or give in without protest
	guile (gīl) n. clever trickery; deceit
	assail (ə-sāl′) v. to attack, either with blows or with words

in every available craft, and a bloody battle <u>ensued</u> in the ships and on the beach. If King Arthur's army were the smaller, their courage was the higher, confident as they were of the righteousness of their cause. Without stint[16] they battled through the burning ships, the screaming wounded, and the corpses floating on the bloodstained waters. Once ashore they put Sir Modred's entire army to flight.

The battle over, King Arthur began a search for his casualties, and on peering into one of the ships found Sir Gawain, mortally wounded. Sir Gawain fainted when King Arthur lifted him in his arms; and when he came to, the king spoke:

"Alas! dear nephew, that you lie here thus, mortally wounded! What joy is now left to me on this earth? You must know it was you and Sir Launcelot I loved above all others, and it seems that I have lost you both."

"My good uncle, it was my pride and my stubbornness that brought all this about, for had I not urged you to war with Sir Launcelot your subjects would not now be in revolt. Alas, that Sir Launcelot is not here, for he would soon drive them out! And it is at Sir Launcelot's hands that I suffer my own death: the wound which he dealt me has reopened. I would not wish it otherwise, because is he not the greatest and gentlest of knights?

"I know that by noon I shall be dead, and I repent bitterly that I may not be reconciled to Sir Launcelot; therefore I pray you, good uncle, give me pen, paper, and ink so that I may write to him."

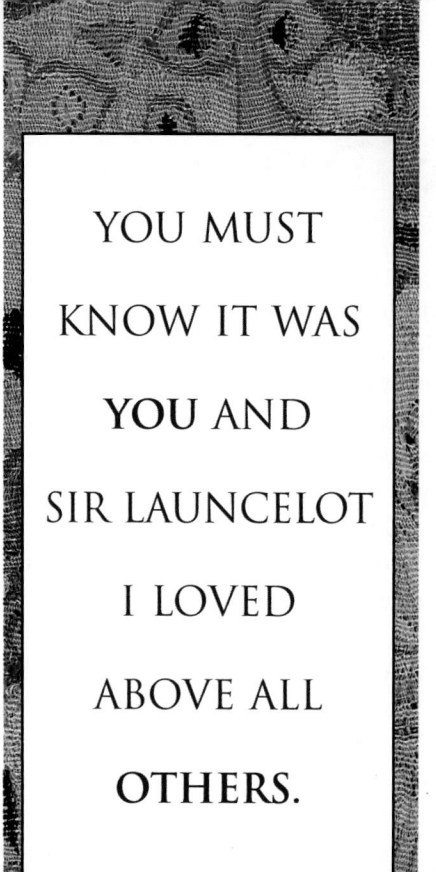

YOU MUST KNOW IT WAS YOU AND SIR LAUNCELOT I LOVED ABOVE ALL OTHERS.

A priest was summoned and Sir Gawain confessed; then a clerk brought ink, pen, and paper, and Sir Gawain wrote to Sir Launcelot as follows:

"Sir Launcelot, flower of the knighthood: I, Sir Gawain, son of King Lot of Orkney and of King Arthur's sister, send you my greetings!

"I am about to die; the cause of my death is the wound I received from you outside the city of Benwick; and I would make it known that my death was of my own seeking, that I was moved by the spirit of revenge and spite to provoke you to battle.

"Therefore, Sir Launcelot, I beseech you to visit my tomb and offer what prayers you will on my behalf; and for myself, I am content to die at the hands of the noblest knight living.

"One more request: that you hasten with your armies across the sea and give <u>succor</u> to our noble king. Sir Modred, his bastard son, has usurped the throne and now holds against him with an army of a hundred thousand. He would have won the queen, too, but she fled to the Tower of London and there charged her loyal supporters with her defense.

"Today is the tenth of May, and at noon I shall give up the ghost; this letter is written partly with my blood. This morning we fought our way ashore, against the armies of Sir Modred, and that is how my wound came to be reopened. We won the day, but my lord King Arthur needs you, and I too, that on my tomb you may bestow your blessing."

---

16. **stint:** holding back.

WORDS TO KNOW

ensue (ĕn-sōō′) *v.* to occur as a result; follow
succor (sŭk′ər) *n.* aid in a time of need; relief

Sir Gawain fainted when he had finished, and the king wept. When he came to he was given extreme unction,[17] and died, as he had anticipated, at the hour of noon. The king buried him in the chapel at Dover Castle, and there many came to see him, and all noticed the wound on his head which he had received from Sir Launcelot.

Then the news reached Arthur that Sir Modred offered him battle on the field at Baron Down. Arthur hastened there with his army, they fought, and Sir Modred fled once more, this time to Canterbury.

When King Arthur had begun the search for his wounded and dead, many volunteers from all parts of the country came to fight under his flag, convinced now of the rightness of his cause. Arthur marched westward, and Sir Modred once more offered him battle. It was assigned for the Monday following Trinity Sunday, on Salisbury Down.

Sir Modred levied fresh troops from East Anglia and the places about London, and fresh volunteers came forward to help Arthur. Then, on the night of Trinity Sunday, Arthur was vouchsafed[18] a strange dream:

He was appareled in gold cloth and seated in a chair which stood on a pivoted scaffold. Below him, many fathoms deep, was a dark well, and in the water swam serpents, dragons, and wild beasts. Suddenly the scaffold tilted and Arthur was flung into the water, where all the creatures struggled toward him and began tearing him limb from limb.

Arthur cried out in his sleep and his squires hastened to waken him. Later, as he lay between waking and sleeping, he thought he saw Sir Gawain, and with him a host of beautiful noblewomen. Arthur spoke:

"My sister's son! I thought you had died; but now I see you live, and I thank the lord Jesu! I pray you, tell me, who are these ladies?"

"My lord, these are the ladies I championed[19] in righteous quarrels when I was on earth. Our lord God has vouchsafed that we visit you and plead with you not to give battle to Sir Modred tomorrow, for if you do, not only will you yourself be killed, but all your noble followers too. We beg you to be warned, and to make a treaty with Sir Modred, calling a truce for a month, and granting him whatever terms he may demand. In a month Sir Launcelot will be here, and he will defeat Sir Modred."

Thereupon Sir Gawain and the ladies vanished, and King Arthur once more summoned his squires and his counselors and told them his vision. Sir Lucas and Sir Bedivere were commissioned to make a treaty with Sir Modred. They were to be accompanied by two bishops and to grant, within reason, whatever terms he demanded.

The ambassadors found Sir Modred in command of an army of a hundred thousand and unwilling to listen to overtures of peace. However, the ambassadors eventually prevailed on him, and in return for the truce granted him suzerainty[20] of Cornwall and Kent, and succession to the British throne when King Arthur died. The treaty was to be signed by King Arthur and Sir Modred the next day. They were to meet between the two armies, and each was to be accompanied by no more than fourteen knights.

Both King Arthur and Sir Modred suspected the other of treachery, and gave orders for their armies to attack at the sight of a naked sword. When they met at the appointed place the treaty was signed and both drank a glass of wine.

---

17. **extreme unction:** a ritual in which a priest anoints and prays for a dying person.
18. **vouchsafed:** granted.
19. **championed:** defended or fought for.
20. **suzerainty** (sōō′zər-ən-tē): the position of feudal lord.

Then, by chance, one of the soldiers was bitten in the foot by an adder[21] which had lain concealed in the brush. The soldier unthinkingly drew his sword to kill it, and at once, as the sword flashed in the light, the alarums[22] were given, trumpets sounded, and both armies galloped into the attack.

"Alas for this fateful day!" exclaimed King Arthur, as both he and Sir Modred hastily mounted and galloped back to their armies. There followed one of those rare and heartless battles in which both armies fought until they were destroyed. King Arthur, with his customary valor, led squadron after squadron of cavalry into the attack, and Sir Modred encountered him unflinchingly. As the number of dead and wounded mounted on both sides, the active combatants continued dauntless until nightfall, when four men alone survived.

King Arthur wept with dismay to see his beloved followers fallen; then, struggling toward him, unhorsed and badly wounded, he saw Sir Lucas the Butler and his brother, Sir Bedivere.

"Alas!" said the king, "that the day should come when I see all my noble knights destroyed! I would prefer that I myself had fallen. But what has become of the traitor Sir Modred, whose evil ambition was responsible for this carnage?"

Looking about him King Arthur then noticed Sir Modred leaning with his sword on a heap of the dead.

"Sir Lucas, I pray you give me my spear, for I have seen Sir Modred."

"Sire, I entreat you, remember your vision—how Sir Gawain appeared with a heaven-sent message to dissuade you from fighting Sir Modred. Allow this fateful day to pass; it is ours, for we three hold the field, while the enemy is broken."

"My lords, I care nothing for my life now! And while Sir Modred is at large I must kill him: there may not be another chance."

"God speed you, then!" said Sir Bedivere.

When Sir Modred saw King Arthur advance with his spear, he rushed to meet him with drawn sword. Arthur caught Sir Modred below the shield and drove his spear through his body; Sir Modred, knowing that the wound was mortal, thrust himself up to the handle of the spear, and then, brandishing his sword in both hands, struck Arthur on the side of the helmet, cutting through it and into the skull beneath; then he crashed to the ground, gruesome and dead.

King Arthur fainted many times as Sir Lucas and Sir Bedivere struggled with him to a small chapel nearby, where they managed to ease his wounds a little. When Arthur came to, he thought he heard cries coming from the battlefield.

"Sir Lucas, I pray you, find out who cries on the battlefield," he said.

Wounded as he was, Sir Lucas hobbled painfully to the field, and there in the moonlight saw the camp followers stealing gold and jewels from the dead, and murdering the wounded. He returned to the king and reported to him what he had seen, and then added:

"My lord, it surely would be better to move you to the nearest town?"

"My wounds forbid it. But alas for the good Sir Launcelot! How sadly I have missed him today! And now I must die—as Sir Gawain warned me I would—repenting our quarrel with my last breath."

Sir Lucas and Sir Bedivere made one further attempt to lift the king. He fainted as they did so. Then Sir Lucas fainted as part of his intestines broke through a wound in the stomach. When the king came to, he saw Sir Lucas lying dead with foam at his mouth.

"Sweet Jesu, give him succor!" he said. "This noble knight has died trying to save my life—alas that this was so!"

Sir Bedivere wept for his brother.

---

21. **adder:** a poisonous snake.
22. **alarums:** calls to arms.

WORDS TO KNOW

dissuade (dĭ-swād') *v.* to divert from a course of action by persuasion

Illustration from an illuminated manuscript showing a wounded Arthur in the foreground waiting for Sir Bedivere, who watches a hand appear from the lake to take King Arthur's sword, Excalibur.

"Sir Bedivere, weep no more," said King Arthur, "for you can save neither your brother nor me; and I would ask you to take my sword Excalibur to the shore of the lake and throw it in the water. Then return to me and tell me what you have seen."

"My lord, as you command, it shall be done."

Sir Bedivere took the sword, but when he came to the water's edge, it appeared so beautiful that he could not bring himself to throw it in, so instead he hid it by a tree, and then returned to the king.

"Sir Bedivere, what did you see?"

"My lord, I saw nothing but the wind upon the waves."

"Then you did not obey me; I pray you, go swiftly again, and this time fulfill my command."

Sir Bedivere went and returned again, but this time too he had failed to fulfill the king's command.

"Sir Bedivere, what did you see?"

"My lord, nothing but the lapping of the waves."

"Sir Bedivere, twice you have betrayed me! And for the sake only of my sword: it is unworthy of you! Now I pray you, do as I command, for I have not long to live."

This time Sir Bedivere wrapped the girdle around the sheath and hurled it as far as he could into the water. A hand appeared from below the surface, took the sword, waved it thrice, and disappeared again. Sir Bedivere re-

turned to the king and told him what he had seen.

"Sir Bedivere, I pray you now help me hence, or I fear it will be too late."

Sir Bedivere carried the king to the water's edge, and there found a barge in which sat many beautiful ladies with their queen. All were wearing black hoods, and when they saw the king, they raised their voices in a piteous lament.

"I pray you, set me in the barge," said the king.

Sir Bedivere did so, and one of the ladies laid the king's head in her lap; then the queen spoke to him:

"My dear brother, you have stayed too long: I fear that the wound on your head is already cold."

Thereupon they rowed away from the land and Sir Bedivere wept to see them go.

"My lord King Arthur, you have deserted me! I am alone now, and among enemies."

"Sir Bedivere, take what comfort you may, for my time is passed, and now I must be taken to Avalon[23] for my wound to be healed. If you hear of me no more, I beg you pray for my soul."

The barge slowly crossed the water and out of sight while the ladies wept. Sir Bedivere walked alone into the forest and there remained for the night.

In the morning he saw beyond the trees of a copse[24] a small hermitage. He entered and found a hermit kneeling down by a fresh tomb. The hermit was weeping as he prayed, and then Sir Bedivere recognized him as the Archbishop of Canterbury, who had been banished by Sir Modred.

"Father, I pray you, tell me, whose tomb is this?"

"My son, I do not know. At midnight the body was brought here by a company of ladies. We buried it, they lit a hundred candles for the service, and rewarded me with a thousand bezants."[25]

"Father, King Arthur lies buried in this tomb."

Sir Bedivere fainted when he had spoken, and when he came to he begged the Archbishop to allow him to remain at the hermitage and end his days in fasting and prayer.

"Father, I wish only to be near to my true liege."

"My son, you are welcome; and do I not recognize you as Sir Bedivere the Bold, brother to Sir Lucas the Butler?"

Thus the Archbishop and Sir Bedivere remained at the hermitage, wearing the habits of hermits and devoting themselves to the tomb with fasting and prayers of contrition.[26]

Such was the death of King Arthur as written down by Sir Bedivere. By some it is told that there were three queens on the barge: Queen Morgan le Fay, the Queen of North Galys, and the Queen of the Waste Lands; and others include the name of Nyneve, the Lady of the Lake who had served King Arthur well in the past, and had married the good knight Sir Pelleas.

In many parts of Britain it is believed that King Arthur did not die and that he will return to us and win fresh glory and the Holy Cross of our Lord Jesu Christ; but for myself I do not believe this, and would leave him buried peacefully in his tomb at Glastonbury, where the Archbishop of Canterbury and Sir Bedivere humbled themselves, and with prayers and fasting honored his memory. And inscribed on his tomb, men say, is this legend:

HIC IACET **ARTHURUS**,
REX **QUONDAM** REXQUE FUTURUS.[27]

---

23. **Avalon:** an island paradise of Celtic legend, where heroes are taken after death.

24. **copse** (kŏps): a grove of small trees.

25. **bezants** (bĕz'ənts): gold coins.

26. **contrition** (kən-trĭsh'ən): sincere regret for wrongdoing.

27. *Hic iacet Arthurus, rex quondam rexque futurus*
(hĭk yä'kĕt är-tōō'rŏŏs räks kwôn'däm räk'skwĕ fōō-tōō'rŏŏs)
Latin: Here lies Arthur, the once and future king.

Connect to the Literature

1. **What Do You Think?**
   What thoughts were in your mind as you finished reading this selection? Share them with the class.

   Comprehension Check
   - What happens when Gawain and Launcelot meet on the field of battle?
   - What is Gawain's secret weakness in combat?
   - What warning does Sir Gawain give to Arthur in a vision?

Think Critically

2. In your opinion, which character in the selection is most admirable, and which is least admirable?

   THINK ABOUT
   - the ways in which Launcelot shows loyalty and disloyalty to the king
   - Arthur's willingness to forget his loyalty to Launcelot and follow Gawain's advice
   - Modred's seizure of the throne
   - Gwynevere's involvement with Launcelot

3. How much choice do you think Arthur has in determining his own fate?

   THINK ABOUT
   - the importance of chivalry to his followers
   - the consequences of his long stay in France
   - the warnings he receives in his dreams

4. If Arthur, Launcelot, and Gawain were given a second chance to resolve their conflicts, what do you think they might do differently?

5. **ACTIVE READING** **UNDERSTANDING CHARACTERIZATION**
   Look again at your ▯ **READER'S NOTEBOOK**. What did you discover about the characterization of Launcelot as you recorded examples of his words and behavior in the cluster diagram?

Extend Interpretations

6. **What If?** Suppose that Sir Launcelot had arrived with his army in time to help Arthur battle Modred. How might things have turned out differently for the major characters?

7. **Connect to Life** Would you say that the forces that end Arthur's reign are the same forces that bring down governments in the real world? Support your answer with examples from local, national, or world history.

Literary Analysis

CHARACTERIZATION The way in which writers guide readers' impressions of characters is called **characterization.** There are four basic methods of developing a character: (1) description of the character's physical appearance; (2) presentation of the character's speech, thoughts, feelings, and actions; (3) presentation of other characters' speech, thoughts, feelings, and actions; and (4) direct comments about the character.

Cooperative Learning Activity With a group of classmates, look back through this selection, identifying passages that help create readers' impressions of Launcelot, Arthur, Gawain, Modred, and Gwynevere. In a chart, record the character, passage, method of characterization, and the qualities of character that are revealed in the passage.

Character	Passage	Method	Qualities
Launcelot	"I will not lead you against . . .	Launcelot's own words	Nobility and honor
Arthur			

REVIEW **ROMANCE** The term **romance** refers to an imaginative adventure concerned with noble heroes, gallant love, a chivalric code of honor, and daring deeds. Romances usually have faraway settings, depict events unlike those of ordinary life, and idealize heroes as well as the eras in which the heroes lived. What characteristics of romance can you find in this excerpt?

Choices & CHALLENGES

Writing Options

Essay on Virtues Many virtues are portrayed in this excerpt from Malory. Write a two-or-three paragraph essay in which you explain which virtues of Malory's characters are most important to you in your life. Place the essay in your **Working Portfolio**. 📁

Sir Thomas Malory
1405?–1471

An Active Life A son of prosperous parents, the Thomas Malory who many scholars think to be the author of *Le Morte d'Arthur* led a surprisingly unsettled life that ended in prison. A native of Warwickshire, England, he fought in the Hundred Years' War, was knighted around 1442, and was elected to Parliament in 1445. Malory then became embroiled in the violent political conflicts that preceded the outbreak of the Wars of the Roses.

Political Turmoil A staunch supporter of the house of Lancaster and its claim to the throne, Malory was imprisoned repeatedly by the Yorkist government on a variety of charges, including robbery, cattle rustling, bribery, and attempted murder. He pleaded innocent to all the charges, and his guilt was never proven. It is possible that his outspoken opposition to the ruling family provoked enemies to accuse him falsely in some instances.

Prisoner and Writer Malory seems to have written *Le Morte d'Arthur* while he served a series of prison terms that began in 1451. He finished the book about two years before his death in 1471. William Caxton, who introduced the art of printing to England, published the first edition of Malory's work in 1485, giving the book the title by which it is known today. *Le Morte d'Arthur* remains the most complete English version of the Arthurian legends and has been the source of many later adaptations of the tales.

Vocabulary in Action

EXERCISE: CONTEXT CLUES Choose the word that could be substituted for the italicized word or phrase in each sentence below.

1. The king's followers began to *attack* his honor.
2. Everyone marveled at the *patience* with which he reacted to the attacks.
3. The king's enemies tried to *unlawfully take over* the throne.
4. The king hoped to *discourage* them from doing harm.
5. The enemies ignored the king's *plea* for peace.
6. They used *trickery* and threats against him.
7. The king had to *agree without protest* to a declaration of war.
8. He felt that it was *laid as a duty* on him to fight for his honor.
9. His army sought *repayment* for crimes against the king.
10. The king knew that after he issued his challenge, a full-scale war would *follow*.
11. His advisers warned that the war would *greatly damage* the land.
12. The number of healthy soldiers began to *decline*.
13. Wounded soldiers were seen *falling back* all over the battlefield.
14. Other kingdoms were asked to give *assistance* to the weakened army.
15. The plundering soldiers caused *damage* and sorrow throughout the land.

WORDS TO KNOW			
	acquiesce	entreaty	
	assail	forbearance	reeling
	depredation	guile	succor
	dissuade	incumbent	usurp
	dwindle	ravage	
	ensue	redress	

Building Vocabulary
For an in-depth study of context clues, see page 938.

from

PREFACE TO THE FIRST EDITION
Le Morte d' Arthur

William Caxton, the first English printer, had a significant impact on the literature of his day. In his preface to the first edition of Malory's *Le Morte d'Arthur*, published in 1485, Caxton describes his anticipated audience and reveals his purpose in publishing the work.

1   I have, after the simple cunning that God hath sent to me, under the favor and correction of all noble lords and gentlemen, enprised to enprint a book of the noble histories of the said King Arthur and of certain of his knights, after a copy unto me delivered, which copy Sir Thomas Malory did take out of certain books of French and reduced it into English.

2   And I, according to my copy, have done set it in enprint to the intent that noble men may see and learn the noble acts of chivalry, the gentle and virtuous deeds that some knights used in tho[se] days, by which they came to honor, and how they that were vicious were punished and oft put to shame and rebuke; humbly beseeching all noble lords and ladies with all other estates, of what estate or degree they been of, that shall see and read in this said book and work, that **3** they take the good and honest acts in their remembrance, and to follow the same; wherein they shall find many joyous and pleasant histories and noble and renowned acts of humanity, gentleness, and chivalries. For herein may be seen noble chivalry, courtesy, humanity, friendliness, hardiness, love, friendship, cowardice, murder, hate, virtue and sin. Do after the good and leave the evil, and it shall bring you to good fame.

Reading for Information

The **preface** to a literary work typically sheds light on why the author wrote the work. Imagine that you are a printer at a time when books are scarce. What might you want to include in your preface to a first edition?

PARAPHRASING AND SUMMARIZING

As you might expect, Caxton's language and syntax are typical of 15th-century English. To unlock the meanings of such challenging texts, you can use the skills of paraphrasing and summarizing. Review the primary source as you complete these activities:

1 **Paraphrase,** or restate in your own words, the first paragraph. What sources does Caxton suggest Malory used?

2 Refer to your paraphrase of the second paragraph. What was Caxton's purpose in publishing *Le Morte d'Arthur?* What virtues does it portray? Who does Caxton expect will be his audience?

3 Look at your paraphrase of "that they take the good and honest acts in their remembrance, and to follow the same." What is Caxton hoping his readers will do?

Summarizing With a partner, summarize Caxton's main points. How has reading Caxton's words affected your understanding of *Le Morte d'Arthur.* In what ways, if any, has your reaction to characters such as Sir Gawain changed?

from the Ramayana

Epic by VALMIKI
Translated and adapted by R. K. NARAYAN

Comparing Literature of the World

Legendary Deeds Across Cultures

Le Morte d'Arthur **and the** *Ramayana* The *Ramayana* was written hundreds of centuries before *Le Morte d'Arthur*. However, both tales contain chivalric **heroes** who clash with their adversaries during **epic battles.** In both cases, the combatants are aided by supernatural elements that enhance their power.

Points of Comparison As you read the *Ramayana,* compare its **characters,** battles, and turn of events with those you recall from *Le Morte d'Arthur.*

[Map showing Afghanistan, Pakistan, China, Nepal, India, Gulf of Oman, Arabian Sea, Bay of Bengal, Sri Lanka]

Build Background

Epic Proportions The great Indian **epic** *Ramayana* was composed in verse by the poet Valmiki, probably between 300 and 200 B.C. Like epics of other cultures, the *Ramayana* celebrates the achievements of both human heroes and divine beings. It is the story of Rama (rä′mə), a royal prince who is the seventh incarnation, or embodiment, of the god Vishnu (vĭsh′nōō). The epic describes Rama's life, love, battles, and hardships. At the point of the story where this excerpt begins, Rama's wife Sita (sē′tä) has been kidnapped by Ravana (rä′və-nə), the 10-headed, 20-armed demon-king of the island of Lanka (ləng′kä). Hanuman (hə′nŏŏ-män), a flying monkey in Rama's army, has located Sita and helped build a bridge to Lanka so that all of Rama's forces can cross over and rescue her.

> WORDS TO KNOW
> **Vocabulary Preview**
>
> esoteric   incarnation
> formidable   invincibility
> impervious   parrying
> imprecation   primordial
> incantation   rampart

Focus Your Reading

LITERARY ANALYSIS **SUPERNATURAL ELEMENTS**

Epics often journey into the realm of the supernatural. Supernatural elements include any beings, powers, or events that are unexplainable by the known forces or laws of nature. In the *Ramayana,* for example, Ravana's son Indrajit is a supernatural being, as this passage suggests.

> *He also created a figure resembling Sita, carried her in his chariot, took her before Rama's army and killed her within their sight.*

Be aware of other supernatural elements as you read this excerpt from the *Ramayana.*

ACTIVE READING **CLASSIFYING CHARACTERS** In this selection, the hero Rama and his followers engage in a major battle with the demon-king Ravana and his allies. As the battle progresses, it will be important for you to keep track of characters by **classifying** them as belonging on either Rama's or Ravana's side of the **conflict.**

READER'S NOTEBOOK As you read, list the participants in groups according to their loyalty to Rama or to Ravana. Beside each name, write down something that will help you remember the **character**—a physical description, a personality trait, or his or her role in the **epic.**

from the

R A M A Y A N A

Sculpture of Hanuman

THE SIEGE OF LANKA

Ravana deployed the pick of his divisions to guard the approaches to the capital and appointed his trusted generals and kinsmen in special charge of key places. Gradually, however, his world began to shrink. As the fight developed he lost his associates one by one. No one who went out returned.

He tried some devious measures in desperation. He sent spies in the garb of Rama's monkey army across to deflect and corrupt some of Rama's staunchest supporters, such as Sugreeva,[1] on whom rested the entire burden of this war. He employed sorcerers to disturb the mind of Sita, hoping that if she yielded, Rama would ultimately lose heart. He ordered a sorcerer to create a decapitated head resembling Rama's and placed it before Sita as evidence of Rama's defeat. Sita, although shaken at first, very soon recovered her composure and remained unaffected by the spectacle.

---

1. **Sugreeva** (sŏŏ-grē′və).

At length a messenger from Rama arrived, saying, "Rama bids me warn you that your doom is at hand. Even now it is not too late for you to restore Sita and beg Rama's forgiveness. You have troubled the world too long. You are not fit to continue as King. At our camp, your brother, Vibishana,[2] has already been crowned the King of this land, and the world knows all people will be happy under him."

Ravana ordered the messenger to be killed instantly. But it was more easily said than done, the messenger being Angada,[3] the son of mighty Vali.[4] When two rakshasas[5] came to seize him, he tucked one of them under each arm, rose into the sky, and flung the rakshasas down. In addition, he kicked and broke off the tower of Ravana's palace, and left. Ravana viewed the broken tower with dismay.

Rama awaited the return of Angada, and, on hearing his report, decided that there was no further cause to hope for a change of heart in Ravana and immediately ordered the assault on Lanka.

As the fury of the battle grew, both sides lost sight of the distinction between night and day. The air was filled with the cries of fighters, their challenges, cheers, and imprecations; buildings and trees were torn up and, as one of his spies reported to Ravana, the monkeys were like a sea overrunning Lanka. The end did not seem to be in sight.

At one stage of the battle, Rama and Lakshmana[6] were attacked by Indrajit,[7] and the serpent darts employed by him made them swoon on the battlefield. Indrajit went back to his father to proclaim that it was all over with Rama and Lakshmana and soon, without a leader, the monkeys would be annihilated.

Ravana rejoiced to hear it and cried, "Did not I say so? All you fools believed that I should surrender." He added, "Go and tell Sita that Rama and his brother are no more. Take her high up in Pushpak Vimana,[8] my chariot, and show her their bodies on the battlefield." His words were obeyed instantly. Sita, happy to have a chance to glimpse a long-lost face, accepted the chance, went high up, and saw her husband lying dead in the field below. She broke down. "How I wish I had been left alone and not brought up to see this spectacle. Ah, me . . . Help me to put an end to my life."

Trijata,[9] one of Ravana's women, whispered to her, "Don't lose heart, they are not dead," and she explained why they were in a faint.

In due course, the effect of the serpent darts was neutralized when Garuda,[10] the mighty eagle, the born enemy of all serpents, appeared on the scene; the venomous darts enveloping Rama and Lakshmana scattered at the approach of Garuda and the brothers were on their feet again.

From his palace retreat Ravana was surprised to hear again the cheers of the enemy hordes outside the ramparts; the siege was on again. Ravana still had about him his commander-in-chief, his son Indrajit, and five or six others on whom he felt he could rely at the last instance. He sent them one by one. He felt shattered when news came of the death of his commander-in-chief.

"No time to sit back. I will myself go and destroy this Rama and his horde of monkeys," he said and got into his chariot and entered the field.

At this encounter Lakshmana fell down in a faint, and Hanuman hoisted Rama on his shoulders and charged in the direction of Ravana.

---

2. **Vibishana** (vĭ-bē'shə-nə).
3. **Angada** (əng'gə-də).
4. **Vali** (və'lē): king of the monkeys.
5. **rakshasas** (räk'shə-səz): demons.
6. **Lakshmana** (lək'shmə-nə).
7. **Indrajit** (ĭn'drə-jēt): Ravana's son.
8. **Pushpak Vimana** (pōōsh'pak vĭ-mä'nə).
9. **Trijata** (trĭ'jə-tä).
10. **Garuda** (gə-rōō'də).

WORDS
TO
KNOW

imprecation (ĭm'prĭ-kā'shən) *n.* a curse
rampart (răm'pärt') *n.* an embankment or wall for defense against attack

The main combatants were face to face for the first time. At the end of this engagement Ravana was sorely wounded, his crown was shattered, and his chariot was broken. Helplessly, bare-handed, he stood before Rama, and Rama said, "You may go now and come back tomorrow with fresh weapons." For the first time in his existence of many thousand years, Ravana faced the humiliation of accepting a concession, and he returned crestfallen to his palace.

He ordered that his brother Kumbakarna,[11] famous for his deep sleep, should be awakened. He could depend upon him, and only on him now. It was a mighty task to wake up Kumba-karna. A small army had to be engaged. They sounded trumpets and drums at his ears and were ready with enormous quantities of food and drink for him, for when Kumbakarna awoke from sleep, his hunger was phenomenal and he made a meal of whomever he could grab at his bedside. They cudgelled, belaboured, pushed, pulled, and shook him, with the help of elephants; at last he opened his eyes and swept his arms about and crushed quite a number among those who had stirred him up. When he had eaten and drunk, he was approached by Ravana's chief minister and told, "My lord, the battle is going badly for us."

"Which battle?" he asked, not yet fully awake.

And they had to refresh his memory. "Your brother has fought and has been worsted; our enemies are breaking in, our fort walls are crumbling. . . ."

Kumbakarna was roused. "Why did not anyone tell me all this before? Well, it is not too late; I will deal with that Rama. His end is come." Thus saying, he strode into Ravana's chamber and said, "Don't worry about anything any more. I will take care of everything."

Ravana spoke with anxiety and defeat in his voice. Kumbakarna, who had never seen him in this state, said, "You have gone on without heeding anyone's words and brought yourself to this pass. You should have fought Rama and

acquired Sita. You were led away by mere lust and never cared for anyone's words. . . . Hm . . . This is no time to speak of dead events. I will not forsake you as others have done. I'll bring Rama's head on a platter."

Kumbakarna's entry into the battle created havoc. He destroyed and swallowed hundreds and thousands of the monkey warriors and came very near finishing off the great Sugreeva himself. Rama himself had to take a hand at destroying this demon; he sent the sharpest of his arrows, which cut Kumbakarna limb from limb; but he fought fiercely with only inches of his body remaining intact. Finally Rama severed his head with an arrow. That was the end of Kumbakarna.

When he heard of it, Ravana lamented, "My right hand is cut off."

One of his sons reminded him, "Why should you despair? You have Brahma's[12] gift of invincibility. You should not grieve." Indrajit told him, "What have you to fear when I am alive?"

Indrajit had the power to remain invisible and fight, and accounted for much destruction in the invader's camp. He also created a figure resembl-ing Sita, carried her in his chariot, took her before Rama's army and killed her within their sight.

This completely demoralized the monkeys, who suspended their fight, crying, "Why should we fight when our goddess Sita is thus gone?" They were in a rout until Vibishana came to their rescue and rallied them again.

—•— —•— —•—

Indrajit fell by Lakshmana's hand in the end. When he heard of his son's death, Ravana shed bitter tears and swore, "This is the time to kill that woman Sita, the cause of all this misery."

---

11. **Kumbakarna** (kŏŏm′bə-kər′nə).

12. **Brahma's** (brä′məz): given by Brahma—in the Hindu religion, the creator of the universe and one of a trinity of gods that make up the Supreme God.

invincibility (ĭn-vĭn′sə-bĭl′ĭ-tē) *n.* a state of being unbeatable

A few encouraged this idea, but one of his councillors advised, "Don't defeat your own purpose and integrity by killing a woman. Let your anger scorch Rama and his brother. Gather all your armies and go and vanquish Rama and Lakshmana, you know you can, and then take Sita. Put on your blessed armour and go forth."

RAMA AND RAVANA IN BATTLE

Every moment, news came to Ravana of fresh disasters in his camp. One by one, most of his commanders were lost. No one who went forth with battle cries was heard of again. Cries and shouts and the wailings of the widows of warriors came over the chants and songs of triumph that his courtiers arranged to keep up at a loud pitch in his assembly hall. Ravana became restless and abruptly left the hall and went up on a tower, from which he could obtain a full view of the city. He surveyed the scene below but could not stand it. One who had spent a lifetime in destruction, now found the gory spectacle intolerable. Groans and wailings reached his ears with deadly clarity; and he noticed how the monkey hordes revelled in their bloody handiwork. This was too much for him. He felt a terrific rage rising within him, mixed with some admiration for Rama's valour. He told himself, "The time has come for me to act by myself again."

He hurried down the steps of the tower, returned to his chamber, and prepared himself for the battle. He had a ritual bath and performed special prayers to gain the benediction of Shiva; donned his battle dress, matchless armour, armlets, and crowns. He had on a protective armour for every inch of his body. He girt his sword-belt and attached to his body his accoutrements for protection and decoration.

When he emerged from his chamber, his heroic appearance was breathtaking. He summoned his chariot, which could be drawn by horses or move on its own if the horses were hurt or killed. People stood aside when he came out of the palace and entered his chariot. "This is my resolve," he said to himself: "Either that woman Sita, or my wife Mandodari,[13] will soon have cause to cry and roll in the dust in grief. Surely, before this day is done, one of them will be a widow."

The gods in heaven noticed Ravana's determined move and felt that Rama would need all the support they could muster. They requested Indra to send down his special chariot for Rama's use. When the chariot appeared at his camp, Rama was deeply impressed with the magnitude and brilliance of the vehicle. "How has this come to be here?" he asked.

"Sir," the charioteer answered, "my name is Matali.[14] I have the honour of being the charioteer of Indra. Brahma, the four-faced god and the creator of the Universe, and Shiva, whose power has emboldened Ravana now to challenge you, have commanded me to bring it here for your use. It can fly swifter than air over all obstacles, over any mountain, sea, or sky, and will help you to emerge victorious in this battle."

Rama reflected aloud, "It may be that the rakshasas have created this illusion for me. It may be a trap. I don't know how to view it." Whereupon Matali spoke convincingly to dispel the doubt in Rama's mind. Rama, still hesitant, though partially convinced, looked at Hanuman and Lakshmana and asked, "What do you think of it?" Both answered, "We feel no doubt that this chariot is Indra's; it is not an illusory creation."

Rama fastened his sword, slung two quivers full of rare arrows over his shoulders, and climbed into the chariot.

The beat of war drums, the challenging cries of soldiers, the trumpets, and the rolling chariots speeding along to confront each other, created a deafening mixture of noise. While Ravana had

---

13. **Mandodari** (mən-dō′də-rē).
14. **Matali** (mä′tə-lē).

instructed his charioteer to speed ahead, Rama very gently ordered his chariot-driver, "Ravana is in a rage; let him perform all the antics he desires and exhaust himself. Until then be calm; we don't have to hurry forward. Move slowly and calmly, and you must strictly follow my instructions; I will tell you when to drive faster."

Ravana's assistant and one of his staunchest supporters, Mahodara[15]—the giant among giants in his physical appearance—begged Ravana, "Let me not be a mere spectator when you confront Rama. Let me have the honour of grappling with him. Permit me to attack Rama."

"Rama is my sole concern," Ravana replied. "If you wish to engage yourself in a fight, you may fight his brother Lakshmana."

Noticing Mahodara's purpose, Rama steered his chariot across his path in order to prevent Mahodara from reaching Lakshmana. Whereupon Mahodara ordered his chariot-driver, "Now dash straight ahead, directly into Rama's chariot."

The charioteer, more practical-minded, advised him, "I would not go near Rama. Let us keep away." But Mahodara, obstinate and intoxicated with war fever, made straight for Rama. He wanted to have the honour of a direct encounter with Rama himself in spite of Ravana's advice; and for this honour he paid a heavy price, as it was a moment's work for Rama to destroy him, and leave him lifeless and shapeless on the field. Noticing this, Ravana's anger mounted further. He commanded his driver, "You will not slacken now. Go." Many ominous signs were seen now—his bow-strings suddenly snapped; the mountains shook; thunders rumbled in the skies; tears flowed from the horses' eyes; elephants with decorated foreheads moved along dejectedly. Ravana, noticing them, hesitated only for a second, saying, "I don't care. This mere mortal Rama is of no account, and these omens do not concern me at all." Meanwhile, Rama

paused for a moment to consider his next step; and suddenly turned towards the armies supporting Ravana, which stretched away to the horizon, and destroyed them. He felt that this might be one way of saving Ravana. With his armies gone, it was possible that Ravana might have a change of heart. But it had only the effect of spurring Ravana on; he plunged forward and kept coming nearer Rama and his own doom.

Rama's army cleared and made way for Ravana's chariot, unable to stand the force of his approach. Ravana blew his conch[16] and its shrill challenge reverberated through space. Following it another conch, called "Panchajanya,"[17] which belonged to Mahavishnu[18] (Rama's original form before his present incarnation), sounded of its own accord in answer to the challenge, agitating the universe with its vibrations. And then Matali picked up another conch, which was Indra's, and blew it. This was the signal indicating the commencement of the actual battle. Presently Ravana sent a shower of arrows on Rama; and Rama's followers, unable to bear the sight of his body being studded with arrows, averted their heads. Then the chariot horses of Ravana and Rama glared at each other in hostility, and the flags topping the chariots—Ravana's ensign of the Veena[19] and Rama's with the whole universe on it—clashed, and one heard the stringing and twanging of bow-strings on both sides, overpowering in volume all other sound. Then followed a shower of arrows from Rama's own bow. Ravana stood gazing at the chariot sent by Indra and swore, "These gods, instead of supporting me, have gone to the support of this

---

15. **Mahodara** (mə-hō′də-rä).

16. **conch** (kŏngk): a large spiral seashell, used as a trumpet.

17. **Panchajanya** (pän′chə-jən′yə).

18. **Mahavishnu** (mə-hä′vĭsh′noō): the Supreme God in Hinduism, who divides himself into the trinity of Brahma, Vishnu, and Shiva.

19. **Veena** (vē′nə): a stringed musical instrument.

---

incarnation (ĭn′kär-nā′shən) *n.* a bodily form taken on by a spirit

petty human being. I will teach them a lesson. He is not fit to be killed with my arrows but I shall seize him and his chariot together and fling them into high heaven and dash them to destruction." Despite his oath, he still strung his bow and sent a shower of arrows at Rama, raining in thousands, but they were all invariably shattered and neutralized by the arrows from Rama's bow, which met arrow for arrow. Ultimately Ravana, instead of using one bow, used ten with his twenty arms, multiplying his attack tenfold; but Rama stood unhurt.

Ravana suddenly realized that he should change his tactics and ordered his charioteer to fly the chariot up in the skies. From there he attacked and destroyed a great many of the monkey army supporting Rama. Rama ordered Matali, "Go up in the air. Our young soldiers are being attacked from the sky. Follow Ravana, and don't slacken."

There followed an aerial pursuit at dizzying speed across the dome of the sky and rim of the earth. Ravana's arrows came down like rain; he was bent upon destroying everything in the world. But Rama's arrows diverted, broke, or neutralized Ravana's. Terror-stricken, the gods watched this pursuit. Presently Ravana's arrows struck Rama's horses and pierced the heart of Matali himself. The charioteer fell. Rama paused for a while in grief, undecided as to his next step. Then he recovered and resumed his offensive. At that moment the divine eagle Garuda was seen perched on Rama's flagpost, and the gods who were watching felt that this could be an auspicious sign.

After circling the globe several times, the duelling chariots returned, and the fight continued over Lanka. It was impossible to be very clear about the location of the battleground as the fight occurred here, there, and everywhere. Rama's arrows pierced Ravana's armour and made him wince. Ravana was so insensible to pain and impervious to attack that for him to wince was a good sign, and the gods hoped that this was a turn for the better. But at this moment, Ravana suddenly changed his tactics. Instead of merely shooting his arrows, which were powerful in themselves, he also invoked several supernatural forces to create strange effects: He was an adept in the use of various asthras[20] which could be made dynamic with special incantations. At this point, the fight became one of attack with supernatural powers, and parrying of such an attack with other supernatural powers.

Ravana realized that the mere aiming of shafts with ten or twenty of his arms would be of no avail because the mortal whom he had so contemptuously thought of destroying with a slight effort was proving formidable, and his arrows were beginning to pierce and cause pain. Among the asthras sent by Ravana was one called "Danda," a special gift from Shiva, capable of pursuing and pulverizing its target. When it came flaming along, the gods were struck with fear. But Rama's arrow neutralized it.

Now Ravana said to himself, "These are all petty weapons. I should really get down to proper business." And he invoked the one called "Maya"—a weapon which created illusions and confused the enemy.

With proper incantations and worship, he sent off this weapon and it created an illusion of reviving all the armies and its leaders—Kumbakarna and Indrajit and the others—and bringing them back to the battlefield. Presently Rama found all those who, he thought, were no

---

20. **asthras** (əs'thrəz): arrows or other weapons powered by supernatural forces.

more, coming on with battle cries and surrounding him. Every man in the enemy's army was again up in arms. They seemed to fall on Rama with victorious cries. This was very confusing and Rama asked Matali, whom he had by now revived, "What is happening now? How are all these coming back? They were dead." Matali explained, "In your original identity you are the creator of illusions in this universe. Please know that Ravana has created phantoms to confuse you. If you make up your mind, you can dispel them immediately." Matali's explanation was a great help. Rama at once invoked a weapon called "Gnana"[21]—which means "wisdom" or "perception." This was a very rare weapon, and he sent it forth. And all the terrifying armies who seemed to have come on in such a great mass suddenly evaporated into thin air.

Ravana then shot an asthra called "Thama," whose nature was to create total darkness in all the worlds. The arrows came with heads exposing frightening eyes and fangs, and fiery tongues. End to end the earth was enveloped in total darkness and the whole of creation was paralysed. This asthra also created a deluge of rain on one side, a rain of stones on the other, a hail-storm showering down intermittently, and a tornado sweeping the earth. Ravana was sure that this would arrest Rama's enterprise. But Rama was able to meet it with what was named "Shivasthra."[22] He understood the nature of the phenomenon and the cause of it and chose the appropriate asthra for counteracting it.

Ravana now shot off what he considered his deadliest weapon—a trident[23] endowed with extraordinary destructive power, once gifted to Ravana by the gods. When it started on its journey there was real panic all round. It came on flaming toward Rama, its speed or course unaffected by the arrows he flung at it.

When Rama noticed his arrows falling down

Rama and Lakshmana fight the demoness Taraka (1587–1598, India, Mughal, school of Akbar), Mushfiq. Leaf from a manuscript, opaque colors and gold on paper, 27.5 cm x 15.2 cm, courtesy of the Freer Gallery of Art, Smithsonian Institution, Washington, D.C. (07.217 35v).

21. **Gnana** (gnä′nə).

22. **Shivasthra** (shĭ-vəs′thrə).

23. **trident** (trīd′nt): a spear with three prongs.

ineffectively while the trident sailed towards him, for a moment he lost heart. When it came quite near, he uttered a certain mantra[24] from the depth of his being and while he was breathing out that incantation, an _esoteric_ syllable in perfect timing, the trident collapsed. Ravana, who had been so certain of vanquishing Rama with his trident, was astonished to see it fall down within an inch of him, and for a minute wondered if his adversary might not after all be a divine being although he looked like a mortal. Ravana thought to himself, "This is, perhaps, the highest God. Who could he be? Not Shiva, for Shiva is my supporter; he could not be Brahma, who is four faced; could not be Vishnu, because of my immunity from the weapons of the whole trinity. Perhaps this man is the _primordial_ being, the cause behind the whole universe. But whoever he may be, I will not stop my fight until I defeat and crush him or at least take him prisoner."

With this resolve, Ravana next sent a weapon which issued forth monstrous serpents vomiting fire and venom, with enormous fangs and red eyes. They came darting in from all directions.

Rama now selected an asthra called "Garuda" (which meant "eagle"). Very soon thousands of eagles were aloft, and they picked off the serpents with their claws and beaks and destroyed them. Seeing this also fail, Ravana's anger was roused to a mad pitch and he blindly emptied a quiverful of arrows in Rama's direction. Rama's arrows met them half way and turned them round so that they went back and their sharp points embedded themselves in Ravana's own chest.

Ravana was weakening in spirit. He realized that he was at the end of his resources. All his learning and equipment in weaponry were of no avail and he had practically come to the end of his special gifts of destruction. While he was going down thus, Rama's own spirit was soaring up. The combatants were now near enough to grapple with each other and Rama realized that this was the best moment to cut off Ravana's heads. He sent a crescent-shaped arrow which sliced off one of Ravana's heads and flung it far into the sea, and this process continued; but every time a head was cut off, Ravana had the benediction of having another one grown in its place. Rama's crescent-shaped weapon was continuously busy as Ravana's heads kept cropping up. Rama lopped off his arms but they grew again and every lopped-off arm hit Matali and the chariot and tried to cause destruction by itself, and the tongue in a new head wagged, uttered challenges, and cursed Rama. On the cast-off heads of Ravana, devils and minor demons, who had all along been in terror of Ravana and had obeyed and pleased him, executed a dance of death and feasted on the flesh.

Ravana was now desperate. Rama's arrows embedded themselves in a hundred places on his body and weakened him. Presently he collapsed in a faint on the floor of his chariot. Noticing his state, his charioteer pulled back and drew the chariot aside. Matali whispered to Rama, "This is the time to finish off that demon. He is in a faint. Go on. Go on."

But Rama put away his bow and said, "It is not fair warfare to attack a man who is in a faint. I will wait. Let him recover," and waited.

When Ravana revived, he was angry with his charioteer for withdrawing, and took out his sword, crying, "You have disgraced me. Those who look on will think I have retreated." But his charioteer explained how Rama suspended the fight and forebore to attack when he was in a faint. Somehow, Ravana appreciated his explanation and patted his back and resumed his attacks. Having exhausted his special weapons, in desperation Ravana began to throw on Rama

24. **mantra** (măn′trə): a word, sound, or phrase used as a prayer or spell.

WORDS
TO
KNOW
esoteric (ĕs′ə-tĕr′ĭk) _adj._ understood only by a chosen few
primordial (prī-môr′dē-əl) _adj._ first existing; original

all sorts of things such as staves, cast-iron balls, heavy rocks, and oddments he could lay hands on. None of them touched Rama, but glanced off and fell ineffectually. Rama went on shooting his arrows. There seemed to be no end of this struggle in sight.

Now Rama had to pause to consider what final measure he should take to bring this campaign to an end. After much thought, he decided to use "Brahmasthra,"[25] a weapon specially designed by the Creator Brahma on a former occasion, when he had to provide one for Shiva to destroy Tripura,[26] the old monster who assumed the forms of flying mountains and settled down on habitations and cities, seeking to destroy the world. The Brahmasthra was a special gift to be used only when all other means had failed. Now Rama, with prayers and worship, invoked its fullest power and sent it in Ravana's direction, aiming at his heart rather than his head; Ravana being vulnerable at heart. While he had prayed for indestructibility of his several heads and arms, he had forgotten to strengthen his heart, where the Brahmasthra entered and ended his career.

Rama watched him fall headlong from his chariot face down onto the earth, and that was the end of the great campaign. Now one noticed Ravana's face aglow with a new quality. Rama's arrows had burnt off the layers of dross,[27] the anger, conceit, cruelty, lust, and egotism which had encrusted his real self, and now his person-ality came through in its pristine form—of one who was devout and capable of tremendous attainments. His constant meditation on Rama, although as an adversary, now seemed to bear fruit, as his face shone with serenity and peace. Rama noticed it from his chariot above and commanded Matali, "Set me down on the ground." When the chariot descended and came to rest on its wheels, Rama got down and commanded Matali, "I am grateful for your services to me. You may now take the chariot back to Indra."

Surrounded by his brother Lakshmana and Hanuman and all his other war chiefs, Rama approached Ravana's body, and stood gazing on it. He noted his crowns and jewellery scattered piecemeal on the ground. The decorations and the extraordinary workmanship of the armour on his chest were blood-covered. Rama sighed as if to say, "What might he not have achieved but for the evil stirring within him!"

At this moment, as they readjusted Ravana's blood-stained body, Rama noticed to his great shock a scar on Ravana's back and said with a smile, "Perhaps this is not an episode of glory for me as I seem to have killed an enemy who was turning his back and retreating. Perhaps I was wrong in shooting the Brahmasthra into him." He looked so concerned at this supposed lapse on his part that Vibishana, Ravana's brother, came forward to explain. "What you have achieved is unique. I say so although it meant the death of my brother."

"But I have attacked a man who had turned his back," Rama said. "See that scar."

Vibishana explained, "It is an old scar. In ancient days, when he paraded his strength around the globe, once he tried to attack the divine elephants that guard the four directions. When he tried to catch them, he was gored in the back by one of the tuskers and that is the scar you see now; it is not a fresh one though fresh blood is flowing on it."

Rama accepted the explanation. "Honour him and cherish his memory so that his spirit may go to heaven, where he has his place. And now I will leave you to attend to his funeral arrange-ments, befitting his grandeur." ❖

---

25. **Brahmasthra** (brə-məs′thrə).

26. **Tripura** (trĭ-pōō′rə).

27. **dross:** waste matter; impurities.

Connect to the Literature

1. **What Do You Think?** What is your reaction to the battle between Rama and Ravana?

> **Comprehension Check**
> • Why does Rama lay siege to Ravana's island?
> • Name some ways in which Ravana uses illusion as a weapon.
> • How does Rama treat Ravana after killing him?

Think Critically

2. Ravana, with his 10 heads and 20 arms, would seem to have an advantage over Rama. Why do you think Rama is able to defeat him?

3. How would you describe Rama's **heroic code** of conduct?

> • the offer he sends to Ravana by messenger
> • the two chances he gives Ravana to recover
> • his strategy and behavior in battle
> • what he tells Ravana's brother after Ravana has been killed

4. Do you think that Ravana is heroic? Use evidence from the epic to support your answer.

5. **ACTIVE READING** **CLASSIFYING CHARACTERS** Look over your chart in your **READER'S NOTEBOOK** and discuss the **characters** with a partner. What generalizations can you make about the characters on each side? Remember that you can form a generalization about a character by making broad judgments based on evidence in the story.

Extend Interpretations

6. **What If?** Suppose that Trijata had let Sita believe that Rama and his brother had been killed. What do you think Sita would have done? What impact might her actions have had on Rama and the battle with Ravana?

7. **Connect to Life** In India, Rama has been celebrated as a **hero** for centuries. Compare Rama's heroic qualities with those displayed by heroes of your own country.

8. **Points of Comparison** Compare Sir Launcelot's refusal to strike Sir Gawain after he falls to the ground in *Le Morte d'Arthur* with Rama's insistence on halting the fight until Ravana comes out of a faint. What does their behavior suggest about their character and code of honor?

Literary Analysis

SUPERNATURAL ELEMENTS
Both Rama and Ravana use **supernatural elements** to try to defeat the other. Supernatural elements go beyond the bounds of reality by involving beings, powers, or events that cannot be explained by the laws of nature. Some of the supernatural elements in this excerpt from the *Ramayana* include the following:

• Indra's chariot, which has the power to "fly swifter than air over all obstacles"
• the ominous signs—mountains shaking, tears flowing from horses' eyes—that herald Ravana's attack on Rama
• asthras—arrows powered by supernatural forces

Supernatural elements are found in the literatures of nearly all cultures. In **epics,** in particular, these elements help make the characters' attributes larger-than-life.

Cooperative Learning Activity With a group of classmates, discuss the supernatural elements in this excerpt from the *Ramayana.* Then think about how the epic would be affected if it didn't include supernatural elements. Choose a scene and rewrite it, deleting those elements. What is lost? What, if anything, is gained?

REVIEW **EPIC** An **epic** is a long narrative poem, presented in an elevated or formal style, that traces the adventures of a great hero. *Beowulf* and the *Iliad* are two other epics you have read. What characteristics do these poems share with the *Ramayana?*

Choices & CHALLENGES

Writing Options

1. Rama's Speech Compose a speech that Rama might deliver to his people following his victory at Lanka. The speech should focus on Rama's own actions, courage, and faith in the face of Ravana's onslaught. Place the entry in your **Working Portfolio.**

2. Points of Comparison Compare the supernatural powers Ravana uses to trick his enemy with those Sir Launcelot wields against Sir Gawain. Then answer the following question in a brief essay: Do you think Ravana and Launcelot would have been able to defeat their opponents if they could have traded supernatural powers? Why or why not?

Activities & Explorations

1. Illustrated Battle Illustrate a battle scene described in the excerpt. You might depict the scene in one illustration or in a series of sketches. ~ **ART**

2. Battle Scene Soundtrack Using sound effects, voices, and passages from recordings, create a soundtrack that captures the mood of a battle scene or other event in the excerpt. ~ **SPEAKING AND LISTENING**

Inquiry & Research

Hidden Temple The sculpture shown on page 241 adorns Angkor Wat, a group of temples in Cambodia that were constructed in the 1100s. Long hidden by forest growth, Angkor Wat was discovered by a French naturalist in 1860. Research to find out more about the history and art of Angkor Wat. Present your findings to the class.

 More Online: Research Starter www.mcdougallittell.com

Vocabulary in Action

EXERCISE: CONTEXT CLUES Write the word that best fits in each blank.

Zing, the hero of the Zoori nation, was an ___1___ of Erg, the god of energy. According to legend, Zing was a ___2___ being, the first and greatest of the Zoori man-gods. He fought bravely from behind a ___3___ when attacked by Zud, the six-fisted demon. The nasty Zud, with his superior weapons, was a ___4___ opponent. Because of his many fists and scaly skin, Zud seemed ___5___ to harm. Zing recited an ___6___, seeking aid from his divine protectors. His words were ___7___ and meant only for heavenly ears. An army of sacred zebras arrived to help Zing in ___8___ the many swords and spears of his foe. Zing and his army proved their ___9___, easily overpowering Zud and his evil followers. Zud shouted a hateful ___10___, shook his six fists, and retired from the battlefield.

WORDS TO KNOW

esoteric	incarnation
formidable	invincibility
impervious	parrying
imprecation	primordial
incantation	rampart

Building Vocabulary For an in-depth study of context clues, see page 938.

Valmiki

First Poet of India According to current versions of the *Ramayana*, the story of Rama was told to the wise man Valmiki by the divine sage Narada. Although little is known about the poet, some scholars believe that Valmiki was indeed a man of genius. They regard him as the "first poet" of India and the inventor of the *sloka*, the poetic meter used in the *Ramayana* and popular in later Indian poetry.

Influential Epic The *Ramayana* pervades the culture of India. Over the centuries, it has been translated and adapted by many authors, including the 20th-century writer R. K. Narayan. According to Narayan, "Everyone of whatever age, outlook, education, or station in life knows the essential part of the epic and adores the main figures in it."

from **The Book of Margery Kempe**

Autobiography by MARGERY KEMPE

Connect to Your Life

Handling Stress Think of a time when you experienced a great deal of stress or anxiety—perhaps a time when you were facing a serious illness or a major change in your life. How did you handle the experience? Did you do anything special to help yourself cope?

Build Background

Religion and the Middle Ages During the Middle Ages, religion influenced all aspects of life, and the clergy was a powerful force in both spiritual and political matters. Like the rest of medieval society, the religious hierarchy was controlled by men. A woman who wished to pursue a spiritual calling was expected to join a convent or to live as a recluse. Margery Kempe did neither. Although a wife and mother, she was determined to devote her life to Christ and, at the age of 40, became a religious visionary, traveling and preaching extensively in England, Europe, and the Holy Land. In the 1430s, Kempe's story of her spiritual life, *The Book of Margery Kempe,* was first set down in manuscript. Kempe dictated the story of her spiritual

life to two different scribes, who then wrote it down. It is the earliest surviving autobiography in the English language. Kempe's account begins with the birth of her first child and describes a deeply troubling experience that would affect the course of her life.

Focus Your Reading

LITERARY ANALYSIS **AUTOBIOGRAPHY**

An **autobiography** is an account of a writer's own life, told in his or her own words. An autobiography provides revealing insights into the following subjects:

- the writer's character
- the writer's attitudes
- the writer's motivations
- the society in which the writer lived

As you read this autobiographical excerpt, be aware of details that suggest how Margery Kempe views herself and her experience.

ACTIVE READING **STRATEGIES FOR READING AUTOBIOGRAPHY**

Typically, writers of autobiographies recount their experiences in the first person, using the pronouns *I* and *me.* Margery Kempe, however, tells her story in the third person, referring to herself as "this creature" and using the pronouns *she* and *her.*

READER'S NOTEBOOK As you read Kempe's account of her experience, think of reasons why she might have chosen to use the third-person point of view and to use such phrases as "this creature." Jot down notes to indicate the effect this has on you as a reader.

from The Book of Margery Kempe

Chapter One *Illness and* Recovery

Woman tending fire and reading, from an illuminated manuscript

When this creature was twenty years of age, or somewhat more, she was married to a worshipful burgess[1] [of Lynn] and was with child within a short time, as nature would have it. And after she had conceived, she was troubled with severe attacks of sickness until the

---

1. **burgess** (bûr′jĭs): a citizen of an English town.

child was born. And then, what with the labor-pains she had in childbirth and the sickness that had gone before, she despaired of her life, believing she might not live. Then she sent for her confessor,[2] for she had a thing on her conscience which she had never revealed before that time in all her life. For she was continually hindered by her enemy—the devil—always saying to her while she was in good health that she didn't need to confess but to do penance by herself alone, and all should be forgiven, for God is merciful enough. And therefore this creature often did great penance in fasting on bread and water, and performed other acts of charity with devout prayers, but she would not reveal that one thing in confession.

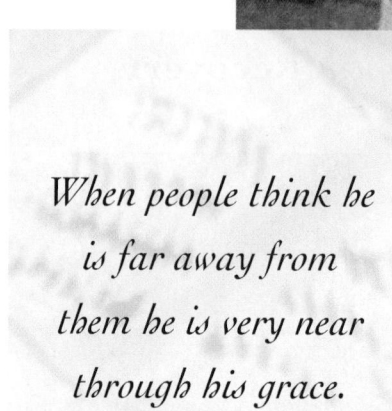

When people think he is far away from them he is very near through his grace.

And when she was at any time sick or troubled, the devil said in her mind that she should be damned, for she was not shriven[3] of that fault. Therefore, after her child was born, and not believing she would live, she sent for her confessor, as said before, fully wishing to be shriven of her whole lifetime, as near as she could. And when she came to the point of saying that thing which she had so long concealed, her confessor was a little too hasty and began sharply to reprove her before she had fully said what she meant, and so she would say no more in spite of anything he might do. And soon after, because of the dread she had of damnation on the one hand, and his sharp reproving of her on the other, this creature went out of her mind and was amazingly disturbed and tormented with spirits for half a year, eight weeks and odd days.

And in this time she saw, as she thought, devils opening their mouths all alight with burning flames of fire, as if they would have swallowed her in, sometimes pawing at her, sometimes threatening her, sometimes pulling her and hauling her about both night and day during the said time. And also the devils called out to her with great threats, and bade her that she should forsake her Christian faith and belief, and deny her God, his mother, and all the saints in heaven, her good works and all good virtues, her father, her mother, and all her friends. And so she did. She slandered her husband, her friends, and her own self. She spoke many sharp and reproving words; she recognized no virtue nor goodness; she desired all wickedness; just as the spirits tempted her to say and do, so she said and did. She would

---

2. **confessor:** spiritual adviser; the priest to whom Margery confessed her sins.

3. **shriven:** absolved; forgiven.

have killed herself many a time as they stirred her to, and would have been damned with them in hell, and in witness of this she bit her own hand so violently that the mark could be seen for the rest of her life. And also she pitilessly tore the skin on her body near her heart with her nails, for she had no other implement, and she would have done something worse, except that she was tied up and forcibly restrained both day and night so that she could not do as she wanted.

And when she had long been troubled by these and many other temptations, so that people thought she should never have escaped from them alive, then one time as she lay by herself and her keepers were not with her, our merciful Lord Christ Jesus—ever to be trusted, worshiped be his name, never forsaking his servant in time of need—appeared to his creature who had forsaken him, in the likeness of a man, the most seemly, most beauteous, and most amiable that ever might be seen with man's eye, clad in a mantle of purple silk, sitting upon her bedside, looking upon her with so blessed a countenance that she was strengthened in all her spirits, and he said to her these words: "Daughter, why have you forsaken me, and I never forsook you?"

And as soon as he had said these words, she saw truly how the air opened as bright as any lightning, and he ascended up into the air, not hastily and quickly, but beautifully and gradually, so that she could clearly behold him in the air until it closed up again.

And presently the creature grew as calm in her wits and her reason as she ever was before, and asked her husband, as soon as he came to her, if she could have the keys of the buttery[4] to get her food and drink as she had done before. Her maids and her keepers advised him that he should not deliver up any keys to her, for they said she would only give away such goods as there were, because she did not know what she was saying, as they believed.

Nevertheless, her husband, who always had tenderness and compassion for her, ordered that they should give her the keys. And she took food and drink as her bodily strength would allow her, and she once again recognized her friends and her household, and everybody else who came to her in order to see how our Lord Jesus Christ had worked his grace in her—blessed may he be, who is ever near in tribulation.[5] When people think he is far away from them he is very near through his grace. Afterwards this creature performed all her responsibilities wisely and soberly enough, except that she did not truly know our Lord's power to draw us to him.[6] ❖

---

4. **buttery:** pantry.

5. **tribulation:** suffering or distress.

6. **did not . . . power:** did not feel the full attraction of God's grace. Kempe is saying that her total devotion to the Lord did not come until later.

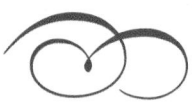

Thinking through the LITERATURE

Connect to the Literature

1. **What Do You Think?**
   How did Margery Kempe's description of her illness affect you? Share your thoughts with the class.

   Comprehension Check
   - Why does Kempe send for her confessor?
   - Why does Kempe tear her skin and bite herself?
   - Why does the vision of Christ restore her senses?

Think Critically

2. On the basis of your reading, how would you describe Margery Kempe?

   THINK ABOUT
   - her reasons for talking to a confessor
   - the way she handles stress and anxiety
   - her response to the spiritual vision

3. Do you think Kempe's account of her illness and recovery is believable? Why or why not?

4. What does Kempe's experience tell you about her society's attitude toward mental illness?

5. **ACTIVE READING** **STRATEGIES FOR READING AUTOBIOGRAPHY**
   Look at your notes in your **READER'S NOTEBOOK**. What might be some of the advantages and disadvantages of writing an autobiography in the third person?

Extend Interpretations

6. **Critic's Corner** A critic has said that Margery Kempe exhibits contradictory qualities, appearing to be both humble and forceful, both devout and arrogant. What evidence do you see in the selection of these contradictory qualities? Be specific in your answer.

7. **Different Perspectives** Assume the role of Margery Kempe's husband and describe her experience from his point of view. What additional information do you think his account might contain?

8. **Connect to Life** Think about modern attitudes toward mental illness. How do you think Margery Kempe's experiences would be viewed today? Explain your opinion.

Literary Analysis

AUTOBIOGRAPHY

An **autobiography** is a writer's account of his or her own life. Autobiographies often convey profound insights as writers recount past events from the perspective of greater understanding and distance.

Paired Activity With a partner, list various reasons why someone might be inspired to write an autobiography. Then decide which of those reasons—or what other possible reasons—might have prompted Kempe to record her life story. Share your ideas with the class.

Kempe's Reasons

Reasons for Writing an Autobiography

1. Reflect on my life
2. Tell interesting stories

Writing Options

1. **Dialogue Script** Write a script for a dialogue in which Kempe and her husband discuss her recovery after more than eight months of mental disturbances.

2. **Narrative on Survival** Think about a time when you recovered from an illness or survived a bad experience in your life. What kept you going during this difficult time? What attitudes and strategies did you use to survive? Write a personal narrative in which you describe the qualities you possess that helped you endure. Place the narrative in your **Working Portfolio.**

Activities & Explorations

1. **Visionary Art** Make a drawing or painting of one of the visions Kempe experienced during her illness. ~ **ART**

2. **Book Jacket** Design and create a book jacket for Kempe's autobiography. Use images from the selection. ~ **ART**

Inquiry & Research

Medieval Medical Care Investigate the nature of medical care during the 14th and 15th centuries. Present your findings in an oral report to the class.

Margery Kempe
1373?–1439?

First Religious Stirrings Margery Kempe was born about 1373 in Lynn—a town in the county of Norfolk, England—where her father served five terms as mayor. Although born to a prominent family, Kempe, like most women of her time, received little education. Around the age of 20, she married John Kempe, a tax collector, with whom she had 14 children. At around the age of 40, Margery Kempe decided to become a "bride of Christ"—to live in chastity and preach her visions to the world. As a vocal, outgoing speaker she was quite an oddity at a time when most women remained at home as wives and mothers. Although many men and women she met considered her a model of human compassion and devotion, many others disapproved of her lifestyle.

A Religious Life Once Kempe had made her commitment to God, she began a series of religious pilgrimages to Jerusalem, Spain, Italy, and Germany. It was in Jerusalem that she received her "gift" of weeping. She would fall into violent fits of crying at unpredictable times throughout the rest of her life, often during church services. Both the clergy and the common people found her hysterical crying at best annoying, at worst heretical. As a result, Kempe encountered a good deal of persecution and ridicule, although she maintained that her tears were a special gift from God, a physical token of her special worth in his eyes. She was also censured by many for dressing all in white, which at the time was a symbol of both chastity and piety.

Her Life Story Her autobiography, *The Book of Margery Kempe,* is important for several reasons. The work serves as a sort of time capsule, preserving for the reader the social customs, speech, and attitudes of the day. It also reveals the singular character of Kempe herself, a strong woman of faith who lived by her convictions despite intense social criticism and opposition. Finally, as an autobiography it is unique in its purpose: Kempe felt her story to be worth the telling not as a record of her life, which she probably thought too unimportant to merit a written account, but as a testament to God's power and his wonderful dealings with "this creature" Margery Kempe.

Author Activity

Words into Print Margery Kempe's autobiography has had an unusual publishing history. Check an encyclopedia, biography, the Internet, or some other reference source to find out how her words made their way into print.

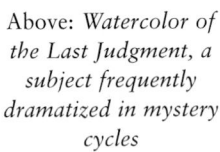

Above: *Watercolor of the Last Judgment, a subject frequently dramatized in mystery cycles*

Above right: *Miniature from a manuscript of* Li Romans d'Alixandre *(about 1340), showing people wearing animal masks, perhaps for an entertainment at court*

Mystery, Miracle, & Morality *Plays*

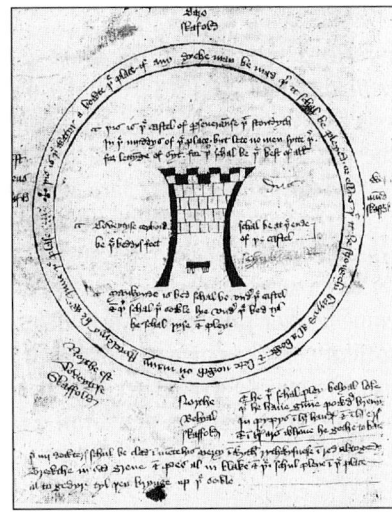

Staging diagram for The Castle of Perseverance, *one of the earliest surviving English morality plays*

During the early Middle Ages, in order to make church teachings accessible to the common people, clergymen began to dramatize stories from the Bible and episodes from the lives of saints. The clerics themselves played the roles in the dramas, bringing sacred history to life as part of church services. These dramatized stories soon became a popular part of church life.

As time passed, these plays developed into more elaborate productions, known as **mystery plays** (the biblical dramas) and **miracle plays** (the dramas of saints' lives), that were unsuitable for performance inside a church. The job of presenting the mystery plays was taken over by trade and craft guilds, or unions. Each guild took responsibility for one or two plays, building a pageant wagon and making costumes, props, and scenery. On a feast day, the guilds would load their props and scenery onto their wagons, form a procession, and take turns performing the plays at prearranged sites. Together, the plays formed what is called a mystery cycle, covering the whole history of the world, from the creation of Adam and Eve to the Last Judgment.

The mystery cycles were fabulous events. They often ran from sunrise to sunset, sometimes for three or more days, and included music, dance, comedy skits, and special effects to create the illusion of rain, lightning, and flying. These spectacular productions whetted the English appetite for drama. By the 1400s, professional acting troupes were traveling the countryside, performing plays of their own—called **morality plays**—that dealt with the moral struggles of everyday people.

Morality plays dramatized the inner conflicts of characters such as Everyman, an average man who is summoned by Death. Everyman tries to soften his fate by appealing to friends with names like Kindred and Fellowship, but in the face of Death they desert him. He can bring only Good Deeds along with him to the grave.

The message, of course, was crystal clear, but the play *Everyman* was more than a sermon or fable. To a large extent, morality plays such as this represented a step away from the religious drama and toward a popular English secular drama. By the 1500s, morality plays were a regular part of street pageants and began to adopt elements of court entertainments, such as mummers plays (pantomimes), tournaments, and masquerades.

As morality plays grew more varied and sophisticated, their popularity increased. The English people became a nation of theatergoers, and a wide range of dramatic entertainments became part of England's cultural life. In this way, the morality plays—like the mystery and miracle plays before them—set the stage for Elizabethan drama and the genius of playwrights like William Shakespeare.

Above:
Woodcut illustrating John Skot's edition of Everyman *(about 1503)*

Left:
In a mystery cycle, a trade or craft guild might produce a play related to its members' occupation. A shipbuilders' guild, for example, might produce a play about Noah's ark.

Writing Workshop — Application Essay

Presenting yourself positively . . .

From Reading to Writing *Le Morte d'Arthur* and *Sir Gawain and the Green Knight* reflect the ideal medieval virtues of honor, courage, and loyalty. Although the characters in these legends do not always achieve their goals, they are generally portrayed in a positive light. One way to present yourself in a positive way is through an **application essay,** often part of applying to college or for a job. Writing an application essay gives you an opportunity to reflect on the meaning of a significant experience in your life and to reveal your interests, achievements, and abilities for others to judge.

For Your Portfolio

WRITING PROMPT Write an application essay in which you reflect on the significance of an important experience or achievement that has special meaning to you.

Purpose: To present information about yourself that would encourage a college to admit you

Audience: Members of a college admissions committee

Basics in a Box

Application Essay at a Glance

Introduction
Begins with a hook, or attention-grabbing detail

Body
• Tells about your significant experience
• Reveals your qualities, interests, and abilities
• Shows that you can organize thoughts and express yourself

Conclusion
Summarizes the effects of the experience on your life

RUBRIC Standards for Writing

A successful application essay should

• reflect a thoughtful response to the application prompt

• identify and describe a significant experience or achievement

• explain what the experience or achievement means to you

• be written honestly in your own voice and from your personal experience

• have an engaging introduction

• reflect careful attention to grammar, style, and organization

Analyzing a Student Model

**Jennifer Talon
Truman High School**

Whomp!

My friends and I have a special word to perfectly describe an "ah hah experience." The word is *Whomp!* We use this word to describe what happens when something really hits us hard. For example: "I left my accounting project at home, and, Whomp!, Mrs. Winslow gave me *six* extra assignments as a consequence!" Or, "I couldn't believe he took her out. Whomp! It's really over between us."

Okay. I hope you now have an idea of the significance of the word. With that as background I can tell you about the biggest Whomp! of my life. It happened early in October of my junior year. I was with a group of friends at a cabin in the hills of eastern Iowa. While I was standing on a balcony approximately thirty-five feet above the rocky terrain, the supports under the balcony gave way. Luckily for me, the ground broke my fall; unluckily, my leg did the same. One minute I was a healthy, mobile sixteen-year-old and, Whomp!, the next I had a leg in about fourteen different pieces, with some of those pieces protruding through a gaping wound.

My memories of the next few days are rather hazy. I can remember my mother's worried face hovering over me from time to time. I remember being told that I'd been through surgery and that they'd (the wondrous orthopedists) packed the bones together and fastened them at each end with pins. "Cool. You'll beep the airport metal detectors, Jen," my brother told me. Well, I'd also have sore armpits (crutches became my best friend and worst brother), and a cast up to my hip for six months. It seemed like an eternity.

Physical pain was the least of my worries. Whomp! People stared at me now. I couldn't take a shower. I couldn't go jogging. I couldn't stand for very long. I couldn't be on the track team. I couldn't get down to the newspaper room at school. I could watch TV—small compensation. I felt totally helpless and very frustrated at times. I needed help getting dressed, and getting to class, and getting into the car. . . .

RUBRIC
IN ACTION

❶ The writer begins with an unusual hook that sets an engaging, humorous tone.

Other Options:
- Begin with a general concept (such as a quote or proverb) that will be tested or proved by your own experience
- Open with a dramatic thesis statement

❷ The writer focuses on the details of one incident, described chronologically.

Other Options:
- Tell several anecdotes that highlight your different qualities
- Describe more recent events first, then tell what led up to them

❸ Uses vivid details and narrative techniques to draw readers into the scene

❹ Brings up extracurricular activities by weaving them into the story

Wait a minute, this cast is only going to be on for six more months. Whomp! Some people are like this for their entire life. Some people have much worse problems that they must deal with every day of their existence with no light at the end of a six-month tunnel.

This really got me thinking. What would it be like to be physically disabled? Dependent your whole life? These insights made me want to get involved. They made me want to do something to make a difference.

Now it's my senior year. Students with disabilities (trainable mentally retarded kids, some with physical disabilities, too) have been brought to Westside for their Special Education classes. I went to see the Department Head of Special Education. Together we devised a club called Peer Advocates, which is like a buddy system between the regular education and special-education kids. We have tried to pair the non-disabled with the disabled students according to interests and personalities. Each pair is required to spend at least four hours a month together. We are also planning several group field trips to places like the zoo and the bowling alley.

Organizing this group has been one of the most meaningful things I've ever done. Now kids of two totally different lifestyles are going out to lunch together and learning things about each other that they could never have learned from reading a book or studying disabilities. We are all learning compassion and tolerance and understanding. As for myself, I feel as though I'm doing something extremely worthwhile. For example, one morning, after a breakfast meeting of the group, a boy with Down's Syndrome named David walked up to me with a huge smile and gave me a great bear hug. He told me that he was so happy to have a special friend at Westside and thanked me. That was all I needed to know that the idea had been a good one.

Breaking my leg and its aftermath of pain and frustration was one experience I'd never want to go through again. But what it taught me was invaluable and I wouldn't change it for the world. It was a definite Whomp!

❺ Repeats the hook to create a transition into the major accomplishment described next

❻ *Shows* through an example that she cares about her subject *and* that the experience was important to her

❼ Concludes with a brief summary of her main point

Writing Your Application Essay

❶ Prewriting

One writes out of one thing only—one's own experience.
James Baldwin

Begin with the directions on your application. Many college-essay prompts invite you to tell about how something or someone affected your life. Try listing turning points in your life and people who have influenced you along the way. See the **Idea Bank** in the margin for more topic suggestions.

   Choose a topic that you truly care about, then consider how you can best use it to represent yourself to the application committee. The important thing is to write about your experiences meaningfully and demonstrate how they contributed to your personal growth. You are more likely to write a forceful, engaging essay if you stay true to your interests and experience.

Planning Your Application Essay

▶ **1. Carefully consider the prompt.** What information should be included in the response? Note that the prompt on page 260 asks you to reflect on the significance of an important experience—not just retell it.

▶ **2. Examine your strengths.** What personal qualities, talents, and accomplishments are you most proud of? What experiences have had special meanings for you?

▶ **3. Think about your experience.** Why is it important to you? What meaning or significance can you draw from it?

▶ **4. Determine a focus.** What is the overall point you want to make? Which of your achievements or experiences best supports your reflections on your own learning and growth?

❷ Drafting

There are many approaches you can take in writing a reflective essay. Like the writer of the student model, you could focus on a particular event and use it to reveal an aspect of yourself. Or, you could show how several similar events have influenced you in significant ways. Whatever the approach, keep it focused—don't try to tell everything about yourself.

   As you draft your essay, include **details, description,** and **dialogue,** if appropriate to engage the readers. Give extra attention to writing a strong beginning. The opening should be engaging and informative without sounding contrived. It needs to catch the interest of an admissions officer, who has to read a stack of applications.

Ask Your Peer Reader

• What experience or achievement is my essay about?

• Why is the experience I talk about important to me?

• What is the most important thing you learn about me from this essay?

• In what places can I improve my voice to avoid sounding contrived?

IDEABank

1. **Your Working Portfolio**
Build on the Writing Options you completed earlier in this unit:
• **Essay On Virtues,** p. 238
• **Rama's Speech,** p. 251
• **Narrative on Survival,** p. 257

2. **Time Line**
Make a time line of your life, listing important events and accomplishments in your past. Look at the time line and identify major turning points.

3. **Notebook**
Write down the essay prompt (or prompts) in a notebook or on an index card. Keep this with you for several days, and write down ideas as you think about the essay.

Have a Question?

See the **Writing Handbook**
Elaboration, p. 1361
Descriptive Writing, pp. 1363–1364

Need help with active and passive voice?

See the **Grammar Handbook,** pp. 1397 and 1426.

❸ Revising

TARGET SKILL ▶ USING THE ACTIVE VOICE Writing sentences in the active voice produces a more lively and engaging style, which helps draw readers in. It also helps place the focus on you as the main achiever in your story. While the passive voice is sometimes necessary, choosing the active voice can make your writing stronger and more fluent.

> *the counselors plan*
> Each day, a new lesson ~~is planned~~ based on events that
> *arose*
> occurred the previous day. For example, if a conflict,
> *the staff might organize*
> between two campers ~~was revealed,~~ a trust activity
> ~~might be done~~ for the next day.

❹ Editing and Proofreading

TARGET SKILL ▶ SUBJECT-VERB AGREEMENT When rewriting from passive to active voice, be sure to check that your subjects and verbs agree, particularly when a word or phrase separates the subject from the verb. Also, keep in mind that a college essay should be a polished piece of work—so edit and proofread everything carefully.

> *Each day*
> Under my guidance, a special group of kids
> *s*
> learn the basics of swimming. In return, I, along with
> the rest of the staff, receives a valuable lesson in
> courage and perseverance.

Uncertain about agreement?

See the **Grammar Handbook,** pp. 1410, 1417, and 1421.

Publishing
IDEAS

- Submit your essay to the college of your choice.
- In a group, read your essays aloud, then role-play the response of an application review committee.

More Online: Publishing Options
www.mcdougallittell.com

❺ Reflecting

FOR YOUR WORKING PORTFOLIO What did you discover about yourself while completing your application essay? How did writing about yourself help you understand your strengths better? Attach your answer to your finished essay. Save your application essay in your **Working Portfolio.**

Read this opening from the first draft of an application essay. The underlined sections include the following kinds of errors:

- **using active and passive voice**
- **subject-verb agreement**
- **verb tense errors**
- **sentence fragments**

For each underlined phrase or sentence, choose the revision that most improves the writing.

It just took two little words to change everything: "We're moving." One simple sentence <u>was uprooting</u> my whole life. <u>How could I have anticipated the</u>
(1)   (2)
<u>challenges? Never predicted the rewards.</u>

Of course, at the beginning I <u>loathe</u> the idea. <u>I was overwhelmed by even</u>
(3)   (4)
<u>the thought of moving.</u> Fourteen years <u>are</u> a long time to live in one house. It
(5)
was hard to imagine coming home to a strange house or doing homework in a
foreign kitchen. <u>You see, change still made me nervous then.</u>
(6)

---

1. **A.** had been uprooting
   B. uprooted
   C. will uproot
   D. Correct as is

2. **A.** How could I have anticipated the challenges or predicted the rewards?
   B. I could never have anticipated the challenges. Never predicted the rewards.
   C. How could I have anticipated the challenges, predicted the rewards.
   D. Correct as is

3. **A.** loathes
   B. loathed
   C. was loathing
   D. Correct as is

4. **A.** I had been overwhelmed by even the thought of moving.
   B. I was being overwhelmed by even the thought of moving.
   C. Even the thought of moving overwhelmed me.
   D. Correct as is

5. **A.** is
   B. is being
   C. are being
   D. will be

6. **A.** You see. Change still made me nervous then.
   B. Then, you see, I was still made nervous by change.
   C. You see, change is still making me nervous then.
   D. Correct as is

Need extra help?

See the **Grammar Handbook**

Active and passive voice, p. 1397

Subject-verb agreement, p. 1410

Verb tenses, p. 1426

Sentence fragments, p. 1409

Matching Meanings to Contexts

Language is constantly evolving to meet the needs of those who use it. As a result, many words have acquired more than one meaning. One such word is *craft*, which comes from the Old English word *cræft*, meaning "strength." Compare the ways in which *craft* is used in the sentences on the right.

In the first sentence, *craft* means "skill in deception or evasion"; in the second, *craft* refers to a boat or small ship. *Craft* can also mean "proficiency, skill, and dexterity" or "to make in a skillful manner by hand." Note that over time the original meaning of the word—"strength"—was extended to refer to various kinds of skill.

> With craft and guile, Sir Modred persuaded the people to turn against their king.

> As King Arthur with his fleet drew into the harbor, Sir Modred and his army launched forth in every available craft.
> —Sir Thomas Malory, *Le Morte d'Arthur*, retold by Keith Baines

Strategies for Building Vocabulary

As you read, be alert to words that do not mean what you'd expect. Then use the following strategies to increase your understanding of the new words.

❶ **Use Context Clues to Determine Meaning** When you encounter a word that is used in an unexpected way, begin by using the sense of the sentences that surround the word to figure out the word's meaning. Read the passage below.

> "Sir Gawain, why these insults? I have the measure of your strength and you can do me but little harm."
> "Come forth, traitor, and this time I shall make good my revenge!" Sir Gawain shouted.
> —*Le Morte d'Arthur*

You can tell from the context that the two men have met before and that the first speaker is not concerned about the abilities of the second. These clues help you determine that in this context, *measure* means "a knowledge of the limits of the other's strength and skill," and that *make good* means "to fulfill."

❷ **Look Up the Word in a Dictionary** Sometimes you may need more help than context clues provide. To determine the appropriate meaning of a word with multiple definitions, locate the word in a dictionary and read through the definitions in order to identify the one that makes the most sense in the sentence.

Occasionally you will discover that a word appears to have two entries in the dictionary. These are actually separate words called **homonyms**—words with the same pronunciation and spelling but different meanings and origins. One such word is *pale*. What meaning does it have in each sentence below?

> Sir Lancelot was banished because his actions were beyond the *pale*.
> As a ruler, Sir Modred was a *pale* substitute for King Arthur.

Be aware that writers, especially poets, may intentionally use words in ways that evoke both literal and symbolic meanings. Note the double meaning of *age* in this quote "Every age has its pleasures." *Age* can be taken to mean the stages in a person's life or a time period in history.

EXERCISE Use a dictionary or context clues to define each underlined word in these passages from *Le Morte d'Arthur*.

1. "The issue of a mare has failed me; but I am the issue of a king and a queen and I shall not fail!" he exclaimed.
2. They were received by the gentle knight Sir Lucas the Butler.
3. "My lord King Arthur, it is with a heavy heart that I set forth to do battle."
4. "Surely our honor demands that we pursue this war to its proper conclusion."
5. "It is too late now to sue for peace."

Grammar from Literature

Expert writers craft sentences that express ideas as efficiently and effectively as possible. Using more advanced sentence structures can help add variety to your writing and show relationships between ideas.

A **compound sentence** is used to connect two ideas of equal importance. It consists of two independent clauses, which are clauses that can stand alone as sentences. The independent clauses in a compound sentence are separated by a semicolon or by a comma and coordinating conjunction such as *and, but,* and *or.*

> independent   independent
> clause   semicolon   clause
> **"Sir Gawain, I have once spared your life; should you not beware of meddling with me again?"**
> —Sir Thomas Malory, *Le Morte d'Arthur*
>
> independent   independent
> clause   conjunction   clause
> **I know your worth and price, and my debt's by no means slight.**
> —*Sir Gawain and the Green Knight*

A **complex sentence** consists of one independent clause and at least one subordinate clause. The independent clause contains the main idea, and the subordinate clause contains a related, less important idea. A subordinate clause is a clause that cannot stand alone as a sentence. A subordinate clause often begins with a subordinating conjunction, such as *if* and *when.*

> subordinate clause   independent clause
> **If you remain within the city, soon everything will be destroyed.**
> —*Le Morte d'Arthur*
>
> independent clause   subordinate clause
> **I never moved a muscle when you came down.**
> —*Sir Gawain and the Green Knight*

The following example shows how you can combine two simple sentences into one complex sentence by adding the subordinating conjunction *when.*

> SEPARATE
> **King Arthur leaves Britain to fight Sir Launcelot. Modred decides to take control of the throne.**
>
> COMBINED
> **When King Arthur leaves Britain to fight Sir Launcelot, Modred decides to take control of the throne.**

Usage Tip If you use a comma between the two independent clauses in a compound sentence, you must also include a coordinating conjunction. Not using a coordinating conjunction results in a type of run-on sentence known as a comma splice.

> INCORRECT
>   no conjunction
> **The Green Knight's head was cut off, it didn't seem to bother him much.**
>
> CORRECT
>   conjunction
> **The Green Knight's head was cut off, but it didn't seem to bother him much.**

Punctuation Tip When a complex sentence begins with a subordinate clause, a comma should appear at the end of the subordinate clause. If the subordinate clause appears at the end of the sentence, it is not preceded by a comma.

> **After she gave birth to her first child, Margery Kempe became seriously ill.**
>
> **Margery Kempe became seriously ill after she gave birth to her first child.**

WRITING EXERCISE Rewrite each sentence or pair of sentences below, following the directions that appear at the end of each exercise.

1. The Green Knight has a big bushy beard. His war horse has a green mane. (Make a compound sentence that includes a conjunction.)
2. The Green Knight issues a challenge. King Arthur's knights at first do not know what to do. (Make a complex sentence that includes the word *when.*)
3. Arthur runs Modred through with a spear. However, then Modred mortally wounds Arthur. (Make a compound sentence, replacing one of the words with the word *but.*)
4. Sir Bedivere must throw Excalibur into the lake, or King Arthur will not be taken to Avalon. (Make a complex sentence beginning with the word *if,* replacing the word *must* with different words and omitting *or.*)
5. If Margery Kempe does not stop seeing demons, she will not be able to take care of her child. (Make a compound sentence by omitting some words and adding the words *or else.*)

The Anglo-Saxon and Medieval Periods

How has reading the selections in this unit added to your understanding of the Anglo-Saxon and medieval periods? What new insights did you gain into life during these times, and how does it compare with life as you know it? Explore these questions by completing one or more options in each of the following sections.

Reflecting on the Unit

OPTION 1

Comparing Challenges Many of the people you have encountered in this unit—both real and fictitious—endure physical, spiritual, and emotional challenges. Select an individual from each of the three parts of the unit, and then write a few paragraphs comparing the ways in which the three people confront their challenges. Explain which person's methods of coping with adversity might be most useful in today's society.

OPTION 2

Resetting the Scene With a small group of classmates, discuss which selections in this unit stand out in your mind as being most representative of life in medieval times. Then choose a scene from one of these selections and perform it as a short skit for the rest of the class. If possible, use costumes and background music to help you convey the feeling of the period.

OPTION 3

Role-Playing With four or five classmates, hold a "meeting of the minds" in which you role-play several heroic individuals from this unit who sit down to reflect on their lives and times. You may wish to have them praise, criticize, or question one another's actions as they are depicted in the selections.

Self ASSESSMENT

📖 **READER'S NOTEBOOK**

Make a list of the impressions you had about people of the Anglo-Saxon and medieval periods before you read the selections in Unit One. Then note whether your reading has confirmed these preconceptions or proved them wrong.

Reviewing Literary Concepts

Understanding the Epic Across Cultures This unit contains excerpts from three epics, each originating in a different culture: *Beowulf* (Anglo-Saxon culture), the *Iliad* (Ancient Greek culture), and the *Ramayana* (Indian culture). Look back at the list of characteristics that most epics share (page 29). In terms of these characteristics, what do the three epics have in common? How would you explain these similarities?

Character	Main Conflict	Type of Conflict
Beowulf	He must battle with Grendel and the fire dragon.	External

OPTION 2

Assessing Conflict The individuals portrayed in this unit become involved in a variety of conflicts, both external and internal. In a chart similar to the one shown, list at least six characters or historical figures from the unit. Describe the main conflict that each faces, and note whether that conflict is external or internal. Are most of the conflicts external, or internal? What kinds of problems would you say the people of these times were concerned with?

📁 Building Your Portfolio

- **Writing Options** Many of the Writing Options in this unit asked you to assume the identities of characters and people depicted in the selections. From your responses, choose two that you think are particularly successful at conveying the individuals' personalities. In a cover note, explain what you think makes each piece of writing so effective. Then add the pieces and the cover notes to your **Presentation Portfolio.** 📁

- **Writing Workshops** In this unit, you wrote a Personality Profile based on a person of interest and an Application Essay in which you focused on a way to present yourself in a positive light. Reread these pieces and assess the quality of the writing. Would you like to keep either or both of these pieces for inclusion in your **Presentation Portfolio?** 📁 If so, attach a note indicating the strengths and weaknesses of the writing.

- **Additional Activities** Think back to any of the assignments you completed under **Activities & Explorations** and **Inquiry & Research.** Keep a record in your portfolio of any assignments that you think are representative of your best work.

Self ASSESSMENT

📖 READER'S NOTEBOOK
On a sheet of paper, copy the following list of literary terms introduced in this unit. Put a question mark next to each term that you do not fully understand. Consult the **Glossary of Literary Terms** (page 1328) to clarify the meanings of the terms you've marked with question marks.

alliteration	plot
simile	conflict
epic simile	ballad
historical writing	romance
kenning	characterization
tone	supernatural elements
moral tale	autobiography
narrator	

Self ASSESSMENT

Review the pieces you have chosen to include so far in your **Presentation Portfolio.** 📁 What generalizations can you make about your writing strengths and interests?

Setting GOALS

As you work through the reading and writing activities in the unit, you probably became aware of areas in which your work could use some improvement. After thinking over the work you did for this unit, create a list of skills or concepts that you would like to work on in the next unit.

LITERATURE CONNECTIONS
Beowulf

Anonymous, translated by Burton Raffel

Read this epic masterpiece in its entirety to find out more about the exploits of the great Anglo-Saxon warrior. Swords and shields, monsters and dragons, sailing ships and spears play an important part in this powerful tale of heroism. Beowulf sails the seas in search of adventure, and by doing great deeds he wins honor and fame for himself and his people. Beowulf and his adventures reveal how the Anglo-Saxons viewed good and evil, life and death.

These thematically related readings are provided along with *Beowulf*:

The Wanderer
ANONYMOUS, TRANSLATED BY
BURTON RAFFEL

Beowulf
BY RICHARD WILBUR

from **Grendel**
BY JOHN GARDNER

Beowulf
BY MAURICE SAGOFF

from **Gilgamesh**
ANONYMOUS, TRANSLATED BY
HERBERT MASON

David and Goliath
from **The King James Bible**

Anger *from*
The Seven Deadly Sins
BY LINDA PASTAN

from **A Gathering of Heroes**
BY GREGORY ALAN-WILLIAMS

And Even *More* . . .

Grendel

JOHN GARDNER

This modern retelling of the *Beowulf* story from Grendel's point of view provides an inside look at the mind of a monster. Told with equal parts of humor and horror, the tale makes the point that even monsters have a story to tell.

Books
Beowulf
GEORGE CLARK
A recent, widely available critical study.

Eaters of the Dead
MICHAEL CRICHTON
The popular author resets *Beowulf* among 10th-century Vikings in a novel disguised as nonfiction.

The Life and Times of Chaucer
JOHN GARDNER
A lively biography of the poet by the author of *Grendel.*

from **The Canterbury Tales**

GEOFFREY CHAUCER

A matchless array of humanity passes before the reader's eyes in Chaucer's brilliant collection of related stories, *The Canterbury Tales*. Chaucer views his pilgrims with a wise tolerance and a gentle humor that communicate his deep understanding of the paths, both crooked and straight, taken by different people. This book expands your enjoyment of Chaucer by offering several more of his classic tales.

These thematically related readings are provided along with *The Canterbury Tales*:

LITERATURE CONNECTIONS

The Canterbury Tales
SELECTED WORKS
Geoffrey Chaucer

and Related Readings

from **The Life and Times of Chaucer**
BY JOHN GARDNER

from **The Author's Introduction to The Decameron**
BY GIOVANNI BOCCACCIO, TRANSLATED BY MARK MUSA AND PETER E. BONDANELLA

from **The Art of Courtly Love**
BY ANDREAS CAPELLANUS, TRANSLATED BY JOHN JAY PARRY

Laüstic (the Nightingale)
BY MARIE DE FRANCE

from **The Romance of Reynard the Fox**
ANONYMOUS FABLE, TRANSLATED BY D. D. R. OWEN

The Second Shepherds' Play *from* The Wakefield Mystery Cycle
EDITED BY MARTIAL ROSE

from **The Autobiography of Malcolm X**
BY MALCOLM X, WITH ALEX HALEY

Chaucer Aboard a Spaceship
BY NAOSHI KORIYAMA

The Hobbit
J.R.R. TOLKIEN
This famous fantasy of Middle Earth draws on the author's profound knowledge of Anglo-Saxon life and literature.

The Aeneid
VIRGIL, TRANSLATED BY ROBERT FITZGERALD
This epic poem about the founding of Rome by the hero Aeneas was modeled on Homer's *Iliad* and *Odyssey*. Virgil's poem illustrates the ancient virtues of heroism, filial devotion, piety, and dedication to Rome.

Other Media
Beowulf
Old English poetry, including "The Wanderer" and passages from *Beowulf*.
(AUDIOCASSETTE)

The Canterbury Tales
Tim Pigott-Smith, Prunella Scales, and other British actors read "The Prologue," "The Pardoner's Tale," and "The Wife of Bath's Tale," as well as other tales in modern English.
(AUDIOCASSETTES)

The Dark Ages: Europe After the Fall of Rome
Includes reenactments of dramatic moments in the development of Medieval Europe.
(VIDEOCASSETTE)

A Prologue to Chaucer
Originally produced in 1986 by the University of California, Berkeley, this video relates characters and themes of *The Canterbury Tales* to everyday life in late 14th-century England.
(VIDEOCASSETTE)

UNIT TWO

No man is an island,
entire of itself;
every man is a piece of the
continent,
a part of the main.

John Donne
poet

1485–1660

The ENGLISH Renaissance

Detail of the altarpiece of the *Virgin of the Navigators* (16th century), Alejo Fernández. Seville, Spain, Reales Alcázares.

The ENGLISH
Renaissance

EVENTS IN BRITISH LITERATURE

1450   **1500**

c. 1495 *Everyman*, earliest morality play, written anonymously (printed c. 1530)

1516 Thomas More publishes *Utopia*, written in Latin (published in English c. 1551) ➤

1557 Tottel's anthology *Miscellany*, originally *Songs and Sonnets*, published, containing 97 poems attributed to Sir Thomas Wyatt

c. 1576 Edmund Spenser writes his first poetry

EVENTS IN BRITAIN

1450   **1500**   **1550**

1485 Henry Tudor defeats Richard III and takes throne as Henry VII

1509 Reign of Henry VIII begins (to 1547) ➤

1534 At insistence of Henry VIII, England breaks with Roman Catholic Church

1536 Henry VIII unites England and Wales

1547 Reign of Edward VI begins

1553 Reign of Mary I begins

1558 Reign of Elizabeth I begins (to 1603) ➤

EVENTS IN THE WORLD

1450   **1500**   **1550**

1492 Columbus sails to Bahamas in Western Hemisphere

c. 1502 First slaves exported from Africa for work in Americas

1517 Martin Luther begins Reformation, creating Protestant Christians

1520 Suleiman I begins reign as Ottoman sultan (to 1566)

1521 Cortés conquers Aztecs in Mexico

1522 Magellan's crew sails around world

PERIOD PIECES

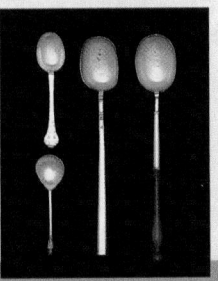

Household items

Early microscope

Engraved floral clock
from mid-17th century

1600   1650

c. 1587 Christopher Marlowe's tragedy *Tamburlaine the Great* establishes blank verse as main form in English drama

c. 1590 Shakespeare, settled in London, begins career as playwright

1597 First edition of Bacon's *Essays* published

1604 James I appoints scholars who begin creating new translation of Bible

c. 1606 Shakespeare's *Macbeth* produced

1633 John Donne's *Poems* published posthumously

1643 John Milton's pamphlet *Areopagitica* attacks press censorship

1658 Milton begins composing *Paradise Lost*

1600   1650

1580 Sir Francis Drake brings great treasures back to England after sailing around world

1588 English navy defeats Spanish Armada

1603 James VI of Scotland becomes king of England as James I (to 1625)

1605 Gunpowder Plot uncovered, saving life of James I

1607 English establish Jamestown colony in Virginia

1620 English Pilgrims establish colony in Plymouth, Massachusetts

1625 Reign of Charles I begins

1642 English Civil War begins (to 1649)

1649 Charles I beheaded

1660 Monarchy restored with accession of Charles II

1600   1650

1543 Theory of Polish astronomer, Nicolaus Copernicus, that earth and other planets revolve around sun, published

1547 Ivan the Terrible seizes power in Russia, becoming first czar (to 1584)

1590 Dutch eyeglass-maker Zacharias Janssen invents microscope

1603 Japan's Tokugawa regime begins (to 1868)

1609 Italian scientist Galileo Galilei studies heavens with telescope

1633 Galileo condemned for supporting Copernicus's theory

1643 Louis XIV begins 72-year reign in France

1644 Ming Dynasty collapses, replaced by the Qing Dynasty, China's last (to 1912)

The ENGLISH

Renaissance
1485–1660

At certain points in history, factors converge to cause dramatic shifts in human values and perceptions. One such shift, beginning in 14th-century Italy, launched the period of European history known as the Renaissance ("rebirth"). During the Renaissance, the medieval world view, focused on religion and the afterlife, was replaced by a more modern view, stressing human life here on earth. Renaissance Europeans delighted in the arts and literature, in the beauty of nature, in human impulses, and in a new sense of mastery over the world. They reinterpreted Europe's pre-Christian past, using the arts and philosophies of ancient Greece and Rome as models for their own achievements. Surging with creative energy, they expanded the scientific, geographical, and philosophical boundaries of the medieval world, often questioning timeworn truths and challenging authority. A new emphasis was placed on the individual and on the development of human potential. The ideal "Renaissance man" was a many-faceted person who cultivated his innate talents to the fullest.

In England, political instability delayed the advent of Renaissance ideas, but they began to penetrate English society after 1485, when the Wars of the Roses ended and Henry Tudor took the throne as Henry VII. A shrewd if colorless monarch, Henry exercised strong authority at home and negotiated favorable commercial treaties abroad. He built up the nation's merchant fleet and financed expeditions that established English claims in the New World. He also engineered a clever political alliance by arranging

Above: Henry VIII
Right: Self-portrait of Leonardo da Vinci, artistic and scientific genius of the Italian Renaissance

for his eldest son, Arthur, to marry Catherine of Aragon, daughter of King Ferdinand and Queen Isabella of Spain, England's greatest New World rival. When Arthur died unexpectedly, the pope granted a special dispensation allowing Arthur's younger brother Henry, the new heir to the throne, to marry Catherine. The marriage would have startling consequences.

Stained-glass panels depicting Henry VIII and Catherine of Aragon

THE REIGN OF HENRY VIII

Henry VIII succeeded his father in 1509. A true Renaissance prince, Henry was a skilled athlete, poet, and musician, well educated in French, Italian, and Latin. During his reign, the Protestant Reformation was sweeping northern Europe, propelled by discontent with church abuses and a growing nationalism that resented the influence of Rome. While many in England sympathized with Protestant reforms, Henry at first remained loyal to Rome.

However, after 18 years of marriage he had only one child, Mary, and he became obsessed with producing a male heir. Insisting that the papal dispensation had been a mistake, he requested that his marriage be annulled so that he could wed Catherine's court attendant Anne Boleyn. When the pope refused to comply, Henry broke with Rome and in 1534 declared himself head of the Church of England, or Anglican Church.

Anne Boleyn

Development of the English Language

During the 1400s, the pronunciation of most English long vowels changed, in what is referred to as the Great Vowel Shift. In addition, the final *e* in words like *take* was no longer pronounced. By 1500, Middle English had evolved into an early form of the modern English spoken today. In spite of the changes in pronunciation, however, early printers continued to use Middle English spellings— retaining, for example, the *k* and *e* in *knave*, even though the letters were no longer pronounced. This practice resulted in many of the inconsistent spellings for which modern English is known.

Printing helped stabilize the language, so that the differences between Renaissance English and our own are comparatively minor. Nevertheless, there are some differences. In the Renaissance, *thou, thee, thy,* and *thine* were used for familiar address, while *you, your,* and *yours* were reserved for more formal and impersonal situations. Renaissance speakers and writers also distinguished between "this tree" (near), "that tree" (farther), and "yon tree" (even farther). They used the verb ending -*est* or -*st* with the second-person singular subject *thou* ("thou leadest," "thou canst") and -*eth* or -*th* with third-person singular subjects ("she looketh," "he doth"). They also used fewer helping verbs, especially in questions ("Saw you the bird?").

The English vocabulary grew as new ideas and discoveries demanded new words. The Renaissance interest in the classics gave rise to new formations from Greek and Latin roots. Trade brought English speakers into contact with languages such as Spanish, Portuguese, Italian, Dutch, and Arabic—as well as various African, Indian, and American languages—and English borrowed words from all of them. The Renaissance spirit also encouraged writers to coin new words. Shakespeare is credited with some 2000 coinages, many involving the use of nouns as verbs and verbs as nouns.

Growing English nationalism and the spread of Protestant ideas brought popular support for Henry's action; those who openly opposed it frequently paid with their lives.

Ironically, Anne Boleyn produced only a daughter, Elizabeth, and eventually Anne was executed on a charge of adultery. A third marriage finally gave Henry his long-sought son, the frail and sickly Edward VI, who in 1547, at the age of nine, succeeded his father. During his six-year reign, the Church of England became more truly Protestant, clarifying its beliefs and establishing its rituals in a landmark publication, the Book of Common Prayer. When Edward died, however, his half-sister Mary took the throne and tried to reintroduce Roman Catholicism. The move was unpopular, as was her marriage to her cousin Philip II of Spain, and her persecution of Protestants earned her the nickname Bloody Mary. On her death in 1558, most welcomed the succession of her half-sister Elizabeth.

Top to bottom: Edward, Prince of Wales, son of Henry VIII and Jane Seymour; Mary, daughter of Henry VIII and Catherine of Aragon; Elizabeth I, daughter of Henry VIII and Anne Boleyn

THE ELIZABETHAN ERA

Elizabeth I, the unwanted daughter of Henry VIII and Anne Boleyn, proved to be one of the ablest monarchs in English history. During her long reign, the English Renaissance reached its full flower, and England enjoyed a time of unprecedented prosperity and international prestige. A practical and disciplined ruler, Elizabeth loved pomp and ceremony but was nevertheless frugal and intent on balancing the national budget. She was also a consummate politician, exercising absolute authority while remaining sensitive to public opinion and respectful of Parliament. In religious matters she steered a middle course. Reestablishing the independent Church of England, she made it a buffer between Roman Catholics and radical Protestants, now often called Puritans because they sought to "purify" the church of all remaining Roman Catholic practices.

In foreign policy, Elizabeth was a shrewd strategist who kept England out of costly wars and ended the unpopular Spanish alliance. Though she never married, for 20 years she used the possibility of her mar-

riage to utmost advantage, feigning interest in one European prince after another. Convinced by advisers that the path to national prosperity lay in New World riches, she encouraged overseas ventures, including Sir Francis Drake's circumnavigation of the globe and Sir Walter Raleigh's attempt to establish a colony in Virginia. In secret, she funded pirate raids against the ships of Spain, while publicly denouncing such "unlawful acts" of plunder.

The quarrel with Catholic Spain intensified in 1587, when Elizabeth reluctantly executed her cousin Mary Stuart, the Roman Catholic queen of Scotland, for conspiracy. Catholics, who questioned the legitimacy of Elizabeth's parents' marriage, had believed Mary to be the rightful heir to the English throne and had participated in a number of foreign-backed plots against Elizabeth. A year after Mary's execution, Spain's Philip II sent a great armada, or fleet of warships, to challenge the English navy. Aided by a violent storm, the smaller, more maneuverable English ships defeated the Spanish Armada, making Elizabeth the undisputed leader of a great military power.

THE RISE OF THE STUARTS

With Elizabeth's death in 1603, the powerful Tudor dynasty came to an end, and the rule of England fell into the hands of the weaker house of Stuart. Elizabeth was succeeded by her cousin James VI of Scotland, son of Mary Stuart, who ascended

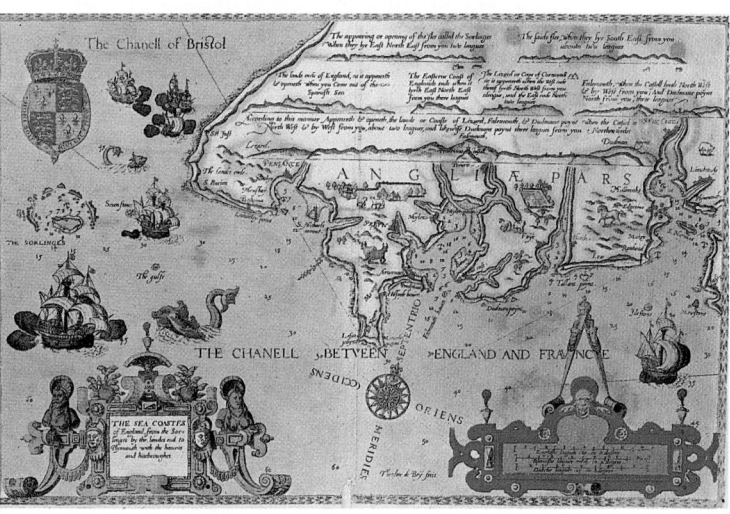

Map published in 1588, depicting the approach of the Spanish Armada

Although the zenith of English Renaissance literature was not reached until Elizabeth's reign, a number of earlier writers paved the way. Among them were Sir Thomas Wyatt and Henry Howard, earl of Surrey, court poets of Henry VIII's reign who introduced into England the Italian verse form called the **sonnet.** During Elizabethan times, the sonnet became the most popular form of love lyric. Sonnets were often published in sequences, such as Edmund Spenser's *Amoretti,* addressed to his future wife. William Shakespeare's magnificent sonnets do not form a clear sequence, but several address a mysterious figure known as the Dark Lady, who some scholars think may have been the poet Amelia Lanier.

Shakespeare left an even clearer mark on drama, which came of age in the Renaissance. Although most plays of medieval times had treated religious themes, Renaissance drama was concerned with the complexities of human life here on earth. Plays were often staged at court, in the homes of wealthy nobles, and in inn yards, where spectators could sit on the ground in front of the stage or in balconies overlooking it. A similar plan was used in England's first theaters, like the famous Globe Theater in London. Most of the plays were written mainly or entirely in verse. Among the era's finest playwrights other than Shakespeare were Christopher Marlowe and Ben Jonson. Jonson was influential in shaping English drama on the basis of classical models, distinguishing clearly between **tragedies,** which end with their heroes' downfall, and **comedies,** which end happily.

the throne of England as James I. Separated from his mother in childhood, James was happy to support the Church of England, but both Roman Catholic and Protestant extremists expected otherwise— Catholics because he was Mary Stuart's son, Puritans because he was king of Presbyterian Scotland. Problems with Roman Catholics arose early in his reign, when a group including Guy Fawkes conspired to kill him and blow up Parliament in the unsuccessful Gunpowder Plot of 1605. Later, James had greater difficulties with the Puritans, and these problems only worsened when his son Charles I took the throne in 1625.

James and Charles lacked the political savvy and frugality of Elizabeth, and both aroused opposition by their belief in the divine right of kings, considering themselves God's representatives in all civil and religious matters. Their contempt for Parliament and their shocking extravagance met with much hostility in the House of Commons, now dominated by Puritans. Even more offensive to the Puritans was the kings' preference for "High-Church" rituals in the Anglican Church—rituals that seemed to smack of Roman Catholicism.

In 1629, with the situation deteriorating, Charles I dismissed Parliament, refusing to summon it again for 11 years. During this time he took strong measures against his political opponents through the royal Courts of the Star Chamber, which operated without trial by jury. The result of these oppressive measures was a deepening of religious, political, and economic unrest. Thousands of English citizens—especially Puritans—emigrated to North America, making the Stuart years England's first period of major colonial expansion. Then, in 1637, Charles's attempt to introduce Anglican prayers and practices in Scotland's Presbyterian churches led to open rebellion there. In need of funds to suppress the Scots, Charles was forced to reconvene Parliament. In a session known as the Long Parliament, many of his powers were stripped. He responded with a show of military force, and England was soon plunged into civil war.

Top: James I
Bottom: Charles I, depicted as a knight on horseback

The Pilgrims begin their voyage to the New World after living in the Netherlands for 12 years.

Oliver Cromwell in his military finery

THE DEFEAT OF THE MONARCHY

The English civil war pitted the Royalists, or supporters of the monarchy—mainly Roman Catholics, Anglicans, and members of the nobility—against the supporters of Parliament, consisting principally of Puritans, smaller landowners, and middle-class town dwellers. Under the skilled leadership of General Oliver Cromwell, the devout, disciplined Puritan army soundly defeated the Royalists in 1645, and the king surrendered a year later. Cromwell's army, now in control of Parliament, ordered stiff retaliatory measures against the Royalists. In 1649, the king himself was executed.

The members of Parliament had difficulty in deciding on an alternative to monarchy. At first they established a commonwealth with Cromwell as head; later they made him "lord protector" for life. Under the Puritan-dominated government, England's theaters were closed and most forms of recreation suspended; Sunday became a day of prayer, when even walking for pleasure was forbidden. A reluctant but able politician, Cromwell curbed quarrels among members of the military, religious leaders, and discontented government officials. When Cromwell died in 1658, his son inherited his title. Richard Cromwell, however, showed little of his father's ability to control the country's political wrangling and increasingly unruly public. Puritan government had proved no less autocratic than the Stuart reign, and in 1660 a new Parliament invited Charles II, son of Charles I, to return from exile and assume the throne. His reign ushered in a new chapter in English history, known as the Restoration.

LITERARY HISTORY

Like Shakespeare, Marlowe and Jonson were fine lyric poets. Marlowe's "The Passionate Shepherd to His Love" is a famous example of **pastoral verse,** which praises the simple joys of rural life. Jonson's lyrics influenced many of the younger poets of the age, such as Robert Herrick and Richard Lovelace. Jonson's contemporary, John Donne, broke with poetic conventions, employing unusual imagery and elaborate metaphors to produce what came to be called **metaphysical poetry.** His blend of passion and intellect was especially influential among younger religious poets, such as George Herbert.

The English Renaissance was also a high point in the history of epic poetry. Edmund Spenser dedicated his action-packed romantic epic *The Faerie Queene* to Elizabeth I. Some decades later, the Puritan poet John Milton penned the lofty epic *Paradise Lost,* retelling the story of the fall of Adam and Eve in the Garden of Eden. The Bible, Milton's main source of inspiration, had been made accessible to all English people in 1611, with the publication of the magnificent King James Bible—the culmination of years of effort by many translators, most notably the Protestant reformer William Tyndale. Although this translation rivals Shakespeare's plays in its use of memorable poetic language, most sections are in fact prose. Among the era's other influential prose works are the essays of Sir Francis Bacon, who pioneered the essay form in English, and the sermons and meditations of John Donne.

The Renaissance was a time of rapid change in the arts, literature, and learning. New ideas were embraced, and old ones–including the concept of love–were examined from different perspectives. In sonnets and other forms of verse, English poets of the period explored the many aspects of love: unrequited love, constant love, timeless love, and love that is subject to change. As you read the poems in this part of Unit Two, compare your own ideas about love with those expressed in these works.

COMPARING LITERATURE: SONNETS OF SPENSER, SHAKESPEARE, AND PETRARCH

The Sonnet Across Cultures: Italy

My Lute, Awake!

Poetry by
SIR THOMAS WYATT

On Monsieur's Departure

Poetry by
ELIZABETH I

(Connect to Your Life)

Dealing with Rejection Suppose that you loved or liked someone who did not return your love or your friendship. How would you react? In your reader's notebook, write a short paragraph describing the effect that such a rejection might have on you.

Build Background

Court Poets and Courtly Love Sir Thomas Wyatt, a diplomat in the service of King Henry VIII, traveled widely and was responsible for introducing various forms of Italian lyric poetry to England. Although this achievement was of great importance to the development of English poetry, many of Wyatt's best poems—including "My Lute, Awake!"—are in the style of the native English dance song, or ballet (băl'ət). The ballet was a lively and forceful kind of verse written to be sung to the accompaniment of the lute, a stringed instrument popular in the 16th century.

The writer of "On Monsieur's Departure," Elizabeth I, was a daughter of Henry VIII and queen of England during the flowering of the English Renaissance. Elizabeth was unusually well educated for a woman of her time and wrote several poems, all of which seem to have been based on events in her life.

One of the popular themes of love poetry in the 16th century was unrequited love—love that is ignored or rejected. In the tradition of earlier European poems of courtly love, such poetry portrayed the rejected lover as desolate and anguished, totally in the power of the beloved. These poems by Wyatt and Elizabeth I are both concerned with the theme of unrequited love. The individuality of each poem lies in the way the poet works subtle variations on the traditional situations and responses.

Focus Your Reading

LITERARY ANALYSIS **RHYME SCHEME** A **rhyme scheme** is the pattern of end rhyme in a poem. Notice the pattern of end rhyme in this stanza from "My Lute, Awake!"

> *Proud of the spoil that thou hast got*
> *Of simple hearts, thorough love's shot;*
> *By whom, unkind, thou hast them won,*
> *Think not he hath his bow forgot,*
> *Although my lute and I have done.*

As you read both poems, be aware of their different rhyme schemes.

ACTIVE READING **CLARIFYING MEANING** Poetry of the Renaissance can be challenging to modern readers. If you find the syntax or the order of the words hard to follow, you can use the following strategies to increase your understanding:

- Use the text annotations and the dictionary to help you define difficult words or phrases.
- Reread the poem several times—aloud and silently.
- Try **paraphrasing** the lines until the sense becomes clear. For example, read these lines from "On Monsieur's Departure."

> *I grieve and dare not show my discontent,*
> *I love and yet am forced to seem to hate, . . .*

You might paraphrase the lines as follows: "I must hide my grief and disguise my love."

READER'S NOTEBOOK As you read these poems, try to paraphrase lines that seem difficult to you.

My Lute, Awake!

Sir Thomas Wyatt

My lute, awake! Perform the last
Labor that thou and I shall waste,
And end that I have now begun;
For when this song is sung and past,
5   My lute, be still, for I have done.

As to be heard where ear is none,
As lead to grave in marble stone,
My song may pierce her heart as soon.
Should we then sigh or sing or moan?
10 No, no, my lute, for I have done.

The rocks do not so cruelly
Repulse the waves continually
As she my suit and affection.
So that I am past remedy,
15 Whereby my lute and I have done.

Proud of the spoil that thou hast got
Of simple hearts, thorough love's shot;
By whom, unkind, thou hast them won,
Think not he hath his bow forgot,
20 Although my lute and I have done.

6–8 as to be heard . . . as soon: My song's having an effect on her emotions is as unlikely as sound being heard without an ear or soft lead carving hard marble.

13 suit: wooing; courtship.

17 thorough love's shot: through the arrow of Cupid, the god of love.

Vengeance shall fall on thy disdain
That makest but game on earnest pain.
Think not alone under the sun
Unquit to cause thy lovers plain,
25 Although my lute and I have done.

Perchance thee lie withered and old
The winter nights that are so cold,
Plaining in vain unto the moon.
Thy wishes then dare not be told.
30 Care then who list, for I have done.

And then may chance thee to repent
The time that thou hast lost and spent
To cause thy lovers sigh and swoon.
Then shalt thou know beauty but lent,
35 And wish and want as I have done.

Now cease, my lute. This is the last
Labor that thou and I shall waste,
And ended is that we begun.
Now is this song both sung and past;
40 My lute, be still, for I have done.

23–24 think not . . . plain: Do not think that you alone under the sun will escape unrevenged for causing your lovers to lament.

30 list: likes; wishes.

Thinking Through the Literature

1. **Comprehension Check** What has happened between the speaker and the subject of the poem?

2. What is your impression of this poem?

3. How would you describe the speaker's attitude toward the woman who is the subject of the poem?

4. If the speaker's wishes came true, what do you think would happen to the woman? Explain your answer.

5. Do you think the speaker is sincere when he says "I have done"? Why or why not?

ELIZABETH I

On Monsieur's Departure

Young Elizabeth

I grieve and dare not show my discontent,
I love and yet am forced to seem to hate,
I do, yet dare not say I ever meant,
I seem stark mute but inwardly do prate.
5   I am and not, I freeze and yet am burned,
        Since from myself another self I turned.

My care is like my shadow in the sun,
Follows me flying, flies when I pursue it,
Stands and lies by me, doth what I have done.
10 His too familiar care doth make me rue it.
        No means I find to rid him from my breast,
        Till by the end of things it be suppressed.

Some gentler passion slide into my mind,
For I am soft and made of melting snow;
15 Or be more cruel, love, and so be kind.
Let me or float or sink, be high or low.
        Or let me live with some more sweet content,
        Or die and so forget what love ere meant.

4 prate: chatter.

6 another self: The man referred to in this poem is thought by some to be a French duke who had been involved in negotiations for marriage to Elizabeth; by others, to be the earl of Essex, a favorite courtier of Elizabeth's who was executed for treason in 1601.
7 care: sorrow.
9 doth . . . done: does all that I do.
10 his too familiar care . . . it: His too easy and superficial sorrow makes me regret my own feelings of sorrow.

Thinking through the LITERATURE

Connect to the Literature

1. What Do You Think?
Do you feel sympathy for the speaker of "On Monsieur's Departure"? Why or why not?

> **Comprehension Check**
> - How does the speaker in "On Monsieur's Departure" feel about the man she refers to?
> - How does the speaker hope to conquer her painful emotions?

Think Critically

2. What **conflicts** does the speaker in "On Monsieur's Departure" seem to be experiencing?

THINK ABOUT
- the contrasts she presents in lines 1–5
- what she says in line 6
- the references to her care and "his too familiar care"

3. Do you think the **speaker** is responsible for the situation she finds herself in? Why or why not?

4. How would you explain the speaker's wish in the last stanza?

5. How does knowing that this poem was written by Queen Elizabeth I affect your interpretation of it?

6. **ACTIVE READING   CLARIFYING MEANING** Choose two lines that you paraphrased in your ▯ READER'S NOTEBOOK as you read the poems. Compare your paraphrase with that of a classmate. What additional understanding did you gain through comparing your work?

Extend Interpretations

7. **Comparing Texts** Compare the portrayals of unrequited love in "My Lute, Awake!" and "On Monsieur's Departure." Think about the attitudes and actions of the man and the woman in each poem, the **tone** of each poem, and the traditional portrayal of unrequited love in courtly-love poetry.

8. **Connect to Life** How is unrequited love portrayed in literature and film today? How do modern **characters** react when they are rejected?

Literary Analysis

RHYME SCHEME The pattern of end rhyme in a poem determines the poem's **rhyme scheme.** The rhyme scheme is charted by assigning a letter of the alphabet, beginning with *a,* to each line. Lines that rhyme are given the same letter. Notice that in "My Lute, Awake!," for example, the rhyme scheme of each stanza is *aabab.*

Proud of the spoil that thou hast got	*a*
Of simple hearts, thorough love's shot;	*a*
By whom, unkind, thou hast them won,	*b*
Think not he hath his bow forgot,	*a*
Although my lute and I have done.	*b*

Be aware, however, that the rhyme may not always be exact. In the first stanza of "My Lute, Awake!" the word *waste* is meant to rhyme with *last* and *past.*

Paired Activity Working with a partner, use the letters *a, b,* and *c* to chart the rhyme scheme of the stanzas of "On Monsieur's Departure."

Choices & CHALLENGES

Writing Options

Letter from a Queen Imagine that you are Elizabeth I and have just read "My Lute, Awake!" Write a letter to a friend, expressing your reaction to Wyatt's poem.

Activities & Explorations

Mood Music Listen to some recordings of Renaissance music, both vocal and instrumental. Select a group of pieces that you think reflect the mood of either "My Lute, Awake!" or "On Monsieur's Departure." Then make a tape recording of the pieces and play it for the class. Explain your choices, and ask for feedback from your classmates. ~ **MUSIC**

Sir Thomas Wyatt
1503–1542

Other Works
"Whoso List to Hunt"
"Blame Not My Lute"
"My Galley Charged with
    Forgetfulness"

At the King's Service As a courtier and diplomat for Henry VIII, Sir Thomas Wyatt was alternately in and out of favor with the whimsical king. Henry ordered Wyatt imprisoned twice, once for quarreling with a duke and once for treason, both times threatening him with execution. Each time, however, Wyatt was pardoned and accepted back into the king's service.

Lyrics for the Lute A skilled musician and amateur poet, Wyatt wrote lyrics in his leisure time to amuse himself and other courtiers. As was usual during the Renaissance, his poems were circulated privately, and only a few were published during his lifetime. Critical opinion of Wyatt's poems varies— some think their rhythm too irregular and rough, while others consider them fresh and vigorous. Most critics agree, however, that his most inventive work is to be found in the songs he wrote for lute accompaniment and that his introduction of the Italian sonnet form into English was a significant contribution to English literature.

Elizabeth I
1533–1603

Other Works
"The Doubt of Future Foes"
"Speech to the Troops at Tilbury"

Lonely Childhood Elizabeth I, daughter of King Henry VIII and Anne Boleyn, had an unsettling and probably lonely childhood. Her father, hoping for a male heir, was disappointed at Elizabeth's birth and two years later ordered her mother executed, supposedly for treason. Despite his bitterness at not having a son, Henry provided Elizabeth with the rigorous education normally given only to boys. She learned Latin, Greek, French, Italian, history, and theology, and her literary output includes speeches, translations, and a small collection of poems focusing on events in her personal life.

Glorious Reign Elizabeth ascended the throne in 1558 and ruled for 45 years. Her reign was a glorious period in English history, a time of great prosperity, artistic achievement, and international prestige. Although she considered a number of marriage proposals, Elizabeth rejected all of them, ignoring the advisers who hoped she would marry and provide an heir to the throne.

 LaserLinks: Background for Reading
Author Background
Music Connection

PREPARING to *Read*

The Passionate Shepherd to His Love
Poetry by CHRISTOPHER MARLOWE

The Nymph's Reply to the Shepherd
Poetry by SIR WALTER RALEIGH

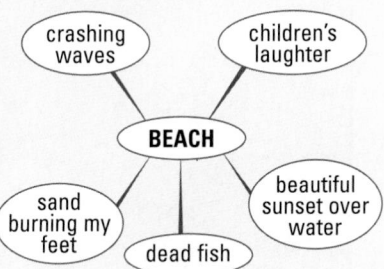

Connect to Your Life

Imagining Paradise Close your eyes and think of a beautiful place you have visited. What images make up your mental picture of the place? Create a cluster diagram similar to the one shown, identifying the place in the center oval and surrounding it with words and phrases that describe the images you associate with the place. Which of your images do you consider realistic? Which would you describe as romantic or idealized?

Build Background

Renaissance Poetry The Renaissance was a time in which knowledge and skills were cultivated in a broad range of fields, from music, art, and literature to science and athletics. According to writers of the time, the ideal "Renaissance man" should develop himself in every possible way.

Included in the ranks of the true Renaissance men were two kindred spirits, Christopher Marlowe and Sir Walter Raleigh. During his short life, Marlowe studied religion, became a talented and recognized poet and playwright, conducted secret government business, and engaged in philosophical discussions with his friend Raleigh. As a statesman, writer, soldier, scientist, adventurer, and explorer, Raleigh lived a life of action as well as contemplation.

Marlowe's poem "The Passionate Shepherd to His Love" became so famous that other poets wrote responses to it. The most notable of these is "The Nymph's Reply to the Shepherd," written by Raleigh. Together, the two poems enact a debate about the realities of love.

Focus Your Reading

LITERARY ANALYSIS **PASTORAL** Renaissance poets used **pastorals** to convey their own thoughts and feelings about love and other subjects. A pastoral is a poem presenting shepherds in rural settings that are usually idealized. Notice the images from a country setting in the following lines:

> *And we will sit upon the rocks,*
> *Seeing the shepherds feed their flocks.*

As you read these poems, notice examples of pastoral life involving shepherds and their rural existence.

ACTIVE READING **COMPARING SPEAKERS IN POETRY**
The two speakers in these poems—the shepherd and the nymph—have very different perspectives on the topic of love. To identify the differences, consider the following:

- each speaker's choice of words when addressing the other person
- evidence of each speaker's motivation
- each speaker's attitude about life

READER'S NOTEBOOK As you read these poems, jot down details that point out the differences between the two speakers on the subject of romantic love.

Christopher Marlowe

THE PASSIONATE SHEPHERD
to HIS LOVE

The Hireling Shepherd (1851), William Holman Hunt. Manchester (U.K.) City Art Gallery/A.K.G., Berlin/Superstock.

Come live with me and be my love,
And we will all the pleasures prove
That valleys, groves, hills, and fields,
Woods, or steepy mountain yields.

5 And we will sit upon the rocks,
Seeing the shepherds feed their flocks,
By shallow rivers to whose falls
Melodious birds sing madrigals.

2 prove: experience.

8 madrigals: songs of a type popular during the Renaissance.

And I will make thee beds of roses
10　And a thousand fragrant posies,
　　A cap of flowers, and a kirtle
　　Embroidered all with leaves of myrtle;

　　A gown made of the finest wool
　　Which from our pretty lambs we pull;
15　Fair lined slippers for the cold,
　　With buckles of the purest gold;

　　A belt of straw and ivy buds,
　　With coral clasps and amber studs:
　　And if these pleasures may thee move,
20　Come live with me, and be my love.

　　The shepherds' swains shall dance and sing
　　For thy delight each May morning:
　　If these delights thy mind may move,
　　Then live with me and be my love.

11 kirtle: skirt.

21 swains: youths.

Thinking Through the Literature

1. What is your opinion of the gifts that the shepherd offers to his beloved?

2. How serious or realistic do you think the shepherd's offer is?

   THINK ABOUT { • the way he describes the setting
   • the gifts he promises

3. Why do you think Marlowe chose the setting described in the poem?

SIR WALTER RALEIGH

THE NYMPH'S Reply *to* THE SHEPHERD

If all the world and love were young,
And truth in every shepherd's tongue,
These pretty pleasures might me move
To live with thee and be thy love.

5   Time drives the flocks from field to fold
When rivers rage and rocks grow cold,
And Philomel becometh dumb;
The rest complains of cares to come.

The flowers do fade, and wanton fields
10 To wayward winter reckoning yields;
A honey tongue, a heart of gall,
Is fancy's spring, but sorrow's fall.

Thy gowns, thy shoes, thy beds of roses,
Thy cap, thy kirtle, and thy posies
15 Soon break, soon wither, soon forgotten—
In folly ripe, in reason rotten.

Thy belt of straw and ivy buds,
Thy coral clasps and amber studs,
All these in me no means can move
20 To come to thee and be thy love.

But could youth last and love still breed,
Had joys no date nor age no need,
Then these delights my mind might move
To live with thee and be thy love.

5 fold: a pen for animals, especially sheep.

7 Philomel: the nightingale; **dumb:** silent.

9 wanton: producing abundant crops; luxuriant.

22 date: ending.

Thinking through the LITERATURE

Connect to the Literature

1. What Do You Think? Were you surprised by the nymph's response in "The Nymph's Reply to the Shepherd"? Share your thoughts with a classmate.

> **Comprehension Check**
> - What images in Marlowe's poem are repeated in Raleigh's poem?
> - Does the nymph in Raleigh's poem agree or disagree with the shepherd's arguments in Marlowe's poem?

Think Critically

2. How would you describe the nymph's attitude toward life?

THINK ABOUT
- the connection she makes between youth and love
- her descriptions of the effects of time

3. Do you agree with the nymph's reasons for not accepting the shepherd's offer? Why or why not?

4. On the basis of the first and last **stanzas,** what do you think might convince the nymph to accept the shepherd's offer?

5. **ACTIVE READING** **COMPARING SPEAKERS IN POETRY**
Look back at the details you noted in your **READER'S NOTEBOOK** about the speakers' perspectives. What is the debate between the two **speakers** of these poems all about? Which of the two speakers' attitudes is closer to your own attitude?

Extend Interpretations

6. Comparing Texts Who do you think would be more likely to share the shepherd's attitude toward love—the speaker of Wyatt's "My Lute, Awake!" or the speaker of Elizabeth I's "On Monsieur's Departure"? Explain your opinion.

7. Connect to Life Think about the different ways love is depicted in current music. Do these depictions usually reflect a romantic or realistic view of love?

Literary Analysis

PASTORAL A **pastoral** is a poem presenting shepherds in rural settings, usually in an idealized manner. The style of pastorals may seem unnatural, since the supposedly simple, rustic characters tend to use very formal, courtly language; however, Renaissance poets were drawn to this form not as a means of accurately portraying rustic life but as a means of conveying their own emotions and ideas in an artistic way. Marlowe's "The Passionate Shepherd to His Love" is a perfect example of a pastoral.

Paired Activity With a partner, decide on the **mood** that the pastoral evokes in you. What are the details that the poet provides to create a pastoral feeling or atmosphere? How do these details help to create the mood? Use a chart like the one below to organize your ideas. Compare your findings with those of your classmates.

	Details	Mood
"The Passionate Shepherd to His Love"		
"The Nymph's Reply to the Shepherd"		

Writing Options

A Modern Parody Write a parody, or humorous imitation, of "The Passionate Shepherd to His Love." In place of the shepherd, substitute a person with a different job (for example, an accountant, a truck driver, a plumber, or a chef) and select an appropriate setting. Place the parody in your **Working Portfolio.**

Activities & Explorations

1. Telephone Dialogue With a partner, act out a modern phone conversation in which the shepherd tries to persuade the nymph to accept his offer.
~ SPEAKING AND LISTENING

2. Drawing Shepherds and Nymphs Create a single drawing or painting that depicts the contrasting scenes described in the two poems. **~ ART**

Christopher Marlowe
1564–1593

Other Works
The Tragedy of Dido, Queen of Carthage
Edward II
Hero and Leander

Talent and Intrigue Christopher Marlowe is best remembered for writing plays in which his use of what Ben Jonson dubbed his "mighty line," or blank verse, transformed the British theater. The son of a shoemaker, Marlowe attended Cambridge University on a scholarship but was almost denied his master's degree because he was suspected of conspiring against the queen. A letter from the queen's Privy Council excused the young man, hinting that he was active in Elizabeth's secret service.

Brief but Influential Life Marlowe wrote his first successful play, *Tamburlaine the Great,* at the age of 23. He lived only six more years but wrote five plays during that time, including *The Jew of Malta* and *Dr. Faustus,* works that would profoundly influence the development of Elizabethan drama. Like his friend Sir Walter Raleigh, Marlowe was a freethinker who was suspected of treasonous and antichurch sentiment. In 1593, at the age of 29, Marlowe was murdered in a tavern, allegedly during an argument over the bill.

Sir Walter Raleigh
1552?–1618

Other Works
"Epitaph of Sir Philip Sidney"
The History of the World

An Active Life Sir Walter Raleigh was a man of action and intellect. He attended Oxford University, studied law, and was widely read in chemistry, mathematics, and medicine. He also wrote history and poetry. By helping to quell an Irish rebellion in 1580, he won the affection of Queen Elizabeth. As the queen's favorite, he was granted land, made a vice-admiral, knighted, and appointed governor of Jersey, an island in the English Channel.

Exploration and Imprisonment Raleigh fell out of favor with the queen in 1592 but continued to pursue ambitious projects. Among his activities were the establishment of the short-lived Roanoke colony in North America and the leading of an expedition to South America in search of gold. In 1603, during the reign of James I, he was charged with treason and imprisoned for 13 years. Afterward, Raleigh led another expedition to South America but fell into disfavor once again when his soldiers burned a local settlement. On his return to London, he was imprisoned and executed.

Sonnet Form

Origins of the Sonnet

A **sonnet** is a 14-line lyric poem with a complicated rhyme scheme and a defined structure. Because of the technical skill required to write a sonnet, the form has challenged English poets ever since it was introduced into England almost 500 years ago.

The sonnet originated in Italy in the 13th century (the word *sonnet* comes from the Italian for "little song"). The great Italian poet Petrarch (1304–1374) perfected the **Italian sonnet,** which is often called the **Petrarchan sonnet** in his honor. Petrarch felt that the sonnet, with its brevity and musical rhymes, was a perfect medium for the expression of emotion, especially love. Although the Italian sonneteers did not restrict themselves to love as a subject, Petrarch wrote over 300 sonnets detailing his devotion to a beautiful but unobtainable lady, whom he called Laura.

The English Sonnet Develops

The story of the English sonnet begins, not surprisingly, with another lovelorn poet, Sir Thomas Wyatt (1503–1542). A diplomat in the court of King Henry VIII, Wyatt was rumored to be in love with the ill-fated queen Anne Boleyn. In the 1530s, Wyatt translated some of Petrarch's love sonnets and wrote a few of his own in a slight modification of the Italian form. By this time, the Renaissance had at last reached England, accompanied by an awakening of interest in Italian literature. Henry VIII, although brutal to his wives, encouraged the poetry of courtly love and so welcomed the sonnet as a poetic form. Another English poet who deserves credit for popularizing the sonnet in England is Henry Howard, earl of Surrey

(1517–1547). Building on Wyatt's modifications, Surrey changed the rhyme scheme of the sonnet to adapt it to the rhyme-poor English language. Surrey's innovations distinguished the English sonnet from the Italian sonnet. The English form ultimately became known as the **Shakespearean sonnet** because William Shakespeare used it with such distinction.

By 1609, when Shakespeare's sonnets were published, the conventions of love sonnets had been firmly established, most notably by Sir Philip Sidney's *Astrophel and Stella* (1591) and Edmund Spenser's *Amoretti* (1595). Surrey's rhyme scheme allowed Shakespeare more freedom in his versification, and he used this freedom to expand sonnet conventions. In some of his sonnets, for example, the object of the speaker's affection is not a divinely beautiful woman but one with all-too-human defects. Instead of limiting himself to the subject of love, he introduced deep philosophical issues and perplexing ironies. Because of his mastery of the sonnet's form and broadening of its content, Shakespeare remains the undisputed master of the English sonnet.

What Makes a Poem a Sonnet?	
Length	14 lines
Subject(s)	a lyrical nature—a focus on personal feelings and thoughts
Meter	iambic pentameter lines (lines containing five metrical units, each consisting of an unstressed syllable followed by a stressed syllable)
Structure and rhyme scheme	a particular structure and rhyme scheme, Petrarchan or Shakespearean (that of the sonnet or another variation)

Sonnet Structure

THE PETRARCHAN FORM What distinguishes the Italian sonnet is its two-part structure: an **octave** (the first eight lines), usually rhyming *abbaabba*, followed by a **sestet** (the last six lines) with the rhyme scheme *cdcdcd* or *cdecde*. Typically, the octave establishes the speaker's situation, and the sestet resolves, draws conclusions about, or expresses a reaction to that situation. The Petrarchan sonnet has been called "organic" in its unity—like an acorn in its cup, the octave and sestet fit together perfectly. Unity is also produced by the rhyme scheme, which involves only four or five different rhyming sounds. The resulting need for many rhyming words makes the Petrarchan sonnet difficult to write in English. Still, plenty of English poets have written them, including John Milton, William Wordsworth, and John Keats to name just a few.

THE SHAKESPEAREAN FORM The English sonnet is divided into three **quatrains** (groups of four lines) and a rhyming **couplet** (two lines).

Generally, the first quatrain introduces a situation, which is explored in the next two quatrains.

Often, a turn, or shift in thought, occurs at the third quatrain or at the couplet.

The couplet resolves the situation. The rhyme scheme follows the pattern: *abab cdcd efef gg.*

> That time of year thou mayst in me behold
> When yellow leaves, or none, or few, do hang
> Upon those boughs which shake against the cold,
> Bare ruined choirs, where late the sweet birds sang.
> In me thou see'st the twilight of such day
> As after sunset fadeth in the west;
> Which by and by black night doth take away,
> Death's second self, that seals up all in rest.
> In me thou see'st the glowing of such fire,
> That on the ashes of his youth doth lie,
> As the deathbed whereon it must expire,
> Consumed with that which it was nourished by.
> This thou perceiv'st, which makes thy love more strong,
> To love that well which thou must leave ere long.
>
> —Shakespeare, *Sonnet 73*

Notice that each quatrain elaborates on a particular image: autumn in the first quatrain, twilight in the second, and the embers of a fire in the third. The final couplet is a concise statement that pulls the sonnet together by shedding new light on the situation developed in the three quatrains. Think of the closing couplet in a Shakespearean sonnet as a "punch line" that gives meaning to the whole.

Strategies for Reading: Sonnet Form

1. Read the sonnet several times.
2. Use letters to label like-sounding words at the end of lines.
3. Identify the major units of thought or feeling.
4. Describe the situation introduced in the first part of the sonnet.
5. Paraphrase the speaker's final resolution of, conclusions about, or reaction to the situation.
6. Study the imagery and figurative language for clues to the emotions expressed.
7. **Monitor** your reading strategies and modify them when your understanding breaks down. Remember to use your Strategies for Active Reading: **predict, visualize, connect, question, clarify,** and **evaluate.**

Sonnet 30 / Sonnet 75

Poetry by EDMUND SPENSER

Comparing Literature of the World

Sonnets of Spenser, Shakespeare, and Petrarch

This lesson and the two that follow present an opportunity for you to compare the work of three sonnet masters: Spenser, Shakespeare, and Petrarch. Specific points of comparison contained in these lessons will help you understand the similarities and differences among sonnet forms and themes.

Connect to Your Life

Romantic Responses Romantic love can generate a variety of intense feelings and conflicting emotions. Recall a character in a book or a movie—or perhaps someone you know—who has seemed to respond to romantic love in an unusually intense way. With a group of classmates, briefly discuss the emotions and reactions of that individual, explaining why you think the individual reacted as he or she did.

Build Background

Tokens of Love During the 16th century, the **sonnet** became one of the most popular poetic forms in England. Originally developed in Italy in the 13th century, the sonnet was used to convey deep and intense amorous feelings, often expressing an idealized love typical of the courtly love of the Middle Ages. In many Renaissance sonnets, the speaker—typically a man—tells of his intense love and of the anxiety and distress he feels as his beloved remains aloof and unreachable.

"Sonnet 30" and "Sonnet 75" by Edmund Spenser are part of a collection of sonnets, or **sonnet sequence,** that he named *Amoretti,* which can be translated roughly as "intimate little tokens of love." Published in 1595, the sonnets in *Amoretti* are arranged in a narrative progression that simulates the ritual and emotions of a courtship. Many of them were written during Spenser's courtship of his second wife, Elizabeth Boyle, and the details and emotions they present are thought to be in part autobiographical.

Focus Your Reading

LITERARY ANALYSIS **SPENSERIAN SONNET** The **Spenserian sonnet** is a variation of the English sonnet, which was introduced on page 295. Both consist of three 4-line units, called **quatrains,** followed by a **couplet** (two rhymed lines), but the Spenserian sonnet has an interlocking **rhyme scheme** linking the quatrains *(abab bcbc cdcd ee)* by the use of rhyming lines.

As you read each of Spenser's sonnets, think about the relationship between the quatrains and couplet and watch for the interlocking rhymes.

ACTIVE READING **SUMMARIZING MAJOR IDEAS IN POETRY**
You can understand the sonnets' **major ideas** by breaking each poem down into its three quatrains and couplet and **summarizing** the meaning expressed in each of the parts.

READER'S NOTEBOOK For each poem, create a chart like the one shown. Jot down the major idea expressed in each part of the sonnet.

"Sonnet 30"	
Part of Poem	**Major Idea**
1st quatrain	
2nd quatrain	
3rd quatrain	
couplet	

SONNET 30

Edmund Spenser

My love is like to ice, and I to fire;
How comes it then that this her cold so great
Is not dissolved through my so hot desire,
But harder grows the more I her entreat?   **4 entreat:** plead with.
5 Or how comes it that my exceeding heat
Is not delayed by her heart-frozen cold:
But that I burn much more in boiling sweat,
And feel my flames augmented manifold?   **8 augmented manifold:** greatly increased.
What more miraculous thing may be told
10 That fire which all things melts, should harden ice:
And ice which is congealed with senseless cold,   **11 congealed:** solidified.
Should kindle fire by wonderful device.
Such is the pow'r of love in gentle mind,
That it can alter all the course of kind.   **14 kind:** nature.

Thinking Through the Literature

1. What are your reactions to the speaker's feelings about love?

2. Why do you think Spenser chose to use the **images** of fire and ice?

    THINK ABOUT { • the characteristics usually associated with fire and ice
   • the characteristics of fire and ice in this sonnet

3. Is this poem a believable description of a love relationship? Explain your opinion.

SONNET 75

Edmund Spenser

One day I wrote her name upon the strand,   **1 strand:** beach.
But came the waves and washéd it away:
Again I wrote it with a second hand,
But came the tide, and made my pains his prey.
5 "Vain man," said she, "that dost in vain assay,   **5 assay:** try.
A mortal thing so to immortalize.
For I myself shall like to this decay,
And eke my name be wipéd out likewise."   **8 eke:** also.
"Not so," quod I, "let baser things devise   **9 quod:** said.
10 To die in dust, but you shall live by fame:
My verse your virtues rare shall eternize,
And in the heavens write your glorious name,
Where whenas death shall all the world subdue,
Our love shall live, and later life renew."

Connect to the Literature

1. **What Do You Think?** What **images** remain in your mind after your reading of "Sonnet 75"?

> **Comprehension Check**
> • How does the woman in the poem react when the speaker writes her name in the sand?
> • Why does the speaker believe that their love will endure?

Think Critically

2. Why do you think the **speaker** in "Sonnet 75" wants to immortalize his love? Explain your thinking.

3. Reread lines 13 and 14. Do you agree with the speaker that love can overcome death?

THINK ABOUT
- • the woman's statement that she and her name will be "wiped out"
- • the speaker's assertion in line 11
- • your own observations about love

4. **ACTIVE READING** **SUMMARIZING MAJOR IDEAS IN POETRY**
With a partner, compare the charts you created in your **READER'S NOTEBOOK** and then discuss what you think are the **major ideas** in each of Spenser's poems. Collaborate on creating a title for each poem, choosing words or phrases that summarize the major ideas and reflect the thoughts and intense feelings of each speaker.

Extend Interpretations

5. **Comparing Texts** Compare Spenser's "Sonnet 30" with Elizabeth I's "On Monsieur's Departure," paying particular attention to similarities and differences in the poets' uses of opposites in their descriptions of love relationships.

6. **Different Perspectives** Suppose that the object of the speaker's love in either "Sonnet 30" or "Sonnet 75" wrote a reply. What do you think would be her view of the speaker and his ideas about love?

7. **Connect to Life** Think back to the character or person you recalled in Connect to Your Life on page 297. Which of the two sonnets most closely expresses how this character or person responded to romantic love?

Literary Analysis

SPENSERIAN SONNET The **Spenserian sonnet,** like the English sonnet, consists of 14 lines of **iambic pentameter** divided into three **quatrains** followed by a **couplet.** However, while the typical **rhyme scheme** of an English sonnet is *abab cdcd efef gg,* a Spenserian sonnet uses the interlocking rhyme scheme *abab bcbc cdcd ee.* This rhyme scheme reinforces the relationship of ideas between the quatrains.

Paired Activity Notice the progression of the speaker's thoughts about the intensity of love in each of Spenser's sonnets. Note, too, the progression of the relationship between the man and woman from one poem to the next. With a partner, write notes for a Spenserian sonnet that might bridge the gap between "Sonnet 30" and "Sonnet 75." Jot down images you could use to express intense feelings of love. Use your notes to write the sonnet, applying the interlocking rhyme scheme as effectively as possible.

REVIEW **ALLITERATION**
Alliteration is the repetition of consonant sounds at the beginnings of words. Read "Sonnet 75" aloud, paying particular attention to the use of alliteration. What effect do you think these repetitions of sounds create?

Writing Options

Natural Comparison In "Sonnet 30," Spenser compares his feelings to fire. Write a paragraph in which you make your own comparison between love and some aspect of nature. Explain the reasons for your comparison.

Writing Handbook
See page 1367: Compare and Contrast.

Activities & Explorations

Opinion Poll Conduct an opinion poll in which you ask ten or more participants to complete the sentence "Love is like . . ." Record their responses on tape or in your notebook. Share any unusual responses with the class.
~ SPEAKING AND LISTENING

Inquiry & Research

Renaissance Courtship and Marriage Find out about more typical courtship and marriage customs of the English Renaissance by answering these questions: What was the average age of the courters? Was love an essential component of the relationship? How long did a typical engagement last?

Edmund Spenser
1552?–1599

Other Works
"Sonnet 26"
"Sonnet 67"
"Sonnet 71"
"Sonnet 72"

Early Ambitions Born to a relatively poor London family, Edmund Spenser was able to work his way through Cambridge University as a "poor scholar." He read extensively, becoming acquainted with Latin, Greek, French, and Italian literature. His earliest publication was of translations of several French poems, written when he was 16 years old. While at Cambridge, Spenser established literary friendships and showed that he had ambitious plans for a poetic career.

Influences and Experimentation After receiving his master of arts degree in 1576, Spenser served as secretary to several influential men, including the earl of Leicester. His employment in Leicester's household was important, for it was there that he met and developed a friendship with Sir Philip Sidney and other court writers who were promoting the new English poetry of the Elizabethan Age. In his own poetry, Spenser often experimented with verse forms and used archaic language for its rustic and musical effect. He was respected and imitated by his contemporaries, as he has been by many later poets.

Literary Achievements One year after publishing his first major work, *The Shepheardes Calender,* which he dedicated to Sidney, Spenser moved to Ireland, where he held various minor government jobs and continued his writing. It was there that he wrote one of the greatest poetic romances in English literature, *The Faerie Queene.* Spenser spent most of his remaining life in Ireland, but after his home near Dublin was destroyed during a civil war, he returned to England, where he died a few years later almost impoverished despite his many years of service to nobility. In honor of his great literary achievements, Spenser was buried near Geoffrey Chaucer—one of his favorite poets—in what is now called the Poets' Corner of Westminster Abbey.

Author Activity

Mystery Queen To learn more about *The Faerie Queene,* find a copy of the work and read a few passages. Investigate its background and structure. To whom did Spenser dedicate the romance? How long is the poem? What, in brief, is it about?

PREPARING to *Read*

Sonnet 29 / Sonnet 116 / Sonnet 130

Poetry by WILLIAM SHAKESPEARE

Comparing Literature of the World

Sonnets of Spenser, Shakespeare, and Petrarch

This lesson, as well as the one before on Spenser and the one following on Petrarch, presents an opportunity for you to compare the work of three sonnet masters: Spenser, Shakespeare, and Petrarch. Specific points of comparison contained in these lessons will help you understand the similarities and differences among sonnet forms and themes.

Connect to Your Life

True Love Think about two people you know who have a strong love relationship that has lasted for many years. Consider the qualities of each of the persons involved in the relationship. Do you think those qualities help explain the strength of the relationship? Share your thoughts with classmates.

Build Background

Shakespeare's Sonnets William Shakespeare, best known for his plays, also wrote nondramatic poetry, including a series of 154 sonnets. In the 1590s many English poets wrote **sonnet sequences,** groups of sonnets related through an overall narrative structure, usually addressed to an idealized but unattainable woman. Typical themes included the woman's great beauty, her coldness and disdain, the suffering of the poet-lover, and the immortality of poetry. Shakespeare almost certainly wrote his sonnets—which were not published until 1609—during the 1590s too, but they differ in some ways from the sonnets written by other poets. First, they are addressed to at least three different people: a young man, whom the poet urges to marry and have children; a "dark lady," who is unlike the ideal beautiful woman of the time; and a rival poet. Second, the themes of Shakespeare's sonnets are more complex and less predictable than those of other poets' sonnets. Shakespeare writes, for example, of time, change, and death as well as of love and beauty. Third, Shakespeare developed the structure of the sonnet form to its highest artistic level; today, the English sonnet is often referred to as the **Shakespearean sonnet.**

Focus Your Reading

LITERARY ANALYSIS   **SHAKESPEAREAN SONNET**

Like Spenser, Shakespeare uses the structure of three **quatrains** and a **couplet** in his sonnets. However, he uses the **rhyme scheme** *abab cdcd efef gg* instead of the interlocking Spenserian pattern *(abab bcbc cdcd ee)*. As you read these three **Shakespearean sonnets,** discuss with your classmates how the rhyme scheme contributes to the meaning and appeal of each poem.

ACTIVE READING   **ANALYZING SENSORY LANGUAGE**

In his sonnets, Shakespeare often chose words that would appeal to the reader's senses. As you read the poems, you will notice language used by the poet that appeals to the five senses: sight, hearing, touch, smell, and taste.

READER'S NOTEBOOK Make a chart like the one shown. As you read each poem, record words or phrases that appeal to one or more of the senses. Note whether any of the senses are not used. Also note that some poems may have more **sensory language** than others.

	Sonnet 29	Sonnet 116	Sonnet 130
Sight			
Hearing			
Touch			
Smell			
Taste			

SONNET 29

W I L L I A M   S H A K E S P E A R E

When in disgrace with Fortune and men's eyes
I all alone beweep my outcast state,
And trouble deaf heaven with my bootless cries,
And look upon myself and curse my fate,
5 Wishing me like to one more rich in hope,
Featur'd like him, like him with friends possess'd,
Desiring this man's art, and that man's scope,
With what I most enjoy contented least;
Yet in these thoughts myself almost despising,
10 Haply I think on thee, and then my state,
Like to the lark at break of day arising
From sullen earth, sings hymns at heaven's gate,
   For thy sweet love rememb'red such wealth brings,
   That then I scorn to change my state with kings.

2 state: condition.

3 bootless: futile; useless.

6 featur'd like him: with his features—that is, handsome.

7 scope: intelligence.

11 lark: the English skylark, noted for its beautiful singing while soaring in flight.

Thinking Through the Literature

1. **Comprehension Check** What changes the speaker's mood in "Sonnet 29"?

2. Can you identify in any way with the speaker of this poem? Share your thoughts with classmates.

3. What do you think are the speaker's strongest feelings in this sonnet? Cite lines from the poem to support your answer.

SONNET 116

WILLIAM SHAKESPEARE

Let me not to the marriage of true minds
Admit impediments; love is not love
Which alters when it alteration finds,
Or bends with the remover to remove.
5 O no, it is an ever-fixéd mark
That looks on tempests and is never shaken;
It is the star to every wand'ring bark,
Whose worth's unknown, although his height be taken.
Love's not Time's fool, though rosy lips and cheeks
10 Within his bending sickle's compass come,
Love alters not with his brief hours and weeks,
But bears it out even to the edge of doom.
　　　If this be error and upon me proved,
　　　I never writ, nor no man ever loved.

2 impediments: obstacles. The traditional marriage service reads in part, "If any of you know cause or just impediment why these persons should not be joined together . . ."
5 mark: seamark—a landmark that can be seen from the sea and used as a guide in navigation.
7 bark: sailing ship.
8 whose . . . height be taken: a reference to the star, whose value is measureless even though its altitude is measured by navigators.
10 within . . . compass: within the range of his curving sickle.
12 bears it out: endures; **doom:** Doomsday; Judgment Day.

Anne of Gonzaga, Nathaniel Hatch. Victoria & Albert Museum, London/Art Resource, New York.

Thinking Through the Literature

1. What is your response to the description of love in this poem?
2. What kind of person might the speaker be?

   THINK ABOUT
   - the likely age of such a person
   - the experiences that such a person might have had

3. Do you think the speaker's concept of love is realistic? Why or why not?

SONNET 130

WILLIAM SHAKESPEARE

Catherine Howard, John Hoskins. Victoria &
Albert Museum, London/Art Resource, New York.

My mistress' eyes are nothing like the sun;
Coral is far more red than her lips' red;
If snow be white, why then her breasts are dun;
If hairs be wires, black wires grow on her head.
5 I have seen roses damask'd, red and white,
But no such roses see I in her cheeks,
And in some perfumes is there more delight
Than in the breath that from my mistress reeks.
I love to hear her speak, yet well I know
10 That music hath a far more pleasing sound;
I grant I never saw a goddess go,
My mistress when she walks treads on the ground.
    And yet, by heaven, I think my love as rare
    As any she belied with false compare.

3 dun: tan.

5 damask'd: with mingled colors.

8 reeks: is exhaled (used here without the word's present reference to offensive odors).

11 go: walk.

14 as . . . compare: as any woman misrepresented by exaggerated comparisons.

Connect to the Literature

1. What Do You Think?
Were you surprised by the **description** in "Sonnet 130"? Share your reactions with your classmates.

> **Comprehension Check**
> • Is the speaker's mistress dark or fair?
> • Do the flaws pointed out by the speaker affect his love for the woman described?

Think Critically

2. In "Sonnet 130," what do you think is the **speaker's** attitude toward the woman he loves?

> **THINK ABOUT**
> • his descriptions of her physical characteristics
> • his description of her voice
> • his conclusion in the **couplet**

3. What do you think might have been Shakespeare's **purpose** in writing this sonnet?

4. Does this poem present a realistic or idealized portrait of the beloved?

5. **ACTIVE READING** **ANALYZING SENSORY LANGUAGE** Review the chart you prepared for your **READER'S NOTEBOOK**. Which sonnet contains the most **sensory language?** How does this language suit the subject? Cite examples in your answer.

Extend Interpretations

6. Critic's Corner One critic, Hallett Smith, has called Shakespeare's sonnets "explorations of the human spirit." Discuss ways in which this interpretation applies to the three sonnets you have read. Use details from the poems to support your conclusions.

7. Connect to Life Renaissance sonnets often focus on the great beauty of the beloved. How important is physical beauty or attractiveness in today's society?

8. Points of Comparison The speaker of "Sonnet 130," like the speaker of Spenser's "Sonnet 75," uses the word *rare* to describe his beloved. Compare the thoughts and emotions of the two **speakers.** Whom would you more likely enjoy meeting? Why?

Literary Analysis

SHAKESPEAREAN SONNET The **Shakespearean sonnet,** also called the English or Elizabethan sonnet, consists of 14 lines of **iambic pentameter** divided into three **quatrains,** or four-line units, and a final **couplet.** The typical **rhyme scheme** is *abab cdcd efef gg.* The couplet provides a final commentary on the subject developed in the three quatrains. There is also usually a **turn,** or shift in thought, in the poem, occurring most often at the couplet or at the beginning of the third quatrain.

Paired Activity With a partner, decide where the turn occurs in each of the three Shakespeare sonnets. In which poem does the turn occur between the second and third quatrains? Does the turn occur at the couplet in any of the poems? What is the effect of each turn?

FIGURATIVE LANGUAGE
Figurative language is language that conveys meaning beyond the literal meanings of the words. **Similes** and **metaphors** are types of figurative language. A simile uses the word *like* or *as* to make a comparison between things. A metaphor makes a comparison without using those words.

Simile: Her hair was bright as gold.

Metaphor: Hope is a light in the dark.

Activity Choose one simile or one metaphor from each of the three sonnets. Explain the comparison and its effect.

Writing Options

1. Love Poem Write a Shakespearean sonnet describing someone you love or greatly admire. Use at least one simile or metaphor. Place the sonnet in your **Working Portfolio.**

2. Character Sketch As the speaker of "Sonnet 116," write a character sketch of the ideal partner in a strong love relationship. Make sure to identify various qualities the person would need to possess.

3. Letter to the Speaker Imagine that you are the woman described in "Sonnet 130." In a letter to the speaker, give your opinion of his description.

4. Opinion Essay Which of the three sonnets do you think expresses the strongest commitment to a love relationship? Write a two- or three-paragraph essay explaining your opinion.

Writing Handbook
See pages 1369–1370: Analysis.

Activities & Explorations

1. Television Talk Show With a partner, stage a television talk show in which the host interviews William Shakespeare about the meaning of love.
~ SPEAKING AND LISTENING

2. Love's Scrapbook Prepare a scrapbook of items—such as photos, drawings, poems, and sayings—that express your conception of a strong love relationship. **~ ART**

3. A Reading of Sonnets With a small group of classmates, investigate some of Shakespeare's other sonnets. Have each group member prepare a reading of his or her favorite sonnet. Discuss the feelings and ideas expressed in each poem, and compare it with one or more of the three sonnets you have read in this lesson.
~ SPEAKING AND LISTENING

4. List of Resources Reread each of the three sonnets, and choose your favorite. Think of films, novels, short stories, works of art, and musical compositions that in some way represent the mood of the poem or the ideas and images in it. List these resources, and share the list with the class.
~ VIEWING AND REPRESENTING

Inquiry & Research

1. Portraits of Women Find books of English Renaissance painting showing portraits of women of the time. Look at several of the portraits and think about whether they seem idealized or realistic. How does the portrayal of women in painting of the period compare with the portrayal of women in Renaissance poetry?

2. What Is Love? For most people, love is one of the most important aspects of life. Investigate some of the definitions and analyses of love in the writings of contemporary psychologists. Share what you find with the class, and discuss any relationships you can see between Shakespeare's views of love and the psychologists' views.

 More Online: Research Starter
www.mcdougallittell.com

Art Connection

Illustrating Poetry Look again at the two small portraits of women on pages 304–305. Why do you think they were chosen to illustrate "Sonnet 116" and "Sonnet 130"? Look for other paintings that you think could be used to illustrate the two poems.

A biography of William Shakespeare appears on pages 314–317.

Sonnet 169 / Sonnet 292

Poetry by **FRANCESCO PETRARCH** (frän-chäs′ kō pē′trärk′)

Comparing Literature of the World

The Sonnet Across Cultures

Sonnets of Spenser, Shakespeare, and Petrarch Long before Spenser and Shakespeare's time, the Italian poet Petrarch played an influential role in the development of the structure as well as the content of the **sonnet**. A brilliant man of the 14th-century Italian Renaissance, Petrarch perfected the sonnet style that 200 years later was used and adapted by Spenser, Shakespeare, and other English poets. Because of this, you will find in Petrarch's writing the same love **themes** that were explored by his followers: unrequited love, desperate love, eternal love, and tragic love.

Points of Comparison As you read these sonnets by Petrarch, compare the poet's treatment of love with that seen in Spenser's and Shakespeare's sonnets.

Build Background

The Sonnet Takes Shape Although sonnets had been written in Italy for nearly 100 years before Petrarch wrote his, it was he who established the **sonnet** as a major poetic form. In addition to his impact on the Elizabethans, Petrarch had a considerable influence on such poets as Michelangelo, Ronsard, and Lope de Vega.

Petrarch's sonnets, the output of a lifetime of work, show his longing for a woman named Laura, with whom he reportedly fell passionately in love on Good Friday, April 6, 1327, after seeing her in church. Even though Laura did not return his love, she was the inspiration for over 300 of Petrarch's poems. Like many of Petrarch's contemporaries, Laura died in the plague that devastated much of Europe in the mid-14th century. "Sonnet 292" was written after her death.

Focus Your Reading

LITERARY ANALYSIS **ITALIAN SONNET** The **Italian sonnet** used by Petrarch is different in form from the English sonnet. The 14 lines of the Italian sonnet are divided into these two parts:

- an octave (the first eight lines)
- a sestet (the last six lines)

Generally, the octave tells a story, introduces a situation, or raises a question. In the sestet, the speaker comments on the story, situation, or question.

As you read these sonnets, notice the relationship between their structure and content.

ACTIVE READING **SUMMARIZING MAJOR IDEAS IN POEMS**
The ideas expressed in a poem can be hard to understand because the language of poetry may be difficult to decipher. The following steps are strategies you can use to determine the major ideas in Petrarch's sonnets:

- Reread the poem two or three times.
- Look for the major idea in each stanza.
- Identify the story or situation introduced in the octave.
- Determine the comment made by the speaker in the sestet.

READER'S NOTEBOOK **Summarize** the major idea of each stanza in the two sonnets.

SONNET 169

Rapt in the one fond thought that makes me stray
from other men and walk this world alone,
sometimes I have escaped myself and flown
to seek the very one that I should flee;

5   so fair and fell I see her passing by
that the soul trembles to take flight again,
so many arméd sighs are in her train,
this lovely foe to Love himself and me!

And yet, upon that high and clouded brow
10 I seem to see a ray of pity shine,
shedding some light across the grieving heart:

so I call back my soul, and when I vow
at last to tell her of my hidden pain,
I have so much to say I dare not start.

Translated by Anthony Mortimer

1 rapt: deeply absorbed.

5 fell: cruel.

7 train: a group of people following in attendance.

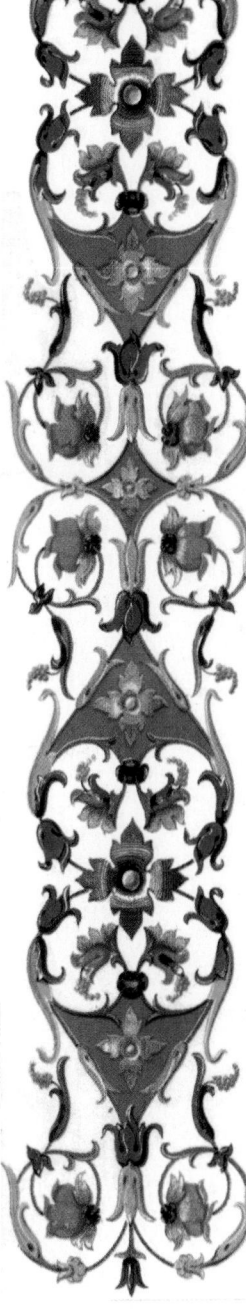

Thinking Through the Literature

1. What are your thoughts about the feelings the speaker expresses in this poem?

2. How would you describe the relationship between the speaker and his beloved?

THINK ABOUT

- the **conflict** the speaker expresses in lines 3–4
- his description of how his soul "trembles to take flight again" (line 6)
- his use of contradictory phrases in describing the beloved, such as "fair and fell" (line 5) and "lovely foe" (line 8)
- the needs he suggests in lines 12–14

FRANCESCO PETRARCH

Portrait of a Man and Woman at a Casement (about 1440–1445), Fra Filippo Lippi. Tempera on wood, 25¼″ × 16½″, The Metropolitan Museum of Art, New York, gift of Henry G. Marquand, 1889, Marquand Collection (89.15.19).

Sonnet 292

The eyes I spoke of once in words that burn,
the arms and hands and feet and lovely face
that took me from myself for such a space
of time and marked me out from other men;

5   the waving hair of unmixed gold that shone,
the smile that flashed with the angelic rays
that used to make this earth a paradise,
are now a little dust, all feeling gone;

and yet I live, grief and disdain to me,
10 left where the light I cherished never shows,
in fragile bark on the tempestuous sea.

Here let my loving song come to a close,
the vein of my accustomed art is dry,
and this, my lyre, turned at last to tears.

Translated by Anthony Mortimer

11 bark: sailing ship;
tempestuous: stormy.

14 lyre (līr): a stringed musical instrument of the harp family, used in ancient Greece.

Connect to the Literature

1. What Do You Think?
What type of music would convey the overall **mood** of "Sonnet 292"?

Comprehension Check
• What has happened to the woman in the poem?
• Who or what is meant by "fragile bark" and "tempestuous sea"?

Think Critically

2. How would you describe the speaker's feelings over the loss of love?

THINK ABOUT

• his description of his beloved's physical attributes
• his attitude toward his own life (lines 9–11)
• what he means by "the vein of my accustomed art is dry" (line 13)

3. **ACTIVE READING** **SUMMARIZING MAJOR IDEAS IN POEMS**
Review the summaries for each stanza that you created in your **READER'S NOTEBOOK**. How would you describe what happens in each poem? Compare your ideas with those of a partner.

Extend Interpretations

4. Critic's Corner Edgar Quinet, a 19th-century French critic, said that "Petrarch's originality consists in having realized, for the first time, that every moment of our existence contains in itself the substance of a poem." Read Petrarch's sonnets again. Do you agree that everyday incidents can in themselves be poetic? Explain your opinion.

5. Connect to Life Think again about the two situations presented in these poems. Do you think it is more difficult to cope with a love that is hopeless or with the death of someone you love? Explain your answer.

6. **Points of Comparison** Compare the attitude toward the beloved in Petrarch's "Sonnet 292" with that in Shakespeare's "Sonnet 130." How does each speaker view his beloved?

7. **Points of Comparison** Compare the treatment of love in Petrarch's "Sonnet 169" with that in Spenser's "Sonnet 30." How are the two poems similar? How do they differ?

Literary Analysis

ITALIAN SONNET The 14 lines of the Italian sonnet are divided into two parts: an octave (the first eight lines) and a sestet (the last six lines). The usual rhyme scheme for the octave is *abbaabba*. The rhyme scheme for the sestet may be *cdecde, cdccdc,* or a similar variation. The octave generally presents a problem or raises a question, and the sestet resolves or comments on the question.

Cooperative Learning Activity
Reread the sonnets by Spenser and those by Shakespeare in this part of Unit Two. Then compare the form of these Italian sonnets with those of Spenser's and Shakespeare's sonnets. Which form do you think gives the writer more liberties? Which seems to you to fit more situations or themes? Jot down your ideas in a chart like the one shown below. Then compare your conclusions with those of your classmates.

Sonnets:		
Spenser's	**Shakespeare's**	**Petrarch's**

Choices & CHALLENGES

Writing Options

1. Soap-Opera Outline Write an outline for a series of soap-opera episodes based on Petrarch's two sonnets. Describe the speaker and the woman he loves. Add details to explain the speaker's "hidden pain" and grief. Place the outline in your **Working Portfolio.**

Main Idea
A
B

2. **Points of Comparison**
Compare the attitude toward love conveyed in the sonnets you have read by Spenser, Shakespeare, and Petrarch. Which approach do you identify with the most? Write a letter to the poet explaining why you appreciate his attitude.

Activities & Explorations

Dance Interpretation Choreograph a dance interpretation of one of Petrarch's sonnets. Create different movements to express the speaker's thoughts and emotions. Perform your dance for the class. ~ **PERFORMING**

Inquiry & Research

Italian Renaissance Research the Italian Renaissance to find out what impact the art and writing of the period had on Europe. What artists and writers led the Renaissance? What themes and ideas were typical of the period?

Francesco Petrarch
1304–1374

Early Years Although born in Italy, Petrarch moved with his family to France, where his father had accepted a job. It was in France that Petrarch, on his father's insistence, began his study of law, later returning to Italy to continue his education. After his father's death in 1326, however, Petrarch abandoned law, a subject for which he had little inclination, to study Greek and Latin literature and to write poetry.

Renaissance Man In the spirit of the Renaissance, Petrarch had varied interests, ranging from the scholarly and literary to a love of and fascination with nature. In 1336, together with his brother, he climbed Mt. Ventoux in the Alps; the climb was quite unusual in an age that showed little interest in nature. He also had a deep interest in religious studies, which led him to join the clergy. The church positions he held provided him not only with a modest means of income but also with much free time to devote to literature. He studied, wrote, and traveled extensively and was highly regarded as a literary and cultural leader of his time.

Wreathed in Laurels In 1340, Petrarch received invitations from both Paris and Rome to become poet laureate. He chose Rome, and in 1341 received the honor of being its first poet laureate since ancient times. Most of the 366 poems in the *Canzoniere* ("Book of Songs"), Petrarch's poetic masterpiece, are written about his love for Laura, who also appears in his *Trionfi* ("Triumphs"). Petrarch never lost his love of writing. He spent the last years of his life composing and revising his literary works, and he died in his study, at work at his desk.

Author Activity

Lady Muse Get together with a small group of classmates and find out what you can about Laura. Divide the following questions among the group members: When did Laura die? Why was the date significant? What else can you find out about her? Present your findings to the class.

During Shakespeare's lifetime there were frequent struggles for political control in and around the court of Elizabeth I and her successor, James I. Many of Shakespeare's history plays as well as his tragedies deal with political conflict and the never-ending struggle to achieve a balance between power, justice, and legitimate authority in society. Shakespeare's play *Macbeth* is one of the definitive studies of the effect of power and ambition on the mind and soul. Who should be king and how political power should be first gained and then secured are among the issues addressed in this play.

Author Study
WILLIAM SHAKESPEARE

"He was not of an age, but for all time!"

—Ben Jonson

HIS LIFE
HIS TIMES

Master Playwright and Poet

With his brilliant poetic language and keen insight into human nature, William Shakespeare is generally regarded as the world's greatest writer in the English language. His plays are more widely translated than any other works except the Bible. Yet his life remains something of a mystery, with many details lost in the swirl of time.

1564–1616

"I COULD A TALE UNFOLD" Shakespeare was born in Stratford-upon-Avon, a busy market town on the Avon River, northwest of London. Though the precise date of his birth is not known, church records indicate that he was baptized on April 26, 1564. Unlike most other writers of his era, he did not come from a noble family with close ties to the English court. The Shakespeares were what today we would call middle class, although his father, a glove maker, once served as the equivalent of mayor of Stratford.

Though no record of Shakespeare's schooling survives, it is assumed that he attended the local grammar school in Stratford. Again unlike most other writers of his day, Shakespeare did not

1564
Is born in
Stratford-
upon-Avon

Tudor
house in
Stratford

1572
Family suffers a
decline in fortune,
loses most land
holdings

| 1560 | 1565 | 1570 | 1575 |

1558
Elizabeth I becomes
queen; England
returns to the
Protestant faith.

Elizabeth I

1572
Protestants
massacred in
Paris on St.
Bartholomew's Day.

go on to a university; instead, at the age of 18, he married Anne Hathaway, with whom he would have three children. After their birth, the documentary record of Shakespeare's life is once again blank for several years. When he can next be placed, he was in London, working as an actor and beginning to be noticed as a playwright.

"THIS REALM, THIS ENGLAND"   The London to which Shakespeare came was at the center of a nation just emerging as a major European power. In 1588, the English defeated the powerful Spanish Armada, a fleet of ships carrying a Spanish invasion force to England. In the wake of this victory, London flourished as a commercial center.

The arts, with the support of Queen Elizabeth I, flourished as well. The queen spent much of her time in London, where celebrated literary figures of the day—the poets Edward Spenser and Sir Philip Sidney, among them—visited the royal court. She also enjoyed pageants and plays, as well as the more sophisticated entertainment of classical literature. Attracted by England's vitality, commercial and artistic people from other countries soon began flocking to London, a bustling city of nearly 200,000 people. London's first public theaters sprang up across the Thames River in suburban Southwark. Both the mighty and the humble became avid theatergoers.

This Elizabethan drawing is believed to be of Anne Hathaway.

LITERARY *Contributions*

Poetic Drama Shakespeare is best known for his **verse drama**, plays in which most of the dialogue is in the form of poetry. In all, he wrote 37 plays, including the following:

All's Well That Ends Well
Antony and Cleopatra
As You Like It
The Comedy of Errors
Hamlet
Henry IV, Parts I and II
Henry V
Julius Caesar
King Lear
Love's Labour's Lost
Macbeth
Measure for Measure
The Merchant of Venice
The Merry Wives of Windsor
A Midsummer Night's Dream
Othello
Richard II
Richard III
Romeo and Juliet
The Taming of the Shrew
The Tempest
Twelfth Night
The Two Gentlemen of Verona
The Winter's Tale

Narrative Poetry In addition to his famous sonnets, Shakespeare wrote two highly regarded narrative poems, ***Venus and Adonis*** (1593) and ***The Rape of Lucrece*** (1594), when the London theaters had to shut down because of an outbreak of plague.

| 1582 Marries Anne Hathaway | 1583 Birth of first child, Susanna | 1585 Birth of twins, Hamnet and Judith | 1590–92 *The Comedy of Errors* and *Henry VI* in London | 1594–96 Joins the Lord Chamberlain's Men | 1596 Death of Hamnet at age 11 |

1580   **1585**   **1590**   **1595**

| 1577–80 English explorer Sir Francis Drake sails around the world. | 1587 Elizabeth executes her cousin Mary, Queen of Scots. | 1588 England defeats the Spanish Armada. | 1591 *Astrophel and Stella* by Sir Philip Sidney is published. | 1592–94 Plague forces closing of London theaters. |

"ALL THE WORLD'S A STAGE" The first extant mention of William Shakespeare's presence on London's literary scene is in a 1592 pamphlet mocking his dramatic efforts. Already famous enough to be criticized (the rival dramatist Robert Greene referred to Shakespeare bitterly as an "upstart crow"), he became a member of the Lord Chamberlain's Men, a company of actors whose patron was an influential member of Elizabeth's court. Shakespeare's plays helped to make the company successful—so successful that the queen herself attended its productions. Although the precise dating of Shakespeare's plays is uncertain, his early masterpieces include *Richard III, The Comedy of Errors, The Taming of the Shrew,* and *Romeo and Juliet.* By 1598, one scholar was praising Shakespeare as England's finest playwright: "As Plautus and Seneca are accounted the best for Comedy and Tragedy among the Latins," wrote Francis Meres, "so Shakespeare among the English is the most excellent in both kinds for the stage."

Shakespeare's fame was accompanied by a financial success that allowed him to become a partner in London's new Globe Theatre and to purchase a fine home, called New Place, in Stratford. He also paid to obtain a coat of arms for his father, perhaps in an effort to improve his family's social position.

When Elizabeth's Scottish cousin James succeeded her in 1603, the Lord Chamberlain's Men became the King's Men, and the company's domination of the London stage continued. In 1608, Shakespeare and the other leading members of the King's Men even leased a second London theater, the Blackfriars, which was better equipped for winter performances.

"OUR REVELS NOW ARE ENDED" After 1608, Shakespeare curtailed his theatrical activities and spent more time back in Stratford. He wrote no plays after 1613; his last complete dramas are believed to be *The Winter's Tale, The Tempest,* and *Henry VIII.* He died in 1616 and was buried in his parish church in Stratford. His famous epitaph, which he may have written himself, reads:

> *Good friend, for Jesus' sake forbear*
> *To dig the dust enclosed here.*
> *Blest be the man that spares these stones,*
> *And curst be he that moves my bones.*

 More Online: Author Link
www.mcdougallittell.com

1600		1605		1610		1615	
	1603 Receives royal license for the King's Men		**1605–6** First performances of *King Lear* and *Macbeth*		**1608** Leases London's Blackfriars Theatre	**1611–12** First performance of *The Tempest*	**1616** Dies on April 23
1600 East India Company receives a royal charter.		**1603** Elizabeth I dies; James VI of Scotland becomes James I of England.			**1611** King James translation of the Bible appears.		

James I

To Be or Not to Be *Shakespeare*

Because documentary evidence of his life is scanty and his origins and education were relatively humble, some people have for centuries speculated that Shakespeare did not write the works attributed to him. Such theories persist even though they have no basis in solid fact and many scholars dispute them. Here are some of the nearly 60 people who have been offered by various sources as the real Shakespeare.

William Stanley Earl of Derby

(1508/09–1572)

A most unlikely candidate, he is not known to have written a single line of blank verse.

Edward de Vere Earl of Oxford

(1550–1604)

De Vere became a candidate simply because he fit someone's profile of qualities that any "Shakespeare" should possess.

Francis Bacon

(1561–1626)

"The Baconian controversy" is the name given to the once-popular belief in some circles that this English philosopher and essayist is the actual author of Shakespeare's plays.

Christopher Marlowe

(1564–1593)

Because some passages from Shakespeare's early work closely resemble Marlowe's work, a theory arose that Marlowe lived abroad to escape his enemies. He may have sent his plays to an actor he knew, Shakespeare.

Queen Elizabeth I

(1533–1603)

Some have speculated that Queen Elizabeth I was the actual author, arguing that only someone of royal background could develop the depth of knowledge required to produce works of such eloquence.

1623
Death of Anne Shakespeare; First Folio publication of Shakespeare's plays

1620	1625	1630	1635

1620
Pilgrims establish the Plymouth Colony in Massachusetts.

1625
James I dies; his son Charles becomes king.

1628
The duke of Buckingham, a favorite of James I, is assassinated.

The English Renaissance Theater

FROM THE COURTYARD TO THE GLOBE

The Renaissance brought to England a heightened interest in drama—at first in the universities, then in the royal court, and finally among the public at large. Although small private stage productions might be held indoors, in schools, royal palaces, and noblemen's homes, public performances demanded more space and access.

Most of the earliest public performances were held in the courtyards of inns, with the spectators watching from the surrounding balconies. The permanent public theater was designed to resemble one of these courtyards. Built by James Burbage, it opened in 1576 in the London suburb of Shoreditch and was called simply the Theatre. Later two other theaters, the Rose and the Swan, opened in the Bankside area of Southwark, just south of central London. This location proved popular, and in 1599, the original Theatre was torn down and rebuilt in the Bankside area as the Globe. By 1600, London had more playhouses than any other European capital.

Because the Globe—which Shakespeare referred to as "this Wooden O" in *Henry V*—was home to the Lord Chamberlain's Men, the acting company with which Shakespeare was affiliated, it is the best known of the Elizabethan public theaters.

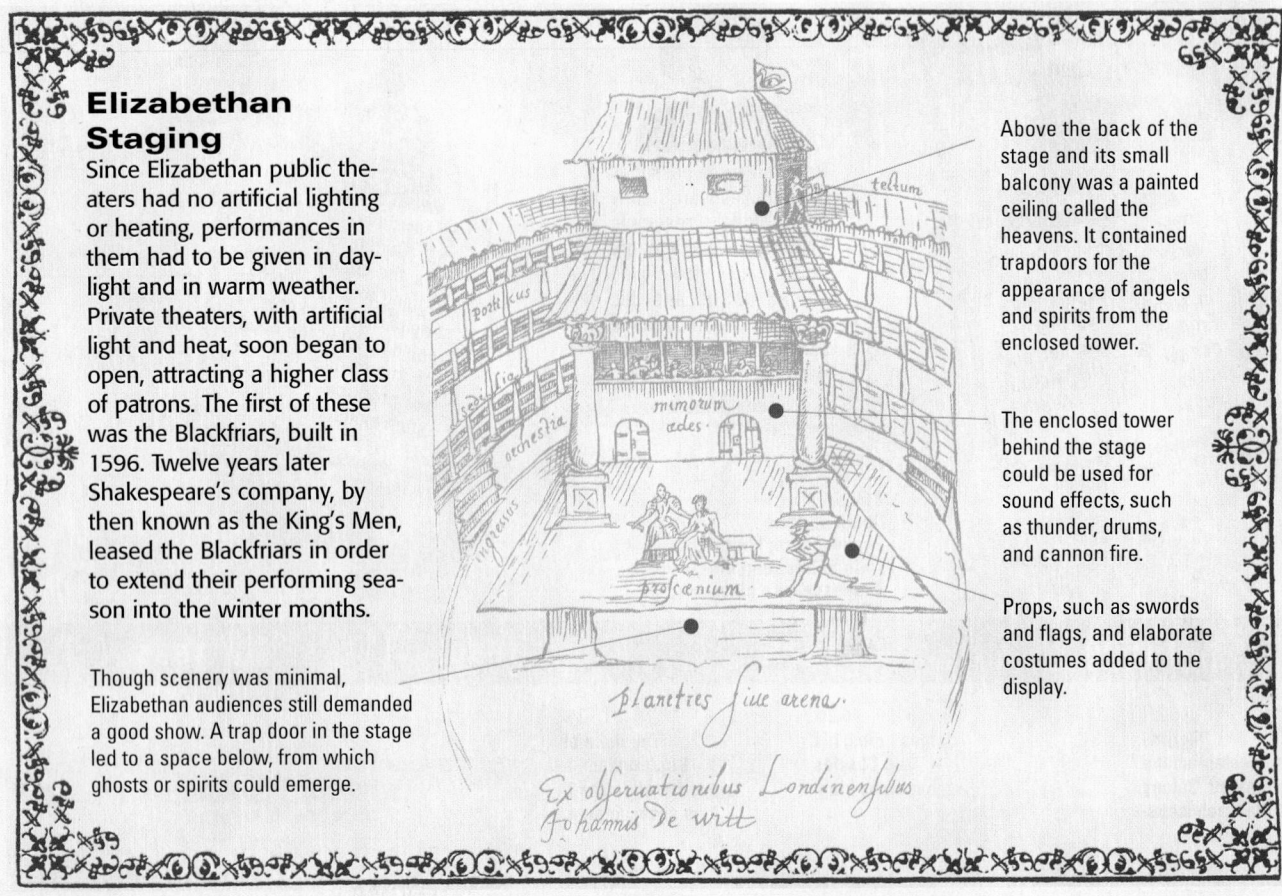

Elizabethan Staging

Since Elizabethan public theaters had no artificial lighting or heating, performances in them had to be given in daylight and in warm weather. Private theaters, with artificial light and heat, soon began to open, attracting a higher class of patrons. The first of these was the Blackfriars, built in 1596. Twelve years later Shakespeare's company, by then known as the King's Men, leased the Blackfriars in order to extend their performing season into the winter months.

Though scenery was minimal, Elizabethan audiences still demanded a good show. A trap door in the stage led to a space below, from which ghosts or spirits could emerge.

Above the back of the stage and its small balcony was a painted ceiling called the heavens. It contained trapdoors for the appearance of angels and spirits from the enclosed tower.

The enclosed tower behind the stage could be used for sound effects, such as thunder, drums, and cannon fire.

Props, such as swords and flags, and elaborate costumes added to the display.

"THIS WOODEN O" The Globe Theatre was a three-story wooden structure that could hold as many as 3,000 people. Plays were performed in the open air on a platform stage that jutted out into a roofless courtyard in the theater's center, where the poorer patrons, or "groundlings," stood to watch the performance. Except for the part directly behind the stage, the theater building consisted of covered galleries where wealthier patrons sat, protected from the elements.

A 17th century drawing of the Globe Theater in its London neighborhood

ELIZABETHAN ACTORS It wasn't easy being an actor in Shakespeare's time. Besides having to memorize their lines, actors had to be able to sing and dance, wrestle and fence, clown and weep. They also had to be able to convey subtle messages with simple gestures or minor changes in voice. Because the stage had no front curtain, the actors always walked on and off the stage in full view of the audience. Plays had to be written so that any character who died on stage could be unobtrusively hauled off.

Actors worked in close proximity to the audience, who either stood around the stage, eating and drinking, or watched from the galleries. If audience members disapproved of certain characters or lines, they would let the actors know by jeering or throwing food. The large crowds also attracted pickpockets and other ruffians. The rowdiness of the audiences caused many towns to label actors as vagrants, lumping them together with rogues, vagabonds, and other undesirables.

Because of the scandalous nature of the Elizabethan theater, women were not allowed to perform. All the actors were male, with young boys usually playing the female roles, from aging matrons to young lovers. Shakespeare himself was an actor as well as a playwright, although it was in the latter capacity that he won fame. The leading tragic actor in Shakespeare's company was Richard Burbage, the son of the man who had built London's first theater.

THE FATE OF THE GLOBE In 1613, the Globe's roof caught fire during a performance of *Henry VIII*, and the theater was destroyed. It was quickly rebuilt at the same location, however this time with a tiled gallery roof. Only 30 years later, Oliver Cromwell and the Puritans suppressed what they considered a frivolous form of entertainment by closing the theater's doors. The Globe was torn down in 1644 and replaced with tenement housing. A lively period in London's history had come to a close.

The Rebirth of the Globe

One of the first performances in the newly restored Globe Theater; *inset:* Queen Elizabeth II views the exterior of the new Globe Theater, 1997.

After more than 300 years, a new Globe Theatre now stands only 200 yards from the original site. A pet project of the American actor Sam Wanamaker and a product of much historical and archaeological research, it opened in June 1997 with a performance of *Henry V.* The new Globe features three levels of wooden benches surrounding an open yard and a platform stage. It seats 1,500 theatergoers—substantially fewer than the 3,000 that the original theater held—because today's audiences prefer not to be crowded as close together as Elizabethan audiences were.

As in its Elizabethan namesake, no formal sets, microphones, or spotlights are used in productions at today's Globe. And another Elizabethan tradition continues: contemporary audiences often mimic their 16th-century predecessors by voicing their reactions, sometimes quite loudly and energetically, to events on the stage.

Shakespearean Tragedy

Renaissance Drama

During the Middle Ages, English drama focused mainly on religious themes, teaching moral lessons or retelling Bible stories to a populace that by and large could not read. With the Renaissance, however, came a rebirth of interest in the dramas of ancient Greece and Rome. First at England's universities and then among graduates of those universities, plays imitating classical models became increasingly popular. These plays fell into two main categories: **comedies** and **tragedies.**

In Renaissance England, comedy was broadly defined as a dramatic work with a happy ending; many comedies contained humor, but humor was not required. A tragedy, in contrast, was a work in which the main character, or tragic hero, came to an unhappy end. In addition to comedies and tragedies, Shakespeare wrote several plays classified as histories—these present stories about England's earlier monarchs. Of all Shakespeare's plays, however, his tragedies are the ones most often cited as his greatest.

The Greek Origins of Tragedy

In the Western tradition, both comedies and tragedies arose in ancient Greece, where they were performed as part of elaborate outdoor festivals. According to the definition of the famous ancient Greek philosopher Aristotle, tragedy arouses pity and fear in the audience—pity for the hero and fear for all human beings, who are subject to character flaws and an unknown destiny. Seeing a tragedy unfold produces a catharsis, or cleansing,

Laurence Fishburne as Othello in the 1995 film directed by Oliver Parker

of these emotions, for by the end the audience is watching in awe as the hero faces defeat with great courage and dignity.

In ancient Greek tragedies, the heroes' tragic flaw was often hubris—an excessive pride that led a tragic hero to challenge the gods. Angered by such hubris, the gods unleashed their retribution, or nemesis, on the hero. Ancient Greek tragedies also made use of a chorus, a group of performers who stood outside the action and commented on the events and characters in a play, often hinting at the doom to come and stressing the fatalistic aspect of the hero's downfall. By Shakespeare's day, the chorus consisted of only one person—a kind of narrator—or was dispensed with entirely.

Characteristics of Tragedy

Shakespearean tragedy differs somewhat from classic Greek tragedy in that Shakespeare's works are not unrelentingly serious. For example, he often eased the intensity of the action by using the device of **comic relief**—the following of a serious scene with a lighter, mildly humorous one. Nevertheless, the following general characteristics are shared by Shakespearean tragedy and classic Greek tragedy:

- The main character, called the **tragic hero,** comes to an unhappy or miserable end.
- The tragic hero is generally a person of importance in society, such as a king or a queen.
- The tragic hero exhibits extraordinary abilities but also a **tragic flaw,** a fatal error in judgment or weakness of character, that leads directly to his or her downfall.

- Outside forces may also contribute to the hero's downfall. If so, the person or force with whom the hero battles is called the **antagonist.**

- A series of causally related events lead inevitably to the **catastrophe,** or tragic resolution. This final stage of the plot usually involves the death of the hero, but other characters may also be affected.

- The tragic hero usually recognizes his or her tragic flaw by the end and so gains the audience's sympathy.

- The tragic hero meets his or her doom with courage and dignity, reaffirming the grandeur of the human spirit.

Shakespeare on the Big Screen

Romeo and Juliet, Shakespeare's first great tragedy, is a tale of teenaged lovers from two feuding families in medieval Verona, Italy. A 1997 film version featured Leonardo Di Caprio and Clare Danes.

Julius Caesar focuses on Roman emperor Brutus, a close friend of Julius Caesar's who reluctantly joins the plot to assassinate him. Marlon Brando played Mark Anthony in the 1953 version.

Leonardo DiCaprio and Clare Danes as Romeo and Juliet, 1997

Hamlet tells the story of a prince of Denmark whose procrastination leads to disaster. Kenneth Branagh directed and starred in the 1996 epic film that uses all of Shakespeare's original script.

Othello focuses on a North African soldier whose great flaw "is the green-eyed monster," jealousy. In 1995, Laurence Fishburne appeared in the title role.

King Lear tells of an aged monarch who fails to distinguish honesty from flattery. *A Thousand Acres,* an update of the King Lear story, became a film in 1997.

Macbeth, which appears in this book (see page 323), is a powerful drama of ambition and murder. Several images appearing throughout the selection are from Orson Welles's 1948 version and Roman Polanski's 1971 version.

YOUR TURN Why do you think that so many of Shakespeare's plays have been adapted to film?

Strategies for Reading: Shakespearean Tragedy

1. Trace the plot's main events, especially the causes and effects that lead to the catastrophe. Watch for the first event that sets the series in motion. At what point is there no turning back?

2. Sort out the antagonists in the play. Who is against whom, and what are the conflicts?

3. Identify the tragic hero. Make sure that you can justify your choice with reasons.

4. Determine the hero's admirable character traits as well as his or her tragic flaw.

5. Analyze how the tragic hero faces destiny. Does he or she show courage and dignity in defeat?

6. **Monitor** your reading strategies and modify them when your understanding breaks down. Remember to use your Strategies for Active Reading: **predict, visualize, connect, question, clarify,** and **evaluate.**

The Tragedy of Macbeth

Verse drama by WILLIAM SHAKESPEARE

Connect to Your Life

Ambitious Goals Lazy people are often blamed for having too little ambition. At the same time, many overachievers are criticized for excessive single-mindedness or for doing the wrong things to achieve their goals. Think about your own ambitions and the people you would describe as ambitious. When is ambition good? When is it undesirable or even evil? Share your ideas in a class discussion.

Build Background

A Scottish Clan Ambition is a driving force in *Macbeth.* The title character is based to some extent on a historical Macbeth, a king of 11th-century Scotland who seized the monarchy after killing his predecessor, Duncan I. The play was written to please King James I, who had been the King of Scotland (as James VI) before the death of his cousin Elizabeth in 1603 brought him to the English throne. King James became the patron, or chief sponsor, of Shakespeare's acting company, thereafter known as the King's Men. *The Tragedy of Macbeth* was probably first performed in the summer of 1606, with James I and the visiting king of Denmark in attendance.

Shakespeare's desire to please King James may account for the prominence of witchcraft in *Macbeth.* The new king was quite interested in the subject, having himself written a book on witchcraft, called *Demonology,* which was published in 1597. Belief in witchcraft was widespread in Shakespeare's day, particularly among less educated people. Members of the nobility, whether or not they truly believed in witches, at times used accusations of witchcraft as a way to get rid of political enemies.

Focus Your Reading: Literary Analysis

LITERARY ANALYSIS **SOLILOQUY/ASIDE** Authors of plays rely on certain conventions to give the audience more information about the characters. Two such conventions are the soliloquy and the aside.

- A **soliloquy** is a speech that a character makes while alone on stage, to reveal his or her thoughts to the audience.
- An **aside** is a remark that a character makes in an undertone to the audience or another character but that others on stage are not supposed to hear. A stage direction clarifies that a remark is an aside; unless otherwise specified, the aside is to the audience. Here is an example:

> **Macbeth.** [*Aside*] Glamis, and Thane of
>   Cawdor!
> The greatest is behind.—[*To* Ross *and* Angus]
>   Thanks for your pains.
> [*Aside to* Banquo] Do you not hope your
>   children shall be kings . . . ?

LITERARY ANALYSIS **BLANK VERSE** Like most plays written before the 20th century, *Macbeth* is a **verse drama,** a play in which the dialogue consists almost entirely of poetry with a fixed pattern of rhythm, or **meter.** Many English verse dramas are written in blank verse, or unrhymed iambic pentameter, a meter in which the normal line contains five stressed syllables, each preceded by an unstressed syllable:

> *Sŏ fóul ănd fáir ă dáy Ĭ háve nŏt séen.*

Blank verse has been a popular medium for drama because it easily accommodates the rhythms of spoken English.

LITERARY ANALYSIS **DRAMATIC IRONY** Irony is based on a contrast between appearance or expectation and reality. In **dramatic irony,** what appears true to one or more characters in a play is seen to be false to the audience. The audience has a more complete picture of the action, because it knows more details. In Act One of *Macbeth,*

dramatic irony can be found in Duncan's words to Lady Macbeth upon his arrival at the Macbeths' castle.

> *Conduct me to mine host. We love him highly*
> *And shall continue our graces toward him.*

Duncan is sure of Macbeth's loyalty and says that he will continue to honor Macbeth with marks of his favor. However, the audience knows that Macbeth is planning to murder Duncan to increase his own power. The audience recognizes the irony of Duncan's trusting remarks.

LITERARY ANALYSIS **FORESHADOWING**

Foreshadowing is a writer's use of hints or clues to suggest what events will occur later in a work. The witches' prophesies are the most explicit hints of what is going to happen in the play. As you read *Macbeth,* list examples of foreshadowing and the events you think they hint at.

Act, Scene, Lines	What the Lines Hint At
Act Two, Scene 1, lines 62–64	Macbeth will murder Duncan.

LITERARY ANALYSIS **THEME** A **theme** is a central idea conveyed by a work of literature. Not to be confused with the work's subject (what it is about in a literal sense), a theme is a general perception about life or human nature. Longer works like *Macbeth* usually contain several themes. As you read the play, take notes about what it has to say about the following topics:

- ambition
- impulses and desires
- marriage
- fate and our efforts to control it
- appearance versus reality
- loyalty
- the supernatural
- reason and mental stability

Focus Your Reading: Active Reading Skills

As you read *Macbeth,* record any of your questions or comments about Shakespeare's use of dramatic conventions or language. For specific suggestions, refer to the Active Reading strategies that follow.

ACTIVE READING **READING DRAMA** The printed text of Shakespeare's *Macbeth,* like that of any drama, consists mainly of **dialogue** spoken by the characters (with labels that show who is speaking) and **stage directions** that specify settings (times and places) and tell how characters behave and speak. The play is divided into **acts,** which are themselves divided into **scenes.** The beginning of a new scene usually involves a change in setting.

Strategies for Reading *Macbeth*

1. Read the opening list of characters—the dramatis personae—to familiarize yourself with the characters.
2. Study the plot summary and stage directions at the beginning of each scene. Try to develop a mental picture of the setting of the scene's action.
3. Pay attention to the labels that show who is speaking and to stage directions that indicate to whom the characters are speaking. Try to envision what each character might look and sound like if you were seeing the play performed on a stage.
4. To get a better sense of what the dialogue might sound like, try reading some of it aloud.

ACTIVE READING **SHAKESPEARE'S LANGUAGE**
Though Shakespeare wrote in modern English, the language of his time was quite different from today's English. Here are some major differences:

- **Grammatical forms:** In Shakespeare's day, people still commonly used the pronouns *thou, thee, thy, thine,* and *thyself* in place of forms of *you.* Verb forms that are now outdated were also in use— *art* for *are* and *cometh* for *comes,* for example.

- **Grammatical structures:** Helping verbs were used far less than they are today. For example, instead of saying "Don't you know he has?" Lady Macbeth says "Know you not he has?"
- **Unusual word order:** Shakespeare often puts verbs before subjects, objects before verbs, and other sentence parts in positions that now seem unusual. For instance, Lady Macbeth says "O, never shall the sun that morrow see!" instead of "O, the sun shall never see that morrow!"
- **Unfamiliar vocabulary:** Shakespeare's vocabulary included many words no longer in use (like *seeling* meaning "blinding") or with meanings different from their meanings today (like *choppy* meaning "chapped"). Shakespeare also coined new words, some of which (like *assassination*) have become a permanent part of the language. The Guide for Reading notes accompanying the play will clarify the meanings of many of the unfamiliar words.

Strategies for Reading Shakespeare's Language

As you read *Macbeth,* you may find it helpful to go through the scenes several times to improve your understanding of the language.

1. Skim each scene quickly to get a general sense of what is going on.
2. Study the Guide for Reading notes for help with the unfamiliar vocabulary and phrasing.
3. Go through the scene again, paraphrasing the lines in your head to clarify their meaning.
4. Read through the scene—or at least the important speeches—one more time, focusing on the figurative language and sensory images (imagery that appeals to the five senses) and the clues they contain about the characters and themes.
5. Focus on the wording of the dialogue, especially asides or soliloquies, to make inferences about the characters' feelings, attitudes, thoughts, and motives.

Orson Welles as Macbeth
(film, directed by Orson Welles, 1948)

SCENE 2

King Duncan's camp near the battlefield.

Duncan, the king of Scotland, waits in his camp for news of the battle. He learns that one of his generals, Macbeth, has been victorious in several battles. Not only has Macbeth defeated the rebellious Macdonwald, but he has also conquered the armies of the king of Norway and the Scottish traitor, the thane of Cawdor. Duncan orders the thane of Cawdor's execution and announces that Macbeth will receive the traitor's title.

[*Alarum within. Enter* Duncan, Malcolm, Donalbain, Lennox, *with* Attendants, *meeting a bleeding* Captain.]

Duncan. What bloody man is that? He can report,
    As seemeth by his plight, of the revolt
    The newest state.

Malcolm.   This is the sergeant
    Who like a good and hardy soldier fought
5   'Gainst my captivity. Hail, brave friend!
    Say to the King the knowledge of the broil
    As thou didst leave it.

Captain.   Doubtful it stood,
    As two spent swimmers that do cling together
    And choke their art. The merciless Macdonwald
10   (Worthy to be a rebel, for to that
    The multiplying villainies of nature
    Do swarm upon him) from the Western Isles
    Of kerns and gallowglasses is supplied;
    And Fortune, on his damned quarrel smiling,
15   Showed like a rebel's whore. But all's too weak;
    For brave Macbeth (well he deserves that name),
    Disdaining Fortune, with his brandished steel,
    Which smoked with bloody execution
    (Like valor's minion), carved out his passage
20   Till he faced the slave;
    Which ne'er shook hands nor bade farewell to him
    Till he unseamed him from the nave to the chops
    And fixed his head upon our battlements.

Duncan. O valiant cousin! worthy gentleman!

25 **Captain.** As whence the sun 'gins his reflection
    Shipwracking storms and direful thunders break,
    So from that spring whence comfort seemed to come
    Discomfort swells. Mark, King of Scotland, mark.
    No sooner justice had, with valor armed,
30   Compelled these skipping kerns to trust their heels

[Stage Direction] **alarum within:** the sound of a trumpet offstage, a signal that soldiers should arm themselves.

5 'gainst my captivity: to save me from capture.
6 broil: battle.

7–9 Doubtful . . . art: The two armies are compared to two exhausted swimmers who cling to each other and thus cannot swim.

9–13 The officer hates Macdonwald, whose evils (**multiplying villainies**) swarm like insects around him. His army consists of soldiers (**kerns and gallowglasses**) from the Hebrides (**Western Isles**).

19 valor's minion: the favorite of valor, meaning the bravest of all.

22 unseamed him . . . chops: split him open from the navel to the jaw. What does this act suggest about Macbeth?

25–28 As whence . . . discomfort swells: As the rising sun is sometimes followed by storms, a new assault on Macbeth began.

But the Norweyan lord, surveying vantage,
With furbished arms and new supplies of men,
Began a fresh assault.

Duncan.   Dismayed not this
Our captains, Macbeth and Banquo?

Captain.   Yes,
35   As sparrows eagles, or the hare the lion.
If I say sooth, I must report they were
As cannons overcharged with double cracks, so they
Doubly redoubled strokes upon the foe.
Except they meant to bathe in reeking wounds,
40   Or memorize another Golgotha,
I cannot tell—
But I am faint; my gashes cry for help.

Duncan. So well thy words become thee as thy wounds
They smack of honor both. Go get him surgeons.

[*Exit* Captain, *attended.*]

[*Enter* Ross *and* Angus.]

45   Who comes here?

Malcolm.   The worthy Thane of Ross.

Lennox. What a haste looks through his eyes! So
     should he look
That seems to speak things strange.

Ross.   God save the King!

Duncan. Whence cam'st thou, worthy thane?

Ross.   From Fife, great King,
Where the Norweyan banners flout the sky
50   And fan our people cold. Norway himself,
With terrible numbers,
Assisted by that most disloyal traitor
The Thane of Cawdor, began a dismal conflict,
Till that Bellona's bridegroom, lapped in proof,
55   Confronted him with self-comparisons,
Point against point, rebellious arm 'gainst arm,
Curbing his lavish spirit; and to conclude,
The victory fell on us.

Duncan.   Great happiness!

Ross.   That now
Sweno, the Norways' king, craves composition;
60   Nor would we deign him burial of his men
Till he disbursed, at Saint Colme's Inch,
Ten thousand dollars to our general use.

Duncan. No more that Thane of Cawdor shall deceive

31–33 the Norweyan . . . assault: The king of Norway took an opportunity to attack.

36 sooth: the truth.

37 double cracks: a double load of ammunition.

39–40 Except . . . memorize another Golgotha: The officer's admiration leads to exaggeration. He claims he cannot decide whether (**except**) Macbeth and Banquo wanted to bathe in blood or make the battlefield as famous as Golgotha, the site of Christ's crucifixion.

45 Thane: a Scottish noble, similar in rank to an English earl.

48–58 Ross has arrived from Fife, where Norway's troops had invaded and frightened the people. There the king of Norway, along with the thane of Cawdor, met Macbeth (described as the husband of **Bellona,** the goddess of war). Macbeth, in heavy armor (**proof**), challenged the enemy, and achieved victory.

59 craves composition: wants a treaty.

60 deign: allow.

61 disbursed, at Saint Colme's Inch: paid at Saint Colme's Inch, an island in the North Sea.

Our bosom interest. Go pronounce his present death
65 And with his former title greet Macbeth.

Ross. I'll see it done.

Duncan. What he hath lost noble Macbeth hath won.

[*Exeunt.*]

63–64 deceive our bosom interest: betray our friendship; **present death:** immediate execution.

65 What reward has the king decided to give to Macbeth?

SCENE 3

A bleak place near the battlefield.

While leaving the battlefield, Macbeth and Banquo meet the witches, who are gleefully discussing the trouble they have caused. The witches hail Macbeth by a title he already holds, thane of Glamis. Then they prophesy that he will become both thane of Cawdor and king. When Banquo asks about his future, they speak in riddles, saying that he will be the father of kings but not a king himself.

After the witches vanish, Ross and Angus arrive to announce that Macbeth has been named thane of Cawdor. The first part of the witches' prophecy has come true, and Macbeth is stunned. He immediately begins to consider the possibility of murdering King Duncan to fulfill the rest of the witches' prophecy to him. Shaken, he turns his thoughts away from this "horrid image."

[*Thunder. Enter the three* Witches.]

First Witch. Where hast thou been, sister?

Second Witch. Killing swine.

Third Witch. Sister, where thou?

First Witch. A sailor's wife had chestnuts in her lap
5   And mounched and mounched and mounched. "Give
        me," quoth I.
    "Aroint thee, witch!" the rump-fed ronyon cries.
    Her husband's to Aleppo gone, master o' the
        "Tiger";
    But in a sieve I'll thither sail
    And, like a rat without a tail,
10   I'll do, I'll do, and I'll do.

Second Witch. I'll give thee a wind.

First Witch. Th' art kind.

Third Witch. And I another.

First Witch. I myself have all the other,
15   And the very ports they blow,
    All the quarters that they know
    I' the shipman's card.

2 Killing swine: Witches were often accused of killing people's pigs.

5 mounched: munched.

6 "Aroint thee, witch!" . . . ronyon cries: "Go away, witch!" the fat-bottomed (**rump-fed**), ugly creature (**ronyon**) cries.

7–8 The woman's husband, the master of a merchant ship (**the "Tiger"**), has sailed to Aleppo, a famous trading center in the Middle East. The witch will pursue him. Witches, who could change shape at will, were thought to sail on strainers (**sieve**).

View and Compare

In what ways do each of these images convey the eerie nature of the witches' scene?

Act 1, Scene 3: Macbeth and Banquo meet one of the witches, *The Throne of Blood* (film, directed by Akira Kurosawa, Japan, 1957)

Act 1, Scene 3: Banquo and the Witches (film, 1961)

I'll drain him dry as hay.
Sleep shall neither night nor day
20   Hang upon his penthouse lid.
He shall live a man forbid.
Weary sev'nights, nine times nine,
Shall he dwindle, peak, and pine.
Though his bark cannot be lost,
25   Yet it shall be tempest-tost.
Look what I have.

Second Witch. Show me! Show me!

First Witch. Here I have a pilot's thumb,
Wracked as homeward he did come.

[*Drum within.*]

30 **Third Witch.** A drum, a drum!
Macbeth doth come.

All. The Weird Sisters, hand in hand,
Posters of the sea and land,
Thus do go about, about,
35   Thrice to thine, and thrice to mine,
And thrice again, to make up nine.
Peace! The charm's wound up.

[*Enter* Macbeth *and* Banquo.]

Macbeth. So foul and fair a day I have not seen.

Banquo. How far is't called to Forres? What are these,
40   So withered, and so wild in their attire,
That look not like the inhabitants o' the earth,
And yet are on't? Live you? or are you aught
That man may question? You seem to understand me,
By each at once her choppy finger laying
45   Upon her skinny lips. You should be women,
And yet your beards forbid me to interpret
That you are so.

Macbeth.   Speak, if you can. What are you?

First Witch. All hail, Macbeth! Hail to thee, Thane of Glamis!

Second Witch. All hail, Macbeth! Hail to thee, Thane of
Cawdor!

50 **Third Witch.** All hail, Macbeth, that shalt be King hereafter!

Banquo. Good sir, why do you start and seem to fear
Things that do sound so fair? I' the name of truth,
Are ye fantastical, or that indeed
Which outwardly ye show? My noble partner
55   You greet with present grace and great prediction

14–23 The witch is going to torture the woman's husband. She controls where the winds blow, covering all points of a compass (**shipman's card**). She will make him sleepless, keeping his eyelids (**penthouse lid**) from closing. Thus, he will lead an accursed (**forbid**) life for weeks (**sev'nights**), wasting away with fatigue.

33 posters: quick riders.

36 Nine was considered a magical number by superstitious people.

42–46 aught: anything; **choppy:** chapped; **your beards:** Beards on women identified them as witches. Banquo vividly describes the witches. What does he notice about them?

48–50 What is surprising about the three titles the witches use to greet Macbeth?

53 Are ye fantastical: Are you (the witches) imaginary?

Of noble having and of royal hope,
That he seems rapt withal. To me you speak not.
If you can look into the seeds of time
And say which grain will grow and which will not,
60 Speak then to me, who neither beg nor fear
Your favors nor your hate.

First Witch. Hail!

Second Witch. Hail!

Third Witch. Hail!

65 **First Witch.** Lesser than Macbeth, and greater.

Second Witch. Not so happy, yet much happier.

Third Witch. Thou shalt get kings, though thou be none.
So all hail, Macbeth and Banquo!

First Witch. Banquo and Macbeth, all hail!

70 **Macbeth.** Stay, you imperfect speakers, tell me more!
By Sinel's death I know I am Thane of Glamis,
But how of Cawdor? The Thane of Cawdor lives,
A prosperous gentleman; and to be King
Stands not within the prospect of belief,
75 No more than to be Cawdor. Say from whence
You owe this strange intelligence, or why
Upon this blasted heath you stop our way
With such prophetic greeting. Speak, I charge you.

[Witches *vanish*.]

Banquo. The earth hath bubbles, as the water has,
80 And these are of them. Whither are they vanished?

Macbeth. Into the air, and what seemed corporal melted
As breath into the wind. Would they had stayed!

Banquo. Were such things here as we do speak about?
Or have we eaten on the insane root
85 That takes the reason prisoner?

Macbeth. Your children shall be kings.

Banquo.   You shall be King.

Macbeth. And Thane of Cawdor too. Went it not so?

Banquo. To the selfsame tune and words. Who's here?

[*Enter* Ross *and* Angus.]

Ross. The King hath happily received, Macbeth,
90 The news of thy success; and when he reads
Thy personal venture in the rebels' fight,
His wonders and his praises do contend

54–57 My noble partner . . . . rapt withal: The witches' prophecies of noble possessions (**having**)—the lands and wealth of Cawdor—and kingship (**royal hope**) have left Macbeth dazed (**rapt withal**). Look for evidence that shows what Macbeth thinks of the prophecies.

65–68 The witches speak in riddles. Though Banquo will be less fortunate (**happy**) than Macbeth, he will be father to (**get**) future kings. What do the witches predict for Banquo? What do you think their predictions mean?

75–76 whence: where. Macbeth wants to know where the witches received their knowledge (**strange intelligence**).

80 whither: where.

81 corporal: physical; real.

84 insane root: A number of plants were believed to cause insanity when eaten.

92–93 His wonders . . . Silenced with that: King Duncan hesitates between awe (**wonders**) and gratitude (**praise**) and is, as a result, speechless.

Which should be thine or his. Silenced with that,
In viewing o'er the rest o' the selfsame day,
95 He finds thee in the stout Norweyan ranks,
Nothing afeard of what thyself didst make,
Strange images of death. As thick as hail
Came post with post, and every one did bear
Thy praises in his kingdom's great defense
100 And poured them down before him.

Angus.   We are sent
To give thee from our royal master thanks;
Only to herald thee into his sight,
Not pay thee.

Ross. And for an earnest of a greater honor,
105 He bade me, from him, call thee Thane of Cawdor;
In which addition, hail, most worthy Thane!
For it is thine.

Banquo.   What, can the devil speak true?

Macbeth. The Thane of Cawdor lives. Why do you dress me
In borrowed robes?

Angus.   Who was the Thane lives yet,
110 But under heavy judgment bears that life
Which he deserves to lose. Whether he was combined
With those of Norway, or did line the rebel
With hidden help and vantage, or that with both
He labored in his country's wrack, I know not;
115 But treasons capital, confessed and proved,
Have overthrown him.

Macbeth.   [*Aside*] Glamis, and Thane of Cawdor!
The greatest is behind.—[*To* Ross *and* Angus] Thanks for
   your pains.
[*Aside to* Banquo] Do you not hope your children shall
   be kings,
When those that gave the Thane of Cawdor to me
120 Promised no less to them?

Banquo. [*Aside to* Macbeth] That, trusted home,
Might yet enkindle you unto the crown,
Besides the Thane of Cawdor. But 'tis strange!
And oftentimes, to win us to our harm,
The instruments of darkness tell us truths,
125 Win us with honest trifles, to betray's
In deepest consequence.—
Cousins, a word, I pray you.

96–97 nothing afeard . . . of death: Although Macbeth left many dead (**strange images of death**), he obviously did not fear death himself.

104 earnest: partial payment.

106 addition: title.

111–116 Whether he was . . . overthrown him: The former thane of Cawdor may have been secretly allied (**combined**) with the king of Norway, or he may have supported the traitor Macdonwald (**did line the rebel**). But he is guilty of treasons that deserve the death penalty (**treasons capital**), having aimed at the country's ruin (**wrack**).

116 aside: a stage direction that means Macbeth is speaking to himself, beyond hearing.

120 home: fully; completely.

121 enkindle you unto: inflame your ambitions.

123–126 to win us . . . consequence: Banquo warns that evil powers often offer little truths to tempt people. The witches may be lying about what matters most (**in deepest consequence**).

Macbeth. [*Aside*] Two truths are told,
As happy prologues to the swelling act
Of the imperial theme.—I thank you, gentlemen.—

130 [*Aside*] This supernatural soliciting
Cannot be ill; cannot be good. If ill,
Why hath it given me earnest of success,
Commencing in a truth? I am Thane of Cawdor.
If good, why do I yield to that suggestion

135 Whose horrid image doth unfix my hair
And make my seated heart knock at my ribs
Against the use of nature? Present fears
Are less than horrible imaginings.
My thought, whose murder yet is but fantastical,

140 Shakes so my single state of man that function
Is smothered in surmise and nothing is
But what is not.

Banquo.   Look how our partner's rapt.

Macbeth. [*Aside*] If chance will have me King, why
    chance may crown me,
Without my stir.

Banquo.   New honors come upon him,

145 Like our strange garments, cleave not to their mold
But with the aid of use.

Macbeth.   [*Aside*] Come what come may,
Time and the hour runs through the roughest day.

Banquo. Worthy Macbeth, we stay upon your leisure.

Macbeth. Give me your favor. My dull brain was wrought

150 With things forgotten. Kind gentlemen, your pains
Are registered where every day I turn
The leaf to read them. Let us toward the King.
[*Aside to* Banquo] Think upon what hath chanced, and, at
    more time,
The interim having weighed it, let us speak

155 Our free hearts each to other.

Banquo.   [*Aside to* Macbeth] Very gladly.

Macbeth. [*Aside to* Banquo] Till then, enough.—Come, friends.

[*Exeunt.*]

144 my stir: my doing anything.

146–147 Come what . . . roughest day: The future will arrive no matter what.

148 stay: wait.

150–152 your pains . . . read them: I will always remember your efforts. The metaphor refers to keeping a diary and reading it regularly.

153–155 at more time . . . other: Macbeth wants to discuss the prophecies later, after he and Banquo have had time to think about them.

SCENE 4

A room in the king's palace at Forres.

King Duncan receives news of the execution of the former thane of Cawdor. As the king is admitting his bad judgment concerning the traitor, Macbeth enters with Banquo, Ross, and Angus. Duncan expresses his gratitude to them and then, in a most unusual action, officially names his own son Malcolm as heir to the throne. To honor Macbeth, Duncan decides to visit Macbeth's castle at Inverness. Macbeth, his thoughts full of dark ambition, leaves to prepare for the king's visit.

[*Flourish. Enter* Duncan, Lennox, Malcolm, Donalbain, *and* Attendants.]

Duncan. Is execution done on Cawdor? Are not
  Those in commission yet returned?

Malcolm.   My liege,
  They are not yet come back. But I have spoke
  With one that saw him die; who did report

5   That very frankly he confessed his treasons,
  Implored your Highness' pardon, and set forth
  A deep repentance. Nothing in his life
  Became him like the leaving it. He died
  As one that had been studied in his death

10   To throw away the dearest thing he owed
  As 'twere a careless trifle.

Duncan.   There's no art
  To find the mind's construction in the face.
  He was a gentleman on whom I built
  An absolute trust.

[*Enter* Macbeth, Banquo, Ross, *and* Angus.]

                   O worthiest cousin,

15   The sin of my ingratitude even now
  Was heavy on me! Thou art so far before
  That swiftest wing of recompense is slow
  To overtake thee. Would thou hadst less deserved,
  That the proportion both of thanks and payment

20   Might have been mine! Only I have left to say,
  More is thy due than more than all can pay.

Macbeth. The service and the loyalty I owe,
  In doing it pays itself. Your Highness' part
  Is to receive our duties; and our duties

2 those in commission: those who have the responsibility for Cawdor's execution.

6 set forth: showed.

8–11 He died as . . . trifle: He died as if he had rehearsed (**studied**) the moment. Though losing his life (**the dearest thing he owed**), he behaved with calm dignity.

14–21 O worthiest . . . pay: The king feels that he cannot repay (**recompense**) Macbeth enough. Macbeth's qualities and accomplishments are of greater value than any thanks or payment Duncan can give.

25 Are to your throne and state children and servants,
Which do but what they should by doing everything
Safe toward your love and honor.

Duncan.   Welcome hither.
I have begun to plant thee and will labor
To make thee full of growing. Noble Banquo,
30 That hast no less deserved, nor must be known
No less to have done so, let me infold thee
And hold thee to my heart.

Banquo.   There if I grow,
The harvest is your own.

Duncan.   My plenteous joys,
Wanton in fullness, seek to hide themselves
35 In drops of sorrow. Sons, kinsmen, thanes,
And you whose places are the nearest, know
We will establish our estate upon
Our eldest, Malcolm, whom we name hereafter
The Prince of Cumberland; which honor must
40 Not unaccompanied invest him only,
But signs of nobleness, like stars, shall shine
On all deservers. From hence to Inverness,
And bind us further to you.

Macbeth. The rest is labor, which is not used for you.
45 I'll be myself the harbinger, and make joyful
The hearing of my wife with your approach;
So, humbly take my leave.

Duncan.   My worthy Cawdor!

Macbeth. [*Aside*] The Prince of Cumberland! That is a step
On which I must fall down, or else o'erleap,
50 For in my way it lies. Stars, hide your fires!
Let not light see my black and deep desires.
The eye wink at the hand; yet let that be,
Which the eye fears, when it is done, to see. [*Exit.*]

Duncan. True, worthy Banquo: he is full so valiant,
55 And in his commendations I am fed;
It is a banquet to me. Let's after him,
Whose care is gone before to bid us welcome.
It is a peerless kinsman.

[*Flourish. Exeunt.*]

28–29 I have . . . growing: The king plans to give more honors to Macbeth. What might Macbeth be thinking now?

33–35 My plenteous . . . sorrow: The king is crying tears of joy.

39 Prince of Cumberland: the title given to the heir to the Scottish throne. Now that Malcolm is heir, how might Macbeth react?

42 Inverness: site of Macbeth's castle, where the king has just invited himself, giving another honor to Macbeth.

45 harbinger: a representative sent before a royal party to make proper arrangements for its arrival.

52–53 The eye . . . to see: Macbeth hopes for the king's murder, although he does not want to see it.

SCENE 5

Macbeth's castle at Inverness.

Lady Macbeth reads a letter from her husband that tells her of the witches' prophecies, one of which has already come true. She is determined that Macbeth will be king. However, she fears that he lacks the courage to kill Duncan. After a messenger tells her the king is coming, she calls on the powers of evil to help her do what must be done. When Macbeth arrives, she tells him that the king must die that night but reminds him that he must appear to be a good and loyal host.

[*Enter* Lady Macbeth *alone, with a letter.*]

Lady Macbeth. [*Reads*] "They met me in the day of
success; and I have learned by the perfect'st report they
have more in them than mortal knowledge. When I
burned in desire to question them further, they made
themselves air, into which they vanished. Whiles I stood
rapt in the wonder of it, came missives from the King,
who all-hailed me Thane of Cawdor, by which title,
before, these Weird Sisters saluted me, and referred me
to the coming on of time with 'Hail, King that shalt
be!' This have I thought good to deliver thee, my
dearest partner of greatness, that thou mightst not lose
the dues of rejoicing by being ignorant of what
greatness is promised thee. Lay it to thy heart, and
farewell."

     Glamis thou art, and Cawdor, and shalt be
What thou art promised. Yet do I fear thy nature.
It is too full o' the milk of human kindness
To catch the nearest way. Thou wouldst be great;
Art not without ambition, but without
The illness should attend it. What thou wouldst highly,
That wouldst thou holily; wouldst not play false,
And yet wouldst wrongly win. Thou'ldst have, great Glamis,
That which cries "Thus thou must do," if thou have it;
And that which rather thou dost fear to do
Than wishest should be undone. Hie thee hither,
That I may pour my spirits in thine ear
And chastise with the valor of my tongue
All that impedes thee from the golden round
Which fate and metaphysical aid doth seem
To have thee crowned withal.

[*Enter* Messenger.]

16–21 Yet do . . . holily: Lady Macbeth fears her husband is too good (**too full o' the milk of human kindness**) to seize the throne by murder (**the nearest way**). Lacking the necessary wickedness (**illness**), he wants to gain power virtuously (**holily**).

What is your tidings?

Messenger. The King comes here tonight.

Lady Macbeth.   Thou'rt mad to say it!
Is not thy master with him? who, were't so,
Would have informed for preparation.

Messenger. So please you, it is true. Our Thane is coming.
One of my fellows had the speed of him,
Who, almost dead for breath, had scarcely more
Than would make up his message.

Lady Macbeth.   Give him tending;
He brings great news.

[*Exit* Messenger.]

                                   The raven himself is hoarse
That croaks the fatal entrance of Duncan
Under my battlements. Come, you spirits
That tend on mortal thoughts, unsex me here,
And fill me, from the crown to the toe, top-full
Of direst cruelty! Make thick my blood;
Stop up the access and passage to remorse,
That no compunctious visitings of nature
Shake my fell purpose nor keep peace between
The effect and it! Come to my woman's breasts
And take my milk for gall, you murd'ring ministers,
Wherever in your sightless substances
You wait on nature's mischief! Come, thick night,
And pall thee in the dunnest smoke of hell,
That my keen knife see not the wound it makes,
Nor heaven peep through the blanket of the dark
To cry "Hold, hold!"

[*Enter* Macbeth.]

                                   Great Glamis! worthy Cawdor!
Greater than both, by the all-hail hereafter!
Thy letters have transported me beyond
This ignorant present, and I feel now
The future in the instant.

Macbeth.   My dearest love,
Duncan comes here tonight.

Lady Macbeth.   And when goes hence?

Macbeth. Tomorrow, as he purposes.

Lady Macbeth.   O, never
Shall sun that morrow see!
Your face, my Thane, is as a book where men
May read strange matters. To beguile the time,

35 had the speed of him: rode
faster than he.

38 raven: The harsh cry of the
raven, a bird symbolizing evil and
misfortune, was supposed to
indicate an approaching death.

40–54 Lady Macbeth calls on the
spirits of evil to rid her of feminine
weakness (**unsex me**) and to block
out guilt. She wants no normal
pangs of conscience (**compunctious
visitings of nature**) to get in the
way of her murderous plan. She
asks that her mother's milk be
turned to bile (**gall**) by the unseen
evil forces (**murd'ring ministers,
sightless substances**) that exist in
nature. Furthermore, she asks that
the night wrap (**pall**) itself in
darkness as black as hell so that no
one may see or stop the crime. Do
you think Lady Macbeth could
actually kill Duncan?

Look like the time; bear welcome in your eye,
Your hand, your tongue; look like the innocent flower,
But be the serpent under't. He that's coming
Must be provided for; and you shall put
This night's great business into my dispatch,
Which shall to all our nights and days to come
Give solely sovereign sway and masterdom.

Macbeth. We will speak further.

Lady Macbeth.   Only look up clear.
To alter favor ever is to fear.
Leave all the rest to me.

[*Exeunt.*]

63–66 **To beguile . . . under't:** To
fool (**beguile**) everyone, act as
expected at such a time, that is, as
a good host. *Who is more like a
serpent, Lady Macbeth or her
husband?*

68 **my dispatch:** my management.

70 **give solely sovereign sway:**
bring absolute royal power.

72 **To alter . . . fear:** To change
your expression (**favor**) is a sign of
fear.

SCENE 6

In front of Macbeth's castle.

*King Duncan and his party arrive, and Lady Macbeth welcomes them.
Duncan is generous in his praise of his hosts and eagerly awaits the
arrival of Macbeth.*

[*Hautboys and torches. Enter* Duncan, Malcolm,
Donalbain, Banquo, Lennox, Macduff, Ross, Angus, *and
Attendants.*]

Duncan. This castle hath a pleasant seat. The air
Nimbly and sweetly recommends itself
Unto our gentle senses.

Banquo.   This guest of summer,
The temple-haunting martlet, does approve
By his loved mansionry that the heaven's breath
Smells wooingly here. No jutty, frieze,
Buttress, nor coign of vantage, but this bird
Hath made his pendent bed and procreant cradle.
Where they most breed and haunt, I have observed
The air is delicate.

[*Enter* Lady Macbeth.]

Duncan.   See, see, our honored hostess!
The love that follows us sometime is our trouble,
Which still we thank as love. Herein I teach you
How you shall bid God 'ield us for your pains
And thank us for your trouble.

Lady Macbeth.   All our service
In every point twice done, and then done double

[Stage Direction] **hautboys:** oboes.

1 **seat:** location.

3–10 **This guest . . . delicate:** The
martin (**martlet**) usually built its
nest on a church (**temple**), where
every projection (**jutty**), sculptured
decoration (**frieze**), support
(**buttress**), and convenient corner
(**coign of vantage**) offered a good
nesting site. Banquo sees the
presence of the martin's hanging
(**pendent**) nest, a breeding
(**procreant**) place, as a sign of
healthy air.

Were poor and single business to contend
Against those honors deep and broad wherewith
Your Majesty loads our house. For those of old,
And the late dignities heaped up to them,
20 We rest your hermits.

Duncan.   Where's the Thane of Cawdor?
We coursed him at the heels and had a purpose
To be his purveyor; but he rides well,
And his great love, sharp as his spur, hath holp him
To his home before us. Fair and noble hostess,
25 We are your guest tonight.

Lady Macbeth.   Your servants ever
Have theirs, themselves, and what is theirs, in compt,
To make their audit at your Highness' pleasure,
Still to return your own.

Duncan.   Give me your hand;
Conduct me to mine host. We love him highly
30 And shall continue our graces towards him.
By your leave, hostess.

[*Exeunt.*]

16 single business: weak service. Lady Macbeth claims that nothing she or her husband can do will match Duncan's generosity.

20 we rest your hermits: we can only repay you with prayers. The wealthy used to hire hermits to pray for the dead.

21 coursed him at the heels: followed him closely.

22 purveyor: one who makes advance arrangements for a royal visit.

23 holp: helped.

25–28 Legally, Duncan owned everything in his kingdom. Lady Macbeth politely says that they hold his property in trust (**compt**), ready to return it (**make their audit**) whenever he wants. Why do you think Lady Macbeth is being especially gracious to Duncan?

Act 1, Scene 6: Duncan at Macbeth's castle (film, 1971)

SCENE 7

A room in Macbeth's castle.

Macbeth has left Duncan in the middle of dinner. Alone, he begins to have second thoughts about his murderous plan. Lady Macbeth enters and discovers that he has changed his mind. She scornfully accuses him of cowardice and tells him that a true man would never back out of a commitment. She reassures him of success and explains her plan. She will make sure that the king's attendants drink too much. When they are fast asleep, Macbeth will stab the king with the servants' weapons.

[*Hautboys. Torches. Enter a* Sewer, *and divers* Servants *with dishes and service over the stage. Then enter* Macbeth.]

[Stage Direction] **Sewer:** the steward, the servant in charge of arranging the banquet and tasting the King's food; **divers:** various.

Macbeth. If it were done when 'tis done, then 'twere well
It were done quickly. If the assassination
Could trammel up the consequence, and catch,
With his surcease, success, that but this blow
5   Might be the be-all and the end-all here,
But here, upon this bank and shoal of time,
We'ld jump the life to come. But in these cases
We still have judgment here, that we but teach
Bloody instructions, which, being taught, return
10 To plague the inventor. This even-handed justice
Commends the ingredience of our poisoned chalice
To our own lips. He's here in double trust:
First, as I am his kinsman and his subject,
Strong both against the deed; then, as his host,
15 Who should against his murderer shut the door,
Not bear the knife myself. Besides, this Duncan
Hath borne his faculties so meek, hath been
So clear in his great office, that his virtues
Will plead like angels, trumpet-tongued, against
20 The deep damnation of his taking-off;
And pity, like a naked new-born babe,
Striding the blast, or heaven's cherubin, horsed
Upon the sightless couriers of the air,
Shall blow the horrid deed in every eye,
25 That tears shall drown the wind. I have no spur
To prick the sides of my intent, but only
Vaulting ambition, which o'erleaps itself
And falls on the other—

[*Enter* Lady Macbeth.]

How now? What news?

1–10 Again, Macbeth argues with himself about murdering the king. If it could be done without causing problems later, then it would be good to do it soon. If Duncan's murder would have no negative consequences and be successfully completed with his death (**surcease**), then Macbeth would risk eternal damnation. He knows, however, that terrible deeds (**bloody instructions**) often backfire.

12–28 Macbeth reminds himself that he is Duncan's relative, subject, and host and that the king has never abused his royal powers (**faculties**). In fact, Duncan is such a good person that there is no possible reason for his murder except Macbeth's own driving ambition.

Act 1, Scene 7: Orson Welles as Macbeth and Jeanette Nolan as Lady Macbeth (film, 1948)

Lady Macbeth. He has almost supped. Why have you left the
    chamber?

30 **Macbeth.** Hath he asked for me?

Lady Macbeth.   Know you not he has?

Macbeth. We will proceed no further in this business.
    He hath honored me of late, and I have bought
    Golden opinions from all sorts of people,
    Which would be worn now in their newest gloss,
35   Not cast aside so soon.

Lady Macbeth.   Was the hope drunk
    Wherein you dressed yourself? Hath it slept since?
    And wakes it now to look so green and pale
    At what it did so freely? From this time
    Such I account thy love. Art thou afeard
40   To be the same in thine own act and valor
    As thou art in desire? Wouldst thou have that
    Which thou esteem'st the ornament of life,
    And live a coward in thine own esteem,
    Letting "I dare not" wait upon "I would,"
45   Like the poor cat i' the adage?

Macbeth.   Prithee peace!
    I dare do all that may become a man.

32–35 I have . . . so soon: The praises that Macbeth has received are, like new clothes, to be worn, not quickly thrown away. What has Macbeth decided?

35–38 Was the hope drunk . . . freely: Lady Macbeth sarcastically suggests that Macbeth's ambition must have been drunk, because it now seems to have a hangover (**to look so green and pale**).

39–45 Such I . . . adage: Lady Macbeth criticizes Macbeth's weakened resolve to secure the crown (**ornament of life**) and calls him a coward. She compares him to a cat in a proverb (**adage**) who wouldn't catch fish because it feared wet feet.

Who dares do more is none.

Lady Macbeth.   What beast was't then
That made you break this enterprise to me?
When you durst do it, then you were a man;
50   And to be more than what you were, you would
Be so much more the man. Nor time nor place
Did then adhere, and yet you would make both.
They have made themselves, and that their fitness now
Does unmake you. I have given suck, and know
55   How tender 'tis to love the babe that milks me.
I would, while it was smiling in my face,
Have plucked my nipple from his boneless gums
And dashed the brains out, had I so sworn as you
Have done to this.

Macbeth.   If we should fail?

Lady Macbeth.   We fail?
60   But screw your courage to the sticking place,
And we'll not fail. When Duncan is asleep
(Whereto the rather shall his day's hard journey
Soundly invite him), his two chamberlains
Will I with wine and wassail so convince
65   That memory, the warder of the brain,
Shall be a fume, and the receipt of reason
A limbeck only. When in swinish sleep
Their drenched natures lie as in a death,
What cannot you and I perform upon
70   The unguarded Duncan? what not put upon
His spongy officers, who shall bear the guilt
Of our great quell?

Macbeth.   Bring forth men-children only,
For thy undaunted mettle should compose
Nothing but males. Will it not be received,
75   When we have marked with blood those sleepy two
Of his own chamber and used their very daggers,
That they have done't?

Lady Macbeth.   Who dares receive it other,
As we shall make our griefs and clamor roar
Upon his death?

Macbeth.   I am settled and bend up
80   Each corporal agent to this terrible feat.
Away, and mock the time with fairest show;
False face must hide what the false heart doth know.

[*Exeunt.*]

54 I have given suck: I have nursed a baby.

60 but . . . place: When each string of a guitar or lute is tightened to the peg (**sticking place**), the instrument is ready to be played.

65–67 that memory . . . a limbeck only: Memory was thought to be at the base of the brain, to guard against harmful vapors rising from the body. Lady Macbeth will get the guards so drunk that their reason will become like a still (**limbeck**), producing confused thoughts.

72 quell: murder.

72–74 Bring forth . . . males: Your bold spirit (**undaunted mettle**) is better suited to raising males than females. Do you think Macbeth's words express admiration?

79–82 I am settled . . . know: Now that Macbeth has made up his mind, every part of his body (**each corporal agent**) is tightened like a bow. He and Lady Macbeth will return to the banquet and deceive everyone (**mock the time**), hiding their evil intent with gracious faces.

Thinking through the LITERATURE

Connect to the Literature

1. What Do You Think?
At this point, what are your impressions of Macbeth and his wife?

> **Comprehension Check**
> - What predictions do the three witches make about Macbeth's future?
> - What do Macbeth and his wife plan to do to make the last prediction come true?
> - What predictions do the witches make about Banquo?

Think Critically

2. What values do you think motivate Macbeth?

3. At this point in the play, who would you say is the more forceful character, Macbeth or Lady Macbeth? Why?

THINK ABOUT
- their ambitions and fears
- their attitudes toward Duncan
- their attitudes toward murder
- their attitudes toward each other

4. Do you think Macbeth would have formed his murderous plan if the witches hadn't made their predictions to him? Explain who you think controls Macbeth's fate.

5. What might the witches' predictions about Banquo mean?

6. ACTIVE READING SHAKESPEARE'S LANGUAGE   In Act One, Scene 7, what does Macbeth mean in the final sentence of his **soliloquy,** lines 25–28? You may want to refer to your READER'S NOTEBOOK for notes you took on the Strategies for Reading Shakespeare's Language.

Extend Interpretations

7. What If? Imagine that you are a friend and adviser of Macbeth and his wife. What advice would you give them? What would you tell them about the three witches' predictions?

8. Critic's Corner According to the critic L. C. Knights, "*Macbeth* defines a particular kind of evil—the evil that results from a lust for power." On the basis of what you have read so far, do you agree? Is excessive ambition the only source of Macbeth's "evil"? Support your opinion with details from Act One.

Literary Analysis

SOLILOQUY/ASIDE   A **soliloquy** is a speech that reveals a character's private thoughts to the audience. An **aside** is a character's remark that others on the stage are not supposed to hear. Although unrealistic, the soliloquy and the aside allow playwrights to reveal characters' thoughts and motives that would otherwise remain hidden.

Paired Activity Working with a partner, identify revealing soliloquies and asides in Act One of *Macbeth,* and explain the thoughts and motives that they reveal. You might fill in a chart like the one below.

Act, Scene, Lines	Soliloquy or Aside?	What It Reveals
Act One, Scene 3, lines 116–117	Aside	Macbeth's ambition and his belief in the witches' prophecies

REVIEW   CHARACTERIZATION
Consider Duncan's speeches and actions, as well as the remarks that Macbeth and others make about him. What sort of person does Duncan seem to be? How good a king is he?

View and Compare

What aspects of Macbeth's character do these images convey?

Laurence Olivier, Memorial Theatre, Stratford-upon-Avon, England (1955)

John Gielgud, Piccadilly Theatre, London (1942)

Toshiro Mifune as Macbeth, *The Throne of Blood* (film, 1957)

Raul Julia, New York Shakespeare Festival

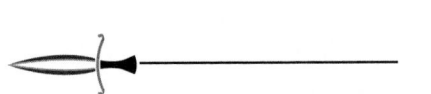

Act 2

SCENE 1

The court of Macbeth's castle.

It is past midnight, and Banquo and his son Fleance cannot sleep. When Macbeth appears, Banquo tells of his uneasy dreams about the witches. Macbeth promises that they will discuss the prophecies later, and Banquo goes to bed. Once alone, Macbeth imagines a dagger leading him toward the king's chamber. When he hears a bell, the signal from Lady Macbeth, he knows it is time to go to Duncan's room.

[*Enter* Banquo, *and* Fleance *with a torch before him.*]

Banquo. How goes the night, boy?

Fleance. The moon is down; I have not heard the clock.

Banquo. And she goes down at twelve.

Fleance.   I take't, 'tis later, sir.

Banquo. Hold, take my sword. There's husbandry in heaven;
5   Their candles are all out. Take thee that too.
       A heavy summons lies like lead upon me,
       And yet I would not sleep. Merciful powers,
       Restrain in me the cursed thoughts that nature
       Gives way to in repose!

[*Enter* Macbeth, *and a* Servant *with a torch.*]

                                        Give me my sword.
10   Who's there?

Macbeth. A friend.

Banquo. What, sir, not yet at rest? The King's abed.
       He hath been in unusual pleasure and
       Sent forth great largess to your offices.
15   This diamond he greets your wife withal
       By the name of most kind hostess, and shut up
       In measureless content.

Macbeth.   Being unprepared,
       Our will became the servant to defect,
       Which else should free have wrought.

Banquo.   All's well.
20   I dreamt last night of the three Weird Sisters.
       To you they have showed some truth.

Macbeth.   I think not of them.
       Yet when we can entreat an hour to serve,

4–5 There's husbandry . . . all out:
The heavens show economy
(**husbandry**) by keeping the lights
(**candles**) out—it is a starless night.

6 heavy summons: desire for
sleep.

14 largess to your offices: gifts to
the servants' quarters.

16 shut up: went to bed.

17–19 Being . . . wrought: Because
we were unprepared, we could not
entertain the king as we would
have liked. Do you believe in
Macbeth's sincerity here?

22 can entreat an hour: both have
the time.

We would spend it in some words upon that business,
If you would grant the time.

Banquo.   At your kind'st leisure.

25 **Macbeth.** If you shall cleave to my consent, when 'tis,
It shall make honor for you.

Banquo.   So I lose none
In seeking to augment it but still keep
My bosom franchised and allegiance clear,
I shall be counseled.

Macbeth.   Good repose the while!

30 **Banquo.** Thanks, sir. The like to you!

[*Exeunt* Banquo *and* Fleance.]

Macbeth. Go bid thy mistress, when my drink is ready,
She strike upon the bell. Get thee to bed.

[*Exit* Servant.]

Is this a dagger which I see before me,
The handle toward my hand? Come, let me clutch thee!
35 I have thee not, and yet I see thee still.
Art thou not, fatal vision, sensible
To feeling as to sight? or art thou but
A dagger of the mind, a false creation,
Proceeding from the heat-oppressed brain?
40 I see thee yet, in form as palpable
As this which now I draw.
Thou marshal'st me the way that I was going,
And such an instrument I was to use.

25–29 If you . . . be counseled:
Macbeth asks Banquo for his
support (**cleave to my consent**),
promising honors in return.
Banquo is willing to increase
(**augment**) his honor provided he
can keep a clear conscience and
remain loyal to the king (**keep my
bosom . . . clear**). How do you
think Macbeth feels about
Banquo's virtuous stand?

33–43 Is this a dagger . . . to use:
Macbeth sees a dagger hanging in
midair before him and questions
whether it is real (**palpable**) or the
illusion of a disturbed (**heat-
oppressed**) mind. The floating,
imaginary dagger, which leads
(**marshal'st**) him to Duncan's room,
prompts him to draw his own
dagger. Is Macbeth losing his
mind?

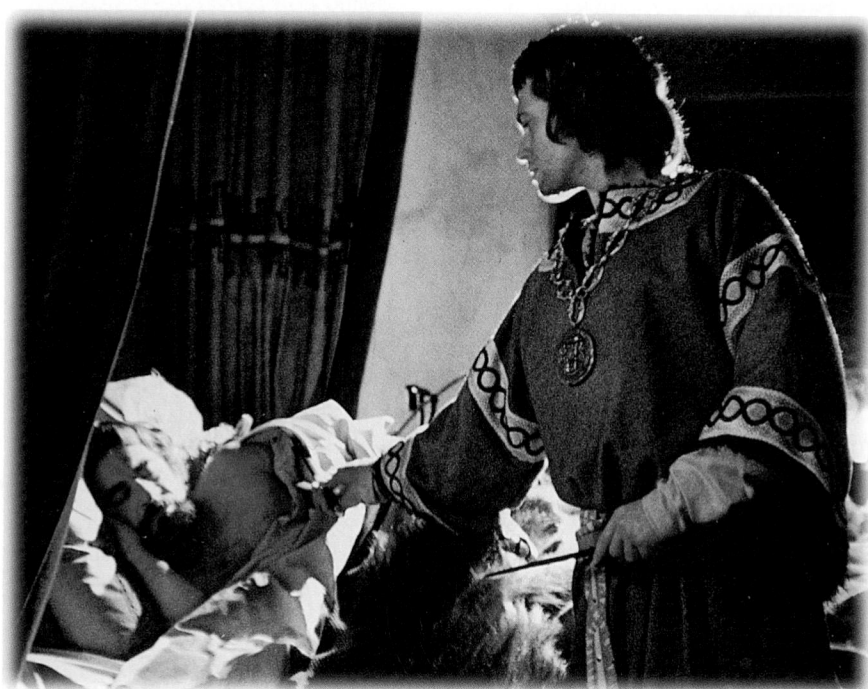

Act 2, Scene 2:
Duncan's murder,
Jon Finch as
Macbeth (film, 1971)

349

Mine eyes are made the fools o' the other senses,
45 Or else worth all the rest. I see thee still;
And on thy blade and dudgeon gouts of blood,
Which was not so before. There's no such thing.
It is the bloody business which informs
Thus to mine eyes. Now o'er the one half-world
50 Nature seems dead, and wicked dreams abuse
The curtained sleep. Witchcraft celebrates
Pale Hecate's offerings; and withered murder,
Alarumed by his sentinel, the wolf,
Whose howl's his watch, thus with his stealthy pace,
55 With Tarquin's ravishing strides, towards his design
Moves like a ghost. Thou sure and firm-set earth,
Hear not my steps which way they walk, for fear
Thy very stones prate of my whereabout
And take the present horror from the time,
60 Which now suits with it. Whiles I threat, he lives;
Words to the heat of deeds too cold breath gives.

[A bell rings.]

I go, and it is done. The bell invites me.
Hear it not, Duncan, for it is a knell
That summons thee to heaven, or to hell.

[Exit.]

44–45 Mine eyes . . . the rest:
Either his eyes are mistaken (**fools**)
or his other senses are.

46 on thy blade . . . blood: drops
of blood on the blade and handle.

60–61 Whiles I . . . gives: Talk
(**threat**) delays action (**deeds**).

63 knell: funeral bell.

SCENE 2

Macbeth's castle.

*As Lady Macbeth waits for her husband, she explains how she
drugged Duncan's servants. Suddenly a dazed and terrified Macbeth
enters, carrying the bloody daggers that he used to murder Duncan.
He imagines a voice that warns, "Macbeth shall sleep no more" and is
too afraid to return to the scene of the crime. Lady Macbeth takes the
bloody daggers back so that the servants will be blamed. Startled by a
knocking at the gate, she hurries back and tells Macbeth to wash off
the blood and change into his nightclothes.*

[*Enter* Lady Macbeth.]

Lady Macbeth. That which hath made them drunk hath made me
  bold;
What hath quenched them hath given me fire. Hark! Peace!
It was the owl that shrieked, the fatal bellman
Which gives the stern'st good-night. He is about it.
5 The doors are open, and the surfeited grooms
Do mock their charge with snores. I have drugged their
  possets,

3 fatal bellman: town crier.

5 surfeited grooms: drunken
servants.

6 possets: drinks.

View and Compare

In the scene portraying Duncan's murder, how do you interpret the dynamics between Macbeth and Lady Macbeth in each photo?

Act 2, Scene 2: After Duncan's murder, Derek Jacobi as Macbeth and Cheryl Campbell as Lady Macbeth, Royal Shakespeare Company (1993)

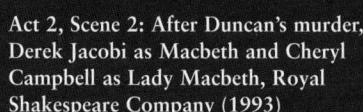

Act 2, Scene 2: After Duncan's murder, Toshiro Mifune as Macbeth and Isuzu Yamada as Lady Macbeth, *The Throne of Blood* (film, 1957)

That death and nature do contend about them
Whether they live or die.

Macbeth. [*Within*] Who's there? What, ho?

Lady Macbeth. Alack, I am afraid they have awaked,
10 And 'tis not done! The attempt, and not the deed,
Confounds us. Hark! I laid their daggers ready;
He could not miss 'em. Had he not resembled
My father as he slept, I had done't.

[*Enter Macbeth.*]

My husband!

Macbeth. I have done the deed. Didst thou not hear a noise?

15 **Lady Macbeth.** I heard the owl scream and the crickets cry.
Did not you speak?

Macbeth. When?

Lady Macbeth. Now.

Macbeth. As I descended?

Lady Macbeth. Ay.

Macbeth. Hark!
Who lies i' the second chamber?

Lady Macbeth. Donalbain.

20 **Macbeth.** This is a sorry sight.

Lady Macbeth. A foolish thought, to say a sorry sight.

Macbeth. There's one did laugh in's sleep, and one cried
"Murder!"
That they did wake each other. I stood and heard them.
But they did say their prayers and addressed them
25 Again to sleep.

Lady Macbeth. There are two lodged together.

Macbeth. One cried "God bless us!" and "Amen!" the other,
As they had seen me with these hangman's hands,
List'ning their fear. I could not say "Amen!"
When they did say "God bless us!"

30 **Lady Macbeth.** Consider it not so deeply.

Macbeth. But wherefore could not I pronounce "Amen"?
I had most need of blessing, and "Amen"
Stuck in my throat.

Lady Macbeth. These deeds must not be thought
After these ways. So, it will make us mad.

35 **Macbeth.** Methought I heard a voice cry "Sleep no more!
Macbeth does murder sleep"—the innocent sleep,

9–10 Why does the sound of Macbeth's voice make his wife so afraid?

11 confounds: destroys. If Duncan survives, they will be killed (as his attempted murderers)

27–28 as they . . . fear: He imagines that the sleepers could see him listening to their exclamations of fear, with his hands bloody like those of an executioner.

28–33 Why is Macbeth so troubled by the fact that he cannot say "Amen"?

Sleep that knits up the raveled sleave of care,
The death of each day's life, sore labor's bath,
Balm of hurt minds, great nature's second course,
40 Chief nourisher in life's feast.

Lady Macbeth.   What do you mean?

Macbeth. Still it cried "Sleep no more!" to all the house;
"Glamis hath murdered sleep, and therefore Cawdor
Shall sleep no more! Macbeth shall sleep no more!"

Lady Macbeth. Who was it that thus cried? Why, worthy Thane,
45 You do unbend your noble strength to think
So brainsickly of things. Go get some water
And wash this filthy witness from your hand.
Why did you bring these daggers from the place?
They must lie there. Go carry them and smear
50 The sleepy grooms with blood.

Macbeth.   I'll go no more.
I am afraid to think what I have done;
Look on't again I dare not.

Lady Macbeth.   Infirm of purpose!
Give me the daggers. The sleeping and the dead
Are but as pictures. 'Tis the eye of childhood
55 That fears a painted devil. If he do bleed,
I'll gild the faces of the grooms withal,
For it must seem their guilt. [*Exit. Knocking within.*]

Macbeth.   Whence is that knocking?
How is't with me when every noise appals me?
What hands are here? Ha! they pluck out mine eyes!
60 Will all great Neptune's ocean wash this blood
Clean from my hand? No. This my hand will rather
The multitudinous seas incarnadine,
Making the green one red. [*Enter* Lady Macbeth.]

Lady Macbeth. My hands are of your color, but I shame
65 To wear a heart so white. [*Knock.*] I hear a knocking
At the south entry. Retire we to our chamber.
A little water clears us of this deed.
How easy is it then! Your constancy
Hath left you unattended. [*Knock.*] Hark! more knocking.
70 Get on your nightgown, lest occasion call us
And show us to be watchers. Be not lost
So poorly in your thoughts.

Macbeth. To know my deed, 'twere best not know myself.
[*Knock.*]
Wake Duncan with thy knocking! I would thou couldst!
[*Exeunt.*]

36–40 the innocent sleep . . . life's feast: Sleep eases worries (**knits up the raveled sleave of care**), relieves the aches of physical work (**sore labor's bath**), soothes the anxious (**hurt minds**), and nourishes like food. Why is Macbeth so concerned about sleep?

47 this filthy witness: the evidence, that is, the blood.

56–57 I'll gild . . . guilt: She'll cover (**gild**) the servants with blood, blaming them for the murder. How is her attitude toward blood different from her husband's?

61–63 This my hand . . . one red: The blood on my hand will redden (**incarnadine**) the seas.

68–69 Your constancy . . . unattended: Your courage has left you.

70–71 lest . . . watchers: in case we are called for and found awake (**watchers**), which would look suspicious.

73 To know . . . myself: To come to terms with what I have done, I must forget about my conscience.

SCENE 3

Within Macbeth's castle, near the gate.

The drunken porter staggers across the courtyard to answer the knocking. After Lennox and Macduff are let in, Macbeth arrives to lead them to the king's quarters. Macduff enters Duncan's room and discovers his murder. Lennox and Macbeth then go to the scene, and Macbeth, pretending to be enraged, kills the two servants. Amid all the commotion, Lady Macbeth faints. Duncan's sons, Malcolm and Donalbain, fearing for their lives, quietly leave, hoping to escape the country.

[*Enter a* Porter. *Knocking within.*]

Porter. Here's a knocking indeed! If a man were porter
of hell gate, he should have old turning the key.
[*Knock.*] Knock, knock, knock! Who's there, i' the name
of Belzebub? Here's a farmer that hanged himself on
5   the expectation of plenty. Come in time! Have napkins
enow about you; here you'll sweat for't. [*Knock.*]
Knock, knock! Who's there, in the other devil's name?
Faith, here's an equivocator, that could swear in both
the scales against either scale; who committed treason
10   enough for God's sake, yet could not equivocate to
heaven. O, come in, equivocator! [*Knock.*] Knock,
knock, knock! Who's there? Faith, here's an English

2 old turning the key: plenty of
key turning. Hell's porter would be
busy because so many people are
ending up in hell these days.

4 Belzebub: a devil.

Act 2, Scene 3: The porter (right), with Lennox and
Macduff, in a stage production of *Macbeth* (1948)

354

tailor come hither for stealing out of a French hose.
Come in, tailor. Here you may roast your goose.

15 [*Knock.*] Knock, knock! Never at quiet! What are you?
But this place is too cold for hell. I'll devilporter it no
further. I had thought to have let in some of all
professions that go the primrose way to the everlasting
bonfire. [*Knock.*] Anon, anon! [*Opens the gate.*] I pray

20 you remember the porter.

[*Enter Macduff and Lennox.*]

Macduff. Was it so late, friend, ere you went to bed,
That you do lie so late?

Porter. Faith, sir, we were carousing till the second cock;
and drink, sir, is a great provoker of three things.

25 **Macduff.** What three things does drink especially
provoke?

Porter. Marry, sir, nose-painting, sleep, and urine.
Lechery, sir, it provokes, and unprovokes: it provokes
the desire, but it takes away the performance.

30 Therefore much drink may be said to be an
equivocator with lechery: it makes him, and it mars
him; it sets him on, and it takes him off; it persuades
him, and disheartens him; makes him stand to, and not
stand to; in conclusion, equivocates him in a sleep, and,

35 giving him the lie, leaves him.

Macduff. I believe drink gave thee the lie last night.

Porter. That it did, sir, i' the very throat on me; but I
requited him for his lie; and, I think, being too strong
for him, though he took up my legs sometime, yet I

40 made a shift to cast him.

Macduff. Is thy master stirring?

[*Enter Macbeth.*]

Our knocking has awaked him; here he comes.

Lennox. Good morrow, noble sir.

Macbeth.   Good morrow, both.

Macduff. Is the King stirring, worthy Thane?

Macbeth.   Not yet.

45 **Macduff.** He did command me to call timely on him;
I have almost slipped the hour.

Macbeth.   I'll bring you to him.

Macduff. I know this is a joyful trouble to you;
But yet 'tis one.

4–13 The porter pretends he is welcoming a farmer who killed himself after his schemes to get rich (**expectation of plenty**) failed, a double talker (**equivocator**) who perjured himself yet couldn't talk his way into heaven, and a tailor who cheated his customers by skimping on material (**stealing out of a French hose**).

23 second cock: early morning, announced by the crow of a rooster.

28–35 The porter jokes that alcohol stimulates lust (**lechery**) but makes the lover a failure.

36–40 More jokes about alcohol, this time described as a wrestler finally thrown off (**cast**) by the porter, who thus paid him back (**requited him**) for disappointment in love. *Cast* also means "to vomit" and "to urinate," two other ways of dealing with alcohol.

45 timely: early.

46 slipped the hour: missed the time.

Macbeth. The labor we delight in physics pain.
50   This is the door.

Macduff.   I'll make so bold to call,
    For 'tis my limited service. [*Exit.*]

Lennox. Goes the King hence today?

Macbeth.   He does; he did appoint so.

Lennox. The night has been unruly. Where we lay,
    Our chimneys were blown down, and, as they say,
55   Lamentings heard i' the air, strange screams of death,
    And prophesying, with accents terrible,
    Of dire combustion and confused events
    New hatched to the woeful time. The obscure bird
    Clamored the livelong night. Some say the earth
60   Was feverous and did shake.

Macbeth.   'Twas a rough night.

Lennox. My young remembrance cannot parallel
    A fellow to it.

[*Enter Macduff.*]

Macduff. O horror, horror, horror! Tongue nor heart
    Cannot conceive nor name thee!

Macbeth and Lennox.   What's the matter?

65 **Macduff.** Confusion now hath made his masterpiece!
    Most sacrilegious murder hath broke ope
    The Lord's anointed temple and stole thence
    The life o' the building!

Macbeth.   What is't you say? the life?

Lennox. Mean you his majesty?

70 **Macduff.** Approach the chamber, and destroy your sight
    With a new Gorgon. Do not bid me speak.
    See, and then speak yourselves.

[*Exeunt Macbeth and Lennox.*]

                    Awake, awake!
    Ring the alarum bell. Murder and treason!
    Banquo and Donalbain! Malcolm! awake!
75   Shake off this downy sleep, death's counterfeit,
    And look on death itself! Up, up, and see
    The great doom's image! Malcolm! Banquo!
    As from your graves rise up and walk like sprites
    To countenance this horror! Ring the bell!

[*Bell rings.*]

[*Enter Lady Macbeth.*]

49 physics: cures.

51 limited service: appointed duty.

53–60 Lennox discusses the strange events of the night, from fierce winds to the continuous shrieking (**strange screams of death**) of an owl (**obscure bird**). The owl's scream, a sign of death, bodes more (**new hatched**) uproar (**combustion**) and confusion.

65–68 Macduff mourns Duncan's death as the destruction (**confusion**) of order and as sacrilegious, violating all that is holy. In Shakespeare's time the king was believed to be God's sacred representative on earth.

71 new Gorgon: Macduff compares the shocking sight of the corpse to a Gorgon, a monster of Greek mythology with snakes for hair. Anyone who saw a Gorgon turned to stone.

75 counterfeit: imitation.

77 great doom's image: a picture like the Last Judgment, the end of the world.

78 sprites: spirits. The spirits of the dead were supposed to rise on Judgment Day.

80 **Lady Macbeth.** What's the business,
That such a hideous trumpet calls to parley
The sleepers of the house? Speak, speak!

Macduff. O gentle lady,
'Tis not for you to hear what I can speak!
The repetition in a woman's ear
85 Would murder as it fell.

[*Enter* Banquo.]

O Banquo, Banquo,
Our royal master's murdered!

Lady Macbeth. Woe, alas!
What, in our house?

Banquo. Too cruel anywhere.
Dear Duff, I prithee contradict thyself
And say it is not so.

[*Enter* Macbeth, Lennox, *and* Ross.]

90 **Macbeth.** Had I but died an hour before this chance,
I had lived a blessed time; for from this instant
There's nothing serious in mortality;
All is but toys; renown and grace is dead;
The wine of life is drawn, and the mere lees
95 Is left this vault to brag of.

[*Enter* Malcolm *and* Donalbain.]

Donalbain. What is amiss?

Macbeth. You are, and do not know't.
The spring, the head, the fountain of your blood
Is stopped, the very source of it is stopped.

Macduff. Your royal father's murdered.

Malcolm. O, by whom?

100 **Lennox.** Those of his chamber, as it seemed, had done't.
Their hands and faces were all badged with blood;
So were their daggers, which unwiped we found
Upon their pillows.
They stared and were distracted. No man's life
105 Was to be trusted with them.

Macbeth. O, yet I do repent me of my fury
That I did kill them.

Macduff. Wherefore did you so?

Macbeth. Who can be wise, amazed, temp'rate, and furious,
Loyal and neutral, in a moment? No man.
110 The expedition of my violent love

81 trumpet calls to parley: She compares the clanging bell to a trumpet used to call two sides of a battle to negotiation.

91–95 for from . . . brag of: From now on, nothing matters (**there's nothing serious**) in human life (**mortality**); even fame and grace have been made meaningless. The good wine of life has been removed (**drawn**), leaving only the dregs (**lees**). Is Macbeth being completely insincere, or does he regret his crime?

101 badged: marked.

Outrun the pauser, reason. Here lay Duncan,
His silver skin laced with his golden blood,
And his gashed stabs looked like a breach in nature
For ruin's wasteful entrance; there, the murderers,
115 Steeped in the colors of their trade, their daggers
Unmannerly breeched with gore. Who could refrain
That had a heart to love and in that heart
Courage to make's love known?

Lady Macbeth.   Help me hence, ho!

Macduff. Look to the lady.

Malcolm. [*Aside to* Donalbain] Why do we hold our tongues,
120   That most may claim this argument for ours?

Donalbain. [*Aside to* Malcolm] What should be spoken here,
Where our fate, hid in an auger hole,
May rush and seize us? Let's away,
Our tears are not yet brewed.

Malcolm.   [*Aside to* Donalbain] Nor our strong sorrow
125   Upon the foot of motion.

Banquo.   Look to the lady.

[Lady Macbeth *is carried out.*]

And when we have our naked frailties hid,
That suffer in exposure, let us meet
And question this most bloody piece of work,
To know it further. Fears and scruples shake us.
130 In the great hand of God I stand, and thence
Against the undivulged pretense I fight
Of treasonous malice.

Macduff.   And so do I.

All.   So all.

Macbeth. Let's briefly put on manly readiness
And meet i' the hall together.

All.   Well contented.

[*Exeunt all but* Malcolm *and* Donalbain.]

135 **Malcolm.** What will you do? Let's not consort with them.
To show an unfelt sorrow is an office
Which the false man does easy. I'll to England.

Donalbain. To Ireland I. Our separated fortune
Shall keep us both the safer. Where we are,
140   There's daggers in men's smiles; the near in blood,
The nearer bloody.

110–111 The . . . reason: He claims his emotions overpowered his reason, which would have made him pause to think before he killed Duncan's servants.

113 breach: a military term to describe a break in defenses, such as a hole in a castle wall.

118 Lady Macbeth faints. Is she only pretending?

119–120 Why do . . . ours: Malcolm wonders why he and Donalbain are silent, since they have the most right to discuss the topic (**argument**) of their father's death.

126–129 Banquo suggests that they all meet to discuss the murder after they have dressed (**our naked frailties hid**), since people are shivering in their nightclothes (**suffer in exposure**).

129–132 Though shaken by fears and doubts (**scruples**), he will fight against the secret plans (**undivulged pretense**) of the traitor. Do you think Banquo suspects Macbeth?

135–137 Malcolm does not want to join (**consort with**) the others because one of them may have plotted the murder.

Malcolm.   This murderous shaft that's shot
Hath not yet lighted, and our safest way
Is to avoid the aim. Therefore to horse!
And let us not be dainty of leave-taking
145 But shift away. There's warrant in that theft
Which steals itself when there's no mercy left.

[*Exeunt.*]

145–146 There's . . . left: There's good reason (**warrant**) to steal away from a situation that promises no mercy.

SCENE 4

Outside Macbeth's castle.

[*Enter* Ross *with an* Old Man.]

Old Man. Threescore and ten I can remember well;
Within the volume of which time I have seen
Hours dreadful and things strange; but this sore night
Hath trifled former knowings.

Ross.   Ah, good father,
5 Thou seest the heavens, as troubled with man's act,
Threaten his bloody stage. By the clock 'tis day,
And yet dark night strangles the traveling lamp.
Is't night's predominance, or the day's shame,
That darkness does the face of earth entomb
10 When living light should kiss it?

Old Man.   'Tis unnatural,
Even like the deed that's done. On Tuesday last
A falcon, tow'ring in her pride of place,
Was by a mousing owl hawked at and killed.

Ross. And Duncan's horses (a thing most strange and certain),
15 Beauteous and swift, the minions of their race,
Turned wild in nature, broke their stalls, flung out,
Contending 'gainst obedience, as they would make
War with mankind.

Old Man.   'Tis said they eat each other.

Ross. They did so, to the amazement of mine eyes
20 That looked upon't.

[*Enter* Macduff.]

                        Here comes the good Macduff.
How goes the world, sir, now?

Macduff.   Why, see you not?

Ross. Is't known who did this more than bloody deed?

1–4 Nothing the old man has seen in seventy years (**threescore and ten**) has been as strange and terrible (**sore**) as this night. It has made other times seem trivial (**hath trifled**) by comparison.

6–10 By the clock . . . kiss it: Though daytime, an unnatural darkness blots out the sun (**strangles the traveling lamp**).

12–13 a falcon . . . and killed: The owl would never be expected to attack a high-flying (**tow'ring**) falcon, much less defeat one.

15 minions: best or favorites.

17 contending 'gainst obedience: The well-trained horses rebelliously fought against all constraints.

Macduff. Those that Macbeth hath slain.

Ross.   Alas, the day!
What good could they pretend?

Macduff.   They were suborned.
25   Malcolm and Donalbain, the King's two sons,
Are stol'n away and fled, which puts upon them
Suspicion of the deed.

Ross.   'Gainst nature still!
Thriftless ambition, that will raven up
Thine own live's means! Then 'tis most like
30   The sovereignty will fall upon Macbeth.

Macduff. He is already named, and gone to Scone
To be invested.

Ross.   Where is Duncan's body?

Macduff. Carried to Colmekill,
The sacred storehouse of his predecessors
35   And guardian of their bones.

Ross.   Will you to Scone?

Macduff. No, cousin, I'll to Fife.

Ross.   Well, I will thither.

Macduff. Well, may you see things well done there. Adieu,
Lest our old robes sit easier than our new!

Ross. Farewell, father.

40   **Old Man.** God's benison go with you, and with those
That would make good of bad, and friends of foes!

[*Exeunt omnes.*]

24 What . . . pretend: Ross wonders what the servants could have hoped to achieve (**pretend**) by killing; **suborned:** hired or bribed.

27–29 He is horrified by the thought that the sons could act contrary to nature (**'gainst nature still**) because of wasteful (**thriftless**) ambition and greedily destroy (**raven up**) their father, the source of their own life (**thine own live's means**).

31–32 to Scone . . . invested: Macbeth went to the traditional site (**Scone**) where Scotland's kings were crowned.

40–41 The old man gives his blessing (**benison**) to Macduff and all those who would restore good and bring peace to the troubled land.

from HOLINSHED'S CHRONICLES

Preparing to Read
Build Background

One of Shakespeare's favorite sources for his plays was the *Chronicles* (1577), a collection of histories and descriptions of the British Isles written by Raphael Holinshed and others. The following passage reveals Macbeth's involvement in Duncan's murder.

1. **laund**: glade.
2. **elder**: ancient.
3. **quarrel**: cause.
4. **pretend**: claim.
5. **lay sore upon him**: pressed him hard.

It fortuned, as Macbeth and Banquo journeyed toward Forres, where the King then lay, they went sporting by the way together without other company save only themselves, passing through the woods and fields, when suddenly, in the midst of a laund,[1] there met them three women in strange and wild apparel, resembling creatures of elder[2] world; whom when they attentively beheld, wondering much at the sight, the first of them spoke and said, "All hail, Macbeth, Thane of Glamis!" (for he had lately entered into that dignity and office by the death of his father Sinel). The second of them said, "Hail, Macbeth, Thane of Cawdor!" But the third said, "All hail, Macbeth, that hereafter shalt be King of Scotland!"

Then Banquo. "What manner of women," saith he, "are you, that seem so little favorable unto me, whereas to my fellow here, besides high offices, ye assign also the kingdom, appointing forth nothing for me at all?" "Yes," saith the first of them, "we promise greater benefits unto thee than unto him, for he shall reign indeed, but with an unlucky end; neither shall he leave any issue behind him to succeed in his place, where contrarily thou indeed shalt not reign at all, but of thee those shall be born which shall govern the Scottish kingdom by long order of continual descent." Herewith the foresaid women vanished immediately out of their sight. . . . Shortly after, the Thane of Cawdor being condemned at Forres of treason against the King committed, his lands, livings, and offices were given of the King's liberality to Macbeth. . . .

Shortly after it chanced that King Duncan, having two sons by his wife (which was the daughter of Siward Earl of Northumberland), he made the elder of them (called Malcolm) Prince of Cumberland, as it were thereby to appoint him his successor in the kingdom immediately after his decease. Macbeth, sore troubled herewith, for that he saw by this means his hope sore hindered . . . he began to take counsel how he might usurp the kingdom by force, having a just quarrel[3] so to do (as he took the matter), for that Duncan did what in him lay to defraud him of all manner of title and claim which he might, in time to come, pretend[4] unto the crown.

The words of the three Weird Sisters also (of whom before ye have heard) greatly encouraged him hereunto; but specially his wife lay sore upon him[5] to attempt the thing, as she that was very ambitious, burning in unquenchable desire to bear the name of a queen. At length, therefore, communicating his purposed intent with his trusty friends, amongst whom Banquo was the chiefest, upon confidence of their promised aid he slew the King at Inverness or (as some say) at Bothgowanan, in the sixth year of his reign.

Thinking through the LITERATURE

Connect to the Literature

1. What Do You Think? What mental picture from this act lingers most in your mind? Jot down words and phrases to describe it.

> **Comprehension Check**
> • Whom do Macbeth and his wife plan to take the blame for Duncan's murder?
> • What prompts people to think that Malcolm and Donalbain may be guilty of killing their father?
> • In the absence of Malcolm and Donalbain, who will become king?

Think Critically

2. How does the nocturnal setting of Act Two, Scene 1, contribute to the scene's overall **mood,** or atmosphere?

THINK ABOUT
{
• the time of night at which the events take place
• Banquo's observations about the night
• Macbeth's remarks about the night

3. Why do you think Macbeth imagines that he sees a dagger at the end of Act Two, Scene 1?

4. **ACTIVE READING** **READING DRAMA** Review any questions about or reactions to stage directions in your **READER'S NOTEBOOK**. What effect do you think each of the following **sound effects** might have on the audience?

- the bell at the end of Scene 1
- the owl referred to in Scene 2
- the knocking that ends Scene 2 and continues in Scene 3
- the "alarum bell" in Scene 3

5. Consider the porter's humorous comments on the types of people who wind up at the gates of hell. How is Macbeth like or unlike the sinners that the porter describes?

6. How does Lady Macbeth compare with her husband at this point in the play? Cite evidence to support your opinion.

7. Do you think the Macbeths are finished with their killing? If so, why? If not, whom do you think they might kill next?

Extend Interpretations

8. What If? Do you think Macbeth would have killed Duncan if his wife had not urged him to do so? Cite evidence from the first two acts to support your opinion.

Literary Analysis

BLANK VERSE One of the most popular verse forms in English, **blank verse** consists of unrhymed iambic pentameter, in which the normal line contains five stressed syllables, each preceded by an unstressed syllable:

> *Wĭll aĺl grĕat Néptŭne's ócĕan wásh thĭs blóod*

Paired Activity Working with a partner, copy a representative passage from *Macbeth,* marking the unstressed (˘) and stressed (´) syllables. Then discuss the following questions:

- Shakespeare sometimes introduces rhyming pairs of lines for emphasis or as signals to the actors, indicating entrances or changes of scene. What are some examples in Act Two?
- Shakespeare sometimes has characters speak in prose. Why do you think he uses prose for the porter's opening remarks in Act Two, Scene 3?

REVIEW **FIGURATIVE LANGUAGE**
Find examples of figurative language that help convey Macbeth's fears and doubts before the murder of Duncan, his horror of the act itself, and the guilt he feels afterward.

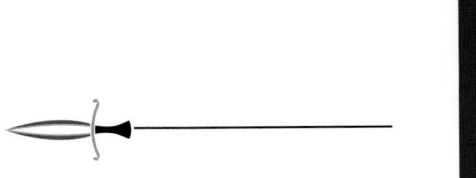

Act 3

SCENE 1

Macbeth's palace at Forres.

Banquo voices his suspicions of Macbeth but still hopes that the prophecy about his own children will prove true. Macbeth, as king, enters to request Banquo's presence at a state banquet. Banquo explains that he will be away during the day with his son Fleance but that they will return in time for the banquet. Alone, Macbeth expresses his fear of Banquo, because of the witches' promise that Banquo's sons will be kings. He persuades two murderers to kill Banquo and his son before the banquet.

[*Enter* Banquo.]

Banquo. Thou hast it now—King, Cawdor, Glamis, all,
As the Weird Women promised; and I fear
Thou play'dst most foully for't. Yet it was said
It should not stand in thy posterity,

5   But that myself should be the root and father
Of many kings. If there come truth from them
(As upon thee, Macbeth, their speeches shine),
Why, by the verities on thee made good,
May they not be my oracles as well

10   And set me up in hope? But, hush, no more!

[*Sennet sounded. Enter* Macbeth, *as King;* Lady Macbeth, *as Queen;* Lennox, Ross, Lords, *and* Attendants.]

Macbeth. Here's our chief guest.

Lady Macbeth.   If he had been forgotten,
It had been as a gap in our great feast,
And all-thing unbecoming.

Macbeth. Tonight we hold a solemn supper, sir,

15   And I'll request your presence.

Banquo.   Let your Highness
Command upon me, to the which my duties
Are with a most indissoluble tie
For ever knit.

Macbeth.   Ride you this afternoon?

Banquo. Ay, my good lord.

20 **Macbeth.** We should have else desired your good advice
(Which still hath been both grave and prosperous)

3–4 it was said . . . posterity: it was predicted that the kingship would not remain in your family.

6–10 If . . . in hope: Banquo is impressed by the truth (**verities**) of the prophecies. He hopes the witches' prediction for him will come true too (**be my oracles as well**).

[Stage Direction] **sennet sounded:** A trumpet is sounded.

14–15 A king usually uses the royal pronoun *we.* Notice how Macbeth switches to *I,* keeping a personal tone with Banquo.

15–18 Banquo says he is duty-bound to serve the king. Do you think his tone is cold or warm here?

21 grave and prosperous: thoughtful and profitable.

In this day's council; but we'll take tomorrow.
Is't far you ride?

Banquo. As far, my lord, as will fill up the time
25 'Twixt this and supper. Go not my horse the better,
I must become a borrower of the night
For a dark hour or twain.

Macbeth.   Fail not our feast.

Banquo. My lord, I will not.

Macbeth. We hear our bloody cousins are bestowed
30 In England and in Ireland, not confessing
Their cruel parricide, filling their hearers
With strange invention. But of that tomorrow,
When therewithal we shall have cause of state
Craving us jointly. Hie you to horse. Adieu,
35 Till you return at night. Goes Fleance with you?

Banquo. Ay, my good lord. Our time does call upon's.

Macbeth. I wish your horses swift and sure of foot,
And so I do commend you to their backs.
Farewell.

[*Exit* Banquo.]

40 Let every man be master of his time
Till seven at night. To make society
The sweeter welcome, we will keep ourself
Till supper time alone. While then, God be with you!

[*Exeunt all but* Macbeth *and a* Servant.]

Sirrah, a word with you. Attend those men
45 Our pleasure?

Servant. They are, my lord, without the palace gate.

Macbeth. Bring them before us.

[*Exit* Servant.]

Macbeth.   To be thus is nothing,
But to be safely thus. Our fears in Banquo
Stick deep, and in his royalty of nature
50 Reigns that which would be feared. 'Tis much he dares,
And to that dauntless temper of his mind
He hath a wisdom that doth guide his valor
To act in safety. There is none but he
Whose being I do fear; and under him
55 My genius is rebuked, as it is said
Mark Antony's was by Caesar. He chid the Sisters
When first they put the name of King upon me,
And bade them speak to him. Then, prophet-like,

25–27 Go not . . . twain: If his horse goes no faster than usual, he'll be back an hour or two (**twain**) after dark.

29 bloody cousins: murderous relatives (Malcolm and Donalbain); **bestowed:** settled.

32 strange invention: lies; stories they have invented. What kinds of stories might they be telling?

33–34 when . . . jointly: when matters of state will require the attention of us both.

40 be master of his time: do what he wants.

43 while: until.

44–45 sirrah: a term of address to an inferior; **Attend . . . pleasure:** Are they waiting for me?

47–48 To be thus . . . safely thus: To be king is worthless unless my position as king is safe.

51 dauntless temper: fearless temperament.

55–56 my genius . . . Caesar: Banquo's mere presence forces back (**rebukes**) Macbeth's ruling spirit (**genius**). In ancient Rome, Octavius Caesar, who became emperor, had the same effect on his rival, Mark Antony.

They hailed him father to a line of kings.
60 Upon my head they placed a fruitless crown
And put a barren scepter in my gripe,
Thence to be wrenched with an unlineal hand,
No son of mine succeeding. If't be so,
For Banquo's issue have I filed my mind;
65 For them the gracious Duncan have I murdered;
Put rancors in the vessel of my peace
Only for them, and mine eternal jewel
Given to the common enemy of man
To make them kings, the seed of Banquo kings!
70 Rather than so, come, Fate, into the list,
And champion me to the utterance! Who's there?

[*Enter* Servant *and two* Murderers.]

Now go to the door and stay there till we call.

[*Exit Servant.*]

Was it not yesterday we spoke together?
Murderers. It was, so please your Highness.

Macbeth.   Well then, now
75 Have you considered of my speeches? Know
That it was he, in the times past, which held you
So under fortune, which you thought had been
Our innocent self. This I made good to you
In our last conference, passed in probation with you
80 How you were borne in hand, how crossed; the instruments;
Who wrought with them; and all things else that might
To half a soul and to a notion crazed
Say "Thus did Banquo."

First Murderer.   You made it known to us.

Macbeth. I did so; and went further, which is now
85 Our point of second meeting. Do you find
Your patience so predominant in your nature
That you can let this go? Are you so gospeled
To pray for this good man and for his issue,
Whose heavy hand hath bowed you to the grave
90 And beggared yours for ever?

First Murderer.   We are men, my liege.

Macbeth. Ay, in the catalogue ye go for men,
As hounds and greyhounds, mongrels, spaniels, curs,
Shoughs, water-rugs, and demi-wolves are clept
All by the name of dogs. The valued file
95 Distinguishes the swift, the slow, the subtle,
The housekeeper, the hunter, every one

60–69 They gave me a childless (**fruitless, barren**) crown and scepter, which will be taken away by someone outside my family (**unlineal**). It appears that I have committed murder, poisoned (**filed**) my mind, and destroyed my soul (**eternal jewel**) all for the benefit of Banquo's heirs.

70–71 Rather . . . utterance: Rather than allowing Banquo's heirs to become kings, he calls upon Fate itself to enter the combat arena (**list**) so that he can fight it to the death (**utterance**). Why does he feel that he needs to fight Fate?

75–83 Macbeth supposedly proved (**passed in probation**) Banquo's role, his deception (**how you were borne in hand**), his methods, and his allies. Even a half-wit (**half a soul**) or a crazed person would agree that Banquo caused their trouble.

87–90 He asks whether they are so influenced by the gospel's message of forgiveness (**so gospeled**) that they will pray for Banquo and his children despite his harshness, which will leave their own families beggars.

According to the gift which bounteous nature
Hath in him closed; whereby he does receive
Particular addition, from the bill
100 That writes them all alike; and so of men.
Now, if you have a station in the file,
Not i' the worst rank of manhood, say't;
And I will put that business in your bosoms
Whose execution takes your enemy off,
105 Grapples you to the heart and love of us,
Who wear our health but sickly in his life,
Which in his death were perfect.

91–100 The true worth of a dog can be measured only by examining the record (**valued file**) of its special qualities (**particular addition**).

103–107 Macbeth will give them a secret job (**business in your bosoms**) that will earn them his loyalty (**grapples you to the heart**) and love. Banquo's death will make this sick king healthy.

Act 3, Scene 1: Macbeth with the murderers (film 1971)

Second Murderer. I am one, my liege,
Whom the vile blows and buffets of the world
have so incensed that I am reckless what
110 I do to spite the world.

First Murderer. And I another,
So weary with disasters, tugged with fortune,
That I would set my life on any chance,
To mend it or be rid on't.

Macbeth. Both of you
Know Banquo was your enemy.

Murderers. True, my lord.

115 **Macbeth.** So is he mine, and in such bloody distance
That every minute of his being thrusts
Against my near'st of life; and though I could
With barefaced power sweep him from my sight
And bid my will avouch it, yet I must not,
120 For certain friends that are both his and mine,
Whose loves I may not drop, but wail his fall
Who I myself struck down. And thence it is
That I to your assistance do make love,
Masking the business from the common eye
125 For sundry weighty reasons.

Second Murderer. We shall, my lord,
Perform what you command us.

First Murderer. Though our lives—

Macbeth. Your spirits shine through you. Within this hour
at most
I will advise you where to plant yourselves,
Acquaint you with the perfect spy o' the time,
130 The moment on't; for't must be done tonight,
And something from the palace (always thought
That I require a clearness), and with him,
To leave no rubs nor botches in the work,
Fleance his son, that keeps him company,
135 Whose absence is no less material to me
Than is his father's, must embrace the fate
Of that dark hour. Resolve yourselves apart;
I'll come to you anon.

Murderers. We are resolved, my lord.

Macbeth. I'll call upon you straight. Abide within.
[*Exeunt* Murderers.]

111 tugged with: knocked about by.

115–117 Banquo is near enough to draw blood, and like a menacing swordsman, his mere presence threatens (**thrusts against**) Macbeth's existence.

119 bid my will avouch it: justify it as my will.

127 Your spirits shine through you: Your courage is evident.

131–132 and something . . . clearness: The murder must be done away from the palace so that I remain blameless (**I require a clearness**).

135 absence: death. Why is the death of Fleance so important?

137 Resolve yourselves apart: Decide in private.

139 straight: soon.

140   It is concluded. Banquo, thy soul's flight,
       If it find heaven, must find it out tonight.

[*Exit.*]

SCENE 2

Macbeth's palace at Forres.

Lady Macbeth and her husband discuss the troubled thoughts and bad dreams they have had since Duncan's murder. However, they agree to hide their dark emotions at the night's banquet. Lady Macbeth tries to comfort the tormented Macbeth, but her words do no good. Instead, Macbeth hints at some terrible event that will occur that night.

[*Enter* Lady Macbeth *and a* Servant]

Lady Macbeth. Is Banquo gone from court?

Servant. Ay, madam, but returns again tonight.

Lady Macbeth. Say to the King I would attend his leisure
     For a few words.

Servant.   Madam, I will.

[*Exit.*]

Lady Macbeth.   Naught's had, all's spent,
5   Where our desire is got without content.
     'Tis safer to be that which we destroy
     Than by destruction dwell in doubtful joy.

[*Enter* Macbeth.]

     How now, my lord? Why do you keep alone,
     Of sorriest fancies your companions making,
10   Using those thoughts which should indeed have died
     With them they think on? Things without all remedy
     Should be without regard. What's done is done.

Macbeth. We have scotched the snake, not killed it.
     She'll close and be herself, whilst our poor malice
15   Remains in danger of her former tooth.
     But let the frame of things disjoint, both the worlds suffer,
     Ere we will eat our meal in fear and sleep
     In the affliction of these terrible dreams
     That shake us nightly. Better be with the dead,
20   Whom we, to gain our peace, have sent to peace,
     Than on the torture of the mind to lie
     In restless ecstasy. Duncan is in his grave;
     After life's fitful fever he sleeps well.
     Treason has done his worst: nor steel nor poison,

4–7 Nothing (**naught**) has been gained; everything has been wasted (**spent**). It would be better to be dead like Duncan than to live in uncertain joy.

8–12 Does Lady Macbeth follow her own advice about forgetting Duncan's murder?

16–22 He would rather have the world fall apart (**the frame of things disjoint**) than be afflicted with such fears and nightmares. Death is preferable to life on the torture rack of mental anguish (**restless ecstasy**).

View and Compare

Compare the facial expressions of these two Lady Macbeths. Which better fits your idea of her attitude as she tries to persuade Macbeth to forget about Duncan?

Act 3, Scene 2: Jon Finch as Macbeth and Francesca Annis as Lady Macbeth (film, 1971)

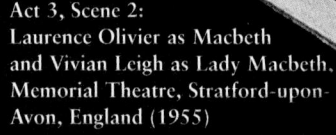

Act 3, Scene 2: Laurence Olivier as Macbeth and Vivian Leigh as Lady Macbeth, Memorial Theatre, Stratford-upon-Avon, England (1955)

25 Malice domestic, foreign levy, nothing,
    Can touch him further.

Lady Macbeth.   Come on.
    Gentle my lord, sleek o'er your rugged looks;
    Be bright and jovial among your guests tonight.

Macbeth. So shall I, love; and so, I pray, be you.
30 Let your remembrance apply to Banquo;
    Present him eminence both with eye and tongue:
    Unsafe the while, that we
    Must lave our honors in these flattering streams
    And make our faces vizards to our hearts,
35 Disguising what they are.

Lady Macbeth   You must leave this.

Macbeth. O, full of scorpions is my mind, dear wife!
    Thou know'st that Banquo, and his Fleance, lives.

Lady Macbeth. But in them Nature's copy's not eterne.

Macbeth. There's comfort yet; they are assailable.
40 Then be thou jocund. Ere the bat hath flown
    His cloistered flight, ere to black Hecate's summons
    The shard-borne beetle with his drowsy hums
    Hath rung night's yawning peal, there shall be done
    A deed of dreadful note.

Lady Macbeth.   What's to be done?

45 **Macbeth.** Be innocent of the knowledge, dearest chuck,
    Till thou applaud the deed. Come, seeling night,
    Scarf up the tender eye of pitiful day,
    And with thy bloody and invisible hand
    Cancel and tear to pieces that great bond
50 Which keeps me pale! Light thickens, and the crow
    Makes wing to the rooky wood.
    Good things of day begin to droop and drowse,
    Whiles night's black agents to their preys do rouse.
    Thou marvell'st at my words; but hold thee still:
55 Things bad begun make strong themselves by ill.
    So prithee go with me.

    [*Exeunt.*]

27 sleek: smooth.

31 present him eminence: pay special attention to him.

33 lave . . . streams: wash (**lave**) our honor in streams of flattery—that is, falsify our feelings.

34 vizards: masks.

38 in them . . . not eterne: Nature did not give them immortality.

40–44 jocund: cheerful; merry; **Ere the bat . . . note:** Before nightfall, when the bats and beetles fly, something dreadful will happen.

45 chuck: chick (a term of affection).

46 seeling: blinding.

49 great bond: Banquo's life.

51 rooky: gloomy; also, filled with crows (rooks).

55 Things brought about through evil need additional evil to make them strong.

SCENE 3

A park near the palace.

The two murderers, joined by a third, ambush Banquo and Fleance, killing Banquo. Fleance manages to escape in the darkness.

[*Enter three* Murderers.]

First Murderer. But who did bid thee join with us?

Third Murderer.   Macbeth.

Second Murderer. He needs not our mistrust, since he delivers
    Our offices, and what we have to do,
    To the direction just.

First Murderer.   Then stand with us.
5   The west yet glimmers with some streaks of day.
    Now spurs the lated traveler apace
    To gain the timely inn, and near approaches
    The subject of our watch.

Third Murderer.   Hark! I hear horses.

Banquo. [*Within*] Give us a light there, ho!

Second Murderer.   Then 'tis he! The rest
10   That are within the note of expectation
    Already are i' the court.

First Murderer.   His horses go about.

Third Murderer. Almost a mile; but he does usually,
    So all men do, from hence to the palace gate
    Make it their walk.

[*Enter* Banquo, *and* Fleance *with a torch*.]

Second Murderer.   A light, a light!

Third Murderer.   'Tis he.

15 **First Murderer.** Stand to't.

Banquo. It will be rain tonight.

First Murderer.   Let it come down!

[*They set upon* Banquo.]

Banquo. O, treachery! Fly, good Fleance, fly, fly, fly!
    Thou mayst revenge. O slave!

[*Dies. Fleance escapes.*]

Third Murderer. Who did strike out the light?

First Murderer.   Was't not the way?

20 **Third Murderer.** There's but one down; the son is fled.

Second Murderer.   We have lost

2–4 He needs . . . just: Macbeth should not be distrustful, since he gave us the orders (**offices**) and we plan to follow his directions exactly.

6 lated: tardy; late.

9 Give us a light: Banquo, nearing the palace, calls for servants to bring a light.

9–11 Then 'tis . . . court: It must be Banquo, since all the other expected guests are already in the palace.

15 Stand to't: Be prepared.

18 Thou mayst revenge: You might live to avenge my death.

19 Was't not the way: Isn't that what we were supposed to do? Apparently, one of the murderers struck out the light, thus allowing Fleance to escape.

Best half of our affair.

First Murderer. Well, let's away, and say how much is done.

[*Exeunt.*]

SCENE 4

The hall in the palace.

As the banquet begins, one of the murderers reports on Banquo's death and Fleance's escape. Macbeth is disturbed by the news and even more shaken when he returns to the banquet table and sees the bloody ghost of Banquo. Only Macbeth sees the ghost, and his terrified reaction startles the guests. Lady Macbeth explains her husband's strange behavior as an illness from childhood that will soon pass. Once the ghost disappears, Macbeth calls for a toast to Banquo, whose ghost immediately reappears. Because Macbeth begins to rant and rave, Lady Macbeth dismisses the guests, fearful that her husband will reveal too much. Macbeth, alone with his wife, tells of his suspicions of Macduff, absent from the banquet. He also says he will visit the witches again and hints at bloody deeds yet to happen.

[*Banquet prepared. Enter* Macbeth, Lady Macbeth, Ross, Lennox, Lords, *and* Attendants.]

Macbeth. You know your own degrees, sit down. At first
   And last the hearty welcome.

Lords.   Thanks to your Majesty.

Macbeth. Ourself will mingle with society
   And play the humble host.

5   Our hostess keeps her state, but in best time
   We will require her welcome.

Lady Macbeth. Pronounce it for me, sir, to all our friends,
   For my heart speaks they are welcome.

[*Enter* First Murderer *to the door.*]

Macbeth. See, they encounter thee with their hearts' thanks.

10   Both sides are even: here I'll sit i' the midst.
   Be large in mirth; anon we'll drink a measure
   The table round. [*Moves toward* Murderer *at door.*]
   There's blood upon thy face.

Murderer. 'Tis Banquo's then.

15   **Macbeth.** 'Tis better thee without than he within.
   Is he dispatched?

Murderer. My lord, his throat is cut. That I did for him.

Macbeth. Thou art the best o' the cutthroats! Yet he's good
   That did the like for Fleance. If thou didst it,

1 your own degrees: where your rank entitles you to sit.

5 keeps her state: sits on her throne rather than at the banquet table.

11 measure: toast. Macbeth keeps talking to his wife and guests as he casually edges toward the door to speak privately with the murderer.

16 dispatched: killed.

20 nonpareil: best.

20   Thou art the nonpareil.

Murderer.   Most royal sir,
    Fleance is scaped.

Macbeth. [*Aside*] Then comes my fit again. I had else been
perfect;
    Whole as the marble, founded as the rock,
    As broad and general as the casing air.
25   But now I am cabined, cribbed, confined, bound in
    To saucy doubts and fears.—But Banquo's safe?

Murderer. Ay, my good lord. Safe in a ditch he bides,
    With twenty trenched gashes on his head,
    The least a death to nature.

Macbeth.   Thanks for that!
30   There the grown serpent lies; the worm that's fled
    Hath nature that in time will venom breed,
    No teeth for the present. Get thee gone. Tomorrow
    We'll hear ourselves again.

[*Exit* Murderer.]

Lady Macbeth.   My royal lord,
    You do not give the cheer. The feast is sold
35   That is not often vouched, while 'tis a-making,
    'Tis given with welcome. To feed were best at home.
    From thence, the sauce to meat is ceremony;
    Meeting were bare without it.

[**Enter the Ghost of** Banquo, *and sits in* Macbeth's *place.*]

22 fit: fever of fear.

24 casing: surrounding.

30 worm: little serpent, that is,
Fleance.

32 no teeth for the present: too
young to cause harm right now.
Contrast this comment with his
privately expressed fears.

33 hear ourselves: talk together.

Act 3, Scene 4: Orson Welles as Macbeth
faces Banquo's ghost (film, 1948)

Macbeth. Sweet remembrancer!
Now good digestion wait on appetite,
40 And health on both!

Lennox. May't please your Highness sit.

Macbeth. Here had we now our country's honor, roofed,
Were the graced person of our Banquo present;
Who may I rather challenge for unkindness
Than pity for mischance!

Ross. His absence, sir,
45 Lays blame upon his promise. Please't your Highness
To grace us with your royal company?

Macbeth. The table's full.

Lennox. Here is a place reserved, sir.

Macbeth. Where?

Lennox. Here, my good lord. What is't that moves your
Highness?

50 **Macbeth.** Which of you have done this?

Lords. What, my good lord?

Macbeth. Thou canst not say I did it. Never shake
Thy gory locks at me.

Ross. Gentlemen, rise. His Highness is not well.

Lady Macbeth. Sit, worthy friends. My lord is often thus,
55 And hath been from his youth. Pray you keep seat.
The fit is momentary; upon a thought
He will again be well. If much you note him,
You shall offend him and extend his passion.
Feed, and regard him not.—Are you a man?

60 **Macbeth.** Ay, and a bold one, that dare look on that
Which might appal the devil.

Lady Macbeth. O proper stuff!
This is the very painting of your fear.
This is the air-drawn dagger which you said
Led you to Duncan. O, these flaws and starts
65 (Impostors to true fear) would well become
A woman's story at a winter's fire,
Authorized by her grandam. Shame itself!
Why do you make such faces? When all's done,
You look but on a stool.

70 **Macbeth.** Prithee see there! behold! look! lo! How say you?
Why, what care I? If thou canst nod, speak too.
If charnel houses and our graves must send

33–38 Macbeth must not forget his duties as host. A feast will be no different from a meal that one pays for unless the host gives his guests courteous attention (**ceremony**), the best part of any meal.

38 sweet remembrancer: a term of affection for his wife, who has reminded him of his duty.

41–44 The best people of Scotland would all be under Macbeth's roof if Banquo were present too. He hopes Banquo's absence is due to rudeness rather than to some accident (**mischance**).

47 Macbeth finally notices that Banquo's ghost is present and sitting in the king's chair. As you read about this encounter, consider how Macbeth's reaction affects his guests.

52 gory: bloody.

54–59 Sit . . . not: Lady Macbeth tries to calm the guests by claiming her husband often has such fits. She says the attack will pass quickly (**upon a thought**) and that looking at him will only make him worse (**extend his passion**). Why does Lady Macbeth make up a story to tell the guests?

61–69 She dismisses his hallucination as utter nonsense (**proper stuff**). His outbursts (**flaws and starts**) are the product of imaginary fears (**impostors to true fear**) and are unmanly, the kind of behavior described in a woman's story. Do you think her appeal to his manhood will work this time?

Those that we bury back, our monuments
Shall be the maws of kites.

[*Exit* Ghost.]

Lady Macbeth.   What, quite unmanned in folly?

75 **Macbeth.** If I stand here, I saw him.

Lady Macbeth.   Fie, for shame!

Macbeth. Blood hath been shed ere now, i' the olden time
Ere humane statute purged the gentle weal;
Ay, and since too, murders have been performed
Too terrible for the ear. The time has been
80 That, when the brains were out, the man would die,
And there an end! But now they rise again,
With twenty mortal murders on their crowns,
And push us from our stools. This is more strange
Than such a murder is.

Lady Macbeth.   My worthy lord,
85 Your noble friends do lack you.

Macbeth.   I do forget.
Do not muse at me, my most worthy friends.
I have a strange infirmity, which is nothing
To those that know me. Come, love and health to all!
Then I'll sit down. Give me some wine, fill full.

[*Enter* Ghost.]

90 I drink to the general joy o' the whole table,
And to our dear friend Banquo, whom we miss.
Would he were here! To all, and him, we thirst,
And all to all.

Lords.   Our duties, and the pledge.

Macbeth. Avaunt, and quit my sight! Let the earth hide thee!
95 Thy bones are marrowless, thy blood is cold;
Thou hast no speculation in those eyes
Which thou dost glare with!

Lady Macbeth.   Think of this, good peers,
But as a thing of custom. 'Tis no other.
Only it spoils the pleasure of the time.

100 **Macbeth.** What man dare, I dare.
Approach thou like the rugged Russian bear,
The armed rhinoceros, or the Hyrcan tiger;
Take any shape but that, and my firm nerves
Shall never tremble. Or be alive again
105 And dare me to the desert with thy sword.

72–74 If burial vaults (**charnel houses**) give back the dead, then we may as well throw our bodies to the birds (**kites**), whose stomachs (**maws**) will become our tombs (**monuments**).

76–79 Macbeth desperately tries to justify his murder of Banquo. Murder has been common from ancient times to the present, though laws (**humane statute**) have tried to rid civilized society (**gentle weal**) of violence.

86 muse: wonder.

92–93 To all . . . to all: Macbeth toasts everyone, including Banquo.

94–97 avaunt: go away. Macbeth sees Banquo again. He tells Banquo that he is only a ghost, with unreal bones, cold blood, and no consciousness (**speculation**).

If trembling I inhabit then, protest me
The baby of a girl. Hence, horrible shadow!
Unreal mock'ry, hence!

[*Exit* Ghost.]

       Why, so! Being gone,
I am a man again. Pray you sit still.

110 **Lady Macbeth.** You have displaced the mirth, broke the good
  meeting
With most admired disorder.

Macbeth.   Can such things be,
And overcome us like a summer's cloud
Without our special wonder? You make me strange
Even to the disposition that I owe,
115 When now I think you can behold such sights
And keep the natural ruby of your cheeks
When mine is blanched with fear.

Ross.   What sights, my lord?

Lady Macbeth. I pray you speak not. He grows worse and worse;
Question enrages him. At once, good night.
120 Stand not upon the order of your going,
But go at once.

Lennox.   Good night, and better health
Attend his Majesty!

Lady Macbeth.   A kind good night to all!

[*Exeunt* Lords *and* Attendants.]

Macbeth. It will have blood, they say: blood will have blood.
Stones have been known to move and trees to speak;
125 Augures and understood relations have
By maggot-pies and choughs and rooks brought forth
The secret'st man of blood. What is the night?

Lady Macbeth. Almost at odds with morning, which is which.

Macbeth. How say'st thou that Macduff denies his person
130 At our great bidding?

Lady Macbeth.   Did you send to him, sir?

Macbeth. I hear it by the way; but I will send.
There's not a one of them but in his house
I keep a servant feed. I will tomorrow
(And betimes I will) to the Weird Sisters.
135 More shall they speak; for now I am bent to know
By the worst means the worst. For mine own good
All causes shall give way. I am in blood
Stepped in so far that, should I wade no more,

100–108 Macbeth would be willing to face Banquo in any other form, even his living self. **If trembling . . . girl:** If I still tremble, call me a girl's doll.

111 admired: astonishing.

111–117 Macbeth is bewildered by his wife's calm. Her reaction makes him seem a stranger to himself (**strange even to the disposition that I owe**): she seems to be the one with all the courage, since he is white (**blanched**) with fear.

120 Stand . . . going: Don't worry about the proper formalities of leaving.

123–127 Macbeth fears that Banquo's murder (**it**) will be revenged by his own murder. Stones, trees, or talking birds (**maggot-pies and choughs and rooks**) may reveal the hidden knowledge (**augures**) of his guilt.

129–130 How say'st . . . bidding: What do you think of Macduff's refusal to come? Why do you think Macbeth is suddenly so concerned about Macduff?

132–133 There's . . . feed: Macbeth has paid (**feed**) household servants to spy on every noble, including Macduff.

134 betimes: early.

135 bent: determined.

136–141 For mine . . . scanned: Macbeth will do anything to protect himself. He has stepped so far into a river of blood that it would make no sense to turn back. He will act upon his unnatural (**strange**) thoughts without having examined (**scanned**) them.

Returning were as tedious as go o'er.
140 Strange things I have in head, that will to hand,
Which must be acted ere they may be scanned.

Lady Macbeth. You lack the season of all natures, sleep.

Macbeth. Come, we'll to sleep. My strange and self-abuse
Is the initiate fear that wants hard use.
145 We are yet but young in deed.

[*Exeunt.*]

142 **season:** preservative.

143–145 His vision of the ghost (**strange and self-abuse**) is only the result of a beginner's fear (**initiate fear**), to be cured with practice (**hard use**).

SCENE 5

A heath.

The goddess of witchcraft, Hecate, scolds the three witches for dealing independently with Macbeth. She outlines their next meeting with him, planning to cause his downfall by making him overconfident. (Experts believe this scene was not written by Shakespeare but rather was added later.)

[*Thunder. Enter the three* Witches, *meeting* Hecate.]

First Witch. Why, how now, Hecate? You look angerly.

Hecate. Have I not reason, beldams as you are,
Saucy and overbold? How did you dare
To trade and traffic with Macbeth
5 In riddles and affairs of death;
And I, the mistress of your charms,
The close contriver of all harms,
Was never called to bear my part
Or show the glory of our art?
10 And, which is worse, all you have done
Hath been but for a wayward son,
Spiteful and wrathful, who, as others do,
Loves for his own ends, not for you.
But make amends now. Get you gone
15 And at the pit of Acheron
Meet me i' the morning. Thither he
Will come to know his destiny.
Your vessels and your spells provide,
Your charms and everything beside.
20 I am for the air. This night I'll spend
Unto a dismal and a fatal end.
Great business must be wrought ere noon.
Upon the corner of the moon
There hangs a vap'rous drop profound.
25 I'll catch it ere it come to ground;

2 **beldams:** hags.

7 **close contriver:** secret inventor.

13 **loves . . . you:** cares only about his own goals, not about you.

15 **Acheron:** a river in hell, according to Greek mythology. Hecate plans to hold their meeting in a hellish place.

20–21 **This . . . end:** Tonight I'm working for a disastrous (**dismal**) and fatal end for Macbeth.

And that, distilled by magic sleights,
Shall raise such artificial sprites
As by the strength of their illusion
Shall draw him on to his confusion.
30   He shall spurn fate, scorn death, and bear
His hopes 'bove wisdom, grace, and fear;
And you all know security
Is mortals' chiefest enemy.

[*Music and a song within. "Come away, come away," etc.*]

Hark! I am called. My little spirit, see,
35   Sits in a foggy cloud and stays for me.

[*Exit.*]

First Witch. Come, let's make haste. She'll soon be back again.

[*Exeunt.*]

23–29 Hecate will obtain a magical drop from the moon, treat it with secret art, and so create spirits (**artificial sprites**) that will lead Macbeth to his destruction (**confusion**).

34–35 Like the other witches, Hecate has a demon helper (**my little spirit**). At the end of her speech, she is raised by pulley to the "Heavens" of the stage.

SCENE 6

The palace at Forres.

Lennox and another Scottish lord review the events surrounding the murders of Duncan and Banquo, indirectly suggesting that Macbeth is both a murderer and a tyrant. It is reported that Macduff has gone to England, where Duncan's son Malcolm is staying with King Edward and raising an army to regain the Scottish throne. Macbeth, angered by Macduff's refusal to see him, is also preparing for war.

[*Enter* Lennox *and another* Lord.]

Lennox. My former speeches have but hit your thoughts,
Which can interpret farther. Only I say
Things have been strangely borne. The gracious Duncan
Was pitied of Macbeth. Marry, he was dead!
5   And the right valiant Banquo walked too late;
Whom, you may say (if't please you) Fleance killed,
For Fleance fled. Men must not walk too late.
Who cannot want the thought how monstrous
It was for Malcolm and for Donalbain
10   To kill their gracious father? Damned fact!
How it did grieve Macbeth! Did he not straight,
In pious rage, the two delinquents tear,
That were the slaves of drink and thralls of sleep?
Was not that nobly done? Ay, and wisely too!
15   For 'twould have angered any heart alive
To hear the men deny't. So that I say
He has borne all things well; and I do think

1–3 My former . . . borne: Lennox and the other lord have shared suspicions of Macbeth.

6–7 whom . . . Fleance fled: Lennox is being ironic when he says that fleeing the scene of the crime must make Fleance guilty of his father's death.

8–10 who . . . father: He says that everyone agrees on the horror of Duncan's murder by his sons. But Lennox has been consistently ironic, claiming to believe in what is obviously false. His words indirectly blame Macbeth.

12 pious: holy.

15–16 For 'twould . . . deny't: Again, he is being ironic. If the servants had lived, Macbeth might have been discovered.

That, had he Duncan's sons under his key
(As, an't please heaven, he shall not), they should find
20 What 'twere to kill a father. So should Fleance.
But peace! for from broad words, and 'cause he failed
His presence at the tyrant's feast, I hear
Macduff lives in disgrace. Sir, can you tell
Where he bestows himself?

Lord.   The son of Duncan,
25 From whom this tyrant holds the due of birth,
Lives in the English court, and is received
Of the most pious Edward with such grace
That the malevolence of fortune nothing
Takes from his high respect. Thither Macduff
30 Is gone to pray the holy King upon his aid
To wake Northumberland and warlike Siward;
That by the help of these (with Him above
To ratify the work) we may again
Give to our tables meat, sleep to our nights,
35 Free from our feasts and banquets bloody knives,
Do faithful homage and receive free honors—
All which we pine for now. And this report
Hath so exasperate the King that he
Prepares for some attempt of war.

Lennox.   Sent he to Macduff?

40 **Lord.** He did; and with an absolute "Sir, not I!"
The cloudy messenger turns me his back
And hums, as who should say, "You'll rue the time
That clogs me with this answer."

Lennox.   And that well might
Advise him to a caution t' hold what distance
45 His wisdom can provide. Some holy angel
Fly to the court of England and unfold
His message ere he come, that a swift blessing
May soon return to this our suffering country
Under a hand accursed!

Lord.   I'll send my prayers with him.

[*Exeunt.*]

---

21 from broad words: because of his frank talk.

24 bestows himself: is staying.

25 from . . . birth: Macbeth keeps Malcolm from his birthright. As the eldest son of Duncan, Malcolm should be king.

27 Edward: Edward the Confessor, king of England from 1042 to 1066, a man known for his virtue and religion.

28–29 that . . . respect: Though Malcolm suffers from bad fortune (the loss of the throne), he is respectfully treated by Edward.

29–37 Thither . . . for now: Macduff wants the king to persuade the people of Northumberland and their earl, Siward, to join Malcolm's cause.

40–43 The messenger, fearing Macbeth's anger, was unhappy (**cloudy**) with Macduff's refusal to cooperate. Because Macduff burdens (**clogs**) him with bad news, he will not hurry back.

from

HOLINSHED'S CHRONICLES

This was but a counterfeit zeal of equity[1] showed by him, partly against his natural inclination, to purchase thereby the favor of the people. Shortly after, he began to show what he was, instead of equity practicing cruelty. For the prick of consciene (as it chanceth ever in tyrants and such as attain to any estate by unrighteous means) caused him ever to fear lest he should be served of the same cup as he had ministered to his predecessor. The words also of the three Weird Sisters would not out of his mind, which as they promised him the kingdom, so likewise did they promise it at the same time unto the posterity of Banquo. He willed therefore the same Banquo, with his son named Fleance, to come to a supper that he had prepared for them; which was indeed, as he had devised, present death at the hands of certain murderers whom he hired to execute that deed, appointing them to meet with the same Banquo and his son without the palace, as they returned to their lodgings, and there to slay them, so that he would not have his house slandered but that in time to come he might clear himself if anything were laid to his charge upon any suspicion that might arise.

It chanced by the benefit of the dark night that, though the father were slain, yet the son, by the help of almighty God reserving him to better fortune, escaped that danger; and afterward, having some inkling (by the admonition of some friends which he had in the court) how his life was sought no less than his father's, who was slain not by chance-medley[2] (as by the handling of the matter Macbeth would have had it to appear) but even upon a prepensed[3] device, whereupon to avoid further peril he fled into Wales.

Thinking Through the Literature

1. Based on this and the preceding selection from Holinshed's *Chronicles*, what can you conclude about politics and power in Macbeth's Scotland?

2. What does the inclusion of the three witches suggest about the historical accuracy of Holinshed's *Chronicles*?

3. **Comparing Texts** Compare the information from Holinshed's *Chronicles* with the **plot** and **characters** so far in *Macbeth*. What events and characters are similar? What differences do you detect? Why do you think Shakespeare portrays King James's ancestor Banquo in a more flattering light than he appears in the *Chronicles*?

1. **equity:** fairness.
2. **chance-medley:** accidental homicide.
3. **prepensed:** premeditated.

Thinking through the LITERATURE

Connect to the Literature

1. **What Do You Think?** How has your impression of Macbeth and Lady Macbeth changed?

   Comprehension Check
   - What suspicions does Banquo voice?
   - Why does Macbeth fear Banquo?
   - What happens to Fleance when Banquo is killed?
   - Where does Banquo's ghost appear?

Think Critically

2. **ACTIVE READING** **SHAKESPEARE'S LANGUAGE** Summarize what Macbeth and Lady Macbeth say to each other in Act Three, Scene 2. What notes did you take in your **READER'S NOTEBOOK** about what these **characters** discuss? How would you restate Lady Macbeth's soliloquy (lines 4–7) in contemporary language?

3. How has the relationship between Macbeth and his wife changed since the death of Duncan?

   THINK ABOUT
   - Macbeth's view of Duncan's murder
   - Lady Macbeth's view of Duncan's murder
   - Macbeth's refusal to tell his wife about his plan to murder Banquo
   - Macbeth's "fit" at the banquet and his wife's reaction to it

4. Why aren't Macbeth and Lady Macbeth happy being king and queen? Cite evidence to support your opinion.

5. Why is the escape of Fleance significant in the light of the witches' earlier predictions?

Extend Interpretations

6. **Critic's Corner** In Act Three, Scene 1, Macbeth meets with two murderers, but three murderers take part in the actual murder in Scene 3. Critics have speculated about the identity of the third murderer, with some thinking that it may be Macbeth himself. How do you explain this situation?

7. **Comparing Texts** What do Macbeth and his wife have in common with the villainous characters in "The Pardoner's Tale" from Chaucer's *Canterbury Tales* (page 141)?

8. **Connect to Life** Think about present-day explanations of the behavior of criminals. In what ways might Macbeth's state of mind and behavior in Act Three be similar to those of criminals today? Cite evidence to explain your response.

Literary Analysis

DRAMATIC IRONY Writers introduce **irony** into their works when they convey a contrast or discrepancy between appearance and reality—between the way things seem and the way they really are. In **dramatic irony,** what appears true to one or more characters in a play is seen to be false by the audience.

Cooperative Learning Activity With a small group of classmates, focus on one of the first three acts of *Macbeth* and analyze at least two remarks or incidents that create dramatic irony. Explain why the remarks or incidents are ironic, detailing the contrast between what characters think and what the audience knows. Then consider how the irony affects your enjoyment of the play. Before presenting your group's ideas to the class, organize your thoughts in a chart.

What Characters Think	What Audience Knows

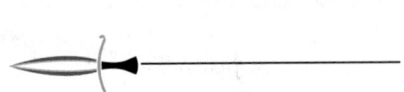  

Act 4

SCENE 1

A cave. In the middle, a boiling cauldron.

The three witches prepare a potion in a boiling kettle. When Macbeth arrives, demanding to know his future, the witches raise three apparitions. The first, an armed head, tells him to beware of Macduff. Next, a bloody child assures Macbeth that he will never be harmed by anyone born of woman. The third apparition tells him that he will never be defeated until the trees of Birnam Wood move toward his castle at Dunsinane. Macbeth, now confident of his future, asks about Banquo's son. His confidence fades when the witches show him a line of kings who all resemble Banquo, suggesting that Banquo's sons will indeed be kings. Macbeth curses the witches as they disappear.

Lennox enters the cave and tells Macbeth that Macduff has gone to the English court. Hearing this, Macbeth swears to kill Macduff's family.

[*Thunder. Enter the three* Witches.]

First Witch. Thrice the brinded cat hath mewed.

Second Witch. Thrice, and once the hedge-pig whined.

Third Witch. Harpier cries; 'tis time, 'tis time.

First Witch. Round about the cauldron go;
5   In the poisoned entrails throw.
Toad, that under cold stone
Days and nights has thirty-one
Swelt'red venom sleeping got,

1–3 Magical signals and the call of the third witch's attending demon (**Harpier**) tell the witches to begin.

The Three Witches (1783), Henry Fuseli. Oil on canvas, Royal Shakespeare Theatre Collection, London.

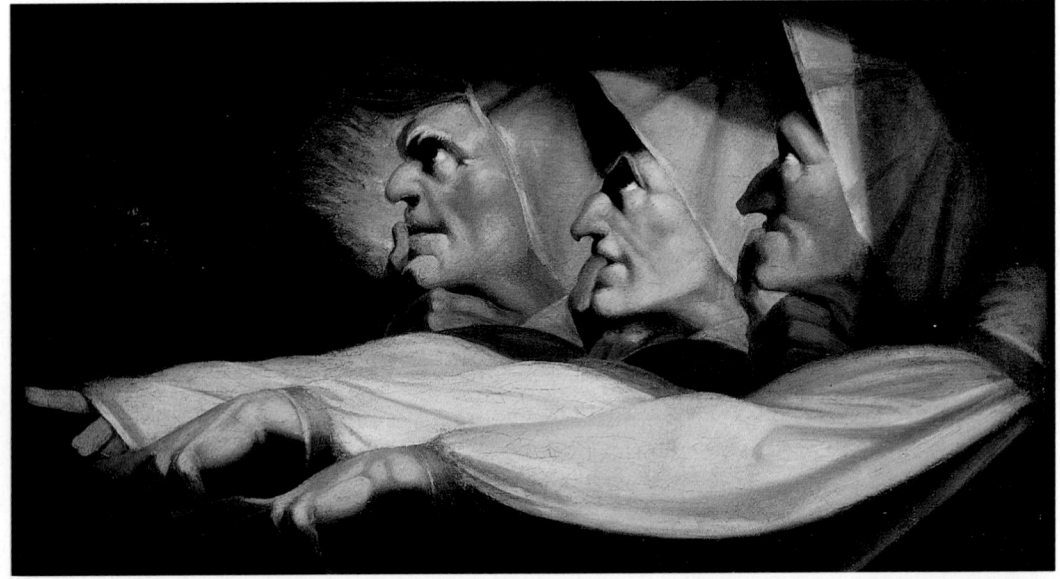

Boil thou first i' the charmed pot.

10   **All.** Double, double, toil and trouble;
         Fire burn, and cauldron bubble.

      Second Witch. Fillet of a fenny snake,
         In the cauldron boil and bake;
         Eye of newt, and toe of frog,
15   Wool of bat, and tongue of dog,
         Adder's fork, and blindworm's sting,
         Lizard's leg, and howlet's wing;
         For a charm of pow'rful trouble
         Like a hell-broth boil and bubble.

20   **All.** Double, double, toil and trouble;
         Fire burn, and cauldron bubble.

      Third Witch. Scale of dragon, tooth of wolf,
         Witch's mummy, maw and gulf
         Of the ravined salt-sea shark,
25   Root of hemlock, digged i' the dark;
         Liver of blaspheming Jew,
         Gall of goat, and slips of yew
         Slivered in the moon's eclipse;
         Nose of Turk and Tartar's lips;
30   Finger of birth-strangled babe
         Ditch-delivered by a drab:
         Make the gruel thick and slab.
         Add thereto a tiger's chaudron
         For the ingredience of our cauldron.

35   **All.** Double, double, toil and trouble;
         Fire burn, and cauldron bubble.

      Second Witch. Cool it with a baboon's blood,
         Then the charm is firm and good.

[*Enter* Hecate *and the other three* Witches.]

      Hecate. O, well done! I commend your pains,
40   And every one shall share i' the gains.
         And now about the cauldron sing
         Like elves and fairies in a ring,
         Enchanting all that you put in.

[*Music and a song, "Black spirit," etc.*]

      Second Witch. By the pricking of my thumbs,
45   Something wicked this way comes.
                         Open locks,
                         Whoever knocks!

[*Enter* Macbeth.]

4–34 The witches are stirring up a magical stew to bring trouble to humanity. Their recipe includes intestines (**entrails, chaudron**), a slice (**fillet**) of snake, eye of salamander (**newt**), snake tongue (**adder's fork**), a lizard (**blindworm**), a baby owl's (**howlet's**) wing, a shark's stomach and gullet (**maw and gulf**), the finger of a baby strangled by a prostitute (**drab**), and other gruesome ingredients. They stir their brew until it is thick and slimy (**slab**).

[Stage Direction] **Enter Hecate . . . :** Most experts believe that the entrance of Hecate and three more witches was not written by Shakespeare. The characters were probably added later to expand the role of the witches, who were favorites of the audience.

Macbeth. How now, you secret, black, and midnight hags?
What is't you do?

All.   A deed without a name.

50 **Macbeth.** I conjure you by that which you profess
(Howe'er you come to know it), answer me.
Though you untie the winds and let them fight
Against the churches; though the yesty waves
Confound and swallow navigation up;
55 Though bladed corn be lodged and trees blown down;
Though castles topple on their warders' heads;
Though palaces and pyramids do slope
Their heads to their foundations; though the treasure
Of nature's germens tumble all together,
60 Even till destruction sicken—answer me
To what I ask you.

First Witch.   Speak.

Second Witch.   Demand.

Third Witch.   We'll answer.

First Witch. Say, if th' hadst rather hear it from our mouths
Or from our masters.

Macbeth.   Call 'em! Let me see 'em.

First Witch. Pour in sow's blood, that hath eaten
65 Her nine farrow; grease that's sweaten
From the murderer's gibbet throw
Into the flame.

All.   Come, high or low;
Thyself and office deftly show!

[*Thunder. First Apparition,* an Armed Head.]

Macbeth. Tell me, thou unknown power—

First Witch.   He knows thy thought.
70 Hear his speech, but say thou naught.

First Apparition. Macbeth! Macbeth! Macbeth! Beware Macduff;
Beware the Thane of Fife. Dismiss me. Enough.

[*He descends.*]

Macbeth. Whate'er thou art, for thy good caution thanks!
Thou hast harped my fear aright. But one word more—

75 **First Witch.** He will not be commanded. Here's another,
More potent than the first.

[*Thunder. Second Apparition,* a Bloody Child.]

Second Apparition. Macbeth! Macbeth! Macbeth!

Macbeth. Had I three ears, I'ld hear thee.

50–61 Macbeth calls upon (**conjure**) the witches in the name of their dark magic (**that which you profess**). Though they unleash winds to topple churches and make foaming (**yesty**) waves to destroy (**confound**) ships, though they flatten wheat (**corn**) fields, destroy buildings, and reduce nature's order to chaos by mixing all seeds (**germens**) together, he demands an answer to his question. How has Macbeth's attitude toward the witches changed from his earlier meetings?

63 masters: the demons whom the witches serve.

65–66 farrow: newborn pigs; **grease . . . gibbet:** grease from a gallows where a murderer was hung.

[Stage Direction] Each of the three apparitions holds a clue to Macbeth's future. What do you think is suggested by the armed head?

74 harped: guessed. The apparition has confirmed Macbeth's fears of Macduff.

[Stage Direction] Whom or what might the bloody child represent?

Act 4, Scene 1: Macbeth meets the second apparition (film 1971)

Second Apparition. Be bloody, bold, and resolute; laugh to scorn
80   The pow'r of man, for none of woman born
        Shall harm Macbeth.

[*Descends.*]

Macbeth. Then live, Macduff. What need I fear of thee?
        But yet I'll make assurance double sure
        And take a bond of fate. Thou shalt not live!
85   That I may tell pale-hearted fear it lies
        And sleep in spite of thunder.

[*Thunder. Third Apparition, a Child Crowned, with a tree in his hand.*]

                            What is this
        That rises like the issue of a king
        And wears upon his baby-brow the round
        And top of sovereignty?

All.   Listen, but speak not to't.

90 **Third Apparition.** Be lion-mettled, proud, and take no care
        Who chafes, who frets, or where conspirers are.
        Macbeth shall never vanquished be until
        Great Birnam Wood to high Dunsinane Hill
        Shall come against him.   [*Descends.*]

Macbeth.   That will never be.

79–81 How do you think this prophecy will affect Macbeth?

83–84 Despite the prophecy's apparent promise of safety, Macbeth decides to seek double insurance. The murder of Macduff will give Macbeth a guarantee (**bond**) of his fate and put his fears to rest.

[Stage Direction] Whom or what might the child crowned represent?

87 issue: child.

88–89 the round and top: the crown.

90–94 The third apparition tells Macbeth to take courage. He cannot be defeated unless Birnam Wood travels the 12-mile distance to Dunsinane Hill, where his castle is located.

95   Who can impress the forest, bid the tree
Unfix his earth-bound root? Sweet bodements, good!
Rebellious dead rise never till the Wood
Of Birnam rise, and our high-placed Macbeth
Shall live the lease of nature, pay his breath
100   To time and mortal custom. Yet my heart
Throbs to know one thing. Tell me, if your art
Can tell so much—shall Banquo's issue ever
Reign in this kingdom?

All.   Seek to know no more.

Macbeth. I will be satisfied. Deny me this,
105   And an eternal curse fall on you! Let me know.
Why sinks that cauldron? and what noise is this?

                                        [Hautboys.]

First Witch. Show!

Second Witch. Show!

Third Witch. Show!

110   **All.** Show his eyes, and grieve his heart!
Come like shadows, so depart!

[A show of eight Kings, the eighth with a glass in his hand, and Banquo last.]

Macbeth. Thou art too like the spirit of Banquo. Down!
Thy crown does sear mine eyeballs. And thy hair,
Thou other gold-bound brow, is like the first.
115   A third is like the former. Filthy hags!
Why do you show me this? A fourth? Start, eyes!
What, will the line stretch out to the crack of doom?
Another yet? A seventh? I'll see no more.
And yet the eighth appears, who bears a glass
120   Which shows me many more; and some I see
That twofold balls and treble scepters carry.
Horrible sight! Now I see 'tis true;
For the blood-boltered Banquo smiles upon me
And points at them for his. *[Apparitions descend.]* What?
    Is this so?
125   **First Witch.** Ay, sir, all this is so. But why
Stands Macbeth thus amazedly?
Come, sisters, cheer we up his sprites
And show the best of our delights.
I'll charm the air to give a sound
130   While you perform your antic round,
That this great king may kindly say
Our duties did his welcome pay.

95 impress: force into service.

96 bodements: prophecies.

97–100 Rebellious . . . custom: Macbeth boasts that he will never again be troubled by ghosts (**rebellious dead**) and that he will live out his expected life span (**lease of nature**). He believes he will die (**pay his breath**) by natural causes (**mortal custom**).

106 Why . . . this: The cauldron is sinking from sight to make room for the next apparition.

[Stage Direction] **A show . . . :** Macbeth next sees a procession (**show**) of eight kings, the last carrying a mirror (**glass**). According to legend, Fleance escaped to England, where he founded the Stuart family. James I of England, the king when this play was first performed, was the eighth Stuart king, the first to rule over both England and Scotland.

112–124 Macbeth is outraged that all eight kings in the procession look like Banquo. The mirror held by the last one shows a future with many more Banquo look-alikes as kings. The twofold balls and treble scepters pictured in the mirror foretell the union of Scotland and England in 1603, the year that James became king of both realms. Banquo, his hair matted (**boltered**) with blood, claims all the kings as his descendants. What do you think is going through Macbeth's mind?

[*Music. The* Witches *dance, and vanish.*]

Macbeth. Where are they? Gone? Let this pernicious hour
Stand aye accursed in the calendar!
135 Come in, without there!

[*Enter* Lennox.]

Lennox.   What's your Grace's will?

Macbeth. Saw you the Weird Sisters?

Lennox.   No, my lord.

Macbeth. Came they not by you?

Lennox.   No indeed, my lord.

Macbeth. Infected be the air whereon they ride,
And damned all those that trust them! I did hear
140 The galloping of horse. Who was't came by?

Lennox. 'Tis two or three, my lord, that bring you word
Macduff is fled to England.

Macbeth.   Fled to England?

Lennox. Ay, my good lord.

Macbeth. [*Aside*] Time, thou anticipat'st my dread exploits.
145 The flighty purpose never is o'ertook
Unless the deed go with it. From this moment
The very firstlings of my heart shall be
The firstlings of my hand. And even now,
To crown my thoughts with acts, be it thought and done!
150 The castle of Macduff I will surprise,
Seize upon Fife, give to the edge o' the sword
His wife, his babes, and all unfortunate souls
That trace him in his line. No boasting like a fool!
This deed I'll do before this purpose cool.
155 But no more sights!—Where are these gentlemen?
Come, bring me where they are.

[*Exeunt.*]

133–135 pernicious: deadly, destructive; **aye:** always. After the witches vanish, Macbeth hears noises outside the cave and calls out.

144–156 Frustrated in his desire to kill Macduff, Macbeth blames his own hesitation, which gave his enemy time to flee. He concludes that one's plans (**flighty purpose**) are never achieved (**o'ertook**) unless carried out at once. From now on, Macbeth promises, he will act immediately on his impulses (**firstlings of my heart**) and complete (**crown**) his thoughts with acts. He will surprise Macduff's castle at Fife and kill his wife and children. Why does Macbeth decide to kill Macduff's family?

SCENE 2

Macduff's castle at Fife.

Ross visits Lady Macduff to assure her of her husband's wisdom and courage. Lady Macduff cannot be comforted, believing that he left out of fear. After Ross leaves she tells her son, who is still loyal to his father, that Macduff was a traitor and is now dead. A messenger warns them to flee but is too late. Murderers sent by Macbeth burst in, killing both wife and son.

[*Enter* Lady Macduff, *her* Son, *and* Ross.]

Lady Macduff. What had he done to make him fly the land?

Ross. You must have patience, madam.

Lady Macduff.   He had none.
His flight was madness. When our actions do not,
Our fears do make us traitors.

Ross.   You know not
5   Whether it was his wisdom or his fear.

Lady Macduff. Wisdom? To leave his wife, to leave his babes,
His mansion, and his titles, in a place
From whence himself does fly? He loves us not,
He wants the natural touch. For the poor wren,
10   (The most diminutive of birds) will fight,
Her young ones in her nest, against the owl.
All is the fear, and nothing is the love,
As little is the wisdom, where the flight
So runs against all reason.

Ross.   My dearest coz,
15   I pray you school yourself. But for your husband,
He is noble, wise, judicious, and best knows
The fits o' the season. I dare not speak much further;
But cruel are the times, when we are traitors
And do not know ourselves; when we hold rumor
20   From what we fear, yet know not what we fear,
But float upon a wild and violent sea
Each way and move—I take my leave of you.
Shall not be long but I'll be here again.
Things at the worst will cease, or else climb upward
25   To what they were before.—My pretty cousin,
Blessing upon you!

Lady Macduff. Fathered he is, and yet he's fatherless.

Ross. I am so much a fool, should I stay longer,
It would be my disgrace and your discomfort.

3–4 When our . . . traitors: Macduff's wife is worried that others will think her husband a traitor because his fears made him flee the country (**our fears do make us traitors**), though he was guilty of no wrongdoing.

9 wants the natural touch: lacks the instinct to protect his family.

12–14 All . . . reason: Lady Macduff believes her husband is motivated entirely by fear, not by love of his family. His hasty flight is contrary to reason.

14–15 coz: cousin (a term used for any close relation); **school:** control; **for:** as for.

17 fits o' the season: disorders of the present time.

18–22 But . . . upon you: Ross laments the cruelty of the times that made Macduff flee. In such times, people are treated like traitors for no reason. Their fears make them believe (**hold**) rumors, though they do not know what to fear and drift aimlessly like ships tossed by a tempest.

Macduff's Castle (film, 1948)

30   I take my leave at once.   [*Exit.*]

Lady Macduff.   Sirrah, your father's dead;
And what will you do now? How will you live?

Son. As birds do, mother.

Lady Macduff.   What, with worms and flies?

Son. With what I get, I mean; and so do they.

Lady Macduff. Poor bird! thou'dst never fear the net nor lime,

28–30 Moved by pity for Macduff's family, Ross is near tears (**my disgrace**). He will leave before he embarrasses himself.

30–31 Why does Lady Macduff tell her son that his father is dead, though the boy heard her discussion with Ross?

35   The pitfall nor the gin.

Son. Why should I, mother? Poor birds they are not set for.
My father is not dead, for all your saying.

Lady Macduff. Yes, he is dead. How wilt thou do for a father?

Son. Nay, how will you do for a husband?

40   **Lady Macduff.** Why, I can buy me twenty at any market.

Son. Then you'll buy 'em to sell again.

Lady Macduff. Thou speak'st with all thy wit; and yet, i' faith,
With wit enough for thee.

Son. Was my father a traitor, mother?

45   **Lady Macduff.** Ay, that he was!

Son. What is a traitor?

Lady Macduff. Why, one that swears, and lies.

Son. And be all traitors that do so?

Lady Macduff. Every one that does so is a traitor and must be
50   hanged.

Son. And must they all be hanged that swear and lie?

Lady Macduff. Every one.

Son. Who must hang them?

Lady Macduff. Why, the honest men.

55   **Son.** Then the liars and swearers are fools; for there are liars
and swearers enow to beat the honest men and hang up
them.

Lady Macduff. Now God help thee, poor monkey! But how wilt
thou do for a father?

60   **Son.** If he were dead, you'd weep for him. If you would
not, it were a good sign that I should quickly have a new
father.

Lady Macduff. Poor prattler, how thou talk'st!

[*Enter a* Messenger.]

Messenger. Bless you, fair dame! I am not to you known,
65   Though in your state of honor I am perfect.
I doubt some danger does approach you nearly.
If you will take a homely man's advice,
Be not found here. Hence with your little ones!
To fright you thus methinks I am too savage;
70   To do worse to you were fell cruelty,
Which is too nigh your person. Heaven preserve you!
I dare abide no longer.   [*Exit.*]

Lady Macduff.   Whither should I fly?
I have done no harm. But I remember now

32–35 The spirited son refuses to be defeated by their bleak situation. He will live as birds do, taking whatever comes his way. His mother responds in kind, calling attention to devices used to catch birds: nets, sticky birdlime (**lime**), snares (**pitfall**), and traps (**gin**).

40–43 Lady Macduff and her son affectionately joke about her ability to find a new husband. She expresses admiration for his intelligence (**with wit enough**).

44–54 Continuing his banter, the son asks if his father is a traitor. Lady Macduff, understandably hurt and confused by her husband's unexplained departure, answers yes.

55–63 Her son points out that traitors outnumber honest men in this troubled time. The mother's terms of affection, *monkey* and *prattler* (childish talker), suggest that his playfulness has won her over.

64–72 The messenger, who knows Lady Macduff is an honorable person (**in your state of honor I am perfect**), delivers a polite but desperate warning, urging her to flee immediately. While he apologizes for scaring her, he warns that she faces a deadly (**fell**) cruelty, one dangerously close (**too nigh**).

I am in this earthly world, where to do harm
75 Is often laudable, to do good sometime
Accounted dangerous folly. Why then, alas,
Do I put up that womanly defense
To say I have done no harm?—What are these faces?

[*Enter* Murderers.]

Murderer. Where is your husband?

80 **Lady Macduff.** I hope, in no place so unsanctified
Where such as thou mayst find him.

Murderer.   He's a traitor.

Son. Thou liest, thou shag-eared villain!

Murderer.   What, you egg!

[*Stabbing him.*]

Young fry of treachery!

Son.   He has killed me, mother.
Run away, I pray you!   [*Dies.*]

[*Exit* Lady Macduff, *crying "Murder!" followed by* Murderers.]

80 **unsanctified:** unholy.

82 **shag-eared:** long-haired. Note how quickly the son reacts to the word *traitor.* How do you think he feels about his father?

83 **young fry:** small fish.

SCENE 3

England. Before King Edward's palace.

Macduff urges Malcolm to join him in an invasion of Scotland, where the people suffer under Macbeth's harsh rule. Since Malcolm is uncertain of Macduff's motives, he tests him to see what kind of king Macduff would support. Once convinced of Macduff's honesty, Malcolm tells him that he has ten thousand soldiers ready to launch an attack. Ross arrives to tell them that some revolts against Macbeth have already begun. Reluctantly, Ross tells Macduff about the murder of his family. Wild with grief, Macduff vows to confront Macbeth and avenge the murders.

[*Enter* Malcolm *and* Macduff.]

Malcolm. Let us seek out some desolate shade, and there
Weep our sad bosoms empty.

Macduff.   Let us rather
Hold fast the mortal sword and, like good men,
Bestride our downfall'n birthdom. Each new morn
5 New widows howl, new orphans cry, new sorrows
Strike heaven on the face, that it resounds
As if it felt with Scotland and yelled out
Like syllable of dolor.

Malcolm.   What I believe, I'll wail;
What know, believe; and what I can redress,
10   As I shall find the time to friend, I will.
What you have spoke, it may be so perchance.
This tyrant, whose sole name blisters our tongues,
Was once thought honest; you have loved him well;
He hath not touched you yet. I am young; but something
15   You may discern of him through me, and wisdom
To offer up a weak, poor, innocent lamb
T' appease an angry god.

Macduff. I am not treacherous.

Malcolm.   But Macbeth is.
A good and virtuous nature may recoil
20   In an imperial charge. But I shall crave your pardon.
That which you are, my thoughts cannot transpose.
Angels are bright still, though the brightest fell.
Though all things foul would wear the brows of grace,
Yet grace must still look so.

Macduff.   I have lost my hopes.

25   **Malcolm.** Perchance even there where I did find my doubts.
Why in that rawness left you wife and child,
Those precious motives, those strong knots of love,
Without leave-taking? I pray you,
Let not my jealousies be your dishonors,
30   But mine own safeties. You may be rightly just,
Whatever I shall think.

Macduff.   Bleed, bleed, poor country!
Great tyranny, lay thou thy basis sure,
For goodness dare not check thee! Wear thou thy wrongs;
The title is affeered! Fare thee well, lord.
35   I would not be the villain that thou think'st
For the whole space that's in the tyrant's grasp
And the rich East to boot.

Malcolm.   Be not offended.
I speak not as in absolute fear of you.
I think our country sinks beneath the yoke;
40   It weeps, it bleeds, and each new day a gash
Is added to her wounds. I think withal
There would be hands uplifted in my right;
And here from gracious England have I offer
Of goodly thousands. But, for all this,
45   When I shall tread upon the tyrant's head
Or wear it on my sword, yet my poor country
Shall have more vices than it had before,

1–8 In response to Malcolm's depression about Scotland, Macduff advises that they grab a deadly (**mortal**) sword and defend their homeland (**birthdom**). The anguished cries of Macbeth's victims strike heaven and make the skies echo with cries of sorrow (**syllable of dolor**).

8–15 Malcolm will strike back only if the time is right (**as I shall find the time to friend**). Macduff may be honorable (**honest**), but he may be deceiving Malcolm to gain a reward from Macbeth (**something you may discern of him through me**).

18–24 Malcolm further explains the reasons for his suspicions. Even a good person may fall (**recoil**) into wickedness because of a king's command (**imperial charge**). If Macduff is innocent, he will not be harmed by these suspicions, which cannot change (**transpose**) his nature (**that which you are**). Virtue cannot be damaged even by those who fall into evil, like Lucifer (the **brightest** angel), and disguise themselves as virtuous (**wear the brows of grace**).

25–31 Malcolm cannot understand how Macduff could leave his family, a source of inspiration (**motives**) and love, in an unprotected state (**rawness**). He asks him not to be insulted by his suspicions (**jealousies**); Malcolm is guarding his own safety.

34 affeered: confirmed.

More suffer and more sundry ways than ever,
By him that shall succeed.

Macduff.   What should he be?

50   **Malcolm.** It is myself I mean; in whom I know
All the particulars of vice so grafted
That, when they shall be opened, black Macbeth
Will seem as pure as snow, and the poor state
Esteem him as a lamb, being compared
55   With my confineless harms.

Macduff.   Not in the legions
Of horrid hell can come a devil more damned
In evils to top Macbeth.

Malcolm.   I grant him bloody,
Luxurious, avaricious, false, deceitful,
Sudden, malicious, smacking of every sin
60   That has a name. But there's no bottom, none,
In my voluptuousness. Your wives, your daughters,
Your matrons, and your maids could not fill up
The cistern of my lust; and my desire
All continent impediments would o'erbear
65   That did oppose my will. Better Macbeth
Than such an one to reign.

Macduff.   Boundless intemperance
In nature is a tyranny. It hath been
The untimely emptying of the happy throne
And fall of many kings. But fear not yet
70   To take upon you what is yours. You may
Convey your pleasures in a spacious plenty,
And yet seem cold—the time you may so hoodwink.
We have willing dames enough. There cannot be
That vulture in you to devour so many
75   As will to greatness dedicate themselves,
Finding it so inclined.

Malcolm.   With this there grows
In my most ill-composed affection such
A stanchless avarice that, were I King,
I should cut off the nobles for their lands,
80   Desire his jewels, and this other's house,
And my more-having would be as a sauce
To make me hunger more, that I should forge
Quarrels unjust against the good and loyal,
Destroying them for wealth.

46–49 yet my . . . succeed: To test Macduff's honor and loyalty, Malcolm begins a lengthy description of his own fictitious vices. He suggests that Scotland may suffer more under his rule than under Macbeth's.

50–55 Malcolm says that his own vices are so plentiful and deeply planted (**grafted**) that Macbeth will seem innocent by comparison.

58 luxurious: lustful.

59 sudden: violent; **smacking:** tasting.

61 voluptuousness: lust.

63 cistern: large storage tank.

63–65 His lust is so great that it would overpower (**o'erbear**) all restraining obstacles (**continent impediments**).

66–76 Macduff describes uncontrolled desire (**boundless intemperance**) as a tyrant of human nature that has caused the early (**untimely**) downfall of many kings. When Malcolm is king, however, his lustful appetite (**vulture in you**) can be satisfied by the many women willing to give (**dedicate**) themselves to a king. Do you think Macduff's prediction is accurate?

76–78 Malcolm adds insatiable greed (**stanchless avarice**) to the list of evils in his disposition (**affection**).

Macduff.   This avarice

85   Sticks deeper, grows with more pernicious root
       Than summer-seeming lust; and it hath been
       The sword of our slain kings. Yet do not fear.
       Scotland hath foisons to fill up your will
       Of your mere own. All these are portable,
90   With other graces weighed.

       Malcolm. But I have none. The king-becoming graces,
       As justice, verity, temp'rance, stableness,
       Bounty, perseverance, mercy, lowliness,
       Devotion, patience, courage, fortitude,
95   I have no relish of them, but abound
       In the division of each several crime,
       Acting it many ways. Nay, had I pow'r, I should
       Pour the sweet milk of concord into hell,
       Uproar the universal peace, confound
100   All unity on earth.

       Macduff.   O Scotland, Scotland!

       Malcolm. If such a one be fit to govern, speak.
       I am as I have spoken.

       Macduff.   Fit to govern?
       No, not to live. O nation miserable,
       With an untitled tyrant bloody-scept'red,
105   When shalt thou see thy wholesome days again,
       Since that the truest issue of thy throne
       By his own interdiction stands accursed
       And does blaspheme his breed? Thy royal father
       Was a most sainted king; the queen that bore thee,
110   Oft'ner upon her knees than on her feet,
       Died every day she lived. Fare thee well!
       These evils thou repeat'st upon thyself
       Have banished me from Scotland. O my breast,
       Thy hope ends here!

       Malcolm.   Macduff, this noble passion,
115   Child of integrity, hath from my soul
       Wiped the black scruples, reconciled my thoughts
       To thy good truth and honor. Devilish Macbeth
       By many of these trains hath sought to win me
       Into his power; and modest wisdom plucks me
120   From over-credulous haste; but God above
       Deal between thee and me! for even now
       I put myself to thy direction and
       Unspeak mine own detraction, here abjure

84–90 Macduff recognizes that greed is a deeper-rooted problem than lust, which passes as quickly as the summer (**summer–seeming**). But the king's property alone (**of your mere own**) offers plenty (**foisons**) to satisfy his desire. Malcolm's vices can be tolerated (**are portable**). Do you think Macduff's position is sensible?

91–95 Malcolm claims that he lacks all the virtues appropriate to a king (**king-becoming graces**). His list of missing virtues includes truthfulness (**verity**), consistency (**stableness**), generosity (**bounty**), humility (**lowliness**), and religious devotion.

102–114 Macduff can see no prospect of relief for Scotland's suffering under a tyrant who has no right to the throne (**untitled**). The rightful heir (**truest issue**), Malcolm, bans himself from the throne (**by his own interdiction**) because of his evil. Malcolm's vices slander his parents (**blaspheme his breed**)—his saintly father and his mother who renounced the world (**died every day**) for the sake of her religion. Since Macduff will not help an evil man to become king, he will not be able to return to Scotland.

The taints and blames I laid upon myself
125 For strangers to my nature. I am yet
Unknown to woman, never was forsworn,
Scarcely have coveted what was mine own,
At no time broke my faith, would not betray
The devil to his fellow, and delight
130 No less in truth than life. My first false speaking
Was this upon myself. What I am truly,
Is thine and my poor country's to command;
Whither indeed, before thy here-approach,
Old Siward with ten thousand warlike men
135 Already at a point was setting forth.
Now we'll together; and the chance of goodness
Be like our warranted quarrel! Why are you silent?

Macduff. Such welcome and unwelcome things at once
'Tis hard to reconcile.

[*Enter a* Doctor.]

140 **Malcolm.** Well, more anon. Comes the King forth, I pray you?

Doctor. Ay, sir. There are a crew of wretched souls
That stay his cure. Their malady convinces
The great assay of art; but at his touch,
Such sanctity hath heaven given his hand,
145 They presently amend.

Malcolm.   I thank you, doctor.

[*Exit* Doctor.]

Macduff. What's the disease he means?

Malcolm.   'Tis called the evil:
A most miraculous work in this good king,
Which often since my here-remain in England
I have seen him do. How he solicits heaven
150 Himself best knows; but strangely-visited people,
All swol'n and ulcerous, pitiful to the eye,
The mere despair of surgery, he cures,
Hanging a golden stamp about their necks,
Put on with holy prayers; and 'tis spoken,
155 To the succeeding royalty he leaves
The healing benediction. With this strange virtue,
He hath a heavenly gift of prophecy,
And sundry blessings hang about his throne
That speak him full of grace.

[*Enter* Ross.]

114–125 Macduff has finally convinced Malcolm of his honesty. Malcolm explains that his caution (**modest wisdom**) resulted from his fear of Macbeth's tricks. He takes back his accusations against himself (**unspeak mine own detraction**) and renounces (**abjure**) the evils he previously claimed.

133–137 Malcolm already has an army, 10,000 troops belonging to old Siward, the earl of Northumberland. Now that Macduff is an ally, he hopes the battle's result will match the justice of their cause (**warranted quarrel**). Why is Macduff left speechless by Malcolm's revelation?

141–159 Edward the Confessor, king of England, could reportedly heal the disease of scrofula (**the evil**) by his saintly touch. The doctor describes people who cannot be helped by medicine's best efforts (**the great assay of art**) waiting for the touch of the king's hand. Edward has cured many victims of this disease. Each time, he hangs a gold coin around their necks and offers prayers, a healing ritual that he will teach to his royal descendants (**succeeding royalty**).

Macduff. See who comes here.

160 **Malcolm.** My countryman; but yet I know him not.

Macduff. My ever gentle cousin, welcome hither.

Malcolm. I know him now. Good God betimes remove
The means that makes us strangers!

Ross. Sir, amen.

Macduff. Stands Scotland where it did?

Ross. Alas, poor country,
165 Almost afraid to know itself! It cannot
Be called our mother, but our grave; where nothing,
But who knows nothing, is once seen to smile;
Where sighs and groans, and shrieks that rent the air,
Are made, not marked; where violent sorrow seems
170 A modern ecstasy. The dead man's knell
Is there scarce asked for who; and good men's lives
Expire before the flowers in their caps,
Dying or ere they sicken.

Macduff. O, relation
Too nice, and yet too true!

Malcolm. What's the newest grief?

175 **Ross.** That of an hour's age doth hiss the speaker;
Each minute teems a new one.

Macduff. How does my wife?

Ross. Why, well.

Macduff. And all my children?

Ross. Well too.

Macduff. The tyrant has not battered at their peace?

Ross. No, they were well at peace when I did leave 'em.

180 **Macduff.** Be not a niggard of your speech. How goes't?

Ross. When I came hither to transport the tidings
Which I have heavily borne, there ran a rumor
Of many worthy fellows that were out;
Which was to my belief witnessed the rather
185 For that I saw the tyrant's power afoot.
Now is the time of help. Your eye in Scotland
Would create soldiers, make our women fight
To doff their dire distresses.

Malcolm. Be't their comfort
We are coming thither. Gracious England hath

162–163 Good God . . . strangers: May God remove Macbeth, who is the cause (**means**) of our being strangers.

164–173 Ross describes Scotland's terrible condition. In a land where screams have become so common that they go unnoticed (**are made, not marked**), violent sorrow becomes a commonplace emotion (**modern ecstasy**). So many have died that people no longer ask for their names, and good men die before their time.

173–174 relation too nice: news that is too accurate.

175–176 If the news is more than an hour old, listeners hiss at the speaker for being outdated; every minute gives birth to a new grief.

179 well at peace: Ross knows about the murder of Macduff's wife and son, but the news is too terrible to report.

181–188 Notice how Ross avoids the subject of Macduff's family. He mentions the rumors of nobles who are rebelling (**out**) against Macbeth. Ross believes the rumors because he saw Macbeth's troops on the march (**tyrant's power afoot**). The presence (**eye**) of Malcolm and Macduff in Scotland would help raise soldiers and remove (**doff**) Macbeth's evil (**dire distresses**).

190 Lent us good Siward and ten thousand men.
An older and a better soldier none
That Christendom gives out.

Ross.   Would I could answer
This comfort with the like! But I have words
That would be howled out in the desert air,
195 Where hearing should not latch them.

Macduff.   What concern they?
The general cause? or is it a fee-grief
Due to some single breast?

Ross.   No mind that's honest
But in it shares some woe, though the main part
Pertains to you alone.

Macduff.   If it be mine,
200 Keep it not from me, quickly let me have it.

Ross. Let not your ears despise my tongue for ever,
Which shall possess them with the heaviest sound
That ever yet they heard.

Macduff.   Humh! I guess at it.

Ross. Your castle is surprised; your wife and babes
205 Savagely slaughtered. To relate the manner
Were, on the quarry of these murdered deer,
To add the death of you.

Malcolm.   Merciful heaven!
What, man! Ne'er pull your hat upon your brows.
Give sorrow words. The grief that does not speak
210 Whispers the o'erfraught heart and bids it break.

Macduff. My children too?

Ross.   Wife, children, servants, all
That could be found.

Macduff.   And I must be from thence?
My wife killed too?

Ross.   I have said.

Malcolm.   Be comforted.
Let's make us med'cines of our great revenge
215 To cure this deadly grief.

Macduff. He has no children. All my pretty ones?
Did you say all? O hell-kite! All?
What, all my pretty chickens and their dam
At one fell swoop?

194 would: should.

195 latch: catch.

196 fee-grief: private sorrow.

197–198 No mind . . . woe: Every honorable (**honest**) person shares in this sorrow.

205–207 To relate . . . of you: Ross won't add to Macduff's sorrow by telling him how his family was killed. He compares Macduff's dear ones to the piled bodies of killed deer (**quarry**).

209–210 The grief . . . break: Silence will only push an overburdened heart to the breaking point.

212 Macduff laments his absence from the castle.

216–219 He has no children: possibly a reference to Macbeth, who has no children to be killed for revenge. Macduff compares Macbeth to a bird of prey (**hell-kite**) who kills defenseless chickens and their mother.

220 **Malcolm.** Dispute it like a man.

Macduff.   I shall do so;
But I must also feel it as a man.
I cannot but remember such things were
That were most precious to me. Did heaven look on
And would not take their part? Sinful Macduff,
225 They were all struck for thee! Naught that I am,
Not for their own demerits, but for mine,
Fell slaughter on their souls. Heaven rest them now!

Malcolm. Be this the whetstone of your sword. Let grief
Convert to anger; blunt not the heart, enrage it.

230 **Macduff.** O, I could play the woman with mine eyes
And braggart with my tongue! But, gentle heavens,
Cut short all intermission. Front to front
Bring thou this fiend of Scotland and myself.
Within my sword's length set him. If he scape,
235 Heaven forgive him too!

Malcolm.   This tune goes manly.
Come, go we to the King. Our power is ready;
Our lack is nothing but our leave. Macbeth
Is ripe for shaking, and the pow'rs above
Put on their instruments. Receive what cheer you may.
240 The night is long that never finds the day.

[*Exeunt.*]

225 naught: nothing.

228 whetstone: grindstone used for sharpening.

230–235 O, I could play . . . him too: Macduff won't act like a woman by crying or like a braggart by boasting. He wants no delay (**intermission**) to keep him from face-to-face combat with Macbeth. Macduff ironically swears that if Macbeth escapes, he deserves heaven's mercy.

236–240 Our troops are ready to attack, needing only the king's permission (**our lack is nothing but our leave**). Like a ripe fruit, Macbeth is ready to fall, and heavenly powers are preparing to assist us. The long night of Macbeth's evil will be broken.

Thinking through the LITERATURE

Connect to the Literature

1. What Do You Think?

Do you have any sympathy for Macbeth at this point in the play? Why or why not?

Comprehension Check

- What three messages does Macbeth receive from the three apparitions?
- What happens to Lady Macduff and her children?
- After learning of his family's fate, what does Macduff vow to do?

Think Critically

2. **ACTIVE READING** **READING DRAMA** Envision Act Four, Scene 1, as it might be performed on a stage. Also, review any notes about this scene that you may have recorded in your **READER'S NOTEBOOK.** What sights and sounds (and perhaps smells) would you expect the **audience** to experience?

3. How would you describe the attitude toward the supernatural expressed in this play?

4. Why do you think Macbeth is so interested in learning about the future?

5. Consider Macduff's reaction to the news of his family's murder. Do you find his behavior realistic? Why or why not?

6. What do you think will happen when Malcolm and Macduff confront Macbeth?

THINK ABOUT
- the predictions of the three apparitions
- the motives of all three men
- Macduff's pledge to fight Macbeth

7. Do you think Malcolm would make a good king? Why or why not?

Extend Interpretations

8. **Comparing Texts** Recall the views of vengeance, heroism, and kingship expressed in *Beowulf* (page 30). Which **characters** in *Macbeth* would you say are most like Beowulf? Which would you say are more like the monsters? Cite details from the two works as support.

9. **Connect to Life** Consider the methods present-day politicians use to gauge public response to their actions and to shape their policies. On which of these methods might Macbeth rely if he were a leader today?

Literary Analysis

FORESHADOWING One way that writers heighten their audiences' interest is by foreshadowing upcoming events. **Foreshadowing** is a writer's use of hints or clues to suggest what events will occur later in a work.

Activity Create a third column in the chart you've been using to keep track of foreshadowing. In the new column, indicate whether each instance of foreshadowing you have listed has actually hinted at what you thought it did, at least as far as you know at this point in the play.

Act, Scene, Lines	What the Lines Hint At	Accurate?
Act Two, Scene 1, lines 62–64	Macbeth will murder Duncan.	yes

View and Compare

What characteristics—costuming, posture, facial expressions—link these images of Lady Macbeth? What qualities set them apart?

Judith Anderson as Lady Macbeth

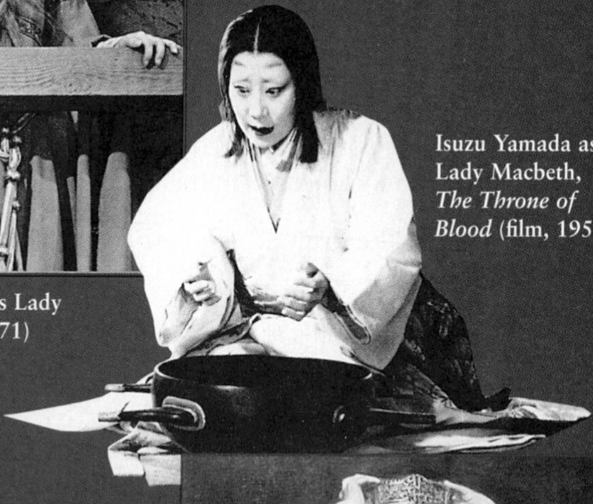

Francesca Annis as Lady Macbeth (film, 1971)

Isuzu Yamada as Lady Macbeth, *The Throne of Blood* (film, 1957)

Ellen Terry as Lady Macbeth (1889), John Singer Sargent, National Portrait Gallery, London

Act 5

SCENE 1

Macbeth's castle at Dunsinane.

A sleepwalking Lady Macbeth is observed by a concerned attendant, or gentlewoman, and a doctor. Lady Macbeth appears to be washing imagined blood from her hands. Her actions and confused speech greatly concern the doctor, and he warns the attendant to keep an eye on Lady Macbeth, fearing that she will harm herself.

[*Enter a* Doctor of Physic *and a* Waiting Gentlewoman.]

Doctor. I have two nights watched with you, but can perceive no truth in your report. When was it she last walked?

Gentlewoman. Since his Majesty went into the field I have
5   seen her rise from her bed, throw her nightgown upon her, unlock her closet, take forth paper, fold it, write upon't, read it, afterwards seal it, and again return to bed; yet all this while in a most fast sleep.

Doctor. A great perturbation in nature, to receive at once
10   the benefit of sleep and do the effects of watching! In this slumb'ry agitation, besides her walking and other actual performances, what (at any time) have you heard her say?

Gentlewoman. That, sir, which I will not report after her.

15   **Doctor.** You may to me, and 'tis most meet you should.

Gentlewoman. Neither to you nor any one, having no witness to confirm my speech.

[*Enter* Lady Macbeth, *with a taper.*]

Lo you, here she comes! This is her very guise, and, upon my life, fast asleep! Observe her; stand close.

20   **Doctor.** How came she by that light?

Gentlewoman. Why, it stood by her. She has light by her continually. 'Tis her command.

Doctor. You see her eyes are open.

Gentlewoman. Ay, but their sense is shut.

25   **Doctor.** What is it she does now? Look how she rubs her hands.

Gentlewoman. It is an accustomed action with her, to

4 went into the field: went to battle.

9–10 A great . . . of watching: To behave as though awake (**watching**) while sleeping is a sign of a greatly troubled nature.

15 meet: appropriate.

16–17 The attendant won't repeat what Lady Macbeth has said, because there are no other witnesses to confirm her report. What is she worried about?

18–19 guise: usual manner; **stand close:** hide yourself.

20 that light: her candle.

21–22 Why might Lady Macbeth want a light by her at all times?

View and Compare

Which of these portrayals of Lady Macbeth's madness do you find more intriguing?

Diana Rigg as Lady Macbeth, National Theatre, London

Isuzu Yamada as Lady Macbeth in
The Throne of Blood (film, 1957)

seem thus washing her hands. I have known her continue in this a quarter of an hour.

Lady Macbeth. Yet here's a spot.

30 **Doctor.** Hark, she speaks! I will set down what comes from her, to satisfy my remembrance the more strongly.

Lady Macbeth. Out, damned spot! out, I say! One; two. Why then 'tis time to do't. Hell is murky. Fie, my lord, fie! a soldier, and afeard? What need we fear who

35 knows it, when none can call our pow'r to accompt? Yet who would have thought the old man to have had so much blood in him?

Doctor. Do you mark that?

Lady Macbeth. The Thane of Fife had a wife. Where is

40 she now? What, will these hands ne'er be clean? No more o' that, my lord, no more o' that! You mar all with this starting.

Doctor. Go to, go to! You have known what you should not.

45 **Gentlewoman.** She has spoke what she should not, I am sure of that. Heaven knows what she has known.

Lady Macbeth. Here's the smell of the blood still. All the perfumes of Arabia will not sweeten this little hand. Oh, oh, oh!

50 **Doctor.** What a sigh is there! The heart is sorely charged.

Gentlewoman. I would not have such a heart in my bosom for the dignity of the whole body.

Doctor. Well, well, well.

Gentlewoman. Pray God it be, sir.

55 **Doctor.** This disease is beyond my practice. Yet I have known those which have walked in their sleep who have died holily in their beds.

Lady Macbeth. Wash your hands, put on your nightgown, look not so pale! I tell you yet again, Banquo's buried.

60 He cannot come out on's grave.

Doctor. Even so?

Lady Macbeth. To bed, to bed! There's knocking at the gate. Come, come, come, come, give me your hand! What's done cannot be undone. To bed, to bed, to bed!

[*Exit.*]

65 **Doctor.** Will she go now to bed?

Gentlewoman. Directly.

32–35 Lady Macbeth refers to hell's darkness, and then she relives how she persuaded her husband to murder Duncan; she had believed that their power would keep them from being held accountable (**accompt**).

39–42 Lady Macbeth shows guilt about Macduff's wife. Then she addresses her husband, as if he were having another ghostly fit (**starting**).

50 sorely charged: heavily burdened.

51–52 The gentlewoman says that she would not want Lady Macbeth's heavy heart in exchange for being queen.

55 practice: skill.

60 on's: of his.

61 What has the doctor learned so far from Lady Macbeth's ramblings?

Doctor. Foul whisp'rings are abroad. Unnatural deeds
    Do breed unnatural troubles. Infected minds
    To their deaf pillows will discharge their secrets.
70   More needs she the divine than the physician.
    God, God forgive us all! Look after her;
    Remove from her the means of all annoyance,
    And still keep eyes upon her. So good night.
    My mind she has mated, and amazed my sight.
75   I think, but dare not speak.

Gentlewoman.   Good night, good doctor.

[*Exeunt.*]

67 Foul whisp'rings are abroad: Rumors of evil deeds are circulating.

70 She needs a priest more than a doctor.

72 annoyance: injury. The doctor may be worried about the possibility of Lady Macbeth's committing suicide.

74 mated: astonished.

SCENE 2

The country near Dunsinane.

The Scottish rebels, led by Menteith, Caithness, Angus, and Lennox, have come to Birnam Wood to join Malcolm and his English army. They know that Dunsinane has been fortified by a furious and brave Macbeth. They also know that his men neither love nor respect him.

[*Drum and Colors. Enter* Menteith, Caithness, Angus, Lennox, Soldiers.]

Menteith. The English pow'r is near, led on by Malcolm,
    His uncle Siward, and the good Macduff.
    Revenges burn in them; for their dear causes
    Would to the bleeding and the grim alarm
5   Excite the mortified man.

Angus.   Near Birnam Wood
    Shall we well meet them; that way are they coming.

Caithness. Who knows if Donalbain be with his brother?

Lennox. For certain, sir, he is not. I have a file
    Of all the gentry. There is Siward's son
10   And many unrough youths that even now
    Protest their first of manhood.

Menteith.   What does the tyrant?

Caithness. Great Dunsinane he strongly fortifies.
    Some say he's mad; others, that lesser hate him,
    Do call it valiant fury; but for certain
15   He cannot buckle his distempered cause
    Within the belt of rule.

Angus.   Now does he feel
    His secret murders sticking on his hands.

3–5 for their dear . . . man: The cause of Malcolm and Macduff is so deeply felt that a dead (**mortified**) man would respond to their call to arms (**alarm**).

10–11 many . . . manhood: many soldiers who are too young to grow beards (**unrough**)—that is, who have hardly reached manhood.

15–16 Like a man so swollen with disease (**distempered**) that he cannot buckle his belt, Macbeth cannot control his evil actions.

Now minutely revolts upbraid his faith-breach.
Those he commands move only in command,
20 Nothing in love. Now does he feel his title
Hang loose about him, like a giant's robe
Upon a dwarfish thief.

Menteith. Who then shall blame
His pestered senses to recoil and start,
When all that is within him does condemn
25 Itself for being there?

Caithness. Well, march we on
To give obedience where 'tis truly owed.
Meet we the med'cine of the sickly weal;
And with him pour we in our country's purge
Each drop of us.

Lennox. Or so much as it needs
30 To dew the sovereign flower and drown the weeds.
Make we our march towards Birnam.

[*Exeunt, marching.*]

18 Every minute, the revolts against Macbeth shame him for his treachery (**faith-breach**).

22–25 Macbeth's troubled nerves (**pestered senses**)—the product of his guilty conscience—have made him jumpy.

25–29 Caithness and the others will give their loyalty to the only help (**med'cine**) for the sick country (**weal**). They are willing to sacrifice their last drop of blood to cleanse (**purge**) Scotland.

29–31 Lennox compares Malcolm to a flower that needs the blood of patriots to water (**dew**) it and drown out weeds like Macbeth.

SCENE 3

Dunsinane. A room in the castle.

Macbeth awaits battle, confident of victory because of what he learned from the witches. After hearing that a huge army is ready to march upon his castle, he expresses bitter regrets about his life. While Macbeth prepares for battle, the doctor reports that he cannot cure Lady Macbeth, whose illness is mental, not physical.

[*Enter* Macbeth, Doctor, *and* Attendants.]

Macbeth. Bring me no more reports. Let them fly all!
Till Birnam Wood remove to Dunsinane,
I cannot taint with fear. What's the boy Malcolm?
Was he not born of woman? The spirits that know
5 All mortal consequences have pronounced me thus:
"Fear not, Macbeth. No man that's born of woman
Shall e'er have power upon thee." Then fly, false thanes,
And mingle with the English epicures.
The mind I sway by and the heart I bear
10 Shall never sag with doubt nor shake with fear.

[*Enter* Servant.]

The devil damn thee black, thou cream-faced loon!
Where got'st thou that goose look?

Servant. There is ten thousand—

Macbeth. Geese, villain?

1 Macbeth wants no more news of thanes who have gone to Malcolm's side.

2–10 Macbeth will not be infected (**taint**) with fear, because the witches (**spirits**), who know all human events (**mortal consequences**), have convinced him that he is invincible. He mocks the self-indulgent English (**English epicures**), then swears that he will never lack confidence.

11–12 loon: stupid rascal; **goose look:** look of fear.

Act 5, Scene 3: Orson Welles as Macbeth with Edgar Barrier as the Servant (film, 1948)

Servant.   Soldiers, sir.

Macbeth. Go prick thy face and over-red thy fear,
15   Thou lily-livered boy. What soldiers, patch?
       Death of thy soul! Those linen cheeks of thine
       Are counselors to fear. What soldiers, whey-face?

Servant. The English force, so please you.

Macbeth. Take thy face hence.

[*Exit* Servant.]

                                        Seyton!—I am sick at heart,
20   When I behold—Seyton, I say!—This push
       Will cheer me ever, or disseat me now.
       I have lived long enough. My way of life
       Is fallen into the sere, the yellow leaf;
       And that which should accompany old age,
25   As honor, love, obedience, troops of friends,
       I must not look to have; but, in their stead,
       Curses not loud but deep, mouth-honor, breath,
       Which the poor heart would fain deny, and dare not.
       Seyton!

[*Enter* Seyton.]

30 **Seyton.** What's your gracious pleasure?

Macbeth.   What news more?

14–17 Macbeth suggests that the servant cut his face so that blood will hide his cowardice. He repeatedly insults the servant, calling him a coward (**lily-livered**) and a clown (**patch**) and making fun of his white complexion (**linen cheeks, whey-face**).

20–28 This push . . . dare not: The upcoming battle will either make Macbeth secure (**cheer me ever**) or dethrone (**disseat**) him. He bitterly compares his life to a withered (**sere**) leaf. He cannot look forward to old age with friends and honor, but only to curses and empty flattery (**mouth-honor, breath**) from those too timid (**the poor heart**) to tell the truth.

Seyton. All is confirmed, my lord, which was reported.

Macbeth. I'll fight, till from my bones my flesh be hacked.
Give me my armor.

Seyton. 'Tis not needed yet.

Macbeth. I'll put it on.

35 Send out mo horses, skirr the country round;
Hang those that talk of fear. Give me mine armor.
How does your patient, doctor?

Doctor. Not so sick, my lord,
As she is troubled with thick-coming fancies
That keep her from her rest.

Macbeth. Cure her of that!

40 Canst thou not minister to a mind diseased,
Pluck from the memory a rooted sorrow,
Raze out the written troubles of the brain,
And with some sweet oblivious antidote
Cleanse the stuffed bosom of that perilous stuff

45 Which weighs upon the heart?

Doctor. Therein the patient
Must minister to himself.

Macbeth. Throw physic to the dogs, I'll none of it!—
Come, put mine armor on. Give me my staff.
Seyton, send out.—Doctor, the thanes fly from me.—

50 Come, sir, dispatch.—If thou couldst, doctor, cast
The water of my land, find her disease,
And purge it to a sound and pristine health,
I would applaud thee to the very echo,
That should applaud again.—Pull't off, I say.—

55 What rhubarb, senna, or what purgative drug,
Would scour these English hence? Hear'st thou of them?

Doctor. Ay, my good lord. Your royal preparation
Makes us hear something.

Macbeth. Bring it after me!
I will not be afraid of death and bane

60 Till Birnam Forest come to Dunsinane.

Doctor. [*Aside*] Were I from Dunsinane away and clear,
Profit again should hardly draw me here.

[*Exeunt.*]

35 mo: more; **skirr:** scour.

39–45 Macbeth asks the doctor to remove the sorrow from Lady Macbeth's memory, to erase (**raze out**) the troubles imprinted on her mind, and to relieve her overburdened heart (**stuffed bosom**) of its guilt (**perilous stuff**). Do you think Macbeth shares his wife's feelings of guilt?

47–54 Macbeth has lost his faith in the ability of medicine (**physic**) to help his wife. Then as he struggles into his armor, he says that if the doctor could diagnose Scotland's disease (**cast . . . land**) and cure it, Macbeth would never stop praising him.

54 Pull't off: referring to a piece of armor.

56 scour: purge; **them:** the English.

58–60 Macbeth leaves for battle, telling Seyton to bring the armor. He declares his fearlessness before death and destruction (**bane**).

SCENE 4

The country near Birnam Wood.

The rebels and English forces have met in Birnam Wood. Malcolm orders each soldier to cut tree branches to camouflage himself. In this way Birnam Wood will march upon Dunsinane.

[*Drum and Colors. Enter* Malcolm, Siward, Macduff, Siward's Son, Menteith, Caithness, Angus, Lennox, Ross, *and* Soldiers, *marching.*]

Malcolm. Cousins, I hope the days are near at hand
   That chambers will be safe.

Menteith.   We doubt it nothing.

Siward. What wood is this before us?

Menteith.   The wood of Birnam.

Malcolm. Let every soldier hew him down a bough
5   And bear't before him. Thereby shall we shadow
   The numbers of our host and make discovery
   Err in report of us.

Soldiers.   It shall be done.

Siward. We learn no other but the confident tyrant
   Keeps still in Dunsinane and will endure
10   Our setting down before't.

Malcolm.   'Tis his main hope;
   For where there is advantage to be given,
   Both more and less have given him the revolt;
   And none serve with him but constrained things,
   Whose hearts are absent too.

Macduff.   Let our just censures
15   Attend the true event, and put we on
   Industrious soldiership.

Siward.   The time approaches
   That will with due decision make us know
   What we shall say we have, and what we owe.
   Thoughts speculative their unsure hopes relate,
20   But certain issue strokes must arbitrate;
   Towards which advance the war.

[*Exeunt, marching.*]

4–7 Malcolm orders his men to cut down tree branches to camouflage themselves. This will conceal (**shadow**) the size of their army and confuse Macbeth's scouts. Consider the prophecy about Birnam Wood. What do you now think the prophecy means?

10 setting down: siege.

10–14 Malcolm says that men of all ranks (**both more and less**) have abandoned Macbeth. Only weak men who have been forced into service remain with him.

14–16 Macduff warns against overconfidence and advises that they attend to the business of fighting.

16–21 Siward says that the approaching battle will decide whether their claims will match what they actually possess (**owe**). Right now, their hopes and expectations are the product of guesswork (**thoughts speculative**); only fighting (**strokes**) can settle (**arbitrate**) the issue.

SCENE 5

Dunsinane. Within the castle.

*Convinced of his powers, Macbeth mocks the enemy; his slaughters
have left him fearless. News of Lady Macbeth's death stirs little emotion,
only a comment on the emptiness of life. However, when a messenger
reports that Birnam Wood seems to be moving toward the castle,
Macbeth grows agitated. Fearing that the prophecies have deceived
him, he decides to leave the castle to fight and die on the battlefield.*

[*Enter* Macbeth, Seyton, *and* Soldiers, *with Drum and Colors.*]

Macbeth. Hang out our banners on the outward walls.
The cry is still, "They come!" Our castle's strength
Will laugh a siege to scorn. Here let them lie
Till famine and the ague eat them up.

5   Were they not forced with those that should be ours,
We might have met them dareful, beard to beard,
And beat them backward home.

[*A cry within of women.*]

                          What is that noise?

Seyton. It is the cry of women, my good lord. [*Exit.*]

Macbeth. I have almost forgot the taste of fears.

10   The time has been, my senses would have cooled
To hear a night-shriek, and my fell of hair
Would at a dismal treatise rouse and stir
As life were in't. I have supped full with horrors.
Direness, familiar to my slaughterous thoughts,

15   Cannot once start me.

[*Enter Seyton.*]

                       Wherefore was that cry?

Seyton. The Queen, my lord, is dead.

Macbeth. She should have died hereafter;
There would have been a time for such a word.
Tomorrow, and tomorrow, and tomorrow

20   Creeps in this petty pace from day to day
To the last syllable of recorded time;
And all our yesterdays have lighted fools
The way to dusty death. Out, out, brief candle!
Life's but a walking shadow, a poor player,

25   That struts and frets his hour upon the stage
And then is heard no more. It is a tale
Told by an idiot, full of sound and fury,
Signifying nothing.

4 ague: fever.

5–7 Macbeth complains that the attackers have been reinforced (**forced**) by deserters (**those that should be ours**), which has forced him to wait at Dunsinane instead of seeking victory on the battlefield.

9–15 There was a time when a scream in the night would have frozen Macbeth in fear and a terrifying tale (**dismal treatise**) would have made the hair on his skin (**fell of hair**) stand on end. But since he has fed on horror (**direness**), it cannot stir (**start**) him anymore.

17–23 Macbeth wishes that his wife had died later (**hereafter**), when he would have had time to mourn her. He is moved to express despair about his own meaningless life: the future promises monotonous repetition (**tomorrow, and tomorrow, and tomorrow**), and the past merely illustrates death's power. He wishes his life could be snuffed out like a candle.

24–28 Macbeth compares life to an actor who only briefly plays a part. Life is senseless, like a tale told by a raving idiot. Do you feel sorry for Macbeth here?

[*Enter a* Messenger.]

    Thou com'st to use thy tongue. Thy story quickly!

30 **Messenger.** Gracious my lord,
    I should report that which I say I saw,
    But know not how to do't.

    Macbeth.   Well, say, sir!

    Messenger. As I did stand my watch upon the hill,
    I looked toward Birnam, and anon methought
35   The wood began to move.

    Macbeth.   Liar and slave!

    Messenger. Let me endure your wrath if't be not so.
    Within this three mile may you see it coming;
    I say, a moving grove.

    Macbeth.   If thou speak'st false,
    Upon the next tree shalt thou hang alive,
40   Till famine cling thee. If thy speech be sooth,
    I care not if thou dost for me as much.
    I pull in resolution, and begin
    To doubt the equivocation of the fiend,
    That lies like truth. "Fear not, till Birnam Wood
45   Do come to Dunsinane!" and now a wood
    Comes toward Dunsinane. Arm, arm, and out!
    If this which he avouches does appear,
    There is nor flying hence nor tarrying here.
    I 'gin to be aweary of the sun,
50   And wish the estate o' the world were now undone.
    Ring the alarum bell! Blow wind, come wrack,
    At least we'll die with harness on our back!

    [*Exeunt.*]

38–52 The messenger's news has dampened Macbeth's determination (**resolution**); Macbeth begins to fear that the witches have tricked him (**to doubt the equivocation of the fiend**). His fear that the messenger tells the truth (**avouches**) makes him decide to confront the enemy instead of staying in his castle. Weary of life, he nevertheless decides to face death and ruin (**wrack**) with his armor (**harness**) on.

SCENE 6

Dunsinane. Before the castle.

Malcolm and the combined forces reach the castle, throw away their camouflage, and prepare for battle.

[*Drum and Colors. Enter* Malcolm, Siward, Macduff, *and their* Army, *with boughs.*]

Malcolm. Now near enough. Your leavy screens throw down
    And show like those you are. You, worthy uncle,
    Shall with my cousin, your right noble son,
    Lead our first battle. Worthy Macduff and we
5   Shall take upon's what else remains to do,

Act 5, Scene 6: The attack on Dunsinane Castle (film, 1961)

According to our order.

Siward.   Fare you well.
Do we but find the tyrant's power tonight,
Let us be beaten if we cannot fight.

Macduff. Make all our trumpets speak, give them all breath,
10   Those clamorous harbingers of blood and death.

[*Exeunt. Alarums continued.*]

1–6 Malcolm commands the troops to put down their branches (**leavy screens**) and gives the battle instructions.

7 power: forces.

10 harbingers: announcers.

SCENE 7

Another part of the battlefield.

Macbeth kills young Siward, which restores his belief that he cannot be killed by any man born of a woman. Meanwhile, Macduff searches for the hated king. Young Siward's father reports that Macbeth's soldiers have surrendered and that many have even joined their attackers.

[*Enter* Macbeth.]

Macbeth. They have tied me to a stake. I cannot fly,
But bearlike I must fight the course. What's he
That was not born of woman? Such a one
Am I to fear, or none.

1–4 Macbeth compares himself to a bear tied to a post (a reference to the sport of bearbaiting, in which a bear was tied to a stake and attacked by dogs).

[*Enter* Young Siward.]

5 **Young Siward.** What is thy name?

Macbeth.   Thou'lt be afraid to hear it.

Young Siward. No; though thou call'st thyself a hotter name
    Than any is in hell.

Macbeth.   My name's Macbeth.

Young Siward. The devil himself could not pronounce a title
    More hateful to mine ear.

Macbeth.   No, nor more fearful.

10 **Young Siward.** Thou liest, abhorred tyrant! With my sword
    I'll prove the lie thou speak'st.

[*Fight, and* Young Siward *slain.*]

Macbeth.   Thou wast born of woman.
    But swords I smile at, weapons laugh to scorn,
    Brandished by man that's of a woman born. [*Exit.*]

[*Alarums. Enter* Macduff.]

Macduff. That way the noise is. Tyrant, show thy face!
15   If thou beest slain and with no stroke of mine,
    My wife and children's ghosts will haunt me still.
    I cannot strike at wretched kerns, whose arms
    Are hired to bear their staves. Either thou, Macbeth,
    Or else my sword with an unbattered edge
20   I sheathe again undeeded. There thou shouldst be.
    By this great clatter one of greatest note
    Seems bruited. Let me find him, Fortune!
    And more I beg not.

[*Exit. Alarums.*]

[*Enter* Malcolm *and* Siward.]

Siward. This way, my lord. The castle's gently rendered:
25   The tyrant's people on both sides do fight;
    The noble thanes do bravely in the war;
    The day almost itself professes yours,
    And little is to do.

Malcolm.   We have met with foes
    That strike beside us.

Siward.   Enter, sir, the castle.

[*Exeunt. Alarum.*]

11–13 Do you think Macbeth is justified in his confidence?

14–20 Macduff enters alone. He wants to avenge the murders of his wife and children and hopes to find Macbeth before someone else has the chance to kill him. Macduff does not want to fight the miserable hired soldiers (**kerns**), who are armed only with spears (**staves**). If he can't fight Macbeth, Macduff will leave his sword unused (**undeeded**).

20–23 After hearing sounds suggesting that a person of great distinction (**note**) is nearby, Macduff exits in pursuit of Macbeth.

24 gently rendered: surrendered without a fight.

27 You have almost won the day.

28–29 During the battle many of Macbeth's men deserted to Malcolm's army.

View and Compare

Which portrayal of Macbeth's death better captures the mood of the scene as you interpret it?

The fallen Macbeth in
The Throne of Blood
(film, 1957)

Macduff and Macbeth fight (film, 1971)

SCENE 8

Another part of the battlefield.

Macduff finally hunts down Macbeth, who is reluctant to fight because he has already killed too many Macduffs. The still-proud Macbeth tells his enemy that no man born of a woman can defeat him, only to learn that Macduff was ripped from his mother's womb, thus not born naturally. Rather than face humiliation, Macbeth decides to fight to the death. After their fight takes them elsewhere, the Scottish lords, now in charge of Macbeth's castle, discuss young Siward's noble death. Macduff returns carrying Macbeth's bloody head, proclaiming final victory and declaring Malcolm king of Scotland. The new king thanks his supporters and promises rewards, while asking for God's help to restore order and harmony.

[*Enter* Macbeth.]

Macbeth. Why should I play the Roman fool and die
On mine own sword? Whiles I see lives, the gashes
Do better upon them.

[*Enter* Macduff.]

Macduff.   Turn, hellhound, turn!

Macbeth. Of all men else I have avoided thee.
5   But get thee back! My soul is too much charged
With blood of thine already.

Macduff.   I have no words;
My voice is in my sword, thou bloodier villain
Than terms can give thee out!

[*Fight. Alarum.*]

Macbeth.   Thou losest labor.
As easy mayst thou the intrenchant air
10   With thy keen sword impress as make me bleed.
Let fall thy blade on vulnerable crests.
I bear a charmed life, which must not yield
To one of woman born.

Macduff.   Despair thy charm!
And let the angel whom thou still hast served
15   Tell thee, Macduff was from his mother's womb
Untimely ripped.

Macbeth. Accursed be that tongue that tells me so,
For it hath cowed my better part of man!
And be these juggling fiends no more believed,
20   That palter with us in a double sense,

1–3 Macbeth vows to continue fighting, refusing to commit suicide in the style of a defeated Roman general.

4–6 Macbeth does not want to fight Macduff, having already killed so many members of Macduff's family. Do you think Macbeth regrets his past actions?

8–13 Macbeth says that Macduff is wasting his effort. Trying to wound Macbeth is as useless as trying to wound the invulnerable (**intrenchant**) air. Macduff should attack other, more easily injured foes, described in terms of helmets (**crests**).

15–16 Macduff . . . untimely ripped: Macduff was a premature baby delivered by cesarean section, an operation that removes the child directly from the mother's womb.

18 cowed my better part of man: made my spirit, or soul, fearful.

That keep the word of promise to our ear
And break it to our hope! I'll not fight with thee!

Macduff. Then yield thee, coward,
And live to be the show and gaze o' the time!
25   We'll have thee, as our rarer monsters are,
Painted upon a pole, and underwrit
"Here may you see the tyrant."

Macbeth.   I will not yield,
To kiss the ground before young Malcolm's feet
And to be baited with the rabble's curse.
30   Though Birnam Wood be come to Dunsinane,
And thou opposed, being of no woman born,
Yet I will try the last. Before my body
I throw my warlike shield. Lay on, Macduff,
And damned be him that first cries "Hold, enough!"

[*Exeunt fighting. Alarums.*]

[*Retreat and flourish. Enter, with Drum and Colors,* Malcolm,
Siward, Ross, Thanes, *and* Soldiers.]

35   **Malcolm.** I would the friends we miss were safe arrived.

Siward. Some must go off; and yet, by these I see,
So great a day as this is cheaply bought.

Malcolm. Macduff is missing, and your noble son.

Ross. Your son, my lord, has paid a soldier's debt.
40   He only lived but till he was a man,
The which no sooner had his prowess confirmed
In the unshrinking station where he fought
But like a man he died.

Siward.   Then he is dead?

Ross. Ay, and brought off the field. Your cause of sorrow
45   Must not be measured by his worth, for then
It hath no end.

Siward.   Had he his hurts before?

Ross. Ay, on the front.

Siward.   Why then, God's soldier be he!
Had I as many sons as I have hairs,
I would not wish them to a fairer death.
50   And so his knell is knolled.

Malcolm.   He's worth more sorrow,
And that I'll spend for him.

Siward.   He's worth no more.
They say he parted well and paid his score,
And so, God be with him! Here comes newer comfort.

19–22 The cheating witches (**juggling fiends**) have tricked him (**palter with us**) with words that have double meanings.

23–27 Macduff scornfully tells Macbeth to surrender so that he can become a public spectacle (**the show and gaze o' the time**). Macbeth's picture will be hung on a pole (**painted upon a pole**) as if he were part of a circus sideshow.

27–34 Macbeth cannot face the shame of surrender and public ridicule. He prefers to fight to the death (**try the last**) against Macduff, even though he knows all hope is gone. What is your opinion of Macbeth's attitude?

[Stage Direction] **Retreat . . . :** The first trumpet call (**retreat**) signals the battle's end. The next one (**flourish**) announces Malcolm's entrance.

36–37 Though some must die (**go off**) in battle, Siward can see that their side does not have many casualties.

44–46 Ross tells old Siward that if he mourns his son according to the boy's value, his sorrow will never end.

46 hurts before: wounds in the front of his body, which indicate he died facing his enemy.

50 knell is knolled: Young Siward's death bell has already rung, meaning there is no need to mourn him further. What do you think of old Siward's refusal to grieve for his son?

[*Enter* Macduff, *with* Macbeth's *head*.]

Macduff. Hail, King! for so thou art. Behold where stands
55   The usurper's cursed head. The time is free.
      I see thee compassed with thy kingdom's pearl,
      That speak my salutation in their minds;
      Whose voices I desire aloud with mine—
      Hail, King of Scotland!

   All.   Hail, King of Scotland!

[*Flourish*.]

60 **Malcolm.** We shall not spend a large expense of time
      Before we reckon with your several loves
      And make us even with you. My Thanes and kinsmen,
      Henceforth be Earls, the first that ever Scotland
      In such an honor named. What's more to do
65   Which would be planted newly with the time—
      As calling home our exiled friends abroad
      That fled the snares of watchful tyranny,
      Producing forth the cruel ministers
      Of this dead butcher and his fiendlike queen,
70   Who (as 'tis thought) by self and violent hands
      Took off her life—this, and what needful else
      That calls upon us, by the grace of Grace
      We will perform in measure, time, and place.
      So thanks to all at once and to each one,
75   Whom we invite to see us crowned at Scone.

[*Flourish. Exeunt omnes.*]

[Stage Direction] Macduff is probably carrying Macbeth's head on a pole.

55–56 The time . . . pearl: Macduff declares that the age (**time**) is now freed from tyranny. He sees Malcolm surrounded by Scotland's noblest men (**thy kingdom's pearl**).

60–75 Malcolm promises that he will quickly reward his nobles according to the devotion (**several loves**) they have shown. He gives the thanes new titles (**henceforth be Earls**) and declares his intention, as a sign of the new age (**planted newly with the time**), to welcome back the exiles who fled Macbeth's tyranny and his cruel agents (**ministers**). Now that Scotland is free of the butcher Macbeth and his queen, who is reported to have killed herself, Malcolm asks for God's help to restore order and harmony. He concludes by inviting all present to his coronation.

THE MACBETH MURDER MYSTERY

by James Thurber

It was a stupid mistake to make," said the American woman I had met at my hotel in the English lake country, "but it was on the counter with the other Penguin books—the little sixpenny ones, you know, with the paper covers—and I supposed of course it was a detective story. All the others were detective stories. I'd read all the others, so I bought this one without really looking at it carefully. You can imagine how mad I was when I found it was Shakespeare." I murmured something sympathetically. "I don't see why the Penguin-books people had to get out Shakespeare's plays in the same size and everything as the detective stories," went on my companion. "I think they have different-colored jackets," I said. "Well, I didn't notice that," she said. "Anyway, I got real comfy in bed that night and all ready to read a good mystery story and here I had 'The Tragedy of Macbeth'—a book for high-school students. Like 'Ivanhoe.'" "Or 'Lorna Doone,'" I said. "Exactly," said the American lady. "And I was just crazy for a good Agatha Christie, or something. Hercule Poirot is my favorite detective." "Is he the rabbity one?" I asked. "Oh, no," said my crime-fiction expert. "He's the Belgian one. You're thinking of Mr. Pinkerton, the one that helps Inspector Bull. He's good, too."

Over her second cup of tea my companion began to tell the plot of a detective story that had fooled her completely—it seems it was the old family doctor all the time. But I cut in on her. "Tell me," I said. "Did you read 'Macbeth'?" "I *had* to read it," she said. "There wasn't a scrap of anything else to read in the whole room." "Did you like it?" I asked. "No, I did not," she said, decisively. "In the first place, I don't think for a moment that Macbeth did it." I looked at her blankly. "Did what?" I asked. "I don't think for a moment that he killed the King," she said. "I don't think the Macbeth woman was mixed up in it, either.

You suspect them the most, of course, but those are the ones that are never guilty—or shouldn't be, anyway." "I'm afraid," I began, "that I—" "But don't you see?" said the American lady. "It would spoil everything if you could figure out right away who did it. Shakespeare was too smart for that. I've read that people never *have* figured out 'Hamlet,' so it isn't likely Shakespeare would have made 'Macbeth' as simple as it seems." I thought this over while I filled my pipe. "Who do you suspect?" I asked, suddenly. "Macduff," she said, promptly. "Good God!" I whispered, softly.

"Oh, Macduff did it, all right," said the murder specialist. "Hercule Poirot would have got him easily." "How did you figure it out?" I demanded. "Well," she said, "I didn't right away. At first I suspected Banquo. And then, of course, he was the second person killed. That was good right in there, that part. The person you suspect of the first murder should always be the second victim." "Is that so?" I murmured. "Oh, yes," said my informant. "They have to keep surprising you. Well, after the second murder I didn't know *who* the killer was for a while." "How about Malcolm and Donalbain, the King's sons?" I asked. "As I remember it, they fled right after the first murder. That looks suspicious." "Too suspicious," said the American lady. "Much too suspicious. When they flee, they're never guilty. You can count on that." "I believe," I said, "I'll have a brandy," and I summoned the waiter. My companion leaned toward me, her eyes bright, her teacup quivering. "Do you know who discovered Duncan's body?" she demanded. I said I was sorry, but I had forgotten. "Macduff discovers it," she said, slipping into the historical present. "Then he comes running downstairs and shouts, 'Confusion has broke open the Lord's anointed temple' and 'Sacrilegious murder has made his masterpiece' and on and on like that." The good lady tapped me on the knee. "All that stuff was *rehearsed*," she said. "You wouldn't say a lot of stuff like that, offhand, would you— if you had found a body?" She fixed me with a glittering eye. "I—" I began. "You're right!" she said. "You wouldn't! Unless you had practiced it in advance. 'My God, there's a body in here!' is what an innocent man would say." She sat back with a confident glare.

I thought for a while. "But what do you make of the Third Murderer?" I asked. "You know, the Third Murderer has puzzled 'Macbeth' scholars for three hundred years." "That's because they never thought of Macduff," said the American lady. "It was Macduff, I'm certain. You couldn't have one of the victims murdered by two ordinary thugs—the murderer always has to be somebody important." "But what about the banquet scene?" I asked, after a moment. "How do you account for Macbeth's guilty actions there, when Banquo's ghost came in and sat in his chair?" The lady leaned forward and tapped me on the knee again. "There wasn't any ghost," she said. "A big, strong man like that doesn't go around seeing ghosts—especially in a brightly lighted banquet hall with dozens of people around. Macbeth was *shielding somebody!*" "Who was he shielding?" I asked. "Mrs. Macbeth, of course," she said. "He thought she did it and he was going to take the rap himself. The husband always does that when the wife is suspected." "But what," I demanded, "about the sleepwalking scene, then?" "The same thing, only the other way around," said my companion. "That time *she* was shielding *him*. She wasn't asleep at all. Do you remember where it says, 'Enter Lady Macbeth with a taper'?" "Yes," I said. "Well, people who walk in their sleep *never carry lights!*" said my fellow-traveler. "They have a second sight. Did you ever hear of a sleepwalker carrying a light?" "No," I said, "I never did." "Well, then, she wasn't asleep. She was acting guilty to shield Macbeth." "I think," I said, "I'll have another brandy," and I called the waiter. When he brought it, I drank it rapidly and rose to go. "I believe," I said, "that you have got hold of something. Would you lend me that 'Macbeth'? I'd like to look it over tonight. I don't feel, somehow, as if I'd ever really read it." "I'll get it for you," she said. "But you'll find that I am right."

Illustration by
James Thurber

"I've found out," I said,
triumphantly, "the name
of the murderer!"

I read the play over carefully that night, and the next morning, after breakfast, I sought out the American woman. She was on the putting green, and I came up behind her silently and took her arm. She gave an exclamation. "Could I see you alone?" I asked, in a low voice. She nodded cautiously and followed me to a secluded spot. "You've found out something?" she breathed. "I've found out," I said, triumphantly, "the name of the murderer!" "You mean it wasn't Macduff?" she said. "Macduff is as innocent of those murders," I said, "as Macbeth and the Macbeth woman." I opened the copy of the play, which I had with me, and turned to Act II, Scene 2. "Here," I said, "you will see where Lady Macbeth says, 'I laid their daggers ready. He could not miss 'em. Had he not resembled my father as he slept, I had done it.' Do you see?" "No," said the American woman, bluntly, "I don't." "But it's simple!" I exclaimed. "I wonder I didn't see it years ago. The reason Duncan resembled Lady Macbeth's father as he slept is that *it actually was her father!*" "Good God!" breathed my companion, softly. "Lady Macbeth's father killed the King," I said, "and, hearing someone coming, thrust the body under the bed and crawled into the bed himself." "But," said the lady, "you can't have a murderer who only appears in the story once. You can't have that."

"I know that," I said, and I turned to Act II, Scene 4. "It says here, 'Enter Ross with an old Man.' Now, that old man is never identified and it is my contention he was old Mr. Macbeth, whose ambition it was to make his daughter Queen. There you have your motive." "But even then," cried the American lady, "he's still a minor character!" "Not," I said, gleefully, "when you realize that he was also *one of the weird sisters in disguise!*" "You mean one of the three witches?" "Precisely," I said. "Listen to this speech of the old man's. 'On Tuesday last, a falcon towering in her pride of place, was by a mousing owl hawk'd at and kill'd.' Who does that sound like?" "It sounds like the way the three witches talk," said my companion, reluctantly. "Precisely!" I said again. "Well," said the American woman, "maybe you're right, but—" "I'm sure I am," I said. "And do you know what I'm going to do now?" "No," she said. "What?" "Buy a copy of 'Hamlet,'" I said, "and solve *that!*" My companion's eyes brightened. "Then," she said, "you don't think Hamlet did it?" "I am," I said, "absolutely positive he didn't." "But who," she demanded, "do you suspect?" I looked at her cryptically. "Everybody," I said, and disappeared into a small grove of trees as silently as I had come.

Connect to the Literature

1. What Do You Think? Were you surprised by the outcome of events for the Macbeths? Why or why not?

Comprehension Check
- What happens to Lady Macbeth in Act Five?
- How do the apparitions' three predictions in Act Four come true?
- Who becomes king of Scotland after Macbeth is killed?

Think Critically

2. How does Lady Macbeth change during the play?

THINK ABOUT

- her early ambition
- her remarks in the sleepwalking scene (Act Five, Scene 1)
- the remarks of the doctor and the gentlewoman as they observe her in the scene

3. **ACTIVE READING** **READING DRAMA** Some playwrights use numerous **stage directions,** but Shakespeare does not. Imagine Lady Macbeth's sleepwalking scene as it might appear on a stage. In what type and color of garment might Lady Macbeth be dressed? How might she speak and move? You may want to refer to any notes you have taken about Lady Macbeth in your 📖 **READER'S NOTEBOOK.**

4. In the play's opening scene, the witches say "Fair is foul, and foul is fair." How is this **paradox,** or apparent contradiction, manifested in Act Five?

5. Do you think Macbeth's downfall is more a result of fate or of his own ambition? Support your response.

6. Even though Macbeth is a villain, how is he also a **tragic hero?** Review the characteristics of tragedy listed on page 321, and use examples of Macbeth's character traits as support.

7. Do you think Lady Macbeth can be considered a **tragic hero?** Why or why not?

Extend Interpretations

8. Critic's Corner In a famous assessment of Shakespeare's plays, the poet and critic Samuel Taylor Coleridge wrote, "The interest in the **plot** is always . . . on account of the **characters,** not vice versa." Do you agree that *Macbeth's* characters are more interesting than its plot? Explain.

9. Connect to Life What aspects of *Macbeth* make it relevant to readers and audiences today? Support your answer.

Literary Analysis

THEME A work of literature usually conveys a central idea about life or human nature, called a **theme.** Longer works like *Macbeth* usually contain several themes.

Cooperative Learning Activity Review your notes about the possible themes you discovered as you read *Macbeth*. Then, with a small group of classmates, discuss what ideas the play conveys about the following topics:

- ambition
- appearance versus reality
- fate and our efforts to control it
- impulses and desires
- loyalty
- marriage
- reason and mental stability
- the supernatural

Then write a sentence stating each theme, and cite specific evidence from the play to support it.

REVIEW **CONFLICT** Identify an external conflict in any act of the play. Then find an example of an internal conflict. How does the outcome of each conflict help convey one or more of the play's themes?

THE AUTHOR'S STYLE
Shakespeare's Poetic Language

Style refers to the particular way in which a work is written. It reflects a writer's unique way of communicating ideas. Shakespeare was a poet as well as a playwright. He is as famous for his powerful poetic language as for his universal themes and keen insight into human behavior.

> ### Key Aspects of Shakespeare's Style
>
> - precise and sometimes lofty diction, or word choice
> - coinage of new words (often by using one part of speech as another) and use of words with double meanings
> - inversions of word order for poetic effect
> - restatements of ideas for emphasis
> - vivid imagery and pairs of images that appeal to more than one of the senses
> - imaginative figurative language, including personifications, metaphors, similes, and hyperboles

Analysis of Style

At the right are four excerpts from *Macbeth*. Study the list above, and read each excerpt carefully. Then do the following:

- Identify an example of each aspect of Shakespeare's style in the excerpts. Notice, for example, the personification in the first line of the second excerpt (sleep's having the ability to knit).

- Look through the play to find three or four additional examples of Shakespeare's stylistic devices.

- Try drawing or describing the images in the examples you identified.

Applications

1. Speaking and Listening Share your examples of Shakespeare's stylistic devices by reading them aloud to a small group of class-mates. Then discuss how the examples illustrate different aspects of Shakespeare's style.

2. Changing Style Choose a famous soliloquy or another famous passage from *Macbeth*, then rewrite it in informal, contemporary language that expresses the same ideas. Share your rewritten version with classmates.

3. Imitating Style Working with a partner, write an additional scene for *Macbeth*—one that takes place just after the actual end of the play. Try to imitate Shakespeare's style. If humor is your strength, try parodying Shakespeare's style in your new scene.

from **Act One, Scene 5**

. . . Come, thick night,
And pall thee in the dunnest smoke of hell,
That my keen knife see not the wound it makes,
Nor heaven peep through the blanket of the dark
To cry "Hold, hold!". . .

from **Act Two, Scene 2**

Sleep that knits up the raveled sleave of care,
The death of each day's life, sore labor's bath,
Balm of hurt minds, great nature's second course,
Chief nourisher in life's feast.

from **Act Two, Scene 2**

You do unbend your noble strength to think
So brainsickly of things. . . .

from **Act Five, Scene 5**

Tomorrow, and tomorrow, and tomorrow
Creeps in this petty pace from day to day
To the last syllable of recorded time;
And all our yesterdays have lighted fools
The way to dusty death. Out, out, brief candle!
Life's but a walking shadow, a poor player,
That struts and frets his hour upon the stage
And then is heard no more. It is a tale
Told by an idiot, full of sound and fury,
Signifying nothing.

Choices & CHALLENGES

Writing Options

1. News Coverage Write three or four news articles covering different events in *Macbeth*, such as Duncan's murder, Macbeth's odd behavior after Banquo's death, and Lady Macbeth's mental breakdown.

Writing Handbook
See page 1368: Cause and Effect.

2. Modern Version Write a synopsis of a modernized version of the play. Focus on keeping the play's major themes while modernizing its plot, setting, and characters. For example, in what present-day arenas might Macbeth compete for higher status?

3. Obituary Write an obituary for one of the victims in *Macbeth.* You might write in the persona of one of the surviving characters.

Activities & Explorations

1. Actors' Workshop With a small group of classmates, perform a scene from *Macbeth.* As in Shakespeare's day, keep the scenery simple, but feel free to use props and costumes. Afterwards, discuss how each actor's interpretation of a character helped to shape the performance. **~ PERFORMING**

2. Video View the movie segment of Act One, Scenes 1 and 3, of *Macbeth* and the video-taped play segment from Act One. Then get together with your classmates to compare the presentations. Which depiction of the witches was more interesting? Create a comparison diagram to record your classmates' opinions.
~ VIEWING AND REPRESENTING

 **Literature in Performance**

Inquiry & Research

History Research Scottish history to learn about the real figures on whom such characters as Macbeth, Duncan, and Banquo were based. Share your findings in a written report. Put the report in your **Working Portfolio.**

William Shakespeare

Author Study Project
CREATING A MAGAZINE

Shakespeare's London Life

Work with a group of classmates to research the London of Shakespeare's day, then present your findings in a special-edition magazine called *London Life.* Your magazine should include illustrations, maps, and articles that provide information about different aspects of London life—for example, religion and politics; theater and literature; science, health, and hygiene; upper-class life; and the London poor. Organize the work equitably, with some group members concentrating on illustrations, others on research, others on writing and editing, and so on.

Primary Sources Investigate editions of letters, diaries, pamphlets, and other writings by people of the time.

Secondary Sources Consult general histories, social histories, and biographies of Shakespeare. Especially useful are books that combine biography and social history, such as Marchette Chute's *Shakespeare of London.* Also consult books on specific subjects, such as the history of the English theater.

World Wide Web Sites Reliable Web sites can provide a wealth of detail, including addresses to which you can write for more information. Consider searching for keywords such as *Shakespeare, Elizabethan society, theater museums,* and *London tourist information.* Also look at the Web sites of English and drama departments at major universities.

 More Online: Research Starter
www.mcdougallittell.com

Writing Workshop

Exploring a topic in depth . . .

From Reading to Writing As you read *Macbeth,* several questions probably came to mind. Was Macbeth a real person? Was treason a serious threat to the monarch in Shakespeare's day? Did Banquo's descendants ever rule Scotland? Out of these questions you might develop a topic for a **research report.** A research report is an academic paper in which you present information you have gathered and synthesized in exploring a subject. The skills you acquire in writing a research report can help you outside of school, too, whether deciding which brand of a particular product to buy or investigating a college or career.

For Your Portfolio

WRITING PROMPT Write a research report on a literary topic or another topic that intrigues you.

Purpose: To share information and draw a conclusion about your topic

Audience: Your classmates, teacher, or someone who shares your interest in the topic

---

Basics in a Box

Research Report at a Glance

THESIS

INTRODUCTION Presents the thesis statement

BODY Presents evidence that **supports the thesis statement**

CONCLUSION Restates the thesis

WORKS CITED Lists the sources of information

RESEARCH

RUBRIC Standards for Writing

A successful research report should

- provide a strong introduction with a clear thesis statement
- use evidence from primary and secondary sources to develop and support ideas
- credit sources of information

- follow a logical pattern of organization, using transitions between ideas
- synthesize ideas with a satisfying conclusion
- provide a correctly formatted Works Cited list at the end of the paper

Analyzing a Student Model

Tom Mendozza

Mendozza 1

Ms. Forrest
English IV
May 15

The Gunpowder Plot of 1605 and <u>Macbeth</u>

On the night of November 4, 1605, an Englishman named Guy Fawkes was found with 36 barrels of gunpowder in a cellar beneath the palace of Westminster (Nicholls 8–9). His intention was to blow up King James I, along with the queen, their eldest son Henry, and the House of Lords during the opening session of Parliament the very next day. Before Fawkes could carry out this plan, he was captured and interrogated by the English government. Under torture, Fawkes revealed that he was part of a conspiracy of English Catholics to murder the king and restore Catholicism to England. This conspiracy came to be known as The Gunpowder Plot (Fraser, <u>Faith and Treason</u> 189).

The attempted assassination of King James and the subsequent trials and executions of the conspirators were widely publicized in Shakespeare's day (Wills 15–19). It is in this highly charged atmosphere of political intrigue that Shakespeare's play <u>Macbeth</u> opened in 1606. Shakespeare was well aware of these political goings-on. In <u>Macbeth</u>, he makes reference to the events of the Gunpowder Plot to add drama to his play.

<u>In order to understand these references in Macbeth, it is first necessary to be aware of the details surrounding the Gunpowder Plot.</u> According to official sources at the time, King James himself helped avert the tragedy. On October 26, several days before the attempted assassination was to take place, Lord Monteagle, a member of the House of Lords, received an anonymous letter warning him not to attend the upcoming session of Parliament. The letter stated that "though there be no appearance of any stir, yet I say they shall receive a terrible blow this Parliament; and yet they shall not see who hurts them" (<u>Faith</u> 150). Monteagle took the letter to Robert Cecil, the chief minister to King James. Cecil did not immediately show the letter to the king, who was away on a hunting expedition at the time. On November 1, the day after King James returned from hunting, Cecil gave Monteagle's letter to the king. James suspected that the warning referred to an explosion because his own father was killed in a plot involving gunpowder (<u>Faith</u> 161; Fraser, <u>King James</u> 19).

RUBRIC
IN ACTION

❶ This writer begins with an engaging fact to capture the reader's attention.

Other Options:
· Begin with an intriguing question
· Start with a quotation

❷ Presents the thesis statement

❸ Uses a transitional sentence between paragraphs to connect ideas

❹ This writer uses a direct quotation to support an idea.

Other Options:
· Paraphrase a quotation
· Summarize the information

❺ Credits the sources of information

On the night of November 4, the king's officials searched the building of Parliament and noticed an unusually large pile of firewood in a storehouse beneath the House of Lords. They reported their findings to the king, who ordered a second, more thorough search. This time the king's officials uncovered the gunpowder and apprehended Guy Fawkes, who was found lurking on the premises. At first, Fawkes gave his name as John Johnson, but after days of interrogation by the English government, he revealed his true identity and eventually named his fellow conspirators (Nicholls 8–9; Parkinson 75–76).

One connection to the Gunpowder Plot and <u>Macbeth</u> involves the use of

> **❻ This writer presents information chronologically.**
> **Another Option:**
> • Arrange ideas by order of importance

Works Cited

Boot, Jeremy. <u>Gunpowder Plot: High Treason in 1605</u>. 16 May 1998
  <http://www.innotts.co.uk/~asperges/fawkes/>.

Fraser, Antonia. <u>Faith and Treason: The Story of the Gunpowder
  Plot</u>. New York: Doubleday, 1996.

---. <u>King James VI of Scotland, I of England</u>. New York: Knopf,
  1974.

Greaves, Richard L. "Gunpowder Plot." <u>The World Book
  Encyclopedia</u>. 1996 ed.

Greenblatt, Stephen. "Toil and Trouble." <u>New Republic</u>
  14 Nov. 1994: 32–37.

"Gunpowder Plot." <u>Britannica Online</u>. Vers. 98.2. Apr. 1998.
  Encyclopaedia Britannica. 16 May 1998
  <http://www.eb.com:180>.

Nicholls, Mark. <u>Investigating Gunpowder Plot</u>. Manchester, England:
  Manchester UP, 1991.

Parkinson, C. Northcote. <u>Gunpowder, Treason and Plot</u>.
  New York: St. Martin's, 1976.

Wills, Garry. <u>Witches and Jesuits: Shakespeare's Macbeth</u>. New
  York: Oxford UP, 1995.

> **Works Cited**
> • Identifies sources of information used in researching a paper
> • Alphabetizes entries by author's last name
> • Lists complete publication information
> • Punctuates entries correctly
> • Double spaces entire list
> • Follows a preferred style

Need help with Works Cited?

See pp. 1376–1378 in the **Writing Handbook**.

IDEABank

1. Your Working Portfolio

Build on the Inquiry & Research activity you completed earlier in this unit:

• **History,** p. 422

2. Reading Literature
What authors or literary works made a strong impression on you? Are you drawn to certain writers or the subjects they address? Choose one as a starting point for your research.

3. Surfing the Net
Browse the Internet for topics that interest you. Explore frequently visited sites or do a subject search using various search engines. Choose one topic and explore it further.

Writing Your Research Report

Writing, like life itself, is a voyage of discovery.

Henry Miller

❶ Prewriting and Exploring

To explore topics, you might begin by looking through the magazine section of the library. Skim several periodicals and jot down interesting subjects. Think of movies you've seen or books you've read. Generate a list of interesting and researchable questions. As you read and write about a topic, you will understand it better. See the **Idea Bank** in the margin for further suggestions on finding a topic.

The steps below will help you choose and narrow your topic and define your goal.

Planning Your Research Report

▶ **1. Choose a topic.** What topic appeals to you most? What would you like to learn about it? You might make a cluster map with a general topic area in the center. Connect related ideas with lines and circles radiating outward.

▶ **2. Narrow your topic.** Is your topic too broad to cover in the research report you plan to write? How can you divide it into smaller subtopics? You may need to do some preliminary research as you narrow your topic.

▶ **3. Set your goal.** What do you want your writing to accomplish? Do you want simply to learn more about your subject, to prove a point, or to elicit a strong response from your audience?

▶ **4. Identify your purpose.** Will your main purpose be to inform, to examine cause and effect, to compare and contrast, to analyze, or a combination of these?

▶ **5. Write a statement of controlling purpose.** What will you focus on in your paper? Your controlling purpose will guide your research and give you direction as you work. Your controlling purpose should be flexible, so you can revise it as you continue your research.

❷ Researching

Research is the process of gathering information on a topic from reliable sources. The best place to begin your search for reliable information is the library. Consider making a list of questions about your topic that will help to guide your research. The information you find will either be in primary or secondary sources. **Primary sources** furnish eyewitness accounts of events. Primary sources include letters, journals, diaries, and historical documents. **Secondary sources** present information that is derived or compiled from other sources. Encyclopedias, many books, newspapers, and magazine articles are examples of secondary sources.

Research TIP

Use primary sources when they are available and easy to read. **Use secondary sources** to explain difficult or hard-to-read material from primary sources.

Evaluate Your Sources

Some sources of information are better than others. Use these guidelines to evaluate your sources.

- **To what extent is the author's viewpoint biased**—that is, influenced by his or her political position, gender, or ethnic background? Be sure to read material from a variety of viewpoints.

- **Is the source up-to-date?** Certain fields such as science, technology, and medicine change rapidly. Use recent information when researching these fields.

- **Is the source reliable?** Supermarket tabloid newspapers, for example, are not reliable sources of information.

- **Who is the intended audience?** Is the source written for young people, for the general public, or for experts in a particular field?

Make Source Cards

When you have found information that is relevant to your topic, you will need to make source cards. Use index cards, like those at the right, to record publishing information for each source you decide to use. Follow the format for each type of source card. Number each source card and refer to it when you take notes. You will use these source cards to credit sources in your report and to write your Works Cited page.

Take Notes

Keeping your controlling purpose in mind, take notes on pertinent information. Use a separate index card for each piece of information and write the number of the source on each note card. You need not document general knowledge—that is, information that is widely known and that your readers would not question. The example below shows ways of noting information.

Internet Tip

Not all sites on the Internet are reliable. Evaluate information found on the Internet as you would print material. Generally, information from a government agency (.gov) or an educational institution (.edu) will be reputable. Material posted to someone's personal web page may or may not be reliable.

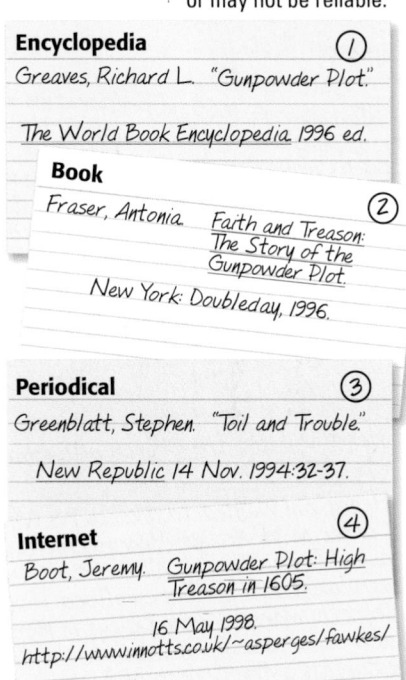

Encyclopedia ①
Greaves, Richard L. "Gunpowder Plot."
The World Book Encyclopedia. 1996 ed.

Book ②
Fraser, Antonia. *Faith and Treason: The Story of the Gunpowder Plot.*
New York: Doubleday, 1996.

Periodical ③
Greenblatt, Stephen. "Toil and Trouble."
New Republic 14 Nov. 1994:32-37.

Internet ④
Boot, Jeremy. *Gunpowder Plot: High Treason in 1605.*
16 May 1998.
http://www.innotts.co.uk/~asperges/fawkes/

Paraphrase. Restate the material in your own words. Paraphrasing is a good choice when your notes need to be detailed.

Source Number.

Note Card

Quotation. Copy the original text word for word, including all punctuation. Use quotations marks to indicate the beginning and end of the quotation. Use this form to emphasize a point or when the author's words are well phrased.

Catholic Priests and Equivocation ②

Catholic priests were forced to make a difficult decision if government agents questioned them about their priesthood. It was against the teachings of the Catholic Church to lie, yet priests could be put to death if they told the truth and admitted they were priests. Therefore, they chose to equivocate. "The underlying principle of equivocation was that the speaker's words were capable of being taken in two ways, only one of which was true." 242

Paraphrase and quotation

More Online:
Research Starter
www.mcdougallittell.com

Organize Your Material

Once you have gathered the information from your sources, you can begin to organize your notes. One way to do this is to make a topic outline. Begin by grouping your note cards into stacks of related material. Determine the main idea of each stack. Next, think about the best way to arrange your stacks of note cards. Chronological order works well for historical or biographical information, although you may wish to try other organizational patterns, such as comparison-and-contrast order or cause-and-effect order. Write your outline based on the order of the main ideas and subpoints in your stacks of notes.

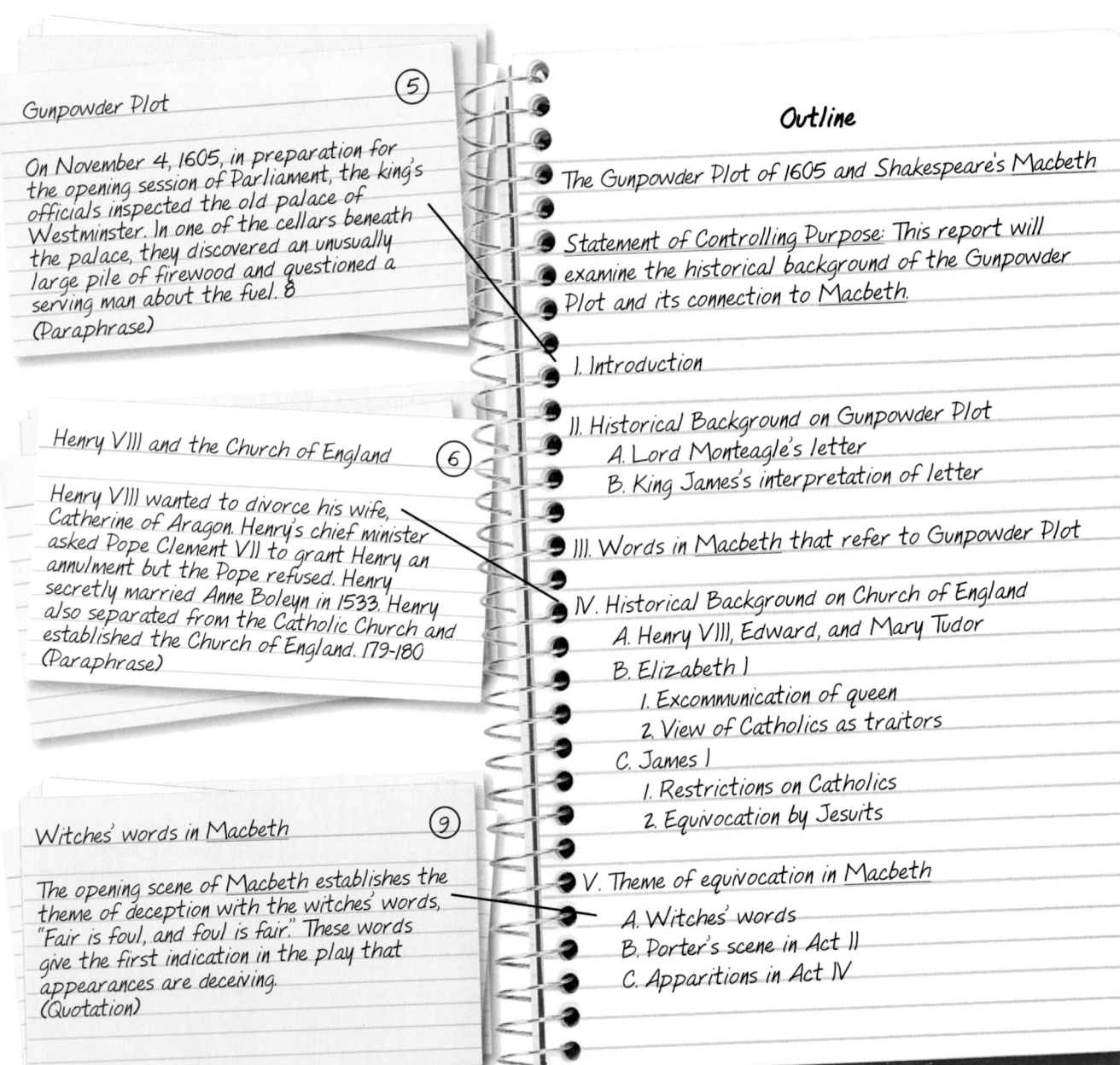

Gunpowder Plot ⑤

On November 4, 1605, in preparation for the opening session of Parliament, the king's officials inspected the old palace of Westminster. In one of the cellars beneath the palace, they discovered an unusually large pile of firewood and questioned a serving man about the fuel. 8
(Paraphrase)

Henry VIII and the Church of England ⑥

Henry VIII wanted to divorce his wife, Catherine of Aragon. Henry's chief minister asked Pope Clement VII to grant Henry an annulment but the Pope refused. Henry secretly married Anne Boleyn in 1533. Henry also separated from the Catholic Church and established the Church of England. 179-180
(Paraphrase)

Witches' words in Macbeth ⑨

The opening scene of Macbeth establishes the theme of deception with the witches' words, "Fair is foul, and foul is fair." These words give the first indication in the play that appearances are deceiving.
(Quotation)

Outline

The Gunpowder Plot of 1605 and Shakespeare's Macbeth

Statement of Controlling Purpose: This report will examine the historical background of the Gunpowder Plot and its connection to Macbeth.

I. Introduction

II. Historical Background on Gunpowder Plot
    A. Lord Monteagle's letter
    B. King James's interpretation of letter

III. Words in Macbeth that refer to Gunpowder Plot

IV. Historical Background on Church of England
    A. Henry VIII, Edward, and Mary Tudor
    B. Elizabeth I
        1. Excommunication of queen
        2. View of Catholics as traitors
    C. James I
        1. Restrictions on Catholics
        2. Equivocation by Jesuits

V. Theme of equivocation in Macbeth
    A. Witches' words
    B. Porter's scene in Act II
    C. Apparitions in Act IV

❸ Drafting

Your report, like many other essays, will begin with an introduction that states your thesis and will end with a conclusion that restates this thesis and summarizes your main points. The largest part of your report, the body, should explain and support your topic.

Develop a Thesis Statement

When you finish your research, you should have a good idea of what you want your report to accomplish. Rework your statement of controlling purpose into a **thesis statement** that expresses the main idea of your report.

Write Your Draft

In the drafting stage, concentrate on getting your ideas on paper using your own voice. Follow your outline and refer to your note cards as you write.

Support your thesis. Use the information from your sources creatively, analyzing, synthesizing, making inferences, and interpreting evidence to reach a conclusion. Use facts, quotations, statistics, and examples from your research to support your thesis. While writing, you may discover that you need to do further research on your topic.

Document your sources. After each quotation, paraphrase, or summary in your paper, write in parentheses the author's name (or the source title, if no name is given) and the page number. Use your note cards and source cards to identify the sources of information used in your report. Failure to credit your sources constitutes **plagiarism**—the unlawful use of another's words or ideas as your own. The Works Cited page at the end of your report will provide complete publishing information for each source used in your report.

Evaluate Your Draft

Think about these questions as you review your draft.

- How could I make my thesis statement clearer?

- What additional support for my thesis can I provide in the body of the report?

- What material can I delete?

- How can I organize my material more effectively?

- What material could I paraphrase rather than quote directly?

- What facts and documentation do I need to check?

- How can I better accomplish my purpose?

Drafting Tip

Remember that your outline is only a tool. Feel free to reorganize your material at any time or collect new information as needed.

Need help documenting sources?

See the **Writing Handbook,** p. 1376.

Ask Your Peer Reader

- What did you like most about my paper?

- What was the most memorable thing you learned about my topic?

- Which parts, if any, seemed confusing or unclear?

- What would you like to know more about?

Need revising help?

Review the **Rubric,** p. 423

Consider **peer reader** comments

Check **Revision Guidelines,** p. 1355

❹ Revising

TARGET SKILL ▶ PARAGRAPH BUILDING Writing has unity when all the sentences in a paragraph support its central idea. As you revise your research report, delete any unrelated ideas.

> At the time of Elizabeth I's death in 1603, many penalties were imposed against English Catholics. Catholics were prohibited from celebrating Mass anywhere in England. Those who violated this restriction were fined and jailed, and some priests were executed. ~~Phillip II, the Catholic king of Spain, wanted to restore Catholicism to England.~~

❺ Editing

TARGET SKILL ▶ SHIFTING VERB TENSE Keep in mind that writers generally avoid shifting verb tense in a paper. However, not all shifts in verb tense are incorrect. A shift in tense may be needed to show when an action occurred in relation to another action.

> Father Garnet ~~wrote~~ *had written* a Treatise of Equivocation before the English government tried and executed him for conspiracy in The Gunpowder Plot. In this treatise, Garnet claim*ed* that a person may, under certain circumstances, avoid telling the complete truth.

❻ Making a Works Cited List

When you have finished revising and editing your report, make a **Works Cited list** and attach it to the end of your paper. See pages 1376–1378 in the **Writing Handbook** for the correct format.

❼ Reflecting

FOR YOUR PORTFOLIO What did you learn about yourself as you worked through the process of writing a research report? Is there anything more you would like to know about your topic? Draw relevant questions for further study from your findings. Attach them to your research report and save them in your **Working Portfolio.**

Publishing IDEAS

• Share your paper with the class as an oral presentation.

More Online: Publishing Options www.mcdougallittell.com

Read this opening from the first draft of a research report. The underlined sections may include the following kinds of errors:

- **unrelated ideas in a paragraph**
- **capitalization errors**
- **incorrect verb tenses**
- **comma errors**

For each underlined phrase or sentence, choose the revision that most improves the writing.

> You shouldn't judge a book by its cover, but you shouldn't ignore the cover either. <u>The dust jacket copy is important, too.</u> One of the most famous book covers
> (1)
> in American fiction appeared on the <u>first edition of F. Scott Fitzgerald's the *Great*</u>
> (2)
> *Gatsby*. <u>Fitzgerald was so pleased with the art that he writes the image into his</u>
> (3)
> book. The mysterious artwork was created by <u>Spanish-born artist Francis Cugat.</u>
> (4)
> It shows a woman's sad face <u>floating, above bright and gaudy city lights.</u> A single
> (5)
> green tear drops from one eye. <u>This poignant design is often reprinted.</u>
> (6)

1. **A.** The dust-jacket copy is important, too.
   B. It is important to judge the dust jacket copy, too.
   C. Delete sentence
   D. Correct as is

2. **A.** First Edition of F. Scott Fitzgerald's *The Great Gatsby*.
   B. first edition of F. Scott Fitzgerald's *The Great Gatsby*.
   C. first edition of F. Scott Fitzgerald's *the Great Gatsby*.
   D. Correct as is

3. **A.** Fitzgerald is so pleased with the art that he wrote the image into his book.
   B. Fitzgerald was so pleased with the art that he had written the image into his book.
   C. Fitzgerald was so pleased with the art that he wrote the image into his book.
   D. Correct as is

4. **A.** Spanish-Born artist Francis Cugat.
   B. Spanish-Born Artist Francis Cugat.
   C. spanish-born artist Francis Cugat.
   D. Correct as is

5. **A.** floating above bright and gaudy city lights.
   B. floating above bright, and gaudy city lights.
   C. floating, above bright, and gaudy, city lights.
   D. Correct as is

6. **A.** As a result, this poignant design is often reprinted.
   B. Because this poignant design beautifully reflects the book's content, it is often reprinted on modern editions.
   C. Cugat often reprints this poignant design.
   D. Correct as is

Need extra help?

See the **Grammar Handbook**
Verb tenses, p. 1396
Capitalization, p. 1415
Commas, p. 1413

Core Meanings

English speakers regularly borrow words from other languages to add to their own. Greek and Latin in particular have been fertile sources of roots for building English words. (A **root** is a core part of a word, to which other word parts, such as prefixes and suffixes, can be added to create new words.) Consider, for instance, the word *intemperance* in the sentence above from *Macbeth.* The Latin root *temper* means "to moderate," the prefix *in-* means "not" or "without," and the suffix *-ance* indicates a condition or action. By putting the meanings of the parts together you can infer that *intemperance* probably means something like "action that is without moderation."

> **Boundless intemperance**
> **In nature is a tyranny.** . . .
> —William Shakespeare, *Macbeth,* Act 4, Scene 3

Strategies for Building Vocabulary

If you know some common Greek and Latin roots and their meanings, you can figure out the meaning of unknown words—even without a dictionary.

Use the Meanings of Roots to Build Word Families
You can expand your knowledge of roots by noting the etymologies of words that you look up in the dictionary. Read the etymology of *horrific* below. What insight into the meaning of the English word does it provide?

> [Latin *horrificus : horrēre,* to tremble + *-ficus,* -fic (causing).]

Once you understand the meaning of the root, you can use it to help you understand other unfamiliar words that also contain that root. The illustration below shows one Greek root, *chron,* and its word family.

chron (time)	*chronology* (the study of time)
	chronic (continuing over time)
	anachronism (something out of chronological order)
	chronical (a record of events over time)
	synchronize (to set time together)

Study the charts that follow to learn the meanings of some other Greek and Latin roots that have given rise to English word families.

Greek Root	Meaning	Word Family
arche	primitive, ancient	archaic, archetype, archaize, archaeologist
bibl	book	bibliography, Bible
cosm	world	cosmic, cosmopolitan,
gnos	know	Gnostic, agnostic, diagnosis
mania	madness	maniac, kleptomania
path	feeling	pathetic, sympathy

Latin Root	Meaning	Word Family
belli	war	bellicose, antebellum, belligerent
cede, ceed	go	proceed, exceed, recede
cide	kill	homicide, insecticide
cla(i)m	shout	proclaim, clamor, exclaim
imag	likeness	image, imagine, imagery
ment	mind	mental, demented, mentality
mor(t)	death	moribund, mortal, mortified
optim	best	optimum, optimist, optimize
sanit	health	sanitary, insanity, sanitarium
viv, vit	alive, life	vital, survive, vivid, vivacious

EXERCISE Use a dictionary to identify the meaning and root of each of these words from *Macbeth.* Use the information you find to create charts like the ones above for the words' Greek and Latin roots.

1. resolute   3. conspirers   5. rhinoceros
2. prediction   4. metaphysical

Grammar from Literature

Look at the lines below from *Macbeth.* Notice the information that the highlighted adverbs add to each sentence.

> SINGLE-WORD ADVERBS
>
>   *time*
> **She has light by her continually.**
>
>   *manner*   *manner*
> **Was not that nobly done? Ay, and wisely too!**

> ADVERB PREPOSITIONAL PHRASES
>
>   *location*
> **Is this a dagger which I see before me?**
>
>   *purpose*
> **He's worth more sorrow, and that I'll spend for him.**
>
>   *degree*
> **I would applaud thee to the very echo.**

Writers use adverbs to tell how, when, or where. These uses are also sometimes referred to as manner, time, location, purpose, and degree.

Adverbs modify verbs, adjectives, and other adverbs. You will notice from the examples above that adverbs can take the form of single words or of phrases.

Using Adverbs in Your Writing You can make your writing more precise by using adverbs to establish details about the how, when, or where of scenes, events, or people's actions. You can also add precision and accuracy by using adverbs to qualify or limit your ideas. Such qualification can improve accuracy.

The following examples show the two different ways you can use adverbs.

> ADD DETAIL
> **Ross says the king has received news of Macbeth's success.**
>
> **Ross says the king has happily received news of Macbeth's success.**

> ADD DETAIL
> **Macduff rejoices that his kingdom is free.**
>
> **In the final scene, Macduff rejoices that his kingdom is finally free from tyranny.**

> QUALIFY OR LIMIT
> **The conflict in Shakespeare's plays centers on how characters resolve moral issues.**
>
> **The conflict in Shakespeare's plays often centers on how characters resolve moral issues.**

Usage Tip Placement of adverbs can affect meaning. If you misplace an adverb, your sentence may not say what you want it to say.

> INCORRECT
> **Before 1603 Shakespeare only wrote four tragedies.**
>
> CORRECT
> **Before 1603 Shakespeare wrote only four tragedies.**

The first example says that Shakespeare did nothing but write tragedies. Placing *only* next to *four* correctly indicates that he wrote a limited number of tragedies.

WRITING EXERCISE Rewrite the following sentences, following the instructions given in parentheses.

1. The three witches appear to Macbeth. (Add one or more single-word adverbs that tell how, when, or where the witches appeared.)
2. Lady Macbeth urges her husband to commit crimes. (Add a prepositional phrase that tells how, when, or where.)
3. Macduff vows to kill Macbeth. (Add a prepositional phrase that indicates purpose.)

4. Shakespeare is called the "bard of Avon" and the "swan of Avon." (Add a single-word adverb or an adverb prepositional phrase to qualify this statement and make it more accurate.)
5. Shakespeare is considered the greatest dramatist of all time. (Add an adverb or an adverb prepositional phrase to qualify this statement and make it more accurate.)

M any people of the Renaissance sought answers to questions about life's limitations. Some found comfort in the lessons of the Bible. Others read works in which writers reflected on love, death, and the role of men and women. You may find that the questions posed are still relevant today.

COMPARING LITERATURE: The Lyrics of the Cavalier Poets
and Omar Khayyám

The Theme of Carpe Diem Across Cultures: Persia

LITERARY LINK

King James Bible
from Ecclesiastes, Chapter 3
Psalm 23
Parable of the Prodigal Son

Connect to Your Life

Time Line Think about events that have occurred in your life. Which of these events stand out in your mind as being particularly important? Create a time line, charting significant events and phases. If appropriate, include times when you made major changes in your attitude and times when you learned valuable lessons about life.

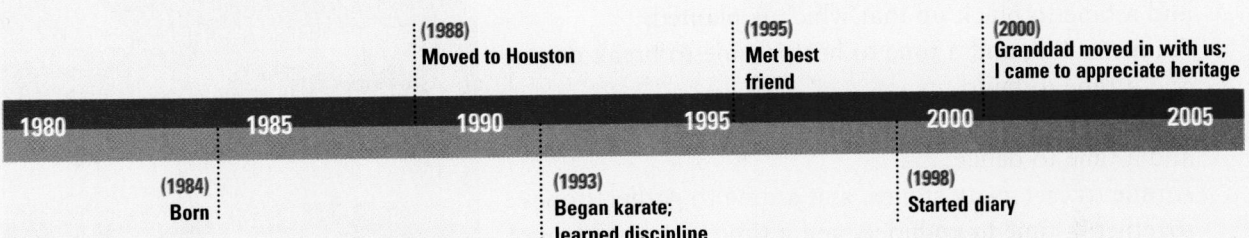

(1988) Moved to Houston

(1995) Met best friend

(2000) Granddad moved in with us; I came to appreciate heritage

1980   1985   1990   1995   2000   2005

(1984) Born

(1993) Began karate; learned discipline

(1998) Started diary

Build Background

The King James Version of the Bible When James I, the successor of Elizabeth I, became king of England in 1603, Puritan leaders petitioned him to support a new translation of the Bible. Although he bore no great love for the Puritans, he agreed that English worshipers needed a translation better than the ones in popular use. In 1604, the king appointed 54 distinguished scholars and clergymen to create a new translation—one that would be more accurate than previous English versions and more beautiful in its use of language. The result—the King James Bible—was the main Protestant Bible in English for over 300 years. Even today, although many other translations are available, it remains the most important and influential of all versions.

The following passages from the King James Bible illustrate different types of scriptural writing, each designed to impart spiritual lessons about life. The selection from Ecclesiastes is an example of what is called wisdom literature—literature intended to help human beings find the meaning of life. The second selection is a psalm, or song of praise. The last is a parable, a brief story that is meant to teach a moral or religious lesson.

Focus Your Reading

LITERARY ANALYSIS   **REPETITION**

Repetition is a technique in which a word or group of words is repeated throughout a selection. As you read the following excerpts from the Bible, notice examples of repetition and the effect they have.

ACTIVE READING   **MAKING INFERENCES**   In order to be able to understand and interpret passages from the Bible, it is important to be able to make inferences from the text about the spiritual lesson being taught. Inferences are ideas and meanings not directly stated in the material. **Making inferences** often means reading between the lines to understand the main idea.

READER'S NOTEBOOK As you read each excerpt from the Bible, try to infer the spiritual lesson or main idea, and then briefly **summarize** it.

from the King James Bible

from Ecclesiastes, Chapter 3

1 To every thing there is a season, and a time to every purpose under the heaven:

2 A time to be born, and a time to die; a time to plant, and a time to pluck up that which is planted;

3 A time to kill, and a time to heal; a time to break down, and a time to build up;

4 A time to weep, and a time to laugh; a time to mourn, and a time to dance;

5 A time to cast away stones, and a time to gather stones together; a time to embrace, and a time to refrain from embracing;

6 A time to get,[1] and a time to lose; a time to keep, and a time to cast away;

7 A time to rend,[2] and a time to sew; a time to keep silence, and a time to speak;

8 A time to love, and a time to hate; a time of war, and a time of peace.

---

1. **get:** gain; win.
2. **rend:** tear or rip.

Month of July from *Très riches heures du duc de Berry* (about 1415), Limbourg brothers. Musée Condé, Chantilly, France. Giraudon/Art Resource, New York.

Thinking Through the Literature

1. What is your overall reaction to this excerpt from Ecclesiastes?

2. Do you agree with the message conveyed in this excerpt?

THINK ABOUT
- the meaning of the statement "To every thing there is a season" (line 1)
- the contrasting examples given throughout the excerpt

3. Which lines do you think have special relevance to contemporary life?

Psalm 23

A Psalm of David

Title page of the first edition of the King James Bible, London, 1611. The Granger Collection, New York.

1 The Lord is my shepherd; I shall not want.[1]

2 He maketh me to lie down in green pastures: he leadeth me beside the still waters.

3 He restoreth my soul: he leadeth me in the paths of righteousness for his name's sake.

4 Yea, though I walk through the valley of the shadow of death, I will fear no evil: for thou art with me; thy rod and thy staff they comfort me.

5 Thou preparest a table before me in the presence of mine enemies: thou anointest my head with oil; my cup runneth over.[2]

6 Surely goodness and mercy shall follow me all the days of my life: and I will dwell in the house of the Lord for ever.

---

1. **want:** be in need.
2. **Thou preparest . . . runneth over:** In this verse, the Lord is presented as a generous host who offers his guest food, oil for grooming, and an overflowing cup of wine. In ancient times, olive oil was used as a cleansing agent and was quite expensive.

Thinking Through the Literature

1. What **images** are you left with after reading this psalm?
2. In your opinion, how might this psalm affect someone trying to cope with life's difficulties or limitations?
3. Psalm 23 is part of a group of psalms often called "songs of trust." Why do you think it is included in this group?

Return of the Prodigal Son (1667–1668), Rembrandt van Rijn. The Hermitage Museum, St. Petersburg, Russia.
Bridgeman Art Library, London/Superstock.

from Luke, Chapter 15

PARABLE OF THE PRODIGAL SON

11 And he said, A certain man had two sons:

12 And the younger of them said to his father, Father, give me the portion of goods that falleth to me. And he divided unto them his living.

13 And not many days after the younger son gathered all together, and took his journey into a far country, and there wasted his substance with riotous living.

14 And when he had spent all, there arose a mighty famine in that land; and he began to be in want.

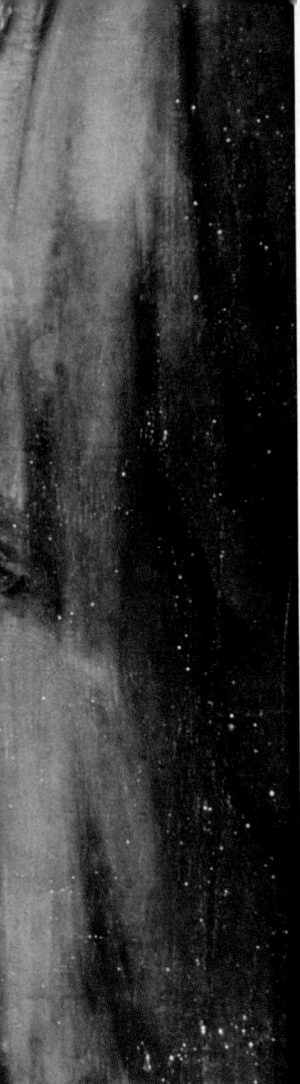

15 And he went and joined himself to a citizen of that country; and he[1] sent him into his fields to feed swine.

16 And he would fain[2] have filled his belly with the husks that the swine did eat: and no man gave unto him.

17 And when he came to himself, he said, How many hired servants of my father's have bread enough and to spare, and I perish with hunger!

18 I will arise and go to my father, and will say unto him, Father, I have sinned against heaven, and before thee,

19 And am no more worthy to be called thy son: make me as one of thy hired servants.

20 And he arose, and came to his father. But when he was yet a great way off, his father saw him, and had compassion, and ran, and fell on his neck, and kissed him.

21 And the son said unto him, Father, I have sinned against heaven, and in thy sight, and am no more worthy to be called thy son.

22 But the father said to his servants, Bring forth the best robe, and put it on him; and put a ring on his hand, and shoes on his feet:

23 And bring hither the fatted calf, and kill it; and let us eat, and be merry:

24 For this my son was dead, and is alive again; he was lost, and is found. And they began to be merry.

25 Now his elder son was in the field: and as he came and drew nigh to the house, he heard musick and dancing.

26 And he called one of the servants, and asked what these things meant.

27 And he said unto him, Thy brother is come; and thy father hath killed the fatted calf, because he hath received him safe and sound.

28 And he was angry, and would not go in: therefore came his father out, and intreated[3] him.

29 And he answering said to his father, Lo, these many years do I serve thee, neither transgressed[4] I at any time thy commandment: and yet thou never gavest me a kid,[5] that I might make merry with my friends:

30 But as soon as this thy son was come, which hath devoured thy living with harlots, thou hast killed for him the fatted calf.

31 And he said unto him, Son, thou art ever with me, and all that I have is thine.

32 It was meet[6] that we should make merry, and be glad: for this thy brother was dead, and is alive again; and was lost, and is found.

---

1. **he:** the citizen.
2. **fain:** gladly.
3. **intreated:** entreated; urged.
4. **transgressed:** violated; broke.
5. **kid:** young goat.
6. **meet:** fitting; proper.

Connect to the Literature

1. What Do You Think? How did you respond to the three **characters** in the parable of the prodigal son?

Comprehension Check
- How does the father feel about the prodigal son's return?
- How does the elder son feel about the return of the prodigal son?

Think Critically

2. If you were in the father's place, would you react to the younger son's return as he does?

THINK ABOUT
- the father's reaction to the words spoken by the younger son upon his return
- the father's explanation to his older son
- your own feelings about forgiveness

3. In your opinion, what is the message or lesson of this **parable**?

4. **ACTIVE READING** | **MAKING INFERENCES** | Look back at your **READER'S NOTEBOOK** for your summary of the spiritual lesson of the parable. What details from the text support your summary? Compare your ideas with those of your classmates.

Extend Interpretations

5. Comparing Texts Look again at the excerpt from *The Book of Margery Kempe* (page 252). Which of the three selections from the Bible do you think would offer the greatest comfort to Kempe?

6. Different Perspectives How might readers of different ages— for example, a teenager and an elderly person—differ in their reactions to the selection from Ecclesiastes, to Psalm 23, or to the parable?

7. Connect to Life Think about the different spiritual lessons presented in the passages from Ecclesiastes, Psalm 23, and the parable of the prodigal son. Do you think it is difficult to put these lessons into practice today? Discuss your ideas.

Literary Analysis

REPETITION Used in both poetry and prose, **repetition** is a technique in which a word or group of words is repeated throughout a selection. Repetition of words and phrases often helps to reinforce meaning and to create an appealing rhythm.

Activity Find examples of repetition in the excerpt from Ecclesiastes and in the parable of the prodigal son. Record them in a chart like the one shown. In which selection do you think repetition plays a more important role? Discuss your conclusions with your classmates.

	Examples of Repetition
Ecclesiastes	
Parable of the Prodigal Son	

PARABLE A **parable** is a brief story that is intended to teach a lesson or illustrate a moral truth. Although the characters, action, and dialogue are simple and direct, they point to fundamental ideas about how humans should live. Think again about the parable of the prodigal son. Do you think a parable is an effective way to present moral teachings?

Writing Options

1. Parable Sequel Decide what might happen next in the parable of the prodigal son. Write a sequel to the story.

2. Modern Parable Think of a simple lesson about life that you would like to teach others. Then write a modern parable, in either a serious or a humorous style, to convey the lesson. Place the parable in your **Working Portfolio.**

Return of the Prodigal Son?

3. Newspaper Editorial Pretend that you work for your local newspaper. Write an editorial relating the message of one of these selections to contemporary life. Tell how a local or world situation might be improved if people took the message to heart.

Writing Handbook
See pages 1369–1370: Analysis.

4. Spiritual Essay The philosopher George Santayana once said that "there is no cure for birth and death save to enjoy the interval." How does his reflection on life compare with the spiritual lessons taught in these three selections? Draft an essay to answer this question, using specific lines or sentences from the three selections to support your opinion.

Activities & Explorations

1. Calendar Design Design a 12-month calendar that contains your favorite lines from the selections. Choose one line for each month. Then find appropriate art to accompany the texts, or use a computer to make your own illustrations.
~ ART

2. Dramatic Soliloquy Imagine that you are the older son in the parable of the prodigal son. Rehearse and perform a dramatic soliloquy—a speech revealing your innermost thoughts—about events in your life. **~ PERFORMING**

3. Biblical Collage Create a collage of images that reflects your understanding of the excerpt from Ecclesiastes. You may use fine art, photographs, illustrations, or a combination of the three. **~ ART**

Inquiry & Research

1. Language Chart Note that the King James Bible contains verb forms ending in -*eth* and -*est.* Look up these endings in a dictionary. How far back do they go in the history of the language? Which ending is used for the second person, and which for the third person? In most dictionaries, terms such as *colloquial, slang, poetic,* and *archaic* are used to describe certain words. Which term is applied to these endings?

2. Music and the Bible Find and share with classmates the Byrds' 1966 recording of the song "Turn, Turn, Turn." Compare the lyrics of the song with the passage from Ecclesiastes that you have read. Then discuss the significance of the song's title.

Art Connection

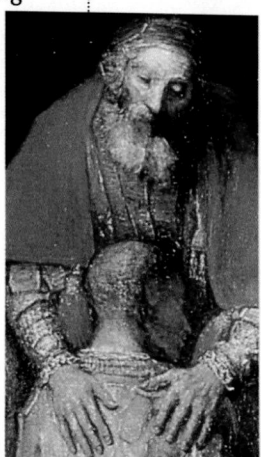

Looking at Rembrandt One critic has stated that Rembrandt's *Return of the Prodigal Son* (page 438) represents the artist's idea of Christian forgiveness and mercy. Look closely at the painting. In addition to the subject matter, what qualities of the painting do you think express the idea of mercy or forgiveness?

from Essays

By SIR FRANCIS BACON

> ### Connect to Your Life
>
> **Burning Issues** Most people have strong opinions about certain topics or issues. Think about an issue that concerns you—perhaps something that affects you personally, such as a school policy or a community problem, or a more universal issue, such as crime, the protection of the environment, or individual rights. Then get together with a group of classmates and explain your stand on the issue, citing reasons that support your position.

Build Background

Opinions on Life Sir Francis Bacon is often called the father of the English **essay.** In 1597, he published ten essays, the first examples of that literary form to gain popularity in England. Bacon actually borrowed the title and concept for his *Essays* from the French author Michel de Montaigne, who had published a similar work, titled *Essais,* in 1580. In contrast with Montaigne's writing—which is light and personal, revealing glimpses of the author's own life and personality—Bacon's essays are more philosophical, offering opinions on the nature of human behavior and motivation and generalizing about what humans do and ought to do. In writing his essays, Bacon had a single purpose in mind—to give instruction and advice to young men who were ambitious to succeed. His first collection included "Of Studies," one of the essays presented on the following pages. His final collection was published in 1625, a year before his death, and included 58 essays on subjects ranging from love, friendship, and beauty to superstition, death, and revenge.

Focus Your Reading

LITERARY ANALYSIS **ESSAY** An **essay** is a brief work of nonfiction that offers an opinion on a subject. The purpose of an essay may be to express ideas and feelings, to inform, to entertain, or to persuade. The main point of an essay is often presented in the opening sentences, as in the first sentence of "Of Studies."

> *Studies serve for delight, for ornament, and for ability.*

As you read the two essays, pay particular attention to the examples, facts, and reasons Bacon uses to support his main points.

ACTIVE READING **EVALUATING OPINION** When you are reading nonfiction, it is important to **evaluate opinions** as you encounter them.

READER'S NOTEBOOK Make two charts like the one shown, one for each of Bacon's essays. As you read each essay, look for statements of opinion. Write each statement in your chart and use a check to indicate whether you agree or disagree with it.

Opinion	Agree	Disagree
To spend too much time in studies is sloth.		

Of Studies

Sir Francis Bacon

wise men use them

Crafty men contemn studies

Abeunt studia in mores

natural abilities are **like natural plants**

Reading maketh a **full** man

Some books **are to be tasted**

simple men admire them

Detail of *Still Life with Old Books* (17th century), unknown French artist. Courtesy of the Musée de Brou, Bourg-en-Bresse, France.

Studies

serve for delight, for ornament, and for ability. Their chief use for delight is in privateness and retiring; for ornament, is in discourse;[1] and for ability, is in the judgment and disposition of business. For expert men can execute, and perhaps judge of particulars, one by one; but the general counsels, and the plots and marshaling of affairs, come best from those that are learned. To spend too much time in studies is sloth; to use them too much for ornament is affectation;[2] to make judgment wholly by their rules is the humor[3] of a scholar. They perfect

---

1. **discourse:** conversation.
2. **affectation:** something done just for show or to give a false impression.
3. **humor:** whim; temperament.

nature, and are perfected by experience; for natural abilities are like natural plants, that need pruning by study; and studies themselves do give forth directions too much at large, except they be bounded in by experience. Crafty men contemn[4] studies, simple men admire them, and wise men use them, for they teach not their own use; but that is a wisdom without them, and above them, won by observation. Read not to contradict and confute,[5] nor to believe and take for granted, nor to find talk and discourse, but to weigh and consider. Some books are to be tasted, others to be swallowed, and some few to be chewed and digested; that is, some books are to be read only in parts; others to be read, but not curiously;[6] and some few to be read wholly, and with diligence and attention. Some books also may be read by deputy and extracts made of them by others, but that would be only in the less important arguments and the meaner sort of books; else[7] distilled[8] books are like common distilled waters,[9] flashy[10] things. Reading maketh a full man, conference[11] a ready man, and writing an exact man. And therefore, if a man write little, he had need have a great memory; if he confer little, he had need have a present wit;[12] and if he read little, he had need have much cunning, to seem to know that he doth not. Histories make men wise; poets, witty; the mathematics, subtle; natural philosophy, deep; moral, grave; logic and rhetoric, able to contend. *Abeunt studia in mores.*[13] Nay, there is no stond[14] or impediment in the wit but may be wrought out by fit studies, like as diseases of the body may

have appropriate exercises. Bowling is good for the stone and reins,[15] shooting for the lungs and breast, gentle walking for the stomach, riding for the head, and the like. So if a man's wit be wandering, let him study the mathematics; for in demonstrations, if his wit be called away never so little, he must begin again. If his wit be not apt to distinguish or find differences, let him study the schoolmen,[16] for they are *cumini sectores.*[17] If he be not apt to beat over[18] matters and to call up one thing to prove and illustrate another, let him study the lawyer's cases. So every defect of the mind may have a special receipt.[19] ❖

---

4. **contemn:** view with contempt, hate.

5. **confute:** prove wrong.

6. **curiously:** carefully or thoroughly.

7. **else:** in other respects.

8. **distilled:** having only the important elements extracted or taken out.

9. **common distilled waters:** herbal home remedies.

10. **flashy:** tasteless; dull.

11. **conference:** conversation.

12. **present wit:** active intelligence.

13. *Abeunt studia in mores* (ă′bĕ-ŏŏnt stōō′dē-ä ĭn mō′rāz) *Latin:* Studies show themselves in manners.

14. **stond:** stoppage.

15. **the stone and reins:** kidney stones and other kidney disorders.

16. **schoolmen:** medieval scholastic philosophers.

17. *cumini sectores* (kōō′mĭ-nē sĕk-tō′rāz) *Latin:* cutters of herbs—that is, people who make extremely fine distinctions; hairsplitters.

18. **beat over:** reason through.

19. **receipt:** remedy; prescription.

Thinking Through the Literature

1. **Comprehension Check** According to Bacon, why should men avoid being too influenced by their studies?

2. What was your first reaction to Bacon's views on studies?

3. Do you think that different kinds of studies can have different effects on you? Give reasons for your opinion.

4. Have Bacon's opinions changed your attitude toward studies or toward the reading of books? Explain your answer.

Of Marriage and Single Life

Sir Francis Bacon

Vetulam suam praetulit immortalitati

single men . . . are more cruel and hard-hearted

single life is liberty

It is often seen that BAD husbands have very *good* wives

Unmarried men are b e s t friends . . . but not always best subjects

wife and children are a kind of discipline of humanity

. . . those that have children should have greatest care of future t i m e s

He that hath wife and children hath given hostages to fortune; for they are impediments to great enterprises, either of virtue or mischief. Certainly the best works, and of greatest merit for the public, have proceeded from the unmarried or childless men, which both in affection and means have married and endowed the public. Yet it were great reason that those that have children should have greatest care of future times, unto which they know they must transmit their dearest pledges. Some there are who, though they lead a single life, yet their thoughts do end with themselves, and account future times impertinences.[1] Nay, there are some other that account wife and children but as bills of charges. Nay more, there are some foolish rich covetous men that take a pride in having no children, because they may be thought so much the richer. For perhaps they have heard some talk, "Such an one is a great rich man," and another except to it, "Yea, but he hath a great charge of children"; as if it were an abatement[2] to his riches. But the most ordinary cause of a single life is liberty, especially in certain self-pleasing and humorous[3] minds, which are so sensible of every restraint, as they will go near to think their girdles and garters to be bonds and shackles. Unmarried men are best friends, best masters, best servants, but not always best subjects, for they are light to run away, and almost all fugitives are of that condition. A single life doth well with churchmen, for charity will hardly water the ground where it must first fill a pool. It is indifferent for judges and magistrates, for if they be facile[4] and corrupt, you shall have a servant five times worse than a wife. For soldiers, I find the generals commonly in their hortatives[5] put men in mind of their wives and children; and I think the despising of marriage amongst the Turks maketh the vulgar[6] soldier more base. Certainly wife and children are a kind of

> A single life doth well with churchmen

discipline of humanity; and single men, though they be many times more charitable, because their means are less exhaust,[7] yet, on the other side, they are more cruel and hard-hearted (good to make severe inquisitors), because their

Wives are young men's mistresses, . . . and old men's nurses

tenderness is not so oft called upon. Grave natures, led by custom, and therefore constant, are commonly loving husbands, as was said of Ulysses, *Vetulam suam praetulit immortalitati.*[8] Chaste women are often proud and froward,[9] as presuming upon the merit of their chastity. It is one of the best bonds, both of chastity and obedience, in the wife if she think her husband wise, which she will never do if she find him jealous. Wives are young men's mistresses, companions for middle age, and old men's nurses, so as a man may have a quarrel[10] to marry when he will. But yet he was reputed one of the wise men that made answer to the question when a man should marry: "A young man not yet, an elder man not at all." It is often seen that bad husbands have very good wives; whether it be that it raiseth the price of their husbands' kindness when it comes, or that the wives take a pride in their patience. But this never fails, if the bad husbands were of their own choosing, against their friends' consent; for then they will be sure to make good their own folly. ❖

---

1. **impertinences** (ĭm-pûr′tn-ən-səz): irrelevant concerns; things not worthy of attention.

2. **abatement** (ə-bāt′mənt): a reduction.

3. **humorous:** whimsical.

4. **facile** (făs′əl): easily influenced or persuaded.

5. **hortatives** (hôr′tə-tĭvz): speeches to encourage troops before battle.

6. **vulgar:** common; ordinary.

7. **exhaust:** depleted; drained.

8. ***Vetulam suam praetulit immortalitati*** (vĕ′tŏŏ-läm sŏŏ′äm prī′tŏŏ-lĭt ĭm-môr-tä′lĭ-tä′tē) *Latin:* He preferred his aged wife to immortality.

9. **froward** (frō′wərd): stubborn.

10. **quarrel:** reason; excuse.

Connect to the Literature

1. What Do You Think? Did any of the statements in "Of Marriage and Single Life" surprise you? Explain why.

Comprehension Check
- According to Bacon, which professions are best suited to unmarried men?
- Describe the importance of marriage to men at different times in their lives.

Think Critically

2. Which do you think Bacon respects more, the married life or the single life? Support your answer with details from the **essay.**

3. How would you describe Bacon's views of men and of women?

 THINK ABOUT
- the assumptions he makes about men and about women
- the different roles he assigns to men and women
- his opinion of the relationship between men and women

4. Think about the aspects of marriage that Bacon describes in his essay. In your opinion, why has he failed to mention love?

5. **ACTIVE READING** **EVALUATING OPINION** Study the opinion charts you completed in your **READER'S NOTEBOOK** as you read the two essays. Beside each statement you disagreed with, write down your own opinion on the subject. Discuss your opinions with a partner.

Extend Interpretations

6. What If? Suppose that Bacon had addressed his essays to young women. What specific advice do you think he would offer?

7. Different Perspectives What advice do you think a female contemporary of Bacon's would give to young men on marriage?

8. Connect to Life Today there is a great deal of discussion about what makes a good marriage. Do you think any of Bacon's views are relevant to contemporary ideas about marriage? Provide supporting details for your conclusions.

Literary Analysis

ESSAY In an **essay,** a writer offers an opinion on a subject. Bacon's essays are **persuasive,** designed to convince the reader to accept his ideas. Some of Bacon's statements are well supported with examples, facts, and reasons. For example, in "Of Marriage and Single Life," Bacon claims that single men produce the best works because they can devote all their energies to a particular task. A married man's wife and children, he suggests, are "impediments to great enterprises." On the other hand, some of Bacon's statements are unsubstantiated. His declaration that chaste women are often proud and stubborn, for instance, is unsupported by any reasons or examples.

Cooperative Learning Activity
Remember that one of Bacon's main purposes in writing his essays was to give advice to young men of the time who wanted to succeed in life. As a class, divide into two groups. With your group, make a list of guidelines from each essay that could be included in a book of "rules for success." Share your list with the class.

Writing Options

1. Letter to Bacon Select one of Bacon's statements with which you disagree. In a letter to the author, give reasons why you do not share his opinion.

2. Persuasive Essay Draft a persuasive essay about the issue you named for the Connect to Your Life on page 442. State your opinion regarding the issue, and give reasons for it. Place the persuasive essay in your **Working Portfolio.**

3. Marriage Questionnaire Create a list of questions for an opinion poll on marriage. Include questions that reflect Bacon's ideas.

Activities & Explorations

1. Image Collection Put together a collection of images—either paintings or photographs—that could be used to illustrate some of the ideas and impressions in "Of Studies" or in "Of Marriage and Single Life." Show your collection to the class and ask them what passage they think each image is related to. Discuss the reasons for your choices.
~ **VIEWING AND REPRESENTING**

2. Opinion Poll With a partner, conduct the opinion poll described in the third activity under "Writing Options." Question both students and adults, and videotape their responses if possible. Show your video to the class. ~ **SPEAKING AND LISTENING**

Inquiry & Research

Brain Calisthenics In Bacon's opinion, a variety of studies is needed to stimulate the different functions of the brain. Investigate current research on the brain and its functions. Report on two or three of the functions, listing activities that can strengthen each of them.

More Online: Research Starter
www.mcdougallittell.com

Sir Francis Bacon
1561–1626

Other Works
"Of Truth"
"Of Great Place"

Rise and Fall Like Marlowe and Raleigh, Francis Bacon was a Renaissance man. His interests extended from law and public service to philosophy and science. Although he entered Cambridge University at the age of 12, he stayed there just two years. He began his legal studies only when faced with financial difficulties, but he became an ambitious public servant and rose steadily in royal service, acting as legal counsel both to Elizabeth I and to James I. Bacon was eventually knighted and in 1618 was appointed to the highest judicial position in England. Three years later, his career ended in scandal when he was charged with—and admitted—accepting bribes.

Deadly Experimentation Banished from public service, Bacon directed his full attention to other interests. He was a prolific writer and produced, in addition to his famous essays, many philosophical and scientific treatises. Unfortunately, his avid interest in scientific discovery led ultimately to his death. Curious about the preservative effects of refrigeration, Bacon killed a hen and carefully stuffed it with snow. Chilled by the experiment, he developed bronchitis, from which he died on April 9, 1626.

Author Activity

Is Bacon the Bard? Some people have claimed that Francis Bacon is actually the author of plays attributed to William Shakespeare. Research these claims and draw your own conclusions. Share your results with the class.

Metaphysical Poetry

Leaving the Elizabethans Behind

If you found the intricacies of the sonnet form and the musical language of Elizabethan love poetry artificial, you aren't alone. During the 17th century, a number of poets rejected the highly ornamented style of late-Elizabethan lyric poetry. They wrote what became known as **metaphysical poetry.**

Metaphysical poetry was written in the manner of everyday speech—the everyday speech, that is, of someone deeply introspective and slightly irreverent. (*Metaphysical* in this usage refers to abstract or theoretical reasoning.) Such a personality is evident throughout the works of John Donne, who is considered the movement's central figure. His down-to-earth yet philosophical approach also characterizes the works of the other metaphysical poets, including Andrew Marvell, George Herbert, Richard Crashaw, and Henry Vaughan.

Portrait of John Donne as a young man (artist unknown)

Experiments with Language

When you first read metaphysical poetry, the ideas expressed in it may seem confusing. The metaphysical poets experimented with language in imaginative ways. One device they used was the **metaphysical conceit,** an extended metaphor that makes a surprising connection between two quite dissimilar things. An example is Donne's description in "A Valediction: Forbidding Mourning" of how two lovers' souls are connected, despite their physical distance:

> If they be two, they are two so
> As stiff twin compasses are two;
> Thy soul, the fixed foot, makes no show
> To move, but doth, if th' other do.
>
> —John Donne, "A Valediction: Forbidding Mourning"

The speaker likens the lovers' souls to the legs of a compass used for drawing circles. One lover is the "fixed foot" that remains home, while the other is the foot that journeys away—but always in a circle. The conceit suggests that, though the lovers are not together, their souls are so joined that they will always be in sympathy with each other. The metaphysical poets' use of such fanciful and extended conceits led the writer and critic Samuel Johnson to complain about their "violent yoking together of heterogeneous ideas."

Another characteristic of metaphysical poetry is **paradox**—a statement that seems contradictory but nevertheless suggests a truth. In his poem "A Fever," Donne ties together the contradictory concepts of love and hate in a startling way:

*R*iddles from Donne

YOUR TURN Try to figure out these comparisons from Donne (answers appear below):

That swimming college, and free hospitall
Of all mankind; that cage and vivary
Of fowls, and beasts . . .

*　　*　　*　　*　　*

In which as in a gallery this mouse
Walk'd, and surveyed the rooms of this vast house,
And to the brain, the souls bedchamber, went,
And gnaw'd the life cords there.

Answers: Noah's ark; Mouse enters elephant through trunk.

> **Oh do not die, for I shall hate**
> **All women so when thou art gone,**
> **That thee I shall not celebrate**
> **When I remember, thou wast one.**
>
> —John Donne, "A Fever"

The speaker's feelings reveal a paradox: he loves a woman so much that he will not praise her if she dies.

YOUR TURN With a partner, come up with a paradox or a conceit of your own using objects from everyday life.

Another characteristic of Donne's poetry is his disruption of poetic meter (the regular pattern of stressed and unstressed syllables). Violating the poetic meter occurs frequently in poetry, but in the eyes of many critics, Donne used this poetic technique too often. Poet Ben Jonson once declared that "Donne, for not keeping of accent, deserved hanging." However, Jonson had to admit that he greatly admired Donne as a poet.

The Critics Respond
As Jonson's comment reveals, metaphysical poetry did have its detractors. In fact, the label "metaphysical poetry" was originally meant as a criticism. In the late 1700s, Samuel Johnson named the group metaphysical poets because he thought that they used their poetry merely to show off their knowledge. Earlier, the writer John Dryden had made a similar criticism of Donne's poetry. Donne, Dryden wrote, "affects the metaphysics . . . [even] in his amorous verses, where nature only should reign."

The metaphysical poets experienced a revival in the early 20th century, thanks in part to poet and critic T. S. Eliot. In a famous essay, Eliot praised the metaphysical poets' ability to unify experience—in particular, to "feel their thought as immediately as the odor of a rose."

Elements of Metaphysical Poetry
Although every metaphysical poet had a unique style, their poetry shares several traits:

- simple, conversational diction
- complex sentence patterns
- themes that are often philosophical
- metaphysical conceits, or extended metaphors comparing very dissimilar things
- paradoxes, or statements that seem to contradict themselves
- disruptions of poetic meter
- witty and imaginative plays on words

Strategies for Reading: Metaphysical Poetry

1. Use the notes that accompany the poems to help you better understand the metaphysical poets' use of language.
2. Study each metaphysical conceit and identify the things being compared.
3. Look for paradoxes and try to determine what deeper meanings they convey.
4. Identify the subject and verb of any problematic clause, and then try to determine the functions of surrounding words or phrases.
5. Paraphrase any dense passages.
6. **Monitor** your reading strategies and modify them when your understanding breaks down. Remember to use your Strategies for Active Reading: **predict, visualize, connect, question, clarify,** and **evaluate.**

A Valediction: Forbidding Mourning
Holy Sonnet 10
from Meditation 17

Poetry and Nonfiction by JOHN DONNE

Connect to Your Life

The Meaning of Life Many writers struggle with life's difficult questions and try to come to terms with their own doubts and fears by writing about them. Think about how you strive to find answers to your most challenging questions about life. How do you express your thoughts and concerns? Share your reflections with others.

Build Background

Poet and Preacher As a young man, John Donne wrote passionate love poems and sought the admiration of numerous women. Later in life, Donne made a notable change. He married, fathered 12 children, entered the ministry, and authored over 160 sermons. "Jack" Donne, the spirited young Renaissance man, became Dr. John Donne, a highly respected preacher and the dean of St. Paul's Cathedral in London.

Donne was an intellectual who contemplated life's most perplexing questions, particularly those involving death—a common literary theme of the time. During the Renaissance, medical knowledge was limited, and effective medicines were rare. It was not unusual for people to die well before the age of 50. Donne's own wife died at the age of 33, shortly after giving birth to their 12th child. Two of his children were stillborn, and others died at the ages of 3, 7, and 19.

"A Valediction: Forbidding Mourning" was written prior to the poet's departure for France in 1611. The poem was intended to console his wife, who was distressed over her husband's impending long absence. "Holy Sonnet 10" reflects Donne's concerns about spiritual matters, particularly death and salvation. Donne wrote "Meditation 17" in 1623 while recovering from a serious illness. He was inspired in part by hearing the ringing of church bells to announce a person's death.

Focus Your Reading

LITERARY ANALYSIS **EXTENDED METAPHOR**

An **extended metaphor,** or **conceit,** compares two unlike things at length and in a number of ways. In "Meditation 17," for example, Donne uses an extended metaphor to compare humanity to a book in which each person makes up a chapter. As you read these selections, be aware of other examples of extended metaphors employed by the writer.

ACTIVE READING **INTERPRETING LANGUAGE STRUCTURES**

In his writing, Donne frequently uses **paradox** (a statement that seems to contradict itself but reveals some element of truth), unusual **imagery,** and surprising **comparisons.** By identifying these elements, you can gain insight into the main ideas in a work and the relationship between those ideas.

READER'S NOTEBOOK As you read these selections by Donne, identify and list unusual images, paradoxes, and comparisons in each work.

FORBIDDINGMOURNING

A Valediction:
FORBIDDING MOURNING

John Donne

As virtuous men pass mildly away,
 And whisper to their souls to go,
Whilst some of their sad friends do say
 The breath goes now, and some say, No;

5 So let us melt, and make no noise,
 No tear-floods, nor sigh-tempests move,
'Twere profanation of our joys
 To tell the laity our love.

Moving of th' earth brings harms and fears,
10 Men reckon what it did and meant;
But trepidation of the spheres,
 Though greater far, is innocent.

5 melt: part; dissolve our togetherness.
7 profanation (prŏf'ə-nā'shən): an act of contempt for what is sacred or respected.
8 laity (lā'ĭ-tē): persons without understanding of the "religion" of love.
9 moving of th' earth: an earthquake.
11 trepidation of the spheres: apparently irregular movements of heavenly bodies.
12 innocent: harmless.

Dull sublunary lovers' love
    (Whose soul is sense) cannot admit
15 Absence, because it doth remove
    Those things which elemented it.

But we by a love so much refined
    That our selves know not what it is,
Inter-assuréd of the mind,
20   Care less, eyes, lips, and hands to miss.

Our two souls therefore, which are one,
    Though I must go, endure not yet
A breach, but an expansion,
    Like gold to airy thinness beat.

25 If they be two, they are two so
    As stiff twin compasses are two;
Thy soul, the fixed foot, makes no show
    To move, but doth, if th' other do.

And though it in the center sit,
30   Yet when the other far doth roam,
It leans and hearkens after it,
    And grows erect, as that comes home.

Such wilt thou be to me, who must
    Like th' other foot, obliquely run;
35 Thy firmness makes my circle just,
    And makes me end where I begun.

---

13 sublunary (sŭb'lōō-nĕr'ē) **lovers' love:** the love of earthly lovers, which, like all things beneath the moon, is subject to change and death.
14 soul: essence; **sense:** sensuality.
16 elemented: composed.

19 inter-assuréd of the mind: confident of each other's love.

22 endure not yet: do not, nevertheless, suffer.

26 twin compasses: the two legs of a compass used for drawing circles.

32 as that comes home: when the moving foot returns to the center as the compass is closed.

34 obliquely (ō-blēk'lē): not in a straight line.
35 firmness: constancy; **just:** perfect.

Thinking Through the Literature

1. **Comprehension Check** To what does the poem compare the speaker and his love?

2. What **image** in this poem made the greatest impression on you? Why did it impress you?

3. How do you think the speaker would define true love?

   THINK ABOUT
   - his description of "sublunary lovers' love" (lines 13–16)
   - the comparison in lines 25–36
   - the title of the poem

4. In your opinion, is the message of this poem still relevant? Explain your answer.

Detail of Nativity of Christ. Stained glass, Abbey Ste. Foy, Conques, France. Giraudon/Art Resource, New York.

Holy Sonnet 10 | *John Donne*

Death, be not proud, though some have calléd thee
Mighty and dreadful, for thou art not so;
For those whom thou think'st thou dost overthrow
Die not, poor Death, nor yet canst thou kill me.
5 From rest and sleep, which but thy pictures be,
Much pleasure; then from thee much more must flow,
And soonest our best men with thee do go,
Rest of their bones, and soul's delivery.
Thou art slave to fate, chance, kings, and desperate men,
10 And dost with poison, war, and sickness dwell,
And poppy or charms can make us sleep as well
And better than thy stroke; why swell'st thou then?
One short sleep past, we wake eternally
And death shall be no more; Death, thou shalt die.

5–6 From rest . . . flow: Since we derive pleasure from rest and sleep, which are only likenesses of death, we should derive much more from death itself.

8 soul's delivery: the freeing of the soul from the body.

11 poppy: opium, a narcotic drug made from the juice of the poppy plant.

12 swell'st: swell with pride.

Thinking Through the Literature

1. What are your thoughts about the **speaker's** attitude toward death? Share your response with your classmates.

2. Why do you think the speaker addresses death as a person?

3. How do you interpret the speaker's statement, "Death, thou shalt die"? Explain your response.

from
Meditation 17

John Donne

Perchance he for whom this bell tolls may be so ill as that he knows not it tolls for him; and perchance I may think myself so much better than I am, as that they who are about me and see my state may have caused it to toll for me, and I know not that. The church is catholic,[1] universal, so are all her actions; all that she does belongs to all. When she baptizes a child, that action concerns me; for that child is thereby connected to that body which is my head too, and ingrafted into that body whereof I am a member.[2] And when she buries a man, that action concerns me: all mankind is of one author and is one volume; when one man dies, one chapter is not torn out of the book, but translated into a better language; and every chapter must be so translated. God employs several translators; some pieces are translated by age, some by sickness, some by war, some by justice; but God's hand is in every translation, and his hand shall bind up all our scattered leaves again for that library where every book shall lie open to one another. As therefore the bell that rings to a sermon calls not upon the preacher only, but upon the congregation to come, so this bell calls us all; but how much more me, who am brought so near the door by this sickness. . . . Who casts not up his eye to the sun when it rises? but who takes off his eye from a comet when that breaks out? Who bends not his ear to any bell which upon any occasion rings? but who can remove it from that bell which is passing a piece of himself out of this world? No man is an island, entire of itself; every man is a piece of the continent, a part of the main.[3] If a clod be washed away by the sea, Europe is the less, as well as if a promontory[4] were, as well as if a manor of thy friend's or of thine own were. Any man's death diminishes me because I am involved in mankind, and therefore never send to know for whom the bell tolls; it tolls for thee. ❖

Nunc lento

sonitu dicunt,
Now this bell tolling
morieris.
softly

for another,

says to me,

Thou must

die.

---

1. **is catholic:** embraces all humankind.
2. **body which is my head . . . member:** Donne likens the church to the head, which controls every part of the body, and to the body itself, because it is made up of interconnected parts (the individuals who compose it).
3. **main:** mainland.
4. **promontory** (prŏm′ən-tôr′ē): a ridge of land jutting out into a body of water.

Thinking through the LITERATURE

Connect to the Literature

1. **What Do You Think?**
   Which part of the excerpt from Donne's "Meditation 17" did you find most thought-provoking? Discuss your choice with your classmates.

   ┌─────────────────────────────────┐
   Comprehension Check
   - What does the ringing church bell announce?
   - Does the writer suggest we should be moved or unmoved by the fate of others?
   └─────────────────────────────────┘

Think Critically

2. **ACTIVE READING** **INTERPRETING LANGUAGE STRUCTURES**
   What do you think Donne is saying in the last three sentences of "Meditation 17"? You may want to review your list of unusual **images, paradoxes,** and **comparisons** from your **READER'S NOTEBOOK**.

3. Donne says that when a person dies, the person's "chapter is not torn out of the book, but translated into a better language." What do you think he means by this statement?

4. In your opinion, how might the thoughts recorded in this meditation help someone to cope with life's limitations?

   THINK ABOUT
   - Donne's statements about how people are connected
   - his views of God and the church

Extend Interpretations

5. **Critic's Corner** The scholar C. S. Lewis commented that much of Donne's writing deals with rather grim **themes.** On the basis of your understanding of these three selections, do you agree or disagree with Lewis? Give evidence to support your answer.

6. **Comparing Texts** Compare Donne's depiction of love in "A Valediction: Forbidding Mourning" with Shakespeare's depiction of love in "Sonnet 116" on page 302. Do the two speakers appear to agree or to disagree? Explain your opinion.

7. **Connect to Life** In their writings, Donne and many of his contemporaries tried to unravel the mysteries of death. Do you think the level of interest in death is as great in today's society? Why or why not?

Literary Analysis

EXTENDED METAPHOR Donne's writing contains several types of figurative language, including extended metaphors, or **conceits.** Like any metaphor, an **extended metaphor** is a comparison between two essentially unlike things that does not contain the word *like* or *as*. A metaphor becomes extended when the two things are compared at length and in a number of ways—perhaps throughout a stanza, a paragraph, or even an entire work.

Cooperative Learning Activity
The comparison of two lovers to the two feet of a draftsman's compass in "A Valediction: Forbidding Mourning" is one of the most famous **conceits** in metaphysical poetry. With classmates, draw up a list of interpretations of what the metaphor might mean.

Conceit: two lovers compared to two feet of a compass

Possible meanings:

Choices & CHALLENGES

Writing Options

1. **Extended Metaphor** Create your own extended metaphor, or conceit, to depict either love or death. You may choose to write your metaphor in the form of a paragraph or a short poem.

2. **Poem of Farewell** Using the title "A Valediction," write a poem of your own in which you describe your thoughts about going away and leaving someone you love behind. Place your poem in your **Working Portfolio.**

Activities & Explorations

1. **Mood Painting/Collage** Using appropriate colors, shapes, and images, create an abstract or representational painting or collage that reflects the mood conveyed by one of the Donne selections. **~ ART**

2. **Dramatic Reading** With a partner, prepare a reading of "A Valediction: Forbidding Mourning." Take turns reading, with one person taking the odd-numbered and the other the even-numbered stanzas. **~ SPEAKING AND LISTENING**

Inquiry & Research

A Modern Novel An important American writer of this century has used a phrase from this meditation of Donne's as the title of one of his novels. Discover the writer, the title of the novel, the year of its publication, and the subject of the book. Then, by reading a summary of the novel, try to figure out the relevance of the title to the subject of the book.

 More Online: Research Starter www.mcdougallittell.com

John Donne
1572–1631

Other Works
"The Canonization"
"The Flea"
"Holy Sonnet 7"

Early Years John Donne was born into a Roman Catholic family at a time when the Protestant majority had no tolerance for religious ideas different from their own. Although he attended Oxford University for several years, he was not eligible for a degree because of his religious beliefs. In 1593, his only brother died while imprisoned for sheltering a Jesuit priest.

Public Career At the age of 25, Donne became the personal secretary of Sir Thomas Egerton, a distinguished official of the royal court. A few years later, he married Egerton's niece, Ann More, secretly and without seeking permission. When the marriage was discovered, Donne lost his job. He was left nearly penniless and battled poverty for many years thereafter. Eventually, King James I recruited the struggling poet to the cause of Protestantism, and

Donne became an Anglican priest in 1615. Within six years, he was named dean of St. Paul's Cathedral, a position he held until his death. Donne was hailed as a dynamic preacher who incorporated wit and poetic language into his sermons.

A Master of Paradox Donne, whose writing is filled with paradoxes, was something of a paradox himself—a poet turned preacher, a sensualist and a scholar, a doubter and a believer. He was both dramatic and introspective, worldly and spiritual. Steeped in medieval learning, he was at the same time open to the fresh currents of 17th-century science and discovery. It is said that Donne "married passion to reason," and his example has influenced writers from his own time to the 20th century.

Author Activity

A Burial Shroud Near the end of his life, Donne had his portrait painted while dressed in his burial shroud. There is also a statue of him in this shroud. Investigate one of these portrayals of Donne and find out how and why he had it made.

On My First Son / Still to Be Neat

Poetry by BEN JONSON

Connect to Your Life

Invalid Assumptions Most of us make various assumptions as we go through life. For example, we might assume that certain events will happen as we have planned or that people will behave as we expect. Do you tend to make assumptions about yourself and others? Can you remember a time when something did not happen the way you assumed it would? With your classmates, discuss assumptions you have made about yourself or others. Which assumptions were valid? Which ones were not?

Build Background

Literary Lion Ben Jonson was a literary giant who knew most of London's important writers, including Francis Bacon, John Donne, and William Shakespeare. Like Shakespeare, Jonson has been remembered chiefly as a great playwright—in fact, his influence on English drama may have been equal to that of his more celebrated contemporary. However, Jonson also wrote some of the finest poetry in the English language.

The selections on the following pages show two of Jonson's varied poetic styles. Each poem deals with a speaker's assumptions about life and people. "On My First Son" is the poet's response to the death of his son, Benjamin. Like John Donne and others in his society, Jonson was forced on more than one occasion to experience the anguish of an untimely death. Both of his children died at very young ages, his son at the age of seven, a victim of the plague, and his daughter, Mary, in infancy. The second poem, "Still to Be Neat," is a song from one of Jonson's major plays, the comedy *Epicene; or, The Silent Woman.* In it, the speaker shares his assumptions about a "neat" woman.

Focus Your Reading

LITERARY ANALYSIS **EPITAPH** An **epitaph** is an inscription placed on a tomb or monument to honor the memory of the person buried there. The term *epitaph* has also been used more loosely to describe a verse, such as "On My First Son," which commemorates someone who has died. Notice the serious tone and somber mood of this line from the poem, as Jonson memorializes his dead son.

> *Farewell, thou child of my right hand, and joy;*
> *My sin was too much hope of thee, loved boy. . . .*

As you read the poem, determine which other lines are especially deserving of the label *epitaph.*

ACTIVE READING **COMPARING SPEAKERS IN POETRY** The speaker in a poem is often thought to be the writer, but in many cases this assumption is not valid. Though a writer may speak with his or her own voice in a poem, the speaker is often a voice or character made up by the writer. Two poems by the same writer may therefore have very different speakers.

READER'S NOTEBOOK As you read these poems by Ben Jonson, note the differences in the two speakers. You might use a Venn diagram to list the speakers' similarities and differences.

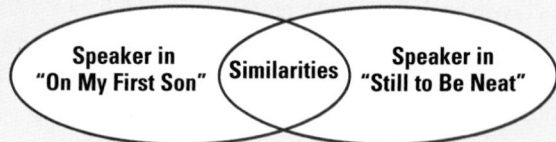

Speaker in "On My First Son"   Similarities   Speaker in "Still to Be Neat"

ON MY FIRST SON

Ben Jonson

Farewell, thou child of my right hand, and joy;
My sin was too much hope of thee, loved boy:
Seven years thou wert lent to me, and I thee pay,
Exacted by thy fate, on the just day.
5   O could I lose all father now! for why
Will man lament the state he should envy,
To have so soon 'scaped world's and flesh's rage,
And, if no other misery, yet age?
Rest in soft peace, and asked, say, "Here doth lie
10 Ben Jonson his best piece of poetry."
For whose sake henceforth all his vows be such
As what he loves may never like too much.

1 child of my right hand: The Hebrew name *Benjamin* means "son of the right hand."

4 just: required.

5 lose all father: lose the feeling of being a father.

Detail of *The Graham Children* (1742), William Hogarth. Oil on canvas. The Granger Collection, New York.

Thinking Through the Literature

1. What is your attitude toward the **speaker** after reading the poem?

2. In your opinion, what are some of the emotions and issues the speaker is grappling with as a result of his son's death?

   THINK ABOUT
   • the "sin" he describes in line 2
   • the comparison he makes in lines 3–4
   • his resolve in lines 11–12

3. The English poet Alfred, Lord Tennyson, once wrote, "'Tis better to have loved and lost / Than never to have loved at all." How do you think Jonson would have responded to Tennyson's statement?

Portrait of Frances Howard, Countess of Essex and Somerset, Isaac Oliver. Victoria & Albert Museum, London/Art Resource, New York.

STILL TO BE NEAT

BEN JONSON

Still to be neat, still to be dressed,
As you were going to a feast;
Still to be powdered, still perfumed;
Lady, it is to be presumed,
5   Though art's hid causes are not found,
All is not sweet, all is not sound.

Give me a look, give me a face
That makes simplicity a grace;
Robes loosely flowing, hair as free;
10   Such sweet neglect more taketh me
Than all th'adulteries of art.
They strike mine eyes, but not my heart.

1 still: always.

11 adulteries: impurities; debasements.

Thinking through the LITERATURE

Connect to the Literature

1. What Do You Think?
Do you agree with the ideas expressed by the speaker of "Still to Be Neat"?

> **Comprehension Check**
> - Why does the speaker object to the lady's "neat" appearance?
> - What look does the speaker in the poem claim to prefer?

Think Critically

2. What do you think the **speaker** assumes about the "powdered" and "perfumed" woman?

THINK ABOUT

- his reference to "art's hid causes" (line 5)
- what he means by "All is not sweet, all is not sound" (line 6)
- his use of the word "adulteries" to describe the ways in which a woman tries to improve her appearance (line 11)

3. On the basis of your reading of the poem, what is your opinion of the speaker of "Still to Be Neat"?

4. **ACTIVE READING** **COMPARING SPEAKERS IN POETRY** Look again at the Venn diagram you completed in your 📖 **READER'S NOTEBOOK**. How are the speakers similar? How do they differ? Discuss your ideas with a partner.

Extend Interpretations

5. Comparing Texts Reread lines 5–8 of "On My First Son." Then compare Jonson's attitude toward death with that of John Donne in "Holy Sonnet 10" on page 454.

6. What If? How do you think the woman addressed in "Still to Be Neat" might respond to the poem's speaker? Consider why she uses powder and perfume and what effect she hopes to achieve.

7. Connect to Life Do you think "Still to Be Neat" could have been written about a contemporary woman? Explain your opinion, keeping in mind the values of today's society.

Literary Analysis

EPITAPH In literature, an **epitaph** is used to describe any verse commemorating someone who has died. Although a few humorous epitaphs have been composed, most are serious in tone. "On My First Son" is considered an epitaph. In Jonson's poem, phrases such as "O could I lose all father now!" and "Rest in soft peace" reflect the poet's deep grief over the death of his son. Such lines effectively convey the poet's sadness to the reader.

Paired Activity With a partner, reread the poem and decide which lines would be the best epitaph to inscribe on a gravestone for Jonson's son, or adapt the poem's language and tone and write your own epitaph for the boy.

REVIEW **REPETITION** Find examples of **repetition** in "Still to Be Neat." Discuss why Jonson might have chosen to repeat certain words. How does the repetition affect your reading of the poem? You might want to use a chart like the one below to organize your thoughts.

Repeated Words	Reasons for Repetition	Effects on Reader

Writing Options

1. Message of Condolence Write a sympathy note to Ben Jonson, offering him advice or comfort on the occasion of the death of his son. You may refer to his poem "On My First Son" in your note and try to help him with some of the issues he raises.

2. Poetic Parody Think of a quality or trait that you particularly dislike in a person. Using that trait as your subject, write a parody, or imitation, of the first stanza of "Still to Be Neat."

Activities & Explorations

1. Monument Design Create a sketch of a tombstone or monument that Jonson might have erected in memory of his son. ~ **ART**

2. Pictorial Essay Put together a pictorial essay depicting the contrast between natural beauty and the "adulteries of art."
~ **VIEWING AND REPRESENTING**

Inquiry & Research

Fashion Sense In "Still to Be Neat," Jonson refers to a woman's efforts to dress for a "feast." Find out what cosmetics and clothes women of the Elizabethan Age wore to a formal gathering. To what extent, if any, did hygiene influence what was worn? Share your findings with the class.

Ben Jonson
1572–1637

Other Works
"Song, to Celia"
"To the Memory of My Beloved, the Author Master William Shakespeare"
"Epitaph on Elizabeth, L. H."

Eclectic Careers In spite of a quarrelsome nature, Ben Jonson was a leader in the literary world and was greatly admired by a group of young poets—including Robert Herrick and Sir John Suckling—who proudly called themselves the "sons of Ben." Although well-educated as a child, Jonson never attended a university. He worked a short time as a bricklayer and then joined the British army. While aiding the Dutch in their war against Spain, Jonson killed the enemy's best soldier in single combat. Returning to England, he pursued a career in the theater, faring poorly as an actor but gaining extensive popularity as a playwright.

Close Calls A man of great bulk, with what he described as a "mountain belly" and a "rocky face," Jonson lived life with gusto. Unfortunately, his volcanic temperament led to occasional scrapes with the law. Once, he barely escaped hanging after killing a fellow actor in a duel. Because a knowledge of Latin was largely confined to clergymen in Renaissance England, Jonson eluded death by reading a "neck verse"—a passage from the Latin Bible—so that he could be tried by a church court rather than a more harsh criminal court. He was, however, branded on the thumb as a convicted felon. He was also twice imprisoned when he offended authorities with his plays.

Literary Works Satire, which was just emerging as a popular dramatic form, was well suited to Jonson's combative nature and scathing wit. He gained fame for his satiric comedies, two of which, *Volpone* and *The Alchemist,* are still staged in theaters today. Many of his plays were performed at the Globe Theater, and Shakespeare himself acted in Jonson's first comedy, *Every Man in His Humor.* In 1616, Jonson published a volume of his plays and poems under the title *Works.* At that time, only more intellectual subjects, such as history and theology, were considered important enough to be presented as "works." The volume therefore became quite controversial, as Jonson undoubtedly had hoped. In his later years, Jonson wrote elaborate entertainments for the royal court and was rewarded with a sizable pension. His tombstone in Westminster Abbey bears the epitaph "O rare Ben Jonson."

PREPARING to *Read*

To the Virgins, to Make Much of Time

Poetry by ROBERT HERRICK

To His Coy Mistress

Poetry by ANDREW MARVELL

To Lucasta, Going to the Wars

Poetry by RICHARD LOVELACE

Comparing Literature of the World

The Lyrics of the Cavalier Poets and Omar Khayyám

This lesson and the one that follows present an opportunity for you to compare the lyrics of the Cavalier poets with the poems of Omar Khayyám. Specific points of comparison in the Khayyám lesson will help you note similarities and differences in the writers' treatments of the *carpe diem* theme.

Connect to Your Life

"Gather Ye Rosebuds While Ye May" The Latin expression *carpe diem* (kär′pĕ dē′ĕm)— "seize the day"—comes from a poem in which the Roman poet Horace advocates enjoying life fully because death is inevitable. This philosophy of life has been embraced by various individuals over the centuries and is still popular with some people today. With a group of classmates, discuss your opinion of this approach to life.

Build Background

The Cavalier Poets The Stuart king Charles I—successor to James I—believed that he had a divine right to rule, independent of Parliament. Tension grew between Charles and members of the legislative body, and in 1629 the king suspended Parliament. Thirteen years later, in 1642, England erupted in a civil war between those who supported the monarchy, who were called Cavaliers, and those who supported Parliament, known as Roundheads. The Cavaliers included a group of poets whose musical, lighthearted verse was popular among members of the royal court. The Cavalier poets focused on themes of love, war, honor, and courtly behavior and frequently advocated the philosophy of *carpe diem*, or living for the moment.

Prominent among the Cavalier poets were Robert Herrick and Richard Lovelace. Another 17th-century poet, Andrew Marvell, although not a Cavalier in political sympathies, is often grouped with the Cavaliers because of his poetic style. His combination of the intellectual depth and wit of the metaphysical poets with the lighthearted and melodious style of the Cavaliers makes him difficult to categorize.

Focus Your Reading

LITERARY ANALYSIS **HYPERBOLE** Figurative language that greatly exaggerates facts or ideas for humorous effect or for emphasis is called **hyperbole** (hī-pûr′ bə-lē). For example, in "To His Coy Mistress," the speaker talks about loving someone for 30,000 years. Look for other instances of hyperbole in Marvell's poem.

ACTIVE READING **COMPARING SPEAKERS IN POETRY** Each of the speakers in these three poems has a slightly different attitude toward love and life. As you read, compare the speakers' feelings as reflected in their words. Remember these points:

- the speaker is the voice in a poem that talks to the reader
- the speaker can be a distant observer or an intimate participant
- the speaker and the poet are not necessarily the same

READER'S NOTEBOOK As you read these poems, jot down a few words or phrases for each that seem to capture the speaker's attitude toward love and life.

TO THE VIRGINS, TO MAKE MUCH OF TIME

Gather ye rosebuds while ye may,
    Old time is still a-flying;
And this same flower that smiles today
    Tomorrow will be dying.

5 The glorious lamp of heaven, the sun,
    The higher he's a-getting,
The sooner will his race be run,
    And nearer he's to setting.

That age is best which is the first,
10   When youth and blood are warmer;
But being spent, the worse, and worst
    Times still succeed the former.

Then be not coy, but use your time,
    And, while ye may, go marry;
15 For, having lost but once your prime,
    You may forever tarry.

Robert Herrick

GUIDE FOR READING

9–12 How does the speaker appear to feel about old age? Do you agree with his opinion?

13 coy: hesitant; modest.

15–16 How do these lines reflect the philosophy of *carpe diem?*
16 tarry: wait.

Thinking Through the Literature

1. What was your overall reaction to this poem? Record your response in your notebook.

2. How would you describe the **speaker's** thoughts about time? Be sure to use examples from the poem to help explain your opinion.

3. Do you agree or disagree with the speaker's idea that "that age is best which is the first" (line 9)? Why or why not?

TO HIS COY MISTRESS

Andrew Marvell

The Proposal (1872), Adolphe-William Bouguereau. Oil on canvas, 64⅜″ × 44″, The Metropolitan Museum of Art, New York, gift of Mrs. Elliot L. Kamen in memory of her father, Bernard R. Armour, 1960 (60.122).

Had we but world enough, and time,
This coyness, lady, were no crime.
We would sit down, and think which way
To walk, and pass our long love's day.
5 Thou by the Indian Ganges' side
Shouldst rubies find; I by the tide
Of Humber would complain. I would
Love you ten years before the flood,
And you should, if you please, refuse

10   Till the conversion of the Jews.
     My vegetable love should grow
     Vaster than empires and more slow;
     An hundred years should go to praise
     Thine eyes, and on thy forehead gaze;
15   Two hundred to adore each breast,
     But thirty thousand to the rest;
     An age at least to every part,
     And the last age should show your heart.
     For, lady, you deserve this state,
20   Nor would I love at lower rate.
          But at my back I always hear
     Time's wingéd chariot hurrying near;
     And yonder all before us lie
     Deserts of vast eternity.
25   Thy beauty shall no more be found,
     Nor, in thy marble vault, shall sound
     My echoing song; then worms shall try
     That long-preserved virginity,
     And your quaint honor turn to dust,
30   And into ashes all my lust:
     The grave's a fine and private place,
     But none, I think, do there embrace.
          Now therefore, while the youthful hue
     Sits on thy skin like morning dew,
35   And while thy willing soul transpires
     At every pore with instant fires,
     Now let us sport us while we may,
     And now, like amorous birds of prey,
     Rather at once our time devour
40   Than languish in his slow-chapped power.
     Let us roll all our strength and all
     Our sweetness up into one ball,
     And tear our pleasures with rough strife
     Thorough the iron gates of life:
45   Thus, though we cannot make our sun
     Stand still, yet we will make him run.

10 till . . . Jews: In Marvell's day, Christians believed that all Jews would convert to Christianity just before the Last Judgment and the end of the world.

11 vegetable love: a love that grows like a plant (an oak tree, for example)—slowly but with the power to become very large.

19 state: dignity.

20 How would you describe the speaker's tone up to this point?

32 Has the speaker's tone changed?

35 transpires: breathes.

37–40 Consider the title of this part of Unit Two, "Facing Life's Limitations." How is the speaker trying to deal with life's limitations?
40 slow-chapped: slow-jawed.

44 thorough: through.

Thinking Through the Literature

1. How do you picture the **speaker** in the poem?

2. Do you think the speaker's argument about time is convincing? Explain your opinion, using support from the poem.

3. In your opinion, is the speaker sincere in his description of the way he would go about loving his mistress if he had more time?

To Lucasta,
GOING TO THE WARS

Tell me not, Sweet, I am unkind
That from the nunnery
Of thy chaste breast and quiet mind,
To war and arms I fly.

5 True, a new mistress now I chase,
The first foe in the field;
And with a stronger faith embrace
A sword, a horse, a shield.

Yet this inconstancy is such
10 As you too shall adore;
I could not love thee, Dear, so much,
Loved I not honor more.

RICHARD
LOVELACE

GUIDE FOR READING

4 Think about the speaker's use of the word *arms*. Why is it especially appropriate for the speaker to talk about flying to arms?

7 What is the "stronger faith" the speaker mentions in this line?

Sir Philip Sidney (about 1576), unknown artist. The Granger Collection, New York.

Thinking through the LITERATURE

Connect to the Literature

1. **What Do You Think?**
Jot down words or phrases that convey your impression of the speaker of "To Lucasta, Going to the Wars." Share them with a partner.

> **Comprehension Check**
> • How does Lucasta feel about the speaker going off to war?
> • What does the speaker love most?

Think Critically

2. Which do you think the speaker prefers, love or war?

> **THINK ABOUT**
> • his description of Lucasta
> • what he means by "stronger faith" in line 7
> • his thoughts about honor

3. Why do you think the speaker uses words like *mistress, embrace, inconstancy,* and *adore* in referring to his duty?

4. If you were the speaker's beloved, how might you react to lines 11–12?

5. **ACTIVE READING** **COMPARING SPEAKERS IN POETRY** Review the words and phrases reflecting the speakers' attitudes that you jotted down in your **READER'S NOTEBOOK.** Then think about the ways in which women are described in "To the Virgins, to Make Much of Time," "To His Coy Mistress," and "To Lucasta, Going to the Wars." Do you think the **speakers** share the same attitude toward women? Explain your opinion.

Extend Interpretations

6. **Comparing Texts** In your opinion, what would each of the speakers of these poems think of the kind of love described in Donne's "A Valediction: Forbidding Mourning"?

7. **Different Perspectives** What if the speaker in "To His Coy Mistress" were the speaker in "To Lucasta, Going to the Wars"? What differences do you think there would be in **theme** and **tone?**

8. **Connect to Life** Think about the philosophy of *carpe diem* as it is expressed in these poems. Are there popular songs today that express the same idea as "seize the day" or "Gather ye rosebuds while ye may"?

Literary Analysis

HYPERBOLE "Saying goodbye felt like the end of the world" is an example of **hyperbole,** figurative language that greatly exaggerates facts or ideas for humorous effect or for emphasis.

Cooperative Learning Activity
What examples of hyperbole can you find in "To His Coy Mistress"? How do they help the speaker develop his argument? In a small group, list all the examples of hyperbole you can find in the poem. Then compare your list with those of other groups.

REVIEW **THEME** Recall that a **theme** is a central idea or message in a work of literature. Sometimes the theme is directly stated; at other times, it is implied. What would you say is the theme in each of the three poems?

REVIEW **METAPHOR** Recall that a **metaphor** is a figure of speech that makes a comparison between two things that are basically unlike but have something in common. In Andrew Marvell's poem "To His Coy Mistress," the phrase "time's wingéd chariot" is a metaphor in which the swift passage of time is compared to a speeding chariot. Look for other striking metaphors in the poems.

Choices & CHALLENGES

Writing Options

1. Comparison of Poems Draft a short comparison-contrast essay in which you compare the poems "To His Coy Mistress" and "To the Virgins, to Make Much of Time," concentrating on their speakers, themes, and styles.

Writing Handbook
See page 1367: Compare and Contrast

2. Exaggerated Speech Write a speech in which you use your own examples of hyperbole to convince your listeners to "seize the day." Place your speech in your **Working Portfolio.**

3. Letter in Time of War Write a letter from Lucasta to her lover after he's left for the war. Be sure to mention how you feel about his choice to leave you and go fight in a war.

Activities & Explorations

1. *Carpe Diem* Banner Arrange images and words to create a classroom banner on the *carpe diem* theme. ~ **VIEWING AND REPRESENTING**

2. Booklet of Quotations Prepare a booklet of quotations about the fleeting nature of time. Be sure to include Marvell's reference to "time's wingéd chariot." ~ **LITERATURE**

3. Cartoons and Poetry Draw single-panel cartoons depicting some of the ideas and objects that are personified in the poems—for example, "old time . . . still a-flying." ~ **ART**

Inquiry & Research

The Reign of Charles I Find out more about life during the reign of Charles I—include court life, the lifestyle of the Cavalier poets, and the events that led up to the civil war.

 More Online: Research Starter www.mcdougallittell.com

Art Connection

Matching the Mood Look again at Adolphe-William Bouguereau's painting *The Proposal* on page 465. In your opinion, does this painting capture the mood of Marvell's poem "To His Coy Mistress"? Give reasons for your answer.

Robert Herrick
1591–1674

Other Works
"Corinna's Going A-Maying"
"Delight in Disorder"
"The Argument of His Book"

Youth and Man-About-Town As a young man, Robert Herrick tried his hand at goldsmithing, the family trade, before going off to Cambridge University. There he received two degrees and, a few years later, was ordained a priest. An ardent admirer of Ben Jonson, Herrick was one of the "sons of Ben" and an active member of London society. He loved the city and was disappointed when assigned to a rural church in Devonshire.

Because of his loyalty to the king, he was deprived of this post for 15 years under the Parliamentary government but was reassigned to Devonshire when the monarchy was restored.

Poet and Priest While in London in 1648, Herrick published his only book, *Hesperides,* which contained over 1,400 poems on both worldly and religious themes. Unfortunately, because of the civil war, society was not very interested in Herrick's light, playful verse, and his work was not much appreciated until the 19th century. After returning to the country, Herrick settled down to his life as a country priest, spending his days in enjoyment of nature and the quiet life and writing no more poetry. Herrick's poetry is greatly appreciated today, and he has been called "the greatest songwriter ever born of English race."

Andrew Marvell
1621–1678

Other Works
"The Mower's Song"
"The Garden"
"On a Drop of Dew"

Richard Lovelace
1618–1657

Other Works
"To Amarantha, That She Would
Dishevel Her Hair"
"To Lucasta, Going Beyond the Seas"
"To Althea, from Prison"

Student and Tutor During his lifetime, Andrew Marvell was known for his political activities rather than his poetry. After receiving a degree from Cambridge University, he traveled abroad for several years before returning to England in 1650 to tutor the daughter of the Parliamentary general Lord Fairfax. It was while living at the Fairfax estate that he wrote most of his nonsatirical poetry. Three years later, Marvell became tutor to Oliver Cromwell's ward, William Dutton.

A Political Poet Marvell wrote a number of poems about Cromwell, including "An Horatian Ode upon Cromwell's Return from Ireland," perhaps the greatest political poem in English. In 1657 he became an assistant to John Milton, the Latin secretary for the Parliamentary government, and in 1659 was himself elected to membership in Parliament, an office he held until his death. After the Restoration, he seems to have been influential in securing Milton's deliverance from prison and from possible execution. During this time he also wrote many political satires attacking the king's policies. Marvell's poetry was not published until after his death, and his true talent as a poet was not fully recognized until the 20th century.

The Perfect Cavalier A courtier, soldier, poet, lover, connoisseur of the arts, and reputedly one of the most handsome men in England—Richard Lovelace had all of the qualities of the perfect Cavalier. He was born into a wealthy military family and was educated at Oxford. On a visit to the university, the king and queen admired him so much that they granted him a master's degree on the spot. Naturally, he fought for the monarchy during the civil war.

Prisoner and Poet Lovelace was imprisoned twice, once for petitioning Parliament in the king's favor and again for his involvement in an uprising against the legislative body. It was while he was imprisoned that he wrote his best and most famous poems, "To Althea, from Prison" and "To Lucasta, Going to the Wars." In 1646, he was badly wounded while fighting the Spanish in France. Lovelace depleted most of his fortune trying to help the king and spent the last years of his life dependent on the charity of friends. During his lifetime, Lovelace's poems were popular and even set to music, but after his death they were forgotten for over 100 years.

from the Rubáiyát (roo′ bē-yät′)

Poetry by OMAR KHAYYÁM (ō′ mär kī-yäm′)
Translated by EDWARD FITZGERALD

Comparing Literature of the World

The Theme of *Carpe Diem* Across Cultures

Poems by Herrick, Marvell, Lovelace, and Omar Khayyám The theme of *carpe diem*—"seize the day"—is dominant in the *Rubáiyát,* just as it is in the poems of the English Cavalier poets and Andrew Marvell. Many of the poems by Herrick, Marvell, Lovelace, and Omar Khayyám feature speakers who warn about the fleeting nature of time and urge their audiences to live in the present. These poets also use metaphors to convey their themes.

Points of Comparison As you read the poems from the *Rubáiyát,* compare their **themes** and **metaphors** with those you encountered in the poems by Herrick, Marvell, and Lovelace.

Build Background

Persian Poetry The *Rubáiyát* is probably the work of Persian literature best known in the West. It has been translated into almost every major language of the world. The word *rubáiyát* is the plural form of *ruba'i,* the name of a Persian poetic form. A ruba'i is a quatrain, or four-line poem, in which the first, second, and fourth lines rhyme.

In its entirety, the *Rubáiyát* contains more than 400 of these quatrains. Each quatrain conveys a single thought about a subject such as beauty, love, death, or the fleeting nature of time. Although at one time all 400 poems were attributed to the 12th-century Persian poet Omar Khayyám, scholars now believe that he perhaps wrote no more than 250.

In 1859, the British writer Edward FitzGerald translated 75 of the poems into English. FitzGerald tried to remain true to Omar's expression of his philosophy of life by respecting the poems' form and individual themes, but he did modify the images to fit the tastes of his Victorian audience. Because the original quatrains were disconnected, FitzGerald rearranged them into a more unified and continuous sequence.

Focus Your Reading

LITERARY ANALYSIS | **THEME AND METAPHOR** As you know, the **theme** of a literary work is a message or insight about life or human nature that the writer wishes to communicate to the reader. You will also recall that a **metaphor** is a comparison that does not contain the word *like* or *as.* This comparison may be stated directly, as in "Life is a broken-winged bird," or it may be implied, as in "the Bird of Time." Metaphors can be an effective means of conveying theme in a literary work. As you read these poems from the *Rubáiyát,* look for metaphors that are used to express theme.

ACTIVE READING | **DRAWING CONCLUSIONS ABOUT TONE** Frequently, a writer relies on **imagery**—words and phrases that appeal to the senses—to convey his or her **tone,** or attitude, toward a subject. The writer's tone, in turn, usually reflects his or her philosophy of life.

READER'S NOTEBOOK As you read these poems, look for imagery that helps establish the tone. Keep track of the images you find by using a chart like the one shown.

Poem	Imagery
1	Field of Night, Shaft of Light
7	
12	

FROM THE
Rubáiyát

Omar

Khayyám

Joy of Wine fresco. Chehel Sotün Palace, Isfahan, Iran. Photo by Roloff Beny, courtesy of the National Archives of Canada (PA-1986-009).

1

Wake! For the Sun, who scatter'd into flight
The Stars before him from the Field of Night,
    Drives Night along with them from Heav'n, and strikes
The Sultán's Turret with a Shaft of Light.

4 Sultán's Turret: a tower in the palace of a Moslem ruler.

7

5 Come, fill the Cup, and in the fire of Spring
Your Winter-garment of Repentance fling:
    The Bird of Time has but a little way
To flutter—and the Bird is on the Wing.

12

A Book of Verses underneath the Bough,
10   A Jug of Wine, a Loaf of Bread—and Thou
         Beside me singing in the Wilderness—
      Oh, Wilderness were Paradise enow!

12 enow: enough.

63

Oh, threats of Hell and Hopes of Paradise!
One thing at least is certain—*This* Life flies;
15   One thing is certain and the rest is Lies;
The Flower that once has blown for ever dies.

64

Strange, is it not? that of the myriads who
Before us pass'd the door of Darkness through,
         Not one returns to tell us of the Road,
20   Which to discover we must travel too.

17 myriads (mĭr′ē-ədz): countless numbers (of people).

68

We are no other than a moving row
Of Magic Shadow-shapes that come and go
         Round with the Sun-illumined Lantern held
In Midnight by the Master of the Show;

69

25   But helpless Pieces of the Game He plays
Upon this Checker-board of Nights and Days;
         Hither and thither moves, and checks, and slays,
And one by one back in the Closet lays.

27 hither and thither: here and there.

96

Yet Ah, that Spring should vanish with the Rose!
30   That Youth's sweet-scented manuscript should close!
         The Nightingale that in the branches sang,
Ah, whence, and whither flown again, who knows!

99

Ah, Love! could you and I with Him conspire
To grasp this sorry Scheme of Things entire,
35   Would not we shatter it to bits—and then
Re-mold it nearer to the Heart's Desire!

Thinking through the LITERATURE

Connect to the Literature

1. What Do You Think?
Freewrite about the thoughts you had after reading these poems.

Comprehension Check
- According to the speaker, what one thing in life is certain?
- What would make life like a paradise for the speaker?

Think Critically

2. How would you describe the philosophy of life expressed by the **speaker**?

> **THINK ABOUT**
> - what he compares time to in poem 7
> - the actions he advocates in poems 1, 7, and 12
> - his view of death in poems 63 and 64
> - what he compares human beings to in poems 68 and 69

3. How do you think the speaker views the relationship between human beings and God?

4. | ACTIVE READING | DRAWING CONCLUSIONS ABOUT TONE |
Look back at the **imagery** chart you kept in your READER'S NOTEBOOK as you read. What conclusions can you draw about the **tone** in each poem?

5. Which **theme** expressed in the poems seems to come closest to your own philosophy of life? Explain your response.

Extend Interpretations

6. Critic's Corner One critic, Gordon S. Haight, stated that the *Rubáiyát* "will always attract some readers by its dark philosophy." What do you think Haight meant by "dark philosophy"? Explain your interpretation.

7. Connect to Life The speaker suggests that happiness can be achieved very simply, with "a Book of verses . . . a Jug of Wine, a Loaf of Bread—and Thou." Do you think most people can be satisfied with such simple pleasures? Give reasons for your opinion.

8. **Points of Comparison** Which of these poems from the *Rubáiyát* seem most closely related to the ideas expressed in Robert Herrick's "To the Virgins, to Make Much of Time" (page 464)? What theme do they share with Herrick's poem?

Literary Analysis

| THEME AND METAPHOR | In poetry, **metaphors** often help convey **themes.** For example, in poem 7, time is compared to a bird that has already completed part of a short journey. This comparison reflects the theme that time is limited and passes quickly.

Paired Activity With a partner, identify at least five other metaphors in these poems. Determine what theme or themes the metaphors help convey.

Poem Number	Metaphor	Theme
1		
7		
12		
63		
64		
68		
69		
96		
99		

Choices & CHALLENGES

Writing Options

1. Paragraph of Explanation In a paragraph, identify the person whom you think the speaker is addressing in these poems. Give reasons for your opinion.

I think the speaker is addressing . . .

2. Letter to Omar Select one poem with which you strongly agree or disagree. Write a letter to Omar Khayyám, explaining your thoughts about his ideas. Place the letter in your **Working Portfolio.**

3. Points of Comparison Compare the metaphors used in the *Rubáiyát* with those in Marvell's "To His Coy Mistress." Then write your own metaphor to express your philosophy of life.

Writing Handbook
See page 1367: Compare and Contrast.

Activities & Explorations

1. Philosophy Report Read other poems from the *Rubáiyát* and choose two to share with classmates. In a brief oral report, tell how you think each poem reflects the speaker's philosophy of life. ~ **SPEAKING AND LISTENING**

2. Poetic Mural Create a mural depicting images or ideas presented in some or all of the poems. ~ **ART**

Inquiry & Research

Omar's Culture Investigate the culture of 12th-century Persia—the culture in which Omar Khayyám wrote his poems. Find information on religion, education, or government, and report your findings to the class.

Omar Khayyám
1050?–1123?

Omar the Tentmaker Omar Khayyám lived in Persia, the region now occupied by the nation of Iran. During his lifetime, he was more famous for his work as a scientist than for his poetry. The name Khayyám means "tentmaker"; thus, the author of the *Rubáiyát* is sometimes called Omar the Tentmaker. It is possible that Omar briefly engaged in this line of work before going on to more scholarly pursuits; however, it is more likely that his father was the tentmaker.

Man of Science Omar was an exceptionally brilliant man who mastered the subjects of mathematics, astronomy, philosophy, history, medicine, and law. He was the author of important works on astronomy, geometry, and algebra as well as poetry. Because of his scientific genius, Omar was asked to make the astronomical calculations that were needed to reform the calendar in use at the time. He was later asked to help in the design and building of an observatory in the city of Isfahan. Despite his many scientific contributions, however, Omar's worldwide reputation is based mainly on his poetry.

Author Activity

Counting the Days Find out about the calendar that Omar helped reform. What was the old calendar based on? What changes were made to the new one? How does the reformed calendar compare with the calendar used today in the Western world?

How Soon Hath Time
When I Consider How My Light Is Spent

Poetry by JOHN MILTON

Connect to Your Life

A Dream Deferred Think about someone you know or have read about—such as a musician or an athlete—who has suffered disappointment in trying to reach a desired goal or realize a dream. Discuss your impressions of how that person reacted to disappointment and how he or she carried on afterward.

Build Background

Life's Disappointments Studious and devout even as a child, John Milton devoted his life to writing about religious issues and dreamed of producing great poetry that would explore humanity's relationship with God. Though he ultimately realized this ambition, his life was marked by a series of disappointments, not the least of which was the political downfall of the Puritans, the faction he supported in the civil warfare that racked mid-17th-century England. The two famous sonnets you will read explore two other disappointments in the writer's life. In the first, composed to mark the occasion of his 23rd birthday, Milton examines the meagerness of his creative output. In the second, he reveals his feelings about his loss of sight at the age of 43.

Focus Your Reading

LITERARY ANALYSIS **ALLUSION** An **allusion** is a brief reference to a historical or fictional person, place, event, or thing with which the reader is assumed to be familiar. A devout Puritan who often wrote on religious topics, Milton frequently alluded to material in the Bible. As you read these sonnets, look for examples of biblical allusions.

ACTIVE READING **CLARIFYING SENTENCE MEANING** Like many other poets, Milton sometimes used unusual word order to make his ideas fit particular patterns of **rhythm** or **rhyme** and to make his lines more memorable. For example, instead of writing "that I am arrived so near to manhood," he wrote:

That I to manhood am arrived so near

READER'S NOTEBOOK As you read these sonnets, be alert to the order of words in Milton's sentences. When the word order in a sentence seems odd, try **paraphrasing** the sentence in a way that sounds more natural and makes sense to you. Record your paraphrases in your notebook.

Milton's sentence:
". . . who best/Bear his mild yoke, they serve him best."

My paraphrase:

HOW SOON HATH TIME

JOHN MILTON

How soon hath Time, the subtle thief of youth,
    Stoln on his wing my three and twentieth year!
    My hasting days fly on with full career,
    But my late spring no bud or blossom show'th.
5 Perhaps my semblance might deceive the truth,
    That I to manhood am arrived so near,
    And inward ripeness doth much less appear,
    That some more timely-happy spirits endu'th.
Yet be it less or more, or soon or slow,
10   It shall be still in strictest measure even
    To that same lot, however mean or high,
Toward which Time leads me, and the will of Heaven;
    All is, if I have grace to use it so,
    As ever in my great Taskmaster's eye.

3 **career:** speed.

5 **semblance:** outward appearance.

8 **more timely-happy spirits:** people who have accomplished more at an early age; **endu'th:** endows.
10 **still:** always; **even:** adequate.
11 **lot:** fate.

14 **ever:** eternally.

Thinking Through the Literature

1. Does this poem seem optimistic or pessimistic to you? Explain your impression.

2. Do you think the 23-year-old speaker would characterize himself as a youth or as a man? Consider the evidence.

   THINK ABOUT
   - his statement that "no bud or blossom show'th"
   - his reference to his appearance in line 5
   - the "inward ripeness" he mentions in line 7

3. What conclusions does the speaker reach by the poem's end?

HOW SOON HATH TIME   **477**

Illustration (about 1856),
Birket Foster.

WHEN I CONSIDER HOW MY LIGHT IS SPENT

John Milton

When I consider how my light is spent
    Ere half my days, in this dark world and wide,
    And that one talent which is death to hide,
    Lodged with me useless, though my soul more bent
5 To serve therewith my Maker, and present
    My true account, lest he returning chide;
    "Doth God exact day-labor, light denied?"
    I fondly ask; but Patience to prevent
That murmur, soon replies, "God doth not need
10   Either man's work or his own gifts; who best
    Bear his mild yoke, they serve him best. His state
Is kingly. Thousands at his bidding speed
    And post o'er land and ocean without rest:
    They also serve who only stand and wait."

3 talent: a reference to the biblical parable of the talents (Matthew 25:14–30), in which a servant who has hidden his one talent (a sum of money) in the earth is reprimanded for not putting it to good use.
8 fondly: foolishly.

12 thousands: here, thousands of angels.

Connect to the Literature

1. What Do You Think?
What are your thoughts about the last line of "When I Consider How My Light Is Spent"? Share your reaction with classmates.

....
Comprehension Check
- What is the speaker's problem?
- What does the speaker ask about God?
....

Think Critically

2. What seems to trouble the speaker most about his loss of sight?

THINK ABOUT

- the **image** conveyed by "this dark world" in line 2
- the reference to his "talent" in lines 3–4
- the question he "fondly" asks in line 8

3. **ACTIVE READING** **CLARIFYING SENTENCE MEANING** Look again at the sentences you paraphrased in your READER'S NOTEBOOK. How would you **paraphrase** Patience's statements in lines 9–14 in everyday English? What would you say is the main point of Patience's speech?

4. Do you think the speaker will be able to follow the advice of Patience? Why or why not?

Extend Interpretations

5. Comparing Texts Compare and contrast the speakers' attitudes in "How Soon Hath Time" and "When I Consider How My Light Is Spent." Pay particular attention to their feelings about their talent and their relationship with God.

6. What If? If Milton had been deaf rather than blind, how might his writing have been different?

7. Connect to Life In what specific situations do you think the advice in either sonnet might be useful to people today? Explain your opinion.

Literary Analysis

ALLUSION Writers often use **allusions** to make their works more meaningful to readers. An allusion is a brief reference to a historical or fictional person, place, event, or thing with which the reader is assumed to be familiar. In "When I Consider How My Light is Spent," Milton alludes to a biblical parable in which a master praises two servants who have made good use of the talents entrusted to them and criticizes a servant who has buried his one talent instead of using it. The first two servants are given rewards, but the third has his talent taken away.

Activity
- Explain the two meanings of the word *talent* in the poem. What, specifically, might the speaker's "one talent" be?
- Explain how the allusion to the biblical parable of the talents adds to the meaning of the poem.

REVIEW **SONNET** These two poems follow the **Italian sonnet** form: an **octave** (eight lines) followed by a **sestet** (six lines). The **rhyme scheme** in the octave is *abbaabba;* in the sestet, it is *cdedce* or *cdecde.* For each of the two sonnets, explain the relationship between the content of the octave and the content of the sestet.

from Paradise Lost

Epic poetry by JOHN MILTON

Connect to Your Life

Masterpiece Imagine that you are a writer, a filmmaker, or a creative artist of some other kind and that you are planning to create your finest work ever. What subject might you choose to explore in your masterpiece? On what great works of the past might you draw? What themes might you hope to express? Jot down ideas for your masterpiece. You might organize them in a cluster diagram like this one.

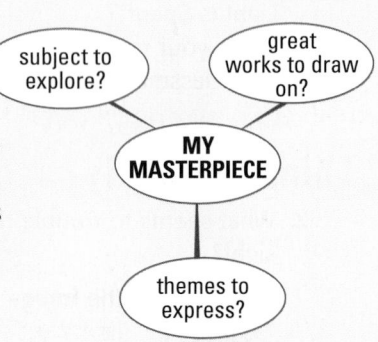

Focus Your Reading

LITERARY ANALYSIS **DICTION** **Diction** is another term for word choice. In *Paradise Lost,* Milton employs the lofty, elevated diction that his exalted **subject** and **themes** demand. Notice how, in the following passage, powerful nouns and verbs are juxtaposed with eloquent adjectives to convey the majestic nature of the event described:

> *. . . Him the Almighty Power*
> *Hurled headlong flaming from th' ethereal*
> *sky*
> *With hideous ruin and combustion down*
> *To bottomless perdition, there to dwell*
> *In adamantine chains and penal fire*

As you read the selection, look for other examples of elevated diction.

ACTIVE READING **CLARIFYING MEANING**
Milton's long, sweeping sentences and elevated diction take some time to appreciate. Here are some obstacles you may encounter, along with suggestions on how to **clarify meaning:**

- **Archaic verb and pronoun forms** (like *dost* for *does* and *thou* for *you*): Think of a familiar word that resembles the unfamiliar form and see if it makes sense in the context; if it does not, consult a dictionary.
- **Obsolete or unfamiliar vocabulary:** See if you can determine meanings from context or from information in the Guide for Reading notes; consult a dictionary when necessary.
- **Allusions** (mainly to people, places, and events in the Bible and in ancient mythology): Use the Guide for Reading notes to help you understand the allusions and their significance.
- **Long, sweeping sentences:** Mentally break each sentence down into parts you can understand; focus on key words, such as the subject and the verb, to get the gist of the sentence's meaning before taking account of qualifiers and interrupters.
- **Unusual word order:** Mentally reorder the words in the sentences so that they sound more natural and make sense to you.

READER'S NOTEBOOK As you encounter difficult passages in this selection, use the strategies suggested above to improve your understanding of them. Write down definitions and explanations to help you remember the meanings of complex lines.

Build Background

Epic Proportions In 1658, when he had been blind for almost a decade, John Milton undertook the composition of his masterpiece, a poem in which he would achieve "things unattempted yet in prose or rhyme." The poem he hoped to create was one that he had had in mind since he was 19, a great Christian epic that would "justify the ways of God to men." It was his hope "that by labor and intent study (which I take to be my portion in this life), joined with the strong propensity of nature, I might perhaps leave something so written to aftertimes, as they should not willingly let it die." In a sense, his whole life was a preparation for this task.

The Blind Milton Dictating to his Daughters (1878), Mihaly von Munkacsy. Oil on canvas, The Granger Collection, New York

Using the biblical account in Genesis as his basic source, he mentally constructed long, flowing sentences in rhythmic blank verse, which he then dictated, 20 or 30 lines at a time, to paid assistants, friends, and relatives, including his three daughters. For seven painstaking years he worked on his ambitious project. The result, *Paradise Lost,* is widely considered to be the finest epic poem in the English language. In it Milton probes the relationships between free will and destiny and between freedom and responsibility. His treatment of these themes is appropriately grand, in the tradition of the ancient epics—Homer's *Iliad* and *Odyssey* and Virgil's *Aeneid*—that were his models.

Rebellion and Its Aftermath Divided into 12 books, *Paradise Lost* is vast in its scope. Milton tells of a heavenly rebellion led by the angel who would come to be known as Satan, who resents God's appointment of his Son to the position of greatest honor and power in Heaven. After the rebel angels are defeated and cast into Hell, Satan vows to corrupt God's latest creation, humanity. This he accomplishes by tempting the first woman, Eve, to disobey God by eating the fruit of the Tree of Knowledge in the Garden of Eden. When Eve and her mate, Adam, realize that they have disobeyed God, they are overcome with grief and despair. Yet they experience God's mercy as well as his wrath and by the end of the epic have some hope for the future: though they have been banished from the Garden of Eden, their exile has been softened by the promise of a Messiah. Milton's *Paradise Regained,* an epic sequel to *Paradise Lost,* presents the fulfillment of that promise.

Engraving by Gustave Doré.

John Milton

from Paradise Lost

*In this excerpt—the opening of Book I—Milton begins his epic like the
ancient epics that were his models, with an invocation of, or call upon,
a Muse, in which the speaker asks for inspiration and sets forth the
subject and themes of the poem. (In Greek mythology, the Muses were
goddesses of learning and the creative arts.) There follows a summary
of how Satan, once among the most powerful of God's angels, was cast
out of Heaven for leading a rebellion against God's rule. Awakening in
Hell alongside Beëlzebub (bē-ĕl′zə-bŭb′), another fallen angel, Satan
considers what he has lost and reaffirms his defiance of God.*

> Of man's first disobedience, and the fruit
> Of that forbidden tree whose mortal taste
> Brought death into the world, and all our woe,
> With loss of Eden, till one greater Man
> 5 Restore us, and regain the blissful seat,
> Sing, Heavenly Muse, that on the secret top
> Of Oreb, or of Sinai, didst inspire
> That shepherd who first taught the chosen seed
> In the beginning how the heavens and earth
> 10 Rose out of Chaos: or, if Sion hill
> Delight thee more, and Siloa's brook that flowed
> Fast by the oracle of God, I thence
> Invoke thy aid to my adventurous song,
> That with no middle flight intends to soar
> 15 Above th' Aonian mount, while it pursues
> Things unattempted yet in prose or rhyme.
> And chiefly thou, O Spirit, that dost prefer
> Before all temples th' upright heart and pure,
> Instruct me, for thou know'st; thou from the first
> 20 Wast present, and with mighty wings outspread
> Dovelike sat'st brooding on the vast abyss,
> And mad'st it pregnant: what in me is dark
> Illumine; what is low, raise and support;

GUIDE FOR READING

4 one greater Man: Jesus Christ.

6 Heavenly Muse: the divine source of Milton's poetic inspiration—here identified with the Spirit of God that the Bible says spoke to Moses (the "shepherd" of line 8).

7 Oreb . . . Sinai: Mounts Horeb and Sinai, on which Moses heard the voice of God.

8 the chosen seed: the Jews.

10–11 Sion Hill . . . Siloa's brook: places in Jerusalem, the holy city of the Jews.

12 fast by the oracle of God: near the Jews' temple in Jerusalem.

15 Aonian (ā-ō′nē-ən) **mount:** Mount Helicon in Greece, which in ancient times was considered sacred to the Muses.

20–22 with mighty wings . . . pregnant: In the Bible, the Spirit of God is described as hovering over the primeval "deep" during the creation of the universe.

That to the height of this great argument
25 I may assert Eternal Providence,
And justify the ways of God to men.
      Say first (for Heaven hides nothing from thy view,
Nor the deep tract of Hell), say first what cause
Moved our grand parents, in that happy state,
30 Favored of Heaven so highly, to fall off
From their Creator, and transgress his will
For one restraint, lords of the world besides?
Who first seduced them to that foul revolt?
      Th' infernal serpent; he it was, whose guile,
35 Stirred up with envy and revenge, deceived
The mother of mankind, what time his pride
Had cast him out from Heaven, with all his host
Of rebel angels, by whose aid aspiring
To set himself in glory above his peers,
40 He trusted to have equaled the Most High,
If he opposed; and with ambitious aim
Against the throne and monarchy of God
Raised impious war in Heaven and battle proud,
With vain attempt. Him the Almighty Power
45 Hurled headlong flaming from th' ethereal sky
With hideous ruin and combustion down
To bottomless perdition, there to dwell
In adamantine chains and penal fire,
Who durst defy th' Omnipotent to arms.
50   Nine times the space that measures day and night
To mortal men, he with his horrid crew
Lay vanquished, rolling in the fiery gulf
Confounded though immortal. But his doom
Reserved him to more wrath; for now the thought
55 Both of lost happiness and lasting pain
Torments him; round he throws his baleful eyes,
That witnessed huge affliction and dismay,
Mixed with obdùrate pride and steadfast hate.
At once, as far as angels ken, he views
60 The dismal situation waste and wild:
A dungeon horrible, on all sides round
As one great furnace flamed; yet from those flames
No light, but rather darkness visible
Served only to discover sights of woe,
65 Regions of sorrow, doleful shades, where peace
And rest can never dwell, hope never comes
That comes to all, but torture without end
Still urges, and a fiery deluge, fed

24 argument: subject.

25 Providence: God's plan for the universe.

26 justify: show the justice of. Milton states his purpose in this line. What assumptions does he make about his own abilities?

29 our grand parents: Adam and Eve.

31 transgress: overstep the limits set by.

32 for: on account of; **besides:** otherwise.

34 th' infernal serpent: Satan, who in the Bible is referred to as "that old serpent" (Revelation 20:2). Later in the poem, it will be in the form of a serpent that Satan will tempt Eve to eat the fruit of the Tree of Knowledge.

36 what time: when.

43 impious (ĭm'pē-əs): showing disrespect for God; sacrilegious.

34–44 These lines introduce the figure of Satan. What is your first impression of him? How does he view God?

45 th' ethereal (ĭ-thîr'ē-əl) **sky:** Heaven.

47 perdition: damnation.

48 adamantine (ăd'ə-măn'tēn'): indestructible; unbreakable.

44–49 What has happened to Satan?

53–54 his doom . . . wrath: fate had more punishment in store for him.

53–56 What is Satan's reaction to his punishment?

58 obdurate (ŏb'dŏō-rĭt): stubborn; unyielding.

62–63 Milton conveys the desolation of hell through a horrifying paradox: flames that give no light, only "darkness visible."

With ever-burning sulphur unconsumed:
70 Such place Eternal Justice had prepared
For those rebellious; here their prison ordained
In utter darkness and their portion set
As far removed from God and light of Heaven
As from the center thrice to th' utmost pole.
75 O how unlike the place from whence they fell!
There the companions of his fall, o'erwhelmed
With floods and whirlwinds of tempestuous fire,
He soon discerns; and, weltering by his side,
One next himself in power, and next in crime,
80 Long after known in Palestine, and named
Beëlzebub. To whom th' arch-enemy,
And thence in Heaven called Satan, with bold words
Breaking the horrid silence thus began:
    "If thou beëst he—but O how fallen! how changed
85 From him who in the happy realms of light
Clothed with transcendent brightness didst outshine
Myriads, though bright! if he whom mutual league,
United thoughts and counsels, equal hope
And hazard in the glorious enterprise,
90 Joined with me once, now misery hath joined
In equal ruin; into what pit thou seest
From what height fallen, so much the stronger proved
He with his thunder: and till then who knew
The force of those dire arms? Yet not for those,
95 Nor what the potent Victor in his rage
Can else inflict, do I repent or change,
Though changed in outward luster, that fixed mind
And high disdain, from sense of injured merit,
That with the Mightiest raised me to contend,
100 And to the fierce contention brought along
Innumerable force of spirits armed,
That durst dislike his reign, and me preferring,
His utmost power with adverse power opposed
In dubious battle on the plains of Heaven,
105 And shook his throne. What though the field be lost?
All is not lost: the unconquerable will,
And study of revenge, immortal hate,
And courage never to submit or yield:
And what is else not to be overcome?
110 That glory never shall his wrath or might
Extort from me. To bow and sue for grace
With suppliant knee, and deify his power
Who from the terror of this arm so late

73–74 as far . . . utmost pole: a reference to a passage in Virgil's *Aeneid,* which states that Tartarus (hell) is twice as far below the surface of the earth as the heavens are above it.

75 What must Heaven be like if it is the opposite of Hell?

78 weltering: writhing; thrashing about.

80 Palestine (păl'ĭ-stīn'): here, the land of the Phoenicians, who worshiped the god Baal.

81 Beëlzebub: a powerful demon, called "the prince of the devils" in the Bible (Matthew 12:24) and identified with the Phoenician god Baal.

81–82 th' arch-enemy . . . Satan: The name *Satan* comes from a Hebrew word meaning "adversary," or "enemy."

84 Who is speaking here, and to whom is he speaking?

94–99 What does Satan refuse to change?

107 study: pursuit.

110 To whom does "his" refer here?

112 with suppliant (sŭp'lē-ənt) **knee:** kneeling in a begging posture.

Doubted his empire—that were low indeed;
That were an ignominy and shame beneath
This downfall; since, by fate, the strength of gods
And this empyreal substance cannot fail;
Since, through experience of this great event,
In arms not worse, in foresight much advanced,
We may with more successful hope resolve
To wage by force or guile eternal war,
Irreconcilable to our grand Foe,
Who now triùmphs, and in th' excess of joy
Sole reigning holds the tyranny of Heaven."
So spake th' apostate angel, though in pain,
Vaunting aloud, but racked with deep despair;
And him thus answered soon his bold compeer:
"O prince, O chief of many thronèd powers,
That led th' embattled seraphim to war
Under thy conduct, and in dreadful deeds
Fearless, endangered Heaven's perpetual King,
And put to proof his high supremacy,
Whether upheld by strength, or chance, or fate!
Too well I see and rue the dire event
That with sad overthrow and foul defeat
Hath lost us Heaven, and all this mighty host
In horrible destruction laid thus low,
As far as gods and heavenly essences
Can perish: for the mind and spirit remains
Invincible, and vigor soon returns,
Though all our glory extinct, and happy state
Here swallowed up in endless misery.
But what if he our Conqueror (whom I now
Of force believe almighty, since no less
Than such could have o'erpowered such force as ours)
Have left us this our spirit and strength entire,
Strongly to suffer and support our pains,
That we may so suffice his vengeful ire,
Or do him mightier service as his thralls
By right of war, whate'er his business be,
Here in the heart of Hell to work in fire,
Or do his errands in the gloomy deep?
What can it then avail though yet we feel
Strength undiminished, or eternal being
To undergo eternal punishment?"
Whereto with speedy words th' arch-fiend replied:
"Fallen cherub, to be weak is miserable,
Doing or suffering: but of this be sure,
To do aught good never will be our task,

114 doubted: feared for.

115 ignominy (ĭg'nə-mĭn'ē): disgrace.

117 this empyreal (ĕm-pîr'ē-əl) **substance:** the heavenly material of which the angels' bodies are made.

125 apostate (ə-pŏs'tāt'): renegade.

126 vaunting: boasting.

127 compeer (kəm-pîr'): companion of equal rank.

128 Who begins speaking here?

129 seraphim (sĕr'ə-fĭm): an order of angels.

144 of force: necessarily.

148 suffice (sə-fīs'): satisfy fully.

149 thralls: slaves.

143–155 Beëlzebub suggests that God has left the fallen angels their strength so that their suffering will be increased or so that he can use them for his own purposes. Then Beëlzebub asks what use in that case ("what can it then avail") the fallen angels' strength and eternal life will be to them.

157 cherub: angel.

160 But ever to do ill our sole delight,
As being the contrary to his high will
Whom we resist. If then his providence
Out of our evil seek to bring forth good,
Our labor must be to pervert that end,
165 And out of good still to find means of evil;
Which ofttimes may succeed, so as perhaps
Shall grieve him, if I fail not, and disturb
His inmost counsels from their destined aim.
But see! the angry Victor hath recalled
170 His ministers of vengeance and pursuit
Back to the gates of Heaven; the sulphurous hail,
Shot after us in storm, o'erblown hath laid
The fiery surge that from the precipice
Of Heaven received us falling; and the thunder,
175 Winged with red lightning and impetuous rage,
Perhaps hath spent his shafts, and ceases now
To bellow through the vast and boundless deep.
Let us not slip th' occasion, whether scorn
Or satiate fury yield it from our Foe.
180 Seest thou yon dreary plain, forlorn and wild,
The seat of desolation, void of light,
Save what the glimmering of these livid flames
Casts pale and dreadful? Thither let us tend
From off the tossing of these fiery waves;
185 There rest, if any rest can harbor there;
And reassembling our afflicted powers,
Consult how we may henceforth most offend
Our enemy, our own loss how repair,
How overcome this dire calamity,
190 What reinforcement we may gain from hope,
If not, what resolution from despair."
　　　Thus Satan talking to his nearest mate
With head uplift above the wave, and eyes
That sparkling blazed; his other parts besides
195 Prone on the flood, extended long and large
Lay floating many a rood, in bulk as huge
As whom the fables name of monstrous size,
Titanian or Earth-born, that warred on Jove,
Briareos or Typhon, whom the den
200 By ancient Tarsus held, or that sea beast
Leviathan, which God of all his works
Created hugest that swim th' ocean-stream.
Him, haply, slumbering on the Norway foam,
The pilot of some small night-foundered skiff,
205 Deeming some island, oft, as seamen tell,

167 fail not: am not mistaken.

172 laid: calmed.

175 impetuous (ĭm-pĕch'ŏŏ-əs): violently forceful.

171–177 What change is Satan describing in these lines?

178 slip th' occasion: miss the chance.

179 satiate (sā'shē-ĭt): satisfied.

186 powers: troops.

190 reinforcement: increase of strength.

180–191 What does Satan propose?

196 rood: a unit of measure, between six and eight yards.

197–200 as whom . . . Tarsus held: In Greek mythology, both the huge Titans—of whom Briareos was one—and the earth-born giant Typhon battled unsuccessfully against Jove (Zeus), just as Satan rebelled against God. Zeus defeated Typhon in Asia Minor, near the town of Tarsus.

201 Leviathan (lə-vī'ə-thən): a huge sea beast mentioned in the Bible—here identified with the whale by Milton.

204 night-foundered: overtaken by the darkness of night.

With fixèd anchor in his scaly rind
Moors by his side under the lee, while night
Invests the sea, and wishèd morn delays:
So stretched out huge in length the arch-fiend lay,
210 Chained on the burning lake; nor ever thence
Had risen or heaved his head, but that the will
And high permission of all-ruling Heaven
Left him at large to his own dark designs,
That with reiterated crimes he might
215 Heap on himself damnation, while he sought
Evil to others, and enraged might see
How all his malice served but to bring forth
Infinite goodness, grace, and mercy shown
On man by him seduced, but on himself
220 Treble confusion, wrath, and vengeance poured.
　　Forthwith upright he rears from off the pool
His mighty stature; on each hand the flames
Driven backward slope their pointing spires, and rolled
In billows, leave i' th' midst a horrid vale.
225 Then with expanded wings he steers his flight
Aloft, incumbent on the dusky air,
That felt unusual weight; till on dry land
He lights, if it were land that ever burned
With solid, as the lake with liquid fire,
230 And such appeared in hue; as when the force
Of subterranean wind transports a hill
Torn from Pelorus or the shattered side
Of thundering Etna, whose combustible
And fuelèd entrails thence conceiving fire,
235 Sublimed with mineral fury, aid the winds,
And leave a singèd bottom all involved
With stench and smoke: such resting found the sole
Of unblest feet. Him followed his next mate,
Both glorying to have 'scaped the Stygian flood
240 As gods, and by their own recovered strength,
Not by the sufferance of supernal power.
　　"Is this the region, this the soil, the clime,"
Said then the lost archangel, "this the seat
That we must change for Heaven? this mournful gloom
245 For that celestial light? Be it so, since he
Who now is sovereign can dispose and bid
What shall be right: farthest from him is best,
Whom reason hath equaled, force hath made supreme
Above his equals. Farewell, happy fields,
250 Where joy forever dwells! Hail, horrors! hail,
Infernal world! and thou, profoundest Hell,

208 invests: covers.

196–209 An **epic simile** is a comparison that extends over a number of lines. What two comparisons does Milton make in these lines?

214 reiterated (rē-ĭt′ə-rā′tĭd): repeated.

220 treble: three times as much.

210–220 What do these lines suggest about how much control Satan has over his own destiny?

226 incumbent on: resting upon.

230–231 the force . . . transports a hill: It was formerly thought that earthquakes were caused by underground winds.

232 Pelorus (pə-lōr′əs): a cape on the coast of Sicily.

233 Etna: a volcano near Pelorus.

235 sublimed: vaporized.

236–237 involved with: wrapped in.

239 the Stygian (stĭj′ē-ən) **flood:** the river Styx—in Greek mythology, one of the rivers of the underworld.

241 sufferance: permission. How do Satan and Beëlzebub view their own power in relation to God's power?

Receive thy new possessor, one who brings
A mind not to be changed by place or time.
The mind is its own place, and in itself
255 Can make a Heaven of Hell, a Hell of Heaven.
What matter where, if I be still the same,
And what I should be, all but less than he
Whom thunder hath made greater? Here at least
We shall be free; th' Almighty hath not built
260 Here for his envy, will not drive us hence.
Here we may reign secure; and in my choice
To reign is worth ambition, though in Hell:
Better to reign in Hell than serve in Heaven.
But wherefore let we then our faithful friends,
265 Th' associates and copartners of our loss,
Lie thus astonished on th' oblivious pool,
And call them not to share with us their part
In this unhappy mansion, or once more
With rallied arms to try what may be yet
270 Regained in Heaven, or what more lost in Hell?"

254–255 Why do you think Satan makes this statement?

257 all but less than: second only to.

264 wherefore: why.

266 astonished: stunned; **th' oblivious pool:** the river Lethe—in Greek mythology, a river of the underworld that causes forgetfulness.

268 mansion: dwelling place.

Engraving by Gustave Doré.

Thinking through the LITERATURE

Connect to the Literature

1. **What Do You Think?**
   What is your overall impression of Satan?

   ....
   Comprehension Check
   - Where do the fallen angels find themselves after their rebellion?
   - Whom does Satan talk to?
   ....

Think Critically

2. **ACTIVE READING** **CLARIFYING MEANING** Whom is the **speaker** addressing in lines 1–26? In order to answer this question, review the suggestions for **clarifying meaning** in the Active Reading feature on page 480. Take special note of the technique for breaking down long, sweeping sentences.

3. Do the **details** in the opening invocation give you the impression that the poet is humble, ambitious, or both? Cite details to explain your evaluation.

4. What human characteristics does Satan display?

   THINK ABOUT
   {
   - his past actions
   - his attitude toward God
   - his views of Heaven and Hell

5. In the light of their past, why would Satan and Beëlzebub find Hell especially painful and horrible?

6. Do you think Satan actually believes the statement he makes in line 263? Why or why not?

Extend Interpretations

7. **Critic's Corner** In an essay on Milton, the Victorian historian and literary critic Thomas Babington Macaulay observed, "Poetry which relates to the beings of another world ought to be at once mysterious and picturesque. That of Milton is so." Do you agree? Cite details from the selection to support your evaluation.

8. **Comparing Texts** Compare and contrast Satan with an **epic hero** (such as Beowulf) and with a **tragic hero** (such as Shakespeare's Macbeth). With which **character** would you say he has more in common? Why?

9. **Connect to Life** Satan is greedy for total power in his world. What historical figures have had a similar kind of greed? What are the effects of such greed?

Literary Analysis

DICTION In *Paradise Lost*, Milton employed the powerful, elevated **diction**, or word choice, that his lofty subject and themes demanded. Consider, for example, lines 230–235 of the selection:

> . . . *as when the force*
> *Of <u>subterranean</u> wind transports*
>   *a hill*
> *Torn from Pelorus or the shattered*
>   *side*
> *Of thundering Etna, whose*
>   *<u>combustible</u>*
> *And fuelèd <u>entrails</u> thence*
>   *conceiving fire,*
> *<u>Sublimed</u> with mineral fury . . .*

Milton could have used words less imposing and elevated than those underlined in the lines above. Instead, he chose words that eloquently convey the majesty of his subject and themes.

Paired Activity Choose a passage from *Paradise Lost*, such as the summary of Satan's fall in lines 34–49 or Satan's speech in lines 242–270. In a chart, list words that exemplify Milton's diction in that passage. Then write a synonym of each word you listed. Discuss how Milton's word choice contributes to his powerful, lofty style.

	Milton's Words	**Synonyms**
Nouns	clime (l. 242)	climate
Verbs	dispose (l. 246)	
Modifiers	celestial (l. 245)	

REVIEW **BLANK VERSE** Milton's long, sweeping sentences are cast in the form of blank verse—unrhymed iambic pentameter. Do you find this verse form appropriate for his lofty subject and themes? Explain.

Writing Options

1. Psychological Profile Write a psychological profile of Satan as he is presented in the excerpt from *Paradise Lost* or of the speaker of either of the two sonnets. Briefly describe your subject's personality traits and attitudes.

2. Descriptive Paragraph Write a paragraph in which you describe Hell as it is presented in the excerpt from *Paradise Lost.*

Activities & Explorations

1. *Paradise Lost* **Illustrated** Paint or draw a picture of Satan as he is depicted in the excerpt from *Paradise Lost.* ~ **ART**

2. Musical Accompaniment Set either of Milton's two sonnets to music—either your original composition or a recording that you find suitable. Perform your musical version of the sonnet in class, or record it on audiotape. ~ **MUSIC**

Inquiry & Research

Researching Angels Research an aspect of the Judeo-Christian concept of angels touched on in *Paradise Lost.* For example, you might find out more about the different orders of angels (seraphim, cherubim, and so on) or about the idea of the fall of rebellious angels led by Satan. Present your findings in an oral report.

 More Online: Research Starter www.mcdougallittell.com

John Milton
1608–1674

Other Works
Comus
"Lycidas"
"L'Allegro"
"Il Penseroso"
Areopagitica

Youthful Dreams A devout youth of scholarly bent, Milton seemed destined for the clergy but instead, while still a teenager, decided to become a writer. He dreamed of producing important poetry dealing with religious themes. To that end, he studied Latin, Greek, Hebrew, and most of the modern European languages. His knowledge of Italian allowed him to read *The Divine Comedy*, the great 14th-century Christian poem by Dante Alighieri.

A Contentious Puritan Milton attended Cambridge University, where he was critical of the curriculum and at one point was briefly suspended for arguing with his tutor. He had adversaries in the political arena as well. When civil war erupted in 1642, he devoted his energies to writing political pamphlets for the Puritan faction, or Roundheads, who supported Parliament over the king. For a time the Roundheads triumphed under Oliver Cromwell, and Milton accepted the post of Cromwell's Latin secretary; but after Cromwell's death and the restoration of the monarchy, Milton was arrested for his earlier political activities. He avoided execution or lengthy imprisonment, however—in part through the intercession of his former protégé, the poet Andrew Marvell.

Crowning Achievements By this time, Milton's progressive blindness had become total, but he still managed to complete his masterpiece, *Paradise Lost.* A 10-book version of the poem was published in 1667, and a revised version, in which the poem was divided into 12 books, appeared in 1674, the year of Milton's death. Milton also composed a sequel, *Paradise Regained,* and a drama, *Samson Agonistes,* which was patterned on the tragedies of ancient Greece.

Author Activity

Courtly Entertainment Milton's *Comus* is a masque, a form of drama popular in the Renaissance. Find out why *Comus* was written, what it is about, and where it was first performed.

Female Orations

Debate by MARGARET CAVENDISH, DUCHESS OF NEWCASTLE

(Connect to Your Life)

Privileged Gender? Have you ever felt that members of the opposite sex have special privileges or advantages not available to members of your sex? Have you ever engaged in a dialogue or debate about this subject with members of your own or the opposite sex? Draw up a list of some of the advantages that you think each sex possesses. Then share your list with the class.

Build Background

A Feminist Pioneer Margaret Cavendish lived at a time when female writers were few and tended to concentrate on such subjects as family, religion, romance, and the responsibilities of keeping a household. Modesty was highly valued as a feminine virtue, so most women writers of the time never published their work. Cavendish was keenly aware of the limitations placed on women in her society, yet she published her unorthodox writings despite them. She became the subject of considerable criticism and scorn for publishing her thoughts on subjects that were considered off-limits to female interpretation. In "Female Orations" she records an imaginary debate between women with differing points of view on the role of women in society.

WORDS TO KNOW
Vocabulary Preview

demeanor   subsistence
eloquently   unconscionable
enticing

Focus Your Reading

LITERARY ANALYSIS | **ARGUMENTATION** | Speech or writing intended to convince an audience that a proposal should be adopted or rejected is called **argumentation.** An argument may be developed in an essay, in a speech, or in a debate like that in "Female Orations." As you read this work, look for the arguments Cavendish presents for and against women's rights.

ACTIVE READING | **ANALYZING THE STRUCTURE OF ARGUMENTS** | The overall structure of "Female Orations" is an imaginary debate in which seven women express different points of view. The arguments of the individual speakers, however, contain examples of other structures. For example, the first speaker uses a **comparison-contrast structure,** comparing the conditions of men and women. The fourth speaker uses a **problem-and-solution structure,** arguing that lack of strength and wit can be overcome by means of exercise and conversation.

1st speaker's argument:

2nd speaker's argument:

3rd speaker's argument:

READER'S NOTEBOOK As you read "Female Orations," take note of the argument set forth by each speaker. Also note other examples of comparison-contrast and problem-solution structures that you find.

Female Orations

MARGARET CAVENDISH,
DUCHESS OF NEWCASTLE

Young Woman Standing at a Virginal (about 1670),
Jan Vermeer. The Granger Collection, New York.

I

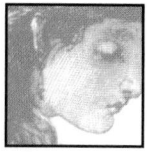

Ladies, gentlewomen, and other inferior women, but not less worthy: I have been industrious to assemble you together, and wish I were so fortunate as to persuade you to make frequent assemblies, associations, and combinations amongst our sex, that we may unite in prudent counsels, to make ourselves as free, happy, and famous as men; whereas now we live and die as if we were produced from beasts, rather than from men; for men are happy, and we women are miserable; they possess all the ease, rest, pleasure, wealth, power, and fame; whereas women are restless with labor, easeless with pain, melancholy for want of pleasures, helpless for want of power, and die in oblivion, for want of fame. Nevertheless, men are so <u>unconscionable</u> and cruel against us that they endeavor to bar us of all sorts of liberty, and will not suffer us freely to associate amongst our own sex; but would fain[1] bury us in their houses or beds, as in a grave. The truth is, we live like bats or owls, labor like beasts, and die like worms.

II

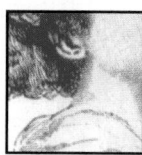

Ladies, gentlewomen, and other inferior women: The lady that spoke to you hath spoken wisely and <u>eloquently,</u> in expressing our unhappiness; but she hath not declared a remedy, or showed us a way to come out of our miseries; but, if she could or would be our guide, to lead us out of the labyrinth men have put us into, we should not only praise and admire her, but adore and worship her as our goddess: but alas! men, that are not only our tyrants but our devils, keep us in the hell of subjection, from whence I cannot perceive any redemption or getting out; we may complain and bewail our condition, yet that will not free us; we may murmur and rail against men, yet they regard not what we say. In short, our words to men are as empty sounds; our sighs, as puffs of winds; and our tears, as fruitless showers; and our power is so inconsiderable, that men laugh at our weakness.

III

Ladies, gentlewomen, and other inferior women: The former orations were exclamations against men, repining[2] at their condition and mourning for our own; but we have no reason to speak against men, who are our admirers and lovers; they are our protectors, defenders, and maintainers; they admire our beauties, and love our persons; they protect us from injuries, defend us from dangers, are industrious for our <u>subsistence,</u> and provide for our children; they swim great voyages by sea, travel long journeys by land, to get us rarities and curiosities; they dig to the center of the earth for gold for us; they dive to the bottom of the sea for jewels for us: they build to the skies houses for us: they hunt, fowl, fish, plant, and reap for food for us. All which, we could not do ourselves; and yet we complain of men, as if they were our enemies, whenas[3] we could not possibly live without them, which shows we are as ungrateful as inconstant.

---

1. **fain:** gladly.
2. **repining:** complaining.
3. **whenas:** when in fact.

495

But we have more reason to murmur against Nature, than against men, who hath made men more ingenious, witty,[4] and wise than women; more strong, industrious, and laborious than women; for women are witless and strengthless, and unprofitable creatures, did they not bear children. Wherefore, let us love men, praise men, and pray for men; for without men, we should be the most miserable creatures that Nature hath made or could make.

IV

Noble ladies, gentlewomen, and other inferior women: The former oratoress says we are witless and strengthless; if so, it is that we neglect the one and make no use of the other, for strength is increased by exercise, and wit is lost for want of conversation. But to show men we are not so weak and foolish as the former oratoress doth express us to be, let us hawk, hunt, race, and do the like exercises that men have; and let us converse in camps,[5] courts, and cities; in schools, colleges, and courts of judicature; in taverns, brothels, and gaming houses; all of which will make our strength and wit known, both to men and to our own selves, for we are as ignorant of ourselves as men are of us. And how should we know ourselves, when we never made a trial of ourselves? Or how should men know us, when they never put us to the proof? Wherefore my advice is, we should imitate men; so will our bodies and minds appear more masculine, and our power will increase by our actions.

V

Noble, honorable, and virtuous women: The former oration was to persuade us to change the custom of our sex, which is a strange and unwise persuasion, since we cannot change the nature of our sex, nor make ourselves men; and to have female bodies, and yet to act masculine parts, will be very preposterous and unnatural. In truth, we shall make ourselves like the defects of Nature, and be hermaphroditical,[6] neither perfect women, nor perfect men, but corrupt and imperfect creatures. Wherefore let me persuade you, since we cannot alter the nature of our persons, not to alter the course of our lives; but to rule so our lives and behaviors that we be acceptable and pleasing to God and men; which is, to be modest, chaste, temperate, humble, patient, and pious; also, be housewifely, cleanly, and of few words. All which will gain us praise from men and blessing from Heaven; love in this world and glory in the next.

VI

Worthy women: The former oratoress's oration endeavored to persuade us that it would not only be a reproach and disgrace, but unnatural, for women in their actions and behavior to imitate men: we may as well say it will be a reproach, disgrace, and unnatural to imitate the gods, which imitation we are commanded both by the gods and their ministers; and shall we neglect the imitation of men, which is more easy and natural than the imitation of the gods? For how can terrestrial[7] creatures imitate celestial deities?[8] Yet one terrestrial may imitate another, although in different sorts of creatures. Wherefore, since all terrestrial imitations ought to ascend to the

---

4. **witty:** intelligent.

5. **camps:** military encampments.

6. **hermaphroditical** (hər-măf′rə-dĭt′ĭ-kəl): having both male and female characteristics in one body.

7. **terrestrial:** earthly.

8. **celestial deities:** heavenly gods.

better and not to descend to the worse, women ought to imitate men, as being a degree in nature more perfect than they themselves; and all masculine women ought to be as much praised as effeminate men to be dispraised; for the one advances to perfection, the other sinks to imperfection; that so, by our industry, we may come, at last, to equal men, both in perfection and power.

VII

 **Noble ladies, honorable gentlewomen, and worthy female-commoners:** The former oratoress's speech was to persuade us out of ourselves and to be that which Nature never intended us to be, to wit, masculine. But why should we desire to be masculine, since our own sex and condition is far the better? For if men have more courage, they have more danger; and if men have more strength, they have more labor than women have; if men are more eloquent in speech, women are more harmonious in voice; if men be more active, women are more graceful; if men have more liberty, women have more safety; for we never fight duels nor battles; nor do we go long travels or dangerous voyages; we labor not in building nor digging in mines, quarries, or pits, for metal, stone, or coals; neither do we waste or shorten our lives with university or scholastical studies, questions, and disputes; we burn not our faces with smiths' forges or chemists'[9] furnaces; and hundreds of other actions which men are employed in; for they would not only fade the fresh beauty, spoil the lovely features, and decay the youth of women, causing them to appear old, when they are young; but would break their small limbs, and destroy their tender lives. Wherefore women have no reason to complain against Nature or the god of Nature, for although the gifts are not the same as they have given to men, yet those gifts they have given to women are much better; for we women are much more favored by Nature than men, in giving us such beauties, features, shapes, graceful <u>demeanor</u>, and such insinuating and <u>enticing</u> attractives, that men are forced to admire us, love us, and be desirous of us; insomuch that rather than not have and enjoy us, they will deliver to our disposals their power, persons, and lives, enslaving themselves to our will and pleasures; also, we are their saints, whom they adore and worship; and what can we desire more than to be men's tyrants, destinies, and goddesses? ❖

---

9. **chemists':** alchemists'.

from Eve's Apology in Defense of Women

Amelia Lanier

Adam Tempted by Eve (1517), Hans Holbein the Younger. Öffentliche Kunstsammlung Basel, Switzerland (313).

In the biblical Book of Genesis, Eve is tempted by a serpent to eat the fruit of the forbidden tree of knowledge, and she, in turn, offers it to Adam. As a result of their disobedience, God expels them from the Garden of Eden, taking away the gift of human immortality. These stanzas are from Amelia Lanier's defense of Eve, in which the poet (1570?–1640?) adopts a position that was quite radical in its time.

But surely Adam cannot be excused;
Her fault though great, yet he was most to blame.
What weakness offered, strength might have refused;
Being lord of all, the greater was his shame;
5 Although the serpent's craft had her abused,
God's holy word ought all his actions frame;
　　For he was lord and king of all the earth,
　　Before poor Eve had either life or breath,

Who being framed by God's eternal hand
10 The perfectest man that ever breathed on earth,
And from God's mouth received that strait command,
The breach whereof he knew was present death;
Yea, having power to rule both sea and land,
Yet with one apple won to lose that breath
15 　　Which God had breathéd in his beauteous face,
　　Bringing us all in danger and disgrace;

And then to lay the fault on patience's back,
That we (poor women) must endure it all;
We know right well he did discretion lack,
20 Being not persuaded thereunto at all.
If Eve did err, it was for knowledge sake;
The fruit being fair persuaded him to fall.
　　No subtle serpent's falsehood did betray him;
　　If he would eat it, who had power to stay him?

25 Not Eve, whose fault was only too much love,
Which made her give this present to her dear,
That what she tasted he likewise might prove,
Whereby his knowledge might become more clear;
He never sought her weakness to reprove
30 With those sharp words which he of God did hear;
　　Yet men will boast of knowledge, which he took
　　From Eve's fair hand, as from a learned book.

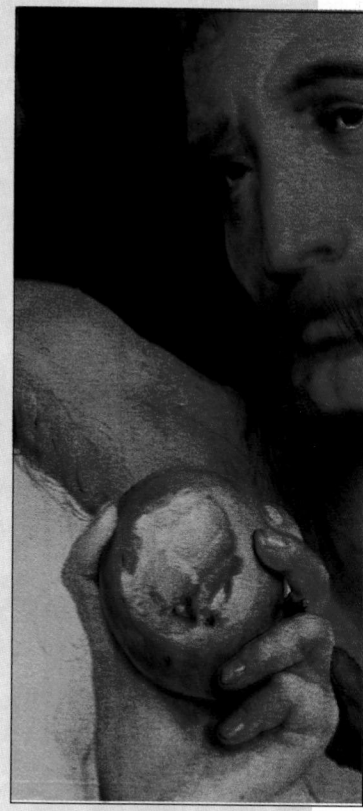

Thinking through the LITERATURE

Connect to the Literature

1. **What Do You Think?** Which of the seven speakers makes the most sense to you?

   Comprehension Check
   - What is the third speaker's attitude toward men?
   - Does the seventh speaker regard women as inferior or superior to men?

Think Critically

2. How does the third speaker's **argument** compare with those of the two preceding speakers?

3. What seems to have been the role of women in the society of the time?

    THINK ABOUT
   - public life
   - family life
   - household management
   - political and military affairs

4. Why do you think Cavendish presented a variety of viewpoints?

5. **ACTIVE READING** **ANALYZING THE STRUCTURE OF ARGUMENTS** Look back at the notes you took in your **READER'S NOTEBOOK**. What examples of comparison-contrast and problem-solution structures did you find?

Extend Interpretations

6. **Comparing Texts** Consider the view of the relationship between men and women expressed in the excerpt from "Eve's Apology in Defense of Women." How is it similar to or different from the view of one or more of the speakers in "Female Orations"?

7. **Different Perspectives** How might a male speaker have responded to the speeches in "Female Orations"?

8. **Connect to Life** Do you think Cavendish believed in equality of the sexes as we understand it today? Support your opinion.

Literary Analysis

> **ARGUMENTATION**

Argumentation is speech or writing intended to convince an audience that a proposal should be adopted or rejected. Most arguments begin with a statement of an idea or opinion, which is then supported with logical evidence. Another technique of argumentation is the anticipation and rebuttal of opposing views. In "Female Orations," Cavendish presents a number of different arguments through the mouths of the seven speakers.

Cooperative Learning Activity With six classmates, read aloud to the rest of the class the seven speeches that make up this imaginary debate. Try to make your reading sound like a real debate, with each speaker directing her response to the preceding speaker.

> **ACTIVE READING** **WRITER'S MOTIVATION AND TEXT STRUCTURE**

A writer's motivation can affect the form, or structure, he or she uses to express ideas. Cavendish examines ideas and arguments about the roles and rights of women in the form of a debate between seven speakers, who voice a variety of opinions. Think about Cavendish's possible motivation for writing about the position of women. Think also about the society in which she lived. Why do you think she cast the orations as debates?

Choices&CHALLENGES

Writing Options

Argument Outline Imagine that you are an eighth speaker in this debate. Write an outline of the main points of your response to the seven speakers who have preceded you. What additional points, not touched on by them, might you wish to address?

Activities & Explorations

Mural Design Sketch a design for a wall mural showing the roles of women in society today. ~ **ART**

Inquiry & Research

Women in the 17th Century Do some research to find out about famous women of the 17th century. What did they do to achieve fame? Choose a woman who interests you and write a two- or three-paragraph summary of her life and achievements.

Vocabulary in Action

EXERCISE: CONTEXT CLUES Read each sentence below. On your paper, indicate whether the boldfaced word is used correctly or incorrectly.

1. One of the speakers in Cavendish's imaginary debate says that the preceding speaker spoke **eloquently** and intelligently.
2. Another of the speakers admires men for their kind and **unconscionable** behavior.
3. There must have been a large **subsistence** of women who were dissatisfied with their lives.
4. Cavendish pitied women whose sole purpose in life was to appear **enticing** to men.
5. In the 17th century, men were sometimes willing to listen to a woman's **demeanor.**

WORDS TO KNOW	demeanor eloquently enticing	subsistence unconscionable

Building Vocabulary
For an in-depth study of context clues, see page 938.

Margaret Cavendish
1623?–1674

Early Years Born Margaret Lucas, Margaret Cavendish was two years old when her father died. Her mother, who assumed control of the family's extensive estate, was regarded as a shrewd and ambitious businessperson and, as a result, was not well liked by her neighbors. The Lucas family further alienated their neighbors by allying themselves with the monarchy during the conflicts between the king and Parliament. Margaret became an attendant to the queen, whom she accompanied to Paris in 1645. There she met and married William Cavendish, the duke of Newcastle.

Civil War and Exile As an English nobleman and supporter of the monarchy, the duke had voluntarily fled to France during England's civil war. As the new duchess of Newcastle, Margaret Cavendish was forced to live in exile as well, and in poverty, until the monarchy was restored. It was during her exile that the childless Cavendish began writing with the intent of publishing her work.

After the Restoration After the restoration of the monarchy, Cavendish and her husband returned to England, where she began to pursue a literary career in earnest. Cavendish wrote about science, mathematics, and philosophy—subjects considered beyond the capacities of women in the 17th century—and produced numerous works of poetry, prose, and drama. Her bold writings and strange manner earned her the nickname Mad Madge of Newcastle. Her husband, however, supported her throughout and at her death wrote that "This Dutches was a wise, wittie and learned Lady, which her many Bookes do well testifie."

John Bunyan

The Pilgrim's Progress

"This Book will make a Traveller of thee." So claims John Bunyan in the Author's Apology to *The Pilgrim's Progress* (1678). The author's promise is all the more striking because he wrote much of this prose masterpiece while in prison. However, the "travel" Bunyan had in mind was not literal: it was a spiritual journey that reflected the author's own religious experiences and beliefs.

These beliefs were formed during a turbulent period in English history—the time of the English civil war and of Oliver Cromwell's Puritan-dominated government, which ruled after the defeat of the monarchy in 1649. During this time, Bunyan, a traveling mender of pots and pans who had little formal education, plunged into a lengthy spiritual crisis. He emerged a devout Christian and lay preacher. When the monarchy was restored in 1660 and Charles II sought to suppress religious dissent, Bunyan was imprisoned for "preaching without a license." He was jailed twice, for a total of nearly 12 years. While in prison, Bunyan worked on his allegorical "travel guide." *The Pilgrim's Progress* dramatizes the process of religious salvation by tracing the progress of a wayfarer named Christian on his journey through a fallen world. Christian's pilgrimage begins when he leaves the City of Destruction without his wife and relatives, all of whom ridicule his visions of a coming apocalypse. He is urged on by Evangelist, a godly man who directs him to keep his eyes on "yonder shining light."

Christian encounters a series of characters who embody outlooks that are obstacles to salvation. Mr. Worldly Wiseman, for example, gives Christian short-sighted advice to quit his

This wood engraving from a 19th-century edition of The Pilgrim's Progress *shows Christian setting out from the City of Destruction.*

"desperate venture" and move into the village of Morality, which offers the safety and friendship of such men as Legality and Civility.

The allegorical nature of Christian's struggles is clear. At one point he and a companion named Hopeful fall asleep on the grounds of Doubting Castle. They are discovered by Giant Despair and locked in the dungeon. Christian is almost driven to suicide, but eventually he opens the door with a key called Promise. Such symbolism can be traced back to the morality plays of the Middle Ages.

Bunyan's rendering of characters and events, however, is so natural and lifelike that his tale "thrilled many generations of children who did not recognize the allegory," according to the 20th-century English critic W. W. Robson. Bunyan's descriptive details about everyday life and his ear for dialogue reflect the rural England of his time, and the beauty of his language and imagery often transcends his allegorical purpose.

The direct, vivid style and the sense of spiritual urgency in *The Pilgrim's Progress* contributed to its instant success with all social classes. It was so popular, in fact, that six years later Bunyan wrote and published a second part, which portrays the journey to salvation of Christian's wife and children.

In all, Bunyan wrote nearly 60 works, mostly doctrinal tracts. He remains best known for *The Pilgrim's Progress,* which was one of the most widely read works in the English language for over two centuries.

❧

Above:
William Blake's portrayal of the encounter between Christian and Mr. Worldly Wiseman. Illustrations to John Bunyan's "The Pilgrim's Progress" (1824–7) by William Blake. The Frick Collection, New York

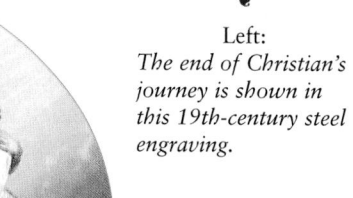

❧

Left:
The end of Christian's journey is shown in this 19th-century steel engraving.

The English Renaissance

From reading this unit, what have you learned about the interests and problems of people who lived during the English Renaissance? What connections have you discovered between life then and your life now? Explore these questions by completing one or more options in each of the following sections.

Reflecting on the Unit

OPTION 1

Drafting an Essay Many of the works in this unit deal with various aspects of the theme of love. Which of these works did you find the most meaningful for life today? Explore this question in a brief essay, drawing connections between the works and experiences you have had, heard about, or witnessed.

OPTION 2

Focusing on Important Issues After reading the selections in this unit, you should be able to identify some of the main issues with which English Renaissance writers were concerned. Develop a list of generalizations about concerns that can be inferred from the selections. To illustrate each generalization, quote a sentence or a line of poetry from the unit. Then, working with your classmates, combine the quotations with appropriate images to create a collage that conveys the spirit of the English Renaissance.

OPTION 3

Interpreting a Quotation Recall the quotation from John Donne at the beginning of this unit: "No man is an island, entire of itself; every man is a piece of the continent, a part of the main." Choose your two favorite writers in this unit (other than Donne himself). Create a diary entry for each of them in which you explore what the writer's reaction to the quotation might be. Then jot down your thoughts about what the quotation means to you.

Self ASSESSMENT

To explore how your understanding of the English Renaissance has developed over the course of the unit, jot down words and phrases that come to mind when you think of this historical period. Then circle at least three words and phrases that you think describe the English Renaissance most accurately. Get together with a partner and compare what the two of you have noted. Feel free to make changes in your own list on the basis of your partner's ideas.

Reviewing Literary Concepts

OPTION 1

Identifying Figurative Language Most of the poetry you have read in this unit contains figurative language, including metaphor, simile, personification, and hyperbole. In a chart like the one shown, name at least two poems in each part of the unit that contain figurative language. Quote an example of figurative language from each poem,

Poems	Example of Figurative Language	Type of Figurative Language
"My Lute, Awake!"	"Perform the last / Labor that thou and I shall waste" (ll. 1–2)	Personification

and note what type of figurative language it is. When you have completed the chart, identify the example of figurative language you find the most interesting or appealing, as well as your reasons for finding it so.

OPTION 2

Shakespearean Drama Review the definitions of *soliloquy, aside, dramatic irony,* and *foreshadowing* on page 324. Then look back through *Macbeth* and find one or two examples of each of these literary techniques. Get together with a partner and compare the examples you chose.

Self ASSESSMENT

Copy the following list of literary terms introduced in this unit. Rank the terms to show your understanding of their meanings, from 1 (the terms that you feel you understand most fully) to 5 (the terms you understand the least). Your ranking should help you decide which concepts you need to review.

rhyme scheme	foreshadowing
pastoral	theme
sonnet	repetition
Spenserian sonnet	parable
	essay
Shakespearean sonnet	extended metaphor
figurative language	epitaph
Italian sonnet	hyperbole
soliloquy	allusion
aside	diction
blank verse	argumentation
dramatic irony	

📁 Building Your Portfolio

- **Writing Options** Several of the Writing Options in this unit asked you to analyze attitudes and ideas presented in the selections. Choose two pieces of writing that you think represent your best attempts at analyzing the literature in this unit. Write a cover note supporting your choices, then add the note and the two pieces to your **Presentation Portfolio.** 📁

- **Writing Workshop** Earlier in this unit, you worked on a Research Report that had you investigate a topic that intrigued you. Look over your report and evaluate your work on the basis of the following:

  Did your writing stay focused on your thesis statement?

  Was your information organized?

  Were your conclusions supported by thorough research?

  Write the answers to these questions on a note that you attach to your report. Then place the report in your **Presentation Portfolio.** 📁

- **Additional Activities** Reflect on the various assignments you completed under **Activities & Explorations** and **Inquiry & Research.** Which activities proved to be the most rewarding? Write a note that explains your choice, and add it to your **Presentation Portfolio.** 📁

Self ASSESSMENT

Now that you have a handful of writing pieces in your portfolio, look them over and decide which are examples of your strongest work. Are there any pieces that you consider weak and may wish to replace as the year goes on?

Setting GOALS

As you worked through the reading and writing activities in this unit, you probably became more aware of your interests and abilities. Are there any skills on which you feel you still need improvement? Are there any particular writers or genres that you would like to investigate further? Create a list of these skills and interests.

LITERATURE CONNECTIONS

HAMLET

WILLIAM SHAKESPEARE

AND RELATED READINGS

McDougal Littell

LITERATURE CONNECTIONS
Hamlet

WILLIAM SHAKESPEARE

Hamlet, Shakespeare's best-known and most frequently performed play, is a tragedy of revenge, betrayal, and inner conflict. Like *Macbeth,* the play involves the murder of a king and the seizing of the crown by an unlawful usurper. Hamlet seeks revenge against his father's murderer in a story involving sword fights, poison, and duels.

These thematically related readings are provided along with *Hamlet:*

from Introduction to Hamlet
BY DAVID BEVINGTON

Father and Son
BY STANLEY KUNITZ

Ophelia
BY ARTHUR RIMBAUD

The Management of Grief
BY BHARATI MUKHERJEE

Tell Them Not to Kill Me!
BY JUAN RULFO

Hamlet
BY YEVGENY VINOKUROV

Japanese Hamlet
BY TOSHIO MORI

And Even *More . . .*

Mary Queen of Scots

ANTONIA FRASER

This heartwarming biography of a queen caught in the political and religious turmoil of Elizabethan England provides not only a vivid picture of the context of Mary's life but a clear portrait of her as a person. Mary was next in line to succeed to the throne of England, held at the time by her cousin, Elizabeth I. Elizabeth suspected Mary of treason and a fatal struggle ensued.

Books
The Succession: A Novel of Elizabeth and James
GEORGE GARRETT
A fictionalized account of political events in England at the time that Shakespeare was writing his plays.

Shakespeare: His Life, Work, and Era
DENNIS KAY
Excellent account of Shakespeare's life, with extensive background.

Light Thickens
NGAIO MARSH
Detective story involving a production of *Macbeth* that is truly cursed.

A Midsummer Night's Dream

WILLIAM SHAKESPEARE

The line between illusion and reality blurs in this fun-filled comedy featuring the escapades of mischievous fairies and spellbound young lovers in an enchanted forest. After a wild night of love potions, magical transformations, and confusion, harmony is restored, love is set right, and weddings are celebrated.

These thematically related readings are provided along with *A Midsummer Night's Dream*:

A Midsummer Night's Dream
BY NORRIE EPSTEIN

The Song of Wandering Aengus
BY WILLIAM BUTLER YEATS

The Sweet Miracle / El Dulce Milagro
BY JUANA DE IBARBOUROU

April Witch
BY RAY BRADBURY

Come. And Be My Baby
BY MAYA ANGELOU

Love's Initiations
BY THOMAS MOORE

The Sensible Thing
BY F. SCOTT FITZGERALD

from **Love and Marriage**
BY BILL COSBY

A Preface to Milton
LOIS POTTER
The author examines Milton's life and work to show his commitment to intellectual freedom and love of learning.

Witches & Jesuits: Shakespeare's *Macbeth*
GARY WILLS
A discussion of the theological and political crises that formed the backdrop for *Macbeth,* in particular the Gunpowder Plot of 1605.

Other Media

English Literature on Video: Shakespeare and the Globe
An educational program that retraces Shakespeare's life and work. Films for the Humanities.
(VIDEOCASSETTE)

Macbeth
This version stars Orson Welles, Jeanette Nolan, and Roddy McDowall. Directed by Orson Welles. NTA Home Entertainment.
(VIDEOCASSETTE)

Metaphysical and Devotional Poetry
Films for the Humanities & Sciences.
(VIDEOCASSETTE)

Shakespeare's Sonnets
Films for the Humanities & Sciences.
(VIDEOCASSETTE)

Throne of Blood
Excellent Japanese film adaptation with a Samurai setting. Directed by Akira Kurosawa. Rental: Films, Inc. Lease: Macmillan Films.
(VIDEOCASSETTE)

Reading&Writing for Assessment

Throughout high school, you will be tested on your ability to read and understand many different kinds of reading selections. These tests will assess your basic understanding of ideas and knowledge of vocabulary. They will also check your ability to analyze and evaluate both the message of the text and the techniques the writer uses in getting that message across.

The following pages will give you test-taking strategies. Practice applying these strategies by working through each of the models provided.

PART 1 How to Read a Test Selection

In many tests, you will read a passage and then answer multiple-choice questions about it. Applying the basic test-taking strategies that follow, taking notes, and highlighting or underscoring passages as you read can help you focus on the information you will need to know.

STRATEGIES FOR READING A TEST SELECTION

▷ **Before you begin reading, skim the questions that follow the passage.** These can help focus your reading.

▷ **Use your active reading strategies such as analyzing, predicting, and questioning.** Make notes in the margin or highlight key words and passages to help you focus your reading. You may do this only if the test directions allow you to mark on the test itself.

▷ **Think about the title.** What does it suggest about the overall message or theme of the selection?

▷ **Look for main ideas.** These are often stated at the beginnings or ends of paragraphs. Sometimes they are implied, not stated. After reading each paragraph, ask "What was this passage about?"

▷ **Note the literary elements and techniques used by the writer.** You might consider the writer's introduction, use of quotations, or descriptive language. Then ask yourself what effect the writer achieves with each choice.

▷ **Unlock word meanings.** Use context clues and word parts to help you unlock the meaning of unfamiliar words.

▷ **Think about the message or theme.** What larger lesson can you draw from the passage? Can you infer anything or make generalizations about other similar situations, human beings, or life in general?

Network Helps Children Cope With Serious Illness
by Catherine Greenman

1   When 16-year-old Thricia DrePaul logged onto Starbright World, a computer network for hospitalized children, she usually chose to be a silver pony, her favorite character of the 40 offered. Although she was comfortable trading messages with any of the other children roaming the three-dimensional landscape, the idea of entering the network's video-conferencing and talking face to face with someone was intimidating to her.

2   **②** But two weeks after her kidney transplant, Thricia decided to give it a shot. She propped herself up in her bed at Mount Sinai Medical Center in New York to look at a computer monitor and exchange a few words with Chris, a 13-year-old asthma patient at Children's Hospital of Pittsburgh. "I don't know what to say," she whispered to Karen Marcinczyk, a therapist in the Child Life program at Mount Sinai who pointed a video camera toward Thricia and handed her a small microphone. "Why don't you say 'Hi,' and ask him what his name is?" she coaxed.

3   Chris, no stranger to Starbright's video-conferencing, stared into his monitor and called out an introduction. He had already met children on line from hospitals in Dallas, Minneapolis, and Seattle. "Hi, I'm Chris," he said. "What are you in the hospital for?" Thricia told him, and he admired a stuffed animal he spotted on her pillow. With slight delays after each giddy sentence, Thricia and Chris continued a conversation that spanned the weather, hospital food, and how long each would be in the hospital. Then Thricia had to say goodbye to have her blood pressure taken. Afterward, she said she was glad she had tried video-conferencing and that she might try to find someone else to talk to the next day.

4   Encounters like this, as well as text- and audio-only chats, occur about 30 times a day within Starbright World, a password-protected service started by the Starbright Foundation. . . .
③ The goal of the network is to create a community on line for seriously ill children that will educate them and help them cope with the difficulties of hospitalization. . . .

5   Because most hospitals in the program have three to five computer terminals in their children's wards to dedicate to Starbright World, computer time is allotted to the children with the most acute needs. "In some cases, such as when a child is in isolation, we roll the computer into the hospital room on a cart, and it stays there for the entire isolation period," said Merri Fishman, manager of the Child Life program at Mount Sinai. Otherwise, the children go to the hospital schoolroom or playroom to log on.

STRATEGIES
IN ACTION

❶ Think about the title.

ONE STUDENT'S THOUGHTS

"If I hadn't read the title I would think this selection was going to be about Thricia DrePaul—but the title suggests it will be about a computer network."

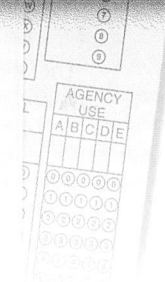

❷ Notice the writer's technique at the beginning.

"By telling me Thricia's story, the writer creates a strong introduction."

YOUR TURN

What other techniques does the writer use to keep you interested?

❸ Look for main ideas.

"This selection is about Starbright World and how it helps seriously ill children."

YOUR TURN

What other key ideas have been introduced so far?

6   Though enough personal computers are not always available, the prospect of communicating with someone in Starbright World can help motivate a child to get out of bed and walk down the hall. Ms. Fishman remembered a time last year when two patients on the same hall started chatting with each other over the network. ❹ "Although they were both immobilized and couldn't meet for a long time, they were really able to cheer each other on," she said.

7   Diane Rode, director of the Child Life program at Mount Sinai, agreed that Starbright World gave hospitalized children a sense of connectedness and a forum for self-expression, but she emphasized the importance of giving them a context in which to express themselves. ❺ "Hooking kids up with other kids in similar situations is not a new idea for us," she said. "It's existed in support groups and over the phone for years. After the initial thrill of seeing and talking to someone on a computer screen goes away, it helps if the kids can share a sense of purpose."

8   For this reason, Ms. Rode uses computer technology in the same way she uses art, music or any other therapeutic medium. "I take issue with, 'Here's a sick child; we'll give him a computer and make his life better,' " she said. "It treats the patient as an object of pity who needs to be given something to make it all better. Any child has absolutely no interest in that idea at all. Whether it's a computer, a box of watercolors, or a musical instrument, they want to learn how to master it and say something meaningful about themselves with it."

9   Based on feedback received from children who have used the network . . . , the Starbright Foundation will introduce a new version of Starbright World. . . . ❻ "Creating a community of peers is by far the most important element of Starbright World," said Nancy Hayes, chief executive of the Starbright Foundation, based in Los Angeles. "So with the new version, we're trying to facilitate as many opportunities for connection between the kids as possible." . . .

10   ❼ "If a child is about to undergo chemotherapy, he or she will be able to enter a chat room and hear what to expect from a child who has gone through it," she said. Another new component, Find a Friend, will match two children of similar age who have similar illnesses. Young patients will be able to view videos about procedures like getting a blood test or being hooked up to an intravenous line.

11   "Kids want more information on health care topics in their own language, not doctor-speak," Ms. Hayes said.

12   The children using Starbright World want contacts with more children on line, so the foundation is working on expanding the network.

13   "After we expand Starbright World, our long-term goal is to make the network accessible to kids after they leave the hospital, by using a password to log on at home," Ms. Hayes said.

❹ **Think about the message.**

"Kids in the hospital are pretty isolated. I guess using a computer doesn't so much improve their computer skills as give them a way to talk to other kids."

❺ **Note techniques used by the writer.**

"This quote helps me to visualize why Starbright World is important—it helps kids meet each other's needs for support."

YOUR TURN
Look at the other quotations in the selection. What purpose does each quotation serve?

❻ **Skim the questions that follow the passage.**

"What is a 'community of peers'? I have to figure out what Ms. Hayes means to answer question 4."

❼ **Read actively— analyze.**

"If kids who have the same illness talk to each other, they can learn more about what to expect."

YOUR TURN
How else might Starbright World be able to help seriously ill children?

Use the strategies in the box and the notes in the side column to help you answer the questions below and on the following pages.

Based on the selection you have just read, choose the best answer for each of the following questions.

1. According to the writer, how does Starbright World help children?

   A. It gives them a way to communicate with other children at a time when they may be physically isolated.

   B. It gives them a way to continue their education at a time when they cannot go to school.

   C. It entertains them at a time when they need cheering up.

   D. It provides them with access to medical sites on the Internet.

2. How does the anecdote in paragraphs 1, 2, and 3 entice readers to read on?

   A. It discusses the services of Starbright World.

   B. It makes readers realize that they themselves might one day need Starbright World.

   C. It adds human interest to the selection.

   D. all of the above

3. How does the writer of this selection use quotations?

   A. to provide information

   B. to add interest

   C. to support the selection's message

   D. all of the above

4. In paragraph 9, the writer quotes Nancy Hayes who says, "Creating a community of peers is by far the most important element of Starbright World." What does she mean?

   A. Learning computer skills helps hospitalized children.

   B. Reaching out to other children and sharing experiences helps hospitalized children.

   C. Hospitalized children need to connect to the local community.

   D. Children need to express feelings about their illnesses.

5. The primary technique this writer uses to keep the reader's interest is to include

   A. comparisons.

   B. descriptive language.

   C. quotations.

   D. chronological structure.

STRATEGIES IN ACTION

Pay attention to choices such as "all of the above."

ONE STUDENT'S THOUGHTS
"The anecdote doesn't discuss the services of Starbright World—it gives an example of one child who used them. So I can eliminate choice A—and that means I can also eliminate choice D. "

YOUR TURN
Which other choice doesn't make sense?

Skim your notes.

ONE STUDENT'S THOUGHTS
"I also noticed the word 'community' in paragraph 4. I don't think learning computer skills is the purpose of Starbright World. I can eliminate choice A."

YOUR TURN
How can you choose the best answer from the three choices that remain?

PART 3

How to Respond in Writing

You may also be asked to write answers to questions about a reading passage. Short-answer questions usually ask you to answer in a sentence or two. Essay questions require a fully developed piece of writing.

Short-Answer Question

STRATEGIES FOR RESPONDING TO SHORT-ANSWER QUESTIONS

▸ **Identify the key words** in the writing prompt that tell you the ideas to discuss. Make sure you know what is meant by each.
▸ **State your response directly** and to the point.
▸ **Support your ideas** by using evidence from the selection.
▸ **Use correct grammar.**

> **Sample Question**
> Answer the following question in one or two sentences.
>
> How does the writer show that children in the hospital are isolated? What details does the writer use as evidence?

STRATEGIES IN ACTION

Support your ideas using evidence from the selection.

ONE STUDENT'S THOUGHTS
"The prompt asks for *details* that show how *isolated* children are when they are in the hospital. For example, I remember that sometimes a computer has to be rolled into a child's room on a cart."

YOUR TURN
What other detail in the selection shows that hospitalized children are isolated?

Essay Question

STRATEGIES FOR ANSWERING ESSAY QUESTIONS

▸ **Look for direction words** in the writing prompt, such as *essay, analyze, describe,* or *compare* and *contrast,* that tell you how to respond directly to the prompt.
▸ **List the points** you want to make before beginning to write.
▸ **Write an interesting introduction** that presents your main point.
▸ **Develop your ideas** by using evidence from the selection that supports the statements you make. Present the ideas in a logical order.
▸ **Write a conclusion** that summarizes your points.
▸ **Check your work** for correct grammar.

> **Sample Prompt**
> How does Starbright World help children cope with their illnesses? Write an essay in which you describe the services offered by Starbright World and analyze how these services could make a difference to a child during his or her recovery.

Look for direction words.

ONE STUDENT'S THOUGHTS
"The key words are *describe* and *analyze*. First I will describe the services that Starbright provides. Then, I will *analyze* how a sick child could benefit from Starbright's services."

YOUR TURN
List the services that Starbright offers to children.

Here is a student's first draft in response to the writing prompt at the bottom of page 512. Read it and answer the multiple-choice questions that follow.

1	Starbright World offers services that help children in the
2	hospital to connect with other children. Through Starbright,
3	children can talk to other children in several ways. They can
4	use chat rooms. They can use video conferences. They can learn
5	what to expect about their illness from other children who
6	have it, too.
7	They can become lonely if they spend most of their time
8	alone. Starbright gives children a way to bring other children
9	into their hospital rooms with them—on line. Starbright also
10	makes being sick less scary giving children a chance to talk to
11	other children with the same illness.

▶ **Read the passage carefully.**
▶ **Note the parts that are confusing** or don't make sense. What kinds of errors would that signal?
▶ **Look for errors** in grammar, usage, spelling, and capitalization. Common errors include:
- run-on sentences
- sentence fragments
- lack of subject-verb agreement
- unclear pronoun antecedents
- lack of transition words

1. What is the BEST way to combine the three sentences in lines 2–4 ("Through Starbright . . . conferences.")?

   A. Through Starbright, children can talk to other children using chat rooms or video conferences.

   B. Chat rooms and video conferences, through Starbright are ways children can talk to other children in several ways.

   C. Several ways that Starbright has can help children to talk to each other, chat rooms or video conferences.

   D. Talking to other children in several ways through Starbright, children can use chat rooms or video conferences.

2. The meaning of the sentence in lines 7–8 ("They . . . alone.") can BEST be improved by changing *They* to

   A. These children

   B. Those children

   C. Children in the hospital

   D. Children using chat rooms

3. What is the BEST change, if any, to make to the sentence in lines 9–11 ("Starbright also . . . same illness.")?

   A. Insert the word *by* between *scary* and *giving*.

   B. Delete the word *giving* between *scary* and *children*.

   C. Insert a period after *scary* and capitalize the first letter of *giving*.

   D. Make no change.

UNIT THREE

The Restoration *and* Enlightenment

1660 — 1798

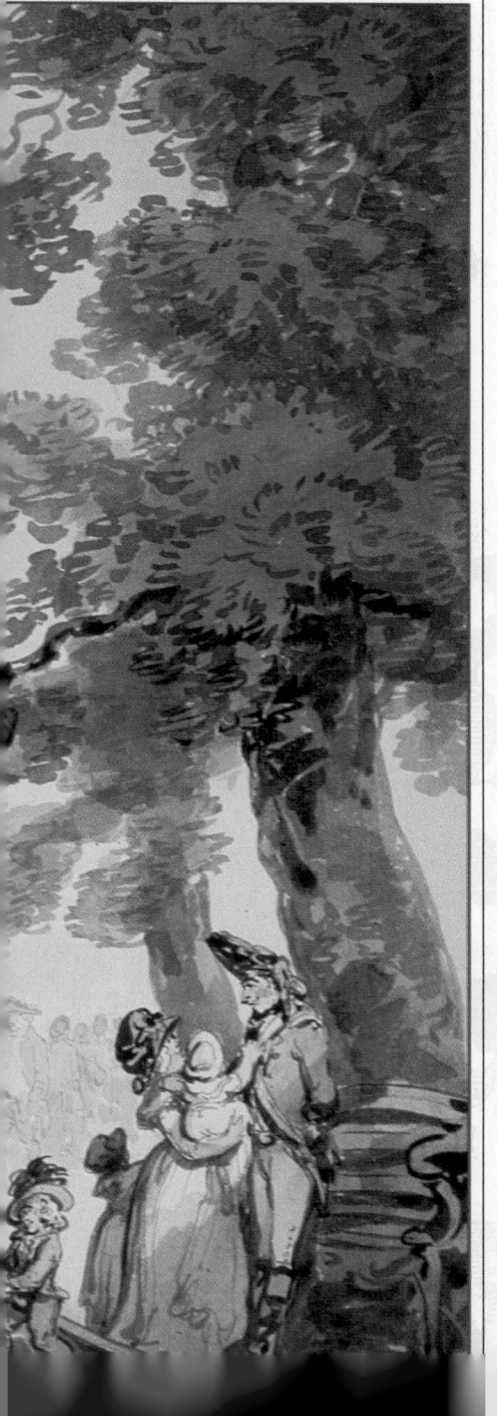

Let observation with extensive view,
Survey mankind, from China to Peru;
Remark each anxious toil, each eager strife
And watch the busy scenes of crowded life.

SAMUEL JOHNSON
critic and scholar

The Restoration *and* Enlightenment

EVENTS IN BRITISH LITERATURE

1650   1700

1660 Samuel Pepys begins diary

1668 John Dryden first official poet laureate

1671 John Milton's *Paradise Regained* published

1690 John Locke publishes essay *Two Treatises on Civil Government* stating natural rights of life, liberty, and property

1695 End of prepublication censorship a victory for press freedom

1709 Richard Steele begins periodical *The Tatler,* to which Joseph Addison contributes articles

1711 Addison and Steele begin *The Spectator*

1719 Daniel Defoe's narrative chronicle *Robinson Crusoe* published, considered by many the first novel in English

EVENTS IN BRITAIN

1650   1700

1665 Great Plague of London kills thousands

1666 Five-day Great Fire of London destroys large section of city

1685 Reign of James II begins (to 1688) ➤

1687 Sir Isaac Newton publishes law of gravity

1689 Parliament passes English Bill of Rights

1702 Reign of Anne, last Stuart monarch, begins (to 1714) ➤

1707 England and Scotland united as Great Britain

1714 Reign of George I, first Hanoverian monarch, begins (to 1727)

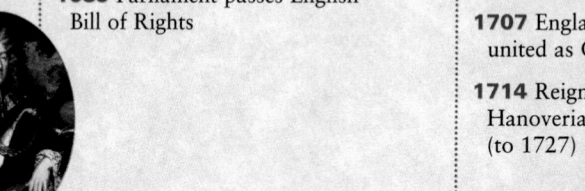

EVENTS IN THE WORLD

1650   1700

1661 Louis XIV begins building grand palace at Versailles near Paris

1699 After 17-year war, Austria negotiates control of east-central Europe, ending Turkish presence in region

1703 Peter the Great begins building city of St. Petersburg

1707 Mughal Empire in India breaks into patchwork of independent states

1721 Edo (Tokyo) becomes world's largest city

1722 Safavid Empire of Persia collapses from Afghan and Ottoman assaults

PERIOD PIECES

Personal cleanliness began to assume more importance. Pictured is a drawing of an 18th-century washstand.

Day-bed, c. 1695

Painted watch dial from latter half of the 18th century

1750

1722 Defoe publishes *A Journal of the Plague Year,* fictional narrative of London's deadly plague of 1665–66

1726 Jonathan Swift arranges anonymous delivery of manuscript of *Gulliver's Travels* to London printer

1740 Samuel Richardson's *Pamela* published, considered by others first novel in English

1746 Samuel Johnson signs contract to prepare *A Dictionary of the English Language* (published 1755)

1763 James Boswell meets Samuel Johnson, forming 21-year friendship

1768 Publication of *Encyclopaedia Britannica* begins in Scotland

1784 William Blake creates "illuminated printing" technique for combining text and illustration

1791 Boswell issues two-volume *Life of Samuel Johnson*

1750

1721 Robert Walpole, first political leader to be called prime minister, takes office

1727 Reign of George II begins (to 1760)

1757 British rule over India begins (to 1947)

1760 Reign of George III begins (to 1820)

1763 Britain defeats France in Seven Years' (French and Indian) War, acquiring French Canada

1775 War with colonies in North America begins (to 1783)

1783 American independence acknowledged in Treaty of Paris

1784 Religious reformer John Wesley, founder of Methodism, officially splits with Church of England

1788 First British settlement in Australia

1793 War with revolutionary France begins (to 1815)

1750

1736 Eventually to lead China to its greatest prosperity, Qian-long becomes emperor (to 1796)

1740 Maria Theresa becomes queen of Austria, Bohemia, and Hungary (to 1780)

1756 Frederick the Great of Prussia starts Seven Years' War fought in Europe, North America, and India

1762 Catherine the Great begins rule of Russia (to 1796)

1789 French Revolution starts (to 1799)

1791 Austrian composer genius Wolfgang Amadeus Mozart dies at age 35

1793 French King Louis XVI executed by guillotine

1795 Napoleon Bonaparte's defense of National Convention delegates from rebels makes him savior of French republic

The Restoration and Enlightenment

1660 - 1798

Charles II wearing finery inspired by the French fashions he saw during his exile

The palace and grounds of Versailles, residence of the French king Louis XIV

After the restoration of the monarchy in 1660, England turned its back on the grim era of Puritan rule and entered a lively period in which the glittering Stuart court set the tone for upper-class social and political life. Charles II had spent much of his long exile in France, absorbing the glamour, elegance, and intrigue of the court of Louis XIV, and after his return to England he and his courtiers tried to emulate the French court's sophistication and splendor. Lords and ladies dressed in rich silks and lace-trimmed finery, wearing elaborate wigs and sparkling jewels. They performed intricate, stately dances at elegant balls and flocked to London's newly reopened theaters. Like Louis XIV, Charles was a patron of the arts and sciences, appointing England's first official poet laureate and chartering the scientific organization known as the Royal Society. Clever and cynical, the king was also extremely self-indulgent, and his excesses both shocked and titillated the English public.

With the Restoration came a return to Anglicanism as England's state religion and a realization that future monarchs would have to share their authority with Parliament, whose influence had increased substantially. An astute

Left: Hand bells were rung to warn of approaching carts filled with victims of the Great Plague of 1665.

Below: Sir Christopher Wren designed the new St. Paul's Cathedral (completed 1710) to replace one that had been destroyed by the Great Fire of London in 1666.

politician, Charles at first won widespread support in Parliament, weathering a series of disasters that included the Great Plague of 1665 and the Great Fire of London a year later. Soon, however, old political rivalries resurfaced, creating two factions that became the nation's chief political parties: the Tories and the Whigs. The Tory party—supporters of royal authority—consisted mainly of landowning aristocrats and conservative Anglicans, who had little tolerance for Protestant dissenters and no desire for war with France. The Whigs, who wanted to limit royal authority, included several powerful nobles as well as wealthy merchants and financiers. Suspicious of the king's Catholic advisers and his pro-French sympathies, the Whigs favored leniency toward Protestant dissenters and sought to curb French expansion in Europe and North America, which they saw as a threat to England's commercial interests.

WILLIAM AND MARY

Political conflict increased when Charles, who had no legitimate children, was succeeded in 1685 by his Catholic brother, James. A blundering, tactless statesman, James II was determined to restore Roman Catholicism as England's state religion, thereby losing the support even of many Tories. As a result, the Whigs in Parliament met with little opposition when they began negotiating to replace James with his Protestant daughter Mary and her husband, the Dutch nobleman William of Orange. In 1688, James was forced to abdicate, and William and Mary took the English throne peacefully in what would become known as the Glorious (or Bloodless)

William and Mary, who ruled England jointly after the Glorious Revolution

Development of the English Language

During the Enlightenment, emphasis on reason and logic led to efforts to stabilize and systematize the English language. In 1693, the influential writer John Dryden complained, "We have yet no prosodia, not so much as a tolerable dictionary or grammar, so that our language is in a manner barbarous," and over the next decades scholars worked to remedy the situation. One such scholar was Samuel Johnson, whose *Dictionary of the English Language* was published in 1755. Although Johnson recognized that language is always changing, he also recognized the importance of a standard for pronunciation, usage, and spelling. Seven years later Robert Lowth published *A Short Introduction to English Grammar,* in which he attempted to establish a system of rules for judging correctness in matters under dispute. Since early grammarians like Lowth based their ideas on Latin, however, their rules often proved inappropriate for English. For example, they considered the infinitive form of an English verb to consist of two words ("to stun"); but because Latin infinitives are single words, they deemed it incorrect to "split" an English infinitive with an adverb ("to completely stun"), thus creating a puzzling "rule" that has bedeviled generations of schoolchildren.

Despite the Enlightenment scholars' search for uniformity and stability, overseas colonization was bringing variety and growth to English. New environments demanded new vocabulary, often borrowed from the native languages of the regions (like *raccoon* and *chipmunk* from Native American tongues and *kangaroo* from the language of Australian Aborigines). In addition, the great distance of the colonies from the homeland and the slow methods of communication allowed differences between the colonists' English and that spoken in Britain to grow.

Revolution—a triumph of Parliamentary rule over the divine right of kings. The next year, Parliament passed the English Bill of Rights, which put specific limits on royal authority. The remaining supporters of James II—and later those who supported the royal claims of his Catholic son, James Edward Stuart—were known as Jacobites (from *Jacobus,* the Latin form of *James*).

As a Dutchman and a Protestant, King William (who ruled alone after Mary died) was a natural enemy of Catholic France and its expansionist threats to Holland. From the first year of his reign, with Whig support, he took every opportunity to oppose the ambitions of Louis XIV with English military power, beginning a series of wars with France that some historians consider a "Second Hundred Years' War." A year before William's death, Parliament passed the Act of Settlement, which permanently barred Catholics from the throne. In 1702, therefore, the crown passed to Mary's Protestant sister, Anne, a somewhat stodgy but undemanding ruler who faithfully tended to her royal duties. During her reign, Scotland officially united with England to form Great Britain, and war with France continued—although Anne, unlike William, sided with the Tories who opposed it. A peace treaty arranged by her Tory ministers, or advisers, in 1713 procured what was to be only a brief lull in British-French antagonisms.

THE HOUSE OF HANOVER

Outliving all 16 of her children, Anne was the last monarch of the house of Stuart. With her death in 1714, the crown passed to a distant cousin of hers—the ruler of Hanover in Germany—who as George I became the first ruler of Britain's house of Hanover. The new king spoke no English and was viewed with contempt by many Tories, some of whom supported James Edward

German-born George I was the first Hanoverian ruler of England.

Portrait of George III with his wife Charlotte and the first 6 of their 15 children

Stuart's bid for the throne in the unsuccessful Jacobite rebellion of 1715. The Whigs, on the other hand, favored the Hanoverian succession and won the new king's loyalty. Because of the language barrier, George I relied heavily on his Whig ministers; and Robert Walpole, the head of the Whig party, emerged as the king's "prime minister" (the first official to be so called)—a position he continued to hold under George II, who succeeded his father in 1727. Toward the end of George II's reign, another able prime minister, William Pitt (the Elder), arose on the political scene. Pitt led the nation to victory over France in the Seven Years' War (called the French and Indian War in America), which resulted in Britain's acquisition of French Canada.

The Seven Years' War was still being fought when George III, grandson of George II, succeeded to the throne in 1760. The first British-born monarch of the house of Hanover, George III sought a more active role in governing the country, but his highhanded ways soon antagonized many. Scornful of the Whigs, George had trouble working with nearly everyone, partly because he suffered from a mental illness that grew worse over the years. During the first few decades of his 60-year reign, he led Britain into a series of political blunders that ultimately resulted in the loss of the American colonies.

In 1770, British soldiers attacked American colonists in the Boston Massacre, one of the events leading to the American Revolution.

LITERARY HISTORY

The literary style that prevailed from the Restoration nearly to the end of the 18th century is called neoclassicism ("new classicism"). Neoclassical writers modeled their works on those of ancient Greece and Rome—especially those of Rome—emulating the supposed restraint, rationality, and dignity of classical writing. Neoclassicists stressed balance, order, logic, sophisticated wit, and emotional restraint, focusing on society and the human intellect and avoiding personal feelings. The neoclassical era in English literature is often divided into three periods: the Restoration (1660–1700), the Augustan Age (1700–1750), and the Age of Johnson (1750–1784).

During the Restoration, drama flourished in England's newly reopened theaters. Influenced by the French "comedy of manners," witty Restoration comedies portrayed and often satirized the artificial, sophisticated society centered in the Stuart court. Equally popular were heroic dramas, tragedies or tragicomedies featuring idealized heroes, dastardly villains, exciting action, and spectacular staging. Although many of the comedies were in prose, the heroic dramas were usually written in heroic couplets (iambic pentameter lines rhyming in pairs), the dominant verse form of the neoclassical period.

Both the Restoration comedies and the heroic dramas appealed primarily to the elite. Attracting a much wider audience was *The Pilgrim's Progress* (1678), a prose allegory by the Puritan John Bunyan, in which he extolled the virtues of faith, hope, and charity and condemned the shallow inhabitants of a worldly place called Vanity Fair. Another great Restoration prose work was the personal diary of Samuel Pepys, not published until 1825.

THE AGE OF REASON

Despite recurring warfare with France and the disaster of the American Revolution, the 18th century was a time of relative stability in Britain. The thought of the time was heavily influenced by the Enlightenment, a philosophical movement inspired by the works of such late-17th-century figures as John Locke, the political philosopher who had provided a logical justification for the Glorious Revolution, and Sir Isaac Newton, the scientist who had provided rational explanations of gravity and motion. Order, balance, logic, and reason were the paramount ideals of the day—so much so that the 18th century is often called the Age of Reason. The methods of scientific inquiry were applied to everything from farming to politics. Religion, the source of so much bloodshed a century earlier, became a far less emotional issue, although John Wesley did lead an evangelical revival that gave rise not only to the new Methodist groups but also to a revivalist movement within the Church of England.

Many British citizens lived well during the 18th century, and a few lived sumptuously. Wealthy aristocrats built lavish country estates filled with furnishings of exquisite craftsmanship and surrounded by beautifully tended lawns and gardens. When Parliament was in session, members relocated to their London townhouses on the spacious new streets and squares that had been laid out after the Great Fire. Writers, artists, politicians, and other educated members of society gathered daily in London's coffeehouses to exchange ideas, conduct business, and gossip. Educated women sometimes held salons, or private gatherings, where they too could participate in the nation's intellectual life.

Sir Isaac Newton is considered the father of modern science.

Women at a salon, about 1780

By producing larger animals, breeding experiments led to an improved diet, with more meat for more people.

ADVANCES AND CHANGES

The spirit of the Enlightenment led to many improvements in living conditions. Early in the century, Lady Mary Wortley Montagu, the wife of a British ambassador, brought back from Turkey the idea of inoculation to prevent smallpox, and by the end of the 1700s, Edward Jenner had developed an effective smallpox vaccination. Dramatic advances in agriculture helped improve Britain's food supply as wealthy landowners developed more productive methods of cultivating and harvesting crops. Breeding experiments resulted in larger animals: by the end of the century, the average weight of sheep and cattle had more than doubled. Unfortunately, putting these improvements into practice drove thousands of peasant farmers off the land. Increasingly, the open fields that had formerly been available to villagers for livestock grazing were being enclosed into large, separate tracts, held by the prosperous landowners who could then make use of the agricultural innovations. Although this enclosure of the land improved farming efficiency and output, it destroyed the traditional way of life of the English village.

Many of the villagers forced off the land sought jobs at the factories that had begun to dot the landscape. Britain, with its wealth of inventions, ample coal and iron, and ready colonial markets, was becoming a pioneer in the use of machines and steam power to manufacture goods that had formerly been made by hand. This Industrial Revolution changed the very fabric of British life. Sleepy towns in the north and west, near the sources of coal, iron, and water power, were transformed into grimy manufacturing centers in which workers—many of them women and children—labored long hours for low pay. By the end of the century, Britain had produced not only a solid commercial and industrial base but also a growing mass of restless, impoverished workers. The stability that had marked 18th-century life was beginning to crumble.

LITERARY HISTORY

Neoclassicism reached its zenith in the Augustan Age—so named because its writers likened their society to that of Rome in the prosperous, stable reign of the emperor Augustus, when the finest Roman literature was produced. An alternative name for the period is the Age of Pope, because Alexander Pope dominated the literary world of the day with his epigrammatic and satiric verses. Satire also characterized the poetry and prose of Jonathan Swift and the essays of Joseph Addison and Richard Steele, which appeared in the early English magazines *The Tatler* and *The Spectator*.

The 18th century also saw the birth of novels as we know them. Early examples of these works of fiction include Daniel Defoe's episodic tale of adventure *Robinson Crusoe,* the sentimental stories of Samuel Richardson, and the comic works of Tobias Smollett and Henry Fielding.

The name "Age of Johnson" is a tribute to Samuel Johnson, Britain's most influential man of letters in the second half of the 18th century. Johnson was at the center of a circle that included his biographer James Boswell, the historian Edward Gibbon, the novelist and diarist Fanny Burney, and the comic dramatist Richard Brinsley Sheridan. Though Johnson and most of his associates affirmed neoclassical ideals, during this time poetry entered a transitional stage in which poets began writing simpler, freer lyrics on subjects close to the human heart. The reflective poetry of Oliver Goldsmith and Thomas Gray and the lyrical songs of Scotland's Robert Burns anticipate the first stirrings of romanticism at the very end of the century.

PART 1 Views of Society

In the late 17th and early 18th centuries, English writers sought to make sense of their world by observing human society and reflecting on both its positive and negative attributes. In this part of Unit Three, some of the writers of the time offer their views on the restored monarchy, human nature, the proper behavior of children, and the role of women in society. As you read the selections, decide what these observations reveal about English society of this era.

from The Diary of Samuel Pepys

By SAMUEL PEPYS (pēps)

Connect to Your Life

Exaggeration and Honesty Many people exaggerate when relating stories about themselves. Think of people you know who exaggerate their own qualities and experiences. Which do they tend to exaggerate most—their good qualities or their bad ones? Do you know any people who always describe their experiences honestly, giving a balanced, candid portrayal of themselves and their activities? Discuss these questions with classmates.

Build Background

Public and Private Events Few descriptions of daily life in any period of history are as vivid as those found in *The Diary of Samuel Pepys*— a rare firsthand account of events that occurred over 300 years ago. Begun in 1660, the historic year of the Restoration, the **diary** not only records the drama of public events but also provides a candid portrayal of the social and domestic life of a middle-class Londoner. Although Samuel Pepys wrote his diary in shorthand to ensure the privacy of his thoughts, he was undoubtedly aware of its immense value to future generations, since he eventually bequeathed his library, including the diary, to Cambridge University.

Pepys had an intimate view of some of the most dramatic events of his time. As personal secretary to a British admiral, he was aboard the ship on which King Charles II returned to England after a long exile in France. He also witnessed the Great Fire of London in 1666, which destroyed more than 13,000 homes, at least 80 churches, and most of London's government buildings.

Focus Your Reading

LITERARY ANALYSIS **DIARY** A **diary** is a writer's personal day-to-day account of his or her experiences and impressions. *The Diary of Samuel Pepys* is an example of a well-written diary of great historical interest. As you read these excerpts from the diary, note how Pepys discusses matters of both personal and public concern.

ACTIVE READING **MAKING INFERENCES ABOUT CHARACTER TRAITS** In reading a diary, one of the things you can **make inferences** about is the dominant **character traits** of the writer of the diary. As you read, certain qualities or characteristics of the person will come to seem particularly important. To make inferences about Pepys's character, note details about his words and actions that seem to reveal something about his character.

READER'S NOTEBOOK Use a chart like the one shown to list the character traits that you think Samuel Pepys possessed. Cite evidence from the selection to support the traits you identify.

Traits	Evidence

from

THE DIARY OF
Samuel Pepys

Samuel Pepys (1666), John Hayls. Oil on canvas. The Granger Collection, New York. *Frame:* The last page of Pepys's diary. Courtesy of The Master and Fellows, Magdalene College, Cambridge, U.K.

SAMUEL PEPYS

The Restoration of Charles II
1660

March 16. . . . To Westminster Hall, where I heard how the Parliament had this day dissolved themselves[1] and did pass very cheerfully through the Hall and the Speaker without his mace.[2] The whole Hall was joyful thereat, as well as themselves; and now they begin to talk loud of the King. . . .

May 22. . . . News brought that the two dukes are coming on board, which, by and by they did in a Dutch boat, the Duke of York in yellow trimming, the Duke of Gloucester in gray and red. My Lord[3] went in a boat to meet them, the captain, myself, and others standing at the entering port. . . .

May 23. . . . All the afternoon the King walking here and there, up and down (quite contrary to what I thought him to have been), very active and stirring. Upon the quarter-deck he fell in discourse of his escape from Worcester.[4] Where it made me ready to weep to hear the stories that he told of his difficulties that he had passed through. As his traveling four days and three nights on foot, every step up to his knees in dirt, with nothing but a green coat and a pair of country breeches on and a pair of country shoes, that made him so sore all over his feet that he could scarce stir. Yet he was forced to run away from a miller and other company that took them for rogues. His sitting at table at one place, where the master of the house, that had not seen him in eight years, did know him but kept it private; when at the same table there was one that had been of his own regiment at Worcester, could not know him but made him drink the King's health and said that the King was at least four fingers higher than he. Another place, he was by some servants of the house made to drink, that they might know him not to be a Roundhead,[5] which they swore he was. In another place, at his inn, the master of the house, as the King was standing with his hands upon the back of a chair by the fire-side, he kneeled down and kissed his hand privately, saying that he would not ask him who he was, but bid God bless him whither that he was going. . . .

The Coronation of the King
1661

April 23. . . . About 4 in the morning I rose. . . . And got to the Abbey,[6] . . . where with a great deal of patience I sat from past 4 till 11 before the King came in. And a pleasure it was to see the Abbey raised in the middle, all covered with red and a throne (that is a chair) and footstool on the top of it. And all the officers of all kinds, so much as the very fiddlers, in red vests. At last comes in the dean and prebends of Westminster with the bishops (many of them in cloth-of-gold copes[7]); and after them the nobility all in their parliament-robes, which was a most magnificent sight. Then

---

1. **Parliament . . . themselves:** This Parliament abolished the government established by Oliver Cromwell and restored the monarchy under Charles II, who had been living in exile in France.

2. **mace:** a staff used as a symbol of authority.

3. **my Lord:** Sir Edward Montagu, Pepys's employer, who was in command of the fleet that brought Charles II back to England.

4. **his escape from Worcester** (wŏŏs′tər): Charles II, at the head of a Scottish army, had been defeated by Cromwell's troops at the Battle of Worcester in 1651. He had gone into hiding, journeyed secretively to the coast, and escaped to France.

5. **Roundhead:** a supporter of Cromwell's Puritan government.

6. **Abbey:** Westminster Abbey, the London church where monarchs are crowned.

7. **copes:** long robes worn by church officials while performing services or rites.

the duke and the King with a scepter (carried by my Lord of Sandwich) and sword and mond[8] before him, and the crown too.

The King in his robes, bare-headed, which was very fine. And after all had placed themselves—there was a sermon and the service. And then in the choir at the high altar he passed all the ceremonies of the coronation—which, to my very great grief, I and most in the Abbey could not see. The crown being put upon his head, a great shout begun. And he came forth to the throne and there passed more ceremonies: as, taking the oath and having things read to him by the bishop, and his lords (who put on their caps as soon as the King put on his crown) and bishops came and kneeled before him. And three times the king-at-arms[9] went to the three open places on the scaffold and proclaimed that if any one could show any reason why Ch. Stuart[10] should not be King of England, that now he should come and speak. And a general pardon also was read by the Lord Chancellor; and medals flung up and down by my Lord Cornwallis—of silver; but I could not come by any.

But so great a noise, that I could make but little of the music; and indeed, it was lost to everybody. . . . I went out a little while before the King had done all his ceremonies and went round the Abbey to Westminster Hall, all the way within rails, and 10,000 people, with the ground covered with blue cloth—and scaffolds all the way. Into the hall I got—where it was very fine with hangings and scaffolds, one upon another, full of brave ladies. And my wife in one little one on the right hand. Here I stayed walking up and down; and at last, upon one of the side-stalls, I stood and saw the King come in with all the persons (but the soldiers) that were yesterday in the cavalcade; and a most pleasant sight it was to see them in their several robes. And the King came in with his crown on and his scepter in his hand—under a canopy borne up by six silver staves, carried by barons of the Cinque Ports[11]—and little bells at every end.

And after a long time he got up to the farther end, and all set themselves down at their several tables—and that was also a rare sight. And the King's first course carried up by the Knights of the Bath. And many fine ceremonies there was of the heralds leading up people before him and bowing; and my Lord of Albemarle going to the kitchen and ate a bit of the first dish that was to go to the Kings's table. . . .

The Great London Fire

1666

September 2. (Lord's day) Some of our maids sitting up late last night to get things ready against our feast today, Jane called us up, about 3 in the morning, to tell us of a great fire they saw in the city. So I rose, and slipped on my nightgown and went to her window, and thought it to be on the back side of Mark Lane at the furthest; but being unused to such fires as followed, I thought it far enough off, and so went to bed again and to sleep. About 7 rose again to dress myself, and there looked out at the window and saw the fire not so much as it was, and further off. So to my closet to set things to rights after yesterday's cleaning. By and by Jane comes and tells me that she hears that above 300 houses have been burned down tonight by the fire we saw, and that it was now burning down all Fish Street by London Bridge. So I made myself ready presently, and walked to the Tower[12] and there got up upon one of the high places, Sir J. Robinson's little son

---

8. **mond:** a sphere with a cross on top, used as a symbol of royal power and justice.

9. **king-at-arms:** one of the chief heralds assigned to make official proclamations.

10. **Ch. Stuart:** Charles Stuart. (Charles II was one of the Stuart line of English monarchs.)

11. **Cinque (sĭngk) Ports:** a group of seaports of southeastern England that formed a defensive association.

12. **Tower:** the Tower of London, a group of buildings built as a fortress and later used as a royal residence and a prison for political offenders.

The Great Fire of London (1666), Dutch school. The Granger Collection, New York.

going up with me; and there I did see the houses at that end of the bridge all on fire, and an infinite great fire on this and the other side the end of the bridge—which, among other people, did trouble me for poor little Michell and our Sarah on the bridge.[13] So down, with my heart full of trouble, to the Lieutenant of the Tower, who tells me that it begun this morning in the King's baker's house in Pudding Lane, and that it hath burned down St. Magnus Church and most part of Fish Street already. So I down to the water-side and there got a boat and through bridge, and there saw a lamentable fire. Poor Michell's house, as far as the Old Swan, already burned that way and the fire running further, that in a very little time it got as far as the steelyard while I was there. Everybody endeavoring to remove their goods, and flinging into the river or bringing them into lighters that lay off. Poor people staying in their houses as long as till the very fire touched them, and then running into boats or clambering from one pair of stair by the water-side to another. And among other things, the poor pigeons I perceive were loath to leave their houses, but hovered about the windows and balconies till they were some of them burned, their wings, and fell down.

. . . At last met my Lord Mayor in Canning Street, like a man spent, with a handkerchief about his neck. To the King's message, he cried like a fainting woman, "Lord, what can I do? I am spent. People will not obey me. I have been pull[ing] down houses. But the fire overtakes us faster than we can do it." That he needed no more soldiers; and that for himself, he must go and refresh himself, having been up all night. So he left me, and I him, and walked home—seeing people all almost distracted and no manner of means used to quench the fire. The houses too, so very thick thereabouts, and full of matter for burning, as pitch and tar, in Thames Street—and warehouses of oil and wines and brandy and other things. . . .

---

13. **on the bridge:** in one of the houses on Old London Bridge. (London was so crowded that this bridge bore an entire superstructure of houses and shops.)

Having seen as much as I could now, I away to Whitehall[14] by appointment, and there walked to St. James's Park, and there met my wife and Creed and Wood and his wife and walked to my boat, and there upon the water again, and to the fire up and down, it still increasing and the wind great. So near the fire as we could for smoke; and all over the Thames,[15] with one's face in the wind you were almost burned with a shower of firedrops—this is very true—so as houses were burned by these drops and flakes of fire, three or four, nay five or six houses, one from another. When we could endure no more upon the water, we to a little alehouse on the bankside over against the Three Cranes, and there stayed till it was dark almost and saw the fire grow; and as it grew darker, appeared more and more, and in corners and upon steeples and between churches and houses, as far as we could see up the hill of the city, in a most horrid malicious bloody flame, not like the fine flame of an ordinary fire. Barbary and her husband away before us. We stayed till, it being darkish, we saw the fire as only one entire arch of fire from this to the other side the bridge, and in a bow up the hill, for an arch of above a mile long. It made me weep to see it. The churches, houses, and all on fire and flaming at once, and a horrid noise the flames made, and the cracking of houses at their ruin. So home with a sad heart, and there find everybody discoursing and lamenting the fire. . . .

September 3. About 4 o'clock in the morning, my Lady Batten sent me a cart to carry away all my money and plate and best things to Sir W. Rider's at Bethnal Green; which I did, riding myself in my nightgown in the cart; and Lord, to see how the streets and the highways are crowded with people, running and riding and getting of carts at any rate to fetch away thing[s]. . . .

September 8. . . . I met with many people undone, and more that have extraordinary great losses. People speaking their thoughts variously about the beginning of the fire and the rebuilding of the city. . . .

September 20. . . . In the afternoon out by coach, my wife with me (which we have not done several weeks now), through all the ruins to show her them, which frets her much—and is a sad sight indeed. . . .

September 25. . . . So home to bed—and all night still mightily troubled in my sleep with fire and houses pulling down.

Domestic Affairs

1663

January 13. So my poor wife rose by 5 o'clock in the morning, before day, and went to market and bought fowl and many other things for dinner—with which I was highly pleased. And the chine of beef was down also before 6 o'clock, and my own jack,[16] of which I was doubtful, doth carry it very well. Things being put in order and the cook come, I went to the office, where we sat till noon; and then broke up and I home—whither by and by comes Dr. Clerke and his lady—his sister and a she-cousin, and Mr. Pierce and his wife, which was all my guest[s].

I had for them, after oysters—at first course, a hash of rabbits and lamb, and a rare chine of beef—next, a great dish of roasted fowl, cost me about 30s, and a tart; and then fruit and cheese. My dinner was noble and enough. I had my house mighty clean and neat, my room below with a good fire in it—my dining-room above, and my chamber being made a withdrawing-chamber, and my wife's a good fire also. I find my new table very proper, and will hold nine or ten people well, but eight with great room. After dinner, the women to cards in my wife's chamber and the doctor [and] Mr. Pierce in mine, because the dining-room smokes unless I keep a good charcoal fire, which I was not then provided with. . . .

---

14. **Whitehall:** a wide road in London, the location of many government offices.

15. **Thames** (tĕmz): the principal river flowing through London.

16. **jack:** a device for roasting meat.

October 21. This evening after I came home, I begun to enter my wife in arithmetic, in order to her studying of the globes,[17] and she takes it very well—and I hope with great pleasure I shall bring her to understand many fine things.

January 7. . . . To the duke's house and saw *Macbeth;* which though I saw it lately, yet appears a most excellent play in all respects, but especially in divertisement,[18] though it be a deep tragedy; which is a strange perfection in a tragedy, it being most proper here and suitable. . . .

May 26. (Lord's day) . . . After dinner, I by water alone to Westminster . . . toward the parish church. . . . I did entertain myself with my perspective glass[19] up and down the church, by which I had the great pleasure of seeing and gazing a great many very fine women; and what with that and sleeping, I passed away the time till sermon was done. . . .

May 27. . . . Stopped at the Bear Garden[20] stairs, there to see a prize fought; but the house so full, there was no getting in there; so forced to [go] through an alehouse into the pit where the bears are baited, and upon a stool did see them fight, which they did very furiously, a butcher and a waterman. The former had the better all along, till by and by the latter dropped his sword out of his hand, and the butcher, whether not seeing his sword dropped or I know not, but did give him a cut over the wrist, so as he was disabled to fight any longer. But Lord, to see how in a minute the whole stage was full of watermen to revenge the foul play, and the butchers to defend their fellow, though most blamed him; and there they all fell to it, to knocking down and cutting many of each side. It was pleasant to see, but that I stood in the pit and feared that in the tumult I might get some hurt. At last the rabble broke up, and so I away. . . .

January 12. . . . This evening I observed my wife mighty dull; and I myself was not mighty fond, because of some hard words she did give me at noon, out of a jealousy at my being abroad this morning; when, God knows, it was upon the business of the office unexpectedly; but I to bed, not thinking but she would come after me; but waking by and by out of a slumber, which I usually fall into presently after my coming into the bed, I found she did not prepare to come to bed, but got fresh candles and more wood for her fire, it being mighty cold too. At this being troubled, I after a while prayed her to come to bed, all my people being gone to bed; so after an hour or two, she silent, and I now and then praying her to come to bed, she fell out into a fury, that I was a rogue and false to her. . . . At last, about 1 o'clock, she came to my side of the bed and drew my curtain open, and with the tongs, red hot at the ends, made as if she did design to pinch me with them; at which in dismay I rose up, and with a few words she laid them down and did by little and little, very sillily, let all the discourse fall; and about 2, but with much seeming difficulty, came to bed and there lay well all night. . . .

---

17. **the globes:** geography (the terrestrial globe) and astronomy (the celestial globe).

18. **divertisement** (dĭ-vûr′tĭs-mənt): diversion; amusement.

19. **perspective glass:** small telescope.

20. **Bear Garden:** an establishment in which bears were chained to a post and tormented by dogs as a form of entertainment. It was also the site of scheduled fights between men.

Connect to the Literature

1. What Do You Think? Which of Pepys's entries was the most interesting?

Comprehension Check
- What is Pepys's attitude toward the return of King Charles II?
- How does Pepys portray the victims of the fire?

Think Critically

2. What do you think might have been Pepys's **purpose** in keeping his diary?

THINK ABOUT
- the variety of events he describes
- what types of people he chooses to describe
- whether his observations are primarily objective or subjective

3. **ACTIVE READING** **MAKING INFERENCES ABOUT CHARACTER TRAITS** On the basis of the entries you have read, what would you say are Pepys's main **character traits?** Support your answer with evidence from the selection. You may want to refer to the chart of personality traits of Pepys that you developed in your **READER'S NOTEBOOK**.

4. Does Pepys seem to you to give a candid portrayal of himself, or do you think he exaggerates his best qualities? Explain your answer.

Extend Interpretations

5. Critic's Corner The author Virginia Woolf once said that the "chief delight" of Pepys's diary might be its revelation of "those very weaknesses and idiosyncrasies which in our own case we would die rather than reveal." What do you think Woolf meant? What effect do Pepys's "weaknesses" have on you as you read the diary?

6. Different Perspectives Imagine that the Lord Mayor of London were writing his account of the great fire and his encounter with Pepys while the fire raged. How might the mayor's account of their conversation differ from Pepys's account?

7. Connect to Life Suppose that Pepys were living today and had witnessed a recent memorable event—for example, an inauguration, a meeting of world leaders, or a natural disaster, such as a hurricane, an earthquake, or a flood. What aspects of the event would he most likely highlight in his **diary?**

Literary Analysis

DIARY Most diaries are private and not intended to be shared. Some, however, have been published because they are well written and provide useful perspectives on historical events or on the everyday life of particular eras. In the following passage from Pepys's diary, notice the glimpse into the writer's domestic life even as he reports the Great Fire of London:

Some of our maids sitting up late last night to get things ready against our feast today, Jane called us up, about 3 in the morning, to tell us of a great fire they saw in the city.

Paired Activity What unique insights into a public event might be found in a diary but not in a more formal account of the event? With a partner, draw up a list of the kinds of insights that might be found in a diary. Include examples from Pepys's diary. Share your list with the class.

ACTIVE READING **EVALUATING CREDIBILITY OF SOURCES**
Diaries can be valuable sources of information about the period in which they are written. To evaluate the credibility of a diary, you need to consider the writer's motivation, the objectivity of observations and descriptions, and the relationship of the diary to other sources of information about the period. How would you describe Pepys's motivation for writing his diary? Do you think the diary would be a reliable source of information about life in England in the late 17th century?

Choices & CHALLENGES

Writing Options

Problem-Solving Essay Write an essay in which you recommend possible solutions to the threat of fires in London. Discuss issues of overcrowding, materials used in construction, fire prevention techniques, and general proposals for reducing the outbreak of fires. You might also suggest strategies for dealing with fires once they occur. Place the essay in your **Working Portfolio.**

Fire Prevention
1. _____
2. _____
3. _____

Writing Handbook
See page 1369: Problem-Solution.

Activities & Explorations

A Movie Set Design a set for a movie depiction of the Great Fire of London. Be sure to include specific details from Pepys's description. ~ **ART**

Inquiry & Research

Commonwealth and Restoration Investigate the events that led to the downfall of the Puritan Commonwealth and the restoration of the English monarchy under Charles II. What was the mood of the people? How was the Parliamentary government overthrown?

More Online: Research Starter
www.mcdougallittell.com

Samuel Pepys
1633–1703

An Insatiable Curiosity The son of a tailor, Samuel Pepys received a scholarship to Cambridge University, where he earned both a bachelor's and a master's degree. Pepys had an insatiable curiosity and strove to learn all that he could about every subject. His interests ranged from music and theater to science, history, and mathematics. It was undoubtedly this fascination with life that inspired him, at the age of 26, to begin keeping the diary in which he would eventually set down more than 1.2 million words. After faithfully making entries for nine years, he was forced to abandon his diary because of poor eyesight.

The Royal Navy Shortly after starting the diary, Pepys became a clerk in the Royal Navy office, where he decided to prove his own worth by becoming a naval expert. His hard work and honesty, as well as his saving of the navy office during the Great Fire of London, led eventually to his appointment as secretary of the admiralty. In that capacity, he doubled the number of battleships and restored the previously weakened Royal Navy as a major sea power.

A Public Life During his years of public service, Pepys enjoyed an active social life amid a circle of friends that included such notables as Sir Isaac Newton and John Dryden. However, Pepys also made enemies in his rise to power. In 1678, some of his adversaries tried unsuccessfully to ruin his reputation. They first tried to implicate Pepys in the murder of a London official, then falsely accused him of treason. Although Pepys was imprisoned briefly, the intervention of King Charles II kept him from further punishment, and in 1683 he returned once again to public service. One tragedy marred Pepys's middle years. His wife, Elizabeth, died in 1669 of a fever. Pepys never remarried.

In Retirement Pepys lived in retirement for the last 14 years of his life. He spent his time amassing a large personal library, collecting material for a history of the navy—which he unfortunately never completed—and corresponding with various artists and scholars. He died at the home of his friend and former servant, William Hewer.

from **An Essay on Man**

Epigrams, *from* **An Essay on Criticism**

Poetry by ALEXANDER POPE

Comparing Literature of the World

Poetry of Alexander Pope and Jean de La Fontaine

This lesson and the one that follows present an opportunity for comparing Pope's observations on society with those of French poet Jean de La Fontaine. Specific Points of Comparison in the La Fontaine lesson will help you note similarities and differences in the two poets' perspectives and themes.

Connect to Your Life

Social Graces Recall some recent social events in which you have participated—parties or dances, perhaps, or more informal get-togethers with friends. Jot down words that describe your attitude or behavior in each situation. Were you friendly or sympathetic on one occasion and hostile or insensitive on another? Did you act wisely one time and foolishly another? If so, how do you account for the contradictions in your behavior?

Build Background

Classic Ideals In England, the literary movement of neoclassicism began about 1660 and persisted throughout much of the 18th century. Neoclassical writers modeled their works on the literature of ancient Greece and Rome, which they believed contained universal truths and rules of form important in writing. Neoclassicists emphasized reason, common sense, good taste, simplicity, emotional restraint, order, and balance. Many writers exposed the contradictions and weaknesses of society; some gave moral instruction.

Two concepts important to neoclassicists were nature and wit. *Nature* generally referred to the universal principles of truth underlying the structure of the world. Nature was viewed as a source of order and harmony both in society and in individual behavior. The word *wit* had a number of meanings, ranging from "intellect" to "imagination" to "cleverness."

Alexander Pope was a neoclassical writer in both thought and style; the two verse essays *An Essay on Man* and *An Essay on Criticism* reflect many of the neoclassical ideals. In *An Essay on Criticism,* which Pope began writing when he was just 17, he made use of the **epigram,** a literary form that had originated in ancient Greece. The epigram developed from simple inscriptions on monuments into a literary genre—a short poem or saying characterized by conciseness, balance, clarity, and wit.

Focus Your Reading

LITERARY ANALYSIS | **HEROIC COUPLET** A **heroic couplet** consists of two rhyming lines written in **iambic pentameter**—a metrical pattern of five feet (units), each of which is made up of two syllables, the first unstressed and the second stressed. The following lines are an example of a heroic couplet:

> Avoid extremes; and shun the fault of such,
> Who still are pleased too little or too much.

As you read, be aware of the meter and content of the heroic couplets in Pope's poetry.

ACTIVE READING | **ANALYZING AN AUTHOR'S IDEAS** In his verse essays, Pope uses contrasting words and statements to express his opinion about weaknesses and contradictions in human nature.

READER'S NOTEBOOK For each poem, create a diagram like the one shown here. As you read, use the diagrams to record the contrasts that Pope presents in each poem. Underline contrasts that point out contradictions in human nature.

An Essay on Man

	Contrasts	
1. darkly		1. wise
2. lord	←→	2. prey
3.		3.

FROM AN ESSAY ON MAN

ALEXANDER POPE

Know then thyself, presume not God to scan;
The proper study of mankind is man.
Placed on this isthmus of a middle state,
A being darkly wise, and rudely great:
5 With too much knowledge for the Skeptic side,
With too much weakness for the Stoic's pride,
He hangs between; in doubt to act, or rest;
In doubt to deem himself a god, or beast;
In doubt his mind or body to prefer;
10 Born but to die, and reasoning but to err;
Alike in ignorance, his reason such,
Whether he thinks too little, or too much:
Chaos of thought and passion, all confused;
Still by himself abused, or disabused;
15 Created half to rise, and half to fall;
Great lord of all things, yet a prey to all;
Sole judge of truth, in endless error hurled:
The glory, jest, and riddle of the world!

3 isthmus (ĭs′məs): a narrow strip of land connecting larger bodies of land.
4 rudely: in a rough or clumsy way.
5 Skeptic side: the Greek philosophy of skepticism, whose adherents held that sure knowledge is unattainable.
6 Stoic's (stō′ĭks) **pride:** the haughty behavior of an adherent of the Greek philosophy of Stoicism, which taught that human beings should be indifferent to all pleasure and pain.
8 deem: judge; consider.

Thinking Through the Literature

1. **Comprehension Check** Identify two examples of contradictions in the poem.

2. What is your reaction to Pope's **style** and manner of writing? Take a few moments to discuss your impressions.

3. Why do you think Pope says that human beings are continually "in doubt" (lines 7–9)? Use evidence from the poem to support your ideas.

EPIGRAMS
from AN ESSAY ON CRITICISM

ALEXANDER POPE

The Sense of Touch (about 1615–1616), Jusepe de Ribera. Oil on canvas, 45⅝″ × 34¾″, The Norton Simon Foundation, Pasadena, California.

First follow Nature, and your judgment frame
By her just standard, which is still the same:
Unerring Nature, still divinely bright,
One clear, unchanged, and universal light,
5   Life, force, and beauty, must to all impart,
At once the source, and end, and test of art.

■

Of all the causes which conspire to blind
Man's erring judgment, and misguide the mind,
What the weak head with strongest bias rules,
10   Is pride, the never-failing vice of fools.

■

Pride, where wit fails, steps in to our defense,
And fills up all the mighty void of sense.
If once right reason drives that cloud away,
Truth breaks upon us with resistless day.
15   Trust not yourself; but your defects to know,
Make use of every friend—and every foe.
A little learning is a dangerous thing;
Drink deep, or taste not the Pierian spring:
There shallow draughts intoxicate the brain,
20   And drinking largely sobers us again.

■

12 void: emptiness; vacuum.

18 Pierian (pī-îr′ē-ən) **spring:** a spring sacred to the Muses and therefore considered a source of inspiration. (In Greek mythology, the Muses—nine daughters of Zeus and Memory—were the goddesses of all artistic and intellectual pursuits.)

19 draughts (drăfts): gulps or swallows.

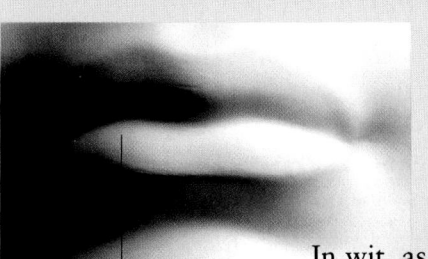

In wit, as Nature, what affects our hearts
Is not th' exactness of peculiar parts;
'Tis not a lip, or eye, we beauty call,
But the joint force and full result of all.

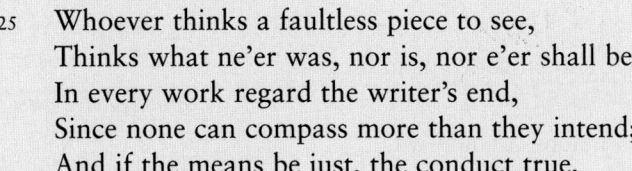

■

25 Whoever thinks a faultless piece to see,
Thinks what ne'er was, nor is, nor e'er shall be.
In every work regard the writer's end,
Since none can compass more than they intend;
And if the means be just, the conduct true,
30 Applause, in spite of trivial faults, is due.

■

True wit is Nature to advantage dressed,
What oft was thought, but ne'er so well expressed;
Something, whose truth convinced at sight we find,
That gives us back the image of our mind.

■

35 True ease in writing comes from art, not chance,
As those move easiest who have learned to dance.
'Tis not enough no harshness gives offense,
The sound must seem an echo to the sense.

■

Avoid extremes; and shun the fault of such,
40 Who still are pleased too little or too much.

■

Regard not then if wit be old or new,
But blame the false, and value still the true.

■

Good nature and good sense must ever join;
To err is human, to forgive, divine.

22 peculiar: individual.

27 end: goal or intention.
28 compass: accomplish.

Connect to the Literature

1. What Do You Think?
Write down two of your favorite epigrams from *An Essay on Criticism,* and share them with another student.

Comprehension Check
• According to Pope, how should one approach learning?
• How should the reader evaluate a writer's work?

Think Critically

2. What seem to be some of Pope's main concerns in these **epigrams?**

THINK ABOUT
• his references to nature, art, and wit
• what he says about pride
• his statements "the sound must seem an echo to the sense" (line 38) and "blame the false, and value still the true" (line 42)

3. ACTIVE READING | ANALYZING AN AUTHOR'S IDEAS | Look back in your 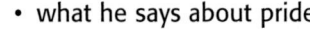 READER'S NOTEBOOK at the diagrams you used to record contrasts in the poems. What ideas about human nature does Pope convey through contrasting words and statements in these epigrams? How does he use contradictions in the epigrams?

4. Do you think Pope is optimistic or pessimistic about human behavior? Support your opinion with details from the poems.

Extend Interpretations

5. Comparing Texts How might the descriptions of events in *The Diary of Samuel Pepys* (page 525) be used to illustrate the contradiction Pope suggests in his statement that a human being is "great lord of all things, yet a prey to all"?

6. Art Connection Look again at the reproduction of the painting *The Sense of Touch* on page 536. Notice that the man's eyes are shut and that a portrait is lying on the table. In what ways might the painting reflect some of the concerns Pope expresses in the epigrams?

7. Connect to Life Compare the views of human nature expressed in the excerpts from *An Essay on Man* and *An Essay on Criticism* with modern views. Do you think Pope's viewpoints are similar to those held today?

Literary Analysis

HEROIC COUPLET | Two rhyming lines written in **iambic pentameter** are referred to as a **heroic couplet.** The couplet is called *heroic* because English poems written in iambic pentameter often have heroic themes and elevated style. Heroic couplets are especially well suited to writing epigrams. Notice the elevated style of this epigram from *An Essay on Criticism.*

Good nature and good sense must ever join;
To err is human, to forgive, divine.

Activity Choose one epigram from *An Essay on Criticism* and note Pope's use of the heroic couplet in it. Read the epigram aloud and then mark the unstressed and stressed syllables. Is the pattern of stresses strictly iambic, or are there some variations? How effective is the form of the heroic couplet in this epigram?

Writing Options

1. Epigram on Human Nature
Convey your own message about human nature in an epigram consisting of one or more heroic couplets.

2. Essay on a Social Problem
Address a social problem or failing raised by Pope in *An Essay on Criticism* and write an essay in which you provide your own solution to the problem. Place the essay in your **Working Portfolio.** 📁

Writing Handbook
See page 1369: Problem-Solution.

Activities & Explorations

Character List Make a list of TV or movie characters who exhibit some of the contradictory qualities suggested in the excerpt from *An Essay on Man.*
~ INTERPRETING

TV characters
1.
2.
3.
Movie characters
1.
2.
3.

Inquiry & Research

Reasonable Ideas In the history of Western thought, the 18th century is often referred to as the Age of Reason or the Enlightenment. Most of the philosophers of the time considered reason to be the only road to truth and were therefore particularly interested in the methods and laws of science and mathematics. Investigate some of the ideas of the Age of Reason, and share your findings with the class. Pay particular attention to ideas that you see reflected in Pope's work.

Alexander Pope
1688–1744

Other Works
The Rape of the Lock
"Epistle to Miss Blount"

Physical Limitations From childhood, Alexander Pope was plagued by ill health. As a result of tuberculosis of the spine, he suffered constant physical pain and grew to a height of only four feet six inches. Although he was therefore severely limited in his physical activities, it is likely that these limitations may have contributed to his early devotion to reading and writing and to his ultimate success as a writer.

Early Genius Pope was raised as a Roman Catholic during a period in England's history when only Protestants could obtain a university education or hold public office. For this reason, he was largely self-taught. He was an exceptional child, however, and his genius as a poet was recognized at an early age. Pope maintained that he began writing verse before the age of 12. By the time he was 17, his poems were being read and admired by many

of England's best literary critics. Unlike most of his predecessors in the literary world, Pope was able to prosper with writing as his sole career. His prosperity was achieved primarily through his translations of Homer's *Iliad* and *Odyssey,* products of an enormous amount of work for which he was handsomely rewarded.

Friends and Enemies Pope's friends included the distinguished writers Richard Steele, Joseph Addison, Jonathan Swift, and John Gay. Along with Swift and Gay, he was a member of the Scriblerus Club, a group devoted to the writing of satires. Because of his sharp tongue, Pope was often the object of criticism by less talented writers, with several of whom he engaged in lifelong feuds.

Author Activity

Roasted and Skewered Read some of the satires Pope wrote as a member of the Scriblerus Club. Who or what were the objects of his satiric wit? What form did his satires take? How did Pope's victims react to his attacks?

The Acorn and the Pumpkin
The Value of Knowledge

Fables by JEAN DE LA FONTAINE (zhän də lə fŏn-tän′)

Comparing Literature of the World

Observing Society Across Cultures

Pope's Verse Essays and La Fontaine's Fables Jean de La Fontaine wrote his poetry in France in the 17th century, and Alexander Pope wrote his poetry in England in the 18th century, but they had a common goal: to observe human nature and society and comment on the manners and morals of their times.

Points of Comparison As you read the following fables by La Fontaine, compare them with Pope's poems in terms of the observations made about human behavior and society.

Build Background

Neoclassicism and Fables In France, the neoclassical movement began around 1600, roughly 60 years before the advent of English neoclassicism. Jean de La Fontaine and other 17th-century French writers, like their later English counterparts, placed great emphasis on reason, intellect, order, and simplicity in thought and actions. Many focused on the flaws in human nature, pointing out society's weaknesses and giving moral instruction.

   Like the English writers of the late 1600s, La Fontaine was inspired by his reading of ancient authors; he borrowed ideas for many of his fables from the tales traditionally ascribed to Aesop, a Greek slave who lived around 600 B.C. In his masterful verse retellings of Aesop's fables, La Fontaine employed a natural, relaxed style that made the tales more appealing to readers, often using humor to reveal human shortcomings and to convey meaningful messages about life. The two poems you are about to read are from his Fables, a collection of over 200 moral tales that have entertained readers for centuries.

Focus Your Reading

LITERARY ANALYSIS **FABLE** A brief tale, in either prose or verse, told to illustrate a moral or teach a lesson is a **fable.** In the following opening lines from "The Acorn and the Pumpkin," La Fontaine makes it clear that the story he is about to tell will teach a lesson:

> *The Lord knows best what He's about.*
> *No need to search for proof throughout*
> *The universe. Look at the pumpkin.*
> *It gives us all the proof we need.*

As you read these fables, be aware of how the details of each tale contribute to the moral, or lesson, the writer seems to be conveying.

ACTIVE READING **MAKING JUDGMENTS** A **fable** persuades or convinces the reader of its moral not by presenting logical arguments but by illustrating the lesson in a brief, entertaining tale. To judge the effectiveness of a fable, use the following criteria:

• Is the tale entertaining?
• How well does the tale illustrate the moral?
• Are you persuaded or convinced by the moral?

READER'S NOTEBOOK Briefly **summarize** the story that is being told by each poem, and then note the moral of each.

The Acorn and the Pumpkin

Jean de La Fontaine

The Lord knows best what He's about.
No need to search for proof throughout
The universe. Look at the pumpkin.
It gives us all the proof we need. To wit:

5   The story of a village bumpkin—
Garo by name—who found one, gazed at it,
And wondered how so huge a fruit could be
Hung from so slight a stem: "It doesn't fit!
    God's done it wrong! If He'd asked me,

10 He'd hang them from those oaks. Big fruit, big tree.
    Too bad someone so smart and strong—
At least that's what the vicar's always saying
    With all his preaching and his praying—
Didn't have me to help His work along!

15 I'd hang the acorn from this vine instead . . .
No bigger than my nail . . . It's like I said:
    God's got things backwards. It's all wrong . . .
Well, after all that weighty thought I'd best
Take me a nap. We thinkers need our rest."

20 No sooner said than done. Beneath an oak
Our Garo laid his head in sweet repose.
Next moment, though, he painfully awoke:
An acorn, falling, hit him on the nose.
    Rubbing his face, feeling his bruises,

25 He finds it still entangled in his beard.
    "A bloody nose from this?" he muses.
"I must say, things aren't quite what they appeared.
    My goodness, if this little nut
Had been a pumpkin or a squash, then what?

30 God knows His business after all, no question!
It's time I changed my tune!" With that suggestion,
    Garo goes home, singing the praise
    Of God and of His wondrous ways.

Translated by Norman R. Shapiro

4 to wit: that is to say (used to introduce an explanation or example).

26 muses: thinks to himself; ponders.

Thinking Through the Literature

1. How did you react to the story of Garo?
2. What is your opinion of the logic that Garo uses? Explain your response.
3. What message do you think the speaker is trying to convey? Support your opinion.

THE VALUE of KNOWLEDGE

Jean de La Fontaine

Betwixt two burghers there arose
A row. One, quick of wit, was poor;
The other, rich, but much the boor.
The latter, twitting, clucks and crows:
5   Surely his bookish rival owes
The likes of him respect, and should—
If he, indeed, had any sense—
Pay homage to his opulence.
("Sense"? Hardly! Rather say "foolhardihood"!
10   For why revere mere wealth without
Real worth? It's meaningless.) "So, brother,"
Brashly the lout would taunt and flout
    The other;
"Doubtless you think yourself my better; but
15   How often do you have your friends to dinner?
What good are books? Will reading fill their gut?
    The wretches just grow poorer, thinner;
Up in their garrets, garbed all year the same;
No servants but their shadows! Fie! For shame!
20   The body politic has little use
For those who never buy. Wealth and excess—
    Luxury, in a word—produce
The greatest deal of human happiness.
    Our pleasures set the wheel a-turning:
25   Earning and spending; spending, earning.

1 burghers: citizens of a town.

3 boor (bŏŏr): a rude, ill-mannered person.
4 twitting: mocking; ridiculing.

8 opulence: wealth.

10 revere: regard with great respect; honor.

12 flout: show contempt for; scorn.

18 garrets: rooms on the top floor of buildings; attics.
19 fie: an interjection used to express disapproval or distaste.
20 body politic: the people of a nation or state.

Each of us, Heaven knows, must play his part:
Spinners and seamsters, fancy beaus and belles
Who buy the finery the merchant sells;
And even you, who with your useless art,
30   Toady to patrons ever quick to pay."
        Our bookman doesn't deign respond:
        There's much too much that he might say.
But still, revenge is his, and far beyond
Mere satire's meager means. For war breaks out,
35   And Mars wreaks havoc round about.
Homeless, our vagabonds must beg their bread.
Scorned everywhere, the boor meets glare and glower;
Welcomed, the wit is plied with board and bed.

So ends their quarrel. Fools take heed: knowledge is power!

Translated by Norman R. Shapiro

27 beaus (bōz) **and belles** (bĕlz): fashionable men and women.

30 toady: act in a subservient way, using flattery to get what one wants.
31 Our bookman . . . respond: Our scholar thinks it beneath his dignity to reply.
35 Mars wreaks (rēks) **havoc:** war causes great destruction. (In Roman mythology, Mars was the god of war.)
38 plied: continually supplied.

Engraving by Gustave Doré.

Connect to the Literature

1. **What Do You Think?**
Were you satisfied with the way "The Value of Knowledge" ended? Share your thoughts with the class.

> **Comprehension Check**
> • Why does the wealthy burgher say that books serve no purpose?
> • How does the poor burgher view the rich burgher?

Think Critically

2. Why do you think the wit is welcomed and the boor rejected at the end of the poem?

THINK ABOUT
- • the description of the boor
- • the conditions after the outbreak of war
- • what the speaker means by the statement that "knowledge is power"

3. Do you agree with any of the rich burgher's opinions? Explain your response.

4. What messages about human nature do you think the poem expresses?

5. **ACTIVE READING** | **MAKING JUDGMENTS** | Review the summaries and notes you made earlier in your **READER'S NOTEBOOK.** Which of the two tales do you think illustrates its moral more effectively? Explain your answer with reference to the criteria on page 540.

Extend Interpretations

6. **Connect to Life** Do you agree or disagree with the morals of these two **fables?** Defend your position with examples from modern life.

7. **Points of Comparison** Compare La Fontaine's poetic fables with the epigrams from Pope's *An Essay on Criticism* (page 534). How do fables and epigrams differ in **style?** in **tone?** Can you think of any situations in which one of these forms of moral instruction might be preferable to the other? Explain your thoughts.

Literary Analysis

FABLE A **fable** is a brief tale, in either prose or verse, told to illustrate a moral or teach a lesson. Often, the moral of a fable appears in a distinct and memorable statement near the tale's beginning or end. Because they draw a clear lesson from a single episode, fables generally contain simple narratives and exaggerated characters. **Humor** is a prominent feature of many fables.

Paired Activity Which of the following elements do you think contribute to the humorous **tone** of these fables? In a chart like the one shown, make a note of any examples you find of the following:

- • humorous situations
- • exaggerated characters
- • humorous language

Then discuss with your partner whether the humorous elements contribute to the lesson each fable is trying to teach. Explain your answer.

Humorous Situations	Exaggerated Characters	Humorous Language

Choices & CHALLENGES

Writing Options

1. An Original Fable Think of a familiar saying or proverb you know, such as "Haste makes waste." Compose an original fable to illustrate the saying. Include it as the moral of your fable.

2. **Points of Comparison**
Write an essay comparing the views of human nature and society found in the excerpt from Pope's *Essay on Man* with the views found in one of La Fontaine's fables.

Writing Handbook
See page 1367: Compare and Contrast.

Activities & Explorations

1. Debate on Lifestyles With several of your classmates, present a debate on the pros and cons of the lifestyles of the two characters in "The Value of Knowledge." Include visual aids, such as charts or diagrams, to help you illustrate your points. Ask the class to vote on which side presents the most logical and effective argument.
~ SPEAKING AND LISTENING

2. Comic Strip Create a comic strip based on the story of Garo in "The Acorn and the Pumpkin."
~ ART

Inquiry & Research

Other Writers of Fables Fables are a popular form of literature. They have their roots in folklore and are found in nearly every culture. Important writers of fables, in addition to La Fontaine and the Greek Aesop, are John Gay in England, Gotthold Lessing in Germany, and Ivan Krylov in Russia. Do some research about the fables written by Gay, Lessing, and Krylov. Share your findings with the class.

 More Online: Research Starter
www.mcdougallittell.com

Jean de La Fontaine
1621–1695

Other Works
"The Crow and the Fox"
"The Stag Who Saw Himself in the Water"
"The Hen Who Laid Golden Eggs"

Youth and Student As a young man, Jean de La Fontaine was rather restless, with no apparent goals in life and little inclination to work. Born into a middle-class family in the Champagne region of France, La Fontaine began studying for the priesthood at the age of 19 but after a very short time switched to the study of law. His father, an inspector of waterways and forests, arranged for his son to take over his position, one that La Fontaine was to occupy—with little interest or attention—for almost 20 years.

A Writing Career Although he read a great deal of poetry, especially the works of classical authors, La Fontaine did not begin writing original poems until

he was in his mid-30s. In 1656, he moved to Paris, where for several years the financial support of a succession of wealthy patrons enabled him to devote his time to writing. He also frequented Parisian literary circles, becoming acquainted with such important French writers as Molière and Racine.

The Fables La Fontaine produced great quantities of prose and poetry, but his lasting fame depends chiefly on his *Fables*. These poetic tales are an important part of French culture and are enjoyed by people of all ages, from small schoolchildren to world-renowned scholars.

Author Activity

The Kindness of Patrons Throughout his career, La Fontaine was able to gain the support of wealthy patrons such as Nicolas Fouquet, the superintendent of finance. Find out what other patrons La Fontaine had. Draw up a list of the names of his more important patrons, along with a little information about each one.

*N*onfiction in the 18th Century

New Ways of Knowing

In recent years, as the pace of technological innovation has seemed to carry with it a promise of continued progress, many people have come to view the future with enthusiasm. A similar enthusiasm was evident among English people as they entered the 18th century. They were seized by a spirit of curiosity and experimentation—a spirit fueled by the movement known as the Enlightenment. In England, the movement was ushered in by the writings of two major political thinkers, John Locke and Thomas Hobbes, who inspired citizens to rethink all aspects of society. The English people found themselves questioning accepted beliefs, exploring new ideas, and applying close scrutiny to nature and society. Other English writers quickly capitalized on this new spirit.

Isaac Biekerstaff, the mythical editor of *The Tatler*

The Growth of Nonfiction

In this rich environment of ideas, **nonfiction** writing became a favored literary form. Though the aristocracy was the primary audience of the Enlightenment writers, the vitality of the period also touched the middle and lower classes. A spread of education in the 17th century had caused the literacy rate in England to soar. The newly literate public's appetite for information grew, and London became home to a number of periodicals. (See the time line below.)

The Development of the Essay

Most of the contents of 18th-century periodicals consisted of essays. The **essay** is a short work of nonfiction that offers a writer's opinion on a particular subject. The essay form became popular after the 16th-century French philosopher Michel de Montaigne published a collection of writings

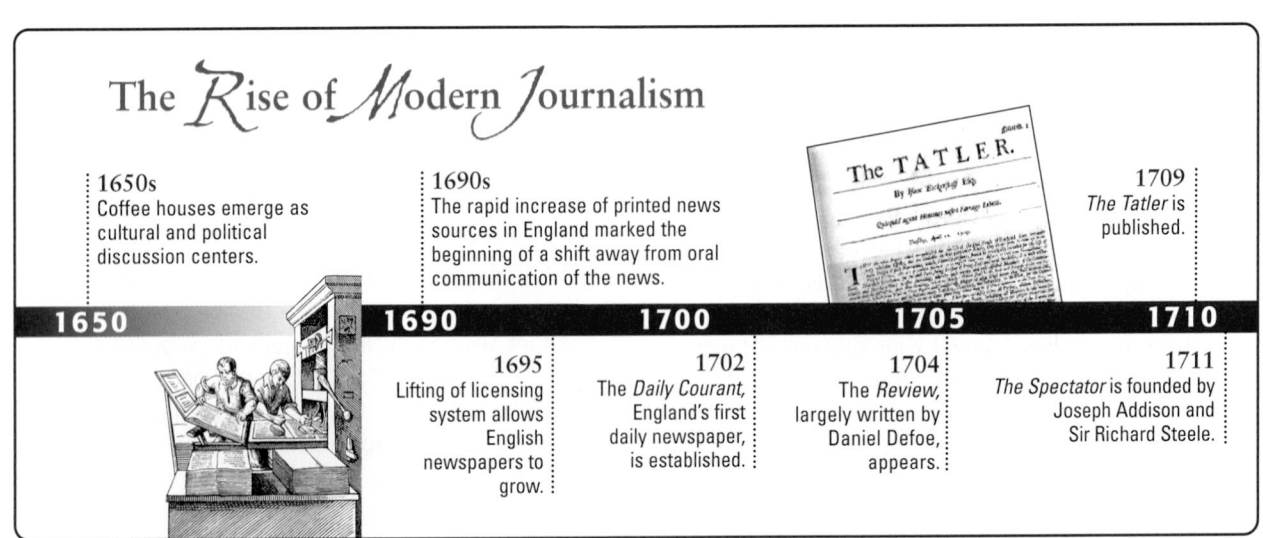

The *R*ise of *M*odern *J*ournalism

1650s
Coffee houses emerge as cultural and political discussion centers.

1690s
The rapid increase of printed news sources in England marked the beginning of a shift away from oral communication of the news.

The TATLER.

1709
The Tatler is published.

| 1650 | 1690 | 1700 | 1705 | 1710 |

1695
Lifting of licensing system allows English newspapers to grow.

1702
The *Daily Courant*, England's first daily newspaper, is established.

1704
The *Review*, largely written by Daniel Defoe, appears.

1711
The Spectator is founded by Joseph Addison and Sir Richard Steele.

with the title *Essais*, which means "attempts." In 1597, Francis Bacon became the first prominent English essayist when he published the first edition of his *Essays*. Works labeled essays were even written in verse, as Alexander Pope's *An Essay on Criticism* shows. The essay became a popular means of expression, a way for English writers to air their views on public matters and to promote social reform.

Informal essays are essays in which writers express their opinions without adopting a completely serious or formal tone. An informal essay can include humor and may deal with an unconventional topic, like these examples:

- Joseph Addison's witty and entertaining commentaries on the morals and manners of the day
- Samuel Johnson's powerfully personal essays in *The Rambler*

Formal essays explore topics in a more serious, thorough, and organized manner than informal essays. Eighteenth-century examples include

- Daniel Defoe's persuasive analysis of female education in "An Academy for Women"
- Mary Wollstonecraft's argument against injustice in *A Vindication of the Rights of Woman*

Other Forms of Nonfiction

Letters and **diaries** often provide personal details of everyday life at the time they were written. You have already read excerpts from Samuel Pepys's diary. This work is important as a record by someone who observed life in its smallest details and then meditated on the meaning of what he had witnessed. Other examples are

- the letters of Lord Chesterfield and Lady Mary Wortley Montagu, which are candid and serious
- the letters in Fanny Burney's *The Diary and Letters of Madame d'Arblay*

Biography is nonfiction in which a writer recounts the events of another person's life. Memoirs, a form of autobiography, are works in which people recall significant events in their own lives. Eighteenth-century examples of these forms include

- James Boswell's biography *The Life of Samuel Johnson,* which gives a full and vivid picture of a great literary figure
- Élisabeth Vigée-Lebrun's memoirs, which tell of her experiences during the upheaval of the French Revolution.

YOUR TURN Find and examine a few modern-day equivalents of any of the nonfiction forms discussed.

Strategies for Reading: Nonfiction

1. Take note of the kind of document you are reading. Is it a formal essay, or is it an informal work with a loose structure?
2. Draw conclusions about the writer's purpose. Was the writer addressing a social problem? What solutions does he or she suggest?
3. Connect to the work by putting yourself in the place and time of the work's original audience.
4. If the writer is giving advice to the reader,

consider its value at the time the work was published and its relevance today.

5. Summarize the main ideas of the work in your own words when you have finished reading it.
6. **Monitor** your reading strategies and modify them when your understanding breaks down. Remember to use your Strategies for Active Reading: **predict, visualize, connect, question, clarify,** and **evaluate.**

from The Spectator

Informal Essays by JOSEPH ADDISON

Connect to Your Life

Popular Bylines Most major newspapers publish daily or weekly feature columns by noted journalists. Many of these columns are extremely popular. Think of some columnists whose articles you have read. What kinds of topics do they usually discuss? Are they concerned with everyday life, or do they focus on other issues? Discuss why these columnists enjoy such a wide readership.

Build Background

Everyday Issues In the late 1600s, England's growing middle class became increasingly concerned with the morals and manners of English society. Responding to this concern, certain writers began to offer moral instruction in periodicals, displaying a casual, good-natured approach to society's ills.

Although hundreds of these periodicals were published before the 18th century, none enjoyed the popularity of those written by Joseph Addison and his friend Richard Steele in the early 1700s. Together, Addison and Steele created a form of writing that has remained popular for nearly three centuries—a predecessor of the articles in modern newsmagazines.

The pair jointly launched *The Spectator,* a periodical dealing with issues of everyday life. It was distributed six days a week for nearly two years. Addison and Steele were the first journalists to write deliberately for women as well as men and to publish letters from both male and female readers.

WORDS TO KNOW	**Vocabulary Preview**		
assiduous	laudable	scruple	temper
disconsolate	lugubrious	speculation	
indulge	reprobate	superficial	

Focus Your Reading

LITERARY ANALYSIS **INFORMAL ESSAY** Through their periodicals, Addison and Steele increased the popularity of the informal essay. An **informal essay** presents an opinion on a subject, but not in a completely serious or formal tone. Characteristics of this type of essay include

- humor
- a personal or confidential approach
- a loose and sometimes rambling style
- a surprising or unconventional topic

As you read the excerpts from *The Spectator,* look for these characteristics of the informal essay.

ACTIVE READING **UNDERSTANDING AUTHOR'S PURPOSE**

An **author's purpose** may be to **entertain,** to **inform,** to **express opinions,** or to **persuade.** An author may fulfill more than one purpose in a piece of writing, but one purpose is usually the most important. To help you understand Addison's purposes, be aware of the following as you read these excerpts:

- the author's **tone**
- the main subject
- the supporting details the author uses to develop his ideas

READER'S NOTEBOOK Use a chart like the one shown to jot down Addison's purposes and the details that support each one.

Title of Excerpt	Purpose(s)	Details Supporting Purpose(s)

from The SPECTATOR

JOSEPH ADDISON

PLAN *and* PURPOSE

I t is with much satisfaction that I hear this great city inquiring day by day after these my papers, and receiving my morning lectures with a becoming seriousness and attention. My publisher tells me that there are already three thousand of them distributed every day. . . . Since I have raised to myself so great an audience, I shall spare no pains to make their instruction agreeable, and their diversion useful. For which reasons I shall endeavor to enliven morality with wit, and to temper wit with morality, that my readers may, if possible, both ways find their account in the speculation of the day. . . . The mind that lies fallow[1] but a single day, sprouts up in follies that are only to be killed by a constant and assiduous culture. It was said of Socrates, that he brought philosophy down from heaven to inhabit among men; and I shall be ambitious to have it said of me, that I have brought philosophy out of closets and libraries, schools and colleges, to dwell in clubs and assemblies, at tea tables and in coffeehouses.

I would therefore in a very particular manner recommend these my speculations to all well-regulated families, that set apart an hour in every morning for tea and bread and butter; and would earnestly advise them for their good to order this paper to be punctually served up and to be looked upon as a part of the tea equipage. . . .[2]

---

1. **lies fallow:** is uncultivated, like a field in which no crops have been sown.

2. **equipage:** equipment.

WORDS
TO
KNOW

temper (tĕm′pər) *v.* to make less intense; moderate
speculation (spĕk′yə-lā′shən) *n.* a consideration of a subject
assiduous (ə-sĭj′ōō-əs) *adj.* steadily and carefully attentive

COUNTRY MANNERS

The first and most obvious reflections which arise in a man who changes the city for the country are upon the different manners of the people whom he meets with in those two different scenes of life. By manners I do not mean morals, but behavior and good breeding, as they show themselves in the town and in the country. . . .

Rural politeness is very troublesome to a man of my temper, who generally takes the chair that is next me and walks first or last, in the front or in the rear, as chance directs. I have known my friend Sir Roger's dinner almost cold before the company could adjust the ceremonial and be prevailed upon to sit down. . . . Honest Will Wimble, who I should have thought had been altogether uninfected with ceremony, gives me abundance of trouble in this particular. Though he has been fishing all the morning, he will not help himself

Patience in a Punt (1792), Henry William Bunbury. Watercolor, 8″ × 12⅛″, The Paul Mellon Collection, Upperville, Virginia.

at dinner till I am served. When we are going out of the hall, he runs behind me; and last night, as we were walking in the fields, stopped short at a stile[3] till I came up to it, and upon my making signs to him to get over, told me, with a serious smile, that sure I believed they had no manners in the country. . . .

On COURTSHIP and MARRIAGE

Before marriage we cannot be too inquisitive and discerning in the faults of the person beloved, nor after it too dim-sighted and superficial. However perfect and accomplished the person appears to you at a distance, you will find many blemishes and imperfections in her humor,[4] upon a more intimate acquaintance, which you never discovered or perhaps suspected. Here therefore discretion and good nature are to show their strength; the first will hinder your thoughts from dwelling on what is disagreeable, the other will raise in you all the tenderness of compassion and humanity, and by degrees soften those very imperfections into beauties. . . .

---

3. **stile:** a set of steps for climbing over a fence.
4. **humor:** disposition; temperament.

LUGUBRIOUS PEOPLE

There are many persons, who, by a natural uncheerfulness of heart, mistaken notions of piety, or weakness of understanding, love to indulge this uncomfortable way of life, and give up themselves a prey to grief and melancholy. Superstitious fears, and groundless scruples, cut them off from the pleasures of conversation, and all those social entertainments which are not only innocent but laudable; as if mirth was made for reprobates, and cheerfulness of heart denied those who are the only persons that have a proper title to it.

Sombrius is one of these sons of sorrow. He thinks himself obliged in duty to be sad and disconsolate. He looks on a sudden fit of laughter, as a breach of his baptismal vow. An innocent jest startles him like blasphemy. Tell him of one who is advanced to a title of honor, he lifts up his hands and eyes; describe a public ceremony, he shakes his head. . . . All the little ornaments of life are pomps and vanities. Mirth is wanton,[5] and wit profane. He is scandalized at youth for being lively, and at childhood for being playful. He sits at a Christening, or a marriage feast, as at a funeral; sighs at the conclusion of a merry story; and grows devout when the rest of the company grow pleasant. . . .

ADVANTAGES *of* MARRIAGE

There is another accidental advantage in marriage, which has likewise fallen to my share; I mean having a multitude of children. These I cannot but regard as very great blessings. When I see my little troop before me, I rejoice in the additions which I have made to my species, to my country, and to my religion, in having produced such a number of reasonable creatures, citizens, and Christians. I am pleased to see myself thus perpetuated, and as there is no production comparable to that of a human creature, I am more proud of having been the occasion of ten such glorious productions, than if I had built a hundred pyramids at my own expense, or published as many volumes of the finest wit and learning. . . . ❖

---

5. **wanton:** immoral or impure.

WORDS TO KNOW

lugubrious (lŏŏ-gōō′brē-əs) *adj.* dismal or gloomy to an exaggerated degree
indulge (ĭn-dŭlj′) *v.* to yield to; devote oneself to
scruple (skrōō′pəl) *n.* an uneasiness about the rightness of an action
laudable (lô′də-bəl) *adj.* praiseworthy
reprobate (rĕp′rə-bāt′) *n.* an immoral person; one without principles
disconsolate (dĭs-kŏn′sə-lĭt) *adj.* unable to be comforted; cheerless and gloomy

Connect to the Literature

1. **What Do You Think?**
   What is your overall impression of these excerpts from *The Spectator?*

   Comprehension Check
   - Why does Addison object to some practices stemming from "rural politeness"?
   - According to Addison, how should you regard your beloved before marriage? after marriage?

Think Critically

2. On the basis of these excerpts, how would you describe Addison?

   THINK ABOUT
   - his goals, as stated under "Plan and Purpose"
   - the kinds of topics he addresses
   - his **tone,** or attitude toward the topics

3. **ACTIVE READING** **UNDERSTANDING AUTHOR'S PURPOSE** With a small group of classmates, discuss Addison's purposes in these excerpts. Consider each possible **purpose,** providing reasons and details from the excerpts to support it. Then come to a group consensus on Addison's main purpose in each essay. During the discussion, you may want to refer to the chart you made in your 📖 **READER'S NOTEBOOK.**

4. What messages about everyday life do you think Addison hoped to convey to his readers?

   THINK ABOUT
   - the lifestyles and manners he praises
   - the types of behavior he criticizes

5. Considering the popularity of Addison's writing when it first appeared, what can you conclude about his **audience?** Give evidence to support your conclusions.

Extend Interpretations

6. **Comparing Texts** Compare the third and fifth excerpts from Addison's essays with Sir Francis Bacon's essay "Of Marriage and Single Life" (page 442). What similarities and differences in subject matter and **tone** do you notice?

7. **Connect to Life** Do you think any of the opinions expressed in the excerpts could be applied to contemporary life? Explain your answer and, if appropriate, support it with examples.

Literary Analysis

INFORMAL ESSAY An **informal essay** presents an opinion on a subject, usually in a light or humorous tone. Other characteristics of this type of essay include a personal approach, a loose rambling style, and often a surprising or unconventional topic. All of these aspects are evident in the following lines from "Lugubrious People":

Sombrius is one of these sons of sorrow. . . . He sits at a Christening, or a marriage feast, as at a funeral; sighs at the conclusion of a merry story; and grows devout when the rest of the company grow pleasant. . . .

Paired Activity With a partner, find other examples from Addison's essays that contain the characteristics mentioned above. List the examples and the characteristics they contain in a chart like the one shown. Then discuss the following question: Why do you think the informal essay was particularly suited to Addison's purpose?

Examples	Characteristics
"Rural politeness is very troublesome to a man of my temper. . . ."	humorous tone, personal approach

Writing Options

Newspaper Column Write a newspaper column about a problem in your school or community, presenting your solution to the problem. Place the column in your **Working Portfolio.**

Writing Handbook
See page 1369: Problem-Solution.

Activities & Explorations

Illustrated Excerpts Illustrate the excerpts from *The Spectator.* You might draw your own sketches or find cartoons or other finished pieces that represent the excerpts. ~ **ART**

Vocabulary in Action

EXERCISE A: SYNONYMS Write the letter of the word that is a synonym of the boldfaced word.

1. **temper:** (a) modify, (b) gratify, (c) explain

2. **assiduous:** (a) critical, (b) diligent, (c) flexible

3. **disconsolate:** (a) forlorn, (b) argumentative, (c) separated

4. **lugubrious:** (a) huge, (b) difficult, (c) mournful

5. **indulge:** (a) praise, (b) submit, (c) ruin

EXERCISE B: MEANING CLUES For each phrase in the first column, write the letter of the rhyming phrase in the second column that has a similar meaning.

1. shame the villain
2. distinct and admirable
3. a shallow administrator
4. greatly increase your ethics
5. a pondering about the economy

a. quadruple your **scruples**
b. humiliate the **reprobate**
c. a **speculation** on inflation
d. audible and **laudable**
e. a **superficial** official

Building Vocabulary
For an in-depth lesson on how to expand your vocabulary, see page 1182.

Joseph Addison
1672–1719

Inseparable Friends Joseph Addison's name is inseparably linked with that of his friend Richard Steele because of their collaboration on *The Spectator.* Addison and Steele's long friendship began when they were teenagers at the same London school. Both attended Oxford University and later became strong supporters of the liberal political party known as the Whigs.

Poet and Statesman At Oxford, Addison received a master's degree and distinguished himself as a master of Latin verse. He later served as a member of the British and Irish parliaments and held several important government posts, including that of secretary of state.

Coffeehouse Philosophy Addison was successful in his attempt to bring philosophy "out of closets and libraries . . . and in[to] coffeehouses," partly because the light, humorous style of *The Spectator* made its moral content acceptable to 18th-century readers. By praising marriage, honesty, and simplicity while ridiculing hypocrisy and pride, Addison and Steele sought to improve the morals and manners of their audience; and by writing about the events and scenes of everyday life, they have given future generations a good idea of how people lived in their time.

Author Activity

More Words of Wisdom Read some other articles written by Addison for *The Spectator.* Select a favorite article and present a summary of it to the class.

from Letters to His Son

By PHILIP STANHOPE, LORD CHESTERFIELD

Letter to Her Daughter

By LADY MARY WORTLEY MONTAGU

Connect to Your Life

Let Me Give You Some Advice Most parents feel that they have a responsibility to advise their children and attempt to do so in various ways. Think about your own response to advice from parents or older family members. What is the most important or helpful advice that a parent can give a child?

Build Background

Collections of Correspondence The popularity of letter writing during the 1700s resulted in collections of correspondence that have become an important part of English literary tradition. Among the most notable are the **letters** written by Philip Stanhope, Lord Chesterfield, to his son and godson and those written by Lady Mary Wortley Montagu to her husband, sister, and daughter. Because these letters were personal and meant to be read only by their recipients, they offer unique perspectives on 18th-century society.

Chesterfield wrote letters nearly every day for more than 30 years, most of them dealing with matters of etiquette and social awareness. An able statesman, he was known as a man of wit and elegance. The published correspondence of Montagu, who traveled widely and was a leading figure in society, consists of almost 900 letters. In them she reveals her views on society, focusing on the lives and education of women. Also the author of poems and essays, Montagu was encouraged in her pursuits by her friend Mary Astell, who argued for a woman's right to a challenging and balanced education.

> WORDS TO KNOW
> **Vocabulary Preview**
>
> contrive
> controverted
> diverting
> edifice
> implacable
>
> inveterate
> inviolably
> mortification
> prepossess
> scrupulous

Focus Your Reading

LITERARY ANALYSIS | **PARALLELISM** | **Parallelism** is the use of similar grammatical constructions to express ideas that are related or equal in importance.

> *No entertainment is so cheap as reading, nor any pleasure so lasting.*

In this example, there are a number of parallel items. *No* is balanced by *nor; entertainment* is balanced by *pleasure; so cheap* is balanced by *so lasting.* As you read these letters, be aware of the writers' use of parallelism.

ACTIVE READING | **MAKING GENERALIZATIONS** | A **generalization** is a broad statement based on several examples. In these letters, the two writers present many details about life in 18th-century England—particularly education, the roles of women and men, and manners of the time. Think about what generalizations you might make about 18th-century English society based on the details you find.

READER'S NOTEBOOK As you read these letters, record evidence about education, the roles of men and women, and manners of the day in a chart like the one shown. Make one generalization for each topic.

Topic	Details from Chesterfield Letters	Details from Montagu Letter	Generalization
1. Education			
2. Roles of men and women			
3. Manners of the day			

George Morland (about 1785–1810), Thomas Rowlandson. British Museum, London, Bridgeman/Art Resource.

from LETTERS to His SON

PHILIP STANHOPE, LORD CHESTERFIELD

SPA, JULY 25, 1741

Dear Boy,

I have often told you in my former letters (and it is most certainly true) that the strictest and most scrupulous honor and virtue can alone make you esteemed and valued by mankind; that parts and learning can alone make you admired and celebrated by them; but that the possession of lesser talents was most absolutely necessary towards making you liked, beloved, and sought after in private life. Of these lesser talents, good-breeding is the principal and most necessary one, not only as it is very important in itself; but as it adds great luster to the more solid advantages both of the heart and the mind.

I have often touched upon good-breeding to you before; so that this letter shall be upon the next necessary qualification to it, which is a genteel, easy manner and carriage, wholly free from those odd tricks, ill habits, and awkwardnesses, which even very many worthy and sensible people have in their behavior. However trifling a genteel manner may sound, it is of very great consequence towards pleasing in private life, especially the women; which, one time or other, you will think worth pleasing; and I have known many a man, from his awkwardness, give people such a dislike of him at first, that all his merit could not get the better of it afterwards. Whereas a genteel manner prepossesses people in your favor, bends them towards you, and makes them wish to like you.

WORDS
TO
KNOW

scrupulous (skro͞o'pyə-ləs) *adj.* showing great strictness and care, especially in matters of right and wrong
prepossess (prē'pə-zĕs') *v.* to influence beforehand; prejudice

Awkwardness can proceed but from two causes; either from not having kept good company, or from not having attended to it. As for your keeping good company, I will take care of that; do you take care to observe their ways and manners, and to form your own upon them. Attention is absolutely necessary for this, as indeed it is for everything else; and a man without attention is not fit to live in the world. When an awkward fellow first comes into a room, it is highly probable that his sword gets between his legs, and throws him down, or makes him stumble at least; when he has recovered this accident, he goes and places himself in the very place of the whole room where he should not; there he soon lets his hat fall down; and, taking it up again, throws down his cane; in recovering his cane, his hat falls a second time; so that he is a quarter of an hour before he is in order again. If he drinks tea or coffee, he certainly scalds his mouth, and lets either the cup or the saucer fall, and spills the tea or coffee in his breeches. At dinner, his awkwardness distinguishes itself particularly, as he has more to do: there he holds his knife, fork, and spoon differently from other people; eats with his knife to the great danger of his mouth, picks his teeth with his fork, and puts his spoon, which has been in his throat twenty times, into the dishes again. If he is to carve, he can never hit the joint; but, in his vain efforts to cut through the bone, scatters the sauce in everybody's face. He generally daubs himself with soup and grease, though his napkin is commonly stuck through a button-hole, and tickles his chin. When he drinks, he infallibly coughs in his glass, and besprinkles the company. Besides all this, he has strange tricks and gestures; such as snuffing up his nose, making faces, putting his fingers in his nose, or blowing it and looking afterwards in his handkerchief, so as to make the company sick. His hands are troublesome to him, when he has not something in them, and he does not know where to put them; but they are in perpetual motion between his bosom and his breeches: he does not wear his clothes, and in short does nothing, like other people. All this, I own, is not in any degree criminal; but it is highly disagreeable and ridiculous in company, and ought most carefully to be avoided by whoever desires to please.

From this account of what you should not do, you may easily judge what you should do; and a due attention to the manners of people of fashion, and who have seen the world, will make it habitual and familiar to you.

There is, likewise, an awkwardness of expression and words, most carefully to be avoided; such as false English, bad pronunciation, old sayings, and common proverbs; which are so many proofs of having kept bad and low company. For example: if, instead of saying that tastes are different, and that every man has his own peculiar one, you should let off a proverb, and say, That what is one man's meat is another man's poison; or else, Every one as they like, as the good man said when he kissed his cow; everybody would be persuaded that you had never kept company with anybody above footmen and housemaids.

Attention will do all this; and without attention nothing is to be done: want of attention, which is really want of thought, is either folly or madness. You should not only have attention to everything, but a quickness of attention, so as to observe, at

AWKWARDNESS CAN PROCEED BUT FROM TWO CAUSES; EITHER FROM NOT HAVING KEPT GOOD COMPANY, OR FROM NOT HAVING ATTENDED TO IT.

once, all the people in the room; their motions, their looks, and their words; and yet without staring at them, and seeming to be an observer. This quick and unobserved observation is of infinite advantage in life, and is to be acquired with care; and, on the contrary, what is called absence, which is a thoughtlessness, and want of attention about what is doing, makes a man so like either a fool or a madman, that, for my part, I see no real difference. A fool never had thought; a madman has lost it; and an absent man is, for the time, without it.

Adieu! Direct your next to me, *chez Monsieur Chabert, Banquier, à Paris;*[1] and take care that I find the improvements I expect at my return.

London, September 5, 1748

Dear Boy,

. . . As women are a considerable, or at least a pretty numerous part, of company; and as their suffrages[2] go a great way towards establishing a man's character in the fashionable part of the world (which is of great importance to the fortune and figure he proposes to make in it), it is necessary to please them. I will therefore, upon this subject, let you into certain *arcana*,[3] that will be very useful for you to know, but which you must, with the utmost care, conceal, and never seem to know.

Women, then, are only children of a larger growth; they have an entertaining tattle and sometimes wit; but for solid, reasoning good-sense, I never in my life knew one that had it, or who reasoned or acted consequentially[4] for four-and-twenty hours together. Some little passion or humor always breaks in upon their best resolutions. Their beauty neglected or <u>controverted</u>, their age increased, or their supposed understandings depreciated, instantly kindles their little passions, and overturns any system of consequential conduct, that in their most reasonable moments they might have been capable of forming. A man of sense only trifles with them, plays with them, humors and flatters them, as he does with a sprightly, forward child; but he neither consults them about, nor trusts them with, serious matters; though he often makes them believe that he does both; which is the thing in the world that they are proud of; for they love mightily to be dabbling in business (which by the way, they always spoil); and being justly distrustful, that men in general look upon them in a trifling light, they almost adore that man, who talks more seriously to them, and who seems to consult and trust them; I say, who seems, for weak men really do, but wise ones only seem to do it. No flattery is either too high or too low for them. They will greedily swallow the highest, and gratefully accept of the lowest; and you may safely flatter any woman, from her understanding down to the exquisite taste of her fan.

Women who are either indisputably beautiful, or indisputably ugly, are best flattered upon the score of their understandings; but those who are in a state of mediocrity, are best flattered upon their beauty, or at least their graces; for every woman who is not absolutely ugly, thinks herself handsome; but, not hearing often that she is so, is the more grateful and the more obliged to the few who tell her so; whereas a decided and conscious beauty looks upon every tribute paid to her beauty, only as her due; but wants to shine, and to be considered on the side of her understanding; and a woman who is ugly enough to know that she is so, knows that she has nothing left for it but her understanding, which is consequently (and probably in more senses than one) her weak side.

But these are secrets which you must keep <u>inviolably</u>, if you would not, like Orpheus, be torn

---

1. *chez* (shā) . . . *à Paris* (ä pä-rē′) *French:* at the house of . . . in Paris. (Chesterfield is giving the address where he can be reached.)

2. **suffrages** (sŭf′rĭ-jĭz): signs of approval.

3. *arcana* (är-kā′nə) *Latin:* secrets; mysteries.

4. **consequentially:** in a logically consistent manner.

WORDS TO KNOW
controverted (kŏn′trə-vûr′tĭd) *adj.* disputed; denied **controvert** *v.*
inviolably (ĭn-vī′ə-lə-blē) *adv.* with absolute security

557

to pieces by the whole sex;[5] on the contrary, a man who thinks of living in the great world, must be gallant, polite, and attentive to please the women. They have, from the weakness of men, more or less influence in all Courts; they absolutely stamp every man's character in the *beau monde*,[6] and make it either current, or cry it down, and stop it in payments. It is, therefore, absolutely necessary to manage, please, and flatter them; and never to discover the least marks of contempt, which is what they never forgive; but in this they are not singular, for it is the same with men; who will much sooner forgive an injustice than an insult. Every man is not ambitious, or covetous, or passionate; but every man has pride enough in his composition to feel and resent the least slight and contempt. Remember, therefore, most carefully to conceal your contempt, however just, wherever you would not make an <u>implacable</u> enemy. Men are much more unwilling to have their weaknesses and their imperfections known, than their crimes; and, if you hint to a man that you think him silly, ignorant, or even ill-bred or awkward, he will hate you more, and longer, than if you tell him plainly that you think him a rogue. Never yield to that temptation, which to most young men is very strong, of exposing other people's weaknesses and infirmities, for the sake either of <u>diverting</u> the

company, or of showing your own superiority. You may get the laugh on your side by it, for the present; but you will make enemies by it for ever; and even those who laugh with you then will, upon reflection, fear, and consequently hate you; besides that, it is ill-natured, and a good heart desires rather to conceal than expose other people's weaknesses or misfortunes. If you have wit, use it to please, and not to hurt: you may shine like the sun in the temperate zones, without scorching. Here it is wished for: under the line[7] it is dreaded.

These are some of the hints which my long experience in the great world enables me to give you; and which, if you attend to them, may prove useful to you in your journey through it. I wish it may be a prosperous one; at least, I am sure that it must be your own fault if it is not.

Make my compliments to Mr. Harte, who, I am very sorry to hear, is not well. I hope by this time he is recovered. ❖

Adieu!

---

5. **like Orpheus** (ôr´fē-əs) . . . **sex:** a reference to a Greek myth in which the musician Orpheus is torn limb from limb by maenads—women frenzied under the influence of the god Dionysus.

6. *beau monde* (bō môɴd) *French:* the fashionable world; high society.

7. **line:** equator.

Thinking Through the Literature

1. What is your reaction to Chesterfield after reading his letters?

2. What attitudes and behavior seem to be most important to Chesterfield? Consider the evidence.

   THINK ABOUT
   - the kind of advice he offers and the examples he gives
   - what he hopes to accomplish
   - his views of men and women

3. How would you describe Chesterfield's relationship with his son? Support your ideas with evidence from the letters.

WORDS TO KNOW
implacable (ĭm-plăk´ə-bəl) *adj.* impossible to appease; unforgiving
diverting (dĭ-vûr´tĭng) *n.* entertaining; amusing **divert** *v.*

Letter to Her Daughter

Lady Mary Wortley Montagu

January 28, 1753

Dear Child,

You have given me a great deal of satisfaction by your account of your eldest daughter. I am particularly pleased to hear she is a good arithmetician; it is the best proof of understanding. The knowledge of numbers is one of the chief distinctions between us and brutes. If there is anything in blood you may reasonably expect your children should be endowed with an uncommon share of good sense. Mr. Wortley's family and mine have both produced some of the greatest men that have been born in England. I mean Admiral Sandwich, and my great-grandfather who was distinguished by the name of Wise William. I have heard Lord Bute's father mentioned as an extraordinary genius (though he had not many opportunities of showing it), and his uncle the present Duke of Argyle has one of the best heads I ever knew.

Lady Mary Wortley Montagu (about 1725), Jonathan Richardson. Private collection, courtesy of the Earl of Harrowby.

world, as it is hers to know how to be easy out of it. It is the common error of builders and parents to follow some plan they think beautiful (and perhaps is so) without considering that nothing is beautiful that is misplaced. Hence we see so many <u>edifices</u> raised that the raisers can never inhabit, being too large for their fortunes. Vistas are laid open over barren heaths, and apartments <u>contrived</u> for a coolness very agreeable in Italy but killing in the north of Britain. Thus every woman endeavors to breed her daughter a fine lady, qualifying her for a station in which she will never appear, and at the same time incapacitating her for that retirement to which she is destined. Learning (if she has a real taste for it) will not only make her contented but happy in it. No entertainment is so cheap as reading, nor any pleasure so lasting. She will not want new fashions nor regret the loss of expensive diversions or variety of company if she can be amused with an author in her closet. To render this amusement extensive, she should be permitted to learn the languages. I have heard it lamented that boys lose so many years in mere learning of words. This is no objection to a girl, whose time is not so precious. She cannot advance herself in any profession, and has therefore more hours to spare; and as you say her memory is good she will be very agreeably employed this way.

There are two cautions to be given on this subject: first, not to think herself learned when she can read Latin or even Greek. Languages are more properly to be called vehicles of learning than learning itself, as may be observed in many schoolmasters, who though perhaps critics in grammar are the most ignorant fellows upon earth. True knowledge consists in knowing things, not words. I would wish her no further a linguist than to enable her to read books in their originals, that are often corrupted and always injured by translations. Two hours application every morning will bring this about much sooner

I will therefore speak to you as supposing Lady Mary not only capable but desirous of learning. In that case, by all means let her be indulged in it. You will tell me, I did not make it a part of your education. Your prospect was very different from hers, as you had no defect either in mind or person to hinder, and much in your circumstances to attract, the highest offers. It seemed your business to learn how to live in the

than you can imagine, and she will have leisure enough beside to run over the English poetry, which is a more important part of a woman's education than it is generally supposed. Many a young damsel has been ruined by a fine copy of verses, which she would have laughed at if she had known it had been stolen from Mr. Waller.[1] I remember when I was a girl I saved one of my companions from destruction, who communicated to me an epistle[2] she was quite charmed with. As she had a natural good taste she observed the lines were not so smooth as Prior's or Pope's,[3] but had more thought and spirit than any of theirs. She was wonderfully delighted with such a demonstration of her lover's sense and passion, and not a little pleased with her own charms, that had force enough to inspire such elegancies. In the midst of this triumph I showed her they were taken from Randolph's *Poems,* and the unfortunate transcriber was dismissed with the scorn he deserved. To say truth, the poor plagiary[4] was very unlucky to fall into my hands; that author, being no longer in fashion, would have escaped anyone of less universal reading than myself. You should encourage your daughter to talk over with you what she reads, and as you are very capable of distinguishing, take care she does not mistake pert folly for wit and humor, or rhyme for poetry, which are the common errors of young people, and have a train of ill consequences.

The second caution to be given her (and which is most absolutely necessary) is to conceal whatever learning she attains, with as much solicitude as she would hide crookedness or lameness. The parade of it can only serve to draw on her the envy, and consequently the most <u>inveterate</u> hatred of all he and she fools, which will certainly be at least three parts in four of all her acquaintance. The use of knowledge in our sex (beside the amusement of solitude) is to moderate the passions and learn to be contented with a small expense, which are the certain effects of a studious life and, it may be, preferable even to that fame which men have engrossed to themselves and will not suffer us to share. You will tell me I have not observed this rule myself, but you are mistaken; it is only inevitable accident that has given me any reputation that way. I have always carefully avoided it, and ever thought it a misfortune.

The explanation of this paragraph would occasion a long digression, which I will not trouble you with, it being my present design only to say what I think useful for the instruction of my granddaughter, which I have much at heart. If she has the same inclination (I should say passion) for learning that I was born with, history, geography, and philosophy will furnish her with materials to pass away cheerfully a longer life than is allotted to mortals. I believe there are few heads capable of making Sir Isaac Newton's calculations, but the result of them is not difficult to be understood by a moderate capacity. Do not fear this should make her affect the character of Lady———, or Lady———, or Mrs.———. Those women are ridiculous not because they have learning but because they have

Christie's Images.

---

1. **Mr. Waller:** the English poet Edmund Waller.
2. **epistle:** letter.
3. **as Prior's or Pope's:** as those of Matthew Prior or Alexander Pope, both English poets.
4. **plagiary:** plagiarist—one who copies someone else's writing and presents it as his or her own.

WORDS TO KNOW   **inveterate** (ĭn-vĕt′ər-ĭt) *adj.* firmly established and deep-rooted

it not. One thinks herself a complete historian after reading Echard's *Roman History*,[5] another a profound philosopher having got by heart some of Pope's unintelligible essays, and a third an able divine[6] on the strength of Whitefield's sermons.[7] Thus you hear them screaming politics and controversy. It is a saying of Thucydides:[8] Ignorance is bold, and knowledge reserved. Indeed it is impossible to be far advanced in it without being more humbled by a conviction of human ignorance than elated by learning.

At the same time I recommend books I neither exclude work nor drawing. I think it as scandalous for a woman not to know how to use a needle, as for a man not to know how to use a sword. I was once extreme fond of my pencil, and it was a great <u>mortification</u> to me when my father turned off my master,[9] having made a considerable progress for the short time I learned. My over-eagerness in the pursuit of it had brought a weakness on my eyes that made it necessary to leave it off, and all the advantage I got was the improvement of my hand. I see by hers that practice will make her a ready writer. She may attain it by serving you for a secretary when your health or affairs make it troublesome to you to write yourself, and custom will make it an agreeable amusement to her. She cannot have too many for that station in life which will probably be her fate. The ultimate end of your education was to make you a good wife (and I have the comfort to hear that you are one); hers ought to be, to make her happy in a virgin state. I will not say it is happier, but it is undoubtedly safer than any marriage. In a lottery where there is (at the lowest computation) ten thousand blanks to a prize it is the most prudent choice not to venture.

I have always been so thoroughly persuaded of this truth that notwithstanding the flattering views I had for you (as I never intended you a sacrifice to my vanity) I thought I owed you the justice to lay before you all the hazards attending matrimony. You may recollect I did so in the strongest manner. Perhaps you may have more success in the instructing your daughter. She has so much company at home she will not need seeking it abroad, and will more readily take the notions you think fit to give her. As you were alone in my family, it would have been thought a great cruelty to suffer you no companions of your own age, especially having so many near relations, and I do not wonder their opinions influenced yours. I was not sorry to see you not determined on a single life, knowing it was not your father's intention, and contented myself with endeavoring to make your home so easy that you might not be in haste to leave it.

I am afraid you will think this a very long and insignificant letter. I hope the kindness of the design will excuse it, being willing to give you every proof in my power that I am your most affectionate mother,

M. Wortley

---

5. **Echard's *Roman History*:** a book by Lawrence Echard, an English historian.

6. **able divine:** knowledgeable religious scholar.

7. **Whitefield's sermons:** the printed sermons of George Whitefield, a famous English preacher.

8. **Thucydides** (thōō-sĭd'ĭ-dēz'): an ancient Greek historian.

9. **turned off my master:** discharged my art instructor.

mortification (môr'tə-fĭ-kā'shən) *n.* extreme embarrassment; humiliation

from

Some Reflections upon Marriage

Mary Astell

According to the rate that young women are educated, according to the way their time is spent, they are destined to folly and impertinence, to say no worse, and, which is yet more inhuman, they are blamed for that ill conduct they are not suffered to avoid, and reproached for those faults they are in a manner forced into; so that if Heaven has bestowed any sense on them, no other use is made of it, than to leave them without excuse. So much, and no more, of the world is shown them, than serves to weaken and corrupt their minds, to give them wrong notions, and busy them in mean pursuits; to disturb, not to regulate their passions; to make them timorous and dependent, and, in a word, fit for nothing else but to act a farce for the diversion of their governors.

Thinking through the LITERATURE

Connect to the Literature

1. What Do You Think? Does Montagu strike you as an appealing person? Explain your opinion.

> **Comprehension Check**
> • What kind of future does Montagu expect for her granddaughter?
> • What advice does Montagu give on distinguishing true knowledge from the mere appearance of knowing?

Think Critically

2. What is your opinion of Montagu's views on education and marriage for women? Explain your opinion.

3. What factors do you think might have influenced Montagu to give this kind of advice about the raising of her granddaughter?

4. How do you think Montagu's granddaughter might have felt about her grandmother's advice?

5. **ACTIVE READING** **MAKING GENERALIZATIONS** Look back at the chart and the **generalizations** you made about 18th-century society in your 📖 **READER'S NOTEBOOK**. What generalization can you make about how much appearances and manners mattered in 18th-century England?

Extend Interpretations

6. Comparing Texts Reread the excerpt from *Some Reflections upon Marriage* on page 563. In what ways might the **letters** of Chesterfield and Montagu be used to support Astell's claims about the treatment of women? Be specific in your answer.

7. What If? Suppose Montagu's granddaughter had no "defect either in mind or person." How do you think Montagu's letter would be different? What advice would she impart regarding her granddaughter?

8. Connect to Life What do you think Montagu and Chesterfield would make of the role of women in society today? Discuss with your classmates.

Literary Analysis

PARALLELISM **Parallelism**—the use of similar grammatical constructions to express ideas that are related or equal in importance—may involve words, phrases, sentences, or paragraphs. The following sentence from Chesterfield's second letter, for example, repeats both words and phrases:

> *Women who are either indisputably beautiful, or indisputably ugly, are best flattered upon the score of their understandings; but those who are in a state of mediocrity, are best flattered upon their beauty. . . .*

There are many such examples in these letters of parallel constructions that reflect the relationship between ideas.

Paired Activity With a partner, exchange letters on a subject of interest to you both—sports or movies, for example—in which you employ parallelism to express your thoughts.

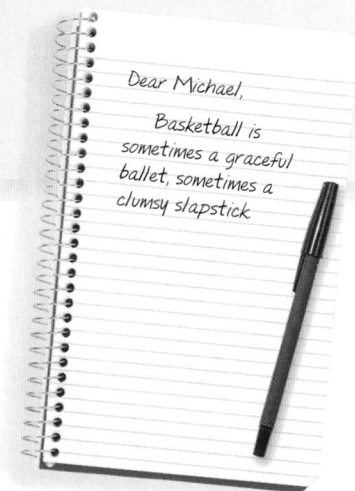

Dear Michael,
   Basketball is sometimes a graceful ballet, sometimes a clumsy slapstick

Choices & CHALLENGES

Writing Options

Essay on Awkwardness
Chesterfield addresses the problem of awkwardness in social relations and proposes ways of dealing with it. Write an essay in which you suggest solutions to social awkwardness in today's world. Place the essay in your **Working Portfolio.**

Writing Handbook
See page 1368: Cause and Effect.

Building Vocabulary
Several Words to Know in this lesson contain prefixes and suffixes. For an in-depth study of word parts, see page 1104.

Vocabulary in Action

EXERCISE: CLUES AND IDIOMS
On your paper, write the vocabulary words that are suggested by the phrases in items 1–5 and by the groups of idioms in items 6–10.

1. how secrets should be kept and deep friendships preserved
2. what you do when you make a friend expect a blind date to be terrific
3. what the White House and Buckingham Palace are examples of
4. the kind of behavior that is so habitual that it can never be changed
5. what inventors, architects, and schemers do
6. nearly die of shame, blow one's cool, be red as a beet, feel like two cents
7. dotting all the *i*'s, being as good as one's word, taking pains, following through
8. no way, on the contrary, have a bone to pick
9. just for laughs, take a break, live a little
10. carry a grudge, heart of stone, hard as nails

WORDS TO KNOW	contrive controverted diverting edifice	implacable inveterate inviolably mortification	prepossess scrupulous

Philip Stanhope, Lord Chesterfield
1694–1773

Diplomat, Writer, Patron of the Arts Philip Stanhope was raised and educated by his grandmother and largely ignored by his aristocratic father. He studied briefly at Cambridge University, then left the university to travel abroad, where he eagerly observed and imitated French manners and culture. He became a capable statesman and diplomat, eventually serving as secretary of state. Chesterfield was a friend of Pope, Swift, and Voltaire, and as a patron of the arts he gave financial assistance to many struggling writers. Although he contributed numerous essays to periodicals, he is remembered chiefly for his letters to his son and godson.

Lady Mary Wortley Montagu
1689–1762

An Adventurous Life Lady Mary Wortley Montagu, a gifted poet and essayist, was acquainted with many literary figures, including Pope, Addison, and Steele. Her first published work was an essay contributed to *The Spectator.* A daughter of London aristocrats, Montagu educated herself in her father's library. In 1712, to escape an arranged marriage, she eloped with Edward Wortley Montagu. When Edward was appointed ambassador to Turkey, Lady Mary accompanied him to Constantinople, where she wrote more than 50 letters describing Turkish culture. Her Turkish letters were published in 1763, but a full edition of her letters was not available until 1967.

Robinson Crusoe

I f you were marooned on a remote and wild island, how would you respond to the challenges of nature? What would you eat? Where would you sleep? Would you go mad from isolation—or use the experience as a chance to grow? These are some of the issues confronted by the hero of Daniel Defoe's masterful adventure story *Robinson Crusoe.*

The plot of *Robinson Crusoe* is based on the true story of Alexander Selkirk, a sailor who had been stranded for 52 months on an uninhabited island near Chile. Defoe capitalized on public interest in Selkirk by producing a memoir of a fictional castaway—Robinson Crusoe—using the first-person narrative, exact details, and precise chronology that would be found in the journal of a seasoned seafarer. The resulting story was so popular that unscrupulous publishers scrambled to produce and sell their own editions. Even today, the book is available in many editions, some lavishly illustrated, and the story of Robinson Crusoe is used as a basis for comic books, feature films, and science fiction adventures.

In his 28 years on the island, Crusoe learns how to make tools, plant seeds, and domesticate animals. Slowly, he turns the untamed land into a secure and productive homestead.

In addition to chronicling the adventures of a castaway, Defoe explored the social and moral values of his time. For example, he portrays Crusoe as a willful son whose disregard for the wishes of his parents leads him into danger, slavery, and shipwreck. He also shows how the experience of life alone on the island leads Crusoe to appreciate the moral and social values back home. Only when Crusoe begins to apply these values, along with his native talents, does he begin to prosper. He teaches himself carpentry, pottery, agriculture, and animal husbandry. He learns the geography of his island. He rescues from cannibals a man whom he names Friday and who becomes his devoted servant. Finally, he saves the captain of a passing ship from mutineers. Leaving the mutineers on the island, Crusoe and the captain sail with Friday to England, where Crusoe assumes a place in English society.

At one time or another, almost everyone has wondered what it would be like to have to survive in a wilderness. In *Robinson Crusoe,* Defoe presents a man who not only survives but thrives—who transforms the wilderness into an expression of humanity. The result is a story that appeals to everyone who yearns for adventure.

Left:
Despite ominous mishaps, including a severe storm, Robinson Crusoe is determined to make his fortune at sea.

Center:
Crusoe, the disheveled castaway

Right:
For 26 of his years on the island, Crusoe's only companions are a dog, some cats, a goat, and his parrot, which he teaches to say "Poor Robin Crusoe! Where are you?"

Writing Workshop

Recommending a Solution . . .

From Reading to Writing In the second half of the 17th century, English writers sought to make sense of their world by observing society and addressing problems that they saw. People today are just as observant and concerned, and they often make suggestions on improving their communities in the form of proposals. A **proposal** is a document or speech that identifies a problem or need, and offers a plan of action to solve the problem or meet the need. You can write a proposal to address issues affecting your family, school, or community.

For Your Portfolio

WRITING PROMPT Write a proposal recommending a solution to a problem or a need.

Purpose: To convince a group or organization to put your plan into practice

Audience: The decision-makers who will be evaluating your proposal

---

Basics in a Box

Proposal at a Glance

> **Summary of Proposal**
>
> Briefly states the purpose of the proposal

> **Need**
>
> - Defines the problem or need
> - States why addressing it is important

> **Proposed Solution**
>
> - Presents a detailed solution
> - Explains its benefits
> - Restates the problem or need and the benefits of the solution

RUBRIC Standards for Writing

A successful proposal should

- target a specific audience
- clearly define a problem or state a need
- present a clear solution, using evidence to demonstrate that the plan is workable
- show how the plan will be implemented and what resources will be required
- demonstrate clearly that the advantages of the plan outweigh possible objections to it

Analyzing a Student Model

Simona Ioffe
Stevenson High School

A Proposal to Enhance Arts Education at Stevenson High School

Summary

This proposal requests approval and support from the faculty and administration of Stevenson High School for creating an arts festival. This festival will increase students' awareness of and appreciation for the arts and will give them a more fully rounded education.

Need

An understanding of the arts is vital because it broadens the horizons of every individual. The Association for the Advancement of Arts Education (AAAE) states that "the arts are necessary at all grade levels for many aspects of students' success in school and in life, as in their careers." The Association further states that "all of the arts help students develop emotionally and socially."

Stevenson High School currently addresses this need by offering several courses in the areas of art and music and by sponsoring student drama and dance clubs. However, many students do not take advantage of these opportunities. A random poll of 50 senior students at Stevenson High School showed that 40 percent had not taken any arts courses throughout their years at the school. Some even stated that "only people who will become actors need to participate in the arts." Other disturbing comments included "the fine arts are a waste of time" and "it's boring!" This poll clearly shows the need for the school to develop a plan that will give all students at least a basic appreciation for the arts.

To solve this problem, members of the faculty have suggested creating an arts requirement for graduation. This idea meets the problem head-on. However, it will take time to plan and may require a restructuring of the arts department. For example, a new survey class covering visual art, theater, music, and dance will have to be developed. Although this would be a good long-term solution, students need an opportunity to experience the arts as soon as possible—and not by reading about them in a textbook.

RUBRIC
IN ACTION

❶ The summary clearly states the purpose of the proposal and identifies the audience.

❷ This writer uses a quotation to show the importance of the issue.
Other Options:
· Give an example or anecdote.
· Cite expert opinions.

❸ This writer defines the problem and supports it with data from her own opinion poll.
Other Options:
· Do library or Internet research.
· Consult authorities.

❹ Points out the weaknesses of a current plan

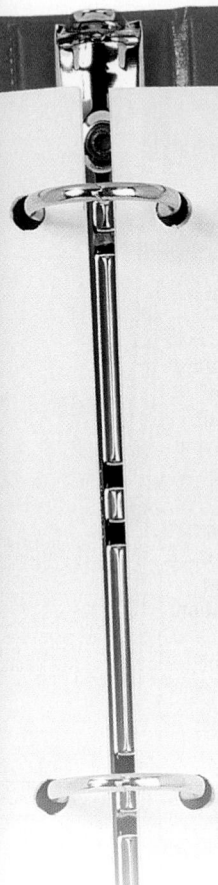

Proposed Solution

My solution is to create an arts festival this spring. The festival would allow students to participate in the arts firsthand and would be a school-wide event involving the entire student body, faculty, and staff. During the two-day festival, Stevenson High School would be completely transformed into a learning facility for the arts. The festival would include performances, visual presentations, and hands-on experiences for every student. Exhibits, classes, workshops, and activities would be held throughout the building.

Students would be allowed to select the events to participate in, but they would be required to experience all four genres of art. The mix of genres and formats would give students broad exposure to the arts.

Implementing this plan would require commitment from the entire school community. The arts department faculty would need to plan events that would be interesting and beneficial for students and manageable for the staff. The administration would handle scheduling and legal issues. The maintenance staff would need to organize the acquisition and distribution of chairs, tables, and other necessary furniture. Student volunteers would do much of the work of making the festival run smoothly. Most of the funding for the fair could probably come from the regular budgets of the administration and art department. However, local businesses could be asked to donate materials; and if necessary, students and faculty could hold fundraising activities such as bake sales or car washes.

Even though an arts festival would shorten the school year by two days, Stevenson High School would be responding to the needs of students. Writer Marcel Proust said, "Only through art can we get outside of ourselves and know another's view of the universe. . . ." An arts festival would give students the opportunity to explore new ways of understanding and experiencing the world.

❺ Explains the details of the solution

❻ This writer describes the general resources needed to implement the plan.

Other Options
· Spell out the steps involved in putting the plan into action
· Identify people who will back or fund the plan
· Estimate the costs

❼ Explains how the advantages of the plan outweigh the disadvantages

Writing Your Proposal

❶ Prewriting

Begin by choosing a problem to be solved or identifying a need to be filled. You might make a **list** of ideas for improving your school or community. You could also try **brainstorming** problems or needs with a group of friends. See the **Idea Bank** in the margin for more suggestions. After you have selected the topic for your proposal, follow the steps below.

Planning your Proposal

▶ **1. Think about your proposal.** Why is the issue important? How will your proposal meet the need?

▶ **2. Consider your audience.** Who will evaluate your proposal? What do they care about? What will persuade them to accept your proposal?

▶ **3. List the details.** What steps are involved? What resources are needed?

▶ **4. Evaluate the workability of your proposal.** How hard will it be to put your plan into effect? What are some of the arguments against it?

▶ **5. Plan your research.** What information will help support the proposal? Where can you find information? Can you conduct some of your own research?

❷ Drafting

A problem well stated is a problem half solved.
Charles Kettering, inventor

You can begin drafting your proposal anywhere—with the summary, the problem or need, or the solution. No matter where you begin, though, you eventually will have to address all these points. As you draft, remember to show both why addressing the problem or need is important and how your proposed solution accomplishes that. Be sure to support your statements with facts, statistics, or expert opinions. Also, define any technical terms your audience might not know and think about objections they might have to your plan. You can improve your draft later with input from your peer readers.

Ask Your Peer Reader

• What other evidence would convince people there is a real problem or need?

• How can obstacles to implementing my plan be overcome?

• What other resources are needed to support my plan?

• Who is likely to oppose my plan and why?

IDEABank

1. Your Working Portfolio 📁
Build on one of the Writing Options you completed earlier in this unit:

• **Problem-Solving Essay,** p. 533

• **Essay on a Social Problem,** p. 539

• **Newspaper Column,** p. 553

• **Essay on Awkwardness,** p. 565

2. Community Issues
Study recent issues of your school or community newsletters to find problems that need solutions.

3. A Friend in Need
Interview friends or neighbors to find out what neighborhood problem bothers them most. What can you think of that would help solve this problem? Choose one solution as the focus for your proposal.

Adding an appendix

Include supporting material such as charts, copies of published articles, letters of support, and other information at the end of your proposal in a section called the appendix.

Need revising help?

Review the **Rubric,** p. 568

Consider **peer reader** comments

Check **Revision Guidelines,** p. 1355.

❸ Revising

TARGET SKILL ▶ TRANSITION WORDS Transition words or phrases show how the ideas in your proposal are related and so make your writing more convincing. You can also use transitions to signal that you are refuting an objection to your plan.

> This poll clearly shows the need for the school to develop a plan that will give all students at least a basic appreciation for the arts. *To solve this problem,* Members of the faculty have suggested creating an arts requirement for graduation. This idea meets the problem head-on. *However,* It will take time and may require a restructuring of the arts department. *For example,* A new survey class covering visual art, theater, music, and dance will have to be developed. *Although* This would be a good long-term solution, students need an opportunity to experience the fine arts as soon as possible—and not by reading about them in a textbook.

Stumped by adverbs?

See the **Grammar Handbook,** p. 1403

❹ Editing and Proofreading

TARGET SKILL ▶ USING ADVERBS CORRECTLY As you edit your proposal, check to see that you have used adverbs correctly. Do not use an adjective when an adverb is needed.

> Student volunteers would do much of the work of making the festival run smooth*ly*. Most of the funding for the *fair* ~~fare~~ could probabl*y* come from the regular budgets of the administration and art department.

Publishing
IDEAS

- Present your proposal orally to the audience for which it was intended.
- Submit your proposal to a school or local newspaper to bring it to the attention of a wider audience.

More Online: Publishing Options www.mcdougallittell.com

❺ Reflecting

FOR YOUR WORKING PORTFOLIO In what ways did your initial idea change during the writing of your proposal? What influences led to the changes? Attach your answer to your proposal. Save your proposal in your **Working Portfolio.**

Read this introduction from the first draft of a student essay. The underlined sections may include the following kinds of errors:

- **run-on sentences**
- **incorrectly used adverb and adjective modifiers**
- **incorrect plural forms**
- **verb tense errors**

For each underlined section, choose the revision that most improves the writing.

Nelson Park played an important role in our region's history; therefore, the park should <u>be granted</u> landmark status by the community board. Without this recognition, commercial development <u>will sure destroy</u> the park. Although small in size, it <u>was</u> loaded with history. In the early part of this century, Susan B. Anthony <u>has led</u> important suffragist rallies at Nelson Park. Later in the century, the park became a focus for the civil rights movement. Many peaceful <u>assemblys</u> took place there. <u>Nelson Park has a proud history it should also have a strong future.</u>

(1) (2) (3) (4) (5) (6)

---

1. A. be granting
　B. granted
　C. have granted
　D. Correct as is

2. A. will, for sure, destroy
　B. sure will destroy
　C. will surely destroy
　D. Correct as is

3. A. is
　B. were
　C. am
　D. Correct as is

4. A. had led
　B. led
　C. leads
　D. Correct as is

5. A. assembles
　B. assembling
　C. assemblies
　D. Correct as is

6. A. Nelson Park has a proud history, it should also have a strong future.
　B. Nelson Park has a proud history. It should also have a strong future.
　C. Nelson Park has a proud, history it should also have a strong, future.
　D. Correct as is

Need extra help?

See the **Grammar Handbook**

Writing Complete Sentences, p. 1409

Modifiers, pp. 1398–1399

Nouns, p. 1392

Verbs, pp. 1395–1398

Expanding Word Choice

Before the 18th century, people lacked many of the reference tools we use to help us in our writing. There was no way to look up unfamiliar English words, no way to determine words' correct usages, and no standard for spelling. Amid this confusion, Samuel Johnson began work on his *Dictionary of the English Language*. When the book was published in 1755, it became an instant bestseller.

Today, many reference tools are available both in print and on-line. One of the most helpful reference tools for writers is a book of synonyms and related words that is called a **thesaurus.**

When to Use a Thesaurus If you are looking for just the right word to express an idea or if you simply want to vary your word choices, a thesaurus can be even more useful than a dictionary. A dictionary entry will give you the meanings of a word, often accompanied by some synonyms (words with similar meanings), but a thesaurus will usually provide you with a more thorough listing of the word's synonyms. Compare the following thesaurus entry for *valuable* with the dictionary entry in your dictionary.

valuable *adjective*	
Of great value: *valuable Georgian silver.*	**Syns:** costly, inestimable, invaluable, precious, priceless, worthy. — *Idioms* beyond price, of great price.
	Near-syns: dear, expensive, pricey; prized, treasured, valued.
	Ants: valueless, worthless.
	—*Roget's II: The New Thesaurus*

The dictionary entry may detail more of the word's shades of meaning, but the thesaurus entry lists a number of synonyms, near synonyms, and antonyms (words opposite in meaning).

Strategies for Building Vocabulary

A thesaurus can help you spice up your writing and speaking and can help you build your vocabulary.

❶ **Find the Precise Word** If you tend to overuse certain words or if you want to make your writing more vivid, a thesaurus can help you convey your thoughts more precisely. Suppose you are looking for a verb to replace *use* in the sentence "Use your brain if you want to succeed in life!" A thesaurus can help. Look at this entry for *use* from *Roget's II: The New Thesaurus.*

use *verb*	
1. To put into action or use: *Use the utmost caution at intersections. He used the money to pay off debts. I used the brakes as quickly as possible. We want to use her talents to our advantage.*	1. **Syns:** actuate, apply, employ, exercise, exploit, implement, practice, utilize. —*Idioms* bring into play, bring to bear, make use of, put into practice, put to use.
2. To control or direct the functioning of.	2. OPERATE.
3. *Informal.* To take advantage of unfairly.	3. ABUSE *verb.*
4. To be depleted.	4. GO *verb.*

Begin by reading the left-hand column to find the meaning that you want to employ. Then refer to the right-hand column for synonyms that reflect that meaning. Which synonym would you choose?

❷ **Use Available Technology** Some word-processing programs have built-in thesauruses. Besides offering a list of synonyms, an electronic thesaurus may also provide other information, such as lists of antonyms and words with similar spellings. Most such thesauruses can also insert into your document any synonym you choose.

❸ **Develop Your Options** Take time to study a thesaurus, jotting down words you find interesting. Try to use those words in conversation until they become part of your vocabulary.

EXERCISE Use a dictionary to determine what parts of speech each of these words can serve as, as well as the word's possible meanings. Write a sentence containing the word; then use a thesaurus to find a synonym that can replace the word in the sentence.

1. beautiful	**3.** profitable	**5.** animate
2. object	**4.** fair	

Grammar from Literature

Writers use adjectives for a variety of reasons:

- To add sensory detail such as description of size, color, and kind.
- To make characters and settings more realistic.
- To make explanations more precise.

Look at the passage below about Lord Chesterfield's views of a person's composition, or personality. Notice how the highlighted adjectives add information to this passage and the other passages below.

> single-word adjectives
> **Every man is not ambitious, or covetous, or passionate; but every man has pride enough in his composition to feel and resent the least slight and contempt.**
> —Lord Chesterfield, *Letters to His Son*

> adjective prepositional phrases
> **The knowledge of numbers is one of the chief distinctions between us and brutes.**
> —Lady Mary Wortley Montagu, letter to her daughter

> participial phrase
> **I hear this great city inquiring day by day after these my papers.**
> —Joseph Addison, *The Spectator*

You may recall that a participle is a verb form that functions as an adjective. A participial phrase consists of a participle and any words that modify the participle.

Using Adjectives in Your Writing Look for places in your writing where you can make the picture in your reader's mind clearer and more accurate. Include adjectives that capture the sights, smells, tastes, and experiences you are recording.

> **Can you imagine yourself stranded on an uninhabited island? Everything around you is strange and unfamiliar. Will that curious orange prickly fruit be your supper tonight, or is it poisonous? This is the situation Robinson Crusoe found himself in.**

Usage Tip Place adjectives as close as possible to the words they modify. Misplaced modifiers can be confusing and at times even humorous.

> INCORRECT
> **Lord Albemarle smelled the fish going to the kitchen.**
> CORRECT
> **Going to the kitchen, Lord Albemarle smelled the fish.**

> INCORRECT
> **The helpful librarian pointed out the copy of Pepys's diary to the boy on the shelf.**
> CORRECT
> **The helpful librarian pointed out the copy of Pepys's diary on the shelf to the boy.**

Punctuation Tip Use a comma after an introductory participial phrase.

> **Reading Pepys's diary, we discover an earlier era.**

WRITING EXERCISE Rewrite these sentences, following the directions in parentheses.

1. The ceremonies surrounding the king's coronation impressed Samuel Pepys. (Add a single-word adjective describing the ceremonies.)
2. I did see the houses and warehouses all on fire. (Add one or more prepositional phrases that tell what kind of houses or warehouses or their location.)
3. Pepys traveled in his boat ∧ to get a good look at the fire. He took the boat up and down the Thames River. (Combine the two sentences, inserting the prepositional phrase from the second sentence into the first sentence at the position shown by the caret.)
4. _____ and _____, the survivors of the fire wandered the streets. (Fill in the blanks with two participles or participial phrases.)

5. People make little show of what they know. These people are truly educated. (Insert the information from the second sentence into the first as a participle. Delete words if necessary.)

GRAMMAR EXERCISE Rewrite the sentences, correcting errors in punctuation and usage.

1. Spectators saw many tragic sights walking the streets of London after the fire.
2. Considered distinguished Montagu's grandfather was known as Wise William.
3. Having a passion for learning Lady Montagu supported education for women.
4. Pope wrote many famous epigrams blessed with a remarkable brain.
5. A lugubrious person takes no joy in life having a sour personality.

Social and economic conditions improved for many people during the Enlightenment. However, the wealth and privilege enjoyed by the middle and upper classes contrasted strikingly with the poverty suffered by the rest of the people. Many writers fought against the injustices they perceived by arguing in favor of social reforms. Some, including several of the essayists in this part of Unit Three, supported equal opportunities for women. Others penned stinging satires attacking the treatment of the poor. As you read the selections, think about what changes you would promote in today's society.

from An Academy for Women

Essay by DANIEL DEFOE

> **(Connect to Your Life)**
>
> **Limits on Learning** In the 17th and early 18th centuries, the only females who received an education were those whose families could afford private lessons, and even they were taught only a few subjects and were barred from attending universities. On the basis of your understanding of history and social customs, why do you think females were prevented from receiving the same education as males? Record your thoughts.

Build Background

Women's Rights Although the education of females in 17th-century England was not entirely neglected, the only schooling available to them was private tutoring, which was usually shared with siblings or cousins. Such tutoring was an option only for the upper classes, and then only if the father or husband allowed it. Despite their limited education, a few women began to express themselves publicly in books, pamphlets, and essays during the 1600s. Some called for more rights for women, including the right to an education. In most circles, however, such ideas were ignored or ridiculed.

Following the Restoration, England experienced a period of growth in social awareness as well as in industry and commerce. More and more individuals looked for practical ways to correct what they perceived as society's flaws. One of those individuals was Daniel Defoe. Best known today as a novelist, Defoe was also involved in both commerce and social reform. One of his first publications, written in 1697, was *An Essay on Projects*, a series of proposals advocating, among other things, the establishment of banks, insurance companies, and credit unions—and, in "An Academy for Women," the education of females.

LaserLinks:
Background
for Reading
Cultural Connection

> WORDS TO KNOW
> **Vocabulary Preview**
>
> cloister   retentive
> degenerate   vie
> manifest

Focus Your Reading

LITERARY ANALYSIS   **PERSUASIVE ESSAY**   In a **persuasive essay,** a writer attempts to convince readers to adopt a particular opinion or to perform a certain action. In the first sentence of his essay, Defoe introduces a general opinion that he hopes to persuade his readers to adopt:

> *I have often thought of it as one of the most barbarous customs in the world . . . that we deny the advantages of learning to women.*

As you read the essay, look for statements of opinion and pay particular attention to the ways in which Defoe supports his opinions.

ACTIVE READING   **ANALYZING A FORMAL ARGUMENT** In a formal argument, a writer makes a proposal and then presents facts, reasons, and examples to support it. The proposal is generally a call to action and usually appears near the beginning of the argument.

READER'S NOTEBOOK   Make a chart like the one shown, and as you read this selection on the education of females, use it to record Defoe's main proposal and supporting details.

Proposal	Supporting Details
	1.
	2.
	3.
	4.

FROM An Academy for WOMEN

Daniel Defoe

I have often thought of it as one of the most barbarous customs in the world, considering us as a civilized and a Christian country, that we deny the advantages of learning to women. We reproach the sex every day with folly and impertinence, while I am confident, had they the advantages of education equal to us, they would be guilty of less than ourselves.

One would wonder, indeed, how it should happen that women are conversible[1] at all, since they are only beholden to natural parts for all their knowledge. Their youth is spent to teach them to stitch and sew or make baubles. They are taught to read indeed, and perhaps to write their names or so, and that is the height of a woman's education. And I would but ask any who slight the sex for their understanding, what is a man (a gentleman, I mean) good for that is taught no more? . . .

The soul is placed in the body like a rough diamond, and must be polished, or the luster of it will never appear: and it is <u>manifest</u> that as the rational soul distinguishes us from brutes, so education carries on the distinction and makes some less brutish than others. This is too evident to need any demonstration. But why then should women be denied the benefit of instruction? If knowledge and understanding had been useless additions to the sex, God Almighty would never have given them capacities, for He made nothing needless. Besides, I would ask such what they can see in ignorance that they should think it a necessary ornament to a woman? or how much worse is a wise woman than a fool? or what has the woman done to forfeit the privilege of being taught? Does she plague us with her pride and impertinence? Why did we not let her learn, that she might have had more wit? Shall we upbraid women with folly,[2] when it is only the error of this inhuman custom that hindered them being made wiser?

The capacities of women are supposed to be greater and their senses quicker than those of the men; and what they might be capable of being bred to is plain from some instances of female wit, which this age is not without; which upbraids us with injustice, and looks as if we denied women the advantages of education for fear they should <u>vie</u> with the men in their improvements.

To remove this objection, and that women might have at least a needful opportunity of

---

1. **conversible:** able to carry on a conversation.
2. **upbraid women with folly:** scold women for foolishness.

Portrait of a Young Woman, called Mademoiselle Charlotte du Val d'Ognes (about 1800), unknown French artist. Oil on canvas, 63½″ × 50⅜″, The Metropolitan Museum of Art, bequest of Isaac D. Fletcher, 1917. Mr. and Mrs. Isaac D. Fletcher Collection (17.120.204). Copyright © 1989 The Metropolitan Museum of Art.

education in all sorts of useful learning, I propose the draft of an academy for that purpose. . . .

The academy I propose should differ but little from public schools, wherein such ladies as were willing to study should have all the advantages of learning suitable to their genius. . . .

The persons who enter should be taught all sorts of breeding suitable to both their genius and their quality, and in particular music and dancing, which it would be cruelty to bar the sex of, because they are their darlings; but besides this, they should be taught languages, as particularly French and Italian; and I would venture the injury of giving a woman more tongues than one.

They should, as a particular study, be taught all the graces of speech and all the necessary air of conversation, which our common education is so defective in that I need not expose it. They should be brought to read books, and especially history, and so to read as to make them understand the world, and be able to know and judge of things when they hear of them.

ACTIVE READING

ANALYZE What reasons does Defoe present to support his **formal argument**?

To such whose genius would lead them to it I would deny no sort of learning; but the chief thing in general is to cultivate the understandings of the sex, that they may be capable of all sorts of conversation; that their parts and judgments being improved, they may be as profitable in their conversation as they are pleasant.

Women, in my observation, have little or no difference in them, but as they are or are not distinguished by education. Tempers indeed may in some degree influence them, but the main distinguishing part is their breeding.

The whole sex are generally quick and sharp. I believe I may be allowed to say generally so, for you rarely see them lumpish and heavy when they are children, as boys will often be. If a woman be well-bred, and taught the proper management of her natural wit, she proves generally very sensible and retentive; and without partiality, a woman of sense and manners is the finest and most delicate part of God's creation; the glory of her Maker, and the great instance of His singular regard to man, His darling creature, to whom He gave the best gift either God could bestow or man receive. And it is the sordidest[3] piece of folly and ingratitude in the world to withhold from the sex the due luster which the advantages of education gives to the natural beauty of their minds.

A woman well-bred and well taught, furnished with the additional accomplishments of knowledge and behavior, is a creature without comparison; her society is the emblem of sublimer[4] enjoyments; her person is angelic and her conversation heavenly; she is all softness and sweetness, peace, love, wit, and delight. She is every way suitable to the sublimest wish, and the man that has such a one to his portion has nothing to do but to rejoice in her and be thankful.

On the other hand, suppose her to be the very same woman, and rob her of the benefit of

The great distinguishing difference which is seen in the world between men and women is in their EDUCATION.

---

3. **sordidest:** most meanly selfish.

4. **sublimer:** more noble or exalted.

WORDS TO KNOW   **retentive** (rĭ-tĕn'tĭv) *adj.* able to retain knowledge or information easily

education, and it follows thus:

If her temper be good, want of education makes her soft and easy.

Her wit, for want of teaching, makes her impertinent and talkative.

Her knowledge, for want of judgment and experience, makes her fanciful and whimsical.

If her temper be bad, want of breeding makes her worse, and she grows haughty, insolent, and loud.

If she be passionate, want of manners makes her termagant[5] and a scold, which is much at one with lunatic.

If she be proud, want of discretion (which still is breeding) makes her conceited, fantastic, and ridiculous.

And from these she degenerates to be turbulent, clamorous, noisy, nasty, and the devil.

Methinks mankind for their own sakes, since, say what we will of the women, we all think fit one time or other to be concerned with them, should take some care to breed them up to be suitable and serviceable, if they expected no such thing as delight from them. Bless us! what care do we take to breed up a good horse and to break him well, and what a value do we put upon him when it is done, and all because he should be fit for our use; and why not a woman? Since all her ornaments and beauty without suitable behavior is a cheat in nature, like the

ACTIVE READING

QUESTION What point is Defoe making in his simile of the false tradesman?

false tradesman who puts the best of his goods uppermost that the buyer may think the rest are of the same goodness. . . .

But to come closer to the business, the great distinguishing difference which is seen in the world between men and women is in their education, and this is manifested by comparing it with the difference between one man or woman and another.

And herein it is that I take upon me to make such a bold assertion that all the world are mistaken in their practice about women; for I cannot think that God Almighty ever made them so delicate, so glorious creatures, and furnished them with such charms, so agreeable and so delightful to mankind, with souls capable of the same accomplishments with men, and all to be only stewards of our houses, *cooks and slaves.*

. . . I remember a passage which I heard from a very fine woman; she had wit and capacity enough, an extraordinary shape and face, and a great fortune, but had been cloistered up all her time, and for fear of being stolen, had not had the liberty of being taught the common necessary knowledge of women's affairs; and when she came to converse in the world, her natural wit made her so sensible of the want of education, that she gave this short reflection on herself: "I am ashamed to talk with my very maids," says she, "for I don't know when they do right or wrong. I had more need to go to school than be married."

I need not enlarge on the loss the defect of education is to the sex, nor argue the benefit of the contrary practice; it is a thing will be more easily granted than remedied. This chapter is but an essay at the thing, and I refer the practice to those happy days, if ever they shall be, when men shall be wise enough to mend it. ❖

---

5. **termagant** (tûr′mə-gənt): a quarrelsome woman.

WORDS
TO
KNOW

degenerate (dĭ-jĕn′ə-rāt′) *v.* to sink to a lower condition; deteriorate
cloister (kloi′stər) *v.* to confine or seclude, as in a convent

581

Thinking through the LITERATURE

Connect to the Literature

1. What Do You Think?
What thoughts came to mind when you finished reading this **essay?**

> **Comprehension Check**
> • What courses would be taught at Defoe's academy?
> • Why does Defoe believe that these areas of study are necessary?

Think Critically

2. How would you describe Defoe's attitude toward women?

THINK ABOUT
{
• the qualities he attributes to women
• the areas of study he proposes for them
• his description of an uneducated woman
• the possible motives behind his proposal

3. **ACTIVE READING** **ANALYZING A FORMAL ARGUMENT** Refer to the chart you created in your **READER'S NOTEBOOK.** In your opinion, does Defoe present a convincing **argument?** Defend your answer.

Extend Interpretations

4. Different Perspectives How might a contemporary defender of women's rights respond to Defoe's essay?

5. Comparing Texts Compare Defoe's opinions on the education of women with those expressed by Lady Mary Wortley Montagu in her **letter** to her daughter (page 554). What opinions do Defoe and Montagu seem to share? On what issues might they disagree?

6. Connect to Life Do you think that any issues related to the education or training of women are still controversial? Explain your answer.

7. Art Connection Look closely at the portrait of Mademoiselle Charlotte du Val d'Ognes on page 579. In your opinion, what specific elements of the painting reflect ideas presented in this selection?

Literary Analysis

PERSUASIVE ESSAY When writing a **persuasive essay,** a writer tries to influence readers to accept an idea, adopt an opinion, or perform an action. The body of evidence a writer uses to convince readers includes the facts, reasons, or examples that support his or her opinion or proposal.

In Defoe's essay, the writer proposes the establishment of an educational academy for women. Statements such as the following support his proposal:

> *If knowledge and understanding had been useless additions to the sex, God Almighty would never have given them capacities. . . .*

> *If a woman be well-bred, and taught the proper management of her natural wit, she proves generally very sensible and retentive. . . .*

Effective persuasion appeals to both the intelligence and the emotions of its intended audience.

Paired Activity With a partner, reread Defoe's essay, looking for details that support his proposal. Of the supporting details that you find, which ones do you think appeal to readers' intelligence? Which appeal to their emotions?

Choices & CHALLENGES

Writing Options

Persuasive Letter Imagine that you are an educated 17th-century woman. Write a letter in which you try to convince educated 17th-century men to support Defoe's proposal. Use humor to persuade your audience. Place the letter in your **Working Portfolio.**

Activities & Explorations

1. Advertisement for the Academy Create an advertisement for Defoe's proposed academy that would encourage women to enroll. ~ **ART**

2. Interview with Defoe With a partner, conduct an interview between Defoe and a contemporary female television or radio talk-show host. ~ **SPEAKING AND LISTENING**

Inquiry & Research

Educational Opportunities Investigate the education of women in England after 1700. What types of formal education were offered to females? What subjects were taught? When were women's colleges founded in the major universities?

Vocabulary in Action

EXERCISE: ASSESSMENT PRACTICE For each group of words below, write the letter of the word that is an antonym of the boldfaced word.

1. **degenerate:** (a) produce, (b) improve, (c) accelerate
2. **retentive:** (a) forgetful, (b) selfish, (c) graceful
3. **vie:** (a) startle, (b) cooperate, (c) lose
4. **cloister:** (a) free, (b) organize, (c) praise
5. **manifest:** (a) hurtful, (b) questionable, (c) timid

Building Vocabulary
For an in-depth lesson on how to use a thesaurus to find a word's synonyms and antonyms, see page 574.

Daniel Defoe
1660–1731

Other Works
Moll Flanders
Roxana
Colonel Jack

Rich Man, Poor Man "No man has tasted differing fortunes more, / And thirteen times I have been rich and poor." In this self-description, Daniel Defoe summarized the many ups and downs of his career. Fascinated with the world of trade, Defoe became a merchant, dealing at different times in an assortment of products, from bricks to insurance. Although he amassed great wealth in many of his ventures, occasional bad investments led him to bankruptcy.

Popular Opinions Defoe wrote many political pamphlets, one of which led to his imprisonment. A devout Presbyterian, his interest in politics stemmed largely from his desire to "purify" the Church of England. His imprisonment included time in the pillory, a wooden device with holes for the prisoner's head and hands. Prisoners in the pillory were usually pelted with rotten fruit and vegetables by onlookers, but Defoe's views were so popular that the public drank to his health and threw flowers instead. One of his political poems, *The True-Born Englishman*, reportedly sold more copies than any poem published in England before that time.

Novel Approach Today Defoe is most recognized for his novels, which he did not begin writing until he was in his late 50s. His most famous novel, *Robinson Crusoe*, was the first book other than the Bible to be widely read by members of all levels of English society.

Satire

Laughter as a Weapon

Satire is a literary technique in which behaviors or institutions are ridiculed for the purpose of improving society. What sets satire apart from other forms of social and political protest is humor. Satirists use irony and exaggeration to poke fun at human faults and foolishness in order to correct human behavior.

A famous example of satire is Alexander Pope's brilliant mock epic *The Rape of the Lock* (1714). The poem, which satirizes the trivial pursuits of the idle wealthy, echoes the openings of ancient epics in its famous first lines:

Gulliver in Lilliput. Illustration by H. J. Ford for an 1891 edition of Swift's *Gulliver's Travels*

> What dire offense from amorous causes springs,
> What mighty contests rise from trivial things,
> I sing— . . .
>
> —Alexander Pope, *The Rape of the Lock*

In the poem, a young lord is so smitten by a lady's beauty that he secretly cuts off a lock of her hair. The lady's offense at this violation takes on epic—or mock-epic—proportions:

> Then flashed the living lightning from her eyes,
> And screams of horror rend the affrighted skies.
> Not louder shrieks to pitying heaven are cast,
> When husbands, or when lapdogs breathe their last;
>
> —Alexander Pope, *The Rape of the Lock*

The exaggeration of the lady's response, plus the ironic aside equating the death of husbands with the death of favorite pets, typifies this satire's charm.

For the most part, a satirist attempts to bring about change by exposing an oddity or a problem in an imaginative, often humorous way. The target is often a social or political one.

A Historical Perspective

Satire began with the ancient Greeks but came into its own in ancient Rome, where the "fathers" of satire, Horace and Juvenal, had their names given to the two basic types of satire:

- **Horatian satire** is playfully amusing and seeks to correct vice or foolishness with gentle laughter and understanding. Alexander Pope's satire is Horatian.
- **Juvenalian satire** provokes a darker kind of laughter. It is often bitter and criticizes corruption or incompetence with scorn and outrage. Swift, in *Gulliver's Travels,* tended toward Juvenalian satire.

The next great flourishing of satire began in Europe in the second half of the 17th century and continued throughout the 18th century. In England, this "golden age" of satire encompassed the talents of the Restoration dramatists, as well as Dryden, Pope, Swift and Samuel Johnson.

The 18th century was dominated by satiric poetry, prose, and drama. Satirists, as guardians of the culture, sought to protect their highly developed civilization from corruption by attacking hypocrisy, arrogance, greed, vanity, and stupidity. "The satirist is to be regarded as our physician, not our enemy," wrote Henry Fielding.

Satire Since 1800

With a few notable exceptions—namely, Lord Byron, William Makepeace Thackeray, and Samuel Butler in England and Mark Twain in America—the popularity of satire faded in the 19th century.

Much of the satire of the 20th century, reacting to warfare and complex social issues, has been Juvenalian in the extreme. George Orwell's political satire *Animal Farm* (1945) departed from this gloomy pattern through the use of fantasy. This seemingly simple animal fable satirizes political systems that claim to be democracies but oppress their citizens. Like *Gulliver's Travels, Animal Farm* portrays a fantasy world with similarities to our own. But unlike Swift's work, some modern satires lack humorous elements to raise them from bleakness and despair.

YOUR TURN Identify other examples of satire in the 20th century that you have read or know about. Add your examples to a class list.

Satire Today

Although some critics lament the scarcity of good literary satire, today satire has permeated all forms of popular culture. Political cartoons, with their caricatures of leaders and parodies of contemporary issues, have always been hallmarks of satire. The satiric spirit also pervades many of today's popular comic strips, such as *Doonesbury, Dilbert,* and *Cathy.* Many national magazines either devote themselves entirely to satire (*National Lampoon* and *Spy*) or dedicate part of their pages to satirizing contemporary life (*The New Yorker* and *Esquire*).

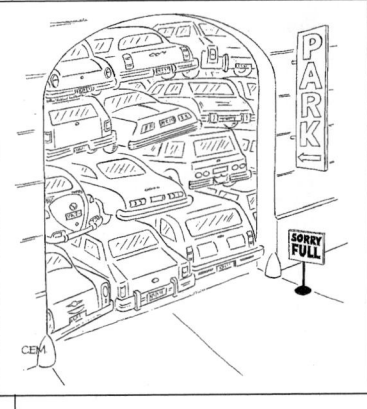

You can also find satire on TV—on programs such as *The Simpsons* and the Saturday late-night comedy shows—and in movie theaters all across the United States. Future historians may look back on the end of the 20th century as the dawn of another great age of satire.

Strategies for Reading: Satire

1. Determine the object of the satire. A writer who encourages you to laugh at a custom, or a person, probably thinks that the object of laughter is an undesirable part of society.

2. Use your knowledge of what the satirist criticizes to infer what he or she believes is right and proper.

3. Watch for irony, which often points directly to the object of the satire.

4. Evaluate whether the satire is more Horatian (playful and sympathetic) or Juvenalian (bitter and critical).

5. Enjoy the humor. Pay attention to what makes you laugh or what sounds ridiculous.

6. **Monitor** your reading strategies and modify them when your understanding breaks down. Remember to use your Strategies for Active Reading: **predict, visualize, connect, question, clarify,** and **evaluate.**

Author Study

JONATHAN SWIFT

OVERVIEW

> "[Swift] stood solitary on the peak of his nature, his scornful eyes raking mankind."
>
> -Carl Van Doren

Jonathan Swift

HIS LIFE
HIS TIMES

The Great Satirist

Jonathan Swift has been called the greatest satirist in the English language. Readers have enjoyed him, and critics have argued about him for centuries. He is one of the few great writers who appeals to children as well as adults.

1667–1745

This Author Study will introduce you to this complicated man—a clergyman and political writer as well as a satirist—who delighted readers even in his bitterest moments.

EARLY LIFE Swift was born of English parents in Dublin. Although his family wasn't rich, the young Swift received the best education available. After graduating from Trinity College, he moved to Surrey in England to accept a position as secretary to a retired diplomat, Sir William Temple.

Swift worked on and off for Temple for approximately ten years—a crucial time in his intellectual and social development. It was also at Temple's estate that Swift met eight-year-old Esther Johnson, whom he nicknamed Stella. She would become Swift's lifelong friend and confidante. By the time Temple died in 1699, Swift had been ordained as an Anglican priest and

1667
Is born
Nov. 30 in
Dublin

1686
Receives
B.A. degree
from Trinity
College,
Dublin

1670

1680

1665
The Great Plague
begins in London
and eventually
kills over 65,000.

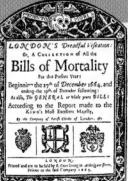

1678
Roman Catholics
in England are
excluded from
serving in
Parliament.

1679
English
political
parties, Whig
and Tory, are
formed.

1683
Antony van
Leeuwenhoek first
observes bacteria
under a
microscope.

become a full-fledged satirist, with two completed works ready for publication.

SATIRE AND POLITICS Swift supported himself as a clergyman and political writer for the Whig party, while he tried out his satire on the public. His first two satires, *The Battle of the Books* and *A Tale of a Tub*, established Swift's biting style. Whether lampooning modern thinkers and scientists (John Locke and Isaac Newton among them), religious abuses, or humans at large, Swift raged at the arrogance, phoniness, and shallowness he saw infecting contemporary intellectual and moral life. He stood for justice, order, moral rectitude, and rational thought.

Both satires were published anonymously. However, as Swift became known for his venomous political writing and his witty contributions to *The Tatler* and *The Spectator*, people recognized Swift's style and ascribed the authorship unofficially to him.

When the Whigs lost power to the Tories in 1710, the Tories courted Swift to join their side. Swift was by nature conservative and so worked enthusiastically for the Tory cause. As a man of principle and a strict moralist, he eventually found himself temperamentally unsuited to the compromises and manipulations of politics. When Queen Anne died in 1714 and the Whigs returned to power, Swift left England a bitter and disappointed man.

1689	1695	1702	1707
In England, becomes secretary to Sir William Temple; first meets Esther Johnson (Stella)	Ordained as Anglican priest	Receives D.D. (doctor of divinity) degree from Trinity College, Dublin	Petitions Queen Anne on behalf of Ireland; becomes friends with Joseph Addison

1690   **1700**

1688	1690	1702
Glorious Revolution overthrowing James II begins; William and Mary become monarchs (1689).	England's population reaches 5 million; John Locke publishes "An Essay Concerning Human Understanding."	The first daily newspaper, *The Daily Courant,* is founded in England.

IRISH PATRIOT Before Queen Anne died, Swift was appointed dean of St. Patrick's Cathedral in Dublin. Stung by his political defeats and far from his London friends—such as John Arbuthnot, Alexander Pope, and John Gay—Swift at first felt exiled in Ireland. He maintained a quiet life of church duties and visits to friends. His friends included Esther Vanhomrigh (nicknamed Vanessa), a young woman who had fallen in love with him in London and followed him to Ireland, and Esther Johnson (nicknamed Stella), who inspired his poetry. After about ten years, however, Swift grew interested in politics again—Irish politics, this time.

Ireland had been reduced to a state of poverty and dependence by England's repressive policies. The Catholic majority could not vote, hold public office, buy land, or receive an education. In addition, Ireland was restricted from trade with the American colonies. Angered by such tyranny, Swift fought back in a series of publications collectively called *The Drapier's Letters:* "Were not the people of Ireland born as free as those of England? . . . Am I a freeman in England, and do I become a slave in six hours by crossing the channel?" Although the letters were published anonymously, most people recognized Swift's indignant voice. Rhetoric such as this had never been raised by an Anglo-Irish voice against the English. For Irish Catholics and Protestants alike, Swift became a hero.

GULLIVER'S SUCCESS Swift's reputation for fierce satire was now legendary in both Ireland and England. Although such impassioned writing won him loyal friends, it also earned him bitter enemies. Two years after *The Drapier's Letters,* Swift anonymously  published his masterful satire *Gulliver's Travels.*

The narration of a fictional voyager allowed Swift to vent his fury at political corruption and his annoyance with the general worthlessness of human beings. "Drown the world!" he exclaimed. "I am not content with despising it, but I would anger it if I could with safety." Anger is what he hoped to achieve with *Gulliver's Travels,* which gets increasingly pessimistic with each voyage. Swift expected the book to offend people; he wanted "to vex the world rather than divert it." Instead, in an ironic twist that Swift himself must have appreciated, the book diverted—entertained—almost everyone.

1710
Begins political activity and writing for the Tory government in London; becomes friends with John Gay, Alexander Pope, John Arbuthnot, and Esther Vanhomrigh (Vanessa)

1713
Appointed dean of St. Patrick's Cathedral in Dublin

1724
Publishes *The Drapier's Letters;* gains reputation as Irish hero

1726
Publishes *Gulliver's Travels* in London

1710   **1720**

1714
Alexander Pope publishes "The Rape of the Lock."

1717
Lady Mary Wortley Montagu introduces smallpox inoculation in England.

1719
Ireland is declared inseparable from England; Daniel Defoe publishes *Robinson Crusoe.*

THE HATE BEHIND THE HUMOR Swift's humor is so light that many readers miss the deep vein of rage that runs throughout his work. In his words: "I have ever hated all nations, professions, and communities, and all my love is towards individuals. . . . But principally I hate and detest that animal called man." Swift's misanthropy, his hatred of humankind, may have grown from his religious conviction. He saw humans as fallen victims of original sin, not the rational creatures that many Enlightenment thinkers believed in.

Swift's last major work about Ireland, "A Modest Proposal," is an outrageous attack on those who mistreated Ireland's poor. Once again, his ferocious satire made people laugh.

THE GREATEST EPITAPH Swift outlived most of his friends. Before succumbing to mental decline, he arranged to be buried next to Esther Johnson in St. Patrick's. He left his remaining fortune to go toward building a mental hospital.

The Literary Coffee House

Coffee houses such as this one were popular with educated men like Swift, who often dined at a coffee house in the evening with his literary friends and political associates. Coffee houses were the center of cultural and political life in London from 1650 to 1860.

W. B. Yeats, the great 20th-century Irish poet, maintained that "Swift sleeps under the greatest epitaph in history." Composed by Swift in Latin, the epitaph is translated as follows:

Here lies the body of
Jonathan Swift, D.D., Dean of this Cathedral.
He has gone where fierce indignation
can lacerate his heart no more.
Go, traveler, and imitate if you can
a man who was an undaunted
champion of liberty.

1728
Long-time friend Esther Johnson (Stella) dies.

1729
Publishes "A Modest Proposal"

1731
Composes "Verses on the Death of Dr. Swift" (published in 1739)

1745
Dies Oct. 19 and is buried in St. Patrick's Cathedral

1730

1740

1729
Johann Sebastian Bach composes "St. Matthew Passion."

1732
Benjamin Franklin publishes *Poor Richard's Almanack.*

1741
George Frederick Handel composes "Messiah."

1742
Swift is declared by court to be "of unsound mind and memory"

from Gulliver's Travels

Fiction by JONATHAN SWIFT

Comparing Literature of the World

Gulliver's Travels, "A Modest Proposal," and *Candide*

To compare satirical writing across cultures, read the excerpt from *Candide* on page 625. Specific points of comparison between the works of Swift and Voltaire will help you examine how each author satirizes 18th-century society.

Connect to Your Life

Giant Size Recall a time when you found yourself in an unfamiliar country or culture. How did you react? Were you frightened and uncomfortable, or did you find the experience exciting? How did people from that country or culture react to you? Write about what your experience as a stranger in an unfamiliar place was like.

Build Background

Out of Place Lilliput, a kingdom of six-inch people, is the first place described in Jonathan Swift's satiric masterpiece *Gulliver's Travels*—originally titled *Travels into Several Remote Nations of the World, in Four Parts, by Lemuel Gulliver, First a Surgeon, and Then a Captain of Several Ships.* Gulliver's second voyage brings him to Brobdingnag, where he finds himself in the opposite position: he is the diminutive human among giants.

Gulliver's Travels is not only a comedy about an ordinary man's adventures in some extraordinary places, but also a **satire** of English society in Swift's day and of humankind in general. Use Strategies for Reading: Satire on page 585 to help you recognize the objects of Swift's satire. You will notice that Gulliver himself is often an object of satire, for his uncritical narration of what he sees reveals that he is naive and, true to his name, totally gullible.

Focus Your Reading

LITERARY ANALYSIS **FANTASY** **Fantasy** is literature in which the limits of reality are purposely disregarded. The aim of fantasy may be to entertain, to make a serious comment about society and human nature, or both. For Swift, the humorous fantasy of *Gulliver's Travels* is a perfect vehicle for his **satire.** What aspects of society could Swift criticize through a fantasy that places a normal human in a country where everyone else is only six inches tall? How might Swift use an opposite fantasy—a normal-sized person living among 70-foot giants—to satirize different qualities of humanity?

ACTIVE READING **VISUALIZING** Forming a mental picture from a verbal or written description—something you do every day—is called **visualizing.** For example, vivid details about a character in a story help the reader form an idea or "picture" of that character. Swift helps readers visualize the setting, characters, and events in *Gulliver's Travels* by providing a number of realistic details.

READER'S NOTEBOOK As you read, keep track of key details that help you visualize by filling in a graphic like the one shown. You might also sketch some scenes that Swift describes.

His Behavior and Treatment

How he is confined

What he eats and drinks; in what amounts

Key Details

Body (including hair) is tied by strings and pegs to the ground

WORDS TO KNOW **Vocabulary Preview**

censure	infallibly	prostrating
civility	morose	recapitulate
conjecture	panegyric	retinue
dexterity	perfidiousness	schism
diminutive	pernicious	solicitation

Jonathan Swift

from **Gulliver's Travels**

Blefuſcu.

Lilliput.

Mendendo

Diſcovered, A.D. 1699.

Map of Lilliput from the first edition
of *Gulliver's Travels*, 1726

from PART 1. **A Voyage to Lilliput**

*The first part of Gulliver's Travels describes Gulliver's
adventures in Lilliput. After going to sea as a ship's
doctor, Gulliver faces disaster as his ship breaks apart
in a storm. He swims toward land, reaches shore,
and falls exhausted on the ground.*

I lay down on the grass, which was very short
and soft, where I slept sounder than ever I
remember to have done in my life, and as I
reckoned, above nine hours; for when I awaked,
it was just daylight. I attempted to rise, but was
not able to stir: for as I happened to lie on my
back, I found my arms and legs were strongly
fastened on each side to the ground; and my hair,
which was long and thick, tied down in the same
manner. I likewise felt several slender ligatures[1]
across my body, from my armpits to my thighs. I
could only look upwards; the sun began to grow
hot, and the light offended my eyes. I heard a
confused noise about me, but in the posture I lay,
could see nothing except the sky. In a little time I
felt something alive moving on my left leg, which
advancing gently forward over my breast, came
almost up to my chin; when bending my eyes

downwards as much as I could, I perceived it to
be a human creature not six inches high, with a
bow and arrow in his hands, and a quiver[2] at his
back. In the meantime, I felt at least forty more
of the same kind (as I conjectured) following the
first. I was in the utmost astonishment, and
roared so loud, that they all ran back in a fright;
and some of them, as I was afterwards told, were
hurt with the falls they got by leaping from my
sides upon the ground. However, they soon
returned; and one of them, who ventured so far
as to get a full sight of my face, lifting up his
hands and eyes by way of admiration, cried out
in a shrill, but distinct voice, *Hekinah Degul:* the
others repeated the same words several times,
but I then knew not what they meant.

I lay all this while, as the reader may believe,
in great uneasiness; at length, struggling to get
loose, I had the fortune to break the strings, and
wrench out the pegs that fastened my left arm to
the ground; for, by lifting it up to my face, I
discovered the methods they had taken to bind

---

1. **ligatures** (lĭg′ə-choŏrz′): cords used to tie something up.

2. **quiver:** a case for carrying arrows.

Ted Danson as Gulliver (*Gulliver's Travels,* NBC, 1996). Photofest.

me; and, at the same time, with a violent pull, which gave me excessive pain, I a little loosened the strings that tied down my hair on the left side; so that I was just able to turn my head about two inches. But the creatures ran off a second time, before I could seize them; whereupon there was a great shout in a very shrill accent; and after it ceased, I heard one of them cry aloud, *Tolgo phonac*; when in an instant I felt above an hundred arrows discharged on my left hand, which pricked me like so many needles; and besides they shot another flight into the air, as we do bombs in Europe, whereof many, I suppose, fell on my body (though I felt them not) and some on my face, which I immediately covered with my left hand. When this shower of arrows was over, I fell a groaning with grief and pain; and then striving again to get loose, they discharged another volley[3] larger than the first, and some of them attempted with spears to stick me in the sides; but, by good luck, I had on me a buff jerkin[4], which they could not pierce. I thought it the most prudent method to lie still; and my design was to continue so till night, when, my

left hand being already loose, I could easily free myself: and as for the inhabitants, I had reason to believe I might be a match for the greatest armies they could bring against me, if they were all of the same size with him that I saw. But fortune disposed otherwise of me.

When the people observed I was quiet, they discharged no more arrows: but by the noise increasing, I knew their numbers were greater; and about four yards from me, over-against my right ear, I heard a knocking for above an hour, like people at work; when turning my head that way, as well as the pegs and strings would permit me, I saw a stage erected about a foot and a half from the ground, capable of holding four of the inhabitants, with two or three ladders to mount it: from whence one of them, who seemed to be a person of quality,[5] made me a long speech, whereof I understood not one syllable. But I should have mentioned, that before the principal

---

3. **volley:** a group of missiles—in this case, arrows—fired simultaneously.
4. **buff jerkin:** a leather jacket.
5. **person of quality:** a high-ranking person.

person began his oration, he cried out three times, *Langro Dehul san:* (these words and the former were afterwards repeated and explained to me). Whereupon immediately about fifty of the inhabitants came, and cut the strings that fastened the left side of my head, which gave me the liberty of turning it to the right, and of observing the person and gesture of him who was to speak. He appeared to be of a middle age, and taller than any of the other three who attended him; whereof one was a page[6] who held up his train, and seemed to be somewhat longer than my middle finger; the other two stood one on each side to support him. He acted every part of an orator, and I could observe many periods of threatenings, and others of promises, pity and kindness. I answered in a few words, but in the most submissive manner, lifting up my left hand and both my eyes to the sun, as calling him for a witness; and being almost famished with hunger, having not eaten a morsel for some hours before I left the ship, I found the demands of nature so strong upon me, that I could not forbear showing my impatience (perhaps against the strict rules of decency) by putting my finger frequently on my mouth, to signify that I wanted food.

The *Hurgo* (for so they call a great lord, as I afterwards learned) understood me very well. He descended from the stage, and commanded that several ladders should be applied to my sides, on which above an hundred of the inhabitants mounted, and walked towards my mouth, laden with baskets full of meat, which had been provided and sent thither by the King's orders upon the first intelligence[7] he received of me. I observed there was the flesh of several animals, but could not distinguish them by the taste. There were shoulders, legs, and loins shaped like those of mutton, and very well dressed, but smaller than the wings of a lark. I eat them by two or three at a mouthful, and took three loaves at a time, about the bigness of musket bullets. They supplied me as fast as they could, showing

a thousand marks of wonder and astonishment at my bulk and appetite. I then made another sign that I wanted drink. They found by my eating that a small quantity would not suffice[8] me; and being a most ingenious people, they slung up with great dexterity one of their largest hogsheads;[9] then rolled it towards my hand, and beat out the top; I drank it off at a draft,[10] which I might well do, for it hardly held half a pint, and tasted like a small wine of Burgundy, but much more delicious. They brought me a second hogshead, which I drank in the same manner, and made signs for more, but they had none to give me. When I had performed these wonders, they shouted for joy, and danced upon my breast, repeating several times as they did at first, *Hekinah Degul.* They made me a sign that I should throw down the two hogsheads, but first warned the people below to stand out of the way, crying aloud, *Borach Mivola,* and when they saw the vessels in the air, there was an universal shout of *Hekinah Degul.*

I confess I was often tempted, while they were passing backwards and forwards on my body, to seize forty or fifty of the first that came in my reach, and dash them against the ground. But the remembrance of what I had felt, which probably might not be the worst they could do; and the promise of honor I made them, for so I interpreted my submissive behavior, soon drove out those imaginations. Besides, I now considered myself as bound by the laws of hospitality to a people who had treated me with so much expense and magnificence. However, in my thoughts I could not sufficiently wonder at the intrepidity[11] of these diminutive mortals, who

---

6. **page:** a youth serving as a personal attendant.

7. **intelligence:** news; information.

8. **suffice:** satisfy.

9. **hogsheads:** large barrels used to store liquids, such as wine or ale.

10. **draft:** a swallow or gulp.

11. **intrepidity** (ĭn-trə-pĭd′ĭ-tē): boldness; courage.

WORDS TO KNOW   **diminutive** (dĭ-mĭn′yə-tĭv) *adj.* tiny

durst[12] venture to mount and walk on my body, while one of my hands was at liberty, without trembling at the very sight of so prodigious a creature as I must appear to them.

After some time, when they observed that I made no more demands for meat, there appeared before me a person of high rank from his Imperial Majesty. His Excellency, having mounted on the small of my right leg, advanced forwards up to my face, with about a dozen of his retinue. And producing his credentials under the Signet Royal,[13] which he applied close to my eyes, spoke about ten minutes, without any signs of anger, but with a kind of determinate resolution; often pointing forwards, which, as I afterwards found, was towards the capital city, about half a mile distant, whither it was agreed by his Majesty in council that I must be conveyed. I answered in a few words, but to no purpose, and made a sign with my hand that was loose, putting it to the other (but over his Excellency's head, for fear of hurting him or his train) and then to my own head and body, to signify that I desired my liberty. It appeared that he understood me well enough; for he shook his head by way of disapprobation,[14] and held his hand in a posture to show that I must be carried as a prisoner. However, he made other signs to let me understand that I should have meat and drink enough, and very good treatment. Whereupon I once more thought of attempting to break my bonds; but again, when I felt the smart of their arrows upon my face and hands, which were all in blisters, and many of the darts still sticking in them; and observing likewise that the number of my enemies increased; I gave tokens to let them know that they might do with me what they pleased. Upon this the *Hurgo* and

his train withdrew, with much civility and cheerful countenances.[15] Soon after I heard a general shout, with frequent repetitions of the words, *Peplom Selan,* and I felt great numbers of the people on my left side relaxing the cords to such a degree, that I was able to turn upon my right, and to ease myself. . . .

My gentleness and good behavior had gained so far on the Emperor and his court, and indeed upon the army and people in general, that I began to conceive hopes of getting my liberty in a short time. I took all possible methods to cultivate this favorable disposition. The natives came by degrees to be less apprehensive of any danger from me. I would sometimes lie down, and let five or six of them dance on my hand. And at last the boys and girls would venture to come and play at hide-and-seek in my hair. I had now made a good progress in understanding and speaking their language. The Emperor had a mind one day to entertain me with several of the country shows; wherein they exceed all nations I have known, both for dexterity and magnificence. I was diverted with none so much as that of the rope-dancers,[16] performed upon a slender white thread, extended about two foot,

> *The boys and girls would venture to come and play at hide-and-seek in my hair.*

---

12. **durst:** dared.

13. **Signet Royal:** the official seal of a king or queen.

14. **disapprobation** (dĭs-ăp′rə-bā′shən): disapproval.

15. **countenances:** facial expressions.

16. **rope-dancers:** acrobats who perform on a tightrope. Here the rope-dancers represent Whig Party politicians at the court of George I, whose "acrobatics"—political maneuverings—were intended to increase their power. (Swift supported the opposing party, the Tories.)

---

and twelve inches from the ground. Upon which I shall desire liberty, with the reader's patience, to enlarge a little.

This diversion is only practiced by those persons who are candidates for great employments, and high favor, at court. They are trained in this art from their youth, and are not always of noble birth, or liberal education. When a great office is vacant either by death or disgrace (which often happens) five or six of those candidates petition the Emperor to entertain his Majesty and the court with a dance on the rope; and whoever jumps the highest without falling, succeeds in the office. Very often the chief ministers themselves are commanded to show their skill, and to convince the Emperor that they have not lost their faculty. Flimnap, The Treasurer,[17] is allowed to cut a caper on the strait rope, at least an inch higher than any other lord in the whole empire. I have seen him do the summerset[18] several times together upon a trencher[19] fixed on the rope, which is no thicker than a common packthread[20] in England. My friend Reldresal, Principal Secretary for Private Affairs, is, in my opinion, if I am not partial, the second after the Treasurer; the rest of the great officers are much upon a par.

These diversions are often attended with fatal accidents, whereof great numbers are on record. I myself have seen two or three candidates break a limb. But the danger is much greater when the ministers themselves are commanded to show their dexterity; for, by contending to excel themselves and their fellows, they strain so far, that there is hardly one of them who hath not received a fall; and some of them two or three. I was assured, that a year or two before my arrival, Flimnap would have <u>infallibly</u> broke his neck, if one of the King's cushions, that accidentally lay on the ground, had not weakened the force of his fall.

There is likewise another diversion, which is only shown before the Emperor and Empress, and first minister, upon particular occasions. The Emperor lays on a table three fine silken threads of six inches long. One is blue, the other red, and the third green.[21] These threads are proposed as prizes for those persons whom the Emperor hath a mind to distinguish by a peculiar mark of his favor. The ceremony is performed in his Majesty's great chamber of state; where the candidates are to undergo a trial of dexterity very different from the former, and such as I have not observed the least resemblance of in any other country of the old or the new world. The Emperor holds a stick in his hands, both ends parallel to the horizon, while the candidates, advancing one by one, sometimes leap over the stick, sometimes creep under it backwards and forwards several times, according as the stick is advanced or depressed. Sometimes the Emperor holds one end of the stick, and his first minister the other; sometimes the minister has it entirely to himself. Whoever performs his part with most agility, and holds out the longest in *leaping* and *creeping,* is rewarded with the blue-colored silk; the red is given to the next, and the green to the third, which they all wear girt[22] twice round about the middle; and you see few great persons about this court who are not adorned with one of these girdles. . . .

I had sent so many memorials and petitions for my liberty, that his Majesty at length mentioned the matter first in the cabinet, and

---

17. **Flimnap, The Treasurer:** a character representing the Whig leader and statesman Sir Robert Walpole, who served as first lord of the treasury from 1715 to 1717 and from 1721 to 1742.

18. **summerset:** somersault.

19. **trencher:** a tray or platter for serving food.

20. **packthread:** a strong twine for tying packages.

21. **three fine silken . . . third green:** The three colored threads represent the Order of the Garter, the Order of the Bath, and the Order of the Thistle—honorary societies revived by Walpole.

22. **girt:** wrapped.

WORDS
TO
KNOW

infallibly (ĭn-făl′ə-blē) *adv.* without fail; certainly

then in a full council; where it was opposed by none, except Skyresh Bolgolam, who was pleased, without any provocation, to be my mortal enemy. But it was carried against him by the whole board, and confirmed by the Emperor. That minister was *Galbet,* or Admiral of the Realm; very much in his master's confidence, and a person well versed in affairs, but of a <u>morose</u> and sour complexion. However, he was at length persuaded to comply; but prevailed that the articles and conditions upon which I should be set free, and to which I must swear, should be drawn up by himself. These articles were brought to me by Skyresh Bolgolam in person, attended by two under-secretaries, and several persons of distinction. After they were read, I was demanded to swear to the performance of them; first in the manner of my own country, and afterwards in the method prescribed by their laws; which was to hold my right foot in my left hand, to place the middle finger of my right hand on the crown of my head, and my thumb on the tip of my right ear. But because the reader may perhaps be curious to have some idea of the style and manner of expression peculiar to that people, as well as to know the articles upon which I recovered my liberty, I have made a translation of the whole instrument, word for word, as near as I was able; which I here offer to the public.

GOLBASTO MOMAREN EVLAME GURDILO SHEFIN MULLY ULLY GUE, most mighty Emperor of Lilliput, delight and terror of the universe, whose dominions extend five thousand blustrugs (about twelve miles in circumference) to the extremities of the globe; Monarch of all Monarchs; taller than the sons of men; whose feet press down to the center, and whose head strikes against the sun; at whose nod the princes of the earth shake their knees; pleasant as the spring, comfortable as the summer, fruitful as autumn, dreadful as winter. His most sublime Majesty proposeth to the Man-Mountain, lately arrived at our celestial dominions, the following articles, which by a solemn oath he shall be obliged to perform.

Ted Danson as Gulliver in Lilliput (NBC, 1996). Photofest.

First, the Man-Mountain shall not depart from our dominions, without our license under our great seal.

Secondly, He shall not presume to come into our metropolis, without our express order; at which time the inhabitants shall have two hours warning, to keep within their doors.

Thirdly, The said Man-Mountain shall confine his walks to our principal high roads; and not offer to walk or lie down in a meadow, or field of corn.

Fourthly, As he walks the said roads, he shall take the utmost care not to trample upon the bodies of any of our loving subjects, their horses, or carriages, nor take any of our said subjects into his hands, without their own consent.

Fifthly, If an express require extraordinary dispatch, the Man-Mountain shall be obliged to

WORDS TO KNOW **morose** (mə-rōs′) *adj.* gloomy

carry in his pocket the messenger and horse, a six days' journey once in every moon, and return the said messenger back (if so required) safe to our Imperial Presence.

Sixthly, He shall be our ally against our enemies in the island of Blefuscu, and do his utmost to destroy their fleet, which is now preparing to invade us.

Seventhly, That the said Man-Mountain shall, at his times of leisure, be aiding and assisting to our workmen, in helping to raise certain great stones, towards covering the wall of the principal park, and other our royal buildings.

Eighthly, That the said Man-Mountain shall, in two moons' time, deliver in an exact survey of the circumference of our dominions by a computation of his own paces round the coast.

Lastly, That upon his solemn oath to observe all the above articles, the said Man-Mountain shall have a daily allowance of meat and drink sufficient for the support of 1,728 of our subjects; with free access to our Royal Person, and other marks of our favor. Given at our palace at Belfaborac the twelfth day of the ninety-first moon of our reign.

I swore and subscribed[23] to these articles with great cheerfulness and content . . . whereupon my chains were immediately unlocked, and I was at full liberty: the Emperor himself in person did me the honor to be by at the whole ceremony. I made my acknowledgements by prostrating myself at his Majesty's feet: but he commanded me to rise; and after many gracious expressions, which, to avoid the censure of vanity, I shall not repeat, he added, that he hoped I should prove a useful servant, and well deserve all the favors he had already conferred upon me, or might do for the future.

> *I made my acknowledgements by prostrating myself at his Majesty's feet.*

The reader may please to observe, that in the last article for the recovery of my liberty, the Emperor stipulates to allow me a quantity of meat and drink, sufficient for the support of 1,728 Lilliputians. Some time after, asking a friend at court how they came to fix on that determinate number, he told me, that his Majesty's mathematicians, having taken the height of my body by the help of a quadrant,[24] and finding it to exceed theirs in the proportion of twelve to one, they concluded from the similarity of their bodies, that mine must contain at least 1,728 of theirs, and consequently would require as much food as was necessary to support that number of Lilliputians. By which, the reader may conceive an idea of the ingenuity of that people, as well as the prudent and exact economy of so great a prince. One morning, about a fortnight after I had obtained my liberty, Reldresal, Principal Secretary (as they style him) of Private Affairs, came to my house, attended only by one servant. He ordered his coach to wait at a distance, and desired I would give him an hour's audience; which I readily consented to, on account of his quality, and personal merits, as well as of the many good offices he had done me during my solicitations at court. I offered to lie down, that he might the more conveniently reach my ear; but he chose rather to let me hold him in my hand during our conversation. He began with compliments on my liberty, said he might pretend to some merit in it; but, however, added, that if it had not been for the present situation of things at court, perhaps I might not have obtained it so soon. For, said he, as flourishing a

---

23. **subscribed:** signed my name.
24. **quadrant:** an instrument for measuring altitudes.

WORDS TO KNOW	**prostrating** (prŏs′trā′tĭng) *v.* kneeling or bowing down **prostrate** *v.*
	censure (sĕn′shər) *n.* criticism; blame
	solicitation (sə-lĭs′ĭ-tā′shən) *n.* a plea or request

condition as we appear to be in to foreigners, we labor under two mighty evils; a violent faction at home, and the danger of an invasion by a most potent enemy from abroad. As to the first, you are to understand, that for above seventy moons past, there have been two struggling parties in the empire, under the names of *Tramecksan,* and *Slamecksan,*[25] from the high and low heels on their shoes, by which they distinguish themselves.

It is alleged indeed, that the high heels are most agreeable to our ancient constitution: but however this be, his Majesty hath determined to make use of only low heels in the administration of the government and all offices in the gift of the crown; as you cannot but observe; and particularly, that his Majesty's imperial heels are lower at least by a *drurr* than any of his court; (*drurr* is a measure about the fourteenth part of an inch). The animosities between these two parties run so high, that they will neither eat nor drink, nor talk with each other. We compute the *Tramecksan,* or High-Heels, to exceed us in number, but the power is wholly on our side. We apprehend his Imperial Highness, the heir to the crown, to have some tendency towards the High-Heels; at least we can plainly discover one of his heels higher than the other, which gives him a hobble in his gait.[26] Now, in the midst of these intestine[27] disquiets, we are threatened with an invasion from the island of Blefuscu,[28] which is the other great empire of the universe, almost as large and powerful as this of his Majesty. For as to what we have heard you affirm, that there are other kingdoms and states in the world, inhabited by human creatures as large as yourself, our philosophers are in much doubt; and would rather conjecture that you dropped from the moon, or one of the stars; because it is certain, that an hundred mortals of your bulk would, in a short time, destroy all the fruits and cattle of his Majesty's dominions. Besides, our histories of six thousand moons make no mention of any other regions, than the two great empires of Lilliput and Blefuscu. Which two mighty powers have, as I was going to tell you, been engaged in a most obstinate war for six and thirty moons past. It began upon the following occasion.

It is allowed on all hands, that the primitive way of breaking eggs before we eat them, was upon the larger end: but his present Majesty's grandfather, while he was a boy, going to eat an egg, and breaking it according to the ancient practice, happened to cut one of his fingers. Whereupon the Emperor his father published an edict, commanding all his subjects, upon great penalties, to break the smaller end of their eggs. The people so highly resented this law, that our histories tell us there have been six rebellions raised on that account; wherein one emperor lost his life, and another his crown.[29] These civil commotions were constantly fomented by the monarchs of Blefuscu; and when they were quelled, the exiles always fled for refuge to that empire. It is computed, that eleven thousand persons have, at several times, suffered death, rather than submit to break their eggs at the smaller end. Many hundred large volumes have been published upon this

---

25. **Tramecksan, and Slamecksan . . . shoes:** The "high heel" party corresponds to the Tory Party, which promoted the "High-Church" (Catholic) aspects of Anglicanism; the "low heel" party corresponds to the Whig Party, which promoted the "Low-Church" (Protestant) aspects.

26. **his Imperial Highness . . . hobble in his gait:** The Prince of Wales, who later reigned as George II, had both Tory and Whig friends.

27. **intestine:** internal.

28. **Blefuscu:** an imaginary country that represents France, Britain's main political rival at the time.

29. **six rebellions . . . his crown:** The dispute over egg breaking corresponds to the conflict between Roman Catholics and Protestants in 17th-century England. The "emperor" who lost his life in the conflict was King Charles I; the one who lost his crown was James II, who fled into exile.

WORDS TO KNOW **conjecture** (kən-jĕk′chər) *v.* to guess or infer

controversy: but the books of the Big-Endians have been long forbidden, and the whole party rendered incapable by law of holding employments. During the course of these troubles, the emperors of Blefuscu did frequently expostulate[30] by their ambassadors, accusing us of making a <u>schism</u> in religion, by offending against a fundamental doctrine of our great prophet Lustrog, in the fifty-fourth chapter of the *Brundecral* (which is their Alcoran). This, however, is thought to be a mere strain upon the text: for the words are these; *That all true believers shall break their eggs at the convenient end:* and which is the convenient end, seems, in my humble opinion, to be left to every man's conscience, or at least in the power of the chief magistrate to determine. Now the Big-Endian exiles have found so much credit in the Emperor of Blefuscu's court, and so much private assistance and encouragement from their party here at home, that a bloody war hath been carried on between the two empires for six and thirty moons with various success; during which time we have lost forty capital ships, and a much greater number of smaller vessels, together with thirty thousand of our best seamen and soldiers; and the damage received by the enemy is reckoned to be somewhat greater than ours. However, they have now equipped a numerous fleet, and are just preparing to make a descent upon us; and his Imperial Majesty, placing great confidence in your valor and strength, hath commanded me to lay this account of his affairs before you.

I desired the Secretary to present my humble duty to the Emperor, and to let him know, that I thought it would not become me, who was a foreigner, to interfere with parties; but I was ready, with the hazard of my life, to defend his person and state against all invaders.

---

30. **expostulate** (ĭk-spŏs′chə-lāt′): raise objections.

Thinking Through the Literature

1. What situation or **character** from Gulliver's adventures in Lilliput did you find especially amusing or interesting? Explain your choice.

2. What is your opinion of the diminutive Lilliputians? Think of three words to describe them and give three examples of their behavior to support your opinion.

3. Name some characteristics of human societies that Swift may be **satirizing** through the Lilliputians.

   THINK ABOUT
   - how the Emperor of Lilliput sees himself
   - how the Emperor selects people for political offices and favors
   - what divides the Lilliputians from each other and from neighboring Blefuscu
   - how the Lilliputians treat Gulliver

4. Considering that Gulliver is physically capable of destroying Lilliput ("I might be a match for the greatest armies they could bring against me"), why do you think he acts so submissively?

5. What do you think of Gulliver at this point in the story? Explain your opinion of him as a person and as a narrator of his travels.

from PART 2. A Voyage to Brobdingnag

The second part of Gulliver's Travels *describes Gulliver's adventures in Brobdingnag. As the story opens, Gulliver has again gone to sea as a ship's doctor. The ship has been blown off course by a storm. When the ship comes in sight of land, the captain sends ashore a boatload of men (including Gulliver) to look for drinking water. While exploring the island, Gulliver is separated from the others, and when he returns to the boat he sees his shipmates rowing in a panic back to the ship, in flight from a huge monster who is chasing them. Gulliver turns back into the interior to hide from the giant.*

I fell into a highroad, for so I took it to be, although it served to the inhabitants only as a footpath through a field of barley. Here I walked on for some time, but could see little on either side, it being now near harvest, and the corn rising at least forty foot. I was an hour walking to the end of this field, which was fenced in with a hedge of at least one hundred and twenty foot high, and the trees so lofty that I could make no computation of their altitude. There was a stile[31] to pass from this field into the next: it had four steps, and a stone to cross over when you came to the utmost. It was impossible for me to climb this stile, because every step was six foot high, and the upper stone above twenty. I was endeavoring to find some gap in the hedge when I discovered one of the inhabitants in the next field advancing towards the stile, of the same size with him whom I saw in the sea pursuing our boat. He appeared as tall as an ordinary spire-steeple, and took about ten yards at every stride, as near as I could guess. I was struck with the utmost fear and astonishment, and ran to hide myself in the corn, from whence I saw him at the top of the stile, looking back into the next field on the right hand; and heard him call in a voice many degrees louder than a speaking trumpet; but the noise was so high in the air that at first I certainly thought it was thunder. Whereupon seven monsters like himself came towards him with reaping hooks in their hands, each hook about the largeness of six scythes. These people were not so well clad as the first, whose servants or laborers they seemed to be.

---

31. **stile:** a set of steps for climbing over a hedge or fence.

Richard Redgrave, *Gulliver Exhibited to the Brobdingnag Farmer;* Victoria and Albert Museum, London.

For, upon some words he spoke, they went to reap the corn in the field where I lay. I kept from them at as great a distance as I could, but was forced to move with extreme difficulty, for the stalks of the corn were sometimes not above a foot distant, so that I could hardly squeeze my body betwixt them. However, I made a shift to go forward till I came to a part of the field where the corn had been laid by the rain and wind; here it was impossible for me to advance a step, for the stalks were so interwoven that I could not creep through, and the beards of the fallen ears so strong and pointed that they pierced through my clothes into my flesh. At the same time I heard the reapers not above an hundred yards behind me. Being quite dispirited with toil, and wholly overcome by grief and despair, I lay down between two ridges and heartily wished I might there end my days. I bemoaned my desolate widow and fatherless children; I lamented my own folly and willfulness in attempting a second voyage against the advice of all my friends and relations. In this terrible agitation of mind, I could not forbear[32] thinking of Lilliput, whose inhabitants looked upon me as the greatest prodigy that ever appeared in the world; where I was able to draw an imperial fleet in my hand, and perform those other actions which will be recorded forever in the chronicles of that empire, while posterity shall hardly believe them,

---

32. **forbear:** refrain from; resist.

although attested by millions. I reflected what a mortification it must prove to me to appear as inconsiderable in this nation as one single Lilliputian would be among us. But this I conceived was to be the least of my misfortunes; for as human creatures are observed to be more savage and cruel in proportion to their bulk, what could I expect but to be a morsel in the mouth of the first among these enormous barbarians who should happen to seize me? Undoubtedly philosophers are in the right when they tell us that nothing is great or little otherwise than by comparison. It might have pleased fortune to let the Lilliputians find some nation where the people were as diminutive with respect to them as they were to me. And who knows but that even this prodigious race of mortals might be equally overmatched in some distant part of the world, whereof we have yet no discovery?

Scared and confounded as I was, I could not forbear going on with these reflections; when one of the reapers approaching within ten yards of the ridge where I lay, made me apprehend that with the next step I should be squashed to death under his foot, or cut in two with his reaping hook. And therefore when he was again about to move, I screamed as loud as fear could make me. Whereupon the huge creature trod short, and looking round about under him for some time, at last espied me as I lay on the ground. He considered a while with the caution of one who endeavors to lay hold on a small dangerous animal in such a manner that it shall not be able either to scratch or to bite him, as I myself have sometimes done with a weasel in England. At length he ventured to take me up behind by the middle between his forefinger and thumb, and brought me within three yards of his eyes, that he might behold my shape more perfectly. . . .

He ventured to take me up behind by the middle between his forefinger and thumb.

Lifting up the lappet[33] of his coat, he put me gently into it, and immediately ran along with me to his master, who was a substantial farmer, and the same person I had first seen in the field.

The farmer having (as I supposed by their talk) received such an account of me as his servant could give him, took a piece of a small straw about the size of a walking staff, and therewith lifted up the lappets of my coat, which it seems he thought to be some kind of covering that nature had given me. He blew my hairs aside to take a better view of my face. He called his hinds[34] about him, and asked them (as I afterwards learned) whether they had ever seen in the fields any little creature that resembled me. He then placed me softly on the ground upon all four; but I got immediately up, and walked slowly backwards and forwards, to let those people see I had no intent to run away. They all sat down in a circle about me, the better to observe my motions. I pulled off my hat, and made a low bow towards the farmer; I fell on my knees, and lifted up my hands and eyes, and spoke several words as loud as I could; I took a purse of gold out of my pocket, and humbly presented it to him. . . .

The farmer by this time was convinced I must be a rational creature. He spoke often to me, but the sound of his voice pierced my ears like that of a water mill, yet his words were articulate enough. I answered as loud as I could in several languages, and he often laid his ear within two yards of me, but all in vain, for we were wholly unintelligible to each other. He then sent his servants to their work, and taking his

---

33. **lappet:** flap or fold.
34. **hinds:** farm servants.

handkerchief out of his pocket, he doubled and spread it on his hand, which he placed flat on the ground with the palm upwards, making me a sign to step into it, as I could easily do, for it was not above a foot in thickness. I thought it my part to obey, and for fear of falling, laid myself at full length upon the handkerchief, with the remainder of which he lapped me up to the head for further security, and in this manner carried me home to his house. . . .

Gulliver lives with the farmer and his family and grows especially close to the farmer's daughter, Glumdalclitch. After a number of adventures in the farmer's house, including an attack on Gulliver by two ferocious rats, he is taken to the metropolis where he is purchased from the farmer by the queen of Brobdingnag, who presents him to the king. Glumdalclitch remains with Gulliver at the royal court as his nurse and instructor. Gulliver becomes a favorite of the king and queen.

It is the custom that every Wednesday (which, as I have before observed, was their Sabbath) the King and Queen, with the royal issue of both sexes, dine together in the apartment of his Majesty, to whom I was now become a favorite; and at these times my little chair and table were placed at his left hand, before one of the salt-cellars. This prince took a pleasure in conversing with me, inquiring into the manners, religion, laws, government, and learning of Europe; wherein I gave him the best account I was able. His apprehension was so clear, and his judgment so exact, that he made very wise reflections and observations upon all I said. But I confess that after I had been a little too copious[35] in talking of my own beloved country, of our trade and wars by sea and land, of our schisms in religion and parties in the state, the prejudices of his education prevailed so far that he could not forbear taking me up in his right hand, and stroking me gently with the other, after an hearty fit of laughing, asked me whether I were a Whig or a Tory. Then turning to his first minister, who waited behind him with a white staff, near as tall as the mainmast of the *Royal Sovereign*,[36] he observed how contemptible a thing was human grandeur, which could be mimicked by such diminutive insects as I: "and yet," said he, "I dare engage, these creatures have their titles and distinctions of honor; they contrive little nests and burrows, that they call houses and cities; they make a figure in dress and equipage; they love, they fight, they dispute, they cheat, they betray." And thus he continued on, while my color came and went several times with indignation to hear our noble country, the mistress of arts and arms, the scourge of France, the arbitress of Europe, the seat of virtue, piety, honor, and truth, the pride and envy of the world, so contemptuously treated.

But as I was not in a condition to resent injuries, so, upon mature thoughts, I began to doubt whether I were injured or no. For, after having been accustomed several months to the sight and converse of this people, and observed every object upon which I cast my eyes to be of proportionable magnitude, the horror I had first conceived from their bulk and aspect was so far worn off that if I had then beheld a company of English lords and ladies in their finery and birthday clothes,[37] acting their several parts in the most courtly manner of strutting and bowing and prating,[38] to say the truth, I should have been strongly tempted to laugh as much at them as this King and his grandees did at me. Neither indeed could I forbear smiling at myself when the Queen used to place me upon her hand towards a looking glass, by which both our persons appeared before me in full view together; and there could be nothing more ridiculous than the comparison; so that I really began to imagine myself dwindled many degrees below my usual size. . . .

---

35. **copious** (kō′pē-əs): wordy; verbose.

36. *Royal Sovereign:* at the time, one of the largest ships of the British navy.

37. **birthday clothes:** elaborate costumes worn by courtiers on the monarch's birthday.

38. **prating** (prā′tĭng): chattering; talking foolishly.

I was frequently rallied by the Queen upon account of my fearfulness, and she used to ask me whether the people of my country were as great cowards as myself. The occasion was this. The kingdom is much pestered with flies in summer, and these odious insects, each of them as big as a Dunstable lark, hardly gave me any rest while I sat at dinner, with their continual humming and buzzing about my ears. They would sometimes alight upon my victuals, and leave their loathsome excrement or spawn behind, which to me was very visible, although not to the natives of that country, whose large optics were not so acute as mine in viewing smaller objects. Sometimes they would fix upon my nose or forehead, where they stung me to the quick, smelling very offensively; and I could easily trace that viscous[39] matter, which our naturalists tell us enables those creatures to walk with their feet upwards upon a ceiling. I had much ado to defend myself against these detestable animals, and could not forbear starting when they came on my face. It was the common practice of the dwarf to catch a number of these insects in his hand, as schoolboys do among us, and let them out suddenly under my nose, on purpose to frighten me, and divert the Queen. My remedy was to cut them in pieces with my knife as they flew in the air, wherein my dexterity was much admired.

I remember one morning when Glumdalclitch had set me in my box upon a window, as she usually did in fair days to give me air (for I durst not venture to let the box be hung on a nail out of the window, as we do with cages in England), after I had lifted up one of my sashes, and sat down at my table to eat a piece of sweet cake for my breakfast, above twenty wasps, allured by the smell, came flying into the room, humming louder than the drones of as many bagpipes. Some of them seized my cake, and carried it piecemeal away; others flew about my head and face, confounding me with the noise, and putting me in the utmost terror of their stings.

However, I had the courage to rise and draw my hanger, and attack them in the air. I dispatched four of them, but the rest got away, and I presently shut my window. These insects were as large as partridges; I took out their stings, found them an inch and a half long, and as sharp as needles. I carefully preserved them all, and having since shown them with some other curiosities in several parts of Europe, upon my return to England I gave three of them to Gresham College,[40] and kept the fourth for myself. . . .

The King, who, as I before observed, was a prince of excellent understanding, would frequently order that I should be brought in my box and set upon the table in his closet. He would then command me to bring one of my chairs out of the box, and sit down within three yards distance upon the top of the cabinet, which brought me almost to a level with his face. In this manner I had several conversations with him. . . . He desired I would give him as exact an account of the government of England as I possibly could; because, as fond as princes commonly are of their own customs (for so he conjectured of other monarchs, by my former discourses), he should be glad to hear of anything that might deserve imitation. . . .

He wondered to hear me talk of such chargeable and extensive wars; that certainly we must be a quarrelsome people, or live among very bad neighbors, and that our generals must needs be richer than our kings.[41] He asked what business we had out of our own islands, unless upon the

---

39. **viscous** (vĭs′kəs): thick and sticky.

40. **Gresham** (grĕsh′əm) **College:** a London college that was the meeting place of the Royal Society (the principal British scientific organization of Swift's day).

41. **our generals . . . our kings:** a reference to the wealth of the Duke of Marlborough, a former general whose palace was larger than the king's.

Gulliver with the king of Brobdingnag. Illustration from a 19th-century edition of *Gulliver's Travels*.

score of trade or treaty or to defend the coasts with our fleet. Above all, he was amazed to hear me talk of a mercenary standing army in the midst of peace, and among a free people. He said if we were governed by our own consent in the persons of our representatives, he could not imagine of whom we were afraid, or against whom we were to fight; and would hear my opinion whether a private man's house might not better be defended by himself, his children, and family, than by half a dozen rascals picked up at a venture[42] in the streets for small wages, who might get an hundred times more by cutting their throats. . . .

He was perfectly astonished with the historical account I gave him of our affairs during the last century, protesting it was only an heap of conspiracies, rebellions, murders, massacres, revolutions, banishments, the very worst effects that avarice, faction, hypocrisy, perfidiousness, cruelty, rage, madness, hatred, envy, lust, malice, or ambition could produce.

His Majesty in another audience was at the pains to recapitulate the sum of all I had spoken; compared the questions he made with the answers I had given; then taking me into his hands, and stroking me gently, delivered himself in these words, which I shall never forget, nor the manner he spoke them in: "My little friend Grildrig, you have made a most admirable panegyric upon your country. You have clearly proved that ignorance, idleness, and vice are the proper ingredients for qualifying a legislator. That laws are best explained, interpreted, and applied by those whose interests and abilities lie in perverting, confounding, and eluding them. I observe among you some lines of an institution which in its original might have been tolerable; but these half erased, and the rest wholly blurred and blotted by corruptions. It doth not appear from all you have said how any one virtue is required towards the procurement of any one station among you; much less that men are ennobled on account of their virtue, that priests are advanced for their piety or learning, soldiers for their conduct or valor, judges for their integrity, senators for the love of their country, or counselors for their wisdom. As for yourself," continued the King, "who have spent the greatest part of your life in traveling, I am well disposed to hope you may hitherto have escaped many vices of your country. But by what I have gathered from your own relation, and the answers I have with much pains wringed and extorted from you, I cannot but conclude the bulk of your natives to be the most pernicious race of little odious vermin that nature ever suffered to crawl upon the surface of the earth." ❖

---

42. **at a venture:** at random.

Thinking through the LITERATURE

Connect to the Literature

1. What Do You Think?
What impressed you most about Gulliver's adventures in Brobdingnag?

> **Comprehension Check**
> • What dangers does Gulliver face in Brobdingnag?
> • In general, how do the Brobdingnagians treat Gulliver?
> • What is the king's opinion of England?

Think Critically

2. What changes of feelings or attitudes does Gulliver experience in Brobdingnag because of his diminutive size?

3. How does Gulliver's opinion of the Brobdingnagians change?

4. What can you infer about the Brobdingnagians and their society from the king's reaction to Gulliver's account of English society?

THINK ABOUT
• why the king is curious about England
• what he thinks about English warfare
• what he thinks about English history

5. **ACTIVE READING** **VISUALIZING** Review the chart of details and any sketches you made in your **READER'S NOTEBOOK** as you read. In your opinion, what is the overall effect of such detailed descriptions of Gulliver's experiences?

Extend Interpretations

6. Comparing Texts Compare the Lilliputians with the Brobdingnagians. Then write a sentence stating the major difference between the two societies.

7. Critic's Corner Swift claimed that he was a misanthrope, one who hates humanity. Critics have debated this issue for centuries, some defending Swift as more moralistic than misanthropic. What do you think? Cite evidence from these excerpts from _Gulliver's Travels_ to support Swift's assertion or to argue against it.

8. Connect to Life If you had been lost in Lilliput and Brobdingnag, in what ways would you have felt or acted differently than Gulliver did? How would you have felt or acted differently than what you described about your own reactions in Connect to Your Life?

Literary Analysis

FANTASY As you know, a **fantasy** is a work of fiction that stretches the limits of reality. However, fantasies often do explore genuine ideas about human life—in fact, effective fantasies usually contain enough realistic details to make them believable.

In _Gulliver's Travels,_ for example, Gulliver remains recognizably human. Moreover, his fantasy account of strange lands was not unlike the authentic accounts of foreign cultures published in Swift's time. Swift's talent lay in making his fantasy both strange and familiar.

Cooperative Learning Activity
Some of the events and feelings described in _Gulliver's Travels_ seem realistic—it's no surprise that a stranger in an unfamiliar land would be treated with suspicion, for example. However, the element of fantasy becomes clear when Swift describes just _who_ has made Gulliver captive. Working in a small group, use a chart similar to this one to sort out the real and fantasy aspects of Gulliver's experiences.

Event/Reaction	Real qualities	Fantasy qualities
Gulliver awakens in Lilliput.	Gulliver is taken captive by inhabitants.	Captors are six inches tall.

REVIEW **SATIRE** Which do you think is the major kind of satire in _Gulliver's Travels_—Horatian satire, which is playful and sympathetic, or Juvenalian satire, which is bitter and critical? Give examples from the text.

Choices & CHALLENGES

Writing Options

1. Satiric Fantasy Using the excerpts from *Gulliver's Travels* as a model, draft a satiric fantasy on a topic of your choice. Think of an issue or experience you want to make fun of—for example, you might satirize the process of applying to colleges or interviewing for a job. Possible formats might include a travel narrative, a children's story, or a comic book.

2. Creating Another Land Create your own fantasy land for Gulliver to visit. Write a journal entry in which you describe this new land.

Writing Handbook
See page 1367: Compare and Contrast.

Activities & Explorations

1. Scene Performance With a partner, choose a scene from *Gulliver's Travels* to perform for the class. Possible scenes: the early communication between Gulliver and the lords of Lilliput or Gulliver's arrival in Brobdingnag. You may need to create additional dialogue based on Gulliver's account. ~ **SPEAKING AND LISTENING**

2. Lilliput on Video Watch the video segment of the Lilliputians' first encounter with Gulliver. Discuss how the camera angles convey both Gulliver's and the Lilliputians' points of view. Do the special effects enhance or detract from Swift's descriptions of the encounter? ~ **VIEWING AND REPRESENTING**

VIDEO Literature in Performance

3. Comparing Size Find details in the story to figure out how tall Gulliver is. How does Swift figure that Gulliver eats as much as 1,728 Lilliputians? Next, calculate how tall the Brobdingnagians are. How many Gullivers would it take to eat as much as one Brobdingnagian? Make a **diagram** of this information and explain it to your classmates. ~ **MATH**

Inquiry & Research

Literary History How did people react to *Gulliver's Travels* when it was first published? Read letters to Swift dated November 1726, a month after the book was published, to find out. Look up letters by John Arbuthnot, Alexander Pope, and John Gay in *The Correspondence of Jonathan Swift,* edited by Harold Williams. Report your findings to the class.

Vocabulary in Action

EXERCISE A: CONTEXT CLUES On your paper, write the word from the list below that is most clearly related to the topic of each sentence.

| censure | prostrating | retinue |
| panegyric | recapitulate | |

1. Gulliver's speech describing the glories of his native land was received with great amusement.
2. The members of the royal court followed their monarch like sheep behind a shepherd.
3. As the emperor appeared, thousands of his subjects fell to the ground in awe and submission.
4. The crowd was so delighted by the story that the sailor was forced to tell it again and again.
5. Gulliver feared that some would criticize him for being too vain.

EXERCISE B: ASSESSMENT PRACTICE On your paper, identify each pair of words as synonyms or antonyms.

1. **morose**—sad
2. **schism**—unification
3. **solicitation**—appeal
4. **diminutive**—huge
5. **civility**—rudeness
6. **pernicious**—evil
7. **infallibly**—doubtfully
8. **perfidiousness**—loyalty
9. **conjecture**—guess
10. **dexterity**—clumsiness

Building Vocabulary
For an in-depth study of context clues, see page 938.

Letter from *Richard Sympson*

PSEUDONYM OF JONATHAN SWIFT

Preparing to Read

Build Background

Because Swift thought the political satire in *Gulliver's Travels* would offend powerful people, especially his political enemies, he took the precaution of having it published anonymously. In August of 1726, Swift sent part of the manuscript by messenger to a London publisher. The manuscript contained the following cover letter written under the fictitious name of "Richard Sympson," supposedly Lemuel Gulliver's cousin, friend, and manager.

Focus Your Reading

As you read this letter, notice the questions Swift/Sympson raises about the manuscript and the cautious nature of his business negotiations.

London, August 8, 1726

Sir,

My cousin, Mr. Lemuel Gulliver, entrusted me some years ago with a copy of his travels, whereof that which I here send you is about a fourth part, for I shortened them very much, as you will find in my Preface to the Reader. I have shown them to several persons of great judgment and distinction, who are confident they will sell very well; and, although some parts of this and the following volumes may be thought in one or two places to be a little satirical, yet it is agreed they will give no offence; but in that you must judge for yourself, and take the advice of your friends, and if they or you be of another opinion, you may let me know it when you return these papers, which I expect shall be in three days at furthest. The good report I have received of you makes me put so great a trust into your hands, which I hope you will give me no reason to repent, and in that confidence I require that you will never suffer these papers to be once out of your sight.

As the printing these Travels will probably be of great value to you, so, as a manager for my friend and cousin, I expect you will give a due consideration for it, because I know the author intends the profit

This portrait of Lemuel Gulliver, printed in the 1726 edition of *Gulliver's Travels*, was part of the effort to make people think that Gulliver was a real person.

for the use of poor seamen, and I am advised to say that two hundred pounds is the least sum I will receive on his account; but if it shall happen that the sale will not answer, as I expect and believe, then whatever shall be thought too much, even upon your own word, shall be duly repaid.

Perhaps you may think this a strange way of proceeding to a man of trade, but since I begin with so great a trust to you, whom I never saw, I think it not hard that you should trust me as much; therefore, if after three days' reading and consulting these papers you think it proper to stand to my agreement, you may begin to print them, and the subsequent parts shall be all sent you one after another in less than a week, provided that immediately upon your resolution to print them you do within three days deliver a bank-bill of two hundred pounds, wrapped up so as to make a parcel, to the hand from whence you receive this, who will come in the same manner exactly at nine o'clock at night on Thursday, which will be the IIth instant.

If you do not approve of this proposal, deliver these papers to the person who will come on Thursday. If you choose rather to send the papers, make no other proposal of your own, but just barely write on a piece of paper that you do not accept my offer. I am, Sir,

Your humble servant,

Richard Sympson

Richard Sympson

Thinking Through the Literature

1. What does Swift as Sympson say about the manuscript that gives a clue to its content?

2. What doubts about the manuscript does he reveal?

3. Swift asked for and eventually received £200 (less than his annual earnings as Dean of St. Patrick's) for *Gulliver's Travels.* That was the only money he ever earned from his writing. How do you think he felt about this payment based on the financial arrangements he stipulates in this letter?

4. **Comparing Texts** Look back over the excerpts from *Gulliver's Travels.* Which sections do you think might have been offensive? Who might have been offended?

A Modest Proposal

Essay by JONATHAN SWIFT

Connect to Your Life

Reacting to Injustice Has there ever been a situation that you witnessed or read about that upset or angered you? How did you react? What did you do? Discuss with classmates ways other people have called attention to a bad situation or an injustice.

Build Background

Ireland in Swift's Day By 1700, Ireland was so completely dominated by England that it seemed like a conquered territory. All the laws governing Ireland came from the English Parliament. The English also strangled the country economically by restricting Irish trade and agriculture so that few jobs were available. Even in the best years, life was harsh for Ireland's poor. When crops failed—as they did several years during the 1720s—many faced starvation. Religious and class divisions fostered by the English added to Ireland's political and economic woes. The vast majority of Irish were Roman Catholics, who according to English law could not own land and consequently had to pay high rents. Most of the landowners and officeholders were Anglo-Irish Anglicans—people like Swift who were of English ancestry and members of the Protestant Church of England.

While he served as dean of St. Patrick's Cathedral in Dublin, Swift wrote several pamphlets to attack English injustices toward Ireland and to encourage the Irish to resist oppression. In 1729, three years after the success of *Gulliver's Travels,* Swift wrote his most famous piece about Ireland, "A Modest Proposal." Instead of reason and argumentation, Swift used savage satire well-suited to the desperation he saw around him.

> **WORDS TO KNOW**
> **Vocabulary Preview**
>
> animosity   expedient
> deference   perpetual
> deplorable   prodigious
> emulation   proficiency
> encumbrance   rudiment

Focus Your Reading

LITERARY ANALYSIS | **IRONY** An important element of satire is **irony,** the contrast between what is expected and what actually happens. For example, it is ironic that the tiny Lilliputians act so aggressively, whereas the giant Gulliver is meek as a kitten. One type of irony that is typical of satirical prose is **verbal irony.** Verbal irony occurs when what is said is not exactly what is meant—as when someone says "Nice day, isn't it?" during a rainstorm. As you read Swift's proposal, watch for the irony in his rational arguments.

ACTIVE READING | **DRAWING CONCLUSIONS** How can you tell what an author really means? One way is to **draw conclusions** by using information you already know. For instance, you know that Swift is a **satirist,** so you can expect him to be ironic. Another way to draw conclusions about an author's purpose is to look for the deeper meaning beneath the surface details.

READER'S NOTEBOOK As you read, use a chart like the one below to record your reactions to Swift's statements in "A Modest Proposal." In the first column, write down a statement from the selection that seems important or surprising to you. In the second column, record your response to that statement.

Statement	My Comments/Reactions
"a boy or girl before twelve years old is no salable commodity"	• The Irish didn't have slaves. • Earlier, Swift wrote about "breeders"—as if people were like livestock.

A Modest

PROPOSAL

FOR PREVENTING THE CHILDREN OF POOR PEOPLE IN IRELAND
FROM BEING A BURDEN TO THEIR PARENTS OR COUNTRY,
AND FOR MAKING THEM BENEFICIAL TO THE PUBLIC

Jonathan Swift

Industry and Idleness: The Idle 'Prentice Executed at Tyburn (1747),
William Hogarth. Steel engraving. The Granger Collection, New York.

It is a melancholy object to those who walk through this great town[1] or travel in the country, when they see the streets, the roads, and cabin doors, crowded with beggars of the female sex, followed by three, four, or six children, all in rags and importuning every passenger for an alms. These mothers, instead of being able to work for their honest livelihood, are forced to employ all their time in strolling to beg sustenance for their helpless infants, who, as they grow up, either turn thieves for want of work, or leave their dear native country

---

1. **this great town:** Dublin.

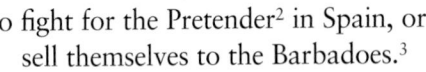

to fight for the Pretender[2] in Spain, or sell themselves to the Barbadoes.[3]

I think it is agreed by all parties that this <u>prodigious</u> number of children in the arms, or on the backs, or at the heels of their mothers, and frequently of their fathers, is in the present <u>deplorable</u> state of the kingdom a very great additional grievance; and therefore whoever could find out a fair, cheap, and easy method of making these children sound, useful members of the commonwealth would deserve so well of the public as to have his statue set up for a preserver of the nation.

But my intention is very far from being confined to provide only for the children of professed beggars; it is of a much greater extent, and shall take in the whole number of infants at a certain age who are born of parents in effect as little able to support them as those who demand our charity in the streets.

As to my own part, having turned my thoughts for many years upon this important subject, and maturely weighed the several schemes of other projectors, I have always found them grossly mistaken in their computation. It is true, a child just dropped from its dam[4] may be supported by her milk for a solar year, with little other nourishment; at most not above the value of two shillings, which the mother may certainly get, or the value in scraps, by her lawful occupation of begging; and it is exactly at one year old that I propose to provide for them in such a manner as instead of being a charge upon their parents or the parish, or wanting food and raiment for the rest of their lives, they shall on the contrary contribute to the feeding, and partly to the clothing, of many thousands.

There is likewise another great advantage in my scheme, that it will prevent those voluntary abortions, and that horrid practice of women murdering their bastard children, alas, too frequent among us, sacrificing the poor innocent babes, I doubt, more to avoid the expense than the shame, which would move tears and pity in the most savage and inhuman breast.

The number of souls in this kingdom being usually reckoned one million and a half, of these I calculate there may be about two hundred thousand couple whose wives are breeders; from which number I subtract thirty thousand couples who are able to maintain their own children, although I apprehend there cannot be so many under the present distresses of the kingdom; but this being granted, there will remain an hundred and seventy thousand breeders. I again subtract fifty thousand for those women who miscarry, or whose children die by accident or disease within the year. There only remain an hundred and twenty thousand children of poor parents annually born. The question therefore is, how this number shall be reared and provided for, which, as I have already said, under the present situation of affairs, is utterly impossible by all the methods hitherto proposed. For we can neither employ them in handicraft or agriculture; we neither build houses (I mean in the country) nor cultivate land. They can very

ACTIVE READING

EVALUATE What tone is conveyed by the speaker's mathematical calculations?

---

2. **Pretender:** James Edward Stuart—the "pretender," or claimant, to the English throne, from which his father, James II, had been deposed in 1688. Because he was Roman Catholic, the common people of Ireland were loyal to him.

3. **sell . . . the Barbadoes** (bär-bā′dōz): To escape extreme poverty, some of the Irish migrated to the West Indies, obtaining money for their passage by agreeing to work in servitude on plantations there for a set time.

4. **dam:** female parent (used almost exclusively of farm animals).

seldom pick up a livelihood by stealing till they arrive at six years old, except where they are of towardly parts;[5] although I confess they learn the <u>rudiments</u> much earlier, during which time they can however be looked upon only as probationers, as I have been informed by a principal gentleman in the county of Cavan, who protested to me that he never knew above one or two instances under the age of six, even in a part of the kingdom so renowned for the quickest <u>proficiency</u> in that art.

I am assured by our merchants that a boy or girl before twelve years old is no salable commodity; and even when they come to this age they will not yield above three pounds, or three pounds and half a crown at most on the Exchange; which cannot turn to account either to the parents or the kingdom, the charge of nutriment and rags having been at least four times that value.

I shall now therefore humbly propose my own thoughts, which I hope will not be liable to the least objection.

I have been assured by a very knowing American of my acquaintance in London, that a young healthy child well nursed is at a year old a most delicious, nourishing, and wholesome food, whether stewed, roasted, baked, or boiled; and I make no doubt that it will equally serve in a fricassee or a ragout.[6]

I do therefore humbly offer it to public consideration that of the hundred and twenty thousand children, already computed, twenty thousand may be reserved for breed, whereof only one fourth part to be males, which is more than we allow to sheep, black cattle, or swine; and my reason is that these children are seldom the fruits of marriage, a circumstance not much regarded by our savages, therefore one male will be sufficient to serve four females. That the remaining hundred thousand may at a year old be offered in sale to the persons of quality and fortune through the kingdom, always advising the mother to let them suck plentifully in the last

month, so as to render them plump and fat for a good table. A child will make two dishes at an entertainment for friends; and when the family dines alone, the fore or hind quarter will make a reasonable dish, and seasoned with a little pepper or salt will be very good boiled on the fourth day, especially in winter.

I have reckoned upon a medium that a child just born will weigh twelve pounds, and in a solar year if tolerably nursed increaseth to twenty-eight pounds.

I grant this food will be somewhat dear, and therefore very proper for landlords, who, as they have already devoured most of the parents, seem to have the best title to the children.

Infant's flesh will be in season throughout the year, but more plentiful in March, and a little before and after. For we are told by a grave author, an eminent French physician,[7] that fish being a prolific[8] diet, there are more children born in Roman Catholic countries about nine months after Lent than at any other season; therefore, reckoning a year after Lent, the markets will be more glutted than usual, because the number of popish[9] infants is at least three to one in this kingdom; and therefore it will have one other collateral advantage, by lessening the number of Papists[10] among us.

I have already computed the charge of nursing a beggar's child (in which list I reckon all

---

5. **are of towardly parts:** have a promising talent.
6. **fricassee** (frĭk′ə-sē′) **. . . ragout** (ră-gōō′): types of meat stews.
7. **grave . . . physician:** François Rabelais (1494?–1553), a French satirist.
8. **prolific:** promoting fertility.
9. **popish** (pō′pĭsh): Roman Catholic.
10. **Papists** (pā′pĭsts): Roman Catholics.

cottagers, laborers, and four fifths of the farmers), to be about two shillings per annum, rags included; and I believe no gentleman would repine to give ten shillings for the carcass of a good fat child, which, as I have said, will make four dishes of excellent nutritive meat, when he hath only some particular friend or his own family to dine with him. Thus the squire will learn to be a good landlord, and grow popular among the tenants; the mother will have eight shillings net profit, and be fit for work till she produces another child.

Those who are more thrifty (as I must confess the times require) may flay the carcass; the skin of which artificially dressed will make admirable gloves for ladies, and summer boots for fine gentlemen.

As to our city of Dublin, shambles[11] may be appointed for this purpose in the most convenient parts of it, and butchers we may be assured will not be wanting; although I rather recommend buying the children alive, and dressing them hot from the knife as we do roasting pigs.

A very worthy person, a true lover of his country, and whose virtues I highly esteem, was lately pleased in discoursing on this matter to offer a refinement upon my scheme. He said that many gentlemen of this kingdom, having of late destroyed their deer, he conceived that the want of venison might be well supplied by the bodies of young lads and maidens, not exceeding fourteen years of age nor under twelve, so great a number of both sexes in every county being now ready to starve for want of work and service; and these to be disposed of by their parents, if alive, or otherwise by their nearest relations. But with due deference to so excellent a friend and so deserving a patriot, I cannot be altogether in his sentiments; for as to the males, my American acquaintance assured me from frequent experience that their flesh was generally tough and lean, like that of our

schoolboys, by continual exercise, and their taste disagreeable; and to fatten them would not answer the charge. Then as to the females, it would, I think with humble submission, be a loss to the public, because they soon would become breeders themselves; and besides, it is not improbable that some scrupulous people might be apt to censure such a practice (although indeed very unjustly) as a little bordering upon cruelty; which, I confess, hath always been with me the strongest objection against any project, how well soever intended.

But in order to justify my friend, he confessed that this expedient was put into his head by the famous Psalmanazar,[12] a native of the island Formosa, who came from thence to London above twenty years ago, and in conversation told my friend that in his country when any young person happened to be put to death, the executioner sold the carcass to persons of quality as a prime dainty; and that in his time the body of a plump girl of fifteen, who was crucified for an attempt to poison the emperor, was sold to his Imperial Majesty's prime minister of state, and other great mandarins of the court, in joints from the gibbet,[13] at four hundred crowns. Neither indeed can I deny that if the same use were made of several plump young girls in this town, who without one single groat[14] to their fortunes cannot stir abroad without a chair, and appear at the playhouse and assemblies in foreign fineries which they never will pay for, the kingdom would not be the worse.

Some persons of a desponding spirit are in great concern about that vast number of poor people

---

11. **shambles:** slaughterhouses.
12. **Psalmanazar** (săl′mə-năz′ər): a French impostor in London, who called himself George Psalmanazar and pretended to be from Formosa (now Taiwan)—where, he said, cannibalism was practiced.
13. **gibbet** (jĭb′ĭt): gallows.
14. **groat:** an old British coin worth four pennies.

who are aged, diseased, or maimed, and I have been desired to employ my thoughts what course may be taken to ease the nation of so grievous an <u>encumbrance</u>. But I am not in the least pain upon that matter, because it is very well known that they are every day dying and rotting by cold and famine, and filth and vermin, as fast as can be reasonably expected. And as to the younger laborers, they are now in almost as hopeful a condition. They cannot get work, and consequently pine away for want of nourishment to a degree that if at any time they are accidentally hired to common labor, they have not strength to perform it; and thus the country and themselves are happily delivered from the evils to come.

I have too long digressed, and therefore shall return to my subject. I think the advantages by the proposal which I have made are obvious and many, as well as of the highest importance.

For first, as I have already observed, it would greatly lessen the number of Papists, with whom we are yearly overrun, being the principal breeders of the nation as well as our most dangerous enemies; and who stay at home on purpose to deliver the kingdom to the Pretender, hoping to take their advantage by the absence of so many good Protestants, who have chosen rather to leave their country than stay at home and pay tithes against their conscience to an Episcopal curate.[15]

Secondly, the poorer tenants will have something valuable of their own, which by law may be made liable to distress,[16] and help to pay their landlord's rent, their corn and cattle being already seized and money a thing unknown.

Thirdly, whereas the maintenance of an hundred thousand children, from two years old and upwards, cannot be computed at less than ten shillings a piece per annum, the nation's stock will be thereby increased fifty thousand pounds per annum, besides the profit of a new dish introduced to the tables of all gentlemen of fortune in the kingdom who have any refinement in taste. And the money will circulate among ourselves, the goods being entirely of our own growth and manufacture.

Fourthly, the constant breeders, besides the gain of eight shillings sterling per annum by the sale of their children, will be rid of the charge of maintaining them after the first year.

Fifthly, this food would likewise bring great custom to taverns, where the vintners will certainly be so prudent as to procure the best receipts for dressing it to perfection, and consequently have their houses frequented by all the fine gentlemen, who justly value themselves upon their knowledge in good eating; and a skillful cook, who understands how to oblige his guests, will contrive

---

15. **Protestants . . . curate:** Swift is referring to Anglo-Irish landowners who lived—and spent the income from their property—in England.

16. **distress:** seizure for the payment of debts.

WORDS TO KNOW **encumbrance** (ĕn-kŭm′brəns) *n.* a burden

to make it as expensive as they please.

Sixthly, this would be a great inducement to marriage, which all wise nations have either encouraged by rewards or enforced by laws and penalties. It would increase the care and tenderness of mothers toward their children, when they were sure of a settlement for life to the poor babes, provided in some sort by the public, to their annual profit instead of expense. We should see an honest <u>emulation</u> among the married women, which of them could bring the fattest child to the market. Men would become as fond of their wives during the time of their pregnancy as they are now of their mares in foal, their cows in calf, or sows when they are ready to farrow; nor offer to beat or kick them (as is too frequent a practice) for fear of a miscarriage.

ACTIVE READING

EVALUATE What effect is the speaker trying to create by listing the advantages of the proposal?

Many other advantages might be enumerated. For instance, the addition of some thousand carcasses in our exportation of barreled beef, the propagation of swine's flesh, and improvement in the art of making good bacon, so much wanted among us by the great destruction of pigs, too frequent at our tables, which are no way comparable in taste or magnificence to a well-grown, fat, yearling child, which roasted whole will make a considerable figure at a lord mayor's feast or any other public entertainment. But this and many others I omit, being studious of brevity.

Supposing that one thousand families in this city would be constant customers for infants' flesh, besides others who might have it at merry meetings, particularly weddings and christenings, I compute that Dublin would take off annually about twenty thousand carcasses, and the rest of the kingdom (where probably they will be sold somewhat cheaper) the remaining eighty thousand.

I can think of no one objection that will possibly be raised against this proposal, unless it should be urged that the number of people will be thereby much lessened in the kingdom. This I freely own, and it was indeed one principal design in offering it to the world. I desire the reader will observe, that I calculate my remedy for this one individual kingdom of Ireland and for no other that ever was, is, or I think ever can be upon earth. Therefore let no man talk to me of other expedients: of taxing our absentees at five shillings a pound: of using neither clothes nor household furniture except what is of our own growth and manufacture: of utterly rejecting the materials and instruments that promote foreign luxury: of curing the expensiveness of pride, vanity, idleness, and gaming in our women: of introducing a vein of parsimony,[17] prudence, and temperance: of learning to love our country, in the want of which we differ even from Laplanders and the inhabitants of Topinamboo:[18] of quitting our <u>animosities</u> and factions, nor acting any longer like the Jews, who were murdering one another at the very moment their city was taken:[19] of being a little cautious not to sell our country and conscience for nothing: of teaching landlords to have at least one degree of

---

17. **parsimony** (pär′sə-mō′nē): frugality; thrift.
18. **Topinamboo** (tŏp′ĭ-năm′bōō): an area in Brazil.
19. **Jews . . . taken:** In A.D. 70, during a Jewish revolt against Roman rule, the inhabitants of Jerusalem, by fighting among themselves, made it easier for the future Roman emperor Titus to capture the city.

WORDS TO KNOW

emulation (ĕm′yə-lā′shən) *n.* an effort to equal or outdo another person; rivalry

animosity (ăn′ə-mŏs′ĭ-tē) *n.* hostility; hatred

mercy toward their tenants: lastly, of putting a spirit of honesty, industry, and skill into our shopkeepers; who, if a resolution could now be taken to buy only our native goods, would immediately unite to cheat and exact upon us in the price, the measure, and the goodness, nor could ever yet be brought to make one fair proposal of just dealing, though often and earnestly invited to it.

ACTIVE READING

QUESTION What might be the speaker's source for the "other expedients" he lists?

Therefore I repeat, let no man talk to me of these and the like expedients,[20] till he hath at least some glimpse of hope that there will ever be some hearty and sincere attempt to put them in practice.

But as to myself, having been wearied out for many years with offering vain, idle, visionary thoughts, and at length utterly despairing of success, I fortunately fell upon this proposal, which, as it is wholly new, so it hath something solid and real, of no expense and little trouble, full in our own power, and whereby we can incur no danger in disobliging England. For this kind of commodity will not bear exportation, the flesh being of too tender a consistence to admit a long continuance in salt, although perhaps I could name a country which would be glad to eat up our whole nation without it.

After all, I am not so violently bent upon my own opinion as to reject any offer proposed by wise men, which shall be found equally innocent, cheap, easy, and effectual. But before something of that kind shall be advanced in contradiction to my scheme, and offering a better, I desire the author or authors will be pleased maturely to consider two points. First, as things now stand, how they will be able to find food and raiment for an hundred thousand useless mouths and backs. And secondly, there being a round million of creatures in human figure throughout this kingdom, whose sole subsistence put into a common stock would leave them in debt two millions of pounds sterling, adding those who are beggars by profession to the bulk of farmers, cottagers, and laborers, with their wives and children who are beggars in effect; I desire those politicians who dislike my overture, and may perhaps be so bold to attempt an answer, that they will first ask the parents of these mortals whether they would not at this day think it a great happiness to have been sold for food at a year old in the manner I prescribe, and thereby have avoided such a perpetual scene of misfortunes as they have since gone through by the oppression of landlords, the impossibility of paying rent without money or trade, the want of common sustenance, with neither house nor clothes to cover them from the inclemencies of the weather, and the most inevitable prospect of entailing the like or greater miseries upon their breed forever.

I profess, in the sincerity of my heart, that I have not the least personal interest in endeavoring to promote this necessary work, having no other motive than the public good of my country, by advancing our trade, providing for infants, relieving the poor, and giving some pleasure to the rich. I have no children by which I can propose to get a single penny; the youngest being nine years old, and my wife past childbearing. ❖

---

20. **let no man . . . expedients:** Swift had, in his writings, suggested the "other expedients" without success.

Connect to the Literature

1. What Do You Think? What was your first reaction to the proposal offered in this essay?

> **Comprehension Check**
> - What is Swift's proposal?
> - What problem in Ireland does the proposal pretend to solve?
> - Name one advantage that the speaker sees in this solution.

Think Critically

2. **ACTIVE READING** **DRAWING CONCLUSIONS** Use the chart you created in your **READER'S NOTEBOOK** to review the statements from "A Modest Proposal" and your responses to their meanings. What can you conclude was Swift's **purpose** in suggesting such a horrible solution? Support your conclusion with evidence from the selection.

3. What response do you think Swift hoped to get from readers of "A Modest Proposal"?

4. Go back through the essay and find at least two places where you think Swift's **satire** is particularly powerful. Explain your choices.

5. How would you describe the **speaker** in the essay? Use details to support your answer.

6. In your opinion, why did Swift have the speaker list "other expedients" to solve Ireland's problems?

> THINK ABOUT
> - the types of proposals the speaker mentions
> - the contrast between those proposals and the "modest proposal"
> - Swift's overall purpose for writing the essay

Extend Interpretations

7. Comparing Texts What major similarities and differences do you see between Gulliver and the speaker in this essay? Support your response with examples from the two works.

8. Connect to Life Poverty and starvation in 18th-century Ireland inspired Swift to write "A Modest Proposal." What are some of the social and political issues that might inspire satirists today? Give reasons for your choices.

Literary Analysis

IRONY **Irony** is the contrast between expectation and reality. **Verbal irony** is a specific kind of irony in which what is said is not what is meant. The title of Swift's essay is an example of verbal irony, for the proposal is hardly "modest"—it's totally outrageous. The verbal irony in the title points to the ironic tone of the essay as a whole. But Swift's irony is not an end in itself; he used it to expose what he saw as deep truths.

Cooperative Learning Activity Work with a small group of classmates to find at least three ironic statements in "A Modest Proposal" that reveal important facts about Ireland's condition in Swift's time. Use graphics like those below to organize your ideas.

> **Ironic Statement**
> 1. "I am assured by our merchants that a boy or girl before twelve years old is no salable commodity." (p. 615)

> **Truth Revealed**
> 1. Irish children are not seen as human beings but as worthless objects.

> **Ironic Statement**
> 2. "This food will be . . . very proper for landlords, who, as they have already devoured most of the parents, seem to have the best title to the children." (p. 615)

> **Truth Revealed**

REVIEW **SATIRE** What kind of person is Swift satirizing with the speaker in this essay?

THE AUTHOR'S STYLE
Swift's Savage Wit

Jonathan Swift's signature style in his great satiric works sets him apart from his more lighthearted contemporaries, such as Alexander Pope, and even from most satirists today. An uncompromising moralist, Swift was continually disappointed by what he saw as humankind's corruption. His passion made him bitter, but his irony gave his bitterness a clever twist.

Key Aspects of Swift's Style

- the use of a persona—a narrator or speaker other than Swift—as an object of satire
- words, phrases, and situations that are shocking or disturbing
- ironic statements and situations that point out human shortcomings and faults
- use of understatement to expose a mindless acceptance of surface facts without regard to their deeper meaning

Analysis of Style

Study the aspects of Swift's style in the chart above. Then read the excerpts at right and complete the following activities:

- Find examples of each stylistic device in the excerpts. Explain who you think is the object of the satire in each excerpt.
- Explain what, if anything, you think is funny about each excerpt, and identify which stylistic device best contributes to this effect.
- Go back through the selections in this Author Study and identify other examples of Swift's satiric style.

Applications

1. **Imitation of Style** Try imitating Swift's style in a written commentary on some human weaknesses that you see around you. Use at least two of his techniques from the chart above.

2. **Changing Style** Go through the selections and paraphrase two or three of Swift's ideas in a straightforward way, without irony. Read your paraphrases along with Swift's original wording to your classmates. Discuss how the use of irony makes a difference.

3. **Speaking and Listening** How do you think Gulliver, the world traveler, would react to "A Modest Proposal"? Working with a partner, create and perform an interview with Gulliver for the amusement of your classmates.

---

from **A Tale of a Tub**

Last week I saw a woman flayed [skinned], and you will hardly believe how much it altered her person for the worse.

from the preface to **The Battle of the Books**

Satire is a sort of glass, wherein beholders do generally discover everybody's face but their own; which is the chief reason for that kind of reception it meets in the world, and that so very few are offended with it.

from **Gulliver's Travels**

The learning of this people [the Brobdingnagians] is very defective, consisting only in morality, history, poetry, and mathematics, wherein they must be allowed to excel. But the last of these is wholly applied to what may be useful in life, to the improvement of agriculture and all mechanical arts; so that among us it would be little esteemed.

from **"A Modest Proposal"**

I rather recommend buying the children alive, and dressing them hot from the knife as we do roasting pigs.

from **"Verses on the Death of Dr. Swift"**

My female Friends, whose tender Hearts,
Have better learn'd to Act their Parts,
Receive the News in *doleful Dumps*,
"The Dean is Dead, *(and what is Trumps?)*
Then Lord have Mercy on his Soul."

Choices & CHALLENGES

Writing Options

1. Editorial Memo Imagine that you are the editor of an 18th-century periodical. To help your staff decide whether to print "A Modest Proposal," write a memo in which you list the pros and cons of publishing it.

pros & cons

2. Ironic Rebuttal In the same spirit of irony, write a response to Swift's proposal in which you argue against his solution to Ireland's problems and propose an equally outrageous one of your own.

3. Another Proposal Draft a satiric essay of your own, titled "A Modest Proposal." Offer a ridiculous proposal for reforming a current social or political problem. Place your draft in your **Working Portfolio.**

Writing Handbook
See page 1369: Problem-Solution.

Activities & Explorations

1. Town Meeting Pretend you're in Dublin in 1729. In a group, organize a town meeting to discuss Ireland's problems as described in "A Modest Proposal." Include Catholics, Protestants, mothers, fathers, children, landowners, beggars, thieves, and English government officials. You might also include Dean Swift himself. Select a moderator and a record keeper. After the meeting, present a list of problems and proposed solutions. ~ **SPEAKING AND LISTENING**

2. Political Cartoon Create a political cartoon that might have appeared in newspapers in response to the original publication of Swift's essay. ~ **ART**

3. "Modest" Diagrams Imagine that Jonathan Swift will be presenting his proposal to a committee of English politicians gathered to solve Ireland's problems. He needs some visual aids to display his calculations and help the committee understand the "logic" of his solution. Create a diagram that he could use in his presentation. In addition to a bar graph to show figures, here is a sample diagram that you could use to highlight Swift's "modest" argument. ~ **VIEWING AND REPRESENTING**

```
        ┌─────────────┐
        │   Problem   │
        │ • Who       │
        │ • What      │
        │ • When      │
        │ • Where     │
        │ • Why       │
        └─────────────┘
              │
              ▼
        ┌─────────────┐
        │  Solution   │
        └─────────────┘
              │
              ▼
      ( Projected Results )
```

Inquiry & Research

1. Literary History How did readers react to "A Modest Proposal" at the time? Did anyone take the proposed solution seriously? Research the reception of Swift's famous essay. Also, find out why Swift stopped writing anything substantial about Ireland after "A Modest Proposal." Report your findings to the class.

2. Irish History Investigate the history of Ireland from the 18th century to the formation of the Irish Republic in 1937. What changes occurred in the relationship between Protestants and Catholics? How did those changes alter the political climate in Ireland? What happened to Ireland's economy? Here are some good places to start your research: a print or online encyclopedia and general histories, such as *History of Ireland* by Edmund Curtis and the *Dictionary of Irish History Since 1800.*

3. Swift Biography Find out more about the women in Swift's life: Esther Johnson, whom he called Stella, and Esther Vanhomrigh, whom he referred to as Vanessa. Also look at Swift's works about these women, the series of letters titled *Journal to Stella* and the long poem *Cadenus and Vanessa.*

Write a short report on Swift's relationship with these two women.

A portrait of Esther Johnson, Swift's Stella

4. Swift Online Check out Swift's web site. Input keyword *Jonathan Swift* in a search engine and see what you find. Write a critical review of online materials about Swift, specifying, for example, what would be useful for students interested in this great 18th-century satirist.

Vocabulary in Action

EXERCISE: ASSESSMENT PRACTICE Decide whether the words in each of the following pairs are synonyms or antonyms. On your paper, write **S** for Synonyms or **A** for Antonyms.

1. **animosity**—admiration
2. **prodigious**—small
3. **perpetual**—temporary
4. **deference**—esteem
5. **expedient**—device
6. **proficiency**—incompetence
7. **deplorable**—wretched
8. **emulation**—cooperation
9. **encumbrance**—asset
10. **rudiment**—basis

Building Vocabulary

For an in-depth lesson on how to use a thesaurus to find a word's synonyms and antonyms, see page 574.

Jonathan Swift

Author Study Project
PRODUCING A TALK SHOW

Working with a group of classmates, create a talk show segment with Jonathan Swift as the primary guest. You will need the following people to perform: a talk show host to conduct the interview; someone to play Swift in character (and in costume, if possible); and secondary guests, such as Swift's male friends, Joseph Addison and Alexander Pope, and his female friends, Stella and Vanessa. You will also need researchers, writers, editors, and, most important, a director who organizes everything. If you'd like to videotape the segment, you'll also need someone to operate the camera. Members of your class can act as the studio audience. Make sure they are prepared to participate in the open question-and-answer section of the program.

Print Resources Research biographies and criticisms of Swift's works for important information about him to use in the interview. Also, if you decide to use costumes, look for illustrations of how Swift and his contemporaries dressed. To accurately capture Swift's distinctive "voice," read more of his satire: for example, more of *Gulliver's Travels* and some of his poetry, especially "Verses on the Death of Dr. Swift," which contains Swift's comments about himself.

Video Watch the latest film version of *Gulliver's Travels* available at your local library or video store. Think about how you could use this video in your talk show.

Computers Encyclopedias on CD-ROM and an Internet search could yield valuable current information on Swift.

More Online: Research Starter
www.mcdougallittell.com

from Candide

Fiction by VOLTAIRE

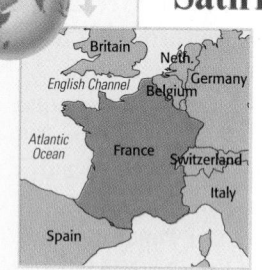

Comparing Literature of the World

Satirical Commentary Across Cultures

Gulliver's Travels* and *Candide According to Jonathan Swift, satirists hold up a mirror to show society its faults. In both *Gulliver's Travels* and *Candide*, the writers use **satire** to ridicule 18th-century society by revealing its hypocrisies, injustices, and follies.

Points of Comparison As you read the excerpt from *Candide*, compare Voltaire's use of exaggeration as a means to criticize society with Swift's. Notice, too, that both writers present their social commentary by recounting the episodic adventures of impressionable characters.

Map labels: Britain, Neth., Germany, Belgium, English Channel, Atlantic Ocean, France, Switzerland, Italy, Spain

Build Background

The Best of All Possible Worlds On a literal level, *Candide* tells the story of a naive young man as he wanders through the world. On a philosophical level, the novel deals with the nature of good and evil. Voltaire wrote *Candide* in response to the influential philosophical optimism of Gottfried Leibniz. A German philosopher, mathematician, and scholar, Leibniz believed that God had created the "best of all possible worlds." According to this theory, people should accept evil simply because it is part of the world. Voltaire, who spent much of his life trying to correct the wrongs he saw in the world, found such a philosophy appalling.

In *Candide*, Voltaire creates a world of horrors and folly and a character who enters that world believing fully that it is the best it can possibly be. After seeing and suffering outrageous misfortunes, Candide finally begins to question philosophical optimism and eventually discovers the secret of happiness.

> **WORDS TO KNOW**
> **Vocabulary Preview**
> condescend
> disposition
> doctrine
> gauntlet
> implicitly

Focus Your Reading

LITERARY ANALYSIS HUMOR **Humor** is the quality possessed by a literary work that entertains by evoking laughter. Humor plays an important part in **satire**. In *Candide*, Voltaire uses a variety of elements to create humor, including exaggeration, absurd reasoning, and irony. Notice the absurdity in the following statement:

> *Observe, for instance, the nose is formed for spectacles, therefore we wear spectacles.*

As you read the excerpt, look for other examples of humor.

ACTIVE READING DRAWING CONCLUSIONS ABOUT CHARACTERS When you **draw conclusions** about characters in literature, you form opinions about their personalities. You should base your conclusions about a character on the character's speech and actions and on descriptions of the character.

READER'S NOTEBOOK As you read the excerpt from *Candide*, record information about the characters in a chart like the one shown.

	Speech	Action	Description
Candide			a most sweet disposition
Baron			
Pangloss	"It is demonstrable that things . . ."		

from Candide

TRANSLATED BY TOBIAS SMOLLETT

Chapter I

How Candide was brought up in a magnificent castle, and how he was driven from thence

In the country of Westphalia, in the castle of the most noble Baron of Thunder-ten-tronckh, lived a youth whom nature had endowed with a most sweet disposition. His face was the true index of his mind. He had a solid judgment joined to the most unaffected simplicity, and hence, I presume, he had his name of Candide.[1] The old servants of the house suspected him to have been the son of the Baron's sister, by a mighty good sort of a gentleman of the neighborhood, whom that young lady refused to marry because he could produce no more than threescore and eleven quarterings[2] in his arms; the rest of the genealogical tree belonging to the family having been lost through the injuries of time.

The Baron was one of the most powerful lords in Westphalia, for his castle had not only a gate but even windows, and his great hall was hung with tapestry. He used to hunt with his mastiffs and spaniels instead of greyhounds; his groom served him for huntsman, and the parson of the parish officiated as grand almoner.[3] He was called "My Lord" by all his people, and he never told a story but everyone laughed at it.

My lady Baroness weighed three hundred and fifty pounds, consequently was a person of no small consideration; and then she did the honors of the house with a dignity that commanded universal respect. Her daughter Cunegund was about seventeen years of age fresh colored, comely, plump, and desirable. The Baron's son seemed to be a youth in every respect worthy of his father. Pangloss[4] the preceptor[5] was the oracle of the family, and little Candide listened to his instructions with all the simplicity natural to his age and disposition.

Master Pangloss taught metaphysico-theologo-cosmolo-nigology.[6] He could prove admirably

---

1. **Candide** (kăn-dēd'): The name is a French word meaning "innocent" or "without guile."

2. **quarterings:** divisions in coat of arms that indicate connections with other noble families. The baron's "threescore and eleven" (71) quarterings are a ridiculously large number.

3. **grand almoner** (ăl'mə-nər): a person in charge of distributing charity to the poor.

4. **Pangloss:** The name of this know-it-all character comes from Greek words meaning "all" and "tongue."

5. **preceptor** (prĭ-sĕp'tər): teacher.

6. **metaphysico-theologo-cosmolo-nigology:** Pangloss teaches a nonsensical subject with a pretentious name. (*Nigology* comes from the French word *nigaud*, meaning "foolish.")

WORDS TO KNOW

disposition (dĭs'pə-zĭsh'ən) *n.* temperament

that there is no effect without a cause, and that, in this best of all possible worlds, the Baron's castle was the most magnificent of all castles and my lady the best of all possible baronesses.

"It is demonstrable," said he, "that things cannot be otherwise than they are; for as all things have been created for some end, they must necessarily be created for the best end. Observe, for instance, the nose is formed for spectacles, therefore we wear spectacles. The legs are visibly designed for stockings, accordingly we wear stockings. Stones were made to be hewn, and to construct castles, therefore my lord has a magnificent castle; for the greatest baron in the province ought to be the best lodged. Swine were intended to be eaten; therefore we eat pork all the year round. And they who assert that everything is good do not express themselves correctly; they should say that everything is for the best."

Candide listened attentively, and believed implicitly; for he thought Miss Cunegund excessively handsome, though he never had the courage to tell her so. He concluded that next to the happiness of being Baron of Thunder-ten-tronckh, the next was that of being Miss Cunegund, the next that of seeing her every day, and the last that of hearing the doctrine of Master

The Stolen Kiss (late 1780s), Jean-Honoré Fragonard. Oil on canvas. Hermitage, St. Petersburg, Russia.

Pangloss, the greatest philosopher of the whole province, and consequently of the whole world.

One day, when Miss Cunegund went to take a walk in a little neighboring wood, which was called a park, . . . she happened to meet Candide; she blushed, he blushed also. She wished him a good morning in a faltering tone; he returned the salute, without knowing what he said. The next day, as they were rising from dinner, Cunegund and Candide slipped behind the screen. She dropped her handkerchief; the young man picked it up. She innocently took hold of his hand, and he as innocently kissed hers with a warmth, a sensibility, a grace—all very extraordinary—their lips met, their eyes sparkled, their knees trembled, their hands strayed. The Baron of Thunder-ten-tronckh chanced to come by; he beheld the cause and effect, and, without hesitation, saluted Candide with some notable kicks on the breech and drove him out of doors. Miss Cunegund fainted away, and, as soon as she came to herself, the Baroness boxed her ears. Thus a general consternation was spread over this most magnificent and most agreeable of all possible castles.

WORDS TO KNOW

implicitly (ĭm-plĭs′ĭt-lē) *adv.* without question or doubt
doctrine (dŏk′trĭn) *n.* the ideas taught by an authority

Chapter II

What befell Candide among the Bulgarians

Candide, thus driven out of this terrestrial paradise, wandered a long time, without knowing where he went; sometimes he raised his eyes, all bedewed with tears, toward Heaven, and sometimes he cast a melancholy look toward the magnificent castle where dwelt the fairest of young baronesses. He laid himself down to sleep in a furrow, heartbroken and supperless. The snow fell in great flakes, and, in the morning when he awoke, he was almost frozen to death; however, he made shift to crawl to the next town, which was called Waldberghoff-trarbk-dikdorff, without a penny in his pocket, and half dead with hunger and fatigue. He took up his stand at the door of an inn. He had not been long there before two men dressed in blue fixed their eyes steadfastly upon him.

"Faith, comrade," said one of them to the other, "yonder is a well-made young fellow, and of the right size."

Thereupon they went up to Candide, and with the greatest civility and politeness invited him to dine with them.

"Gentlemen," replied Candide, with a most engaging modesty, "you do me much honor, but, upon my word, I have no money."

"Money, sir!" said one of the men in blue to him. "Young persons of your appearance and merit never pay anything. Why, are not you five feet five inches high?"

"Yes, gentlemen, that is really my size," replied he with a low bow.

"Come then, sir, sit down along with us. We will not only pay your reckoning,[7] but will never

suffer such a clever young fellow as you to want money. Mankind were born to assist one another."

"You are perfectly right, gentlemen," said Candide; "that is precisely the doctrine of Master Pangloss; and I am convinced that everything is for the best."

His generous companions next entreated him to accept a few crowns, which he readily complied with, at the same time offering them his note for the payment, which they refused, and sat down to table.

"Have you not a great affection for—"

"Oh, yes!" he replied. "I have a great affection for the lovely Miss Cunegund."

"Maybe so," replied one of the men, "but that is not the question! We are asking you whether you have not a great affection for the King of the Bulgarians?"

"For the King of the Bulgarians?" said Candide. "Not at all. Why, I never saw him in my life."

"Is it possible! Oh, he is a most charming king! Come, we must drink his health."

"With all my heart, gentlemen," Candide said, and he tossed off his glass.

"Bravo!" cried the blues. "You are now the support, the defender, the hero of the Bulgarians; your fortune is made; you are on the high road to glory." So saying, they put him in irons and carried him away to the regiment. There he was made to wheel about to the right, to the left, to draw his ramrod,[8] to return his ramrod, to present, to fire, to march, and they gave him thirty blows with a cane. The next day he performed his exercise a little better, and they gave him but twenty. The day following he came off with ten and was looked upon as a young fellow of surprising genius by all his comrades.

---

7. **reckoning:** bill.

8. **ramrod:** a rod used to ram gunpowder and bullets into a musket.

Candide was struck with amazement and could not for the soul of him conceive how he came to be a hero. One fine spring morning, he took it into his head to take a walk, and he marched straight forward, conceiving it to be a privilege of the human species as well as of the brute creation, to make use of their legs how and when they pleased. He had not gone above two leagues[9] when he was overtaken by four other heroes, six feet high, who bound him neck and heels, and carried him to a dungeon. A court-martial[10] sat upon him, and he was asked which he liked best, either to run the gauntlet six and thirty times through the whole regiment, or to have his brains blown out with a dozen musket balls. In vain did he remonstrate to them that the human will is free, and that he chose neither. They obliged him to make a choice, and he determined, in virtue of that divine gift called free will, to run the gauntlet six and thirty times. He had gone through his discipline twice, and the regiment being composed of two thousand men, they composed for him exactly four thousand strokes, which laid bare all his muscles and nerves, from the nape of his neck to his rump. As they were preparing to make him set out the third time, our young hero, unable to support it any longer, begged as a favor they would be so obliging as to shoot him through the head. The favor being granted, a bandage was tied over his eyes, and he was made to kneel down. At that very instant, his Bulgarian Majesty, happening to pass by, inquired into the delinquent's crime, and being a prince of great penetration, he found, from what he heard of Candide, that he was a young metaphysician,[11] entirely ignorant of the world. And, therefore, out of his great clemency, he condescended to pardon him, for which his name will be celebrated in every journal, and in every age. A skillful surgeon made a cure of Candide in three weeks by means of emollient unguents[12] prescribed by Dioscorides.[13] His sores were now skinned over, and he was able to march when the King of the Bulgarians gave battle to the King of the Abares. ❖

Anonymous print (1700s). Recruiting officers in 18th-century Europe often took men by force.

---

9. **two leagues:** about five or six miles.

10. **court-martial:** military tribunal.

11. **metaphysician** (mĕt′ə-fĭ-zĭsh′ən): one who is skilled in metaphysics, the branch of philosophy that investigates the nature of reality.

12. **emollient unguents** (ĭ-mŏl′yənt ŭng′gwənts): soothing ointments.

13. **Dioscorides** (dī′ə-skôr′ĭ-dēz′): a Greek physician of the first century A.D., who wrote an influential book about the medicinal properties of plants.

WORDS TO KNOW

gauntlet (gônt′lĭt) *n.* a punishment in which a person is forced to run between two lines of people who beat the person as he or she passes

condescend (kŏn′dĭ-sĕnd′) *v.* to do something considered to be beneath one's dignity

Connect to the Literature

1. **What Do You Think?**
   What was your reaction to Candide's experiences?

   Comprehension Check
   - Why is Candide thrown out of the castle by the Baron?
   - How is Candide drafted into the Bulgarian army?

Think Critically

2. What happens to Candide when he tries to live according to Master Pangloss's teachings?

   THINK ABOUT

   - the "cause and effect" Candide engages in with Cunegund
   - his assertion to the men in blue that "everything is for the best"
   - Candide's decision to "make use of [his] legs" while a soldier in the Bulgarian army

3. Why do you suppose the Baron appreciates Pangloss's philosophy?

4. What is the effect of statements like "Thus a general consternation was spread over this most magnificent and most agreeable of all possible castles"?

5. Do you think that Candide will reject the teachings of Pangloss after his experience with the Bulgarian army? Why or why not?

6. **ACTIVE READING** **DRAWING CONCLUSIONS ABOUT CHARACTERS** With a classmate, discuss the information you recorded in your **READER'S NOTEBOOK.** Based on this information, what **conclusions** can you draw about the nature of Candide, Pangloss, and other **characters** in the selection?

Extend Interpretations

7. **Connect to Life** Voltaire uses **satire** to point out weaknesses in 18th-century society. What examples can you think of in which writers and filmmakers today use satire to criticize flaws in modern life?

8. **Points of Comparison** Compare Candide's relationship to Pangloss with Gulliver's relationship to the leaders of the Lilliputians and the Brobdingnagians. How are the relationships similar? What do they suggest about Candide and Gulliver?

Literary Analysis

HUMOR There are three basic types of **humor,** all of which may involve exaggeration or irony.

- **Humor of situation** usually involves exaggerated events or **situational irony.** Candide's exaggerated punishment at the hands of the Bulgarian army is an example of this type of humor.
- **Humor of character** often involves exaggerated personality traits or characters who, ironically, don't recognize their own failings. Pangloss, with his self-serving philosophy, reflects this type of humor.
- **Humor of language** may include sarcasm, exaggeration, puns, absurdity, or **verbal irony.** The descriptions of the Baron, the Baroness, and their son are examples of this type of humor.

Paired Activity With a partner, choose a passage of the story that you find particularly funny, and discuss the types of humor it contains. How does the humor contribute to the **satire** in *Candide?* You might use a chart like the one shown to organize your ideas.

Passage	Types of Humor	How Humor Contributes to Satire

Writing Options

Points of Comparison

Think about the use of satire in *Gulliver's Travels* and *Candide*. In which is satire used more effectively? Write an essay explaining your ideas.

Satire in Gulliver

Satire in Candide

Inquiry & Research

Enlightened Ideas

Voltaire was attracted to the ideas of the philosopher John Locke and the scientist Sir Isaac Newton. Learn about Locke's and Newton's ideas and their impact on Voltaire.

Vocabulary in Action

EXERCISE: CONTEXT CLUES Write the vocabulary word that best answers each riddle.

1. I am a group activity that inflicts harm on one person.
2. Some people live their lives in accordance with me.
3. I am what a snob might do.
4. I am different in each person.
5. I am a way in which you might believe or trust.

WORDS TO KNOW		
condescend	gauntlet	
disposition	implicitly	
doctrine		

Building Vocabulary

For an in-depth study of context clues, see page 938.

Voltaire
1694–1778

Other Works
Philosophical Dictionary
Zadig
Zaïre

Early Success François Marie Arouet chose the pen name Voltaire shortly after *Oedipe,* his first major play, achieved success in 1718. Other successes followed. He became independently wealthy in his early 30s and enjoyed the status of an honored celebrity at the court of King Louis XV.

English Influence Circumstances changed abruptly when Voltaire insulted a young nobleman in 1726. Given the option of imprisonment or exile, Voltaire chose exile in England. During his three years there, Voltaire met the English writers Alexander Pope and Jonathan Swift. After Voltaire returned to Paris in 1729, he wrote a book praising English customs and institutions. However, the book was thought to be critical of the French government, and Voltaire was forced to flee Paris again.

Exile and Return During his years of exile, Voltaire produced a steady flow of books, plays, pamphlets, and letters. Many addressed religious intolerance and persecution. Although Voltaire enjoyed a triumphant return to Paris at age 83, the excitement of the trip proved too much for him and he died shortly thereafter. Because of his criticism of the Catholic Church, Voltaire was denied burial in church ground. However, in 1791, his remains were moved to the Panthéon in Paris, where many of France's most famous citizens are buried.

from A Vindication of the Rights of Woman

Essay by MARY WOLLSTONECRAFT

(Connect to Your Life)

Women's Rights Women's rights have been debated for centuries. From your knowledge of history, what has caused this debate? Do you think that women's rights are still a controversial issue in our society? Why or why not? Jot down your thoughts.

Build Background

Radical Views Although a number of 18th-century British writers discussed the role of women in society, none became as celebrated for their feminist views as Mary Wollstonecraft. Early in her life, Wollstonecraft learned the value of independence and became openly critical of a society that treated females as inferior creatures who were socially, financially, and legally dependent on men. Her concern for humanity was not limited to compassion for downtrodden women; she advocated the equality and independence of all human beings. In 1790, Wollstonecraft had written a defense of the French Revolution entitled *A Vindication of the Rights of Men.* It was controversial not only for its radical ideas but for being a woman's venture into political writing. In 1792, Wollstonecraft continued the controversy with her publication of *A Vindication of the Rights of Woman,* in which she called for an end to the prevailing injustices against females. Although her opinions on women's rights may seem conservative by modern standards, they were radical in 18th-century Britain, where most women accepted their inferior status or at least refrained from expressing their discontent.

> WORDS TO KNOW
> **Vocabulary Preview**
> affectation
> concurring
> feign
> grovel
> ignoble
> languid
> solicitude
> specious
> subordinate
> vivacity

Focus Your Reading

LITERARY ANALYSIS | ARGUMENTATION

Argumentation is speech or writing intended to convince an audience that a proposal should be adopted or rejected. Most argumentation begins with a statement of an idea or opinion, which is then supported with logical evidence. Wollstonecraft states her opinion in the first paragraph of her essay:

> *. . . the neglected education of my fellow-creatures is the grand source of the misery I deplore. . . .*

As you read this **persuasive essay,** consider the evidence Wollstonecraft uses to support her opinion.

ACTIVE READING | RECOGNIZING LOGICAL PERSUASION

In her essay, Wollstonecraft uses persuasive techniques that appeal to logic and reason rather than to emotion. For example, the writer uses the technique of anticipation and rebuttal of opposing views. That is, she foresees the opposition's argument in her **essay** and logically responds to it.

READER'S NOTEBOOK As you read the essay, list in a chart like the one shown opposing views that Wollstonecraft identifies. Jot down briefly how she responds to each view.

Opposing Views	Response

FROM A VINDICATION OF THE RIGHTS OF WOMAN

MARY WOLLSTONECRAFT

FROM THE INTRODUCTION

After considering the historic page, and viewing the living world with anxious solicitude, the most melancholy emotions of sorrowful indignation have depressed my spirits, and I have sighed when obliged to confess, that either nature has made a great difference between man and man, or that the civilization which has hitherto taken place in the world has been very partial. I have turned over various books written on the subject of education, and patiently observed the conduct of parents and the management of schools; but what has been the result?—a profound conviction that the neglected education of my fellow-creatures is the grand source of the misery I deplore; and that women, in particular, are rendered weak and wretched by a variety of concurring causes, originating from one hasty conclusion. The conduct and manners of women, in fact, evidently prove that their minds are not in a healthy state; for, like the flowers which are planted in too rich

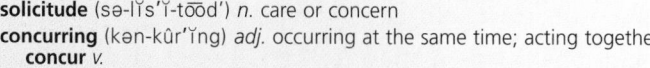

a soil, strength and usefulness are sacrificed to beauty; and the flaunting leaves, after having pleased a fastidious eye, fade, disregarded on the stalk, long before the season when they ought to have arrived at maturity. One cause of this barren blooming I attribute to a false system of education, gathered from the books written on this subject by men who, considering females rather as women than human creatures, have been more anxious to make them alluring mistresses than affectionate wives and rational mothers; and the understanding of the sex has been so bubbled by this specious homage, that the civilized women of the present century, with a few exceptions, are only anxious to inspire love, when they ought to cherish a nobler ambition, and by their abilities and virtues exact respect.

In a treatise,[1] therefore, on female rights and manners, the works which have been particularly written for their improvement must not be overlooked; especially when it is asserted, in direct terms, that the minds of women are enfeebled by false refinement; that the books of instruction, written by men of genius, have had the same tendency as more frivolous productions; and that . . . they are treated as a kind of subordinate beings, and not as a part of the human species, when improvable reason is allowed to be the dignified distinction which raises men above the brute creation, and puts a natural scepter in a feeble hand.

Yet, because I am a woman, I would not lead my readers to suppose that I mean violently to agitate the contested question respecting the quality or inferiority of the sex; but as the subject lies in my way, and I cannot pass it over without subjecting the main tendency of my reasoning to misconstruction, I shall stop a moment to deliver, in a few words, my opinion. In the government of the physical world it is observable that the female in point of strength is, in general, inferior to the male. This is the law of nature; and it does not appear to be suspended or abrogated[2] in favor of

woman. A degree of physical superiority cannot, therefore, be denied—and it is a noble prerogative! But not content with this natural pre-eminence, men endeavor to sink us still lower merely to render us alluring objects for a moment; and women, intoxicated by the adoration which men, under the influence of their senses, pay them, do not seek to obtain a durable interest in their hearts, or to become the friends of the fellow creatures who find amusement in their society.

I am aware of an obvious inference: from every quarter have I heard exclamations against masculine women; but where are they to be found? If by this appellation men mean to inveigh against their ardor[3] in hunting, shooting, and gaming, I shall most cordially join in the cry; but if it be against the imitation of manly virtues, or, more properly speaking, the attainment of those talents and virtues, the exercise of which ennobles the human character, and which raise females in the scale of animal being, when they are comprehensively termed mankind; all those who view them with a philosophic eye must, I should think, wish with me, that they may every day grow more and more masculine. . . .

My own sex, I hope, will excuse me, if I treat them like rational creatures, instead of flattering their

---

1. **treatise** (trē′tĭs): a formal, detailed article or book on a particular subject.
2. **abrogated** (ăb′rə-gā′tĭd): canceled; repealed.
3. **if by . . . ardor**: if by this word (that is, *masculine*) men mean to condemn some women's enthusiasm.

WORDS TO KNOW
specious (spē′shəs) *adj.* attractive in a deceptive or insincere way
subordinate (sə-bôr′dn-ĭt) *adj.* less important; lower in rank

fascinating graces, and viewing them as if they were in a state of perpetual childhood, unable to stand alone. I earnestly wish to point out in what true dignity and human happiness consists—I wish to persuade women to endeavor to acquire strength, both of mind and body, and to convince them that the soft phrases, susceptibility of heart, delicacy of sentiment, and refinement of taste, are almost synonymous with epithets[4] of weakness, and that those beings who are only the objects of pity and that kind of love, which has been termed its sister, will soon become objects of contempt. . . .

The education of women has, of late, been more attended to than formerly; yet they are still reckoned a frivolous sex, and ridiculed or pitied by the writers who endeavor by satire or instruction to improve them. It is acknowledged that they spend many of the first years of their lives in acquiring a smattering of accomplishments; meanwhile strength of body and mind are sacrificed to libertine[5] notions of beauty, to the desire of establishing themselves—the only way women can rise in the world—by marriage. And this desire making mere animals of them, when they marry they act as such children may be expected to act: they dress; they paint, and nickname God's creatures. Surely these weak beings are only fit for a seraglio![6] Can they be expected to govern a family with judgment, or take care of the poor babes whom they bring into the world?

If then it can be fairly deduced from the present conduct of the sex, from the prevalent fondness for pleasure which takes place of ambition and those nobler passions that open and enlarge the soul; that the instruction which women have hitherto received has only tended, with the constitution of civil society, to render

them insignificant objects of desire—mere propagators of fools!—if it can be proved that in aiming to accomplish them, without cultivating their understandings, they are taken out of their sphere of duties, and made ridiculous and useless when the short-lived bloom of beauty is over, I presume that *rational* men will excuse me for endeavoring to persuade them to become more masculine and respectable.

Indeed the word masculine is only a bugbear:[7] there is little reason to fear that women will acquire too much courage or fortitude; for their apparent inferiority with respect to bodily strength, must render them, in some degree, dependent on men in the various relations of life; but why should it be increased by prejudices that give a sex to virtue, and confound simple truths with sensual reveries?[8]

FROM CHAPTER 2

Youth is the season for love in both sexes; but in those days of thoughtless enjoyment provision should be made for the more important years of life, when reflection takes place of sensation. But Rousseau, and most of the male writers who have followed his steps, have warmly inculcated[9] that the whole tendency of female education ought to be directed to one point: to render them pleasing.

Let me reason with the supporters of this opinion who have any knowledge of human nature, do they imagine that marriage can

---

4. **epithets:** descriptive terms.
5. **libertine** (lĭb′ər-tēn′): indecent or unseemly.
6. **seraglio** (sə-răl′yō): harem.
7. **bugbear:** an object of exaggerated fear.
8. **confound . . . reveries:** confuse simple truths with sexual daydreams.
9. **inculcated** (ĭn-kŭl′kā′tĭd): taught.

eradicate the habitude of life? The woman who has only been taught to please will soon find that her charms are oblique sunbeams, and that they cannot have much effect on her husband's heart when they are seen every day, when the summer is passed and gone. Will she then have sufficient native energy to look into herself for comfort, and cultivate her dormant faculties? or, is it not more rational to expect that she will try to please other men; and, in the emotions raised by the expectation of new conquests, endeavor to forget the mortification her love or pride has received? When the husband ceases to be a lover—and the time will inevitably come, her desire of pleasing will then grow languid, or become a spring of bitterness; and love, perhaps, the most evanescent[10] of all passions, gives place to jealousy or vanity.

I now speak of women who are restrained by principle or prejudice; such women, though they would shrink from an intrigue with real abhorrence, yet, nevertheless, wish to be convinced by the homage of gallantry that they are cruelly neglected by their husbands; or, days and weeks are spent in dreaming of the happiness enjoyed by congenial souls till their health is undermined and their spirits broken by discontent. How then can the great art of pleasing be such a necessary study? it is only useful to a mistress; the chaste wife, and serious mother, should only consider her power to please as the polish of her virtues, and the affection of her husband as one of the comforts that render her talk less difficult and her life happier. But, whether she be loved or neglected, her first wish should be to make herself respectable, and not to rely for all her happiness on a being subject to like infirmities with herself.

The worthy Dr. Gregory fell into a similar error. I respect his heart; but entirely disapprove of his celebrated Legacy to his Daughters. . . .

He actually recommends dissimulation,[11] and advises an innocent girl to give the lie to her feelings, and not dance with spirit, when gaiety of heart would make her feet eloquent without making her gestures immodest. In the name of truth and common sense, why should not one woman acknowledge that she can take more exercise than another? or, in other words, that she has a sound constitution; and why, to damp innocent vivacity, is she darkly to be told that men will draw conclusions which she little thinks of? Let the libertine draw what inference he pleases; but, I hope, that no sensible mother will restrain the natural frankness of youth by instilling such indecent cautions. Out of the abundance of the heart the mouth speaketh; and a wiser than Solomon hath said, that the heart should be made clean, and not trivial ceremonies observed, which it is not very difficult to fulfil with scrupulous exactness when vice reigns in the heart.

Women ought to endeavor to purify their heart; but can they do so when their uncultivated understandings make them entirely dependent on their senses for employment and amusement, when no noble pursuit sets them above the little vanities of the day, or enables them to curb the wild emotions that agitate a reed over which every passing breeze has power? To gain the affections of a virtuous man, is affectation necessary? Nature has given woman a weaker frame than man; but, to ensure her husband's

ACTIVE READING

ANALYZE How does Wollstonecraft suggest that a woman "make herself respectable"?

---

10. **evanescent** (ĕv´ə-nĕs´ənt): quickly vanishing; fleeting.

11. **dissimulation:** a concealing of one's true feelings; pretense.

WORDS
TO
KNOW

languid (lăng´gwĭd) *adj.* sluggish; weak
vivacity (vĭ-văs´ĭ-tē) *n.* liveliness
affectation (ăf´ĕk-tā´shən) *n.* unnatural behavior; conduct intended to give a false impression

affections, must a wife, who by the exercise of her mind and body whilst she was discharging the duties of a daughter, wife, and mother, has allowed her constitution to retain its natural strength, and her nerves a healthy tone, is she, I say, to condescend to use art and <u>feign</u> a sickly delicacy in order to secure her husband's affection? Weakness may excite tenderness, and gratify the arrogant pride of man; but the lordly caresses of a protector will not gratify a noble mind that pants for, and deserves to be respected. Fondness is a poor substitute for friendship! . . .

Besides, the woman who strengthens her body and exercises her mind will, by managing her family and practicing various virtues, become the friend, and not the humble dependent of her husband; and if she, by possessing such substantial qualities, merit his regard, she will not find it necessary to conceal her affection, nor to pretend to an unnatural coldness of constitution to excite her husband's passions. . . .

ACTIVE READING

EVALUATE What type of marriage is Wollstonecraft condemning?

If all the faculties of woman's mind are only to be cultivated as they respect her dependence on man; if, when a husband be obtained, she have arrived at her goal, and meanly proud rests satisfied with such a paltry crown, let her <u>grovel</u> contentedly, scarcely raised by her employments above the animal kingdom; but, if, struggling for the prize of her high calling, she look beyond the present scene, let her cultivate her understanding without stopping to consider what character the husband may have whom she is destined to marry. Let her only determine, without being too anxious about present happiness, to acquire the qualities that ennoble a rational being, and a rough inelegant husband may shock her taste without destroying her peace of mind. She will not model her soul to suit the frailties of her companion, but to bear with them: his character may be a trial, but not an impediment to virtue. . . .

These may be termed Utopian dreams. Thanks to that Being who impressed them on my soul, and gave me sufficient strength of mind to dare to exert my own reason, till, becoming dependent only on him for the support of my virtue, I view, with indignation, the mistaken notions that enslave my sex.

I love man as my fellow; but his scepter, real, or usurped, extends not to me, unless the reason of an individual demands my homage; and even then the submission is to reason, and not to man. In fact, the conduct of an accountable being must be regulated by the operations of its own reason; or on what foundation rests the throne of God?

It appears to me necessary to dwell on these obvious truths, because females have been insulated, as it were; and, while they have been stripped of the virtues that should clothe humanity, they have been decked with artificial graces that enable them to exercise a short-lived tyranny. Love, in their bosoms, taking place of every nobler passion, their sole ambition is to be fair, to raise emotion instead of inspiring respect; and this <u>ignoble</u> desire, like the servility in absolute monarchies, destroys all strength of character. Liberty is the mother of virtue, and if women be, by their very constitution, slaves, and not allowed to breathe the sharp invigorating air of freedom, they must ever languish like exotics,[12] and be reckoned beautiful flaws in nature.

---

12. **languish like exotics:** wilt like plants grown away from their natural environment.

WORDS   **feign** (fān) *v.* to give a false appearance of; simulate or counterfeit
TO   **grovel** (grŏv′əl) *v.* to behave with exaggerated submission or humility
KNOW   **ignoble** (ĭg-nō′bəl) *adj.* not noble; degrading; contemptible

Connect to the Literature

1. **What Do You Think?**
   Would you like to hear Wollstonecraft speak on women's rights? Explain why or why not.

Comprehension Check
- How does a woman's lack of education affect her husband and children?
- Why does the author encourage women to strengthen their bodies?

Think Critically

2. In your opinion, what "manly virtues" does Wollstonecraft want women to imitate?

3. How do you think Wollstonecraft would describe a good marriage?

   > **THINK ABOUT**
   > - the kinds of female behavior she criticizes
   > - her complaints about the attitude of men toward women
   > - the qualities she would like women to acquire
   > - her reasons for encouraging women to strengthen their minds

4. Do you think Wollstonecraft believes in the complete equality of men and women?

5. **ACTIVE READING** **RECOGNIZING LOGICAL PERSUASION** With a partner, use the chart in your 📖 **READER'S NOTEBOOK** to discuss Wollstonecraft's specific responses to opposing views. Do you think this technique is an effective tool against the opposition? Why or why not?

Extend Interpretations

6. **Comparing Texts** Compare Wollstonecraft's views with those expressed by Defoe in "An Academy for Women" (page 577). How are their attitudes toward women alike? How are they different?

7. **Connect to Life** In your opinion, what social issues would concern Wollstonecraft today? Would she still feel a need to defend women's rights? Discuss your ideas.

Literary Analysis

ARGUMENTATION Writing that seeks to convince readers to adopt or reject an idea or proposal is referred to as **argumentation.** In *A Vindication of the Rights of Woman*, Wollstonecraft attempts to convince her readers that women should receive a better education. The writer supports her proposal with logical evidence. In the following excerpt, for example, Wollstonecraft reasons against limiting a woman's education to the simple goal of rendering her pleasing to a husband.

The woman who has only been taught to please will soon find that her charms are oblique sunbeams, and that they cannot have much effect on her husband's heart when they are seen every day, when the summer is passed and gone.

Cooperative Learning Activity With a small group of classmates, evaluate the evidence Wollstonecraft uses to support her opinion on the education of women. What points do you think are most convincing? What additional points would have strengthened her argument? Use a chart like the one below to keep track of your ideas.

Convincing Evidence	Additional Points

Writing Options

1. **Opinion Paper** Draft an opinion paper on the importance of cultivating one's mind. Use any of Wollstonecraft's reasons with which you agree, but also add some of your own.

2. **Questions and Answers** Create a set of questions you would like to ask Wollstonecraft, and then write what you think her answers would be.

Vocabulary in Action

EXERCISE: MEANING CLUES Use your knowledge of the boldfaced words to answer the following questions.

1. Are people who **feign** friendship being loyal, being rude, or being phony?

2. Is a person who displays **vivacity** showing conceit, showing pep, or showing wealth?

3. Is a **specious** statement a truth, a mistake, or a lie?

4. Which is a sign of **solicitude**—a salute, a yawn, or a pat on the shoulder?

5. Would a person who feels **subordinate** speak forcefully, moderately, or timidly?

6. Would a person who's feeling **languid** be most likely to want to sit on the beach, to climb a mountain, or to dig at an archaeological site?

7. Are people who **grovel** while asking for something most likely to ask on their knees, with their noses in the air, or while shaking their fists?

8. Is an **ignoble** man most likely to be described as a prince of a fellow, a giant in his field, or a real rat?

9. If you felt that someone was displaying **affectation,** would you say that the person was cracking the whip, was putting on airs, or was looking on the bright side?

10. If you can't take Beginning Art and Advanced Drama because they are **concurring** classes, is your problem due to a scheduling conflict, a lack of training, or a lack of space?

Building Vocabulary

For an in-depth lesson on how to expand your vocabulary, see page 1182.

Mary Wollstonecraft
1759–1797

Other Works
A Vindication of the Rights of Men

Difficult Childhood Mary Wollstonecraft's unusual and difficult childhood taught her to question conventional attitudes about women. Her family moved frequently as her alcoholic father pursued a series of unsuccessful farming ventures in which he used up the family's money, including the money promised to his daughters by their grandfather. In this impoverished, chaotic household, Wollstonecraft received only six or seven years of formal education and was mostly self-taught.

Self-Made Woman At age 19, Wollstonecraft left home to take a job as companion to a rich widow. When she was 22, she opened a private school near London, and although the project was short-lived, it introduced her to important friends who encouraged her to write. Wollstonecraft had taught herself French and German, and in 1787 she was hired as a translator for a journal. She often participated in discussions with the journal's publisher, Joseph Johnson, and his circle of intellectual friends, including political essayist Thomas Paine, the poet William Blake, and the philosopher William Godwin.

Brief Happiness Wollstonecraft later developed a close friendship with Godwin and, at the age of 37, married him. Their happy but brief relationship ended unexpectedly when Wollstonecraft died less than a year later from inept medical care following childbirth. The couple's daughter—the future Mary Wollstonecraft Shelley—was to become famous in her own right as the author of *Frankenstein* and the wife of the poet Percy Bysshe Shelley.

Using Humor to Persuade . . .

From Reading to Writing In "A Modest Proposal," Jonathan Swift uses wit and irony to draw attention to the serious social problems in 18th-century Ireland. Swift was a master of achieving biting social criticism through **satire,** a form of persuasive writing that uses humor to attack human vice or folly. By using satire, a writer can expose problems or argue for change in a way that is powerful but not preachy.

Basics in a Box

Satire at a Glance

Object of Satire

Takes aim at a particular person, institution, or idea to call attention to a problem, folly, or vice.

Uses humor, wit, and irony to attack the problem.

Criticism

Humor

RUBRIC Standards for Writing

A successful satire should

- poke fun at people, ideas, customs, or institutions to persuade readers to change

- use a tone that matches the goal

- use humor, exaggeration, understatement, and specific examples to reveal the subject in a more critical light

- make clear the object of the satire, but make the reader discover the writer's true perspective on the issue

- use a form that enhances the writer's purpose

Analyzing a Professional Model

Ellen Goodman
Columnist, the *Boston Globe*

A New "Modest Proposal"

Now that we have repealed welfare, I have a modest proposal. Let's go all the way and rescind childhood.

Childhood has become far too burdensome for the American public to bear. It isn't good for the country. It isn't even good for children who are captured in an unwholesome and prolonged state of dependency.

The whole idea of childhood, it should be remembered, is nothing but an anachronistic leftover from the original liberals. Before the so-called Enlightenment, before Rousseau, before the left-wing conspiracy of 18th-century do-gooders, the young dressed, worked and were looked upon as short adults.

Children existed, but they didn't have their own 'hood—a place where they were supposed to be educated and nurtured until they reached maturity. Adolescence, for that matter, wasn't invented until the early 20th century. Nor was the concept of juvenile as in delinquency, nor the notion of teen-age as in pregnancy.

But now we are stuck with this useless thing called childhood, a drain on the private and public exchequers. Not to mention a merciless drag on the private and public conscience.

Consider what happened when Congress passed and the president approved the "Personal Responsibility and Work Opportunity Act" (a.k.a. welfare reform). The only teensy-weensy reservations about cutting $56 billion from the poorest Americans, ending the federal guarantee of assistance to poor families and launching them into the unknown, had to do with children.

There are still a handful of people troubled by the fact that America has the highest child poverty rates of any industrialized country and that when this "reform" clicks in, a million more children are expected to become poor.

Why not eliminate all this messy, counterproductive guilt? Why not apply the same principles of "personal responsibility" and "work opportunity" to our youngest citizens?

I am not alone in my plan, though perhaps I am the first to put it quite so baldly. But we are already erasing the line between childhood and adulthood whenever we want to.

1 Sets a humorous, ironic tone with a seemingly preposterous proposal

2 This writer uses the form of a persuasive essay.
Another Option:
· Use another format such as a narrative, poem, drama, letter, or cartoon.

3 Uses exaggeration to make point

4 This writer introduces the real object of her satire after establishing the overall tone.
Other Option:
· Identify the object of satire up-front.

At the Olympics, we had 14-year-old gymnasts on the "Women's Team." In the states, we now have plans to try 13-year-old lawbreakers as adults. In Congress they are considering doing away with juvenile jails and "mainstreaming" kids with older criminals. Across the world, the "new economy" is using kids as a way to meet global competition.

Most Americans already recognize that childhood is simply not cost-effective. If children were once economic assets, they are now deficits, unlikely to ever pay back our investments. So only a third of our households have anyone under 18 in them today. Communities that once felt a collective responsibility for the next generation now often regard children as private property to be exclusively maintained by their owners.

If we eliminated the entire notion of childhood we wouldn't have to worry about children having children. Or about child care. Or after-school care. Or school. Child labor would become another "work opportunity."

Of course, we could retain childhood as a luxury item for those who could afford it. Sort of like an Ivy League college. The rest, the poor especially, will have to do without childhood the way they do without so much else. . . .

The last great evil in America today is dependency. The last remaining "culture of dependency" is, of course, childhood. Is it any wonder that it has to go?

If my modest proposal seems too harsh, may I remind you of the one Jonathan Swift offered in 1729: "A Modest Proposal for Preventing the Children of Poor People in Ireland from Being a Burden to Their Parents or Country and for Making Them Beneficial to the Public."

Swift proposed, modestly and satirically, that the Irish young be sold and eaten. They would be as well off as growing up in poverty under British policy.

I would never suggest such a thing. But come to think of it, this reckless "reform" is also cutting food stamps by about a fifth. Maybe Swift was just ahead of his time.

5 Cites specific examples to expose the absurdity of the situation

6 Uses exaggeration to reinforce point

7 This writer departs from satire by allowing her own voice to be heard.
Another Option:
· Stay in the satirical mode through the end of the piece.

1. Your Working Portfolio ▱
Build on one of the Writing Options you completed earlier in this unit:

- **Persuasive Letter,** p. 583
- **Another Proposal,** p. 622

2. Community Action
With a small group of classmates, make a list of problems in your school or community. Choose one problem as the subject of your satire.

3. Sound Bites
Many magazines and newspapers list "quotes of the week." These are oftentimes ironic or absurd. Choose one of these quotations as the basis for your satire.

Writing Your Satire

❶ Prewriting

What really bugs you? Make a list of everything from your personal pet peeves to global concerns. Include such things as rude drivers, ridiculous dress codes, gender stereotyping, air pollution, and ethnic wars. Scan newspapers and magazines to jog your memory about topics important to you. Then think carefully about each topic on your list. Which topics evoke strong feelings in you? See the **Idea Bank** for more suggestions. After you select your topic, follow the steps below.

Planning Your Satire

▶ **1. Dissect your victim.** Satire depends on a careful analysis and evaluation of the target subject. Pick apart those aspects of your subject that seem weak or absurd and plan to highlight these in your piece.

▶ **2. Choose a form.** Satire comes in all sizes, shapes, and forms. It can be a letter, a proposal, an advice column, a report, an essay, a speech, or a story. Select a form that you think fits your subject.

▶ **3. Match your tone with your goal.** Do you want to poke gentle fun or offer biting criticism? Your goal should determine your tone.

▶ **4. Flaunt your attitude.** Satire enables writers to go too far. You can make absurd and ridiculous suggestions. You can **exaggerate** the importance of trivial events or facts. You can **understate** critical truths. It's all part of your attitude, and with the right use of satirical techniques you can pull it off.

❷ Drafting

Freewriting can help you discover your satirical **voice.** Just start writing and don't worry about how it sounds yet. Keep going until you begin to develop a sense of who is talking and how your ideas are taking shape. You can go back later and revise your piece so the voice is consistent throughout.

Keep in mind that satire needs to hit the topic hard so your readers have no doubt about the issue you are addressing. You want, however, to be subtle and indirect about where you really stand on this issue. Let your readers mull over your ideas and figure out your true feelings.

Have a question?

See Satire in the Glossary of Literary Terms, p. 1348.

Ask Your Peer Reader

- What subject or issue is being addressed?
- How would you state my true feelings about it?
- Is it clear that the work is satiric? Why or why not?
- What parts work best? How would you improve the piece?

❸ Revising

TARGET SKILL ▶ **USING APPROPRIATE DICTION** Keep in mind that diction—the words you choose—helps set the tone for your satire. Diction can be formal or informal, technical or general, depending on the purpose. As you revise, choose words that best suit your tone and subject. In general, avoid wordiness, clichés, and jargon. In this model, the writer uses an informal tone.

Need revising help?

Review the **Rubric,** p. 639

Consider **peer reader** comments

Check **Revision Guidelines,** p. 1355.

> The federal government warns us that our national parks are being "loved to death." ~~Each and~~ every year, more ~~individuals~~ *people* visit the parks. ~~Accommodations and transportation facilities are utilized~~ *Campgrounds fill up. Traffic clogs the roads.* ~~beyond capacity. On the flip side,~~ *Yet* park fees do not bring in enough revenue to pay for park maintenance. ~~Someone has to pay the piper.~~ What to do? It's simple: ~~Give the reins~~ *Turn the parks over* to one of the giant entertainment companies and let it run them.

❹ Editing and Proofreading

TARGET SKILL ▶ **PRONOUN-ANTECEDENT AGREEMENT** Now check to see that all personal pronouns agree with their antecedents in number (singular or plural), gender (masculine, feminine, or neuter), and person (first, second, or third).

Stumped by pronoun-antecedent agreement?

See **Pronoun Agreement,** p. 1393

> Just think what a company that runs theme parks could do if ~~they~~ *it* ran the national parks. First, quadruple the entrance fees. Make *a* visitor*s* think twice before they come to a park. Of course, everyone *people* would expect more than scenery for your *their* money. An entertainment company could add your *its* usual mix of thrilling rides and activities. Imagine the sensation of being whisked down the Grand Canyon on a high-speed roller coaster. Park patrons might miss a bit of the scenery, but that's nothing compared to the thrill you'll *they'll* experience.

Publishing IDEAS

- Use your satire as a broadcast news commentary for a classroom radio or TV show.
- Adapt your satire as a comedy skit or make it part of a magazine featuring your class's satires.

❺ Reflecting

FOR YOUR WORKING PORTFOLIO How did others respond to your satire? Do you think your writing could help correct the situation you satirized? Why or why not? Attach your answer to your finished work. Save your satire in your **Working Portfolio.**

More Online: Publishing Options www.mcdougallittell.com

Read this paragraph from the first draft of a satire. The underlined sections include the following kinds of errors:

- **fragments**
- **double negatives**
- **lack of pronoun-antecedent agreement**
- **misplaced modifiers**

For each underlined phrase or sentence, choose the revision that most improves the writing.

> Computers are no longer just an option for students: <u>those</u> are an essential
> (1)
> tool. <u>Today no student can learn without these electronic brains.</u> When is the
> (2)
> right time for a first computer? Children should have mastered <u>computer</u>
> (3)
> <u>basics. By the time</u> they enter kindergarten. Education specialist Dr.
> Gwendolyn Flugelhorn <u>states that children should receive their first computers</u>
> (4)
> <u>as infants in her published paper.</u> These computers will be lifelong tutors. <u>They</u>
> (5)
> will help children think efficiently. Annoying distractions such as daydreams
> and idle thoughts will no longer be problems. <u>Children raised by this strategy</u>
> (6)
> <u>won't hardly even need to go to school.</u>

1. **A.** them
   B. they
   C. those
   D. Correct as is

2. **A.** No student today can fail to learn without these electronic brains.
   B. No student today can hardly learn without these electronic brains.
   C. No students today can learn without these electronic brains.
   D. Correct as is

3. **A.** computer basics by the time
   B. computer basics, by the time
   C. computer basics, basics, by the time
   D. Correct as is

4. **A.** states in her published paper that children should receive their first computers as infants.
   B. states that children in her published paper should receive their first computers as infants.
   C. states that children should receive their first computers in her published paper as infants.
   D. Correct as is

5. **A.** it
   B. them
   C. their
   D. Correct as is

6. **A.** Children raised by this strategy won't barely need to go to school.
   B. Children raised by this strategy will need to go to school.
   C. Children raised by this strategy won't never need to go to school.
   D. Children raised by this strategy will hardly even need to go to school.

Need extra help?

See the **Grammar Handbook**

Writing Complete Sentences, pp. 1408–1409

Pronouns, p. 1398

Misplaced modifiers, p. 1403

Selecting the Right Word

> The number of souls in this kingdom being usually reckoned one million and a half, of these I calculate there may be about two hundred thousand couple whose wives are breeders.
>
> —Jonathan Swift, "A Modest Proposal"

Words have the power to impress and influence people on several different levels. In addition to their precise meanings, called **denotations**, words have implied meanings and overtones, called **connotations**. Writers often choose words with particular connotations in order to elicit emotional responses from readers. For example, what was your reaction to the use of the word *breeders* in the sentence on the left from "A Modest Proposal"?

Although the word *breeder* has the denotation "one that produces offspring," the word's most common application is to livestock, a connotation that Swift exploits throughout his essay. Swift chose the word for its emotional impact, because his purpose in writing the satirical "A Modest Proposal" was to persuade his readers that the policies he was attacking were inhuman.

Strategies for Building Vocabulary

Because readers are influenced by words' connotations as well as their denotations, you need to be aware of the layers of meaning that are implied, but not directly stated, when you read and when you write.

❶ **Read Beyond the Literal Meaning** Connotations play an important role in revealing a writer's attitude toward his or her subject—that is, in establishing the tone of a work. They can also help in enlisting readers' sympathies. As you read a work, consider the writer's purpose and the audience for which the work was intended. How, for example, does this excerpt from *A Vindication of the Rights of Woman* reveal Mary Wollstonecraft's opinion of the treatment of women in her society?

> It is acknowledged that they [women] spend many of the first years of their lives in acquiring a smattering of accomplishments.

Here the word *smattering* was probably chosen for its negative connotations. Wollstonecraft might have used *set* or *collection,* but those words would not have conveyed such associations of triviality. The persuasive power of her sentence would therefore have been diminished.

❷ **Choose Words Carefully** Although synonyms have similar meanings, they may have very different connotations. When you write, always evaluate the connotations of the words you choose, especially when your purpose is to persuade. To see the full range of synonyms and antonyms of a word, consult a thesaurus. If you wanted, for example, to find a word similar in meaning to *strong* but with a particular connotation, you could choose from the words listed in this entry, adapted from *Roget's II: The New Thesaurus:*

strong *adjective*
Having great physical strength: *It takes two strong men to move a piano.*

Syns: brawny, lusty, mighty, potent, powerful, puissant.

If you are still unsure of the connotations of a word, look up the word in a dictionary.

EXERCISE Rewrite each sentence, substituting a synonym for the underlined word. Then, with a partner, decide how the connotations of the new word affect the meaning of the sentence.

1. Landowners <u>used</u> peasants to make their farms profitable.
2. In the 18th century, a woman was expected to <u>defer</u> to her husband in all matters.
3. Wollstonecraft <u>deplored</u> the way women were treated.
4. Swift's proposal is a <u>brilliant</u> example of satire.
5. Both Swift and Wollstonecraft used their writings to <u>encourage</u> social change.

Grammar from Literature

One way to include several pieces of information in a single sentence is to link elements—nouns, verbs, modifiers, phrases, or clauses—in a series. A series usually includes three elements, with the items separated by commas and, usually, at least one coordinating conjunction. Notice the examples below. The writers have improved precision and established relationships by listing items in series.

> series of nouns
> **There were shoulders, legs, and loins shaped like those of mutton.**
> —Jonathan Swift, *Gulliver's Travels*
>
> series of adjectives
> **Want of discretion . . . makes her conceited, fantastic, and ridiculous.**
> —Daniel Defoe, *An Academy for Women*
>
> series of prepositional phrases
> **I think it is agreed by all parties that this prodigious number of children in the arms, or on the backs, or at the heels of their mothers, and frequently of their fathers is . . . a very great additional grievance.**
> —Swift, "A Modest Proposal"

Using Series in Your Writing Listing items allows you to combine ideas. Look for places where listing will help you reduce repetition. Notice how creating a series eliminates wordiness in the following examples at the top of the next column.

> WORDY
> **Mary Wollstonecraft says that men apply the term *masculine* to women interested or skilled in hunting. This is also true of women good at shooting or gaming.**
>
> REVISED
> **Mary Wollstonecraft says that men apply the term *masculine* to women interested or skilled in hunting, shooting, or gaming.**

Usage Tip In a series, items that are parallel in meaning should be parallel in structure.

> INCORRECT
> adjective adjective
> **In Brobdingnag, Gulliver is talkative, cooperative,**
> independent clause
> **and he entertains the people.**

In the sentence above, the last item in the series is not grammatically parallel with the other two items.

> CORRECT
> adjective adjective
> **In Brobdingnag, Gulliver is talkative, cooperative,**
> adjective
> **and entertaining.**

Punctuation Tip When a series interrupts a sentence, you may use dashes to set it off.

> **Three activities—getting dressed, painting, and naming animals—dominate women's lives, writes Defoe.**

WRITING EXERCISE Combine each group of sentences below by creating a sentence containing a series.

1. The king of Brobdingnag is wise. He is curious. Also, he is gentle.
2. The Lilliputians tie Gulliver down. Then they shoot arrows at him, and they realize he is not dangerous.
3. In "A Modest Proposal" Swift wrote that poor Irish children could be seen in cabin doorways. They could also be seen on city streets and along country roads.
4. Daniel Defoe believed that a women's academy should teach music, dance, speech, history. He also thought that the students should learn foreign languages.
5. A lack of a good education caused problems for women, according to Mary Wollstonecraft. So did an emphasis on physical appearance. In addition suppression of emotion was problematic.

GRAMMAR EXERCISE Rewrite the sentences below, correcting any errors in parallelism. Insert dashes where needed.

1. Three important people in Lilliput the emperor, the empress, and the first minister observe the ceremony of the silken threads.
2. Giant Brobdingnagian flies buzz around Gulliver's ears, spoil his food, and they sting him on the nose.
3. Swift's purpose in writing his proposal was to draw attention to England's neglect, mistreatment, and its disapproval of the Irish people.
4. Defoe says that women are taught three things to stitch, sewing, and making baubles—during their youth.
5. Wollstonecraft says that men value women for being modest, their beauty, and acting affectionately.

PART 3 Revelations About Human Nature

In this part of Unit Three, the people of the 18th century come to life in biographical sketches, essays, letters, and poems that offer interesting perspectives on the human condition. The writers of the selections reveal their thoughts on everything from bad habits and other everyday concerns to such universal topics as war, aging, and death. Some even take a humorous look at themselves and the people around them. As you read these writings, you may find yourself confronted with aspects of your own nature.

PREPARING to *Read*

On Spring
from The Rambler

On Idleness
from The Idler

Essays *by* SAMUEL JOHNSON

> (**Connect to Your Life**)
>
> **Human Nature** "It's human nature" is an expression often used to justify the behavior of an individual or a group. Describe an experience that gave you valuable insights into human nature. What did the experience tell you about the way people sometimes think or act?

Build Background

The Age of Johnson Among students of English literature, the years 1750–1784 are often called the Age of Johnson—a tribute to the influence of Samuel Johnson, the literary leader of his day. Although known today chiefly for his *Dictionary of the English Language,* Johnson was also a talented poet, essayist, and critic. Perhaps even more famous than Johnson's literary achievements, however, was his witty conversation. He met regularly with a circle of friends, whom he often entertained with his profound wisdom and outrageous opinions. Much of Johnson's own writing was prompted by financial problems. Even while compiling his dictionary, he relied on journalistic writing to help pay his bills. Two of his journalistic **essays,** one from *The Rambler* and one from *The Idler,* appear on the following pages. Johnson launched *The Rambler,* a twice-weekly periodical, in 1750. Each issue consisted of a single essay, often laced with moral instruction. In 1758, he began writing *The Idler,* a weekly feature that appeared for two years in a London newspaper. His keen insights into human nature revealed a recognition of his own shortcomings as well. Many scholars consider the character Mr. Sober to be Johnson's caricature of himself.

WORDS TO KNOW	
Vocabulary Preview	
clemency	paradox
languish	procure
malevolence	propitious
obviate	solace
ostentation	suffer

Focus Your Reading

LITERARY ANALYSIS | **APHORISM** An **aphorism** is a brief statement that expresses a general observation about life in a clever or forceful way. The following statement from "On Spring" is an aphorism:

> *When a man cannot bear his own company there is something wrong.*

As you read these essays, be on the lookout for statements that might be regarded as aphorisms.

ACTIVE READING | **STRATEGIES FOR CLARIFYING MEANING** Many of the sentences in Johnson's essays are quite lengthy. His insights into human nature, though perceptive, are often embedded in a series of related thoughts. You might want to approach these selections by using the following strategies:

- Read each sentence slowly, looking for the main idea. **Paraphrase** the main idea in your own words.
- **Take notes** as you read to help unravel the meaning of complex passages.
- Use the **dictionary** to find the meaning of unfamiliar words.
- Read a difficult sentence or passage again, concentrating on phrases or clauses that add meaning to the main point.

READER'S NOTEBOOK Write down two lengthy sentences from each essay that you find challenging. Then use the strategies listed above to decipher the meaning.

ON Spring

TUESDAY, *April 3,* 1750

ET NUNC OMNIS AGER, NUNC OMNIS PARTURIT ARBOS,
NUNC FRONDENT SILVAE, NUNC FORMOSISSIMUS ANNUS.

VIRGIL, *Eclogues* [1] 3.56–57

Now ev'ry field, now ev'ry tree is green;
Now genial nature's fairest face is seen. [2]

Elphinston

Every man is sufficiently discontented with some circumstances of his present state, to suffer his imagination to range more or less in quest of future happiness, and to fix upon some point of time, in which, by the removal of the inconvenience which now perplexes him, or acquisition of the advantage which he at present wants, he shall find the condition of his life very much improved.

When this time, which is too often expected with great impatience, at last arrives, it generally comes without the blessing for which it was desired; but we solace ourselves with some new prospect, and press forward again with equal eagerness.

It is lucky for a man, in whom this temper prevails, when he turns his hopes upon things wholly out of his own power; since he forbears then to precipitate his affairs, [3] for the sake of the great event that is to complete his felicity, [4] and waits for the blissful hour, with less neglect of the measures necessary to be taken in the mean time.

I have long known a person of this temper, who indulged his dream of happiness with less hurt to himself than such chimerical [5] wishes commonly produce, and adjusted his scheme with such address, that his hopes were in full bloom three parts of the year, and in the other part never

1. *Eclogues* (ĕk′lôgz′): a book of pastoral poems by the Roman poet Virgil.
2. **Now ev'ry . . . is seen:** a free translation of Virgil's lines.
3. **forbears . . . affairs:** refrains from acting rashly or impetuously.
4. **felicity:** happiness.
5. **chimerical** (kī-mĕr′ĭ-kəl): unrealistic and fantastic; fanciful.

WORDS
TO
KNOW

suffer (sŭf′ər) *v.* to allow; permit
solace (sŏl′ĭs) *v.* to console; comfort

wholly blasted.[6] Many, perhaps, would be desirous of learning by what means he procured to himself such a cheap and lasting satisfaction. It was gained by a constant practice of referring the removal of all his uneasiness to the coming of the next spring; if his health was impaired, the spring would restore it; if what he wanted was at a high price, it would fall in value in the spring.

The spring, indeed, did often come without any of these effects, but he was always certain that the next would be more propitious; nor was ever convinced that the present spring would fail him before the middle of summer; for he always talked of the spring as coming till it was past, and when it was once past, everyone agreed with him that it was coming.

By long converse with this man, I am, perhaps, brought to feel immoderate pleasure in the contemplation of this delightful season; but I have the satisfaction of finding many, whom it can be no shame to resemble, infected with the same enthusiasm; for there is, I believe, scarce any poet of eminence, who has not left some testimony of his fondness for the flowers, the zephyrs,[7] and the warblers of the spring. Nor has the most luxuriant imagination been able to describe the serenity and happiness of the golden age, otherwise than by giving a perpetual spring, as the highest reward of uncorrupted innocence.

There is, indeed, something inexpressibly pleasing, in the annual renovation of the world, and the new display of the treasures of nature. The cold and darkness of winter, with the naked deformity of every object on which we turn our eyes, make us rejoice at the succeeding season, as well for what we have escaped, as for what we may enjoy; and every budding flower, which a warm situation brings early to our view, is considered by us as a messenger to notify the approach of more joyous days.

The spring affords to a mind, so free from the disturbance of cares or passions as to be vacant to calm amusements, almost every thing that our present state makes us capable of enjoying. The variegated verdure[8] of the fields and woods, the succession of grateful odors, the voice of pleasure pouring out its notes on every side, with the gladness apparently conceived by every animal, from the growth of his food, and the clemency of the weather, throw over the whole earth an air of gaiety, significantly expressed by the smile of nature.

Yet there are men to whom these scenes are able to give no delight, and who hurry away from all the varieties of rural beauty, to lose their hours, and divert their thoughts by cards, or assemblies, a tavern dinner, or the prattle of the day.

It may be laid down as a position which will seldom deceive, that when a man cannot bear his own company there is something wrong. He must fly from himself, either because he feels a

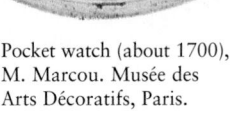

Pocket watch (about 1700), M. Marcou. Musée des Arts Décoratifs, Paris.

---

6. **blasted:** shriveled; withered.

7. **zephyrs** (zĕf'ərz): gentle breezes.

8. **variegated verdure** (vâr'ē-ĭ-gā'tĭd vûr'jər): greenery of many hues.

Sandleford Priory (1744), Edward Haytley. Oil on canvas, The Leger Galleries Ltd., London.

tediousness in life from the equipoise[9] of an empty mind, which, having no tendency to one motion more than another but as it is impelled by some external power, must always have recourse to foreign objects; or he must be afraid of the intrusion of some unpleasing ideas, and, perhaps, is struggling to escape from the remembrance of a loss, the fear of a calamity, or some other thought of greater horror.

Those whom sorrow incapacitates to enjoy the pleasures of contemplation, may properly apply to such diversions, provided they are innocent, as lay strong hold on the attention; and those, whom fear of any future affliction chains down to misery, must endeavor to <u>obviate</u> the danger.

My considerations shall, on this occasion, be turned on such as are burthensome[10] to themselves merely because they want subjects for reflection, and to whom the volume of nature is thrown open, without affording them pleasure or instruction, because they never learned to read the characters.

A French author has advanced this seeming <u>paradox</u>, that *very few men know how to take a walk;* and, indeed, it is true, that few know how to take a walk with a prospect of any other pleasure, than the same company would have afforded them at home.

There are animals that borrow their color from the neighboring body, and, consequently, vary their hue as they happen to change their place. In like manner it ought to be the endeavor of every man to derive his reflections from the objects about him; for it is to no purpose that he alters his position, if his attention continues fixed to the same point. The mind should be kept open to the access of every new idea, and so far disengaged from the predominance of particular thoughts, as easily to accommodate itself to occasional entertainment.

A man that has formed his habit of turning every new object to his entertainment, finds in the productions of nature an inexhaustible stock of materials upon which he can employ himself, without any temptations to envy or <u>malevolence</u>; faults, perhaps, seldom totally avoided by those, whose judgment is much exercised upon the works of art. He has always a certain prospect of discovering new reasons for adoring the sovereign

---

9. **equipoise:** state of balance; lack of direction.

10. **burthensome:** an obsolete spelling of *burdensome.*

WORDS TO KNOW	**obviate** (ŏb′vē-āt′) *v.* to prevent; avert **paradox** (păr′ə-dŏks′) *n.* a statement that appears to be self-contradictory or contrary to common sense but may nevertheless be true **malevolence** (mə-lĕv′ə-ləns) *n.* wickedness; ill will

author of the universe, and probable hopes of making some discovery of benefit to others, or of profit to himself. There is no doubt but many vegetables and animals have qualities that might be of great use, to the knowledge of which there is not required much force of penetration, or fatigue of study, but only frequent experiments, and close attention. What is said by the chemists of their darling mercury,[11] is, perhaps, true of everybody through the whole creation, that if a thousand lives should be spent upon it, all its properties would not be found out.

Mankind must necessarily be diversified by various tastes, since life affords and requires such multiplicity of employments, and a nation of naturalists is neither to be hoped, or desired; but it is surely not improper to point out a fresh amusement to those who <u>languish</u> in health, and repine[12] in plenty, for want of some source of diversion that may be less easily exhausted, and to inform the multitudes of both sexes, who are burthened with every new day, that there are many shows which they have not seen.

He that enlarges his curiosity after the works of nature, demonstrably multiplies the inlets to happiness; and, therefore, the younger part of my readers, to whom I dedicate this vernal[13] speculation, must excuse me for calling upon them, to make use at once of the spring of the year, and the spring of life; to acquire, while their minds may be yet impressed with new images, a love of innocent pleasures, and an ardor for useful knowledge; and to remember, that a blighted spring makes a barren year, and that the vernal flowers, however beautiful and gay, are only intended by nature as preparatives to autumnal fruits. ❖

---

11. **chemists . . . mercury:** The properties (characteristics) of mercury and its compounds made the silvery liquid metal fascinating to early chemists.

12. **repine:** feel dissatisfied; complain.

13. **vernal:** having to do with spring.

■ ■ ■

Thinking Through the Literature

1. **Comprehension Check** In Johnson's opinion, why is spring particularly pleasing?

2. What is your overall impression of this essay?

3. Why do you think Johnson, in the last paragraph, dedicates his essay to "the younger part of my readers"? Consider the evidence.

 THINK ABOUT
- his recommended approach to life
- the types of behavior he condemns
- the hope he expresses for those in "the spring of life"

WORDS TO KNOW   **languish** (lăng′gwĭsh) *v.* to be weak or depressed

Mr. and Mrs. Andrews (late 1700s), Thomas Gainsborough. National Gallery, London. Bridgeman/Art Resource.

On Idleness

SAMUEL JOHNSON

Saturday, November 18, 1758

Many moralists have remarked, that Pride has of all human vices the widest dominion, appears in the greatest multiplicity of forms, and lies hid under the greatest variety of disguises; of disguises, which, like the moon's veil of brightness, are both its luster and its shade, and betray it to others, though they hide it from ourselves.

It is not my intention to degrade Pride from this pre-eminence of mischief, yet I know not whether Idleness may not maintain a very doubtful and obstinate competition.

*T*here are some that profess Idleness in its full dignity, who call themselves the Idle, as Busiris in the play[1] "calls himself the Proud"; who boast that they do nothing, and thank their stars that they have nothing to do; who sleep every night till they can sleep no longer, and rise only that exercise may enable them to sleep again; who prolong the reign of darkness by double curtains, and never see the sun but to "tell him how they hate his beams"; whose whole labor is to vary the postures of indulgence, and whose day differs from their night but as a couch or chair differs from a bed.

These are the true and open votaries[2] of Idleness, for whom she weaves the garlands of poppies, and into whose cup she pours the waters of oblivion;[3] who exist in a state of unruffled stupidity, forgetting and forgotten; who have long ceased to live, and at whose death the survivors can only say, that they have ceased to breathe.

But Idleness predominates in many lives where it is not suspected; for being a vice which terminates in itself, it may be enjoyed without injury to others; and is therefore not watched like Fraud, which endangers property, or like Pride, which naturally seeks its gratifications in another's inferiority. Idleness is a silent and peaceful quality, that neither raises envy by <u>ostentation</u>, nor hatred by opposition; and therefore nobody is busy to censure or detect it.

As Pride sometimes is hid under humility, Idleness is often covered by turbulence and hurry. He that neglects his known duty and real employment, naturally endeavors to crowd his mind with something that may bar out the remembrance of his own folly, and does any thing but what he ought to do with eager diligence, that he may keep himself in his own favor.

Some are always in a state of preparation, occupied in previous measures, forming plans, accumulating materials, and providing for the

IDLENESS IS A SILENT AND PEACEFUL QUALITY, THAT NEITHER RAISES ENVY BY OSTENTATION, NOR HATRED BY OPPOSITION.

main affair. These are certainly under the secret power of Idleness. Nothing is to be expected from the workman whose tools are forever to be sought. I was once told by a great master, that no man ever excelled in painting, who was eminently curious about pencils and colors.

---

1. **Busiris** (byo͞o-sī'rĭs) **in the play:** a reference to the play *Busiris, King of Egypt* by the English poet Edward Young. A figure in Greek mythology, Busiris put to death all strangers who entered his kingdom and was himself killed by Hercules.

2. **votaries:** worshipers; devotees.

3. **waters of oblivion:** in Greek mythology, the waters of the river Lethe, which produce forgetfulness

WORDS TO KNOW

ostentation (ŏs'tĕn-tā'shən) *n.* a showy display, especially of wealth or knowledge; boastful showiness

There are others to whom Idleness dictates another expedient, by which life may be passed unprofitably away without the tediousness of many vacant hours. The art is, to fill the day with petty business, to have always something in hand which may raise curiosity, but not solicitude, and keep the mind in a state of action, but not of labor.

This art has for many years been practiced by my old friend Sober, with wonderful success. Sober is a man of strong desires and quick imagination, so exactly balanced by the love of ease, that they can seldom stimulate him to any difficult undertaking; they have, however, so much power, that they will not suffer him to lie quite at rest, and though they do not make him sufficiently useful to others, they make him at least weary of himself.

*M*r. Sober's chief pleasure is conversation; there is no end of his talk or his attention; to speak or to hear is equally pleasing; for he still fancies that he is teaching or learning something, and is free for the time from his own reproaches.

But there is one time at night when he must go home, that his friends may sleep; and another time in the morning, when all the world agrees to shut out interruption. These are the moments of which poor Sober trembles at the thought. But the misery of these tiresome intervals, he has many means of alleviating. He has persuaded himself that the manual arts are undeservedly overlooked; he has observed in many trades the effects of close thought, and just ratiocination.[4]

From speculation he proceeded to practice, and supplied himself with the tools of a carpenter, with which he mended his coalbox very successfully, and which he still continues to employ, as he finds occasion.

*H*e has attempted at other times the crafts of the shoemaker, tinman, plumber, and potter; in all these arts he has failed, and resolves to qualify himself for them by better information. But his daily amusement is chemistry. He has a small furnace, which he employs in distillation,[5] and which has long been the solace of his life. He draws oils and waters, and essences and spirits, which he knows to be of no use; sits and counts the drops as they come from his retort,[6] and forgets that, whilst a drop is falling, a moment flies away.

Poor Sober! I have often teased him with reproof, and he has often promised reformation; for no man is so much open to conviction as the Idler, but there is none on whom it operates so little. What will be the effect of this paper I know not; perhaps he will read it and laugh, and light the fire in his furnace; but my hope is that he will quit his trifles, and betake himself to rational and useful diligence. ❖

---

4. **ratiocination** (răsh′ē-ŏs′ə-nā′shən): systematic and logical thought.

5. **distillation:** the separation of parts of a liquid mixture by condensing and collecting the vapors produced when it is heated.

6. **retort:** a vessel used for distilling liquids.

Connect to the Literature

1. What Do You Think?
What were your reactions to Johnson's essay "On Idleness"? Discuss with a classmate.

> **Comprehension Check**
> • What is Johnson's definition of an idler?
> • What quality does Mr. Sober represent?

Think Critically

2. Do you think Johnson views idleness as a serious character flaw?

THINK ABOUT
{
• the **tone** of the essay
• his examples of idleness
• his expectations regarding Sober's reformation
}

3. What insights about himself do you think Johnson reveals through the character of Mr. Sober?

4. According to Johnson, idleness is "a vice which terminates in itself" and therefore can be indulged in "without injury to others." Do you agree? Explain your opinion.

5. Would you say that Johnson's **tone** is the same in "On Spring" and "On Idleness"? Support your answer.

6. **ACTIVE READING** | **STRATEGIES FOR CLARIFYING MEANING**
Look again at your ▯ **READER'S NOTEBOOK.** What sentence in each essay seemed most difficult to understand and what strategies did you use to unravel the meaning? How does Johnson's complex sentence structure reinforce his ideas?

Extend Interpretations

7. Comparing Texts Compare these **essays** of Johnson's with the excerpts from Joseph Addison's *Spectator* essays (page 548). Which of Johnson's essays is more similar in tone to Addison's writing? Support your answer with details from the essays.

8. Different Perspectives How do you think Mr. Sober might defend idleness? Be specific in your answer.

9. Connect to Life What do you think would be good examples of idleness that are common in the world today? Explain.

Literary Analysis

APHORISM Unlike proverbs, which stem from oral folk tradition, **aphorisms** are created by individual authors. Because they are generalizations, aphorisms are meaningful even when taken out of their original contexts. "A blighted spring makes a barren year," in the last sentence of "On Spring," is an example of a statement that is an aphorism. What other aphorisms can you find in these essays?

Cooperative Learning Activity With three or four classmates, try to come up with aphorisms of your own creation. Choose topics that interest the group and then write a couple of aphorisms for each topic. Present your aphorisms to the rest of the class.

REVIEW | **INFORMAL ESSAY** An **informal essay** presents an opinion on a subject, but not in a completely serious or formal tone. Informal essays include a personal approach and a somewhat loose style. They also are often humorous, and they frequently address an unconventional topic. With a partner, look for characteristics of an informal essay in "On Spring" and in "On Idleness." List examples of the characteristics you find, and discuss how effectively you think Johnson uses the informal essay to express his ideas.

Writing Options

Friendly Anecdote Write an anecdote about someone you know who exhibits one or more of the traits Johnson describes in these essays.

Activities & Explorations

Personality Caricature Draw a caricature portraying one of the personality types described by Johnson in these essays. ~ **ART**

Vocabulary in Action

EXERCISE A: ANTONYMS For each Word to Know in the first column, write the letter of the best antonym in the second column.

1. **procure**   a. thrive
2. **languish**   b. forbid
3. **obviate**   c. lose
4. **malevolence**   d. permit
5. **suffer**   e. kindness

EXERCISE B: CONTEXT CLUES Write the Word to Know described by each sentence below.

1. "It was the best of times, it was the worst of times" is an example of this.
2. "Red sky at night, sailor's delight" means that a red sunset is a sign of this kind of weather on the next day.
3. "Peacock, look at your legs!" is a reminder that this can be foolish.
4. "When in disgrace with Fortune and men's eyes / I all alone beweep my outcast state" shows that the speaker of the sonnet needs someone to do this to him.
5. "Power can do by gentleness what violence fails to accomplish" indicates that this can be an effective quality.

WORDS TO KNOW	clemency ostentation	paradox propitious	solace

Building Vocabulary

For an in-depth lesson on how to use a thesaurus to find a word's synonyms and antonyms, see page 574.

Samuel Johnson
1709–1784

Other Works
Lives of the Poets
"Preface" in *A Dictionary of the English Language*

Youth and Education Born in Lichfield, England, Samuel Johnson was the son of a prominent but impoverished bookseller. During infancy, he contracted scrofula, a tubercular infection that left him with a disfigured face and impaired vision and hearing. He attended public schools until he was 17 and read widely in his father's shop, but Johnson's family could not afford to give him the higher education he craved. Although a small inheritance of his mother's allowed him to enroll in Oxford University in 1728, he was forced to leave after only 13 months when the money ran out.

Teacher, Translator, Writer For many years, Johnson earned a meager income by teaching and by translating books. Then, at the age of 27, determined to make a name for himself, he walked to London to seek a career in writing. Within a year he had published his first significant poem and had begun to gain recognition as a literary talent.

Literary Achievements Johnson's literary achievements during the next 30 years—particularly his dictionary, an edition of Shakespeare's works, and a series of critical biographies of English poets in which he proves himself a forerunner of modern literary critics—earned him fame, as well as honorary doctorates from Oxford University and Trinity College in Dublin. Nevertheless, he was still on the brink of poverty in 1756, when he was briefly imprisoned for his many debts. In 1762, Johnson's financial woes finally ended when the king awarded him an annual pension.

from A DICTIONARY OF THE ENGLISH LANGUAGE

Samuel Johnson

ADU′LT. A person above the age of infancy, or grown to some degree of strength; sometimes full grown: a word used chiefly by medicinal writers.

❶ TO A′MBLE. To move easily, without hard shocks, or shaking.

APE. A kind of monkey remarkable for imitating what he sees.

CORN. The seeds which grow in ears, not in pods; such as are made into bread.

DULL. Not exhilarating; not delightful; as, *to make dictionaries is dull work.*

FISH. An animal that inhabits the water.

TO HISS. To utter a noise like that of a serpent and some other animals. It is remarkable, that this word cannot be pronounced without making the noise which it signifies.

LOUSE. A small animal, of which different species live on the bodies of men, beasts, and perhaps of all living creatures.

MI′SER. A wretched person; one overwhelmed with calamity.

MOULD. A kind of concretion on the top or outside of things kept, motionless and damp; now discovered by microscopes to be perfect plants.

MOUSE. The smallest of all beasts; a little animal haunting houses and corn fields, destroyed by cats.

NO′VEL. A small tale, generally of love.

POP. A small smart quick sound. It is formed from the sound.

RE′CIPE. A medical prescription.

RI′VER. A land current of water bigger than a brook.

❷ TO SLU′BBER. To do any thing lazily, imperfectly, or with idle hurry.

SUN. The luminary that makes the day.

❸ TE′MPEST. The utmost violence of the wind; the names by which the wind is called according to the gradual increase of its force seems to be, a breeze; a gale; a gust; a storm; a tempest.

WA′RREN. A kind of park for rabbits.

Reading for Information

In creating the first comprehensive dictionary in the English language, Johnson compiled 40,000 entries from the most reputable sources of his time. Like every other dictionary, Johnson's dictionary reflects the meaning and usage of words at the time it was written.

DENOTATION AND CONNOTATION

Remember that a word's **denotation** is its literal meaning, whereas its **connotations** are the feelings associated with it. To explore this excerpt from Johnson's dictionary, complete the activities below.

❶ Determining Denotations Look up the word *amble.* How is its definition similar to and different from Johnson's?

❷ Archaic Language Over time, some words may cease to be used at all. Such words are classified as **archaic language**—that is, words that are no longer current. Johnson's word *slubber,* for example, is not included in most modern dictionaries.

❸ Clarifying Connotation The words *tempest* and *storm* have similar denotations but may have different connotations. How would you compare tempestuous weather and stormy weather?

from The Life of Samuel Johnson

Biography by JAMES BOSWELL

Connect to Your Life

Lives of the Rich and Famous People have always been curious about the lives of famous people. Think of a current celebrity who interests you. What kinds of things would you like to know about this person? Where would you go to find such information? Discuss your ideas with a partner.

Build Background

When Boswell Met Johnson Samuel Johnson was one of the most extraordinary scholars and personalities of his time. Despite years of struggle and hardship, he pursued his literary and intellectual interests and eventually became respected as a poet, essayist, journalist, and critic. He also devoted ten years of his life to compiling a massive dictionary. Though Johnson was a leading figure of his day, his opinions were controversial and often inspired heated reactions.

James Boswell, 31 years younger than Johnson, was a university-trained lawyer from a wealthy Scottish family. He had a lifelong fascination with London and the variety of experiences to be found there. He also had a great desire to meet the famous Samuel Johnson. In 1763, when Boswell was only 22, he was unexpectedly introduced to Johnson in the back room of a bookseller's shop in London. Although Johnson was at first annoyed by Boswell's questions and impertinences, he quickly warmed to the young man.

During the next 21 years, Boswell chronicled in great detail his conversations, experiences, and travels with Johnson. After Johnson's death in 1784, Boswell spent 7 years writing the great man's biography. Unlike earlier biographies, which emphasized the positive aspects of their subjects' lives and were often excessively flattering, Boswell's presents a full and accurate portrait that includes both the good and the bad, giving the reader a vivid sense of Johnson as a real person.

WORDS TO KNOW
Vocabulary Preview

corporal	temperate
discernment	vehement
impunity	

Focus Your Reading

LITERARY ANALYSIS **BIOGRAPHY** A **biography** is an account of a person's life written by another person. In a good biography, the presentation of the subject's life is comprehensive, clear, unified, and accurate. As you read these excerpts from Boswell's biography, decide whether each passage creates a clear impression of Johnson.

ACTIVE READING **ANALYZING THE BIOGRAPHER'S PERSPECTIVE**

A biographer's **perspective** may be influenced by his or her own views, prejudices, or relationship to the subject. Boswell's friendship with Johnson helped him gain intimate knowledge of his subject, but it also affected his perception of the man. Evidence of Boswell's perspective is signaled by the following:

- the use of the pronoun *I*
- anecdotes and dialogue that involve the biographer
- the writer's tone

READER'S NOTEBOOK As you read each excerpt, look for evidence of Boswell's perspective. List examples in which Boswell's relationship to Johnson influences the writing.

Examples
"Yet I have heard him. . . ."

On Eating (1763)

At supper this night he talked of good eating with uncommon satisfaction. "Some people (said he,) have a foolish way of not minding, or pretending not to mind, what they eat. For my part, I mind my belly very studiously, and very carefully; for I look upon it, that he who does not mind his belly will hardly mind anything else."

He now appeared to me *Jean Bull philosophe,*[1] and he was, for the moment, not only serious but <u>vehement</u>. Yet I have heard him, upon other occasions, talk with great contempt of people who were anxious to gratify their palates; and the 206th number of his *Rambler* is a masterly essay against gulosity.[2] His practice, indeed, I must acknowledge, may be considered as casting the balance of his different opinions upon this subject; for I never knew any man who relished good eating more than he did. When at table, he was totally absorbed in the business of the moment; his looks seemed riveted to his plate; nor would he, unless when in very high company, say one word, or even pay the least attention to what was said by others, till he had satisfied his appetite, which was so fierce, and indulged with such intenseness, that while in the act of eating, the veins of his forehead swelled, and generally a strong perspiration was visible. To those whose sensations were delicate, this could not but be disgusting; and it was doubtless not very suitable to the character of a philosopher, who should be distinguished by self-command. But it must be owned, that Johnson,

though he could be rigidly *abstemious,*[3] was not a *temperate* man either in eating or drinking. He could refrain, but he could not use moderately. He told me, that he had fasted two days without inconvenience, and that he had never been hungry but once. They who beheld with wonder how much he ate upon all occasions when his dinner was to his taste, could not easily conceive what he must have meant by hunger; and not only was he remarkable for the extraordinary quantity which he ate, but he was, or affected to be, a man of very nice <u>discernment</u> in the science of cookery. He used to descant[4] critically on the dishes which had been at table where he had dined or supped, and to recollect very minutely what he had liked. . . .

When invited to dine, even with an intimate friend, he was not pleased if something better than a plain dinner was not prepared for him. I have heard him say on such an occasion, "This was a good dinner enough, to be sure; but it was not a dinner to *ask* a man to." On the other hand, he was wont to express, with great glee, his satisfaction when he had been entertained quite to his mind.

---

1. *Jean Bull philosophe* (zhäɴ′ bool′ fē-lô-zôf′) *French:* John Bull philosopher. (John Bull is a figure representing the typical Englishman—honest, hearty, and gruff.)
2. **gulosity** (gyoo-lŏs′ĭ-tē): excessive appetite; gluttony.
3. **abstemious** (ăb-stē′mē-əs): self-denying; abstinent.
4. **descant** (dĕs′kănt′): speak at length.

WORDS TO KNOW

vehement (vē′ə-mənt) *adj.* forceful in expression or feeling; intense
temperate (tĕm′pər-ĭt) *adj.* moderate; restrained
discernment (dĭ-sûrn′mənt) *n.* good judgment

SAMUEL JOHNSON

JAMES BOSWELL

Oliver Goldsmith, James Boswell, and Dr. Samuel Johnson at the Mitre Tavern, London (19th century), unknown artist. Colored engraving, The Granger Collection, New York.

On Equality of the Sexes (1778)

Mrs. Knowles affected to complain that men had much more liberty allowed them than women.

JOHNSON. "Why, Madam, women have all the liberty they should wish to have. We have all the labor and the danger, and the women all the advantage. We go to sea, we build houses, we do everything, in short, to pay our court to the women."

MRS. KNOWLES. "The Doctor reasons very wittily, but not convincingly. Now, take the instance of building; the mason's wife, if she is ever seen in liquor, is ruined; the mason may get himself drunk as often as he pleases, with little loss of character; nay, may let his wife and children starve."

JOHNSON. "Madam, you must consider, if the mason does get himself drunk, and let his wife and children starve, the parish will oblige him to find security for their maintenance. We have different modes of restraining evil. Stocks for the men, a ducking-stool for women, and a pound for beasts. If we require more perfection from women than from ourselves, it is doing them honor. And women have not the same temptations that we have: they may always live in virtuous company;

Johnson and Boswell (late 1700s), engraving by unknown artist. Copyright © British Museum.

men must mix in the world indiscriminately. If a woman has no inclination to do what is wrong being secured from it is no restraint to her. I am at liberty to walk into the Thames; but if I were to try it, my friends would restrain me in Bedlam,[5] and I should be obliged to them."

MRS. KNOWLES. "Still, Doctor, I cannot help thinking it a hardship that more indulgence is allowed to men than to women. It gives a superiority to men, to which I do not see how they are entitled."

JOHNSON. "It is plain, Madam, one or other must have the superiority. As Shakespeare says, 'If two men ride on a horse, one must ride behind.'"

DILLY. "I suppose, Sir, Mrs. Knowles would have them to ride in panniers,[6] one on each side."

JOHNSON. "Then, Sir, the horse would throw them both."

MRS. KNOWLES. "Well, I hope that in another world the sexes will be equal."

BOSWELL. "That is being too ambitious, Madam. *We* might as well desire to be equal with the angels. *We* shall all, I hope, be happy in a future state, but we must not expect to be all happy in the same degree. It is enough if we be happy according to our several capacities. A worthy carman[7] will get to heaven as well as Sir Isaac Newton.[8] Yet, though equally good, they will not have the same degrees of happiness."

JOHNSON. "Probably not."

On the Fear of Death (1769)

I mentioned to him that I had seen the execution of several convicts at Tyburn,[9] two days before, and that none of them seemed to be under any concern.

JOHNSON. "Most of them, Sir, have never thought at all."

BOSWELL. "But is not the fear of death natural to man?"

JOHNSON. "So much so, Sir, that the whole of life is but keeping away the thoughts of it."

He then, in a low and earnest tone, talked of his meditating upon the awful hour of his own dissolution,[10] and in what manner he should conduct himself upon that occasion: "I know not (said he,) whether I should wish to have a friend by me, or have it all between God and myself." . . .

When we were alone, I introduced the subject of death, and endeavored to maintain that the fear of it might be got over. I told him that David Hume[11] said to me, he was no more uneasy to think he should *not be* after this life, than that he *had not been* before he began to exist.

JOHNSON. "Sir, if he really thinks so, his perceptions are disturbed; he is mad: if he does not think so, he lies. He may tell you, he holds his finger in the flame of a candle, without feeling pain; would you believe him? When he dies, he at least gives up all he has."

BOSWELL. "Foote,[12] Sir, told me, that when he was very ill he was not afraid to die."

JOHNSON. "It is not true, Sir. Hold a pistol to Foote's breast, or to Hume's breast, and threaten to kill them, and you'll see how they behave."

BOSWELL. "But may we not fortify our minds for the approach of death?"

Here I am sensible[13] I was in the wrong, to bring before his view what he ever looked upon with horror; for although when in a celestial frame, in his "Vanity of Human Wishes," he has supposed death to be "kind Nature's signal for retreat," from this state of being to "a happier seat," his thoughts upon this awful change were in general full of dismal apprehensions. His mind

---

5. **Bedlam:** a London institution for the mentally ill.
6. **panniers** (păn′yərz): a pair of baskets hung across the back of a pack animal.
7. **carman:** carriage driver.
8. **Sir Isaac Newton:** a famous English mathematician.
9. **Tyburn:** the former site of public hangings in London.
10. **awful . . . dissolution:** awe-inspiring hour of his own death.
11. **David Hume:** a Scottish philosopher and historian.
12. **Foote:** Samuel Foote, an actor and dramatist.
13. **sensible:** aware.

resembled the vast amphitheater, the Colosseum at Rome. In the center stood his judgment, which, like a mighty gladiator, combated those apprehensions that, like the wild beasts of the *Arena,* were all around in cells, ready to be let out upon him. After a conflict, he drove them back into their dens; but not killing them, they were still assailing him. To my question, whether we might not fortify our minds for the approach of death, he answered, in a passion, "No, Sir, let it alone. It matters not how a man dies, but how he lives. The act of dying is not of importance, it lasts so short a time." He added, (with an earnest look,) "A man knows it must be so, and submits. It will do him no good to whine."

I attempted to continue the conversation. He was so provoked, that he said, "Give us no more of this"; and was thrown into such a state of agitation, that he expressed himself in a way that alarmed and distressed me; showed an impatience that I should leave him, and when I was going away, called to me sternly, "Don't let us meet to-morrow."

On Johnson's Physical Courage (1775)

♦ ♦ ♦ No man was ever more remarkable for personal courage. He had, indeed, an awful dread of death, or rather, "of something after death"; and what rational man, who seriously thinks of quitting all that he has ever known, and going into a new and unknown state of being, can be without that dread? But his fear was from reflection; his courage natural. His fear, in that one instance, was the result of philosophical and religious consideration. He feared death, but he feared nothing else, not even what might occasion death. Many instances of his resolution may be mentioned. One day, at Mr. Beauclerk's house in the country, when two large dogs were fighting, he went up to them, and beat them till they separated; and at another time, when told of the danger there was that a gun might burst if charged with many balls, he put in six or seven, and fired it off against a wall. Mr. Langton told

me, that when they were swimming together near Oxford, he cautioned Dr. Johnson against a pool, which was reckoned particularly dangerous; upon which Johnson directly swam into it. He told me himself that one night he was attacked in the street by four men, to whom he would not yield, but kept them all at bay, till the watch came up, and carried both him and them to the roundhouse.[14] In the playhouse at Lichfield, as Mr. Garrick informed me, Johnson having for a moment quitted a chair which was placed for him between the side-scenes, a gentleman took possession of it, and when Johnson on his return civilly demanded his seat, rudely refused to give it up; upon which Johnson laid hold of it, and tossed him and the chair into the pit. Foote, who so successfully revived the old comedy, by exhibiting living characters, had resolved to imitate Johnson on the stage, expecting great profits from his ridicule of so celebrated a man. Johnson being informed of his intention, and being at dinner at Mr. Thomas Davies's the bookseller, from whom I had the story, he asked Mr. Davies "what was the common price of an oak stick"; and being answered sixpence, "Why then, Sir, (said he,) give me leave to send your servant to purchase me a shilling one. I'll have a double quantity; for I am told Foote means to *take me off,* as he calls it, and I am determined the fellow shall not do it with impunity." Davies took care to acquaint Foote of this, which effectually checked the wantonness of the mimic. Mr. Macpherson's menaces[15] made Johnson provide himself with the same implement of defense; and had he been attacked, I have no doubt that, old as he was, he would have made his corporal prowess be felt as much as his intellectual. ❖

---

14. **roundhouse:** jail.

15. **Mr. Macpherson's menaces:** the threats of James Macpherson, a Scottish poet whose "translations" of alleged third-century poems had been exposed as frauds by Johnson.

impunity (ĭm-pyōō′nĭ-tē) *n.* freedom from punishment or penalty
corporal (kôr′pər-əl) *adj.* bodily; physical

Thinking through the LITERATURE

Connect to the Literature

1. What Do You Think? Which of these excerpts did you find most interesting?

> **Comprehension Check**
> - What was Johnson's attitude toward food and drink?
> - Why did Johnson become angry with Boswell?

Think Critically

2. Do you think that Johnson's opinions are fair and based on adequate evidence? Support your conclusion with details from the selection.

3. How do you account for Johnson's willingness to risk his life despite his great fear of death?

THINK ABOUT
- Johnson's response to a challenge
- his forcefulness in expressing himself
- Boswell's statement that Johnson's "fear was from reflection; his courage natural"

4. What do you think might account for Johnson's becoming such a well-known figure in his time?

5. **ACTIVE READING   ANALYZING THE BIOGRAPHER'S PERSPECTIVE** Review the examples you listed in your ▮▮**READER'S NOTEBOOK** that reveal Boswell's perspective. Do you think Boswell was a credible chronicler of Johnson's life? Why or why not?

Extend Interpretations

6. Comparing Texts Compare Johnson's **description** of Mr. Sober in "On Idleness" (page 655) with Boswell's depiction of Johnson. Which characteristics of Mr. Sober do you think could be used to describe Johnson?

7. Writer's Style In his **biography** of Samuel Johnson, Boswell recounts many humorous moments and conversations. Look for two or three examples of **humor** in the excerpts you have read. What part does humor seem to play in Boswell's portrayal of Johnson's personality?

8. Connect to Life The four subjects treated in these excerpts—eating, the equality of men and women, death, and courage—are still important issues. Choose one of the four subjects and compare the aspects of it that concerned Johnson with the aspects that are most commonly discussed today.

Literary Analysis

BIOGRAPHY In a good **biography,** the reader is provided with a full picture of the subject's personality. The skilled biographer synthesizes information from many sources and strives for a balanced portrayal through detailed anecdotes, reconstructed dialogue, description, quotations, and interpretive passages. Notice how Boswell uses description and interpretation to convey Johnson's attitude toward eating.

- *When at table, he was totally absorbed in the business of the moment; his looks seemed riveted to his plate. . . .*

- *He could refrain, but he could not use moderately.*

Cooperative Learning Activity In a small group, discuss some of the details, conversations, and incidents Boswell includes in these excerpts. What can you infer about Johnson's character from these accounts?

ACTIVE READING   EVALUATING SOURCES For a piece of writing to be a valid source of information, it must be both **credible** and **appropriate.** A work may contain reliable facts about its subject, but the type of information or the way it is presented may not be appropriate for particular research tasks and objectives. Think about the content and how it is presented in Boswell's biography of Johnson. In what situations would the biography be an appropriate source of information? When inappropriate?

Choices & CHALLENGES

Writing Options

Biography Outline Think about the famous person you identified for the Connect to Your Life on page 659. Write a brief proposal outlining your ideas for a biography of the person.

Activities & Explorations

Scene in Pantomime Work with classmates to present in pantomime one of the scenes from these excerpts. Use gestures and facial expressions to convey the characters' personalities. ~ VIEWING AND REPRESENTING

Building Vocabulary
For in-depth study of context clues, see page 938.

Vocabulary in Action

EXERCISE: CONTEXT CLUES Write the word that best completes each sentence.

1. When Johnson was attacked physically or verbally, he was likely to respond in a _____ manner.
2. Surely Johnson's threatening to take a stick to an actor who made fun of him was not the reaction of a _____ man.
3. Johnson frequently used biting sarcasm to attack people who offended him, but at times his attack would be more _____.
4. People quickly found that they could not be rude to Johnson with _____.
5. Clearly, a person with a reasonable amount of _____ would have hesitated to insult or offend Johnson unnecessarily.

WORDS TO KNOW			
	corporal	impunity	vehement
	discernment	temperate	

James Boswell
1740–1795

Other Works
The Journal of a Tour to the Hebrides, with Samuel Johnson, LL.D.
Boswell's London Journal: 1762–1763

A Reluctant Lawyer Born in Edinburgh, Scotland, James Boswell was the oldest son of Lord Auchinleck, a wealthy landowner and prominent judge. Under his father's prodding, young Boswell reluctantly took up the study of law, and he did eventually practice law, marry, raise a family, and manage the Auchinleck estate; but his real passion was London—its zest, elegance, and wit. Because he was charming and had a gift for friendship, he became well-known and widely liked in the city.

The Odd Couple His most famous friendship, of course, was with Samuel Johnson, though the two men could not have been more different. Whereas Johnson was learned, deeply religious, and revered for the logic, seriousness, and elegance of his writings, Boswell was gregarious, insatiably curious, and frivolous. Beneath Boswell's apparent superficiality, however, lay a great ability to listen to other people and to record their words and behavior in astonishing detail.

Biographer and Diarist Extraordinaire Boswell began keeping a diary at about the age of 16. It was thought for many years that his personal papers had been destroyed, but during the 1920s and 1930s, in a series of events that read like a detective story, 8,000 pages of Boswell's journal came to light. The diary reveals the extent of Boswell's genius. With a prodigious memory for detail, he described events, recorded impressions, and reconstructed entire conversations with unparalleled immediacy and vividness. Ironically, Boswell died thinking himself a failure, never to know that he would be acclaimed as both the world's greatest biographer and a brilliant diarist.

Author Activity

The Life of James Boswell Locate a copy of Boswell's *Journal* and read some of the entries. What impression do the entries convey of Boswell? How does this impression compare with the image you formed of him after reading the excerpts from *The Life of Samuel Johnson?*

Elegy Written in a Country Churchyard

Poetry by THOMAS GRAY

Connect to Your Life

Thoughts of Final Things Think about times when you have traveled past or visited a cemetery. What thoughts and feelings did you have? Did you feel sad? Did you wonder about the lives of the people buried there? With a group of classmates, explore your reactions by completing a cluster diagram similar to the one shown.

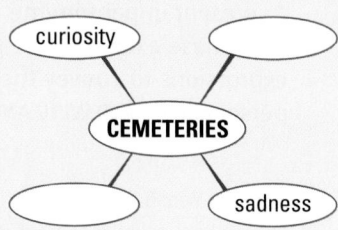

curiosity

CEMETERIES

sadness

Build Background

A Preromantic Poet Thomas Gray is one of the transitional poets sometimes called preromantic. These poets typically employed the elaborate, stately diction of the neoclassicists but used it to treat different subjects and explore new outlooks. Whereas many neoclassical writers often focused on city life, for example, Gray usually found his subject matter in the country and in nature. Neoclassicists emphasized simplicity and emotional restraint, but Gray dared to describe intense personal feelings.

Gray began "Elegy Written in a Country Churchyard" after his close friend Richard West died at the age of 26. The melancholy and depression Gray suffered as a result of this loss inspired some portions of the elegy, which he spent eight years writing and revising. Although the sense of loss it expresses may be personal, the poem nevertheless clearly has relevance to the lives of all people. This universal appeal has made it one of the most-quoted poems in English literature.

Focus Your Reading

LITERARY ANALYSIS   PERSONIFICATION   Personification is a type of figurative language in which human qualities are attributed to an object, animal, or idea. Notice how Gray personifies the ideas of honor, flattery, and death in the following lines:

> *Can Honor's voice provoke the silent dust,*
> *Or Flattery soothe the dull cold ear of Death?*

As you read this poem, look for other examples of personification used by the poet.

ACTIVE READING   MAKING INFERENCES FROM DETAILS You can **make inferences** about the people Gray writes about by paying attention to the **descriptive details** he provides. As you read, notice details related to the following categories:

- the villagers' values—what they believe
- the conditions of their lives
- their dreams and ambitions

READER'S NOTEBOOK Create a list of details about the villagers. Next to each detail, cite the line or lines of the poem that convey the information.

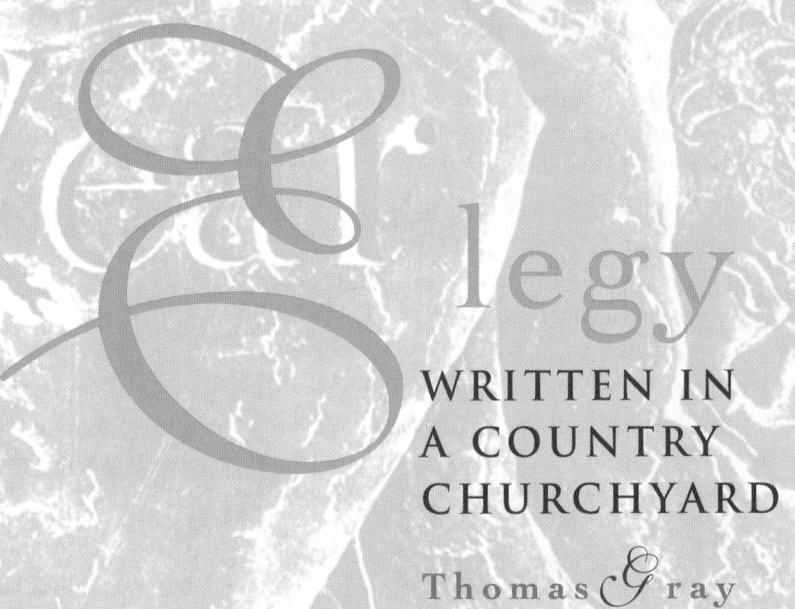

Elegy
WRITTEN IN A COUNTRY CHURCHYARD

Thomas Gray

The curfew tolls the knell of parting day,
   The lowing herd wind slowly o'er the lea,
The plowman homeward plods his weary way,
   And leaves the world to darkness and to me.

5 Now fades the glimmering landscape on the sight,
   And all the air a solemn stillness holds,
Save where the beetle wheels his droning flight,
   And drowsy tinklings lull the distant folds;

Save that from yonder ivy-mantled tower
10   The moping owl does to the moon complain
Of such, as wandering near her secret bower,
   Molest her ancient solitary reign.

GUIDE FOR READING

2 lea (lē): meadow.

Beneath those rugged elms, that yew tree's shade,
　　Where heaves the turf in many a moldering heap,
15　Each in his narrow cell forever laid,
　　The rude forefathers of the hamlet sleep.

The breezy call of incense-breathing Morn,
　　The swallow twittering from the straw-built shed,
The cock's shrill clarion, or the echoing horn,
20　　No more shall rouse them from their lowly bed.

For them no more the blazing hearth shall burn,
　　Or busy housewife ply her evening care;
No children run to lisp their sire's return,
　　Or climb his knees the envied kiss to share.

25　Oft did the harvest to their sickle yield,
　　Their furrow oft the stubborn glebe has broke;
How jocund did they drive their team afield!
　　How bowed the woods beneath their sturdy stroke!

Let not Ambition mock their useful toil,
30　　Their homely joys, and destiny obscure;
Nor Grandeur hear with a disdainful smile
　　The short and simple annals of the poor.

The boast of heraldry, the pomp of power,
　　And all that beauty, all that wealth e'er gave,
35　Awaits alike the inevitable hour.
　　The paths of glory lead but to the grave.

Nor you, ye proud, impute to these the fault,
　　If Memory o'er their tomb no trophies raise,
Where through the long-drawn aisle and fretted vault
40　　The pealing anthem swells the note of praise.

Can storied urn or animated bust
　　Back to its mansion call the fleeting breath?
Can Honor's voice provoke the silent dust,
　　Or Flattery soothe the dull cold ear of Death?

16 rude: unsophisticated; rustic. Where is the speaker?

26 glebe: soil; earth.
27 jocund (jŏk'ənd): merry.

32 annals: descriptive records; history. What is the speaker's attitude toward the dead?

33 heraldry: noble birth.

35 What is meant by "the inevitable hour"?

37 impute . . . fault: assign the blame to them.

38 trophies: sculptures depicting the achievements of the deceased.

39 fretted vault: space enclosed under a decorated arched ceiling.

41 storied . . . bust: an urn for the ashes of the deceased, decorated with scenes from the person's life, or a lifelike portrait sculpture.

43 provoke: call forth.

45 Perhaps in this neglected spot is laid
      Some heart once pregnant with celestial fire;
Hands that the rod of empire might have swayed,
      Or waked to ecstasy the living lyre.

But Knowledge to their eyes her ample page
50   Rich with the spoils of time did ne'er unroll;
Chill Penury repressed their noble rage,
      And froze the genial current of the soul.

Full many a gem of purest ray serene,
      The dark unfathomed caves of ocean bear:
55 Full many a flower is born to blush unseen,
      And waste its sweetness on the desert air.

Some village Hampden, that with dauntless breast
      The little tyrant of his fields withstood;
Some mute inglorious Milton here may rest,
60   Some Cromwell guiltless of his country's blood.

The applause of listening senates to command,
      The threats of pain and ruin to despise,
To scatter plenty o'er a smiling land,
      And read their history in a nation's eyes,

65 Their lot forbade: nor circumscribed alone
      Their growing virtues, but their crimes confined;
Forbade to wade through slaughter to a throne,
      And shut the gates of mercy on mankind,

The struggling pangs of conscious truth to hide,
70   To quench the blushes of ingenuous shame,
Or heap the shrine of Luxury and Pride
      With incense kindled at the Muse's flame.

Far from the madding crowd's ignoble strife,
      Their sober wishes never learned to stray;
75 Along the cool sequestered vale of life
      They kept the noiseless tenor of their way.

48 lyre: a small harplike musical instrument used in ancient Greece to accompany the singing of poetry and therefore frequently used as a symbol of the poetic art.

51–52 penury (pĕn'yə-rē): extreme poverty; **genial current:** warm, life-giving power. Why has poverty held back their "noble rage" and "genial current"?

57 Hampden: John Hampden, a 17th-century English politician who opposed the "tyrant" Charles I over unjust taxation.

60 Cromwell: Oliver Cromwell, leader of the Parliamentary forces in the English Civil War and head of the English government from 1653 to 1658.

65 circumscribed: limited; confined.

69 conscious truth: conscience.

72 incense . . . flame: poetic praise.

73 madding: wildly excited; disorderly.

75 sequestered: isolated; secluded.

76 tenor: unwavering course.

Yet even these bones from insult to protect
    Some frail memorial still erected nigh,
With uncouth rhymes and shapeless sculpture decked,
80   Implores the passing tribute of a sigh.

Their name, their years, spelt by the unlettered Muse,
    The place of fame and elegy supply:
And many a holy text around she strews,
    That teach the rustic moralist to die.

85 For who to dumb Forgetfulness a prey,
    This pleasing anxious being e'er resigned,
Left the warm precincts of the cheerful day,
    Nor cast one longing lingering look behind?

On some fond breast the parting soul relies,
90   Some pious drops the closing eye requires;
Even from the tomb the voice of Nature cries,
    Even in our ashes live their wonted fires.

For thee, who mindful of the unhonored dead
    Dost in these lines their artless tale relate;
95 If chance, by lonely contemplation led,
    Some kindred spirit shall inquire thy fate,

Haply some hoary-headed swain may say,
    "Oft have we seen him at the peep of dawn
Brushing with hasty steps the dews away
100   To meet the sun upon the upland lawn.

"There at the foot of yonder nodding beech
    That wreathes its old fantastic roots so high,
His listless length at noontide would he stretch,
    And pore upon the brook that babbles by.

105 "Hard by yon wood, now smiling as in scorn,
    Muttering his wayward fancies he would rove,
Now drooping, woeful wan, like one forlorn,
    Or crazed with care, or crossed in hopeless love.

81 unlettered Muse: the "inspiration" of the uneducated stonecutters who carved the inscriptions on the tombstones.

85–88 For who . . . behind?: For who has ever accepted that he will be forgotten, leaving the warmth of earthly life without any regret?

90 drops: tears.

92 wonted (wôn'tĭd): accustomed.

93 thee: that is, Gray himself.

97 hoary-headed swain: white-haired peasant.

104 pore: to gaze intently.

"One morn I missed him on the customed hill,
110   Along the heath and near his favorite tree;
Another came; nor yet beside the rill,
         Nor up the lawn, nor at the wood was he;

"The next with dirges due in sad array
         Slow through the churchway path we saw him borne.
115 Approach and read (for thou canst read) the lay,
         Graved on the stone beneath yon aged thorn."

111 rill: brook.

113 dirges: funeral hymns.

115 lay: poem.
116 thorn: hawthorn.

The Epitaph

Here rests his head upon the lap of Earth
         A youth to fortune and to Fame unknown.
Fair Science frowned not on his humble birth,
120   *And Melancholy marked him for her own.*

Large was his bounty, and his soul sincere,
         Heaven did a recompense as largely send:
He gave to Misery all he had, a tear,
         He gained from Heaven ('twas all he wished) a friend.

125 *No farther seek his merits to disclose,*
         Or draw his frailties from their dread abode
(There they alike in trembling hope repose),
         The bosom of his Father and his God.

117–128 What do you learn about Gray from this epitaph?

Connect to the Literature

1. What Do You Think?
What were your impressions of the speaker by the end of the poem?

> **Comprehension Check**
> • What kind of people are buried in the churchyard?
> • What does the speaker suggest can compensate for unhappiness in life?

Think Critically

2. `ACTIVE READING` `MAKING INFERENCES FROM DETAILS`
Review the list of details you made in your **READER'S NOTEBOOK** about the people Gray describes. What **inferences** can you make about the lives of the villagers based upon these details? Be specific in your answer.

3. How do you think Gray feels about the society he portrays? Explain your answer.

4. Review the cluster diagram you created for the Connect to Your Life on page 666. How does your reaction to cemeteries compare with Gray's?

5. How would you describe Gray's attitude toward death?

> **THINK ABOUT**
> • your answer to question 2
> • Gray's description of what someone might say about his own death (lines 98–116)
> • his inclusion of his own epitaph

Extend Interpretations

6. Comparing Texts Compare the **speakers** of "Elegy Written in a Country Churchyard," Ben Jonson's "On My First Son" (page 458), and Donne's "Holy Sonnet 10" (page 451). Do you notice any similarities or differences in their attitudes toward death? Discuss your observations with your classmates, and compare your ideas with theirs.

7. Different Perspectives Consider how different readers might react to this poem. For example, how might the reaction of a 20-year-old reader differ from that of a 70-year-old reader?

8. Connect to Life In your opinion, does this poem have relevance to the lives of people today? Why or why not?

Literary Analysis

`PERSONIFICATION` Gray makes frequent use of **personification** in this poem. In line 117 of the elegy, for example, Earth is personified as a motherly figure upon whose lap the dead may rest their heads. Thus, human qualities of nurturing, affection, and love are attributed to an object.

Paired Activity With a partner, find some other examples of personification in the poem. Make a list of the examples you find and then compare your examples with those found by others. Discuss why you think personification is such a popular figure of speech among poets.

`ELEGY` Gray's "Elegy Written in a Country Churchyard" is one of the most famous elegies in English literature. An **elegy** is an extended meditative poem in which the speaker reflects upon death—often in tribute to a person who has died recently—or upon an equally serious subject. Most elegies are written in formal, dignified language and are serious in tone. List the purposes you think Gray had for writing his elegy. Give evidence to support your ideas.

Choices & CHALLENGES

Writing Options

1. Explanatory Paragraph In a paragraph, explain what you think is meant by "Full many a flower is born to blush unseen, / And waste its sweetness on the desert air" (lines 55–56).

Writing Handbook
See page 1369–1370: Analysis.

2. Alternative Title Give the poem a new title that conveys either the poem's mood or an aspect of its subject.

Activities & Explorations

Background Music Create a recording of background music to accompany an oral reading of the poem. For the recording, select an instrumental work or a song (or excerpts from several pieces) that you think complements the poem's mood. Play your recording as you read the poem aloud for your classmates.
~ SPEAKING AND LISTENING

Inquiry & Research

King Charles I Investigate Gray's allusions, in lines 57–60, to events of the reign of Charles I. What circumstances caused the king to be viewed as a "tyrant"? How was he challenged?

 More Online: Research Starter
www.mcdougallittell.com

Thomas Gray
1716–1771

Other Works
"Ode on a Distant Prospect of Eton College"
"Ode on the Spring"

Boyhood The only one of his parents' 12 children to survive past infancy, Thomas Gray was rather delicate and frail as a child. Although his mother adored and sheltered her son, his ill-tempered, abusive father frequently vented his rage on the family. Gray was able to escape his uneasy, frightening home life, however, when at the age of 8 he entered boarding school at Eton College. A studious, sensitive boy, he disliked boisterous games and sports and chose friends who shared his scholarly interests. Among these were Horace Walpole—the son of Britain's most prominent Whig leader—and Richard West, a fellow poet.

University and the Grand Tour At about the age of 18, Gray entered Cambridge University. There he embarked upon the study of law, but after several years he abandoned his studies to accompany his friend Walpole on a tour of Europe. The trip ended in a bitter quarrel, which severed their friendship for many years.

A Scholarly Life In 1742, the year of Richard West's early death, Gray returned to Cambridge. There he continued his studies, obtained his degree, and wrote a number of carefully crafted poems. In 1757, the government was ready to offer him the position of poet laureate; however, not wanting to write poems on request and always hesitant to publish his poetry, he declined. Gray remained at Cambridge, rarely leaving its grounds, for the rest of his life. He died at the age of 55 and was buried beside his mother in the rural churchyard at Stoke Poges in Buckinghamshire, the setting of his famous elegy.

Author Activity

A Life of Gray Samuel Johnson, in his *Lives of the Poets*, wrote an essay on Gray. Look at Johnson's essay and find his comments on "Elegy Written in a Country Churchyard." What does Johnson think of the poem? Discuss Johnson's opinions with your classmates.

from The Diary and Letters of Madame d'Arblay

By FANNY BURNEY

Comparing Literature of the World

The Diary and Letters of Madame d'Arblay and *Memoirs of Madame Vigée-Lebrun*

This lesson and the one that follows present an opportunity for comparing Fanny Burney's personal experiences and observations about life in 18th-century England with those of Madame Vigée-Lebrun about life in 18th-century France. Specific points of comparison in the Vigée-Lebrun lesson will help you note similarities and differences in the writers' comments on human nature and their portrayals of life in their times.

Connect to Your Life

First Impressions Think about your initial conversation with a person you met recently. Did the conversation leave you with a distinct impression of the person? In your opinion, what personality traits can be revealed in a brief conversation? Share your thoughts with your classmates.

Build Background

The Art of Conversation Conversation was a fashionable activity in London throughout the 18th century, but after 1750 the preferred setting for conversation changed from coffeehouses to private homes. Parties intended chiefly as occasions for conversation were often hosted by women, particularly the members of a literary group known as the bluestockings.

One of London's most prominent social hostesses was Hester Thrale, whose prestigious guests included the renowned author Samuel Johnson, the playwright Richard Brinsley Sheridan, the painter Joshua Reynolds, the actor David Garrick, the philosopher Edmund Burke, and a young writer named Fanny Burney. At the age of 26, Burney had anonymously published her first novel, *Evelina,* an instant success.

Although Burney (known after her marriage as Madame d'Arblay) achieved immediate fame through her novels, readers today are more familiar with her **diary,** which she began when she was 15 and wrote in regularly for 70 years. A number of the entries are copies of letters to relatives and close friends, including Burney's sister and best friend, Susan Burney Phillips.

> WORDS TO KNOW
> **Vocabulary Preview**
>
> ascribed   loquacious
> complacently   transport
> inducement

Focus Your Reading

LITERARY ANALYSIS | **DIALOGUE** Written conversation between two or more people, in either fiction or nonfiction, is called **dialogue.** Writers use dialogue to bring characters to life and to give readers insights into the characters' qualities, personality traits, and reactions to other people. Notice how the following dialogue brings Lady Say and Sele to life:

> *"I think it's the most elegant novel I ever read in my life. Such a style! I am quite surprised at it. I can't think where you got so much invention!"*

As you read Burney's letter, be aware of how dialogue reveals the speakers' personalities.

ACTIVE READING | **EFFECT OF WORD CHOICE ON TONE**
Writers choose words that best convey their ideas, delineate their characters, and set a particular mood. The writer's choice of words also helps establish a work's **tone,** the attitude a writer takes toward a subject. As you read Burney's letter, pay attention to the words she uses to describe the people she meets at the party.

READER'S NOTEBOOK Make a list of all the people Burney encounters. As you read, jot down words used to describe each person.

FROM *The Diary and Letters of* MADAME D'ARBLAY

FANNY BURNEY

Letter to Mrs. Phillips, Her Sister

I thank you most heartily for your two sweet letters, my ever dearest Susy, and equally for the kindness they contain and the kindness they accept. And, as I have a frank[1] and a subject, I will leave my *bothers,* and write you and my dear brother Molesworth a little account of a *rout*[2] I have just been at, at the house of Mr. Paradise.

You will wonder, perhaps, in this time of hurry, why I went thither; but when I tell you Pacchierotti[3] was there, you will not think it surprising.

There was a crowd of company; Charlotte and I went together; my father came afterwards. Mrs. Paradise received us very graciously, and led me immediately up to Miss Thrale, who was sitting by the Pac.[4] The Miss Kirwans, you may be sure, were not far off, and so I did pretty well. There was nobody else I knew but Dr. Solander, Mr. Coxe, the traveler, Sir Sampson and Lady Gideon (Streatham acquaintances), Mr. Sastres, and Count Zenobia, a noble Venetian, whom I have often met lately at Mrs. Thrale's.

We were very late, for we had waited cruelly for the coach, and Pac. had sung a song out of *Artaxerxes,*[5] composed for a tenor, which we lost, to my infinite regret. Afterwards he sang "Dolce speme," set by Bertoni, less elegantly than by Sacchini, but more expressively for the words. He sang it delightfully. It was but the second time I have heard him in a room since his return to England.

---

1. **frank:** an envelope marked by an official so that it can be mailed without postage.
2. **rout:** party.
3. **Pacchierotti** (päk´yĕ-rôt´tē): a well-known operatic singer of the time.
4. **Pac.:** an abbreviation of *Pacchierotti.*
5. *Artaxerxes* (är´tə-zûrk´sēz´): an opera by the 18th-century British composer Thomas Arne.

The Porten Family, Gawen Hamilton. Museum of Fine Arts, Springfield, Massachusetts, James Philip Gray Collection.

After this he went into another room, to try if it would be cooler; and Mrs. Paradise, leaning over the Kirwans and Charlotte, who hardly got a seat all night for the crowd, said she begged to speak to me. I squeezed my great person out, and she then said,

"Miss Burney, Lady Say and Sele[6] desires the honor of being introduced to you."

Her ladyship stood by her side. She seems pretty near fifty—at least turned forty; her head was full of feathers, flowers, jewels, and geegaws, and as high as Lady Archer's; her dress was trimmed with beads, silver, persian sashes, and all sort of fine fancies; her face is thin and fiery, and her whole manner spoke a lady all alive.

"Miss Burney," cried she, with great quickness, and a look all curiosity, "I am very happy to see you; I have longed to see you a great while; I have read your performance, and I am quite delighted with it. I think it's the most elegant novel I ever read in my life. Such a style!

I am quite surprised at it. I can't think where you got so much invention!"

You may believe this was a reception not to make me very <u>loquacious</u>. I did not know which way to turn my head.

"I must introduce you," continued her ladyship, "to my sister; she'll be quite delighted to see you. She has written a novel herself; so you are sister authoresses. A most elegant thing it is, I assure you; almost as pretty as yours, only not quite so elegant. She has written two novels, only one is not so pretty as the other. But I shall insist upon your seeing them. One is in letters, like yours, only yours is prettiest; it's called the *Mausoleum of Julia!*"

What unfeeling things, thought I, are *my* sisters! I'm sure I never heard them go about thus praising *me!*

---

6. **Lady Say and Sele:** the title of the wife of Baron Say and Sele.

loquacious (lō-kwā′shəs) *adj.* very talkative

Mrs. Paradise then again came forward, and taking my hand, led me up to her ladyship's sister, Lady Hawke, saying aloud, and with a courteous smirk, "Miss Burney, ma'am, authoress of *Evelina*."

"Yes," cried my friend, Lady Say and Sele, who followed me close, "it's the authoress of *Evelina*; so you are sister authoresses!"

Lady Hawke arose and curtsied. She is much younger than her sister, and rather pretty; extremely languishing, delicate, and pathetic; apparently accustomed to be reckoned the genius of her family, and well contented to be looked upon as a creature dropped from the clouds.

I was then seated between their ladyships, and Lady S. and S., drawing as near to me as possible, said,

"Well, and so you wrote this pretty book!— and pray did your papa know of it?"

"No, ma'am; not till some months after the publication."

"So I've heard; it's surprising! I can't think how you invented it!—there's a vast deal of invention in it! And you've got so much humor, too! Now my sister has no humor—hers is all sentiment. You can't think how I was entertained with that old grandmother and her son!"

I suppose she meant Tom Branghton for the son.

"How much pleasure you must have had in writing it; had not you?"

"Y—e—s, ma'am."

"So has my sister; she's never without a pen in her hand; she can't help writing for her life. When Lord Hawke is traveling about with her, she keeps writing all the way."

"Yes," said Lady Hawke; "I really can't help writing. One has great pleasure in writing the things; has not one, Miss Burney?"

"Y—e—s, ma'am."

"But your novel," cried Lady Say and Sele, "is in such a style!—so elegant! I am vastly glad you made it end happily. I hate a novel that don't end happy."

"Yes," said Lady Hawke, with a languid smile,

"I was vastly glad when she married Lord Orville. I was sadly afraid it would not have been."

"My sister intends," said Lady Say and Sele, "to print her *Mausoleum*, just for her own friends and acquaintances."

"Yes," said Lady Hawke, "I have never printed yet."

"I saw Lady Hawke's name," quoth I to my first friend, "<u>ascribed</u> to the play of *Variety*."

"Did you indeed?" cried Lady Say, in an ecstasy. "Sister! do you know Miss Burney saw your name in the newspapers, about the play!"

"Did she?" said Lady Hawke, smiling <u>complacently</u>. "But I really did not write it; I never wrote a play in my life."

"Well," cried Lady Say, "but do repeat that sweet part that I am so fond of—you know what I mean; Miss Burney *must* hear it,—out of your novel, you know!"

Lady H.—No I can't; I have forgot it.

Lady S.—Oh no! I am sure you have not; I insist upon it.

Lady H.—But I know you can repeat it yourself; you have so fine a memory; I am sure you can repeat it.

Lady S.—Oh, but I should not do it justice! that's all,—I should not do it justice!

Lady Hawke then bent forward, and repeated— "'If, when he made the declaration of his love, the sensibility that beamed in his eyes was felt in his heart, what pleasing sensations and soft alarms might not that tender avowal awaken!'"

"And from what, ma'am," cried I, astonished, and imagining I had mistaken them, "is this taken?"

"From my sister's novel!" answered the delighted Lady Say and Sele, expecting my raptures to be equal to her own; "it's in the *Mausoleum,*—did not you know that? Well, I can't think how you can write these sweet novels! And it's all just like that part. Lord Hawke himself says it's all poetry. For my part, I'm sure I never could write so. I suppose, Miss

WORDS
TO
KNOW

ascribed (ə-skrībd′) *adj.* assigned; referred to as a source **ascribe** *v.*
complacently (kəm-plā′sənt-lē) *adv.* in a contented, self-satisfied way; smugly

Burney, you are producing another,— a'n't you?"

"No, ma'am."

"Oh, I daresay you are. I daresay you are writing one at this very minute!"

Mrs. Paradise now came up to me again, followed by a square man, middle-aged, and humdrum, who, I found, was Lord Say and Sele, afterwards from the Kirwans; for though they introduced him to me, I was so confounded by their vehemence and their manners, that I did not hear his name.

"Miss Burney," said Mrs. P., presenting me to him, "authoress of *Evelina.*"

"Yes," cried Lady Say and Sele, starting up, "'tis the authoress of *Evelina!*"

"Of what?" cried he.

"Of *Evelina.* You'd never think it,—she looks so young, to have so much invention, and such an elegant style! Well, I could write a play, I think, but I'm sure I could never write a novel."

"Oh yes, you could, if you would try," said Lady Hawke.

"Oh no, I could not," answered she; "I could not get a style—that's the thing—I could not tell how to get a style! and a novel's nothing without a style, you know!"

"Why no," said Lady Hawke; "that's true. But then you write such charming letters, you know!"

"Letters!" repeated Lady S. and S., simpering; "do you think so? Do you know I wrote a long letter to Mrs. Ray just before I came here, this very afternoon,—quite a long letter! I did, I assure you!"

Here Mrs. Paradise came forward with another gentleman, younger, slimmer, and smarter, and saying to me, "Sir Gregory Page Turner," said to him, "Miss Burney, authoress of *Evelina.*"

At which Lady Say and Sele, in fresh transport, again arose, and rapturously again repeated—"Yes, she's authoress of *Evelina!* Have you read it?"

"No; is it to be had?"

"Oh dear, yes! it's been printed these two years! You'd never think it! But it's the most elegant novel I ever read in my life. Writ in such a style!"

"Certainly," said he, very civilly; "I have every inducement to get it. Pray where is it to be had? everywhere, I suppose?"

"Oh, nowhere, I hope!" cried I, wishing at that moment it had been never in human ken.[7]

My *square* friend, Lord Say and Sele, then putting his head forward, said, very solemnly, "I'll purchase it!"

His lady then mentioned to me a hundred novels that I had never heard of, asking my opinion of them, and whether I knew the authors; Lady Hawke only occasionally and languidly joining in the discourse: and then Lady S. and S., suddenly arising, begged me not to move, for she should be back again in a minute, and flew to the next room.

I took, however, the first opportunity of Lady Hawke's casting down her eyes, and reclining her delicate head, to make away from this terrible set; and, just as I was got by the piano-forte,[8] where I hoped Pacchierotti would soon present himself, Mrs. Paradise again came to me, and said,

"Miss Burney, Lady Say and Sele wishes vastly to cultivate your acquaintance, and begs to know if she may have the honor of your company to an assembly at her house next Friday?—and I will do myself the pleasure to call for you, if you will give me leave."

"Her ladyship does me much honor, but I am unfortunately engaged," was my answer, with as much promptness as I could command. ❖

---

7. **ken:** range of vision; sight.

8. **piano-forte** (pē-ăn′ō-fôr′tā): piano.

WORDS TO KNOW

transport (trăns′pôrt′) *n.* a state of being carried away by emotion; a state of bliss
inducement (ĭn-dōōs′mənt) *n.* a motive for action; incentive

Connect to the Literature

1. What Do You Think? Jot down your impression of Burney's experience at the party.

Comprehension Check
- Why is Lady Say and Sele so anxious to meet Burney?
- Why does Burney want to escape from Lady Say and Sele and her sister, Lady Hawke?

Think Critically

2. In your opinion, what different aspects of human nature are illuminated by the **dialogue** Burney recounts?

 THINK ABOUT
- the reasons for Burney's popularity
- the conduct of Mrs. Paradise
- the sentiments expressed by Lady Say and Sele
- the attitude of Lady Hawke

3. **ACTIVE READING** **EFFECT OF WORD CHOICE ON TONE** Compare your list of descriptive words in your **READER'S NOTEBOOK** with that of a partner. What **tone** do Burney's word choices help establish? What descriptive words might the writer have used if she had wanted to set an altogether different tone?

4. What kind of person does Fanny Burney seem to be? Cite details from the letter to support your answer.

Extend Interpretations

5. Comparing Texts Compare the ways in which Fanny Burney and Samuel Pepys describe social gatherings. How do they differ in the types of details they record? What do the differences reveal about the writers? Justify your answers with examples from their selections in this book.

6. Different Perspectives Imagine that Lady Say and Sele writes a gossip column for the society page of her local newspaper. What might she report about her meeting with Fanny Burney? How would her account differ from Burney's?

7. Connect to Life Have you ever met or observed a person who behaved like Lady Say and Sele? What do you think motivated the person's behavior?

Literary Analysis

DIALOGUE **Dialogue**—the written conversation between two or more people—helps bring characters to life by providing insights into their qualities and personality traits. It also shows the relationships between characters. Read the following dialogue between Lady Say and her sister:

"Well," cried Lady Say, "but do repeat that sweet part that I am so fond of—you know what I mean; Miss Burney must hear it,—out of your novel, you know!"

Lady H.—No I can't; I have forgot it.

Lady S.—Oh no! I am sure you have not; I insist upon it.

Lady H.—But I know you can repeat it yourself; you have so fine a memory; I am sure you can repeat it.

Lady S.—Oh, but I should not do it justice! that's all,—I should not do it justice!

The dialogue reveals Lady Say's excessive admiration for her sister and her sister's complacent acceptance of it.

Cooperative Learning Activity Do you think Burney's account of the party would have been as effective without dialogue? With a group of classmates, rewrite a scene from the party, replacing the dialogue with description. How does the removal of the dialogue affect your perception of the characters?

Writing Options

1. Party Script Create a script for the scene Burney describes. Be sure to include any stage directions and director's notes that you think are needed to flesh out the scene.

2. Diary Entry Use a conversation that you recently took part in or overheard as the basis for a diary entry written, like Burney's, as a letter to a friend or sibling. Place the entry in your **Working Portfolio.**

Activities & Explorations

1. Caricature of a Lady Draw a humorous caricature of Lady Say and Sele, based on the information revealed in this selection. Try to capture her personality as well as her appearance. ~ **ART**

2. Photo Essay Create a photo essay called "Conversations." Include pictures that show a variety of facial expressions and gestures.
~ **VIEWING AND REPRESENTING**

Inquiry & Research

Literary Ladies Research the origin of the term *bluestocking.* What role did the bluestockings play in the history of English literature? Did they change society's attitudes toward women?

Vocabulary in Action

EXERCISE: IDIOMS Write the word suggested by each of the following sets of idioms.

1. on cloud nine, walking on air
2. rattle on, run off at the mouth
3. point the finger, give credit where it's due
4. dangle a carrot in front of, light a fire under
5. without batting an eye, not give a hoot

WORDS TO KNOW		
ascribed		loquacious
complacently		transport
inducement		

Building Vocabulary
Several Words to Know in this lesson contain prefixes and suffixes. For an in-depth study of word parts, see page 1104.

Fanny Burney
1752–1840

Timid Child Largely self-taught, Fanny Burney was an avid reader who, by the time she was ten, had begun writing stories, poems, and plays. As a girl, she stood timidly in the background at her father's parties, listening closely to the guests; her remarkable memory allowed her to recall conversations word for word. Even after becoming a successful novelist, she remained modest around her ardent admirers.

Influential Author Burney's novels influenced a number of later female novelists, particularly Jane Austen. *Evelina* was a forerunner of the "novel of manners," a genre in which the customs and conventions of social life occupy a prominent place. None of Burney's other novels had the success of *Evelina,* although Austen was to find both the title and the theme for her *Pride and Prejudice* in Burney's second novel, *Cecilia.*

Working Woman In 1786, Burney's life took a new direction when she reluctantly accepted a position at the court of King George III. It was an unpleasant experience that allowed her little time to write, and she left the court after five years. At age 41, she married Alexandre d'Arblay, a French general who had fled to England during the French Revolution. Although d'Arblay was poor, the proceeds from Burney's third novel, *Camilla,* enabled them to live comfortably. In 1802, a visit to France became a ten-year exile for the d'Arblays and their son when the country suddenly became engaged in war with England. During her later years, back in London, Burney published her father's memoirs. Her own diary was not published until long after her death.

from Memoirs of Madame Vigée-Lebrun

By ÉLISABETH VIGÉE-LEBRUN (vē-zhā′ lə-brœn′)

Comparing Literature of the World

Personal Narratives Across Cultures

The Diary and Letters of Madame d'Arblay and **Memoirs of Madame Vigée-Lebrun** Like Fanny Burney, Vigée-Lebrun was a keen observer of human nature and offers a unique perspective on some of the famous as well as the ordinary people of her day. Burney and Vigée-Lebrun were writing during the same period, one in England and one in France.

Points of Comparison As you read this memoir, compare how Vigée-Lebrun and Burney paint vivid portraits of their particular time and place through their use of telling detail and attention to daily life.

Build Background

A Painter and Writer In these excerpts from her **memoirs,** Élisabeth Vigée-Lebrun—a gifted artist who painted portraits of the French nobility—recalls events of her own life amidst the turmoil of the French Revolution, which began in 1789. Before the Revolution, France was ruled by a king, who had almost unlimited authority, and by the privileged nobility and clergy. These groups obtained most of the money they needed to maintain their rich lifestyles by taxing peasant farmers and other poor workers. In 1789, the French government's finances were in a shambles. Peasants and farmers were angry because their requests for a voice in government had been denied. Facing economic hardships, they revolted and stormed the Bastille, a Paris fortress-prison that was a hated symbol of royal authority and oppression.

A long period of violence ensued, during which King Louis XVI and his wife, Marie Antoinette, were imprisoned and later executed—the king in January 1793 and the queen in October. The most horrific months of the Revolution, the Reign of Terror, came in late 1793 and 1794, when thousands of citizens were imprisoned and executed.

> WORDS TO KNOW
> **Vocabulary Preview**
> amiability   fortitude
> consternation   mien
> execrable

Focus Your Reading

LITERARY ANALYSIS **DESCRIPTION** **Description** is writing that helps a reader to picture scenes, events, and characters. Notice, for example, how Vigée-Lebrun describes Marie Antoinette in the following passage:

> *Her nose was slender and pretty, and her mouth not too large, though her lips were rather thick.*

As you read, be aware of the writer's use of vivid description to bring to life the people and events that she describes.

ACTIVE READING **INTERPRETING DETAILS** Élisabeth Vigée-Lebrun includes many **details** in her **descriptions.** These details help to create rich and rounded portraits of the various people she encounters in her world.

READER'S NOTEBOOK As you read Vigée-Lebrun's memoirs, use a chart like the one shown to note the details she uses to describe the people whom she encounters.

Person	Details
Marie Antoinette	brilliant complexion

f r o m

MEMOIRS OF
MADAME VIGÉE-LEBRUN

It was in the

year 1779 that

I painted the Queen

for the

first time; she was then in the heyday of her youth and beauty. Marie
Antoinette was tall and admirably built, being somewhat stout, but not
excessively so. Her arms were superb, her hands small and perfectly
formed, and her feet charming. She had the best walk of any woman in
France, carrying her head erect with a dignity that stamped her queen

in the midst of her whole court, her majestic mien, however, not in the least diminishing the sweetness and amiability of her face. To anyone who has not seen the Queen it is difficult to get an idea of all the graces and all the nobility combined in her person. Her features were not regular; she had inherited that long and narrow oval peculiar to the Austrian nation. Her eyes were not large; in color they were almost blue, and they were at the same time merry and kind. Her nose was slender and pretty, and her mouth not too large, though her lips were rather thick. But the most remarkable thing about her face was the splendor of her complexion. I never have seen one so brilliant, and brilliant is the word, for her skin was so transparent that it bore no umber[1] in the painting. Neither could I render the real effect of it as I wished. I had no colors to paint such freshness, such delicate tints, which were hers alone, and which I had never seen in any other woman.

At the first sitting the imposing air of the Queen at first frightened me greatly, but Her Majesty spoke to me so graciously that my fear was soon dissipated. It was on that occasion that I began the picture representing her with a large basket, wearing a satin dress, and holding a rose in her hand. This portrait was destined for her brother, Emperor Joseph II, and the Queen ordered two copies besides—one for the Empress of Russia, the other for her own apartments at Versailles or Fontainebleau.[2]

I painted various pictures of the Queen at different times. In one I did her to the knees, in a pale orange-red dress, standing before a table on which she was arranging some flowers in a vase. It may be well imagined that I preferred to paint her in a plain gown and especially without a wide hoopskirt. She usually gave these portraits to her friends or to foreign diplomatic envoys. One of them shows her with a straw hat on, and a white muslin dress, whose sleeves are turned up, though quite neatly. When this work was exhibited at the Salon,[3] malignant folk did not fail to make the remark that the Queen had been painted in her chemise,[4] for we were then in 1786, and calumny[5] was already busy concerning her. Yet in spite of all this the portraits were very successful.

Toward the end of the exhibition a little piece was given at the Vaudeville Theater, bearing the title, I think, "The Assembling of the Arts." Brongniart,[6] the architect, and his wife, whom the author had taken into his confidence, had taken a box on the first tier, and called for me on the day of the first performance. As I had no suspicion of the surprise in store for me, judge of my emotion when Painting appeared on the scene and I saw the actress representing that art copy me in the act of painting a portrait of the Queen. The same moment everybody in the parterre[7] and the boxes turned toward me and applauded to bring the roof down. I can hardly believe that anyone was ever more moved and more grateful than I was that evening.

I was so fortunate as to be on very pleasant terms with the Queen. When she heard that I had something of a voice we rarely had a sitting without singing some duets by Grétry[8] together, for she was exceedingly fond of music, although she did not sing very true. As for her conversation, it would be difficult for me to convey all its charm, all its affability. I do not think that Queen Marie Antoinette ever missed an opportunity of saying something pleasant to those who had the honor of being presented to her, and the

---

1. **umber:** a brown pigment.
2. **Versailles** (věr-sī′) . . . **Fontainebleau** (fôn-těn-blō′): sites of royal palaces.
3. **Salon:** an annual French art exhibition.
4. **chemise** (shə-mēz′): a woman's loose-fitting undergarment.
5. **calumny** (kăl′əm-nē): the making of false statements intended to injure a person's reputation; slander.
6. **Brongniart** (brôn-nyär′).
7. **parterre** (pär-târ′): the seating area nearest the stage on the main floor of a theater.
8. **Grétry** (grā-trē′): an 18th-century French composer of operas.

kindness she always bestowed upon me has ever been one of my sweetest memories.

One day I happened to miss the appointment she had given me for a sitting; I had suddenly become unwell. The next day I hastened to Versailles to offer my excuses. The Queen was not expecting me; she had had her horses harnessed to go out driving, and her carriage was the first thing I saw on entering the palace yard. I nevertheless went upstairs to speak with the chamberlains on duty. One of them, M. Campan, received me with a stiff and haughty manner, and bellowed at me in his stentorian voice, "It was yesterday, madame, that Her Majesty expected you, and I am very sure she is going out driving, and I am very sure she will give you no sitting today!" Upon my reply that I had simply come to take Her Majesty's orders for another day, he went to the Queen, who at once had me conducted to her room. She was finishing her toilet,[9] and was holding a book in her hand, hearing her daughter repeat a lesson. My heart was beating violently, for I knew that I was in the wrong. But the Queen looked up at me and said most amiably, "I was waiting for you all the morning yesterday; what happened to you?"

"I am sorry to say, Your Majesty," I replied, "I was so ill that I was unable to comply with Your Majesty's commands. I am here to receive more now, and then I will immediately retire."

"No, no! Do not go!" exclaimed the Queen. "I do not want you to have made your journey for nothing!" She revoked the order for her carriage and gave me a sitting. I remember that, in my confusion and my eagerness to make a fitting response to her kind words, I opened my paint-box so excitedly that I spilled my brushes on the floor. I stooped down to pick them up. "Never mind, never mind," said the Queen, and, for aught I could say, she insisted on gathering them all up herself.

When the Queen went for the last time to Fontainebleau, where the court, according to custom, was to appear in full gala, I repaired there to enjoy that spectacle. I saw the Queen in her grandest dress; she was covered with diamonds, and as the brilliant sunshine fell upon her she seemed to me nothing short of dazzling. Her head, erect on her beautiful Greek neck, lent her as she walked such an imposing, such a majestic air, that one seemed to see a goddess in the midst of her nymphs. During the first sitting I had with Her Majesty after this occasion I took the liberty of mentioning the impression she had made upon me, and of saying to the Queen how the carriage of her head added to the nobility of her bearing. She answered in a jesting tone, "If I were not Queen they would say I looked insolent, would they not?"

The Queen neglected nothing to impart to her children the courteous and gracious manners which endeared her so to all her surroundings. I once saw her make her six-year-old daughter dine with a little peasant girl and attend to her wants. The Queen saw to it that the little visitor was served first, saying to her daughter, "You must do the honors."

The last sitting I had with Her Majesty was given me at Trianon, where I did her hair for the large picture in which she appeared with her children. After doing the Queen's hair, as well as separate studies of the Dauphin,[10] Madame Royale, and the Duke de Normandie, I busied myself with my picture, to which I attached great importance, and I had it ready for the Salon of 1788. The frame, which had been taken there alone, was enough to

---

9. **toilet:** the process of dressing or grooming oneself.
10. **Dauphin** (dō-făn′): the eldest son of the king of France.

evoke a thousand malicious remarks. "That's how the money goes," they said, and a number of other things which seemed to me the bitterest comments. At last I sent my picture, but I could not muster up the courage to follow it and find out what its fate was to be, so afraid was I that it would be badly received by the public. In fact, I became quite ill with fright. I shut myself in my room, and there I was, praying to the Lord for the success of my "Royal Family," when my brother and a host of friends burst in to tell me that my picture had met with universal acclaim. After the Salon, the King, having had the picture transferred to Versailles, M. d'Angevilliers,[11] then minister of the fine arts and director of royal residences, presented me to His Majesty. Louis XVI vouchsafed[12] to talk to me at some length and to tell me that he was very much pleased. Then he added, still looking at my work, "I know nothing about painting, but you make me like it."

The picture was placed in one of the rooms at Versailles, and the Queen passed it going to mass and returning. After the death of the Dauphin, which occurred early in the year 1789, the sight

Marie Antoinette and Her Children (about 1785), Élisabeth Vigée-Lebrun. Chateau Versailles, France. Giraudon/Art Resource, New York.

of this picture reminded her so keenly of the cruel loss she had suffered that she could not go through the room without shedding tears. She then ordered M. d'Angevilliers to have the picture taken away, but with her usual consideration she informed me of the fact as well, apprising me of her motive for the removal. It is really to the Queen's sensitiveness that I owed the preservation of my picture, for the fishwives[13] who soon afterward came to Versailles for Their Majesties would certainly have destroyed it, as they did the Queen's bed, which was ruthlessly torn apart.

I never had the felicity of setting eyes on Marie Antoinette after the last court ball at Versailles. The ball was given in the theater, and the box where I was seated was so situated that I could hear what the Queen said. I observed that she was

---

11. **d'Angevilliers** (dänzh-vēl-yā′).

12. **vouchsafed** (vouch-sāft′): granted in a gracious manner; condescended.

13. **fishwives:** women who sell fish (a derogatory reference to the common women who supported the French Revolution).

very excited, asking the young men of the court to dance with her, such as M. Lameth, whose family had been overwhelmed with kindness by the Queen, and others, who all refused, so that many of the dances had to be given up. The conduct of these gentlemen seemed to me exceedingly improper; somehow their refusal likened a sort of revolt—the prelude to revolts of a more serious kind. The Revolution was drawing near; it was, in fact, to burst out before long. . . .

It was in 1786 that I went for the first time to Louveciennes,[14] where I had promised to paint Mme. Du Barry. She might then have been about forty-five years old. She was tall without being too much so; she had a certain roundness, her throat being rather pronounced but very beautiful; her face was still attractive, her features were regular and graceful; her hair was ashy, and curly like a child's. But her complexion was beginning to fade. She received me with much courtesy, and seemed to me very well behaved, but I found her more spontaneous in mind than in manner: her glance was that of a coquette,[15] for her long eyes were never quite open, and her pronunciation had something childish which no longer suited her age.

She lodged me in a part of the building where I was greatly put out by the continual noise. Under my room was a gallery, sadly neglected, in which busts, vases, columns, the rarest marbles, and a quantity of other valuable articles were displayed without system or order. These remains of luxury contrasted with the simplicity adopted by the mistress of the house, with her dress and her mode of life. Summer and winter Mme. Du Barry wore only a dressing-robe of cotton cambric or white muslin, and every day, whatever the weather might be, she walked in her park, or outside of it, without ever incurring disastrous consequences, so sturdy had her health become through her life in the country.

She had maintained no relations with the numerous court that surrounded her so long. In the evening we were usually alone at the fireside, Mme. Du Barry and I. She sometimes talked to me about Louis XV and his court. She showed herself a worthy person by her actions as well as her words, and did a great deal of good at Louveciennes, where she helped all the poor. Every day after dinner we took coffee in the pavilion which was so famous for its rich and tasteful decorations. The first time Mme. Du Barry showed it to me she said: "It is here that Louis XV did me the honor of coming to dinner. There was a gallery above for musicians and singers who performed during the meal."

When Mme. Du Barry went to England, before the Terror, to get back her stolen diamonds, which, in fact, she recovered there, the English received her very well. They did all they could to prevent her from returning to France. But it was not long before she succumbed to the fate in store for everybody who had some possessions. She was informed against and betrayed by a little Negro called Zamore, who is mentioned in all the memoirs of the period as having been overwhelmed with kindness by her and Louis XV. Being arrested and thrown into prison, Mme. Du Barry was tried and condemned to death by the Revolutionary tribunal at the end of 1793. She was the only woman, among all who perished in those dreadful days, unable to face the scaffold with firmness; she screamed, she sued for pardon to the hideous mob surrounding her, and that mob became moved to such a degree that the executioner hastened to finish his task. This has always confirmed my belief that if the victims of that

---

14. **Louveciennes** (lōōv-syĕn′): an estate given to Madame Du Barry by Louis XV.

15. **coquette** (kō-kĕt′): a woman who tries to get men to notice and admire her; a flirt.

period of execrable memory had not had the noble pride of dying with fortitude the Terror would have ceased long before it did.

I made three portraits of Mme. Du Barry. In the first I painted her at half length, in a dressing-gown and straw hat. In the second she is dressed in white satin; she holds a wreath in one hand, and one of her arms is leaning on a pedestal. The third portrait I made of Mme. Du Barry is in my own possession. I began it about the middle of September, 1789. From Louveciennes we could hear shooting in the distance, and I remember the poor woman saying, "If Louis XV were alive I am sure this would not be happening." I had done the head, and outlined the body and arms, when I was obliged to make an expedition to Paris. I hoped to be able to return to Louveciennes to finish my work, but heard that Berthier and Foulon[16] had been murdered. I was now frightened beyond measure, and thenceforth thought of nothing but leaving France. The fearful year 1789 was well advanced, and all decent people were already seized with terror. I remember perfectly that one evening when I had gathered some friends about me for a concert, most of the arrivals came into the room with looks of consternation; they had been walking at Longchamps that morning, and the populace assembled at the Étoile gate had cursed at those who passed in carriages in a dreadful manner. Some of the wretches had clambered on the carriage steps, shouting, "Next year you will be behind your carriages and we shall be inside!" and a thousand other insults.

As for myself, I had little need to learn fresh details in order to foresee what horrors impended. I knew beyond doubt that my house in the Rue Gros Chenet, where I had settled but three months since, had been singled out by the criminals. They threw sulphur into our cellars through the airholes. If I happened to be at my window, vulgar ruffians would shake their fists at me. Numberless sinister rumors reached me from every side; in fact, I now lived in a state of continual anxiety and sadness. My health became sensibly affected, and two of my best friends, the architect Brongniart and his wife, when they came to see me, found me so thin and so changed that they besought me to come and spend a few days with them, which invitation I thankfully accepted. Brongniart had his lodgings at the Invalides, whither I was conducted by a physician attached to the Palais Royal, whose servants wore the Orléans livery,[17] the only one then held in any respect. There I was given everything of the best. As I was unable to eat, I was nourished on excellent Burgundy wine and soup, and Mme. Brongniart was in constant attendance upon me. All this solicitude ought to have quieted me, especially as my friends took a less black view of things than I did. Nevertheless, they did not succeed in banishing my evil forebodings. "What is the use of living; what is the use of taking care of oneself?" I would often ask my good friends, for the fears that the future held over me made life distasteful to me. But I must acknowledge that even with the furthest stretch of my imagination I guessed only at a fraction of the crimes that were to be committed. . . .

---

16. **Berthier** (bĕr-tyā´): a French aristocrat; **Foulon** (fōō-lôn´): a government minister of war and finance who increased his own wealth at the expense of the poor.

17. **livery:** the uniform of a servant.

WORDS TO KNOW

execrable (ĕk´sĭ-krə-bəl) *adj.* detestable; hateful
fortitude (fôr´tĭ-tōōd´) *n.* the strength to bear misfortune or pain calmly and patiently; firm courage
consternation (kŏn´stər-nā´shən) *n.* a sudden fear or amazement that makes one feel helpless; dismay

Self-Portrait (late 1700s), Élisabeth Vigée-Lebrun. Oil on canvas, Uffizi, Florence, Italy. Scala/Art Resource, New York.

I had made up my mind to leave France. For some years I had cherished the desire to go to Rome. The large number of portraits I had engaged to paint had, however, hindered me from putting my plan into execution. But I could now paint no longer; my broken spirit, bruised with so many horrors, shut itself entirely to my art. Besides, dreadful slanders were pouring upon my friends, my acquaintances and myself, although, Heaven knows, I had never hurt a living soul. I thought like the man who said, "I am accused of having stolen the towers of Notre Dame; they are still in their usual place, but I am going away, as I am evidently to blame." I left several portraits I had begun, among them Mlle. Contat's. At the same time I refused to paint Mlle. de Laborde (afterward Duchess de Noailles),[18] brought to me by her father. She was scarcely sixteen, and very charming, but it was no longer a question of success or money—it was only a question of saving one's head. I had my carriage loaded, and my passport ready, so that I might leave next day with my daughter and her governess, when a crowd of national guardsmen burst into my room with their muskets. Most of them were drunk and shabby, and had terrible faces. A few of them came up to

me and told me in the coarsest language that I must not go, but that I must remain. I answered that since everybody had been called upon to enjoy his liberty, I intended to make use of mine. They would barely listen to me, and kept on repeating, "You will not go, citizeness; you will not go!" Finally they went away. I was plunged into a state of cruel anxiety when I saw two of them return. But they did not frighten me, although they belonged to the gang, so quickly did I recognize that they wished me no harm. "Madame," said one of them, "we are your neighbors, and we have come to advise you to leave, and as soon as possible. You cannot live here; you are changed so much that we feel sorry for you. But do not go in your carriage: go in the stage-coach; it is much safer." I thanked them with all my heart, and followed their good advice. I had three places reserved, as I still wanted to take my daughter, who was then five or six years old, but was unable to secure them until a fortnight later, because all who exiled themselves chose the stage-coach, like myself. At last came the long-expected day.

It was the 5th of October, and the King and Queen were conducted from Versailles to Paris surrounded by pikes. The events of that day filled me with uneasiness as to the fate of Their Majesties and that of all decent people, so that I was dragged to the stage-coach at midnight in a dreadful state of mind. I was very much afraid of the Faubourg Saint Antoine, which I was obliged to traverse to reach the Barrière du Trône.[19] My brother and my husband escorted me as far as this gate without leaving the door of the coach for a moment; but the suburb that I was so frightened of was perfectly quiet. All its inhabitants, the workmen and the rest, had been to Versailles after the royal family, and fatigue kept them all in bed.

Opposite me in the coach was a very filthy man, who stunk like the plague, and told me quite simply that he had stolen watches and

18. **Noailles** (nô-ī′).

19. **Faubourg Saint Antoine** (fō-bōōr′ săN äN-twän′) . . . **Barrière de Trône** (bä-ryĕr′ də trōn′).

other things. Luckily he saw nothing about me to tempt him, for I was only taking a small amount of clothing and eighty louis for my journey. I had left my principal effects and my jewels in Paris, and the fruit of my labors was in the hands of my husband, who spent it all. I lived abroad solely on the proceeds of my painting.

Not satisfied with relating his fine exploits to us, the thief talked incessantly of stringing up such and such people on lamp-posts, naming a number of my own acquaintances. My daughter thought this man very wicked. He frightened her, and this gave me the courage to say, "I beg you, sir, not to talk of killing before this child." That silenced him, and he ended by playing at battle with my daughter. On the bench I occupied there also sat a mad Jacobin[20] from Grenoble, about fifty years old, with an ugly, bilious[21] complexion, who each time we stopped at an inn for dinner or supper made violent speeches of the most fearful kind. At all of the towns a crowd of people stopped the coach to learn the news from Paris. Our Jacobin would then exclaim: "Everything is going well, children! We have the baker and his wife safe in Paris. A constitution will be drawn up, they will be forced to accept it, and then it will be all over." There were plenty of ninnies and flatheads who believed this man as if he had been an oracle. All this made my journey a very melancholy one. I had no further fears for myself, but I feared greatly for everybody else—for my mother, for my brother, and for my friends. I also had the gravest apprehensions concerning Their Majesties, for all along the route, nearly as far as Lyons, men on horseback rode up to the coach to tell us that the King and Queen had been killed and that Paris was on fire. My poor little girl got all a-tremble; she thought she saw her father dead and our house burned down, and no sooner had I succeeded in reassuring her than another horseman appeared and told us the same stories.

I cannot describe the emotions I felt in passing over the Beauvoisin[22] Bridge. Then only did I breathe freely. I had left France behind, that France which nevertheless was the land of my birth, and which I reproached myself with quitting with so much satisfaction. The sight of the mountains, however, distracted me from all my sad thoughts. I had never seen high mountains before; those of the Savoy[23] seemed to touch the sky, and seemed to mingle with it in a thick vapor. My first sensation was that of fear, but I unconsciously accustomed myself to the spectacle, and ended by admiring it. A certain part of the road completely entranced me; I seemed to see the "Gallery of the Titans,"[24] and I have always called it so since. Wishing to enjoy all these beauties as fully as possible, I got down from the coach, but after walking some way I was seized with a great fright, for there were explosions being made with gunpowder, which had the effect of a thousand cannon shots, and the din echoing from rock to rock was truly infernal.

I went up Mount Cenis, as other strangers were doing, when a postilion[25] approached me, saying, "The lady ought to take a mule; to climb up on foot is too fatiguing." I answered that I was a work-woman and quite accustomed to walking. "Oh! no!" was the laughing reply. "The lady is no work-woman; we know who she is!" "Well, who am I, then?" I asked him. "You are Mme. Lebrun, who paints so well, and we are all very glad to see you safe from those bad people." I never guessed how the man could have learned my name, but it proved to me how many secret agents the Jacobins must have had. Happily I had no occasion to fear them any longer. ❖

Mme Lebrun

---

20. **Jacobin:** radical revolutionary.
21. **bilious** (bĭl′yəs): sickly yellow.
22. **Beauvoisin** (bō-vwä-zăn′).
23. **the Savoy:** the mountainous region along the border between France and Italy.
24. **Titans:** a group of giants in Greek mythology.
25. **postilion:** a person who helps guide a coach by riding on one of the lead horses.

Connect to the Literature

1. What Do You Think?
As you read, how did you feel about the situation Vigée-Lebrun found herself in? Share your reactions with your classmates.

Comprehension Check
- What was the author's occupation?
- Describe Vigée-Lebrun's relationship with the Queen of France.

Think Critically

2. Explain Vigée-Lebrun's feelings about the French Revolution, as revealed in her comments about the rich and the poor.

 THINK ABOUT
- the encounters she has with aristocrats and with revolutionaries
- the terms that she uses to refer to the aristocracy and the revolutionaries
- her acceptance by the French aristocracy

3. **ACTIVE READING** **INTERPRETING DETAILS** Review the chart in your **READER'S NOTEBOOK** that lists **details** about people Vigée-Lebrun encounters. What impression of Marie Antoinette do you think Vigée-Lebrun wished to convey? Why might she have wanted to convey that impression? Use details from the selection to support your opinions.

4. Do you find Vigée-Lebrun a sympathetic person? Why or why not?

Extend Interpretations

5. Different Perspectives How do you think Vigée-Lebrun's fellow stagecoach passenger, the "mad Jacobin from Grenoble," would describe her?

6. Connect to Life Problems between the rich and the poor continue to exist in modern life. Think about how the rich and the poor view one another in contemporary American society. What do you think would be the best ways of resolving misunderstandings and conflicts between the two groups?

7. **Points of Comparison** Compare this excerpt from Vigée-Lebrun's **memoir** with the excerpt from Fanny Burney's **diary.** What details of daily life does each portray? How do these details affect the **tone** of each work?

Literary Analysis

DESCRIPTION Descriptive writing helps readers understand exactly what someone or something is like by allowing them to picture scenes, events, and characters in their minds. An effective **description** is often like a good painting: it provides visual details of color, size, texture, and shape that give the reader a clear impression of the person, place, object, or event being described.

Paired Activity With a partner, review the excerpt from Vigée-Lebrun's *Memoirs* and decide what descriptive passage in the selection you think is the most effective. Explain your choice.

ACTIVE READING **EVALUATING SOURCES**

In recounting her experiences, Vigée-Lebrun offers a glimpse of life in France at the outbreak of the French Revolution. Do you think her motives for writing the memoirs affect the **credibility** of her account in any way? Do you think her memoirs would be an **appropriate** source of information for understanding the causes and consequences of the French Revolution? List the reasons for your conclusions.

Writing Options

Points of Comparison Write an essay in which you compare the portrayal of people in Fanny Burney's diary with that in Vigée-Lebrun's memoir. As you develop your comparison, consider the techniques used by each author, the relationship of the author to the people being described, and the relative importance of the wider social setting in each work.

Writing Handbook
See page 1367: Compare and Contrast.

Vocabulary in Action

EXERCISE: CONTEXT CLUES On your paper, write the word that best completes each sentence.

1. It was reported that Marie Antoinette, when told that the poor had no bread, responded, "Let them eat cake," and such a response was thought to be truly _____.

2. That story fit the common perception of the queen as haughty and uncaring; Madame Vigée-Lebrun, on the other hand, praises her for her _____.

3. What many of the French people saw as an air of arrogance, Vigée-Lebrun viewed as a majestic _____.

4. Whatever the queen's character, her awareness that her power was gone and that she faced death must have filled her with _____.

5. Even after the king was executed, however, she showed composure and courage in prison—surely a sign of _____.

WORDS TO KNOW	amiability	fortitude
	consternation	mien
	execrable	

Building Vocabulary
For an in-depth study of context clues, see page 938.

Élisabeth Vigée-Lebrun
1755–1842

A Budding Young Artist As a child, Élisabeth Vigée-Lebrun drew miniature portraits in the margins of her schoolbooks and even on the dormitory walls of the convent school she attended in Paris. She received some instruction from her father, a minor painter, and from artist friends, but she was mainly self-taught. When she was 13, her father died, and Vigée-Lebrun began supporting her mother and brother by painting portraits.

Painter of the Nobility The young artist quickly gained a following, and her reputation as a portrait painter of the nobility was established by the time she was 19. At the age of 24, she was invited to do her first portrait of Marie Antoinette. The many portraits of the queen that followed are among the artist's most famous works.

Painting and Politics Because she painted and mingled with the aristocracy, Vigée-Lebrun felt especially threatened by the events leading up to the French Revolution. After she fled Paris in 1789, she traveled and lived in various parts of Europe and England and was sought as a painter wherever she went. She returned to France in 1810 and published her memoirs in the 1830s.

Portrait of an Age During her long and illustrious career, Vigée-Lebrun created more than 800 paintings, including more than 600 portraits. Although her portraits of women were usually flattering—undoubtedly one reason for her popularity—her talent and the stature of her work are undisputed.

The Restoration and Enlightenment

As you read the selections in this unit, what did you learn about the ways people in the 17th and 18th centuries viewed themselves and others? What did they see clearly? In what areas did they have blind spots? Did you learn anything about yourself and the ways people today view themselves and others? Explore these questions by completing one or more of the options in each of the following sections.

Reflecting on the Unit

Gaining Insights Some of the writers represented in this unit portrayed life as it was in the late 17th century and the 18th century, whereas others portrayed life as they thought it should be. Choose two of the writers—one to represent each perspective. What does the work of each reveal about how people see themselves and others? Which had the greater impact on your understanding of human nature and society? Explain your choices in one or two paragraphs.

OPTION 2

Examining Form and Content The selections in this unit include essays, poetry, a diary, letters, biography, and autobiography. Which kind of writing did you enjoy reading the most? Which do you think gives the clearest, most objective view of human nature? Make a chart in which you list the literary forms and identify at least one example of each among the selections in this unit. Then jot down one strength and one weakness of each form.

OPTION 3

Evaluating the Issues The selections in this unit reveal a variety of human weaknesses and problems. How clearly did the people of the time understand their own faults and those of others? Which of their concerns seem trivial? Which seem significant? Are any of their concerns important to people today? Get together with some of your classmates to discuss your conclusions.

Self ASSESSMENT

To explore what you have learned about human nature from this unit, create a three-column chart. In the first column, list four insights you have gained into how people view themselves and others; in the second, identify the source of each insight; in the third, rank the insights according to how important each is to you.

Reviewing Literary Concepts

OPTION 1

Analyzing Essays Several of the prose selections in this unit are informal or persuasive essays. Make a chart like the one shown, listing the selections that are essays and identifying each as informal or persuasive. Briefly explain the purpose of each essay and evaluate how effectively the purpose is carried out.

Selection	Type of Essay	Purpose	Effectiveness
from *The Spectator*	informal	entertainment, mild criticism of human weaknesses	enjoyable humor, accurate perceptions of human nature

OPTION 2

Recognizing Irony and Satire Writers often use irony and satire to reveal human defects and weaknesses. Think about the selections that you read from this unit that use these techniques. Which examples are most effective? Why? Compare your choices with those of your classmates and discuss any differences in your opinions.

🗂 Building Your Portfolio

- **Writing Options** Many of the Writing Options in this unit asked you to observe and comment on aspects of human behavior. Look over your work for these assignments and pick two pieces that you think contain your most perceptive ideas. Write a brief cover note in which you explain why these pieces show particularly clear insights, and add them, along with the note, to your **Presentation Portfolio**. 🗂

- **Writing Workshops** In this unit you wrote a Proposal recommending a solution to a problem. You also wrote a Satire that made use of humor to persuade your readers. Reread these pieces and decide which is more successful at convincing your readers to adopt a particular viewpoint. Explain your choice in a note attached to the preferred one. Place the piece in your **Presentation Portfolio**. 🗂

- **Additional Activities** Think back to any of the assignments you completed under **Activities & Explorations** and **Inquiry & Research.** Keep a record in your portfolio of any assignments that you would like to do further work on in the future.

Self ASSESSMENT

On a piece of paper, copy the following list of literary terms introduced in this unit. Put checks next to those you understand well and question marks next to those that are still unclear to you. Then find a partner and exchange lists. Take turns defining the terms that one of you understands well but the other is having difficulty with. Work together to define any terms whose meanings you are both unsure of.

diary	humor
heroic couplet	argumentation
fable	aphorism
informal essay	biography
parallelism	personification
persuasive essay	elegy
	dialogue
fantasy	description
irony	

Self ASSESSMENT

You are now beginning to build up a variety of writing pieces in your portfolio. Look through them. Do you find a stronger sense of confidence in your more recent writing? What is your favorite piece so far?

Setting GOALS

As you reviewed your work for this unit, you probably noticed some aspects of your writing that are not as strong as others. Identify the weak areas that need continued attention and the skills that need practice. Keep these in mind as you work through the next unit.

A Tale of Two Cities

CHARLES DICKENS

Set against the raging upheaval of the French Revolution, this novel examines what it means to be a true hero. *A Tale of Two Cities* explores questions about revolutions, the abuse of power, the nature of justice and loyalty, and the ability of love to triumph over hatred.

These thematically related readings are provided along with *A Tale of Two Cities:*

Declaration of the Rights of Man and of the Citizen, August 27, 1789

Declaration of the Rights of Women
BY OLYMPE DE GOUGES

A Last Letter from Prison
BY OLYMPE DE GOUGES

In Defense of the Terror
BY MAXIMILIEN ROBESPIERRE

from **Hind Swarj or Indian Rule**
BY MOHANDAS K. GANDHI

from **Guillotine: Its Legend and Lore**
BY DANIEL GEROULD

Five Men
BY ZBIGNIEW HERBERT

The Pit and the Pendulum
BY EDGAR ALLAN POE

from **Darkness at Noon**
BY SIDNEY KINGSLEY (BASED ON THE NOVEL BY ARTHUR KOESTLER)

The Strike
BY TILLIE OLSEN

And Even *More* . . .

The Letters of James Boswell

EDITED BY C. B. TINKER

Boswell's letters to his friends give the reader a glimpse of the customs, beliefs, and occupations of 18th-century England. In addition to being the biographer of Samuel Johnson, Boswell led a busy life as a lawyer, a literary critic, and a traveler. All in all, his letters provide a richly detailed portrait of an age.

Books

Isaac Newton and the Scientific Revolution
GALE E. CHRISTIANSON
A compelling description of the genius of Isaac Newton and the absolutely central role he played in the history of science.

The Age of Reason Begins
WILL AND ARIEL DURANT
A history of the Enlightenment from 1558 to 1648.

Robinson Crusoe

DANIEL DEFOE

This riveting tale of shipwreck and survival portrays the adventures of a man isolated on an island for 24 years. Crusoe displays great ingenuity in making the best of his situation. A practical man, he applies his intelligence to contriving various means of improving his physical comfort and security. The novel illustrates the various skills and virtues needed to survive in the face of adversity.

Gulliver's Travels

JONATHAN SWIFT

This satiric work traces the travels of a man who encounters strange and fantastic worlds. In addition to the land of Lilliput, populated by tiny people, and Brobdingnag, peopled by giants, Lemuel Gulliver visits a land where the Houyhnhnms (horse-like, rational creatures) rule over Yahoos, who resemble humans. He also encounters Laputa, a flying island ruled by experts and pedants. Fantasy, science fiction, and satire combine in this compelling story of a stranger who visits strange lands.

Johnson and Boswell
PAT ROGERS
A dual biography of the most famous pair in English literature, written by one of the leading scholars of the period.

Vindication
FRANCES SHERWOOD
Mary Wollstonecraft is portrayed vividly in this fictionalized treatment of her life and times.

Other Media

A Tale of Two Cities
British production of the Dickens classic about the French Revolution, starring Dirk Bogarde. Social Studies School Service.
(VIDEOCASSETTE)

Gulliver's Travels
Dove Audio.
(AUDIOCASSETTES)

The Age of Reason: Europe After the Renaissance
Knowledge Unlimited.
(VIDEOCASSETTE)

The Age of Enlightenment
Cambridge Social Studies.
(VIDEOCASSETTE)

To see a world in a grain of sand

And a heaven in a wild flower,

Hold infinity in the palm of your hand

And eternity in an hour.

William Blake

POET AND ARTIST

The Lake, Petworth: Sunset, Fighting Bucks
(about 1828), Joseph Mallord William
Turner. Clore Collection, Tate Gallery,
London/Art Resource, New York.

696

1798-1832

1798-1832

THE FLOWERING OF
Romanticism

THE FLOWERING OF Romanticism

EVENTS IN BRITISH LITERATURE

1790   1800   1810

1798 William Wordsworth and Samuel Taylor Coleridge publish "Tintern Abbey" and "The Rime of the Ancient Mariner" anonymously in book *Lyrical Ballads*

1800 Dorothy Wordsworth begins keeping *Grasmere Journals*

1811 Jane Austen's *Sense and Sensibility* published anonymously

1812 Lord Byron wins fame with first two sections of *Childe Harold's Pilgrimage*

1813 Jane Austen's *Pride and Prejudice* published anonymously

1814 Sir Walter Scott anonymously publishes *Waverly*

EVENTS IN BRITAIN

1790   1800   1810

1799 British diplomats assemble Second Coalition (Britain, Austria, and Russia) hoping to drive Napoleon from power in France

1800 Act of Union passed, creating United Kingdom of Great Britain and Ireland

1805 British fleet defeats Napoleon's navy in Battle of Trafalgar off Spanish coast, ending Napoleon's hopes of invading Britain

1807 British slave trade abolished

1811 George III declared permanently insane; eldest son George, Prince of Wales, named regent

1812 Britain fights United States in War of 1812

1815 British and Prussian armies under British leader Wellington defeat Napoleon at Waterloo

EVENTS IN THE WORLD

1790   1800   1810

1799 Coup d'état establishes Napoleon dictator of France (crowned emperor in 1804)

1803 U.S. president Jefferson buys Louisiana Territory from France

1804 Haiti gains independence from France

1805 Napoleon begins conquering most of Europe (to 1812); Muhammad Ali begins rule and modernization of Egypt (to 1849)

1808 U.S. abolishes slave trade

1814 Congress of Vienna opens, seeking to remake Europe after Napoleon's downfall and prevent spread of French ideals of democracy (to 1815)

PERIOD PIECES

Combination night lamp and tea warmer

Iron in which heated brick was inserted

Twelve-month equation clock

1820   1830

1818 Mary Shelley's *Frankenstein* published anonymously

1819 Percy Bysshe Shelley writes "Ode to the West Wind"; John Keats writes "Ode on a Grecian Urn" and "To Autumn"

1821 John Keats, age 25, dies of tuberculosis

1822 Percy Bysshe Shelley, age 29, drowns off coast of Italy

1823 Lord Byron joins Greek war for liberation from Turks

1824 Byron, age 36, dies of fever

1820   1830

1818 Crossing of Atlantic Ocean by steamship

1819 "Peterloo Massacre"— 11 killed in St. Peter's Field, Manchester, when cavalry charges social reformers

1820 Regency ends with death of George III and crowning of Prince of Wales as George IV

1821 Engineer George Stephenson begins work on world's first railroad line (passenger service starts in 1825)

1829 First water-purification plant built in London; Catholic Emancipation Act passed, freeing Catholics from restrictions

1830 George IV dies; reign of brother, William IV, begins (to 1837)

1832 First Reform Bill extends voting rights to middle-class men but affects only 5 percent of population

1820   1830

c. 1816 Zulu chief Shaka begins rule over large kingdom in southeastern Africa (to 1828)

1817 Ludwig van Beethoven, nearly deaf, begins composing monumental Ninth Symphony (to 1823)

1821 Spain's Latin American empire begins collapse as Mexico, several Central American states, and Venezuela win independence

1823 U.S. president Monroe issues *Monroe Doctrine* to keep Europe out of Latin America

1824–25 Simón Bolívar liberates last Spanish colonies in Latin America

1829 Greece wins full independence from Ottoman Turks

HISTORICAL BACKGROUND

The Flowering of Romanticism

1798-1832

Great change swept the Western world at the end of the 18th century. A successful revolution in America and an ongoing one in France shattered the political stability of the day. In Britain, revolutions in industry and agriculture rocked the social and economic structure of the nation. Reflecting and responding to these dramatic changes was a movement that came to be called romanticism, which dominated Western intellectual and artistic life in the early 19th century.

Romanticism was an outgrowth of 18th-century neoclassicism as well as a reaction against it. The spiritual father of the movement was the French Enlightenment thinker Jean Jacques Rousseau. Rousseau's argument that human society is based on a contract between the government and the governed echoed earlier ideas of England's John Locke and helped inspire the French Revolution. Rousseau attributed evil not to human nature but to society, insisting that in the natural state a human being was essentially good and happy—a "noble savage." This idealization of nature and human beings became basic tenets of romantic thinking. Also basic was an emphasis on the individual, the personal, and the emotional—in sharp contrast to the emphasis on soci-

Top: Portrait of Jean Jacques Rousseau (1753), Maurice Quentin de La Tour. Musée d'Art et d'Histoire, Geneva, Switzerland, Giraudon/Art Resource, New York.
Bottom: Taking of the Bastille on July 14, 1789 (about 1789–1800), unknown French artist. Giraudon/Art Resource, New York.

ety, science, and reason that had been at the root of neoclassical thought.

Literary romanticism was pioneered in Germany by Johann Wolfgang von Goethe and in Britain by William Wordsworth and Samuel Taylor Coleridge. However, unlike the artistic ideals of neoclassicism, those of romanticism did not reflect the mainstream views of British society. During its peak period from 1798 to 1832, while the political instability and violence emanating from continental Europe prompted a conservative reaction throughout most levels of British society, romanticism flowered mainly as a movement of protest—a powerful expression of a desire for personal freedom and radical reform.

WILLIAM PITT THE YOUNGER

In the 1780s, before the conservative reaction set in, the need for reform was apparent not only to members of Britain's more liberal Whig party but also to the new Tory prime minister, William Pitt the Younger (son of the prime minister who led Britain through the Seven Years' War). The nation's growing cities were beset with a host of problems, including crime and poor sanitation. Child labor and other factory abuses were not being addressed, the emerging industrial centers in the north and west had no representation in Parliament, and archaic laws denied rights to many religious groups, including the Catholic majority in Ireland. Britain had lost its American colonies, primarily because of incompetent management, and the rest of its overseas empire faced a number of difficulties, ranging from corruption in India to the evils of the slave trade.

Although Pitt came to power as a reformer, his reform plans were pushed aside when the French Revolution erupted in 1789. Initial British sympathy for the revolution soon died down when France's revolutionary moderates fell from power. The Whig politician Edmund Burke, who had supported the American

Development of the English Language

The democratic attitudes of romanticism helped broaden the concept of "acceptable" English and narrow the gap between the language of scholars and aristocrats and that of the common people. In their efforts to create literature based on natural speech, romantic writers sometimes employed regional dialects, colloquialisms, and even slang—to the dismay of more conservative critics. Romantic writers who were interested in capturing the flavor of the legendary past sometimes even used archaic language (*quoth* instead of *said,* for example).

In the aftermath of the American Revolution, British and American English grew further apart. A major figure in the development of American English was Connecticut-born Noah Webster, who patriotically set about proving that the new nation's language was as good as its mother tongue. His *American Spelling Book* went through over 300 editions from 1788 to 1829, and his 1828 *American Dictionary of the English Language* became a national institution. It was in part through Webster's influence that Americans dropped the *k* at the end of words like *publick* and *traffick;* eliminated the *u* in words such as *colour, flavour,* and *splendour* (but not, for some reason, in *glamour*); and changed the British *re* to *er* in words like *centre.*

William Pitt Addressing the House of Commons in 1793, Karl Anton Hickel. Oil on canvas, The Granger Collection, New York.

Revolution, was among the first to attack the excesses of the increasingly radical government of France. Burke's attacks created a rift within the Whig party, leaving the party's leader, Charles James Fox, with little support. As the violence of the French radicals increased, so did the British reaction, especially when France began exporting revolution beyond its borders. In 1793, after French troops invaded Holland, Britain entered upon a war with France that would ultimately last for over 25 years. Pitt was forced to succumb to fearful voices equating all reform efforts with revolution and arguing for domestic repression to keep Britain from falling victim to the violence and anarchy seen in France.

Near the end of the century, rebellious Irishmen, encouraged by the promise of French assistance, rose up against their British masters. Though this rebellion was quelled after poor weather prevented a major French landing, the threat of a French invasion of Britain by way of Ireland remained. To combat the threat, Pitt offered to sponsor various reforms, including the granting of voting rights to Roman Catholics, if the Irish Parliament would agree to dissolve itself and join politically with the British Parliament. The passage of the Act of Union in 1800 formalized this arrangement, creating the United Kingdom of Great Britain and Ireland, but George III—still on the throne despite his periodic bouts of madness—refused to allow voting rights for Catholics. Pitt was forced to resign, just when his nation needed him most—when the brilliant Corsican general Napoleon Bonaparte had emerged as the dominant force on the French political scene.

Above: Napoleon Bonaparte Crossing the Alps (about 1801), Jacques Louis David. Chateau de Malmaison, Rueil-Malmaison, France, Giraudon/Art Resource, New York.

THE RISE AND FALL OF NAPOLEON

In late 1799, when Napoleon had taken control of France's revolutionary government, his charisma and acceptance of democratic principles had won him the admiration of reform-minded intellectuals throughout Europe. Soon, however, his hunger for power became clear. In 1804 he crowned himself

Created as a symbol of the union of Great Britain and Ireland, this flag—known as the Union Jack—has served as the national flag of the United Kingdom since 1801. It consists of elements taken from earlier flags of England (red cross on white), Scotland (diagonal white cross on blue), and Ireland (diagonal red cross on white).

emperor of France, and over the next several years his military and political maneuvers allowed him to establish control over most of continental Europe. Called back to power in 1804, Pitt tried to prepare Britain for a seemingly inevitable French invasion. Fortunately, in 1805 the British fleet under Horatio Nelson succeeded in destroying the French navy in the Battle of Trafalgar off the coast of Spain, ending the threat of invasion. The victory was bittersweet, however, for Nelson himself was killed in the battle, and within months Pitt was also gone, dying of over-work at the age of 46.

His plans of invasion thwarted, Napoleon tried to break Britain economically by closing the ports of continental Europe to British trade. Tightening his grip on the Iberian Peninsula (Spain and Portugal), Napoleon deposed the Spanish king and placed his brother Joseph on the throne. In the "Peninsular War" that followed, British troops—commanded first by Sir John Moore (killed in action in 1809) and then by Sir Arthur Wellesley—gradually liberated the Iberian Peninsula from French control.

In 1811, with the Peninsular War in full swing, George III was declared insane and his eldest son and heir—George, Prince of Wales—became Britain's regent, or acting ruler. A spendthrift with loose per-sonal morals, Prince George had been a gambling buddy of the now-deceased Whig leader Charles James Fox and (unlike George III) had always favored the Whigs. Now, however, he abandoned them and sided with the Tories, once again quashing hopes of domestic reform. Anyone who criticized the regent too openly became subject to arrest and imprisonment.

In 1812, Napoleon made the mistake of invading Russia, a nation with which he had enjoyed an uneasy peace. Though his army got as far as Moscow, the brutal Russian winter forced it into a retreat during which starvation, the freezing weather, and Cossack raids managed to kill off most of the French troops. Meanwhile, Wellesley's British forces were closing in on France from the south. At the Battle of Leipzig in 1813, the nations allied against Napoleon dealt him what seemed a death blow. When the allied forces entered Paris a year later,

LITERARY HISTORY

Although the beginning of Britain's romantic period is traditionally assigned to the year 1798, aspects of romanti-cism are evident in earlier British litera-ture. Writing in the dialect of Lowland Scotland, Robert Burns, who died in 1796, produced heartfelt lyrics about love, nature, and the Scottish past, many of which were meant to be sung to familiar tunes. William Blake, who began publishing in the 1780s, expressed his rebellious spirit and his mystical view of the nature of good and evil in such works as *The French Revolution, The Marriage of Heaven and Hell,* and the contrasting poems of *Songs of Innocence* and *Songs of Experience.*

Nevertheless, the real flowering of romanticism came with the 1798 publi-cation of William Wordsworth and Samuel Taylor Coleridge's landmark col-lection *Lyrical Ballads.* The two men, who had first met in 1795, were united by their shared desire to explore new modes of literary expression. Wordsworth, who had visited France when the revolution began, was deeply committed to the common people and sought to express individual human experiences in a natural language. Coleridge, in poems like "Kubla Khan," focused on more exotic experiences, letting his imagination wander in realms of mystery and the supernatural. Both poets rejected the world of sci-ence and industry, feeling that insight into human experience flows most freely from communion with nature. With Wordsworth's sister, Dorothy—whose diaries reveal much about the two poets' personalities—they spent a good deal of their time in the rural Lake District of northwestern England, so that they and their friend Robert Southey are sometimes referred to as the Lake Poets.

Above: Early 19th-century improvements in public hygiene included the construction of sewers.

Napoleon was captured and exiled to the island of Elba; but while allied ministers met to decide Europe's fate at the Congress of Vienna, Napoleon escaped and returned to the French throne for the so-called Hundred Days. He was finally defeated at the Battle of Waterloo in Belgium in 1815 and exiled to the more remote island of St. Helena. Wellesley (recently ennobled as the duke of Wellington), who commanded the British troops that bore the brunt of the battle, was the hero of the hour, and "to meet one's waterloo" became synonymous with "to suffer a decisive defeat."

THE AFTERMATH OF THE WAR

The end of the war with France did not mean an immediate end to reactionary British domestic policies, for the fear of revolution still remained strong. To Britain's growing mass of restless laborers were added thousands of discharged veter-

In August 1819, workers met in St. Peter's Fields, Manchester, to peacefully demonstrate their discontent with Britain's economic and labor policies and to call for reform. The local militia, ordered to arrest the protest's leader, instead launched an attack that resulted in 11 deaths and hundreds of injuries. The incident, likened to the Battle of Waterloo, became known as the Peterloo Massacre.

ans returning to a nation in which jobs were scarce, wages low, and poverty widespread. Large landowners successfully pressured the Tory government to continue the Corn Laws, which barred cheap foreign grain from British markets and so kept the price of food high. Industry, in contrast, operated under the economic philosophy of laissez-faire capitalism, which held that government should not interfere in private enterprise. Thus, workers remained at the mercy of factory owners. They were even forbidden from banding together in labor unions that might pressure owners into improving work conditions and wages.

The Regency ended in 1820, when George III died and the Prince of Wales officially took the throne as George IV. Over the next several years, the Tories gradually began to institute some of the reforms that the nation so sorely needed. Sir Robert Peel revamped Britain's harsh criminal code and organized the nation's first professional civilian police force. The duke of Wellington, now serving as prime minister, pushed the Catholic Emancipation Act through Parliament in 1829, just in time to allow the newly elected Irish Catholic political leader Daniel O'Connell to take his seat in the House of Commons. Wellington's more conservative fellow Tories opposed the bill, however, and like Pitt before him, he was forced to resign over the issue. Thus, the passage of the Reform Bill of 1832, which more fairly distributed seats in Parliament and extended the vote to middle-class men, would be a Whig effort, not a Tory one. This landmark bill marks the end of the romantic period and the start of the mainstream reform efforts that characterized the dawning Victorian era.

Above: Although certain reforms were made in the education of females, mid-century educational policies were still extremely limiting.

LITERARY HISTORY

Wordsworth and Coleridge belonged to the so-called first generation of romantic writers. The leading poets of the second generation, which rose to prominence during the Regency, were Lord Byron, Percy Bysshe Shelley, and John Keats. Byron, in both his poetry and his personal life, helped popularize the brooding, self-absorbed romantic figure now sometimes known as the Byronic hero. Both he and his friend Shelley, a brilliant lyric poet, were members of the upper class whose radical politics and personal affairs eventually made them figures of scandal, leading to their self-imposed exile from Britain. The equally brilliant John Keats, a less-well-born acquaintance of Shelley's, also left Britain, seeking a cure for his tuberculosis in the warmer climate of Italy. All three poets died young while living abroad.

Though best known for poetry, the romantic period also was a time when many memorable works of prose were produced. The romantic emphasis on personal experience is evident in the fine personal essays of Charles Lamb, William Hazlitt, and Thomas De Quincey, many of which first appeared in literary journals. Sir Walter Scott, the most popular novelist of the day, pioneered the historical novel in his best-selling *Waverley* (1814), set in his native Scotland. Also popular were gothic novels of mystery and horror, such as *Frankenstein* (1818) by Mary Wollstonecraft Shelley, the wife of Percy Bysshe Shelley and the daughter of Mary Wollstonecraft (see page 638). Jane Austen, on the other hand, remained in many ways a neoclassical writer, penning ironic novels of manners such as *Pride and Prejudice* (1813) and *Emma* (1815). Nevertheless, Austen's introduction of more dialogue into fiction helped pave the way for the realistic novels of the Victorian era.

PART 1   Seeking Truth

The poets of the romantic period turned their attention from the common experience of society in order to focus on the experiences of the individual, believing that emotion was more important than reason as a way of understanding life. Many rejected the formal style of the neoclassicists and instead employed more lyrical poetic forms to express themselves. Romantic poets looked in particular to the natural world as a source of truth and inspiration, as you will see in this part of Unit Four.

Romanticism

Have you ever read a poem that had a surprisingly strong impact upon you? Maybe, in an inspired moment, you yourself have written a poem to express your feelings. English poet William Wordsworth described such poetry as the "spontaneous overflow of powerful feelings." The kind of poetry we are most familiar with today reflects many of the qualities in the personal, emotional, and meditative poetry written by Wordsworth and other romantic poets.

According to the romantics, the common man was a worthy subject for poetry.

In the British literary tradition, **romanticism** refers to a historical period dominated by Wordsworth and five other poets: William Blake, Samuel Taylor Coleridge, Lord Byron, Percy Bysshe Shelley, and John Keats. While critics often mark the start of European romanticism around the French Revolution in 1789, they mark the start of the romantic literary movement in England around the publication of the poetry collection *Lyrical Ballads* by Wordsworth and Coleridge in 1798.

Revolt Against Neoclassicism

In his famous Preface to *Lyrical Ballads*, Wordsworth declared the poems as "experiments" in poetic language and subject matter. He deliberately chose language and subjects taken from "common life" instead of upper-class life. The second generation of romantic poets—Byron, Shelley, and Keats—added their unique voices and visions to Wordsworth's foundation, yet took their poetry in slightly different directions. Despite their differences, however, the English romantics were united in rebellion against their Enlightenment forebears, which included John Dryden, Alexander Pope, and Samuel Johnson. Reflecting the revolutionary spirit of the age, the romantics

broke neoclassical conventions and expressed a new sensibility of freedom and self-expression. Where the neoclassical writers—also called the Augustans—admired and imitated classical forms, the romantics looked to nature for inspiration. Where the Augustans prized reason, the romantics celebrated strong emotions. Where the Augustans wrote witty satires ridiculing others, the romantics wrote serious lyric poems about their own experiences.

Neoclassical Writers	Romantic Writers
• Stressed reason and common sense	• Stressed emotions and imagination
• Wrote about objective issues that concerned society as a whole, such as politics and religion	• Wrote about subjective experiences of the individual, such as desires, hopes, and dreams
• Respected human institutions of church and state	• Exalted nature in all its creative and destructive forces
• Believed in order in all things	• Believed in spontaneity of thought and action
• Maintained traditional standards	• Believed in experimentation
• Focused on adult concerns, primarily those of the ruling class	• Reflected on the experiences of childhood, primitive societies, and the common man
• Exercised controlled wit and urbanity	• Celebrated intense passion and vision
• Followed formal rules and diction in poetry	• Sought a more natural poetic diction and form

Romantic Poetry's Defining Features

"There was a mighty ferment in the heads of statesmen and poets, kings and people. . . . It was a time of promise, a renewal of the world," wrote essayist William Hazlitt in 1825 to describe his age of revolution and change. Critics and

historians have tried to pin down the characteristics of this "mighty ferment" ever since. Here are five features of English romanticism, taken largely from Wordsworth's preface to *Lyrical Ballads*.

A New Concept of Poetry Wordsworth's emphases on personal experience and on the glorification of the individual are very different from earlier poets' emphasis on the greater world of human behavior. To some degree, all romantic poets wrote about the intricate workings of their own minds and the complexities of their emotions.

A New Spontaneity and Freedom Spontaneity is part of Wordsworth's definition of poetry. The romantics were critical of the artificiality they saw in much neoclassical literature, and they placed a high value on emotional outbursts: "I fall upon the thorns of life! I bleed!" wails Shelley in "Ode to the West Wind." This emotional freedom is matched by the free play of imagination. In his poem "Kubla Khan," Coleridge describes an elaborate palace that existed only in his mind.

Love of Nature Romantic poetry is often dubbed "nature poetry" because of its subject matter. But the romantics rarely use nature for its own sake; rather, they look to nature as a stimulus for their own thinking. For instance, a "beauteous evening" for Wordsworth is an occasion for spiritual contemplation.

YOUR TURN Explain some ways that you think nature could stimulate spiritual thoughts.

The Importance of the Commonplace Wordsworth wanted to enlarge the province of poetry to include "incidents and situations from common life." Although Byron was the only aristocrat among his contemporary poets and didn't quite accept such a lowering of standards, the other romantics often chose humble subjects. They celebrated with Wordsworth the ordinary things—an early morning stroll, a field of daffodils, or a change of seasons.

Fascination with the Supernatural and the Exotic While Wordsworth concentrated mostly on ordinary life, Coleridge introduced mystery and magic into English romantic poetry. From the wonderfully strange journey in "The Rime of the Ancient Mariner" to the "stately pleasure dome" of "Kubla Khan," Coleridge opened up to poetry the realm of the supernatural and the exotic. A preoccupation with the supernatural already characterized Gothic novels of the 18th century, but the romantic poets added a touch of elegance and alluring beauty to the terrors of the unknown.

YOUR TURN Why do you think the romantics were attracted to the supernatural?

Strategies for Reading: Romantic Poetry

1. Compare the tone and the language used in romantic poetry with comparable elements in Augustan poetry by writers like Alexander Pope.

2. Notice how the romantic poets freely embrace such subjects as life, death, love, and nature.

3. Pay attention to the extensive use of imagery and figurative language.

4. Watch for elements of the supernatural and the exotic in the poetry.

5. **Monitor** your reading strategies and modify them when your understanding breaks down. Remember to use your strategies for Active Reading: **predict, visualize, connect, question, clarify,** and **evaluate.**

Selected Poems

By WILLIAM BLAKE

Connect to Your Life

An Author's Inspiration Have you ever wondered what inspired an author to write a particular story or poem? Briefly describe to the class one of your favorite novels, short stories, or poems. Then share your thoughts and speculations about the source of the author's inspiration.

Build Background

The Visionary World of Blake William Blake was an artist, a poet, and a visionary. His work was so incompatible with the taste of his day that his contemporaries could not appreciate his accomplishments. Some believed him to be inspired but irrational; others thought him to be mad. Throughout his life, Blake saw visions—from angels sitting in a tree to messages from his dead brother—which he attributed not to a supernatural source but to the interaction of his imagination with the world and with infinity, or God. This interaction was the inspiration for both his poetry and his art. His work reflects highly original interpretations of human experience and of the relationship between the human and the divine.

In 1789, using his own method of producing books with hand-colored illustrations, Blake published his first major work, *Songs of Innocence*, a group of poems modeled on the street ballads and rhymes sung by London's children. In 1794, he added to these poems a group of contrasting poems called *Songs of Experience*. Many of the poems in *Songs of Innocence* have matching poems in *Songs of Experience*—for example, "The Lamb" is paired with "The Tyger." In the subtitle for this combined edition of the two collections, Blake indicated that his purpose in putting them together was to show "the two contrary states of the human soul."

Focus Your Reading

LITERARY ANALYSIS **SYMBOL** A **symbol** is a person, place, object, or activity that stands for something beyond itself. A heart, for example, is a symbol frequently used to stand for love. As you read these examples of Blake's poetry, think about what the subject of each poem might symbolize.

ACTIVE READING **DRAWING CONCLUSIONS** A reader might be easily tempted to think of Blake's poems as simple descriptions of people and other living things in the natural world. It is important, however, to look beyond the obvious—to try to **draw conclusions** about the possible deeper meaning of Blake's work. As you read, keep in mind the following questions:

- What **details** does Blake include about the subject of each poem?
- What seems to be Blake's **tone,** or attitude, in each poem?
- Why might Blake have chosen a lamb, a tiger, etc., as the subject of each poem?
- What might each subject **symbolize**?

READER'S NOTEBOOK First, read each poem in its entirety. Then go back and read each poem again, pausing after each stanza to jot down any observations you have made about the subject of the poem. See if you can answer any of the above questions.

from **S** o **n** g **s** o **f**

W i l l i a m
B l a k e

The Lamb

Little Lamb, who made thee?
　　Dost thou know who made thee?
Gave thee life & bid thee feed,
By the stream & o'er the mead;[1]
5　Gave thee clothing of delight,
Softest clothing wooly bright;
Gave thee such a tender voice,
Making all the vales[2] rejoice!
　　Little Lamb, who made thee?
10　Dost thou know who made thee?

Little Lamb, I'll tell thee,
　　Little Lamb, I'll tell thee!
He is callèd by thy name,
For he calls himself a Lamb:[3]
15　He is meek & he is mild,
He became a little child:
I a child & thou a lamb,
We are callèd by his name.
　　Little Lamb, God bless thee.
20　Little Lamb, God bless thee.

---

1. **mead:** meadow.

2. **vales:** valleys.

3. In the New Testament, Jesus is
   sometimes referred to as the Lamb
   of God.

The Little Boy *Lost*

Detail of title page of *Songs of Innocence* (1789), William Blake. The Granger Collection, New York.

"Father, father, where are you going?
O do not walk so fast.
Speak father, speak to your little boy,
Or else I shall be lost."

5   The night was dark, no father was there;
The child was wet with dew;
The mire[1] was deep, & the child did weep,
And away the vapor[2] flew.

---

1. **mire:** wet, swampy ground.
2. **vapor:** mist; fog.

The Little Boy *Found*

The little boy lost in the lonely fen,[1]
Led by the wand'ring light,
Began to cry, but God ever nigh,
Appear'd like his father in white.

5   He kissed the child & by the hand led
And to his mother brought,
Who in sorrow pale, thro' the lonely dale,
Her little boy weeping sought.

---

1. **fen:** swamp; marsh.

Thinking Through the Literature

1. What thoughts went through your mind as you were reading these poems? Describe your reactions to a classmate.

2. What ideas about life do you think the speaker expresses?

   THINK ABOUT
   - his thoughts about the lamb's creation
   - what happens to the lost boy

3. Do you think the title *Songs of Innocence* is appropriate for these poems? Explain your answer.

from Songs of

SONGS

W i l l i a m   B l a k e

The TYGER

Tyger! Tyger! burning bright
In the forests of the night,
What immortal hand or eye
Could frame thy fearful symmetry?

5   In what distant deeps or skies
Burnt the fire of thine eyes?
On what wings dare he aspire?
What the hand dare seize the fire?

And what shoulder, & what art,
10   Could twist the sinews of thy heart?
And when thy heart began to beat,
What dread hand? & what dread feet?

What the hammer? what the chain?
In what furnace was thy brain?
15   What the anvil? what dread grasp
Dare its deadly terrors clasp?

When the stars threw down their spears
And water'd heaven with their tears,
Did he smile his work to see?
20   Did he who made the Lamb make thee?

Tyger! Tyger! burning bright
In the forests of the night,
What immortal hand or eye
Dare frame thy fearful symmetry?

4 symmetry: balance of form.

7 he: the tiger's creator; **aspire:** soar; ascend; aim for something great.

10 sinews (sĭn'yo͞oz): tendons.

The Fly

Little Fly,
Thy summer's play
My thoughtless hand
Has brush'd away.

5 Am not I
A fly like thee?
Or art not thou
A man like me?

For I dance
10 And drink & sing,
Till some blind hand
Shall brush my wing.

If thought is life
And strength & breath,
15 And the want
Of thought is death,

Then am I
A happy fly
If I live
20 Or if I die.

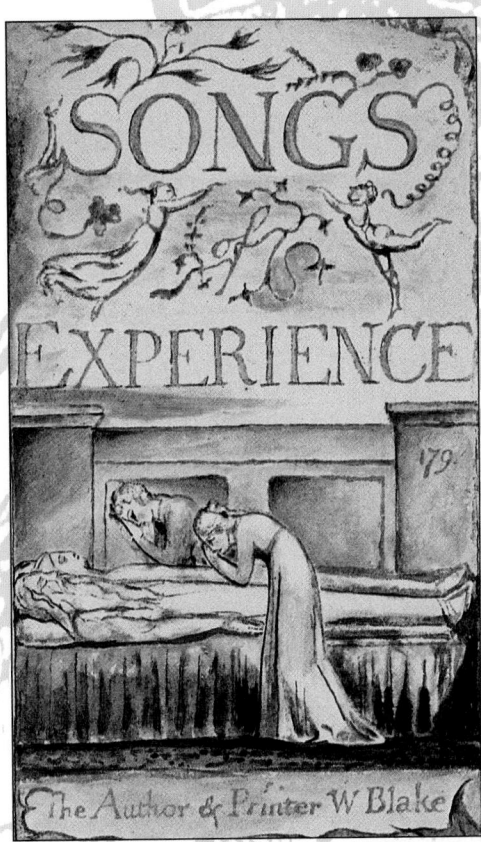

Title page of *Songs of Experience* (1794), William Blake. The Granger Collection, New York.

from Songs of Experience

William Blake

The Sick Rose

O Rose, thou art sick.
The invisible worm
That flies in the night
In the howling storm

5   Has found out thy bed
Of crimson joy,
And his dark secret love
Does thy life destroy.

Thinking through the LITERATURE

Connect to the Literature

1. What Do You Think? Discuss some of the **images** that came to mind as you read "The Tyger," "The Fly," and "The Sick Rose."

Think Critically

2. What view of experience do you think is reflected in these *Songs of Experience*?

THINK ABOUT
- the questions the **speaker** asks about the tiger
- the reasons the speaker compares himself to a fly
- the **image** of the worm in the rose

3. What seems to be the **tone,** or attitude, of the speaker in each of these poems?

4. **ACTIVE READING** **DRAWING CONCLUSIONS** Review any notes you took in your 📖 **READER'S NOTEBOOK** while reading the poems in *Songs of Experience*. What conclusions can you reach about Blake's choice of a tiger, a fly, and a rose as the subjects of these poems?

Extend Interpretations

5. Comparing Texts Compare the attitudes of the speakers in *Songs of Innocence* with those of the speakers in *Songs of Experience*. Consider similarities as well as differences.

6. Comparing Texts Compare the views of life expressed in these poems from *Songs of Innocence* and *Songs of Experience* with the views of life presented in the excerpts from the King James Bible in Unit Two. What similarities and differences do you see?

7. Connect to Life What do you think might have been the sources of Blake's inspiration for these two sets of poems? Consider feelings and thoughts as well as aspects of the external world.

8. Art Connection Look at the two illustrations of Blake's on pages 711 and 713. How do the scenes depicted reflect the themes of innocence and experience?

Literary Analysis

SYMBOL As you know, a person, place, object, or activity that stands for something beyond itself is called a **symbol.** Literary symbols take on meaning within the context of the works in which they occur, and sometimes literary symbols have more than one meaning. For example, the rose in Blake's poem might symbolize goodness, innocence, or all of humanity.

Cooperative Learning Activity In a chart like the one shown, identify the qualities of the lamb and the tiger and tell what you think each animal symbolizes. Then identify any other objects in the six Blake poems that you think might be considered symbols.

Object	Qualities	Symbol of...
Lamb		
Tiger		

Choices & CHALLENGES

Writing Options

1. Blake Critique Think back to Blake's statement (quoted on page 709) that he paired *Songs of Innocence* with *Songs of Experience* to show "the two contrary states of the human soul." Write a critique of the two groups of poems, in which you evaluate how well they fulfill that purpose. Place the critique in your **Working Portfolio.**

2. Discussion Questions Think about some of the issues about life and death that Blake raises in these six poems. Then prepare a set of questions that could be used to lead a discussion of the main themes in *Songs of Innocence* and *Songs of Experience*.

Activities and Explorations

Ideas through Art Create a montage—a composite picture made up of a variety of photos or parts of photos—to illustrate Blake's concept of innocence. Then create a similar montage to illustrate his concept of experience. ~ **ART**

William Blake
1757–1827

Other Works
"Introduction" and "The Chimney Sweeper" in *Songs of Innocence*
"Introduction" and "The Chimney Sweeper" in *Songs of Experience*

Innocence and Experience William Blake's life was at once extraordinary and uneventful. Although his imaginative life was rich and astonishingly creative, his everyday life was lived in obscurity and near poverty. The son of a London clothing merchant, Blake showed an early flair for drawing and began attending art school when he was only 10. He spoke of having visions from the time he was a young child, and he was already writing poetry by the age of 12. When he was 14 he entered a seven-year apprenticeship to an engraver, after which he studied engraving at the Royal Academy of Arts.

Printer and Illustrator When Blake was 24, he married Catherine Boucher, a poor and illiterate young woman. Blake taught her to read, and she later helped him in his engraving and printing work. In 1784, Blake opened his own print shop, where he developed an engraving technique that

he called "illuminated printing." The method involved printing both text and illustration on a page at the same time, then coloring the illustration by hand. *Songs of Innocence* was one of the first works he printed in this manner. Because the process was time-consuming, Blake produced only a few copies of each of his books, undoubtedly one of the reasons that his works were not widely known during his lifetime.

Originality and Obscurity Blake's later works were on a grand scale, marked by prophetic and mythic visions, richly illustrated and difficult to understand. These complex works were almost totally ignored by readers in his own day. During his 60s, Blake stopped writing poetry and devoted all his time to pictorial art. He finally gained the recognition of a small group of artists who admired his work, and it was during this period that he created some of his best designs, including illustrations for Dante's *Divine Comedy* and designs for the book of Job. Blake died three months before his 70th birthday, confident of the value of his work but still relatively unknown, his stunning originality as a poet and artist not to be recognized until well into the 20th century.

Haiku

Poetry by MATSUO BASHŌ (măt-sŏŏ'ō bă'shō)
and KOBAYASHI ISSA (kō-bă-yă'shē ēs'să)

Comparing Literature of the World

Nature Poetry Across Cultures

The Poetry of William Blake and the Haiku Poets Despite differences in location, culture, and time period, the Japanese haiku poets, like William Blake, found nature to be an important source of inspiration.

Points of Comparison As you read the haiku poems in this lesson, compare them with those of Blake. Look for similarities and differences in subject matter, style of writing, ideas expressed, and attitude toward nature.

China Russia
North Korea Sea of Japan
South Korea Japan
Pacific Ocean

Build Background

Haiku and Its Masters Haiku (hī'kōō) is a form of poetry that evolved during the Tokugawa period in Japan (1603–1867). Although it began as a comic style of verse, it eventually became a serious art form, largely due to the efforts and artistry of Matsuo Bashō. Bashō, a 17th-century teacher of haiku, was idolized in his own lifetime and is still regarded as the greatest of all Japanese haiku poets. Kobayashi Issa, who composed nearly 20,000 haiku, achieved fame a century later.

Focus Your Reading

LITERARY ANALYSIS HAIKU **Haiku** is a form of Japanese poetry that embodies three qualities greatly valued in Japanese art: precision, economy, and delicacy. The rules of haiku are strict—in only 17 syllables, arranged in 3 lines of 5, 7, and 5 syllables, the poet must create a clear picture of a single aspect of nature that evokes a strong emotional response in the reader. Although Bashō and Issa followed the strict requirements of the haiku form, the exact number and pattern of syllables in their poems cannot usually be reproduced in English versions, as you may notice when you read these translations.

ACTIVE READING **INTERPRETING IMAGES AND IDEAS** In order to appreciate the full impact of haiku, make sure to read each poem slowly, allowing a mental **image** to form based on the **details** provided. Then read each poem a second time, stopping to ponder the idea implied.

READER'S NOTEBOOK As you read each haiku, jot down words or phrases that describe your mental image. Also record any ideas that you think the haiku imply.

Haiku

Autumn—
even the birds
and clouds look old.

Bashō

Wintry day,
on my horse
a frozen shadow.

Bashō

Skylark
sings all day,
and day not long enough.

Bashō

Nightingale's song
this morning,
soaked with rain.

Issa

What a world,
where lotus flowers
are ploughed into a field.

Issa

Autumn wind—
mountain's shadow
wavers.

Issa

Translated by Lucien Stryk and Takashi Ikemoto

Thinking through the LITERATURE

Connect to the Literature

1. **What Do You Think?** Which of these haiku did you enjoy the most? As a class, discuss reasons for your choice.

Think Critically

2. How would you describe the overall **mood** of the haiku poems?

3. What impressions of nature do the two haiku poets seem to share?

4. **ACTIVE READING** **INTERPRETING IMAGES AND IDEAS** Review what you recorded in your **READER'S NOTEBOOK** about the images and ideas you found in the haiku, and compare them with those recorded by a classmate. Are there more similarities or more differences?

Extend Interpretations

5. **What If?** If the two haiku about autumn were about spring instead, what images might be used?

6. **Critic's Corner** Donald Keene, a scholar of Japanese literature, wrote that Bashō was able "to capture at once the eternal and the momentary" in his haiku. Briefly explain what you think Keene meant by this characterization of Bashō's poems. Then explain why you agree or disagree with the comment.

7. **Connect to Life** On the basis of your reading of these poems, do you think haiku have relevance for all cultures and times, or are they more relevant to a specific culture or era? Support your answer with evidence from the poems.

8. **Points of Comparison** Compare the haiku of Bashō and Issa with the poems of William Blake. Use the following criteria as your points of comparison:

THINK ABOUT {
- the subject matter of the poems
- the poets' **style** of writing
- the ideas expressed in the poems

Literary Analysis

HAIKU Through the use of precision, economy, and delicacy, **haiku** poetry has the ability to appeal to both the emotions and intelligence of its readers. The brevity of haiku can be misleading; their powerful effect comes as much from what is suggested as from what is directly said.

Cooperative Learning Activity With two other classmates, rate each haiku on a scale of 1 to 10 (10 being highest)—first, according to its emotional appeal and second, according to its appeal in terms of ideas expressed. Use a chart like the one below to record your ratings. Then compare the ratings with those of other groups. Analyze whether one or two of the poems had particular appeal to the class.

	Emotional Appeal	Ideas Expressed
Bashō		
Autumn . . .		
Wintry day . . .		
Skylark . . .		
Issa		
Nightingale . . .		
Lotus flowers . . .		
Autumn wind . . .		

Choices & CHALLENGES

Writing Options

1. Modern Haiku Think about various aspects of nature that have strong appeal to you. Then write an original haiku that conveys your reaction to this aspect of nature. Place the poem in your **Working Portfolio**.

2. Points of Comparison In a brief essay, discuss whether you think Blake and the haiku poets viewed nature in the same way. Cite evidence to support your opinion.

Inquiry & Research

Japanese Art Explore the Japanese arts of woodblock printing, calligraphy, painting, and pottery. What do these arts have in common with haiku? Create a bulletin-board display to illustrate the connections.

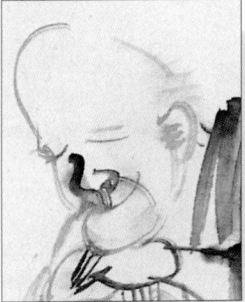

Matsuo Bashō
1644–1694

Humble Beginnings Bashō was born to a family of modest means. Early in life, he became friends with the son of a noble family, whose connections allowed Bashō to study with a prominent teacher of haiku. After his friend died, Bashō pursued a career as a professional haiku poet.

Writer and Teacher Around 1677, Bashō started his own school of haiku and by 1680 was the most famous Japanese poet of his day. In 1684, he began the first of many journeys through Japan—journeys that provided inspiration for much of his poetry. Teaching wherever he traveled, he had more than 2,000 students by the time of his death.

Legendary Figure One day, according to legend, a student announced that he had thought of a poem: "Pluck off the wings of a bright red dragonfly and there a pepper pod will be." Bashō informed him that he would never be a poet. A poet, according to Bashō, would have said: "Add but the wings to a bright red pepper pod and there a dragonfly will be." Whether or not the story is true, it reflects a compassion for living things that, along with his superb technical skills as a poet, has made Bashō a major figure in world literature.

Kobayashi Issa
1763–1828

Promising Student After leaving home at the age of 14, Kobayashi Issa studied under Chikua, a prominent haiku poet. When Chikua died in 1790, Issa took over as head of his school. Issa is known for simple, personal poetry that often touches upon two subjects: his love for insects and small animals and his poverty. Like Bashō, Issa traveled to many parts of Japan and was honored by leading poets of the day.

Poverty and Grief Issa dealt with adversity all his life. In spite of his talent, he lived most of his life in poverty, occasionally being forced to rely on friends for shelter. In 1813, a small inheritance from his family may have given Issa, then in his 50s, the means to marry for the first time. His first four children died in infancy, and his wife eventually died in childbirth. Issa's second marriage ended unhappily, and his only healthy child, the offspring of a third marriage, was born after the poet's death.

Author Study
William Wordsworth

> "He is the first poet
> to try to examine
> the human mind
> from a psychological
> viewpoint."
>
> —Margaret Drabble

England's Greatest Nature Poet

1770–1850

Outliving all the other major English romantic poets, William Wordsworth was a conservative figure by the time of his death in 1850. Yet five decades before, with his friend Samuel Taylor Coleridge, Wordsworth had ushered in a revolution in English poetry, championing the literary philosophy now called romanticism. Viewed as a nature poet, Wordsworth saw nature as a source of spiritual comfort to human beings. His romantic philosophy valued imagination and emotion over reason and stressed the importance of the individual. It also placed poetry at the very center of human experience.

CHILDHOOD TRAGEDY As a child, Wordsworth spent his free time taking in the sights and sounds of the Lake District in northern England, where his father worked as an estate manager. These happy times lasted only until he was seven, when his mother's death began a family breakup that continued with his father's death just five years later. Placed in the care of uncles, the young Wordsworth was sent to the finest schools,

1770	1778	1787	1795
Is born in the Lake District of northern England	Death of mother and break up family	Begins attending Cambridge University	Is reunited with his sister Dorothy; meets Samuel Taylor Coleridge

S.T. Coleridge

HIS LIFE
HIS TIMES

1770   **1780**   **1790**

1769	1776	1789
James Watt perfects the steam engine.	American colonies declare independence.	The French Revolution begins.

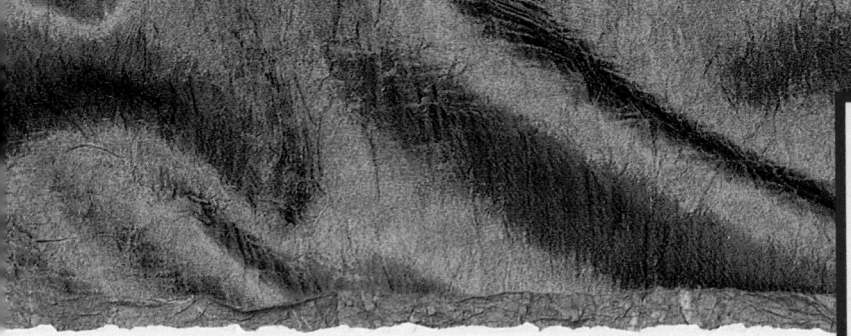

including Cambridge University, but he took little joy in them. He had already developed a deep appreciation for nature; by contrast, he found school life stifling and artificial.

ROMANCE AND REVOLUTION During a summer break from Cambridge in 1790, Wordsworth and a friend hiked through France and witnessed firsthand the effects of its recent revolution. Excited by the changes he saw, Wordsworth returned to France a year later, where he fell in love with a young woman named Annette Vallon. But before the two could marry, the outbreak of war between Britain and France forced Wordsworth to return home abruptly. The growing violence and steady erosion of democratic principles in France turned Wordsworth away from his ardent support of the revolution; and with France an enemy nation, for years he could do little to help the child Annette had borne him. The entire situation filled him with guilt and anxiety.

DOROTHY AND DORSETSHIRE One bright spot of Wordsworth's return to England was his reunion with his sister Dorothy, from whom he had been separated since childhood. Resolving not to be parted again, he and Dorothy moved to the western English county of Dorset. They lived near the poet Samuel Taylor Coleridge, whom Wordsworth had recently met. There the two men began

LITERARY *Contributions*

Hugely popular in the decades after his death, Wordsworth is still widely regarded as one of England's finest poets.

Lyric Poems Wordsworth is best known for lyric poetry of moderate length, including
> "Composed upon Westminster Bridge"
> "I Wandered Lonely as a Cloud"
> "I Traveled Among Unknown Men"
> "It Is a Beauteous Evening"
> "Lines Composed a Few Miles Above Tintern Abbey"
> "Lines Written in Early Spring"
> "London, 1802" (also called "To Milton")
> "My Heart Leaps Up"
> "Nuns Fret Not"
> "Ode: Intimations of Immortality"
> "She Dwelt Among the Untrodden Ways"
> "She Was a Phantom of Delight"
> "A Slumber Did My Spirit Seal"
> "The Solitary Reaper"
> "Strange Fits of Passion Have I Known"
> "Surprised by Joy"
> "The Tables Turned"
> "Three Years She Grew in Sun and Shower"
> "The World Is Too Much with Us"

Other Works Of Wordsworth's longer works, the most famous probably are the following:
> *The Excursion* (philosophical poem)
> *The Prelude* (autobiographical poem)
> Prefaces to *Lyrical Ballads* (prose)

| 1798 Publishes first edition of *Lyrical Ballads* with Coleridge | 1802 Marries Mary Hutchinson | 1805 Death by drowning of brother John; begins writing *The Prelude* | 1813 Wins appointment as revenue collector in the Lake District | 1820 Gains critical and public popularity with *The River Duddon* |

1800   **1810**   **1820**

Napoleon Bonaparte

| 1799 Napoleon Bonaparte comes to power in France. | 1808 German romantic poet Goethe publishes first part of *Faust*. | 1815 Napoleon is defeated at Waterloo; Parliament passes the Corn Laws. | 1816 Workers protest factory layoffs by destroying machinery. | 1829 London police force is established. |

the famous collaboration that would result in the publication of *Lyrical Ballads*. The poems in the collection, with their simple language and subject matter drawn largely from nature and common life, represented a sharp departure from the more formally crafted poetry of the day. Though now considered a cornerstone of England's romantic movement, *Lyrical Ballads* was praised by only a handful of critics when it was first published in 1798.

BACK TO THE LAKES A year later, Wordsworth and his sister settled in the Lake District of their childhood, with Coleridge for a time taking lodgings nearby. In 1802, Wordsworth married Mary Hutchinson, whom he had known since childhood, and over the next several years he continued to labor to win mainstream acceptance as a poet. Gradually, his reputation improved, enough so that by 1813 he was offered the post of local revenue collector, a patronage job showing appreciation for his literary achievements. By the 1820s, he was hugely popular, and in 1843 he was named Britain's poet laureate, succeeding his friend Robert Southey. Wordsworth died on April 23, 1850, and was buried in the Grasmere Churchyard.

More Online: Author Link
www.mcdougallittell.com

The Lake District

The Lake District, where Wordsworth was born and to which he returned in 1799, is a picturesque hilly area of northern England near the Scottish border. The names of many of the area's small lakes (and the towns on their banks) end in *mere*, from the Old English word for "pond": *Windermere* and *Grasmere,* for example. At the right is a photo of Dove Cottage, the house in Grasmere where Wordsworth lived, first with his sister, Dorothy, and later also with his wife and children.

Queen Victoria

1842
Publishes
Poems, Chiefly of Early and Late Years

1843
Succeeds Robert Southey as Britain's poet laureate

Robert Southey

1850
Dies at Rydal Mount, Westmoreland; publication of *The Prelude*

1830   **1840**   **1850**

1830
First railway opens between Manchester and Liverpool.

1832
First Reform Bill expands voting rights.

1837
Victoria becomes queen.

1845–46
Potato famine devastates Ireland.

PREPARING to *Read*

Selected Poems

By WILLIAM WORDSWORTH

Connect to Your Life

A Sense of Place Think about the places you have visited in your life. Which place made the strongest impression on you? What images leap to mind? Briefly describe the setting that so impressed you and the thoughts and feelings it inspired. Organize your details on a web diagram.

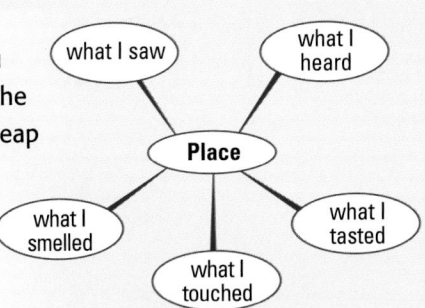

Build Background

Evocative Settings In almost all of the poems on the upcoming pages, Wordsworth describes a specific setting and expresses his thoughts and feelings about it. In "Lines Composed a Few Miles Above Tintern Abbey," he captures an outdoor scene in the Wye River Valley near the English-Welsh border, not far from the ruins of an old abbey. "Composed upon Westminster Bridge" expresses his feelings on seeing the city of London early one morning from a bridge spanning the River Thames. "It Is a Beauteous Evening" also focuses on a specific time of day and the feelings it evokes in the speaker. In "I Wandered Lonely as a Cloud," Wordsworth describes the daffodils he saw on a walk in England's Lake District, not far from the village of Grasmere, where he then lived.

Focus Your Reading

LITERARY ANALYSIS **IMAGERY** To capture the scenes he describes, Wordsworth makes frequent use of **imagery,** words and phrases that create a vivid sensory experience for the reader. The majority of images are visual, but imagery may also appeal to the senses of smell, hearing, taste, and touch. As you read Wordsworth's poetry, look for examples of imagery that help you imagine being in the scene he describes.

ACTIVE READING **DRAWING CONCLUSIONS** When you **draw conclusions,** you use information you already know as well as details in the poems to make logical statements about themes, attitudes, and feelings that are not directly stated. For example, read Wordsworth's description of London in early morning, when the city seems closest to nature:

> *This City now doth, like a garment, wear*
> *The beauty of the morning; silent, bare,*
> *Ships, towers, domes, theaters, and temples lie*
> *Open unto the fields, and to the sky;*
> *All bright and glittering in the smokeless air.*

The images describing the city's beauty also give you an idea of what London must be like after it has awakened, when the smoke, noise, and bustle of human activity (in the "ships, towers, domes, theaters, and temples") displace the early morning calm. You can then draw conclusions about Wordsworth's attitude toward nature in general and London in particular.

READER'S NOTEBOOK As you read Wordsworth's poems, use details in the poems—especially the imagery—plus your own experience with nature to draw conclusions about Wordsworth's reactions to nature. Record your conclusions.

William Wordsworth

Lines Composed
a Few Miles Above
Tintern Abbey

Five years have passed; five summers, with the length
Of five long winters! and again I hear
These waters, rolling from their mountain-springs
With a soft inland murmur. Once again
5 Do I behold these steep and lofty cliffs,
That on a wild secluded scene impress
Thoughts of more deep seclusion; and connect
The landscape with the quiet of the sky.
The day is come when I again repose
10 Here, under this dark sycamore, and view
These plots of cottage ground, these orchard tufts,
Which at this season, with their unripe fruits,
Are clad in one green hue, and lose themselves
'Mid groves and copses. Once again I see
15 These hedgerows, hardly hedgerows, little lines
Of sportive wood run wild; these pastoral farms,
Green to the very door; and wreaths of smoke
Sent up, in silence, from among the trees!
With some uncertain notice, as might seem
20 Of vagrant dwellers in the houseless woods,
Or of some Hermit's cave, where by his fire
The Hermit sits alone.

         These beauteous forms,
Through a long absence, have not been to me
As is a landscape to a blind man's eye;
25 But oft, in lonely rooms, and 'mid the din
Of towns and cities, I have owed to them,

GUIDE FOR READING

9 repose: lie at rest.

14 copses (kŏp'sĭz): thickets of small trees.

16 pastoral (păs'tər-əl): rural and serene.

20 vagrant: wandering.

The Seine at Giverny, Morning Mists (1897), Claude Monet. North Carolina Museum of Art, Raleigh, purchased with funds from the Sarah Graham Kenan Foundation and the North Carolina Art Society (Robert F. Phifer Bequest).

In hours of weariness, sensations sweet,
Felt in the blood, and felt along the heart;
And passing even into my purer mind,
30　With tranquil restoration—feelings too
Of unremembered pleasure; such, perhaps,
As have no slight or trivial influence
On that best portion of a good man's life,
His little, nameless, unremembered, acts
35　Of kindness and of love. Nor less, I trust,
To them I may have owed another gift,
Of aspect more sublime; that blessed mood,
In which the burthen of the mystery,
In which the heavy and the weary weight
40　Of all this unintelligible world,
Is lightened—that serene and blessed mood,
In which the affections gently lead us on—
Until, the breath of this corporeal frame
And even the motion of our human blood
45　Almost suspended, we are laid asleep
In body, and become a living soul;
While with an eye made quiet by the power
Of harmony, and the deep power of joy,
We see into the life of things.

　　　　　　　　　　　　　　If this
50　Be but a vain belief, yet, oh! how oft—
In darkness and amid the many shapes
Of joyless daylight; when the fretful stir
Unprofitable, and the fever of the world,
Have hung upon the beatings of my heart—
55　How oft, in spirit, have I turned to thee,
O sylvan Wye! thou wanderer through the woods,
How often has my spirit turned to thee!

38 burthen: burden.

43 corporeal (kôr-pôr′ē-əl): bodily.

56 sylvan: located in a wood or forest; **Wye:** a river in Wales and England.

22–57 What effect do you think the memory of the "beauteous forms" has on the speaker?

And now, with gleams of half-extinguished thought
With many recognitions dim and faint,
60 And somewhat of a sad perplexity,
The picture of the mind revives again;
While here I stand, not only with the sense
Of present pleasure, but with pleasing thoughts
That in this moment there is life and food
65 For future years. And so I dare to hope,
Though changed, no doubt, from what I was when first
I came among these hills; when like a roe
I bounded o'er the mountains, by the sides
Of the deep rivers, and the lonely streams,
70 Wherever nature led—more like a man
Flying from something that he dreads than one
Who sought the thing he loved. For nature then
(The coarser pleasures of my boyish days,
And their glad animal movements all gone by)
75 To me was all in all.—I cannot paint
What then I was. The sounding cataract
Haunted me like a passion; the tall rock,
The mountain, and the deep and gloomy wood,
Their colors and their forms, were then to me
80 An appetite; a feeling and a love,
That had no need of a remoter charm,
By thought supplied, nor any interest
Unborrowed from the eye.—That time is past,
And all its aching joys are now no more,
85 And all its dizzy raptures. Not for this
Faint I, nor mourn nor murmur; other gifts
Have followed; for such loss, I would believe,
Abundant recompense. For I have learned
To look on nature, not as in the hour
90 Of thoughtless youth; but hearing oftentimes
The still, sad music of humanity,
Nor harsh nor grating, though of ample power
To chasten and subdue. And I have felt
A presence that disturbs me with the joy
95 Of elevated thoughts; a sense sublime
Of something far more deeply interfused,
Whose dwelling is the light of setting suns,
And the round ocean and the living air,
And the blue sky, and in the mind of man:

64–65 What does the speaker suggest by saying "there is life and food / For future years"?

67 roe: deer.

76 cataract: waterfall.

67–83 Notice how the speaker formerly responded to nature.

88 recompense: compensation. Here the speaker begins to describe what he has received in place of the "aching joys" and "dizzy raptures" of youth.

93 chasten (chā′sən): scold; make modest.

100 A motion and a spirit, that impels
All thinking things, all objects of all thought,
And rolls through all things. Therefore am I still
A lover of the meadows and the woods,
And mountains; and of all that we behold
105 From this green earth; of all the mighty world
Of eye, and ear—both what they half create,
And what perceive; well pleased to recognize
In nature and the language of the sense
The anchor of my purest thoughts, the nurse,
110 The guide, the guardian of my heart, and soul
Of all my moral being.

              Nor perchance,
If I were not thus taught, should I the more
Suffer my genial spirits to decay:
For thou art with me here upon the banks
115 Of this fair river; thou my dearest Friend,
My dear, dear Friend; and in thy voice I catch
The language of my former heart, and read
My former pleasures in the shooting lights
Of thy wild eyes. Oh! yet a little while
120 May I behold in thee what I was once,
My dear, dear Sister! and this prayer I make,
Knowing that Nature never did betray
The heart that loved her; 'tis her privilege,
Through all the years of this our life, to lead
125 From joy to joy: for she can so inform
The mind that is within us, so impress
With quietness and beauty, and so feed
With lofty thoughts, that neither evil tongues,
Rash judgments, nor the sneers of selfish men,
130 Nor greetings where no kindness is, nor all
The dreary intercourse of daily life,
Shall e'er prevail against us, or disturb
Our cheerful faith, that all which we behold
Is full of blessings. Therefore let the moon
135 Shine on thee in thy solitary walk;
And let the misty mountain winds be free
To blow against thee: and, in after years,
When these wild ecstasies shall be matured
Into a sober pleasure; when thy mind
140 Shall be a mansion for all lovely forms,
Thy memory be as a dwelling place
For all sweet sounds and harmonies; oh! then,

115 thou my dearest Friend:
Wordsworth's sister, Dorothy.

119–120 The speaker sees in his sister's response to nature a mirror of his own youthful response.

121 Note the "prayer" the speaker has made. What does he hope for his sister?

If solitude, or fear, or pain, or grief
Should be thy portion, with what healing thoughts
145 Of tender joy wilt thou remember me,
And these my exhortations! Nor, perchance—
If I should be where I no more can hear
Thy voice, nor catch from thy wild eyes these gleams
Of past existence—wilt thou then forget
150 That on the banks of this delightful stream
We stood together; and that I, so long
A worshiper of Nature, hither came
Unwearied in that service; rather say
With warmer love—oh! with far deeper zeal
155 Of holier love. Nor wilt thou then forget,
That after many wanderings, many years
Of absence, these steep woods and lofty cliffs,
And this green pastoral landscape, were to me
More dear, both for themselves and for thy sake!

146 exhortations: words of encouraging advice.

Thinking Through the Literature

1. Use details provided by the visual imagery to sketch a memorable scene depicted in the poem. Share your sketch with classmates.

2. What effect does nature seem to have on the speaker in the present, and how is that different from its effect in the past? Use details from the poem to support your answer.

3. Do you think the speaker regrets his loss of youth? Explain.

   - the way he reacted to nature as a youth in lines 67–83
   - his reference to "other gifts" in line 86
   - his reaction to his sister's presence

4. Considering what you know about Wordsworth and his feelings expressed in this poem, what conclusions can you draw about his relationship with his sister? Why does showing her the scene a few miles above Tintern Abbey have special meaning for him?

William Wordsworth

Composed upon Westminster Bridge,
September 3, 1802

The Thames Below Westminster (1871), Claude Monet. National Gallery, London, Bridgeman/Art Resource, New York.

Earth has not anything to show more fair:
Dull would he be of soul who could pass by
A sight so touching in its majesty;
This City now doth, like a garment, wear
5   The beauty of the morning; silent, bare,
Ships, towers, domes, theaters, and temples lie
Open unto the fields, and to the sky;
All bright and glittering in the smokeless air.
Never did sun more beautifully steep
10   In his first splendor, valley, rock, or hill;
Ne'er saw I, never felt, a calm so deep!
The river glideth at his own sweet will:
Dear God! the very houses seem asleep;
And all that mighty heart is lying still!

GUIDE FOR READING

4 this City: London.

9 steep: soak; saturate.

12 the river: the Thames (tĕmz)— the principal river in London.

13 houses: Westminster Bridge is next to the Houses of Parliament; this word may therefore have a double meaning.

14 What do you think "that mighty heart" might be?

William Wordsworth

The World Is
Too Much with Us

The world is too much with us; late and soon,
Getting and spending, we lay waste our powers;
Little we see in Nature that is ours;
We have given our hearts away, a sordid boon!
5   This Sea that bares her bosom to the moon,
The winds that will be howling at all hours,
And are up-gathered now like sleeping flowers,
For this, for everything, we are out of tune;
It moves us not.—Great God! I'd rather be
10 A Pagan suckled in a creed outworn;
So might I, standing on this pleasant lea,
Have glimpses that would make me less forlorn;
Have sight of Proteus rising from the sea;
Or hear old Triton blow his wreathéd horn.

GUIDE FOR READING

2–3 What does the speaker say alienates us from nature?

4 sordid boon: selfish or ignoble gift.

10 a Pagan: a non-Christian (in this case, a worshiper of the gods of ancient Greece). In the following lines, note what the speaker thinks a pagan could do that he cannot.

11 lea: meadow.

13–14 Proteus (prō'tē-əs) . . . **Triton** (trīt'n): sea gods of Greek mythology. Why do you think the speaker considers it an advantage to be able to see Proteus or hear Triton?

Thinking Through the Literature

1. What words came to mind when you read these two **sonnets?** Discuss your reactions with a partner.

2. In "Composed upon Westminster Bridge," the speaker praises the beauty of the city; but in "The World Is Too Much with Us," the speaker finds more value in the natural world. How do you explain this apparent contradiction?

3. With which of these two poems' speakers do you identify more strongly? Explain your response.

Mortlake Terrace (1827), Joseph Mallord William Turner. Oil on canvas,
36¼″ × 48⅛″, National Gallery of Art, Washington, D.C.,
Andrew W. Mellon Collection. Photo by Richard Carafelli.

IT IS A BEAUTEOUS EVENING

It is a beauteous evening, calm and free,
The holy time is quiet as a Nun
Breathless with adoration; the broad sun
Is sinking down in its tranquility;
5   The gentleness of heaven broods o'er the Sea:
Listen! the mighty Being is awake,
And doth with his eternal motion make
A sound like thunder—everlastingly.
Dear Child! dear Girl! that walkest with me here,
10 If thou appear untouched by solemn thought,
Thy nature is not therefore less divine:
Thou liest in Abraham's bosom all the year,
And worship'st at the Temple's inner shrine,
God being with thee when we know it not.

GUIDE FOR READING

5 broods: hovers protectively.

9 dear Child: Wordsworth's
daughter Caroline.

12 in Abraham's bosom: in the
presence of God.

10–14 Why does the speaker say
that the child's less thoughtful
response to the evening does not
imply a less divine nature?

William Wordsworth

I WANDERED LONELY
As
A CLOUD

I wandered lonely as a cloud
That floats on high o'er vales and hills,
When all at once I saw a crowd,
A host, of golden daffodils;
5   Beside the lake, beneath the trees,
Fluttering and dancing in the breeze.

Continuous as the stars that shine
And twinkle on the milky way,
They stretched in never-ending line
10 Along the margin of a bay:
Ten thousand saw I at a glance,
Tossing their heads in sprightly dance.

The waves beside them danced; but they
Outdid the sparkling waves in glee;
15 A poet could not but be gay,
In such a jocund company;
I gazed—and gazed—but little thought
What wealth the show to me had brought:

For oft, when on my couch I lie
20 In vacant or in pensive mood,
They flash upon that inward eye
Which is the bliss of solitude;
And then my heart with pleasure fills,
And dances with the daffodils.

GUIDE FOR READING

16 jocund (jŏk'ənd): merry.

20 pensive: dreamily thoughtful.

21 What do you think the speaker is referring to when he speaks of "that inward eye"?

DOROTHY WORDSWORTH

from the

Grasmere Journals

Build Background

Much of Wordsworth's inspiration for his poetry came during his frequent walks with his sister Dorothy, first in western England and later in the picturesque Lake District. In her journals, Dorothy recorded her own observations about the sights and sounds they encountered. It was not unusual for Wordsworth to read and borrow from the descriptions in his sister's journal, particularly when he was writing a poem about a scene that they had observed months, or even years, before. This excerpt from Dorothy's journals kept at Grasmere, in the Lake District, records the same scene that inspired Wordsworth's "I Wandered Lonely as a Cloud."

Focus Your Reading

PRIMARY SOURCES JOURNAL

Private journals, like personal letters, are valuable **primary sources** that offer insights into the everyday lives of historical figures. As you read this journal entry, think about what it tells you about both brother and sister.

Apr. 15.

It was a threatening misty morning—but mild. We [Dorothy and William] set off after dinner from Eusemere.

Mrs. Clarkson went a short way with us but turned back. The wind was furious and we thought we must have returned. We first rested in the large Boat-house, then under a furze Bush opposite Mr. Clarkson's. Saw the plough going in the field. The wind seized our breath the Lake was rough. There was a Boat by itself floating in the middle of the Bay below Water Millock. We rested again in the Water Millock Lane. The hawthorns are black and green, the birches here and there greenish but there is yet more of purple to be seen on the Twigs. We got over into a field to avoid some cows—people working, a few primroses by the roadside, wood-sorrel flower, the anemone, scentless violets, strawberries, and that starry yellow flower which Mrs. C. calls pile wort. When we were in the woods beyond Gowbarrow park we saw a few daffodils close to the water side. We fancied that the lake had floated the seeds ashore and that the little colony had so sprung up. But as we went along there were more and yet more and at last under the boughs

of the trees, we saw that there was a long belt of them along the shore, about the breadth of a country turnpike road. I never saw daffodils so beautiful they grew among the mossy stones about and about them, some rested their heads upon these stones as on a pillow for weariness and the rest tossed and reeled and danced and seemed as if they verily laughed at the wind that blew upon them over the lake, they looked so gay ever glancing ever changing. This wind blew directly over the lake to them. There was here and there a little knot and a few stragglers a few yards higher up but they were so few as not to disturb the simplicity and unity and life of that one busy high- way. We rested again and again. The Bays were stormy, and we heard the waves at different distances and in the middle of the water like the sea.

Thinking Through the Literature

1. What did you learn about Dorothy Wordsworth while reading her journal entry?

2. What, if any, insights into William Wordsworth did this journal entry give you?

3. **Comparing Texts** How does Dorothy's response to the daffodils compare with her brother's? What similarities do you see in the **imagery** and the feelings expressed?

Thinking through the LITERATURE

Connect to the Literature

1. What Do You Think? What images remain in your mind after reading "It Is a Beauteous Evening" and "I Wandered Lonely as a Cloud"?

Comprehension Check
- To what religious figure does Wordsworth compare the beauteous evening?
- What does the speaker come across unexpectedly in "I Wandered Lonely as a Cloud"?
- When does the speaker think of the daffodils again?

Think Critically

2. How would you describe the **speakers** of the two poems?

THINK ABOUT

- each speaker's comments about nature
- the speaker's comments about his daughter in lines 10–14 of "It Is a Beauteous Evening"
- the reference to "that inward eye" in line 21 of "I Wandered Lonely as a Cloud"

3. **ACTIVE READING** **DRAWING CONCLUSIONS** Recall the conclusions you reached in your **READER'S NOTEBOOK** about Wordsworth's reactions to nature. What did nature mean to Wordsworth? Refer to the **imagery, figurative language,** and direct statements in Wordsworth's poems.

4. In what way is the scene described in "It Is a Beauteous Evening" similar to the scene in "Composed upon Westminster Bridge"? How are they different?

5. How is the experience described in the last stanza of "I Wandered Lonely as a Cloud" similar to that in "Lines Composed a Few Miles Above Tintern Abbey"?

Extend Interpretations

6. Comparing Texts Compare Wordsworth's treatment of innocence and experience with that of William Blake. How do the two poets differ in their attitudes toward experience and loss of youth?

7. Critic's Corner Samuel Taylor Coleridge praised Wordsworth for capturing "the perfect truth of nature in his images and descriptions." Do you agree with this assessment of Wordsworth's writing? Support your answer with examples.

8. Connect to Life If Wordsworth were alive today, what do you think he would say about our treatment of the environment and such scientific experiments as cloning? Explain.

Literary Analysis

IMAGERY Among the many tools of poets, few are more important than **imagery,** the use of words and phrases that create vivid sensory experiences for the reader. Imagery can appeal to all five senses: sight, smell, hearing, taste, and touch. Notice how the image in these lines from "Tintern Abbey" appeals to both sight and hearing:

These waters, rolling from their
   mountain-springs
With a soft inland murmur.

Cooperative Learning Activity With a small group of classmates, list three examples of imagery from Wordsworth's poems in a chart like the one below. Discuss how the imagery helps create a particular mood or convey a particular idea or emotion.

Image	Poem/Line(s)	Sense(s) Appealed to
These waters . . . inland murmur	"Tintern Abbey"	sight, hearing

REVIEW **SIMILE** The statement, "I wandered lonely as a cloud," uses a simile to add deeper meaning to the speaker's experience. For example, the simile connects the speaker to nature and emphasizes the harmony between them; the simile also sets up a lighthearted, carefree mood that complements the pleasurable images and feelings in the poem. Find three more similes in Wordsworth's poems and analyze how they add to the meaning of the poems.

THE AUTHOR'S STYLE
Wordsworth's Romantic Style

Wordsworth stated the poetic philosophy of romanticism in his preface to *Lyrical Ballads* in 1798. In subsequent editions of the book, he continued to revise his preface to further clarify what he was trying to do. The aspects of his style, therefore, come not only from his own poetry but from his statements about poetry as well.

Key Aspects of Wordsworth's Style

- images drawn from nature to show connections between humans and the natural world
- direct statements of emotions
- philosophical statements of personal beliefs
- ordinary experiences, objects, and people transformed by the imagination and presented in an unusual way
- simple diction, or word choice, to express complicated feelings and abstract concepts

---

Analysis of Style

Study the aspects of Wordsworth's style and read the samples of his poetry at the right. Then complete these activities:

- Find examples of each aspect of Wordsworth's style in the samples.

- Point out other characteristics in the samples that you think distinguish Wordsworth's poetry from other types of poetry.

- Go back through the poems in this Author Study and find further examples that illustrate these key aspects of Wordsworth's style.

Applications

1. **Imitating Style** Imitate Wordsworth's style in either a short poem or a paragraph. Try to capture Wordsworth's simplicity of subject matter and language, while expressing deep emotion and/or thought. Share your work with your classmates.

2. **Changing Style** With a partner, paraphrase, or restate in your own words, three of Wordsworth's philosophical explanations in poems such as "Tintern Abbey," "The World Is Too Much with Us," and "It Is a Beauteous Evening." What gets lost in the paraphrase?

3. **Analyzing Wordsworth's Sonnet Style** All three sonnets in this Author Study are Petrarchan. With a small group of classmates, review the structure of the Petrarchan sonnet on page 308, and then analyze one of Wordsworth's sonnets by (a) tracing the rhyme scheme, (b) paraphrasing the issue or the emotional response set up in the octave, and (c) explaining the conclusions drawn in the sestet.

---

from **"She Dwelt Among the Untrodden Ways"**

She dwelt among the untrodden ways
  Beside the springs of Dove,
A Maid whom there were none to praise
  And very few to love;

A violet by a mossy stone
  Half hidden from the eye!
—Fair as a star, when only one
  Is shining in the sky.

"My Heart Leaps Up"

My heart leaps up when I behold
  A rainbow in the sky:
So was it when my life began;
So is it now I am a man;
So be it when I shall grow old,
  Or let me die!
The Child is father of the Man;
And I could wish my days to be
Bound each to each by natural piety.

---

from **"Lines Composed a Few Miles Above Tintern Abbey"**

  And I have felt
A presence that disturbs me with the joy
Of elevated thoughts; a sense sublime
Of something far more deeply interfused,
Whose dwelling is the light of setting suns,
And the round ocean and the living air,
And the blue sky, and in the mind of man:
A motion and a spirit, that impels
All thinking things, all objects of all thought,
And rolls through all things.

Choices & CHALLENGES

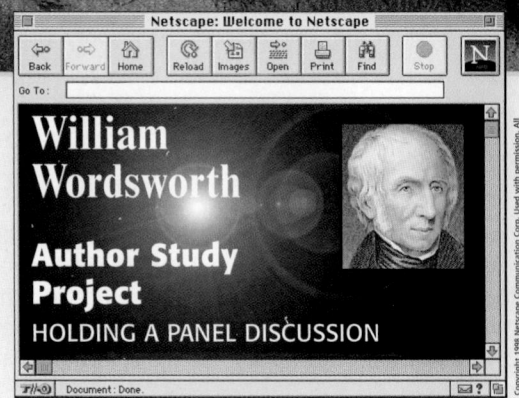

Writing Options

1. Dorothy's Journal Write the journal entry that Dorothy Wordsworth might have written after visiting the area near Tintern Abbey with her brother.

2. Poem About a Place Write a poem about the setting you described for Connect to Your Life on page 725. Describe the setting and your feelings about it.

3. Poetic Comparison Write a paragraph or two comparing "Lines Composed a Few Miles Above Tintern Abbey" and "I Wandered Lonely as a Cloud." Discuss the experiences in both poems as well as the view of nature expressed.

You might use a Venn diagram like this one to organize your ideas. Place the comparison in your **Working Portfolio.**

Writing Handbook
See page 1367: Compare and Contrast.

Activities & Explorations

1. Poem in Pictures Working with several classmates or alone, illustrate the scene described in one of Wordsworth's poems. Use the visual imagery to help you capture the scene in a drawing, a collage, or even a large mural to decorate your classroom. **~ ART**

2. Nature Debate With a partner, debate the view of nature depicted in Wordsworth's poetry. One of you should support Wordsworth's view; the other might refute it by discussing the more threatening side of nature or by stressing the value of science and reason over nature.
~ SPEAKING AND LISTENING

Inquiry & Research

Social History Report Research and report on the early Industrial Revolution and the accompanying revolution in agriculture that were changing the English landscape in Wordsworth's day. Create a poster or other visual to illuminate the romantic poet's turn to nature.

William Wordsworth

Author Study Project

HOLDING A PANEL DISCUSSION

How was *Lyrical Ballads* received by other writers? What did contemporary figures other than writers—such as King George IV, the artist J. M. W. Turner, the influential duke of Wellington, the inventor James Watt, and the political philosopher Jeremy Bentham—think of Wordsworth? Research the answers to these and related questions, and present your findings in a panel discussion in which each participant takes the role of a different person famous in the romantic period (1798–1832). Before the discussion starts, the panelists should introduce themselves and give a brief summary of their achievements. One student should serve as moderator, asking questions when necessary to keep the discussion moving.

Primary Print Sources Consult reviews and other literary criticism of the day, including works by famous romantic prose writers Samuel Taylor Coleridge, William Hazlitt, Thomas De Quincey, and Charles Lamb. Also consider Dorothy Wordsworth's journals and personal writing by later romantic writers, such as Sir Walter Scott, Lord Byron, Percy Bysshe Shelley, Mary Shelley, and John Keats.

Secondary Sources Consult histories, articles in literary journals, historical and biographical entries in reference works, and biographies of different personalities from Wordsworth's era.

Web Sites Reliable Web sites could provide useful information on Wordsworth and the romantic period. Also consider scholarly Web sites maintained by university English departments and established poetry societies.

More Online: Research Starter
www.mcdougallittell.com

Kubla Khan

Poetry by SAMUEL TAYLOR COLERIDGE

Connect to Your Life

Dream a Little Dream Have you ever had a dream so vivid that you wanted to write it down or tell someone about it? Were you able to recapture the mood of your dream when you described it? Discuss your experience with your classmates.

Build Background

Dream Vision Samuel Taylor Coleridge was an influential poet, critic, and philosopher who, like his good friend William Wordsworth, was a leading figure in the English romantic movement. Like other poets of the era, Coleridge responded to nature with intense emotion. In poems such as "Kubla Khan," he wrote enthusiastically not only about the beauty and serenity of nature but also about its savagery and wildness.

The circumstances surrounding the composition of "Kubla Khan" are almost as well-known as the poem itself. According to Coleridge, he had been reading about the building of a summer palace for Kublai Khan, the great 13th-century Mongol ruler, when he fell asleep in his chair as a result of a painkilling drug he had taken. In his sleep, Coleridge later reported, the images of the poem "rose up before him as *things*, . . . without any sensation or consciousness of effort." When he awoke, he began writing the poem down, but at line 54 he was interrupted by a visitor who needed to see him on business. When he returned to the poem, he was unable to remember the rest of his dream. Coleridge therefore called the lines he had written a "fragment" and "a vision in a dream."

Focus Your Reading

LITERARY ANALYSIS ONOMATOPOEIA **Onomatopoeia** (ŏn′ə-măt′ə-pē′ə) is the use of words whose sounds suggest their meanings—such as *buzz* and *murmur*—or of language that echoes the sound of what is being described. In "Kubla Khan," Coleridge made use of onomatopoeia and many other **sound devices.** As you read, be aware of the musical quality that these devices add to the poem.

ACTIVE READING ANALYZING STRUCTURE **Structure** is the organization of details in a literary work—the way in which the parts of the work are put together. Understanding a work's structure can help you understand its meaning. "Kubla Khan" is divided into three parts, which might be called the **thesis,** the **antithesis,** and the **synthesis:**

- thesis—presents a vision
- antithesis—presents a contrasting vision
- synthesis—pulls together the two visions

READER'S NOTEBOOK
As you read, use a diagram similar to the one shown to note where these parts begin and end and what each part of the poem describes.

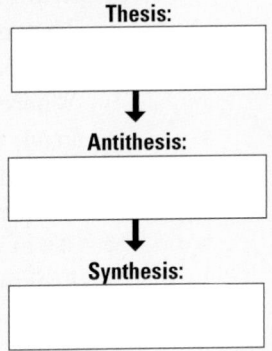

Thesis:

Antithesis:

Synthesis:

Samuel Taylor Coleridge
Kubla

In Xanadu did Kubla Khan
A stately pleasure dome decree:
Where Alph, the sacred river, ran
Through caverns measureless to man
5   Down to a sunless sea.
So twice five miles of fertile ground
With walls and towers were girdled round:
And there were gardens bright with sinuous rills,
Where blossomed many an incense-bearing tree;
10 And here were forests ancient as the hills,
Enfolding sunny spots of greenery.

But oh! that deep romantic chasm which slanted
Down the green hill athwart a cedarn cover!
A savage place! as holy and enchanted
15 As e'er beneath a waning moon was haunted
By woman wailing for her demon lover!
And from this chasm, with ceaseless turmoil seething,
As if this earth in fast thick pants were breathing,
A mighty fountain momently was forced:
20 Amid whose swift half-intermitted burst
Huge fragments vaulted like rebounding hail,
Or chaffy grain beneath the thresher's flail:
And 'mid these dancing rocks at once and ever
It flung up momently the sacred river.
25 Five miles meandering with a mazy motion
Through wood and dale the sacred river ran,
Then reached the caverns measureless to man,
And sank in tumult to a lifeless ocean:
And 'mid this tumult Kubla heard from far
30 Ancestral voices prophesying war!
    The shadow of the dome of pleasure
    Floated midway on the waves;
    Where was heard the mingled measure
    From the fountain and the caves.
35 It was a miracle of rare device,
A sunny pleasure dome with caves of ice!

    A damsel with a dulcimer
    In a vision once I saw:

It was an Abyssinian maid,
40   And on her dulcimer she played,
    Singing of Mount Abora.
Could I revive within me
Her symphony and song,
To such a deep delight 'twould win me,
45 That with music loud and long,
I would build that dome in air,
That sunny dome! those caves of ice!
And all who heard should see them there,
And all should cry, Beware! Beware!
50 His flashing eyes, his floating hair!
Weave a circle round him thrice,
And close your eyes with holy dread,
For he on honeydew hath fed,
And drunk the milk of Paradise.

39 Abyssinian: from Abyssinia, now called Ethiopia.

41 Mount Abora: a legendary earthly paradise like Kubla Khan's.

46 What would the speaker do if he were able? What do you think the Abyssinian maid symbolizes?

48 Note in the following lines what effect the speaker's song and appearance will have on others.

53 honeydew: an ideally sweet or luscious substance.

54 What kind of experience would it be to drink "the milk of Paradise"?

In a Harem Garden (about 1765), attributed to Faiz Allah of Faizabad, Mughal empire. Opaque watercolor on paper. The David Collection, Copenhagen, Denmark.

Connect to the Literature

1. What Do You Think? What **image** in the poem did you find most striking? Compare your opinion with a classmate's.

> **Comprehension Check**
> • Who orders a dome built in Xanadu?
> • What do ancestral voices prophesy to Kubla Khan?

Think Critically

2. How would you describe the world of Kubla Khan as it is depicted in this poem?

THINK ABOUT

> • the description of the **setting** (lines 1–11)
> • the **details** about the chasm (lines 12–16)
> • the description of the river (lines 17–28)

3. This poem contains a curious blend of **contrasting images**—images of lush natural beauty and images of sinister, dark mystery. Why do you think the poet used such contradictory images?

4. Which do you think contributes more to the beauty of Kubla Khan's pleasure dome—human effort or nature?

5. Reread lines 37–54. Why would those who heard the speaker's music cry "Beware, beware"?

6. **ACTIVE READING** **ANALYZING STRUCTURE** Consult the diagram you created in your **📖 READER'S NOTEBOOK.** How do the three parts of the poem work together to create a unified whole?

Extend Interpretations

7. Critic's Corner Algernon Charles Swinburne, a noted 19th-century English poet and critic, wrote, "In reading it ["Kubla Khan"] we seem rapt into that paradise . . . where music and color and perfume were one, where you could hear the hues and see the harmonies of heaven." Do you agree? Defend your position.

8. Connect to Life The world depicted in "Kubla Khan" is strange and exotic, even magical. Think about modern movies, books, and television shows that feature magical or unusual situations. Do you think people are still fascinated by the exotic?

Literary Analysis

ONOMATOPOEIA In its simplest form, **onomatopoeia** is the use of words—such as *crash, groan,* and *boom*—whose sounds suggest their meanings. Onomatopoeia can, however, involve more than the use of such words. Skilled writers, especially poets, choose words whose sounds suggest both their **denotations** and their **connotations.** For example, in this line from "Kubla Khan," the **rhythm** and the repeated *m* and *n* sounds suggest the sound of the lazily winding river that is being described:

Five miles meandering with a mazy motion

Paired Activity With a partner, take turns reading aloud lines 12–24, listening for examples of onomatopoeia. Record your observations, then compare your notes with those of other pairs.

REVIEW **ALLITERATION AND RHYME**

Find examples of **alliteration**—the repetition of consonant sounds at the beginning of words—in "Kubla Khan." Notice, too, patterns of **rhyme** in the poem. Jot down examples of alliteration, and note the variations you observe in the rhyme. How do these **sound devices** affect your reading of the poem?

observations about rhyme:

examples of alliteration:

The Rime of the Ancient Mariner

Narrative Poetry by SAMUEL TAYLOR COLERIDGE

Connect to Your Life

Long Day's Journey Think of the worst trip you ever took. What made the journey so unpleasant? Was it bad traffic, a vehicle breakdown, or something far more dangerous? Whatever it was, how did you feel when you finally reached your destination? Discuss your experience with your classmates.

Build Background

Partners in Rhyme Coleridge and his neighbor William Wordsworth collaborated on the writing of the poems in *Lyrical Ballads.* "It was agreed," Coleridge later wrote, "that my endeavors should be directed to persons and characters supernatural, or at least romantic. . . . Mr. Wordsworth, on the other hand, was to propose to himself as his object, to give the charm of novelty to things of every day." One of the "supernatural" poems that Coleridge created for the book was "The Rime of the Ancient Mariner." According to Wordsworth, *The Ancient Mariner* was founded on a strange dream, which a friend of Coleridge had, who fancied he saw a skeleton ship, with figures in it. . . . I had very little share in the composition of it." Wordsworth did in fact contribute a few lines to the poem and suggested several details of its plot. The italicized marginal explanations were added by Coleridge in later printings of the poem.

At Sea Before the advent of steamships in the early 19th century, sea voyages were quite dangerous. Traveling at the mercy of winds and currents, sailing ships sometimes took months or even years to reach their destinations. In "The Rime of the Ancient Mariner," an old mariner, or sailor, tells an exciting tale about a perilous voyage in which his ship was blown into waters near the South Pole and then into the Pacific Ocean. To capture the flavor of an earlier era, Coleridge used a number of obsolete words and word forms, such as *stoppeth, swounds,* and *eftsoons.*

Focus Your Reading

LITERARY ANALYSIS LITERARY BALLAD

Originally, a **ballad** was a narrative poem that was intended to be sung. Although traditional **folk ballads** were written by unknown authors and handed down orally, **literary ballads** are the products of writers' conscious efforts to imitate the folk-ballad style. The literary ballad became popular during the romantic period. As you read "The Rime of the Ancient Mariner," listen for its musical qualities.

ACTIVE READING READING NARRATIVE POETRY

Like all ballads, "The Rime of the Ancient Mariner" is a **narrative poem**—a poem that tells a story. It thus contains many of the basic elements of a prose story: **plot, conflict, setting, character, point of view,** and **theme.**

READER'S NOTEBOOK While reading "The Rime of the Ancient Mariner," jot down notes to help you answer the following questions:

- In what **setting** do the events unfold?
- Who are the **characters?**
- From whose **point of view** is the story told?
- How would you summarize the **plot?**
- What are the major **conflicts?**
- What **themes** are central to the poem?

The RIME of the ANCIENT MARINER

S a m u e l   T a y l o r   C o l e r i d g e

How a Ship, having first sailed to the Equator, was driven by storms to the cold Country towards the South Pole; how the Ancient Mariner cruelly and in contempt of the laws of hospitality killed a Seabird and how he was followed by many strange Judgments; and in what manner he came back to his own Country.

Engravings by Gustave Doré

PART I

It is an ancient Mariner,
And he stoppeth one of three.
"By thy long grey beard and glittering eye,
Now wherefore stopp'st thou me?

5   The Bridegroom's doors are opened wide,
And I am next of kin;
The guests are met, the feast is set:
May'st hear the merry din."

He holds him with his skinny hand,
10 "There was a ship," quoth he.
"Hold off! unhand me, grey-beard loon!"
Eftsoons his hand dropped he.

He holds him with his glittering eye—
The Wedding-Guest stood still,
15 And listens like a three years' child:
The Mariner hath his will.

The Wedding-Guest sat on a stone:
He cannot choose but hear;
And thus spake on that ancient man,
20 The bright-eyed Mariner.

"The ship was cheered, the harbor cleared,
Merrily did we drop
Below the kirk, below the hill,
Below the lighthouse top.

25 The Sun came up upon the left,
Out of the sea came he!
And he shone bright, and on the right
Went down into the sea.

Higher and higher every day,
30 Till over the mast at noon—"
The Wedding-Guest here beat his breast,
For he heard the loud bassoon.

The bride hath paced into the hall,
Red as a rose is she;
35 Nodding their heads before her goes
The merry minstrelsy.

An ancient Mariner meeteth three Gallants bidden to a wedding feast, and detaineth one.

4 wherefore: why.

12 eftsoons: quickly.

The Wedding Guest is spellbound by the eye of the old seafaring man, and constrained to hear his tale.

23 kirk: church.

The Mariner tells how the ship sailed southward with a good wind and fair weather, till it reached the Line.

30 over . . . noon: The ship has reached the equator, or "Line."

The Wedding Guest heareth the bridal music; but the Mariner continueth his tale.

36 minstrelsy: group of musicians.

The Wedding-Guest he beat his breast,
Yet he cannot choose but hear;
And thus spake on that ancient man,
40 The bright-eyed Mariner.

"And now the Storm-blast came, and he
Was tyrannous and strong:
He struck with his o'ertaking wings,
And chased us south along.

45 With sloping masts and dipping prow,
As who pursued with yell and blow
Still treads the shadow of his foe,
And forward bends his head,
The ship drove fast, loud roared the blast,
50 And southward aye we fled.

And now there came both mist and snow,
And it grew wondrous cold:
And ice, mast-high, came floating by,
As green as emerald.

55 And through the drifts the snowy clifts
Did send a dismal sheen:
Nor shapes of men nor beasts we ken—
The ice was all between.

The ice was here, the ice was there,
60 The ice was all around:
It cracked and growled, and roared and howled,
Like noises in a swound!

At length did cross an Albatross,
Thorough the fog it came;
65 As if it had been a Christian soul,
We hailed it in God's name.

It ate the food it ne'er had eat,
And round and round it flew.
The ice did split with a thunder-fit;
70 The helmsman steered us through!

And a good south wind sprung up behind;
The Albatross did follow,
And every day, for food or play,
Came to the mariners' hollo!

The ship driven by a storm toward the South Pole.

The land of ice, and of fearful sounds where no living thing was to be seen.

55 clifts: cliffs.

57 ken: perceive.

62 swound: swoon; fainting fit.

Till a great sea bird, called the Albatross, came through the snow-fog, and was received with great joy and hospitality.

63 Albatross (ăl′bə-trôs′): a large, web-footed ocean bird common in the Southern Hemisphere.

And lo! the Albatross proveth a bird of good omen, and followeth the ship as it returned northward through fog and floating ice.

74 hollo (hä′lō): call.

75　In mist or cloud, on mast or shroud,
　　It perched for vespers nine;
　　Whiles all the night, through fog-smoke white,
　　Glimmered the white moonshine."

　　"God save thee, ancient Mariner,
80　From the fiends, that plague thee thus!—
　　Why look'st thou so?"—With my crossbow
　　I shot the Albatross.

PART II

　　The Sun now rose upon the right:
　　Out of the sea came he,
85　Still hid in mist, and on the left
　　Went down into the sea.

　　And the good south wind still blew behind,
　　But no sweet bird did follow,
　　Nor any day for food or play
90　Came to the mariners' hollo!

　　And I had done a hellish thing,
　　And it would work 'em woe:
　　For all averred I had killed the bird
　　That made the breeze to blow.
95　Ah wretch! said they, the bird to slay,
　　That made the breeze to blow!

　　Nor dim nor red, like God's own head,
　　The glorious Sun uprist:
　　Then all averred I had killed the bird
100　That brought the fog and mist.
　　'Twas right, said they, such birds to slay,
　　That bring the fog and mist.

　　The fair breeze blew, the white foam flew,
　　The furrow followed free;
105　We were the first that ever burst
　　Into that silent sea.

　　Down dropped the breeze, the sails dropped down,
　　'Twas sad as sad could be;
　　And we did speak only to break
110　The silence of the sea!
　　All in a hot and copper sky,

75 shroud: one of the ropes that support a ship's mast.

76 vespers nine: nine evenings.

The ancient Mariner inhospitably killeth the pious bird of good omen.

83 The Sun . . . right: The rising of the sun on the right indicates that the ship is now heading northward.

His shipmates cry out against the ancient Mariner, for killing the bird of good luck.

93 averred (ə-vûrd'): declared; asserted.

But when the fog cleared off, they justify the same, and thus make themselves accomplices in the crime.

98 uprist: rose.

The fair breeze continues; the ship enters the Pacific Ocean, and sails northward, even till it reaches the Line.

The ship hath been suddenly becalmed.

The bloody Sun, at noon,
Right up above the mast did stand,
No bigger than the Moon.

115 Day after day, day after day,
We stuck, nor breath nor motion;
As idle as a painted ship
Upon a painted ocean.

Water, water, everywhere,
120 And all the boards did shrink;
Water, water, everywhere
Nor any drop to drink.

*And the Albatross begins to be
avenged.*

The very deep did rot: O Christ!
That ever this should be!
125 Yea, slimy things did crawl with legs
Upon the slimy sea.

About, about, in reel and rout
The death-fires danced at night;
The water, like a witch's oils,
130 Burnt green, and blue, and white.

127 in reel and rout: with dizzying,
unpredictable motion.

128 death-fires: dim flamelike
lights reportedly seen above
decomposing matter.

And some in dreams assuréd were
Of the Spirit that plagued us so;
Nine fathom deep he had followed us
From the land of mist and snow.

*A Spirit had followed them; one of
the invisible inhabitants of this planet,
neither departed souls nor angels;
concerning whom the learned Jew,
Josephus, and the Platonic
Constantinopolitan, Michael Psellus,
may be consulted. They are very
numerous, and there is no climate or
element without one or more.*

133 nine fathom: 54 feet.

135 And every tongue, through utter drought,
Was withered at the root;
We could not speak, no more than if
We had been choked with soot.

Ah! well a-day! what evil looks
140 Had I from old and young!
Instead of the cross, the Albatross
About my neck was hung.

*The shipmates, in their sore distress,
would fain throw the whole guilt on
the ancient Mariner: in sign whereof
they hang the dead sea bird round his
neck.*

PART III

There passed a weary time. Each throat
Was parched, and glazed each eye.
145 A weary time! a weary time!
How glazed each weary eye!
When, looking westward, I beheld
A something in the sky.

At first it seemed a little speck,
150 And then it seemed a mist;
It moved and moved, and took at last
A certain shape, I wist.

A speck, a mist, a shape, I wist!
And still it neared and neared:
155 As if it dodged a water-sprite,
It plunged, and tacked and veered.

With throats unslaked, with black lips baked,
We could nor laugh nor wail;
Through utter drought all dumb we stood!
160 I bit my arm, I sucked the blood,
And cried, A sail! a sail!

With throats unslaked, with black lips baked,
Agape they heard me call:
Gramercy! they for joy did grin,
165 And all at once their breath drew in,
As they were drinking all.

See! see! (I cried) she tacks no more!
Hither to work us weal—
Without a breeze, without a tide,
170 She steadies with upright keel!

The western wave was all aflame,
The day was wellnigh done!
Almost upon the western wave
Rested the broad, bright Sun;
175 When that strange shape drove suddenly
Betwixt us and the Sun.

And straight the Sun was flecked with bars
(Heaven's Mother send us grace!),
As if through a dungeon-grate he peered
180 With broad and burning face.

The ancient Mariner beholdeth a sign in the element afar off.

152 wist: perceived; discerned.

155 water sprite: a mythical being living in water.

156 tacked and veered: zigzagged.

At its nearer approach, it seemeth him to be a ship; and at a dear ransom he freeth his speech from the bonds of thirst.

A flash of joy;

164 gramercy (grə-mûr'sē): an exclamation of gratitude.

And horror follows. For can it be a ship that comes onward without wind or tide?

168 hither to work us weal: in this direction to help us.

171 The western wave was all aflame: that is, the water to the west was reflecting the light of the setting sun.

It seemeth him but the skeleton of a ship.

178 Heaven's Mother: the Virgin Mary.

Alas! (thought I, and my heart beat loud)
How fast she nears and nears!
Are those her sails that glance in the Sun,
Like restless gossameres?

185 Are those her ribs through which the Sun
Did peer, as through a grate?
And is that Woman all her crew?
Is that a Death? and are there two?
Is Death that Woman's mate?

190 Her lips were red, her looks were free,
Her locks were yellow as gold:
Her skin was as white as leprosy,
The Nightmare Life-in-Death was she,
Who thicks man's blood with cold.

195 The naked hulk alongside came,
And the twain were casting dice;
"The game is done! I've won! I've won!"
Quoth she, and whistles thrice.

The Sun's rim dips; the stars rush out:
200 At one stride comes the dark;
With far-heard whisper, o'er the sea,
Off shot the spectre-bark.

We listened and looked sideways up!
Fear at my heart, as at a cup,
205 My life-blood seemed to sip!
The stars were dim, and thick the night,
The steersman's face by his lamp gleamed white;
From the sails the dew did drip—
Till clomb above the eastern bar
210 The hornéd Moon, with one bright star
Within the nether tip.

One after one, by the star-dogged Moon,
Too quick for groan or sigh,
Each turned his face with a ghastly pang,
215 And cursed me with his eye.

Four times fifty living men
(And I heard nor sigh nor groan),
With heavy thump, a lifeless lump,
They dropped down one by one.

And its ribs are seen as bars on the face of the setting Sun.

184 gossameres (gŏs'ə-mērz'): cobwebs floating in the air.

The Specter-Woman and her Deathmate, and no other on board the skeleton ship.

Like vessel, like crew!

192 leprosy (lĕp'rə-sē): a disease marked by spreading patches of discoloration on the skin and by deformities of the limbs and other parts of the body.

Death and Life-in-Death have diced for the ship's crew, and she (the latter) winneth the ancient Mariner.

No twilight within the courts of the Sun.

202 spectre-bark: ghost ship.

At the rising of the Moon,

209 clomb (klōm): climbed.
210 hornéd Moon: crescent moon.

One after another,

His shipmates drop down dead.

220　The souls did from their bodies fly—
　　They fled to bliss or woe!
　　And every soul, it passed me by
　　Like the whizz of my crossbow!

But Life-in-Death begins her work on the ancient Mariner.

PART IV

　　"I fear thee, ancient Mariner!
225　I fear thy skinny hand!
　　And thou art long, and lank, and brown,
　　As is the ribbed sea-sand.

The Wedding Guest feareth that a Spirit is talking to him;

　　I fear thee and thy glittering eye,
　　And thy skinny hand so brown."—
230　Fear not, fear not, thou Wedding-Guest!
　　This body dropped not down.

But the ancient Mariner assureth him of his bodily life, and proceedeth to relate his horrible penance.

　　Alone, alone, all, all alone
　　Alone on a wide, wide sea!
　　And never a saint took pity on
235　My soul in agony.

　　The many men, so beautiful!
　　And they all dead did lie:
　　And a thousand thousand slimy things
　　Lived on; and so did I.

He despiseth the creatures of the calm,

240　I looked upon the rotting sea,
　　And drew my eyes away;
　　I looked upon the rotting deck,
　　And there the dead men lay.

And envieth that they should live, and so many lie dead.

　　I looked to heaven, and tried to pray;
245　But or ever a prayer had gushed,
　　A wicked whisper came, and made
　　My heart as dry as dust.

　　I closed my lids, and kept them close,
　　And the balls like pulses beat;
250　But the sky and the sea, and the sea and the sky,
　　Lay like a load on my weary eye,
　　And the dead were at my feet.

249 balls: eyeballs.

　　The cold sweat melted from their limbs,
　　Nor rot nor reek did they:

But the curse liveth for him in the eye of the dead men.

255   The look with which they looked on me
    Had never passed away.

    An orphan's curse would drag to hell
    A spirit from on high;
    But oh! more horrible than that
260   Is the curse in a dead man's eye!
    Seven days, seven nights, I saw that curse,
    And yet I could not die.

    The moving Moon went up the sky,
    And nowhere did abide;

265 Softly she was going up,
And a star or two beside—

Her beams bemocked the sultry main,
Like April hoar-frost spread;
But where the ship's huge shadow lay,
270 The charméd water burnt alway
A still and awful red.

Beyond the shadow of the ship,
I watched the water-snakes:
They moved in tracks of shining white,
275 And when they reared, the elfish light
Fell off in hoary flakes.

Within the shadow of the ship
I watched their rich attire:
Blue, glossy green, and velvet black,
280 They coiled and swam; and every track
Was a flash of golden fire.

O happy living things! no tongue
Their beauty might declare:
A spring of love gushed from my heart,
285 And I blessed them unaware:
Sure my kind saint took pity on me,
And I blessed them unaware.

The selfsame moment I could pray;
And from my neck so free
290 The Albatross fell off, and sank
Like lead into the sea.

PART V

O sleep! it is a gentle thing,
Beloved from pole to pole!
To Mary Queen the praise be given!
295 She sent the gentle sleep from Heaven,
That slid into my soul.

The silly buckets on the deck,
That had so long remained,
I dreamt that they were filled with dew;
300 And when I awoke, it rained.

In his loneliness and fixedness he yearneth towards the journeying Moon, and the stars that still sojourn, yet still move onward; and everywhere the blue sky belongs to them, and is their appointed rest, and their native country and their own natural homes, which they enter unannounced, as lords that are certainly expected and yet there is a silent joy at their arrival.

267 bemocked . . . main: scornfully defied the hot ocean (because the moon's pale light made the sea appear cool).

By the light of the Moon he beholdeth God's creatures of the great calm.

268 hoar-frost: frozen dew.

276 fell off in hoary flakes: that is, glittered on water droplets falling from the snakes.

Their beauty and their happiness.

He blesseth them in his heart.

The spell begins to break.

294 Mary Queen: the Virgin Mary.

By grace of the holy Mother, the ancient Mariner is refreshed with rain.

My lips were wet, my throat was cold.
My garments all were dank;
Sure I had drunken in my dreams,
And still my body drank.

305 I moved, and could not feel my limbs:
I was so light—almost
I thought that I had died in sleep,
And was a blessèd ghost.

And soon I heard a roaring wind:
310 It did not come anear;
But with its sound it shook the sails,
That were so thin and sere.

The upper air burst into life;
And a hundred fire-flags sheen;
315 To and fro they were hurried about!
And to and fro, and in and out,
The wan stars danced between.

And the coming wind did roar more loud,
And the sails did sigh like sedge;
320 And the rain poured down from one black cloud;
The Moon was at its edge.

The thick black cloud was cleft, and still
The Moon was at its side;
Like waters shot from some high crag,
325 The lightning fell with never a jag,
A river steep and wide.

The loud wind never reached the ship,
Yet now the ship moved on!
Beneath the lightning and the Moon
330 The dead men gave a groan.

They groaned, they stirred, they all uprose,
Nor spake, nor moved their eyes;
It had been strange, even in a dream,
To have seen those dead men rise.

335 The helmsman steered, the ship moved on;
Yet never a breeze up-blew;

The mariners all 'gan work the ropes,
Where they were wont to do;
They raised their limbs like lifeless tools—
340 We were a ghastly crew.

The body of my brother's son
Stood by me, knee to knee:
The body and I pulled at one rope,
But he said naught to me.

345 "I fear thee, ancient Mariner!"
Be calm, thou Wedding-Guest:
'Twas not those souls that fled in pain,
Which to their corses came again,
But a troop of spirits blest:

350 For when it dawned—they dropped their arms,
And clustered round the mast;
Sweet sounds rose slowly through their mouths,
And from their bodies passed.

Around, around, flew each sweet sound,
355 Then darted to the Sun;
Slowly the sounds came back again,
Now mixed, now one by one.

Sometimes a-dropping from the sky
I heard the skylark sing;
360 Sometimes all little birds that are,
How they seemed to fill the sea and air
With their sweet jargoning!

And now 'twas like all instruments,
Now like a lonely flute;
365 And now it is an angel's song,
That makes the Heavens be mute.

It ceased; yet still the sails made on
A pleasant noise till noon,
A noise like of a hidden brook
370 In the leafy month of June,
That to the sleeping woods all night
Singeth a quiet tune.

Till noon we quietly sailed on,
Yet never a breeze did breathe:

338 wont: accustomed.

But not by the souls of the men, nor by demons of earth or middle air, but by a blessed troop of angelic spirits, sent down by the invocation of the guardian saint.

348 corses: bodies.

362 jargoning: warbling.

375 Slowly and smoothly went the ship,
     Moved onward from beneath.

     Under the keel nine fathom deep,
     From the land of mist and snow,
     The Spirit slid: and it was he
380 That made the ship to go.
     The sails at noon left off their tune,
     And the ship stood still also.

     The Sun, right up above the mast,
     Had fixed her to the ocean:
385 But in a minute she 'gan stir,
     With a short uneasy motion—

*The lonesome Spirit from the South
Pole carries on the ship as far as the
Line, in obedience to the angelic
troop, but still requireth vengeance.*

Backwards and forwards half her length
With a short uneasy motion.

Then like a pawing horse let go,
390 She made a sudden bound:
It flung the blood into my head,
And I fell down in a swound.

How long in that same fit I lay,
I have not to declare;
395 But ere my living life returned,
I heard, and in my soul discerned
Two voices in the air.

"Is it he?" quoth one, "is this the man?
By Him who died on cross,
400 With his cruel bow he laid full low
The harmless Albatross.

The Spirit who bideth by himself
In the land of mist and snow,
He loved the bird that loved the man
405 Who shot him with his bow."

The other was a softer voice,
As soft as honey-dew:
Quoth he, "The man hath penance done,
And penance more will do."

PART VI

First Voice:
410 "But tell me, tell me! speak again,
Thy soft response renewing—
What makes that ship drive on so fast?
What is the Ocean doing?"

Second Voice:
"Still as a slave before his lord,
415 The Ocean hath no blast;
His great bright eye most silently
Up to the Moon is cast—

If he may know which way to go;
For she guides him smooth or grim.

394 have not: am not able.

The Polar Spirit's fellow demons, the invisible inhabitants of the element, take part in his wrong; and two of them relate, one to the other, that penance long and heavy for the ancient Mariner hath been accorded to the Polar Spirit, who returneth southward.

399 Him who died on cross: Jesus Christ.

408 penance (pĕn'əns): suffering in repayment for a sin.

420 See, brother, see! how graciously
     She looketh down on him."

First Voice:
"But why drives on that ship so fast,
Without or wave or wind?"

Second Voice:
"The air is cut away before,
425 And closes from behind.

Fly, brother, fly! more high, more high!
Or we shall be belated:
For slow and slow that ship will go,
When the Mariner's trance is abated."

430 I woke, and we were sailing on
As in a gentle weather:
'Twas night, calm night, the Moon was high;
The dead men stood together.

All stood together on the deck,
435 For a charnel-dungeon fitter:
All fixed on me their stony eyes,
That in the Moon did glitter.

The pang, the curse, with which they died,
Had never passed away:
440 I could not draw my eyes from theirs,
Nor turn them up to pray.

And now this spell was snapped: once more
I viewed the ocean green,
And looked far forth, yet little saw
445 Of what had else been seen—

Like one that on a lonesome road
Doth walk in fear and dread,
And having once turned round, walks on,
And turns no more his head;
450 Because he knows a frightful fiend
Doth close behind him tread.

But soon there breathed a wind on me,
Nor sound nor motion made:

The Mariner hath been cast into a trance; for the angelic power causeth the vessel to drive northward faster than human life could endure.

The supernatural motion is retarded; the Mariner awakes, and his penance begins anew.

435 for . . . fitter: more suitable for a burial vault.

The curse is finally expiated.

450 fiend: demon.

Its path was not upon the sea,
455   In ripple or in shade.

It raised my hair, it fanned my cheek
Like a meadow-gale of spring—
It mingled strangely with my fears,
Yet it felt like a welcoming.

460   Swiftly, swiftly flew the ship,
Yet she sailed softly too:
Sweetly, sweetly blew the breeze—
On me alone it blew.

O dream of joy! is this indeed
465   The lighthouse top I see?
Is this the hill? is this the kirk?
Is this mine own countree?

And the ancient Mariner beholdeth his native country.

We drifted o'er the harbor-bar,
And I with sobs did pray—
470   O let me be awake, my God!
Or let me sleep alway.

The harbor-bay was clear as glass,
So smoothly it was strewn!
And on the bay the moonlight lay,
475   And the shadow of the Moon.

The rock shone bright, the kirk no less
That stands above the rock:
The moonlight steeped in silentness
The steady weathercock.

479 weathercock: weathervane.

480   And the bay was white with silent light
Till rising from the same,
Full many shapes, that shadows were,
In crimson colors came.

The angelic spirits leave the dead bodies,

A little distance from the prow
485   Those crimson shadows were:
I turned my eyes upon the deck—
O Christ! what saw I there!

And appear in their own forms of light.

Each corse lay flat, lifeless and flat,
And, by the holy rood!

489 the holy rood (rōōd): the cross on which Christ was crucified.

490	A man all light, a seraph-man,
	On every corse there stood.

490 **seraph** (sĕr′əf) **man:** angel.

This seraph-band, each waved his hand:
It was a heavenly sight!
They stood as signals to the land,
495   Each one a lovely light;

This seraph-band, each waved his hand,
No voice did they impart—
No voice; but O, the silence sank
Like music on my heart.

500 But soon I heard the dash of oars,
I heard the Pilot's cheer;
My head was turned perforce away,
And I saw a boat appear.

502 **perforce:** of necessity.

The Pilot and the Pilot's boy,
505   I heard them coming fast:
Dear Lord in Heaven! it was a joy
The dead men could not blast.

507 **blast:** destroy.

I saw a third—I heard his voice:
It is the Hermit good!
510   He singeth loud his godly hymns
That he makes in the wood.
He'll shrieve my soul, he'll wash away
The Albatross's blood.

512 **shrieve** (shrēv): absolve from
sin; pardon.

PART VII

This hermit good lives in that wood
515 Which slopes down to the sea.
How loudly his sweet voice he rears!
He loves to talk with marineres
That come from a far countree.

He kneels at morn, and noon, and eve—
520 He hath a cushion plump.
It is the moss that wholly hides
The rotted old oak-stump.

The skiff-boat neared: I heard them talk,
"Why, this is strange, I trow!
525 Where are those lights so many and fair,
That signal made but now?"

"Strange, by my faith!" the Hermit said—
"And they answered not our cheer!
The planks look warped! and see those sails,
530 How thin they are and sere!
I never saw aught like to them,
Unless perchance it were
Brown skeletons of leaves that lag
My forest-brook along;
535 When the ivy-tod is heavy with snow,
And the owlet whoops to the wolf below,
That eats the she-wolf's young."

"Dear Lord! it hath a fiendish look—
(The Pilot made reply)
540 I am a-fear'd."—"Push on, push on!"
Said the Hermit cheerily.

The boat came closer to the ship,
But I nor spake nor stirred;
The boat came close beneath the ship,
545 And straight a sound was heard.

Under the water it rumbled on
Still louder and more dread:
It reached the ship, it split the bay;
The ship went down like lead.

550 Stunned by that loud and dreadful sound,
Which sky and ocean smote,

The Hermit of the Wood

524 trow: believe.

Approacheth the ship with wonder.

535 tod: clump.

The ship suddenly sinketh.

551 smote: struck.

The ancient Mariner is saved in the Pilot's boat.

Like one that hath been seven days drowned
My body lay afloat;
But swift as dreams, myself I found
555 Within the Pilot's boat.
Upon the whirl, where sank the ship,
The boat spun round and round;
And all was still, save that the hill
Was telling of the sound.

560 I moved my lips—the Pilot shrieked
And fell down in a fit;
The holy Hermit raised his eyes,
And prayed where he did sit.

I took the oars: the Pilot's boy,
565 Who now doth crazy go,
Laughed loud and long, and all the while
His eyes went to and fro.
"Ha! ha!" quoth he, "full plain I see
The Devil knows how to row."

570 And now, all in my own countree,
I stood on the firm land!
The Hermit stepped forth from the boat,
And scarcely he could stand.

"O shrieve me, shrieve me, holy man!"
575 The Hermit crossed his brow.
"Say quick," quoth he, "I bid thee say—
What manner of man art thou?"

Forthwith this frame of mine was wrenched
With a woeful agony,
580 Which forced me to begin my tale;
And then it left me free.

Since then, at an uncertain hour,
That agony returns:
And till my ghastly tale is told,
585 This heart within me burns.

I pass, like night, from land to land;
I have strange power of speech;
That moment that his face I see,
I know the man that must hear me:
590 To him my tale I teach.

559 telling of: echoing.

575 crossed his brow: made the sign of the cross on his forehead.

The ancient Mariner earnestly entreateth the Hermit to shrieve him; and the penance of life falls on him.

And ever and anon throughout his future life an agony constraineth him to travel from land to land;

What loud uproar bursts from that door!
The wedding-guests are there:
But in the garden-bower the bride
And bride-maids singing are:
595 And hark, the little vesper bell,
Which biddeth me to prayer!

O Wedding-Guest! this soul hath been
Alone on a wide, wide sea:
So lonely 'twas, that God Himself
600 Scarce seeméd there to be.

O sweeter than the marriage-feast,
'Tis sweeter far to me,
To walk together to the kirk
With a goodly company!—

605 To walk together to the kirk,
And all together pray,
While each to his great Father bends,

607 his great Father: God.

Old men, and babes, and loving friends,
And youths and maidens gay!

610 Farewell, farewell! but this I tell
To thee, thou Wedding-Guest!
He prayeth well, who loveth well
Both man and bird and beast.

And to teach, by his own example, love and reverence to all things that God made and loveth.

He prayeth best, who loveth best
615 All things both great and small;
For the dear God who loveth us,
He made and loveth all.

The Mariner, whose eye is bright,
Whose beard with age is hoar,

619 hoar: gray.

620 Is gone: and now the Wedding-Guest
Turned from the bridegroom's door.

He went like one that hath been stunned,
And is of sense forlorn:
A sadder and a wiser man
625 He rose the morrow morn.

Thinking through the LITERATURE

Connect to the Literature

1. **What Do You Think?**
   What adjectives would you use to describe the mariner's voyage?

   Comprehension Check
   - In what direction does the ship travel after leaving its home port?
   - After the mariner kills the albatross, what happens to the rest of the crew?

Think Critically

2. **ACTIVE READING | READING NARRATIVE POETRY** Look back at the notes you jotted down in your **READER'S NOTEBOOK** in response to the questions listed on page 745. On what **conflicts** do the events of the **plot** focus? How are these conflicts related to the **setting?**

3. What do you think is the mariner's attitude toward the albatross when he kills it?

4. What might the albatross **symbolize,** or represent?

   THINK ABOUT
   - the effect the arrival of the albatross seems to have on the ship's voyage
   - the consequences that follow from the mariner's killing of the bird
   - the mariner's statement in lines 612–617

5. What are the consequences of the mariner's being won by Life-in-Death (lines 190–198) rather than by Death? Cite evidence from the poem in your answer.

6. Why do you think the mariner tells his story at a wedding?

Extend Interpretations

7. **Comparing Texts** Since early times, the English have been a seagoing people, and they have a long tradition of poetry about the dangers and mystery of ocean voyaging. Compare "The Rime of the Ancient Mariner" with the Anglo-Saxon poem "The Seafarer" (page 84). How are the experiences and world views of Coleridge's mariner and the Anglo-Saxon seafarer similar? How do they differ?

8. **The Writer's Style** Coleridge used **sensory language** to help the reader visualize the scenes and characters he described. To which of your five senses did the poem appeal most? Cite examples from the poem in your answer.

9. **Connect to Life** From your consideration of the poem's **details,** what do you think the expression "to have an albatross around one's neck" means today?

Literary Analysis

LITERARY BALLAD "The Rime of the Ancient Mariner" is a famous example of a **literary ballad,** a poem by a known writer that imitates the style of an anonymous **folk ballad.** Typically, a folk ballad

- is a brief **narrative poem** intended to be set to music
- opens abruptly
- recounts a single dramatic—often a tragic—episode
- contains supernatural elements
- implies more than it actually tells
- includes dialogue, often without directly stating who is speaking
- contains repetitions of lines or stanzas, sometimes with the wording varied slightly
- is made up of four-line stanzas in which the first and third lines contain four stressed syllables, the second and fourth lines contain three stressed syllables, and the second and fourth lines rhyme

Cooperative Learning Activity With classmates, use the list of ballad characteristics above to determine to what extent "The Rime of the Ancient Mariner" conforms to typical ballad style. Compare your findings with those of other groups.

REVIEW | SIMILE A **simile** is a **figure of speech** in which the word *like* or *as* is used to make a comparison. Find several particularly effective similes in the poem. Do most of the similes seem to be used to describe characters, to establish settings, or to advance the plot?

Choices & CHALLENGES

Writing Options

1. Poetry of Dreams Write your own poem or fragment of a poem based on a dream that you remember. Place the poem in your **Working Portfolio.**

2. Analytical Essay Write a brief essay in which you compare the attitudes toward the natural and supernatural worlds expressed in "Kubla Khan" and "The Rime of the Ancient Mariner." Be sure to include ample evidence from the poems to support your thesis, or general statement.

Writing Handbook
See page 1367: Compare and Contrast.

Activities & Explorations

1. Choral Reading With a group of classmates, prepare a choral reading of a portion of "The Rime of the Ancient Mariner." Perform it for the rest of the class. ~ **SPEAKING AND LISTENING**

2. Video Visions View the video of "Kubla Khan," in which the poem is interpreted through oral reading and images. What connections do you see between the imagery in the poem and the images in the video? Do the oral and visual interpretations work well together?

With a partner, list what you think are the most effective sections of the video presentation. ~ **VIEWING AND REPRESENTING**

 **Literature in Performance**

Inquiry & Research

Multimedia Report Research the real Kublai Khan, and present your findings in a multimedia report that includes photocopies of artworks illustrating the achievements of his reign.

 More Online: Research Starter
www.mcdougallittell.com

Samuel Taylor Coleridge
1772–1834

Other Works
Biographia Literaria
"Christabel"
"Dejection: An Ode"
"Frost at Midnight"
"Work Without Hope"

A Restless Youth As a schoolboy, Coleridge was precocious, reading for amusement the most difficult passages of the ancient Roman poet Virgil. Although already a devoted scholar when he entered Cambridge University, Coleridge did not care for college life and at one point left to enlist in a cavalry unit called the Light Dragoons. When his escapade was discovered by his brothers, he was promptly returned to school; but he left Cambridge in 1794 without having received a degree.

Utopian Dream That year, Coleridge met the author Robert Southey, and together they dreamed about establishing an ideal community on the banks of the Susquehanna River in the United States. Their community was to be a pantisocracy—a society in which all members rule equally. Southey backed out of the project, however, and their dream was never realized.

Literary Friendship In 1795 Coleridge had the extraordinary good fortune to meet William Wordsworth. They became close friends, traveling and writing together and often helping each other with their poetry. *Lyrical Ballads,* the joint collection they published in 1798, included Coleridge's famous poem "The Rime of the Ancient Mariner."

Critic and Sage Most of Coleridge's best poetry was written early in his career. Later, he turned to philosophy and literary criticism, becoming the most influential literary theorist of the romantic movement in Britain. In his later years, Coleridge moved into the home of a Dr. Gilman in Highgate, north of London. The doctor helped him control an addiction to opium, and Coleridge seemed more at peace with himself. His rooms became a center of conversation for an admiring crowd that dubbed him the Sage of Highgate.

PRIDE & PREJUDICE

The Cloakroom, Clifton Assembly Rooms,
*Rolinda Sharples (1794–1838). City of Bristol
Museum and Art Gallery, Bristol, Great Britain.*

magine that you are living in England around the turn of the 19th century, standing on the threshold of adulthood. You are a woman, so your only career option is marriage. The match you make will reflect your values and desires—and determine the manner in which you spend the rest of your life.

This is the world of *Pride and Prejudice,* Jane Austen's insightful and clever examination of English manners and morals. The novel centers on the roundabout courtship of a proud young man, Fitzwilliam Darcy, and a spirited but judgmental young woman, Elizabeth Bennet, who fall in dislike at first sight. Elizabeth's and Darcy's friends and families provide a cast of characters whose traits Jane Austen depicts with irony and humor. For example, the silly schemes with which Elizabeth's mother—who has no real understanding of good manners, good breeding, or good sense—tries to ensure that her daughters will marry well cause Elizabeth no end of painful embarrassment. Elizabeth's good-natured

Painting of Jane Austen by her sister, 1804. Robert Harding Picture Library.

but ineffectual father contributes to the near ruin of the family by neglecting to rein in his wife and younger daughters. Elizabeth's best friend astonishes her when she agrees to marry a pompous suitor of Elizabeth's not for love, or even riches, but for security.

In the course of the novel, Austen exposes the ever-changing nature of public opinion, ridicules the assumed superiority of the upper class, and shows how prejudice can lead to premature and even dangerous conclusions. She gently but firmly chides two young lovers who are so mild and polite in expressing their feelings that they almost lose each other, and she celebrates the independent spirit that leads two unlikely lovers to forge a bond of enduring joy.

Soon after *Pride and Prejudice* was published, critics began comparing Jane Austen to Shakespeare. They admired her command of language, her use of comic fools, and her dramatic presentation of characters in action. In addition, they noticed a kinship between the hard-won affection of Elizabeth and Darcy and the reluctant love of Beatrice and Benedick in Shakespeare's *Much Ado About Nothing*.

Unlike Shakespeare's lovers, however, Austen's characters are not tricked into love. Instead, they hammer out their own romance, allowing for shared values and mutual respect. Their integrity, independence, and well-deserved love has made *Pride and Prejudice* a perennial favorite among novels as well as a classic celebration of joyous love between independent equals.

A Darcy-like character wearing gentleman's clothing typical of the day

PART 2 Embracing the Imagination

Romantic poets passionately embraced the concept of creative self-expression, giving free rein to their imaginations in an effort to convey their personal visions of love and life. In this part of Unit Four, you will read poems in which writers imagine what it would be like to embody the ocean's majesty, to soar and sing like a bird, and to defy the ravages of time. As you read these poems, consider what images your own imagination might conjure up as a means of creative self-expression.

COMPARING LITERATURE: The Poetry of Percy Bysshe Shelley
and Heinrich Heine
Romanticism Across Cultures: Germany

Form and Meaning in Poetry

The Organizing Principles

Poets from every era have toyed with poetic form and language to create unique expressions of meaning, and the romantic poets were no exception. **Form** in poetry refers to the principles of arrangement in a poem—the ways in which words and images are organized, including the length of lines, the placement of lines, and the grouping of lines.

Hand-colored illustrations from Blake's *Songs of Experience*

Some poems follow a **fixed form,** which uses a conventional stanza pattern or a defined rhyme scheme. Other poems follow an **irregular form,** which is not defined by any traditional poetic structure. Samuel Taylor Coleridge wrote extensively about the relationship between content and form in his *Biographia Literaria* (1817). He believed that the form and the content of a poem, like the roots and the leaves of a growing plant, do not develop independently but develop simultaneously. The romantics favored this **organic form**—a form that, as Coleridge explains, "is innate; it shapes, as it develops, itself from within." In other words, the shape of the poem is intimately tied to the poem's meaning.

The Shape of a Poem

The most basic element of poetic form—and the one that first catches the reader's eye—is the physical arrangement of words on the page. Poets use lines and stanzas to shape their poems, and these lines and stanzas can vary significantly, as shown in the examples below.

End-stopped lines are lines in which the end of the line is the end of a thought, a clause, or a sentence. End-stopped lines are signaled by a period, hyphen, or semicolon, as this line from "The World Is Too Much with Us" illustrates:

> *Getting and spending, we lay waste our powers;*

Run-on lines are lines in which the thought continues into the next line or further. Notice the run-on lines in this excerpt from "Lines Composed a Few Miles Above Tintern Abbey":

> The day is come when I again repose
> Here, under this dark sycamore, and view
> These plots of cottage ground, these orchard tufts,
> Which at this season, with their unripe fruits,
> Are clad in one green hue, and lose themselves
> 'Mid groves and copses. . . .

YOUR TURN What is the effect of the run-on lines in this stanza?

A **stanza** conveys a particular idea or a set of related ideas and is usually characterized by a common pattern of rhythm, rhyme, and number of lines. Some stanzas are named for the number of lines they contain. For example, a **couplet** is a two-line stanza, a **tercet** is a three-line stanza, a **quatrain** is a four-line stanza, and a **cinquain** is a five-line stanza. The romantics experimented with the verse paragraph form they inherited from the poetry of Dryden and Milton. In a **verse paragraph,** lines of blank verse are grouped according to content, like a paragraph, rather than according to a fixed stanza form. In "Lines Composed a Few Miles Above Tintern Abbey," for example, Wordsworth uses both long and short verse paragraphs: 22 lines in the first stanza, 28 lines in the second, and 9 lines in the third.

Lyric Forms

The romantic poets experimented with a number of traditional lyric forms—including both **Petrarchan** and **Shakespearean** sonnets—and adapted them to suit the contemplative nature of their poetry. For example, Wordsworth followed the Petrarchan sonnet form in "It Is a Beauteous Evening."

Wordsworth, Coleridge, Shelley, and Keats all used the ode form in some of their poems. Originally a choral Greek form that lent itself to dramatic poetry, an **ode** is an exalted, complex lyric that develops a dignified theme and may include an elaborate stanza pattern. In addition, the metrical pattern of an ode quickens and slows to match the emotional intensity of the idea being expressed. The romantic poets favored an irregular form of the ode, which allowed greater freedom of stanza pattern, rhyme scheme, and metrical movement.

The Combination of Poetic Ingredients

The elements of form explained above work together with **sound devices**—such as alliteration, assonance, consonance, onomatopoeia, and repetition—and other **poetic elements** to convey meaning and create a total experience for the reader. This is especially true of the romantic poets. The following excerpt from William Blake's "The Lamb" shows how various literary elements can combine to create meaning—and how form and meaning become an inseparable part of the whole:

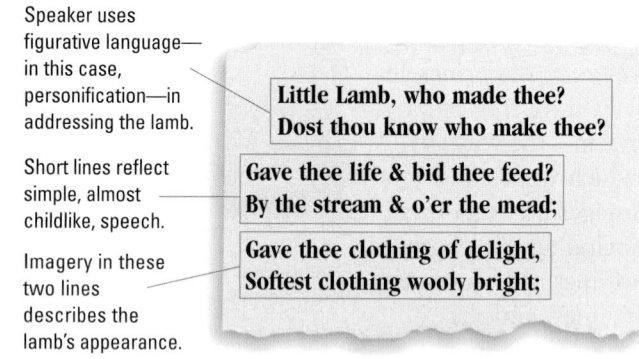

Speaker uses figurative language—in this case, personification—in addressing the lamb.

> Little Lamb, who made thee?
> Dost thou know who make thee?

Short lines reflect simple, almost childlike, speech.

> Gave thee life & bid thee feed?
> By the stream & o'er the mead;

Imagery in these two lines describes the lamb's appearance.

> Gave thee clothing of delight,
> Softest clothing wooly bright;

Rhythm, rhyme, and repetition create a lyrical, musical quality throughout the entire poem.

YOUR TURN What view of life is presented in the poem, and how is it reinforced by the poem's form?

Strategies for Reading: Form and Meaning in Poetry ....

1. Read the poem at least three times to clarify the meaning. Also read the poem aloud to hear its music.

2. Analyze the poem's form. Study the way the poet arranges lines and stanzas and uses patterns of rhyme, rhythm, and other sound devices. Is the poem fixed or irregular?

3. Visualize the setting and the situation. As you read, use details and your imagination to help you "see" what is happening.

4. Identify the speaker. Determine whether the poet has created a speaker with a distinctive identity.

5. Determine the theme. What important ideas does the poem convey about life or human nature?

6. **Monitor** your reading strategies and modify them when your understanding breaks down. Remember to use your Strategies for Active Reading: **predict, visualize, connect, question, clarify,** and **evaluate.**

Selected Poems

By GEORGE GORDON, LORD BYRON

Connect to Your Life

The Power of Emotions Think of someone in your family, school, or community who conveys strong emotions when speaking. Does the person usually express the emotions in ordinary conversation, or does he or she do so in speeches, sermons, or other public presentations? Do you think the ability to express powerful emotions is an advantage or a disadvantage? Discuss these questions with a group of classmates.

Build Background

"A Young Gentleman of Tumultuous Passions" During the romantic period, no English poet achieved greater popularity than George Gordon, Lord Byron. Because the heroes he created in many of his works were rebellious, moody figures of great passion and strong will, Byron was viewed during most of the 19th century as the ideal example of the romantic spirit. He attracted admirers throughout Europe, and his influence was felt not only in the poetry of his many imitators but in art and music as well.

Even though Byron became a symbol of romanticism, his poetry was rooted in 18th-century forms, as is evident in the first two poems that you will read. He avoided, and actually scorned, the experimental poetry of his contemporaries; but he was nevertheless decidedly romantic in his emphasis on freedom and the individual and in his expression of powerful emotions. In the words of one of his university instructors, Byron was "a young gentleman of tumultuous passions."

Byron's immense popularity originated with the publication of the first two sections of his poetic travelogue *Childe Harold's Pilgrimage* in 1812. The young poet acquired the material for this work and several other poems during an adventurous two-year excursion through Portugal, Spain, Malta, Greece, and Asia Minor. For 19th-century readers, part of the appeal of *Childe Harold's Pilgrimage* was the excitement of reading about countries or scenery they had never seen.

Focus Your Reading

LITERARY ANALYSIS APOSTROPHE

An **apostrophe** is a figure of speech in which an object, an abstract quality, or an absent or imaginary person is addressed directly, as if present and able to understand. The excerpt from *Childe Harold's Pilgrimage* on the following pages contains an apostrophe to the ocean. As you read it, be aware of this device and contemplate why Byron chose to use it.

ACTIVE READING COMPARING SPEAKERS

The **speaker** in a poem—the voice that "talks" to the reader—is not necessarily the voice of the poet; poets sometimes create a speaker other than themselves in order to achieve a particular effect. For this reason, two poems by the same poet can have speakers that convey different personalities.

READER'S NOTEBOOK As you read each of Byron's poems, keep track of the emotions, thoughts, and wishes of the speaker in a chart similar to the one shown. Be prepared to discuss similarities and differences.

"She Walks in Beauty"		
Emotions	Thoughts	Wishes

SHE WALKS IN BEAUTY

GEORGE GORDON, LORD BYRON

Comus, Disguised as a Rustic, Addresses the Lady in the Wood
(1801-1802), William Blake. Henry E. Huntington Library and Art
Gallery, San Marino, California.

She walks in beauty, like the night
    Of cloudless climes and starry skies;
And all that's best of dark and bright
    Meet in her aspect and her eyes:
5 Thus mellowed to that tender light
    Which heaven to gaudy day denies.

One shade the more, one ray the less,
    Had half impaired the nameless grace
Which waves in every raven tress,
10   Or softly lightens o'er her face;
Where thoughts serenely sweet express
    How pure, how dear their dwelling place.

And on that cheek, and o'er that brow,
    So soft, so calm, yet eloquent,
15 The smiles that win, the tints that glow,
    But tell of days in goodness spent,
A mind at peace with all below,
    A heart whose love is innocent!

2 climes: regions; climates.

4 aspect: appearance.

9 tress: lock of hair.

When We Two Parted

When we two parted
    In silence and tears,
Half broken-hearted
    To sever for years,
5   Pale grew thy cheek and cold,
    Colder thy kiss;
Truly that hour foretold
    Sorrow to this.

The dew of the morning
10   Sunk chill on my brow—
It felt like the warning
    Of what I feel now.
Thy vows are all broken,
    And light is thy fame;
15 I hear thy name spoken,
    And share in its shame.

They name thee before me,
    A knell to mine ear;
A shudder comes o'er me—
20   Why wert thou so dear?
They know not I knew thee,
    Who knew thee too well—
Long, long shall I rue thee,
    Too deeply to tell.

25 In secret we met—
    In silence I grieve,
That thy heart could forget,
    Thy spirit deceive.
If I should meet thee
30   After long years,
How should I greet thee?—
    With silence and tears.

18 knell: the ringing of a bell to announce a death.

23 rue: remember with feelings of sorrow; regret.

Thinking Through the Literature

1. Did you identify with the situation in one of these poems more than the other? Explain your response.

2. What kinds of relationships does the poet seem to be presenting in the two poems? Support your answer with details from the poems.

3. How would you describe the different emotions expressed by the **speakers** of these poems?

Childe Harold's

from

Snow Storm: Steam-Boat off a Harbour's Mouth (1842), Joseph Mallord William Turner. Clore Collection, Tate Gallery, London/Art Resource, New York.

Pilgrimage

George Gordon, Lord Byron

Apostrophe to the Ocean

There is a pleasure in the pathless woods,
There is a rapture on the lonely shore,
There is society where none intrudes,
By the deep Sea, and music in its roar:
5   I love not Man the less, but Nature more,
From these our interviews, in which I steal
From all I may be or have been before,
To mingle with the Universe, and feel
What I can ne'er express, yet can not all conceal.

10   Roll on, thou deep and dark blue Ocean, roll!
Ten thousand fleets sweep over thee in vain;
Man marks the earth with ruin, his control
Stops with the shore; upon the watery plain
The wrecks are all thy deed, nor doth remain
15   A shadow of man's ravage, save his own,
When, for a moment, like a drop of rain,
He sinks into thy depths with bubbling groan,
Without a grave, unknell'd, uncoffin'd, and unknown.

His steps are not upon thy paths, thy fields
20   Are not a spoil for him,—thou dost arise
And shake him from thee; the vile strength he wields
For earth's destruction thou dost all despise,
Spurning him from thy bosom to the skies,
And send'st him, shivering in thy playful spray
25   And howling, to his Gods, where haply lies
His petty hope in some near port or bay,
And dashest him again to earth:—there let him lay.

15 ravage: destruction.

18 unknell'd: with no announcement of his death.

25 haply: perhaps.

The armaments which thunderstrike the walls
Of rock-built cities, bidding nations quake
And monarchs tremble in their capitals,
The oak leviathans, whose huge ribs make
Their clay creator the vain title take
Of lord of thee and arbiter of war,—
These are thy toys, and, as the snowy flake,
They melt into thy yeast of waves, which mar
Alike the Armada's pride or spoils of Trafalgar.

Thy shores are empires, changed in all save thee—
Assyria, Greece, Rome, Carthage, what are they?
Thy waters wash'd them power while they were free,
And many a tyrant since; their shores obey
The stranger, slave, or savage; their decay
Has dried up realms to deserts:—not so thou,
Unchangeable save to thy wild waves' play;
Time writes no wrinkle on thine azure brow;
Such as creation's dawn beheld, thou rollest now.

Thou glorious mirror, where the Almighty's form
Glasses itself in tempests; in all time,
Calm or convulsed—in breeze, or gale, or storm,
Icing the pole, or in the torrid clime
Dark-heaving;—boundless, endless, and sublime—
The image of Eternity—the throne
Of the Invisible; even from out thy slime
The monsters of the deep are made; each zone
Obeys thee; thou goest forth, dread, fathomless, alone.

And I have loved thee, Ocean! and my joy
Of youthful sports was on thy breast to be
Borne, like thy bubbles, onward. From a boy
I wanton'd with thy breakers—they to me
Were a delight; and if the freshening sea
Made them a terror—'t was a pleasing fear,
For I was as it were a child of thee,
And trusted to thy billows far and near,
And laid my hand upon thy mane—as I do here.

31 oak leviathans: large ships.

32 their clay creator: humankind.

33 arbiter: a person with the power of judging or ruling.

35 yeast: turbulent froth.

36 Armada's . . . Trafalgar (trə-făl′gər): The mighty Spanish Armada was defeated by the British fleet in 1588; Trafalgar is a Spanish cape, the site of a great British naval victory over the French and Spanish in 1805.

38 Assyria . . . Carthage: four powerful ancient civilizations.

44 azure (ăzh′ər): sky blue.

47 glasses itself: is reflected.

49 torrid clime: the intensely hot regions near the equator.

53 zone: one of the five climatic regions of the earth.

54 fathomless: too deep to be measured; also, beyond comprehension.

58 wanton'd: frolicked playfully; **breakers:** large waves.

Connect to the Literature

1. What Do You Think? Describe your reaction to this excerpt from *Childe Harold's Pilgrimage.*

Think Critically

2. What aspects of the ocean do you think the **speaker** admires most? Cite specific examples to support your answer.

3. What different emotions does the ocean seem to inspire in the speaker?

THINK ABOUT

- his **description** of the ocean's relationship to humanity
- what he means when he calls the ocean "the throne / Of the Invisible" (lines 51–52)
- his remembrance of his youth

4. How would you describe the ocean's relationship to other aspects of nature mentioned in the excerpt?

5. **ACTIVE READING** **COMPARING SPEAKERS** Review the charts you created in your **READER'S NOTEBOOK.** What seem to be the main character traits of each speaker? What are their similarities? differences?

Extend Interpretations

6. The Writer's Style "She Walks in Beauty" was written to be set to music. What elements of the poem do you think give it a musical quality? Compare your ideas with those of your classmates.

7. Comparing Texts Which of the three poems—"She Walks in Beauty," "When We Two Parted," or the excerpt from *Childe Harold's Pilgrimage*—do you think conveys the strongest emotions? Give evidence to support your opinion.

8. Connect to Life According to the speaker of *Childe Harold's Pilgrimage,* "Man marks the earth with ruin, his control / Stops with the shore." Do you think a contemporary environmentalist would agree? Why or why not?

Literary Analysis

APOSTROPHE The romantic poets frequently used **apostrophe,** a literary device associated with the expression of powerful emotions. In *Childe Harold's Pilgrimage,* the extended apostrophe addresses the ocean as if it were capable of understanding what is being said and of taking credit for its own characteristics and actions, as the following example illustrates:

> *Roll on, thou deep and dark blue Ocean, roll!*
> *Ten thousand fleets sweep over thee in vain . . .*

Paired Activity Reread the excerpt from *Childe Harold's Pilgrimage,* looking for at least two other passages that you think are strong illustrations of apostrophe. Then discuss with your partner why Byron might have chosen to use apostrophe rather than simply describing the ocean's magnificence. In a chart like the one below, record the examples of apostrophe you choose and your explanations of why Byron used apostrophe.

1st passage:

Why Byron used:

2nd passage:

Why Byron used:

Choices & CHALLENGES

Writing Options

1. Romantic Character Sketch
Write a character sketch conveying your impression of the woman described in "She Walks in Beauty."

2. Imaginary Dialogue Write dialogue for an imaginary conversation between the speaker of "When We Two Parted" and the person he addresses.

3. Weekly Opinion Column As the speaker of *Childe Harold's Pilgrimage,* write an opinion column for a weekly newsmagazine, expressing your views on the foibles of society.

Activities & Explorations

1. Illuminated Manuscript Create border designs for an illuminated manuscript of "She Walks in Beauty." ~ **ART**

2. Interview with the Poet With a partner, plan and conduct an imaginary interview with Lord Byron. Include questions, based on your reading of the excerpt from *Childe Harold's Pilgrimage,* about his attitudes toward society. ~ **SPEAKING AND LISTENING**

Art Connection

Artistic Reflections Look again at the Turner seascape on page 776. What aspects of the excerpt from *Childe Harold's Pilgrimage* do you see reflected in the painting?

Inquiry & Research

The Battle of Trafalgar Research the Battle of Trafalgar. Who was involved in the battle? What were its causes? What long-range effects did it have? Report your findings to the class.

George Gordon, Lord Byron
1788–1824

Other Works
"So We'll Go No More A-Roving"
"On This Day I Complete My Thirty-Sixth Year"

In Pursuit of Adventure Lord Byron is one of the most handsome and daring figures in literary history. Born into a family of hot-tempered soldiers, seamen, and fighters, he lived a dramatic life. He had a fierce determination to test himself physically—a response, in part, to his having been born with a clubfoot that gave him a slight limp throughout his life. At school, Byron enthusiastically engaged in vigorous sports, including swimming, boxing, riding, and fencing. Later, while traveling in Europe, he frequently sought out dangerous ventures that frightened his companions.

Fame and Fortune At the age of 10, Byron inherited an ancestral estate from his great-uncle—and with it the title of sixth Baron Byron. He was only in his 20s when the first parts of *Childe Harold's Pilgri-*

mage were published and, as he put it, "I awoke one morning and found myself famous." Unfortunately, he had a reckless and dissipated lifestyle that often left him in debt and suffering from extreme melancholy. He entered into many romantic alliances throughout his life, but his one marriage lasted only a year. The rumors arising from its failure caused a decline in Byron's popularity in England, and in 1816 he left the country for good, living first in Switzerland and then for several years in Italy, where he began work on what was to be his masterpiece, *Don Juan.* In 1823, impelled by his love of the Greek people, he embarked on a mission to help them in their war for independence from Turkish rule. While training soldiers, he contracted a fever and died shortly thereafter, just after his 36th birthday. Byron is still regarded as a national hero in Greece, not for his poetry but for his dedication to the country's revolution.

Selected Poems

By PERCY BYSSHE SHELLEY

Comparing Literature of the World

The Poetry of Percy Bysshe Shelley and Heinrich Heine

This lesson and the one that follows present an opportunity for comparing the English romantic poetry of Percy Bysshe Shelley with the German romantic poetry of Heinrich Heine. Specific points of comparison in the Heine lesson will help you contrast Shelley's verse with that of his German contemporary.

(**Connect to Your Life**)

Aiming High What aspirations do people your age tend to have? Survey ten students in your class to find out some of their hopes and dreams for the future. Compare their responses. Are their aspirations practical and realistic? lofty and idealistic? Discuss your findings with your classmates.

Build Background

An Idealistic Life Percy Bysshe Shelley was an idealist and a nonconformist who passionately opposed all injustice and dreamed of changing the world through love, imagination, and poetry. Now ranked among the greatest of the English romantic poets, Shelley was rebuked by his contemporaries for his radical views.

As a young man, Shelley fiercely opposed the oppression and poverty he saw in places like Ireland and Wales. When his efforts at reform met with resistance and failure, however, he turned to poetry as a means of expressing and fulfilling his aspirations. He wrote with the conviction that through the imagination of the poet and the power of love, humanity could perceive and transcend the evils of society.

Shelley was a skillful craftsman who explored a wide array of poetic forms and rhythmic patterns in his work. "Ozymandias" is a **sonnet** in which he experiments with **rhyme** and **rhythm.** "Ode to the West Wind" and "To a Skylark" are examples of the **ode**—an exalted, complex lyric that develops a dignified **theme.**

Focus Your Reading

LITERARY ANALYSIS | **RHYTHMIC PATTERNS IN POETRY** | Three important terms to keep in mind as you study poetry of this period include the following:

Meter—the regular repetition of a rhythmic unit in a line of poetry

Foot—a unit of meter consisting of one stressed syllable and one or two unstressed syllables

Iambic pentameter—a type of meter in which the line is made up of five feet, each consisting of an unstressed syllable followed by a stressed syllable.

Ĭ mét ă trávelér fróm ăn ántiqŭe lánd

Rhythmic patterns, along with **structural elements** and other **sound devices,** help to complement and enhance a poem's meaning.

ACTIVE READING | **DRAWING CONCLUSIONS ABOUT THEME** | In order to **draw conclusions** about the **theme** of a poem, use the following strategies:

- Read the poem several times, stopping to ask yourself at the end of each reading what insights you might have gained. Make sure that at least one of your readings is aloud, so that you are able to hear **rhythmic patterns;** these often help to enhance the meaning of the poem.
- Think about the **subject** of the poem. By choosing this particular subject, what theme might the poet be trying to convey?
- Analyze the speaker's **tone,** or attitude toward his or her subject.
- Think about how you would describe the **mood,** or feeling, of the poem; this can also offer clues to the theme.

READER'S NOTEBOOK As you read each poem, jot down notes about rhythmic patterns, subject, tone, and mood. Be ready to discuss your conclusions about theme.

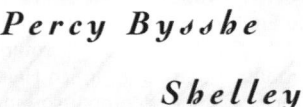

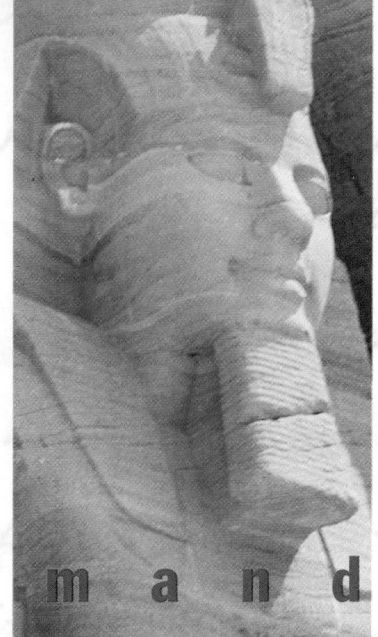

Percy Bysshe

Shelley

O z y m a n d i a s

I met a traveler from an antique land
Who said: Two vast and trunkless legs of stone
Stand in the desert . . . Near them, on the sand,
Half sunk, a shattered visage lies, whose frown,
5 And wrinkled lip, and sneer of cold command,
Tell that its sculptor well those passions read
Which yet survive, stamped on these lifeless things,
The hand that mocked them, and the heart that fed:
And on the pedestal these words appear:
10 "My name is Ozymandias, king of kings:
Look on my works, ye Mighty, and despair!"
Nothing beside remains. Round the decay
Of that colossal wreck, boundless and bare
The lone and level sands stretch far away.

GUIDE FOR READING

2 trunkless legs: legs separated from the rest of the body.

4 visage (vĭz′ĭj): face.

6 those passions: that is, Ozymandias' passions.

8 This line may be paraphrased as "The sculptor's hand, which mocked the passions of the king, and the king's heart, which fed those passions."

10 Ozymandias (ŏz′ĭ-măn′dē-əs): the Greek form of "Usermare," a title of the Egyptian pharaoh Rameses II, who reigned from 1304 to 1237 B.C.

11 What is ironic about the boast inscribed on the pedestal?

Thinking Through the Literature

1. **Comprehension Check** Based on this poem, who was Ozymandias?

2. Does this poem remind you of anything you have seen in your own experience? Explain your response.

3. What **theme,** or message about life, do you think is conveyed in this poem?

THINK ABOUT

- the words Ozymandias had carved on the pedestal
- the aspirations Ozymandias seems to have had
- what has happened to the statue

Ode to the West Wind

Percy Bysshe Shelley

Detail of *Cloud Study* (about 1821), John Constable, R.A. Oil on canvas,
Victoria and Albert Museum, London/Art Resource, New York.

I

O wild West Wind, thou breath of Autumn's being,
Thou, from whose unseen presence the leaves dead
Are driven, like ghosts from an enchanter fleeing,

Yellow, and black, and pale, and hectic red,
5 Pestilence-stricken multitudes: O thou,
Who chariotest to their dark wintry bed

The wingéd seeds, where they lie cold and low,
Each like a corpse within its grave, until
Thine azure sister of the Spring shall blow

10 Her clarion o'er the dreaming earth, and fill
(Driving sweet buds like flocks to feed in air)
With living hues and odors plain and hill:

Wild Spirit, which art moving everywhere;
Destroyer and preserver; hear, oh, hear!

4 hectic: feverish.

9 sister . . . Spring: the reviving south wind of spring.

10 clarion: a trumpet with a clear, ringing tone.

II

¹⁵ Thou on whose stream, mid the steep sky's commotion,
Loose clouds like earth's decaying leaves are shed,
Shook from the tangled bough of Heaven and Ocean,

Angels of rain and lightning: there are spread
On the blue surface of thine aëry surge,
²⁰ Like the bright hair uplifted from the head

Of some fierce Maenad, even from the dim verge
Of the horizon to the zenith's height,
The locks of the approaching storm. Thou dirge

Of the dying year, to which this closing night
²⁵ Will be the dome of a vast sepulcher,
Vaulted with all thy congregated might

Of vapors, from whose solid atmosphere
Black rain, and fire, and hail will burst: oh, hear!

III

Thou who didst waken from his summer dreams
³⁰ The blue Mediterranean, where he lay,
Lulled by the coil of his crystálline streams,

Beside a pumice isle in Baiae's bay,
And saw in sleep old palaces and towers
Quivering within the wave's intenser day,

³⁵ All overgrown with azure moss and flowers
So sweet, the sense faints picturing them! Thou
For whose path the Atlantic's level powers

Cleave themselves into chasms, while far below
The sea-blooms and the oozy woods which wear
⁴⁰ The sapless foliage of the ocean, know

Thy voice, and suddenly grow gray with fear,
And tremble and despoil themselves: oh, hear!

IV

If I were a dead leaf thou mightest bear;
If I were a swift cloud to fly with thee;
⁴⁵ A wave to pant beneath thy power, and share

18 angels: messengers.

19 aëry: airy.

20–23 The speaker is saying that the clouds lie in streaks, looking like the streaming hair of a maenad (mē′năd′)—a wildly dancing female worshiper of Dionysus, the Greek god of wine.

23 dirge: funeral song.

25 sepulcher (sĕp′əl-kər): tomb.

31 crystálline (krĭs-tăl′ĭn) **streams:** the different-colored transparent currents of the Mediterranean Sea.

32 pumice (pŭm′ĭs): a light volcanic rock; **Baiae's** (bī′ēz′) **bay:** the Bay of Naples, site of the ancient Roman resort of Baiae.

37 level powers: surface.

The impulse of thy strength, only less free
Than thou, O uncontrollable! If even
I were as in my boyhood, and could be

The comrade of thy wanderings over Heaven,
50 As then, when to outstrip thy skyey speed
Scarce seemed a vision; I would ne'er have striven

As thus with thee in prayer in my sore need.
Oh, lift me as a wave, a leaf, a cloud!
I fall upon the thorns of life! I bleed!

55 A heavy weight of hours has chained and bowed
One too like thee: tameless, and swift, and proud.

V

Make me thy lyre, even as the forest is:
What if my leaves are falling like its own!
The tumult of thy mighty harmonies

60 Will take from both a deep, autumnal tone,
Sweet though in sadness. Be thou, Spirit fierce,
My spirit! Be thou me, impetuous one!

Drive my dead thoughts over the universe
Like withered leaves to quicken a new birth!
65 And, by the incantation of this verse,

Scatter, as from an unextinguished hearth
Ashes and sparks, my words among mankind!
Be through my lips to unawakened earth

The trumpet of a prophecy! O Wind,
70 If Winter comes, can Spring be far behind?

50 thy skyey (skī′ē) **speed:** the swiftness of clouds moving quickly across the sky.

51 vision: here, something impossible to achieve.

57 lyre: here, a reference to the Aeolian harp, an instrument whose strings make musical sounds when the wind blows over them.

62 impetuous (ĭm-pĕch′ōō-əs): violently forceful; impulsive.

65 incantation: recitation, as of a magic spell.

Thinking Through the Literature

1. With a partner, discuss the **image** left in your mind after reading "Ode to the West Wind."

2. How would you describe the **speaker's** feelings about the wind? Cite evidence.

3. What aspirations does the speaker appear to have?

THINK ABOUT { • what he means by "the thorns of life" in line 54
• his request in lines 63–67

T o a S k y l a r k

PERCY BYSSHE SHELLEY

Hail to thee, blithe Spirit!
   Bird thou never wert,
That from Heaven, or near it,
   Pourest thy full heart
5 In profuse strains of unpremeditated art.

   Higher still and higher
     From the earth thou springest
Like a cloud of fire;
     The blue deep thou wingest,
10 And singing still dost soar, and soaring ever singest.

   In the golden lightning
     Of the sunken sun,
O'er which clouds are bright'ning,
     Thou dost float and run;
15 Like an unbodied joy whose race is just begun.

   The pale purple even
     Melts around thy flight;
Like a star of Heaven,
     In the broad daylight
20 Thou art unseen, but yet I hear thy shrill delight,

   Keen as are the arrows
     Of that silver sphere,
Whose intense lamp narrows
     In the white dawn clear
25 Until we hardly see—we feel that it is there.

5 unpremeditated (ŭn′prĭ-mĕd′ĭ-tā′tĭd): natural; not planned out ahead of time.

16 even: evening.

22 silver sphere: the planet Venus, often called the morning star because it is visible in the east just before daybreak.

All the earth and air
With thy voice is loud,
As, when night is bare,
From one lonely cloud
30 The moon rains out her beams, and Heaven is overflowed.

What thou are we know not;
What is most like thee?
From rainbow clouds there flow not
Drops so bright to see
35 As from thy presence showers a rain of melody.

Like a Poet hidden
In the light of thought,
Singing hymns unbidden,
Till the world is wrought
40 To sympathy with hopes and fears it heeded not:

Like a high-born maiden
In a palace tower
Soothing her love-laden
Soul in secret hour
45 With music sweet as love, which overflows her bower:

45 bower: private room; boudoir.

Like a glowworm golden
In a dell of dew,
Scattering unbeholden
Its aërial hue
50 Among the flowers and grass, which screen it from the view!

Like a rose embowered
In its own green leaves,
By warm winds deflowered,
Till the scent it gives
55 Makes faint with too much sweet those heavy-wingéd thieves:

53 deflowered: fully opened.

55 thieves: the warm winds.

Sound of vernal showers
On the twinkling grass,
Rain-awakened flowers,
All that ever was
60 Joyous, and clear, and fresh, thy music doth surpass:

56 vernal: spring.

Detail of *Cloud Study* (1821), John Constable, R.A. Oil on paper laid on board, 9¾″ × 11⅞″,
Yale Center for British Art, Paul Mellon Collection (B1981.25.155).

Teach us, Sprite or Bird,
    What sweet thoughts are thine:
I have never heard
    Praise of love or wine
65 That panted forth a flood of rapture so divine.

Chorus Hymeneal,
    Or triumphal chant,
Matched with thine would be all
    But an empty vaunt,
70 A thing wherein we feel there is some hidden want.

What objects are the fountains
    Of thy happy strain?
What fields, or waves, or mountains?
    What shapes of sky or plain?
75 What love of thine own kind? what ignorance of pain?

66 chorus Hymeneal (hī′mə-nē′əl):
a wedding song.

69 vaunt: boast.

71 fountains: sources.

With thy clear keen joyance
    Languor cannot be:
Shadow of annoyance
    Never came near thee:
80 Thou lovest—but ne'er knew love's sad satiety.

    Waking or asleep,
        Thou of death must deem
    Things more true and deep
        Than we mortals dream,
85 Or how could thy notes flow in such a crystal stream?

    We look before and after,
        And pine for what is not:
    Our sincerest laughter
        With some pain is fraught;
90 Our sweetest songs are those that tell of saddest thought.

    Yet if we could scorn
        Hate, and pride, and fear;
    If we were things born
        Not to shed a tear,
95 I know not how thy joy we ever should come near.

    Better than all measures
        Of delightful sound,
    Better than all treasures
        That in books are found,
100 Thy skill to poet were, thou scorner of the ground!

    Teach me half the gladness
        That thy brain must know,
    Such harmonious madness
        From my lips would flow
105 The world should listen then—as I am listening now.

77 languor (lăng′gər): lack of energy; listlessness.

80 satiety (sə-tī′Ĭ-tē): the weariness or disgust caused by having a desire fulfilled to excess.

82 deem: know.

91 if: even if.

Connect to the Literature

1. **What Do You Think?** What words or phrases convey your impressions of "To a Skylark"?

Think Critically

2. How would you describe the attitude of the **speaker** toward the skylark? Consider the evidence provided in the poem.

3. How do you think the speaker might like to change his own life?

THINK ABOUT

- the qualities he seems to admire most in the bird
- what he means by "Such harmonious madness / From my lips would flow" (lines 103–104)

4. **ACTIVE READING** **DRAWING CONCLUSIONS ABOUT THEME**
Review the notes in your **READER'S NOTEBOOK**. What conclusions did you reach about the **theme** of each poem? What evidence can you cite to support each conclusion? Compare your findings with those of your classmates.

Extend Interpretations

5. **Comparing Texts** Compare "Ozymandias," "Ode to the West Wind," and "To a Skylark." In your opinion, which poem best conveys the power of nature? Defend your position.

6. **Comparing Texts** Compare Shelley's "To a Skylark" with Matsuo Bashō's haiku about a skylark (page 718). Are there any similarities in the poems' **themes?**

7. **Connect to Life** If you were to write a poem that expressed one of your personal aspirations, what element in nature—a tree, a lake, or a season, for example—might you choose as a **symbol?**

Literary Analysis

RHYTHMIC PATTERNS IN POETRY

Meter is the repetition of a regular rhythmic unit in a line of poetry. The meter emphasizes the musical quality of the language and often relates directly to the subject of the poem. Each unit of meter is known as a **foot,** with each foot having one stressed and one or two unstressed syllables. The most common meter used in English poetry is **iambic pentameter,** in which the line is made up of five feet (called **iambs),** each consisting of an unstressed syllable followed by a stressed syllable.

The lone and level sands stretch far away.

"Ozymandias" is written in iambic pentameter. However, poets use different meters, as well as variations within a regular metrical pattern, to create the effects they want and to reinforce meaning. Typically, this involves adding an extra syllable or reversing the stressed and unstressed syllables in a foot.

Cooperative Learning Activity With a group of classmates, choose another line from "Ozymandias" and two lines each from "Ode to the West Wind" and "To a Skylark." Mark the stressed and unstressed syllables, and then compare the meters and variations. Discuss the effects Shelley creates with different rhythmic patterns.

Choices & CHALLENGES

Writing Options

1. Performance Notes Think about how you might turn your interpretation of one of Shelley's poems into a performance. Write up your ideas in the form of notes, and place the notes in your **Working Portfolio.**

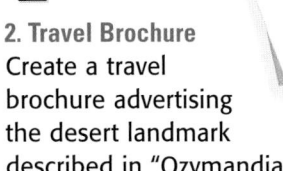

"To a Skylark" Play different pieces of music during performance.

2. Travel Brochure Create a travel brochure advertising the desert landmark described in "Ozymandias."

Activities & Explorations

1. Portrait of a King Design and create a clay statue of Ozymandias, based on your impression of the king as he is portrayed in Shelley's poem. ~ **ART**

2. Poet's Soliloquy In the role of either the speaker of "Ode to the West Wind" or the speaker of "To a Skylark," deliver a soliloquy expressing your aspirations and frustrations as a poet. ~ **SPEAKING AND LISTENING**

Inquiry & Research

Shelley's Poetic Theories Do research on Shelley's critical work titled *A Defense of Poetry.* When did he write it? How was the work received by other writers of the day?

 Related Reading An excerpt of *A Defense of Poetry* can be found on page 792.

Percy Bysshe Shelley
1792–1822

Other Works
"Hymn to Intellectual Beauty"/ "The Cloud"/ "To Night"/ "Love's Philosophy"/ "Adonais"

The Early Years Percy Bysshe Shelley led a driven and tumultuous life that ended prematurely. Born into an aristocratic and wealthy family, he was sent away to boarding school at the age of ten. There, he endured bullying and teasing from the other boys, painful experiences that fueled his hatred of injustice. As an adolescent, Shelley embraced many radical views, including atheism, and rejected most of the institutions of society. When he was expelled from Oxford University during his first year for circulating an essay defending atheism, his family was scandalized, especially his father.

Love and Romance In 1811, a few months after leaving Oxford, Shelley eloped to Scotland with Harriet Westbrook, who was only 16. Their relationship was not a strong one, and in 1814, despite the fact that Harriet was expecting their second child, Shelley abandoned her for Mary Wollstonecraft

Godwin, the daughter of the philosopher William Godwin and the feminist author Mary Wollstonecraft.

The Poet as Outcast Shelley's radical ideas and personal behavior drew criticism from his family and friends, and he began to view himself as an outcast. In 1818, following the death of Harriet, Shelley finally married Mary Godwin, and they moved permanently to Italy. In 1819, despite his despair at the deaths of his two infant children within a period of nine months, he produced much of his greatest poetry, including "Ode to the West Wind" and his masterpiece, the verse drama *Prometheus Unbound.*

A Tragic Ending The years 1820–1822 were ones of relative stability, during which Shelley wrote many fine lyrics, including "To a Skylark" and "Adonais," an elegy in memory of John Keats. In the last stanza of this poem, he speaks of his spirit as a ship "borne darkly, fearfully, afar." On July 8, 1822, Shelley and a friend were drowned when their boat capsized in a sudden storm. Shelley's ashes were buried in Rome, near the graves of John Keats and Shelley's son William.

from

A DEFENSE OF
Poetry

Percy Bysshe Shelley

**After reading a composition in which a friend and fellow
poet jokingly claimed that poetry no longer had a place in
society, Percy Bysshe Shelley was troubled. It seemed to
him possible that this view was in fact becoming widely
held. In response, he wrote *A Defense of Poetry*. As you
read this excerpt, note how he made his case for the value
of poets and poetry.**

1 Poetry is indeed something divine. It is at once the center and
circumference of knowledge; . . . Poetry is not like reasoning, a
power to be exerted according to the determination of the will.
A man cannot say, "I will compose poetry." The greatest poet
2 even cannot say it; for the mind in creation is as a fading coal,
which some invisible influence, like an inconstant wind,
awakens to transitory brightness; this power arises from within,
like the color of a flower which fades and changes as it is
developed, and the conscious portions of our natures are
unprophetic either of its approach or its departure. . .

---

1. **potable** (pō′tə-bəl): drinkable.

Percy Bysshe Shelley

Poetry turns all things to loveliness; it exalts the beauty of that which is most beautiful, and it adds beauty to that which is most deformed; it marries exultation and horror, grief and pleasure, eternity and change; it subdues to union under its light yoke all irreconcilable things. It transmutes all that it touches, and every form moving within the radiance of its presence is changed by wondrous sympathy to an incarnation of the spirit which it breathes; its secret alchemy turns to potable[1] gold the poisonous waters which flow from death through life; it strips the veil of familiarity from the world, and lays bare the naked and sleeping beauty which is the spirit of its forms.

❸

Reading for Information

Has something that you feel passionately about been attacked or insulted? If so, you may have tried to defend your position in writing, as Shelley did.

IDENTIFYING PERSUASIVE TECHNIQUES

What techniques can a writer use to persuade others to adopt his or her point of view? To explore Shelley's persuasive techniques, use the questions and activities that follow.

❶ **Hyperbole** is an intentional exaggeration for effect. Shelley's claim that poetry is "something divine" can be seen as hyperbole, but it probably expresses his true opinion. Identify some instances in which you think Shelley was deliberately hyperbolic.

❷ Writers use **figurative language,** which includes **similes** and **metaphors,** to create specific impressions in readers' minds. When Shelley wrote that "the mind in creation is as a fading coal," he used a simile to illuminate the creative forces that shape poetry. How does his use of figurative language contribute to his argument?

❸ **Parallelism** is the repetition of a grammatical structure in order to emphasize an idea or concept, as in Shelley's series of clauses beginning with *it* ("it exalts . . . it adds . . . "). Identify other examples of parallelism in the excerpt.

The Lotus-Blossom Cowers

Poetry by HEINRICH HEINE (hīn′rĭk hī′nə)

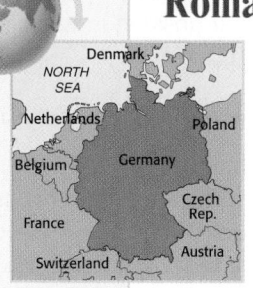

Comparing Literature of the World

Romanticism Across Cultures

The Poetry of Shelley and Heine Although English poet Percy Bysshe Shelley and German poet Heinrich Heine were from different countries and cultures, both were key figures in the romantic movement during the late 18th and early 19th centuries.

Points of Comparison As you read Heine's poem, compare it with Shelley's poetry in terms of the following:

- the **imagery** used by each poet
- the **tone** each poet conveys in his work
- the **themes** conveyed by each poet about life

Build Background

The Literature of Heinrich Heine In Germany, the romantic period extended from approximately 1790 to 1830. In literature, it was characterized by an interest in folksongs, fables, and medieval romances and by an outpouring of poetry dealing with the themes of love, melancholy, and the beauty of nature.

The early poetry of Heinrich Heine exemplifies the style of the period. In 1827, Heine published *The Book of Songs,* a large collection of lyric poems that includes "The Lotus-Blossom Cowers." Containing love songs, ballads, and sonnets—many of which were later set to music—this volume was responsible for Heine's international reputation as a respected and influential poet.

Eventually, Heine turned from composing love poems to writing poetry and essays about political and social issues. Like the English romantic poet Percy Bysshe Shelley, Heine was an outspoken and often bitter critic of social injustice who was rejected in his homeland for expressing radical and unpopular opinions. Unlike Shelley, however, Heine was not a romantic in spirit. He was skeptical of the power of the imagination and did not believe that romantic idealism was the answer to society's ills. Despite this, his earlier love poems are definitely romantic in style, and in this way are representative of the German romantic movement.

Focus Your Reading

LITERARY ANALYSIS **MOOD** **Mood** is the feeling or atmosphere that a writer creates for the reader. Notice the mood evoked by the following example:

> *The lotus-blossom cowers*
> *Under the sun's bright beams . . .*

As you read Heine's poem, consider which aspects of the poem contribute to the mood it establishes.

ACTIVE READING **UNDERSTANDING AND APPRECIATING POETRY** When studying a poem, it is important to read the poem more than once. Each time you reread it, you may discover **images** or **ideas** you missed in a previous reading.

READER'S NOTEBOOK In order to understand and fully appreciate "The Lotus-Blossom Cowers," read the poem three times. After each reading, note images and your reactions to specific lines in a chart similar to the one shown.

"The Lotus-Blossom Cowers"
1st Reading:
2nd Reading:
3rd Reading:

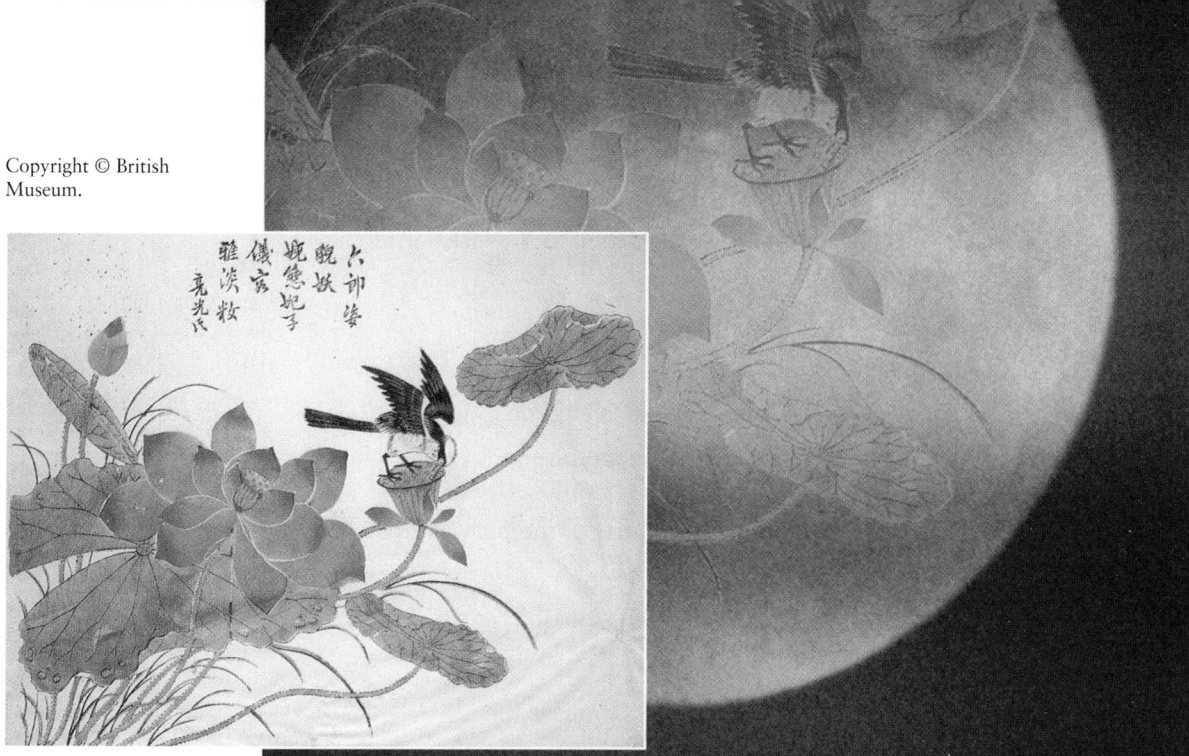

The Lotus-Blossom Cowers

Heinrich Heine

The lotus-blossom cowers
    Under the sun's bright beams;
Her forehead drooping for hours,
    She waits for the night among dreams.

5 The Moon, he is her lover,
    He wakes her with his gaze;
To him alone she uncovers
    The fair flower of her face.

She glows and grows more radiant,
10   And gazes mutely above;
Breathing and weeping and trembling
    With love—and the pain of love.

Translated by Louis Untermeyer

Connect to the Literature

1. **What Do You Think?** What is your reaction to the last stanza of the poem?

Think Critically

2. How would you describe the **speaker's** attitude toward love?

THINK ABOUT

- the way the lotus-blossom responds to the moon
- what the speaker means by "the pain of love" (line 12)

3. Why do you think Heine chose a lotus-blossom as the **subject** of this poem?

4. **ACTIVE READING** **UNDERSTANDING AND APPRECIATING POETRY** Compare the impressions you recorded in your 📖 **READER'S NOTEBOOK** after each reading of the poem. How did they change? After your second the third readings, did you discover any **images** or **ideas** that you hadn't noticed in your first reading? Share your findings.

Extend Interpretations

5. **The Writer's Style** Heine wrote his poems in German, his native language, but they have been translated into English numerous times. What difficulties would you expect a writer to encounter in translating a poem from one language to another? What aspects of a poem might be changed in the process of translation?

6. **Connect to Life** Do you think pain is an integral part of every love relationship? Why or why not?

7. **Points of Comparison** Compare the imagery in "The Lotus-Blossom Cowers" with that in Shelley's "To a Skylark" (page 786). What similarities can you find? In your opinion, which poet paints a more vivid or striking picture? Give reasons for your answer.

Literary Analysis

MOOD The feeling or atmosphere that a writer creates for the reader is referred to as **mood.** One element that contributes to the mood of a poem is **imagery**—the words and phrases that re-create sensory experiences for the reader.

Activity In the center of a word web, describe the mood of Heine's poem. Then, in the surrounding circles, list words or images that contribute to the mood. If you think the poem has more than one mood, complete a word web for each mood you identify.

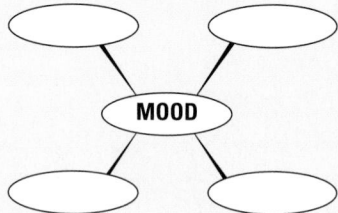
MOOD

REVIEW **PERSONIFICATION** Heine makes use of **personification** when he gives human qualities to a flower. Working with a partner, rewrite "The Lotus-Blossom Cowers," eliminating all instances of personification. How does the absence of personification change the poem?

REVIEW **RHYME SCHEME** A **rhyme scheme** is the pattern of end rhyme in a poem. Reread "The Lotus-Blossom Cowers," and then chart the poem's rhyme scheme. What is the pattern in the first two stanzas? How does the pattern change in the third stanza? Why do you think it changes?

Choices & CHALLENGES

Writing Options

1. **Haiku, Heine Style** Compose a haiku based on an idea or image in Heine's poem.

2. **A Definition of Love** Imagining yourself to be the speaker of "The Lotus-Blossom Cowers," write your definition of love.

3. **Points of Comparison**
Write an essay in which you compare Shelley's and Heine's poems in terms of the tone each poet conveys and the themes about life that each poet imparts to the reader.

Writing Handbook
See page 1367: Compare and Contrast.

Activities & Explorations

Musical Interpretation Look for a musical recording that in your opinion conveys the mood and emotions of the poem. Play the recording for your class.
~ INTERPRETING

Inquiry & Research

Botany Lesson As a group, research the habitat and characteristics of the lotus, or water lily. What unique qualities of the plant might have inspired Heinrich Heine to write "The Lotus-Blossom Cowers"? Discuss your findings with the class.

Heinrich Heine
1797–1856

Other Works
The Book of Songs
Poems of Heinrich Heine

Career Pursuits Born in Düsseldorf, Germany (then Prussia), to Jewish parents, Heinrich Heine was greatly influenced by an uncle who tried unsuccessfully to push his nephew into business. When he was 17, Heine began to halfheartedly pursue a series of apprenticeships, but he succeeded at none. His uncle finally agreed to provide him with a university education, and although the young man was more interested in writing poetry, he eventually received a degree in law. Intent on finding a job, Heine reluctantly converted to Protestantism because government positions were not open to Jews at the time; but his conversion was in vain, for he was never offered any of the jobs he desired.

Critic of Society During his university days, Heine became concerned about political and social injustice. Throughout his life, he searched for a solution to such injustice, exploring ideas ranging from various forms of socialism to the communism espoused by his acquaintance Karl Marx. None of these options totally satisfied Heine, however, for he always worried that any radical changes in social order might destroy the literature, art, and music that he so dearly loved.

Ex-Patriot In 1831, Heine moved to Paris, which at the time was a haven for freethinkers. He was heartily welcomed into French social and literary circles, where he found many admirers of his work. In his essays, he began speaking out against the governments of both France and Germany, but these works were poorly received in his homeland. Many Germans considered him unpatriotic, and the government attempted to ban all of his works. This hostility toward Heine lasted for a long time. Many years after his death, efforts to erect memorials to the poet in Germany were met with violent protests that in some cities erupted into riots.

Declining Health In 1848, a serious illness left Heine partially paralyzed, and for eight years the poet was confined to his bed—or as he termed it, his "mattress grave." Although often in tremendous pain, he continued to write until his death, producing some of his best poetry during the last years of his life.

PREPARING to *Read*

Selected Poetry

By JOHN KEATS

(Connect to Your Life)

Facing Death Think of someone you've either known or heard of who, because of illness, was forced to face death at an early age. What was the person's attitude? How did he or she spend whatever time that was left? Discuss with your classmates.

Build Background

A Brief but Fruitful Life Although John Keats died of tuberculosis at a tragically young age, he was one of the most gifted English romantic poets. Keats began writing poetry at age 18, and by the time of his death at age 25 he had written poems that would establish him as a major poet. In 1819 alone—a year of extreme emotional distress—Keats composed a series of masterpieces, including a narrative poem, numerous sonnets, and five odes. Four of those poems appear on the following pages.

Although his work reflects the powerful emotions typically found in romantic poetry, Keats did not share the social and political concerns of many of his contemporaries. He was not influenced by the revolutionary ideals of the time and did not, like Percy Bysshe Shelley or Heinrich Heine, search for solutions to society's ills. Keats was more concerned with the qualities of beauty and with the private emotions of the individual, such as the joys or pains of love and the anxieties inspired by an uncertain future.

Focus Your Reading

LITERARY ANALYSIS **SOUND DEVICES** **Assonance** is the repetition of a vowel sound within words—for example, the repetition of the long *e* sound in the following line:

> *When I have fears that I may cease*
>   *to be*

Consonance is the repetition of consonant sounds within and at the ends of words, like that of the *st* and *z* sounds in this line:

> *Thou watchest the last oozings*
>   *hours by hours.*

As you read Keats's poems, listen for his use of both sound devices.

ACTIVE READING **ANALYZING AN AUTHOR'S MOTIVATION** All authors have a reason, or **motivation,** for creating their works, and Keats is no exception. As you read each of the four poems that follow, try to analyze his motivation. Ask yourself: Why did Keats choose this particular **subject?** What seems to be his **tone,** or attitude? What **theme,** or message, is being conveyed? Given what you know about his life, what conclusions might you draw about his motivation?

READER'S NOTEBOOK As you read, jot down notes that reflect your thoughts about Keats's motivation for writing each poem. Also write down specific lines from each poem that you think are evidence of his motivation.

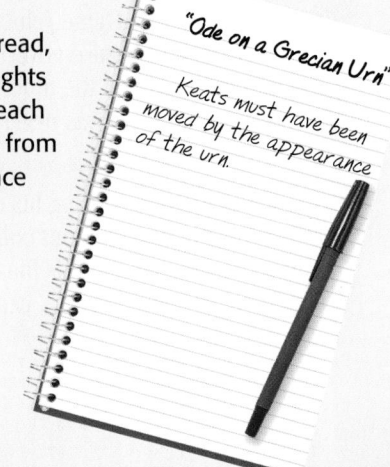

"Ode on a Grecian Urn"

Keats must have been moved by the appearance of the urn.

ODE
ON A GRECIAN URN

Courtesy of the Keats-Shelley Memorial House, Rome.

John Keats

Thou still unravish'd bride of quietness,
    Thou foster-child of silence and slow time,
Sylvan historian, who canst thus express
    A flowery tale more sweetly than our rhyme:
5 What leaf-fring'd legend haunts about thy shape
    Of deities or mortals, or of both,
      In Tempe or the dales of Arcady?
    What men or gods are these? What maidens loath?
What mad pursuit? What struggle to escape?
10   What pipes and timbrels? What wild ecstasy?

Heard melodies are sweet, but those unheard
    Are sweeter; therefore, ye soft pipes, play on;
Not to the sensual ear, but, more endear'd,
    Pipe to the spirit ditties of no tone:
15 Fair youth, beneath the trees, thou canst not leave
    Thy song, nor ever can those trees be bare;
      Bold lover, never, never canst thou kiss,
Though winning near the goal—yet, do not grieve;
      She cannot fade, though thou hast not thy bliss,
20   For ever wilt thou love, and she be fair!

GUIDE FOR READING

1 Do you think *still* means "as yet" or "motionless" here?

3 sylvan: pertaining to trees or woods.

5 haunts about: surrounds.

7 Tempe (tĕm'pē') . . . **Arcady** (är'kə-dē): two places in Greece that are traditional settings in literary works dealing with idealized rustic life. Tempe is a beautiful valley; Arcady (Arcadia) is a mountainous region.

8 loath: unwilling; reluctant.

10 timbrels: tambourines.

11–12 Why might unheard melodies be sweeter than heard ones?

Ah, happy, happy boughs! that cannot shed
　　Your leaves, nor ever bid the spring adieu;
And, happy melodist, unweariéd,
　　For ever piping songs for ever new;
25　More happy love! more happy, happy love!
　　For ever warm and still to be enjoyed,
　　　　For ever panting, and for ever young;
All breathing human passion far above,
　　That leaves a heart high-sorrowful and cloy'd,
30　　　　A burning forehead, and a parching tongue.

29 cloy'd: having had too much of something; oversatisfied.

Who are these coming to the sacrifice?
　　To what green altar, O mysterious priest,
Lead'st thou that heifer lowing at the skies,
　　And all her silken flanks with garlands drest?
35　What little town by river or sea shore,
　　Or mountain-built with peaceful citadel,
　　　　Is emptied of this folk, this pious morn?
And, little town, thy streets for evermore
　　Will silent be; and not a soul to tell
40　　　　Why thou art desolate, can e'er return.

38–40 Why do you think the speaker says that the little town will be forever silent and desolate?

O Attic shape! Fair attitude! with brede
　　Of marble men and maidens overwrought,
With forest branches and the trodden weed;
　　Thou, silent form, dost tease us out of thought
45　As doth eternity: Cold Pastoral!
　　When old age shall this generation waste,
　　　　Thou shalt remain, in midst of other woe
Than ours, a friend to man, to whom thou say'st,
"Beauty is truth, truth beauty,"—that is all
50　　　　Ye know on earth, and all ye need to know.

41 Attic: pure and classical, in the Athenian style; brede: interwoven design.

45 pastoral (păs'tər-əl): an artistic work that portrays rural life in an idealized way. Why do you suppose the speaker calls it "cold"?

Thinking Through the Literature

1. What does the **speaker** seem to admire most about the urn?

2. What role do you think the speaker's imagination plays in his thoughts?

　THINK ABOUT { • his reference to unheard melodies
　　　　　　　　• what has inspired his questions about the "little town"

3. What **themes** about life do you think the poem conveys?

To Autumn

Autumn Leaves, Sir John Everett Millais (1829–1896). Copyright © Manchester (Great Britain) City Art Galleries.

John Keats

GUIDE FOR READING

1 Note the bounty of the harvest the speaker describes in this line and those that follow.

Season of mists and mellow fruitfulness,
   Close bosom-friend of the maturing sun;
Conspiring with him how to load and bless
   With fruit the vines that round the thatch-eaves run;
5 To bend with apples the mossed cottage-trees,

And fill all fruit with ripeness to the core;
    To swell the gourd, and plump the hazel shells
With a sweet kernel; to set budding more,
And still more, later flowers for the bees,
10 Until they think warm days will never cease,
    For Summer has o'er-brimmed their clammy cells.

Who hath not seen thee oft amid thy store?
    Sometimes whoever seeks abroad may find
Thee sitting careless on a granary floor,
15   Thy hair soft-lifted by the winnowing wind;
Or on a half-reaped furrow sound asleep,
    Drowsed with the fume of poppies, while thy hook
      Spares the next swath and all its twinéd flowers:
And sometimes like a gleaner thou dost keep
20   Steady thy laden head across a brook;
Or by a cider-press, with patient look,
    Thou watchest the last oozings hours by hours.

Where are the songs of Spring? Aye, where are they?
    Think not of them, thou hast thy music too—
25 While barred clouds bloom the soft-dying day,
    And touch the stubble-plains with rosy hue;
Then in a wailful choir the small gnats mourn
    Among the river sallows, borne aloft
      Or sinking as the light wind lives or dies;
30 And full-grown lambs loud bleat from hilly bourn;
    Hedge crickets sing; and now with treble soft
The redbreast whistles from a garden croft;
    And gathering swallows twitter in the skies.

12 Whom does the speaker seem to be addressing?

15 winnowing (wĭn′ō-ĭng): separating chaff from grain by blowing the chaff away.

17 hook: scythe (a tool with a long curved blade used for mowing and reaping).

18 swath: a row of grain to be cut.

28 sallows: willow trees.

30 bourn: region.

32 croft: a small enclosed field.

Thinking Through the Literature

1. What parts of Keats's **description** of autumn appeal most to you?

2. Why do you think Keats addresses autumn as though it were a person?

3. How would you describe the **mood** of this poem?

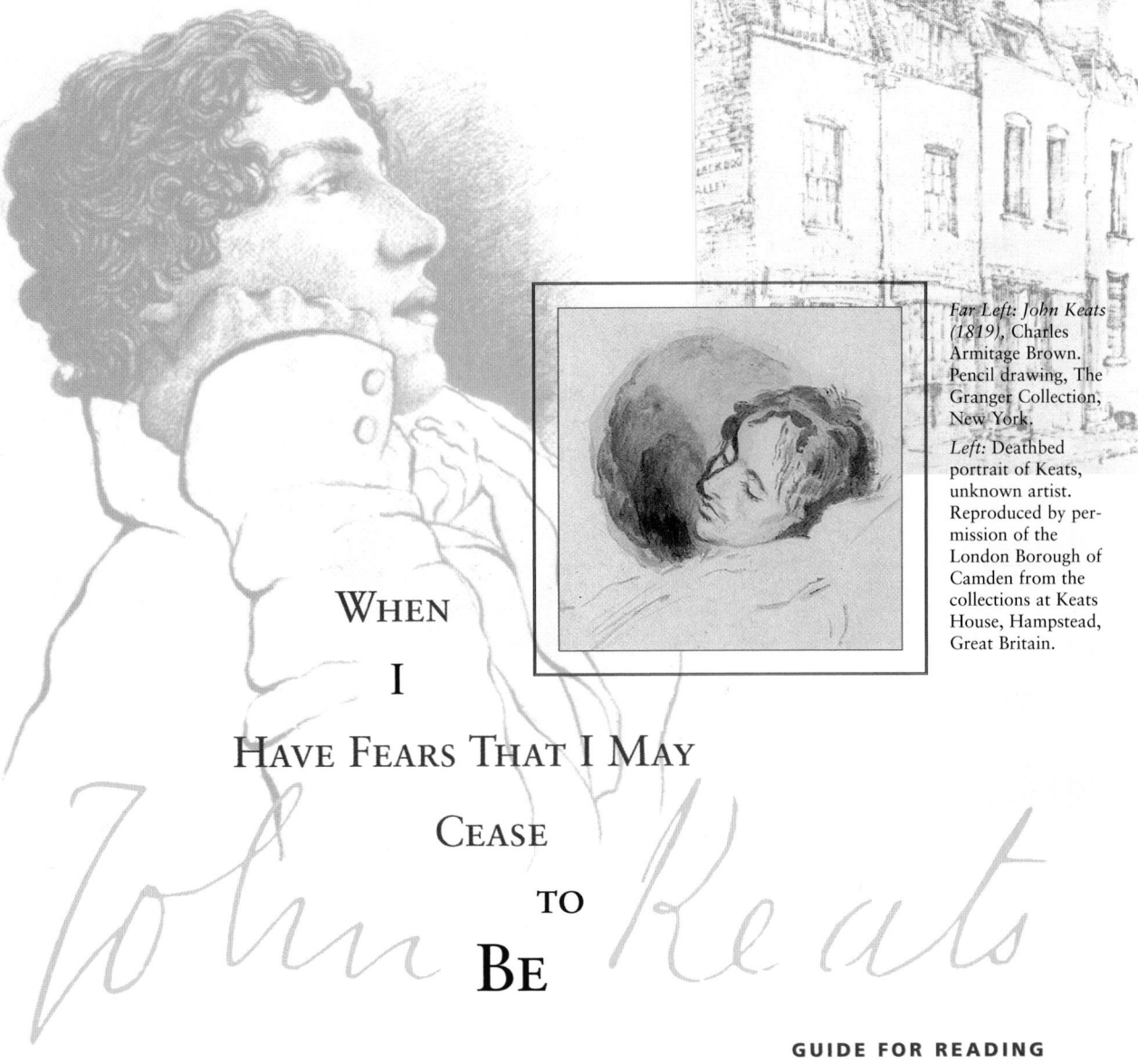

Far Left: *John Keats (1819)*, Charles Armitage Brown. Pencil drawing, The Granger Collection, New York.

Left: Deathbed portrait of Keats, unknown artist. Reproduced by permission of the London Borough of Camden from the collections at Keats House, Hampstead, Great Britain.

WHEN I HAVE FEARS THAT I MAY CEASE TO BE

When I have fears that I may cease to be
    Before my pen has glean'd my teeming brain,
Before high piled books, in charactry,
    Hold like rich garners the full ripen'd grain;
5 When I behold, upon the night's starr'd face,
    Huge cloudy symbols of a high romance,
And think that I may never live to trace
    Their shadows, with the magic hand of chance;
And when I feel, fair creature of an hour,
10   That I shall never look upon thee more,
Never have relish in the fairy power
    Of unreflecting love;—then on the shore
Of the wide world I stand alone, and think
Till love and fame to nothingness do sink.

GUIDE FOR READING

1 Note, in the lines that follow, the reasons for the speaker's fear.

3 charactry: handwriting.

4 garners: storage bins.

9 Why is the "fair creature" described as "of an hour"?

Bright STAR, Would I Were Steadfast As Thou Art

JOHN KEATS

Bright STAR, would I were steadfast as thou art—
    Not in lone splendor hung aloft the night
And watching, with eternal lids apart,
    Like nature's patient, sleepless Eremite,
5 The moving waters at their priestlike task
    Of pure ablution round earth's human shores,
Or gazing on the new soft fallen mask
    Of snow upon the mountains and the moors—
No—yet still steadfast, still unchangeable,
10   Pillowed upon my fair love's ripening breast,
To feel forever its soft fall and swell,
    Awake forever in a sweet unrest,
Still, still to hear her tender-taken breath,
And so live ever—or else swoon to death.

4 Eremite (âr′ə-mīt′): hermit.

6 ablution (ə-bloo′shən): a ritual washing of the body.

The Starry Night (1889), Vincent van Gogh. Oil on canvas, 29″ × 36¼″, The Museum of Modern Art, New York, acquired through the Lillie P. Bliss Bequest. Photo Copyright © 1995 The Museum of Modern Art, New York.

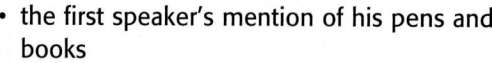

Thinking through the LITERATURE

Connect to the Literature

1. **What Do You Think?** How would you describe the **moods** expressed in "When I Have Fears That I May Cease to Be" and "Bright Star, Would I Were Steadfast as Thou Art"? Share your thoughts with a classmate.

Think Critically

2. What specific concerns does each **speaker** appear to have?

THINK ABOUT
- the first speaker's mention of his pens and books
- what the first speaker fears he'll "never live to trace" (lines 6–8)
- the ways in which the second speaker wishes he were like the star
- each speaker's mention of a loved one

3. How do you interpret the last lines of each poem?

4. **ACTIVE READING** | **ANALYZING AN AUTHOR'S MOTIVATION** Look over the notes you made in your **READER'S NOTEBOOK.** What conclusions can you reach about Keats's motivation for writing these poems? How does his motivation affect the **tone** of the poems?

Extend Interpretations

5. **Comparing Texts** Compare all four poems by Keats. Do you think any of them convey similar **themes** about life?

6. **Critic's Corner** The famous American writer Edgar Allan Poe praised the work of Keats, saying, "Beauty is always his aim." Cite examples of lines from the four poems that help support this claim.

7. **Connect to Life** Think again about the person you discussed in the Connect to Your Life activity on page 798. How did this person's attitude toward life and death compare with the attitude portrayed by Keats in his poetry?

Literary Analysis

SOUND DEVICES Poets often use **sound devices** to emphasize certain words, impart a musical quality, create a mood, or unify a passage. As you recall, **assonance** is the repetition of a vowel sound within words; **consonance** is the repetition of consonant sounds within and at the ends of words. Consonance is different from **rhyme** in that the vowels preceding or following the repeated consonant differ.

Paired Activity With a partner, find examples of assonance and consonance in the four poems. For each example, discuss what effect the sound device has on the passage.

REVIEW **ALLITERATION** Keats also uses **alliteration,** or the repetition of consonant sounds at the beginning of words. Find examples of alliteration in the four poems. Of the three devices—alliteration, assonance, and consonance—which is used the most?

REVIEW **RHYTHMIC PATTERNS IN POETRY**
Meter, the repetition of a regular rhythmic unit in poetry, emphasizes the musical quality of a poem's language. The poems you have read by Keats are written in **iambic pentameter.** However, the poet used variations in rhythmic patterns to create effects. Look at the rhythmic patterns in each poem. What effect does Keats create with the rhythmic variations he used?

Choices & CHALLENGES

Writing Options

1. Seasonal Poetry Rewrite one stanza from "To Autumn," using images that portray another season of the year.

2. Interpretive Essay Draft an essay in which you explain your interpretation of the statement "Beauty is truth, truth beauty."

Writing Handbook.
See pages 1369–1370: Analysis.

Activities & Explorations

1. Autumnal Collage With a partner, design and create a collage that captures the mood of "To Autumn." You might want to use a variety of forms and materials, including drawings, photographs, leaf rubbings, dried leaves and grasses, nuts, seeds, and so on.
~ ART

2. Dramatic Reading In a dramatic oral reading of one of the poems, try to convey the intense emotions that might have inspired the poet.
~ SPEAKING AND LISTENING

Inquiry & Research

Grecian Art Investigate the art of ancient Greece. Try to locate illustrations of the kinds of vases and sculptures that inspired Keats's "Ode on a Grecian Urn." What kinds of designs typically adorn these early works of art?

John Keats
1795–1821

Other Works
"Ode to a Nightingale"
"Solitude"
"On First Looking into Chapman's Homer"
"La Belle Dame Sans Merci"

A Passionate Beginning John Keats's life was brief but intense. As a young child, he was indifferent to his studies and high-spirited. When he was about 13, however, he developed a passion for reading and within a short time read every book in his school library. He was strongly encouraged by a teacher, Charles Cowden Clarke, who remained a friend and literary influence in his life.

A Career as Poet Keats's father had died when Keats was 8, and his mother died when he was 14. He was then taken out of school by his guardian and apprenticed to a surgeon. When he was 18 he began writing poetry, which became the driving force of his life. Although he qualified to practice surgery, by 1817 he had abandoned medicine for the less certain career of poet. He was not immediately successful. In fact, an early narrative poem, *Endymion,* was savagely attacked by London critics. Although Keats was painfully disappointed, fortunately he did not allow the reviews to deter him from continuing his work.

Illness and Poverty Beginning in 1818, Keats had to confront a series of physical and emotional crises. During the summer he developed the early symptoms of tuberculosis, the same disease that had killed his mother. His brother Tom was also suffering from tuberculosis and died in the autumn of 1818. After his brother's death, Keats moved to a friend's house and fell passionately in love with an 18-year-old neighbor, Fanny Brawne. Although he became engaged to Fanny, he was prevented by poverty and poor health from marrying her, a situation that added greatly to his distress. Amazingly, in the midst of this great emotional turmoil, Keats produced his greatest works, which were received with more favorable critical recognition than *Endymion* had been.

An Early End In the fall of 1820, as his illness progressed, Keats followed the advice of friends and moved to Italy in search of a milder climate. He died less than six months later and was buried in Rome under an epitaph he had composed for himself: "Here lies one whose name was writ in water."

Frankenstein

What if you discovered the secret of creation? Suddenly, you would know how to generate life. You could invent a new kind of being, eliminate aging, perhaps conquer death! You might give life to a new species, which would credit you forever as its creator. Would you be willing to dedicate your energy and intellect, forsake your friends, and give up your youth for the sake of such an experiment?

And what if—after all your sacrifice and sweat—your work didn't turn out quite as planned? What if your creation turned out to be ugly, frightful, or grotesque? Would you find it in your heart to embrace your creation—or would you flee from it in terror? These are some of the issues Mary Wollstonecraft Shelley raised when she wrote her classic horror novel *Frankenstein; or, The Modern Prometheus.*

The daughter of the authors William Godwin and Mary Wollstonecraft and the second wife of

the poet Percy Bysshe Shelley, Mary Shelley was keenly aware of the close relationship between life and danger, even death. Her mother had died while giving birth to her. Her own first child, born prematurely, died after two weeks. When Lord Byron first proposed that she write a ghost story, Mary Shelley was only 18 years old, pregnant with her second child, and haunted by suicides in both her husband's family and her own. It is little to be wondered at that she responded by writing a novel of creation gone awry.

Published in 1818, *Frankenstein* received strong, albeit mixed, reviews. One magazine, for example, declared the story "excellent," whereas another called it a "tissue of horrible and disgusting absurdity." Most everyone, however, was struck by the terrifying and pathetic monster created by the scientist Victor Frankenstein. Beginning life as an affectionate creature, the monster became evil only after he was cruelly rejected by Frankenstein and other human beings. Throughout the years, his creator has been compared to Prometheus, Percy Bysshe Shelley, the biblical Adam, and the spirit of science itself.

Today, in our scientific age, Mary Shelley's novel is best known as a tale of scientific horror. Whether on paper or on film, the monster still finds significance and meaning in people's imaginations and hearts.

Top:
Frontispiece from an 1831 edition of Mary Wollstonecraft Shelley's Frankenstein
Middle:
Charles Ogle as Frankenstein's monster in the first movie version, 1910. British Film Institute.
Bottom:
Boris Karloff as the monster, 1931. Photofest.

Communication Workshop — Performance Presentation

Interpreting literature through performance . . .

From Reading to Performing The romantic poets let their imaginations soar as they spoke to the ocean, to the wind, to the folly and arrogance of humankind. Poetry is filled with sounds and images that do not always come through fully for the reader who is alone with the text. A **performance presentation,** using some combination of speakers, images, sounds, movement, and props, can reveal and heighten the meaning of a piece of literature and add to the pleasure of those experiencing the work.

For Your Portfolio

WRITING PROMPT Create a script to interpret and present a literary text.

Purpose: To enrich the audience's experience of the text
Audience: Classmates, teachers, families

Basics in a Box

Performance Presentation at a Glance

GUIDELINES & STANDARDS

A useful script will
- present an overall description of the setting, props, and costumes if any
- include stage directions to indicate the specific gestures, movements, and tone of voice performers should use

A successful presentation will
- make and support a valid interpretation of a literary text
- use voice, movement, and facial expressions to enhance the performance and establish a mood
- use props and costumes, if appropriate, to enrich the audience's experience of the literary work

A successful performance presentation needs
- a literary work chosen for its performance possibilities
- a script marked for the performance
- performers committed to a particular interpretation
- optional costumes, props, sound effects, music, and visuals

Analyzing a Performance Presentation

Interpretive Reading of
"Ozymandias"

PROPS

2 large banners suggesting "two vast and trunkless legs of stone"
    mounted on poles
1 giant, cracked mask showing Ozymandias's sneering face
1 large pedestal
1 drum with drumstick

PERFORMERS

3 speakers: the poet (also plays drum), the traveler, Ozymandias
    (carries mask)
2 people to carry banners

SCRIPT: "Ozymandias"

Stage is empty except for pedestal.

POET. *(carrying drum, <u>enters</u> stage and speaks)*
    Imagine yourself a man who is feared by the world, a man ready
to conquer whoever stands in your way. Who can stop you? What can
bring you down? After all, you are Ozymandias! And yet . . .

    <u>*Poet begins to play a soft, steady rhythm on the drum.*</u>

POET. I met a traveler from an antique land
      Who said:
Traveler and two banner carriers enter. Traveler stands behind pedestal.
Banner carriers circle stage, then stand near the pedestal. Banners sway
slightly as the traveler speaks.

TRAVELER. *(speaks in a conversational style)*
    Two vast and trunkless legs of stone
    Stand in the desert . . . Near them, on the sand,
    Half sunk, a shattered visage lies, whose frown,
    And wrinkled lip, and sneer of cold command,

    Ozymandias enters, holding mask, and marches about aggressively.
Ozymandias stops, feet apart, between the two banner carriers.
Ozymandias faces the audience.

    Tell that its sculptor well those passions read
    Which yet survive, stamped on these lifeless things,

GUIDELINES IN ACTION

❶ Lists performers and props at the top of the script

❷ Stage directions provide detailed cues for performers to follow.

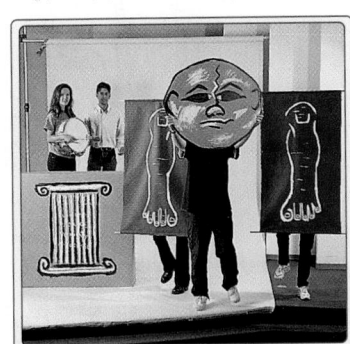

❸ Performance includes music, movement, and art, based on the interpretation of the literature.

The hand that mocked them, and the heart that fed:
And on the pedestal these words appear:

*Poet/Drummer shifts to a steady, heavy beat just before
Ozymandias begins to speak, then stops playing suddenly.*

OZYMANDIAS. *(speaks in loud, harsh, almost angry voice)*
    "My name is Ozymandias, king of kings:
Look on my works, ye Mighty, and despair!"

*Poet/Drummer beats out crescendo, then there is silence for a few
seconds. Ozymandias wilts to floor. As Traveler begins to speak
again, drummer begins playing the soft, steady beat again.*

TRAVELER.
    Nothing beside remains. Round the decay
Of that colossal wreck, boundless and bare
The lone and level sands stretch far away.

Poet/Drummer, traveler, Ozymandias, and banner carriers bow.

FADEOUT

❹ Performers use cardboard, fabric, and mop-handle props, with simple staging.

❺ This scriptwriter notes the music, gestures, and tone of voice needed to introduce a dramatic moment.

Creating Your Performance Presentation

❶ Planning Your Performance

> *One ought, every day at least, to hear a little song,*
> *read a good poem, see a fine picture, and, if it were possible,*
> *to speak a few reasonable words.*
> **Johann Wolfgang von Goethe, German writer and poet**

When choosing a literary work for your performance presentation, you might consider selecting a work that includes one or more of the following:

- dramatic action
- rhythmic or musical language
- opportunities for collaboration with one or more classmates
- compelling characters or setting

See the **Idea Bank** in the margin for more suggestions. Once you have made your choice, follow the steps below.

Developing Your Performance Presentation

▶ **1. Decide on the purpose of your performance.** Is it to add depth to the literature's exact wording? Is it to introduce another point of view? For example, you could present a dialogue between the subject and the writer of "When We Two Parted" to give the woman a chance to defend herself. Or you might want to stage a debate between Truth and Beauty, based on "Ode on a Grecian Urn."

▶ **2. Decide on the mood and texture of the performance.** Do you want your audience to get a sense of anger? joy? beauty? sadness?

▶ **3. Choose strategies for conveying your message.** Will you use props? lighting? music? dance? other forms of communication? How will the strategies you use emphasize your interpretation?

▶ **4. Consider your audience.** What is their level of familiarity with the text? How long is their attention span? What special interests do they have?

▶ **5. Think of what must be included in your script.** For example, if you use music, can you vary the selections or must there be one specific melody? How will you handle entrances and exits if any are needed?

❷ Practicing and Presenting

Follow these steps as you prepare for your performance:

- Memorize your presentation.
- Practice each gesture, tone of voice, facial expression, and movement.
- If your script calls for props, be sure they are available when you practice.
- Time your presentation. Don't wait until you are standing in front of an audience to find out if something is too long, too short, or awkward.

IDEABank

1. Your Working Portfolio 📁
Look for ideas in the **Writing Option** you completed earlier in this unit:

- **Performance Notes,** p. 791

2. Interpretive Movement
Choose a piece of literature—a poem, story, or scene from a novel—and create a dance to accompany a reading of the work.

3. Art Link
Recall a favorite piece of literature from your childhood and develop a slide or video presentation that reflects your interpretation of the piece.

Have a question?

See the
**Communication
Handbook**

Speaking and Listening,
pp.1386–1388

- Practice with the music or other sounds you've planned.
- Get feedback from peers you invite to your practices. If they don't understand your interpretation, you may wish to make some changes before the performance.

With thoughtful planning and adequate practice, your performance presentation will give your audience pleasure and greater understanding of the work.

Ask Your Peer Reviewers

- What is my overall interpretation of this piece?
- What is the most memorable part of my presentation for you?
- What parts of my presentation—sound, movement, voice, props—do I need to change or replace?
- How did your understanding of this piece change as a result of my presentation?

❸ Refining Your Performance

TARGET SKILL ▶ EVALUATING YOUR INTERPRETIVE CHOICES After you have practiced your performance presentation, think about your peer reviewers' comments. Are all the elements you included appropriate for your interpretation of the selection? Do they fit the mood and audience? Make any necessary changes.

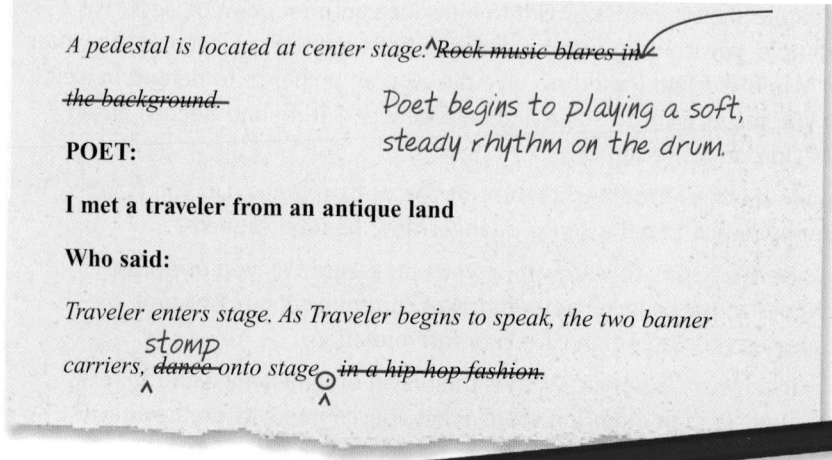

> *A pedestal is located at center stage.* ~~Rock music blares in the background.~~ Poet begins to playing a soft, steady rhythm on the drum.
>
> **POET:**
>
> **I met a traveler from an antique land**
>
> **Who said:**
>
> *Traveler enters stage. As Traveler begins to speak, the two banner carriers,* stomp ~~dance~~ onto stage, ~~in a hip-hop fashion.~~

**Presentation
IDEAS**

- Present it to your classmates or video-tape it and show it to your families.
- Ask your local library about performing a collection of your classmates' work for your community.
- Present it to your drama club or to other youth groups.

**More Online:
Publishing Options**
www.mcdougallittell.com

❹ Reflecting

FOR YOUR WORKING PORTFOLIO How did others respond to your presentation? How did working with the literature affect your appreciation or understanding of it? Attach your answers to your finished work. Save your script in your **Working Portfolio.**

Read this paragraph from the first draft of a student essay. The underlined sections may include the following kinds of errors:

- **misplaced modifiers**
- **comma errors**
- **lack of subject-verb agreement**
- **sentence fragments**

For each underlined section, choose the revision that most improves the writing.

Today I attended an interpretive performance of <u>the poem, "Ode on a Grecian Urn," by John Keats.</u> The students' interpretation <u>were</u> wonderful. They used <u>music, costumes, props and movement</u> to dramatize Keats's philosophical musings. The performance began with Keats staring at a large urn and reciting the first few lines of the poem. <u>Then performers danced onto the stage dressed like Greek gods and goddesses.</u> One performer played a simple melody on a penny whistle. <u>As the last stanza was recited. The performers danced off the stage.</u> Finally, Keats was alone again with the urn. Performances like this one <u>make</u> poetry come alive.

(1) (2) (3) (4) (5) (6)

---

1. **A.** the poem, "Ode on a Grecian Urn" by John Keats.
   B. the poem "Ode on a Grecian Urn" by, John Keats.
   C. the poem "Ode on a Grecian Urn" by John Keats.
   D. Correct as is

2. **A.** are
   B. am
   C. was
   D. Correct as is

3. **A.** music costumes, props, and movement
   B. music, costumes, props, and movement
   C. music, costumes, props and movement,
   D. Correct as is

4. **A.** Then, dressed like Greek gods and goddesses, performers danced onto the stage.
   B. Then performers danced, dressed like Greek gods and goddesses, onto the stage.
   C. Then performers dressed like Greek gods and goddesses danced onto the stage.
   D. Correct as is

5. **A.** As the last stanza was recited; the performers danced off the stage.
   B. As the last stanza was recited, the performers danced off the stage.
   C. As the last stanza was recited and the performers danced off the stage.
   D. Correct as is

6. **A.** makes
   B. has made
   C. can makes
   D. Correct as is

Need extra help?

See the **Grammar Handbook**

Correcting Fragments, p. 1409

Punctuation Chart, pp. 1413–1414

Subject-Verb Agreement, p. 1410

Using modifiers correctly, p. 1399

Words with Similar Sounds and Spellings

For centuries people have complained about the unsystematic nature of English spelling. Many words with the same spelling have different meanings and different origins, like *bear* and *bear*, while some words that sound the same have different spellings, such as *soul* and *sole*. In the excerpt on the right, which words sound the same as other words with different spellings and meanings?

> Roll on, thou deep and dark blue Ocean, roll!
> Ten thousand fleets sweep over thee in vain;
> Man marks the earth with ruin, his control
> Stops with the shore; upon the watery plain
> The wrecks are all thy deed . . .
> —Lord Byron, *Childe Harold's Pilgrimage*

Words with the same pronunciation but different spellings and meanings are called **homophones**. The word *role*, meaning "the part a character assumes in a play," is a homophone of *roll* in the first line of the excerpt. Other homophones of words in the excerpt include *blew (blue)*, *vein (vain)*, and *plane (plain)*.

Strategies for Building Vocabulary

In addition to homophones, words called homonyms and homographs further complicate English vocabulary. Use the information below to help you identify and distinguish homophones, homonyms, and homographs.

❶ **Homophones** The word *homophone* comes from two Greek words: *homos*, meaning "same," and *phonē*, meaning "sound." Unfortunately, there is no easy way of remembering the different spellings of homophones. Only familiarity and practice will help you remember the different spellings and meanings of words like *aisle* and *isle*, *plain* and *plane*, *sore* and *soar*, and *bough* and *bow*.

❷ **Homonyms** One effective way to build your knowledge of **homonyms**—words with the same pronunciation and spelling but different meanings— is to use a dictionary. Consider the word *grave* in the lines "The wingéd seeds, where they lie cold and low, / Each like a corpse within its grave" from Percy Shelley's "Ode to the West Wind." If you look up *grave* in a dictionary, you will find several separate entries, each containing a different set of meanings. Some of these words evolved from unrelated words in different languages; others evolved along different paths from a common source. For example, *grave* meaning "burial place" is from Old English *græf*, whereas *grave* meaning "serious" is from Latin *gravis* ("heavy").

	Examples	Alike in	Different in
Homophones	*eye* and *I*	pronunciation	spelling and meaning
Homonyms	*strain* (ancestry), *strain* (draw tight), and *strain* (physical or mental tension)	pronunciation and spelling	meaning
Homographs	*tear* (water from the eye) and *tear* (rip)	spelling	meaning and pronunciation

❸ **Homographs** Like sets of homonyms, sets of homographs are found together in a dictionary, at the beginning of separate entries. They can be identified by their different pronunciations. Practice will help you remember the pronunciations and meanings of homographs like *desert* (dĕz'ərt) and *desert* (dĭ-zûrt') and *live* (lĭv) and *live* (līv).

EXERCISE Look up each pair of nouns in a dictionary, pronounce each word, and identify its meanings and origins. Then classify the pair as homophones, homonyms, or homographs and use each word in a sentence.

1. *mint* and *mint*
2. *knight* and *night*
3. *gnome* and *gnome*
4. *row* and *row*
5. *complement* and *compliment*

Grammar from Literature

Experienced writers use subordinate clauses to make relationships between ideas clear and to achieve vivid description. Subordinate clauses express ideas that are related to, but less important than, the main idea of a sentence. Notice the highlighted passages below. These show two kinds of subordinate clauses: adjective clauses and noun clauses. As you can see, both prose writers and poets use subordinate clauses.

> adjective clause
> **Our sweetest songs are those** that tell of saddest thought.
> —Percy Bysshe Shelley, "To a Skylark"
>
> noun clauses
> **We fancied** that the lake had floated the seeds ashore **and** that the little colony had so sprung up.
> —Dorothy Wordsworth, *Grasmere Journals*
>
> **I have never heard**
>   **Praise of love or wine**   adjective clause
> That painted forth a flood of rapture so divine.
> —Percy Bysshe Shelley, "To a Skylark"

You may recall that a clause is a group of words containing a subject and a predicate. There are two main types of clauses: independent clauses and subordinate clauses. An independent clause can stand alone as a sentence. A subordinate clause cannot stand alone as a sentence and is usually signaled by a subordinating conjunction such as *who, whom, whose, that,* and *which.*

Using Clauses in Your Writing You can use clauses when you want to join ideas or add detail to a thought. Look at the example at the top of the next column.

> SEPARATE
> **In Greece Byron is celebrated as a hero. He helped Greece win independence.**
>
> COMBINED   adjective clause
> **In Greece, Lord Byron is celebrated as a hero** who helped Greece win independence.

Usage Tip *Who* is a nominative form pronoun. *Whom* is an objective form. The decision about whether to use *who* or *whom* in a subordinate clause should be based on whether the pronoun is used as a subject or an object within the clause.

> subject
> **Shelley was an idealist** who opposed injustice.
>
> direct object
> **Keats is a poet** whom critics admire.

Punctuation Tip An adjective clause that provides information needed to complete the intended meaning of a sentence is called an **essential** adjective clause. An adjective clause that just adds additional information to a sentence in which the meaning is already complete is called **nonessential.** Place a comma before and after a nonessential clause. Do not set off an essential clause with commas.

> essential
> **"Ode on a Grecian Urn" is a poem** that is considered one of the most famous works of British literature.
>
> nonessential
> **"Ode on a Grecian Urn,"** which John Keats wrote, **is one of the most famous works of British literature.**

WRITING EXERCISE Combine each pair of sentences into a single sentence by changing one of the sentences into a subordinate clause. Omit underlined words. Follow the directions given in parentheses.

1. "She Walks in Beauty" may have been inspired by Lord Byron's young cousin. <u>She</u> was dressed in a mourning gown. (Change the second sentence into a subordinate clause that begins with the word *who.*)

2. A reader of "Ozymandias" realizes <u>something important</u>. Fame is fleeting. (Change the second sentence into a subordinate clause that begins with the word *that.*)

3. In "Ode on a Grecian Urn," Keats suggests <u>an idea</u>. Perhaps anticipation or imagination is better than actual experience. (Change the second sentence into a subordinate clause that begins with *that.*)

4. The Greek children seem to jump and dance to the music of the merry piper. <u>This is the piper</u> Keats describes. (Change the second sentence into a subordinate clause that begins with *whom.*)

5. Friends surrounded the gravely ill young poet. <u>These people</u> acted like loyal subjects around a dying king. (Change the second sentence into a subordinate clause beginning with *who.* Place the clause after *friends.*)

The Flowering of Romanticism

What new understanding of the romantic poets have you gained by reading and discussing the poetry in this unit? In your opinion, how do the romantics' views of nature and love compare with the views held by people today? Explore these questions by completing one or more options in each of the following sections.

Reflecting on the Unit

OPTION 1

Analyzing Similarities Recall the quotation from William Blake at the beginning of this unit:

> *To see the world in a grain of sand*
> *And heaven in a wild flower,*
> *Hold infinity in the palm of your hand*
> *And eternity in an hour.*

Working with a small group of classmates, discuss what you think this quotation means. Then, with your group, create a graph indicating how similar the messages of five of the poems in the unit are to the message of Blake's lines.

	Slightly Similar ➡ ➡ Very Similar	
"The World Is Too Much with Us"		

OPTION 2

Comparing Times Many of the romantic poets were inspired to write about their observations of, and powerful responses to, the natural world. From each part of the unit, select one poem in which the observations and responses are, in your opinion, especially pertinent to issues in today's world. In a paragraph or two, explain how the two poems affected you and how the messages or truths they convey relate to contemporary issues.

OPTION 3

Defining Romanticism How would you define the term *romanticism?* With a group of classmates, create a list of words and phrases that you associate with the romantic movement. Highlight the words and phrases that you think are particularly relevant to the era. Compare your list with those of other groups.

Self ASSESSMENT

📖 **READER'S NOTEBOOK**

Review your understanding of the poems in this unit by creating a two-column chart. In the first column, list your five favorites among the poems, in order of your preference. In the second, summarize each poem's message and tell why you like the poem.

Reviewing Literary Concepts

OPTION 1

Examining Imagery, Symbol, and Mood The poets represented in this unit all share a purpose: to express themselves through their poetry. Although some of the poems focus on feelings and others on ideas, all of them depend to some degree on imagery—and many depend on symbols—to convey moods and to present the poets' attitudes toward their subjects. Select six or more of the poems in this unit. Decide what mood each evokes, and identify at least two images or symbols that help sustain the mood. Share your conclusions with a partner.

OPTION 2

Appreciating Sound and Meter Think again about some of the elements—such as rhythm, rhyme, alliteration, consonance, and assonance—that work together to create a total experience for readers of poetry. In what passages of the poems in this unit do you think sound and meter are employed in particularly interesting ways? Identify ten noteworthy examples in various poems; then, with a small group, create a list of the five most effective uses of sound and meter.

Building Your Portfolio

- **Writing Options** Several Writing Options in this unit asked you to recall your own experiences with nature or your impressions of nature—a particular place, an element of nature, a season. Select two pieces of your writing that you think successfully recreate your impressions or experiences. Write a cover note explaining your choices. Then add the note and the two pieces to your **Presentation Portfolio.**

- **Communication Workshop** Earlier in this unit, you explored your insights into a work of literature by creating an Interpretive Presentation. Evaluate your presentation. If you had to do it over again, what might you change? Respond to this question in a note to be included in your **Presentation Portfolio.**

- **Additional Activities** Reflect on the different assignments you completed from the **Activities & Explorations** and **Inquiry & Research** sections of the lessons in this unit. Which of these projects do you think was most successful? Include a note in your portfolio that explains your choice.

Self ASSESSMENT

READER'S NOTEBOOK

The following literary terms were discussed in Unit Four. Copy the list in your notebook, circling any terms that you do not completely understand. Use the **Glossary of Literary Terms** (page 1328) to check the definitions of the circled terms.

symbol	haiku
imagery	simile
onomatopoeia	alliteration
assonance	consonance
rhyme	rhythm
literary ballad	form
apostrophe	meter
foot	iambic pentameter

Self ASSESSMENT

Look over the writing that you have chosen for your portfolio so far. Create a list in which you rank the pieces according to how pleased you are with the results. On the list, note any particular writing strengths you have discovered, along with any skills you want to work on in subsequent units. Date your list and add it to your **Presentation Portfolio.**

Setting GOALS

As you worked through this unit, you very likely developed a deeper understanding of the nature of poetry. Are there any poets you studied in this unit whose work you would like to read more of? Do you have any ideas for poetry of your own? Do you still feel that you are reluctant to read poetry? Develop a list of goals for enhancing your own knowledge and appreciation of poetry.

LITERATURE CONNECTIONS
Pride and Prejudice

JANE AUSTEN

In the funniest and sharpest of Jane Austen's novels, strangers who take an instant dislike of one another overcome their first impressions, discover the truth about each other, and fall in love. Austen's deft comic touch and sharp wit are very much on display in this novel.

These thematically related readings are provided along with *Pride and Prejudice*:

from **What Jane Austen Ate and Charles Dickens Knew: From Fox Hunting to Whist—the Facts of Daily Life in 19th-Century England**
BY DANIEL POOL

Mademoiselle Pearl
BY GUY DE MAUPASSANT

You Have What I Look For
BY JAIME SABINES

The Magic Barrel
BY BERNARD MALAMUD

About Marriage
BY DENISE LEVERTOV

from **Jane Austen**
BY VIRGINIA WOOLF

The Princess and the Tin Box
BY JAMES THURBER

And Even *More* . . .

Letters to Alice on First Reading Jane Austen

FAY WELDON

In these fictional letters inspired by letters Austen wrote to her own niece, Weldon tries to teach an 18-year-old how to appreciate Jane Austen's novels.

Books
William Wordsworth: A Biography
MARY MOORMAN
This two-volume work gives full breadth to the life of this great romantic poet.

The Poet Dying: Heinrich Heine's Last Years in Paris
ERNST PAWEL
A vivid and memorable rendering of the remarkable life of one of the great German poets.

Frankenstein

MARY WOLLSTONECRAFT SHELLEY

Victor Frankenstein, a brilliant and precocious scientist, attempts to probe the deepest secrets of nature in order to create life. Toiling in his laboratory, he creates a monster, which is soon loosed upon the world. This tale of fantasy and horror has stimulated the imaginations of generations of readers.

The Letters of John Keats

EDITED BY ROBERT GITTINGS

Offering one of the most complete portraits available of any English poet, this collection of letters by Keats reflects the intellect, imagination, and curiosity of his poetic genius. Ideas and opinions fly from the pen of this brilliantly gifted young poet, who was fated to die at the age of 25.

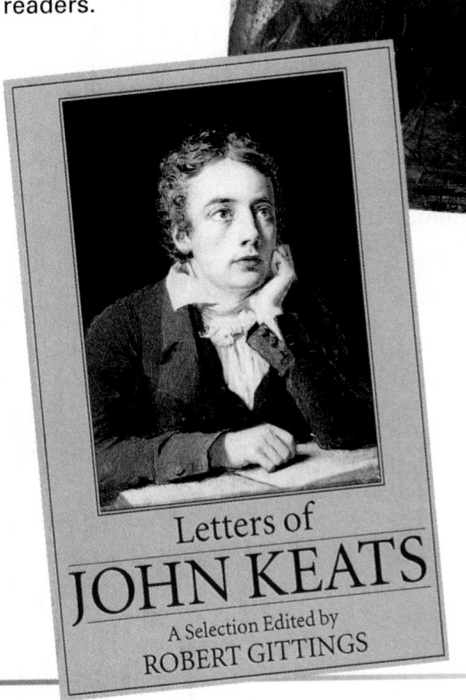

Lord Byron: Selected Letters and Journals
EDITED BY LESLIE MARCHAND
Byron, the prototype of the romantic hero, comes to life in this collection of his personal prose.

Recollections of the Last Days of Shelley and Byron
EDWARD J. TRELAWNY
These two famous friends and fellow poets are examined in this biographical work.

Other Media

Frankenstein: The Making of the Monster: The World of Mary Shelley
Library Video Company.
(VIDEOCASSETTES)

Jane Austen and Her World
Films for the Humanities and Sciences, 1995.
(VIDEOCASSETTES)

Pride and Prejudice
Abridged. Read by Glenda Jackson. Dove Audio, 1995.
(AUDIOCASSETTE)

The Rime of the Ancient Mariner and Other Great Poems
Listening Library, 1987. Narrated by Christopher Plummer and Bramwell Fletcher. Includes "Rime" and "Kubla Khan" by Coleridge as well as poems by Blake, Burns, Wordsworth, Byron, Shelley, and Keats.
(AUDIOCASSETTE)

The Glorious Romantics
Monterey Home Video.
(VIDEOCASSETTE)

Reading & Writing for Assessment

When you studied strategies for reading a test selection on pages 508–513, you practiced techniques for success on reading and writing assessments. These kinds of tests are often important end-of-course examinations.

The following pages will give you more test-taking strategies. You will have a chance to apply them in the practice activities that follow the selection.

PART 1 How to Read a Test Selection

Here are the basic strategies you studied earlier along with several new ones based on a different type of reading selection. Applying these strategies, taking notes, and highlighting or underscoring passages as you read can help you focus on the information you will need to know.

STRATEGIES FOR READING A TEST SELECTION

▶ **Before you begin reading, skim the questions that follow the passage.** These can help focus your reading.

▶ **Unlock word meanings.** Use context clues and word parts to help you unlock the meaning of unfamiliar words.

▶ **Use your active reading strategies such as analyzing, predicting, and questioning.** Make notes in the margin to help you focus your reading. You may do this only if the test directions allow you to mark on the test itself.

▶ **Look for main ideas.** These are often stated at the beginnings or ends of paragraphs. Sometimes they are implied, not stated. After reading each paragraph, ask "What was this passage about?"

▶ **Note the literary elements and techniques used by the writer.** You might consider the tone (writer's attitude toward the subject), figurative language, descriptive language, or use of techniques like comparison and contrast. Then ask yourself what effect the writer achieves with each choice.

▶ **Examine the sequence of ideas.** Are the ideas developed in chronological order, presented in order of importance, or organized in some other way? What does the sequence of ideas suggest about the writer's message?

▶ **Think about the message and writer's purpose.** What questions does the selection answer? What new questions does it imply? Can you make any generalizations?

Reading Selection

Why Leaves Turn Color in the Fall
by Diane Ackerman

1   The stealth of autumn catches one unaware. Was that a goldfinch perching in the early September woods, or just the first turning leaf? A red-winged blackbird or a sugar maple closing up shop for the winter? Keen-eyed as leopards, we stand still and squint hard, looking for signs of movement. Early-morning frost sits heavily on the grass, and turns ❶ barbed wire into a string of stars. On a distant hill, a small square of yellow appears to be a lighted stage. At last the truth dawns on us: Fall is staggering in, right on schedule, with its baggage of chilly nights, macabre holidays, and spectacular, heart-stoppingly beautiful leaves. Soon the leaves will start cringing on the trees, and roll up in clenched fists before they actually fall off. Dry seedpods will rattle like tiny gourds. But first there will be weeks of gushing color so bright, so pastel, so confettilike, that people will travel up and down the East Coast just to stare at it—a whole season of leaves.

2   ❷ Where do the colors come from? Sunlight rules most living things with its golden edicts. When the days begin to shorten, soon after the summer solstice on June 21, a tree reconsiders its leaves. All summer it feeds them so they can process sunlight, but in the dog days of summer the tree begins pulling nutrients back into its trunk and roots, pares down, and gradually chokes off its leaves. A corky layer of cells forms at the leaves' slender petioles, then scars over. Undernourished, the leaves stop producing the pigment chlorophyll, and photosynthesis ceases. Animals can migrate, hibernate, or store food to prepare for winter. But where can a tree go? It survives by dropping its leaves, and by the end of autumn only a few fragile threads of fluid-carrying xylem hold leaves to their stems.

3   ❸ A turning leaf stays partly green at first, then reveals splotches of yellow and red as the chlorophyll gradually breaks down. Dark green seems to stay longest in the veins, outlining and defining them. During the summer, chlorophyll dissolves in the heat and light, but it is also being steadily replaced. In the fall, on the other hand, no new pigment is produced, and so we notice the other colors that were always there, right in the leaf, although chlorophyll's shocking green hid them from view. With their camouflage gone, we see these colors for the first time all year, and marvel, but they were always there, hidden like a vivid secret beneath the hot glowing greens of summer.

4   The most spectacular range of fall foliage occurs in the northeastern United States and in eastern China, where the leaves are robustly colored thanks in part to a rich climate. European maples don't achieve the same flaming reds as their

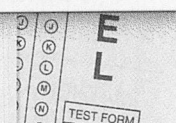

American relatives, which thrive on cold nights and sunny days. In Europe, the warm, humid weather turns the leaves brown or mildly yellow. ❹ Anthocyanin, the pigment that gives apples their red and turns leaves red or red-violet, is produced by sugars that remain in the leaf after the supply of nutrients dwindles. Unlike the carotenoids, which color carrots, squash, and corn, and turn leaves orange and yellow, anthocyanin varies from year to year, depending on the temperature and amount of sunlight. The fiercest colors occur in years when the fall sunlight is strongest and the nights are cool and dry (a state of grace scientists find vexing to forecast). This is also why leaves appear dizzyingly bright and clear on a sunny fall day: The anthocyanin flashes like a marquee. . . .

5   But how do the colored leaves fall? As a leaf ages, the growth hormone, auxin, fades, and cells at the base of the petiole divide. Two or three rows of small cells, lying at right angles to the axis of the petiole, react with water, then come apart, leaving the petioles hanging on by only a few threads of xylem. A light breeze, and the leaves are airborne. They glide and swoop, rocking in invisible cradles. They are all wing and may flutter from yard to yard on small whirlwinds or updrafts, swiveling as they go. Firmly tethered to earth, we love to see things rise up and fly—soap bubbles, balloons, birds, fall leaves. They remind us that the end of a season is capricious, as is the end of life. We especially like the way leaves rock, careen, and swoop as they fall. Everyone knows the motion. Pilots sometimes do a maneuver called a "falling leaf," in which the plane loses altitude quickly and on purpose, by slipping first to the right, then to the left. The machine weighs a ton or more, but in one pilot's mind it is a weightless thing, a falling leaf. She has seen the motion before, in the Vermont woods where she played as a child. Below her the trees radiate gold, copper, and red. Leaves are falling, although she can't see them fall, as she falls, swooping down for a closer view.

6   ❺ At last the leaves leave. But first they turn color and thrill us for weeks on end. Then they crunch and crackle underfoot. They shush, as children drag their small feet through leaves heaped along the curb. Dark, slimy mats of leaves cling to one's heels after a rain. A damp, stuccolike mortar of semidecayed leaves protects the tender shoots with a roof until spring, and makes a rich humus. An occasional bulge or ripple in the leafy mounds signals a shrew or a field mouse tunneling out of sight. ❻ Sometimes one finds in fossil stones the imprint of a leaf, long since disintegrated, whose outlines remind us how detailed, vibrant, and alive are the things of this earth that perish.

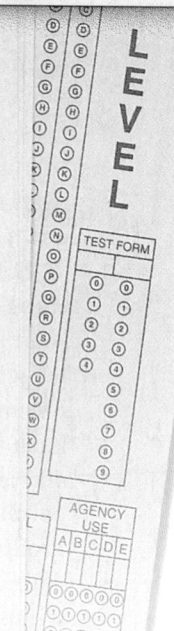

STRATEGIES
IN ACTION

❹ Unlock word meanings

"Anthocyanin and carotenoids must be substances that produce color since they are associated with reds and oranges. Besides, carotenoid looks like it is related to the word carrot."

❺ Note literary elements, like use of descriptive language.

"The descriptions here are neat. They use the senses like sight, sound, and touch."

❻ Think about the message and writer's purpose.

"The writer seems to suggest that we can learn something about life—and death—by watching the leaves turn color and fall."

PART 2

How to Answer Multiple-Choice Questions

Use the strategies in the box and the notes in the side column to help you answer the questions below and on the following pages.

Based on the selection you have just read, choose the best answer for each of the following questions.

1. In paragraph 1, the writer personifies leaves when she says that
   A. they are heart-stoppingly beautiful.
   B. they start cringing on the trees.
   C. their colors will be bright, like confetti.
   D. at first they look like birds perching in the trees.

2. In which of the following passages does the writer adopt a scientific tone?
   A. "Fall is staggering in, right on schedule"
   B. "A corky layer of cells forms at the leaves' slender petioles"
   C. "we see these colors for the first time all year, and marvel"
   D. "a state of grace scientists find vexing to forecast"

3. In paragraph 1, what metaphor does the writer use to suggest what the beginning of fall is like?
   A. a person tiptoeing
   B. a leopard jumping
   C. a lighted stage
   D. a festival

4. What does the writer mean when she says, "Sunlight rules most living things with its golden edicts"?
   A. Most living things could not survive without sunlight.
   B. Most living things enjoy basking in sunlight.
   C. Most living things prefer summer to winter.
   D. The sun determines the actions of plants and animals.

5. Which of the following might be a lesson the writer intends to draw from the falling of leaves?
   A. People should find out more about why leaves change color.
   B. People should try to be more like trees.
   C. Life is a cycle and death is part of life.
   D. Nature appears vibrant but is actually malevolent.

STRATEGIES FOR ANSWERING MULTIPLE-CHOICE QUESTIONS

▶ **Ask questions** that help you eliminate some of the choices.
▶ **Pay attention to choices** such as "all of the above" or "none of the above." To eliminate them, all you need to find is one answer that doesn't fit.
▶ **Skim your notes.** Details you noticed as you read may provide answers.

STRATEGIES IN ACTION

Skim your notes.

ONE STUDENT'S THOUGHTS
"The writer says that we are like leopards as we look for the fall, not that the fall is like a leopard. *So I can eliminate choice B.*"

YOUR TURN
What words does the writer use to describe the beginning of fall?

Ask questions.
Does the writer hope to persuade or describe?

ONE STUDENT'S THOUGHTS
"The writer doesn't seem to be telling people what they should do. She is just describing the process by which leaves fall. *So I can eliminate choices A and B.*"

YOUR TURN
What other choice can you eliminate?

PART 3 **How to Respond in Writing**

You may also be asked to write answers to questions about a reading passage. **Short-answer questions** usually ask you to answer in a sentence or two. **Essay questions** require a fully developed piece of writing.

Short-Answer Question

STRATEGIES FOR RESPONDING TO SHORT-ANSWER QUESTIONS

▶ **Identify the key words** in the writing prompt that tell you the ideas to discuss. Make sure you know what is meant by each.
▶ **State your response** directly and to the point.
▶ **Support your ideas** by using evidence from the selection.
▶ **Use correct grammar.**

> **Sample Prompt**
>
> Answer the following question in two or three sentences.
>
> How does this writer use figurative language to help readers understand her subject? Give several examples of figurative language from the essay and explain why use of such language is an effective technique.

Essay Question

STRATEGIES FOR ANSWERING ESSAY QUESTIONS

▶ **Look for direction words** in the writing prompt, such as *essay, analyze, describe,* or *compare* and *contrast,* that tell you how to respond directly to the prompt.
▶ **List the points** you want to make before beginning to write.
▶ **Write an interesting introduction** that presents your main point.
▶ **Develop your ideas** by using evidence from the selection that supports the statements you make. Present the ideas in a logical order.
▶ **Write a conclusion** that summarizes your points.
▶ **Check your work** for correct grammar.

> **Sample Prompt**
>
> This writer switches back and forth between a poetic and a scientific tone. Write an essay in which you use examples from the text to compare and contrast the two tones.

STRATEGIES IN ACTION

Identify the key words in the writing prompt.

ONE STUDENT'S THOUGHTS

"The key words are *figurative language, example,* and *explain.* I will have to find examples of figurative language in the selection and then explain why the writer uses them. Maybe I can find a metaphor in the selection to use as one example."

YOUR TURN

Go back to the selection and find a metaphor, simile, or another examples of figurative language.

Look for direction words.

ONE STUDENT'S THOUGHTS

"The prompt is asking me to *compare* and *contrast* the passages from the selection that have a poetic tone with the ones that sound more scientific. I'll have to explain how the two tones are alike and how they are different."

YOUR TURN

Make a list of scientific passages and poetic passages in this selection. How are they similar? How are they different?

Here is a student's first draft in response to the writing prompt at the bottom of page 826. Read it and answer the multiple-choice questions that follow.

STRATEGIES FOR
REVISING, EDITING,
AND PROOFREADING

1	This writer uses a poetic tone to present her own point of view
2	about the leaves changing color. She uses a scientific tone to
3	describe simple facts. The author uses a poetic tone to describe
4	her feeling that fall tends to sneak upon us. She says that people
5	observing the signs of fall are leopards and fall is a guest
6	staggering in right on schedule and bringing baggage. But she
7	uses scientific language to tell why leaves actually change color
8	giving the names of pigments like anthocyanin and telling us the
9	fact that the presence of anthocyanin depends on the
10	temperature and quantity of sunlight.

▶ **Read the passage carefully.**
▶ **Note the parts that are confusing** or don't make sense. What kinds of errors would that signal?
▶ **Look for errors** in grammar, usage, spelling, and capitalization. Common errors include:
  • run-on sentences
  • sentence fragments
  • lack of subject-verb agreement
  • unclear pronoun antecedents
  • lack of transition words

1. What is the BEST transition to add to the beginning of the sentence in lines 3–4 ("The author . . . sneak up on us.")?

   A. Furthermore,

   B. Yet

   C. For example,

   D. And

2. What is the BEST change, if any, to make to the sentence in lines 4–6 ("She says that . . . bringing baggage.")?

   A. Change *the signs of fall* to *leaves*.

   B. Add the word *like* between *are* and *leopards*.

   C. Delete the words *staggering in right on schedule*.

   D. Make no change.

3. What is the BEST change, if any, to make to the sentence in lines 6–10 ("But she uses . . . quantity of sunlight.")?

   A. Add a colon after *color*.

   B. Add a semicolon after *color*.

   C. Add a comma after *color*.

   D. Make no change.

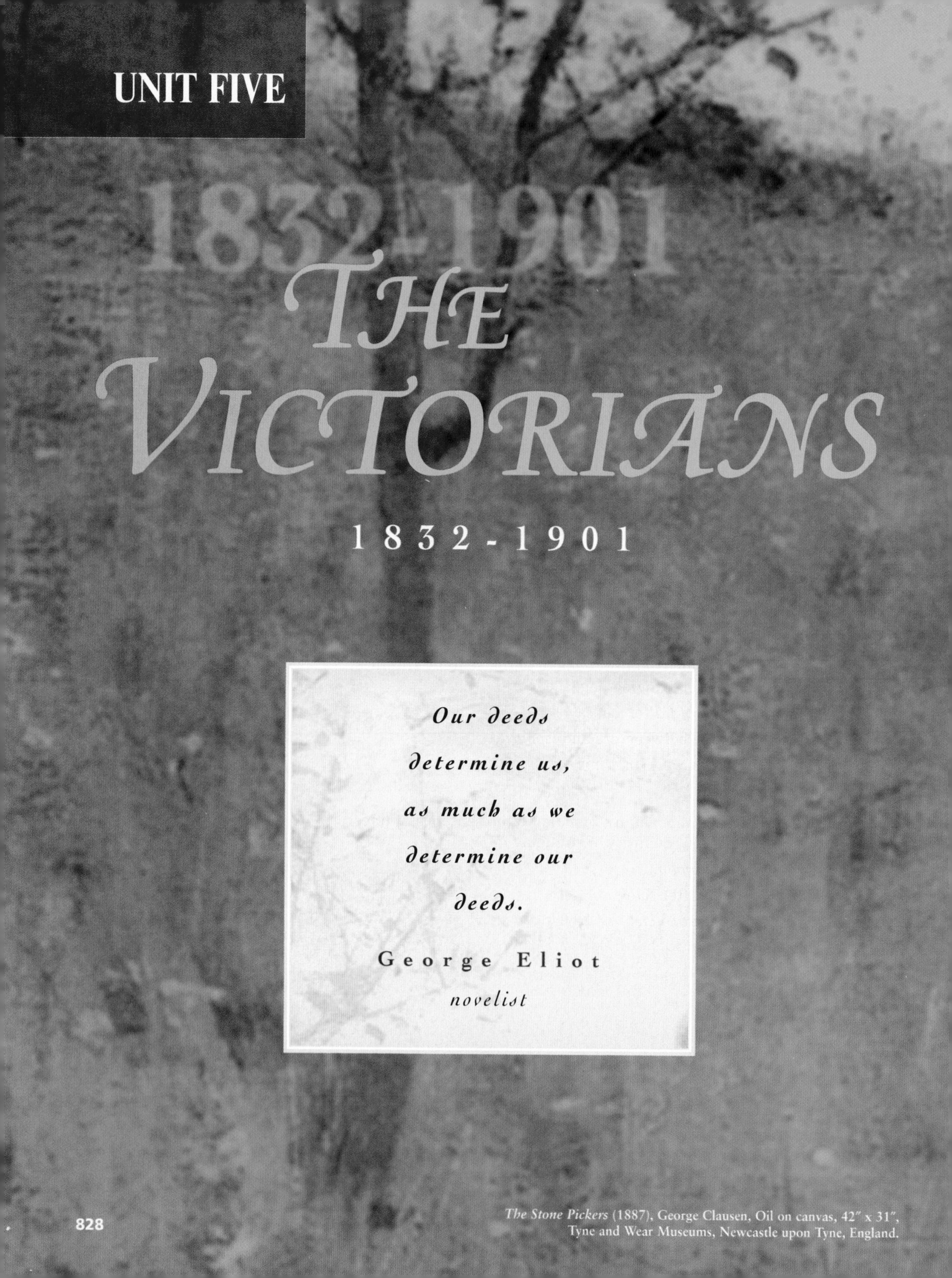

1832-1901

THE VICTORIANS

1832-1901

> Our deeds
> determine us,
> as much as we
> determine our
> deeds.
>
> George Eliot
> *novelist*

The Stone Pickers (1887), George Clausen, Oil on canvas, 42″ x 31″, Tyne and Wear Museums, Newcastle upon Tyne, England.

THE VICTORIANS

EVENTS IN BRITISH LITERATURE

1830   **1845**   **1860**

1833 Alfred, Lord Tennyson, begins writing long poem *In Memoriam*

1843 Charles Dickens publishes short novel *A Christmas Carol*

1846 Poets Robert Browning and Elizabeth Barrett elope and move to Italy

1847 Charlotte Brontë publishes *Jane Eyre;* sister Emily publishes *Wuthering Heights*

1850 Elizabeth Barrett Browning publishes love poems *Sonnets from the Portuguese*

1860 Dickens publishes first magazine installment of *Great Expectations*

1861 George Eliot publishes *Silas Marner*

1865 Lewis Carroll publishes *Alice's Adventures in Wonderland*

1868 Gerard Manley Hopkins enters Jesuit religious order and stops writing poetry

EVENTS IN BRITAIN

1830   **1845**   **1860**

1833 Factory Act bans factory work for children under nine; slavery abolished in British Empire

1837 William IV dies and is succeeded by 18-year-old niece Victoria, ushering in Britain's age of greatest prosperity

1842 Opium War with China settled, with Britain claiming Hong Kong

1845 Irish potato famine begins, killing more than a million people (to 1851)

1848 University of London grants admission to women students

1854 Crimean War—in which Britain, Turkey, France, and Austria fight Russia—begins

1859 Charles Darwin publishes *On the Origin of Species*

1860 Florence Nightingale founds school for nurses

1861 Prince Albert dies ➤

1867 Reform Bill doubles number of voters by including working-class men

1870 Local governments establish public schools; Married Women's Act gives women economic rights

EVENTS IN THE WORLD

1830   **1845**   **1860**

1839 American Charles Goodyear invents process for making rubber strong and elastic

1844 Samuel F. B. Morse sends first long-distance telegraph message

1848 Ethnic uprisings erupt throughout Europe; Karl Marx and Friedrich Engels publish *Communist Manifesto*

1851 Widespread hunger and government corruption lead to China's Taiping Rebellion (to 1864)

1853 U.S. Commodore Matthew Perry sails four ships into Tokyo harbor, ending Japan's self-imposed isolation

1861 Civil war erupts in United States (to 1865); Alexander II frees serfs in Russia

1862 During American civil war, Abraham Lincoln's Emancipation Proclamation symbolically frees slaves in Confederate territory

1869 Suez Canal opens

1874 Alexander Graham Bell develops telephone

PERIOD PIECES

The Benz
Viktoria, 1893

Mangle, used to squeeze
water from laundry

Big Ben, tower clock
installed in Houses
of Parliament, 1859

1875   **1890**   **1900**

1875 Hopkins resumes writing

1883 Robert Louis Stevenson publishes adventure novel *Treasure Island* ➤

1887 Sir Arthur Conan Doyle publishes *A Study in Scarlet*, introducing detective Sherlock Holmes

1891 Thomas Hardy publishes *Tess of the D'Urbervilles*; Oscar Wilde's novel, *A Picture of Dorian Gray*, shocks Victorian England with its theme of corruption of wealth

1895 H. G. Wells publishes landmark science fiction novel *The Time Machine*

1896 Reaction to Thomas Hardy's novel *Jude the Obscure* is so negative that thereafter he writes only poetry

1901 Kipling publishes novel *Kim*, detailing life in India

1875   **1890**   **1900**

1875 Public Health Act expands sanitary laws; new sewer system is installed in London

1876 Disraeli secures title "Empress of India" for Victoria; collective bargaining by trade unions legalized

1879 Ireland pressures for home rule

1884 Reform Bill gives vote to almost all adult males

1899 Boer War against Dutch South African settlers begins (to 1902)

1901 Queen Victoria dies after 64-year rule

1875   **1890**   **1900**

1876 Korea becomes independent nation

1879 Thomas Edison invents first practical light bulb

1884 Berlin Conference of 14 European nations sets rules for dividing Africa into colonies

1893 Henry Ford develops gasoline-powered automobile; France conquers Indochina; New Zealand first country to grant women suffrage

1895 Italian Guglielmo Marconi invents first radio

1896 First modern Olympic Games held in Athens, Greece

1898 Spanish-American War

1900 Austrian psychiatrist Sigmund Freud publishes *The Interpretation of Dreams*

HISTORICAL BACKGROUND

THE VICTORIANS

1832-1901

Britain's Victorian era was a time of overseas expansion and domestic reform. During this period of growth and change, the numbers of the middle class swelled, the lives of the working class improved, and the nation was set on the road to democracy. Its advances included the laying of a transatlantic telegraph cable and the advent of the automobile, electric lighting, and antiseptic medicine. Nevertheless, for many people today the term *Victorian* implies only stuffy complacency, hypocrisy, and prudishness. These characteristics did exist, but they by no means sum up the era.

Victoria was only 18 when she began her reign in 1837. Mindful of the scandalous conduct of her royal uncles, George IV and William IV, the queen placed great emphasis on moral behavior and was scrupulous in the performance of her royal duties. Ably tutored by the Whig prime minister Lord Melbourne, the young queen accepted—as her predecessors had not— the idea of a constitutional monarchy in which the monarch gave advice rather than orders. In 1840 Melbourne helped arrange the marriage of Victoria and her German cousin Prince Albert of Saxe-Coburg-Gotha, to whom she became deeply devoted. After Albert died in 1861, Victoria mourned him for the rest of her life, retiring even further from the daily affairs of government. Fortunately, during Victoria's 64-year reign (the longest in British history) she and the nation would be served by a number of talented prime ministers—including, in addition to Melbourne, Sir Robert Peel in the early Victorian years, Lord Palmerston in the mid-Victorian era, and the rival politicians Benjamin Disraeli and William E.

Top: Portrait of Queen Victoria, painted in the year of her marriage
Above: The Great Exhibition of 1851, held in London's Crystal Palace, celebrated industry and technology.
Left: An Indian floral pattern of the sort that had a major influence on Victorian design
Right: Removal of Irish tenants during the potato famine

Gladstone in later Victorian times. These leaders helped guide Britain through a remarkable period of social, economic, and political change.

AN ERA OF REFORM

Under Lord Melbourne and the Whigs, who held power throughout much of the 1830s, many long-sought reforms were passed, including the abolition of slavery in the British Empire and the first restrictions on child labor in factories. Nevertheless, the Whigs' goal was not democracy but an enlightened government by an educated upper class. Their best-known achievement, the Reform Bill of 1832, expanded voting rights only to men with a certain amount of property. When members of the working-class movement called Chartism demanded universal male suffrage, the demand went unheeded.

After the 1841 election brought Sir Robert Peel and the Tories to power, gradual reform continued, with new laws addressing safety in the mines and factories. Peel, however, faced agitation from both Chartists and the Anti-Corn Law League, which sought to repeal the laws protecting British farmers from foreign competition. The league's cause was advanced by the devastating rains of 1845, which ruined England's wheat crop and allowed disease to wipe out Ireland's harvest of potatoes, the staple

Development of the *English Language*

In Victorian times, as education spread and people entering the middle class attempted to speak "proper" English, the English language became more homogeneous. Increased literacy also stabilized English, since the written language tends to change more slowly than the spoken. The period also saw the beginning of an effort to compile a definitive record of the histories, uses, and meanings of English words, resulting in the massive *Oxford English Dictionary,* the first volume of which was published in 1884. This landmark work, not completed until 1928 and revised several times since, traces each word's changes in meaning from its first recorded use to the present.

Victorian advances in the natural and social sciences spurred the coinage of new words, such as *telephone, photography, psychiatrist,* and *feminist.* As the new fields of study developed their own jargons, their specialized and technical vocabulary began to infiltrate everyday speech. Euphemisms—mild, indirect, or vague terms substituted for ones considered harsh or offensive— also grew more popular as Victorian propriety made certain words taboo. A chicken breast became "white meat"; its legs, "drumsticks." Even words that today seem rather benign—such as *belly, buck,* and *stallion*—were prudishly avoided.

Although "proper" circles frowned on slang, it was widely used among the lower classes as a means of conversing safely in the presence of outsiders, including the police. The Cockneys of London's East End developed an elaborate system of rhyming slang in early Victorian times—using, for example, *loaf* to mean "head" because *loaf* is the first word in the expression *loaf of bread,* which rhymes with *head.* The expression "use your loaf" is still common in the East End today.

food of the Irish poor. With famine stalking Ireland, Peel agreed that foreign grain could ease conditions and introduced a bill to abolish the Corn Laws. The bill passed too late to help most of the Irish, but it did mark the beginning of free trade in Britain.

INTERNATIONAL AFFAIRS

The free-trade issue divided the Tories and led some of them to join the Whigs to form a new political party, the Liberal party. During this realignment, the dominant political figure was the independent Lord Palmerston, a moderate Whig who served as foreign minister for much of the 1830s and 1840s. In that capacity he had successfully overseen the expansion of Britain's empire—including, in 1840, the annexation of New Zealand and the beginning of a war with China that led to the British acquisition of Hong Kong two years later. Palmerston's clever diplomacy, backed up by the British fleet, had also kept France out of Egypt and Russia out of Turkey. Then, in 1854, with Turkey again threatened and Palmerston out of office, Britain joined the fight against Russia in the Crimean War. By the next year, after a series of British military blunders and defeats, the public was clamoring for change. At this point Palmerston became prime minister, and it was he who received credit for ending the war with the 1856 treaty ensuring Turkish sovereignty. Two years later, following a mutiny by native troops in British India, Palmerston's government attempted to end corruption there by removing control of the colony from the hands of the East India Company. This change had mixed results but was generally applauded in Britain.

Top: Disraeli and Gladstone
Above: Florence Nightingale caring for wounded soldiers
Left: Portrait of Nightingale
Below: The advent of the railroad revolutionized the transportation of both people and goods.

PROSPERITY AND ADVANCES

Though Palmerston showed little interest in domestic reform, free trade and the expansion of empire helped make the mid-Victorian period a prosperous time in Britain, both for aristocrats and for the growing middle class. Despite the repeal of the Corn Laws, the

introduction of the McCormick reaper from America prevented an agricultural decline. Textile exports were booming, and industry in general benefited from Henry Bessemer's new steel-making process. Steamships and railways revolutionized the transportation of goods and people, making travel quicker, cheaper, and far more comfortable than ever before. Communications improved with the advent of the telegraph. Growing literacy and improvements in printing spurred the publication of books, magazines, and newspapers. Advances in medicine included the introduction of antiseptic surgery by Joseph Lister and the founding of the first modern nursing school by Florence Nightingale, who had become famous as a volunteer nurse in the Crimean War.

Nightingale's volunteer spirit was echoed in the foundation of the YMCA, the Salvation Army, and a host of new charitable organizations. In mid-Victorian Britain—a society at once deeply religious and highly materialistic—most people viewed charity as a Christian duty and shared an optimistic faith in humanity's ability to achieve happiness through economic and material progress. John Stuart Mill, the most influential economist of the period, argued for gradual, steady social reform and for the abandonment of the strict laissez-faire (government-noninterference) policies of earlier British liberals. Many of Mill's ideas were put into practice after Palmerston's death, when Gladstone and Disraeli rose on the political scene.

GLADSTONE AND DISRAELI

As head of the new Liberal party, Gladstone wore the mantle of reform, but Disraeli also realized the importance of political and social reforms in attracting working-class support for his revitalized Tory party. Gladstone won passage of bills for land reform in Ireland and for the establishment of public schools and secret balloting in elections. Disraeli won passage of the landmark Second Reform Bill of 1867, which extended the vote to working-class males, as well

LITERARY HISTORY

Though no longer the radical movement it once was, **romanticism** continued to influence Victorian writing; but a new movement, called **realism,** increasingly began to take hold. Realism sought to capture everyday life as it really was lived. Instead of turning away from science and industry as romanticism had done, realism focused on the effects of the Industrial Revolution, often bringing social problems to public attention. Many early Victorian novels blend romanticism and realism. Charles Dickens, the era's most popular storyteller, produced entertaining novels with farfetched plots that nevertheless exposed real social problems—such as the plight of orphans in *Oliver Twist* (1837–1839) and *Nicholas Nickleby* (1838–1839). In *Wuthering Heights* (1847), Emily Brontë, one of a growing number of women writers, set a melodramatic plot with a Byronic hero against a realistic Yorkshire landscape; in *Jane Eyre* (1847), her sister Charlotte blended gothic elements with realistic social details. Realism is an even stronger element in the novels of William Makepeace Thackeray and Anthony Trollope.

Later in the century, new ideas in the natural and social sciences prompted the style known as **psychological realism,** which focused not on external realities but on the inner realities of the mind, and **naturalism,** an offshoot of realism that viewed nature and society as forces indifferent to human suffering. One of the pioneering psychological realists was the novelist George Meredith. The beginnings of naturalism are evident in the novels of George Eliot (Mary Ann Evans), but even more strongly naturalistic is the pessimistic fiction of Thomas Hardy, set in the author's native Wessex.

as bills that improved housing and sanitation, legalized trade unions, and reformed factory conditions. Where the two rivals differed most was in their personal styles and their attitudes toward British imperialism. A staid, morally righteous figure, Gladstone was a "Little Englander" who believed that Britain should take care of its own problems rather than involve itself in costly expansion abroad. The more flamboyant Disraeli linked prosperity to colonial expansion and patriotically equated imperialism with Britain's destiny. In 1875 he secretly negotiated the British government's purchase of a large interest in the newly completed Suez Canal in Egypt, which cut thousands of miles off the sea trip to India. A year later, he maneuvered Parliament into conferring the title "Empress of India" on Victoria. He also acquired the Mediterranean island of Cyprus and annexed the Transvaal, a South African republic that had been established by the Boers, settlers of mostly Dutch descent. Disraeli's policies enjoyed the support of the queen, who could not conceal her dislike for the self-righteous Gladstone.

Fascinated by the heroic exploits of their explorers, missionaries, and empire builders in Africa and Asia, most British citizens also supported Disraeli's imperialism, although by the time of his death in 1881, that support was waning. Disraeli's effort to prevent a Russian domination of Afghanistan, which threatened British India, resulted in two years of costly warfare there. Similarly, his annexation of the Transvaal led to conflicts with the native Zulu and with the Boers, who regained control of the Transvaal in 1881. Events such as these introduced the nation to the downside of imperialism, much as Gladstone had warned.

NEW DIRECTIONS

During the last decades of the Victorian era, the confident optimism of earlier times was tinged with an undercurrent of anxiety. To be sure, most people patriotically celebrated Victoria's Golden Jubilee, marking 50 years of her

Top: Boer War soldiers
Above: Charles Darwin; *inset:* detail from Darwin's notebooks
Right: Portrait of an older Queen Victoria
Far right: Victorian bicycle

rule, in 1887, and her Diamond Jubilee a decade later. Nevertheless, the complacency of mid-Victorian times was beginning to shatter as new ideas took hold. The writings of the scientist Charles Darwin created a rift between liberal Christians, whose interpretation of the Bible allowed the acceptance of Darwin's theory of evolution, and fundamentalist Christians, whose interpretation did not. Applying Darwin's ideas to human society, the philosopher Herbert Spencer coined the phrase "survival of the fittest," which conservatives—called social Darwinists—used to justify a return to government noninterference, saying that nature should be allowed to weed out the "unfit." This thinking brought the social Darwinists into conflict with the increasingly socialist labor movement, which supported industrial reform through government control and ownership. The socialism of the labor movement also frayed its ties to moderate Liberals just as the Liberal party was falling into disarray over the issue of Irish home rule. Then, in 1899, British colonial expansion in Africa resulted in the Boer War, which galvanized public patriotism and further weakened the anti-imperialist Liberal party. A new party formed in 1900—the Labor party— would become a dominant political force in the new century, and the Boer War would be a prelude to the far more devastating warfare of the modern age.

Extremely popular in Victorian times, novels often were serialized in magazines aimed at the growing middle class. Toward the 19th century's end the short story also grew popular, in hands such as those of Rudyard Kipling, who championed British imperialism in rousing tales drawn from his experiences in India, and Sir Arthur Conan Doyle, creator of the master detective Sherlock Holmes. The Victorian emphasis on family life also spurred a boom in children's literature, including Lewis Carroll's *Alice's Adventures in Wonderland* (1865) and *Through the Looking Glass* (1872).

Poetry also thrived during Victorian times. Alfred, Lord Tennyson, who became poet laureate in 1850, wrote musical public verse like "The Charge of the Light Brigade," as well as more personal poetry such as that of *In Memoriam* (1850). Elizabeth Barrett Browning produced a bestseller with *Sonnets from the Portuguese* (1850), a volume of love poems to her husband Robert, who himself pioneered the verse form called the dramatic monologue. Poets of the Pre-Raphaelite movement, such as Dante Gabriel Rossetti and his sister Christina, repudiated Victorian excess and sought to return to the clarity of medieval Italian works. The more pessimistic mood of late Victorian times is evident in the verse of Thomas Hardy and A. E. Housman. Gerard Manley Hopkins is noted for his modern experiments in poetic rhythm.

The Victorian era was not an age of great drama, although Oscar Wilde wrote some fine comedies in the 1890s. The era's most enduringly popular stage creations are the comic operas of W. S. Gilbert and Arthur Sullivan, which ridicule social pretense with a vitality that is still admired today.

PART 1　Personal Relationships

During the Victorian era, the Industrial Revolution brought increased productivity and economic growth to much of England. However, it also brought poverty, overcrowding, and appalling work conditions to the many people who had flocked to the cities from rural areas, hoping for a better life. As the world became a confusing and often brutal place, personal relationships—love, marriage, friendship—became especially important to the Victorians. Of course, as the writers in this part of Unit Five suggest, not all such relationships provide comfort. Some, twisted by jealousy, turn dark—even criminal. In these selections, you may encounter experiences and questions that continue to concern people.

COMPARING LITERATURE: The Miracle of Purun Bhagat
and What Men Live By
Moral Lessons Across Cultures: Russia

The Lady of Shalott
Ulysses
from In Memoriam
Crossing the Bar

Poetry by ALFRED, LORD TENNYSON

Connect to Your Life

The Role of the Poet What comes to mind when you think of the word *poet?* Do you imagine someone secluded from the world? Someone who is a popular figure? Someone who expresses deep personal feelings? Discuss your thoughts with some of your classmates.

Build Background

The Voice of His Age Alfred, Lord Tennyson, was a true spokesperson for middle-class Victorians. His poetry reflected many of the prevailing attitudes of the day, especially the moral and religious concerns of individuals living in a universe redefined by scientific discoveries. His output was diverse, ranging from optimistic verse written to please the public, to wistful, melancholy poems expressing his own thoughts and feelings.

In 1833, Tennyson was overwhelmed with grief by the sudden death of his best friend, Arthur Henry Hallam, who had recently become engaged to Tennyson's sister and was just 22 years old. He expressed part of his response to this loss in his poetry. In the two months after his friend's death, Tennyson wrote "Ulysses," in which he describes the restless longing of the now aged hero for one last adventure. He also began writing the lyrics that were to become *In Memoriam,* an elegy mourning the death of a greatly talented man cut off before he is able to fulfill the promise of his youth. Written over a period of 17 years, the poem consists of 132 sections, 3 of which are included in the selection presented here. An early poem, "The Lady of Shalott" is a dreamlike narrative based on the Arthurian legends. "Crossing the Bar" was written by Tennyson near the end of his life; he directed that the poem be printed at the end of all collections of his poetry.

Focus Your Reading

LITERARY ANALYSIS **SPEAKER** As you know, the **speaker** in a poem is the voice that "talks" to the reader, like the narrator in fiction. In Tennyson's poetry, the speaking voice varies from poem to poem, from a main character speaking in the first-person point of view to a neutral, objective voice that describes events in the third-person point of view. As you read each of these poems, think about what is revealed about the speaker.

ACTIVE READING **ANALYZING SPEAKER AND TONE**

Tennyson's use of a different **speaker** in each poem allows him to convey a different **tone,** or attitude, about the subject matter of each work. In one poem, for example, Tennyson might use a speaker that helps convey a serious tone; in another poem, the speaker might observe the subject matter from a distance and therefore convey a tone of formality.

READER'S NOTEBOOK As you read the four poems, use a chart like the one shown to briefly describe each speaker and the tone that the speaker helps to impart.

Speaker	Speaker's Tone

The Lady of Shalott

Alfred, Lord Tennyson

Detail, see p. 843.

PART I

On either side the river lie
Long fields of barley and of rye,
That clothe the wold and meet the sky;
And through the field the road runs by
5 To many-towered Camelot;
And up and down the people go,
Gazing where the lilies blow
Round an island there below,
    The island of Shalott.

10 Willows whiten, aspens quiver,
Little breezes dusk and shiver
Through the wave that runs forever
By the island in the river
    Flowing down to Camelot.
15 Four gray walls, and four gray towers,
Overlook a space of flowers,
And the silent isle imbowers
    The Lady of Shalott.

By the margin, willow-veiled,
20 Slide the heavy barges trailed
By slow horses; and unhailed
The shallop flitteth silken-sailed
    Skimming down to Camelot:
But who hath seen her wave her hand?
25 Or at the casement seen her stand?
Or is she known in all the land,
    The Lady of Shalott?

3 wold: rolling plain.

7 blow: bloom.

17 imbowers: encloses; surrounds.

22 shallop (shăl′əp): a small open boat.

25 casement: a hinged window that opens outward.

Only reapers, reaping early
In among the bearded barley,
30   Hear a song that echoes cheerly
From the river winding clearly,
        Down to towered Camelot;
And by the moon the reaper weary,
Piling sheaves in uplands airy,
35   Listening, whispers "'Tis the fairy
Lady of Shalott."

PART II

There she weaves by night and day
A magic web with colors gay.
She has heard a whisper say,
40   A curse is on her if she stay
        To look down to Camelot.
She knows not what the curse may be,
And so she weaveth steadily,
And little other care hath she,
45   The Lady of Shalott.

And moving through a mirror clear
That hangs before her all the year,
Shadows of the world appear.
There she sees the highway near
50   Winding down to Camelot;
There the river eddy whirls,
And there the surly village churls,
And the red cloaks of market girls,
        Pass onward from Shalott.

55   Sometimes a troop of damsels glad,
An abbot on an ambling pad,
Sometimes a curly shepherd lad,
Or long-haired page in crimson clad,
        Goes by to towered Camelot;
60   And sometimes through the mirror blue
The knights come riding two and two:
She hath no loyal knight and true,
        The Lady of Shalott.

But in her web she still delights
65   To weave the mirror's magic sights,
For often through the silent nights

52 surly village churls: rude members of the lower class in a village.

55 damsels: young, unmarried women.

56 abbot . . . pad: the head monk in a monastery on a slow-moving horse.

58 page: a boy in training to be a knight.

A funeral, with plumes and lights
    And music, went to Camelot;
Or when the moon was overhead,
70 Came two young lovers lately wed:
"I am half sick of shadows," said
    The Lady of Shalott.

PART III

A bowshot from her bower eaves,
He rode between the barley sheaves,
75 The sun came dazzling through the leaves,
And flamed upon the brazen greaves
    Of bold Sir Lancelot.
A red-cross knight forever kneeled
To a lady in his shield,
80 That sparkled on the yellow field,
    Beside remote Shalott.

The gemmy bridle glittered free,
Like to some branch of stars we see
Hung in the golden Galaxy.
85 The bridle bells rang merrily
    As he rode down to Camelot;
And from his blazoned baldric slung
A mighty silver bugle hung,
And as he rode his armor rung,
90   Beside remote Shalott.

All in the blue unclouded weather
Thick-jeweled shone the saddle leather,
The helmet and the helmet-feather
Burned like one burning flame together,
95   As he rode down to Camelot;
As often through the purple night,
Below the starry clusters bright,
Some bearded meteor, trailing light,
    Moves over still Shalott.

100 His broad clear brow in sunlight glowed;
On burnished hooves his war horse trode;
From underneath his helmet flowed
His coal-black curls as on he rode,
    As he rode down to Camelot.
105 From the bank and from the river

73 bowshot: the distance an arrow can be shot; **bower** (bou′ər) **eaves:** the part of the roof that extends above the lady's private room.

76 brazen greaves: metal armor protecting the legs below the knees.

78–79 red-cross . . . shield: the red cross was a symbol worn by knights who fought in the Crusades, a series of holy wars between European Christians and the Muslim conquerors of Jerusalem and other parts of the Holy Land. Sir Lancelot's shield bears a picture of such a knight kneeling to honor a lady.

82 gemmy: studded with gems.

87 blazoned (blā′zənd) **baldric:** a decorated leather belt, worn across the chest to support a sword, or as in this case, a bugle.

He flashed into the crystal mirror,
"Tirra lirra," by the river
    Sang Sir Lancelot.

She left the web, she left the loom,
110 She made three paces through the room,
She saw the water lily bloom,
She saw the helmet and the plume,
    She looked down to Camelot.
Out flew the web and floated wide;
115 The mirror cracked from side to side;
"The curse is come upon me," cried
    The Lady of Shalott.

The Lady of Shalott (1888) by J. W. Waterhouse (1849–1917), Tate Gallery, London/Art Resource, New York.

PART IV

In the stormy east wind straining,
The pale yellow woods were waning,
120 The broad stream in his banks complaining,
Heavily the low sky raining
    Over towered Camelot;
Down she came and found a boat
Beneath a willow left afloat,
125 And round about the prow she wrote
    The Lady of Shalott.

And down the river's dim expanse
Like some bold seër in a trance,
Seeing all his own mischance—
130 With a glassy countenance
    Did she look to Camelot.
And at the closing of the day
She loosed the chain, and down she lay;
The broad stream bore her far away,
135   The Lady of Shalott.

Lying, robed in snowy white
That loosely flew to left and right—
The leaves upon her falling light—
Through the noises of the night
140   She floated down to Camelot;
And as the boat-head wound along
The willowy hills and fields among,
They heard her singing her last song,
    The Lady of Shalott.

145 Heard a carol, mournful, holy,
Chanted loudly, chanted lowly,
Till her blood was frozen slowly,
And her eyes were darkened wholly,
    Turned to towered Camelot.
150 For ere she reached upon the tide
The first house by the waterside,
Singing in her song she died,
    The Lady of Shalott.

Under tower and balcony,
155 By garden wall and gallery,
A gleaming shape she floated by,

128 seër (sē′ər): someone who can see into the future; a prophet.

150 ere (âr): before.

Dead-pale between the houses high,
　　Silent into Camelot.
Out upon the wharfs they came,
160　Knight and burgher, lord and dame,
And round the prow they read her name,
　　The Lady of Shalott.

Who is this? and what is here?
And in the lighted palace near
165　Died the sound of royal cheer;
And they crossed themselves for fear,
　　All the knights at Camelot:
But Lancelot mused a little space;
He said, "She has a lovely face;
170　God in his mercy lend her grace,
　　The Lady of Shalott."

160 **burgher:** a middle-class citizen of a town.

Thinking Through the Literature

1. **Comprehension Check** Summarize the main events in the poem's **plot.**

2. What is your impression of the Lady of Shalott?

3. What is her relationship to the outside world?

   THINK ABOUT
   - what the reapers hear and say
   - the curse she lives under
   - what she sees in the "mirror clear" (line 46)
   - what she weaves in her "magic web" (lines 38, 64–65)

4. Why do you think she says in line 71 that she is "half sick of shadows"?

5. How would you describe her actions after the mirror cracks? Do you think she could have responded differently? Explain your answer.

ULYSSES

Alfred, Lord Tennyson

It little profits that an idle king,
By this still hearth, among these barren crags,
Match'd with an aged wife, I mete and dole
Unequal laws unto a savage race,
That hoard, and sleep, and feed, and know not me.

I cannot rest from travel: I will drink
Life to the lees: all times I have enjoy'd
Greatly, have suffer'd greatly, both with those
That loved me, and alone; on shore, and when
Thro' scudding drifts the rainy Hyades
Vext the dim sea: I am become a name;
For always roaming with a hungry heart
Much have I seen and known; cities of men
And manners, climates, councils, governments,
Myself not least, but honor'd of them all;
And drunk delight of battle with my peers,
Far on the ringing plains of windy Troy.
I am a part of all that I have met;
Yet all experience is an arch wherethro'
Gleams that untravell'd world, whose margin fades
For ever and for ever when I move.
How dull it is to pause, to make an end,
To rust unburnish'd, not to shine in use!
As tho' to breathe were life. Life piled on life
Were all too little, and of one to me
Little remains: but every hour is saved
From that eternal silence, something more,
A bringer of new things; and vile it were
For some three suns to store and hoard myself,
And this gray spirit yearning in desire
To follow knowledge like a sinking star,
Beyond the utmost bound of human thought.

This is my son, mine own Telemachus,
To whom I leave the sceptre and the isle—
Well-loved of me, discerning to fulfil
This labor, by slow prudence to make mild
A rugged people, and thro' soft degrees
Subdue them to the useful and the good.
Most blameless is he, centred in the sphere

3 mete (mēt) **and dole:** give and distribute.

7 to the lees: to the dregs or bottom of the cup; completely.

10 scudding drifts: wind-blown rainclouds; **Hyades:** a constellation whose rising was believed to signify the coming of rain.

17 Troy: an ancient city (in what is now Turkey), conquered by the Greeks in the Trojan War in about 1200 B.C. Ulysses (also called Odysseus) was a major character in the *Iliad,* Homer's epic poem about the Trojan War, written in about 800 B.C.

29 three suns: three years.

34 sceptre: a staff held by a king or a queen as a symbol of royal authority.

Above: *Head of Ulysses,* Rhodian Brothers, 1st CE, Sperlonga/Erich Lessing/Art Resource, New York.

40　Of common duties, decent not to fail
　　In offices of tenderness, and pay
　　Meet adoration to my household gods,　　　　　　　　42 **meet:** appropriate.
　　When I am gone. He works his work, I mine.
　　　　　There lies the port; the vessel puffs her sail:
45　There gloom the dark broad seas. My mariners,
　　Souls that have toil'd, and wrought, and thought with me—
　　That ever with a frolic welcome took　　　　　　　　47 **frolic:** merry.
　　The thunder and the sunshine, and opposed
　　Free hearts, free foreheads—you and I are old;
50　Old age hath yet his honor and his toil;
　　Death closes all: but something ere the end,
　　Some work of noble note, may yet be done,
　　Not unbecoming men that strove with Gods.
　　The lights begin to twinkle from the rocks;
55　The long day wanes; the slow moon climbs; the deep
　　Moans round with many voices. Come, my friends,
　　'Tis not too late to seek a newer world.
　　Push off, and sitting well in order smite
　　The sounding furrows; for my purpose holds
60　To sail beyond the sunset, and the baths　　　　　　60–61 **baths . . . stars:** the Ancient
　　Of all the western stars, until I die.　　　　　　　Greeks believed the earth was
　　It may be that the gulfs will wash us down:　　　　surrounded by an outer ocean or
　　It may be we shall touch the Happy Isles,　　　　　river, into which the stars
　　And see the great Achilles, whom we knew.　　　　descended.
65　Tho' much is taken, much abides; and tho'　　　　　63–64 **Happy Isles . . . Achilles:** the
　　We are not now that strength which in old days　　Islands of the Blessed, where the
　　Moved earth and heaven; that which we are, we are;　souls of heroes, like Achilles, dwelt
　　One equal temper of heroic hearts,　　　　　　　　after death.
　　Made weak by time and fate, but strong in will
70　To strive, to seek, to find, and not to yield.

Thinking Through the Literature

1. What type of person does Ulysses seem to be?

THINK ABOUT
- his attitude toward his present life
- his attitude toward aging and death
- his motive for taking one last voyage

2. What contrast does Ulysses draw between his own role and that of his son, Telemachus?

3. What seems to be Tennyson's **tone,** or attitude, toward Ulysses?

FROM

IN MEMORIAM

ALFRED, LORD TENNYSON

27

I envy not in any moods
    The captive void of noble rage,
    The linnet born within the cage,
That never knew the summer woods;

5 I envy not the beast that takes
    His license in the field of time,
    Unfettered by the sense of crime,
To whom a conscience never wakes;

Nor, what may count itself as blest,
10   The heart that never plighted troth
    But stagnates in the weeds of sloth;
Nor any want-begotten rest.

I hold it true, whate'er befall;
    I feel it, when I sorrow most;
15   'Tis better to have loved and lost
Than never to have loved at all.

2 void of: lacking in.

3 linnet: a kind of small songbird.

6 license: freedom of action; liberty.

7 unfettered: unrestricted.

9–12 nor, what . . . rest: nor do I envy the supposed peace of mind that arises from remaining sunk in inaction, never pledging one's love, or from any deficiency.

May Day (1960), Andrew Wyeth. Watercolor. Copyright © 1995 Andrew Wyeth.

Portrait of Lord Tennyson (about 1856–1859), George Frederick Watts. National Gallery of Victoria, Melbourne, Australia.

54

O, yet we trust that somehow good
    Will be the final goal of ill,
    To pangs of nature, sins of will,
20 Defects of doubt, and taints of blood;

That nothing walks with aimless feet;
    That not one life shall be destroyed,
    Or cast as rubbish to the void,
When God hath made the pile complete;

25 That not a worm is cloven in vain;
    That not a moth with vain desire
    Is shriveled in a fruitless fire,
Or but subserves another's gain.

Behold, we know not anything;
30   I can but trust that good shall fall
    At last—far off—at last, to all,
And every winter change to spring.

So runs my dream; but what am I?
    An infant crying in the night;
35   An infant crying for the light,
And with no language but a cry.

19 pangs of nature: physical pain.

20 taints of blood: inherited faults.

23 void: empty space.

25 cloven: split.

28 subserves: promotes or assists.

Thy voice is on the rolling air;
   I hear thee where the waters run;
   Thou standest in the rising sun,
40 And in the setting thou art fair.

What are thou then? I cannot guess;
   But though I seem in star and flower
   To feel thee some diffusive power,
I do not therefore love thee less.

45 My love involves the love before;
   My love is vaster passion now;
   Though mixed with God and Nature
   thou,
I seem to love thee more and more.

Far off thou art, but ever nigh;
50   I have thee still, and I rejoice;
   I prosper, circled with thy voice;
I shall not lose thee though I die.

43 diffusive: scattered about.

49 nigh: nearby.

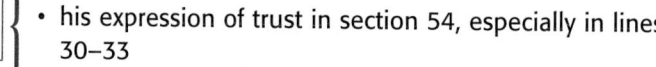

Thinking Through the Literature

1. With your classmates, discuss your thoughts after reading these sections of *In Memoriam*.

2. What different reactions to grief and loss does the **speaker** seem to experience?

   THINK ABOUT
   - the last stanza of section 27
   - the feelings he expresses in lines 34–36
   - his expression of trust in section 54, especially in lines 30–33
   - his thoughts leading up to the statement, "I have thee still, and I rejoice" in line 50

3. What, in the speaker's mind, is the relationship between the deceased loved one and nature?

4. What is your opinion of the speaker's comment that it is "better to have loved and lost / Than never to have loved at all" (lines 15–16)?

Fisherman at Sea (1796), J. M. W. Turner, Clore Collection, Tate Gallery, London/Art Resource.

Crossing the Bar

ALFRED, LORD TENNYSON

Sunset and evening star,
    And one clear call for me!
And may there be no moaning of the bar,
    When I put out to sea,

5   But such a tide as moving seems asleep,
    Too full for sound and foam,
When that which drew from out the boundless deep
    Turns again home.

Twilight and evening bell,
10   And after that the dark!
And may there be no sadness of farewell,
    When I embark;

For though from out our bourne of Time and Place
    The flood may bear me far,
15 I hope to see my Pilot face to face
    When I have crossed the bar.

3 moaning of the bar: the sad, mournful sound of the ocean waves pounding against a sand bar at the mouth of a harbor.

9 evening bell: a ship's bell rung to announce the changing of the watch.

13 from out our bourne of Time and Place: beyond the boundary of our lifetimes.

14 flood: ocean.

Connect to the Literature

1. What Do You Think? With your classmates, discuss your thoughts after reading "Crossing the Bar."

> **Comprehension Check**
> • What is the **setting** of the poem?
> • What sort of bar is being described?

Think Critically

2. To what does the **extended metaphor** of the sea voyage refer?

> • the speaker's reference in line 5 to a tide that "as moving seems asleep"
> • the speaker's wish in lines 11–12 that there be no sadness when he embarks
> • the remark in lines 13–14 that the flood may take the speaker beyond "our bourne of Time and Place"

3. Who might the Pilot represent?

4. How would you describe the **speaker's** attitude toward death?

5. **ACTIVE READING** **ANALYZING SPEAKER AND TONE** Review the chart you created in your **READER'S NOTEBOOK** to identify the **speaker** and the **tone** in each poem. How does the tone differ from poem to poem? How does the speaker affect the tone in each case?

Extend Interpretations

6. Comparing Texts Compare the excerpts from *In Memoriam* with Ben Jonson's "On My First Son" (page 458). What differences do you see in the two speakers' ways of coping with their grief? Share your thoughts with the class.

7. Connect to Life Tennyson wrote both "Ulysses" and *In Memoriam* in response to the death of a friend. Do you think writing a poem or a story or producing other kinds of art would be an effective way of responding to difficulty or loss? Explain your answer.

Literary Analysis

SPEAKER The **speaker** of a poem and the poet are not usually identical, although in some poems the speaker is closely identified with the poet. Often a poet creates a speaker with a distinct identity in order to achieve a particular effect.

Cooperative Learning Activity With a group of classmates, analyze how a different speaker might affect each poem. What if, for example, the speaker of "Ulysses" were his son, Telemachus? Write down your ideas in a chart like the one shown. Then share your conclusions with the rest of the class.

Poem	New Speaker	Effect
"The Lady of Shalott"	Lady of Shalott	
"Ulysses"		
In Memoriam		
"Crossing the Bar"		

REVIEW **BLANK VERSE** **Blank verse** is unrhymed poetry written in **iambic pentameter.** Because iambic pentameter resembles the natural rhythm of spoken English, it has been considered the most suitable meter for dramatic verse in English. Determine which of Tennyson's four poems is written in blank verse.

Choices & CHALLENGES

Writing Options

1. Analysis Essay Write an essay in which you analyze Ulysses' ideas about what constitutes a good and useful life. As a start, think about these questions: What comparison and contrast does Ulysses draw between his life and that of his son? What moral lessons does the poem seem to be teaching? Place the essay in your **Working Portfolio.**

Writing Handbook
See page 1369: Analysis.

2. Three Titles Write individual titles for the three sections of *In Memoriam.* Make sure that each title reflects the principal theme of the section to which it applies.

Activities & Explorations

1. Lancelot's Shield Draw your interpretation of Lancelot's shield as it is described in the first stanza of Part III of "The Lady of Shalott." ~ **ART**

2. The Lady on Film Watch the video "The Lady of Shalott," which features an oral reading and illustrations of the poem. Discuss how the film helps bring the poem to life. How did the video interpretation help convey the mood of the poem? ~ **VIEWING AND REPRESENTING**

 Literature in Performance

Inquiry & Research

Grief and Loss Research current theories of grief and loss. What are the normal stages of the grieving process? Share your findings in a brief oral report to the class.

Alfred, Lord Tennyson
1809–1892

Other Works
"The Charge of the Light Brigade"
Idylls of the King

Childhood The fourth son in a family of twelve children, Alfred Tennyson grew up in Somersby, England, where his father was a clergyman. Even as a child, Tennyson displayed an interest in poetry. He began learning to write poems at age eight by imitating the styles of Milton, Byron, and others. While a teenager, he collaborated with his brother on a collection of poems, which they published in 1826. Although Tennyson's father tutored his children to prepare them for a university education, family life at Somersby was problematic. The Reverend Dr. Tennyson's dissatisfaction with his profession led to periods of drunkenness that caused his family distress. Tensions in the family were increased by the opium addiction of one child and the severe mental illness of another.

University Life In 1827, Tennyson entered Cambridge University, where he won a poetry contest in his first year. His achievements caught the attention of a group of gifted undergraduates who called themselves the Apostles. Under the leadership of Arthur Henry Hallam, the Apostles urged Tennyson to pursue a career as a poet. Unfortunately, lack of funds forced the promising young poet to leave the university in 1831 and return home without taking a degree.

The Writing Life In the following years, Tennyson endured many difficulties, including the calamity of Hallam's death, financial problems, and an engagement complicated by the disapproval of his future wife's father. Throughout this time, however, he persisted with his writing, and in 1850 *In Memoriam* was published to impressive reviews. Tennyson had at last received literary recognition, and later that year he was invited by Queen Victoria to succeed Wordsworth as poet laureate. Tennyson lived a long life, during which he became a living legend—one of the most beloved figures of the Victorian era. In 1884, at the government's urging, he accepted the rank of baron and, along with it, the title *Lord.*

PREPARING to *Read*

My Last Duchess / Porphyria's Lover

Poetry by ROBERT BROWNING

Connect to Your Life

Green with Envy Consider the potential consequences of jealousy in a love relationship. Do you think jealousy is normal in such a relationship? Are there different degrees of this emotion? Share your thoughts with classmates.

Build Background

Playwright and Poet Although Robert Browning is best known as one of the greatest of Victorian poets, he actually devoted many years to writing plays. The techniques he learned as a playwright undoubtedly led to his mastery of the **dramatic monologue**—a type of poem in which a fictional speaker addresses a silent listener about a critical experience in his or her life. "My Last Duchess" and "Porphyria's (pôr-fîr´yəz) Lover" are among Browning's best dramatic monologues.

"My Last Duchess" takes place in 16th-century Italy and reflects the esteem for art that characterized the Italian Renaissance. Loosely based on actual events in the life of Alfonso II, duke of Ferrara, the poem presents a single episode in the duke's negotiations to marry the daughter of a powerful count. As the poem begins, the duke is showing a portrait of his former wife to the count's agent. The painting of the duchess "looking as if she were alive" is typical of Renaissance portraits, in which painters endeavored to portray their sitters as accurately and realistically as possible.

"Porphyria's Lover" first appeared with another dramatic monologue under the title *Madhouse Cells,* a title that reveals the poet's fascination with abnormal states of mind. Though Browning was a respectable, well-balanced person, the fictional speakers in his poems—ranging from corrupt bishops to insanely jealous lovers—often display abnormal behavior.

Focus Your Reading

LITERARY ANALYSIS DRAMATIC MONOLOGUE

In a **dramatic monologue,** the speaker describes a crucial experience to one or more listeners who remain silent. As you read these poems, consider how the use of dramatic monologue affects your knowledge of the speakers.

ACTIVE READING MAKING INFERENCES

An **inference** is a logical guess based on evidence. You often need to make inferences to figure out what is unstated yet implied in a literary work. You might, for example, use clues provided by a writer to infer—simply from the way a character acts—that the character is jealous of another character.

📖 **READER'S NOTEBOOK** As you read each of these poems, use a chart like the one shown to jot down any inferences you make about the speaker, the woman he describes, the setting, or past events.

	Inferences	
	"My Last Duchess"	**"Porphyria's Lover"**
Speaker		
Woman		
Setting		
Past events		

My Last Duchess

Robert Browning

Vespertina Quies (1893), Sir Edward Burne-Jones. Oil on canvas 120.6 cm × 62.2 cm, bequeathed by Miss Maud Beddington, 1940, Tate Gallery, London/Art Resource, New York.

That's my last Duchess painted on the wall,
Looking as if she were alive. I call
That piece a wonder, now: Frà Pandolf's hands
Worked busily a day, and there she stands.
5 Will't please you sit and look at her? I said
"Frà Pandolf" by design, for never read
Strangers like you that pictured countenance,
The depth and passion of its earnest glance,
But to myself they turned (since none puts by
10 The curtain I have drawn for you, but I)
And seemed as they would ask me, if they durst,
How such a glance came there; so, not the first
Are you to turn and ask thus. Sir, 'twas not
Her husband's presence only, called that spot
15 Of joy into the Duchess' cheek: perhaps
Frà Pandolf chanced to say "Her mantle laps
Over my lady's wrist too much," or "Paint
Must never hope to reproduce the faint
Half-flush that dies along her throat": such stuff
20 Was courtesy, she thought, and cause enough
For calling up that spot of joy. She had
A heart—how shall I say?—too soon made glad,
Too easily impressed; she liked whate'er
She looked on, and her looks went everywhere.

GUIDE FOR READING

1 What can you infer from the duke's use of the word *last*?

3 Frà Pandolf's: of Brother Pandolf, a fictitious friar-painter.

7 countenance: face.

9–10 What might it mean that no one save the duke draws the curtain?

11 durst: dared. (Note the hint that the strangers feel some sense of fear about questioning the duke.)

16 mantle: cloak.

21–24 How do you think the duke feels about the duchess's tendency to be easily pleased?

25   Sir, 'twas all one! My favor at her breast,
    The dropping of the daylight in the West,
    The bough of cherries some officious fool
    Broke in the orchard for her, the white mule
    She rode with round the terrace—all and each
30   Would draw from her alike the approving speech,
    Or blush, at least. She thanked men—good! but thanked
    Somehow—I know not how—as if she ranked
    My gift of a nine-hundred-years-old name
    With anybody's gift. Who'd stoop to blame
35   This sort of trifling? Even had you skill
    In speech—(which I have not)—to make your will
    Quite clear to such an one, and say, "Just this
    Or that in you disgusts me; here you miss,
    Or there exceed the mark"—and if she let
40   Herself be lessoned so, nor plainly set
    Her wits to yours, forsooth, and made excuse
    —E'en then would be some stooping; and I choose
    Never to stoop. Oh sir, she smiled, no doubt,
    Whene'er I passed her; but who passed without
45   Much the same smile? This grew; I gave commands;
    Then all smiles stopped together. There she stands
    As if alive. Will't please you rise? We'll meet
    The company below, then. I repeat,
    The Count your master's known munificence
50   Is ample warrant that no just pretense
    Of mine for dowry will be disallowed;
    Though his fair daughter's self, as I avowed
    At starting, is my object. Nay, we'll go
    Together down, sir. Notice Neptune, though,
55   Taming a sea horse, thought a rarity,
    Which Claus of Innsbruck cast in bronze for me!

27 officious: offering unwanted services; meddling.

35 trifling: actions of little importance.

41 forsooth: in truth; indeed.

46 What do you think happened to make the smiles stop?

49 munificence (myo͞o-nĭf′ĭ-səns): generosity.

50 just pretense: legitimate claim.

51 dowry (dou′rē): a financial settlement given to a groom by the bride's father.

53–54 The count's agent has gestured for the duke, because of his higher social status, to descend first. The duke responds that they will go down together. In your opinion, is the duke's graciousness in ignoring social differences genuine?

54 Neptune: in Roman mythology, the god of the sea.

55 What comparison can you draw between the duke and duchess's relationship and Neptune's taming the sea horse?

56 Claus of Innsbruck: a fictitious Austrian sculptor. What can you infer from the last two words of the poem?

Thinking Through the Literature

1. Describe your reaction to this poem.

2. What do you think happened to the duchess? Why do you suppose the poet never tells us exactly what happened to her?

3. How would you describe the speaker's attitude toward his former wife?

> THINK ABOUT
> - where he keeps his wife's picture
> - his reaction to the courtesy Frà Pandolf shows her
> - how he feels about her response to his "gift of a nine-hundred-years-old name" (line 33)
> - why he chooses "never to stoop" (line 43)

PORPHYRIA'S LOVER

ROBERT BROWNING

The Model (1939), Georges Braque. Oil on canvas, 100 cm × 100 cm, private collection, New York. Copyright © 1995 Artists Rights Society (ARS), New York/ADAGP, Paris.

The rain set early in tonight,
    The sullen wind was soon awake,
It tore the elm-tops down for spite,
    And did its worst to vex the lake:
5   I listened with heart fit to break.
When glided in Porphyria; straight
    She shut the cold out and the storm,
And kneeled and made the cheerless grate
    Blaze up, and all the cottage warm;
10   Which done, she rose, and from her form
Withdrew the dripping cloak and shawl,
    And laid her soiled gloves by, untied
Her hat and let the damp hair fall,
    And, last, she sat down by my side
15   And called me. When no voice replied,

GUIDE FOR READING

4 vex: to disturb; trouble the surface of.

6 straight: immediately.

6–9 What do you think Porphyria's first actions reveal about her?

8 grate: fireplace.

15 Although the speaker has heard Porphyria, he does not reply. Why do you think he remains silent?

She put my arm about her waist,
    And made her smooth white shoulder bare,
And all her yellow hair displaced,
    And, stooping, made my cheek lie there,
20   And spread, o'er all, her yellow hair,
Murmuring how she loved me—she
    Too weak, for all her heart's endeavor,
To set its struggling passion free
    From pride, and vainer ties dissever,
25   And give herself to me forever.
But passion sometimes would prevail,
    Nor could tonight's gay feast restrain
A sudden thought of one so pale
    For love of her, and all in vain:
30   So, she was come through wind and rain.
Be sure I looked up at her eyes
    Happy and proud; at last I knew
Porphyria worshiped me: surprise
    Made my heart swell, and still it grew
35   While I debated what to do.
That moment she was mine, mine, fair,
    Perfectly pure and good: I found
A thing to do, and all her hair
    In one long yellow string I wound
40   Three times her little throat around,
And strangled her. No pain felt she;
    I am quite sure she felt no pain.
As a shut bud that holds a bee,
    I warily oped her lids: again
45   Laughed the blue eyes without a stain.
And I untightened next the tress
    About her neck; her cheek once more
Blushed bright beneath my burning kiss:
    I propped her head up as before,
50   Only, this time my shoulder bore
Her head, which droops upon it still:
    The smiling rosy little head,
So glad it has its utmost will,
    That all it scorned at once is fled,
55   And I, its love, am gained instead!
Porphyria's love: she guessed not how
    Her darling one wish would be heard.
And thus we sit together now,
    And all night long we have not stirred,
60   And yet God has not said a word!

22–25 What is Porphyria unable to do? What might the "vainer ties" be?

27–30 Porphyria has left a party in order to be with the speaker.

35 Note that the speaker feels that he must make a decision.

44 In your opinion, why does the speaker open Porphyria's eyes "warily" (cautiously)?

52–55 The speaker here claims that he knows Porphyria's mind.

56–57 What is the speaker claiming?

Thinking through the LITERATURE

Connect to the Literature

1. What Do You Think? Were you surprised by the events presented in "Porphyria's Lover"? Explain.

> **Comprehension Check**
> • How do Porphyria and the speaker feel about each other?
> • How does the speaker kill Porphyria?

Think Critically

2. Why do you think the **speaker** kills Porphyria?

THINK ABOUT
> • what the speaker expects in a love relationship
> • his opinion of Porphyria's activities
> • what he hopes to achieve by his action

3. Do you think the speaker feels guilty about what he has done?

THINK ABOUT
> • the **tone** in which he speaks
> • his reason for strangling Porphyria
> • his attempt to make her look as she did before the murder (lines 44–49)
> • his comment about God's response to the deed (line 60)

4. How would you describe the **mood** of the speaker throughout the poem?

5. **ACTIVE READING** **MAKING INFERENCES** With a small group of classmates, discuss the chart you completed in your **READER'S NOTEBOOK** as you read the poems. Use the information to make **inferences** about the love relationships in "My Last Duchess" and "Porphyria's Lover." How are the relationships alike? How are they different?

Extend Interpretations

6. Comparing Texts Contrast the speakers of "My Last Duchess" and "Porphyria's Lover" with the speaker of Lord Byron's "She Walks in Beauty" (page 773). How do the speakers differ in their attitudes toward women?

7. Critic's Corner The 19th-century novelist George Eliot stated that Browning "sets our thoughts at work rather than our emotions." What do you think she meant? Do you agree with her? Cite evidence from these two poems to support your answer.

8. Connect to Life In books and movies, jealous lovers are most often presented in a negative light. Do you think jealousy is ever a positive emotion?

Literary Analysis

DRAMATIC MONOLOGUE

A **dramatic monologue** is a lyric poem in which a speaker describes a crucial experience to a silent or absent listener. The effect on the reader is that of hearing just one side of a conversation. Dramatic monologue allows the poet to take the reader inside the speaker's mind by revealing his or her feelings, personality, and motivations. In "Porphyria's Lover," for example, the following lines reveal the speaker's exultation after Porphyria's declaration of love. They also provide a glimpse of the speaker's obsession and, perhaps, prepare the reader for what is to come.

> *That moment she was*
> *   mine, mine, fair,*
> *Perfectly pure and good. . . .*

Paired Activity The speaker of a dramatic monologue often reveals to the reader characteristics or feelings of which the speaker is unaware. For each of these poems, make a Venn diagram like the one shown to compare your own opinion of the speaker with his apparent view of himself. Then share and discuss your diagrams with a partner.

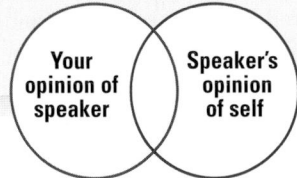

Your opinion of speaker | Speaker's opinion of self

Choices & CHALLENGES

Writing Options

1. Questions for the Duke Imagine that you are the silent listener in "My Last Duchess" and write a list of questions you would like to ask the speaker.

2. Television Mystery Write a synopsis of a television mystery in which the incident described in "Porphyria's Lover" is either the first or the last scene.

Act 1, Scene 1

Activities & Explorations

1. Murder Trial With a group of classmates, conduct a trial of Porphyria's lover on the charge of murder. Students acting as lawyers should question the defendant, and after deliberating, a jury should deliver its verdict.
~ SPEAKING AND LISTENING

2. Portrait of a Madman In a pencil or oil portrait, try to convey some of the charac-teristics of one of the poem's speakers. Your portrait may be realistic or abstract. ~ **ART**

Inquiry & Research

Roots of Jealousy Research theories on jealousy, looking for answers to these questions: What causes some people to be more jealous than others? What is the relationship between jealousy and self-esteem? Can feelings of jealousy be avoided or overcome? Report your findings to the class.

Robert Browning
1812–1889

Other Works
"Count Gismond"
"The Bishop Orders His Tomb at St. Praxed's Church"
"Home Thoughts, from Abroad"
"Prospice"
"The Pied Piper of Hamelin"

Early Criticism Born and raised near London, Robert Browning lived with his parents until he married at the age of 34. Although he attended the University of London for a brief period, his real education took place at home, where he was tutored in literature, history, and music, as well as boxing and horsemanship. At the age of 21 he published his first poem, "Pauline," which was savagely criticized for displaying too much emotion. The criticism embarrassed the young poet, who vowed to keep his writing totally objective, free from personal feelings, in the future. It was at this time that he began to write plays and dramatic monologues. His plays were not well received, and for many years critics claimed that his poetry was too difficult to read.

Happiness and Recognition In 1845, Browning met the poet Elizabeth Barrett, six years his senior, and began a famous romance that has been memorialized in both film and literature. The couple eloped in 1846 and moved to Italy. Although Browning wrote very little during his marriage, he lived happily for the next 15 years. After his wife's death in 1861, he returned to London and concentrated on the writing of *The Ring and the Book,* a series of dramatic monologues based on the records of a 17th-century Roman murder trial. The publication of *The Ring and the Book* made Browning famous and finally obtained for his poetry the recognition it deserved.

Author Activity

The Brownings on Film With a classmate, view one of the films that dramatizes the romance between Browning and Elizabeth Barrett. Then discuss the film by addressing these questions: How does the film portray the two poets? What insight does it provide into their character? their relationship? their writing?

PREPARING to *Read*

Sonnet 43

Poetry by ELIZABETH BARRETT BROWNING

A Warning Against Passion

Letter by CHARLOTTE BRONTË

(**Connect to Your Life**)

Reason and Romance The two selections you are about to read express very different attitudes toward romantic relationships. How would you describe your approach to romance? Try judging yourself on the four scales shown. For each pair of opposite qualities, decide at approximately which point of the scale you think your romantic personality falls.

Idealistic	Adventurous	Emotional	Open
Practical	Cautious	Rational	Reserved

Build Background

Secret Poems Elizabeth Barrett and Robert Browning were one of Victorian England's most famous couples. When they met, Elizabeth, an invalid, was a well-known poet, but Robert—six years her junior—was still struggling to gain recognition. Elizabeth's overprotective father strongly opposed Robert's attentions; the couple, however, married without his knowledge and moved to Italy, where Elizabeth's health improved and her career flourished. During their courtship, Elizabeth had secretly written a group of sonnets, including "Sonnet 43," about her romance with Robert, but she did not show them to him until after they were married. She titled them *Sonnets from the Portuguese* and published them as translations of another poet's work to hide her identity as the author.

Novelist and Letter Writer Charlotte Brontë, the author of the famous romantic novel *Jane Eyre,* reveals some of her attitudes toward love in a personal letter to her close friend Ellen Nussey. Ellen, or Nell, had asked Brontë for advice in handling the attentions of a Mr. Vincent, whom she was thinking of marrying, even though she did not know him well and was not strongly attracted to him. Brontë offers her friend several perspectives on the situation.

WORDS TO KNOW
Vocabulary Preview

deferential   precept
discourse   repugnance
foible

Focus Your Reading

LITERARY ANALYSIS   **AUTHOR'S PURPOSE**

An **author's purpose** may be to entertain, to inform, to express opinions or emotions, or to persuade. The following passage from "A Warning Against Passion" is a direct statement of purpose:

> *Now, Nell, I am about to write thee a discourse and a piece of advice which thou must take as if it came from thy grandmother. . . .*

As you read these selections, be aware of both explicit statements and more subtle clues that help indicate an author's purpose in writing.

ACTIVE READING   **COMPARING AUTHOR'S VIEWS**

Elizabeth Barrett Browning and Charlotte Brontë had different views of love. To compare two authors' views on the same subject, you need to identify the individual ideas that make up each author's understanding of the subject.

READER'S NOTEBOOK Make a cluster diagram, like the one shown, for each selection. Record the aspects of love that you think would be important elements in each writer's definition of the emotion.

passion

Sonnet 43

SONNET 43

Elizabeth Barrett Browning

How do I love thee? Let me count the ways.
I love thee to the depth and breadth and height
My soul can reach, when feeling out of sight
For the ends of Being and ideal Grace.
5 I love thee to the level of everyday's
Most quiet need, by sun and candlelight.
I love thee freely, as men strive for Right;
I love thee purely, as they turn from Praise.
I love thee with the passion put to use
10 In my old griefs, and with my childhood's faith.
I love thee with a love I seemed to lose
With my lost saints,—I love thee with the breath,
Smiles, tears, of all my life!—and, if God choose,
I shall but love thee better after death.

Thinking Through the Literature

1. **Comprehension Check** What question does the **speaker** of "Sonnet 43" pose and answer?

2. What is your impression of the romantic relationship described in this sonnet? Share your thoughts with your classmates.

3. Do you think it is desirable to love or be loved in this way? Explain your answer.

4. Look again at the Connect to Your Life on page 861. On each of the scales shown, where would you place the speaker of the sonnet?

Warning

Against

Passion

Charlotte Brontë

November 20th, 1840.

My dearest Nell,—That last letter of thine treated of matters so high and important I cannot delay answering it for a day—

Now, Nell, I am about to write thee a discourse and a piece of advice which thou must take as if it came from thy grandmother—but in the first place—before I begin with thee, I have a word to whisper in the ear of Mr. Vincent and I wish it could reach him.

In the name of St. Chrysostom, St. Simon and St. Jude,[1] why does not that amiable young gentleman come forward like a man and say all that he has to say to yourself personally—instead of trifling with kinsmen and kinswomen? "Mr. Vincent," I say—"walk or ride over to Brookroyd . . . and say, 'Miss Ellen, I want to speak to you.' Miss Ellen will of course civilly answer, 'I'm at your service, Mr. Vincent' and then when the room is cleared of all but *yourself* and *herself* just take a chair near her, insist upon her laying down that silly . . . basketwork, and listening to *you*. Then begin in a clear, distinct, deferential, but determined voice—'Miss Ellen, I have a question to put to you, a very important question—will you take me as your husband, for better for worse? I am not a rich man, but I have sufficient to support us—I am not a great man, but I love you honestly and truly—Miss Ellen, if you knew the world better you would see that this is an offer not to be despised—a kind attached heart, and a moderate competency.'[2] Do this, Mr. Vincent, and you may succeed—go on writing sentimental and love-sick letters to Henry[3] and I would not give sixpence for your suit."[4]

So much for Mr. Vincent—now, Nell, your turn comes to swallow the black bolus[5]—called a friend's advice. . . . Is the man a fool? is he a knave,[6] a humbug, a hypocrite, a ninny, a noodle? If he is any or all of these things, of course there is no sense in trifling with him—cut him short at once—Blast his hopes with lightning rapidity and keenness.

I hope you will not have the romantic folly to wait for the awakening of what the French call "Une grande *passion*"—My good girl, "une grande passion" is "*une* grande *folie*."

Is he something better than this? has he at least common sense—a good disposition, a manageable temper? Then, Nell, consider the matter. You feel a disgust towards him *now,* an utter repugnance—very likely—but be so good as to remember you don't know him—you have only had three or four days' acquaintance with him—longer and closer intimacy might reconcile you to a wonderful extent. And now I'll tell you a word of truth at which you may be offended or not as you like—From what I know of your character—and I think I know it pretty well—I should say you will never *love before* marriage—After that ceremony is over, and after you have had some months to settle down, and to get accustomed to the creature you have taken for your worse half—you will probably make a most affectionate and happy wife—even if the individual should not prove all you could wish—you will be indulgent towards his little follies and foibles—and will not feel much annoyance at them. This will especially be the case if he should have sense sufficient to allow you to guide him in important matters. Such being the case, Nell, I hope you will not have the romantic folly to wait for the awakening of what the French call "Une grande *passion*"—My good girl, "une grande passion" is "*une* grande *folie*."[7] . . .

---

1. **St. Chrysostom** (krĭs′əs-təm), **St. Simon, and St. Jude:** saints known for their honesty, sincerity, and courage.
2. **competency:** income or means sufficient to meet one's needs.
3. **Henry:** Ellen Nussey's brother.
4. **suit:** courtship.
5. **black bolus:** a round, bitter medicinal preparation, larger than an ordinary pill.
6. **knave:** an unprincipled, crafty fellow.
7. **"Une grande *passion*"** (ün gräɴd′ pä-syôɴ′) . . . **"*une* grande *folie*"** (ün gräɴd′ fô-lē′) *French:* a great passion . . . a great foolishness.

Mediocrity[8] in all things is wisdom—mediocrity in the sensations is superlative wisdom. When you are as old as I am, Nell— (I am sixty at least being your grandmother) you will find that the majority of those worldly precepts—whose seeming coldness shocks and repels us in youth—are founded in wisdom. Did you not once say to me in all childlike simplicity, "I thought, Charlotte—no young ladies should fall in love, till the offer was actually made." . . . The maxim is just . . . I will even extend and confirm it—no young lady should fall in love till the offer has been made, accepted—the marriage ceremony performed and the first half year of wedded life has passed away—a woman may then begin to love, but with great precaution—very coolly—very moderately—very rationally—if she ever loves so much that a harsh word or a cold look from her husband cuts her to the heart—she is a fool—if she ever loves so much that her husband's will is her law—and that she has got into a habit of watching his looks in order that she may anticipate his wishes she will soon be a neglected fool.

Couple in a Garden (about 1840), H. Robinson. Engraving after a Daniel Maclise illustration for a Thomas Moore poem, Mary Evans Picture Library, London.

*D*id I not once tell you of an instance of a relative of mine who cared for a young lady till he began to suspect that she cared more for him and then instantly conceived a sort of contempt for her?[9] . . .

I have two studies—*you* are my study for the success, the credit, and the respectability of a quiet, tranquil character. Mary is my study—for the contempt, the remorse—the misconstruction which follow the development of feelings in themselves noble, warm—generous—devoted and profound—but which being too freely revealed—too frankly bestowed—are not estimated at their real value. . . . I never hope to see in this world a character more truly noble—she would *die* willingly for one she loved—her intellect and her attainments are of the very highest standard, yet I doubt whether Mary will ever marry. . . . ❖

---

8. **mediocrity** (mē′dē-ŏk′rĭ-tē): a state of being midway between two extremes. (The word is used here without any negative connotation.)

9. **relative of mine . . . contempt for her:** a reference to a failed romance between another friend, Mary Taylor, and Brontë's brother, Branwell.

Connect to the Literature

1. What Do You Think? What is your opinion of Brontë's advice in "A Warning Against Passion"?

Comprehension Check
- Why is Brontë annoyed with Mr. Vincent?
- According to Brontë, when should a young woman allow herself to fall in love?

Think Critically

2. How would you **summarize** the main points of Brontë's advice about love and marriage?

THINK ABOUT
- her proposed advice to Mr. Vincent
- her view of falling in love
- her view of possible relationships between husbands and wives

3. How would you describe Brontë's views of men and women?

4. **ACTIVE READING** **COMPARING AUTHOR'S VIEWS** What do you think Brontë and Barrett Browning would say about each other's attitude toward romantic relationships? Look back at the cluster diagrams you created in your **READER'S NOTEBOOK** to help you identify each writer's attitude.

Extend Interpretations

5. Comparing Texts Reread Spenser's "Sonnet 30" (page 297) and Shakespeare's "Sonnet 116" (page 302). Compare these two sonnets with Barrett Browning's "Sonnet 43." Which of the three poems expresses the emotion of love most convincingly for you? Support your opinion.

6. Different Perspectives Suppose that Elizabeth Barrett Browning wrote a reply to Ellen Nussey. What advice do you think Barrett Browning would offer Nell?

7. Connect to Life Issues relating to love and marriage continue to be of great concern to people. Do you think Brontë's advice has relevance today?

Literary Analysis

AUTHOR'S PURPOSE Although a writer can fulfill a number of **purposes** in a work—to entertain, to inform, to express opinions or emotions, or to persuade—one purpose is usually the most important. In "Sonnet 43," the reader can assume that Barrett Browning's main purpose was to express love. In "A Warning Against Passion," Brontë's main purpose appears to have been to persuade her friend to approach marriage cautiously.

Paired Activity "Sonnet 43" and "A Warning Against Passion" have seemingly different main purposes. However, do they share any purposes? Jot down your ideas. Then discuss and compare your findings with your partner's conclusions.

"Sonnet 43"
Purposes:
1. to persuade her beloved of the intensity of her feelings
2.
3.

"A Warning Against Passion"
Purposes:
1. to express an opinion about love
2.
3.

Choices & CHALLENGES

Writing Options

A Letter in Response Write a letter in which Ellen Nussey responds to Brontë's advice. Tell Charlotte Brontë which ideas of hers you agree with and which you disagree with. Tell her what moral lessons you think you can draw from your experience with Mr. Vincent. Place the letter in your **Working Portfolio.**

Activities & Explorations

Imaginary Conversation With a partner, stage an imaginary conversation between Ellen Nussey and Mr. Vincent after Nussey has read the letter from Brontë. ~ **PERFORMING**

Vocabulary in Action

EXERCISE: MEANING CLUES On your paper, choose the word that is most closely related to each of the following sets.

1. lecture, speech, persuasive essay
2. bowing to a queen, giving someone else first choice of a seat
3. walking out of a movie, boycotting a product
4. "Waste not, want not," "Act in haste, repent at leisure."
5. being late all the time, forgetting to return borrowed items

WORDS TO KNOW	deferential	precept
	discourse	repugnance
	foible	

Elizabeth Barrett Browning
1806–1861

Other Works
"Sonnet 22"
The Cry of the Children

Life in Her Parents' House Elizabeth Barrett was the oldest of 11 children in a prosperous family. A precocious child, she read constantly and had her first poem published by the time she was 14. She became ill when she was about 15, and from that time until she eloped with Robert Browning in 1846, she lived the life of an invalid.

Married Life During the 15 years of her marriage, Barrett Browning was intensely happy. She gave birth to a son, wrote a wide variety of poems, and ardently supported such causes as the abolition of slavery, the reform of child labor practices, and women's rights. The Brownings' home in Florence, Italy, became a gathering place for people prominent in politics and the arts. Barrett Browning's most ambitious poem, the verse novel *Aurora Leigh*, was the first work by an Englishwoman in which the main character is herself a writer.

Charlotte Brontë
1816–1855

Other Works
Shirley
Villette

A Writing Family One of six children, Charlotte Brontë grew up in the remote Yorkshire village of Haworth. After the death of her mother and her two oldest sisters, she and her sisters Emily and Anne and her brother, Branwell, became inseparable companions. They wrote constantly through childhood into adulthood, and in 1846 they tried to publish some of their work. Their first efforts received little attention, but when Charlotte's novel *Jane Eyre* appeared in 1847, it was an immediate success.

Decline and Fall Sadly, Charlotte's triumph was soon eclipsed by tragedy. During the next two years, Branwell, Emily, and Anne died, leaving Charlotte heartbroken and lonely. In 1854 she married her father's assistant, but within a year she was dead as a result of pregnancy complications.

The Growth and Development of Fiction

The Novel's Beginning

Although the Internet has been in use for several years, its popularity began to soar in the 1990s. As the general public became more familiar with the Internet, people began to regard it as an "information highway," a new medium of communication that could benefit society. Over a century ago in Victorian England, another medium of communication generated a similar response. English writers began to see this new medium not only as a form of artistic expression, but also as an exciting way to affect the lives of people from all walks of life. It was called the **novel.**

The novel as we think of it came into being after Daniel Defoe published *Robinson Crusoe* in 1719. During this time, the novel was viewed primarily as a form of entertainment. In the mid-18th century, a few steps forward in the development of plot and characterization were taken in the novels *Pamela* (1740) and *Clarissa* (1747–1748) by Samuel Richardson and *Tom Jones* (1749) by Henry Fielding. *The Life and Opinions of Tristram Shandy, Gentleman* (1760–1767), a highly original work by Laurence Sterne, focused on characters' conversations and remembrances instead of on action. These writers inspired other writers to take the novel form in new directions.

The Novel Comes of Age

The Victorian period (1832–1901) is often called "the Age of the Novel." Victorian novels are known for their **realism**—the detailed presentation of everyday life. Through the novel, the Victorians wanted to document the lives and the *values* of the

Charles Dickens (1812–1870) used the novel to promote social reform.

English, including the lower classes. As the Victorian era continued, social concerns began playing a greater role in the general society. The novel became a tool for exposing society's ills. No other writer used this tool as effectively as did Charles Dickens. His novels *Oliver Twist* (1838), *A Christmas Carol* (1843), *David Copperfield* (1850), and *Bleak House* (1853), described in riveting detail the troubling state of England's lower classes. (See Milestones in British Literature, pp. 870–871.)

New Forms Emerge

In the 19th century, a remarkable variety of English novels were written, giving rise to new sub-genres. Here are several of the most popular forms:

HISTORICAL NOVELS This type of fiction combines historical facts with imagination to re-create the spirit of a past age. Charles Dickens based *A Tale of Two Cities* (1859) on historical accounts of the French Revolution.

GOTHIC NOVEL Horror tales became extremely popular in England near the turn of the 19th century. *Frankenstein* (1818) by Mary Shelley is the best known example of gothic fiction.

DETECTIVE NOVEL Mystery is a major ingredient of detective fiction. Sir Arthur Conan Doyle mastered this form in the late 1800s and created Sherlock Holmes, still the world's most famous detective.

NEWGATE NOVEL Stories focusing on criminals and their motives

a growing audience. Newgate fiction—which drew its name from a famous London prison—explored the nature of crime and violence. One example of a Newgate novel is Charles Dickens's *Barnaby Rudge* (1841), which looks at the effects of civil unrest and riot on the lives of a host of characters.

YOUR TURN For any of the popular forms described, offer an example of a similar modern-day version.

The Shift to Naturalism

After about 1880, realism began to be replaced by **naturalism**, a movement arising in France that promoted a grimmer, more "scientific" approach to fiction. Naturalistic writing was an attempt to depict the human condition as objectively as scientific writings depicted the processes of nature. In *Tess of the D'Urbervilles* (1891), an example of the naturalistic novel, Thomas Hardy portrayed a hostile world in which only the "fittest" prospered. This movement would extend into the early 20th century.

Jane Austen
1775–1817
- *Sense and Sensibility*
- *Pride and Prejudice*
- *Emma*

Elizabeth Gaskell
1810–1865
- *Mary Barton*
- *Cranford*
- *North and South*

George Eliot
(Mary Ann Evans)
1819–1880
- *Middlemarch*
- *The Mill on the Floss*
- *Silas Marner*

Emily Brontë
(Ellis Bell)
1818–1848
- *Wuthering Heights*

Charlotte Brontë
(Currer Bell)
1816–1855
- *Jane Eyre*
- *The Professor*
- *Shirley*

Women Novelists

As the reading public became increasingly female and middle class, female writers emerged. Romantic writer Jane Austen led the way with "novels of manners," works known for their focus on courtship, parental authority, and other "domestic" issues.

Victorian women writers were determined to overcome the commonly accepted view that writing was strictly a man's profession. The topics of many of their works often extended far beyond the home. For example, Elizabeth Cleghorn Gaskell, in both novels and short stories, detailed the plight of the industrial lower class.

Strategies for Reading: Victorian Fiction

1. Connect to the times. Many Victorian writers were middle class, and they wrote fiction for a middle-class audience. Notice what middle-class values the writer seems to uphold.

2. Look for evidence of the writer's social concerns. This might either be expressed directly or be woven into the conflict or characterization.

3. Get a sense of how each of the major characters relates to the plot. Pay particular attention to how characters with different backgrounds and values come into conflict.

4. Judge the work as a whole. What important theme has the Victorian writer conveyed?

5. Try to predict the end of the story as you read along.

6. As you read, list the distinctive qualities that you think characterize the writer's style.

7. **Monitor** your reading strategies and modify them when your understanding breaks down. Remember to use your Strategies for Active Reading: **predict, visualize, connect, question, clarify,** and **evaluate.**

THE NOVELS OF
CHARLES DICKENS

"It was the best of times, it was the worst of times": so begins Charles Dickens's novel *A Tale of Two Cities,* set at the time of the French Revolution. In many respects, this description can also be applied to Dickens's own era. Depending on one's perspective, Victorian Britain was the bright new dawning of the Industrial Revolution, or it was a filthy, brutal, and dehumanizing period best gotten over with. Dickens was able to see and comment upon both views of 19th-century life. With humor and intensity, his work shed light on London's criminals, businessmen, and working poor.

Born in Portsmouth but raised in London from the age of two, Dickens used events from his own life as starting points for many of his novels. His early career as a newspaper reporter sharpened his eye for detail and his ear for dialogue, giving him an uncanny ability to make his stories spring to life.

Dickens's first literary success was *The Posthumous Papers of the Pickwick Club*—usually known as *The Pickwick Papers*—in which he chronicled the humorous misadventures of eccentric characters in London and the countryside. The novel was an immediate

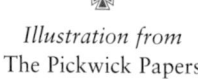

Illustration from
The Pickwick Papers

W. C. Fields and Freddie Bartholomew
in the 1935 film version of David Copperfield

success, catapulting Dickens into sudden and lasting fame. After this lighthearted bestseller, Dickens wrote 14 other novels, as well as numerous short stories and works of nonfiction.

Although Dickens's early novels, including *Oliver Twist* and *Nicholas Nickleby,* address such serious topics as crime, greed, and the mistreatment of children, they are also filled with lighter, humorous moments. His later novels, such as *Bleak House* and *A Tale of Two Cities,* present a grimmer, harsher world, and are etched with irony and satire. In the midst of this later phase of his literary output, however, Dickens also created two celebrated tales of youth and discovery—*David Copperfield,* a largely autobiographical work, and *Great Expectations,* considered by many to be his finest work.

Although Dickens died at the age of 58, his popularity did not. To this day, his works are enjoyed both in their original form and in adaptations as films and plays. An eight-hour stage production of *Nicholas Nickleby* recently enjoyed widespread popularity, and *A Christmas Carol* has become a delightful part of the Christmas tradition in countries around the world. Dickens's novels are an indispensable part of our literary landscape—and our modern social conscience as well.

Upper left:
Dickens's study
Lower left:
*Earliest known photograph
of Dickens, 1852. Photofest.*

Christmas Storms and Sunshine

Short Story by ELIZABETH CLEGHORN GASKELL

Connect to Your Life

Cold Shoulder Treatment Have you ever given someone you didn't know very well the "cold shoulder"? Think about what might have prompted you to act this way. Were your actions based on sound reasoning? Were they based on a mere first impression of the person or on what someone else had said? Get together with a few other students and share your experiences.

Build Background

Rising Middle Class The early Victorian era was a time of political reform, as the old aristocracy reluctantly gave way to a more democratic system. The First Reform Bill, passed in 1832, gave voting rights to the middle class and, as a result, made the upper class less powerful. The Tories, a political party that had controlled the government for almost 50 years, represented the interests of wealthy landowners and opposed the democratic reforms. The Tories were conservative, and they scorned their opponents, the "Radical" Whigs, for supporting reforms that gradually allowed the middle class to become a major force in England's economy.

Many Victorian writers focused on topics that appealed to the growing number of readers in the newly powerful middle class, writing about the social and personal relationships of ordinary people. The popular Victorian novelist Elizabeth Cleghorn Gaskell wrote about the manners and morals of upper- and middle-class Victorian society as well as the living and working conditions of the lower class. The story you are about to read involves the relationship between two families who rent rooms in the same house.

WORDS TO KNOW
Vocabulary Preview

affronted   pompous
allude   propensity
mortal

Focus Your Reading

LITERARY ANALYSIS | **THIRD-PERSON OMNISCIENT POINT OF VIEW**

Many stories are told from the **third-person point of view**—that is, by a narrator who is outside the action of the story. Occasionally, a story is told from an omniscient, or all-knowing, third-person point of view. In stories told from the **omniscient point of view,** the narrator sees into the minds of more than one character. As you read "Christmas Storms and Sunshine," be aware of the information provided by the story's omniscient narrator.

ACTIVE READING | **ANALYZING CAUSES AND EFFECTS**

Noting the **causes** and **effects** in a narrative helps you understand the relationships between events. In Gaskell's story, many of the events result in particular emotional responses. For example, when the cat eats Mrs. Hodgson's mutton, she feels intense anger. As you read the story, identify the different emotions experienced by Mrs. Hodgson and Mrs. Jenkins. Try to determine the cause of each emotion.

READER'S NOTEBOOK Use a chart like the one shown to record your observations about each character's emotions.

Mrs. Hodgson	
Event (cause)	Emotion (effect)
Cat eats cold mutton.	intense anger

Christmas
Storms and Sunshine

ELIZABETH CLEGHORN GASKELL

In the town of — (no matter where) there circulated two local newspapers (no matter when). Now the *Flying Post* was long-established and respectable—alias bigoted and Tory; the *Examiner* was spirited and intelligent—alias newfangled and democratic. Every week these newspapers contained articles abusing each other, as cross and peppery as articles could be, and evidently the production of irritated minds, although they seemed to have one stereotyped commencement[1]—"Though the article appearing in our

---

1. stereotyped commencement: a beginning that was repeatedly used without variation.

last week's *Post* (or *Examiner*) is below contempt, yet we have been induced," &c. &c.; and every Saturday the Radical shopkeepers shook hands together, and agreed that the *Post* was done for by the slashing, clever *Examiner*; while the more dignified Tories began by regretting that Johnson should think that low paper, only read by a few of the vulgar, worth wasting his wit upon; however, the *Examiner* was at its last gasp.

It was not, though. It lived and flourished; at least it paid its way, as one of the heroes of my story could tell. He was chief compositor, or whatever title may be given to the headman of the mechanical part of a newspaper. He hardly confined himself to that department. Once or twice, unknown to the editor, when the manuscript had fallen short, he had filled up the vacant space by compositions of his own; announcements of a forthcoming crop of green peas in December; a grey thrush having been seen, or a white hare, or such interesting phenomena; invented for the occasion, I must confess; but what of that? His wife always knew when to expect a little specimen of her husband's literary talent by a peculiar cough, which served as prelude; and, judging from this encouraging sign, and the high-pitched and emphatic voice in which he read them, she was inclined to think, that an "Ode to an Early Rosebud," in the corner devoted to original poetry, and a letter in the correspondence department, signed "Pro Bono Publico,"[2] were her husband's writing, and to hold up her head accordingly.

I never could find out what it was that occasioned the Hodgsons to lodge in the same house as the Jenkinses. Jenkins held the same office in the Tory Paper as Hodgson did in the *Examiner,* and, as I said before, I leave you to give it a name. But Jenkins had a proper sense of his position, and a proper reverence for all in authority, from the king down to the editor and sub-editor. He would as soon have thought of borrowing the king's crown for a nightcap, or the king's scepter for a walking-stick as he would have thought of filling up any spare corner with any production of his own; and I think it would have even added to his contempt of Hodgson (if that were possible), had he known of the "productions of his brain," as the latter fondly alluded to the paragraphs he inserted, when speaking to his wife.

Jenkins had his wife too. Wives were wanting[3] to finish the completeness of the quarrel which existed one memorable Christmas week, some dozen years ago, between the two neighbors, the two compositors. And with wives, it was a very pretty, a very complete quarrel. To make the opposing parties

---

2. **"Pro Bono Publico"** (prō bō′nō pŭb′lĭ-kō′): a Latin phrase meaning "for the public good."

3. **wanting:** required; needed.

WORDS TO KNOW **allude** (ə-lōōd′) *v.* to make an indirect reference

still more equal, still more well-matched, if the Hodgsons had a baby ("such a baby!—a poor, puny little thing"), Mrs. Jenkins had a cat ("such a cat! a great, nasty, miowling tom-cat, that was always stealing the milk put by for little Angel's supper"). And now, having matched Greek with Greek, I must proceed to the tug of war.[4] It was the day before Christmas; such a cold east wind! such an inky sky! such a blue-black look in people's faces, as they were driven out more than usual, to complete their purchases for the next day's festival.

Before leaving home that morning, Jenkins had given some money to his wife to buy the next day's dinner.

"My dear, I wish for turkey and sausages. It may be a weakness, but I own I am partial to sausages. My deceased mother was. Such tastes are hereditary. As to the sweets—whether plum-pudding or mince-pies—I leave such considerations to you; I only beg you not to mind expense. Christmas comes but once a year."

And again he called out from the bottom of the first flight of stairs, just close to the Hodgsons' door ("such ostentatiousness," as Mrs. Hodgson observed), "You will not forget the sausages, my dear!"

"I should have liked to have had something above common, Mary," said Hodgson, as they too made their plans for the next day; "but I think roast beef must do for us. You see, love, we've a family."

"Only one, Jem! I don't want more than roast beef, though, I'm sure. Before I went to service,[5] mother and me would have thought roast beef a very fine dinner."

"Well, let's settle it, then, roast beef and a plum-pudding; and now, good-bye. Mind and take care of little Tom. I thought he was a bit hoarse this morning."

And off he went to his work.

Now, it was a good while since Mrs. Jenkins and Mrs. Hodgson had spoken to each other, although they were quite as much in possession of the knowledge of events and opinions as though they did. Mary knew that Mrs. Jenkins despised her for not having a real lace cap, which Mrs. Jenkins had; and for having been a servant, which Mrs. Jenkins had not; and the little occasional pinchings which the Hodgsons were obliged to resort to, to make both ends meet, would have been very patiently endured by Mary, if she had not winced under Mrs. Jenkins's knowledge of such economy. But she had her revenge. She had a child, and Mrs. Jenkins had none. To have had a child, even such a puny baby as little Tom, Mrs. Jenkins would have worn commonest caps, and cleaned grates, and drudged her fingers to the bone. The great unspoken disappointment of her life soured her temper, and turned her thoughts inward, and made her morbid and selfish.

"Hang that cat! he's been stealing again! he's gnawed the cold mutton in his nasty mouth till it's not fit to set before a Christian; and I've nothing else for Jem's dinner. But I'll give it him now I've caught him, that I will!"

So saying, Mary Hodgson caught up her husband's Sunday cane, and despite pussy's cries and scratches, she gave him such a beating as she hoped might cure him of his thievish propensities; when, lo! and behold, Mrs. Jenkins stood at the door with a face of bitter wrath.

"Aren't you ashamed of yourself, ma'am, to abuse a poor dumb animal, ma'am, as knows no better than to take food when he sees it, ma'am?

---

4. **having matched . . . tug of war:** a reference to the proverb "When Greek meets Greek, then comes the tug of war," meaning that when evenly matched opponents fight, the battle will be fierce.

5. **went to service:** took employment as a servant.

He only follows the nature which God has given, ma'am; and it's a pity your nature, ma'am, which I've heard is of the stingy saving species, does not make you shut your cupboard door a little closer. There is such a thing as law for brute animals. I'll ask Mr. Jenkins, but I don't think them Radicals has done away with that law yet, for all their Reform Bill, ma'am. My poor precious love of a Tommy, is he hurt? and is his leg broke for taking a mouthful of scraps, as most people would give away to a beggar—if he'd take 'em!" wound up Mrs. Jenkins, casting a contemptuous look on the remnant of a scrag end of mutton.

Mary felt very angry and very guilty. For she really pitied the poor limping animal as he crept up to his mistress, and there lay down to bemoan himself; she wished she had not beaten him so hard, for it certainly was her own careless way of never shutting the cupboard-door that had tempted him to his fault. But the sneer at her little bit of mutton turned her penitence to fresh wrath, and she shut the door in Mrs. Jenkins's face, as she stood caressing her cat in the lobby, with such a bang, that it wakened little Tom, and he began to cry.

Everything was to go wrong with Mary today. Now baby was awake, who was to take her husband's dinner to the office? She took the child in her arms and tried to hush him off to sleep again, and as she sung she cried, she could hardly tell why,— a sort of reaction from her violent angry feelings. She wished she had never beaten the poor cat; she wondered if his leg was really broken. What would her mother say if she knew how cross and cruel her little Mary was getting? If she should live to beat her child in one of her angry fits?

It was of no use lullabying while she sobbed so; it must be given up, and she must just carry her baby in her arms, and take him with her to the office, for it was long past dinner-time. So she pared the mutton carefully, although by so doing she reduced the meat to an infinitesimal quantity, and taking the baked potatoes out of the oven, she popped them piping hot into her basket, with the etceteras of plate, butter, salt, and knife and fork.

It was, indeed, a bitter wind. She bent against it as she ran, and the flakes of snow were sharp and cutting as ice. Baby cried all the way, though she cuddled him up in her shawl. Then her husband had made his appetite up for a potato pie, and (literary man as he was) his body got so much the better of his mind, that he looked rather black at the cold mutton. Mary had no appetite for her own dinner when she arrived at home again. So, after she had tried to feed baby, and he had fretfully refused to take his bread and milk, she laid him down as usual on his quilt, surrounded by playthings, while she sided away, and chopped suet for the next day's pudding. Early in the afternoon a parcel came, done up first in brown paper, then in such a white, grass-bleached, sweet-smelling towel, and a note from her dear, dear mother; in which quaint writing she endeavored to tell her daughter that she was not forgotten at Christmas time; but that, learning that Farmer Burton was killing his pig, she had made interest for some of his famous pork, out of which she had manufactured some sausages, and flavored them just as Mary used to like when she lived at home.

"Dear, dear mother!" said Mary to herself. "There never was any one like her for remembering other folk. What rare sausages she used to make! Home things have a smack with 'em no bought things can ever have. Set them up with their sausages! I've a notion if Mrs. Jenkins had

ever tasted mother's she'd have no fancy for them townmade things Fanny took in just now."

And so she went on thinking about home, till the smiles and the dimples came out again at the remembrance of that pretty cottage, which would look green even now in the depth of winter, with its pyracanthus,[6] and its hollybushes, and the great Portugal laurel that was her mother's pride. And the back path through the orchard to Farmer Burton's, how well she remembered it! The bushels of unripe apples she had picked up there and distributed among his pigs, till he had scolded her for giving them so much green trash!

She was interrupted—her baby (I call him a baby, because his father and mother did, and because he was so little of his age, but I rather think he was eighteen months old,) had fallen asleep some time before among his playthings; an uneasy, restless sleep; but of which Mary had been thankful, as his morning's nap had been too short, and as she was so busy. But now he began to make such a strange crowing noise, just like a chair drawn heavily and gratingly along a kitchen floor! His eyes were open, but expressive of nothing but pain.

"Mother's darling!" said Mary, in terror, lifting him up. "Baby, try not to make that noise. Hush, hush, darling; what hurts him?" But the noise came worse and worse.

"Fanny! Fanny!" Mary called in <u>mortal</u> fright, for her baby was almost black with his gasping breath, and she had no one to ask for aid or sympathy but her landlady's daughter, a little girl of twelve or thirteen, who attended to the house in her mother's absence, as daily cook in gentlemen's families. Fanny was more especially considered the attendant of the upstairs lodgers (who paid for the use of the kitchen, "for Jenkins could not abide the smell of meat cooking"), but just now she was fortunately sitting at her afternoon's work of darning stockings, and hearing Mrs. Hodgson's cry of terror, she ran to her sitting-room, and understood the case at a glance.

"He's got the croup![7] O Mrs. Hodgson, he'll die as sure as fate. Little brother had it, and he died in no time. The doctor said he could do nothing for him—it had gone too far. He said if we'd put him in a warm bath at first, it might have saved him; but, bless you! he was never half so bad as your baby." Unconsciously there mingled in her statement some of a child's love of producing an effect; but the increasing danger was clear enough.

"Oh, my baby! my baby! Oh, love, love! don't look so ill! I cannot bear it. And my fire so low!"

---

6. **pyracanthus** (pī'rə-kăn'thəs): a thorny evergreen shrub.

7. **croup** (kro͞op): a respiratory disease in children, marked by difficulty in breathing and a sharp cough.

WORDS TO KNOW **mortal** (môr'tl) *adj.* intense or severe

Detail, *Newgate* (late 1800s), Frank Holl. Royal Holloway and Bedford Collection, New College, Egham, Surrey, Great Britain. Bridgeman/Art Resource, New York.

There, I was thinking of home, and picking currants, and never minding the fire. O Fanny! what is the fire like in the kitchen? Speak."

"Mother told me to screw it up, and throw some slack[8] on as soon as Mrs. Jenkins had done with it, and so I did. It's very low and black. But, oh, Mrs. Hodgson! let me run for the doctor— I cannot abear to hear him, it's so like little brother."

Through her streaming tears Mary motioned her to go; and trembling, sinking, sick at heart, she laid her boy in his cradle, and ran to fill her kettle.

Mrs. Jenkins, having cooked her husband's snug little dinner, to which he came home; having told him her story of pussy's beating, at which he was justly and dignifiedly (?) indignant, saying it was all of a piece with that abusive *Examiner*; having received the sausages, and turkey, and mince pies, which her husband had ordered; and cleaned up the room, and prepared everything for tea, and coaxed and duly bemoaned her cat (who had pretty nearly forgotten his beating, but very much enjoyed the petting); having done all these and many other things, Mrs. Jenkins sat down to get up the real lace cap. Every thread was pulled out separately, and carefully stretched: when—what was that? Outside, in the street, a chorus of piping children's voices sang the old carol she had heard a hundred times in the days of her youth—

"As Joseph was a walking he heard an angel sing,

'This night shall be born our heavenly King.

He neither shall be born in housen nor in hall,

Nor in the place of Paradise, but in an ox's stall.

He neither shall be clothed in purple nor in pall,

But all in fair linen, as were babies all:

He neither shall be rocked in silver nor in gold,

But in a wooden cradle that rocks on the mould,' " &c.

She got up and went to the window. There, below, stood the group of black little figures, relieved[9] against the snow, which now enveloped everything. "For old sake's sake," as she phrased it, she counted out a halfpenny apiece for the singers, out of the copper bag, and threw them down below.

The room had become chilly while she had been counting out and throwing down her money, so she stirred her already glowing fire, and sat down right before it—but not to stretch her lace; like Mary Hodgson, she began to think over long past days, on softening remembrances of the dead and gone, on words long forgotten, on holy stories heard at her mother's knee.

"I cannot think what's come over me tonight," said she, half aloud, recovering herself by the sound of her own voice from her train of thought—"My head goes wandering on them old times. I'm sure more texts have come into my head with thinking on my mother within this last half-hour, than I've thought on for years and years. I hope I'm not going to die. Folks says, thinking too much on the dead betokens we're going to join 'em; I should be loth[10] to go just yet—such a fine turkey as we've got for dinner tomorrow too!"

Knock, knock, knock, at the door, as fast as knuckles could go. And then, as if the comer could not wait, the door was opened, and Mary Hodgson stood there as white as death.

"Mrs. Jenkins!—oh, your kettle is boiling, thank God! Let me have the water for my baby, for the love of God! He's got croup, and is dying!"

Mrs. Jenkins turned on her chair with a wooden, inflexible look on her face, that (between ourselves) her husband knew and dreaded for all his pompous dignity.

---

8. **slack**: fragments of coal.
9. **relieved**: set off by contrast.
10. **loth** (lōth): unwilling; reluctant.

"I'm sorry I can't oblige you, ma'am; my kettle is wanted for my husband's tea. Don't be afeared, Tommy, Mrs. Hodgson won't venture to intrude herself where she's not desired. You'd better send for the doctor, ma'am, instead of wasting your time in wringing your hands, ma'am—my kettle is engaged."

Mary clasped her hands together with passionate force, but spoke no word of entreaty to that wooden face—that sharp, determined voice; but, as she turned away, she prayed for strength to bear the coming trial, and strength to forgive Mrs. Jenkins.

Mrs. Jenkins watched her go away meekly, as one who has no hope, and then she turned upon herself as sharply as she ever did on any one else.

"What a brute I am, Lord forgive me! What's my husband's tea to a baby's life? In croup, too, where time is everything. You crabbed old vixen, you!—any one may know you never had a child!"

She was downstairs (kettle in hand) before she had finished her self-upbraiding;[11] and when in Mrs. Hodgson's room, she rejected all thanks (Mary had not the voice for many words), saying, stiffly, "I do it for the poor baby's sake, ma'am, hoping he may live to have mercy to poor dumb beasts, if he does forget to lock his cupboards."

But she did everything, and more than Mary, with her young inexperience, could have thought of. She prepared the warm bath, and tried it with her husband's own thermometer (Mr. Jenkins was as punctual as clockwork in noting down the temperature of every day). She let his mother place her baby in the tub, still preserving the same rigid, affronted aspect, and then she went upstairs without a word. Mary longed to ask her to stay, but dared not; though, when she left the room, the tears chased each other down her cheeks faster than ever. Poor young mother! how she counted the minutes till the doctor should come. But, before he came, down again stalked Mrs. Jenkins, with something in her hand.

"I've seen many of these croup-fits, which, I take it, you've not, ma'am. Mustard plasters[12] is very sovereign,[13] put on the throat; I've been up and made one, ma'am, and, by your leave, I'll put it on the poor little fellow."

Mary could not speak, but she signed her grateful assent.

It began to smart while they still kept silence; and he looked up to his mother as if seeking courage from her looks to bear the stinging pain; but she was softly crying to see him suffer, and her want of courage reacted upon him, and he began to sob aloud. Instantly Mrs. Jenkins's apron was up, hiding her face: "Peep-bo, baby," said she, as merrily as she could. His little face brightened, and his mother having once got the cue, the two women kept the little fellow amused, until his plaster had taken effect.

"He's better—oh, Mrs. Jenkins, look at his eyes! how different! And he breathes quite softly"—

As Mary spoke thus, the doctor entered. He examined his patient. Baby was really better.

"It has been a sharp attack, but the remedies you have applied have been worth all the Pharmacopoeia[14] an hour later.—I shall send a powder," &c. &c.

Mrs. Jenkins stayed to hear this opinion; and (her heart wonderfully more easy) was going to leave the room, when Mary seized her hand and kissed it; she could not speak her gratitude.

Mrs. Jenkins looked affronted and awkward, and as if she must go upstairs and wash her hand directly.

But, in spite of these sour looks, she came softly down an hour or so afterwards to see how baby was.

---

11. **self-upbraiding:** self-scolding.

12. **mustard plaster:** a paste made of powdered mustard, water, and vinegar that causes localized irritation when applied to the skin and is intended to relieve inflamed tissues.

13. **sovereign** (sŏv′ər-ĭn): effective.

14. **Pharmacopoeia** (fär′mə-kə-pē′ə): all the medicinal drugs listed in the standard reference work on the subject.

WORDS TO KNOW

affronted (ə-frŭn′tĭd) *adj.* offended **affront** *v.*

The little gentleman slept well after the fright he had given his friends; and on Christmas morning, when Mary awoke and looked at the sweet little pale face lying on her arm, she could hardly realize the danger he had been in.

When she came down (later than usual), she found the household in a commotion. What do you think had happened? Why, pussy had been traitor to his best friend, and eaten up some of Mr. Jenkins's own especial sausages; and gnawed and tumbled the rest so, that they were not fit to be eaten! There were no bounds to that cat's appetite! he would have eaten his own father if he had been tender enough. And now Mrs. Jenkins stormed and cried—"Hang the cat!"

Christmas Day, too! and all the shops shut! "What was turkey without sausages?" gruffly asked Mr. Jenkins.

"O Jem!" whispered Mary, "hearken what a piece of work he's making about sausages—I should like to take Mrs. Jenkins up some of mother's; they're twice as good as bought sausages."

"I see no objection, my dear. Sausages do not involve intimacies, else his politics are what I can no ways respect."

"But, oh, Jem, if you had seen her last night about baby! I'm sure she may scold me forever, and I'll not answer. I'd even make her cat welcome to the sausages." The tears gathered to Mary's eyes as she kissed her boy.

"Better take 'em upstairs, my dear, and give them to the cat's mistress." And Jem chuckled at his saying.

Mary put them on a plate, but still she loitered.

"What must I say, Jem? I never know."

"Say—I hope you'll accept of these sausages, as my mother—no, that's not grammar;—say what comes uppermost, Mary, it will be sure to be right."

So Mary carried them upstairs and knocked at the door; and when told to "come in," she looked very red, but went up to Mrs. Jenkins, saying, "Please take these. Mother made them." And was away before an answer could be given.

Just as Hodgson was ready to go to church, Mrs. Jenkins came downstairs, and called Fanny. In a minute, the latter entered the Hodgsons' room, and delivered Mr. and Mrs. Jenkins's compliments, and they would be particular glad if Mr. and Mrs. Hodgson would eat their dinner with them.

"And carry baby upstairs in a shawl, be sure," added Mrs. Jenkins's voice in the passage, close to the door, whither she had followed her messenger. There was no discussing the matter, with the certainty of every word being overheard.

Mary looked anxiously at her husband. She remembered his saying he did not approve of Mr. Jenkins's politics.

"Do you think it would do for baby?" asked he.

"Oh, yes," answered she eagerly; "I would wrap him up so warm."

"And I've got our room up to sixty-five already, for all it's so frosty," added the voice outside.

Now, how do you think they settled the matter? The very best way in the world. Mr. and Mrs. Jenkins came down into the Hodgsons' room and dined there. Turkey at the top, roast beef at the bottom, sausages at one side, potatoes at the other. Second course, plum pudding at the top, and mince pies at the bottom.

And after dinner, Mrs. Jenkins would have baby on her knee, and he seemed quite to take to her; she declared he was admiring the real lace on her cap, but Mary thought (though she did not say so) that he was pleased by her kind looks and coaxing words. Then he was wrapped up and carried carefully upstairs to tea, in Mrs. Jenkins's room. And after tea, Mrs. Jenkins, and Mary, and her husband, found out each other's mutual liking for music, and sat singing old glees and catches,[15] till I don't know what o'clock, without one word of politics or newspapers.

Before they parted, Mary had coaxed pussy on to her knee; for Mrs. Jenkins would not part with baby, who was sleeping on her lap.

"When you're busy bring him to me. Do, now, it will be a real favor. I know you must have a deal to do, with another coming; let him come up to me. I'll take the greatest of cares of him; pretty darling, how sweet he looks when he's asleep!"

When the couples were once more alone, the husbands unburdened their minds to their wives.

Mr. Jenkins said to his— "Do you know, Burgess tried to make me believe Hodgson was such a fool as to put paragraphs into the *Examiner* now and then; but I see he knows his place, and has got too much sense to do any such thing."

Hodgson said— "Mary, love, I almost fancy from Jenkins's way of speaking (so much civiler than I expected), he guesses I wrote that 'Pro Bono' and the 'Rosebud,'—at any rate, I've no objection to your naming it, if the subject should come uppermost; I should like him to know I'm a literary man."

Well! I've ended my tale; I hope you don't think it too long; but, before I go, just let me say one thing.

If any of you have any quarrels, or misunderstandings, or coolnesses, or cold shoulders, or shynesses, or tiffs, or miffs, or huffs, with anyone else, just make friends before Christmas,—you will be so much merrier if you do.

I ask it of you for the sake of that old angelic song, heard so many years ago by the shepherds, keeping watch by night, on Bethlehem Heights. ❖

---

15. **glees and catches:** types of unaccompanied part songs for several voices.

Connect to the Literature

1. **What Do You Think?** Which character in the story is most appealing to you? Share your thoughts with your classmates.

Comprehension Check
- Why did Mary Hodgson beat Mrs. Jenkins's cat?
- What did Mrs. Hodgson do when her baby got the croup?
- How did Mrs. Jenkins help the baby?

Think Critically

2. How would you describe the characters' first impressions of one another?

- Mr. Hodgson's and Mr. Jenkins's jobs
- the makeup of each family
- the personal opinions and feelings each character reveals
- the social attitudes or class consciousness each character exhibits

3.  **ACTIVE READING** **ANALYZING CAUSES AND EFFECTS**
   Compare the chart you created in your 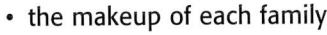 **READER'S NOTEBOOK** for each character and trace how the **characters** and their relationship changed as the story progressed. What event causes each character to change toward the other? After that point, how do their emotions reflect their changing relationship?

4. Do you find the events in the latter part of the story believable? Support your response with details from the story.

Extend Interpretations

5. **Critic's Corner** A student reviewer, Dan Birdsall, thought that "the irony of the ending was cool—it seems like the two families would end up enemies again after a while." Do you agree that the new friendship of the Hodgsons and the Jenkinses is unlikely to last?

6. **What If?** Suppose "Christmas Storms and Sunshine" didn't take place at Christmas. How might the outcome of the story be different? Give reasons for your answer.

7. **Connect to Life** Mr. Jenkins and Mr. Hodgson have opposing political views. Do you think strong political differences always create difficulties in a personal relationship? Support your answer with examples or reasons.

Literary Analysis

THIRD-PERSON OMNISCIENT POINT OF VIEW

In a story told from the **third-person omniscient point of view,** the narrator is all-knowing. This kind of narrator provides the reader with insights into the thoughts, motivations, and responses of all the characters, as well as access to events that may be occurring simultaneously. In the following passage from "Christmas Storms and Sunshine," notice the insight the narrator provides into each character's jealous response to the other:

Mary knew that Mrs. Jenkins despised her for not having a real lace cap, which Mrs. Jenkins had. . . . But she had her revenge. She had a child, and Mrs. Jenkins had none. To have had a child, even such a puny baby as little Tom, Mrs. Jenkins would have worn commonest caps. . . .

Paired Activity The narrator often includes parenthetical remarks about characters and events, as in the clause ". . . I think it would have even added to his contempt of Hodgson (if that were possible) . . ." With a partner, look for other examples of this technique in the story. What kinds of information does the narrator usually convey in parentheses? How does this technique reflect the power of the omniscient narrator?

PLOT AND CONFLICT The events in a narrative's **plot** progress because of a **conflict,** a struggle between opposing forces. What main conflict drives the plot of "Christmas Storms and Sunshine"?

Choices & CHALLENGES

Writing Options

1. Letter to Mary's Mother Pretend that you are Mary Hodgson. In a letter to your mother, describe the experience you have just had with the Jenkinses.

Dear Mother,

2. Mr. Hodgson's Editorial Imagine that you are Mr. Hodgson and write a brief editorial for the *Examiner*. Based on what you have learned over the Christmas holiday, analyze the importance of living in harmony with your neighbors. Place the paragraph in your **Working Portfolio.**

3. Dialogue Between the Jenkinses Suppose that the Jenkinses discover that Mr. Hodgson really does put his own compositions into the *Examiner*. Write the dialogue that might occur between Mr. and Mrs. Jenkins after this revelation.

Activities & Explorations

1. Story Dramatization With a partner or group, plan a dramatic interpretation of one or more scenes from the story. Determine how to portray each character and what lines and actions you will use. Then rehearse your presentation, and give your final performance for the entire class. **~ PERFORMING**

2. Set Design Create a drawing or model of the set design you would use for a dramatized version of "Christmas Storms and Sunshine." **~ ART**

3. Improvisation With a partner, improvise a conversation in which Mary Hodgson tells her son, who is now a teenager, about the incidents described in this story. **~ SPEAKING AND LISTENING**

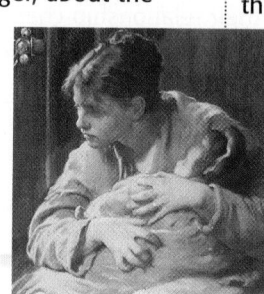

Inquiry & Research

City Life Look up information on life in English industrial cities—such as Manchester—during the early 19th century. What kind of housing was available? What were the popular social activities? How did life differ for various social classes? What were working conditions like in the factories?

Victorian Dailies Find out what the leading newspapers were in 19th-century England. What were their names, their prices, their political leanings? How were they received by the people of their time?

Art Connection

Character Sketches What thoughts come to mind when you look at the woman in *Newgate* on page 878? How do these thoughts relate to your impression of Mrs. Hodgson in "Christmas Storms and Sunshine"? Discuss your ideas with your classmates.

Vocabulary in Action

EXERCISE: CONTEXT CLUES Write the word that best completes each of the following sentences.

1. Since it is always easier to see things from one's own point of view, Mrs. Hodgson and Mrs. Jenkins have a _____ to blame each other for any quarrel they have.

2. Mrs. Jenkins might be shocked to discover that what she thinks is simple self-respect and good breeding could be seen by Mrs. Hodgson as _____ haughtiness.

3. Mrs. Hodgson might be surprised to find out that while Mrs. Jenkins is behaving coldly and showing _____ indignation, she is really quite worried about the Hodgson baby.

4. After all, the Hodgson baby is in serious, even _____, danger, and Mrs. Jenkins has humanity's normal protective impulses toward helpless babies.

5. A bitter memory makes Mrs. Jenkins _____ to an earlier quarrel by saying, "I do it for the poor baby's sake, ma'am, hoping he may live to have mercy to poor dumb beasts, if he does forget to lock his cupboards."

WORDS	affronted	pompous
TO	allude	propensity
KNOW	mortal	

Elizabeth Cleghorn Gaskell
1810–1865

Other Works
"My Lady Ludlow"
"Cousin Phillis"
"Half a Life-Time Ago"

Hard Lessons Elizabeth Cleghorn, only 13 months old when her mother died, was taken from her London home to be raised by her mother's sister in a rural village. In this calm, country setting she learned to appreciate and carefully observe all the details of the natural world. At the age of 12, she was sent to boarding school, where she developed a love of reading and a sympathetic nature. Occasionally she saw her father, who had remained in London and remarried, and from his intensive tutoring she gained a proficiency in languages. These early experiences combined to provide her with a lifelong concern for the less fortunate and the desire and skill to write about their lives.

Married Life In 1831, while visiting relatives in Manchester, she met William Gaskell, a Unitarian minister, and the following year they married. As a minister's wife, she devoted much time to helping those in need. She was also kept busy raising and educating four daughters. Her first serious efforts at writing, however, did not occur until she was in her thirties and recovering from the death in 1845 of her infant son.

The Writing Life Gaskell drew upon her firsthand experiences with the poor in writing her first novel, *Mary Barton*, which was extremely successful and won her the approval of such literary figures as Charles Dickens and Charlotte Brontë. On Dickens's urging, Gaskell contributed stories to his new periodical, *Household Words*, in which two of her novels, *Cranford* and *North and South*, would be published in weekly installments. Gaskell and Brontë admired each other's work and eventually became close friends. Shortly after her dear friend's untimely death, and at the request of Brontë's father, Gaskell wrote her first and only biography, *The Life of Charlotte Brontë*. Gaskell herself died quite suddenly at the age of 55, while having tea and conversing with her family at the country home where she planned one day to retire with her husband.

Victorian Crusader Gaskell was committed to raising the social awareness of her readers. Since some Victorians did not consider it proper to discuss or write about social problems, Gaskell created controversy in her time by honestly depicting the appallingly squalid housing of the poor and vividly portraying working-class life.

Author Activity

Fighting for Reforms Find out what reforms Gaskell recommended to improve the living and working conditions of the lower class. What, if any, of her recommendations were eventually adopted? What impact did her writing have on instituting reforms?

Charlotte and Emily Brontë

The Brontë Novels

"*Wuthering Heights* was hewn in a wild workshop, with simple tools, out of homely materials," wrote Charlotte Brontë in an introduction to her sister Emily's novel. The same could be said of Charlotte's masterpiece *Jane Eyre,* for although these novels were published in 1847, when Charlotte was 31 and Emily 29, the imaginations that inspired them were developed at an early age and evident in the childhood games they played in their father's parsonage on the Yorkshire moors. Using wooden soldiers and a toy village, the six Brontë children created a world called the Great Glass Town Confederacy, consisting of tiny kingdoms inhabited by characters based on their favorite heroes. All of them, but especially Charlotte and Emily, wrote everything down—composing stories, essays, and songs about

Left:
Photograph of the Yorkshire moor where the Brontë children grew up
Above:
The Brontë children wrote their tiny books by hand on folded sheets of paper measuring about 2 inches by 1½ inches. The covers were made of paper from sugar bags or wrapping paper from local shops.

their kingdoms and binding the writings into tiny books. As the children grew, the Glass Town games fell off, but the Brontë girls continued to write, their works springing from the worlds they continued to create within.

As a young adult, Charlotte discovered a stack of Emily's poems. Elated at their high quality, she convinced Emily and Anne, another sister, to combine their poems with hers in a single volume. The three sisters, adopting the pseudonyms "Currer Bell," "Ellis Bell," and "Acton Bell," published their book in 1846. Although only two copies were sold, the young Brontës were not deterred from continuing to write.

It was with their novels that the sisters would achieve their greatest success, even though when Emily's *Wuthering Heights* was published, it was largely ignored. Nevertheless, this fierce, brooding story—set on the moors—of the star-crossed love between Heathcliff and Catherine eventually came to be considered one of the most original novels of all time. Charlotte's *Jane Eyre* became an immediate critical and popular success as readers fell in love with her noble and passionately independent heroine.

Soon afterward, when Anne published *The Tenant of Wildfell Hall*, rumors circulated that Acton, Currer, and Ellis Bell were all the same man; so the sisters revealed their true identities, and their public literary life began. The triumph was muted, however, by their brother Branwell's sudden death, followed closely by the deaths of Emily and Anne. By the time Charlotte was 33, she was the sole survivor of the six Brontë children. Still, she continued to write.

The Brontës' novels, most notably Charlotte's *Jane Eyre* and Emily's *Wuthering Heights,* have remained popular works of literature for nearly 150 years. Through them, readers can experience the imaginations of two women who, despite the male domination of the Victorian literary world, were able to make their voices heard.

Top:
Painting by Thomas Davidson, depicting the scene from Jane Eyre *in which Jane meets Rochester*
Bottom:
Watercolor by Emily of her pet hawk, 1841. All of the Brontë children drew and painted.

The King Is Dead, Long Live the King

Short Story by MARY E. COLERIDGE

> ## Connect to Your Life
>
> **Know Thyself** How do you think you are perceived by others? Do you think other people's perceptions generally coincide with your own opinion of yourself? Get together with a classmate. While you list words and phrases to describe your partner, your partner should do the same for you. Then trade your lists. Do you think the description is accurate?

Build Background

In the Shadow of Greatness A moderately successful writer during the late 19th century, Mary E. Coleridge is probably better known as the great-grandniece of the romantic poet Samuel Taylor Coleridge. In several of her works—including this story—she, like her more famous relation, touches upon themes of fantasy and the supernatural. Both shared a love for the strange and the unearthly. This similarity once inspired a critic to call Mary Coleridge "the tail of the comet S. T. C."

Although Mary Coleridge was a prolific poet, she never aspired to the great literary world which she believed Samuel Coleridge inhabited. Resigned to live in his shadow, she once wrote: "I have no fairy godmother but lay claim to a fairy great-great-uncle, which is perhaps the reason that I am condemned to wander restlessly around the Gates of Fairyland, although I have never yet passed them."

Royal Rule In a monarchy, the laws of succession attempt to maintain stability: If people know that a monarch will automatically be succeeded by the next family member in line for the throne, they can feel reasonably sure that the transition will be a smooth one. The proclamation "The king is dead, long live the king!" reflects the desire for an orderly succession. The first part announces that one monarch has died; the second honors the new monarch, underscoring the continuity of the monarchy despite the passing of one individual.

> **WORDS TO KNOW**
> **Vocabulary Preview**
> malicious   reprieve
> malignant   sentiment
> presently

Focus Your Reading

LITERARY ANALYSIS **SITUATIONAL IRONY** **Irony** is a contrast between expectation and reality. **Situational irony** occurs when what happens is not what a character or the reader expects. Suppose, for example, that the detective in a murder mystery turns out to be the murderer. This incongruity is a case of situational irony. Look for examples of situational irony as you read "The King Is Dead, Long Live the King."

ACTIVE READING **PREDICTING** When you read, you often make **predictions** about what will happen next. The following can help you make predictions:

- details about **characters, setting,** and **events** in the story
- **foreshadowing,** or hints about what is going to happen
- your personal knowledge of human behavior and experiences

READER'S NOTEBOOK As you read Coleridge's story, jot down predictions about what is going to happen each time the king is about to go see a particular person or group of people. In making your predictions, you might use a chart like the one shown.

Person or Group King Is About to See	Your Prediction	Basis of Your Prediction

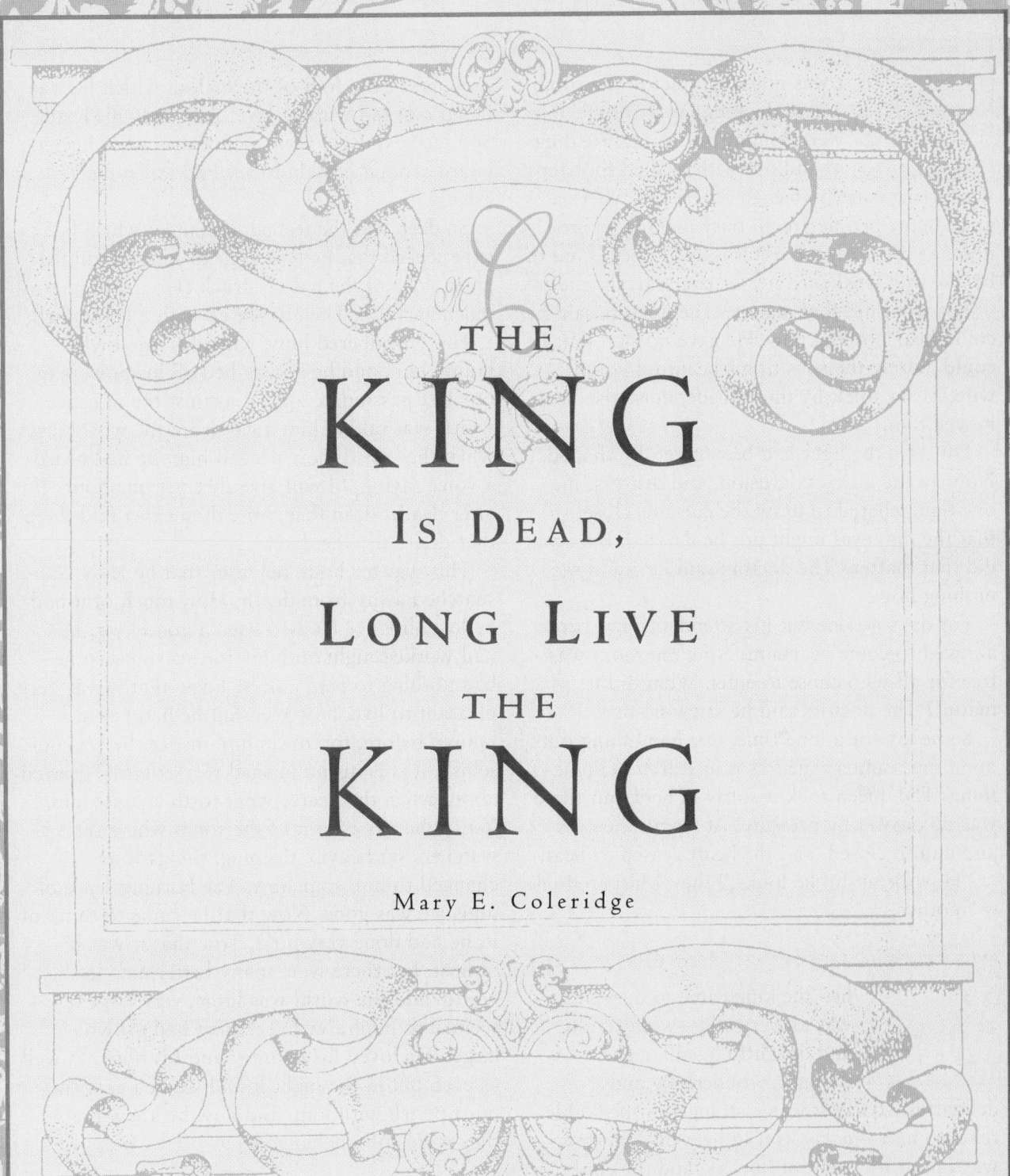

THE
KING
IS DEAD,
LONG LIVE
THE
KING

Mary E. Coleridge

I t was not very quiet in the room where the king lay dying. People were coming and going, rustling in and out with hushed footsteps, whispering eagerly to each other; and where a great many people are all busy making as little noise as possible, the result is apt to be a kind of bustle, that weakened nerves can scarcely endure.

But what did that matter? The doctors said he could hear nothing now. He gave no sign that he could. Surely the sobs of his beautiful young wife, as she knelt by the bedside, must else have moved him.

For days the light had been carefully shaded. Now, in the hurry, confusion, and distress, no one remembered to draw the curtains close, so that the dim eyes might not be dazzled. But what did that matter? The doctors said he could see nothing now.

For days no one but his attendants had been allowed to come near him. Now the room was free for all who chose to enter. What did it matter? The doctors said he knew no one.

So he lay for a long time, one hand flung out upon the counterpane,[1] as if in search of something. The queen took it softly in hers, but there was no answering pressure. At length the eyes and mouth closed, and the heart ceased to beat.

"How beautiful he looks," they whispered one to another.

hen the king came to himself it was all very still—wonderfully and delightfully still, as he thought, wonderfully and delightfully dark. It was a strange, unspeakable relief to him—he lay as if in heaven. The room was full of the scent of flowers, and the cool night air came pleasantly through an open window. A row of wax tapers burned with soft radiance at the foot of the bed on which he was lying, covered with a velvet pall, only his head and face exposed. Four or five men were keeping guard around him, but they had fallen fast asleep.

So deep was the feeling of content which he experienced that he was loth[2] to stir. Not till the great clock of the palace struck eleven, did he so much as move. Then he sat up with a light laugh.

He remembered how, when his mind was failing him, and he had rallied all his powers in one last passionate appeal against the injustice which was taking him away from the world just when the world most needed him, he had heard a voice saying, "I will give thee yet one hour after death. If, in that time, thou canst find three that desire thy life, live!"

This was his hour, his hour that he had snatched away from death. How much of it had he lost already? He had been a good king; he had worked night and day for his subjects: he had nothing to fear, and he knew that it was very pleasant to live, how pleasant he had never known before, for, to do him justice, he was not selfish; it was his unfinished work that he grieved about when the decree went forth against him. Yet, as he passed out of the room where the watchers sat heavily sleeping, things were changed to him somehow. The burning sense of injustice was gone. Now that he came to think of it, he had done very little. True that it was his utmost, but there were many better men in the world, and the world was large, very large it seemed to him now. Everything had grown larger. He loved his country and his home as well as ever, but in the night it had seemed as if they must perish with him, and now he knew that they were still unchanged.

---

1. **counterpane:** bedspread.
2. **loth** (lōth): unwilling.

utside the door he paused a moment, hesitating whither to go first. Not to the queen. The very thought of her grief unnerved him. He would not see her till he could once more clasp her in his arms, and bid her weep tears of joy only because he was come again. After all, he had but an hour to wait. Before the castle clock struck twelve, he would be back again in life, remembering these things only as a dream. He sighed a little to think of it.

"All that to do over again some day," he said, as he recalled his last moments.

Almost he turned again to the couch he had so lately left.

"But I have never yet done anything through fear," said the king.

And he smiled as he thought of the terms of the compact. His city lay before him in the moonlight.

"I could find three thousand as easily as three," he said. "Are they not all my friends?"

As he passed out of the gate, he saw a child sitting on the steps, crying bitterly.

"What is the matter, little one?" said the sentinel on guard, stopping a moment.

"Father and mother have gone to the castle, because the king's dead," sobbed the child, "and they've never come back again; and I'm so tired and so hungry! And I've had no supper, and my doll's broken. Oh! I do wish the king were alive again!"

And she burst into a fresh storm of weeping. It amused the king not a little.

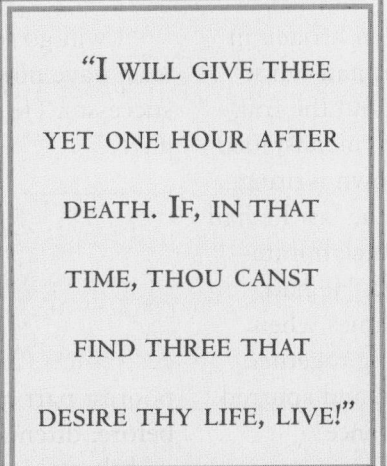

"I WILL GIVE THEE YET ONE HOUR AFTER DEATH. IF, IN THAT TIME, THOU CANST FIND THREE THAT DESIRE THY LIFE, LIVE!"

"So this is the first of my subjects that wants me back!" he said.

He had no child of his own. He would have liked to try and comfort the little maiden, but there were other calls upon him just then. He was on his way to the house of his great friend, the man whom he loved more than all others. A kind of <u>malicious</u> delight possessed him, as he pictured to himself the deep dejection he should find him in.

"Poor Amyas!" he said. "I know what I should be feeling in his place. I am glad he was not taken. I could not have borne his loss."

As he entered the courtyard of his friend's house, lights were being carried to and fro, horses were being saddled, an air of bustle and excitement pervaded the place. Look where he might, he could not see the face he knew so well. He entered at the open door. His friend was not in the hall. Room after room he vainly traversed —they were all empty. A sudden horror took him. Surely Amyas was not dead of grief?

e came at length to a small private apartment, in which they had spent many a happy, busy hour together; but his friend was not here either, though, to judge by appearances, he could only just have left it. Books and papers were tumbled all about in strange confusion, and bits of broken glass strewed the floor.

A little picture was lying on the ground. The king picked it up, and recognized a miniature of

himself, the frame of which had been broken in the fall. He let it drop again, as if it had burnt him. The fire was blazing brightly, and the fragments of a half-destroyed letter lay, unconsumed as yet, in the fender.[3] It was in his own writing. He snatched it up, and saw it was the last he had written, containing the details of an elaborate scheme which he had much at heart. He had only just thrown it back into the flames when two people entered the room, talking together, one a lady, the other a man, booted and spurred as though he came from a long distance.

"Where is Amyas?" he asked.

"Gone to proffer[4] his services to the new king, of course," said the lady. "We are, as you may think, in great anxiety. He has none of the ridiculous notions of his predecessor,[5] who, indeed, hated him cordially. The very favor Amyas has hitherto enjoyed will stand in his way at the new court. I only hope he may be in time to make his peace. He can, with trust, say that he utterly disapproved of the foolish reforms which his late master was bent on making. Of course, he was fond of him in a way; but we must think of ourselves, you know. People in our position have no time for <u>sentiment</u>. He started almost immediately after the king's death. I am sending his retinue[6] after him."

"Quite right," said the gentleman, whom the king now knew as one of his ambassadors. "I shall follow him at once. Between you and me, it is no bad thing for the country. That poor boy had no notion of statesmanship. He forced me to conclude a peace which would have been disastrous to all our best interests. Happily, we shall have war directly now. Promotions in the army would have been at a standstill if he had had his way."

The king did not stay to hear more.

"I will go to my people," he said. "They at least have no interest to make peace with my successor. He will but take from them what I gave."

He heard the clock strike the first quarter as he went. He was, indeed, a very remarkable king, for he knew his way to the poorest part of his dominions. He had been there before, often and often, unknown to any one; and the misery which he had there beheld had stirred and steeled him to attempt what had never before been attempted.

No one about the palace knew where he had caught the <u>malignant</u> fever which carried him off. He had a shrewd suspicion himself, and he went straight to that quarter.

"Fevers won't hurt me now," he said laughing. The houses were as wretched, the people looked as sickly and squalid[7] as ever. They were standing about in knots in the streets, late though it was, talking together about him. His name was in every mouth. The details of his illness, and the probable day of his funeral, seemed to interest them more than anything else.

Five or six men were sitting drinking round a table in a disreputable-looking public-house,[8] and he stopped to overhear their conversation.

"And a good riddance, too!" said one of

---

3. **fender:** a short metal screen in front of a fireplace.
4. **proffer** (prŏf′ər): to offer for acceptance.
5. **predecessor:** the former holder of an office or position.
6. **retinue** (rĕt′n-o͞o′): a group of attendants; entourage.
7. **squalid** (skwŏl′ĭd): dirty and wretched from poverty or lack of care.
8. **public-house:** tavern.

WORDS TO KNOW

sentiment (sĕn′tə-mənt) *n.* tender or nostalgic feeling
malignant (mə-lĭg′nənt) *adj.* extremely harmful

Romance (about 1924), Maxfield Parrish. Cover lining for *The Knave of Hearts* by Louise Saunders, oil on panel, courtesy of New York Graphic Society Ltd. Photo by Allen Photography.

them, whom he knew well. "What's the use of a king as never spends a farthing more than he can help? It gives no impetus[9] to trade, it don't. The new fellow's a very different sort. We shall have fine doings soon."

"Ay!" struck in another, "a meddlesome, priggish[10] sort of chap, he was, always aworritting us about clean houses, and such like. What right's he got to interfere, I'd like to know?"

"Down with all kings! says I," put in a third: "but if we're to have 'em, let 'em behave as sich. I like a young fellow as isn't afraid of his missus, and knows port wine from sherry."

"Wanted to abolish capital punishment, he did!" cried a fourth. "Thought he'd get more work out of the poor fellows in prison, I

suppose? Depend on it, there's some reason like that at the bottom of it. We ain't so very perticular about the lives of our subjects for nothing, we ain't"; an expression of opinion in which all the rest heartily concurred. The clock struck again as the king turned away; he felt as if a storm of abuse from some one he had always hated would be a precious balm[11] just then. He entered the state prison, and made for the condemned cell. Capital punishment was not abolished yet, and in this particular instance he had certainly felt glad of it.

---

9. **impetus** (ĭm′pĭ-təs): incentive; stimulus.
10. **priggish:** irritatingly concerned with proper behavior.
11. **balm:** something that soothes, heals, or comforts.

The cell was tenanted only by a little haggard[12] looking man, who was writing busily on his knee. The king had only seen him once before, and he looked at him curiously.

Presently, the jailer entered, and with him the first councillor, a man whom his late master had greatly loved and esteemed. The convict looked up quickly.

"It was not to be till to-morrow," he said. Then, as if afraid he had betrayed some cowardice, "but I am ready at any moment. May I ask you to give this paper to my wife?"

"The king is dead," said the first councillor gravely. "You are reprieved. His present majesty has other views. You will, in all probability, be set at large to-morrow."

"Dead?" said the man with a stunned look.

"Dead!" said the first councillor, with the impressiveness of a whole board.

The man stood up, passing his hand across his brow.

"Sir," he said earnestly, "I respected him. For all he was a king, he treated me like a gentleman. He, too, had a young wife. Poor fellow, I wish he were alive again!"

There were tears in the man's eyes as he spoke.

he third quarter struck as the king left the prison. He felt unutterably humiliated. The pity of his foe was harder to bear than the scorn of his friends. He would rather have died a thousand deaths than owe his life to

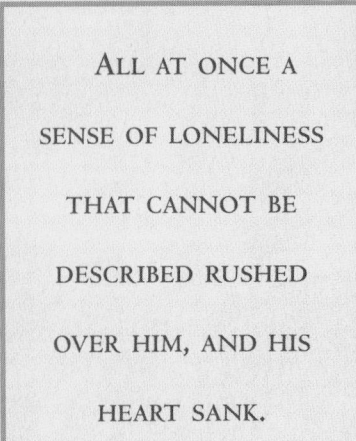
ALL AT ONCE A SENSE OF LONELINESS THAT CANNOT BE DESCRIBED RUSHED OVER HIM, AND HIS HEART SANK.

such a man. And yet, because he was himself noble, he could not but rejoice to find nobility in another. He said to himself sternly that it was not worth what he had gone through. He reviewed his position in no very self-complacent[13] mood. The affection he had so confidently relied upon was but a dream. The people he was fain[14] to work for were not ripe for their own improvement. A foolish little child, a generous enemy, these were his only friends. After all, was it worth while to live? Had he not better go back quietly and submit, making no further effort? He had learnt his lesson; he could "lie down in peace, and sleep, and take his rest." The eternal powers had justified themselves. What matter though every man had proved a liar? The bitterness had passed away, and he seemed to see clearly.

Thick clouds had gathered over the moon, and the cold struck through him. All at once a sense of loneliness that cannot be described rushed over him, and his heart sank. Was there really no one who cared—no one? He would have given anything at that moment for a look, a single word of real sympathy. He longed with sick longing for the assurance of love.

There were yet a few moments left. How had he borne to wait so long? This, at least, he was sure of, and this was all the world to him. He began to find comfort and consolation in the thought; he forgave—indeed he almost forgot—

12. **haggard:** worn and exhausted in appearance.

13. **self-complacent:** self-satisfied; smug.

14. **fain:** ready and willing.

the rest. Yet he had fallen very low, for, as he stood at the door of his wife's room, he hesitated whether to go in. What if this, too, were an illusion? Had he not best go back before he knew?

"But I have never yet done anything through fear," said the king.

His wife was sitting by the fire alone, her face hidden, her long hair falling round her like a veil. At the first sight of her, a pang of self-reproach shot through him. How could he ever have doubted?

She was wearing a ring that he had given her—a ring she wore always, and the light sparkled and flashed from the jewel. Except for this, there was nothing bright in the room.

He ardently desired to comfort her. He wondered why all her ladies had left her. Surely one might have stayed with her on this first night of her bereavement?[15] She seemed to be lost in thought. If she would only speak, or call his name! But she was quite silent.

A slight noise made the king start. A secret door in the wall opened, the existence of which he had thought was known only to himself and his queen, and a man stood before her.

She put her finger to her lips, as though to counsel silence, and then threw herself into his arms.

"You have come," she said— "Oh, I am so glad! I had to hold his hand when he was dying. I was frightened sitting here by myself. I thought his ghost would come back, but he will never come back any more. We may be happy always now," and drawing the ring from her finger, she kissed it, weeping, and gave it to him.

hen midnight struck, the watchers wakened with a start, to find the king lying stark and stiff, as before, but a great change had come over his countenance.[16]

"We must not let the queen see him again," they said. ❖

---

15. **bereavement:** the loss of a loved one to death.
16. **countenance:** face.

Thinking through the LITERATURE

Connect to the Literature

1. What Do You Think? What did you like best about this story? What did you like least?

Comprehension Check
- What must the king find in the one hour after his death?
- Which two people want him to live?
- What startling discovery does the king make about the queen?

Think Critically

2. **ACTIVE READING** **PREDICTING** Look over the **predictions** you made about the story in your **READER'S NOTEBOOK**. How accurate were they? What evidence was most important in making accurate predictions?

3. In your opinion, what kind of person was the king?

THINK ABOUT
- his view of himself and others
- the reason he wants to live
- the reforms he tried to promote during his life
- what others say about him

4. The narrator does not describe the expression on the king's face at the end of the story. How do you think he looks? Give reasons for your response.

5. What view of human nature does the story convey? Do you think this view is overly pessimistic or simply realistic? Cite evidence to support your opinion.

Extend Interpretations

6. Comparing Texts Compare and contrast the quest in this story with the knight's quest in "The Wife of Bath's Tale" by Geoffrey Chaucer (page 154). In what ways are the circumstances of the two quests similar and different? How do the outcomes of the quests compare?

7. What If? Suppose the king found three people who wanted him to live—and then visited his wife. Do you think he would have chosen to live? Why or why not?

8. Connect to Life How do you think people today regard their leaders? Do you think people generally support their elected officials, or do people tend to be cynically suspicious of the leaders' motivations?

Literary Analysis

SITUATIONAL IRONY In **situational irony,** the character or the reader expects one thing to happen, but something else actually occurs. Coleridge's story is filled with situational irony. For example, the king expects Amyas, his closest friend, to be saddened by his death. Instead he finds that Amyas is already busy trying to win favor with the new monarch. On the other hand, the king expects his jailed enemy to be gleeful about his death, but instead he overhears his enemy expressing regret.

Cooperative Learning Activity With a small group of classmates, create a chart like the one below and list the ironic situations in the story. Then discuss the following questions: What do the king's overturned expectations suggest about his relationship with other characters? How does the title help underscore the irony?

Expected Situation	Actual Situation
Amyas mourns king's death.	Amyas is preoccupied with flattering new monarch.

REVIEW **PLOT** As you know, the **plot** in a narrative usually includes the following stages: **exposition, rising action, climax,** and **falling action.** Create a graph in which you identify these stages in "The King Is Dead, Long Live the King."

Writing Options

1. Letter from Amyas Write a letter in which Amyas declares his allegiance to the new king and denounces the dead king.

2. Obituaries for the King Compose three obituaries for the king. Write each one from the standpoint of a different character in the story.

Activities & Explorations

Dramatic Scene With a group of classmates, dramatize a scene from the story. Rehearse your scene and then present it to the class.
~ PERFORMING

Inquiry & Research

Long Live the Queen Research the laws of succession for English monarchs, and then study Queen Victoria's ascension to the throne. Use an abbreviated family tree or another graphic to demonstrate how Queen Victoria came to succeed her uncle, William IV.

 More Online: Research Starter
www.mcdougallittell.com

Vocabulary in Action

EXERCISE: MEANING CLUES For each boldfaced word, choose the topic in which the word might be used in a discussion

1. malicious
a. the king's enemy
b. the king's friend
c. a small child

2. sentiment
a. the moat of a castle
b. building a castle
c. admiration for the king

3. malignant
a. the queen's maid
b. the king's advisers
c. a deadly disease

4. presently
a. winning a war
b. waiting for a doctor's arrival
c. an ancient law

5. reprieve
a. a prisoner facing execution
b. a newly appointed minister
c. a royal banner

Mary E. Coleridge
1861–1907

Other Works
Gathered Leaves
The Collected Poems of Mary Coleridge

A Literary Life Although she never achieved the fame of her ancestor, Mary Coleridge was a talented writer in a variety of literary forms, including novels, short stories, poetry, and essays. Born in London, Coleridge received an excellent education at home and, according to one of her friends, could read French, Italian, German, and Hebrew by the time she was 19 years old. Her father was a well-read lawyer who often entertained noted authors, including the poets Tennyson and Browning. Coleridge herself studied both literature and philosophy, eventually obtaining a job as an instructor of English literature at the Working Women's College, a position she held for the last 12 years of her life. She never married and lived with her family until her death at age 45.

A Retiring Writer Coleridge did not publish her first major work until she was in her 30s. Although her first novel, *The Seven Sleepers of Ephesus,* was not generally well received, it was praised by Robert Louis Stevenson, and several of Coleridge's subsequent novels became quite popular. In addition, she regularly contributed stories and essays to various journals, including *Cornhill Magazine* and the *Times Literary Supplement.* As a poet, she was reluctant to publish, or even talk about, her own work. At the urging of a family friend—the poet Robert Bridges—she eventually allowed two small collections of her poems to be published under the pseudonym Anodos. The rest were not made public until after her death. Bridges said of her poems, "They are both beautiful and original, and often exhibit imagination of a very rare kind, conveyed by the identical expression of true feeling and artistic insight."

The Novels of
GEORGE ELIOT

W ho is George Eliot? This question tantalized the literary world and tormented townspeople throughout 1858, the year John Blackwood published Eliot's two-volume *Scenes of Clerical Life.* Critics admired the work; literary figures discussed it; Warwickshire residents were shocked to recognize themselves in print. Then, in 1859, when Blackwood published a novel by Eliot, *Adam Bede,* the rumors fairly flew. Celebrities clamored to know the author, whom critics declared one of the "masters of the art." Townspeople searched for and found a local man to promote as Eliot unmasked.

Meanwhile, the true author, Mary Ann Evans, and her partner George Lewes were doing all they could to keep people off the track. When Blackwood guessed Eliot's identity, she begged him to keep the secret, and he agreed. Evans wanted her work to be judged on its merits, not on the basis of its author's gender. However, the similarities between her characters and real-life people and places made continued anonymity nearly impossible. Within two years, the secret was out.

Armed with knowledge of Eliot's gender, critics reexamined her work and found it deeply immoral. One critic even accused George Eliot of destroying "all comfortable notions of right and wrong, true and false." These complaints distressed Eliot, but she had this consolation: although Mary Ann Evans's reviews were terrible, George Eliot's had been good. It's little wonder, therefore, that she retained her pen name.

The complaining critics seem to have been unable to see that Eliot's novels actually have a strong moral tone. In *The Mill on the Floss*, for example, a sister rejected by her judgmental brother nevertheless saves his life at the cost of her own. In *Silas Marner*, an alienated miser adopts a foundling and gains for himself both love and redemption. In *Middlemarch*, one of the greatest novels of the 19th century, a woman who must choose between security and love gives up everything—and finds that she is glad she did. These heroes, torn by conflicting desires, struggle mightily to do what's right, and whether or not they succeed, good always wins in the end.

Now that Eliot's gender is not an issue, critics and readers alike enjoy the power and suspense of her novels. She has become respected and admired for the unfailing idealism and tough realism she showed both in her novels and in her life.

Top:
"My new story," wrote Eliot in 1857, *"will be a country story— full of the breath of the cows and the scent of hay."* Adam Bede *richly celebrates the vanishing world of the rural community, as depicted by John Constable in his painting* The Hay Wain. *The Hay Wain, (1821) John Constable. National Gallery, London/Bridgeman Art Library, London/Superstock.*

Above:
Scene from the production of Middlemarch *broadcast by PBS in 1994*

Left:
Manuscript page of "Legend of St. Ogg"

The Miracle of Purun Bhagat

Short Story by RUDYARD KIPLING

Comparing Literature of the World

"The Miracle of Purun Bhagat" and "What Men Live By"

This lesson and the one that follows present an opportunity for comparing the moral teachings that can be inferred in Rudyard Kipling's story "The Miracle of Purun Bhagat" with those that can be inferred in Leo Tolstoy's story "What Men Live By." Specific points of comparison in the Tolstoy lesson will help you note similarities and differences in the way each writer develops the moral teachings of his story.

Connect to Your Life

Changing Ways Do you know or have you read about someone who decided to change his or her life in a major way? Perhaps the person took a new job, moved, or married. What kinds of things did this person value most before and after the change in his or her lifestyle? Share your thoughts with your classmates.

Build Background

British India England's first settlements in India were trading posts established during the 1600s. Taking advantage of a weak Indian government, British agents were in control of India by 1774. Although Indian soldiers revolted against foreign rule in 1857, British forces successfully quelled the rebellion. Shortly thereafter, Queen Victoria appointed a viceroy to head India's government and to carry out the wishes of Parliament. Most Indian princes agreed to abide by British law, and government posts were given to a few Indians who supported the British presence. During the late 19th century, the British changed many of India's laws and constructed both railroad and telegraph systems to improve what they viewed as a primitive, or backward, civilization.

A number of British citizens moved to India during its years as a British colony. Among them were the parents of the writer Rudyard Kipling, who was born in India in 1865. Even as a child, Kipling was fascinated by Indian culture and values; later, he would vividly depict Indian life in his stories.

Most Indians are Hindus, and for them Hinduism is not only a religion but a way of life. Hindus are divided into castes, or social classes, and according to Hindu laws, a person can never leave the caste into which he or she is born. Each person's lifestyle—including eating habits, employment, and choice of friends and a marriage partner—is determined by his or her caste.

Focus Your Reading

LITERARY ANALYSIS **SETTING** The **setting** of a story is the time and place of the action. Setting often plays an important role in a story's events.

> *. . . he had held before him his dream of peace and quiet—the long, white, dusty Indian road, printed all over with bare feet, the incessant, slow-moving traffic, and the sharp-smelling wood-smoke curling up under the fig-trees in the twilight, where the wayfarers sat at their evening meal.*

As you read this story, be aware of the descriptions of setting and the interaction between the setting and the story's meaning.

ACTIVE READING **ANALYZING DETAILS** By including many vivid **details,** such as those in the above excerpt, Kipling creates for the reader a strong impression of the different characters, actions, and places in "The Miracle of Purun Bhagat."

READER'S NOTEBOOK As you read this story, notice scenes in the story that stand out vividly. Jot down specific details about the characters, actions, and places in two or three of these scenes.

THE MIRACLE OF
PURUN BHAGAT

RUDYARD KIPLING

There was once

a man in India

who was

Prime Minister

of one of the

semi-independent

native States

in the north-western

part of the country.

La coupe de mystère [The chalice of mystery] (1890), Odilon Redon. Oil on paper mounted on linen, 22½″ × 14″, collection of the Walker Art Center, Minneapolis, Minnesota, gift of Alexander M. Bing, 1953 (53.53).

He was a Brahmin,[1] so high-caste that caste ceased to have any particular meaning for him; and his father had been an important official in the gay-colored tag-rag and bob-tail[2] of an old-fashioned Hindu Court. But as Purun Dass grew up he realized that the ancient order of things was changing, and that if any one wished to get on he must stand well with the English, and imitate all the English believed to be good. At the same time a native official must keep his own master's favor. This was a difficult game, but the quiet, close-mouthed young Brahmin, helped by a good English education at a Bombay University, played it coolly, and rose, step by step, to be Prime Minister of the kingdom. That is to say, he held more real power than his master, the Maharajah.[3]

When the old king—who was suspicious of the English, their railways and telegraphs—died, Purun Dass stood high with his young successor, who had been tutored by an Englishman; and between them, though he always took care that his master should have the credit, they established schools for little girls, made roads, and started State dispensaries[4] and shows of agricultural implements, and published a yearly blue-book on the "Moral and Material Progress of the State," and the Foreign Office and the Government of India were delighted. Very few native States take up English progress without reservations, for they will not believe, as Purun Dass showed he did, that what is good for the Englishman must be twice as good for the Asiatic. The Prime Minister became the honored friend of Viceroys[5] and Governors, and Lieutenant-Governors, and medical missionaries, and common missionaries, and hard-riding English officers who came to shoot in the State preserves, as well as of whole hosts of tourists who travelled up and down India in the cold weather, showing how things ought to be managed. In his spare time he would endow scholarships for the study of medicine and manufactures on strictly English lines, and write letters to the *Pioneer*, the greatest Indian daily paper, explaining his master's aims and objects.

At last he went to England on a visit, and had to pay enormous sums to the priests when he came back; for even so high-caste a Brahmin as Purun Dass lost caste by crossing the black sea. In London he met and talked with every one worth knowing—men whose names go all over the world—and saw a great deal more than he said. He was given honorary degrees by learned universities, and he made speeches and talked of Hindu social reform to English ladies in evening dress, till all London cried, "This is the most fascinating man we have ever met at dinner since cloths were first laid!"

When he returned to India there was a blaze of glory, for the Viceroy himself made a special visit to confer upon the Maharajah the Grand Cross of the Star of India—all diamonds and ribbons and enamel; and at the same ceremony, while the cannon boomed, Purun Dass was made a Knight Commander of the Order of the Indian Empire; so that his name stood Sir Purun Dass, K.C.I.E.

That evening at dinner in the big Viceregal[6] tent he stood up with the badge and the collar of the Order on his breast, and replying to the toast of his master's health, made a speech that few Englishmen could have surpassed.

Next month, when the city had returned to its sun-baked quiet, he did a thing no Englishman would have dreamed of doing, for, so far as the world's affairs went, he died. The jeweled order of his knighthood returned to the Indian Government, and a new Prime Minister was appointed to the charge of affairs, and a great game of General Post[7] began in all the subordinate

---

1. **Brahmin:** a member of the highest Hindu caste.
2. **tag-rag and bob-tail:** a phrase meaning "a diverse and disorderly assemblage of people."
3. **Maharajah** (mä´hə-rä´jə): an Indian king or prince.
4. **dispensaries:** medical clinics.
5. **Viceroys** (vīs´roiz´): officials ruling as representatives of the sovereign.
6. **Viceregal** (vīs-rē´gəl): belonging to the viceroy.
7. **General Post:** a game in which, at a summons, all players change places.

appointments. The priests knew what had happened and the people guessed; but India is the one place in the world where a man can do as he pleases and nobody asks why; and the fact that Dewan Sir Purun Dass, K.C.I.E., had resigned position, palace, and power, and taken up the begging-bowl and ochre-colored dress of a Sunnyasi[8] or holy man, was considered nothing extraordinary. He had been, as the Old Law recommends, twenty years a youth, twenty years a fighter—though he had never carried a weapon in his life—and twenty years head of a household. He had used his wealth and his power for what he knew both to be worth; he had taken honor when it came his way; he had seen men and cities far and near, and men and cities had stood up and honored him. Now he would let these things go, as a man drops the cloak he needs no longer.

Behind him, as he walked through the city gates, an antelope skin and brass-handled crutch under his arm, and a begging-bowl of polished brown *coco-de-mer*[9] in his hand, barefoot, alone, with eyes cast on the ground—behind him they were firing salutes from the bastions[10] in honor of his happy successor. Purun Dass nodded. All that life was ended; and he bore it no more ill-will or good-will than a man bears to a colorless dream of the night. He was a Sunnyasi—a houseless, wandering

NOW HE

WOULD LET

THESE THINGS

GO, AS A MAN

DROPS THE

CLOAK HE NEEDS

NO LONGER.

❀

mendicant,[11] depending on his neighbors for his daily bread; and so long as there is a morsel to divide in India neither priest nor beggar starves. He had never in his life tasted meat, and very seldom eaten even fish. A five-pound note would have covered his personal expenses for food through any one of the many years in which he had been absolute master of millions of money. Even when he was being lionized[12] in London he had held before him his dream of peace and quiet—the long, white, dusty Indian road, printed all over with bare feet, the incessant, slow-moving traffic, and the sharp-smelling wood-smoke curling up under the fig-trees in the twilight, where the wayfarers sat at their evening meal.

When the time came to make that dream true the Prime Minister took the proper steps, and in three days you might more easily have found a bubble in the trough of the long Atlantic seas than Purun Dass among the roving, gathering, separating millions of India.

---

8. **Sunnyasi** (sŭn-yä′sē).

9. *coco-de-mer* (kō′kō-də-mâr′): the shell of a huge nut, resembling two joined coconut shells.

10. **bastions:** projecting parts of a fortification.

11. **mendicant** (mĕn′dĭ-kənt): beggar.

12. **lionized:** treated as a celebrity.

ACTIVE READING

ANALYZE What **details** in the paragraph help to create a vivid scene?

At night his antelope skin was spread where the darkness overtook him—sometimes in a Sunnyasi monastery by the roadside; sometimes by a mud pillar shrine of Kala Pir, where the Jogis, who are another misty division of holy men, would receive him as they do those who know what castes and divisions are worth; sometimes on the outskirts of a little Hindu village, where the children would steal up with the food their parents had prepared; and sometimes on the pitch of the bare grazing-grounds where the flame of his stick fire waked the drowsy camels. It was all one to Purun Dass—or Purun Bhagat,[13] as he called himself now. Earth, people, and food were all one. But, unconsciously, his feet drew him northward and eastward; from the south to Rohtak; from Rohtak to Kurnool; from Kurnool to ruined Samanah, and then up-stream along the dried bed of the Gugger river that fills only when the rain falls in the hills, till, one day, he saw the far line of the great Himalayas.

Then Purun Bhagat smiled, for he remembered that his mother was of Rajput Brahmin birth, from Kulu way—a Hill-woman, always homesick for the snows—and that the least touch of Hill blood draws a man in the end back to where he belongs.

"Yonder," said Purun Bhagat, breasting the lower slopes of the Sewaliks, where the cacti stand up like seven-branched candlesticks, "yonder I shall sit down and get knowledge"; and the cool wind of the Himalayas whistled about his ears as he trod the road that led to Simla.

The last time he had come that way it had been in state, with a clattering cavalry escort, to visit the gentlest and most affable of Viceroys; and the two had talked for an hour together about mutual friends in London, and what the Indian common folk really thought of things. This time Purun Bhagat paid no calls, but leaned on the rail of the Mall,[14] watching the glorious view of the Plains spread out forty miles below, till a native Mohammedan policeman told him he was obstructing traffic; and Purun Bhagat salaamed[15] reverently to the Law, because he knew the value of it, and was seeking for a Law of his own. Then he moved on, and slept that night in an empty hut at Chota Simla, which looks like the very last end of the earth, but it was only the beginning of his journey. He followed the Himalaya-Thibet[16] road, the little ten-foot track that is blasted out of solid rock, or strutted out on timbers over gulfs a thousand feet deep; that dips into warm, wet, shut-in valleys, and climbs across bare, grassy hill-shoulders where the sun strikes like a burning-glass; or turns through dripping, dark forests where the tree-ferns dress the trunks from head to heel, and the pheasant calls to his mate. And he met Thibetan herdsmen with their dogs and flocks of sheep, each sheep with a little bag of borax on his back,[17] and wandering wood-cutters, and cloaked and blanketed Lamas[18] from Thibet, coming into India on pilgrimage, and envoys[19] of little solitary Hill-states, posting furiously on ring-streaked and piebald ponies, or the cavalcade[20] of a Rajah paying a visit, or else for a long, clear day he would see nothing more than a black bear grunting and rooting down below in the valley. When he first started, the roar of the

ACTIVE READING

CLARIFY What kind of "Law" might Purun Bhagat be seeking?

---

13. **Bhagat** (bəg'ət): The Hindi word *bhagat* means "a devout person or saint."

14. **Mall:** a major roadway in Simla.

15. **salaamed** (sə-lämd'): bowed deeply, with the right palm pressed to the forehead, to show respect.

16. **Thibet:** a variant form of *Tibet*.

17. **borax on his back:** Tibet was the first important source of borax, a mineral with many industrial uses. In Tibet, sheep are often used as beasts of burden.

18. **Lamas:** Buddhist monks.

19. **envoys** (ĕn'voiz'): government representatives or agents.

20. **cavalcade:** a procession of riders on horseback or in horse-drawn carriages.

world he had left still rang in his ears, as the roar of a tunnel rings a little after the train has passed through; but when he had put the Mutteeanee Pass behind him that was all done, and Purun Bhagat was alone with himself, walking, wondering, and thinking, his eyes on the ground, and his thoughts with the clouds.

One evening he crossed the highest pass he had met till then—it had been a two days' climb—and came out on a line of snow-peaks that belted all the horizon—mountains from fifteen to twenty thousand feet high, looking almost near enough to hit with a stone, though they were fifty or sixty miles away. The pass was crowned with dense, dark forest—deodar, walnut, wild cherry, wild olive, and wild pear but mostly deodar, which is the Himalayan cedar; and under the shadow of the deodars stood a deserted shrine to Kali—who is Durga, who is Sitala, who is sometimes worshipped against the smallpox.[21]

Purun Dass swept the stone floor clean, smiled at the grinning statue, made himself a little mud fireplace at the back of the shrine, spread his antelope skin on a bed of fresh pine needles, tucked his *bairagi*—his brass-handled crutch—under his armpit, and sat down to rest.

Immediately below him the hillside fell away, clean and cleared for fifteen hundred feet, to where a little village of stone-walled houses, with roofs of beaten earth, clung to the steep tilt. All round it tiny terraced fields lay out like aprons of patchwork on the knees of the mountain, and cows no bigger than beetles grazed between the smooth stone circles of the threshing-floors. Looking across the valley the eye was deceived by the size of things, and could not at first realize that what seemed to be low scrub, on the opposite mountain-flank, was in truth a forest of hundred-foot pines. Purun Bhagat saw an eagle swoop across the enormous hollow, but the great bird dwindled to a dot ere it was half-way over. A few bands of scattered clouds strung up and down the valley, catching on a shoulder of the hills, or rising up and dying out when they were

level with the head of the pass. And "Here shall I find peace," said Purun Bhagat.

Now, a Hill-man makes nothing of a few hundred feet up or down, and as soon as the villagers saw the smoke in the deserted shrine, the village priest climbed up the terraced hillside to welcome the stranger.

When he met Purun Bhagat's eyes—the eyes of a man used to control thousands—he bowed to the earth, took the begging-bowl without a word, and returned to the village, saying, "We have at last a holy man. Never have I seen such a man. He is of the plains—but pale colored—a Brahmin of the Brahmins." Then all the housewives of the village said, "Think you he will stay with us?" and each did her best to cook the most savory meal for the Bhagat. Hill-food is very simple, but with buckwheat and Indian corn, and rice and red pepper, and little fish out of the stream in the little valley, and honey from the flue-like hives built in the stone walls, and dried apricots, and turmeric,[22] and wild ginger, and bannocks[23] of flour, a devout woman can make good things; and it was a full bowl that the priest carried to the Bhagat. Was he going to stay? asked the priest. Would he need a *chela*—a disciple—to beg for him? Had he a blanket against the cold weather? Was the food good?

Purun Bhagat ate, and thanked the giver. It was in his mind to stay. That was sufficient, said the priest. Let the begging-bowl be placed outside the shrine, in the hollow made by those two twisted roots, and daily should the Bhagat be fed; for the village felt honored that such a man—he looked timidly into the Bhagat's face—should tarry among them.

That day saw the end of Purun Bhagat's

---

21. **Kali . . . smallpox:** In Hinduism, the supreme goddess Devi takes many forms; one of these is Kali, goddess of destruction, who is also identified with the goddesses Durga (another deity of destruction) and Sitala (the deity of smallpox).

22. **turmeric** (tŭr′mər-ĭk): a spice made from the roots of the turmeric plant.

23. **bannocks:** flat loaves of unleavened bread.

wanderings. He had come to the place appointed for him—the silence and the space. After this, time stopped, and he, sitting at the mouth of the shrine, could not tell whether he were alive or dead; a man with control of his limbs, or a part of the hills, and the clouds, and the shifting rain, and sunlight. He would repeat a Name softly to himself a hundred hundred times, till, at each repetition, he seemed to move more and more out his body, sweeping up to the doors of some tremendous discovery; but, just as the door was opening, his body would drag him back, and, with grief, he felt he was locked up again in the flesh and bones of Purun Bhagat.

Every morning the filled begging-bowl was laid silently in the crotch of the roots outside the shrine. Sometimes the priest brought it; sometimes a Ladakhi[24] trader, lodging in the village, and anxious to get merit, trudged up the path; but, more often, it was the woman who had cooked the meal overnight; and she would murmur, hardly above her breath: "Speak for me before the gods, Bhagat. Speak for such an one, the wife of so-and-so!" Now and then some bold child would be allowed the honor, and Purun Bhagat would hear him drop the bowl and run as fast as his little legs could carry him, but the Bhagat never came down to the village. It was laid out like a map at his feet. He could see the evening gatherings held on the circle of the threshing-floors, because that was the only level ground; could see the wonderful unnamed green of the young rice, the indigo blues of the Indian corn; the dock-like patches of buckwheat, and, in its season, the red bloom of the amaranth, whose tiny seeds, being neither grain nor pulse,[25] make a food that can be lawfully eaten by Hindus in time of fasts.

When the year turned, the roofs of the huts were all little squares of purest gold, for it was on the roofs that they laid out their cobs of the corn to dry. Hiving and harvest, rice-sowing and husking, passed before his eyes, all embroidered down there on the many-sided fields, and he thought of them all, and wondered what they all led to at the long last.

Even in populated India a man cannot a day sit still before the wild things run over him as though he were a rock; and in that wilderness very soon the wild things, who knew Kali's Shrine well, came back to look at the intruder. The *langurs*, the big gray-whiskered monkeys of the Himalayas, were, naturally, the first, for they are alive with curiosity; and when they had upset the begging-bowl, and rolled it round the floor, and tried their teeth on the brass-handled crutch, and made faces at the antelope skin, they decided that the human being who sat so still was harmless. At evening, they would leap down from the pines, and beg with their hands for things to eat, and then swing off in graceful curves. They liked the warmth of the fire, too, and huddled round it till Purun Bhagat had to push them aside to throw on more fuel; and in the morning, as often as not, he would find a furry ape sharing his blanket. All day long, one or other of the tribe would sit by his side, staring out at the snows, crooning and looking unspeakably wise and sorrowful.

After the monkeys came the *barasingh*, that big deer which is like our red deer, but stronger. He wished to rub off the velvet of his horns against the cold stones of Kali's statue, and stamped his feet when he saw the man at the shrine. But Purun Bhagat never moved, and, little by little, the royal stag edged up and nuzzled his shoulder. Purun Bhagat slid one cool hand along the hot antlers, and the touch soothed the fretted beast, who bowed his head, and Purun Bhagat very softly rubbed and ravelled off the velvet. Afterwards, the *barasingh* brought his doe and fawn—gentle things that mumbled on the holy man's blanket—or would come alone at night, his eyes green in the fire-flicker, to take his share of fresh walnuts. At last, the musk-deer, the

---

24. **Ladakhi** (lǝ-dä′kē): from Ladakh, a region in the upper Indus River valley—at the time, part of northwestern India.

25. **pulse:** the edible seeds of certain pod-bearing plants, such as peas and beans.

shyest and almost the smallest of the deerlets, came, too, her big, rabbity ears erect; even brindled, silent *mushick-nabha* must needs find out what the light in the shrine meant, and drop her moose-like nose into Purun Bhagat's lap, coming and going with the shadows of the fire. Purun Bhagat called them all "my brothers," and his low call of *"Bhai! Bhai!"* would draw them from the forest at noon if they were within earshot. The Himalayan black bear, moody and suspicious—Sona, who has the V-shaped white mark under his chin—passed that way more than once; and since the Bhagat showed no fear, Sona showed no anger, but watched him, and came closer, and begged a share of the caresses, and a dole of bread or wild berries. Often, in the still dawns, when the Bhagat would climb to the very crest of the notched pass to watch the red day walking along the peaks of the snows, he would find Sona shuffling and grunting at his heels, thrusting a curious forepaw under fallen trunks, and bringing it away with a *whoof* of impatience; or his early steps would wake Sona where he lay curled up, and the great brute, rising erect, would think to fight, till he heard the Bhagat's voice and knew his best friend.

Nearly all hermits and holy men who live apart from the big cities have the reputation of being able to work miracles with the wild things, but all the miracle lies in keeping still, in never making a hasty movement, and, for a long time, at least, in never looking directly at a visitor. The villagers saw the outlines of the *barasingh* stalking like a shadow through the dark forest behind the shrine; saw the *minaul*, the Himalayan pheasant, blazing in her best colors before Kali's statue; and the *langurs* on their haunches, inside, playing with the walnut shells. Some of the children, too, had heard Sona singing to himself, bear-fashion, behind the fallen rocks, and the Bhagat's reputation as miracle-worker stood firm.

Yet nothing was further from his mind than miracles. He believed that all things were one big Miracle, and when a man knows that much he knows something to go upon. He knew for a certainty that there was nothing great and nothing little in this world; and day and night he strove to think out his way into the heart of things, back to the place whence his soul had come.

So thinking, his untrimmed hair fell down about his shoulders, the stone slab at the side of the antelope-skin was dented into a little hole by the foot of his brass-handled crutch, and the place between the tree-trunks, where the begging-bowl rested day after day, sunk and wore into a hollow almost as smooth as the brown shell itself; and each beast knew his exact place at the fire. The fields changed their colors with the seasons; the threshing-floors filled and emptied, and filled again and again; and again and again, when winter came, the *langurs* frisked among the branches feathered with light snow, till the mother-monkeys brought their sad-eyed little babies up from the warmer valleys with the spring. There were few changes in the village. The priest was older, and many of the little children who used to come with the begging-dish sent their own children now; and when you asked of the villagers how long their holy man had lived in Kali's Shrine at the head of the pass, they answered, "Always."

ACTIVE READING

EVALUATE How would you describe the relationship between the villagers and Purun Bhagat?

Then came such summer rains as had not been known in the Hills for many seasons. Through three good months the valley was wrapped in cloud and soaking mist—steady, unrelenting downfall, breaking off into thunder-shower after thunder-shower. Kali's Shrine stood above the clouds, for the most part, and there was a whole month in which the Bhagat never caught a glimpse of his village. It was packed away under a white floor of cloud that swayed and shifted and rolled on itself and bulged upward, but never broke from its piers—the streaming flanks of the valley.

All that time he heard nothing but the sound of a million little waters, overhead from the trees, and underfoot along the ground, soaking

through the pine-needles, dripping from the tongues of draggled fern, and spouting in newly-torn muddy channels down the slopes. Then the sun came out, and drew forth the good incense of the deodars and the rhododendrons, and that far-off, clean smell the Hill People call "the smell of the snows." The hot sunshine lasted for a week, and then the rains gathered together for their last downpour, and the water fell in sheets that flayed off the skin of the ground and leaped back in mud. Purun Bhagat heaped his fire high that night, for he was sure his brothers would need warmth; but never a beast came to the shrine, though he called and called till he dropped asleep, wondering what had happened in the woods.

It was in the black heart of the night, the rain drumming like a thousand drums, that he was roused by a plucking at his blanket, and, stretching out, felt the little hand of a *langur*. "It is better here than in the trees," he said sleepily, loosening a fold of blanket; "take it and be warm." The monkey caught his hand and pulled hard. "Is it food, then?" said Purun Bhagat. "Wait awhile, and I will prepare some." As he kneeled to throw fuel on the fire the *langur* ran to the door of the shrine, crooned, and ran back again, plucking at the man's knee.

"What is it? What is thy trouble, Brother?" said Purun Bhagat, for the *langur's* eyes were full of things that he could not tell. "Unless one of thy caste be in a trap—and none set traps here—I will not go into that weather. Look, Brother, even the *barasingh* comes for shelter."

ACTIVE READING

PREDICT The animals are behaving strangely. What might be happening?

The deer's antlers clashed as he strode into the shrine, clashed against the grinning statue of Kali. He lowered them in Purun Bhagat's direction and stamped uneasily, hissing through his half-shut nostrils.

"Hai! Hai! Hai!" said the Bhagat, snapping his fingers. "Is *this* payment for a night's lodging?" But the deer pushed him towards the door, and as he did so Purun Bhagat heard the sound of something opening with a sigh, and saw two slabs of the floor draw away from each other, while the sticky earth below smacked its lips.

"Now I see," said Purun Bhagat. "No blame to my brothers that they did not sit by the fire to-night. The mountain is falling. And yet—why should I go?" His eye fell on the empty begging-bowl, and his face changed. "They have given me good food daily since—since I came, and, if I am not swift, tomorrow there will not be one mouth in the valley. Indeed, I must go and warn them below. Back there, Brother! Let me get to the fire."

The *barasingh* backed unwillingly as Purun Bhagat drove a torch deep into the flame, twirling it till it was well lit. "Ah! ye came to warn me," he said, rising. "Better than that we shall do, better than that. Out, now, and lend me thy neck, Brother, for I have but two feet."

He clutched the bristling withers[26] of the *barasingh* with his right hand, held the torch away with his left, and stepped out of the shrine into the desperate night. There was no breath of wind, but the rain nearly drowned the torch as the great deer hurried down the slope, sliding on his haunches. As soon as they were clear of the forest more of the Bhagat's brothers joined them. He heard, though he could not see, the *langurs* pressing about him, and behind them the *uhh! uhh!* of Sona. The rain matted his long white hair into ropes; the water splashed beneath his bare feet, and his yellow robe clung to his frail old body, but he stepped down steadily, leaning against the *barasingh*. He was no longer a holy man, but Sir Purun Dass, K.C.I.E., Prime Minister of no small State, a man accustomed to command, going out to save life. Down the steep plashy path they poured all together, the Bhagat and his brothers, down and down till the deer clicked and stumbled on the wall of a threshing-floor, and snorted because he smelt Man. Now they were at the head of the one crooked village

---

26. **withers:** the high part of the deer's back, between the shoulder blades.

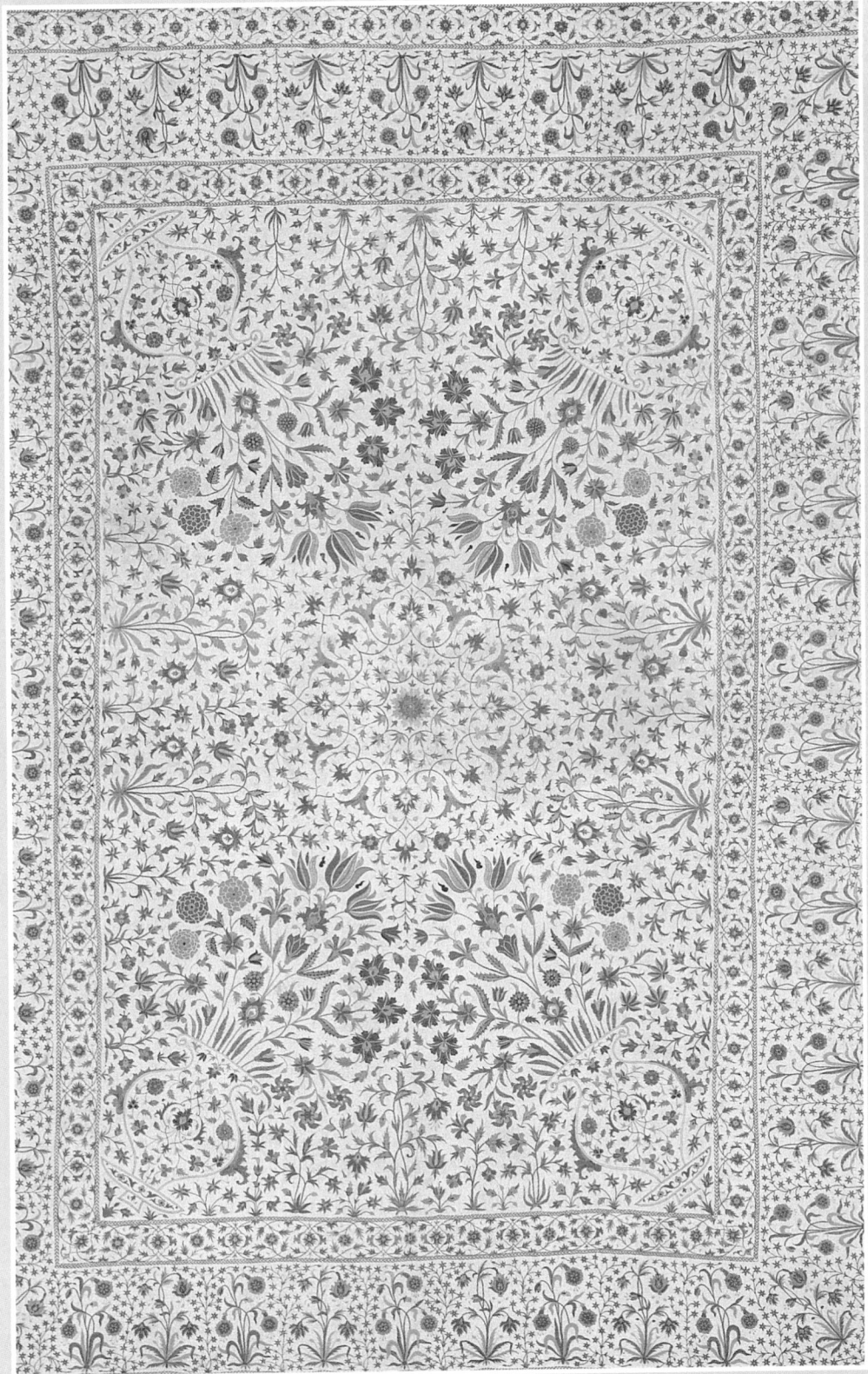

Mughal floorspread (about 1700). Cotton embroidered with silk, 269 cm × 203 cm, Victoria and Albert Museum, London/Art Resource, New York.

street, and the Bhagat beat with his crutch at the barred windows of the blacksmith's house as his torch blazed up in the shelter of the eaves. "Up and out!" cried Purun Bhagat; and he did not know his own voice, for it was years since he had spoken aloud to a man. "The hill falls! The hill is falling! Up and out, oh, you within!"

"It is our Bhagat," said the blacksmith's wife. "He stands among his beasts. Gather the little ones and give the call."

It ran from house to house, while the beasts, cramped in the narrow way, surged and huddled round the Bhagat, and Sona puffed impatiently.

The people hurried into the street—they were no more than seventy souls all told—and in the glare of their torches they saw their Bhagat holding back the terrified *barasingh*, while the monkeys plucked piteously at his skirts, and Sona sat on his haunches and roared.

"Across the valley and up the next hill!" shouted Purun Bhagat. "Leave none behind! We follow!"

Then the people ran as only Hill-folk can run, for they knew that in a landslip you must climb for the highest ground across the valley. They fled, splashing through the little river at the bottom, and panted up the terraced fields on the far side, while the Bhagat and his brethren followed. Up and up the opposite mountain they climbed, calling to each other by name—the roll-call of the village—and at their heels toiled the big

HIS INSTINCT,

THAT HAD

WARNED HIM OF

THE COMING

SLIDE, TOLD HIM

HE WOULD BE

SAFE HERE.

❀

barasingh, weighted by the failing strength of Purun Bhagat. At last the deer stopped in the shadow of a deep pine-wood, five hundred feet up the hillside. His instinct, that had warned him of the coming slide, told him he would be safe here.

Purun Bhagat dropped fainting by his side, for the chill of the rain and that fierce climb was killing him; but first he called to the scattered torches ahead, "Stay and count your numbers;" then, whispering to the deer as he saw the lights gather in a cluster: "Stay with me, Brother. Stay—till—I—go!"

There was a sigh in the air that grew to a mutter, and a mutter that grew to a roar, and a roar that passed all sense of hearing, and the hillside on which the villagers stood was hit in the darkness, and rocked to the blow. Then a note as steady, deep, and true as the deep C of the organ drowned everything for perhaps five minutes, while the very roots of the pines quivered to it. It died away, and the sound of the rain falling on miles of hard ground and grass changed to the muffled drums of water on soft earth. That told its own tale.

Never a villager—not even the priest—was bold enough to speak to the Bhagat who had saved their lives. They crouched under the pines and waited till the day. When it came they looked across the valley, and saw that what had been forest, and terraced field, and track-threaded

grazing-ground was one raw, red, fan-shaped smear, with a few trees flung head-down on the scarp.[27] That red ran high up the hill of their refuge, damming back the little river, which had begun to spread into a brick-colored lake. Of the village, of the road to the shrine, of the shrine itself, and the forest behind, there was no trace. For one mile in width and two thousand feet in sheer depth the mountain-side had come away bodily, planed clean from head to heel.

And the villagers, one by one, crept through the wood to pray before their Bhagat. They saw the *barasingh* standing over him, who fled when they came near, and they heard the *langurs* wailing in the branches, and Sona moaning up the hill; but their Bhagat was dead, sitting cross-legged, his back against a tree, his crutch under his armpit, and his face turned to the north-east.

The priest said: "Behold a miracle after a miracle, for in this very attitude must all Sunnyasis be buried! Therefore, where he now is we will build the temple to our holy man."

They built the temple before a year was ended, a little stone and earth shrine, and they called the hill the Bhagat's Hill, and they worship there with lights and flowers and offerings to this day. But they do not know that the saint of their worship is the late Sir Purun Dass, K.C.I.E., D.C.L.,[28] Ph.D., etc., once Prime Minister of the progressive and enlightened state of Mohiniwala, and honorary or corresponding member of more learned and scientific societies than will ever do any good in this world or the next. ❖

---

27. **scarp:** escarpment—a steep slope or cliff separating two level areas of different elevations.

28. **K.C.I.E., D.C.L.:** abbreviations of the titles *Knight Commander of the Indian Empire* and *Doctor of Civil Law.*

Connect to the Literature

1. **What Do You Think?** What is your impression of Purun and his actions?

> **Comprehension Check**
> - Why does Purun Dass change his name?
> - Why do the animals wake Purun Bhagat?

Think Critically

2. Do you admire Purun more in his role as Purun Dass or in his role as Purun Bhagat? Explain your answer.

3. Why do you think Purun changes his life so drastically?

THINK ABOUT

- his cultural heritage
- his values as a young man
- his accomplishments as prime minister
- the values he expresses as he begins his new life

4. What, in your opinion, is the miracle of Purun Bhagat? Share your ideas with your classmates.

5. **ACTIVE READING** **ANALYZING DETAILS** Review the details you jotted down in your **READER'S NOTEBOOK**. What scenes stand out most vividly in your mind? How do the details describing characters, actions, and events work together to create this vivid effect?

6. What moral lesson do you consider to be one of the story's main **themes**? Support your answer with examples from the text.

Extend Interpretations

7. **Comparing Texts** The heroic code of Rama, as depicted in the *Ramayana* (page 240), is revered by all Hindus and serves as a model of devotion and duty for Hindu men. Do you think that Purun lives his whole life in accordance with that code? Give reasons to support your answer.

8. **Connect to Life** Early in the story, Purun Dass seems to believe that "what is good for the Englishman must be twice as good for the Asiatic." How do you think most people would respond to that type of thinking today?

Literary Analysis

> **SETTING** The time and place of the action of a short story, novel, play, narrative poem, or nonfiction narrative is referred to as the **setting.** Note the details of setting in the following excerpt:

At night his antelope skin was spread where the darkness overtook him—sometimes in a Sunnyasi monastery by the roadside; sometimes by a mud pillar shrine of Kala Pir, where the Jogis, who are another misty division of holy men, would receive him as they do those who know what castes and divisions are worth; sometimes on the outskirts of a little Hindu village, where the children would steal up with the food their parents had prepared; and sometimes on the pitch of the bare grazing-grounds where the flame of his stick fire waked the drowsy camels.

In addition to time and place, setting may include the social and moral environment that form the background for a narrative. Setting is one of the main elements in fiction and often plays an important role in what happens and why.

Cooperative Learning Activity How important do you think the setting of "The Miracle of Purun Bhagat" is? Discuss with your classmates how the events of the story might have been different if Purun Bhagat had become a Sunnyasi but remained in the city. Share your conclusions with the class.

Choices & CHALLENGES

Writing Options

1. Purun Bhagat Obituary Using details from the story, write an obituary of Purun Bhagat for an Indian newspaper.

2. Essay Analyzing Values Write an essay in which you analyze the life-style and values chosen by Purun Dass when he becomes Purun Bhagat. What does he give up? What does he gain? Place the essay in your **Working Portfolio.**

Activities & Explorations

1. Sculpture Tribute Create a design or model of a statue that honors Purun by reflecting both phases of his life. ~ **ART**

2. Dramatic Dialogue With a partner, present a dramatic dialogue in which Purun Dass and Purun Bhagat discuss the pros and cons of their lifestyles. ~ **PERFORMING**

Inquiry & Research

Caste System Find out more about India's caste system and its effects on the lifestyle of the Indian people. What constitutes a caste? What kinds of rules govern each caste? Have any low caste members achieved high political office in India? Share your findings with your classmates.

 More Online: Research Starter
www.mcdougallittell.com

Rudyard Kipling
1865–1936

Other Works
"The Man Who Would Be King"
"The Strange Ride of
    Morrowbie Jukes"
"The Maltese Cat"
"The King's Ankus"
"The Return of Imray"

A Childhood in England and India Although born in Bombay, Joseph Rudyard Kipling spent many of his childhood years in England, unhappily separated from his family. His English parents had moved to India shortly after their marriage, when his father was assigned to a teaching position at an art school. At that time, it was customary for British residents in India to send their children back to Britain for schooling. When Kipling was 6 years old, therefore, his parents took him and his younger sister to Southsea, England, and placed them in a foster home for the next five years. Kipling felt abandoned and later described his stay in Southsea as a period of extreme unhappiness and anxiety. At the age of 12, Kipling was sent to the United Services College, an inexpensive boarding school in Devon, England. Although Kipling later recalled the bullying and unruliness of the students, his school experiences were generally pleasant enough, and his assignment as editor of the school magazine eventually led him to a career in journalism.

Reporter and Writer In 1882, at the age of 16,

Kipling returned to India, where he worked as a newspaper reporter for the next seven years. Many of his early stories were published in a series of paperback books that were sold in train stations. International travelers soon spread word of his work beyond the boundaries of India, and when he returned to England in 1889, his reputation as a great writer had preceded him. He very quickly became one of England's favorite writers.

Marriage and America In 1892, Kipling married an American, Carrie Balestier, and moved with her to the United States. The couple settled in Vermont, but Kipling was never able to adjust to the American way of life. Four years later they were back in England, where Kipling would live the rest of his life. Even though his stay in America was not particularly satisfying, Kipling wrote many of his most famous stories and novels in the United States, including *The Jungle Books* and *Captains Courageous*.

Lifetime Achievement Kipling was an accomplished novelist and poet, as well as the author of over 300 short stories. He is perhaps best known today for his children's stories, particularly the widely read *Just So Stories.* Many of his works—including his most famous novel, *Kim*—reveal his lifelong fascination with the people and animals of India. In 1907, he became the first English writer to be awarded the Nobel Prize for literature.

What Men Live By

Short Story by LEO TOLSTOY

Comparing Literature of the World

Observing Moral Lessons Across Cultures

Russia

Kazakhstan

Russia

Ukraine

Uzbekistan

Turkmenistan

"The Miracle of Purun Bhagat" and "What Men Live By" Many of Kipling's stories describe his lifelong fascination with India. Most of Leo Tolstoy's stories are set in Russia. Despite the differences in language and setting in the two stories included in this book, both writers deal with the moral issue of what constitutes a good and meaningful life. Further, both stories are concerned with the ways in which a simple life can make virtue more attainable.

Points of Comparison As you read the following story by Tolstoy, compare it with Kipling's story in terms of the moral lesson that can be drawn from it.

Build Background

The Aristocrat and the Peasants During the 19th century, the peasants of Russia were poor and struggling. Russia was still a Christian nation then, and it was ruled by an emperor called the czar. Although the peasants were freed from serfdom, a form of slavery, during the 1800s, their standard of living remained far lower than that of the wealthy landowners.

Even though Leo Tolstoy was himself an aristocrat and a wealthy landowner, he became a leader in the fight to change society and educate the peasant class. Like the British authors Elizabeth Gaskell and Charles Dickens, Tolstoy often used his writing to call attention to social and moral issues—especially the plight of the poor. Toward the end of his writing career, he began writing down and adapting the folk tales through which peasants conveyed **themes** about the meaning of life. He believed that these themes revealed truths that could improve the quality of life for all. In "What Men Live By," you will read about a 19th-century Russian peasant and his encounter with a stranger in need.

Focus Your Reading

LITERARY ANALYSIS **FOLK TALE** "What Men Live By" is a version of a Russian **folk tale**—a story that is handed down, usually by word of mouth, from generation to generation. Folk tales often show how the people in a particular region live and what their values are. As you read, be aware of what the story reveals about people's values and way of life.

ACTIVE READING **SUMMARIZING TEXT** Briefly **summarizing** a story can help you to understand the relationships between events and to identify the most important points in a story. It is often useful as you read to pause occasionally and restate the important information in the text.

READER'S NOTEBOOK This story can be divided into four main parts (sections I–V, sections VI–VII, sections VIII–IX, and sections X–XII). As you read,

summarize briefly the main points of each of these four parts. Include only what you consider to be the most important information.

Part	Summary
I–V	
VI–VII	
VIII–IX	
X–XII	

What Men Live By

LEO TOLSTOY

I

A shoemaker named Simon, who
had neither house nor land of his
own, lived with his wife and
children in a peasant's hut and
earned his living by his work.
Work was cheap but bread was
dear, and what he earned he
spent for food. The man and
his wife had but one sheep-skin
coat between them for winter wear,
and even that was worn to tatters, and
this was the second year he had been
wanting to buy sheep-skins for a new coat.
Before winter Simon saved up a little money: a
three-ruble note[1] lay hidden in his wife's box,
and five rubles and twenty kopeks[2] were owed
him by customers in the village.

---

1. **three-ruble** (r$\overline{oo}$′bəl) **note:** a piece of paper money. The
   ruble is the main monetary unit of Russia.
2. **kopeks:** one-hundredths of a ruble.

So one morning he prepared to go to the village to buy the sheep-skins. He put on over his shirt his wife's wadded nankeen[3] jacket, and over that he put his own cloth coat. He took the three-ruble note in his pocket, cut himself a stick to serve as a staff, and started off after breakfast. "I'll collect the five rubles that are due to me," thought he, "add the three I have got, and that will be enough to buy sheep-skins for the winter coat."

He came to the village and called at a peasant's hut, but the man was not at home. The peasant's wife promised that the money should be paid next week, but she would not pay it herself. Then Simon called on another peasant, but this one swore he had no money, and would only pay twenty kopeks which he owed for a pair of boots Simon had mended. Simon then tried to buy the sheep-skins on credit, but the dealer would not trust him.

"Bring your money," said he, "then you may have your pick of the skins. We know what debt-collecting is like."

So all the business the shoemaker did was to get the twenty kopeks for boots he had mended and to take a pair of felt boots a peasant gave him to sole with leather.

Simon felt downhearted. He spent the twenty kopeks on vodka and started homewards without having bought any skins. In the morning he had felt the frost; but now, after drinking the vodka, he felt warm even without a sheep-skin coat. He trudged along, striking his stick on the frozen earth with one hand, swinging the felt boots with the other, and talking to himself.

"I'm quite warm," said he, "though I have no sheep-skin coat. I've had a drop and it runs through my veins. I need no sheep-skins. I go along and don't worry about anything. That's the sort of man I am! What do I care? I can live without sheep-skins. I don't need them. My wife will fret, to be sure. And, true enough, it *is* a shame; one works all day long and then does not get paid. Stop a bit! If you don't bring that money along, sure enough I'll skin you, blessed if I don't. How's that? He pays twenty kopeks at a time!

What can I do with twenty kopeks? Drink it—that's all one can do! Hard up, he says he is! So he may be—but what about me? You have house, and cattle, and everything; I've only what I stand up in! You have corn of your own growing, I have to buy every grain. Do what I will, I must spend three rubles every week for bread alone. I come home and find the bread all used up and I have to work out another ruble and a half. So just you pay up what you owe, and no nonsense about it!"

By this time he had nearly reached the shrine at the bend of the road. Looking up, he saw something whitish behind the shrine. The daylight was fading, and the shoemaker peered at the thing without being able to make out what it was. "There was no white stone here before. Can it be an ox? It's not like an ox. It has a head like a man, but it's too white; and what could a man be doing there?"

He came closer, so that it was clearly visible. To his surprise it really was a man, alive or dead, sitting naked, leaning motionless against the shrine. Terror seized the shoemaker, and he thought, "Some one has killed him, stripped him, and left him here. If I meddle I shall surely get into trouble."

So the shoemaker went on. He passed in front of the shrine so that he could not see the man. When he had gone some way he looked back, and saw that the man was no longer leaning against the shrine but was moving as if looking towards him. The shoemaker felt more frightened than before, and thought, "Shall I go back to him or shall I go on? If I go near him something dreadful may happen. Who knows who the fellow is? He has not come here for any good. If I go near him he may jump up and throttle me, and there will be no getting away. Or if not, he'd still be a burden on one's hands. What could I do with a naked man? I couldn't give him my last clothes. Heaven only help me to get away!"

So the shoemaker hurried on, leaving the shrine

---

3. **nankeen:** a sturdy, cotton cloth.

behind him—when suddenly his conscience smote[4] him and he stopped in the road.

"What are you doing, Simon?" said he to himself. "The man may be dying of want, and you slip past afraid. Have you grown so rich as to be afraid of robbers? Ah, Simon, shame on you!"

So he turned back and went up to the man.

II

Simon approached the stranger, looked at him and saw that he was a young man, fit, with no bruises on his body, but evidently freezing and frightened, and he sat there leaning back without looking up at Simon, as if too faint to lift his eyes. Simon went close to him and then the man seemed to wake up. Turning his head, he opened his eyes and looked into Simon's face. That one look was enough to make Simon fond of the man. He threw the felt boots on the ground, undid his sash, laid it on the boots, and took off his cloth coat.

"It's not a time for talking," said he. "Come, put this coat on at once!" And Simon took the man by the elbows and helped him to rise. As he stood there, Simon saw that his body was clean and in good condition, his hands and feet shapely, and his face good and kind. He threw his coat over the man's shoulders, but the latter could not find the sleeves. Simon guided his arms into them, and drawing the coat on well, wrapped it closely about him, tying the sash round the man's waist.

Simon even took off his cap to put it on the man's head, but then his own head felt cold and he thought: "I'm quite bald, while he has long curly hair." So he put his cap on his own head again. "It will be better to give him something for his feet," thought he; and he made the man sit down and helped him to put on the felt boots, saying, "There, friend, now move about and warm yourself. Other matters can be settled later on. Can you walk?"

The man stood up and looked kindly at Simon but could not say a word.

"Why don't you speak?" said Simon. "It's too cold to stay here, we must be getting home. There now, take my stick, and if you're feeling weak lean on that. Now step out!"

The man started walking and moved easily, not lagging behind.

As they went along, Simon asked him, "And where do you belong to?"

"I'm not from these parts."

"I thought as much. I know the folks here-abouts. But how did you come to be there by the shrine?"

"I cannot tell."

"Has some one been ill-treating you?"

"No one has ill-treated me. God has punished me."

"Of course God rules all. Still, you'll have to find food and shelter somewhere. Where do you want to go to?"

"It is all the same to me."

Simon was amazed. The man did not look like a rogue, and he spoke gently, but yet he gave no account of himself. Still Simon thought, "Who knows what may have happened?" And he said to the stranger: "Well then, come home with me and at least warm yourself awhile."

So Simon walked towards his home, and the stranger kept up with him, walking at his side. The wind had risen and Simon felt it cold under his shirt. He was getting over his tipsiness by now and began to feel the frost. He went along sniffling and wrapping his wife's coat round him, and he thought to himself: "There now—talk about sheep-skins! I went out for sheep-skins and come home without even a coat to my back, and what is more, I'm bringing a naked man along with me. Matrëna won't be pleased!" And when he thought of his wife he felt sad, but when he looked at the stranger and remembered how he had looked up at him at the shrine, his heart was glad.

ACTIVE READING

PREDICT How do you think Simon's wife will react to the stranger?

---

4. **smote:** dealt a blow to; sharply affected.

Nightfall at Hradčany (1909–1913), Jakub Schikaneder. Oil on canvas, 33.7″ × 41.9″, National Gallery, Prague, Czech Republic.

III

Simon's wife had everything ready early that day. She had cut wood, brought water, fed the children, eaten her own meal, and now she sat thinking. She wondered when she ought to make bread: now or tomorrow? There was still a large piece left.

"If Simon has had some dinner in town," thought she, "and does not eat much for supper, the bread will last out another day."

She weighed the piece of bread in her hand again and again and thought: "I won't make any more today. We have only enough flour left to bake one batch. We can manage to make this last out till Friday."

So Matrëna put away the bread and sat down at the table to patch her husband's shirt. While she worked she thought how her husband was buying skins for a winter coat.

"If only the dealer does not cheat him. My good man is much too simple; he cheats nobody, but any child can take him in. Eight rubles is a lot of money—he should get a good coat at that price. Not tanned skins, but still a proper winter coat. How difficult it was last winter to get on without a winter coat. I could neither get down to the river nor go out anywhere. When he went out he put on all we had, and there was nothing left for me. He did not start very early today, but still it's time he was back. I only hope he has not gone on the spree!"

Hardly had Matrëna thought this than steps were heard on the threshold and some one entered. Matrëna stuck her needle into her work and went out into the passage. There she saw two men: Simon, and with him a man without a hat and wearing felt boots.

Matrëna noticed at once that her husband smelt of spirits. "There now, he has been drinking," thought she. And when she saw that he was coatless, had only her jacket on, brought no parcel, stood there silent, and seemed ashamed, her heart

was ready to break with disappointment. "He has drunk the money," thought she, "and has been on the spree with some good-for-nothing fellow whom he has brought home with him."

Matrëna let them pass into the hut, followed them in, and saw that the stranger was a young, slight man, wearing her husband's coat. There was no shirt to be seen under it, and he had no hat. Having entered, he stood neither moving nor raising his eyes, and Matrëna thought: "He must be a bad man—he's afraid."

Matrëna frowned, and stood beside the stove looking to see what they would do.

Simon took off his cap and sat down on the bench as if things were all right.

"Come, Matrëna; if supper is ready, let us have some."

Matrëna muttered something to herself and did not move but stayed where she was, by the stove. She looked first at the one and then at the other of them and only shook her head. Simon saw that his wife was annoyed, but tried to pass it off. Pretending not to notice anything, he took the stranger by the arm.

"Sit down, friend," said he, "and let us have some supper."

The stranger sat down on the bench.

"Haven't you cooked anything for us?" said Simon.

Matrëna's anger boiled over. "I've cooked, but not for you. It seems to me you have drunk your wits away. You went to buy a sheep-skin coat but come home without so much as the coat you had on and bring a naked vagabond home with you. I have no supper for drunkards like you."

"That's enough, Matrëna. Don't wag your tongue without reason! You had better ask what sort of man—"

"And you tell me what you've done with the money?"

Simon found the pocket of the jacket, drew out the three-ruble note, and unfolded it.

"Here is the money. Trifonov did not pay, but promises to pay soon."

Matrëna got still more angry; he had bought no sheep-skins but had put his only coat on some naked fellow and had even brought him to their house.

She snatched up the note from the table, took it to put away in safety, and said: "I have no supper for you. We can't feed all the naked drunkards in the world."

"There now, Matrëna, hold your tongue a bit. First hear what a man has to say—!"

"Much wisdom I shall hear from a drunken fool. I was right in not wanting to marry you—a drunkard. The linen my mother gave me you drank; and now you've been to buy a coat—and have drunk it too!"

Simon tried to explain to his wife that he had only spent twenty kopeks; tried to tell how he had found the man—but Matrëna would not let him get a word in. She talked nineteen to the dozen[5] and dragged in things that had happened ten years before.

Matrëna talked and talked, and at last she flew at Simon and seized him by the sleeve.

"Give me my jacket. It is the only one I have, and you must needs take it from me and wear it yourself. Give it here, you mangy dog, and may the devil take you."

Simon began to pull off the jacket, and turned a sleeve of it inside out; Matrëna seized the jacket and it burst its seams. She snatched it up, threw it over her head, and went to the door. She meant to go out, but stopped undecided—she wanted to work off her anger, but she also wanted to learn what sort of a man the stranger was.

IV

Matrëna stopped and said: "If he were a good man he would not be naked. Why, he hasn't even a shirt on him. If he were all right, you would say where you came across the fellow."

"That's just what I am trying to tell you," said

---

5. **talked nineteen to the dozen:** chattered on excessively.

Simon. "As I came to the shrine I saw him sitting all naked and frozen. It isn't quite the weather to sit about naked! God sent me to him or he would have perished. What was I to do? How do we know what may have happened to him? So I took him, clothed him, and brought him along. Don't be so angry, Matrëna. It is a sin. Remember, we must all die one day."

Angry words rose to Matrëna's lips, but she looked at the stranger and was silent. He sat on the edge of the bench, motionless, his hands folded on his knees, his head drooping on his breast, his eyes closed, and his brows knit as if in pain. Matrëna was silent, and Simon said: "Matrëna, have you no love of God?"

Matrëna heard these words, and as she looked at the stranger, suddenly her heart softened towards him. She came back from the door, and going to the stove she got out the supper. Setting a cup on the table, she poured out some kvas.[6] Then she brought out the last piece of bread and set out a knife and spoons.

"Eat, if you want to," said she.

Simon drew the stranger to the table.

"Take your place, young man," said he.

Simon cut the bread, crumbled it into the broth, and they began to eat. Matrëna sat at the corner of the table, resting her head on her hand and looking at the stranger.

And Matrëna was touched with pity for the stranger and began to feel fond of him. And at once the stranger's face lit up; his brows were no longer bent, he raised his eyes and smiled at Matrëna.

When they had finished supper, the woman cleared away the things and began questioning the stranger. "Where are you from?" said she.

"I am not from these parts."

"But how did you come to be on the road?"

"I may not tell."

"Did some one rob you?"

"God punished me."

"And you were lying there naked?"

"Yes, naked and freezing. Simon saw me and had pity on me. He took off his coat, put it on

me, and brought me here. And you have fed me, given me drink, and shown pity on me. God will reward you!"

Matrëna rose, took from the window Simon's old shirt she had been patching, and gave it to the stranger. She also brought out a pair of trousers for him.

"There," said she, "I see you have no shirt. Put this on, and lie down where you please, in the loft or on the stove."[7]

ACTIVE READING

QUESTION Why do you think Matrëna's attitude toward the stranger has changed?

The stranger took off the coat, put on the shirt, and lay down in the loft. Matrëna put out the candle, took the coat, and climbed to where her husband lay on the stove.

Matrëna drew the skirts of the coat over her and lay down but could not sleep; she could not get the stranger out of her mind.

When she remembered that he had eaten their last piece of bread and that there was none for tomorrow and thought of the shirt and trousers she had given away, she felt grieved; but when she remembered how he had smiled, her heart was glad.

Long did Matrëna lie awake, and she noticed that Simon also was awake—he drew the coat towards him.

"Simon!"

"Well?"

"You have had the last of the bread and I have not put any to rise. I don't know what we shall do tomorrow. Perhaps I can borrow some of neighbor Martha."

"If we're alive we shall find something to eat."

The woman lay still awhile, and then said, "He seems a good man, but why does he not tell us who he is?"

---

6. **kvas** (kväs): a Russian drink, similar to beer, made from fermented grains.

7. **on the stove:** The large stoves and ovens in Russian peasant homes often had tops large enough to sleep on for extra warmth.

"I suppose he has his reasons."

"Simon!"

"Well?"

"We give; but why does nobody give us anything?"

Simon did not know what to say; so he only said, "Let us stop talking" and turned over and went to sleep.

V

n the morning Simon awoke. The children were still asleep; his wife had gone to the neighbor's to borrow some bread. The stranger alone was sitting on the bench, dressed in the old shirt and trousers, and looking upwards. His face was brighter than it had been the day before.

Simon said to him, "Well, friend; the belly wants bread and the naked body clothes. One has to work for a living. What work do you know?"

"I do not know any."

This surprised Simon, but he said, "Men who want to learn can learn anything."

"Men work and I will work also."

"What is your name?"

"Michael."

"Well, Michael, if you don't wish to talk about yourself, that is your own affair; but you'll have to earn a living for yourself. If you will work as I tell you, I will give you food and shelter."

"May God reward you! I will learn. Show me what to do."

Simon took yarn, put it round his thumb and began to twist it.

Grain Harvest (1908), Natalia Sergeevna Goncharova. Oil on canvas, 96 cm × 103 cm, The State Russian Museum, St. Petersburg, Russia.

"It is easy enough—see!"

Michael watched him, put some yarn round his own thumb in the same way, caught the knack, and twisted the yarn also.

Then Simon showed him how to wax the thread. This also Michael mastered. Next Simon showed him how to twist the bristle in, and how to sew, and this, too, Michael learned at once.

Whatever Simon showed him he understood at once, and after three days he worked as if he had sewn boots all his life. He worked without stopping and ate little. When work was over he sat silently, looking upwards. He hardly went into the street, spoke only when necessary, and neither joked nor laughed. They never saw him smile, except that first evening when Matrëna gave him supper.

VI

Day by day and week by week the year went round. Michael lived and worked with Simon. His fame spread till people said that no one sewed boots so neatly and strongly as Simon's workman, Michael; from all the district round people came to Simon for their boots, and he began to be well off.

One winter day, as Simon and Michael sat working, a carriage on sledge-runners, with three horses and with bells, drove up to the hut. They looked out of the window; the carriage stopped at their door; a fine servant jumped down from the box and opened the door. A gentleman in a fur coat got out and walked up to Simon's hut. Up jumped Matrëna and opened the door wide. The gentleman stooped to enter the hut, and when he drew himself up again his head nearly reached the ceiling and he seemed quite to fill his end of the room.

Simon rose, bowed, and looked at the gentleman with astonishment. He had never seen any one like him. Simon himself was lean, Michael was thin, and Matrëna was dry as a bone, but

this man was like some one from another world: red-faced, burly, with a neck like a bull's, and looking altogether as if he were cast in iron.

The gentleman puffed, threw off his fur coat, sat down on the bench, and said, "Which of you is the master bootmaker?"

"I am, your Excellency," said Simon, coming forward.

Then the gentleman shouted to his lad, "Hey, Fédka, bring the leather!"

The servant ran in, bringing a parcel. The gentleman took the parcel and put it on the table.

"Untie it," said he. The lad untied it.

The gentleman pointed to the leather.

"Look here, shoemaker," said he, "do you see this leather?"

"Yes, your honor."

"But do you know what sort of leather it is?"

Simon felt the leather and said, "It is good leather."

"Good, indeed! Why, you fool, you never saw such leather before in your life. It's German and cost twenty rubles."

Simon was frightened and said, "Where should I ever see leather like that?"

"Just so! Now, can you make it into boots for me?"

"Yes, your Excellency, I can."

Then the gentleman shouted at him: "You *can*, can you? Well, remember whom you are to make them for, and what the leather is. You must make me boots that will wear for a year, neither losing shape nor coming unsewn. If you can do it, take the leather and cut it up; but if you can't, say so. I warn you now, if your boots come unsewn or lose shape within a year I will have you put in prison. If they don't burst or lose shape for a year, I will pay you ten rubles for your work."

Simon was frightened and did not know what to say. He glanced at Michael and nudging him with his elbow, whispered: "Shall I take the work?"

Michael nodded his head as if to say, "Yes, take it."

Simon did as Michael advised and undertook

to make boots that would not lose shape or split for a whole year.

Calling his servant, the gentleman told him to pull the boot off his left leg, which he stretched out.

"Take my measure!" said he.

Simon stitched a paper measure seventeen inches long, smoothed it out, knelt down, wiped his hands well on his apron so as not to soil the gentleman's sock, and began to measure. He measured the sole, and round the instep, and began to measure the calf of the leg, but the paper was too short. The calf of the leg was as thick as a beam.

"Mind you don't make it too tight in the leg."

Simon stitched on another strip of paper. The gentleman twitched his toes about in his sock looking round at those in the hut, and as he did so he noticed Michael.

"Whom have you there?" asked he.

"That is my workman. He will sew the boots."

"Mind," said the gentleman to Michael, "remember to make them so that they will last me a year."

Simon also looked at Michael and saw that Michael was not looking at the gentleman, but was gazing into the corner behind the gentleman, as if he saw some one there. Michael looked and looked, and suddenly he smiled, and his face became brighter.

"What are you grinning at, you fool?" thundered the gentleman. "You had better look to it that the boots are ready in time."

"They shall be ready in good time," said Michael.

"Mind it is so," said the gentleman, and he put on his boots and his fur coat, wrapped the latter round him, and went to the door. But he forgot to stoop, and struck his head against the lintel.[8]

He swore and rubbed his head. Then he took his seat in the carriage and drove away.

When he had gone, Simon said: "There's a figure of a man for you! You could not kill him with a mallet. He almost knocked out the lintel, but little harm it did him."

And Matrëna said: "Living as he does, how should he not have grown strong? Death itself can't touch such a rock as that."

VII

Then Simon said to Michael: "Well, we have taken the work, but we must see we don't get into trouble over it. The leather is dear, and the gentleman hot-tempered. We must make no mistakes. Come, your eye is truer and your hands have become nimbler than mine, so you take this measure and cut out the boots. I will finish off the sewing of the vamps."[9]

Michael did as he was told. He took the leather, spread it out on the table, folded it in two, took a knife and began to cut out.

Matrëna came and watched him cutting and was surprised to see how he was doing it. Matrëna was accustomed to seeing boots made, and she looked and saw that Michael was not cutting the leather for boots, but was cutting it round.

She wished to say something, but she thought to herself: "Perhaps I do not understand how gentlemen's boots should be made. I suppose Michael knows more about it—and I won't interfere."

When Michael had cut up the leather he took a thread and began to sew not with two ends, as boots are sewn, but with a single end, as for soft slippers.

Again Matrëna wondered, but again she did not interfere. Michael sewed on steadily till noon. Then Simon rose for dinner, looked around, and saw that Michael had made slippers out of the gentleman's leather.

"Ah!" groaned Simon, and he thought, "How is it that Michael, who has been with me a whole year and never made a mistake before, should do

---

8. **lintel:** the horizontal beam at the top of a door frame.
9. **vamps:** the upper parts of shoes or boots, covering the instep or the instep and the toes.

such a dreadful thing? The gentleman ordered high boots, welted,[10] with whole fronts, and Michael has made soft slippers with single soles and has wasted the leather. What am I to say to the gentleman? I can never replace leather such as this."

And he said to Michael, "What are you doing, friend? You have ruined me! You know the gentleman ordered high boots, but see what you have made!"

Hardly had he begun to rebuke Michael, when "rat-tat" went the iron ring hung at the door. Some one was knocking. They looked out of the window; a man had come on horseback and was fastening his horse. They opened the door, and the servant who had been with the gentleman came in.

"Good day," said he.

"Good day," replied Simon. "What can we do for you?"

"My mistress has sent me about the boots."

"What about the boots?"

"Why, my master no longer needs them. He is dead."

"Is it possible?"

"He did not live to get home after leaving you but died in the carriage. When we reached home and the servants came to help him alight, he rolled over like a sack. He was dead already, and so stiff that he could hardly be got out of the carriage. My mistress sent me here, saying: 'Tell the boot-maker that the gentleman who ordered boots of him and left the leather for them no longer needs the boots, but that he must quickly make soft slippers for the corpse. Wait till they are ready and bring them back with you.' That is why I have come."

Michael gathered up the remnants of the leather; rolled them up, took the soft slippers he had made, slapped them together, wiped them down with his apron, and handed them and the roll of leather to the servant, who took them and said: "Good-bye, masters, and good day to you!"

ACTIVE READING

SUMMARIZE Summarize in a sentence or two what happens in sections VI and VII of this story.

VIII

Another year passed, and another, and Michael was now living his sixth year with Simon. He lived as before. He went nowhere, only spoke when necessary, and had only smiled twice in all those years—one when Matrëna gave him food, and a second time when the gentleman was in their hut. Simon was more than pleased with his workman. He never now asked him where he came from and only feared lest Michael should go away.

They were all at home one day. Matrëna was putting iron pots in the oven; the children were running along the benches and looking out of the window; Simon was sewing at one window and Michael was fastening on a heel at the other.

One of the boys ran along the bench to Michael, leant on his shoulder, and looked out of the window.

"Look, Uncle Michael! There is a lady with little girls! She seems to be coming here. And one of the girls is lame."

When the boy said that, Michael dropped his work, turned to the window, and looked out into the street.

Simon was surprised. Michael never used to look out into the street, but now he pressed against the window, staring at something. Simon also looked out and saw that a well-dressed woman was really coming to his hut, leading by the hand two little girls in fur coats and woolen shawls. The girls could hardly be told one from the other, except that one of them was crippled in her left leg and walked with a limp.

The woman stepped into the porch and entered the passage. Feeling about for the entrance she found the latch, which she lifted, and opened the door. She let the two girls go in first, and followed them into the hut.

"Good day, good folk!"

---

10. **welted:** with a leather strip stitched between the sole and the upper.

"Pray come in," said Simon. "What can we do for you?"

The woman sat down by the table. The two little girls pressed close to her knees, afraid of the people in the hut.

"I want leather shoes made for these two little girls, for spring."

"We can do that. We never have made such small shoes, but we can make them; either welted or turnover shoes, linen lined. My man, Michael, is a master at the work."

Simon glanced at Michael and saw that he had left his work and was sitting with his eyes fixed on the little girls. Simon was surprised. It was true the girls were pretty, with black eyes, plump, and rosy-cheeked, and they wore nice kerchiefs and fur coats, but still Simon could not understand why Michael should look at them like that—just as if he had known them before. He was puzzled but went on talking with the woman and arranging the price. Having fixed it, he prepared the measure. The woman lifted the lame girl on to her lap and said: "Take two measures from this little girl. Make one shoe for the lame foot and three for the sound one. They both have the same-sized feet. They are twins."

Simon took the measure and, speaking of the lame girl, said: "How did it happen to her? She is such a pretty girl. Was she born so?"

"No, her mother crushed her leg."

Then Matrëna joined in. She wondered who this woman was and whose the children were, so she said: "Are not you their mother, then?"

"No, my good woman; I am neither their mother nor any relation to them. They were quite strangers to me, but I adopted them."

"They are not your children and yet you are so fond of them?"

"How can I help being fond of them? I fed them both at my own breasts. I had a child of my own, but God took him. I was not so fond of him as I now am of these."

"Then whose children are they?"

IX

The woman, having begun talking, told them the whole story.

"It is about six years since their parents died, both in one week: their father was buried on the Tuesday, and their mother died on the Friday. These orphans were born three days after their father's death, and their mother did not live another day. My husband and I were then living as peasants in the village. We were neighbors of theirs, our yard being next to theirs. Their father was a lonely man, a wood-cutter in the forest. When felling trees one day they let one fall on him. It fell across his body and crushed his bowels out. They hardly got him home before his soul went to God; and that same week his wife gave birth to twins—these little girls. She was poor and alone; she had no one, young or old, with her. Alone she gave them birth, and alone she met her death.

"The next morning I went to see her, but when I entered the hut, she, poor thing, was already stark and cold. In dying she had rolled on to this child and crushed her leg. The village folk came to the hut, washed the body, laid her out, made a coffin, and buried her. They were good folk. The babies were left alone. What was to be done with them? I was the only woman there who had a baby at the time. I was nursing my first-born—eight weeks old. So I took them for a time. The peasants came together, and thought and thought what to do with them; and at last they said to me: 'For the present, Mary, you had better keep the girls, and later on we will arrange what to do for them.' So I nursed the sound one at my breast, but at first I did not feed this crippled one. I did not suppose she would live. But then I thought to myself, why should the poor innocent suffer? I pitied her and began to feed her. And so I fed my own boy and these two—the three of them—at my own breast. I was young and strong and had good food, and God gave me so much milk that at times it even overflowed. I used sometimes to feed two at a time, while the third was waiting. When one had had enough I nursed

Photo by Kari Haavisto.

the third. And God so ordered it that these grew up, while my own was buried before he was two years old. And I had no more children, though we prospered. Now my husband is working for the corn merchant at the mill. The pay is good and we are well off. But I have no children of my own, and how lonely I should be without these little girls! How can I help loving them! They are the joy of my life!"

ACTIVE READING

CLARIFY How were the twins able to survive after their mother's death?

She pressed the lame little girl to her with one hand, while with the other she wiped the tears from her cheeks.

And Matrëna sighed, and said: "The proverb is true that says, 'One may live without father or mother, but one cannot live without God.' "

So they talked together, when suddenly the whole hut was lighted up as though by summer lightning from the corner where Michael sat. They all looked towards him and saw him sitting, his hands folded on his knees, gazing upwards and smiling.

The woman went away with the girls. Michael rose from the bench, put down his work, and took off his apron. Then, bowing low to Simon and his wife, he said: "Farewell, masters. God has forgiven me. I ask your forgiveness, too, for anything done amiss."

And they saw that a light shone from Michael. And Simon rose, bowed down to Michael, and said: "I see, Michael, that you are no common man, and I can neither keep you nor question you. Only tell me this: how is it that when I found you and brought you home, you were gloomy, and when my wife gave you food you smiled at her and became brighter? Then when the gentleman came to order the boots, you smiled again and became brighter still? And now, when this woman brought the little girls, you smiled a third time and have become as bright as day? Tell me, Michael, why does your face shine so, and why did you smile those three times?"

And Michael answered: "Light shines from me because I have been punished, but now God has pardoned me. And I smiled three times, because God sent me to learn three truths, and I have learnt them. One I learnt when your wife pitied me, and that is why I smiled the first time. The second I learnt when the rich man ordered the boots, and then I smiled again. And now, when I saw those little girls, I learnt the third and last, and I smiled the third time."

And Simon said, "Tell me, Michael, what did God punish you for? and what were the three truths? that I, too, may know them."

And Michael answered: "God punished me for disobeying him. I was an angel in heaven and disobeyed God. God sent me to fetch a woman's

soul. I flew to earth and saw a sick woman lying alone who had just given birth to twin girls. They moved feebly at their mother's side but she could not lift them to her breast. When she saw me, she understood that God had sent me for her soul, and she wept and said: 'Angel of God! My husband has just been buried, killed by a falling tree. I have neither sister, nor aunt, nor mother: no one to care for my orphans. Do not take my soul! Let me nurse my babes, feed them, and set them on their feet before I die. Children cannot live without father or mother.' And I hearkened to her. I placed one child at her breast and gave the other into her arms, and returned to the Lord in heaven. I flew to the Lord, and said: 'I could not take the soul of the mother. Her husband was killed by a tree; the woman has twins and prays that her soul may not be taken. She says: "Let me nurse and feed my children, and set them on their feet. Children cannot live without father or mother." I have not taken her soul.' And God said: 'Go—take the mother's soul, and learn three truths: Learn *What dwells in man, What is not given to man,* and *What men live by.* When thou hast learnt these things, thou shalt return to heaven.' So I flew again to earth and took the

ACTIVE READING

CLARIFY For what was Michael punished?

mother's soul. The babes dropped from her breasts. Her body rolled over on the bed and crushed one babe, twisting its leg. I rose above the village, wishing to take her soul to God, but a wind seized me and my wings drooped and dropped off. Her soul rose alone to God, while I fell to earth by the roadside."

XI

And Simon and Matrёna understood who it was that had lived with them and whom they had clothed and fed. And they wept with awe and with joy. And the angel said: "I was alone in the field, naked. I had never known human needs, cold and hunger, till I became a man. I was famished, frozen, and did not know what to do. I saw, near the field I was in, a shrine built for God, and I went to it hoping to find shelter. But the shrine was locked and I could not enter. So I sat down behind the shrine to shelter myself at least from the wind. Evening drew on, I was hungry, frozen, and in pain. Suddenly I heard a man coming along the road. He carried a pair of boots and was talking to himself. For the first time since I became a man I saw the mortal face of a man, and his face seemed terrible to me and I turned from it. And I heard the man talking to himself of how to cover his body from the cold in winter, and how to feed wife and children. And I thought: 'I am perishing of cold and hunger and here is a man thinking only of how to clothe himself and his wife, and how to get bread for themselves. He cannot help me.' When the man saw me he frowned and became still more terrible and passed me by on the other side. I despaired; but suddenly I heard him coming back. I looked up and did not recognize the same man: before, I had seen death in his face; but now he was alive and I recognized in him the presence of God. He came up to me, clothed me, took me with him, and brought me to his home. I entered the house; a woman came to meet us and began to speak. The woman was still more terrible than the man had been; the spirit of death came from her mouth; I could not breathe for the stench[11] of death that spread around her. She wished to drive me out into the cold, and I knew that if she did so she would die. Suddenly her husband spoke to her of God, and the woman changed at once. And when she brought me food and looked at me, I glanced at her and saw that death no longer dwelt in her; she had become alive, and in her too I saw God.

"Then I remembered the first lesson God had set me: *'Learn what dwells in man.'* And I understood that in man dwells Love! I was glad that God had already begun to show me what He had promised, and I smiled for the first time.

---

11. **stench:** foul smell.

But I had not yet learnt all. I did not yet know *What is not given to man,* and *What men live by.*

"I lived with you and a year passed. A man came to order boots that should wear for a year without losing shape or cracking. I looked at him, and suddenly, behind his shoulder, I saw my comrade—the angel of death. None but me saw that angel; but I knew him, and knew that before the sun set he would take the rich man's soul. And I thought to myself, 'The man is making preparation for a year and does not know that he will die before evening.' And I remembered God's second saying, '*Learn what is not given to man.*'

"What dwells in man I already knew. Now I learnt what is not given him. It is not given to man to know his own needs. And I smiled for the second time. I was glad to have seen my comrade angel—glad also that God had revealed to me the second saying.

"But I still did not know all. I did not know *What men live by.* And I lived on, waiting till God should reveal to me the last lesson. In the sixth year came the girl-twins with the woman; and I recognized the girls and heard how they had been kept alive. Having heard the story, I thought, 'Their mother besought[12] me for the children's sake, and I believed her when she said that children cannot live without father or mother; but a stranger has nursed them and has brought them up.' And when the woman showed her love for the children that were not her own and wept over them, I saw in her the living God, and understood *What men live by.* And I knew that God had revealed to me the last lesson and had forgiven my sin. And then I smiled for the third time."

XII

And the angel's body was bared, and he was clothed in light so that eye could not look on him; and his voice grew louder, as though it came not from him but from heaven above. And the angel said: "I have learnt that all men live not by care for themselves, but by love.

"It was not given to the mother to know what her children needed for their life. Nor was it given to the rich man to know what he himself needed. Nor is it given to any man to know whether, when evening comes, he will need boots for his body or slippers for his corpse.

"I remained alive when I was a man, not by care of myself but because love was present in a passer-by and because he and his wife pitied and loved me. The orphans remained alive not because of their mother's care, but because there was love in the heart of a woman, a stranger to them, who pitied and loved them. And all men live not by the thought they spend on their own welfare, but because love exists in man.

"I knew before that God gave life to men and desires that they should live; now I understood more than that.

"I understood that God does not wish men to live apart, and therefore he does not reveal to them what each one needs for himself; but he wishes them to live united, and therefore reveals to each of them what is necessary for all.

"I have now understood that though it seems to men that they live by care for themselves, in truth it is love alone by which they live. He who has love, is in God, and God is in him, for God is love."

And the angel sang praise to God, so that the hut trembled at his voice. The roof opened, and a column of fire rose from earth to heaven. Simon and his wife and children fell to the ground. Wings appeared upon the angel's shoulders and he rose into the heavens.

And when Simon came to himself the hut stood as before, and there was no one in it but his own family. ❖

Translated by Louise and Aylmer Maude

---

12. **besought** (bĭ-sôt′): begged.

Connect to the Literature

1. **What Do You Think?** What is your reaction to Michael's explanation of what men live by?

   Comprehension Check
   - Why did Simon need to buy some sheepskins?
   - What was Matrëna's initial reaction to Michael?

Think Critically

2. Do you think Simon and Matrëna are basically similar or basically different? Explain your answer.

   THINK ABOUT
   - their initial reactions to Michael and their later attitudes toward him
   - how each of them copes with poverty
   - the role of God in each of their lives

3. Do you think Michael has deserved to be punished by God? Give reasons for your opinion.

4. How would you explain the relationship between the three lessons Michael learns?

5. **ACTIVE READING** **SUMMARIZING TEXT** Review the summaries you created in your ▮▮ **READER'S NOTEBOOK**. What subtitle would you give to each of the four parts? Compare your subtitles with those of a partner, and discuss which you think are most appropriate.

Extend Interpretations

6. **Connect to Life** What do you think would happen if Michael appeared in your neighborhood as a stranger in need of food, clothing, and shelter? Do you think it would be possible for him to learn the same lessons? Give reasons for your answers.

7. **Points of Comparison** Both Tolstoy's story and Kipling's story "The Miracle of Purun Bhagat" are concerned with the qualities of a good and moral life. What similarities and differences do you think there are between the moral lessons that can be inferred from each story? Do you think the **theme** of either story is valid as a principle for living today? Explain your opinion.

Literary Analysis

FOLK TALE A **folk tale** is a story that is handed down, usually by word of mouth, from generation to generation. In addition to showing how the inhabitants of a region live and what their values are, most folk tales have some or all of the following characteristics:

- They usually suggest or explicitly state a moral.
- Many folk tales involve supernatural elements.
- Often, things happen in threes in folk tales.

Cooperative Learning Activity With three or four classmates, list the elements of folk tales that are featured in Tolstoy's story. Then discuss what elements Tolstoy adds that make this more than just a retelling of a traditional tale.

REVIEW **AUTHOR'S PURPOSE**
Although a writer may fulfill more than one **purpose** in a work, one is usually the most important. What do you think might have been Tolstoy's main purpose for writing "What Men Live By"? What other purposes does the story fulfill?

REVIEW **SETTING** **Setting,** the time and place of a narrative's action, can have an important impact on what happens and why. Think about the relationship between the setting and the events in "What Men Live By." Do you think the story could have taken place in a large, modern city? Why or why not?

*Choices&*CHALLENGES

Writing Options

1. New Episode Write an episode that occurs in the lives of Simon and Matrëna after Michael has left them. Imitate the style of the story, and try to show how Michael has affected the couple's life.

2. Maxims for Living Write your own three maxims that embody ideas that might help people lead more meaningful and rewarding lives. Feel free to include ideas that are very different from those in the story.

3. Newspaper Report As a reporter for the local newspaper, write a news story on Michael's mysterious ascent to heaven. Include eyewitness accounts from Simon and Matrëna, as well as information from the neighbors and local residents.

4. Analytical Essay Write an essay in which you analyze the difficulty of leading a good life in a consumer society. What problems does a person today face in leading a simple life in a materialistic world? Place the essay in your **Working Portfolio.**

5. ▮ Points of Comparison ▮ Michael learns his lesson while living with a simple peasant family, and Purun Bhagat in Kipling's "The Miracle of Purun Bhagat" deliberately chooses a simple lifestyle. Write an essay in which you compare the ways in which these stories extol the virtues of a simple life. How is simplicity of life connected to the moral lesson of each story?

Writing Handbook
See page 1367: Compare and Contrast.

Activities & Explorations

1. Storyboard Illustrations Design a storyboard, or series of sketches, for one part of the story. Each sketch should show the setting and the actions of the characters. Display your storyboard in class. **~ ART**

2. Newspaper Display Near the end of the story, Michael says, "I have learnt that all men live not by care for themselves, but by love." With your classmates, collect and create a display of newspaper columns that could serve to illustrate Michael's comment by showing that people still help one another. **~ VIEWING AND REPRESENTING**

3. Commemorative Monument Design a monument to be placed at the spot where the angel first appeared to Simon. Try to visually convey the lesson that Michael learned during his time with Simon. **~ ART**

4. Alternate Titles The title of a literary work often contains important clues to the content, tone, and theme of the work. In a group, try to come up with alternate titles for Tolstoy's story that manage to convey its central themes. **~ SPEAKING AND LISTENING**

Inquiry & Research

1. Rich and Poor Find out about the differences between the economic conditions of Russian aristocrats and peasants in the 19th century. What were the causes of the huge economic gap between the rich and the poor? Report your findings to the class.

2. Angels on the Loose Compile a list of movies, television shows, and works of literature that feature angels who descend to earth. How would you account for the recent increased interest in angels?

Art Connection

Reflected Mood Look again at the painting *Nightfall at Hradčany* on page 918. In your opinion, how closely does this painting reflect the mood of the story?

Leo Tolstoy
1828–1910

Other Works
War and Peace
Anna Karenina
"How Much Land Does a Man Need?"
"Three Questions"
"Two Old Men"
"Alyosha Gorshok"

Youth and Young Adulthood Although Leo Tolstoy was orphaned as a young child, his early years were rather uneventful. He was raised by relatives and lived most of his life on the family estate, Yasnaya Polyana, about 100 miles south of Moscow. At the age of 16, he entered a university, but he returned home after a few years to educate himself. In 1852, determined to change his rather aimless lifestyle, he joined the army and began to spend much of his free time writing. When his stories based on his experiences during the Crimean War were well received, his literary career was launched.

Marriage and the Writing Life In the late 1850s, Tolstoy returned to his family estate and, unhappy with the education available to the peasants there, developed his own school, eliminating all grades, punishments, and rewards. In 1862 he married, and for the next 15 years he devoted his time to his wife, his 13 children, and the writing of his two greatest works, *War and Peace* and *Anna Karenina*. It took him 7 years to complete *War and Peace*, now regarded as one of the greatest novels in world literature.

Spiritual Crisis In spite of his relative success in life, Tolstoy began to suffer a spiritual and emotional crisis during his middle years. He found comfort in Christian principles and decided that he must shed his worldly possessions, give away his wealth, and live the honest, simple life of a Russian peasant. His resolve was not shared by his family, however, and bitter quarrels ensued. To appease them, Tolstoy signed his entire estate over to his wife, thereafter devoting his time to writing essays and stories dealing with religious, social, and moral issues. He dressed in the clothes of a peasant, gave up drinking and smoking, and became a vegetarian. He simplified his life as much as possible but remained unsatisfied. Finally, at the age of 82, accompanied by his youngest daughter and a doctor, Tolstoy left home to search for a simpler existence. He died of pneumonia in a train station a few days later.

Author Activity

War Reporter Research Tolstoy's activities as a reporter during the Crimean War, when Russian forces battled against a coalition of English, French, and Turkish troops. Find out about the outcome of the war, as well as the contribution that Tolstoy's wartime experiences may have made to his ability to write war scenes in his great novel of Napoleon's invasion of Russia, *War and Peace*.

Writing Workshop

Examining the parts of a subject . . .

From Reading to Writing Manners and proper social behavior are concerns to people in any age—from the Victorians to present-day experts such as Miss Manners. Although social customs change over time, kindness and courtesy never go out of fashion. The essay on the next page **analyzes** the lack of manners in contemporary society and expresses the writer's concern over this matter. In an analysis the writer breaks down a subject into its individual parts and studies how the parts fit together. Analysis can be applied to various subjects from science to history to literature.

For Your Portfolio

WRITING PROMPT Write an essay in which you present an analysis of the subject of your choice.

> **Purpose:** To explain the parts of a subject and how they work together
>
> **Audience:** Your classmates, friends, family, or a larger audience

---

Basics in a Box

Subject Analysis at a Glance

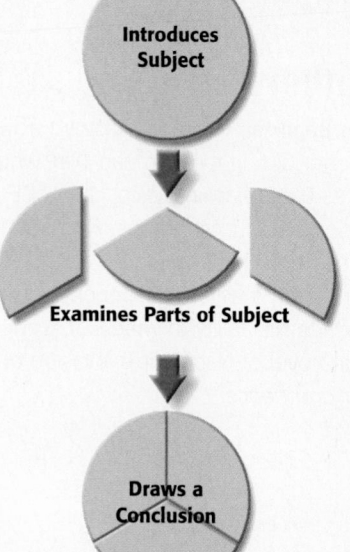

Introduces Subject

Examines Parts of Subject

Draws a Conclusion

RUBRIC Standards for Writing

A successful subject analysis should

- introduce the subject in an interesting, informative manner
- identify the parts that compose the subject
- examine and explain each part
- present information in a logical order
- show how the parts relate to the whole subject and support the main idea or thesis
- include an effective introduction, body, and conclusion

Analyzing a Professional Model

L. A. Wilson
Freelance Writer

No One Stops to Say "Thank You" Anymore

I am sitting in a local restaurant offering takeout homestyle meals, surrounded by exhausted but happy shoppers, families out for Friday night dinner, and students taking a break from college exams. The warm room buzzes with conversation. A well-known local homeless man—very scruffy but clean—comes in, places an order, pays for it, then sits quietly waiting for his dinner. All talk stops. No one looks at him and several diners leave. He is aware of the general discomfort his presence has caused. When his takeout is ready, he gathers up his numerous bags and his dinner and, laden down, advances to the door to go back to the streets. Just as he reaches the door and begins to shift bundles to free a hand, a well-dressed man coming to the restaurant steps aside and holds the door for him. The homeless man stops and says, "Thank you very much."

What struck me about this Dickensian encounter was not the wealthier man helping out the less fortunate one. It was the homeless man stopping to thank him despite being desperate to escape a room full of disapproving people. No doubt he also thanked whoever had given him the money to buy dinner. No one had thanked the young people behind the counter who dished up mashed potatoes for them. Had I taken a poll of the room, though, I bet everyone there would have considered themselves as having more manners than a person who lives on the streets.

But how many of us are truly well mannered? <u>Some observations have been surprising.</u>

When I let someone into my lane of traffic, men almost always acknowledge this courtesy with a wave of the hand; women (the "polite" sex) hardly ever do. More women than men (the "chivalrous" sex) hold open doors for those behind them; teenage boys commit this nicety the least. And I no longer see mothers instructing a child, boy or girl, to hold open a door when several people are approaching—something expected of all boys when I was growing up.

<u>Manners are a tool to remind us of others around us. Our actions affect each other; there is always give and take. However, if youth today are any indication, we are truly destined to become a society of people who think only of themselves.</u> . . .

I have yet to receive an apology from a child who just ran over my foot while chasing a sibling, and only half the time have the parents apologized. Often they simply gather up the children, making no eye contact, and take them to another part of the store to run around. If a child isn't made to deal with a minor situation, how will one ever handle a major *faux pas* (which we all inevitably commit at some point)?

I have noticed that children are not even being schooled in social

---

❶ This writer introduces the subject with an interesting anecdote.

Other Options:
- Pose a question.
- Present a startling, unusual or interesting fact.

❷ Uses contrast to examine the meaning in the anecdote

❸ Signals the organizational structure

❹ Identifies the first observation: everyday courtesies

❺ States the main idea or thesis

❻ Examines a second observation— inadequate parenting—and supports the analysis with examples

graces. At a Sunday brunch, a clown was making balloon animals for the children. My friend's daughter, Sarah, stood by me waiting her turn. One by one the children grabbed their balloons and—yes—ran. I was the only adult present who prompted "What do you say?" when the clown handed Sarah her balloon. The clown beamed at us, grateful he had actually been acknowledged.

I don't blame the children, <u>however.</u> They emulate what they see. And what they are seeing is a society focused solely on acquisition—be it the dream house or another drink in a restaurant or a space on a crowded freeway—without ever stopping to thank the source.

Rude language is now so commonplace it is accepted behavior. And I'm not talking about the obviously blue vocabulary in books and movies. I'm referring to inconsiderate word choice. For example, while discussing a story idea with an editor, a very young staff member asked if I was the "chick" who had called for information. I said nothing, knowing that a show of displeasure would have labeled *me* oversensitive rather than *him* rude.

Most people today feel proud to have built a society that treats the races, sexes, and economic classes more equally than ever before. And, yes, we have made real strides in these areas. But isn't it ironic that these same people don't find it necessary to say "Excuse me" to an older couple walking very slowly in front of them, before zooming around the couple?

It's not necessary to provide yet another analysis of the disintegration of the family or the breakdown of the social fabric or the price of democracy to explain what has happened to our society. The matter at hand is simply to thank the next person who provides a helping hand when needed.

In a crowded world, manners are of vital importance. Small, friendly human interactions help ease the everyday stress of having to hurry, trying to squeeze onto a crowded thoroughfare, standing in one more line to deal with a clerk of some kind, or calling a customer-service representative for the third time about a mistake on a bill. Manners make us aware that everything we have derives from a source. <u>Are we really so pressured that we cannot stop to observe simple courtesy?</u>

❼ Uses a transition to connect the lack of manners in children with poor manners in adults.

❽ Examines a third element—inappropriate language.

❾ Examines the last part—lack of respect for the aged

❿ This writer concludes with a question to make the reader think about the issues raised.

Other Options:
· Summarize the parts to explain how they work together.
· Draw a general conclusion from specific information presented.

Writing Your Analysis

❶ Prewriting

There are no dull subjects. There are only dull writers.
H. L. Mencken

You might begin your search for a topic by listing problems or issues that you want to understand better. For example, you might analyze issues that interest you, such as curfew laws, new rules involving teenage drivers, or censorship on the Internet. See the **Idea Bank** for more suggestions. After you have chosen your topic, follow the steps below.

Planning Your Analysis

▶ **1. Explore the topic.** What do you know about the topic? What do you need to know? Make a list of questions about your subject. What are good sources of information—books? magazines? reference materials? interviews?

▶ **2. Think about your purpose and audience.** Do you want to inform readers? prove a point? persuade them to a course of action? What will your audience already know about the subject? What background should you provide? What terms must you define? What tone and voice will be appropriate?

▶ **3. Write a thesis statement.** What is the main idea that you want to communicate? Write one or two sentences that state your main idea.

▶ **4. Break the subject into parts.** When you analyze, you break down the subject into its parts. Will your analysis include steps in a process, characteristics, stages of development, or other elements?

❷ Drafting

To begin your **draft,** try to set down everything you want to say, keeping your overall purpose in mind. You can always add details later or take out what you don't need. You may find that what you write causes you to change your thesis or main idea statement.

Now you are ready to **organize** your ideas. Although your topic will determine how you proceed, follow the steps below to guide the organizational form of your analysis:

- Provide a **provocative introduction** that quickly attracts reader interest.
- **Identify the subject** you plan to analyze in a sentence or short paragraph.
- **Describe the parts** that make up your subject.
- **Examine each part** in relationship to other parts or to the subject as a whole.

IDEABank

1. Your Working Portfolio
Build on one of the **Writing Options** you completed earlier in this unit:

- **Analysis Essay,** p. 853
- **A Letter in Response,** p. 867
- **Mr. Hodgson's Editorial,** p. 884
- **Essay Analyzing Values,** p. 913
- **Analytical Essay,** p. 930

2. Virtual Field Trip
Explore a museum site on the Internet. Choose a topic to analyze based on your online visit.

3. Television Guide
Look through your local television guide for programs on scientific or social topics that interest you. Watch one of these shows and jot down ideas for an analysis.

Ask Your Peer Reader

- What were the key points of my analysis? Which terms, if any, should I define?
- Describe the structure of my analysis.
- What could I change or add to make my analysis clearer?

Think about how you can **elaborate** on your ideas so they are clear to your readers. You might try one or more of the following strategies.

- **Description** Describe each part in detail.
- **Comparison** Show how your subject or one of its parts resembles or differs from another relevant subject. For instance, *a teenager in love is like a traveler on a fog-shrouded street.*
- **Definition** Define key parts, characteristics, or terms for difficult or technical subjects.

❸ Revising

Need revising help?

Review the **Rubric,** p. 932

Consider **peer reader** comments

Check **Revision Guidelines,** p. 1355

TARGET SKILL ▶ **KEEPING SIMILAR IDEAS PARALLEL** As you break down your subject into its components, be sure that sentence parts which are parallel in meaning are also parallel in structure. One error in parallel construction occurs when *and* is used to join unequal constructions. Remember, join nouns with nouns, verbs with verbs, and phrases with phrases.

> Good table manners allow you and your guests to enjoy a meal and ~~be appreciating~~ *to appreciate* each other's company. It is disrespectful to others to ~~be gobbling~~ *gobble* your food and rush away from the table while others are still eating. As you dine, remember to eat slowly and ~~no~~ chewing your food with your mouth ~~open~~ *closed*.

❹ Editing and Proofreading

Confused by Comparisons?

See the **Grammar Handbook,** pp. 1398–1399

TARGET SKILL ▶ **CORRECT COMPARISONS** In writing an analysis, you may make a number of comparisons. Be careful to avoid double comparisons. A double comparison results when you use *more* and *-er* or *most* and *-est* together.

> If the phone rings during dinner, you might breifly answer it and politely explain that you'll call back after you finish ~~you're~~ *your* meal. Perhaps a ~~more~~ better solution is to let the answering machine take the call.

Publishing IDEAS

- Submit your work to your school or community newspaper.
- Make your analysis into a script for a radio interview. Work with a classmate who will be the interviewer, and present the interview to your class.

More Online: Publishing Options www.mcdougallittell.com

❺ Reflecting

FOR YOUR WORKING PORTFOLIO How did writing your analysis affect your thinking about your subject? How might you pursue your topic further? Attach your answer to your finished work. Save your analysis in your **Working Portfolio.**

Assessment Practice Revising & Editing

Read this passage from the first draft of a student essay. The underlined sections may include the following kinds of errors:

- **lack of parallel structure**
- **punctuation errors**
- **errors in comparative forms**
- **correctly written sentences that should be combined**

For each underlined phrase or sentence, choose the revision that most improves the writing.

Is free verse poetry? <u>Some critics don't think so. Some poets don't think so.</u>
(1)
Both groups feel that poetry requires <u>form, rhyme, and structure.</u> Robert Frost
(2)
said that <u>writing free verse is like tennis without a net.</u> I disagree. Free verse is
(3)
more like a cage without the bars.

These critics seem to believe that a trite rhyme is <u>more better than no</u>
(4)
<u>rhyme at all.</u> Personally, I would rather read <u>a poem without rhyme than with a</u>
<u>tired old rhyme.</u> In fact, most free verse isn't really free. As T. S. Eliot
(5)
<u>recommended, The</u> ghost of some simple meter should lurk behind the arras
(6)
[curtains] in even the 'freest' verse."

---

1. **A.** Some critics and some poets, too, don't think so.
   B. Some critics don't think so; some poets think not.
   C. Some critics and poets don't think so.
   D. Some don't think so.

2. **A.** forms, rhyming, and structure
   B. form, rhyming, and structuring
   C. forms, rhymes, and structure
   D. Correct as is

3. **A.** writing free verse is like playing tennis without a net.
   B. writing free verse is like doing without a net.
   C. writing free verse is tennis without a net.
   D. Correct as is

4. **A.** more than no rhyme at all.
   B. better than no rhyme at all.
   C. best than no rhyme at all.
   D. Correct as is

5. **A.** a poem without rhyme than a tired old rhyming idea.
   B. a poem without rhyme than a tired old one.
   C. a poem without rhyme than one with a tired old rhyme.
   D. Correct as is

6. **A.** recommended; The
   B. recommended. "The
   C. recommended, "The
   D. Correct as is

Need extra help?

See the **Grammar Handbook**
Punctuation Chart, pp. 1413–1414
Structure of Sentences, p. 1409

Clues from Context

As you expand the scope of your reading, you are bound to encounter unfamiliar words and terms. Although you can look up an unfamiliar word in a dictionary or glossary, you can often infer its meaning from clues in the words that surround it—that is, its **context.**

Look at the poem on the right. What clues in these opening lines from "Porphyria's Lover" help you understand the meaning of *vex?*

> The rain set early in tonight,
>   The sullen wind was soon awake,
> It tore the elm-tops down for spite,
>   And did its worst to vex the lake:
>   —Robert Browning, "Porphyria's Lover"

Browning describes the wind as sullen, destructive, and spiteful. The phrase "did its worst" also has negative implications. Together, these details might lead you to conclude that *vex* means "to upset or disturb." A careful reading of the context provides clues to the meaning of the unfamiliar word.

Strategies for Building Vocabulary

There are a number of different types of context clues. Here are a few.

❶ **Definition or Restatement Clue** This type of clue involves a writer's restating an idea in a different way. Words that signal restatements include *or, that is, in other words,* and *also called.* A restatement clue may also be in the form of an **appositive**—a phrase that redefines a word or idea. Consider, for example, the statement "You feel a disgust towards him *now,* an utter repugnance," from Charlotte Brontë's "A Warning Against Passion." Because the phrase "an utter repugnance" is in apposition to *disgust,* you can conclude that *repugnance* is a synonym of *disgust.*

❷ **Comparison Clue** Sometimes the ideas expressed by unfamiliar words are compared to ideas that are easier to understand. Words that may signal such comparison clues are *like, as, similar to, related,* and *than.* A comparison clue can also be a simile or a metaphor. For example, in the sentence "The landslide left a scarp like a deep, red wound on the mountainside," a simile is used to convey a picture of the aftermath of a landslide. From the simile, you can guess that *scarp* refers to a bare slope of soil or rock produced by erosion.

❸ **Contrast Clue** A contrast clue is the opposite of a comparison clue—it explains an unfamiliar word by means of a contrast with another idea. Contrast clues are often signaled by words such as *but, however, yet, on the other hand, different from,* and *in contrast.* Note the use of the signal word *although* in this sentence: "Although the English had expected the prime minister to be a pompous man, he turned out to be humble and unpretentious." Here *although* signals a contrast between the word *pompous* and the words *humble* and *unpretentious.*

❹ **Inference Clue** A word's meaning can sometimes be deduced from details embedded in the larger context of a sentence or a paragraph. A sensitive reader might also pick up clues from the mood or tone of a passage. What clues in the following passage suggest the meaning of *confer?*

> When he returned to India there was a blaze of glory, for the Viceroy himself made a special visit to confer upon the Maharajah the Grand Cross of the Star of India.
> —Rudyard Kipling, "The Miracle of Purun Bhagat"

The tone of this passage is one of triumph: there is a "blaze of glory," the Viceroy makes a "special visit," the Maharajah receives a glorious honor—"the Grand Cross of the Star of India." Together these details suggests that *confer* means "to bestow or award."

EXERCISE Choose five of the Words to Know in this part of Unit Five. For each word, write a sentence containing both the word and a clue to its meaning. Have a classmate identify the context clues that can be used to determine the words' meanings.

Grammar from Literature

Look at the passages below. Notice the kinds of information and detail the highlighted sections provide.

> adverb clause showing time
> **When he first started,** the roar of the world he had left still rang in his ears.
> > —Rudyard Kipling, "The Miracle of Purun Bhagat"
>
> adverb clause showing place
> At night his antelope skin was spread **where the darkness overtook him.**
> > —Rudyard Kipling, "The Miracle of Purun Bhagat"
>
> adverb clause showing condition
> Baby cried all the way, **though she cuddled him up in her shawl.**
> > —Elizabeth Cleghorn Gaskell, "Christmas Storms and Sunshine"

The blue sections are adverb clauses: clauses that modify verbs, adjectives, and other adverbs. Writers use adverb clauses to show relationships between ideas. Notice the words that introduce the clauses. They indicate how the information in the clause is related to the rest of the sentence. These introductory words are called **subordinating conjunctions.** In the following list, some subordinating conjunctions are classified according to the relationships they show.

Cause: *because, since, so that*
Condition: *although, as if, if, though, unless*
Place: *where*
Time: *after, as, before, since, until, when, while*

Using Adverb Clauses in Your Writing As you revise, examine how you have shown relationships between ideas. Look for places where an adverb clause with a well-chosen subordinating conjunction would make relationships between ideas clearer.

> In "My Last Duchess," the duke was troubled. His wife may have had an eye toward romance elsewhere.
>
> adverb clause
> In "My Last Duchess," the duke was troubled **because his wife may have had an eye toward romance elsewhere.**

Usage Tip When you use a pronoun in a subordinate clause that follows an independent clause, make sure there is no confusion about which noun the pronoun is replacing. In other words, make sure the antecedent of the pronoun is clear.

> UNCLEAR
> unclear antecedent   pronoun
> Ulysses **may see** Achilles **if** he **reaches the Happy Isles**

In the sentence above, it is not clear whether it is Ulysses or Achilles who may reach the Happy Isles. The problem can be solved by restructuring the sentence.

> CLEAR
> antecedent   pronoun
> If Ulysses **reaches the Happy Isles,** he **may see Achilles**

WRITING EXERCISE Combine each pair of sentences by changing one into an adverb clause. You may wish to use joining words from the list of subordinating conjunctions above. Follow the directions in parentheses. Omit underlined words.

1. The Lady of Shalott sang her last song. <u>Then</u> she died. (Change the first sentence to an adverb clause showing time.)

2. A silly man went into an orchard. <u>There</u> he broke off a cherry branch for the duchess. (Make the second sentence an adverb clause of place.)

3. Mrs. Hodgson beats the cat. She herself left the cupboard open. (Make the second sentence a clause of condition.)

4. The king must find three people who miss him. Then he can live again. (Make the first sentence a clause of condition.)

5. The Bhagat had given up his important government position. He wanted to live a more spiritual life. (Make the second sentence a clause showing cause.)

GRAMMAR EXERCISE Rewrite the sentences below so that there are no unclear pronoun antecedents.

1. The reapers hear sweet melodies as they approach the island of Shalott.

2. Charlotte Brontë wrote a letter to Nell when she needed advice about marriage.

3. Mr. Hodgson holds Mr. Jenkins in contempt because of his democratic beliefs.

4. The king sees a man enter the queen's room, and she gives him her ring.

5. Purun Dass and the Maharajah made decisions together in the kingdom, where he served as prime minister.

PART 2   New Voices, New Directions

Industrial growth, social upheaval, and a new interest in science changed the direction of Victorian life. A prosperous middle class emerged even as the problems of the poor increased, and scientific theories challenged traditional religious beliefs. Some poets, reflecting on the loss of old certainties, wrote thoughtful poems about human-kind's isolation and the fleeting nature of youth, beauty, and fame. Other writers satirized conventional values and inconsistencies in human behavior. As you read the selections in this part of Unit Five, compare the fears and foibles of Victorian society with those of today's world.

COMPARING LITERATURE: The Poetry of A. E. Housman
and Rabindranath Tagore
The Role of the Poet Across Cultures: India

Dover Beach

To Marguerite—Continued

Poetry by MATTHEW ARNOLD

Connect to Your Life

Lonely Versus Alone What comes to mind when you hear the word *isolation?* Think about situations that might cause a person to experience feelings of isolation. Do you think such feelings occur only when a person is physically separated from other people? Share your thoughts with your classmates.

Build Background

New Science and Old Beliefs In Great Britain, the Victorian era was a time of rapid change in social, economic, and religious life. The growth of industrialization and commercialism created both increasing prosperity and social unrest. The development of new scientific theories challenged traditional beliefs and eroded old assumptions about the nature of the world. Matthew Arnold, who was a social and literary critic as well as a poet, was concerned throughout his life with the questions and struggles of his time. As a critic, he was also disturbed by what he perceived as the complacency of much of society toward the emerging changes and toward the importance of beauty and culture.

In his poetry Arnold deals with the loneliness of humankind in an indifferent universe, bereft of old certainties. Although Arnold thought that religion was an essential part of culture, his poems nonetheless reflect his personal sense of isolation, doubt, and at times even despair. In his poem "Stanzas from the Grande Chartreuse," he speaks of himself as "Wandering between two worlds, one dead, / The other powerless to be born." "Dover Beach," possibly written just after the poet's visit to Dover, England, on his honeymoon in 1851, is probably the most famous of his poems. "To Marguerite—Continued" is one of a series of poems believed to have been written to a woman he met in the 1840s.

Focus Your Reading

LITERARY ANALYSIS **CONTROLLING IMAGE**

A **controlling image** is a single image or comparison that extends throughout a literary work and shapes its meaning. In "Dover Beach," for example, the sound of the sea is an example of imagery that is developed throughout the poem.

> *But now I only hear*
> *Its melancholy, long, withdrawing*
> > *roar. . . .*

As you read these poems, be aware of controlling images and how they are elaborated upon in each work.

ACTIVE READING **DRAWING CONCLUSIONS ABOUT MOOD**

Mood is the feeling, or atmosphere, that a writer creates for the reader. The mood of a poem may be happy, sad, lonely, angry, and so on. **Descriptive details** and careful word choice help a writer create a particular mood.

READER'S NOTEBOOK As you read each of Arnold's poems, record any descriptive details that you find particularly striking. Then draw conclusions about the mood created by each poem.

Dover Beach

Matthew Arnold

The sea is calm tonight.
The tide is full, the moon lies fair
Upon the straits—on the French coast the light
Gleams and is gone; the cliffs of England stand,
5 Glimmering and vast, out in the tranquil bay.
Come to the window, sweet is the night air!
Only, from the long line of spray
Where the sea meets the moon-blanched land,
Listen! you hear the grating roar
10 Of pebbles which the waves draw back, and fling,
At their return, up the high strand,
Begin, and cease, and then again begin,
With tremulous cadence slow, and bring
The eternal note of sadness in.

3 straits: the Strait of Dover, a narrow channel separating England and France, at the northern end of the English Channel.

8 moon-blanched: shining palely in the moonlight.

13 tremulous cadence: trembling rhythm.

15   Sophocles long ago
       Heard it on the Aegean, and it brought
       Into his mind the turbid ebb and flow
       Of human misery; we
       Find also in the sound a thought,
20   Hearing it by this distant northern sea.

       The Sea of Faith
       Was once, too, at the full, and round earth's shore
       Lay like the folds of a bright girdle furled.
       But now I only hear
25   Its melancholy, long, withdrawing roar,
       Retreating, to the breath
       Of the night wind, down the vast edges drear
       And naked shingles of the world.

       Ah, love, let us be true
30   To one another! for the world, which seems
       To lie before us like a land of dreams,
       So various, so beautiful, so new,
       Hath really neither joy, nor love, nor light,
       Nor certitude, nor peace, nor help for pain;
35   And we are here as on a darkling plain
       Swept with confused alarms of struggle and flight,
       Where ignorant armies clash by night.

15 Sophocles (sŏf'ə-klēz'): an ancient Greek writer of tragic plays.

16 Aegean (ĭ-jē'ən): the Aegean Sea—part of the Mediterranean Sea, between Greece and Turkey.

17 turbid: in a state of turmoil; muddled.

21 Sea of Faith: traditional religious beliefs about God and the world, long viewed as true and unshakable.

23 girdle: a belt or sash worn around the waist.

27 drear: dreary.

28 shingles: pebbly beaches.

Thinking Through the Literature

1. **Comprehension Check** What did the sound of the sea suggest to Sophocles?

2. What **images** stand out in your mind after reading the poem?

3. How would you describe the speaker's view of the world?

    THINK ABOUT
       • his responses to what he sees and hears at the beach
       • what he says about the Sea of Faith
       • the images in lines 35–37

4. Why do you think the poem is addressed to the speaker's loved one?

To Marguerite
—Continued

Matthew Arnold

Am Meer [By the sea]
(1875), Anselm Feuerbach.
Kunstmuseum Düsseldorf
im Ehrenhof, Germany.

Yes! in the sea of life enisled,
With echoing straits between us thrown,
Dotting the shoreless watery wild,
We mortal millions live *alone*.
5   The islands feel the enclasping flow,
And then their endless bounds they know.

But when the moon their hollows lights,
And they are swept by balms of spring,
And in their glens, on starry nights,
10   The nightingales divinely sing;
And lovely notes, from shore to shore,
Across the sounds and channels pour—

Oh! then a longing like despair
Is to their farthest caverns sent;
15   For surely once, they feel, we were
Parts of a single continent!
Now round us spreads the watery plain—
Oh might our marges meet again!

Who ordered that their longing's fire
20   Should be, as soon as kindled, cooled?
Who renders vain their deep desire?—
A God, a God their severance ruled!
And bade betwixt their shores to be
The unplumbed, salt, estranging sea.

1 enisled (ĕn-īld′): separated, like islands.

6 bounds: limits or boundaries.

8 balms: soothing scents and airs.
9 glens: valleys.

12 sounds: long, wide bodies of water, larger than channels.

18 marges: margins.

22 severance: separation.
24 unplumbed: unmeasured; **estranging** (ĭ-strān′jĭng): alienating.

Thinking through the LITERATURE

Connect to the Literature

1. What Do You Think? What is your reaction to the speaker in this poem?

> **Comprehension Check**
> • Who are the "mortal millions"?
> • Who, according to the poem, separates Marguerite from the speaker?

Think Critically

2. What seems to be the **theme,** or message, of this poem?

> **THINK ABOUT**
> • the reference to living alone in line 4
> • the imagery of islands
> • the statement that "a God their severance ruled" (line 22)

3. How do you think the speaker would describe his relationship with Marguerite?

4. **ACTIVE READING** **DRAWING CONCLUSIONS ABOUT MOOD** Look back at the notes you recorded in your 📖 **READER'S NOTEBOOK.** What **descriptive details** contribute to the **mood** of each poem? How would you compare these moods?

Extend Interpretations

5. Comparing Texts Compare the attitudes toward life expressed in "Dover Beach" and "To Marguerite—Continued" with the attitude expressed by Tennyson in the excerpt from *In Memoriam* (page 839). In your opinion, which of the three poems reflects the most positive attitude toward the future?

6. Critic's Corner In an essay on "Dover Beach," the American poet and novelist James Dickey speaks of the "subtlety, force, and conviction" of the poem. Look for evidence in the poem to support or refute his comments.

7. Connect to Life Do you think Arnold would express similar ideas if he were writing poetry today? Explain your opinion.

Literary Analysis

CONTROLLING IMAGE Poets often use a **controlling image** to convey their thoughts or feelings. A controlling image is a single image or comparison that extends throughout a literary work and shapes its meaning. Often, the controlling image is an **extended metaphor,** a comparison of two unlike things at some length and in several ways.

Paired Activity With a partner, reread "To Marguerite—Continued" and identify the extended metaphor that acts as a controlling image. Jot down the extended metaphor, and note what objects and ideas are being compared. Then compare your conclusions with those of another group.

> Extended Metaphor:
> Objects and ideas being compared:
> 1.
> 2.
> 3.

REVIEW **ALLUSION** "Dover Beach" contains an **allusion,** or reference, to a well-known literary figure. What is the allusion? What is its function in the poem?

Choices & CHALLENGES

Writing Options

1. Lecture Notes Write lecture notes in which you either support or refute the idea, stated in "To Marguerite—Continued," that "we mortal millions live *alone.*"

2. Beloved's Diary Imagine that you are the "love" addressed in line 29 of "Dover Beach." Write a diary entry expressing your reaction to what the speaker has said. Place the entry in your **Working Portfolio.**

Activities & Explorations

1. Imaginative Illustration Create a drawing or painting to illustrate one of the images in either poem ~ **ART**

2. Set Design Make a set design for a dance based on one of the poems. Include brief notes describing the mood you hope to create. ~ **VIEWING AND REPRESENTING**

Inquiry & Research

Music and Poetry Locate and play a recording of the musical composition "Dover Beach" by Samuel Barber, which was based on Arnold's poem. Conduct a class discussion addressing whether the music effectively conveys the feelings and ideas expressed in the poem.

Matthew Arnold
1822–1888

Other Works
"Isolation: To Marguerite"
"The Buried Life"
"Lines Written in Kensington
   Gardens"
"A Summer Night"

School Days Matthew Arnold grew up under the scholarly influence of his father, a well-known clergyman and renowned headmaster of the distinguished Rugby School. Unlike his father, however, the younger Arnold was high-spirited and mischievous. At Oxford University, he spent more time socializing than studying and, as a result, barely passed his exams. He did, however, win a prestigious award for one of his poems.

Poet and Civil Servant In 1847, Arnold became the private secretary to an English lord. With the help of his employer, he later acquired a job as inspector of schools, a post he held for 35 years. The position required Arnold to travel constantly and gave him the opportunity to observe English culture and society closely. Arnold wrote during his spare time and published his first poems anonymously. His growing reputation as a poet led to his

appointment in 1857 as professor of poetry at Oxford, a part-time post that he retained for 10 years.

Writer and Social Critic After 1867, Arnold devoted most of his efforts to writing critical essays on poetry and on problems in English society. He attacked the provincialism of his time and argued for a broader intellectual life and a greater awareness and appreciation of the arts. Arnold also wrote extensively on the religious controversies of his time. He thought that traditional religious views and institutions needed examination. Finally, Arnold made significant efforts to improve English education by visiting schools in Europe and writing forceful reports on his ideas for reform. He died suddenly at the age of 66 and was buried next to three sons who had preceded him in death.

Author Activity

Inspector of Schools Arnold spent most of his working life as an inspector of schools in Great Britain. Do some research in biographies, encyclopedia articles, and on the Internet to find out more about Arnold's career as a civil servant.

Pied Beauty

Spring and Fall: To a Young Child

Poetry by GERARD MANLEY HOPKINS

Connect to Your Life

Art Versus Nature Think about a time when you closely examined a single leaf or flower. What unique details do you remember observing? Do you think it is possible to convey the unique qualities of a natural object in a poem or a painting? Share your thoughts with your classmates.

Build Background

Revolutionary Style Gerard Manley Hopkins was an innovator whose poetry was not published or understood until decades after his death. Hopkins developed a revolutionary style, one unlike that of his contemporaries or of any poet before him. He experimented with language and form, inventing new words, using inverted word order, and developing nontraditional rhythmic patterns, which he called **sprung rhythm.** Hopkins is now regarded as a major poet of the Victorian era, whose work became a pivotal influence in the development of modern poetry.

Hopkins responded with intensity to the natural world. He invented a word, *inscape,* to describe the qualities of nature he tried to convey in his poems. Generally, inscape seems to be an inner landscape of meaning, derived from the unique qualities of natural objects, that one can experience through close observation. For almost eight years, Hopkins recorded his impressions of the natural world in a journal, which he illustrated with detailed drawings of flowers and trees. Descriptions from his journal often appeared later in his poetry. Hopkins was an aspiring painter and talented musician as well as a poet, and his talent in both art and music is reflected in his poems.

Focus Your Reading

LITERARY ANALYSIS **SPRUNG RHYTHM** In order to approximate the rhythms of natural speech in his poetry, Hopkins ignored traditional patterns of rhythm, instead using what he called **sprung rhythm.** The lines of a poem written in sprung rhythm have fixed numbers of stressed syllables but varying numbers of unstressed syllables. As you read the poems, think about which lines come closest to reproducing the rhythms of natural speech.

ACTIVE READING **RECOGNIZING COINED WORDS** Hopkins frequently coined, or invented, words to capture his impressions of nature's special qualities. In some cases, the coined word is actually a compound made by joining two familiar words in an unfamiliar arrangement, as in "couple-color."

READER'S NOTEBOOK As you read the poems, use a chart like the one shown to make a list of the **coined words** that you discover. Also jot down the **image** or feeling that you think each word conveys. The annotations will help you with the meaning of some words.

Coined Words	Image or Feeling

Pied Beauty

GERARD MANLEY HOPKINS

Glory be to God for dappled things—
　　For skies of couple-color as a brinded cow;
　　　　For rose-moles all in stipple upon trout that swim;
Fresh-firecoal chestnut-falls; finches' wings;
5　　　Landscape plotted and pieced—fold, fallow, and plough;
　　　　And áll trádes, their gear and tackle and trim.

All things counter, original, spare, strange;
　　Whatever is fickle, freckled (who knows how?)
　　　　With swift, slow; sweet, sour; adazzle, dim;
10　He fathers-forth whose beauty is past change:
　　　　　Praise him.

1 dappled: spotted or splashed with color.

2 brinded: brindled—streaked or spotted with a darker color.

3 rose-moles . . . stipple: spots of pink in flecks or speckles.

4 fresh-firecoal chestnut-falls: fallen chestnuts that are the color of glowing coals.

5 fold: a pen for animals; **fallow:** land left unseeded.

6 trim: equipment.

7 counter: opposing.

10 fathers-forth: creates.

Thinking Through the Literature

1. **Comprehension Check** What are some of the "dappled things" that Hopkins admires?

2. Describe one **image** that remains in your mind from your reading of "Pied Beauty."

3. Why do you think the speaker is so fascinated by "dappled things"?

   THINK ABOUT
   - the details the speaker describes
   - the question in parentheses in line 8
   - the references to God in lines 1, 10, and 11

4. Why do you think Hopkins includes "all trades" with the details from nature?

Spring (late 1800s), Frederick Walker. Victoria and Albert Museum, London/Art Resource, New York.

SPRING and FALL:

To a Young Child

GERARD MANLEY HOPKINS

Márgarét, are you gríeving
Over Goldengrove unleaving?
Leáves, líke the things of man, you
With your fresh thoughts care for, can you?
5   Ah! ás the heart grows older
It will come to such sights colder
By and by, nor spare a sigh
Though worlds of wanwood leafmeal lie;
And yet you *will* weep and know why.
10 Now no matter, child, the name:
Sórrow's springs áre the same.
Nor mouth had, no nor mind, expressed
What heart heard of, ghost guessed:
It ís the blight man was born for,
15 It is Margaret you mourn for.

1 Hopkins often included stress marks in his poems to indicate the rhythms he intended.

2 **unleaving:** losing its leaves.

3–4 **Leaves . . . can you?:** Do you in your innocence grieve about falling leaves as though they were equal to human loss?

8 **wanwood:** faded woodland; **leafmeal:** dry, ground-up leaves.

12 **nor:** neither.

13 **ghost:** spirit; soul.

14 **blight:** a condition that stops growth and brings withering and death.

Connect to the Literature

1. What Do You Think?
What impressions of Margaret do you have after reading this poem? Share your reactions with your classmates.

> **Comprehension Check**
> - What is Margaret grieving over?
> - How does the speaker believe Margaret will react to fall when she grows older?

Think Critically

2. How would you describe the **speaker's** relationship to Margaret?

THINK ABOUT

- the speaker's two questions
- the prediction in lines 5–8
- the statements in lines 9 and 11

3. How does the speaker seem to interpret Margaret's grieving?

4. Compare the speakers of "Pied Beauty" and "Spring and Fall: To a Young Child." What similarities and differences do you find in their **tone,** or attitude?

5. **ACTIVE READING** **RECOGNIZING COINED WORDS** With a small group of classmates, discuss the list of **coined words** you made in your **READER'S NOTEBOOK.** What **images** or feelings do the words convey? How do the words affect meaning in each poem?

Extend Interpretations

6. Critic's Corner One critic has observed that for Hopkins "words are a means of possessing nature." Think about what this statement might mean. Look for words in the two poems that might be a "means of possessing nature."

7. Comparing Texts Compare Hopkins's two poems with Wordsworth's "Lines Composed a Few Miles Above Tintern Abbey" (page 726), Shelley's "To a Skylark" (page 786), and Keats's "To Autumn" (page 801). Identify any attitudes toward nature that you think Hopkins shares with the three romantic poets.

8. Connect to Life In "Spring and Fall: To a Young Child," Hopkins explores and brings insight into the experience of a young girl. Think of a time, either in your own life or in the life of a **character** in a book or movie, when a childhood experience led to an important understanding of life.

Literary Analysis

SPRUNG RHYTHM Hopkins used **sprung rhythm** to approximate the rhythms of natural speech in his poetry. The lines of a poem written in sprung rhythm have fixed numbers of stressed syllables but varying numbers of unstressed syllables. As in the example below, a line may contain several consecutive stressed syllables, or a stressed syllable may be followed by one, two, or even three unstressed syllables.

*Lándscăpe plótted ănd pieced—
fold, fallow, and plough;*

*Ănd áll trádes, theĭr geár ănd
tackle and trim.*

Paired Activity With a partner, read "Pied Beauty" and "Spring and Fall: To a Young Child" aloud. Then work together to mark the stressed and unstressed syllables in one of the poems.

REVIEW **ALLITERATION** Notice the many examples of **alliteration,** or repetition of initial consonant sounds, in both poems. Why do you think Hopkins used alliteration so extensively?

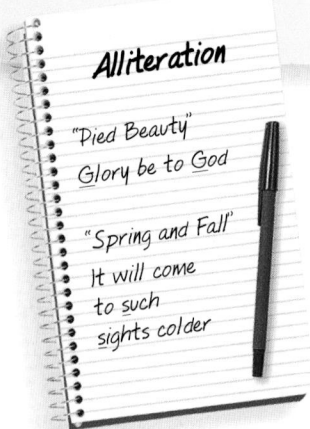

Alliteration

"Pied Beauty"
Glory be to God

"Spring and Fall"
It will come
to such
sights colder

Choices & CHALLENGES

Writing Options

1. Nature Poem Write a short poem in which you express your enthusiasm for a unique quality or pattern in nature.

2. Journal Entry Write an entry for a nature journal, recording your close observations and impressions of one aspect of the natural world. Place the entry in your **Working Portfolio.**

3. Dictionary of Coined Words Create a dictionary of your own coined words to describe details related to a particular subject or area of interest, such as music, sport, dance, city life, and so on.

Activities & Explorations

Nature Mural Work with a partner to create a watercolor mural depicting some of the images in these two poems. Display your finished mural in the classroom. **~ ART**

Inquiry & Research

Natural Patterns Choose an animal or plant characterized by spots or "dappled" splashes of color. What is the function of such markings? Discuss your findings with classmates.

Gerard Manley Hopkins
1844–1889

Other Works
"God's Grandeur"
"Hurrahing in Harvest"
"Binsey Poplars"

Poet and Priest Gerard Manley Hopkins grew up in a family of writers and artists and showed early promise as both a poet and painter. He won a prize for his poetry while still a teenager and continued to write while attending Balliol College at Oxford University, where he was a brilliant student. It was also at Oxford that the deeply religious young man began struggling with his Protestant faith and, in 1866, joined the Roman Catholic Church. This action alienated him from his parents, who could never understand their son's decision. The rift grew even wider when Hopkins joined the Jesuit order and was eventually ordained a priest.

Early Decline Hopkins preached and taught for many years at a number of parishes in England and Scotland. In 1884, he was assigned to teach Greek literature at University College in Dublin, where he would spend his last years. Hopkins did not enjoy his assignment in Ireland, however, because he was overworked and in declining health. At age 44, he died of typhoid fever.

Conflicting Commitments As a young man, Hopkins experienced a continuing conflict between his desire to write poetry and his religious commitment. He burned most of his early poems when he entered the Jesuit order, and he did not write poetry again for seven years, although he did continue to write in his journal. In 1874, Hopkins went to a Jesuit college in rural Wales to study theology. He was deeply happy during his three years there, and with encouragement from his superiors, he eventually returned to writing poetry. When he tried to get his first major poem published, however, it was rejected, and after that he showed his work to only a few friends. A collection of Hopkins's poetry was published in 1918, but it was not until 1930, when a second edition appeared, that his work finally received full recognition.

Author Activity

Word Images Read one or two of Hopkins's other poems and list the coined words he uses in them. Share with the class the images the words convey.

from

Journal

Gerard Manley Hopkins

The priest and poet Gerard Manley Hopkins diligently kept a journal for eight years. As you read the journal excerpt below, see if you recognize any ideas or language that also appear in his poems.

❶ *September 17, 1868*—Fine.—Chestnuts as bright as coals or spots of vermilion.[1]

❷ *July 8, 1871*—After much rain, some thunder, and no summer as yet, the river swollen and golden and, where charged with air, like ropes and hills of melting candy, there was this day a thunderstorm on a greater scale—huge rocky clouds lit with livid[2] light, hail and rain that flooded the garden, and thunder ringing and echoing round like brass. . . .

June 16, 1873— . . . I saw [a pigeon] up on the eaves of the roof: as it moved its head a crush of satin green came and went, a wet or soft flaming of the light. . . .

August 9, 1873— . . . From the cliffs I saw the sea paved with wind—clothed and purpled all over with ribbons of wind. . . .

October 17, 1873— . . . At the end of the month hard frosts. Wonderful downpour of leaf: when the morning sun began to melt the frost they fell at one touch and in a few minutes a whole tree was flung of them; they lay masking and papering the ground at the foot. . . .

August 8, 1874— . . . All the west country seems to me to have soft maroon or rosy cocoa-dust-colored handkerchiefs or ploughfields, sometimes delicately combed with rows of green, their hedges bending in flowing outlines and now misted a little by the beginning of twilight run down into it upon the shoulders of the hills; in the bottom crooked rows of rich tall elms. . . .

---

1. **vermilion:** bright red.
2. **livid:** ashen or pale.

Reading for Information

Of the incidents and thoughts in your everyday experience, what kinds do you think are worth recording? Generally, people keep journals to remember particular events, to recapture feelings, or to record their lives for later generations. Writers often use what they have written in their journals as raw material for their imaginative works.

UNDERSTANDING A WRITER'S ATTITUDE AND IDEAS

Reading a writer's journal can be a revelation. The entries often give you new insight into the sources of ideas and images that you have encountered in the writer's finished works. Use the activities that follow to study the excerpts from Hopkins's journal.

❶ In the entry for September 17, 1868, Hopkins remarks on chestnuts "as bright as coals." Find a similar phrase in "Pied Beauty." Locate another instance in which Hopkins used a journal entry as a source of imagery for a poem.

❷ In the July 8, 1871, entry, Hopkins described a "river swollen and golden." From the two Hopkins poems you've read, choose three examples of description of nature. Then summarize Hopkins's attitude toward nature.

Comparing Texts After reading Hopkins's journal and poems, which sense would you say he relied on most in his experiencing of nature—sight, hearing, or touch? Cite examples to support your answer.

The Man He Killed

Ah, Are You Digging on My Grave?

The Convergence of the Twain

(Lines on the Loss of the *Titanic*)

Poetry by THOMAS HARDY

Connect to Your Life

Life's Twists and Turns Think about a time, either in your own life, a friend's life, or in current world events, when something unexpected occurred. What happened? What reactions did you or others have to this change? Share your thoughts with your classmates.

Build Background

Novelist and Poet Thomas Hardy is one of the most widely recognized authors of the Victorian era. As a novelist, he focused on the bitter and often disastrous ironies of life. Most of his contemporaries thought he was overly pessimistic, but Hardy once denied the charge, calling himself a "meliorist"—someone who thinks humanity has the ability to make the world better. Although known primarily as a novelist, Hardy was also a gifted poet. After devoting the first 25 years of his literary career to writing fiction, including 14 novels, he turned his attention almost completely to writing poetry. Hardy's life spanned 88 years, and although his novels were composed during the Victorian era, most of his poetry was actually written in the 20th century.

Hardy's **style** of poetry is unlike that of most of his contemporaries. In fact, his departure from the typical language and form of Victorian poetry led some of his contemporaries to complain that his poems seemed more like prose than poetry. Characteristics of the novel that might be observed in some of his poems include the use of **dialogue;** a relaxed narrative style; simple, unadorned language; and the framework of a **plot,** often with interaction between **characters, dramatic moments,** and **unexpected twists.**

Focus Your Reading

LITERARY ANALYSIS | **SATIRE IN LYRIC POETRY** | **Satire** is a literary technique in which ideas, customs, behaviors, or institutions are ridiculed for the purpose of improving society. The **tone** of satire may be gently witty, mildly abrasive, or bitterly ironic. As you read these poems, look for the satiric tone in each and try to identify what is being satirized.

ACTIVE READING | **MAKING INFERENCES ABOUT A SPEAKER'S ATTITUDE** | As you know, the **speaker** in a poem may be intimately involved in the subject of the poem or may be a detached observer. To understand the speaker's stance, or attitude, you must look not only for what is stated directly but also for what can be **inferred,** or guessed, on the basis of clues in the poems.

READER'S NOTEBOOK As you read each poem, note your impressions of each speaker's attitude by jotting down answers to the following questions and the reasons for your answers.

1. Does the speaker "talk" to the reader in the **first person** or the **third person?**
2. Are any **details** about the speaker's life or personality revealed in the poem?
3. Does the speaker reveal any of his or her emotions?

THE MAN HE KILLED
Thomas Hardy

"Had he and I but met
By some old ancient inn,
We should have sat us down to wet
Right many a nipperkin!

5   "But ranged as infantry,
And staring face to face,
I shot at him as he at me,
And killed him in his place.

4 nipperkin: a container holding about half a pint of beer or ale.

"I shot him dead because—
10 Because he was my foe,
Just so: my foe of course he was;
 That's clear enough; although

"He thought he'd 'list, perhaps,
 Off-hand like—just as I—
15 Was out of work—had sold his traps—
 No other reason why.

"Yes; quaint and curious war is!
 You shoot a fellow down
You'd treat if met where any bar is,
20 Or help to half-a-crown."

13 'list: enlist.

15 traps: personal belongings.

20 half-a-crown: an old British coin.

Thinking Through the Literature

1. Does the **speaker** of this poem react to killing an enemy in a way that you would expect?

2. Do you think the speaker is satisfied with the reason he provides for killing his enemy?

   THINK ABOUT
   - his repetition of the word *because* (lines 9–10)
   - his repetition of his reason for shooting the man (lines 10–11)
   - the emphasis on the word *although* (line 12)

3. Does the **theme,** or message, of this poem have relevance in today's world?

Ah, Are You Digging on My Grave?

Thomas Hardy

"Ah, are you digging on my grave,
    My loved one?—planting rue?"
—"No: yesterday he went to wed
One of the brightest wealth has bred.
5 'It cannot hurt her now,' he said,
    'That I should not be true.' "

2 rue: an herb that, because its
name is identical to the word *rue*
(meaning "sorrow" or "regret"), is
often used as a symbol of
repentance.

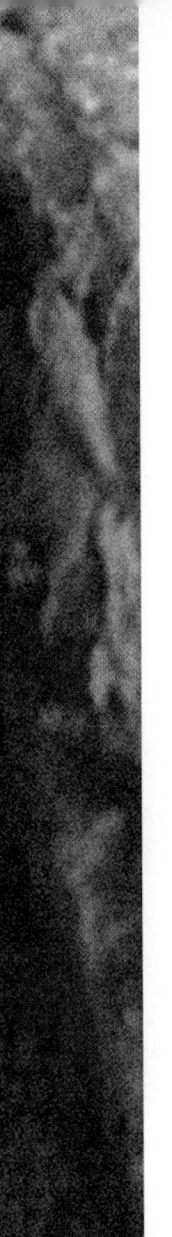

"Then who is digging on my grave?
    My nearest dearest kin?"
—"Ah, no: they sit and think, 'What use!
10 What good will planting flowers produce?
No tendance of her mound can loose
    Her spirit from Death's gin.'"

"But someone digs upon my grave?
    My enemy?—prodding sly?"
15 —"Nay: when she heard you had passed the Gate
That shuts on all flesh soon or late,
She thought you no more worth her hate,
    And cares not where you lie."

"Then, who is digging on my grave?
20   Say—since I have not guessed!"
—"O it is I, my mistress dear,
Your little dog, who still lives near,
And much I hope my movements here
    Have not disturbed your rest?"

25 "Ah yes! *You* dig upon my grave . . .
    Why flashed it not on me
That one true heart was left behind!
What feeling do we ever find
To equal among human kind
30   A dog's fidelity!"

"Mistress, I dug upon your grave
    To bury a bone, in case
I should be hungry near this spot
When passing on my daily trot.
35 I am sorry, but I quite forgot
    It was your resting place."

11 tendance: attendance; watchful care.

12 gin: a snare or trap.

30 fidelity: faithfulness.

Thinking Through the Literature

1. **Comprehension Check** Who are the two speakers conducting a dialogue in this poem?

2. What was your reaction to the unexpected twist in this poem?

3. What reactions to her death does the first speaker seem to expect?

4. Why do you think the poet conceals the identity of the second speaker until the fourth **stanza?**

Thomas Hardy

The Convergence of the Twain

(LINES ON THE LOSS OF THE *TITANIC*)

1

In a solitude of the sea
Deep from human vanity,
And the Pride of Life that planned her, stilly couches she.

2

Steel chambers, late the pyres
5   Of her salamandrine fires,
Cold currents thrid, and turn to rhythmic tidal lyres.

3

Over the mirrors meant
To glass the opulent
The sea-worm crawls—grotesque, slimed, dumb, indifferent.

3 stilly couches she: quietly she lies.

5 salamandrine fires: extremely hot flames. (The name *salamander* was formerly applied to a mythical lizardlike animal that could live unharmed in fire.)

6 thrid: pass through; thread; **lyres:** stringed instruments of the harp family.

The *Titanic* in Southampton, England, just before sailing on her maiden voyage on 10 April 1912

4

10   Jewels in joy designed
        To ravish the sensuous mind
Lie lightless, all their sparkles bleared and black and blind.

5

      Dim moon-eyed fishes near
        Gaze at the gilded gear
15 And query: "What does this vaingloriousness down here?" . . .

6

      Well: while was fashioning
        This creature of cleaving wing,
The Immanent Will that stirs and urges everything

15 vaingloriousness: vain display; ostentation.

18 Immanent Will: Hardy's name for a force that determines the course of events in the world.

7

Prepared a sinister mate
20   For her—so gaily great—
A Shape of Ice, for the time far and dissociate.

21 dissociate: unrelated.

8

And as the smart ship grew
In stature, grace, and hue,
In shadowy silent distance grew the Iceberg too.

9

25   Alien they seemed to be:
No mortal eye could see
The intimate welding of their later history,

10

Or sign that they were bent
By paths coincident
30   On being anon twin halves of one august event,

30 anon: soon; **august:** grand; majestic.

11

Till the Spinner of the Years
Said "Now!" And each one hears,
And consummation comes, and jars two hemispheres.

31 Spinner of the Years: a personification of the "Immanent Will" of line 18.

The wreck of the *Titanic* lies on the ocean floor, 13,000 feet beneath the surface of the sea.

Thinking through the LITERATURE

Connect to the Literature

1. What Do You Think?
What are your thoughts about the sinking of the *Titanic* after reading "The Convergence of the Twain"?

Comprehension Check
- Who or what are the "twain" (two) referred to in the title?
- Who or what crawls over the surface of the ship's mirrors at the bottom of the ocean?

Think Critically

2. What view of human nature do you think Hardy reveals as he describes the sunken *Titanic?*

 THINK ABOUT
- the phrase "the Pride of Life that planned her" (line 3)
- the lifestyle suggested by the words *mirrors, jewels,* and *gilded gear*
- the meaning of "vaingloriousness" (line 15)

3. What **extended metaphor** is developed in stanzas 6 through 11? Why do you think Hardy might have chosen to use this metaphor?

4. **ACTIVE READING** | **MAKING INFERENCES ABOUT A SPEAKER'S ATTITUDE**
Review the answers you wrote down in your **READER'S NOTEBOOK.** How would you describe the attitude of each speaker? What differences do you see between the attitudes of the three?

Extend Interpretations

5. Different Perspectives In "The Man He Killed," what do you think the man who was killed might say in reply to the speaker of the poem?

6. Critic's Corner Lytton Strachey, a well-known biographer and a contemporary of Thomas Hardy, described one of Hardy's poems as depicting a scene that might easily be "the turning point in a realistic psychological novel." Do you think Strachey's description fits any of the Hardy poems you have read? Give reasons to support your answer.

7. Connect to Life The sinking of the *Titanic* still shocks and fascinates people, almost 100 years after the event. Think of a major disaster that has occurred in your lifetime. How did people react to it? What do you think are the reasons for how people respond to such events?

Literary Analysis

SATIRE IN LYRIC POETRY | **Satire** almost always casts light on foibles and failings that are universal to human experience. These human weaknesses can range from individual actions and attitudes to those belonging to an entire nation. Satire often uses exaggeration to make its point, and it always involves some type of **irony.** Satire can be harsh and biting, as in Jonathan Swift's essay "A Modest Proposal," or it can be quiet and restrained, as in Hardy's poems.

Cooperative Learning Activity
With two classmates, compare the object of the satire and the satiric **tone** in each of Hardy's poems. Use a chart like the one shown to list your ideas. Which poem do you think has the most forceful satire? What view of human nature is suggested by the satire in each poem? Share your conclusions with the class.

Title	Object of Satire	Satiric Tone

REVIEW | **SITUATIONAL IRONY**
The responses to the questions posed by the first speaker in "Ah, Are You Digging on My Grave?" and the final revelation create a shattering irony in the poem. This is an example of **situational irony**—the reader or a **character** expects one thing to happen but something else happens instead. Look for examples of situational irony in the other two poems. How does the irony contribute to the satire in each poem?

Choices & CHALLENGES

Writing Options

1. Short Story Summary Write a summary of a short story based on the situation described in "The Man He Killed." Include events before and after the time of the poem.

2. Gravestone Epitaph Write the epitaph that the first speaker in "Ah, Are You Digging on My Grave?" might have wished were on her gravestone.

3. Poem About *Titanic* Write your own poem about the sinking of the *Titanic.* You may base your poem on what you know about the sinking of the ship from television documentaries or movies depicting the 1912 disaster. Place the poem in your **Working Portfolio.**

Activities & Explorations

1. War Poster Draw a war poster that the speaker of "The Man He Killed" might have designed. ~ **ART**

2. Dramatic Reading With a partner, practice and present a dramatic reading of "Ah, Are You Digging on My Grave?" in which you try to convey the attitude of each speaker. Be sure to pay attention to the punctuation as an indicator of shifts between speakers. ~ **SPEAKING AND LISTENING**

Inquiry & Research

Ship Sinks! In order to better appreciate the impact of the sinking of the *Titanic,* do some research in magazines and newspapers of the time to read about the famous disaster. Try to find newspaper headlines about the sinking, and make a list of the most dramatic ones. Share your list of headlines with the class.

More Online: Research Starter
www.mcdougallittell.com

Thomas Hardy
1840–1928

Other Works
"The Darkling Thrush"
"Channel Firing"
The Return of the Native
Tess of the D'Urbervilles
Jude the Obscure

Architect and Writer The son of a builder, Thomas Hardy was reared and educated in southwestern England, a setting he later used in his novels. Apprenticed to a local architect at the age of 15, he left six years later for London, where he studied and worked as an architect for many years. During his stay in London, he began to write both poetry and fiction, and his first published novel appeared anonymously in 1871. Although the response to it was lukewarm, Hardy continued to write, finally achieving success with *Far from the Madding Crowd,* published in 1874. The popularity of that novel inspired him to give up architecture and devote his life to writing.

Novelist As a novelist, Hardy produced a series of mostly successful works, including *The Return of the Native,* considered one of the best novels in English literature. In 1891, however, his novel *Tess of the D'Urbervilles* was harshly criticized for its sympathetic treatment of what many readers viewed as immoral behavior. His next novel, *Jude the Obscure,* also met with hostility and was censored by one of England's most prominent bookstores. Disgusted by these reactions, Hardy abandoned the novel form altogether and turned to writing poetry.

Poet As a poet, Hardy created ironic anecdotes in verse, often using the rhythm of the ballad to emphasize the timelessness of his themes. His poetry has none of the self-pity so common in Victorian verse; his tone is stern and unflinching, his poetry straightforward and authentic—attributes still admired by critics and readers.

Author Activity

Imaginary County Hardy created an imaginary area called Wessex as the setting for his novels. Find out what you can about what actual county in England Wessex most likely corresponds to and what that part of England is like.

When I Was One-and-Twenty

To an Athlete Dying Young

Poetry by A. E. HOUSMAN

Comparing Literature of the World

The Poetry of A. E. Housman and Rabindranath Tagore

This lesson and the one that follows present an opportunity for comparing Housman's role as a poet with the role played by the Indian Nobel Prize-winning poet Rabindranath Tagore. Specific points of comparison in the Tagore lesson will help you contrast the different messages the two poets convey about life and mortality.

Connect to Your Life

Bygone Days Think of conversations you have heard in which older adults, perhaps some of your family members, talked about their youth. What aspects of their younger days did they recall? Share your thoughts with the class.

Build Background

Young Poet, Youthful Themes A. E. Housman composed most of his poems in his early 20s. Although not a prolific poet, he was nevertheless an influential literary figure, admired by many other poets who emulated his concisely crafted short lyrics, and by the public, who appreciated his universal themes and grace of style.

The two poems in this lesson are from Housman's first collection of poetry, *A Shropshire Lad*. In the 63 poems of that book, Housman disguised any autobiographical points by creating an imaginary **speaker**—a young farmer named Terence Hearsay. Like most of Housman's poems, these focus on youth.

Focus Your Reading

LITERARY ANALYSIS **STANZA STRUCTURE** There are three elements that make up **stanza structure,** the way a group of lines that form a unit in a poem are patterned or organized:

- number of **lines**
- **rhyme scheme,** the pattern of end rhyme
- **meter,** the regular rhythmic pattern in a line

In most poetry, rhythm and rhyme work together to create a particular effect. As you read, notice the stanza structure Housman uses in each poem and the effect created by the rhythm and rhyme in each stanza.

ACTIVE READING **INFERRING MEANING** When you read a poem, you usually need to **infer** its meaning. An inference about a poem is a guess based on clues in the work. You can make inferences about the subject of a poem by noting the **details** used to describe the subject. The Housman poems deal primarily with the advantages and disadvantages of youth and aging. As you read the poems, look for the details that give you clues about what Housman is saying.

READER'S NOTEBOOK. For each poem, create a chart like the one shown to record details used to describe the advantages and disadvantages of youth and aging.

"When I Was One-and-Twenty"	
Advantages	**Disadvantages**
Youth:	Youth:
Aging:	Aging:

When I Was
One-and-Twenty

A. E. Housman

When I was one-and-twenty
    I heard a wise man say,
"Give crowns and pounds and guineas
    But not your heart away;
5 Give pearls away and rubies
    But keep your fancy free."
But I was one-and-twenty,
    No use to talk to me.

When I was one-and-twenty
10   I heard him say again,
"The heart out of the bosom
    Was never given in vain;
'Tis paid with sighs a plenty
    And sold for endless rue."
15 And I am two-and-twenty,
    And oh, 'tis true, 'tis true.

3 crowns . . . guineas: British units of money.

14 rue: sorrow; regret.

Thinking Through the Literature

1. **Comprehension Check** What does the wise man say is "sold for endless rue"?

2. What is your reaction to the words of the wise man?

3. What do you think could account for the change in the **speaker's** attitude? Give reasons for your answer.

4. What message do you think the speaker is trying to convey?

TO AN ATHLETE DYING YOUNG

A. E. HOUSMAN

The time you won your town the race
We chaired you through the market-place;
Man and boy stood cheering by,
And home we brought you shoulder-high.

2 chaired: carried publicly on a chair or seat, in triumph.

5　Today, the road all runners come,
Shoulder-high we bring you home,
And set you at your threshold down,
Townsman of a stiller town.

Smart lad, to slip betimes away
10　From fields where glory does not stay
And early though the laurel grows
It withers quicker than the rose.

9 betimes: early.

11 laurel: Wreaths made of leaves of the laurel tree were worn by victorious athletes in ancient times as a token of honor and glory.

Eyes the shady night has shut
Cannot see the record cut,
15　And silence sounds no worse than cheers
After earth has stopped the ears:

14 cut: broken.

Now you will not swell the rout
Of lads that wore their honors out,
Runners whom renown outran
20 And the name died before the man.

So set, before its echoes fade,
The fleet foot on the sill of shade,
And hold to the low lintel up
The still-defended challenge-cup.

25 And round that early-laurelled head
Will flock to gaze the strengthless dead,
And find unwithered on its curls
The garland briefer than a girl's.

17 **rout** (rout): crowd.

22 **sill**: threshold.
23 **lintel**: the beam across the top of a door frame.

28 **garland**: a wreath or woven chain of leaves or flowers.

Thinking through the LITERATURE

Connect to the Literature

1. What Do You Think?
What are your thoughts after reading "To an Athlete Dying Young"? Share them with your classmates.

Comprehension Check
- Why did the townspeople "chair" the athlete through the town in triumph?
- What disappointment does the speaker claim the athlete will never know?

Think Critically

2. How would you describe the **speaker's** response to the young man's death?

- his reference to the athlete as a "smart lad" (line 9)
- what the eyes and ears will not see or hear (lines 13–16)
- his reference to a name's dying "before the man" (line 20)
- the **images** he presents in the last two stanzas

3. Do you agree with the speaker's ideas about fame? Why or why not?

4. 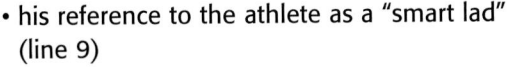 In a small group, discuss the charts you made for the poems in your 📖 **READER'S NOTEBOOK**. Based on the details you listed for each one, what can you **infer** about the advantages and disadvantages of youth and aging?

Extend Interpretations

5. Comparing Texts Compare and contrast the portrayals of youth in the two Housman poems. Cite lines in each to support your ideas.

6. Critic's Corner In 1936, the American poet Conrad Aiken commented that the thoughts expressed in Housman's poetry have an "adolescent note," or "boyishness." Would you use the word *adolescent* or *mature* to describe the thoughts expressed in "To an Athlete Dying Young" and "When I Was One-and-Twenty"? Cite evidence to support your answer.

7. Connect to Life Think about how people today typically respond to the untimely death of a famous athlete. Do you think this poem would comfort them?

Literary Analysis

STANZA STRUCTURE A **stanza** is a group of lines that form a unit in a poem. Stanzas are roughly comparable to paragraphs in prose. Each one deals with a single idea that supports the poem's major idea. In "When I Was One-and-Twenty," for example, each stanza tells what the wise man says and gives the speaker's response to it.

The elements of structure in a stanza—the number of **lines, rhyme scheme, rhythm,** and **meter**—work together to reinforce meaning. They may also affect a poem's **mood.** A slow rhythm and longer lines may convey a sad or mysterious mood, for example. A quicker rhythm and shorter lines may create a more light-hearted mood.

Paired Activity Copy the first stanza of each of these poems on a sheet of paper. With a partner, read each stanza aloud, then mark the meter of each. How do the meters of the poems differ? In which poem do you think the rhythm and rhyme are more obvious? What effect do you think the rhythm and rhyme create in each poem? Write down your observations in a chart like the one below.

	Meter	Rhythm and Rhyme
"When I Was One-and-Twenty"		
"To an Athlete Dying Young"		

Choices & CHALLENGES

Writing Options

1. Personal Anecdote Reflecting on "When I Was One-and-Twenty," write a personal anecdote in which you describe a time when you did not heed the warning of another person, only to learn later that the warning was justified. Place the anecdote in your **Working Portfolio.**

2. Essay on Poetry Echoing the ideas of romanticism, Housman maintained that poetry cannot be explained or analyzed because it is an experience not of intellect but of emotion. Draft an essay explaining

Agree: Poetry is felt--an experience for the senses . . . Disagree: A poem is a tightly constructed piece of writing . . .

whether you agree or disagree with Housman's theory.

Writing Handbook
See page 1367–1370: Explanatory Writing.

Activities & Explorations

1. Rebuttal of Poetic Views Practice and present a rebuttal of the views expressed in "When I Was One-and-Twenty." ~ **SPEAKING AND LISTENING**

2. Poetic Illustration Use pencil or charcoal to create a drawing illustrating an image or idea in one of Housman's poems. ~ **ART**

3. Sculpture of the Runner Create a clay or wire sculpture that reflects your impression of the runner described in "To an Athlete Dying Young." ~ **ART**

Inquiry & Research

Poetic Soundtracks Some of Housman's poems have been set to music by composers such as Ralph Vaughan Williams, George Butterworth, John Ireland, and Arnold Bax. Which poems did they use? How did they happen to write music for these poems? If possible, locate recordings of some of the compositions and play them for the class.

A. E. Housman
1859–1936

Other Works
"Bredon Hill"
"Is My Team Ploughing?"
"Loveliest of Trees"
"On Moonlit Heath and Lonesome Bank"

Early Interests and Setbacks Alfred Edward Housman spent more years working on scholarly Latin translations than writing poetry. His interest in classical studies began in grammar school, where he studied Greek and Latin and developed a skill of creating remarkably clear translations. Although he displayed intellectual prowess early in life, periods of emotional distress plagued his youth and may have contributed to the melancholy later reflected in his poetry. His mother's death when he was just 12 years old upset him greatly. While a student at Oxford University, he faced further personal anxieties that left him in a state of emotional turmoil and caused him to fail his final exams. After leaving the university without a

degree, Housman worked in London as a clerk in the patent office for 10 years.

Scholarly Pursuits During his years as a clerk, Housman continued to study Latin on his own, wrote articles for journals, and eventually earned recognition as a brilliant scholar and critic of Latin texts. In 1892, he was made professor of Latin at University College in London, where he taught until 1911. He then became a professor at Cambridge University, teaching there until shortly before his death. In his later years, Housman turned down various awards and honors, including the government's coveted Order of Merit and an appointment as England's poet laureate.

Author Activity

More About Terence Hearsay Read some more poems from *A Shropshire Lad.* How do their images and themes compare with those in "When I Was One-and-Twenty" and "To an Athlete Dying Young"?

1996

Poetry by RABINDRANATH TAGORE

The Role of the Poet Across Cultures

The Poetry of A. E. Housman and Rabindranath Tagore Although A. E. Housman and Indian poet Rabindranath Tagore were separated by both physical and cultural distances, the two lived as contemporaries, each witnessing tremendous change between the 19th and 20th centuries.

Points of Comparison As you read Tagore's poem "1996," think about how he views his role as a poet at the turn of the century. Compare Tagore's view with the role of the poet that Housman seems to imply. Also compare the **themes** used by each poet and the **images** used to help convey these themes.

Build Background

East Meets West During the 19th century, British colonial rule brought dramatic changes to India's educational system as well as its government. Parliament insisted that Indian schools offer instruction not only in the English language but also in English literature. Although this directive displeased many Indians, the people living in the eastern province of Bengal were generally receptive to learning about the culture of their English rulers.

Born in India in 1861, the Bengali poet Rabindranath Tagore was influenced by the works of both English and Bengali authors. Although the Tagore family welcomed the opportunity to study Western culture, they also promoted Bengali arts and traditions. They read widely in English literature, but when writing their own poems, plays, and stories, they wrote in Bengali. It was not until Rabindranath Tagore was in his 50s that he began translating his poems into English, reluctantly honoring a promise he had made to an English admirer. In 1913, shortly after his translations reached the Western world, Tagore was awarded the Nobel Prize in literature, becoming the first Asian to receive that honor.

Tagore looked for the best in every culture and advocated for his own country a balance between the traditions of East and West. He worried about the tensions between cultures and wondered how they would affect the future of the world. It may have been this contemplation of the future that inspired Tagore to write in 1896 the poem you are about to read, called "1996."

Focus Your Reading

LITERARY ANALYSIS **TITLE** The **title** of a literary work introduces readers to the piece and usually reveals something about its subject or theme. Although some poems are merely identified by their first line, most literary works have been carefully and deliberately titled. Before you read "1996," think about what the poem's **theme** might be. Keep your thoughts and predictions in mind as you read the poem.

ACTIVE READING **ANALYZING STRUCTURE** Tagore's "1996" is structured around three questions. The first question occurs in the first two lines of the poem:

> *Who are you reading curiously this*
> *poem of mine*
> *a hundred years from now?*

READER'S NOTEBOOK As you read "1996," notice how Tagore uses questions to structure his poem. Jot down the poem's other two questions and note how the poet responds to each one.

1 9 9 6

Rabindranath Tagore

Who are you reading curiously this poem of mine
a hundred years from now?
Shall I be able to send to you
—steeped in the love of my heart—
5 the faintest touch of this spring morning's joy,
the scent of a flower,
a bird-song's note,
a spark of today's blaze of color
a hundred years from now?

10 Yet, for once, open your window on the south
and from your balcony

Rabindranath Tagore, 1896

gaze at the far horizon.
Then, sinking deep in fancy
think of the ecstasies of joy
15 that came floating down
from some far heaven of bliss
to touch the heart of the world
a hundred years ago;
think of the young spring day
20 wild, impetuous and free;
and of the south wind
—fragrant with the pollen of flowers—
rushing on restless wings to paint the earth
with the radiant hues of youth
25 a hundred years before your day.

And think, how his heart aflame,
his whole being rapt in song,
a poet was awake that day
to unfold like flowers
30 his myriad thoughts
with what wealth of love!—
one morning a hundred years ago.

A hundred years from now
who is the new poet singing his songs to you?
35 Across the years I send him
the joyous greeting of this spring.
May my song echo for a while,
on your spring day,
in the beating of your heart,
40 in the murmur of bees,
in the rustling of leaves,—
a hundred years from today.

February, 1896

20 impetuous (ĭm-pĕch′o͞o-əs):
impulsive.

27 rapt: deeply absorbed.

30 myriad (mĭr′ē-əd): countless.

Connect to the Literature

1. **What Do You Think?** What impressions of Rabindranath Tagore do you have after reading this poem?

> **Comprehension Check**
> - Who does Tagore address in his poem?
> - What does the poet hope will happen in 100 years?

Think Critically

2. How do you think Tagore would explain the **purpose** of his poem?

> **THINK ABOUT**
> - what he hopes to "send" to the reader (line 3)
> - why he wants the reader to "gaze at the far horizon" (line 12)
> - his desire "to unfold like flowers / his myriad thoughts" (lines 29–30)

3. How would you describe the **mood** Tagore creates in his poem?

4. Do you think Tagore expects the world to change much in 100 years? Use evidence from the poem to support your answer.

5. **ACTIVE READING** **ANALYZING STRUCTURE** With a classmate, review the notes you wrote down in your **READER'S NOTEBOOK** about the questions in "1996." How do the questions relate to each other? How do they link Tagore, the reader, and the poet writing "a hundred years from today"?

Extend Interpretations

6. **The Writer's Style** In "1996," Tagore addresses the reader directly. What is your reaction to this technique? What effect do you think the poet is trying to achieve?

7. **Connect to Life** Think about the message that Tagore sends to his future readers. Do you think a contemporary poet might send a similar message to future readers? Why or why not?

8. **Points of Comparison** Compare Housman's message about mortality in "To an Athlete Dying Young" with the **theme** of rebirth in Tagore's poem. What **images** do the poets use to support their themes?

Literary Analysis

TITLE The **titles** of some literary works are straightforward, stating exactly what the reader can expect to discover in the work. Others merely tickle the imagination, perhaps hinting at the subject and forcing the reader to search for deeper meaning. The title of Tagore's poem gives readers a direct clue about its subject. In addition, the text of the poem repeatedly recalls the title with its reference at the end of each stanza to "a hundred years." Deeper understanding of the title is provided by the poem's **theme**—the passage and effect of time—and by its hopeful **tone.**

Cooperative Learning Activity Get together with a small group of your classmates and plan what you would say in a poem titled "2096." In a chart like the one shown here, compare Tagore's "1996" with the poem you would compose. How would your poem differ from Tagore's in theme and tone? Share your ideas with the rest of the class.

	Theme	Tone
Tagore's "1996"		
My "2096"		

Choices & CHALLENGES

Writing Options

1. Spring Images Jot down some images that come to mind when you think of a spring day. Place a check beside those that might appeal to Tagore.

2. Points of Comparison Think again about the poems you've read by Tagore and Housman and the themes these works convey to the reader. If Tagore and Housman had met, would they have had similar ideas about the role of the poet? Freewrite your ideas.

Activities & Explorations

1. Poetry Anthology Prepare an anthology of contemporary poetry as an answer to Tagore's question "Who is the new poet?" ~ **INTERPRETING**

2. Triptych of Tagore's World With classmates, prepare a triptych—an artwork in three panels—to illustrate your impressions of the world in Tagore's time, the world today, and the world as it might appear 100 years from now. ~ **ART**

Inquiry & Research

Jewel in the Crown Research to find out about some of the political, social, and economic changes brought about in India by the British in the 19th century. Share your findings with the class.

 More Online: Research Starter
www.mcdougallittell.com

Rabindranath Tagore
1861–1941

Other Works
Gitanjali (Song Offerings)
The Crescent Moon
"The Cabuliwallah"
"The Babus of Nayanjore"

A Literary Bent Born into one of the most intellectual and talented Indian families of the time, Rabindranath Tagore wrote his first poem at the age of 8. By the time he was 15, he had published one poem and was reading his work aloud at public gatherings. In spite of his thirst for learning, Tagore disliked his childhood school experiences and rebelled against his rigidly institutionalized education. At the age of 17, he traveled to London, enrolled at University College, and, following his family's wishes, began to study law. Two years later, however, he gave up his studies and returned to India to devote his life to literary pursuits.

Rural Life Although born in the city of Calcutta, Tagore seemed to prefer life in the rural areas of Bengal. He had a fascination with nature that was strengthened during a boyhood trip to northern India and the Himalayas. In later years, he managed his family's estates and composed numerous literary works in rural Bengal, where he eventually founded his own school. In an effort to blend the best of Indian and Western traditions, he introduced many new educational techniques, including coeducation and the elimination of all caste, or class, distinctions. After World War I, he expanded his local school into an international university.

Artist and Activist By the time of his death at the age of 80, Tagore had composed numerous short stories, novels, and plays, as well as 60 volumes of poetry. He was also a gifted painter and musician and had set many of his poems to music. Reflected in some of his best poetry is the intense sadness he experienced after the deaths of his wife, a daughter, and a son within a five-year period. Much of his writing was also inspired by a deep concern for India's poor and by a desire for social and political reforms. Besides being a leader in the arts, Tagore was one of India's leading activists for independence. His death came six years before his country gained its freedom from British rule.

The Victorians

How has reading the selections in this unit helped you understand the Victorian era? Have you discovered any links between your life and the lives of people you have read about? Choose one or more of the options in each section to help you explore these questions.

Reflecting on the Unit

OPTION 1

Considering Relationships In this unit you have read about many kinds of personal relationships. Which of these relationships did you find the most inspiring? the most frightening? the most saddening? Which of the relationships seemed like ones that you might encounter today? Discuss your opinions with a classmate.

OPTION 2

Reflecting on Life's Ironies In several of the selections in this unit, you encountered speakers and narrators who reflect on life and its ironies. In a paragraph, compare two selections that you found ironic, exploring the speakers' or narrators' attitudes and circumstances. Then reflect on some of the ironies you have experienced in your own life.

OPTION 3

Looking at Character Think about the quotation from George Eliot at the beginning of this unit: "Our deeds determine us, as much as we determine our deeds." With a partner, choose a character or speaker from each part of the unit and brainstorm some ways in which each has been "determined" by his or her deeds. Then, for the class, role-play a conversation in which the two individuals discuss the quotation.

Self ASSESSMENT

READER'S NOTEBOOK

To explore how your understanding of the Victorian era has developed over the course of this unit, make a before-and-after chart. In it, show how your ideas about the lives and relationships of some Victorians have changed as a result of reading the selections.

Reviewing Literary Concepts

OPTION 1

Understanding an Author's Purpose You have learned that an author's purpose may be to entertain, to inform, to express opinions, or to persuade. In a chart like the one shown, group this unit's selections according to their authors' purposes. Do any seem to fall under more than one heading? Are there any headings under which no selection fits?

Compare your groupings with a partner's, and discuss any differences between the two.

To Entertain	To Inform	To Express Opinions	To Persuade

OPTION 2

Analyzing Setting In both fiction and poetry, setting often plays an important role—though the settings of poems are frequently implied rather than stated directly. From each part of this unit, choose three selections in which settings are either obvious or implied. List their titles, and describe, next to each, as much as you know about that work's setting. Then rank the selections according to how important you think setting is in them, with 1 representing the selection in which setting plays the most crucial role. Discuss your rankings with the rest of the class.

Self ASSESSMENT

In addition to *setting* and *author's purpose,* the following literary terms were discussed in Unit Five. In your 📖 READER'S NOTEBOOK copy the following list. Next to each term, write W (for "well"), S (for "somewhat"), or N (for "not at all") to indicate how well you think you understand it. Review the terms you are not sure about in the **Glossary of Literary Terms** (page 1328).

speaker

blank verse

author's
 purpose

third-person
 omniscient
 point of view

mood

sprung rhythm

satire

title

tone

dramatic
 monologue

situational irony

setting

folk tale

controlling image

allusion

alliteration

stanza structure

🗂 Building Your Portfolio

- **Writing Options** Several Writing Options in this unit asked you to present your responses to the messages, or themes, of selections. Choose one of your pieces in which you think you explored your reactions to themes most thoroughly. Then write a cover note describing why you found the piece particularly insightful, and add the note, along with the piece, to your **Presentation Portfolio.** 🗂

- **Writing Workshop** In this unit you chose a topic that interested you and then wrote a Subject Analysis about it. Reread this piece and assess the quality of the writing. Then decide if you would like to keep this piece in your **Presentation Portfolio.** 🗂

- **Additional Activities** Review the assignments you completed under **Activities & Explorations** and **Inquiry & Research.** Keep a record in your portfolio of any assignments that you think are representative of your best work.

Self ASSESSMENT

Compare what you have chosen for your **Presentation Portfolio** 🗂 during Unit Five with what was already in your portfolio. Do you see any progress in your work? In what areas? Jot down your thoughts and observations in your 📖 READER'S NOTEBOOK.

Setting GOALS

You have read short stories, poems, and nonfiction in this unit. At this point, which of these genres of literature appeals to you the most, and why? What other works belonging to that genre would you like to read this year? Explore these questions in a paragraph or two.

LITERATURE CONNECTIONS

Jane Eyre

CHARLOTTE BRONTË

In 19th-century England, Jane is an orphan, a teacher, and a governess who, although plain in appearance, is fiercely independent and moral in spirit. These qualities are tested and ultimately bring her the happiness she has searched for. Charlotte Brontë was raised on the English moors, and her novel reflects the influence of this dark and brooding landscape.

These thematically related readings are provided along with *Jane Eyre:*

Sonnet 141
BY WILLIAM SHAKESPEARE

Beauty: When the Other Dancer Is the Self
BY ALICE WALKER

The Governess
BY DANIEL POOL

The Little Governess
BY KATHERINE MANSFIELD

I see, I see the crescent moon
BY ANNA AKHMATOVA

Signs and Symbols
BY VLADIMIR NABOKOV

A Home for Hope
BY RON ARIAS

Seventh House
BY R. K. NARAYAN

In the Evening
BY ANNA AKHMATOVA

And Even *More* . . .

The Importance of Being Earnest

OSCAR WILDE

In this classic farce, Oscar Wilde paints a satirical picture of the values and concerns of Victorian England. The play is famous for its witty lines and absurd comic situations in which paradox is used to undermine convention.

Books
Silas Marner
GEORGE ELIOT
This classic novel, described by the author as "a story of old-fashioned village life," portrays a miserly social outcast who comes to adopt a poor orphan and wins redemption.

The Return of the Native
THOMAS HARDY
In this novel, published in 1878, individuals strive through their relationships to overcome the indifferent forces of fate.

Tess of the d'Urbervilles

THOMAS HARDY

The values of 19th-century society run head-on with the personal life of Tess Durbeyfield, a 16-year-old girl from a poor English family. In this tragic tale of love and betrayal, a father's discovery of his royal ancestry sets in motion a chain of events that spells disaster.

These thematically related readings are provided along with *Tess of the d'Urbervilles*:

Life's Tragedy
BY PAUL LAURENCE DUNBAR

Disappointment Is the Lot of Woman
BY LUCY STONE

The Paris Gown
BY ESTELA PORTILLO TRAMBLEY

The Ruined Maiden
BY THOMAS HARDY

Yesterday He Still Looked in My Eyes
BY MARINA TSVETAYEVA

A Complaint
BY LADY CHWANG KËANG

The Royal Family
BY GARRISON KEILLOR

Design
BY ROBERT FROST

The Brontës and Their World
PHYLLIS BENTLEY
The work provides a solid introduction to the Brontë sisters.

The Nineteenth Century
ASA BRIGGS
This extensive, encyclopedic work on the period contains hundreds of illustrations.

Other Media

The Victorian Age: Browning, Tennyson and Arnold
Listening Library.
(FILMSTRIP WITH CASSETTE)

Victorian Poetry
Caedmon. Several actors read selections by major poets of the era, including Matthew Arnold, Christina Rossetti, Gerard Manley Hopkins, Thomas Hardy, and A. E. Housman.
(AUDIOCASSETTES)

Jane Eyre
Fox Video. A Hollywood production of the novel, starring Joan Fontaine and Orson Welles.
(VIDOECASSETTE)

Tess of the d'Urbervilles
Chivers North America. An unabridged reading of the novel by actor Peter Firth, who played Angel Clare in the 1979 film adaptation.
(AUDIOCASSETTES)

UNIT SIX

1901-1950

1901-1950

Emerging

Modernism

I feel suddenly attached not to the past

but to the future.

Virginia Woolf
novelist, critic, and essayist

Emerging

Modernism

EVENTS IN BRITISH LITERATURE

1900   **1920**

1902 Joseph Conrad's novella, *Heart of Darkness,* published

1913 George Bernard Shaw's play *Pygmalion* produced

1914 James Joyce begins writing controversial novel *Ulysses* (to 1921)

1921 T. S. Eliot writes groundbreaking long poem *The Waste Land*

1922 Katherine Mansfield's *The Garden Party and Other Stories* published; Virginia Woolf's experimental *Jacob's Room* published

1926 D. H. Lawrence writes "The Rocking-Horse Winner"

EVENTS IN BRITAIN

1900   **1920**

1901 Queen Victoria dies and is succeeded by son Edward VII

1903 Emmeline Pankhurst founds Women's Social and Political Union to promote women's suffrage in Britain

1907 Britain, France, and Russia form alliance known as Triple Entente to counter Germany

1910 Edward VII dies and is succeeded by son George V

1912 More than 1,500 drown when *Titanic* sinks in Atlantic

1914 Britain enters World War I after Germany invades Belgium

1918 British military deaths total about 750,000 at World War I's end; British women over 30 allowed to vote

1921 Irish Free State established, while Northern Ireland remains in union with Great Britain

1926 General strike protests national lockout of coal miners

1932 At depth of global depression, British unemployment rate is 23 percent

EVENTS IN THE WORLD

1900   **1920**

1903 U.S. Wright brothers fly first engine-powered airplane

1905 Russian soldiers fire on petitioning citizens in St. Petersburg, starting brief first Russian Revolution

1912 Last emperor of Qing Dynasty, rulers of China since 1644, overthrown

1913 Ford revolutionizes auto industry with assembly-line production

1914 Assassination of Archduke Franz Ferdinand sparks World War I

1917 V. I. Lenin leads Bolshevik Revolution that topples Russian czar

1918 Allies, with U.S. help, defeat Central Powers, ending World War I; Bolsheviks renamed Communist Party

1919 Allies and Germany sign Treaty of Versailles; Gandhi becomes leader of Indian independence movement

1920 Hitler takes control of new National Socialist German Workers' (Nazi) Party; American women gain right to vote

1927 Charles Lindbergh flies solo from New York to Paris; first "talking" movie released in U.S.

1928 Joseph Stalin becomes dictator of Communist Russia

1929 U.S. stock market crashes, initiating global depression

PERIOD PIECES

California Clipper,
mid-1930s

Telephone,
1920s–1930s

Clock in style known
as Art Deco, c. 1925

1940

1927 Yeats's "Sailing to Byzantium" published; T. S. Eliot becomes British citizen

1932 Aldous Huxley's novel *Brave New World*, warning of scientifically controlled future society, published

1934 Dylan Thomas, 20-year-old Welsh poet, publishes *Eighteen Poems*

1940 W. H. Auden publishes poem "Musée des Beaux Arts"

1941 Depression and despair drive Woolf to suicide

1945 George Orwell publishes classic anti-utopian fable *Animal Farm;* Elizabeth Bowen publishes short-story collection *The Demon Lover*

1946 Auden becomes U.S. citizen

1949 Orwell publishes *1984*, nightmarish vision of future totalitarian England

1940

1936 George V dies; son Edward VIII renounces throne; Edward's younger brother becomes king as George VI

1937 Prime minister claims "peace in our time" after giving Hitler part of Czechoslovakia

1939 Britain joins France in declaring war on Germany

1940 Britain suffers daily German bombing but is unconquered in Battle of Britain (to 1941)

1945 At end of war, British military and civilian losses total 360,000; socialist program creates British welfare state (to 1951)

1947 India and Pakistan given independence

1949 Britain helps found NATO; Irish Free State becomes Republic of Ireland

1940

1930 Nationalists and Communists begin civil war in China (to 1949)

1932 Kingdom of Saudi Arabia declared

1933 Hitler and Nazis seize dictatorial control of Germany

1937 Japan invades China

1939 Germany invades Poland and World War II begins

1941 Attack on Pearl Harbor in Hawaii causes U.S. to declare war on Japan

1942 Nazis initiate "Final Solution" stage of murdering unwanted civilians, mostly Jews (to 1945)

1945 World War II ends; United Nations formed

1946 Cold War between U.S. and Soviet Union begins (to 1991)

1948 Israel becomes nation; South African policy of apartheid begins

1949 Communists win civil war to gain control of China

Far left: George V, Victoria, Edward VII, and Edward VIII. *Above:* Women demanding the right to vote.

Emerging
Modernism

1901 - 1950

From the accession of Edward VII in 1901 until the outbreak of World War I, Britain remained the dominant political, economic, and military power in the world. The world, however, was rapidly changing. Recent advances, including electric power and the automobile, were completely transforming everyday life. Through strikes and the emergence of the Labor party, British workers were obtaining economic and political power. Women were growing increasingly vocal in public demonstrations, demanding the right to vote. In Ireland, as well as India and other British colonies, nationalist movements were gaining momentum. At the same time, colonial and commercial rivalries were driving European powers into competing alliances, such as the Triple Entente of Britain, France, and Russia, formed in 1907. These rivalries would escalate into World War I, shattering the Victorian way of life forever.

WORLD WAR I

Known at the time as the Great War, World War I was precipitated by the assassination of Archduke Francis Ferdinand, heir to the throne of Austria-Hungary, by a Serbian nationalist in Sarajevo on June 28, 1914. Austria's demands for satisfaction from Serbia were impossibly harsh, and when Serbia was unable to meet them, Austria declared war on Serbia. The Russian czar came to the aid of his fellow Slavs in Serbia, mobilizing troops along the border of Austria's strongest ally,

Scenes of World War I trench warfare.
Right: Body armor.

Germany, which proceeded to declare war on Russia and France. A German invasion of neutral Belgium prompted Britain, already committed by the Triple Entente, to join the war on the side of France and Russia. After British and French forces halted the Germans' westward advance at the First Battle of the Marne in September 1914, both sides dug in, locked together in bloody trench warfare—a chaos of mud, barbed wire, exploding shells and hand grenades, machine guns, tanks, and poison gas. This stalemate would drag on for four years, with massive propaganda intensifying the bitterness and leaders refusing to admit that the carnage and devastation were in vain.

In 1917 disillusionment with the failures of the war effort led to revolution in Russia. A moderate government was formed to replace the czar, but it was soon overthrown by Lenin's Bolsheviks, who promptly established a

Communist state, agreed to a separate peace with Germany, and withdrew from the war. By then, however, the United States had entered it, tipping the balance in favor of Britain and France and forcing Germany to sue for peace. In the subsequent negotiations, French fears and anti-German sentiment resulted in the highly punitive Treaty of Versailles. To help defuse future crises, the treaty established the League of Nations, brainchild of the U.S. president Woodrow Wilson. The moderating U.S. influence was lost, however, when Congress refused to sign the treaty and join the league.

AFTERMATH OF THE WAR

Through the provisions of the Treaty of Versailles, Britain acquired several former German colonies in Africa and became "trustee" of large chunks of the Middle East that had been part of the Turkish (or Ottoman) Empire, a German ally. With France a war-torn shambles, Russia ravaged by internal conflict, and the United States abandoning the international scene, Britain seemed to be the war's greatest victor. However, the nation had lost almost an

Development of the *English Language*

In the 20th century, the English language has increasingly reflected the fads and fancies of popular culture. The horrors of World War I made the delicacies of Victorian usage seem inappropriate, and by the 1920s a spirit of "anything goes" had made slang and colloquial

language far more acceptable. Modern warfare generated new words—*blimp* and *camouflage* in World War I, for example, and *radar* and *blitz* in World War II—as did new technologies, the terminologies of which sometimes differed from one side of the Atlantic to the other. Thus, what Americans called the *phonograph* and the *radio* were known as the *gramophone* and the *wireless* by their British counterparts. Later, when Americans watched *TV,* Britons were watching the *telly*. Despite these verbal differences, the main effect of the two world wars and the communications revolution was to bring speakers of English even closer together. In Britain, U.S. soldiers, Hollywood films, and recordings of American music all helped to spread American popular culture, including its distinctive vocabulary.

entire generation of young men—over 750,000 killed and
more than twice as many wounded—including a
disproportionate number from the upper class, which
had traditionally provided military leadership.

The casualties resulting from trench warfare had
been so great, in fact, that halfway through the war
the British government had been forced to make
military service compulsory for the first time. Meanwhile, with so many of the nation's men fighting in
France, British women had been forced to take on
traditionally male jobs. Their contribution was
acknowledged in 1918, when women over 30 were
granted the right to vote.

Also acknowledged after the war was the military
support supplied by Canada, Australia, New Zealand,
and South Africa. By 1931, these former colonies, already
largely self-governing, had been granted equal footing
with Britain in the British Commonwealth of Nations.
Britain moved more slowly with India, however, where
nonviolent resistance to British rule, under the direction of
the spiritual leader Mohandas K. Gandhi, was making
Britain look bad in the eyes of the world. Britain did reach
a compromise of sorts with Ireland, however. During the
war, Irish republican extremists had courted German
support, and on Easter Monday, 1916, they had launched
an armed rebellion, seizing the General Post Office in
Dublin. Although the rebellion had quickly been
crushed, the British government's brutal punishment of
its leaders led to widespread sympathy for their cause.
In 1921, Britain succeeded in negotiating a partition with
a group of Irish delegates, establishing the Irish Free State
but allowing northern Ireland, with its Protestant majority
loyal to the crown, to remain in the United Kingdom.
The Irish Free State later became the Republic of Ireland.

While Britain was facing these problems, political
turmoil was rocking nations dissatisfied with the terms
of the Treaty of Versailles. Italy fell into the hands of
the dictator Benito Mussolini, whose Fascist movement
was based on an ideal of military glory. In the Soviet
Union—the Communist successor of the Russian empire—
another dictator, Joseph Stalin, came to power. The fear
and confusion caused by the global economic depression

Top to bottom: Winston Churchill giving "victory" sign;
World War II Spitfires; war poster asking for volunteers in
war effort; London residents with gas masks

that began in 1929 also favored the rise of dictators. Germany's postwar experiment with democracy ended abruptly in 1933, when its parliament gave dictatorial powers to Adolf Hitler, leader of the Nazi party and advocate of German racial and military supremacy. Soon Hitler was rebuilding the German army (in violation of the Treaty of Versailles) and constructing concentration camps where he secretly planned to exterminate Jews and other "racial undesirables."

In the wake of World War I, the Western democracies had little stomach for further violent confrontations. In 1931, when Japan invaded the Chinese region of Manchuria, China's appeals to the West were largely ignored. Four years later, when Italy invaded Ethiopia, the League of Nations invoked only mild economic sanctions. In the Spanish civil war of 1936, Fascists aided by Italy and Germany defeated the democratic loyalists, whose pleas for formal aid from the Western democracies went unheeded. Two years later, when Hitler forcibly annexed Austria and marched into Czechoslovakia, Britain and France maintained their policy of appeasement. Only when Hitler—after signing a secret pact with Stalin—invaded Poland on September 1, 1939, did Britain and France declare war on Germany. Italy and Japan soon allied themselves with Germany. World War II had begun.

WORLD WAR II

For a year after the fall of France in June 1940, Britain stood alone. With its entire population mobilized, civilian volunteers acted as plane spotters, firefighters, and rescue workers. All citizens endured severe shortages and rationing. Londoners slept in subways while bombs rained on the city above. During this period, known as the Battle of Britain, a handful of well-trained fighter pilots battered away at the German bombers. Prime Minister Winston Churchill praised these heroes of the Royal

LITERARY HISTORY

During the first decade of the 20th century—known as the Edwardian era—the major literary movements of Victorian times continued to flourish. The novelists John Galsworthy and Arnold Bennett; the short story writers W. Somerset Maugham, P. G. Wodehouse, and Saki; and the playwright George Bernard Shaw, among others, explored the changes and conflicts in the British class system in a realistic and often witty style. At the same time, a strong romantic spirit marked the work of Rupert Brooke, John Masefield, and other Edwardian poets. Romanticism was also evident in the early poetry of William Butler Yeats, the writings of Lady Gregory, and other works of the Irish Literary Renaissance—a movement propelled by the growing Irish nationalism and a renewed interest in the Celtic myths and legends of Ireland's past.

By 1910, however, Victorian ideas were yielding to the spirit of modernism, the movement that would dominate Western literature in the first half of the 20th century. Modernists stressed innovation as they attempted to create a new kind of literature for a new age. Such modernist poets as T. S. Eliot—and later Yeats—abandoned traditional patterns of stanza and meter for the more natural flow of **free verse.** Influenced by the French symbolists, they discarded the refined sentiment of the 19th century, preferring to convey emotions by means of strong images and unusual symbols. The works of modernist fiction writers—including Joseph Conrad, Katherine Mansfield, E. M. Forster, and D. H. Lawrence—began to reflect the new psychological theories of Sigmund Freud and Carl Jung.

Shaw

Yeats

Mansfield

Lawrence

LITERARY HISTORY

Psychology also had a major impact on the pioneering fiction of James Joyce and Virginia Woolf. In different ways, each became a master of **stream of consciousness,** a narrative technique that attempts to depict the leaps and associations of the human mind.

The excitement of early modernism, however, crumbled into disillusionment for many of the writers who survived the devastation of World War I. In the aftermath of the war, writers tended to see the world as bleak and fragmentary—a Waste Land like that presented by T. S. Eliot in his most famous poem. The tone of many writers became bitter, expressing the cynicism of what has come to be called the Lost Generation. Others turned away from society altogether, exploring private concerns, personal experience, and the role of the artist.

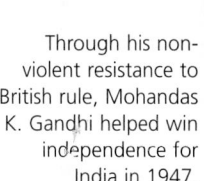

Auden

In the 1930s and 1940s, the growth of fascism and communism and the trauma of World War II prompted many British writers to focus again on social concerns. W. H. Auden and Stephen Spender examined and criticized society in much of their poetry; Aldous Huxley, Graham Greene, and George Orwell did likewise in their fiction. Aspects of modernism were increasingly accepted as they became more familiar, and mere novelty played a less important role in literature than before. Free verse remained popular, but such poets as Auden and Dylan Thomas were equally at home with more traditional forms. In fiction, the use of the stream-of-consciousness technique became more widespread and less obscure.

Air Force, stating that "never in the field of human conflict was so much owed by so many to so few."

In 1941, Hitler broke his pact with Stalin and invaded the Soviet Union. Later that year Japan bombed Pearl Harbor, and the United States entered the war. With these new allies, Britain was able to persevere until the war ended in 1945. Nearly 50 million people died in World War II, including over 10 million in concentration camps and almost a quarter million British civilians. The war also drained Britain financially.

After the war, devastated by widespread poverty and in desperate need of refashioning their social order, Britons turned to the nation's young liberals, electing a Parliament overwhelmingly dominated by Labor members. Over the next few years, the Labor government transformed Britain into a welfare state, setting up a national health-care system and nationalizing such industries as steel, coal, and railroads. Britain also began slowly to relinquish its colonies. In the climate of the cold war, with the United States assuming a leading role in international affairs, Britain was no longer to be the world's greatest power.

LaserLinks: Background for Reading
Historical Literary Connection

Through his non-violent resistance to British rule, Mohandas K. Gandhi helped win independence for India in 1947.

The profound changes of the first half of the 20th century gave rise to a sharpened anxiety and sense of irony. In this part of Unit Six, you will encounter writers who began to experiment with new and highly personal forms to express these feelings. As you read, consider whether their new images of reality express any ideas similar to your own.

The Second Coming
Sailing to Byzantium

Poetry by WILLIAM BUTLER YEATS

Connect to Your Life

Hopes and Fears Most people have concerns and questions about the future—both their own and the world's. What are your main hopes and fears for the future? Do your friends and relatives have similar hopes and fears? Share some of your thoughts with your classmates.

Build Background

Yeats's Beliefs William Butler Yeats, considered by many the greatest poet of the 20th century, was a visionary who developed his own set of beliefs to answer his questions about life and help him interpret the uncertainties of the future. Among these beliefs was the view that history occurs in 2,000-year cycles and that as each era comes to an end, another era—its opposite—is ushered in by a momentous occurrence. Yeats wrote "The Second Coming" at what might be seen as such a time of upheaval in world history—he wrote the poem in January 1919, not long after the Russian Revolution of 1917 and the end of World War I in 1918. In the poem, Yeats employed a cyclical view of history to explain what he and many others saw as a breakdown of society at the beginning of the 20th century.

In the 1920s, Yeats became fascinated with the history and art of medieval Byzantium. This interest is reflected in his 1926 poem "Sailing to Byzantium," one of his most celebrated and closely studied poems. He later commented, "Byzantium was the center of European civilization and the source of its spiritual philosophy, so I symbolize the search for spiritual life by a journey to that city."

Focus Your Reading

LITERARY ANALYSIS | **SYMBOLS** | **Symbols**—persons, places, objects, or actions that stand for things beyond themselves—are a central element in Yeats's poetry. In the two poems you are about to read, there are a number of symbols including a falcon, a beast, fire, and gold. As you read the poems, consider what these and other symbols might represent.

ACTIVE READING | **CLARIFYING MEANING IN POETRY** | When reading complex poems, you may encounter some unfamiliar ideas and images. If a poem seems obscure, it may help to read it several times. Use the following steps as strategies for your reading:

- On your first reading, refer to the explanations in the notes and think about each poem's **subject.**
- The next time you read the poem, note any **images** that stand out in your mind.
- On subsequent readings, be aware of any **lines** that you think are especially difficult.

Don't expect to understand a complex poem immediately, but do expect to discover new insights each time you read it.

READER'S NOTEBOOK As you read, use the strategies listed above to clarify the meaning of the two poems. Using a chart like the one shown, briefly describe the general subject of each poem. Then jot down images and lines that you want to focus on.

Title:	
Subject:	
Images	**Lines**

THE SECOND COMING

Turning and turning in the widening gyre
The falcon cannot hear the falconer;
Things fall apart; the center cannot hold;
Mere anarchy is loosed upon the world,
5   The blood-dimmed tide is loosed, and everywhere
The ceremony of innocence is drowned;
The best lack all conviction, while the worst
Are full of passionate intensity.

Surely some revelation is at hand;
10   Surely the Second Coming is at hand.
The Second Coming! Hardly are those words out
When a vast image out of *Spiritus Mundi*
Troubles my sight: somewhere in sands of the desert
A shape with lion body and the head of a man,
15   A gaze blank and pitiless as the sun,
Is moving its slow thighs, while all about it
Reel shadows of the indignant desert birds.
The darkness drops again; but now I know
That twenty centuries of stony sleep
20   Were vexed to nightmare by a rocking cradle,
And what rough beast, its hour come round at last,
Slouches towards Bethlehem to be born?

1 gyre (jīr): spiral. (Yeats, however, pronounced this word with a hard *g* [gīr].)

2 falcon: a hawklike bird of prey; **falconer:** a person who uses trained falcons to hunt small game.

6 ceremony of innocence: the rituals (such as the rites of baptism and marriage) that give order to life.

10 Second Coming: Christ's return to earth, predicted in the New Testament as an event preceded by a time of terror and chaos.

12 *Spiritus Mundi* (spîr′ĭ-tōōs mōōn′dē) *Latin:* Spirit of the World. Yeats used this term to refer to the collective unconscious, a supposed source of images and memories that all human beings share.

14 This image suggests the Great Sphinx in Egypt, built more than 40 centuries ago.

20 rocking cradle: a reference to the birth of Christ.

Thinking Through the Literature

1. Describe the image from this poem that remains most vivid in your mind.

2. What concerns does the poem's speaker seem to be expressing?

3. How would you describe the speaker's view of the future?

THINK ABOUT

- the speaker's apparent attitude toward the Second Coming
- the speaker's feelings about the "rough beast"
- the effect of the rocking cradle

William Butler Yeats

SAILING TO BYZANTIUM

That is no country for old men. The young
In one another's arms, birds in the trees
—Those dying generations—at their song,
The salmon-falls, the mackerel-crowded seas,
5   Fish, flesh, or fowl, commend all summer long
Whatever is begotten, born, and dies.
Caught in that sensual music all neglect
Monuments of unaging intellect.

An aged man is but a paltry thing,
10 A tattered coat upon a stick, unless
Soul clap its hands and sing, and louder sing
For every tatter in its mortal dress,
Nor is there singing school but studying
Monuments of its own magnificence;
15 And therefore I have sailed the seas and come
To the holy city of Byzantium.

4 salmon-falls: the rapids in rivers that salmon swim up to spawn.

13 but: except for.

14 its: the soul's.

16 Byzantium (bĭ-zăn′shē-əm): a city of southeastern Europe (now Istanbul, Turkey) that was a center of European civilization, especially art and religion, in the Middle Ages.

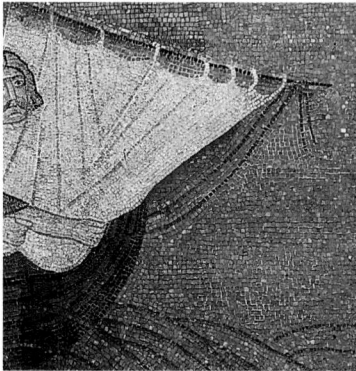

Saint Mark arriving in Venice (about A.D. 800–1000). Byzantine mosaic from San Marco, Venice, Italy, Scala/Art Resource, New York.

III

O sages standing in God's holy fire
As in the gold mosaic of a wall,
Come from the holy fire, perne in a gyre,
20 And be the singing-masters of my soul.
Consume my heart away; sick with desire
And fastened to a dying animal
It knows not what it is; and gather me
Into the artifice of eternity.

17 **sages:** wise people; saints.

18 **gold mosaic of a wall:** artwork in an ancient church.

19 **perne** (pûrn) **in a gyre:** whirl in a spiral.

23 **it:** the speaker's heart.
24 **artifice:** skilled craftsmanship.

IV

25 Once out of nature I shall never take
My bodily form from any natural thing,
But such a form as Grecian goldsmiths make
Of hammered gold and gold enameling
To keep a drowsy Emperor awake;
30 Or set upon a golden bough to sing
To lords and ladies of Byzantium
Of what is past, or passing, or to come.

29 **Emperor:** the ninth-century Byzantine emperor Theophilus, said to have possessed a golden sculpture of a tree with mechanical singing birds on its branches.

Thinking through the LITERATURE

Connect to the Literature

1. What Do You Think?
What impressions of growing old do you have after reading "Sailing to Byzantium"?

> **Comprehension Check**
> • Is the speaker young or old?
> • To whom does the speaker go for spiritual guidance?

Think Critically

2. What **conflict** does the speaker seem to be facing at the start of the poem?

3. Why do you think the speaker decides to go to Byzantium?

> **THINK ABOUT**
> • what the speaker might mean by "monuments of unaging intellect"
> • the possible meanings of *singing*
> • the references to sages, holy fire, and gold mosaic

4. What do you think the speaker expects from the future?

5. Compare and contrast the ways in which the speakers of "The Second Coming" and "Sailing to Byzantium" view the future. Do they share any attitudes or expectations? Explain your answer.

6. **ACTIVE READING** **CLARIFYING MEANING IN POETRY**
Review the charts you completed in your **READER'S NOTEBOOK**. Choose an **image** or **line** from each poem that you think is particularly striking or important to the meaning of the poem. Explain your choice to a partner.

Extend Interpretations

7. Writer's Style Yeats once wrote, "I tried to make the language of poetry coincide with that of passionate, normal speech." Keeping in mind the importance of both **word choice** and **rhythm,** comment on how successful you think Yeats was in his attempt to reflect "passionate, normal speech" in these two poems.

8. Connect to Life Some people see uncertainty and change as a challenge; others, as a threat. What kinds of uncertainties and changes do you think people will face in the 21st century? Do you think these two poems offer any perspectives that might be useful in today's world?

Literary Analysis

SYMBOLS Yeats uses **symbols**—persons, places, objects, or actions that stand for things beyond themselves—to convey major ideas and themes in his poetry. One of his most important symbols is the *gyre,* or spiral, which he uses to express his view of history and his belief that life repeats itself even as it moves forward.

Activity In a chart like the one below, list other possibly symbolic details in the two poems, noting what each symbol might represent.

"The Second Coming"		"Sailing to Byzantium"	
Symbol	What It Represents	Symbol	What It Represents
gyre	repetition in life		

REVIEW **IMAGERY** As you know, **imagery** refers to words or phrases that create vivid sensory experiences. With a partner, read through each poem, making a list of the visual images that you think are essential to the poem's meaning. Decide what feelings or ideas each image conveys and how it contributes to the meaning of the whole poem. Then discuss your list and thoughts with the whole class. Be prepared to defend your interpretation of the images you selected from the text.

Choices & CHALLENGES

Writing Options

1. Stanza Titles Compose subtitles for the four stanzas of "Sailing to Byzantium." Try to make each subtitle reflect your interpretation of the stanza it applies to.

2. Symbolic Description Write a symbolic description of a major event or change in the world or in your life. Use an original symbol that you think captures the intensity or significance of the event.

Activities & Explorations

1. Dance Interpretation Work with a partner to prepare a reading-and-dance presentation of one of these poems. As one of you reads the poem, the other should use gesture and movement to interpret the images and the development of ideas in the poem.
~ PERFORMING

2. Sculpture Design Draw a design for a sculpture that conveys your interpretation of part or all of either poem. **~ ART**

Inquiry & Research

Byzantine Art Research the art of medieval Byzantium. What was the style of Byzantine art like? What materials were used? Look in art history books for photographs of Byzantine art, and share some of the best examples with the class. Discuss why you think Yeats felt drawn to this culture.

 More Online: Research Starter
www.mcdougallittell.com

William Butler Yeats
1865–1939

Other Works
"No Second Troy"
"A Prayer for My Daughter"
"Byzantium"
"Under Ben Bulben"

Early Years Born in Dublin of Protestant parents, William Butler Yeats was educated in large part by his father, a portrait painter. After a brief period at an art school, Yeats decided to write instead of paint. He published his first poems in 1885, and from that time until the end of his life, he was constantly writing—producing drama and criticism as well as poetry.

Patriotic Feelings Yeats was passionately committed to Ireland—its people, culture, and political destiny. At the age of 24, he met and fell in love with the actress Maud Gonne, a fiery Irish patriot. Although Gonne refused to marry him, she inspired some of his finest lyrics and deepened his commitment to Irish nationalism. In 1896, he met Lady Gregory, an Irish aristocrat; together they worked to create a national drama for Ireland, founding Dublin's Abbey Theatre in 1904. Their work was vital to the 20th-century revival of Irish literature.

Yeats's Mysticism Throughout his life, Yeats had an intense interest in mysticism and the supernatural—an interest that received a fresh impetus after his marriage in 1917, when he discovered that his wife could apparently convey "spirit messages" by means of automatic writing. Yeats used the metaphors and symbols he found in these messages to pursue new directions in his poetry and to create his mythological system. Many of his best works were produced in the following decade.

Resting Place In 1923, Yeats received the Nobel Prize in literature. He died in France in January 1939, but after World War II his remains were reburied in Ireland, as he had wished.

Author Activity

Mystical Beliefs Find out more about Yeats's beliefs in mysticism. What elements of these beliefs are reflected in the poems you have just read?

The Rising of the Moon

Drama by LADY ISABELLA AUGUSTA GREGORY

> **(Connect to Your Life)**
>
> **Facing a Dilemma** This play focuses on a moral dilemma—a man must choose between two opposing sides, each of which seems to be right. Think of a time when you had to make a hard choice between two sides of an issue. Describe your experience and tell how you made your decision.

Build Background

Fight for Independence When *The Rising of the Moon* was first performed in 1907, the Irish were struggling to gain independence from Great Britain, and individual citizens found themselves in the position of having to take sides. Some patriots worked for gradual change through peaceful means; others were willing to use violence to obtain an immediate separation from Great Britain. Set in the late 1800s, this play is about the search for an Irish rebel who has plotted to overthrow the British.

Two popular revolutionary songs are important in the play. The song "The Rising of the Moon" celebrates a famous Irish rebellion in 1798. It describes a gathering of rebels at moonrise, armed and ready to fight, and ends with thanks to God that there are still men "who would follow in their footsteps at the rising of the moon." In the other song, "Granuaile" (grän'ōō-āl'), Ireland is portrayed as a maiden who has been brutalized by the "ruffian band" of the English. At one time, when the English outlawed even the speaking of the name of Ireland, *Granuaile* was one of the many metaphorical names that Irish patriots applied to their homeland.

Focus Your Reading

LITERARY ANALYSIS **SUSPENSE** A writer may purposely leave readers uncertain about what will happen in a story or play in order to create **suspense**—that is, a feeling of tension or excitement. For example, reading this passage from the play, the reader wonders what the character has heard out on the moonlit water and what might follow:

> **Sergeant.** *Oh! What's that? . . . I thought it might be a boat.*

As you read, look for other statements and events that add to the suspense.

ACTIVE READING **ANALYZING DIALECT** This play reflects the **dialect** of County Galway in western Ireland. In this dialect, longer vowel sounds and differences in grammar, sentence structure, and idiom—such as the use of *me* for *my*—give a musical quality to the language. A writer may use dialect to make **dialogue** seem authentic or to give a musical quality to the language. Dialect can also be used to give clues about **characters'** backgrounds and beliefs.

READER'S NOTEBOOK As you read this play about a man who takes sides in the Irish-English conflict, use a chart like the one below to jot down interesting examples of dialect.

Example of Dialect	Page, Column, Character
"it's little chance we'd have . . ."	996, col. 1, Sergeant

LaserLinks:
Background for Reading
Historical Connection
Literary Connection

THE RISING OF THE MOON

Lady Isabella Augusta Gregory

Scene: *Side of a quay[1] in a seaport town. Some posts and chains. A large barrel. Enter three policemen. Moonlight.*

Sergeant, who is older than the others, crosses the stage to right and looks down steps. The others put down a pastepot and unroll a bundle of placards.[2]

---

1. **quay** (kē): a landing place for boats; wharf.
2. **placards** (plăk´ärdz´): posters.

Policeman B. I think this would be a good place to put up a notice. (*He points to barrel.*)

Policeman X. Better ask him. (*calls to* Sergeant) Will this be a good place for a placard? (*no answer*)

Policeman B. Will we put up a notice here on the barrel? (*no answer*)

Sergeant. There's a flight of steps here that leads to the water. This is a place that should be minded well. If he got down here, his friends might have a boat to meet him; they might send it in here from outside.

Policeman B. Would the barrel be a good place to put a notice up?

Sergeant. It might; you can put it there. (*They paste the notice up.*)

Sergeant (*reading it*). Dark hair—dark eyes, smooth face, height five feet five—there's not much to take hold of in that—It's a pity I had no chance of seeing him before he broke out of jail. They say he's a wonder, that it's he makes all the plans for the whole organization. There isn't another man in Ireland would have broken jail the way he did. He must have some friends among the jailers.

Policeman B. A hundred pounds is little enough for the Government to offer for him. You may be sure any man in the force that takes him will get promotion.

Sergeant. I'll mind this place myself. I wouldn't wonder at all if he came this way. He might come slipping along there (*points to side of quay*), and his friends might be waiting for him there (*points down steps*), and once he got away it's little chance we'd have of finding him; it's maybe under a load of kelp³ he'd be in a fishing boat, and not one to help a married man that wants it to the reward.

Policeman X. And if we get him itself, nothing but abuse on our heads for it from the people, and maybe from our own relations.

Sergeant. Well, we have to do our duty in the force. Haven't we the whole country depending on us to keep law and order? It's those that are down would be up and those that are up would be down, if it wasn't for us. Well, hurry on, you have plenty of other places to placard yet, and come back here then to me. You can take the lantern. Don't be too long now. It's very lonesome here with nothing but the moon.

Policeman B. It's a pity we can't stop with you. The Government should have brought more police into the town, with *him* in jail, and at assize⁴ time too. Well, good luck to your watch. (*They go out.*)

Sergeant (*walks up and down once or twice and looks at placard*). A hundred pounds and promotion sure. There must be a great deal of spending in a hundred pounds. It's a pity some honest man not to be the better of that. (*A ragged man appears at left and tries to slip past. Sergeant suddenly turns.*)

Sergeant. Where are you going?

Man. I'm a poor ballad singer, your honor. I thought to sell some of these (*holds out bundle of ballads*) to the sailors. (*He goes on.*)

Sergeant. Stop! Didn't I tell you to stop? You can't go on there.

Man. Oh, very well. It's a hard thing to be poor. All the world's against the poor!

Sergeant. Who are you?

Man. You'd be as wise as myself if I told you, but I don't mind. I'm one Jimmy Walsh, a ballad singer.

Sergeant. Jimmy Walsh? I don't know that name.

Man. Ah, sure, they know it well enough in Ennis. Were you ever in Ennis, Sergeant?

Sergeant. What brought you here?

Man. Sure, it's to the assizes I came, thinking I might make a few shillings here or there. It's in

---

3. **kelp:** a seaweed used to keep fish fresh until they get to market.

4. **assize** (ə-sīz′): in Britain, a court session held periodically in a county.

the one train with the judges I came.

Sergeant. Well, if you came so far, you may as well go farther, for you'll walk out of this.

Man. I will, I will; I'll just go on where I was going. (*goes toward steps*)

Sergeant. Come back from those steps; no one has leave to pass down them tonight.

Man. I'll just sit on the top of the steps till I see will some sailor buy a ballad off me that would give me my supper. They do be late going back to the ship. It's often I saw them in Cork carried down the quay in a handcart.

Sergeant. Move on, I tell you. I won't have anyone lingering about the quay tonight.

Man. Well, I'll go. It's the poor have the hard life! Maybe yourself might like one, Sergeant. Here's a good sheet now. (*turns one over*) "Content and a pipe"—that's not much. "The Peeler[5] and the Goat"—you wouldn't like that. "Johnny Hart"—that's a lovely song.

Sergeant. Move on.

Man. Ah, wait till you hear it. (*sings*)
There was a rich farmer's daughter lived near the town of Ross;
She courted a Highland soldier, his name was Johnny Hart;
Says the mother to her daughter, "I'll go distracted mad
If you marry that Highland soldier[6] dressed up in Highland plaid."

Sergeant. Stop that noise. (Man *wraps up his ballads and shuffles toward the steps.*)

Sergeant. Where are you going?

Man. Sure you told me to be going, and I am going.

Sergeant. Don't be a fool. I didn't tell you to go that way; I told you to go back to the town.

Man. Back to the town, is it?

Sergeant (*taking him by the shoulder and shoving him before him*). Here, I'll show you the way. Be off with you. What are you stopping for?

Man (*who has been keeping his eye on the notice, points to it*). I think I know what you're waiting for, Sergeant.

Sergeant. What's that to you?

Man. And I know well the man you're waiting for—I know him well—I'll be going. (*He shuffles on.*)

Sergeant. You know him? Come back here. What sort is he?

Man. Come back is it, Sergeant? Do you want to have me killed?

Sergeant. Why do you say that?

Man. Never mind. I'm going. I wouldn't be in your shoes if the reward was ten times as much. (*goes on offstage to left*) Not if it was ten times as much.

Sergeant (*rushing after him*). Come back here, come back. (*drags him back*) What sort is he? Where did you see him?

Man. I saw him in my own place, in the County Clare. I tell you you wouldn't like to be looking at him. You'd be afraid to be in the one place with him. There isn't a weapon he doesn't know the use of, and as to strength, his muscles are as hard as that board. (*slaps barrel*)

Sergeant. Is he as bad as that?

Man. He is then.

Sergeant. Do you tell me so?

Man. There was a poor man in our place, a sergeant from Ballyvaughan.[7]—It was with a lump of stone he did it.

Sergeant. I never heard of that.

Man. And you wouldn't, Sergeant. It's not everything that happens gets into the papers. And

---

5. **Peeler:** policeman (from the name of the British politician Robert Peel, who established the Irish constabulary in the early 1800s).

6. **If you marry that Highland soldier:** Scottish soldiers were hated by the Irish because of Scotland's close ties to England.

7. **Ballyvaughan** (băl′ē-vôn′).

there was a policeman in plain clothes, too . . . It is in Limerick he was. . . . It was after the time of the attack on the police barrack at Kilmallock. . . . Moonlight . . . just like this . . . waterside. . . . Nothing was known for certain.

Sergeant. Do you say so? It's a terrible county to belong to.

Man. That's so, indeed! You might be standing there, looking out that way, thinking you saw him coming up this side of the quay (*points*), and he might be coming up this other side (*points*), and he'd be on you before you knew where you were.

Sergeant. It's a whole troop of police they ought to put here to stop a man like that.

Man. But if you'd like me to stop with you, I could be looking down this side. I could be sitting up here on this barrel.

Sergeant. And you know him well, too?

Man. I'd know him a mile off, Sergeant.

Sergeant. But you wouldn't want to share the reward?

Man. Is it a poor man like me, that has to be going the roads and singing in fairs, to have the name on him that he took a reward? But you don't want me. I'll be safer in the town.

Sergeant. Well, you can stop.

Man (*getting up on barrel*). All right, Sergeant. I wonder, now, you're not tired out, Sergeant, walking up and down the way you are.

Sergeant. If I'm tired I'm used to it.

Man. You might have hard work before you tonight yet. Take it easy while you can. There's plenty of room up here on the barrel, and you see farther when you're higher up.

Sergeant. Maybe so. (*Gets up beside him on barrel, facing right. They sit back to back, looking different ways.*) You made me feel a bit queer with the way you talked.

Man. Give me a match, Sergeant (*He gives it and Man lights pipe.*); take a draw yourself? It'll

quiet you. Wait now till I give you a light, but you needn't turn round. Don't take your eye off the quay for the life of you.

Sergeant. Never fear, I won't. (*Lights pipe. They both smoke.*) Indeed it's a hard thing to be in the force, out at night and no thanks for it, for all the danger we're in. And it's little we get but abuse from the people, and no choice but to obey our orders, and never asked when a man is sent into danger, if you are a married man with a family.

Man (*sings*).

As through the hills I walked to view the hills and shamrock plain,
I stood awhile where nature smiles to view the rocks and streams,
On a matron fair I fixed my eyes beneath a fertile vale,
As she sang her song it was on the wrong of poor old Granuaile.

Sergeant. Stop that; that's no song to be singing in these times.[8]

Man. Ah, Sergeant, I was only singing to keep my heart up. It sinks when I think of him. To think of us two sitting here, and he creeping up the quay, maybe, to get to us.

Sergeant. Are you keeping a good lookout?

Man. I am; and for no reward too. Amn't I the foolish man? But when I saw a man in trouble, I never could help trying to get him out of it. What's that? Did something hit me? (*rubs his heart*)

Sergeant (*patting him on the shoulder*). You will get your reward in heaven.

Man. I know that. I know that, Sergeant, but life is precious.

Sergeant. Well, you can sing if it gives you more courage.

---

8. **that's no song . . . these times:** "Granuaile" is an anti-British revolutionary anthem.

Man (*sings*).

> Her head was bare, her hands and feet with
> iron bands were bound,
> Her pensive[9] strain and plaintive[10] wail mingles
> with the evening gale,
> And the song she sang with mournful air, I am
> old Granuaile.
> Her lips so sweet that monarchs kissed . . .

Sergeant. That's not it. . . . "Her gown she wore was stained with gore." . . . That's it—you missed that.

Man. You're right, Sergeant, so it is; I missed it. (*repeats line*) But to think of a man like you knowing a song like that.[11]

Sergeant. There's many a thing a man might know and might not have any wish for.

Man. Now, I daresay, Sergeant, in your youth, you used to be sitting up on a wall, the way you are sitting up on this barrel now, and the other lads beside you, and you singing "Granuaile"? . . .

Sergeant. I did then.

Man. And the "Shan Bhean Bhocht"?[12] . . .

Sergeant. I did then.

Man. And the "Green on the Cape"?

Sergeant. That was one of them.

Man. And maybe the man you are watching for tonight used to be sitting on the wall, when he was young, and singing those same songs. . . . It's a queer world.

Sergeant. Whisht! . . . I think I see something coming. . . . It's only a dog.

Man. And isn't it a queer world? . . . Maybe it's one of the boys you used to be singing with that time you will be arresting today or tomorrow, and sending into the dock.[13]

Sergeant. That's true indeed.

Man. And maybe one night, after you had been singing, if the other boys had told you some plan they had, some plan to free the country, you might have joined with them . . . and maybe it is you might be in trouble now.

Sergeant. Well, who knows but I might? I had a great spirit in those days.

Man. It's a queer world, Sergeant, and it's little any mother knows when she sees her child creeping on the floor what might happen to it before it has gone through its life, or who will be who in the end.

Sergeant. That's a queer thought now, and a true thought. Wait now till I think it out. . . . If it wasn't for the sense I have, and for my wife and family, and for me joining the force the time I did, it might be myself now would be after breaking jail and hiding in the dark, and it might be him that's hiding in the dark and that got out of jail would be sitting up where I am on this barrel. . . . And it might be myself would be creeping up trying to make my escape from himself, and it might be himself would be keeping the law, and myself would be breaking it, and myself would be trying maybe to put a bullet in his head, or to take up a lump of a stone the way you said he did . . . no, that myself did. . . . Oh! (*gasps; after a pause*) What's that? (*grasps* Man's *arm*)

Man (*jumps off barrel and listens, looking out over water*). It's nothing, Sergeant.

Sergeant. I thought it might be a boat. I had a notion there might be friends of his coming about the quays with a boat.

Man. Sergeant, I am thinking it was with the people you were, and not with the law you were, when you were a young man.

---

9. **pensive:** thoughtful in a serious or sad way.

10. **plaintive:** mournful; melancholy.

11. **to think of . . . song like that:** Since the sergeant is a police officer, paid to uphold British laws, the man is surprised that he is familiar with an anti-British song.

12. **"Shan Bhean Bhocht"** (shăn′ văn′ vôкнт′): a revolutionary song from the 1798 rebellion. Its title (meaning "the poor old woman"), like that of "Granuaile," is a reference to Ireland.

13. **dock:** the place where the accused person stands in a criminal court.

Captain Ned Bishop with Officers on the Bridge of the SS Eagle (1969), David Blackwood. Original etching.

Sergeant. Well, if I was foolish then, that time's gone.

Man. Maybe, Sergeant, it comes into your head sometimes, in spite of your belt and your tunic, that it might have been as well for you to have followed Granuaile.

Sergeant. It's no business of yours what I think.

Man. Maybe, Sergeant, you'll be on the side of the country yet.

Sergeant (*gets off barrel*). Don't talk to me like that. I have my duties and I know them. (*looks round*) That was a boat; I hear the oars. (*goes to the steps and looks down*)

Man (*sings*).
Oh then tell me, Shawn O'Farrell,
Where the gathering is to be.
In the old spot by the river
Right well known to you and me!

Sergeant. Stop that! Stop that, I tell you!

Man (*sings louder*).
One word more, for signal token,
Whistle up the marching tune,
With your pike upon your shoulder,
At the Rising of the Moon.

Sergeant. If you don't stop that, I'll arrest you. (*A whistle from below answers, repeating the air.*)

Sergeant. That's a signal. (*stands between him and steps*) You must not pass this way. . . . Step farther back. . . . Who are you? You are no ballad singer.

Man. You needn't ask who I am; that placard will tell you. (*points to placard*)

Sergeant. You are the man I am looking for.

Man (*takes off hat and wig.* Sergeant *seizes them*). I am. There's a hundred pounds on my head. There is a friend of mine below in a boat. He knows a safe place to bring me to.

Sergeant (*looking still at hat and wig*). It's a pity!

It's a pity. You deceived me. You deceived me well.

Man. I am a friend of Granuaile. There is a hundred pounds on my head.

Sergeant. It's a pity, it's a pity!

Man. Will you let me pass, or must I make you let me?

Sergeant. I am in the force. I will not let you pass.

Man. I thought to do it with my tongue. (*puts hand in breast*) What is that?

(*Voice of* Policeman X *outside*) Here, this is where we left him.

Sergeant. It's my comrades coming.

Man. You won't betray me . . . the friend of Granuaile. (*slips behind barrel*)

(*Voice of* Policeman B) That was the last of the placards.

Policeman X (*as they come in*). If he makes his escape it won't be unknown he'll make it. (Sergeant *puts hat and wig behind his back.*)

Policeman B. Did anyone come this way?

Sergeant (*after a pause*). No one.

Policeman B. No one at all?

Sergeant. No one at all.

Policeman B. We had no orders to go back to the station; we can stop along with you.

Sergeant. I don't want you. There is nothing for you to do here.

Policeman B. You bade us to come back here and keep watch with you.

Sergeant. I'd sooner be alone. Would any man come this way and you making all that talk? It is better the place to be quiet.

Policeman B. Well, we'll leave you the lantern anyhow. (*hands it to him*)

Sergeant. I don't want it. Bring it with you.

Policeman B. You might want it. There are clouds coming up and you have the darkness of the night before you yet. I'll leave it over here on the barrel. (*goes to barrel*)

Sergeant. Bring it with you I tell you. No more talk.

Policeman B. Well, I thought it might be a comfort to you. I often think when I have it in my hand and can be flashing it about into every dark corner (*doing so*) that it's the same as being beside the fire at home, and the bits of bogwood blazing up now and again. (*flashes it about, now on the barrel, now on* Sergeant)

Sergeant (*furious*). Be off the two of you, yourselves and your lantern! (*They go out.* Man *comes from behind barrel. He and* Sergeant *stand looking at one another.*)

Sergeant. What are you waiting for?

Man. For my hat, of course, and my wig. You wouldn't wish me to get my death of cold? (Sergeant *gives them.*)

Man (*going toward steps*). Well, good night, comrade, and thank you. You did me a good turn tonight, and I'm obliged to you. Maybe I'll be able to do as much for you when the small rise up and the big fall down . . . when we all change places at the Rising (*waves his hand and disappears*) of the Moon.

Sergeant (*turning his back to audience and reading placard*). A hundred pounds reward! A hundred pounds! (*turns toward audience*) I wonder, now, am I as great a fool as I think I am?

Connect to the Literature

1. **What Do You Think?** Jot down words and phrases that describe your reaction to this play.

   Comprehension Check
   - Who are the policemen looking for?
   - Who does the singer reveal himself to be?

Think Critically

2. Do you think the sergeant does the right thing by allowing the man to escape?

   THINK ABOUT
   - Policeman X's statement that "the people" might give them "nothing but abuse" if they catch the man
   - what the reward might do for the sergeant's family
   - the sergeant's duty to enforce the law

3. Think about the different strategies the man uses to persuade the sergeant to let him go. Which do you think works best?

   THINK ABOUT
   - the man's stories about the dangerousness of the escapee
   - the songs he sings
   - how he compares the sergeant to himself

4. Which of the two characters do you admire more? Give reasons for your answer.

5. **ACTIVE READING** **ANALYZING DIALECT** Look back at the examples of dialect you noted in your **READER'S NOTEBOOK.** Why do you think the writer uses dialect in this play? Explain your answer.

6. What would you say was Lady Gregory's **purpose** in writing this play?

Extend Interpretations

7. **What If?** Imagine that Policeman B discovers the revolutionary's disguise and hiding place. How do you think the play might end if this were so?

8. **Connect to Life** The sergeant breaks the law by letting the man escape. What are your feelings about breaking the law for the sake of a cause?

Literary Analysis

SUSPENSE **Suspense**—the tension or excitement readers feel as they are drawn into a story—is created when a writer purposely leaves readers uncertain or apprehensive about what will happen. Writers rely on suspense to entertain their audiences and to hold the audiences' interest. Lady Gregory uses suspense-building techniques such as the interactions between the sergeant and the unidentified man, unexpected sounds and actions, and the songs the man sings.

Paired Activity With a partner, make a chart like the one shown below. Look through the play for other statements and events that add to the suspense. Then for each one, note why the statement or event is suspenseful.

Statement/Event	Why Statement/Event Is Suspenseful
The man sings "Granuaile."	The man's singing of outlawed ballads makes us wonder about his identity.

Writing Options

1. Dramatic Scene Write a scene in which the sergeant tells his wife about his encounter with the man. Try to convey his concern for his family as well as for the nationalist cause. Place the scene in your **Working Portfolio**.

2. Story Outline What might the future hold for the two main characters? Will the sergeant's life go on as usual? Will the man stay out of trouble? Write an outline of a short story that explains what happens to each man in the weeks following their encounter.

3. Political Ballad Write an original ballad that tells the story of the sergeant and the rebel.

Activities & Explorations

1. Classroom Debate Stage a debate in which you present arguments about whether the sergeant was right or wrong to let the man get away. ~ **SPEAKING AND LISTENING**

2. First Night Poster *The Rising of the Moon* opened in 1907 at the Abbey Theatre in Dublin. Create an advertising poster for the play. Draw an appropriate picture and write an attention-getting caption. ~ **VIEWING AND REPRESENTING**

Inquiry & Research

A Divided Nation Although much of Ireland gained independence in 1922, organizations such as Sinn Fein and the Irish Republican Army have continued to fight for the independence of Northern Ireland, which is still part of the United Kingdom. Research the recent activities of these groups and the current status of English-Irish relations. Share your findings with the class.

Lady Isabella Augusta Gregory
1852–1932

Other Works
Spreading the News
The Workhouse Ward

Late Starter The pastoral life of a titled Irish gentlewoman seems far removed from Isabella Gregory's eventual achievements as a dramatist, Irish partisan, and "godmother" of Dublin's Abbey Theatre. Lady Gregory did not take an active interest in literature until after the death of her husband in 1892. When her son told her that he wanted to learn to speak with the people who lived on their estate, she began to study Gaelic (gā´lĭk), the language of the Celtic people of Ireland, and became fascinated with Gaelic myths, legends, and folk tales.

Irish Literary Revival Her interest in Irish traditions led her to a close friendship with William Butler Yeats, Ireland's foremost poet. The two became leading figures in the Irish Literary Revival, which sought to preserve and renew the country's cultural traditions. It was her son whom Yeats commemorated in his poem "An Irish Airman Foresees His Death" (page 1107). Together, Lady Gregory and Yeats helped found the Abbey Theatre expressly for the purpose of staging works such as *The Rising of the Moon*. The theater provided a forum for works celebrating the speech, history, and spirit of the Irish people.

Prolific Career After writing her first play at the age of 52, Lady Gregory went on to write or translate 40 more plays. She also published three collections of Irish oral histories and legends, based on what she called her "imperfect, stumbling" knowledge of Gaelic. These efforts to bring Irish tales and legends to English-speaking readers met with high critical acclaim when they were published and are still highly regarded today.

Author Activity

Abbey Theatre Find out more about Lady Gregory's involvement with the Abbey Theatre. Share your findings with your classmates.

Irony in *Modern* Literature

Unsinkable Irony

To think about irony, let's consider the *Titanic* at three points in history: first, in 1912 when the magnificent ship went down in the North Atlantic and 1,500 lives were tragically lost; second, in 1986 with the exciting discovery of the *Titanic's* wreckage; and third, in 1997 with the release of the blockbuster movie *Titanic*, the largest-grossing motion picture to date. The ghost of irony continues to haunt the great ship in several respects. It is ironic that the largest, strongest ship ever built would be brought down by an iceberg—and on its maiden voyage. It is also ironic that this tragedy at the beginning of the century would become, by the end of the century, a source of popular entertainment and titanic sums of money. Such is the nature of modern irony.

As with irony, there is more to an iceberg than what appears on the surface.

Irony as a Literary Technique

Irony in literature works very much like irony in everyday life. Simply put, irony is the contrast, often great, between expectation or appearance and reality. Generally, irony in literature is classified in three ways:

Verbal irony occurs when a writer says one thing but means another. Jonathan Swift's title for his satiric essay, "A Modest Proposal" (p. 611), is an example.

Situational irony occurs when a character or the reader expects one thing to happen but something entirely different happens. In Mary Coleridge's story, "The King Is Dead, Long Live the King" (p. 888), the king discovers the opposite of what he and the reader expect: his trusted friends and his wife are hypocrites and his enemy is a friend.

Dramatic irony is the difference between what a character knows and what the reader or audience knows. This type of irony is commonly used in drama: think of Duncan's expression of trust in Macbeth, just after the audience has heard Macbeth's desire to murder him. Dramatic irony also occurs in fiction when a character has a limited view of the events (or no view at all), but the reader is fully aware of what is going on.

A Short History of Irony

Irony has been present in European literature since ancient times. You can find examples of verbal, situational, and dramatic irony in Homer's *Odyssey*, the great Greek dramas, *Beowulf*, and the Old Testament. But ironically, the concept was not really named until the 18th century. The great 18th-century satirists primarily defined irony as a figure of speech: "saying the opposite of what you mean." You can see how Swift relies primarily on verbal irony in his satire.

At the end of the 18th century and the beginning of the 19th century, the concept of irony began to take on new meaning. This shift was consistent with the philosophical shift in worldview from the Enlightenment to the Romantic Age. The former meaning of irony as primarily verbal (an intentional manipulation of language) now took on the added idea that irony is something that happens in life (something unintentional but real). For example, in the 18th century, Swift used verbal irony in "A Modest Proposal" to ridicule British policy in Ireland. In the 19th century, Shelley used situational irony in "Ozymandias" (p. 781) to expose the vanity of tyrants by contrasting the "colossal wreck" of the ruler's statue with its arrogant inscription— "Look on my works, ye Mighty, and despair!"

Modern Irony: Less Is More

Over the last century, irony has again undergone a transformation in meaning. For modernist writers—W. B. Yeats, T. S. Eliot, D. H. Lawrence, James Joyce, Virginia Woolf, and others—irony became something larger than a literary technique; it became an attitude infusing the whole of a novel, a story, a poem, or a play.

This new ironic attitude of the modernists is seen as detached and questioning. Its source was the uncertainty that many felt at the core of modern life. Modernists refused to assume an all-knowing attitude. Instead, they aimed for complete objectivity in presenting ideas without commenting on meaning. Modernists regarded such restraint as an appropriate response to the complexities of modern life.

YOUR TURN With a couple of classmates, brainstorm ironic situations that you've encountered in your daily life.

A Study in Contrasts: Shelley and Yeats

Percy
Bysshe Shelley

Readers of Shelley's "Ozymandias" understand the irony because of the clear contrast between Ozymandias's arrogant expectation and the inevitability of what actually happens. Shelley, like Swift before him, speaks with the authority of righteousness on his side, and readers agree that Ozymandias gets what he deserves. The irony in W. B. Yeats's "Sailing to Byzantium" is not so easily grasped. The poet's certainty is gone. In one way, the old man in Yeats's poem is similar to Ozymandias in his desire for "unaging" monuments. Yet, the old man is not a tyrannical king but a "tattered coat upon a stick." The reader tends to sympathize with him because he is lost and defeated by the reality around him. The contrast is not so much between expectation and reality, but between different aspects of reality—the living (and therefore "dying") generations of humanity and the monuments of the past (art, religion, and history).

William
Butler Yeats

Notice that Yeats's irony is much more paradoxical, or contradictory, and less emotionally satisfying than Shelley's. In much of Yeats's poetry and the modernist literature that follows in this unit, irony is not just something that occasionally happens; it has become the nature of reality itself.

Strategies for Reading: Irony in Modern Literature

1. Be alert to anything in a work that seems contradictory or inconsistent with your expectations.

2. Keep the date of the work in mind. Consider how the early decades of the 20th century, with World War I and technological changes, may have shaped the views of a modern writer.

3. Draw conclusions about the type of irony that is used. Is the irony obvious so that you can point it out, or is the irony more subtle and a matter of tone and atmosphere?

4. Question what is actually the object of the writer's concern. Is the writer mocking or sympathetic to one attitude or behavior? Or, does he or she seem to be looking at things from multiple perspectives?

5. **Monitor** your reading strategies and modify them when your understanding breaks down. Remember to use your Strategies for Active Reading: **predict, visualize, connect, question, clarify,** and **evaluate.**

The Rocking-Horse Winner

Short Story by D. H. LAWRENCE

Connect to Your Life

Best of Luck What do you think of when you hear the word *luck?* Are good luck and bad luck always what they appear to be? With a group of classmates, discuss your thoughts about luck, sharing any notable examples of good luck or bad luck you can think of.

Build Background

Horseracing In England, where this story is set, horseracing dates back more than 800 years. Two of the five great annual horseraces in England are the St. Leger Stakes and the Derby. Other notable English races mentioned in this story are the Grand National, the Ascot Gold Cup, and the Lincolnshire.

Large sums of money are bet on horseraces. The amount a bettor can win depends on the odds. The odds on each horse are expressed as a ratio—3 to 1, for example—and are determined by what proportion of the total amount bet on the race is bet on that horse. The more money bet on a horse, the lower the odds and the lower the payoff. For example, the odds on a "favorite" (a horse that many people have bet on) might be 2 to 1; if that horse wins, each person who has bet on the horse receives 2 dollars for every dollar bet. The odds on a "long shot" (a horse that few people have bet on) might be 20 to 1; if that horse wins, each person who has bet on the horse wins 20 dollars for every dollar bet.

Bettors can wager on horses to win, to place, or to show. A holder of a win ticket collects only if the horse finishes first. A holder of a place ticket collects if the horse comes in first or second, and a holder of a show ticket collects if the horse comes in first, second, or third; but holders of place and show bets on a winning horse receive smaller payoffs than holders of win tickets.

WORDS TO KNOW
Vocabulary Preview
career
inconsiderable
obscure
parry
remonstrate

Focus Your Reading

LITERARY	FORESHADOWING
ANALYSIS	IN FICTION

In a short story a writer may use hints or clues at one point in the narrative to suggest events that will occur later. This technique, called **foreshadowing,** creates suspense and prepares readers for what is to come. As you read, look for clues about what will occur later in the story.

ACTIVE READING **DRAWING CONCLUSIONS**

In "The Rocking-Horse Winner," luck plays a signif-icant role in the characters' lives, though Lawrence does not always explicitly state that role. To **draw conclusions** about the role of luck in the story, you must combine the facts that are stated in the text, the facts you must **infer,** and your own **prior knowledge.**

READER'S NOTEBOOK Use a chart like the one shown to note both the stated facts and the inferred facts about each character's experiences with luck.

Characters	Stated Facts	Inferred Facts
Paul		
Paul's mother		
Oscar		

The Rocking-Horse

WINNER

D. H. Lawrence

There was a woman who was beautiful, who started with all the advantages, yet she had no luck. She married for love, and the love turned to dust. She had bonny[1] children, yet she felt they had been thrust upon her, and she could not love them. They looked at her coldly, as if they were finding fault with her. And hurriedly she felt she must cover up some fault in herself. Yet what it was that she must cover up she never knew. Nevertheless, when her children were present, she always felt the center of her heart go hard. This troubled her, and in her manner she was all the more gentle and anxious for her children, as if she loved them very much. Only she herself knew that at the center of her heart was a hard little place that could not feel love, no, not for anybody. Everybody else said of her: "She is such a good mother. She adores her children." Only she herself, and her children themselves, knew it was not so. They read it in each other's eyes.

---

1. **bonny:** pretty.

There were a boy and two little girls. They lived in a pleasant house, with a garden, and they had discreet servants, and felt themselves superior to anyone in the neighborhood.

Although they lived in style, they felt always an anxiety in the house. There was never enough money. The mother had a small income, and the father had a small income, but not nearly enough for the social position which they had to keep up. The father went into town to some office. But though he had good prospects, these prospects never materialized. There was always the grinding sense of the shortage of money, though the style was always kept up.

At last the mother said: "I will see if *I* can't make something." But she did not know where to begin. She racked[2] her brains, and tried this thing and the other, but could not find anything successful. The failure made deep lines come into her face. Her children were growing up, they would have to go to school. There must be more money, there must be more money. The father, who was always very handsome and expensive in his tastes, seemed as if he never *would* be able to do anything worth doing. And the mother, who had a great belief in herself, did not succeed any better, and her tastes were just as expensive.

And so the house came to be haunted by the unspoken phrase: *There must be more money! There must be more money!* The children could hear it all the time, though nobody said it aloud. They heard it at Christmas, when the expensive and splendid toys filled the nursery. Behind the shining modern rocking-horse, behind the smart doll's house, a voice would start whispering: "There *must* be more money! There *must* be more money!" And the children would stop playing, to listen for a moment. They would look into each other's eyes, to see if they had all heard. And each one saw in the eyes of the other two that they too had heard. "There *must* be more money! There *must* be more money!"

It came whispering from the springs of the still-swaying rocking-horse, and even the horse, bending his wooden, champing head, heard it. The big doll, sitting so pink and smirking in her new pram,[3] could hear it quite plainly, and seemed to be smirking all the more self-consciously because of it. The foolish puppy, too, that took the place of the teddy bear, he was looking so extraordinarily foolish for no other reason but that he heard the secret whisper all over the house: "There *must* be more money!"

Yet nobody ever said it aloud. The whisper was everywhere, and therefore no one spoke it. Just as no one ever says: "We are breathing!" in spite of the fact that breath is coming and going all the time.

"Mother," said the boy Paul one day, "why don't we keep a car of our own? Why do we always use uncle's, or else a taxi?"

"Because we're the poor members of the family," said the mother.

"But why *are* we, mother?"

"Well—I suppose," she said slowly and bitterly, "it's because your father has no luck."

The boy was silent for some time.

"Is luck money, mother?" he asked, rather timidly.

"No, Paul. Not quite. It's what causes you to have money."

"Oh!" said Paul vaguely. "I thought when Uncle Oscar said *filthy lucker,* it meant money."

"*Filthy lucre*[4] does mean money," said the mother. "But it's lucre, not luck."

"Oh!" said the boy. "Then what *is* luck, mother?"

"It's what causes you to have money. If you're lucky you have money. That's why it's better to

---

2. **racked:** strained; tortured.

3. **pram:** baby carriage (a shortened form of *perambulator*).

4. **filthy lucre** (lo͞o′kər): money, especially that obtained through fraud or greed (an expression from the King James Bible [Titus 1:11] that has passed into familiar usage).

be born lucky than rich. If you're rich, you may lose your money. But if you're lucky, you will always get more money."

"Oh! Will you? And is father not lucky?"

"Very unlucky, I should say," she said bitterly.

The boy watched her with unsure eyes.

"Why?" he asked.

"I don't know. Nobody ever knows why one person is lucky and another unlucky."

"Don't they? Nobody at all? Does *nobody* know?"

"Perhaps God. But He never tells."

"He ought to, then. And aren't you lucky either, mother?"

"I can't be, if I married an unlucky husband."

"But by yourself, aren't you?"

"I used to think I was, before I married. Now I think I am very unlucky indeed."

"Why?"

"Well—never mind! Perhaps I'm not really," she said.

The child looked at her to see if she meant it. But he saw, by the lines of her mouth, that she was only trying to hide something from him.

"Well, anyhow," he said stoutly,[5] "I'm a lucky person."

"Why?" said his mother, with a sudden laugh.

He stared at her. He didn't even know why he had said it.

"God told me," he asserted, brazening it out.

"I hope He did, dear!" she said, again with a laugh, but rather bitter.

"He did, mother!"

"Excellent!" said the mother, using one of her husband's exclamations.

The boy saw she did not believe him; or rather, that she paid no attention to his assertion. This angered him somewhere, and made him want to compel her attention.

He went off by himself, vaguely, in a childish way, seeking for the clue to "luck." Absorbed, taking no heed of other people, he went about

with a sort of stealth, seeking inwardly for luck. He wanted luck, he wanted it, he wanted it. When the two girls were playing dolls in the nursery, he would sit on his big rocking-horse, charging madly into space, with a frenzy that made the little girls peer at him uneasily. Wildly the horse <u>careered</u>, the waving dark hair of the boy tossed, his eyes had a strange glare in them. The little girls dared not speak to him.

When he had ridden to the end of his mad little journey, he climbed down and stood in front of his rocking-horse, staring fixedly into its lowered face. Its red mouth was slightly open, its big eye was wide and glassy-bright.

"Now!" he would silently command the snorting steed. "Now, take me to where there is luck! Now take me!"

And he would slash the horse on the neck with the little whip he had asked Uncle Oscar for. He *knew* the horse could take him to where there was luck, if only he forced it. So he would mount again and start on his furious ride, hoping at last to get there. He knew he could get there.

"You'll break your horse, Paul!" said the nurse.

"He's always riding like that! I wish he'd leave off!" said his elder sister Joan.

But he only glared down on them in silence. Nurse gave him up. She could make nothing of him. Anyhow, he was growing beyond her.

One day his mother and his Uncle Oscar came in when he was on one of his furious rides. He did not speak to them.

"Hallo, you young jockey! Riding a winner?" said his uncle.

"Aren't you growing too big for a rocking-horse? You're not a very little boy any longer, you know," said his mother.

But Paul only gave a blue glare from his big, rather close-set eyes. He would speak to nobody

---

5. **stoutly:** bravely; firmly.

when he was in full tilt.[6] His mother watched him with an anxious expression on her face.

At last he suddenly stopped forcing his horse into the mechanical gallop and slid down.

"Well, I got there!" he announced fiercely, his blue eyes still flaring, and his sturdy long legs straddling apart.

"Where did you get to?" asked his mother.

"Where I wanted to go," he flared back at her.

"That's right, son!" said Uncle Oscar. "Don't you stop till you get there. What's the horse's name?"

"He doesn't have a name," said the boy.

"Gets on without all right?" asked the uncle.

"Well, he has different names. He was called Sansovino last week."

"Sansovino, eh? Won the Ascot. How did you know his name?"

"He always talks about horse races with Bassett," said Joan.

The uncle was delighted to find that his small nephew was posted with all the racing news. Bassett, the young gardener, who had been wounded in the left foot in the war and had got his present job through Oscar Cresswell, whose batman[7] he had been, was a perfect blade of the "turf."[8] He lived in the racing events, and the small boy lived with him.

Oscar Cresswell got it all from Bassett.

"Master Paul comes and asks me, so I can't do more than tell him, sir," said Bassett, his face terribly serious, as if he were speaking of religious matters.

"And does he ever put anything on a horse he fancies?"

"Well—I don't want to give him away—he's a young sport,[9] a fine sport, sir. Would you mind asking him himself? He sort of takes a pleasure in it, and perhaps he'd feel I was giving him away, sir, if you don't mind."

Bassett was serious as a church.

The uncle went back to his nephew and took

him off for a ride in the car.

"Say, Paul, old man, do you ever put anything on a horse?" the uncle asked.

The boy watched the handsome man closely.

"Why, do you think I oughtn't to?" he <u>parried</u>.

---

6. **in full tilt:** moving at full speed.

7. **batman:** in Britain, a soldier who acts as an officer's servant.

8. **blade of the "turf":** one who is very knowledgeable about horseracing.

9. **sport:** good fellow.

WORDS
TO
KNOW

parry (păr´ē) *v.* to respond by turning aside or evading (a question or argument)

The Races at Longchamp (1866), Édouard Manet. Oil on canvas, 43.9 cm × 84.5 cm, The Art Institute of Chicago, Mr. and Mrs. Potter Palmer Collection (1922.424). Photo Copyright © 1994 The Art Institute of Chicago, all rights reserved.

"Not a bit of it! I thought perhaps you might give me a tip for the Lincoln."

The car sped on into the country, going down to Uncle Oscar's place in Hampshire.

"Honor bright?"[10] said the nephew.

"Honor bright, son!" said the uncle.

"Well, then, Daffodil."

"Daffodil! I doubt it, sonny. What about Mirza?"

"I only know the winner," said the boy. "That's Daffodil."

"Daffodil, eh?"

There was a pause. Daffodil was an <u>obscure</u> horse comparatively.

"Uncle!"

"Yes, son?"

"You won't let it go any further, will you? I promised Bassett."

"Bassett be damned, old man! What's he got to do with it?"

---

10. **honor bright:** an expression meaning "on your (or my) honor."

"We're partners. We've been partners from the first. Uncle, he lent me my first five shillings,[11] which I lost. I promised him, honor bright, it was only between me and him; only you gave me that ten-shilling note I started winning with, so I thought you were lucky. You won't let it go any further, will you?"

The boy gazed at his uncle from those big, hot, blue eyes, set rather close together. The uncle stirred and laughed uneasily.

"Right you are, son! I'll keep your tip private. Daffodil, eh? How much are you putting on him?"

"All except twenty pounds,"[12] said the boy. "I keep that in reserve."

The uncle thought it a good joke.

"You keep twenty pounds in reserve, do you, you young romancer? What are you betting, then?"

"I'm betting three hundred," said the boy gravely. "But it's between you and me, Uncle Oscar! Honor bright?"

The uncle burst into a roar of laughter.

"It's between you and me all right, you young Nat Gould,"[13] he said, laughing. "But where's your three hundred?"

"Bassett keeps it for me. We're partners."

"You are, are you! And what is Bassett putting on Daffodil?"

"He won't go quite as high as I do, I expect. Perhaps he'll go a hundred and fifty."

"What, pennies?" laughed the uncle.

"Pounds," said the child, with a surprised look at his uncle. "Bassett keeps a bigger reserve than I do."

Between wonder and amusement Uncle Oscar was silent. He pursued the matter no further, but he determined to take his nephew with him to the Lincoln races.

"Now, son," he said, "I'm putting twenty on Mirza, and I'll put five on for you on any horse you fancy. What's your pick?"

"Daffodil, uncle."

"No, not the fiver on Daffodil!"

"I should if it was my own fiver," said the child.

"Good! Good! Right you are! A fiver for me and a fiver for you on Daffodil."

The child had never been to a race-meeting before, and his eyes were blue fire. He pursed his mouth tight and watched. A Frenchman just in front had put his money on Lancelot. Wild with excitement, he flayed his arms up and down, yelling *"Lancelot! Lancelot!"* in his French accent.

Daffodil came in first, Lancelot second, Mirza third. The child, flushed and with eyes blazing, was curiously serene. His uncle brought him four five-pound notes, four to one.

"What am I to do with these?" he cried, waving them before the boy's eyes.

"I suppose we'll talk to Bassett," said the boy. "I expect I have fifteen hundred now; and twenty in reserve; and this twenty."

His uncle studied him for some moments.

"Look here, son!" he said. "You're not serious about Bassett and that fifteen hundred, are you?"

"Yes, I am. But it's between you and me, uncle. Honor bright?"

"Honor bright all right, son! But I must talk to Bassett."

"If you'd like to be a partner, uncle, with Bassett and me, we could all be partners. Only, you'd have to promise, honor bright, uncle, not to let it go beyond us three. Bassett and I are lucky, and you must be lucky, because it was your ten shillings I started winning with. . . ."

Uncle Oscar took both Bassett and Paul into Richmond Park for an afternoon, and there they talked.

---

11. **shillings:** coins formerly used in Britain. (There were 20 shillings in a pound.)

12. **twenty pounds:** the equivalent of about $1,000 in today's dollars. (In the mid-1920s, a pound was worth about $5, and the purchasing power of a dollar was about 10 times what it is now.)

13. **Nat Gould:** a well-known British horseracing authority and writer.

"It's like this, you see, sir," Bassett said. "Master Paul would get me talking about racing events, spinning yarns, you know, sir. And he was always keen on knowing if I'd made or if I'd lost. It's about a year since, now, that I put five shillings on Blush of Dawn for him: and we lost. Then the luck turned, with that ten shillings he had from you: that we put on Singhalese. And since that time, it's been pretty steady, all things considering. What do you say, Master Paul?"

"We're all right when we're sure," said Paul. "It's when we're not quite sure that we go down."

"Oh, but we're careful then," said Bassett.

"But when are you *sure?*" smiled Uncle Oscar.

"It's Master Paul, sir," said Bassett in a secret, religious voice. "It's as if he had it from heaven. Like Daffodil, now, for the Lincoln. That was as sure as eggs."[14]

"Did you put anything on Daffodil?" asked Oscar Cresswell.

"Yes, sir. I made my bit."

"And my nephew?"

Bassett was obstinately silent, looking at Paul.

"I made twelve hundred, didn't I, Bassett? I told uncle I was putting three hundred on Daffodil."

"That's right," said Bassett, nodding.

"But where's the money?" asked the uncle.

"I keep it safe locked up, sir. Master Paul he can have it any minute he likes to ask for it."

"What, fifteen hundred pounds?"

"And twenty! And *forty,* that is, with the twenty he made on the course."

"It's amazing!" said the uncle.

"If Master Paul offers you to be partners, sir, I would, if I were you: if you'll excuse me," said Bassett.

Oscar Cresswell thought about it.

"I'll see the money," he said.

They drove home again, and, sure enough, Bassett came round to the garden-house with fifteen hundred pounds in notes. The twenty pounds reserve was left with Joe Glee, in the Turf Commission deposit.[15]

"You see, it's all right, uncle, when I'm *sure!* Then we go strong, for all we're worth. Don't we, Bassett?"

"We do that, Master Paul."

"And when are you sure?" said the uncle, laughing.

"Oh, well, sometimes I'm *absolutely* sure, like about Daffodil," said the boy; "and sometimes I have an idea; and sometimes I haven't even an idea, have I, Bassett? Then we're careful, because we mostly go down."

"You do, do you! And when you're sure, like about Daffodil, what makes you sure, sonny?"

"Oh, well, I don't know," said the boy uneasily. "I'm sure, you know, uncle; that's all."

"It's as if he had it from heaven, sir," Bassett reiterated.

"I should say so!" said the uncle.

But he became a partner. And when the Leger was coming on Paul was "sure" about Lively Spark, which was a quite <u>inconsiderable</u> horse. The boy insisted on putting a thousand on the horse, Bassett went for five hundred, and Oscar Cresswell two hundred. Lively Spark came in first, and the betting had been ten to one against him. Paul had made ten thousand.

"You see," he said, "I was absolutely sure of him."

Even Oscar Cresswell had cleared two thousand.

"Look here, son," he said, "this sort of thing makes me nervous."

"It needn't, uncle! Perhaps I shan't be sure again for a long time."

---

14. **as sure as eggs:** absolutely certain (a shortened form of the expression "as sure as eggs is eggs").

15. **Turf Commission deposit:** a bank where bettors keep money for future bets.

WORDS TO KNOW   **inconsiderable** (ĭn′kən-sĭd′ər-ə-bəl) *adj.* not worth consideration; insignificant

"But what are you going to do with your money?" asked the uncle.

"Of course," said the boy, "I started it for mother. She said she had no luck, because father is unlucky, so I thought if I was lucky, it might stop whispering."

"What might stop whispering?"

"Our house. I *hate* our house for whispering."

"What does it whisper?"

"Why—why"—the boy fidgeted—"why, I don't know. But it's always short of money, you know, uncle."

"I know it, son, I know it."

"You know people send mother writs,[16] don't you, uncle?"

"I'm afraid I do," said the uncle.

"And then the house whispers, like people laughing at you behind your back. It's awful, that is! I thought if I was lucky—"

"You might stop it," added the uncle.

The boy watched him with big blue eyes, that had an uncanny cold fire in them, and he said never a word.

"Well, then!" said the uncle. "What are we doing?"

"I shouldn't like mother to know I was lucky," said the boy.

"Why not, son?"

"She'd stop me."

"I don't think she would."

"Oh!"—and the boy writhed in an odd way—"I *don't* want her to know, uncle."

"All right, son! We'll manage it without her knowing."

They managed it very easily. Paul, at the other's suggestion, handed over five thousand pounds to his uncle, who deposited it with the family lawyer, who was then to inform Paul's mother that a relative had put five thousand pounds into his hands, which sum was to be paid out a thousand pounds at a time, on the mother's birthday, for the next five years.

"So she'll have a birthday present of a thousand pounds for five successive years," said Uncle Oscar. "I hope it won't make it all the harder for her later."

Paul's mother had her birthday in November. The house had been "whispering" worse than ever lately, and, even in spite of his luck, Paul could not bear up against it. He was very anxious to see the effect of the birthday letter, telling his mother about the thousand pounds.

When there were no visitors, Paul now took his meals with his parents, as he was beyond the nursery control. His mother went into town nearly every day. She had discovered that she had an odd knack of sketching furs and dress materials, so she worked secretly in the studio of a friend who was the chief "artist" for the leading drapers.[17] She drew the figures of ladies in furs and ladies in silk and sequins for the newspaper advertisements. This young woman artist earned several thousand pounds a year, but Paul's mother only made several hundreds, and she was again dissatisfied. She so wanted to be first in something, and she did not succeed, even in making sketches for drapery advertisements.

She was down to breakfast on the morning of her birthday. Paul watched her face as she read her letters. He knew the lawyer's letter. As his mother read it, her face hardened and became more expressionless. Then a cold, determined look came on her mouth. She hid the letter under the pile of others, and said not a word about it.

"Didn't you have anything nice in the post for your birthday, mother?" said Paul.

"Quite moderately nice," she said, her voice cold and absent.

She went away to town without saying more.

But in the afternoon Uncle Oscar appeared. He said Paul's mother had had a long interview

---

16. **writs:** legal documents (in this case, demands for the payment of debts).

17. **drapers:** in Britain, dealers in cloth and dry goods.

with the lawyer, asking if the whole five thousand could not be advanced at once, as she was in debt.

"What do you think, uncle?" said the boy.

"I leave it to you, son."

"Oh, let her have it, then! We can get some more with the other," said the boy.

"A bird in the hand is worth two in the bush, laddie!" said Uncle Oscar.

"But I'm sure to *know* for the Grand National; or the Lincolnshire; or else the Derby. I'm sure to know for *one* of them," said Paul.

So Uncle Oscar signed the agreement, and Paul's mother touched[18] the whole five thousand. Then something very curious happened. The voices in the house suddenly went mad, like a chorus of frogs on a spring evening. There were certain new furnishings, and Paul had a tutor. He was *really* going to Eton, his father's school, in the following autumn. There were flowers in the winter, and a blossoming of the luxury Paul's mother had been used to. And yet the voices in the house, behind the sprays of mimosa and almond-blossom, and from under the piles of iridescent[19] cushions, simply trilled and screamed in a sort of ecstasy: "There *must* be more money!

Oh-h-h; there *must* be more money. Oh, now, now-w! Now-w-w—there *must* be more money!—more than ever! More than ever!"

It frightened Paul terribly. He studied away at his Latin and Greek with his tutor. But his intense hours were spent with Bassett. The Grand National had gone by: he had not "known," and had lost a hundred pounds. Summer was at hand. He was in agony for the Lincoln. But even for the Lincoln he didn't "know," and he lost fifty pounds. He became wild-eyed and strange, as if something were going to explode in him.

"Let it alone, son! Don't you bother about it!" urged Uncle Oscar. But it was as if the boy couldn't really hear what his uncle was saying.

"I've got to know for the Derby! I've got to know for the Derby!" the child reiterated, his big blue eyes blazing with a sort of madness.

His mother noticed how overwrought he was.

"You'd better go to the seaside. Wouldn't you like to go now to the seaside, instead of waiting?

18. **touched:** took.

19. **iridescent** (ĭr´ĭ-dĕs´ənt): shining with a rainbowlike display of colors.

Spotted rocking horse, late 1800s.
Wood with polychrome, 29″ × 53″,
courtesy of Ricco Moresca Gallery.

I think you'd better," she said, looking down at him anxiously, her heart curiously heavy because of him.

But the child lifted his uncanny blue eyes.

"I couldn't possibly go before the Derby, mother!" he said. "I couldn't possibly!"

"Why not?" she said, her voice becoming heavy when she was opposed. "Why not? You can still go from the seaside to see the Derby with your Uncle Oscar, if that's what you wish. No need for you to wait here. Besides, I think you care too much about these races. It's a bad sign. My family has been a gambling family, and you won't know till you grow up how much damage it has done. But it has done damage. I shall have to send Bassett away, and ask Uncle Oscar not to talk racing to you, unless you promise to be reasonable about it: go away to the seaside and forget it. You're all nerves!"

"I'll do what you like, mother, so long as you don't send me away till after the Derby," the boy said.

"Send you away from where? Just from this house?"

"Yes," he said, gazing at her.

"Why, you curious child, what makes you care about this house so much, suddenly? I never knew you loved it."

He gazed at her without speaking. He had a secret within a secret, something he had not divulged, even to Bassett or to his Uncle Oscar.

But his mother, after standing undecided and a little bit sullen for some moments, said:

"Very well, then! Don't go to the seaside till after the Derby, if you don't wish it. But promise me you won't let your nerves go to pieces. Promise you won't think so much about horse-racing and *events,* as you call them!"

"Oh no," said the boy casually. "I won't think much about them, mother. You needn't worry. I wouldn't worry, mother, if I were you."

"If you were me and I were you," said his mother, "I wonder what we *should* do!"

"But you know you needn't worry, mother, don't you?" the boy repeated.

"I should be awfully glad to know it," she said wearily.

"Oh, well, you *can,* you know. I mean, you *ought* to know you needn't worry," he insisted.

"Ought I? Then I'll see about it," she said.

Paul's secret of secrets was his wooden horse, that which had no name. Since he was emancipated from a nurse and a nursery-governess, he had had his rocking-horse removed to his own bedroom at the top of the house.

"Surely you're too big for a rocking-horse!" his mother had <u>remonstrated</u>.

"Well, you see, mother, till I can have a *real* horse, I like to have *some* sort of animal about," had been his quaint answer.

"Do you feel he keeps you company?" she laughed.

"Oh yes! He's very good, he always keeps me company, when I'm there," said Paul.

So the horse, rather shabby, stood in an arrested prance in the boy's bedroom.

The Derby was drawing near, and the boy grew more and more tense. He hardly heard what was spoken to him, he was very frail, and his eyes were really uncanny. His mother had sudden strange seizures of uneasiness about him. Sometimes, for half an hour, she would feel a sudden anxiety about him that was almost anguish. She wanted to rush to him at once, and know he was safe.

Two nights before the Derby, she was at a big party in town, when one of her rushes of anxiety about her boy, her first-born, gripped her heart till she could hardly speak. She fought with the feeling, might and main,[20] for she believed in common sense. But it was too strong. She had to

---

20. **might and main:** with all her strength.

WORDS
TO
KNOW

remonstrate (rĭ-mŏn′strāt′) *v.* to protest or object

leave the dance and go downstairs to telephone to the country. The children's nursery-governess was terribly surprised and startled at being rung up in the night.

"Are the children all right, Miss Wilmot?"

"Oh yes, they are quite all right."

"Master Paul? Is he all right?"

"He went to bed as right as a trivet.[21] Shall I run up and look at him?"

"No," said Paul's mother reluctantly. "No! Don't trouble. It's all right. Don't sit up. We shall be home fairly soon." She did not want her son's privacy intruded upon.

"Very good," said the governess.

It was about one o'clock when Paul's mother and father drove up to their house. All was still. Paul's mother went to her room and slipped off her white fur cloak. She had told her maid not to wait up for her. She heard her husband downstairs, mixing a whisky and soda.

And then, because of the strange anxiety at her heart, she stole upstairs to her son's room. Noiselessly she went along the upper corridor. Was there a faint noise? What was it?

She stood, with arrested muscles, outside his door, listening. There was a strange, heavy, and yet not loud noise. Her heart stood still. It was a soundless noise, yet rushing and powerful. Something huge, in violent, hushed motion. What was it? What in God's name was it? She ought to know. She felt that she knew the noise. She knew what it was.

Yet she could not place it. She couldn't say what it was. And on and on it went, like a madness.

Softly, frozen with anxiety and fear, she turned the door handle.

The room was dark. Yet in the space near the window, she heard and saw something plunging to and fro. She gazed in fear and amazement.

Then suddenly she switched on the light, and saw her son, in his green pajamas, madly surging on the rocking-horse. The blaze of light suddenly lit him up, as he urged the wooden horse, and lit her up, as she stood, blonde, in her dress of pale green and crystal, in the doorway.

"Paul!" she cried. "Whatever are you doing?"

"It's Malabar!" he screamed in a powerful, strange voice. "It's Malabar!"

His eyes blazed at her for one strange and senseless second, as he ceased urging his wooden horse. Then he fell with a crash to the ground, and she, all her tormented motherhood flooding upon her, rushed to gather him up.

But he was unconscious, and unconscious he remained, with some brain-fever. He talked and tossed, and his mother sat stonily by his side.

"Malabar! It's Malabar! Bassett, Bassett, I *know!* It's Malabar!"

So the child cried, trying to get up and urge the rocking-horse that gave him his inspiration.

"What does he mean by Malabar?" asked the heart-frozen mother.

"I don't know," said the father stonily.

"What does he mean by Malabar?" she asked her brother Oscar.

"It's one of the horses running for the Derby," was the answer.

And, in spite of himself, Oscar Cresswell spoke to Bassett, and himself put a thousand on Malabar: at fourteen to one.

The third day of the illness was critical: they were waiting for a change. The boy, with his rather long, curly hair, was tossing ceaselessly on the pillow. He neither slept nor regained consciousness, and his eyes were like blue stones. His mother sat, feeling her heart had gone, turned actually into a stone.

In the evening, Oscar Cresswell did not come, but Bassett sent a message, saying could he come up for one moment, just one moment? Paul's mother was very angry at the intrusion, but on second thoughts she agreed. The boy was the same. Perhaps Bassett might bring him to consciousness.

---

21. **as right as a trivet:** in perfect condition.

The gardener, a shortish fellow with a little brown mustache and sharp little brown eyes, tiptoed into the room, touched his imaginary cap to Paul's mother, and stole to the bedside, staring with glittering, smallish eyes at the tossing, dying child.

"Master Paul!" he whispered. "Master Paul! Malabar came in first all right, a clean win. I did as you told me. You've made over seventy thousand pounds, you have; you've got over eighty thousand.[22] Malabar came in all right, Master Paul."

"Malabar! Malabar! Did I say Malabar, mother? Did I say Malabar? Do you think I'm lucky, mother? I knew Malabar, didn't I? Over eighty thousand pounds! I call that lucky, don't you, mother? Over eighty thousand pounds! I knew, didn't I know I knew? Malabar came in all right. If I ride my horse till I'm sure, then I tell you, Bassett, you can go as high as you like. Did you go for all you were worth, Bassett?"

"I went a thousand on it, Master Paul."

"I never told you, mother, that if I can ride my horse, and *get there*, then I'm absolutely sure—oh, absolutely! Mother, did I ever tell you? I *am* lucky!"

"No, you never did," said his mother.

But the boy died in the night.

And even as he lay dead, his mother heard her brother's voice saying to her: "My God, Hester, you're eighty-odd thousand to the good, and a poor devil of a son to the bad. But, poor devil, poor devil, he's best gone out of a life where he rides his rocking-horse to find a winner." ❖

---

22. **eighty thousand:** the equivalent of about $4 million in today's dollars.

Connect to the Literature

1. **What Do You Think?** What scene or image in the story did you find most memorable?

Comprehension Check
- What happens when Paul rides his rocking horse?
- What does he do with his winnings?
- Why doesn't Paul want to leave before the Derby?

Think Critically

2. Why do you think Paul becomes obsessed with horseracing?

THINK ABOUT
- his mother's attitude toward money
- the "voices" in the house
- what happens when he rides the rocking horse

3. How would you describe the relationship between Paul and his mother?

THINK ABOUT
- his mother's view of herself and her family
- what she says about luck
- what Paul wants to do for his mother

4. Why do you think the voices get louder after Paul's mother receives the 5,000 pounds?

5. Who, if anyone, do you think is to blame for Paul's death? Support your answer with evidence from the story.

6. **ACTIVE READING** **DRAWING CONCLUSIONS** Based on the chart in your **READER'S NOTEBOOK**, what **conclusions** would you draw about the role of luck in the lives of Paul, his mother, and his uncle Oscar? For each **character,** is luck a negative, a positive, or a neutral force?

Extend Interpretations

7. **What If?** How might the outcome of the story have been different if Paul's predictions had started to fail?

8. **Connect to Life** Popular culture today is full of suggestions that people can achieve happiness by acquiring possessions. What do you think of this approach to life?

Literary Analysis

FORESHADOWING IN FICTION

A writer's use of hints or clues that suggest events and consequences that will appear later in a narrative is known as **foreshadowing.** The use of foreshadowing points readers to significant developments in the story and creates a **mood** of suspense. Early in "The Rocking-Horse Winner," the strange frenzy with which Paul rides his rocking horse foreshadows the tragedy of his final ride.

Cooperative Learning Activity Working with a small group of classmates, use a chart like the one shown to list other examples of foreshadowing in the story. Note how each one prepares readers for the tragic ending.

Example of Foreshadowing	How Suggests Ending
Paul charging madly on his horse while his sisters watch	Foreshadows final mad ride

REVIEW **IRONY** Lawrence uses **irony**—a contrast between expectation and reality—to explore the meaning of luck for the story's characters. For example, Paul's mother's statement "If you're lucky you have money" (page 1008) is ironic when read in the light of the story's ending. List other examples of irony, explaining how each contributes to Lawrence's exploration of luck.

Choices & CHALLENGES

Writing Options

1. Advice Column Imagine you are Paul's mother. Write a letter to an advice columnist, asking for advice about Paul's odd behavior. Then write the columnist's response.

2. Alternative Ending Write a new ending for this story, in which Paul does not predict the winner of the Derby and does not die.

3. Detective's Report As a police detective, write a report of your investigation into Paul's death. Include statements from witnesses and a list of evidence gathered at the scene, as well as your own conclusions about the death.

Activities & Explorations

1. Radio Play Work with a small group of classmates to rewrite a scene from this story in the form of a radio dramatization. Remember that a radio dramatization relies heavily upon dialogue, and be sure to include sound effects. You might also include descriptive passages for a narrator to read. Collaborate with other groups to tape-record a performance of the entire story. ~ **PERFORMING**

2. Story to Movie Watch the video of an excerpt from a movie adaptation of Lawrence's story. What elements of the story have been changed? Discuss why you think the filmmakers might have made the changes they did. ~ **VIEWING AND REPRESENTING**

VIDEO **Literature in Performance**

3. Abstract Painting Think about the emotions you had as you read this story. Create an abstract painting that expresses one or more of your feelings. Use colors that convey the intensity of your emotions. ~ **ART**

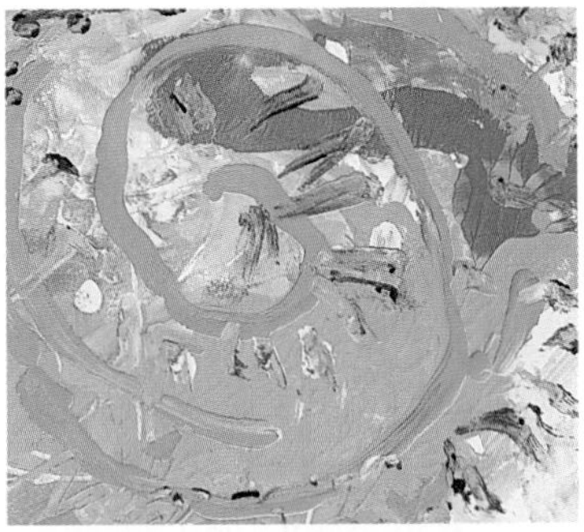

Inquiry & Research

Horseracing Research the career of a professional jockey. Find out what physical characteristics, skills, and education a jockey must have. You could investigate the entrance of women into the profession. Report your findings to the class.

Vocabulary in Action

EXERCISE A: ASSESSMENT PRACTICE For each pair of words, indicate whether the words are **synonyms** or **antonyms.**

1. **remonstrate**—agree
2. **career**—speed
3. **parry**—avoid
4. **obscure**—illustrious
5. **inconsiderable**—outstanding

EXERCISE B In groups of five, take turns pantomiming the meaning of each Word to Know. Choose the person who you think best conveyed the meaning of his or her word. Challenge members of other groups to guess which word is being pantomimed as the person repeats the performance.

WORDS TO KNOW	career	inconsiderable	obscure	parry	remonstrate

Building Vocabulary

For an in-depth lesson on how to use a thesaurus to find a word's synonyms and antonyms, see page 574.

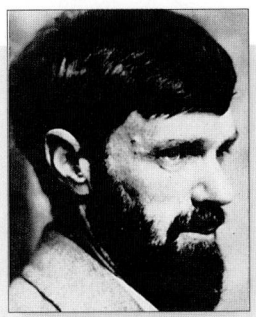

D. H. Lawrence
1885–1930

Other Works
Sons and Lovers
Women in Love
"Tickets, Please"
"Odor of Chrysanthemums"

A Miner's Son One of five children, David Herbert Lawrence was born in a coal-mining village in the central English county of Nottinghamshire. His early semiautobiographical novel *Sons and Lovers* (1913) is set in this region and reflects the conflict between his mother, who had been a teacher and poet, and his father, an uneducated miner. Lawrence was often ill as a child, and his mother, determined to keep him out of the mines, encouraged him in school, where he remained until he was 15, when financial problems forced him to take a job as a clerk and then as an elementary school teacher. After earning a teaching certificate at the University of Nottingham, he taught school in London for four years. He had already begun writing poetry and fiction, and his first novel, *The White Peacock,* was published when he was 26.

Controversy Strikes Although Lawrence was recognized as brilliant and imaginative, the passionate, sensual nature of his work made him one of the most controversial writers of the early 20th century. He not only broke literary conventions but also fought against the restrictive social, political, and moral conventions of his day. Many of his novels, short stories, and books of poetry were destroyed or had their publication delayed because censors objected to his treatment of relationships between men and women.

The "Here and Now" of Life Despite censorship, chronic poverty, and advancing tuberculosis, Lawrence wrote a remarkable number of stories, poems, and novels. He and his wife, Frieda, lived all over the world, trying to discover a better way to relate, live, and grow with other people. Later in his life, Lawrence wrote that "the magnificent here and now of life in the flesh is ours, and ours alone, and ours only for a time. We ought to dance with rapture that we should be alive." Today, Lawrence is studied and admired for the fresh perspective and style he brought to literature and living.

Author Activity

Questioning Conventions Critics have observed that much of Lawrence's fiction expresses a dissatisfaction with the values and limited viewpoint of conventional middle-class people. What evidence for this attitude can you find in "The Rocking-Horse Winner"?

PREPARING to *Read*

Araby

Short Story by JAMES JOYCE

(Connect to Your Life)

Moment of Truth Try to recall a time in your childhood or adolescence when you came to a sudden realization about yourself or someone close to you. Perhaps you discovered that you had a hidden talent, or maybe you suddenly understood why a friend was treating you a certain way. Share the insight with your classmates, explaining the impact it had on you.

Build Background

Joyce's Dublin The Irish writer James Joyce is best known for his novel *Ulysses,* published in 1922. (See pages 1032–1033.) In writing it and his other works, Joyce called upon his own remembrances of Dublin at the turn of the century. Financial problems forced the Joyce family to move frequently, each time to a poorer and shabbier section of the city, and Joyce thus became acquainted with many facets of Dublin society. As a young man, Joyce was critical of the "paralysis," or immobility, of the Irish people, and he left the country to live abroad. Nevertheless, his mind was preoccupied with the people of Dublin, and the life of the city became the focal point of all his fiction. For example, there actually was a charity bazaar called *Araby* which came to Dublin when Joyce was a child.

"Araby" is one of a series of short stories that Joyce began writing in 1904 and that were eventually published in the collection *Dubliners.* The events in each story lead up to what Joyce called an **epiphany**—an ordinary moment or situation in which an important truth about a character's life is suddenly revealed.

WORDS TO KNOW
Vocabulary Preview

garrulous   luxuriate
imperturbable   pervade
litany

Focus Your Reading

LITERARY ANALYSIS   POINT OF VIEW   **Point of view** refers to the narrative method used in a literary work. "Araby" is told from the **first-person point of view**—the **narrator** is a character in the story and so participates in the events he recounts. Readers see everything through the narrator's eyes, and his comments and descriptions convey the intensity of his situation.

> *I could not call my wandering thoughts together. I had hardly any patience with the serious work of life. . . .*

As you read, be aware of what Joyce's use of the first-person point of view reveals about the narrator.

ACTIVE READING   MAKING INFERENCES   **Making inferences** about **characters** involves using clues in the text and "reading between the lines" to understand why characters think and act as they do.

READER'S NOTEBOOK   As you read this story, try to infer how the narrator feels during the various events he recalls. Use a chart similar to the one shown here.

Narrator's Situation	Narrator's Feelings
before talking to Mangan's sister	longing, amazement
during conversation with Mangan's sister	
at school	

ARABY

JAMES

JOYCE

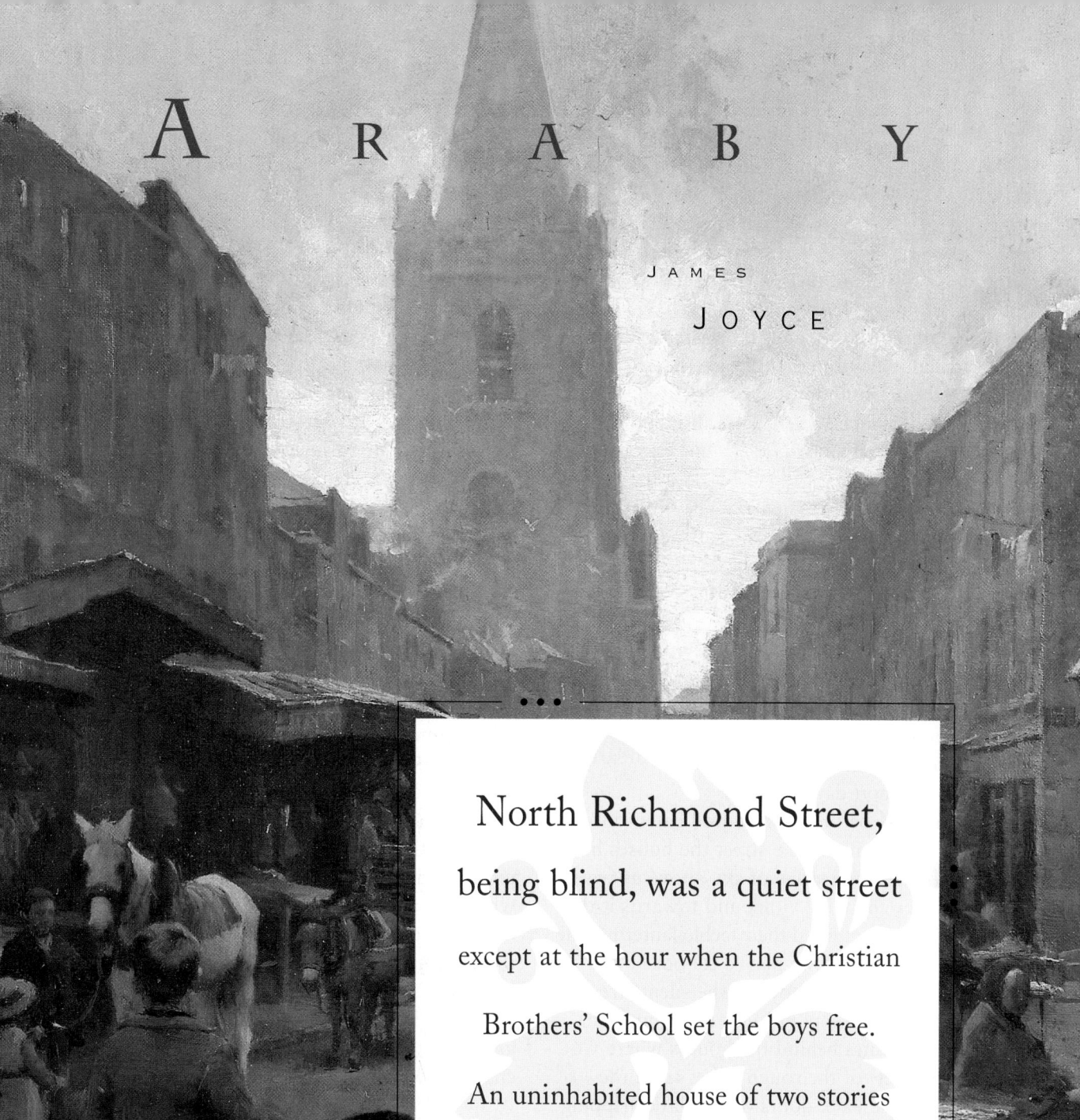

North Richmond Street,

being blind, was a quiet street

except at the hour when the Christian

Brothers' School set the boys free.

An uninhabited house of two stories

stood at the blind end, detached

from its neighbors in a square ground.

The other houses of the street, conscious of decent lives within them, gazed at one another with brown imperturbable faces.

The former tenant of our house, a priest, had died in the back drawing-room. Air, musty from having been long enclosed, hung in all the rooms, and the waste room behind the kitchen was littered with old useless papers. Among these I found a few paper-covered books, the pages of which were curled and damp: *The Abbot*, by Walter Scott, *The Devout Communicant* and *The Memoirs of Vidocq*.[1] I liked the last best because its leaves were yellow. The wild garden behind the house contained a central apple-tree and a few straggling bushes under one of which I found the late tenant's rusty bicycle-pump. He had been a very charitable priest; in his will he had left all his money to institutions and the furniture of his house to his sister.

When the short days of winter came dusk fell before we had well eaten our dinners. When we met in the street the houses had grown somber. The space of sky above us was the color of ever-changing violet and towards it the lamps of the street lifted their feeble lanterns. The cold air stung us and we played till our bodies glowed. Our shouts echoed in the silent street. The career of our play brought us through the dark muddy lanes behind the houses where we ran the gantlet[2] of the rough tribes from the cottages, to the back doors of the dark dripping gardens where odors arose from the ashpits, to the dark odorous stables where a coachman smoothed and combed the horse or shook music from the buckled harness. When we returned to the street, light from the kitchen windows had filled the areas. If my uncle was seen turning the corner we hid in the shadow until we had seen him safely housed. Or if Mangan's sister came out on the doorstep to call her brother in to his tea we watched her from our shadow peer up and down the street. We waited to see whether she would remain or go in and, if she remained, we left our shadow and walked up to Mangan's steps resignedly. She was waiting for us, her figure defined by the light from the half-opened door. Her brother always teased her before he obeyed and I stood by the railings looking at her. Her dress swung as she moved her body and the soft rope of her hair tossed from side to side.

Every morning I lay on the floor in the front parlor watching her door. The blind was pulled down to within an inch of the sash so that I could not be seen. When she came out on the

> When she came out on the doorstep my heart leaped.

doorstep my heart leaped. I ran to the hall, seized my books and followed her. I kept her brown figure always in my eye and, when we came near the point at which our ways diverged, I quickened my pace and passed her. This happened morning after morning. I had never spoken to her, except for a few casual words, and yet her name was like a summons to all my foolish blood.

Her image accompanied me even in places the most hostile to romance. On Saturday evenings when my aunt went marketing I had to go to carry some of the parcels. We walked through the flaring streets, jostled by drunken men and bargaining women, amid the curses of laborers, the shrill litanies of shopboys who stood on guard by the barrels of pigs' cheeks, the nasal chanting of street-singers, who sang a *come-all-*

---

1. *The Abbot . . . Vidocq* (vē-dôk′): three widely varying 19th-century works—the first a historical novel, the second a book of religious instruction, and the third an autobiography of a French police detective.

2. **ran the gantlet:** passed through an area of hostility or attack. (A gantlet [or gauntlet] is a punishment in which a person is made to run between two rows of people who strike him with clubs.)

imperturbable (ĭm′pər-tûr′bə-bəl) *adj.* not easily disturbed; calm
litany (lĭt′n-ē) *n.* a repetitive chant or recital

you about O'Donovan Rossa, or a ballad about the troubles in our native land. These noises converged in a single sensation of life for me: I imagined that I bore my chalice safely through a throng of foes. Her name sprang to my lips at moments in strange prayers and praises which I myself did not understand. My eyes were often full of tears (I could not tell why) and at times a flood from my heart seemed to pour itself out into my bosom. I thought little of the future. I did not know whether I would ever speak to her or not or, if I spoke to her, how I could tell her of my confused adoration. But my body was like a harp and her words and gestures were like fingers running upon the wires.

One evening I went into the back drawing-room in which the priest had died. It was a dark rainy evening and there was no sound in the house. Through one of the broken panes I heard the rain impinge[3] upon the earth, the fine incessant needles of water playing in the sodden beds. Some distant lamp or lighted window gleamed below me. I was thankful that I could see so little. All my senses seemed to desire to veil themselves and, feeling that I was about to slip from them, I pressed the palms of my hands together until they trembled, murmuring: *O love! O love!* many times.

At last she spoke to me. When she addressed the first words to me I was so confused that I did not know what to answer. She asked me was I going to *Araby.* I forgot whether I answered yes or no. It would be a splendid bazaar, she said; she would love to go.

—And why can't you? I asked.

While she spoke she turned a silver bracelet round and round her wrist. She could not go, she said, because there would be a retreat that week in her convent. Her brother and two other boys were fighting for their caps and I was alone at the railings. She held one of the spikes, bowing her head towards me. The light from the lamp opposite our door caught the white curve of her neck, lit up her hair that rested there and, falling, lit up the hand upon the railing. It fell over one side of her dress and caught the white border of a petticoat, just visible as she stood at ease.

—It's well for you, she said.

—If I go, I said, I will bring you something.

What innumerable follies laid waste my waking and sleeping thoughts after that evening! I wished to annihilate the tedious intervening days. I chafed against the work of school. At night in my bedroom and by day in the classroom her image came between me and the page I strove to read. The syllables of the word *Araby* were called to me through the silence in which my soul <u>luxuriated</u>, and cast an Eastern enchantment over me. I asked for leave to go to the bazaar on Saturday night.

My aunt was surprised and hoped it was not some Freemason[4] affair. I answered few questions in class. I watched my master's face pass from amiability to sternness; he hoped I was not beginning to idle. I could not call my wandering thoughts together. I had hardly any patience with the serious work of life which, now that it stood between me and my desire, seemed to me child's play, ugly monotonous child's play.

On Saturday morning I reminded my uncle that I wished to go to the bazaar in the evening. He was fussing at the hallstand,

---

3. **impinge** (ĭm-pĭnj′): hit; strike.

4. **Freemason:** having to do with the Free and Accepted Masons, a worldwide charitable and social organization. (Freemasonry has often been opposed by Roman Catholics and other religious groups, in part because of its secret rituals and signs.)

1026

looking for the hat-brush, and answered me curtly:

—Yes, boy, I know.

As he was in the hall I could not go into the front parlor and lie at the window. I left the house in bad humor and walked slowly towards the school. The air was pitilessly raw and already my heart misgave[5] me.

When I came home to dinner my uncle had not yet been home. Still it was early. I sat staring at the clock for some time and, when its ticking began to irritate me, I left the room. I mounted the staircase and gained the upper part of the house. The high cold empty gloomy rooms liberated me and I went from room to room singing. From the front window I saw my companions playing below in the street. Their cries reached me weakened and indistinct and, leaning my forehead against the cool glass, I looked over at the dark house where she lived. I may have stood there for an hour, seeing nothing but the brown-clad figure cast by my imagination, touched discreetly by the lamp-light at the curved neck, at the hand upon the railings and at the border below the dress.

When I came downstairs again I found Mrs. Mercer sitting at the fire. She was an old garrulous woman, a pawnbroker's widow, who collected used stamps for some pious purpose. I had to endure the gossip of the tea table. The meal was prolonged beyond an hour and still my uncle did not come. Mrs. Mercer stood up to go: she was sorry she couldn't wait any longer, but it was after eight o'clock and she did not like to be out late, as the night air was bad for her. When she had gone I began to walk up and down the room, clenching my fists. My aunt said:

—I'm afraid you may put off your bazaar for this night of Our Lord.

At nine o'clock I heard my uncle's latchkey in the hall-door. I heard him talking to himself and heard the hall-stand rocking when it had received the weight of his overcoat. I could interpret these signs. When he was midway through his dinner I asked him to give me the money to go to the bazaar. He had forgotten.

—The people are in bed and after their first sleep now, he said.

I did not smile. My aunt said to him energetically:

—Can't you give him the money and let him go? You've kept him late enough as it is.

My uncle said he was very sorry he had forgotten. He said he believed in the old saying: *All work and no play makes Jack a dull boy.* He asked me where I was going and, when I had told him a second time he asked me did I know *The Arab's Farewell to His Steed*. When I left the kitchen he was about to recite the opening lines of the piece to my aunt.

I held a florin[6] tightly in my hand as I strode down Buckingham Street towards the station. The sight of the streets thronged with buyers and glaring with gas[7] recalled to me the purpose of my journey. I took my seat in a third-class carriage of a deserted train. After an intolerable delay the train moved out of the station slowly. It crept onward among ruinous houses and over the twinkling river. At Westland Row Station a crowd of people pressed

---

5. **misgave:** caused to feel doubt or anxiety.

6. **florin:** a former British coin worth 2 shillings (24 pence).

7. **gas:** gaslight.

to the carriage doors; but the porters moved them back, saying that it was a special train for the bazaar. I remained alone in the bare carriage. In a few minutes the train drew up beside an improvised wooden platform. I passed out on to the road and saw by the lighted dial of a clock that it was ten minutes to ten. In front of me was a large building which displayed the magical name.

I could not find any sixpenny entrance and, fearing that the bazaar would be closed, I passed in quickly through a turnstile, handing a shilling to a weary-looking man. I found myself in a big hall girdled at half its height by a gallery. Nearly all the stalls were closed and the greater part of the hall was in darkness. I recognized a silence like that which <u>pervades</u> a church after a service. I walked into the center of the bazaar timidly. A few people were gathered about the stalls which were still open. Before a curtain, over which the words *Café Chantant*[8] were written in colored lamps, two men were counting money on a salver.[9] I listened to the fall of the coins.

Remembering with difficulty why I had come I went over to one of the stalls and examined porcelain vases and flowered tea-sets. At the door of the stall a young lady was talking and laughing with two young gentlemen. I remarked their English accents and listened vaguely to their conversation.

—O, I never said such a thing!
—O, but you did!
—O, but I didn't!
—Didn't she say that?
—Yes. I heard her.
—O, there's a . . . fib!

Observing me the young lady came over and asked me did I wish to buy anything. The tone of her voice was not encouraging; she seemed to have spoken to me out of a sense of duty. I

I allowed the two pennies to fall against the sixpence in my pocket.

looked humbly at the great jars that stood like eastern guards at either side of the dark entrance to the stall and murmured:
—No, thank you.

The young lady changed the position of one of the vases and went back to the two young men. They began to talk of the same subject. Once or twice the young lady glanced at me over her shoulder.

I lingered before her stall, though I knew my stay was useless, to make my interest in her wares seem the more real. Then I turned away slowly and walked down the middle of the bazaar. I allowed the two pennies to fall against the sixpence in my pocket. I heard a voice call from one end of the gallery that the light was out. The upper part of the hall was now completely dark.

Gazing up into the darkness I saw myself as a creature driven and derided by vanity; and my eyes burned with anguish and anger. ❖

8. *Café Chantant* (kä-fä′ shäN-täN′): a café providing musical entertainment.

9. **salver:** serving tray.

St. Patrick's Close, Dublin (1887), Walter Frederick Osborne. Oil on canvas, 27 ¼″ × 20″. National Gallery of Ireland, Dublin.

WORDS TO KNOW   **pervade** (pər-vād′) *v.* to spread throughout; completely fill

Thinking through the LITERATURE

Connect to the Literature

1. **What Do You Think?**
Do you agree with the narrator's opinion that he was "driven and derided by vanity"? Why or why not?

> **Comprehension Check**
> - What is Araby?
> - Why does the narrator want to go there?
> - Why doesn't the narrator buy anything?

Think Critically

2. How would you describe the relationship between the narrator and Mangan's sister?

3. What aspects of this story do you think might be considered **ironic**?

THINK ABOUT
- the way the narrator expresses his feelings for Mangan's sister
- his expectations and excitement about going to the bazaar
- his experiences at the bazaar

4. What epiphany, or sudden awareness, does the narrator seem to experience?

5. **ACTIVE READING** **MAKING INFERENCES** Review the chart you completed in your **READER'S NOTEBOOK**. Consider the narrator's emotions at different points of the story. What can you infer about him? Support your answer with examples.

Extend Interpretations

6. **Critic's Corner** According to the American poet and critic Ezra Pound, one of Joyce's merits is that "he carefully avoids telling you a lot that you don't want to know." Similarly, Eva Tanner, a student reviewer, praised "Araby" for its "simplicity" and thoughtful use of **detail**. Do you agree that Joyce is frugal in his use of detail? Use evidence from this story to support your opinion.

7. **Comparing Texts** Compare and contrast the portrayals of adults in "Araby" and D. H. Lawrence's "The Rocking-Horse Winner."

8. **Connect to Life** Do you think the narrator's actions and feelings are typical of a boy's behavior? Why or why not?

Literary Analysis

POINT OF VIEW A literary work's **point of view** is the perspective from which it is told. "Araby" is told from a **first-person point of view;** that is, by a narrator who participates in the story's action. First-person narration imparts an immediacy to the narrative and usually leads to involvement with the narrating **character.**

Paired Activity With a partner, look through the story and choose a passage that you find particularly revealing about the narrator. Rewrite the passage from a third-person point of view. What effect on the passage do you think the shift in point of view has? Then discuss why you think Joyce wrote the story from the first-person point of view.

> Every morning he lay on the floor in the front parlor watching her door.

REVIEW **SETTING** The importance of **setting**—the time and place in which a story's action occurs—varies from story to story. It may play a major role in what happens, contributing to the story's **mood, tone,** or **theme,** or it may be only incidental. Think about the different settings described in "Araby," and discuss what they add to the story.

Choices & CHALLENGES

Writing Options

1. Childhood Diary Imagine that you are the narrator. Write a diary entry in which you express your thoughts after arriving home from the bazaar.

2. Dramatic Scene Write a dramatic scene showing the narrator's next encounter with Mangan's sister. Place the scene in your **Working Portfolio.**

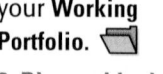

The next day I saw her leave her house.

3. Biographical Sketch Write a biographical sketch of the narrator as a child, based on the information given about him and his family in the story. Feel free to add missing pieces of information.

4. Explanatory Paragraph The images that Joyce uses add a rich layer of intensity and interest to his stories. Sometimes a single image will occur several times in a story. Choose your favorite images in "Araby," and write a brief explanation of why you selected them and what impact you think they have on the story.
Writing Handbook
See pages 1369–1370: Analysis.

Activities & Explorations

1. Interpretation in Pantomime Practice and perform a pantomime of the narrator's actions on the day and evening of the bazaar. **~ PERFORMING**

2. Araby Ad Design an advertisement for Araby that reflects the narrator's anticipation of what the bazaar will be like. **~ ART**

3. Photo Gallery Look through books to find photographs illustrating your impression of the early-20th century city life portrayed in "Araby." Display them in the classroom.
~ VIEWING AND REPRESENTING

Art Connection

Photo Images Look again at the photograph of the boy on page 1027. Does his appearance match your mental image of the narrator of this story? Discuss your impressions with a partner.

Inquiry & Research

Irish History Find out more about Dublin life in the early 1900s. Write a brief report describing the class structure, schooling, clothing, housing, occupations, religious practices, and transportation of the city's residents.

Vocabulary in Action

EXERCISE : MEANING CLUES Write the word that is best described by each clue.

1. Joy, light, or a fragrance can do this to a group or a place.

2. A person who is this is someone you don't want to have a conversation with when you're in a hurry.

3. You might do this in a hot bath on a cold day or in a cool lake on a hot day.

4. It can require great patience not to interrupt this, because you're tempted to say, "So you've said . . . and said and said!"

5. A person who is this might gaze serenely from the stands while the rest of the fans are leaping to their feet to cheer a home run.

WORDS TO KNOW	garrulous	imperturbable	litany	luxuriate	pervade

Building Vocabulary
For an in-depth study of context clues, see page 938.

James Joyce
1882–1941

Other Works
Ulysses
Dubliners
Finnegans Wake
"An Encounter"
"The Sisters"
"Eveline"
"Counterparts"

A Childhood of Poverty James Joyce overcame many handicaps to become one of the greatest novelists of the 20th century. Born into a large Dublin family, he began feeling the effects of poverty as a young child. His father was extremely irresponsible and drank heavily, and during Joyce's childhood the family sank further and further into debt. The children grew accustomed to bill collectors, frequent moves, and the loss of family possessions. At one point, Joyce was forced to leave a grammar school when his parents could no longer afford the tuition. After two years of trying to educate himself at home, he finally had his tuition fees waived so that he might finish his formal education.

His Varied Career In 1902, Joyce graduated from University College in Dublin, where he first began to write seriously. Writing, however, was not the only interest that Joyce pursued—he had a fine voice and as a young man considered a singing career. When he finally did focus his attention on writing, he knew that it was an uncertain profession and that he would probably need another source of income. He began the study of medicine but quickly abandoned it because he had neither the tuition nor the proper educational background. During his lifetime, he tried his hand at various other jobs and enterprises, including teaching, banking, and the movie-theater business.

Self-imposed Exile In June 1904, Joyce met Nora Barnacle, a young girl from Galway, and a few months later the couple moved to Austria-Hungary. Over the next few years, they lived in several European cities—including Trieste, Paris, and Zurich—but never returned to Ireland. Throughout much of his adult life, Joyce faced financial disaster but managed to continue writing with assistance from friends. He also faced serious problems with his vision, undergoing eye surgery 25 times between 1917 and 1930. While working on his last novel, *Finnegans Wake*, he was occasionally forced to write in crayon on large sheets of paper in order to see his own work.

Author Activity

Life in Literature The house in "Araby" is based on one in which Joyce lived as a boy. Find out more about the author's early life to learn what other elements in "Araby," or other short stories by Joyce, are drawn from the author's own life.

ULYSSES

⚛
Above:
*Images of Dublin, early
20th century*

Is it possible to write an epic set in the modern world? Where could one find characters of suitably heroic dimensions? The Irish writer James Joyce faced these questions after leaving his homeland, which he believed to be too narrow in its cultural and religious views, to live in self-imposed exile in Trieste, Zurich, and Paris. From 1914 to 1921, impoverished and struggling to support his family, he produced his masterwork, *Ulysses*, probably the most influential novel of the 20th century.

On one level the plot of *Ulysses* reflects the events recounted in Homer's *Odyssey*—the return of the Greek hero Odysseus (in Latin, Ulysses) to his faithful wife, Penelope, and his son,

Telemachus, after ten years of wandering throughout the Mediterranean after the Trojan War. In typical Joycean fashion, however, the Greek epic is turned on its ear. The hero of *Ulysses* is Leopold Bloom, a middle-aged advertising salesman who lives in Dublin with his unfaithful wife, Molly. He wanders about the city on a single day—June 16, 1904—beginning and ending his journey at his home in Eccles Street. During the course of his wanderings, he encounters Stephen Dedalus, a 22-year-old poet who was the protagonist of Joyce's first novel, *A Portrait of the Artist as a Young Man.* As their lives intersect, the two men form a bond, and in a way Stephen becomes a son to Bloom—a Telemachus to Bloom's Odysseus.

What elevates the story to truly epic proportions is Joyce's presentation of the amazing inner life of his characters through interior monologues. Their thoughts, including the most intimate ones, come rushing by in a stream of consciousness. In the following passage, for example, Bloom, having just attended the funeral of Patrick Dignam, is in a pub, deciding what to have for lunch. Notice how, in the space of a few lines, his thoughts range from sensory experience to a biblical pun to an advertising slogan to Dignam's corpse to a flight of fancy:

> Sardines on the shelves. Almost taste them by looking. Sandwich? Ham and his descendants musterred and bred there. Potted meats. What is home without Plumtree's potted meat? Incomplete. What a stupid ad! Under the obituary notices they stuck it. All up a plumtree. Dignam's potted meat. Cannibals would with lemon and rice. . . .

In addition to the Homeric parallels, allusions to Shakespeare and Dante abound, along with references to the Roman Catholic Church, music, psychology, philosophy, pulp fiction, and a multitude of other topics. Every imaginable aspect of a day in the life of a 20th-century Odysseus, Penelope, and Telemachus is captured in exacting detail, as if their thoughts were our very own.

It is ironic that Joyce, a man who spent his lifetime wandering about Europe, searching for a home, should have spent so much time writing about the very homeland he rejected. Once, when asked if he had plans to return to Ireland at some point, Joyce replied, "Have I ever left?"

Below:
Ulysses and the Sirens (third century A.D.), unknown artist. Musée National du Bardo, Le Bardo, Tunisia, Giraudon/Art Resource, New York.

A Cup of Tea

Short Story by KATHERINE MANSFIELD

(Connect to Your Life)

A Touch of Class Although class distinctions based on wealth are not as pronounced in the United States as they once were, they do still exist. Make three lists, noting what seem to you to be (1) typically upper-class, (2) typically middle-class, and (3) typically lower-class places, events, and institutions. Discuss your lists with classmates.

Build Background

British Society In the early 1900s, when "A Cup of Tea" was written, class distinctions were quite evident in Britain. The best schools and neighborhoods were typically reserved for the rich, who also tended to shop in separate stores on exclusive streets and to avoid contact with people of lower classes whenever possible. An upper-class wife never worked, either inside or outside the home—instead spending her days shopping, visiting, and entertaining. It was considered improper for her to associate with people of lower classes unless they were serving her in some way. In "A Cup of Tea," Mansfield portrays a character named Rosemary who belongs to this pampered upper class.

Focus Your Reading

LITERARY ANALYSIS **REALISM** "A Cup of Tea" is a work of **realism**— that is, one that attempts to give a truthful representation of actual life, without sentimentality or idealism. Mansfield's portrayal of the wealthy Rosemary and her lifestyle employs many details of daily life that were contemporary when the story was written. As you read, be aware of the realistic elements in Mansfield's depiction of Rosemary's character and lifestyle.

ACTIVE READING **ANALYZING PLOT** Most **plots** include the following stages:

- The **exposition** introduces the characters, setting, and major conflict.
- In the **rising action,** complications develop.
- The **climax** is the turning point of the story.
- The **falling action**—sometimes called the **resolution**—consists of the events after the climax.

READER'S NOTEBOOK As you read the story, plot the sequence of events, using a diagram like the one shown. Identify the most important events, and note where you think the four stages of the plot occur.

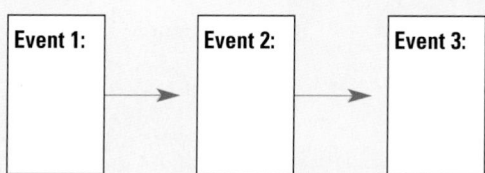

A Cup of Tea

Katherine Mansfield

Rosemary Fell was not exactly beautiful. No, you couldn't have called her beautiful. Pretty? Well, if you took her to pieces . . . But why be so cruel as to take anyone to pieces? She was young, brilliant, extremely modern, exquisitely well dressed, amazingly well read in the newest of the new books, and her parties were the most delicious mixture of the really important people and . . . artists— quaint creatures, discoveries of hers, some of them too terrifying for words, but others quite presentable and amusing.

Rosemary had been married two years. She had a duck[1] of a boy. No, not Peter—Michael. And her husband absolutely adored her. They were rich, really rich, not just comfortably well off, which is odious and stuffy and sounds like one's grandparents. But if Rosemary wanted to shop she would go to Paris as you and I would go to Bond Street.[2] If she wanted to buy flowers, the car pulled up at that perfect shop in Regent Street, and Rosemary inside the shop just gazed in her dazzled, rather exotic way, and said: "I want those and those and those. Give me four bunches of those. And that jar of roses. Yes, I'll have all the roses in the jar. No, no lilac. I hate lilac. It's got no shape." The attendant bowed and put the lilac out of sight, as though this was only too true; lilac was dreadfully shapeless. "Give me those stumpy little tulips. Those red and white ones." And she was followed to the car by a thin shopgirl staggering under an immense white paper armful that looked like a baby in long clothes. . . .

One winter afternoon she had been buying something in a little antique shop in Curzon Street. It was a shop she liked. For one thing, one usually had it to oneself. And then the man who kept it was ridiculously fond of serving her. He beamed whenever she came in. He clasped his hands; he was so gratified he could scarcely speak. Flattery, of course. All the same, there was something . . .

"You see, madam," he would explain in his low respectful tones, "I love my things. I would rather not part with them than sell them to someone who does not appreciate them, who has not that fine feeling which is so rare. . . ." And, breathing deeply, he unrolled a tiny square of blue velvet and pressed it on the glass counter with his pale fingertips.

Today it was a little box. He had been keeping it for her. He had shown it to nobody as yet. An exquisite little enamel box with a glaze so fine it looked as though it had been baked in cream.

On the lid a minute creature stood under a flowery tree, and a more minute creature still had her arms around his neck. Her hat, really no bigger than a geranium petal, hung from a branch; it had green ribbons. And there was a pink cloud like a watchful cherub[3] floating above their heads. Rosemary took her hands out of her long gloves. She always took off her gloves to examine such things. Yes, she liked it very much. She loved it; it was a great duck. She must have it. And, turning the creamy box, opening and shutting it, she couldn't help noticing how charming her hands were against the blue velvet. The shopman, in some dim cavern of his mind, may have dared to think so too. For he took a pencil, leaned over the counter, and his pale bloodless fingers crept timidly towards those rosy, flashing ones, as he murmured gently: "If I may venture to point out to madam, the flowers on the little lady's bodice."[4]

"Charming!" Rosemary admired the flowers. But what was the price? For a moment the shopman did not seem to hear. Then a murmur reached her. "Twenty-eight guineas,[5] madam."

"Twenty-eight guineas." Rosemary gave no sign. She laid the little box down; she buttoned her gloves again. Twenty-eight guineas. Even if one is rich . . . She looked vague. She stared at a plump teakettle like a plump hen above the shopman's head, and her voice was dreamy as she answered: "Well, keep it for me—will you? I'll . . ."

But the shopman had already bowed as though keeping it for her was all any human being could ask. He would be willing, of course, to keep it for her forever.

---

1. **duck:** in British usage, a darling person or thing.
2. **Bond Street:** one of London's main business streets.
3. **cherub:** an angel depicted as a chubby child with wings.
4. **bodice** (bŏd′ĭs): the upper part of a dress.
5. **guineas** (gĭn′ēz): units of British money (equal to 21 shillings each), used mainly for pricing luxury items.

he discreet door shut with a click. She was outside on the step, gazing at the winter after-noon. Rain was falling, and with the rain it seemed the dark came too, spinning down like ashes. There was a cold bitter taste in the air, and the new-lighted lamps looked sad. Sad were the lights in the houses opposite. Dimly they burned as if regretting something. And people hurried by, hidden under their hateful umbrellas. Rosemary felt a strange pang.[6] She pressed her muff to her breast; she wished she had the little box, too, to cling to. Of course, the car was there. She'd only to cross the pavement. But still she waited. There are moments, horrible moments in life, when one emerges from shelter and looks out, and it's awful. One oughtn't to give way to them. One ought to go home and have an extra-special tea. But at the very instant of thinking that, a young girl, thin, dark, shad-owy—where had she come from?—was standing at Rosemary's elbow and a voice like a sigh, almost like a sob, breathed: "Madam, may I speak to you a moment?"

"Speak to me?" Rosemary turned. She saw a little battered creature with enormous eyes, someone quite young, no older than herself, who clutched at her coat-collar with reddened hands, and shivered as though she had just come out of the water.

"M-madam," stammered the voice. "Would you let me have the price of a cup of tea?"

"A cup of tea?" There was something simple, sincere in that voice; it wasn't in the least the voice of a beggar. "Then have you no money at all?" asked Rosemary.

"None, madam," came the answer.

"How extraordinary!" Rosemary peered through the dusk, and the girl gazed back at her. How more than extraordinary! And suddenly it seemed to Rosemary such an adventure. It was like something out of a novel by Dostoyevsky,[7] this meeting in the dusk. Supposing she took the girl home? Supposing she did do one of those things she was always reading about or seeing

The Mirror (1890), Dennis Miller Bunker. Oil on canvas, 50⅜″ × 40⅜″, Terra Foundation for the Arts, Daniel J. Terra Collection (43.1980). Photo Copyright © 1995 courtesy of Terra Museum of American Art, Chicago.

on the stage, what would happen? It would be thrilling. And she heard herself saying afterwards to the amazement of her friends: "I simply took her home with me," as she stepped forward and said to that dim person beside her: "Come home to tea with me."

The girl drew back startled. She even stopped shivering for a moment. Rosemary put out a hand and touched her arm. "I mean it," she said, smiling. And she felt how simple and kind her smile was. "Why won't you? Do. Come home with me now in my car and have tea."

"You—you don't mean it, madam," said the girl, and there was pain in her voice.

---

6. **pang:** a sudden sharp pain or feeling.

7. **Dostoyevsky** (dŏs′tə-yĕf′skē): Feodor Dostoyevsky, a 19th-century Russian writer of novels and short stories. He wrote a number of works dealing with the lives of the poor and the underprivileged.

The First Cloud (1887), Sir William Quiller Orchardson. Tate Gallery, London/Art Resource, New York.

"But I do," cried Rosemary. "I want you to. To please me. Come along."

The girl put her fingers to her lips and her eyes devoured Rosemary. "You're—you're not taking me to the police station?" she stammered.

"The police station!" Rosemary laughed out. "Why should I be so cruel? No, I only want to make you warm and to hear—anything you care to tell me."

Hungry people are easily led. The footman held the door of the car open, and a moment later they were skimming through the dusk.

"There!" said Rosemary. She had a feeling of triumph as she slipped her hand through the velvet strap. She could have said, "Now I've got you," as she gazed at the little captive she had netted. But of course she meant it kindly. Oh,

more than kindly. She was going to prove to this girl that—wonderful things did happen in life, that—fairy godmothers were real, that—rich people had hearts, and that women *were* sisters. She turned impulsively, saying: "Don't be frightened. After all, why shouldn't you come back with me? We're both women. If I'm the more fortunate, you ought to expect . . ."

But happily at that moment, for she didn't know how the sentence was going to end, the car stopped. The bell was rung, the door opened, and with a charming, protecting, almost embracing movement, Rosemary drew the other into the hall. Warmth, softness, light, a sweet scent, all those things so familiar to her she never even thought about them, she watched that other receive. It was fascinating. She was like the little

rich girl in her nursery with all the cupboards to open, all the boxes to unpack.

"Come, come upstairs," said Rosemary, longing to begin to be generous. "Come up to my room." And, besides, she wanted to spare this poor little thing from being stared at by the servants; she decided as they mounted the stairs she would not even ring for Jeanne, but take off her things by herself. The great thing was to be natural!

And "There!" cried Rosemary again, as they reached her beautiful big bedroom with the curtains drawn, the fire leaping on her wonderful lacquer furniture, her gold cushions and the primrose and blue rugs.

The girl stood just inside the door; she seemed dazed. But Rosemary didn't mind that.

"Come and sit down," she cried, dragging her big chair up to the fire, "in this comfy chair. Come and get warm. You look so dreadfully cold."

"I daren't, madam," said the girl, and she edged backwards.

"Oh, please,"—Rosemary ran forward—"you mustn't be frightened, you mustn't, really. Sit down, and when I've taken off my things we shall go into the next room and have tea and be cozy. Why are you afraid?" And gently she half pushed the thin figure into its deep cradle.

But there was no answer. The girl stayed just as she had been put, with her hands by her sides and her mouth slightly open. To be quite sincere, she looked rather stupid. But Rosemary wouldn't acknowledge it. She leaned over her, saying: "Won't you take off your hat? Your pretty hair is all wet. And one is so much more comfortable without a hat, isn't one?"

There was a whisper that sounded like "Very good, madam," and the crushed hat was taken off.

"Let me help you off with your coat, too," said Rosemary.

The girl stood up. But she held on to the chair with one hand and let Rosemary pull. It was quite an effort. The other scarcely helped her at all. She seemed to stagger like a child, and the thought came and went through Rosemary's mind, that if people wanted helping they must respond a little, just a little, otherwise it became very difficult indeed. And what was she to do with the coat now? She left it on the floor, and the hat too. She was just going to take a cigarette off the mantelpiece when the girl said quickly, but so lightly and strangely: "I'm very sorry, madam, but I'm going to faint. I shall go off, madam, if I don't have something."

"Good heavens, how thoughtless I am!" Rosemary rushed to the bell.

"Tea! Tea at once! And some brandy immediately!"

The maid was gone again, but the girl almost cried out. "No, I don't want no brandy. I never drink brandy. It's a cup of tea I want, madam." And she burst into tears.

It was a terrible and fascinating moment. Rosemary knelt beside her chair.

"Don't cry, poor little thing," she said. "Don't cry." And she gave the other her lace handkerchief. She really was touched beyond words. She put her arm round those thin, birdlike shoulders.

Now at last the other forgot to be shy, forgot everything except that they were both women, and gasped out: "I can't go on no longer like this. I can't bear it. I shall do away with myself. I can't bear no more."

"You shan't have to. I'll look after you. Don't cry anymore. Don't you see what a good thing it was that you met me? We'll have tea and you'll tell me everything. And I shall arrange something. I promise. *Do* stop crying. It's so exhausting. Please!"

The other did stop just in time for Rosemary to get up before the tea came. She had the table placed between them. She plied the poor little creature with everything, all the sandwiches, all the bread and butter, and every time her cup was

empty she filled it with tea, cream and sugar. People always said sugar was so nourishing. As for herself she didn't eat; she smoked and looked away tactfully so that the other should not be shy.

And really the effect of that slight meal was marvelous. When the tea table was carried away a new being, a light, frail creature with tangled hair, dark lips, deep, lighted eyes, lay back in the big chair in a kind of sweet languor,[8] looking at the blaze. Rosemary lit a fresh cigarette; it was time to begin.

"And when did you have your last meal?" she asked softly.

But at that moment the door-handle turned.

"Rosemary, may I come in?" It was Philip.

"Of course."

He came in. "Oh, I'm so sorry," he said, and stopped and stared.

"It's quite all right," said Rosemary smiling. "This is my friend, Miss—"

"Smith, madam," said the languid figure, who was strangely still and unafraid.

"Smith," said Rosemary. "We are going to have a little talk."

"Oh, yes," said Philip. "Quite," and his eye caught sight of the coat and hat on the floor. He came over to the fire and turned his back to it. "It's a beastly afternoon," he said curiously, still looking at that listless figure, looking at its hands and boots, and then at Rosemary again.

"Yes, isn't it?" said Rosemary enthusiastically. "Vile."[9]

Philip smiled his charming smile. "As a matter of fact," said he, "I wanted you to come into the library for a moment. Would you? Will Miss Smith excuse us?"

The big eyes were raised to him, but Rosemary answered for her. "Of course she will." And they went out of the room together.

"I say," said Philip, when they were alone. "Explain. Who is she? What does it all mean?"

Rosemary, laughing, leaned against the door and said: "I picked her up in Curzon Street.

Really. She's a real pick-up. She asked me for the price of a cup of tea, and I brought her home with me."

"But what on earth are you going to do with her?" cried Philip.

"Be nice to her," said Rosemary quickly. "Be frightfully nice to her. Look after her. I don't know how. We haven't talked yet. But show her—treat her—make her feel—"

"My darling girl," said Philip, "you're quite mad, you know. It simply can't be done."

"I knew you'd say that," retorted Rosemary. "Why not? I want to. Isn't that a reason? And besides, one's always reading about these things. I decided—"

"But," said Philip slowly, and he cut the end of a cigar, "she's so astonishingly pretty."

"Pretty?" Rosemary was so surprised that she blushed. "Do you think so? I—I hadn't thought about it."

"Good Lord!" Philip struck a match. "She's absolutely lovely. Look again, my child. I was bowled over when I came into your room just now. However . . . I think you're making a ghastly mistake. Sorry, darling, if I'm crude and all that. But let me know if Miss Smith is going to dine with us in time for me to look up *The Milliner's Gazette*."[10]

"You absurd creature!" said Rosemary, and she went out of the library, but not back to her bedroom. She went to her writing-room and sat down at her desk. Pretty! Absolutely lovely! Bowled over! Her heart beat like a heavy bell. Pretty! Lovely! She drew her checkbook towards her. But no, checks would be no use, of course. She opened a drawer and took out five pound notes, looked at them, put two back, and holding the three squeezed in her hand, she went back to her bedroom.

---

8. **languor** (lăng′gər): a dreamy, lazy mood.

9. **vile:** unpleasant; highly disagreeable.

10. ***The Milliner's Gazette:*** an imaginary newsletter for working-class women. (A milliner is a maker of women's hats.)

Half an hour later Philip was still in the library, when Rosemary came in.

"I only wanted to tell you," said she, and she leaned against the door again and looked at him with her dazzled exotic gaze, "Miss Smith won't dine with us tonight."

Philip put down the paper. "Oh, what's happened? Previous engagement?"

Rosemary came over and sat down on his knee. "She insisted on going," said she, "so I gave the poor little thing a present of money. I couldn't keep her against her will, could I?" she added softly.

Rosemary had just done her hair, darkened her eyes a little, and put on her pearls. She put up her hands and touched Philip's cheeks.

"Do you like me?" said she, and her tone, sweet, husky, troubled him.

"I like you awfully," he said, and he held her tighter. "Kiss me."

There was a pause.

Then Rosemary said dreamily, "I saw a fascinating little box today. It cost twenty-eight guineas. May I have it?"

Philip jumped her on his knee. "You may, little wasteful one," said he.

But that was not really what Rosemary wanted to say.

"Philip," she whispered, and she pressed his head against her bosom, "am I *pretty?*" ❖

Connect to the Literature

1. **What Do You Think?**
   What is your reaction to Rosemary's question at the end of the story? Share your thoughts with a classmate.

   Comprehension Check
   • What plans for Miss Smith does Rosemary have at first?
   • How does Philip react toward Miss Smith?
   • What does Rosemary give to Miss Smith?

Think Critically

2. Why do you think Rosemary invites Miss Smith home?

   THINK ABOUT
   • Rosemary's mood when she meets Miss Smith
   • her thoughts when Miss Smith asks her for money
   • the reasons she gives to Miss Smith and to Philip

3. **ACTIVE READING** **ANALYZING PLOT** Review the plot sequence chart you made in your **READER'S NOTEBOOK**. Which event do you think is the **climax**, or turning point, of the story? Explain your choice.

4. Why do you think Miss Smith doesn't stay for dinner? Support your answer with evidence from the story.

5. How might Rosemary's conversation with Philip at the end of the story be considered an example of **dramatic irony?** Explain your answer.

6. What is your opinion of Rosemary, Philip, and the upper-class lifestyle presented in this story?

Extend Interpretations

7. **Different Perspectives** How do you think Miss Smith would describe her encounter with Rosemary? Bear in mind what might have made the strongest impression on Miss Smith, the differences between her and Rosemary, and the separate worlds they inhabit.

8. **Connect to Life** Some people help others out of a true sense of compassion, whereas others have strictly self-serving motives for lending a helping hand. With a partner, discuss which motive you think is more prevalent.

Literary Analysis

REALISM **Realism** in fiction is a truthful representation of actual life. In a realistic work, ordinary, everyday events are presented in clear, direct prose. Detailed **characterization,** focusing on characters' thoughts and values, is also an important element of realism. John Middleton Murry, the critic who became Katherine Mansfield's husband, praised her work for its realism, recalling the judgment of a printer who remarked after reading a manuscript of hers, "But these kids are real!"

Activity Do you agree with this view of the realism in Mansfield's work? Why or why not? Find two or three passages from "A Cup of Tea" to support your answer.

REVIEW **TONE** **Tone** is the expression of a writer's attitude toward his or her subject. Throughout "A Cup of Tea," Mansfield suggests her view of Rosemary through her choice of words and through details describing Rosemary's appearance, actions, and thoughts. After looking through the story to find details that reveal Mansfield's attitude, try to formulate a description of the story's overall tone.

Writing Options

1. Concluding Paragraph The story ends before Philip answers Rosemary's final question. Write a concluding paragraph in which he gives an answer. Try to match Mansfield's writing style and Philip's manner of speech.

2. Missing Scene Write a brief dramatic scene showing what takes place between Rosemary and Miss Smith just before Miss Smith leaves. Try to make the dialogue reflect the social class of each character. Place the scene in your **Working Portfolio.**

Activities & Explorations

1. Contemporary Version With a small group of classmates, brainstorm ideas for a contemporary version of the scene in which Rosemary first meets Miss Smith. You could begin by writing a list of what details would make the scene a work of realism set in modern times. Choose two students to play the characters and have them perform the scene for the class. ~ **SPEAKING AND LISTENING/PERFORMING**

2. Party Invitation Imagine that, having decided to make Miss Smith her protégée, Rosemary wants to throw a party to introduce the woman to her rich friends. Design an invitation she might send, including a description of Miss Smith and of the evening's entertainment. **~ ART**

Inquiry & Research

Class in Britain Research and report on the British class system today. Is it as rigid as it was at the time of this story? If not, how has it changed?

Katherine Mansfield
1888–1923

Other Works
Bliss and Other Stories
Something Childish and Other Stories
The Garden Party and Other Stories

Around the World Although she lived to be only 34 years old, Katherine Mansfield was a master of the short story who developed a distinctive prose style characterized by mood and suggestion rather than dramatic action. Born Kathleen Mansfield Beauchamp in Wellington, New Zealand, she published her first story when she was 9. In 1903 she was sent to college in London, where she played the cello and edited the college literary magazine. On her return to New Zealand, she was so unhappy that her father sent her back to London, where her interest quickly shifted from music to literature. She married in 1909 but left her husband after a few days and began reviewing and writing short stories.

Married Life In 1911, Mansfield met the English critic John Middleton Murry, and they began a creative but stormy relationship. In 1919, after she obtained a divorce from her first husband, she and Murry were married. The couple stayed some weeks with Frieda and D. H. Lawrence, and Lawrence loosely based the main characters in his novel *Women in Love* on the four of them.

Early Death Mansfield suffered from ill health and traveled often in search of a favorable climate. During her last years, although she was at the height of her powers as a writer, she lived as an invalid, fighting a losing battle with tuberculosis. Despite the shortness of her writing career, she is considered a major contributor to the form and style of the modern short story.

Author Activity

Mansfield and Lawrence Find out more about the friendship, and later falling-out, between Mansfield and D. H. Lawrence. How did Lawrence portray Mansfield and her husband when he used them as models for characters in *Women in Love*?

The Novels of

Graham Greene

A stranger arrives in Vienna, or Vietnam, or Cuba—
a scene of conflict and intrigue. He intends to live
quietly, but trouble soon finds him. Torn between
conscience and friendship, duty and love, evidence and
faith, the stranger must betray one or the other. Which
will he choose?

Situations such as this fascinated Graham Greene, who
used them as frameworks for many of his novels. First and
foremost, Greene saw himself as an entertainer, even
characterizing some of his books as "entertainments"
rather than novels. A number of his works, including *Our
Man in Havana* and *Brighton Rock,* have been made into
films; one, *The Third Man,* was actually conceived as a
film before it was published as a novel. Greene's style is
itself basically cinematic, sometimes displaying a wide
view from a distance, sometimes zooming in for a close-up
of details. It is a style that has had a tremendous influence
on other writers, especially writers of the spy novel—
brimming with suspense, danger, and international
intrigue—a form of which Greene was a master.

The settings of Greene's novels tend to be the world's
trouble spots, including such far-flung places as Africa,
Mexico, London, South America, and Haiti. Most of these
exotic locales are places Greene knew well. *The Ministry
of Fear* grew out of his wartime service in West Africa,
and *The Heart of the Matter* evolved from his experiences

in Freetown, Sierra Leone. Similarly, a visit to Vienna resulted in *The Third Man,* and trips to Vietnam, Cuba, and South America provided material for *The Quiet American, Our Man in Havana,* and *The Honorary Consul.*

Like his settings, the themes of Greene's novels spring from personal experience. The web of conflicting loyalties in which his characters are caught resembles his own boyhood sense of dual loyalty—to his head-master father on the one hand and to his school chums on the other. His concern with moral dilemmas reflects his personal interest in spiritual growth as well as his conversion to Roman Catholicism. His political themes reflect his lifelong involvement in world affairs and his experience as a spy.

Recognizing these various influences, critics have labeled Graham Greene a Catholic novelist, a political novelist, and a spy novelist. He is all of these, of course, and more. Despite their varied themes and settings, Greene's novels essentially center on complex, unpredictable people. Like real people, they refuse to be classified or pigeon-holed. Instead, they live as best they know how in a world that is in turmoil.

•

Far top left:
The giant Ferris wheel in Vienna used in filming The Third Man. Photofest.
Top right:
Freetown, Sierra Leone, one of the many places Greene lived in and wrote about.
Middle right:
Joseph Cotton and Orson Welles in The Third Man. Photofest.
Bottom right:
Greene in Havana.

PREPARING to *Read*

The Duchess and the Jeweller

Short Story by VIRGINIA WOOLF

Connect to Your Life

Hard Bargain Have you ever agreed to do something unpleasant in return for a favor? What was the driving force that moved you to accept the bargain? Looking back on the situation, do you think you made the right decision? Explore your thoughts with a classmate.

Build Background

Woolf and the Bloomsbury Group Virginia Woolf was one of the most celebrated members of the Bloomsbury group, a circle of intellectual writers, painters, and philosophers who met and conversed frequently from about 1907 to 1930. Many in the group lived in the Bloomsbury district of London, and they often met in Woolf's house. Members questioned existing ideas and sought ways of improving not only their literary and artistic expression but society in general. They rejected many 19th-century views about literature, art, politics, and social issues and supported writers and artists who were breaking new ground.

Woolf continually experimented with the form of the novel and excelled at revealing the inner thoughts and feelings of her characters. In her essay "Modern Fiction," she wrote that "everything is the proper stuff of fiction, every feeling, every thought; every quality of brain and spirit is drawn upon; no perception comes amiss." Her brilliantly original fiction has won wide acclaim from prominent literary figures, including the novelist E. M. Forster (also a member of the Bloomsbury group), whose comments on Woolf appear on page 1057.

WORDS TO KNOW
Vocabulary Preview

arrogance	forge	obsequiously
astute	lissome	

Focus Your Reading

LITERARY ANALYSIS **STYLE** An important element of Woolf's **style** is her use of **stream of consciousness,** a technique of presenting, in a series of loosely connected associations, the flow of thoughts and sensations in a character's mind:

> *He looked past her, at the backs of the houses in Bond Street. But he saw not the houses in Bond Street, but a dimpling river; and trout rising and salmon; and the Prime Minister; and himself too; in white waistcoats; and then, Diana.*

As you read, be aware of Woolf's use of this stylistic technique.

ACTIVE READING **MAKING INFERENCES**

Understanding what impels a **character** is often the key to understanding an entire story. Sometimes the character's **motivation**—the driving force behind his or her thoughts, feelings, and actions—is obvious; at other times it must be **inferred** from clues buried within the story.

READER'S NOTEBOOK As you read Woolf's story, record the motivations of both the duchess and the jeweller in a diagram like the one shown here.

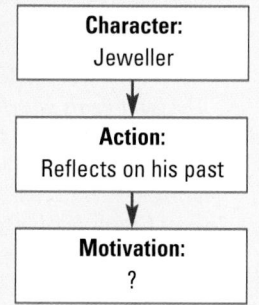

Character:
Jeweller

↓

Action:
Reflects on his past

↓

Motivation:
?

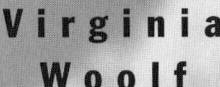

Virginia
Woolf

The Duchess and the Jeweller

*O*liver Bacon lived at the top of a house overlooking the Green Park. He had a flat; chairs jutted out at the right angles—chairs covered in hide. Sofas filled the bays of the windows—sofas covered in tapestry. The windows, the three long windows, had the proper allowance of discreet net and figured satin.[1] The mahogany sideboard bulged discreetly with the right brandies, whiskeys and liqueurs. And from the middle window he looked down upon the glossy roofs of fashionable cars packed in the narrow straits of Piccadilly.[2] A more central position could not be imagined. And at eight in the morning he would have his breakfast brought in on a tray by a manservant; the manservant would unfold his crimson dressing gown; he would rip his letters open with his long pointed nails and would extract thick white cards of invitation upon which the engraving stood up roughly from duchesses, countesses, viscountesses[3] and Honorable Ladies. Then he would wash; then he would eat his toast; then he would read his paper by the bright burning fire of electric coals.

"Behold Oliver," he would say, addressing himself. "You who began life in a filthy little alley, you who . . ." and he would look down at his legs, so shapely in their perfect trousers; at his boots; at his spats. They were all shapely, shining; cut from the best cloth by the best scissors in Savile Row.[4] But he dismantled himself[5] often and became again a little boy in a dark alley. He had once thought that[6] the height of his ambition—selling stolen dogs to fashionable women in Whitechapel.[7] And once he had been done.[8] "Oh, Oliver," his mother had wailed. "Oh, Oliver! When will you have sense, my son?" . . . Then he had gone behind a counter; had sold cheap watches; then he had taken a wallet to Amsterdam. . . . At that

memory he would chuckle—the old Oliver remembering the young. Yes, he had done well with the three diamonds; also there was the commission on the emerald. After that he went into the private room behind the shop in Hatton Garden;[9] the room with the scales, the safe, the thick magnifying glasses. And then . . . and then . . . He chuckled. When he passed through the knots of jewellers in the hot evening who were discussing prices, gold mines, diamonds, reports from South Africa, one of them would lay a finger to the side of his nose and murmur, "Hum–m–m," as he passed. It was no more than a murmur; no more than a nudge on the shoulder, a finger on the nose, a buzz that ran through the cluster of jewellers in Hatton Garden on a hot afternoon—oh, many years ago now! But still Oliver felt it purring down his spine, the nudge, the murmur that meant, "Look at him—young Oliver, the young jeweller—there he goes." Young he was then. And he dressed better and better; and had, first a hansom cab;[10] then a car; and first he went up to the dress circle,

---

1. **discreet net and figured satin:** curtains made of lace that is not showy and satin with a design woven into it.

2. **Piccadilly** (pĭk′ə-dĭl′ē): one of London's main business streets.

3. **viscountesses** (vī′koun′tĭs-ĭz): noblewomen ranking below duchesses and countesses but above baronesses.

4. **Savile** (săv′ĭl) **Row:** a London street in which many exclusive men's clothing stores are located.

5. **dismantled himself:** took himself apart (that is, mentally removed the outer symbols of success in order to see the person he once was).

6. **that:** The word is used as a pronoun here, referring to the selling of stolen dogs mentioned later in the sentence.

7. **Whitechapel:** a seedy area in eastern London.

8. **done:** British slang meaning "arrested and charged with a crime."

9. **Hatton Garden:** the center of London's jewelry trade.

10. **hansom cab:** a two-wheeled horse-drawn carriage.

then down into the stalls.[11] And he had a villa at Richmond, overlooking the river, with trellises of red roses; and Mademoiselle used to pick one every morning and stick it in his buttonhole.

"So," said Oliver Bacon, rising and stretching his legs. "So . . ."

And he stood beneath the picture of an old lady on the mantelpiece and raised his hands. "I have kept my word," he said, laying his hands together, palm to palm, as if he were doing homage to her. "I have won my bet." That was so; he was the richest jeweller in England; but his nose, which was long and flexible, like an elephant's trunk, seemed to say by its curious quiver at the nostrils (but it seemed as if the whole nose quivered, not only the nostrils) that he was not satisfied yet; still smelt something under the ground a little further off. Imagine a giant hog in a pasture rich with truffles;[12] after unearthing this truffle and that, still it smells a bigger, a blacker truffle under the ground further off. So Oliver snuffed always in the rich earth of Mayfair[13] another truffle, a blacker, a bigger further off.

Now then he straightened the pearl in his tie, cased himself in his smart blue overcoat; took his yellow gloves and his cane; and swayed as he descended the stairs and half snuffed, half sighed through his long sharp nose as he passed out into Piccadilly. For was he not still a sad man, a dissatisfied man, a man who seeks something that is hidden, though he had won his bet?

He swayed slightly as he walked, as the camel at the zoo sways from side to side when it walks along the asphalt paths laden with grocers and their wives eating from paper bags and throwing little bits of silver paper crumpled up on to the path. The camel despises the grocers; the camel is dissatisfied with its lot; the camel sees the blue lake and the fringe of palm trees in front of it. So

For was he not still a sad man, a dissatisfied man, a man who seeks something that is hidden, though he had won his bet?

the great jeweller, the greatest jeweller in the whole world, swung down Piccadilly, perfectly dressed, with his gloves, with his cane; but dissatisfied still, till he reached the dark little shop, that was famous in France, in Germany, in Austria, in Italy, and all over America—the dark little shop in the street off Bond Street.[14]

As usual he strode through the shop without speaking, though the four men, the two old men, Marshall and Spencer, and the two young men, Hammond and Wicks, stood straight behind the counter as he passed and looked at him, envying him. It was only with one finger of the amber-colored glove, waggling, that he acknowledged their presence. And he went in and shut the door of his private room behind him.

Then he unlocked the grating that barred the window. The cries of Bond Street came in; the purr of the distant traffic. The light from reflectors at the back of the shop struck upwards. One tree waved six green leaves, for it was June. But Mademoiselle had married Mr. Pedder of the local brewery—no one stuck roses in his buttonhole now.

"So," he half sighed, half snorted, "so . . ."

Then he touched a spring in the wall and slowly the paneling slid open, and behind it were the steel safes, five, no, six of them, all of burnished steel. He twisted a key; unlocked one; then another. Each was lined with a pad of deep

---

11. **dress circle . . . stalls:** In a theater or concert hall, the dress circle is a section of seats—usually in the first balcony—that are expensive but available to all. The stalls are seats near the stage that are usually reserved for royalty or others of very high rank.

12. **truffles:** edible fungi that grow underground, considered a rare delicacy. (Hogs are often used to sniff them out.)

13. **Mayfair:** a fashionable residential section of London.

14. **Bond Street:** a main business street passing through the jewelers' district in London.

A Dinner Table at Night (The Glass of Claret) (1884), John Singer Sargent. Oil on canvas, 20¼″ × 26¼″, The Fine Arts Museums of San Francisco, gift of the Atholl McBean Foundation (73.12).

crimson velvet; in each lay jewels—bracelets, necklaces, rings, tiaras, ducal coronets;[15] loose stones in glass shells; rubies, emeralds, pearls, diamonds. All safe, shining, cool, yet burning, eternally, with their own compressed light.

"Tears!" said Oliver, looking at the pearls.

"Heart's blood!" he said, looking at the rubies.

"Gunpowder!" he continued, rattling the diamonds so that they flashed and blazed.

"Gunpowder enough to blow up Mayfair—sky high, high, high!" He threw his head back and made a sound like a horse neighing as he said it.

The telephone buzzed <u>obsequiously</u> in a low muted voice on his table. He shut the safe.

"In ten minutes," he said. "Not before." And he sat down at his desk and looked at the heads of the Roman emperors that were graved[16] on his sleeve links. And again he dismantled himself and became once more the little boy playing marbles in the alley where they sell stolen dogs on Sunday. He became that wily <u>astute</u> little boy, with lips like wet cherries.

---

15. **ducal** (do͞o′kəl) **coronets:** small crowns worn by dukes and duchesses.

16. **graved:** engraved.

He dabbled his fingers in ropes of tripe;[17] he dipped them in pans of frying fish; he dodged in and out among the crowds. He was slim, lissome, with eyes like licked stones. And now—now—the hands of the clock ticked on. One, two, three, four . . . The Duchess of Lambourne waited his pleasure; the Duchess of Lambourne, daughter of a hundred Earls. She would wait for ten minutes on a chair at the counter. She would wait his pleasure. She would wait till he was ready to see her. He watched the clock in its shagreen[18] case. The hand moved on. With each tick the clock handed him—so it seemed—pâté de foie gras;[19] a glass of champagne; another of fine brandy; a cigar costing one guinea. The clock laid them on the table beside him, as the ten minutes passed. Then he heard soft slow footsteps approaching; a rustle in the corridor. The door opened. Mr. Hammond flattened himself against the wall.

"Her Grace!" he announced.

And he waited there, flattened against the wall.

And Oliver, rising, could hear the rustle of the dress of the Duchess as she came down the passage. Then she loomed up, filling the door, filling the room with the aroma, the prestige, the arrogance, the pomp, the pride of all the Dukes and Duchesses swollen in one wave. And as a wave breaks, she broke, as she sat down, spreading and splashing and falling over Oliver Bacon the great jeweller, covering him with sparkling bright colors, green, rose, violet; and odors; and iridescences;[20] and rays shooting from fingers, nodding from plumes, flashing from silk; for she was very large, very fat, tightly girt[21] in pink taffeta, and past her prime. As a parasol with many flounces,[22] as a peacock with many feathers, shuts its flounces, folds its feathers, so she subsided and shut herself as she sank down in the leather armchair.

"Good morning, Mr. Bacon," said the Duchess. And she held out her hand which came through the slit of her white glove. And Oliver bent low as he shook it. And as their hands touched the link was forged between them once more. They were friends, yet enemies; he was master, she was mistress; each cheated the other, each needed the other, each feared the other, each felt this and knew this every time they touched hands thus in the little back room with the white light outside, and the tree with its six leaves, and the sound of the street in the distance and behind them the safes.

"And today, Duchess—what can I do for you today?" said Oliver, very softly.

The Duchess opened; her heart, her private heart, gaped wide. And with a sigh, but no words, she took from her bag a long wash-leather pouch—it looked like a lean yellow ferret.[23] And from a slit in the ferret's belly she dropped pearls—ten pearls. They rolled from the slit in the ferret's belly—one, two, three, four—like the eggs of some heavenly bird.

"All that's left me, dear Mr. Bacon," she moaned. Five, six, seven—down they rolled, down the slopes of the vast mountainsides that fell between her knees into one narrow valley—the eighth, the ninth, and the tenth. There they lay in the glow of the peach-blossom taffeta. Ten pearls.

---

17. **tripe:** the stomach lining of a cow or calf, used as a food.
18. **shagreen** (shə-grēn′): untanned leather, often dyed green.
19. **pâté de foie gras** (pä-tā′ də fwä grä′): a delicacy made from goose liver.
20. **iridescences** (ĭr′ĭ-děs′ən-sĭz): brilliant displays of changing, rainbowlike colors.
21. **girt:** wrapped; encircled.
22. **parasol with many flounces:** umbrella with many ruffles.
23. **ferret:** a small weasel-like mammal.

WORDS   **lissome** (lĭs′əm) *adj.* easy and graceful in movement
TO   **arrogance** (ăr′ə-gəns) *n.* overbearing pride; exaggerated self-importance
KNOW   **forge** (fôrj) *v.* to form, shape, or produce

"From the Appleby cincture,"[24] she mourned. "The last . . . the last of them all."

Oliver stretched out and took one of the pearls between finger and thumb. It was round, it was lustrous. But real was it, or false? Was she lying again? Did she dare?

She laid her plump padded finger across her lips. "If the Duke knew . . ." she whispered. "Dear Mr. Bacon, a bit of bad luck . . ."

Been gambling again, had she?

"That villain! That sharper!"[25] she hissed.

The man with the chipped cheek bone? A bad 'un. And the Duke was straight as a poker; with side whiskers; would cut her off, shut her up down there if he knew—what I know, thought Oliver, and glanced at the safe.

"Araminta, Daphne, Diana," she moaned. "It's for *them*."

The Ladies Araminta, Daphne, Diana—her daughters. He knew them; adored them. But it was Diana he loved.

"You have all my secrets," she leered. Tears slid; tears fell; tears, like diamonds, collecting powder in the ruts of her cherry-blossom cheeks.

"Old friend," she murmured, "old friend."

"Old friend," he repeated, "old friend," as if he licked the words.

"How much?" he queried.

She covered the pearls with her hand.

"Twenty thousand," she whispered.

But was it real or false, the one he held in his hand? The Appleby cincture—hadn't she sold it already? He would ring for Spencer or Hammond. "Take it and test it," he would say. He stretched to the bell.

"You will come down tomorrow?" she urged, she interrupted. "The Prime Minister—His Royal Highness . . ." She stopped. "And Diana," she added.

Oliver took his hand off the bell.

He looked past her, at the backs of the houses in Bond Street. But he saw, not the houses in Bond Street, but a dimpling river; and trout rising and salmon; and the Prime Minister; and himself too; in white waistcoats; and then, Diana. He looked down at the pearl in his hand. But how could he test it, in the light of the river, in the light of the eyes of Diana? But the eyes of the Duchess were on him.

"Twenty thousand," she moaned. "My honor!"

---

24. **cincture** (sĭngk′chər): an ornamental belt.

25. **sharper:** a cheating gambler.

The honor of the mother of Diana! He drew his checkbook towards him; he took out his pen.

"Twenty," he wrote. Then he stopped writing. The eyes of the old woman in the picture were on him—of the old woman, his mother.

"Oliver!" she warned him. "Have sense! Don't be a fool!"

"Oliver!" the Duchess entreated—it was "Oliver" now, not "Mr. Bacon." "You'll come for a long weekend?"

Alone in the woods with Diana! Riding alone in the woods with Diana!

"Thousand," he wrote, and signed it.

"Here you are," he said.

And there opened all the flounces of the parasol, all the plumes of the peacock, the radiance of the wave, the swords and spears of Agincourt,[26] as she rose from her chair. And the two old men and the two young men, Spencer and Marshall, Wicks and Hammond, flattened themselves behind the counter envying him as he led her through the shop to the door. And he

> The eyes of the old woman in the picture were on him —of the old woman, his mother.

waggled his yellow glove in their faces, and she held her honor—a check for twenty thousand pounds with his signature—quite firmly in her hands.

"Are they false or are they real?" asked Oliver, shutting his private door. There they were, ten pearls on the blotting paper on the table. He took them to the window. He held them under his lens to the light. . . . This, then, was the truffle he had routed out of the earth! Rotten at the center—rotten at the core!

"Forgive me, oh my mother!" he sighed, raising his hands as if he asked pardon of the old woman in the picture. And again he was a little boy in the alley where they sold dogs on Sunday.

"For," he murmured, laying the palms of his hands together, "it is to be a long weekend." ❖

---

26. **Agincourt** (ăj′ĭn-kôrt′): a French village where, in 1415, Henry V's English forces defeated a much larger French army in what is considered one of England's most glorious victories.

Thinking through the LITERATURE

Connect to the Literature

1. **What Do You Think?**
Is the jeweller someone you would like to know? Give reasons for your response.

Comprehension Check
- What kind of childhood did Oliver have?
- Why does he buy the pearls without having them tested?
- What does he discover about the pearls?

Think Critically

2. Why do you think the jeweller is dissatisfied with his life?

THINK ABOUT
- what has been the driving force in his life
- the image of him as a hog searching for truffles
- the references to Mademoiselle and the red roses

3. Why do you think the jeweller keeps thinking about his mother and his past?

4. How would you describe the relationship between the jeweller and the duchess?

THINK ABOUT
- what motive he might have for making her wait ten minutes
- his concerns about the pearls
- what motivates her to mention the prime minister and Diana

5. **ACTIVE READING** **MAKING INFERENCES** Review the diagrams you made in your **READER'S NOTEBOOK.** In a single sentence, how would you describe the jeweller's motivation for his actions in the story? the duchess's motivation for her actions?

6. Would you call the jeweller a winner or a loser in his transactions with the duchess? Support your answer.

Extend Interpretations

7. **Critic's Corner** A student reviewer, Sarah Slezak, said that she enjoyed the **characters** in this story because they "seemed very realistic." Do you agree or disagree? Support your opinion with **details** from the story.

8. **Connect to Life** What do you think are some of the main driving forces that motivate successful businesspeople today? Do you think there are pros and cons to achieving great success? Explain your answer.

Literary Analysis

STYLE The **style** of a literary work is the distinctive way in which it is written—not what is said but how it is said. Many elements contribute to style, including **word choice, tone, figurative language,** and **point of view.** Virginia Woolf uses with great skill a style of writing called **stream of consciousness,** which presents the flow of thoughts and sensations in a character's mind. In this kind of writing, ideas and images occur as loosely connected associations rather than in a logical progression. A character's stream of consciousness is often expressed as an **interior monologue,** a record of the total workings of the character's mind and emotions.

Paired Activity Find a passage in "The Duchess and the Jeweller" (other than the one identified in Focus Your Reading on page 1046) that records Oliver Bacon's stream of consciousness. What does it tell you about his character?

REVIEW **FIGURATIVE LANGUAGE**
Similes and **metaphors** are types of **figurative language** in which basically unlike things are compared. Look through the story to find at least three examples of similes and metaphors involving animals. What two things are compared in each figure of speech? How does each influence your understanding of the story?

Choices & CHALLENGES

Writing Options

1. Alternative Ending Write a new ending for this story—one that the jeweller's mother might prefer.

2. Profile of Oliver Imagine that you are the jeweller's psychologist. Write a psychological profile for your records, in which you describe the forces motivating him and the conflicts in his personality.

3. Imaginary Dialogue Compose a dialogue in which the duchess tells her daughter Diana the truth about her encounter with the jeweller and advises Diana how to behave during his impending visit.

4. Paragraph Analysis Woolf uses many precise details in her descriptions of the characters. Choose one descriptive passage and discuss how the use of detail contributes to your understanding of the character.

Writing Handbook
See pages 1369–1370: Analysis.

Activities & Explorations

1. Caricature of a Shrewd Pair Draw a caricature that depicts the duchess and the jeweller conducting their business deal. Share your work with the class. **~ ART**

2. Duchess's Soliloquy As the duchess, deliver a stream-of-consciousness soliloquy in which you reveal your thoughts and feelings as you wait to see the jeweller. **~ SPEAKING AND LISTENING/PERFORMING**

3. Discussion of Greed With a small group of classmates, hold a roundtable discussion in which you consider whether the jeweller is a greedy person. **~ SPEAKING AND LISTENING**

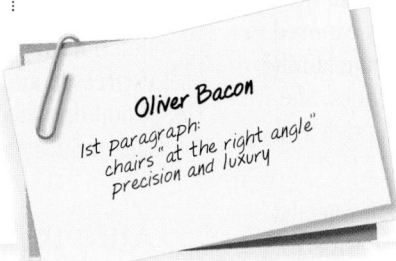

Oliver Bacon
1st paragraph:
chairs "at the right angle"
precision and luxury

Inquiry & Research

1. Bloomsbury Group Locate more information on the Bloomsbury group, and find the names of three of its members (other than Virginia Woolf, Leonard Woolf, and E. M. Forster). Share your findings with the class, briefly describing the contributions each of the three persons made to society.

 More Online: Research Starter
www.mcdougallittell.com

2. Precious Jewels Collect information on the production and sale of precious jewels. Research the production process from the finding of the raw stones to the creation of the highest-quality jewels for sale. Include information about the characteristics that make some gems more valuable than others, as well as details about famous jewels of the past and present. Report to the class on your findings.

Vocabulary in Action

EXERCISE A: MEANING CLUES Use your knowledge of the Words to Know to answer the following questions.

1. If you **forge** an agreement, are you making it, breaking it, or shaking it?

2. Is an **astute** person one who is conceited, one who is honest, or one who is bright?

3. Is being **lissome** most necessary for a lawyer, for a gymnast, or for a weight lifter?

4. Would someone known for **arrogance** be considered appealing, obnoxious, or wise?

5. Does a person who behaves **obsequiously** give the impression of being proud, of being meek, or of being trustworthy?

EXERCISE B Work with four classmates to develop a short scene involving five characters. The scene can deal with any situation—the important thing is to portray the characters in such a way that, by the end of the scene, each has become associated with one of the five vocabulary words. Do not use the words themselves in the scene; develop the associations through the characters' actions and dialogue.

WORDS TO KNOW	arrogance	lissome
	astute	obsequiously
	forge	

Building Vocabulary
For an in-depth study of context clues, see page 938.

Virginia Woolf
1882–1941

Other Works
A Haunted House and Other Short Stories
To the Lighthouse
A Room of One's Own
Flush

Unusual Education Childhood experiences greatly influenced the path Virginia Woolf would take as an adult. Born Adeline Virginia Stephen and raised in a cultured upper-middle-class family, whose friends included leading artists and thinkers of the late Victorian era, she was writing by the time she was nine. Although her parents encouraged her literary efforts, they adhered to the Victorian custom of sending only their sons to school. While her brothers went off to private schools and to Cambridge University, she remained at home with tutors. Although she would never forget this injustice, she fortunately had free access to her father's vast library and was continually exposed to the brilliant ideas and conversation of the family's intellectual friends. Through these avenues, she managed to gain an education that was rich and varied, though unusual.

Literary First As a young woman, Woolf rejected the restrictions of Victorian society and eagerly embraced the free-thinking ideas of her brothers' university friends, who eventually formed the nucleus of the Bloomsbury group. In 1912 she married Leonard Woolf, a member of the group, with whom she founded the Hogarth Press and

began to publish her own fiction as well as the poetry of T. S. Eliot and the short stories of Katherine Mansfield. Throughout her life, Woolf was also an articulate feminist. Her long essay *A Room of One's Own* is considered by many to be the first major literary achievement in the movement for female equality in England.

Battle with Illness The death of Woolf's mother when Woolf was 13 contributed to the first of many battles with mental illness that the author would face during her lifetime. At the start of World War II, her anxieties about a German invasion of England compounded her already deteriorating mental health. In 1941, deeply depressed and fearful that she was going insane, Woolf drowned herself in the river Ouse at the age of 59.

Author Activity

Landmark Essay Find and read a copy of Woolf's essay *A Room of One's Own*. Why do you think some people consider this essay a landmark in the British movement for female equality?

from

Virginia Woolf

by E. M. Forster

E. M. Forster was, like Virginia Woolf, a member of the Bloomsbury group. He built his fame as a novelist and a writer of literary criticism. Shortly after Woolf died, Forster wrote a critical review of her work. In this excerpt he describes her process of writing.

❶ She liked receiving sensations—sights, sounds, tastes—passing them through her mind, where they encountered theories and memories, and then bringing them out again, through a pen, on to a bit of paper. Now began **❷** the higher delights of authorship. For these pen-marks on paper were only the prelude to writing, little more than marks on a wall. They had to be combined, arranged, emphasized here, eliminated there, new

relationships had to be generated, new penmarks born, and out of the interactions, something, one thing, one, arose. This one thing, whether it was a novel or an essay or a short story or a biography or a private paper to be read to her friends, was, if it was successful, itself analogous to a sensation. Although it was so complex and intellectual, although it might be large and heavy with facts, it was akin to the very simple things which had started it off, to the sights, sounds, tastes. It could be best **❸** described as we describe them. For it was not about something. It was something.

SUMMARIZING AND EVALUATING

Summarizing is the process of condensing a work into fewer words. This process will help you better understand and remember what you read. Use the following suggestions and activities as you explore Forster's comments.

❶ Identifying Main Ideas Forster explains that Woolf absorbed sensations that ultimately found expression in her writing. But what happened to the sensations along the way? You might think of the process like this:

> New sensations
> + Woolf's knowledge ("theories") and memories
> ─────────────────
> = a literary work

❷ Forster writes, "Now began the higher delights of authorship." According to Forster, what seems to have delighted Woolf about writing?

❸ Summarizing Summarize the review in a few sentences.

Evaluating involves making judgments about a work. How accurately do you think Forster's comments apply to "The Duchess and the Jeweller" (p. 1046)?

THE NOVELS OF
Virginia Woolf

"Life is not a series of gig-lamps symmetrically arranged; life is
a luminous halo, a semi-transparent envelope surrounding us
from the beginning of consciousness to the end," wrote
Virginia Woolf in her essay "Modern Fiction." Although her vision of
life and art seemed clear in her mind, the problem for Woolf was how
to re-create this luminous halo in her art. After her early efforts in
fiction, she found herself less interested in using the traditional devices
of the novel, such as chronological plot structure and conventional
point of view, and more in portraying the subtle web of impressions
that she believed constituted true reality.

Woolf found her reality in the "world within." Instead of simply
writing about surface actions, events, and settings in the orderly fashion
that most Victorians had done before her, Woolf became a master of

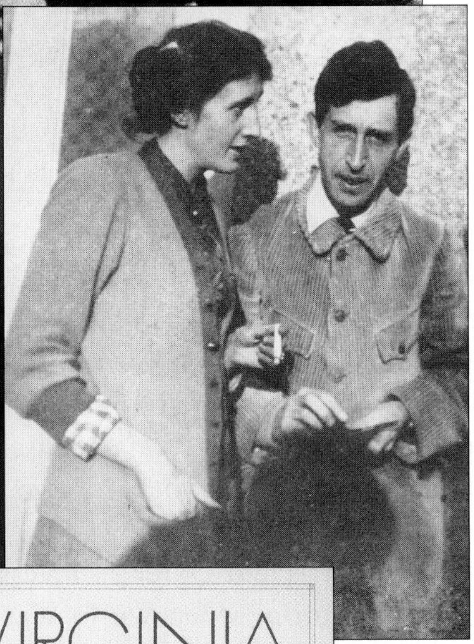

interior monologue and stream of consciousness in order to "record the atoms [of thought] as they fall upon the mind." Believing that one flash of insight could be a more powerful reflection of reality than line after line of literal description, she wove the evocative details and flowing rhythms of lyric poetry into her fiction.

Mrs. Dalloway was the first novel in which Woolf displayed mastery of this distinctive prose style. It depicts a single day in the life of a middle-class Englishwoman preparing to give a party. The novel's reality, however, is composed of the characters' memories and thoughts about life, loved ones, and even strangers—thoughts that create a delicate montage of impressions as they rise to the surface. In similar fashion, *To the Lighthouse* explores the thoughts of a family and their friends on holiday. In the process, one glimpses aspects of daily life that reveal subtle truths about love, death, and art.

In the novel *Orlando,* employing a very different time span, Woolf displays her fascination with male and female identity and with the interplay of past and present. At the opening of the novel, Orlando is a young man in Elizabethan times, but by the work's midpoint, Orlando has become a young woman in the 1920s. *The Waves,* Woolf's most experimental novel, consists almost entirely of interior monologues representing the thoughts of its six major characters from childhood through old age.

In addition to these and other novels, Woolf's literary contributions included numerous reviews and critical essays, as well as the journals that she kept throughout her life. Her most remarkable offerings, however, were undoubtedly her novels, which challenged the existing structures and traditions of literature and inspired future generations of writers to share in her luminous vision of reality.

✳

Top:
The recent film version of the novel Orlando *used lush visuals, music, and voice-overs to convey Orlando's inner life.* Photofest.
Middle:
Leonard and Virginia Woolf.
Left:
Cover of Woolf's novel Mrs. Dalloway

VIRGINIA WOOLF
MRS. DALLOWAY

A HARVEST BOOK

WITH A FOREWORD BY MAUREEN HOWARD

Author Study
T. S. Eliot

"Mr. Eliot does not write for the lazy, the stupid, or the gross. Literature is to him a serious affair."

—E. M. Forster

T. S. Eliot

HIS LIFE
HIS TIMES

A Modern Voice

1888–1965

Claimed by his native America as well as his adopted homeland of Britain, T. S. Eliot was one of the giants of 20th-century literature. As a poet, playwright, and influential literary critic, Eliot helped to define the contours of modern poetry in the early 20th century.

AN INTERNATIONAL EDUCATION

Thomas Stearns Eliot grew up in St. Louis, Missouri, where his grandfather had founded Washington University. Education was a top priority in his family, and he was sent to private schools in Missouri and Massachusetts before attending Harvard University, where he obtained his bachelor's degree in three years. Pursuing further studies at the Sorbonne in Paris and Oxford University in England, he was caught in Europe when World War I broke out, and he eventually married and settled in

1888
Is born in St. Louis, Missouri

Eliot's birthplace in St. Louis, Missouri

1898
Enters Smith Academy in St. Louis

1906
Begins attending Harvard University

1890   **1895**   **1900**   **1905**

1893
Karl Benz builds his first four-wheel car.

1899
Sigmund Freud publishes *The Interpretation of Dreams.*

1906
Pablo Picasso experiments with cubism.

England. A quiet, cultured man, Eliot supported himself and his wife by working successively as a teacher, a bank clerk, and an editor at a London publishing firm while trying to make a name for himself as a writer.

MAKE IT NEW! The years leading up to World War I were a time of social, scientific, and economic changes that radically altered everyday life. This transition into the modern age was both difficult and invigorating. Many European artists and writers, including Eliot, lamented the alienating effects of modern industrial society, with its masses of people crowded into cities and working in monotonous factory jobs. At the same time, however, they energetically seized the opportunity to cast off 19th-century traditions and find new forms of expression to mirror the new realities of modern life. In Paris, Pablo Picasso and Georges Braque developed cubism in painting by breaking up images into geometric parts, sometimes showing different sides of a face in a single portrait. Eliot's American friend and fellow poet Ezra Pound headed a group of poets called the imagists, who aimed at the creation of clear, precise images rather than at the presentation of ideas in their poems. "Make it new!" was Pound's rallying cry for his generation.

LITERARY *Contributions*

Modernist Poetry With Ireland's William Butler Yeats and America's Ezra Pound, T. S. Eliot is considered by many to be one of the three most influential 20th-century poets in English. His most famous poems include

"Ash Wednesday"
Four Quartets
"Gerontion"
"The Hollow Men"
"Journey of the Magi"
"The Love Song of J. Alfred Prufrock"
"Preludes"
"Rhapsody on a Windy Night"
"Sweeney Among the Nightingales"
The Waste Land
"Whispers of Immortality"

On Stage After 1930, Eliot also won fame as a dramatist. Among his plays are

The Cocktail Party
Murder in the Cathedral

Literary Criticism Eliot's literary essays had an enormous influence on the literary criticism of the 20th century. They include

"Hamlet and His Problems"
"The Metaphysical Poets"
"Tradition and the Individual Talent"

1910
Studies at the Sorbonne in Paris

Ezra Pound

1914
Meets the poet Ezra Pound

1915
Marries Vivien Haigh-Wood

1917
Publishes *Prufrock and Other Observations*

1922
Publishes *The Waste Land*

1927
Joins the Church of England and becomes a British citizen

1910   **1915**   **1920**   **1925**

1913
Igor Stravinsky's modernist ballet *The Rite of Spring* premieres in Paris.

1914
World War I begins.

1917
Russian Revolution brings Communists to power.

1922
Irish author James Joyce publishes the modernist novel *Ulysses.*

A VAST WASTELAND Although Eliot was never called upon to fight, World War I seemed to him a total breakdown of 2,000 years of European civilization. The war destroyed the old order that had held European culture together, and Eliot had little faith that the technological and social changes of the 20th century were going to improve the situation. He felt that modern life was a shattered confusion, without a center. William Butler Yeats's prophesy in "The Second Coming"—"Things fall apart; the center cannot hold"—seemed to have come true. "The ordinary man's experience is chaotic, irregular, and fragmentary," Eliot wrote in an essay in 1921. It was, he thought, up to the poet to bring the fragments together into a meaningful whole.

BUILDING A LEGACY In 1917, encouraged by Ezra Pound, Eliot published his first collection of poems, *Prufrock and Other Observations,* which included the now famous poems "The Love Song of J. Alfred Prufrock" and "Preludes." The volume's revolutionary impact has been compared to that of Wordsworth and Coleridge's publication in 1798 of *Lyrical Ballads,* in that it ushered in a new era of poetry.

Still working at his "day job" as a bank clerk to support himself and his wife, Eliot poured all his other energies into his writing. In 1919, he published another volume of verse, and the next year saw the publication of *The Sacred Wood,* a book of literary criticism in which he explained his view of modern poetry. In 1921, he completed most of *The Waste Land,* a long, highly complex poem. Published in 1922 with Pound's help, the poem's expression of the spiritual infirmities of the age echoed throughout the literary world. Today, it is still viewed as one of the definitive modernist statements of the human condition.

REDEMPTION AND RENEWAL Eliot gradually put the disillusionment expressed in *The Waste Land* and in poems such as "The Hollow Men" behind him and turned to religion for spiritual comfort. In 1927, he joined the Church of England; he also became a British citizen, officially adopting England's cultural heritage as well as its state religion. Thereafter, religious themes and symbols came to pervade Eliot's work, notably in "Ash Wednesday" (1930) and *Four Quartets* (1943). *Murder in the Cathedral,* one of Eliot's best-known plays, also reflected his

1929
Publishes his famous critical study of *Dante*

1933
Separates from his wife

1935
First staging of *Murder in the Cathedral*

1939
Publishes *Old Possum's Book of Practical Cats*

FOUR
QUARTETS
T. S. ELIOT

1943
Publishes *Four Quartets* (portions of which appeared earlier)

1947
Vivien Eliot dies

1930 **1935** **1940** **1945**

1929
U.S. stock market crash starts worldwide economic depression.

1936
Fascist forces battle democratic factions in Spanish Civil War.

1939
German troops invade Poland, starting World War II.

1945
World War II ends; United Nations is established.

Winston Churchill

newfound religious convictions. A verse drama first staged in 1935, it presents the story of the slaying of Thomas à Becket, the archbishop of Canterbury whose shrine was visited by Chaucer's pilgrims.

FINAL HONORS In 1925, Eliot became an editor in the London publishing house of Faber & Faber and from that position wielded extensive influence on the English literary scene. After World War II, he was awarded one of literature's highest honors, the Nobel Prize.

 More Online: Author Link
www.mcdougallittell.com

Eliot on Broadway

The London and Broadway musical *Cats* is based on Eliot's surprisingly witty *Old Possum's Book of Practical Cats* and some of his other poetry. The play contains a musical version of the poem "The

 Naming of Cats" (page 1070), as well as the popular song "Memory," which features images and lines from "Preludes" (page 1065) and other Eliot poems.

Modernism: Without Rhyme or Reason

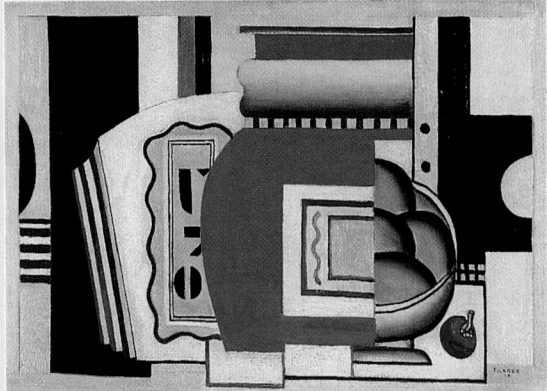

Still Life, first state (1925), Fernand Legér. The Menil Collection, Houston.

Eliot's modernist poetry differs from most 19th-century poetry as greatly as Picasso's cubism differs from Monet's impressionism:

- Eliot often wrote free verse, without regular patterns of rhyme and rhythm—perhaps the poetic equivalent of modern art's break from the limits of realism.

- Eliot's poetry, like much modern art, isn't pretty. He took his images from the gritty urban streets rather than the pastoral lakes and woods favored by most romantic poets.

- Both Eliot's poetry and modern art are hard for most people to understand. Like the imagist poets, Eliot eliminated connections between his images and gave the reader no explanation of the images' meaning.

1948	1949		1957		1965
Wins the Nobel Prize for literature	Enjoys popular success with his play *The Cocktail Party*		Marries Valerie Fletcher		Dies in London on Jan. 4

1950   **1955**   **1960**   **1965**

	1949	1952		1961	
	Communist government is established in mainland China.	Irish-born Samuel Beckett's "absurdist" play *Waiting for Godot* premieres in Paris.		Beatles become a popular rock 'n' roll band in Liverpool, England.	

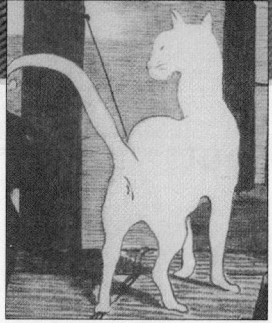

PREPARING to *Read*

Selected Poems

Lyric Poetry by T. S. ELIOT

Connect to Your Life

A Failure to Communicate People today often speak of being alienated from one another. Many people don't know their neighbors, for example, and commuters spend hours with strangers on planes, trains, and buses. Create a chart, like the one shown here, to explore the causes and consequences of alienation today. Then discuss your observations with your classmates.

Examples of Alienation	Causes of Alienation	Immediate Consequences	Long-Term Effects
bus riders ignoring each other	fear of strangers	tension, nervousness	feeling of isolation

Build Background

The Urban Wasteland The first two of the poems you are about to read—"Preludes" and "The Hollow Men" —reflect Eliot's alienation during World War I and his despair at the decay of Western civilization. In both, Eliot used a patchwork of images and allusions to capture his sense of modern life, replacing the authoritative voice of the 19th-century poet with a speaker who is suffering the same spiritual losses as the rest of society. When reading "Preludes," keep in mind that a prelude is a short musical piece based on a recurrent theme.

The last poem, "The Naming of Cats," shows the whimsical, witty side of T. S. Eliot after he came to terms with the modern age. Always fond of the humorous verse of Lewis Carroll and Edward Lear, Eliot tried his hand at humor in a series of cat poems published as *Old Possum's Book of Practical Cats,* from which "The Naming of Cats" is taken.

Focus Your Reading

LITERARY ANALYSIS **RHYTHM IN MODERN VERSE** Rhythm is the pattern of stressed and unstressed syllables in a line of poetry. When such a pattern is repeated throughout a poem, the poem is said to have a meter. T. S. Eliot and other modernist poets felt that the demands of writing in a meter too often forced poets to dilute their meaning. They began experimenting with free verse, poetry with no fixed rhythmic pattern, as in these lines:

> *Wipe your hand across your mouth, and laugh;*
> *The worlds revolve like ancient women*
> *Gathering fuel in vacant lots.*

As you read Eliot's poetry, think about the rhythm of each poem. Do any of the poems have a meter? In which of the free-verse poems is the rhythm especially strong, even if it is not regular?

ACTIVE READING **STRATEGIES FOR READING MODERN VERSE**
Modern poetry can be difficult to understand. Follow these guidelines as you read Eliot's poems.
- Read each section of the poem aloud, lingering over images that engage your attention or evoke strong feelings in you.
- Try to make connections between the images by noticing which ones are similar, which are contrasting, and which are repeated.
- Use the sidenotes to help you understand unfamiliar allusions.
- Try paraphrasing passages that you find puzzling.
- Reread the poem several times, and discuss your impressions with your classmates.

READER'S NOTEBOOK After using the guidelines above, jot down ideas you form about the poems' interpretations.

PRELUDES

T. S. ELIOT

I

The winter evening settles down
With smell of steaks in passageways.
Six o'clock.
The burnt-out ends of smoky days.
5   And now a gusty shower wraps
The grimy scraps
Of withered leaves about your feet
And newspapers from vacant lots;
The showers beat
10   On broken blinds and chimney-pots,
And at the corner of the street
A lonely cab-horse steams and stamps.
And then the lighting of the lamps.

II

The morning comes to consciousness
15   Of faint stale smells of beer
From the sawdust-trampled street
With all its muddy feet that press
To early coffee-stands.
With the other masquerades
20   That time resumes,
One thinks of all the hands
That are raising dingy shades
In a thousand furnished rooms.

GUIDE FOR READING

2 steaks: In the early 20th century, steaks (usually cheap cuts from low-grade beef) were primarily a food of the working class.

7 As you read, note how pronouns are used and how they affect the point of view.

10 What picture do you have of the place being described?

14 Why do you think morning is personified?

18 early coffee-stands: stands of venders who cater to early-morning pedestrians.

23 furnished rooms: one-room apartments with furniture included, usually cheap and rundown.

III

You tossed a blanket from the bed,
25 You lay upon your back, and waited;
You dozed, and watched the night revealing
The thousand sordid images
Of which your soul was constituted;
They flickered against the ceiling.
30 And when all the world came back
And the light crept up between the shutters
And you heard the sparrows in the gutters,
You had such a vision of the street
As the street hardly understands;
35 Sitting along the bed's edge, where
You curled the papers from your hair,
Or clasped the yellow soles of feet
In the palms of both soiled hands.

27 sordid: wretched; dirty; morally degraded.

IV

His soul stretched tight across the skies
40 That fade behind a city block,
Or trampled by insistent feet
At four and five and six o'clock;
And short square fingers stuffing pipes,
And evening newspapers, and eyes
45 Assured of certain certainties,
The conscience of a blackened street
Impatient to assume the world.

I am moved by fancies that are curled
Around these images, and cling:
50 The notion of some infinitely gentle
Infinitely suffering thing.

Wipe your hand across your mouth, and laugh;
The worlds revolve like ancient women
Gathering fuel in vacant lots.

33–38 Lines 35–36 suggest that the person being addressed is a woman. What kind of vision do you think she had?

39 his: the street's. Think about why the street is personified.

42 A reference to afternoon and early evening.

48–49 What metaphor is used here?

50–51 Note the rhythm of these lines.

53–54 What aspect of the women's activity is focused on in this simile?

Thinking Through the Literature

1. Jot down any questions that this poem raised in your mind.

2. How would you describe the **setting** of the poem?

3. What impressions do you have of the people mentioned in the poem?

THE Hollow MEN

T. S. Eliot

Mistah Kurtz—he dead.
A penny for the Old Guy

We are the hollow men
We are the stuffed men
Leaning together
Headpiece filled with straw. Alas!
5   Our dried voices, when
We whisper together
Are quiet and meaningless
As wind in dry grass
Or rats' feet over broken glass
10 In our dry cellar

Shape without form, shade without colour,
Paralysed force, gesture without motion;

Those who have crossed
With direct eyes, to death's other Kingdom
15 Remember us—if at all—not as lost
Violent souls, but only
As the hollow men
The stuffed men.

Eyes I dare not meet in dreams
20 In death's dream kingdom
These do not appear:
There, the eyes are
Sunlight on a broken column
There, is a tree swinging
25 And voices are
In the wind's singing
More distant and more solemn
Than a fading star.

GUIDE FOR READING

[Epigraphs] **Mistah . . . dead:** a quotation from Joseph Conrad's *Heart of Darkness,* in which Kurtz is a character whose descent into evil makes him akin to the "lost violent souls" mentioned in lines 15–16 of the poem; **A penny . . . Guy:** a cry that English children use when collecting money to buy fireworks for Guy Fawkes Day—a yearly celebration of the failure of an attempt, by Guy Fawkes and other conspirators, to blow up Parliament in 1605. The celebration also traditionally includes the burning of straw effigies of Fawkes.

4 headpiece . . . straw: The speaker likens himself and his companions, with their empty and meaningless lives, to the straw effigies prepared for Guy Fawkes Day.

14 death's other Kingdom: perhaps heaven (as opposed to hell, where the "lost violent souls" go).

Let me be no nearer
30 In death's dream kingdom
Let me also wear
Such deliberate disguises
Rat's coat, crowskin, crossed staves
In a field
35 Behaving as the wind behaves
No nearer—

Not that final meeting
In the twilight kingdom

III
40 This is the dead land
This is cactus land
Here the stone images
Are raised, here they receive
The supplication of a dead man's hand
Under the twinkle of a fading star.

45 Is it like this
In death's other kingdom
Waking alone
At the hour when we are
Trembling with tenderness
50 Lips that would kiss
Form prayers to broken stone.

IV
The eyes are not here
There are no eyes here
In this valley of dying stars
55 In this hollow valley
This broken jaw of our lost kingdoms

In this last of meeting places
We grope together
And avoid speech
60 Gathered on this beach of the tumid river

Sightless, unless
The eyes reappear
As the perpetual star
Multifoliate rose
65 Of death's twilight kingdom
The hope only
Of empty men.

33 staves: poles—here, those used as a support for a scarecrow.

43 supplication: begging; plea.

60 tumid (tōō′mĭd): swollen.

64 multifoliate (mŭl′tĭ-fō′lē-ĭt) **rose:** a reminiscence of the multifoliate (many-petaled) rose formed by the souls of the blessed in Dante's *Divine Comedy*.

61–67 What hope is possible for the hollow men?

V

Here we go round the prickly pear
Prickly pear prickly pear
70 Here we go round the prickly pear
At five o'clock in the morning.

Between the idea
And the reality
Between the motion
75 And the act
Falls the Shadow

        For Thine is the Kingdom

Between the conception
And the creation
80 Between the emotion
And the response
Falls the Shadow

            Life is very long

Between the desire
85 And the spasm
Between the potency
And the existence
Between the essence
And the descent
90 Falls the Shadow

        For Thine is the Kingdom

For Thine is
Life is
For Thine is the

95   *This is the way the world ends*
This is the way the world ends
This is the way the world ends
Not with a bang but a whimper.

68–71 Here . . . morning: a variation of the children's rhyme "Here We Go Round the Mulberry Bush" appropriate to the "cactus land" of line 40. (A prickly pear is a type of cactus.)

77 For . . . Kingdom: the beginning of a sentence appended to the Lord's Prayer by many Christians. The "Kingdom" referred to is the kingdom of God.

90 How do you interpret the "Shadow" mentioned here and in lines 76 and 82?

Thinking Through the Literature

1. Which lines and **images** in this poem do you find the most memorable? Describe your reactions.

2. How would you describe the lives of the "hollow men"?

3. How do you interpret part V of the poem? What do you think keeps the hollow men from fulfillment on earth and salvation after death?

from The Book of Practical Cats

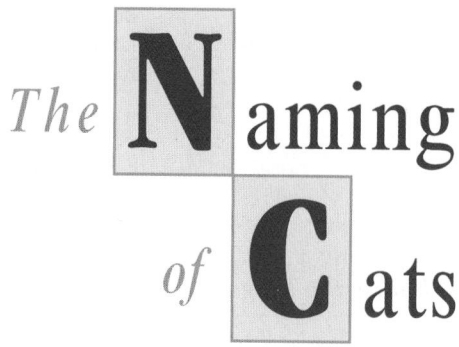

The Naming of Cats

T. S. Eliot

The Naming of Cats is a difficult matter,
    It isn't just one of your holiday games;
You may think at first I'm as mad as a hatter
When I tell you, a cat must have THREE DIFFERENT NAMES.
5 First of all, there's the name that the family use daily,
    Such as Peter, Augustus, Alonzo or James,
Such as Victor or Jonathan, George or Bill Bailey—
    All of them sensible everyday names.
There are fancier names if you think they sound sweeter,
10   Some for the gentlemen, some for the dames:
Such as Plato, Admetus, Electra, Demeter—
    But all of them sensible everyday names.
But I tell you, a cat needs a name that's particular,
    A name that's peculiar, and more dignified,
15 Else how can he keep up his tail perpendicular,
    Or spread out his whiskers, or cherish his pride?
Of names of this kind, I can give you a quorum,
    Such as Munkustrap, Quaxo, or Coricopat,
Such as Bombalurina, or else Jellylorum—
20   Names that never belong to more than one cat.
But above and beyond there's still one name left over,
    And that is the name that you never will guess;
The name that no human research can discover—
    But THE CAT HIMSELF KNOWS, and will never confess.
25 When you notice a cat in profound meditation,
    The reason, I tell you, is always the same:
His mind is engaged in a rapt contemplation
    Of the thought, of the thought, of the thought of his name:
      His ineffable effable
30   Effanineffable
Deep and inscrutable singular Name.

Peter

Augustus

Alonzo

James

Victor

Jonathan

George

Bill Bailey

Plato

Admetus

Electra

Demeter

Munkustrap

Quaxo

Coricopat

Bombalurina

Jellylorum

from

"Prufrock and Other Observations": A Criticism

Book Review by MAY SINCLAIR

Preparing to Read

Build Background

In 1917 the English novelist May Sinclair wrote a review of Eliot's first poetry collection, *Prufrock and Other Observations* (which included "Preludes"). In her review, she compared the poetry of the relatively unknown Eliot with the Victorian poetry of Robert Browning and W. E. Henley.

Focus Your Reading

LITERARY ANALYSIS **BOOK REVIEW**

A **book review** is a kind of opinion essay. In a careful review, well-informed arguments are supported with appropriate examples. A good reviewer is not afraid to be outspoken and leaves no doubt in the reader's mind about his or her opinion of the book being reviewed. As you analyze this excerpt from Sinclair's review, compare her opinion of Eliot's poetry with your own.

Mr. Eliot is not in any tradition at all; not even in Browning's and Henley's tradition. . . . His difference is twofold; a difference of method and technique; a difference of sight and aim. He does not see anything between him and reality, and he makes straight for the reality he sees; he cuts all his corners and his curves; and this directness of method is startling and upsetting to comfortable, respectable people accustomed to going superfluously in and out of corners and carefully round curves. Unless you are prepared to follow with the same nimbleness and straightness you will never arrive with Mr. Eliot at his meaning. . . .

The comfortable and respectable mind loves conventional beauty, and some of the realities that Mr. Eliot sees are not beautiful. He insists on your seeing very vividly, as he sees them, the streets of his "Preludes" and "Rhapsody." . . . And these things are ugly. The comfortable mind turns away from them in disgust. It identifies Mr. Eliot with a modern tendency; it labels him securely "Stark Realist," so that lovers of "true poetry" may beware.

It is nothing to the comfortable mind that Mr. Eliot is

> *. . . moved by fancies that are curled*
> *Around these images, and cling:*
> *The notion of some infinitely gentle*
> *Infinitely suffering thing.*

It is nothing to it that the emotion he disengages from his ugliest image is unbearably poignant. His poignancy is as unpleasant as his ugliness, disturbing to comfort.

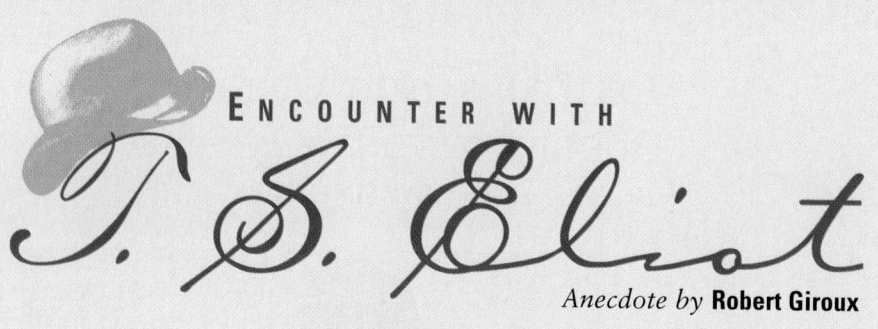

ENCOUNTER WITH T. S. Eliot

Anecdote by **Robert Giroux**

Preparing to Read

Build Background

This anecdote—recorded in 1966 by Robert Giroux, then editor in chief of the New York publishing firm of Farrar, Straus & Giroux—provides a personal glimpse of T. S. Eliot. When he first met Eliot, Giroux was a struggling young editor with Eliot's American publisher, and Eliot was both a world-famous author and an influential editor in the London publishing world.

I first met T. S. Eliot in 1946, when I was an editor at Harcourt, Brace, under Frank Morley. I was just past thirty, and Eliot was in his late fifties. . . .

We went across the street to the old Ritz-Carlton. It was a lovely spring day and the courtyard restaurant—I think it was called the Japanese Garden—had just been opened for the season. For some reason I was astonished at the sight of newly hatched ducklings swimming in the center pond, perhaps because they seemed to embody the odd and improbable quality the occasion had for me.

Eliot could have not found a kinder, or more effective, way of putting me at my ease. As we sat down, he said, "Tell me, as one editor to another, do you have much author trouble?" I could not help laughing, he laughed in return—he had a *booming* laugh—and that was the beginning of our friendship. His most memorable remark of the day occurred when I asked him if he agreed with the definition that most editors are failed writers, and he replied: "Perhaps, but so are most writers."

Thinking through the LITERATURE

Connect to the Literature

1. **What Do You Think?**
Would you have thought it likely that "The Naming of Cats" was the work of the same person who wrote "Preludes" and "The Hollow Men"? Why or why not?

   Comprehension Check
   - According to the poem, how many names must a cat have?
   - What are the different uses of the names?

Think Critically

2. What impression of cats do you think Eliot wanted to convey?

   THINK ABOUT
   - the names given as examples
   - the feline activities mentioned in lines 15–16
   - cats' "deep and inscrutable" secret names

3. How does Eliot's **diction**, or word choice, contribute to the poem's humor?

4. In what way are the details in this poem like and unlike the details in the other two Eliot poems?

5. **ACTIVE READING** **READING MODERN POETRY** Review the poems' interpretations in your **READER'S NOTEBOOK.** How did you use the Active Reading guidelines on page 1064 to help you develop those interpretations? Share your experiences with classmates.

Extend Interpretations

6. **Critic's Corner** A conservative man, Eliot characterized himself as "classicist in literature, royalist in politics, and Anglo-Catholic in religion." Yet the British author Anthony Burgess observed that Eliot "was most radical when he was most conservative." How do you think Burgess's comment might apply to the form and content of Eliot's poems?

7. **Comparing Texts** Compare "Preludes" and "The Hollow Men" with William Wordsworth's poems on pages 725–735. How different are they in **imagery, subject matter, mood, tone,** and **form?**

8. **Connect to Life** Is the worldview underlying "Preludes" and "The Hollow Men" relevant today? Explain why or why not.

Literary Analysis

RHYTHM IN MODERN POETRY

In the early 20th century, many poets abandoned the strictures of regular rhythms, or **meters,** to produce **free verse**—poetry with no fixed rhythm.

By writing lines that corresponded to natural units of thought, they hoped to emphasize the meanings, rather than just the sounds, of their words. Notice, for example, how the lines in this passage of "Preludes" represent natural units of thought and highlight the shifts from image to image:

> *The morning comes to consciousness*
> *Of faint stale smells of beer*
> *From the sawdust-trampled street*
> *With all its muddy feet that press*
> *To early coffee-stands.*

Paired Activity With a partner, examine the rhythm of one section of "The Hollow Men," focusing on the lengths of the lines and the patterns of stressed syllables in them. Does the irregular rhythm contribute to the poem's meaning? How does the rhythm of "The Naming of Cats" differ from that of "The Hollow Men"? Discuss the different effects of irregular and regular rhythmic patterns.

REVIEW **MOOD** The **imagery** in a poem usually contributes to its **mood**—the feeling or atmosphere the writer creates. How would you describe the mood of "Preludes"? of "The Hollow Men"? How is the mood of "The Naming of Cats" different from the other two poems' moods?

THE AUTHOR'S STYLE
Eliot's Modernist Style

Before the 20th century, most British poetry had regular patterns of rhyme and rhythm, dealt with their subjects in a "realistic" way, and contained easily understood images and direct statements of ideas and emotions. T. S. Eliot, as a pioneer of modernism, often broke with these traditions.

Key Aspects of Eliot's Style

- an openness to everyday language, including slang and references to popular culture

- a focus on ordinary, often unpleasant, experiences

- a frequent use of free verse, in which the rhythms fall into no fixed pattern

- the conveying of ideas and feelings by means of complex images and symbols, rather than by means of explicit statements

- a patchwork of images, symbols, and allusions, in which the reader must supply the connections

---

Analysis of Style

At the right are the opening lines of two of Eliot's most famous poems. Study the list of stylistic features above, and read each excerpt carefully. Then complete the following activities:

- Find examples of each aspect of Eliot's style in the two excerpts.
- Reread "Preludes" and "The Hollow Men," noting examples of each stylistic feature.
- Explain how "The Naming of Cats" differs in style from the other two poems and from the two excerpts.

Applications

1. Changing Style Choose a section of "Preludes" or "The Hollow Men," and rewrite it—either as poetry or as prose—in a different style. You could, for example, recast the section in rhyming couplets. Your rewriting should express the same ideas as the original passage. Read your version aloud to your classmates.

2. Imitating Style Working with a partner, imitate Eliot's style by writing an additional section for "Preludes" or "The Hollow Men."

3. Comparing Styles Compare Eliot's style with that of his older contemporary William Butler Yeats. Review Yeats's poems on pages 989–991, and compare his style to Eliot's.

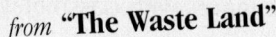

from **"The Love Song of J. Alfred Prufrock"**

Let us go then, you and I,
When the evening is spread out against
    the sky
Like a patient etherized upon a table;
Let us go, through certain half-deserted
    streets,
The muttering retreats
Of restless nights in one-night cheap hotels
And sawdust restaurants with oyster-shells:
Streets that follow like a tedious argument
Of insidious intent
To lead you to an overwhelming
    question . . .
Oh, do not ask, "What is it?"
Let us go and make our visit.

from **"The Waste Land"**

April is the cruelest month, breeding
Lilacs out of the dead land, mixing
Memory and desire, stirring
Dull roots with spring rain.
Winter kept us warm, covering
Earth in forgetful snow, feeding
A little life with dried tubers.
Summer surprised us, coming over the
    Starnbergersee
With a shower of rain; we stopped in the
    colonnade,
And went on in sunlight, into the Hofgarten,
And drank coffee, and talked for an hour.

Choices & CHALLENGES

Writing Options

1. Dramatic Skit Write a short dramatic work based on one of Eliot's poems. For example, you might create characters to reveal the personalities behind some of the names in "The Naming of Cats." Place the dramatic skit in your **Working Portfolio.**

2. Armchair Analysis Write an essay explaining the worldview underlying "Preludes" and "The Hollow Men." Use a graphic like this one to note specific lines from each poem.

Writing Handbook See pages 1369–1370: Analysis.

Name of Poem	Revealing Lines	Worldview Expressed

Activities & Explorations

1. Poetic Collage Capture the fragmentary nature of "Preludes" or "The Hollow Men" by creating a collage of images corresponding to the images in the poem. ~ **ART**

2. Dramatic Reading With two or three classmates, rehearse and perform a dramatic reading of one of the three Eliot poems in a manner appropriate to its mood and tone. ~ **SPEAKING AND LISTENING**

Inquiry & Research

1. Urban Poverty Research the living conditions in the poorer sections of London in Eliot's day. In a written report, compare them with the conditions in poor neighborhoods today.

2. Contemporary Issues Find songs and poems that comment on life in America or Britain today. How do the images and issues in the works compare with those in Eliot's poems? Present your conclusions in a panel discussion before the class.

T. S. Eliot

Author Study Project

DRAMATIZING A DAY IN THE LIFE

What was life like for Eliot as an expatriate American living in England in the early 20th century? Who were his friends and acquaintances? What kind of social life did he have? What was his courtship and marriage like? With a group of classmates, research the answers to these and related questions. Present your findings in a dramatization of a typical day, a revealing incident, or an important conversation in Eliot's life during the period 1910–1930. One group member should play T. S. Eliot; the others should play important figures in Eliot's life, such as his wife Vivien, Bertrand Russell, Ezra Pound, and Virginia Woolf.

Primary Print Sources Consult newspaper and magazine articles, and perhaps even fiction set in the period. Consider investigating memoirs, diaries, autobiographies, and collections of letters by such writers as Ezra Pound, Bertrand Russell, E. M. Forster, Virginia Woolf, James Joyce, Ford Madox Ford, Wyndham Lewis, I. A. Richards, and Eliot himself.

Secondary Print Sources Consult biographies and historical and biographical entries in reference works. Also look in the 20th-century sections of literary histories of England and America.

Computer Resources Reliable Web sites can provide useful information on Eliot and the modernists. Consider sites maintained by university English departments and by established poetry societies.

 More Online: Research Starter www.mcdougallittell.com

Musée des Beaux Arts
The Unknown Citizen

Poetry by W. H. AUDEN

Connect to Your Life

Who Cares? Create a bar graph like the one shown, indicating the extent to which you think other people are concerned about your personal well-being. In addition to groups with whom you are both directly involved—family members, friends, teachers, coaches, employers, doctors—include some with whom you are involved more indirectly, such as store clerks or bus drivers.

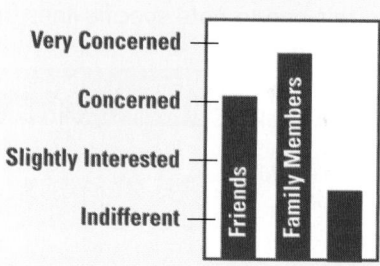

Build Background

Auden's Poetry Generally regarded as one of the foremost modern English poets, W. H. Auden produced a large and complex body of work. At times obscure, his poetry defies easy description or categorization, for it is at times religious, at times lyrical, and frequently satirical. His interest in the problems of modern society and the psychological aspects of human existence is revealed throughout his writing.

Auden, who wanted the style of his poetry to reflect his concern for the common person, strove to write simply and avoid the finery of "grand poetry." He believed that his role as a poet was to present ordinary aspects of human existence in a way that readers could understand and relate to their lives.

The two poems you are about to read reveal Auden's knack for simplicity of style and biting satire. "Musée des Beaux Arts" was inspired by a trip to Brussels, where Auden viewed the paintings in the Royal Museum of Fine Arts, including several by the 16th-century Flemish artist Pieter Breughel (broi'gəl) the Elder. In "The Unknown Citizen," Auden explores the quality of life in the 20th century.

Focus Your Reading

LITERARY ANALYSIS **IRONY IN MODERN POETRY** Both of the poems you are about to read contain ironic elements.

- **Situational irony** is a contrast between what readers expect and what actually happens.
- **Verbal irony** is a speaker's or writer's saying one thing and meaning another.

As you read these poems, watch for examples of irony.

ACTIVE READING **DRAWING CONCLUSIONS** A work's **theme** is a central idea or message that conveys a perception about life or human nature. Poems do not usually state their themes explicitly, but you can discover theme by paying attention to poetic elements that help to convey it—for example, **imagery** and **tone**. In order to **draw conclusions** about a poem's theme, you need to combine what is implied or stated in the poem with your own prior knowledge.

READER'S NOTEBOOK As you read each poem, note down phrases, images, or lines that you think help to convey Auden's ideas about human nature and life.

Landscape with the Fall of Icarus (about 1560), Pieter Brueghel the Elder. Musée Royaux des Beaux Arts de Belgique, Brussels, Belgium/Superstock.

Musée des Beaux Arts

W. H. AUDEN

About suffering they were never wrong,
The Old Masters: how well they understood
Its human position; how it takes place
While someone else is eating or opening a window or just
    walking dully along;
5 How, when the aged are reverently, passionately waiting
For the miraculous birth, there always must be

2 Old Masters: great European artists of the 16th–18th centuries.

Children who did not specially want it to happen, skating
On a pond at the edge of the wood:
They never forgot
10 That even the dreadful martyrdom must run its course
Anyhow in a corner, some untidy spot
Where the dogs go on with their doggy life and the
    torturer's horse
Scratches its innocent behind on a tree.

In Breughel's *Icarus*, for instance: how everything turns
    away
15 Quite leisurely from the disaster; the ploughman may
Have heard the splash, the forsaken cry,
But for him it was not an important failure; the sun shone
As it had to on the white legs disappearing into the green
Water; and the expensive delicate ship that must have seen
20 Something amazing, a boy falling out of the sky,
Had somewhere to get to and sailed calmly on.

14 Breughel's *Icarus* (ĭk′ər-əs): the painting *Landscape with the Fall of Icarus* by Pieter Brueghel (also spelled *Bruegel* and *Breughel*). In Greek mythology, Icarus and his father, Daedalus (dĕd′l-əs), escape imprisonment by flying away on wings crafted of wax and feathers. When Icarus flies too near the sun, the wax melts and he falls into the sea and drowns.

Thinking Through the Literature

1. **Comprehension Check** What incident in the Icarus legend is depicted in Breughel's painting and alluded to by the **speaker** of the poem?

2. What words or phrases best describe your reaction to this poem?

3. Do you agree with the speaker's ideas about suffering and indifference? Give reasons for your answer.

4. How would you describe the **tone** of this poem?

Golconde [Golconda] (1953),
René Magritte. Oil on canvas,
31½″ × 39½″, The Menil Collection,
Houston. Photo by Hickey-Robertson.

THE
Unknown Citizen

(To JS/07/M/378
This Marble Monument
Is Erected by the State)

W. H. AUDEN

He was found by the Bureau of Statistics to be
One against whom there was no official complaint,
And all the reports on his conduct agree
That, in the modern sense of an old-fashioned word, he was a saint,
5   For in everything he did he served the Greater Community.
Except for the War till the day he retired
He worked in a factory and never got fired,
But satisfied his employers, Fudge Motors Inc.
Yet he wasn't a scab or odd in his views,

9 scab: a worker who
refuses to support a
union strike and crosses a
picket line.

10 For his Union reports that he paid his dues,
(Our report on his Union shows it was sound)
And our Social Psychology workers found
That he was popular with his mates and liked a drink.
The Press are convinced that he bought a paper every day
15 And that his reactions to advertisements were normal in
    every way.
Policies taken out in his name prove that he was fully insured,
And his Health-card shows he was once in hospital but left it cured.
Both Producers Research and High-Grade Living declare
He was fully sensible to the advantages of the Installment Plan
20 And had everything necessary to the Modern Man,
A phonograph, a radio, a car and a frigidaire.
Our researchers into Public Opinion are content
That he held the proper opinions for the time of year;
When there was peace, he was for peace; when there was
    war, he went.
25 He was married and added five children to the population,
Which our Eugenist says was the right number for a parent
    of his generation,
And our teachers report that he never interfered with their
    education.
Was he free? Was he happy? The question is absurd:
Had anything been wrong, we should certainly have heard.

21 frigidaire: refrigerator.

26 Eugenist (yo͞o′jə-nĭst): a scientist who tries to improve the human race by controlling hereditary factors.

La grande guerre [The great war] (1964), René Magritte. Private collection, Giraudon/Art Resource, New York. Copyright © 1996 Herscovici/Artists Rights Society (ARS), New York.

Connect to the Literature

1. **What Do You Think?** What is your opinion of the person memorialized in "The Unknown Citizen"? Share your thoughts with your classmates.

Think Critically

2. How would you describe the **tone** of the poem?

THINK ABOUT

- the dedication in parentheses at the beginning of the poem
- the types of accomplishments cited by the speaker
- the speaker's conclusions

3. Do you think the unknown citizen was free and happy? Explain why or why not.

4. **ACTIVE READING** **DRAWING CONCLUSIONS** Review the notes you made in your **READER'S NOTEBOOK** relating to the theme of each poem. What perception about life or human nature do you think is conveyed in each of these poems?

5. After reading "Musée des Beaux Arts" and "The Unknown Citizen," how would you describe Auden's view of the average person?

Extend Interpretations

6. **Critic's Corner** The literary critic Richard Hoggart has remarked on the conversational **style** of Auden's poems, saying that reading them is like "listening to the poet thinking aloud." Do you agree with Hoggart? Cite examples from both poems to support your answer.

7. **Connect to Life** Refer to the graph you created on page 1076. Compare any indifference you noted with the types of indifference portrayed in the two poems. Do you think indifference is an inevitable fact of life?

8. **Art Connection** Look at the reproduction of Brueghel's painting *Landscape with the Fall of Icarus* on page 1077.

Why do you think Auden chose this particular painting as the focus of "Musée des Beaux Arts"?

Literary Analysis

IRONY IN MODERN POETRY In a literary work, **situational irony** is a contrast between what readers expect and what actually happens. **Verbal irony** is a character's or writer's saying one thing and meaning another.

Paired Activity Jot down examples of situational irony in "Musée des Beaux Arts" and verbal irony in "The Unknown Citizen." Then give your interpretation of Auden's use of irony in both poems, citing lines from each one to support your ideas. With your partner, speculate on how the two poems might be different if they contained no irony.

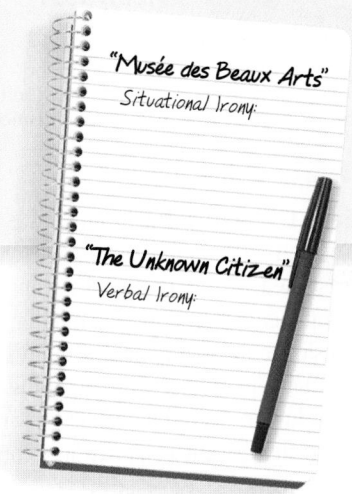

"Musée des Beaux Arts"
Situational Irony:

"The Unknown Citizen"
Verbal Irony:

Choices & CHALLENGES

Writing Options

1. Newspaper Editorial Write an editorial in which you urge average citizens to cast aside the kinds of indifference portrayed in these two poems.

2. Comparison of Workers Draft a short essay in which you compare Auden's depiction of the unknown citizen with your impression of workers in today's society.

Writing Handbook
See page 1367: Compare and Contrast.

Activities & Explorations

1. Police Interview With a partner, role-play an interview in which a police officer asks either the plowman or the captain of the ship in Brueghel's *Landscape with the Fall of Icarus* for more details about the boy's accident. **~ PERFORMING**

2. Census Forms Create two census forms for the Bureau of Statistics—one that seeks only the kind of information presented in "The Unknown Citizen" and one that might elicit a more in-depth picture of people. **~ SOCIOLOGY**

Inquiry & Research

The 1930s Working with a small group of classmates, research political and social developments in the world during the 1930s. Then list some ideas expressed in these poems that readers in the 1930s may have seen as reflections of new realities.

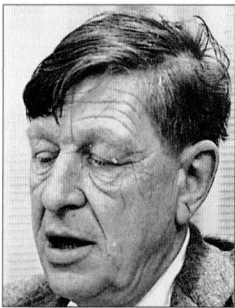

W. H. Auden
1907–1973

Other Works
"On This Island"
"Their Lonely Betters"
"In Praise of Limestone"

Early Life Wystan Hugh Auden was born in York, England, the son of a doctor. His earliest interest was science, and as a boy he planned to become a mining engineer. From his mother, who loved music, he derived a lifelong interest in many kinds of music, particularly opera. At the age of 15, however, he discovered his talent for writing poetry; thereafter, he knew that writing would be his career.

Oxford Years While a student at Oxford University, Auden exerted a significant influence on a group of young writers who would become the literary leaders of the 1930s. Later known as the Auden Generation, this group included Stephen Spender, who in 1928 printed Auden's first published book of poems on a hand-operated press. Auden's genius was also encouraged by the poet T. S. Eliot, then an editor at the publishing firm of Faber & Faber.

American Years Auden assumed various other roles during his lifetime, including those of teacher, playwright, documentary filmmaker, critic, and editor. In 1939 he moved to New York City, becoming a U.S. citizen in 1946. He spent most of his literary career in the United States, where he regularly taught and lectured at colleges and universities, including Yale, Swarthmore, Penn State, and the University of Michigan.

Eccentric Lifestyle Even after becoming a renowned literary figure who mingled with the rich and famous, Auden chose to live the life of an eccentric, residing in messy, rundown apartments; dressing in shabby attire; and frequently appearing in public wearing jeans and bedroom slippers. Although disordered in his daily life, he maintained a strict sense of order in his poetry.

Return to Oxford Auden never had a family of his own, but he appreciated home life and liked to be surrounded by friends and their families. Extremely clever and witty, he hosted parties that were attended by guests from all walks of life. In 1972, a year before his death, his college at Oxford offered him a rent-free residence, and he returned to England to live his remaining days in security and comfort on the Oxford campus.

What I Expected

Poetry by STEPHEN SPENDER

Connect to Your Life

Dashed Hopes Recall a time when what you hoped or dreamed for didn't turn out the way you wanted. How did you react to the disappointment? What realities were you forced to face? Share your thoughts with a classmate.

Build Background

The Auden Generation When he entered Oxford University in 1928, Stephen Spender had already decided that he wanted to be a famous poet. There, he showed his poems to W. H. Auden, a slightly older student who had already achieved recognition within the school for his poetic genius. Auden approved of Spender's work, and a famous literary alliance was formed. The two poets were key members of a small group of Oxford students—the so-called Auden Generation—who became prominent literary figures during the 1930s. In addition to Auden and Spender, the group included the poets Louis MacNeice and C. Day Lewis and the novelist Christopher Isherwood.

The 1930s were turbulent years in European history—the time of the Great Depression, the Spanish civil war, and the start of World War II. Many English writers, particularly those of the Auden Generation, were appalled by what they saw taking place in the world. Sharing a hatred of war and a disgust for the deplorable living conditions endured by the swelling ranks of England's unemployed, they believed that it was their job to reflect the political and social concerns of the time in their writings. Although Spender did notable work as a critic, editor, translator, and travel writer, it is for his political poetry that he is best known. In "What I Expected," written during the early 1930s, he deals with the realities he faced during that period.

Focus Your Reading

LITERARY ANALYSIS **IMAGERY IN MODERN POETRY**

A striking element of "What I Expected" is its **imagery.** Images such as "smoke before wind" and "the faceted crystal" create vivid sensory experiences for the reader. As with much modern poetry, the poem uses patterns of imagery that imply meaning rather than state it. As you read the poem, consider the meaning and effect of each image.

ACTIVE READING **DETERMINING MAJOR IDEAS IN POETRY**

The vivid **images** of "What I Expected" help to convey the poem's major ideas. Some of these images describe the speaker's expectations; others describe the realities the speaker must face. As you read the poem, consider why each image is being used.

READER'S NOTEBOOK In a chart like the one shown, distinguish between the images that express the speaker's expectations and those that express the reality the speaker has had to face. Decide what different impressions the two types of images convey.

Images That Describe Expectations	Images That Describe Reality
1.	1.
2.	2.

WHAT I EXPECTED

Stephen Spender

What I expected, was
Thunder, fighting,
Long struggles with men
And climbing.
5 After continual straining
I should grow strong;
Then the rocks would shake
And I rest long.

What I had not foreseen
10 Was the gradual day
Weakening the will
Leaking the brightness away,
The lack of good to touch,
The fading of body and soul
15 Smoke before wind,
Corrupt, unsubstantial.

The wearing of Time,
And the watching of cripples pass
With limbs shaped like questions
20 In their odd twist,
The pulverous grief
Melting the bones with pity,
The sick falling from earth—
These, I could not foresee.

25 Expecting always
Some brightness to hold in trust
Some final innocence
Exempt from dust,
That, hanging solid,
30 Would dangle through all
Like the created poem,
Or the faceted crystal.

Detail of *1933 (St. Rémy-Provence)* (1933), Ben Nicholson.
Copyright © 1995 Mrs. Angela Verren-Taunt/Licensed by VAGA,
New York/DACS, London.

21 pulverous: devastating; crushing.

32 faceted: having flat, smooth surfaces.

Connect to the Literature

1. **What Do You Think?** Which **images** from "What I Expected" linger in your mind?

Think Critically

2. Summarize what you think the **speaker** expected to feel at this point in his life. Cite details from the poem to support your ideas.

3. In your own words, tell what you think the speaker "had not foreseen." Compare your thoughts with those of your classmates.

4. **ACTIVE READING** | **DETERMINING MAJOR IDEAS IN POETRY**
   With a partner, review the contrasting **images** chart you created in your 📖**READER'S NOTEBOOK.** In what ways do the images contribute to the poem's major ideas?

5. In your opinion, what **theme,** or message, is expressed in this poem?

   > **THINK ABOUT**
   - the speaker's reference to fighting (lines 2–7)
   - what the speaker says about "brightness" (lines 12 and 26)
   - the **image** of "smoke before wind" (line 15)
   - the reference to "Time" (line 17)

Extend Interpretations

6. **Comparing Texts** Do you think the speaker of Gerard Manley Hopkins's "Spring and Fall: To a Young Child" (page 947) would agree with the depiction of reality in "What I Expected"? Why or why not?

7. **Critic's Corner** The critic Geoffrey Thurley considers "What I Expected" to be one of Spender's best poems. He says that Spender conceived the poem "as an act, rather than as a statement" and that for this reason the reader "experiences the poem." Explain what you think Thurley means and tell how you experienced the poem.

8. **Connect to Life** Think of the realities that the speaker acknowledges in the poem. Do you think most people come to similar realizations during the course of their lives?

Literary Analysis

IMAGERY IN MODERN POETRY

The term **imagery** refers to words and phrases that create vivid sensory experiences for the reader. Most images are visual, but imagery may also appeal to the senses of smell, hearing, taste and touch.

Activity Look again at the imagery charts you created on page 1083. Select two or three images that you find especially striking or powerful. In a chart like the one shown, list the senses each one appeals to. Then explain to your classmates why you find these images effective.

Image	Senses
cripples with twisted limbs	

REVIEW | **FREE VERSE** | Most of Spender's poems are written in **free verse**—verse without regular patterns of **rhythm** and **rhyme.** Although free verse lacks conventional meter, it may contain various rhythmic effects and other sound effects—such as recurring syllables or words. Free verse can also contain rhyme, but if so, it is used with great freedom. How would you characterize the overall rhythm of "What I Expected"? How does the rhythm relate to the content of the poem?

Writing Options

1. Diary Entries Imagine that you are the speaker of "What I Expected." Rewrite each stanza as an individual diary entry.

2. Opinion Paper Write an opinion paper in which you disagree with the speaker's attitude toward life. Be sure to support your opinions with reasons.

Activities & Explorations

1. Dramatic Reading With a small group of classmates, stage and present a dramatic reading of the poem for your class. Select appropriate background music and prepare a simple cloth backdrop or screen to enhance your performance. ~ **PERFORMING**

2. Interpretive Montage Create a montage that conveys your interpretation of "What I Expected." Include lines from the poem as well as illustrations or photographs. If you have access to a computer, use it to create designs or to set lines of the poem in different sizes and fonts. ~ **ART**

Art Connection

Visual-Verbal Images In your opinion, how do the visual images in the painting *1933 (St. Rémy-Provence)* on page 1084 relate to the verbal images in "What I Expected"?

Inquiry & Research

Crystals Read about the properties of crystals. What significant qualities, shapes, and uses do they have? In the last lines of "What I Expected," the speaker equates a "created poem" with a "faceted crystal." How do you think the properties of a crystal might be like those of a poem?

Stephen Spender
1909–1995

Other Works
"The Vase of Tears"
"Two Armies"
"Moving Through the Silent Crowd"
"Dark and Light"
"Fall of a City"

Social Writer Throughout his career, Stephen Spender had a reputation for creating humanistic works that struck a balance between bleak pessimism and unfailing optimism. A modest and sometimes shy man, Spender nevertheless enjoyed a camaraderie with his fellow writers. He eagerly accepted invitations to visit the gatherings of London's numerous literary circles, where he met such writers as Virginia Woolf and T. S. Eliot. In later years his reputation for witty conversation made him a popular guest in the homes of the socially prominent both in Britain and in the United States.

Cultural Ambassador Spender's strong interest in humanity was reflected not only in his writing but in his other activities. For approximately 20 years, he acted as a cultural ambassador, lecturing throughout the world on the importance of the artistic and intellectual dimensions of life. From 1970 to 1975, he was a full-time professor of English at University College in London, and he also served as a visiting professor at many universities in the United States and as poetry consultant to the Library of Congress. In 1983 Spender was knighted for his many contributions to literature.

Author Activity

Propaganda War During the Spanish civil war, Spender did propaganda work for the democratic forces that remained loyal to the Spanish Republic and fought against General Franco's Fascist rebels. Find out more about this conflict and the part Spender played in it. How might the war have affected Spender's outlook?

Do Not Go Gentle into That Good Night

In My Craft or Sullen Art

Poetry by DYLAN THOMAS

Comparing Literature of the World

The Poetry of Dylan Thomas and Octavio Paz

This lesson and the one that follows offer an opportunity to compare poems about the nature and process of writing poetry by the Welsh poet Dylan Thomas and the Mexican poet Octavio Paz. Specific points of comparison in the Paz lesson will help you note similarities and differences in the poets' perceptions of their desire to write and the directions they take.

Connect to Your Life

Source of Inspiration If you were a poet, what topics would you be inspired to write about? What personal events would motivate you to take pen in hand? As you read these two poems by Dylan Thomas, compare your own ideas about topics for poems with the topics that he treats.

Build Background

One-of-a-Kind Poet The poetry of Dylan Thomas has provoked strong and widely divergent reactions. The style of his poems, which are unique and difficult to classify but also quite lyrical and moving, seemed bold, unconventional, and unfamiliar to readers in the 1930s and 1940s and aroused responses ranging from adoration to contempt.

In the late 1940s and early 1950s, while critics argued over the merit of his writing, adoring fans flocked to hear the poet read his works. Not all of them fully understood his poetry, but they loved to listen to it—to hear its sounds. In explaining why he began writing, Thomas once said, "I wanted to write poetry in the beginning because I had fallen in love with words. . . . What the words stood for, symbolized, or meant, was of very secondary importance. What mattered was the sound of them." Like the 19th-century poet Gerard Manley Hopkins, Thomas frequently experimented with language, playing with sound devices, coining new words, and creating fresh images.

Thomas wrote about the things closest to his heart, calling his poetry "the record of my individual struggle from darkness towards some measure of light." He was motivated not by social and political issues but by his own experiences, writing about topics such as childhood, holidays, nature, and death. The intensely personal nature of his writing is revealed in both of the poems that you are about to read. In "Do Not Go Gentle into That Good Night," Thomas reacts to his father's deteriorating health; in "In My Craft or Sullen Art," he explores his fundamental motivation for writing.

Focus Your Reading

LITERARY ANALYSIS **CONSONANCE AND ASSONANCE** The following line from "Do Not Go Gentle into That Good Night" illustrates Thomas's love of the sound of words:

> *Blind eyes could blaze like meteors and be gay . . .*

The repetition of the final *z* sound in *eyes, blaze,* and *meteors* is an example of **consonance**, the repetition of consonant sounds within and at the ends of words. The line also provides examples of **assonance**, a repetition of vowel sounds in words—the long *i* in *blind, eyes,* and *like* and the long *a* in *blaze* and *gay*. As you read the poems, look for other examples of these techniques.

ACTIVE READING **VISUALIZING SETTING IN POETRY** Although neither of these poems is what would normally be considered a narrative poem, each poem's topic implies a **setting.** As you read these poems, try to visualize a time and place for each speaker. Consider the relevance of the settings to the meaning of the poems.

READER'S NOTEBOOK Jot down words and phrases that you think suggest the setting of each poem.

Do Not Go Gentle into That Good Night

Dylan Thomas

Do not go gentle into that good night,
Old age should burn and rave at close of day;
Rage, rage against the dying of the light.

Though wise men at their end know dark is right,
5 Because their words had forked no lightning they
Do not go gentle into that good night.

Good men, the last wave by, crying how bright
Their frail deeds might have danced in a green bay,
Rage, rage against the dying of the light.

10 Wild men who caught and sang the sun in flight,
And learn, too late, they grieved it on its way,
Do not go gentle into that good night.

Grave men, near death, who see with blinding sight
Blind eyes could blaze like meteors and be gay,
15 Rage, rage against the dying of the light.

And you, my father, there on the sad height,
Curse, bless, me now with your fierce tears, I pray.
Do not go gentle into that good night.
Rage, rage against the dying of the light.

Portrait of Father III (1972), Leon Kossoff. Oil on board, 60″ × 48″, private collection.

Thinking Through the Literature

1. **Comprehension Check** What does the **speaker** mean by the phrase "that good night"?

2. Jot down two or three phrases that convey your reaction to this poem.

3. How would you describe the speaker's attitude toward death? Give evidence from the poem to support your answer.

4. What can you **infer** about the relationship between the speaker and his father?

In My Craft or Sullen Art

Dylan Thomas

In my craft or sullen art
Exercised in the still night
When only the moon rages
And the lovers lie abed
5   With all their griefs in their arms,
I labor by singing light
Not for ambition or bread
Or the strut and trade of charms
On the ivory stages
10   But for the common wages
Of their most secret heart.

Not for the proud man apart
From the raging moon I write
On these spindrift pages
15   Nor for the towering dead
With their nightingales and psalms
But for the lovers, their arms
Round the griefs of the ages,
Who pay no praise or wages
20   Nor heed my craft or art.

14 spindrift: spray blown up from the sea by the wind.

Les amoureux aux fleurs [Lovers with flowers] (1927), Marc Chagall. Israel Museum (IDAM), Jerusalem, Israel, Giraudon/Art Resource, New York. Copyright © 1996 Artists Rights Society (ARS), New York/ADAGP, Paris.

Connect to the Literature

1. What Do You Think?
What **images** linger in your mind after your reading of "In My Craft or Sullen Art"?

Comprehension Check
- To what practice does the title of "In My Craft or Sullen Art" refer?
- For whom does the speaker say he practices his craft?

Think Critically

2. How would you describe the speaker?

> **THINK ABOUT**
> - why he refers to writing as his "sullen art"
> - his use of the words *labor* (line 6) and *wages* (line 10)
> - his fascination with lovers
> - what he might mean by "the towering dead / With their nightingales and psalms" (lines 15–16)

3. The verb *rage* appears in both "Do Not Go Gentle into That Good Night" and "In My Craft or Sullen Art." Why do you think Thomas chose to include this word in both poems?

4. **ACTIVE READING** | **VISUALIZING SETTING IN POETRY**
Review the notes about **setting** that you made in your **READER'S NOTEBOOK.** How would you describe the setting of each poem? Do you consider the setting important? Explain your answer.

Extend Interpretations

5. Comparing Texts Do you think the speaker of A. E. Housman's "To an Athlete Dying Young" (page 965) shares the attitude toward life expressed by the speaker of "Do Not Go Gentle into That Good Night"? Why or why not?

6. Critic's Corner According to the poet and critic Karl Shapiro, Thomas's poems are characterized by "a fatal pessimism . . . offset by a few bursts of joy and exuberance." Do you detect pessimism, joy, or exuberance in these poems—or perhaps all three? Support your answer with examples.

7. Connect to Life Think back to the Connect to Your Life activity on page 1087. How do the topics of these poems compare with your own notions of topics that might inspire a poet?

Literary Analysis

CONSONANCE AND ASSONANCE Thomas's love of the sound of words is reflected in his use of **consonance** (a repetition of consonant sounds within and at the ends of words) and **assonance** (a repetition of vowel sounds in words). He uses both assonance and consonance to emphasize particular words, to create **mood,** and to add a musical quality to poems.

Paired Activity In both poems, find examples of consonance and assonance that you think are particularly effective. Practice reading the lines aloud. Then explain to your partner why you chose the examples you did.

VILLANELLE "Do Not Go Gentle into That Good Night" is an example of an intricate verse form of French origin called the **villanelle.** Its structure includes the following characteristics:

- It is a 19-line poem comprised of five **tercets,** or three-line stanzas, followed by a **quatrain,** or four-line stanza.
- The **rhyme scheme** is *aba* for each tercet and then *abaa* for the quatrain.
- Line 1 is repeated as a **refrain** at the ends of the second and fourth stanzas. The last line of the first stanza is repeated at the ends of the third and fifth stanzas. Both lines reappear at the final two lines of the poem.
- Villanelles in English often use **iambic pentameter.**

How closely does Thomas's poem follow the villanelle form? How effective is the form in conveying ideas and emotions?

Writing Options

1. Letter to the Poet Write a letter to Dylan Thomas, explaining your opinion of the view of death expressed in "Do Not Go Gentle into That Good Night."

2. Interpretive Notes Reread the poems, writing down any words, phrases, or sentences that you think are used in unusual or ambiguous ways—for example, "spindrift pages" in line 14 of "In My Craft or Sullen Art." Then write a brief interpretation of each word, phrase, or sentence, based on its use in the poem. Share your interpretations with the class.

Activities & Explorations

1. Inspiring Speech Write and deliver a speech that the speaker of "In My Craft or Sullen Art" might give to a class of aspiring poets. **~ SPEAKING AND LISTENING**

2. The Poet's Voice Locate a recording of Dylan Thomas reading his poetry. After playing the recording for the class, discuss the effect of hearing the works in the poet's own voice.
~ SPEAKING AND LISTENING

Inquiry & Research

Welsh Literary Tradition Wales has a long and rich literary history. Although Dylan Thomas did not speak the Welsh language, his work is part of a poetic tradition that began in the sixth century. Find out more about Wales's literary history and traditions. Report your findings to the class.

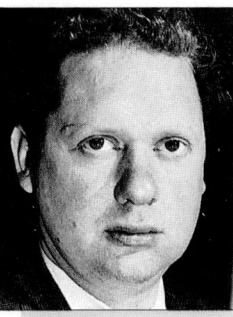

Dylan Thomas
1914–1953

Other Works
"And Death Shall Have No
   Dominion"
"Fern Hill"
"Poem in October"
Portrait of the Artist as a Young Dog
Under Milk Wood
A Child's Christmas in Wales

Welsh Roots Dylan Thomas was considered by many the most original English poet since Yeats and Eliot. He was born in Swansea in southwestern Wales, and his writing is rooted in the countryside and culture of his homeland. Although he did not learn to speak the Welsh language, he captured its cadences and word sequences in both his poetry and prose.

Teenage Poet Thomas attended Swansea Grammar School, where his father taught English and where Thomas performed poorly in every subject but literature. At the age of 16, he quit school and went to work as a newspaper reporter. Already, he had become a prolific poet. By the time he was 20, his first book of poems had been published.

Money Trouble In the late 1930s, Thomas moved to London to look for more lucrative writing assignments and began writing fewer poems and more short stories, radio scripts, and screenplays. Unfortunately, Thomas had no business sense and was always in dire financial straits. He fell behind on his taxes and had to borrow money to support his wife and family. In 1949, Thomas and his family moved back to Wales. The following year, in an attempt to improve his finances, he booked his first series of poetry readings in the United States.

Self-Destructive Streak Thomas captivated audiences with dramatic readings of his own works as well as those of earlier poets. To his many fans in America and Great Britain, he personified the typical image of the bohemian poet—reckless and romantic. Sadly, he was also self-destructive. Thomas had a serious drinking problem, and at the age of 39, in the midst of his fourth American tour, he died in a hotel room from complications of alcoholism. He nevertheless left a legacy of innovative, lyrical work that helped set a new standard for modern poetry.

Author Activity

Celebrated Reader When Thomas began visiting American colleges, he soon became renowned for his dramatic readings. Find out whose poetry he performed in addition to his own work. Why do you think he chose these poets?

Writing/Escritura

Poetry by OCTAVIO PAZ

Poetry Across Cultures

Poems of Dylan Thomas and Octavio Paz In their writing, both Octavio Paz and Dylan Thomas have reflected upon their own cultures—Mexican and Welsh respectively. However, both poets explore subjects that reflect the universal human condition and so have appealed to people in all countries.

Points of Comparison   As you read Paz's poem, compare it with Dylan Thomas's poetry in terms of the following:

- the use of **imagery**
- each poet's **purpose** for writing poetry
- each poet's view of the creative process

Build Background

Writing About Writing Although the history of English poetry extends back many centuries, poetry did not become a popular literary genre in the Spanish-speaking countries of Latin America until the late 19th century and did not flourish until after World War I. In 1933, when a 19-year-old Mexican writer named Octavio Paz published his first volume of poetry, he began a literary career that spanned more than 60 years. Paz achieved widespread recognition for both his poetry and his prose, including the 1990 Nobel Prize in literature.

In his writing, Paz explores the creative process—what it means to be a poet and what steps lead to a finished work. According to Paz, the meaning of a poem depends entirely on the way a reader interprets the work; thus, the reader's response is a part of the creative process.

Focus Your Reading

LITERARY ANALYSIS **PARADOX** "Writing/Escritura" contains examples of **paradoxes**—statements that seem contradictory but nevertheless express truths. Because a paradox is often surprising, it draws the reader's attention to what is being said. As you read Paz's poem, look for seeming contradictions. Consider the meaning and effect of each one.

ACTIVE READING **ANALYZING POETIC LANGUAGE** In addition to paradox, Paz integrates opposites in a number of other ways in his work. For example, he frequently juxtaposes contrasting **images,** such as fire and ice. As you read, be aware of the poet's use of contrast.

READER'S NOTEBOOK Look for examples of contrasting images in "Writing/Escritura." Note them in a chart similar to the one below.

Image	Contrasting Image
fire	ice

Writing

Octavio Paz

When over the paper the pen goes writing
in any solitary hour,
who drives the pen?
To whom is he writing, he who writes for me,
5 this shore made of lips, made of dream,
a hill of stillness, abyss,
shoulder on which to forget the world forever?

Someone in me is writing, moves my hand,
hears a word, hesitates,
10 halted between green mountain and blue sea.
With icy fervor
contemplates what I write.
All is burned in this fire of justice.
But this judge is nevertheless the victim
15 and in condemning me condemns himself:
He writes to anyone, he calls nobody,
to his own self he writes, and in himself forgets,
and is redeemed, becoming again me.

Translated by Muriel Rukeyser

11 fervor: heat; intensity of feeling.

Escritura

Octavio Paz

Cuando sobre el papel la pluma escribe,
a cualquier hora solitaria,
¿quién la guía?
¿A quién escribe el que escribe por mí,
5 orilla hecha de labios y de sueño,
quieta colina, golfo,
hombro para olvidar al mundo para siempre?

Alguien escribe en mí, mueve mi mano,
escoge una palabra, se detiene,
10 duda entre el mar azul y el monte verde.
Con un ardor helado
contempla lo que escribo.
Todo lo quema, fuego justiciero.
Pero este juez también es víctima
15 y al condenarme, se condena:
no escribe a nadie, a nadie llama,
a sí mismo se escribe, en sí se olvida,
y se rescata, y vuelve a ser yo mismo.

Connect to the Literature

1. What Do You Think? What words or phrases best describe your response to this poem?

> **Comprehension Check**
> • What answer does the speaker give to the question, "Who drives the pen?"

Think Critically

2. **ACTIVE READING** **ANALYZING POETIC LANGUAGE** Review the chart in your **READER'S NOTEBOOK** about contrasting **images** and words. Which juxtaposition of opposites in the poem do you find the most striking? Explain why you think it is effective.

3. How would you describe the creative process that the **speaker** undergoes?

> **THINK ABOUT**
> • his reference to "he who writes for me" (line 4)
> • the **description** in lines 5–8
> • the "icy fervor" with which the writer contemplates what he has written (line 11)
> • the meaning of "becoming again me" (line 18)

4. What would you say is the speaker's attitude toward this process?

Extend Interpretations

5. Critic's Corner The critic John M. Fein has suggested that Octavio Paz's poetry might seem "unconcluded" to a reader who does not realize that Paz "invites him to feel his own version of the poem." Explain what you think Fein means and why you agree or disagree with him.

6. Connect to Life Over the centuries, many poets have written about writing. Why do you think this is so?

7. **Points of Comparison** Compare the ideas conveyed in "Writing" and in Dylan Thomas's "In My Craft or Sullen Art." Do you think their **purpose** for writing poetry is similar? Use evidence from the poems to support your answer.

Literary Analysis

PARADOX The use of **paradox**— a statement that seems to contradict itself but, in fact, reveals some element of truth—is one way in which Paz integrates opposites. For example, in the following lines, how can the judge be the victim?

But this judge is nevertheless the victim / and in condemning me condemns himself

This important component of Paz's literary style enables him to express ideas in a concise and memorable way.

Cooperative Learning Activity Working with a small group of classmates, look back at the poem for other examples of paradox. Complete a chart, similar to the one below, in which you note the paradoxical statement and give your interpretation of the truth it expresses. When you have completed the chart, discuss with your classmates how effective you consider this stylistic device to be.

Paradox	Meaning
this judge is . . . the victim (l. 14)	the writer is his own critic; he suffers from self-criticism

Writing Options

1. Creative Definition Write a definition of the word *creativity* from the perspective of this poem's speaker.

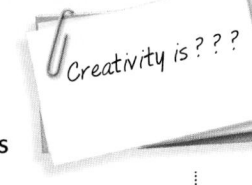

Creativity is ? ? ?

2. Interior Monologue Write a monologue to represent the thoughts of the poem's "he" during the creative process.

3. Points of Comparison Basing your views on the ideas expressed in "In My Craft or Sullen Art" and "Writing/ Escritura," write the draft for an essay in which you discuss whether or not Paz and Dylan

Thomas share a similar vision of the creative process.

Writing Handbook See page 1367: Compare and Contrast.

Activities & Explorations

1. Stamp Design Create a design for a postage stamp commemorating the art of writing. ~ **ART**

2. Multimedia Presentation With a group of classmates, look for books, essays, and interviews in which well-known writers explore the creative process. Then create a flowchart plan for a multimedia presentation called "Writers on Writing," in which you

include inspirational quotations from those works. ~ **TECHNOLOGY/ SPEAKING AND LISTENING**

Inquiry & Research

Translating Poetry In an essay entitled "On Translation," Paz wrote that "to a certain extent every translation is an original invention and thus constitutes a unique text." Locate the work of several different translators who have translated Paz's poems. If possible, find different translations of the same poems. Compare the translations, and, in the light of your comparison, discuss your thoughts about Paz's statement.

Octavio Paz
1914–1998

Other Works
"Two Bodies"
"Wind and Water and Stone"
"Fable"
"The Spoken Word"
"Nightfall"

Mexican Heritage Octavio Paz was born on the outskirts of Mexico City during the Mexican Revolution. The war left his family in financial ruin, and Paz remembers that as a child he lived in a large house that was gradually crumbling to the ground. In spite of these circumstances, he had a fairly pleasant childhood, spending many hours in his grandfather's extensive library. After attending the National Autonomous University of Mexico, he traveled extensively in Spain, France, and the United States, becoming immersed in the literature, history, art, and philosophy of other nations. His experiences are reflected in his writing, which embraces a diversity of topics, including politics, Eastern philosophy, psychology, art, and anthro-

pology. Despite his interest in travel and other cultures, however, Paz never forgot his heritage: his first book of prose, *The Labyrinth of Solitude*, was an exploration of Mexican culture and thought. Published in 1950, it was well-received and brought Paz international recognition.

Varied Career Paz also worked as an ambassador, editor, and teacher. In 1946, he joined the Mexican diplomatic corps and served for 22 years in such countries as France, Switzerland, Japan, and India. He founded and was editor of several literary magazines and, after resigning from his diplomatic post in 1968, taught at various universities, including the Universities of Texas and California, Harvard, and Cambridge.

Author Activity

Cultural Interests Paz was interested in pre-Columbian Mexican history, and this interest is reflected in his work. Find out about his long poem, *Piedra de Sol*, which is about the Aztec calendar. Present your findings to the class in an oral report.

Writing Workshop

Literature through performance . . .

From Reading to Writing In *The Rising of the Moon*, Lady Gregory chose to tell her story in the form of a **drama,** or play. Plays have many of the same elements as narratives—characters, setting, plot, conflict. But in a play, dialogue and stage directions are used to reveal character traits and setting, and to move the plot forward. Drama is the format used for skits, television programs, theater productions, and movies.

For Your Portfolio

WRITING PROMPT Write a dramatic scene based on a piece of fiction or on an incident you create.

Purpose: To entertain

Audience: Your classmates or anyone who will read it or see it performed

---

Basics in a Box

Dramatic Scene at a Glance

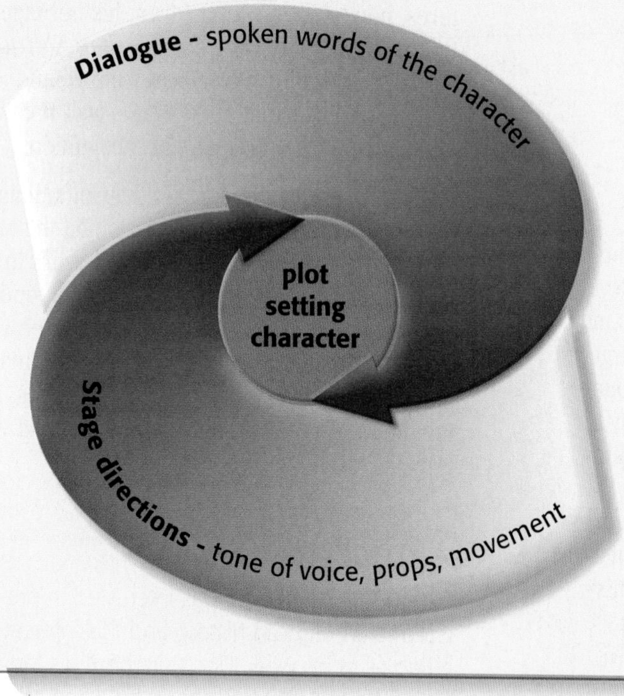

Dialogue - spoken words of the character

plot
setting
character

Stage directions - tone of voice, props, movement

RUBRIC Standards for Writing

A successful dramatic scene should

- introduce the setting and characters in the opening stage directions
- use the setting and characters to create a convincing world
- develop a clear and interesting situation or conflict
- reveal the personalities of the characters through the dialogue
- use actions as well as dialogue to advance the story
- include stage directions as necessary

Analyzing a Student Model: Dramatic Scene

Ana Woody
Gobles High School

Two Characters on a Bus

Characters: <u>**Josh**</u> *is a 16-year-old runaway;*
<u>**Gretta**</u> *is an uneducated older woman traveling alone.*

Setting: *It is summer, and Josh and Gretta are strangers seated next to each other on a cross-country bus. Gretta is going to visit a friend. Josh is headed north to his great-aunt's house. As lights come up, Josh and Gretta are in the middle of a conversation.*

Gretta. Where ya goin' all by yourself? (*Josh doesn't answer.*) Well, ya know we're goin' t'be together on this bus for a long time, boy. Why don't ya just tell me why ya look so sad. It's not hard once ya start.

Josh (*quietly*). It's about my family, my so-called family. But I don't really want to talk about it.

Gretta (*pats his leg*). Sometimes it helps to talk 'bout it to someone. <u>I may be old, but I got good ears to listen with and a quick mind to understand.</u>

Josh (*sad*). After my mom left, my dad was mad all the time. At me, at everyone. He wouldn't talk to me. He said he wished my "no-good mother" would've taken me with her. But she couldn't.

Gretta (*softly*). Why couldn't she take ya with her?

Josh. She didn't have a job, and she was goin' to live with her aunt. She promised to come and get me when she could. It's already been over a year, and I can't wait any longer. Not with him. He's just too mean to live with. (*Gretta hands him a tissue. Josh blows his nose.*)

Josh. Yesterday I told him I was goin' to stay at my friend's house and he got so mad. He yelled that I couldn't go anywhere. When I asked why, he just started mumbling to himself that I was just like my mother. (<u>*hesitates*</u>)

Gretta (<u>*puts hand on his knee*</u>). Go on, child, it hurts, but it'll help.

Josh. I went upstairs to my room and packed all the stuff I could in my bag and snuck out last night. I had some money saved for a car, so I took that along with the money he had stashed for going out on the weekends.

Gretta (*nodding*). And ya bought a bus ticket with it.

Josh. I had to get away. I just hate the way he acts.

Gretta (*with a concerned smile*). What're ya gonna do, Josh? You're too young to be out in the world all alone.

Josh. Well, I plan to go to my great-aunt's house and find out where my mother is and what she's doing. If I tell my great-aunt what I've been dealin' with, she won't send me back. At least I hope not.

Gretta. I'm sure she won't, honey. If'n she's a good-hearted woman, she'll do what she can to help ya.

---

❶ Introduces the characters and setting in the opening stage directions

❷ This writer has the character reveal information about herself through dialogue.
Other Options:
· Reveal information through the character's actions.
· Reveal information through a narrator or another character.

❸ Uses the stage directions to indicate attitudes and body movements

Josh (*smiles for the first time*). I never told anyone about my dad. I just hope he's okay. (*pauses for a beat*) What about you, Gretta? What's your life like?

Gretta (*laughs a little*). I've had a pretty quiet life, I guess. (*closes eyes*) I ain't seen any real trouble, but I seen a good many beautiful and unexplainable things.

Josh (*encouragingly*). Like what?

Gretta (*opens eyes*). Oh, flowers in the middle of a snowy field, rainbows on dry days, green waterfalls, angels in my garden, and such.

Josh (*amazed*). Wha-at? How? Why?

Gretta (*wistfully*). I guess the good Lord saw fit to show me those things along with other things. I never really had anyone on earth to guide me on my life's path, so I figure heaven stepped in. Maybe so I could guide others.

Josh (*shakes head*). I wish my life was like yours.

Gretta. Ya got it wrong if'n ya think it's easy. This world can be a hard place. Ya got ta make do with what ya have, and share what ya can. It's hard work bein' a good person to more than just yourself.

Josh. Do you think it got too hard for my dad to be good to me? When I was young, I thought he was the greatest man alive. But now I see him differently. Maybe he's just a normal person with problems, and no one to help him. No one to listen.

Gretta (*nods*). I think ya just might have learned somethin'. How did ya feel when ya got on this bus?

Josh. I felt bad, like I hated my life. And lonely. I hated my dad, too. Well, thought I did, anyway. You know the right things to say. I feel older. Is that strange?

Gretta (*looking for something in her bag*). No, honey, it ain't strange. It's just sad. You shouldn't have to worry about your dad and his problems. Sometimes people have to grow up a little faster than normal. Happens to the best of us. (*puts bag on floor, smiles*)

Josh. Yeah, I get it. . . . Maybe everything is gonna work out.

(*The bus driver's voice booms out from offstage: Everybody out for Clarksburg!*)

Josh. Here's where I get off. (*stands up to leave*) Thanks for listening. I won't forget you.

Gretta. I'm proud to hear that. Remember, be a good listener and ask the right questions. A fool always has somethin' to say and a wise man hardly speaks. (*laughs again*) Ya take care of ya self.

Josh (*waves as he steps off the bus*).

Gretta (*moves over to the window seat, smiling*).

> **4** Develops the character through specific details

> **5** Advances story entirely without action

> **6** Uses action, stage directions, and dialogue to resolve the situation

Writing Your Dramatic Scene

❶ Prewriting

The secret of playwriting can be given in two maxims:
stick to the point and whenever you can, cut.
W. Somerset Maugham, British novelist and playwright

Begin by thinking about a character or situation that interests you and involves a problem or conflict. Another option is to adapt material from books, movies, magazines, or even songs. For example, you could retell a well-known myth in dramatic form. See the **Idea Bank** in the margin for more suggestions. After you select an idea for your scene, follow the steps below.

IDEABank

1. Your Working Portfolio 📁
Build on one of the **Writing Options** you completed earlier in this unit:
• **Dramatic Scene,** p. 1030.
• **Missing Scene,** p. 1043.
• **Dramatic Skit,** p. 1075.

2. From the Headlines
Borrow an idea for your scene from the headlines, or check a newspaper for human interest stories or news events.

3. Conflict Chart
List conflicts that you or people you know have experienced. Build your scene around one of these conflicts.

Planning Your Dramatic Scene

▶ **1. Consider the basic elements of your scene.** Fill out a chart like the one below to help you identify the elements you need to include.

Characters	Setting	Plot	Stage Directions
Who are the characters? How do they interact?	When and where does the scene take place?	What events will happen? In what sequence will they occur?	How will the characters speak? What is the pace of the scene?

▶ **2. Think about your audience.** Who will read or view your dramatic scene? What language is appropriate for them? What background will they need to understand the setting, characters, and action?

▶ **3. Decide on a mood.** What general emotional atmosphere do you want to convey? What basic elements of character, setting, and action will help contribute to that mood?

▶ **4. Explore your scene.** How will your characters interact and speak? You might write an outline of your scene or jot down bits of dialogue.

❷ Drafting

As you write a script for your dramatic scene, keep the following points in mind:
• Introduce the **characters** and establish the **setting** of your scene. You might begin by putting a character in a situation and having him or her talk with another character.
• Use **dialogue** and **action** to advance the plot. You might collaborate with a partner to think of various actions and situations you could include.

- Use **dialogue** to reveal details about the characters—personalities, interests, attitudes, and beliefs.
- Use **stage directions** to describe setting, costumes, lighting, sound effects, and props. Stage directions can also indicate mood through use of gestures, tone of voice, and characters' body movements.

Ask Your Peer Reader

- What do you think of the way the scene begins? How could this be improved?
- How would you describe the characters?
- Which part of the scene, if any, is not clear to you?

Need help with dialogue?

See the **Writing Handbook,** p. 1365

❸ Revising

TARGET SKILL ▶ USING DIALOGUE EFFECTIVELY Your characters' words should sound natural when spoken, so read your dialogue aloud. Use contractions and sentence fragments to mimic actual speech. Indicate tone of voice or emotion with precise stage directions, such as *mumbles, with a sob,* or *thoughtfully.*

> **Gretta.** ~~I have~~ *(laughs a little).* I've had a ~~fairly~~ *pretty* quiet life. *(closes eyes)* I *guess.* ~~have never~~ *ain't*
>
> seen any real trouble, but I ~~have~~ seen *a good* many beautiful and
>
> unexplainable things.
>
> **Josh.** *(encouragingly) Like what?* ~~What kinds of things have you seen?~~

❹ Editing and Proofreading

TARGET SKILL ▶ FORMATS FOR SCRIPTS Although the format for stage scripts differs from the format for television and film scripts, there are some common conventions to follow.

- Dialogue does not have quotation marks.
- The name of each speaker is set off so actors can find their lines easily.
- Speaking directions follow the name of the character.
- Directions for movements appear in the script where the action happens.
- General directions for props, lighting, or sound effects for a whole scene appear in a separate paragraph.

❺ Reflecting

FOR YOUR WORKING PORTFOLIO What did you learn about writing dialogue for a dramatic scene? How could you make your characters and situation more realistic next time? Attach your answers to your finished work. Save your dramatic scene in your **Working Portfolio.**

Publishing IDEAS

- Choose several scenes from your class to produce and present to other classes.
- Videotape your scene to show to family members and friends.

More Online: Publishing Options www.mcdougallittell.com

Read this paragraph from the first draft of a drama review. The underlined sections may include the following kinds of errors:

- **lack of pronoun-antecedent agreement**
- **punctuation errors**
- **run-on sentences**
- **incorrect possessive forms**

For each underlined section, choose the revision that most improves the writing.

The Littletown Community <u>Players</u> current revue, *Watch It!*, is an
(1)
irreverent and playful look at time. <u>The set is elegantly simple, a large clock</u>
<u>hangs over the stage.</u> As the show opens, the clock chimes six A.M. <u>The cast of</u>
(2)
<u>four engaging performers wake up and begin his or her day.</u> This is a
(3)
convenient device for the cast to sing some old standby songs about time. <u>My</u>
<u>favorites included "Rock Around the Clock," "Five O'clock World," and "Nine to</u>
(4)
<u>Five."</u> The show closes with a sensational performance by Martha Ryan. The
entire audience was caught up in <u>Ryans'</u> stirring version of <u>"Time After Time"</u>.
(5)   (6)

---

1. A. Players's
  B. Player's
  C. Players'
  D. Correct as is

2. A. The set is elegantly simple a large clock hangs over the stage.
  B. The set is elegantly simple; a large clock hangs over the stage.
  C. The set is elegantly simple a large clock, hangs over the stage.
  D. The set is elegantly simple. A large clock hangs, over the stage.

3. A. The cast of four engaging performers wake up and begin their day.
  B. Each member of the engaging cast wakes up and begin their day.
  C. The cast of four, each an engaging performer, wakes up and begins his or her day.
  D. Correct as is

4. A. My favorites included "Rock Around the Clock, Five O'clock World, and Nine to Five."
  B. My favorites included "Rock Around the Clock," Five O'clock World, and "Nine to Five."
  C. My favorites included Rock Around the Clock, Five O'clock World, and Nine to Five.
  D. Correct as is

5. A. Ryan's
  B. Ryans
  C. Ryan'
  D. Correct as is

6. A. "Time After Time.".
  B. Time After Time.
  C. "Time After Time."
  D. "Time After Time"

Need extra help?

See the **Grammar Handbook**

Possessive Nouns, p. 1392

Pronoun Agreement, p. 1393

Punctuation Chart, pp. 1413–1414

Correcting run-on Sentences, p. 1409

Building New Words

Part of what makes English a flexible language is the ease with which new words can be created by adding word parts to the beginning or end of existing words. The lines from William Butler Yeats's "The Second Coming" at the right contain an example—*falconer*.

Knowing the meaning and function of the word part *-er* can help you understand the word *falconer*. One meaning of *-er* is "one who," signifying a person occupationally associated with the thing named by the word to which it is attached. A falconer, therefore, is someone who works with falcons.

> Turning and turning in the widening gyre
> The falcon cannot hear the falconer;
> —W. B. Yeats, "The Second Coming"

Strategies for Building Vocabulary

Roots and base words form the foundation of almost all complex words. **Roots** are core word parts that cannot stand alone, like *dict,* a Latin root meaning "speak." **Base words** are simple complete words, like *turn.* In order to produce words with various meanings, word parts called affixes, such as *anti-* and *-er,* are added to roots and base words. Learning the meanings of affixes can help you decode unfamiliar words and create new words.

❶ **Look for Prefixes** Affixes added to the beginning of base words and roots are called **prefixes.** For example, adding the prefix *anti-,* meaning "against," to the base word *social* creates the word *antisocial,* meaning "shunning the society of others."

Prefixes Expressing Direction

Prefix	Meaning	Words
ab-	away from	abscond, abhor, abstract
circum-	around	circumference, circumspect
inter-	among, between	interject, intercede

Prefixes Expressing Quantity

Prefix	Meaning	Words
equi-	equal	equinox, equilibrium
over-	too much	overbearing, overindulge
poly-	many	polyglot, polyester

❷ **Look for Suffixes** Affixes added to the end of roots and base words are called **suffixes.** There are two types of suffixes: inflectional suffixes and derivational suffixes. An **inflectional suffix** shows a change in number (*falcon/falcons*), tense (*reiterate/reiterated*), or degree of comparison (*livelier/liveliest*). A **derivational suffix** changes a word's part of speech and may add meaning. For example, adding the negative suffix *-less* to the noun *expression* creates the adjective *expressionless,* meaning "without expression."

Noun Suffixes

Suffix	Meaning	Words
-ance	state or action of	repentance
-ation	process of	indoctrination, emancipation
-mony	product of	testimony, ceremony

Adjective Suffixes

Suffix	Meaning	Words
-ent	causing	absorbent, fraudulent
-ose	full of, having a quality of	comatose, verbose
-ous	characterized by	contemptuous, fallacious

Verb Suffixes

Suffix	Meaning	Words
-ate	to engage in the action of	decimate, infiltrate
-fy	to make	amplify, stultify
-ize	to treat as	dramatize, marginalize

EXERCISE Identify the base word in each word below. Then use a dictionary to identify the meanings of the affixes. Classify each suffix as inflectional or derivational.

1. dissatisfied
2. extraordinarily
3. prehistoric
4. semidarkness
5. inconsiderable

Grammar from Literature

Writers use sentence closers for a variety of reasons.
- To provide concrete details.
- To produce sentence variety and interesting sentence rhythms.

A sentence closer can be a word, phrase, or clause. It is called a closer because it appears at the end of a sentence—after the main idea. Many types of words, phrases, and clauses can be used as closers. Some types of closers are shown below, in examples from D. H. Lawrence's "The Rocking-Horse Winner."

> single word
> "That's right," said Bassett, nodding.

> prepositional phrase
> "Oh, well, sometimes I'm absolutely sure, like about Daffodil."

> So he would mount again and start on his furious ride,
> participial phrase
> hoping at last to get there.

> adverb clause
> He became wild-eyed and strange, as if something were going to explode in him.

Writers sometimes combine several elements in closers.

> appositive
> He had a secret within a secret, something he had not
> adverbial phrase
> divulged, even to Bassett or to his Uncle Oscar.

> adverb   prepositional phrase
> He went off by himself, vaguely, in a childish way,
> participial phrase
> seeking for the clue to "luck."

Using Sentence Closers in Your Writing Sentence closers provide a way to add detail to your writing and to vary your sentence structures. Sometimes during revision, you may think of an additional word or phrase that, added as a closer, will make an idea clearer. At other times, you may notice that you can express an idea in fewer words if you create a sentence closer by combining two sentences.

> ORIGINAL
> She invited the young woman to her home.

> REWRITTEN
> She invited the young woman to her home, but not out of total selflessness.

> ORIGINAL
> The Derby is named for the twelfth Earl of Derbyshire. The earl founded the race in 1780.

> REWRITTEN
> The Derby is named for the twelfth Earl of Derbyshire, who founded the race in 1780.

Usage Tip As you add closers to your sentences, be sure to use the word *like* properly. *Like* may be used to introduce a prepositional phrase. *Like* may not be used to introduce a clause. Use *as,* or as *if,* to introduce a clause.

> CORRECT
> I enjoy stories with a touch of suspense, like this story.

> INCORRECT
> The mother tries to act like she adores her children.

> CORRECT
> The mother tries to act as if she adores her children.

WRITING EXERCISE Combine each sentence pair, adding the underlined portion as a closer to the first sentence. Omit words in italics. Punctuate correctly.

1. The voices in the house grow louder. *They were so loud they were* frightening Paul.
2. Paul worries about his mother. *He can see that she is* a bitter, unhappy woman.
3. Paul rides the rocking horse. *He moves* as if he were in a trance.
4. Paul believes Bassett is someone who is *trustworthy. Bassett is* trustworthy enough to keep the money.
5. At the end Paul dies. *Clearly, he is* exhausted.

GRAMMAR EXERCISE Rewrite the sentences below, correcting errors involving the use of the word *like.* If there is no error, write *Correct.*

1. Like Paul's mother says, the family has had no luck.
2. Voices in the house make it seem like the house were alive.
3. Children like Paul should not have to worry about money.
4. At first Uncle Oscar acts like Paul can't know anything about horse racing.
5. Paul is lucky to have a loyal friend like Bassett.

PART 2 Shocking Realities

The first half of the 20th century was one of the most violent times in human history. The bloodshed and atrocities of two world wars shocked people everywhere and altered the course of British life. Throughout the century, many writers have explored the purposes, experiences, and consequences of war. The selections in this part of Unit Six will challenge you to define your own views and beliefs.

An Irish Airman Foresees His Death

Poetry by WILLIAM BUTLER YEATS

The Soldier

Poetry by RUPERT BROOKE

Dreamers

Poetry by SIEGFRIED SASSOON

(Connect to Your Life)

Call to Arms What if your country were suddenly engaged in a full-scale war with another country? Would you volunteer for military service? Would your decision depend on what caused the war, where it was fought, or who the enemy was? Share your thoughts.

Build Background

World War I At the start of the 20th century, the British were for the most part optimistic. Few anticipated a major conflict. However, a feverish sense of nationalism—the belief that loyalty to one's nation comes before all other loyalties—had led the British government and the governments of other nations to stockpile weapons and to issue increasingly alarming threats to their rivals. Tension mounted between countries with opposing goals, and the assassination of an Austrian archduke in 1914 ignited a war that quickly pulled in all the major powers of Europe. The war, known at the time as the Great War and later as World War I, was a devastating four-year conflict that spread to the Middle East, Africa, Asia, and the Pacific, although most of the major battles were fought in Europe. The casualty count was enormous—more than 8.5 million soldiers killed and approximately 21 million wounded.

Perhaps because World War I affected a large portion of the British population, it inspired an abundance of British literature. The military ranks included not only professional soldiers like those who had fought in previous wars but also civilian volunteers and draftees, most of whom were unprepared for the grim realities of warfare. Many experienced changes in attitude during the course of the war, with the patriotism and enthusiasm of the first two years turning into disillusionment and despair as the war dragged on. Rupert Brooke and Siegfried Sassoon were among those who set off to defend their nation.

Focus Your Reading

LITERARY ANALYSIS **SPEAKER** As you know, the **speaker** of a poem—the voice that "talks" to the reader—may be either a distant observer not directly involved in the situation he or she describes or a participant in the situation presented in the poem. In either case, the speaker should not necessarily be identified with the poet. As you read, be aware of details that indicate how involved each speaker is with the situation described.

ACTIVE READING **MAKING INFERENCES** These poems present three different perspectives on World War I, though the speakers do not directly state their attitudes. To fully appreciate these perspectives, you must read between the lines, or **make inferences,** about what each speaker says.

READER'S NOTEBOOK Create a chart like the one shown, recording words and phrases that you think help to convey each speaker's attitude toward war.

Poem	Attitude Toward War
"An Irish Airman . . ."	
"The Soldier"	
"Dreamers"	

Detail of *The Bombing of El-Afuleh Railway Junction*, C. R. Fleming-Williams.
Imperial War Museum, London.

William Butler Yeats

An Irish Airman Foresees His Death

I know that I shall meet my fate
Somewhere among the clouds above;
Those that I fight I do not hate,
Those that I guard I do not love;
5   My country is Kiltartan Cross,
My countrymen Kiltartan's poor,
No likely end could bring them loss
Or leave them happier than before.
Nor law, nor duty bade me fight,
10   Nor public men, nor cheering crowds.
A lonely impulse of delight
Drove to this tumult in the clouds;
I balanced all, brought all to mind,
The years to come seemed waste of breath,
15   A waste of breath the years behind
In balance with this life, this death.

4 Those that I guard . . . love:
Many of the Irish—even those who
fought beside the English against
the Germans—resented their
English rulers.

5 Kiltartan: a district in the west
of Ireland.

Thinking Through the Literature

1. Jot down words that come to mind when you think about the
speaker of this poem.

2. How do you think the speaker feels each time he gets into his plane?

3. What factors may have influenced the speaker's decision to go to war?

The Soldier

Rupert Brooke

Wounded in the Chest: "Just Out of the Trenches near Arras," Sir William Orpen. Imperial War Museum, London.

If I should die, think only this of me,
    That there's some corner of a foreign field
That is forever England. There shall be
    In that rich earth a richer dust concealed,
5 A dust whom England bore, shaped, made aware,
    Gave, once, her flowers to love, her ways to roam,
A body of England's, breathing English air,
    Washed by the rivers, blest by suns of home.

And think, this heart, all evil shed away,
10   A pulse in the Eternal mind, no less
        Gives somewhere back the thoughts by England given,
    Her sights and sounds; dreams happy as her day;
        And laughter, learnt of friends; and gentleness,
            In hearts at peace, under an English heaven.

Thinking Through the Literature

1. After reading this poem, what thoughts or questions do you have?
2. How would you describe the **tone** of the poem?
3. In your opinion, would the sentiments expressed in this poem console the speaker's loved ones? Explain your view.

Dreamers

Siegfried Sassoon

Soldiers are citizens of death's gray land,
    Drawing no dividend from time's tomorrows.
In the great hour of destiny they stand,
    Each with his feuds, and jealousies, and sorrows.
5 Soldiers are sworn to action; they must win
    Some flaming, fatal climax with their lives.
Soldiers are dreamers; when the guns begin
    They think of firelit homes, clean beds and wives.

I see them in foul dugouts, gnawed by rats,
10   And in the ruined trenches, lashed with rain,
Dreaming of things they did with balls and bats,
    And mocked by hopeless longing to regain
Bank holidays, and picture shows, and spats,
    And going to the office in the train.

Connect to the Literature

1. **What Do You Think?** What images were left in your mind after you read "Dreamers"?

> **Comprehension Check**
> • What do the soldiers dream about?

Think Critically

2. What contrasts are made in "Dreamers"? How do you think these contrasts contribute to the poem's impact?

3. Do you think the **speaker** expects that the soldiers' dreams will be fulfilled? Give reasons to support your opinion.

4. **ACTIVE READING** **MAKING INFERENCES** Based on the chart you created in your 📖**READER'S NOTEBOOK** , explain how you think the speakers' attitudes toward war differ in these three poems.

5. Which poem, "The Soldier" or "Dreamers," was most likely written at the start of the war? Cite evidence to support your answer.

Extend Interpretations

6. **Writer's Style** All three of these poems contain parallelism—the use of similar grammatical structures to express related or equally important ideas—and repetition. Find examples of parallelism or repetition in the three poems. Compare and contrast the ways in which these devices contribute to the overall effect of each poem.

7. **Comparing Texts** In your opinion, which speaker in these three war poems would be most likely to share the feelings expressed by the speaker of Thomas Hardy's "The Man He Killed" (page 953)? Give reasons for your choice.

8. **Connect to Life** Do you think any of the thoughts expressed in these three poems would be relevant to soldiers fighting in wars today? Explain your opinion.

Literary Analysis

SPEAKER In each of these three poems, the **speaker** is intimately involved with the situation being described. In two of the poems, the speakers speculate on their own fates, as in the opening lines of "An Irish Airman Foresees His Death":

I know that I shall meet my fate /
Somewhere among the clouds
*   above;*

As you know, the speaker is not necessarily to be identified with the poet. Yeats himself was not an air-man; he modeled the speaker after a real pilot he knew.

Paired Activity Create a chart like the one shown and note details about each speaker. Then compare your chart with a partner's. How important is the identity of each speaker? How would each poem be different if the speaker were a distant observer?

Poem	Speaker's Identity	Speaker's Participation in Events	Speaker's Character
"An Irish Airman Foresees His Death"			
"The Soldier"			
"Dreamers"			

Writing Options

1. Wartime Epitaphs Compose brief epitaphs for the speakers of "An Irish Airman Foresees His Death," "The Soldier," and "Dreamers." In each epitaph, include details that convey the unique qualities of the individual who is its subject.

2. Letter to a Soldier If you were sending a "CARE package" to one of the speakers, what might you include in it? Write a letter to accompany the package, explaining what you are sending and why you chose those things.

3. Multimedia Notes Make notes for an online multimedia presentation on poetry about World War I. Sketch a flowchart that shows how the different parts of your presentation would be connected. Place the notes and chart in your **Working Portfolio.**

4. Bumper Stickers If the speakers of these three poems chose to express their attitudes toward war on bumper stickers, what sentiments might they express? Write messages for three different bumper stickers, one for each speaker.

Activities & Explorations

1. Role Play With a partner, role-play a counseling session in which you offer advice to the speaker of either "An Irish Airman Foresees His Death" or "Dreamers." ~ **PERFORMING**

2. Soldier Rating With a group of classmates, discuss the qualities—both strengths and weaknesses—of the speaker of each poem, and decide how those qualities might affect his performance as a soldier. In an informal vote, choose the speaker you think would make the best soldier; then give a brief rationale for your choice.
~ **SPEAKING AND LISTENING**

3. Choral Reading With a small group of classmates, plan and present a dramatic choral reading of the three poems. Use special effects—such as lighting, background music, and costumes—to help convey the moods and messages of the poems.

As you are preparing, work with your classmates to develop criteria for evaluating a literary performance.

After the choral reading, have classmates use the criteria to analyze, evaluate, and critique your performance.
~ **SPEAKING AND LISTENING**

4. War Diorama Create a miniature diorama depicting the setting presented in one of the three poems. ~ **ART**

Inquiry & Research

World War I Songs Locate printed versions or recordings of songs that were popular during World War I. Read the lyrics or play a few of the songs for the class. As you listen to the lyrics of each song, try to answer these questions: What message about war does the song convey? How might wartime listeners have reacted to the message?

William Butler Yeats 1865–1939 A biography of William Butler Yeats appears on page 993.

Rupert Brooke
1887–1915

Other Works
"The Dead"
"Peace"
"Safety"
"The Old Vicarage"
"Grantchester"

Youthful Promise Rupert Brooke, an extraordinarily handsome and intelligent young man who excelled at both athletics and academics while attending Cambridge University, was regarded as one of Britain's most promising poets. During his brief life, he mingled with such prominent figures as Virginia Woolf and Winston Churchill. At the outbreak of World War I, he joined the Royal Navy and began training for combat. During this time he wrote *1914,* a series of five war sonnets that included "The Soldier."

Victim of War The young poet saw very little wartime action, however, for he fell victim to blood poisoning on the way to his first major conflict. He died at the age of 27 on a hospital ship in the Aegean Sea and was buried on the Aegean island of Skíros. Upon learning of Brooke's death, Churchill, then first lord of the admiralty, recalled that the poet-soldier was "joyous, fearless, versatile . . . all one could wish England's noblest sons to be."

Author Activity

Poet of Youth In an essay written in 1919, the British poet Walter de la Mare referred to the "life-giving youthfulness" of Brooke's poetry. Read several of Brooke's other poems, and discuss what you think of de la Mare's assessment.

Siegfried Sassoon
1886–1967

Other Works
"Absolution"
"To Victory"
"To My Brother"
"Golgotha"
"A Working Party"

From Student to Soldier Although Siegfried Sassoon began writing poetry as a child, he was more interested in sports than in scholastic achievement. Born to a prosperous family in Kent, he attended Cambridge University but left without a degree. He joined the army just a few days before England declared war and, while serving as an infantry officer in France, was wounded several times and received the Military Cross for bravery.

From Soldier to Pacifist Sassoon's experiences in trench warfare affected him profoundly, however, and his early idealism turned to bitter disillusionment as the war progressed. In 1917, having become a pacifist, he wrote his commanding officer a letter protesting the continuation of the war. The letter might have led to a court-martial, but Sassoon was instead briefly hospitalized for shell shock, then sent back to the battlefield, where he was wounded in the head. His wartime experiences were not easily forgotten, and he continued to write about them long after the conflict ended.

Author Activity

Brothers in Arms Find out more about Sassoon's influence on another poet who wrote about World War I, Wilfred Owen. How did the two meet? What part did Sassoon play in securing public recognition of Owen's poetry?

from Testament of Youth

Memoir by VERA BRITTAIN

Small Obligation → Great Obligation

Family
Friends
Community
Society
Myself

Weighing Obligations Most of us live in a web of relationships. We have ties to our families, to friends, to the communities in which we live, and to society as a whole. How committed are you to your family? your friends? society? yourself? Make a bar graph like the one shown, rating your senses of obligation to the different groups in your life. Then, with your classmates, discuss times when a person might experience conflicting obligations.

Build Background

Brittain's Life Vera Brittain's autobiographical *Testament of Youth* is a rare account of World War I from the perspective of a young woman. Brittain lived at a time when options for women were limited. Her childhood was sheltered and comfortable, yet she grew up to find few opportunities for personal and professional growth. Although she had a close relationship with her brother, Edward, Brittain was well aware that many choices open to him were denied to her. For example, Brittain's father—like many people of the time—thought that a university education was valuable for a son but wasted on a daughter. Yet Brittain convinced her father to let her attend Somerville College at Oxford University. She entered in 1914, shortly after World War I broke out in Europe.

Although the war seemed somewhat remote to Brittain at first, it soon changed her life. After her fiancé, Roland Leighton, was sent to the front lines, and then as news of war casualties began to come through, Brittain felt a sense of obligation to join the war effort. She interrupted her education to train as an army nurse—nursing being one of the few war-related jobs available to women. In 1915, while caring for wounded soldiers in London, Brittain learned that her fiancé had been killed by enemy fire. In 1916, she requested duty near the front lines, and she was eventually assigned to a field hospital near Étaples (ā-täp' lə), France. This selection begins during Brittain's time in Étaples.

WORDS TO KNOW
Vocabulary Preview

awry	incessant
bravado	insoluble
dissipation	quiescence
ethereal	semblance
excruciating	travesty

Focus Your Reading

| LITERARY ANALYSIS | MEMOIR | *Testament of Youth* is a **memoir**—a form of autobiographical writing in which a person recalls significant events in his or her life. Brittain's memoir deals with an important historical event—World War I—but this is presented from the writer's personal perspective. For example, instead of simply giving facts about bombing raids, Brittain writes:

> *I knew that I was more frightened than I had ever been in my life, yet all the time a tense, triumphant pride . . . held me to the semblance of self-control.*

As you read, be aware of the writer's personal perspective.

| ACTIVE READING | DISTINGUISHING FACT FROM OPINION | Because memoirs often include the writers' feelings and opinions about historical events, they give readers insight into the impact of history on people's lives. Be sure to distinguish Brittain's feelings and opinions from the historical facts she presents.

📖 **READER'S NOTEBOOK** Keep two lists as you read this selection. In one, record the historical information that Brittain provides; in the other, record Brittain's personal feelings and opinions.

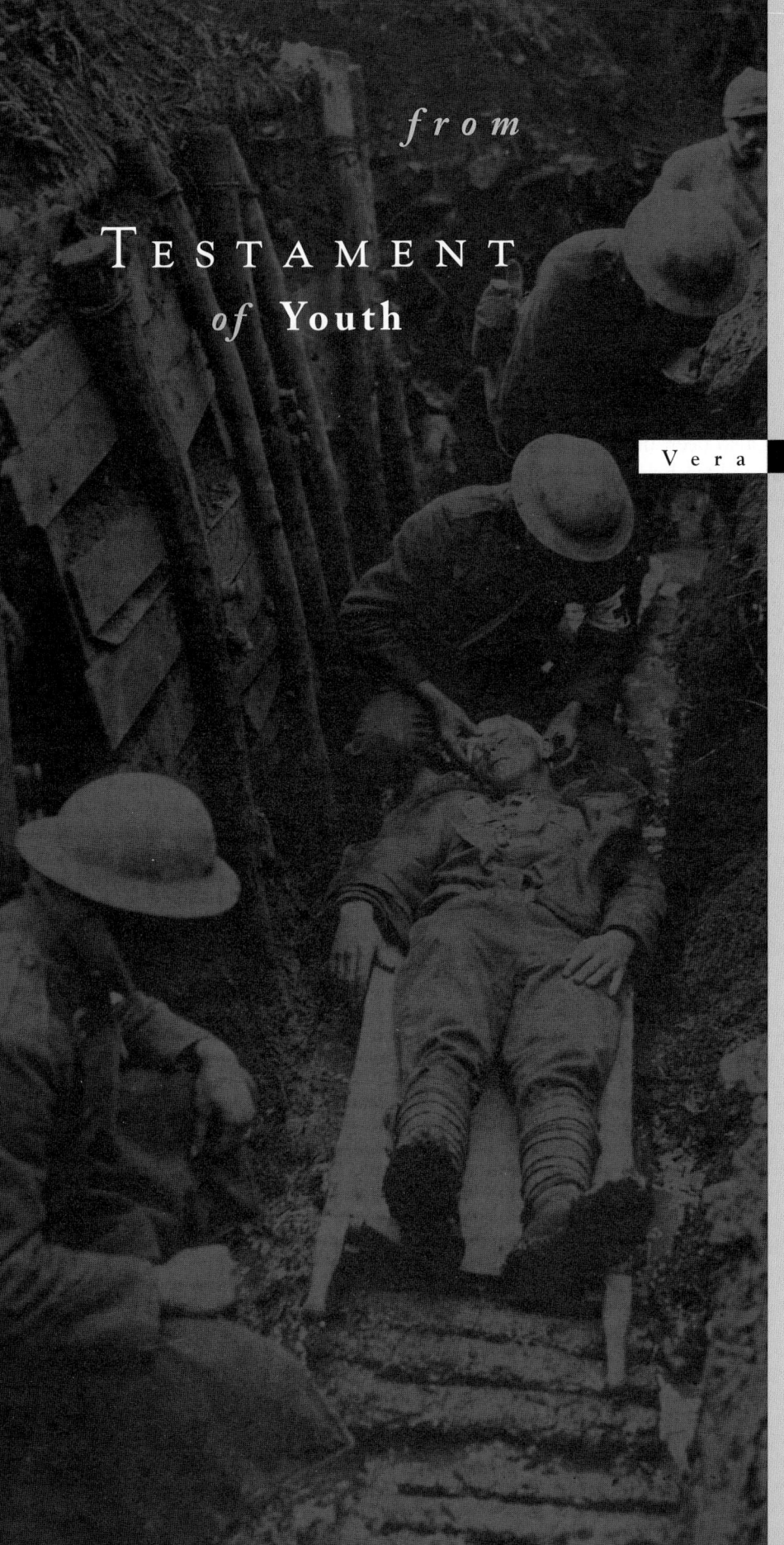

from

TESTAMENT
of Youth

Vera   Brittain

After
days of
continuous
heavy duty

and scamped,[1] inadequate meals, our nerves were none too reliable, and I don't suppose I was the only member of the staff whose teeth chattered with sheer terror as we groped our way to our individual huts in response to the order to scatter. Hope Milroy and I, thinking that we might as well be killed together, sat glassy-eyed in her small, pitch-black room. Suddenly, intermittent flashes half blinded us, and we listened frantically in the deafening din for the bugle call which we knew would summon us to join the night staff in the wards if bombs began to fall on the hospital.

---

1. **scamped:** hurried.

One young Sister,[2] who had previously been shelled at a Casualty Clearing Station, lost her nerve and rushed screaming through the Mess;[3] two others seized her and forcibly put her to bed, holding her down while the raid lasted to prevent her from causing a panic. I knew that I was more frightened than I had ever been in my life, yet all the time a tense, triumphant pride that I was not revealing my fear to the others held me to the <u>semblance</u> of self-control.

When a momentary lull came in the booms and the flashes, Hope, who had also been under fire at a C.C.S., gave way to the sudden <u>bravado</u> of rushing into the open to see whether the raiders had gone; she was still wearing her white cap, and a dozen trembling hands instantly pulled her indoors again, a dozen shakily shrill voices scolded her indiscretion. Gradually, after another brief burst of firing, the camp became quiet, though the lights were not turned on again that night. Next day we were told that most of the bombs had fallen on the village; the bridge over the Canche,[4] it was reported, had been smashed, and the train service had to be suspended while the engineers performed the exciting feat of mending it in twelve hours. . . .

. . . Within the next few weeks a good night's rest proved impossible for most of us. The liability to be called up for late convoys[5] had already induced a habit of light, restless dozing, and the knowledge that the raiders meant business and might return at any moment after sunset did not help us to settle down quietly and confidently during the hours of darkness. Whenever a particularly tiring day had battered our exhausted nerves into indifference, the lights went out as the result of alarming reports from Abbeville or Camiers[6] and revived our apprehensions. Rumor declared that we were all to be issued with steel helmets, and further spasmodic efforts were made to provide us with trenches in case of emergency.

Three weeks of such days and nights, lived without respite or off-duty time under the permanent fear of defeat and flight, reduced the staffs of the Étaples hospitals to the negative conviction that nothing mattered except to end the strain. England, panic-stricken, was frantically raising the military age to fifty and agreeing to the appointment of Foch[7] as Commander-in-Chief, but to us with our blistered feet, our swollen hands, our wakeful, reddened eyes, victory and defeat began—as indeed they were afterwards to prove—to seem very much the same thing. . . .

Just when the Retreat had reduced the strip of coast between the line and the sea to its narrowest dimensions, the summons came that I had subconsciously dreaded ever since my uncomfortable leave.

> Victory and defeat began—as indeed they were afterwards to prove—to seem very much the same thing. . . .

Early in April a letter arrived from my father to say that my mother had "crocked up" and had been obliged, owing to the inefficiency of the domestic help then available, to go into a nursing home. What exactly was wrong remained unspecified, though phrases referred to

---

2. **Sister:** nurse.

3. **Mess:** mess hall—the place where people in the armed forces eat meals.

4. **Canche** (känsh): the river on which Étaples is located.

5. **convoys:** groups of vehicles traveling with protective escorts (here, they are bringing wounded soldiers).

6. **reports from Abbeville** (äb-vēl′) **or Camiers** (kä-myä′): In March 1918, the Germans were advancing on these French towns, which lie directly between Étaples and Paris. As the British retreated toward the coast, it was feared that Étaples itself might be captured or cut off.

7. **Foch** (fôsh): Ferdinand Foch, a French general who in March 1918 became commander of all Allied forces on the western front.

WORDS
TO
KNOW

semblance (sĕm′bləns) *n.* an outward appearance
bravado (brə-vä′dō) *n.* a reckless or false show of courage

"toxic heart" and "complete general break-down." My father had temporarily closed the flat and moved into a hotel, but he did not, he told me, wish to remain there. "As your mother and I can no longer manage without you," he concluded, "it is now your duty to leave France immediately and return to Kensington."[8]

I read these words with real dismay, for my father's interpretation of my duty was not, I knew only too well, in the least likely to agree with that of the Army, which had always been singularly unmoved by the worries of relatives. What was I to do? I wondered desperately. There was my family, confidently demanding my presence, and here was the offensive, which made every pair of experienced hands worth ten pairs under normal conditions. I remembered how the hastily imported VADs had gone sick at the 1st London[9] during the rush after the Somme;[10] a great push was no time in which to teach a tyro[11] her job. How much of my mother's breakdown was physical and how much psychological—the cumulative result of pessimism at home? It did not then occur to me that my father's sense of emergency was probably heightened by a subconscious determination to get me back to London before the Germans reached the Channel ports,[12] as everyone in England felt certain they would. I only knew that no one in France would believe a domestic difficulty to be so insoluble; if I were dead, or a male, it would have to be settled without me. I should merely be thought to have "wind-up,"[13] to be using my mother's health as an excuse to escape the advancing enemy or the threatening air raids.

Half-frantic with the misery of conflicting obligations, I envied Edward his complete power-lessness to leave the Army whatever happened at home. . . . What exhausts women in wartime is not the strenuous and unfamiliar tasks that fall upon them, nor even the hourly dread of death for husbands or lovers or brothers or sons; it is the incessant conflict between personal and national claims which wears out their energy and breaks their spirit.

That night, dizzy from work and indecision, I sat up in bed listening for an air raid and gazing stupidly at the flickering shadows cast by the candle lantern which was all the illumination that we were now allowed. Through my brain ran perpetually a short sentence which—having become, like the men, liable to sudden light-headed intervals—I could not immediately identify with anything that I had read.

" 'The strain all along,' " I repeated dully, " 'is very great . . . very great.' " What exactly did those words describe? The enemy within shelling distance—refugee Sisters crowding in with nerves all awry—bright moonlight, and airplanes carrying machine guns—ambulance trains jolting noisily into the siding, all day, all night—gassed men on stretchers, clawing the air—dying men, reeking with mud and foul green-stained bandages, shrieking and writhing in a grotesque travesty of manhood—dead men with fixed, empty eyes and shiny, yellow faces. . . . Yes, perhaps the strain all along *had* been very great. . . .

Then I remembered; the phrase came out of my father's letter, and it described, not the offensive in France, but the troubles at home. The next day I went to the Matron's[14] office and interviewed the successor to the friendly Scottish Matron who had

---

8. **Kensington:** a residential section of London.

9. **VADs . . . at the 1st London:** Voluntary Aid Detachment nurses at another Étaples hospital.

10. **the Somme** (sŏm): In July 1916, the Allies had launched what turned into a devastating, months-long battle along the Somme River; it resulted in more than a million casualties.

11. **tyro** (tī′rō): beginner.

12. **Channel ports:** seaports on the English Channel.

13. **"wind-up"** (wĭnd′ŭp′): a British slang term meaning "nervousness" or "anxious excitement."

14. **Matron's:** head nurse's.

WORDS TO KNOW

insoluble (ĭn-sŏl′yə-bəl) *adj.* incapable of being solved
incessant (ĭn-sĕs′ənt) *adj.* never ceasing; constant
awry (ə-rī′) *adj.* twisted; faulty; disordered
travesty (trăv′ĭ-stē) *n.* a distorted, bizarre imitation

1117

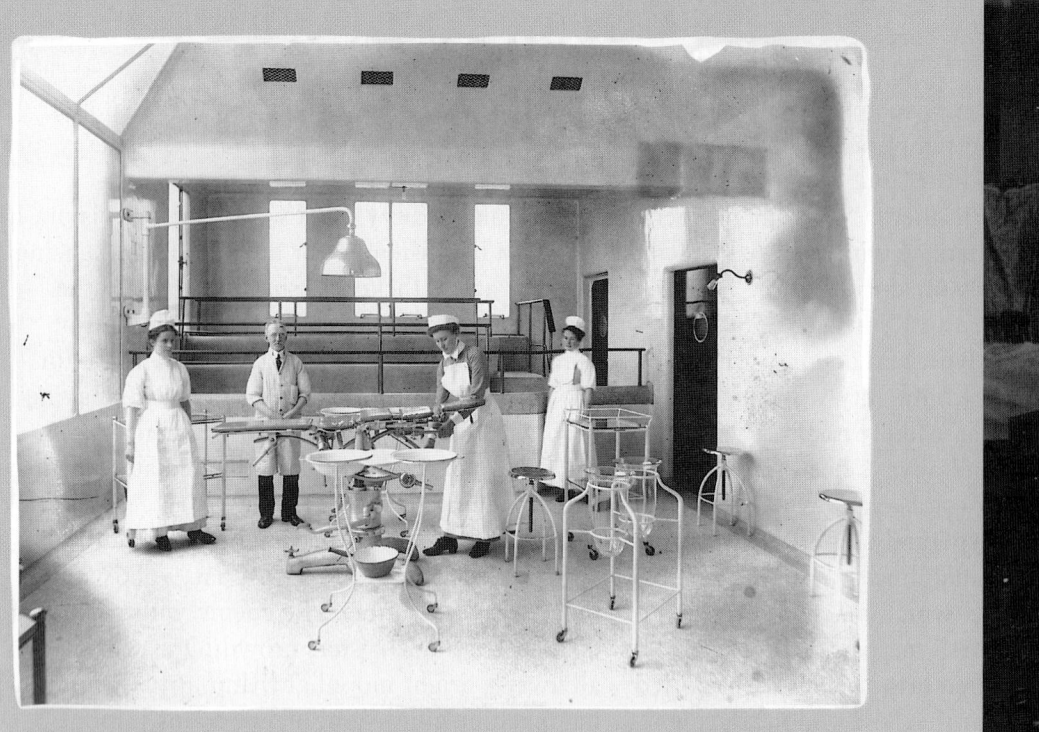
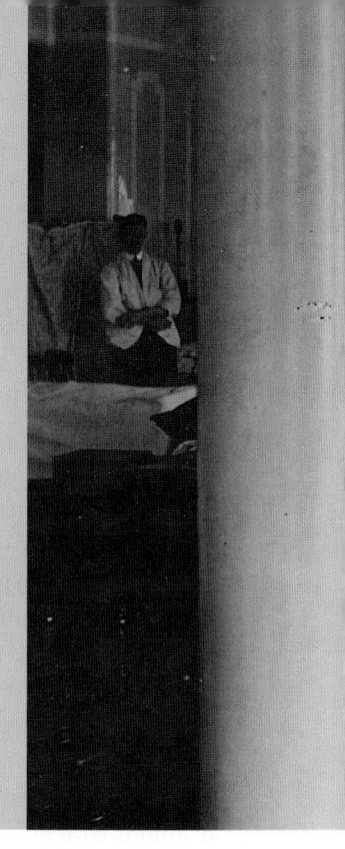

sent me on leave, and whose health had obliged her to leave Étaples and return to the calmer conditions of home service. The new Matron was old and charitable, but she naturally did not welcome my problem with enthusiasm. The application for long leave which I had hoped to put in would have, she said, no chance at all while this push was on; the only possibility was to break my contract, which I might be allowed to do if I made conditions at home sound serious enough.

"I'm giving you this advice against my will," she added. "I'm already short of staff and I can't hope to replace you."

So, with a sinking heart, I asked for leave to break my contract owing to "special circumstances," and returned to my ward feeling a cowardly deserter. Only to Edward could I express the explosive misery caused by my dilemma, and he replied with his usual comprehending sympathy.

"I can well understand how exasperating it must be for you to have to go home now . . . when you have just been in the eddying backwater of the sternest fight this War has known; it

is one of those little ironies which life has ready to offer at a most inopportune moment. I suppose that the Armentières[15] push will have affected you more nearly still as it is not so very far away. . . ."

I was glad that my orders did not come through until almost the end of April, when the offensive against the British had slackened, and we knew for certain that we had not yet lost the War.

Early one morning I bade a forlorn farewell to my friends and went down alone in an ambulance to the station. . . . As the train passed through Hardelot,[16] I noticed that the woods on either side of the line were vivid with a golden green latticework of delicate leaves. For a whole month in which off-duty time had been impossible, I had ceased to be aware of the visible world of the French countryside; my eyes had seen nothing but the wards and the dying, the dirt and dried blood, the obscene wounds of

---

15. **Armentières** (är-mäN-tyĕr′): a town, only 40 miles from Étaples, taken by the Germans in April 1918.
16. **Hardelot** (är-də-lō′).

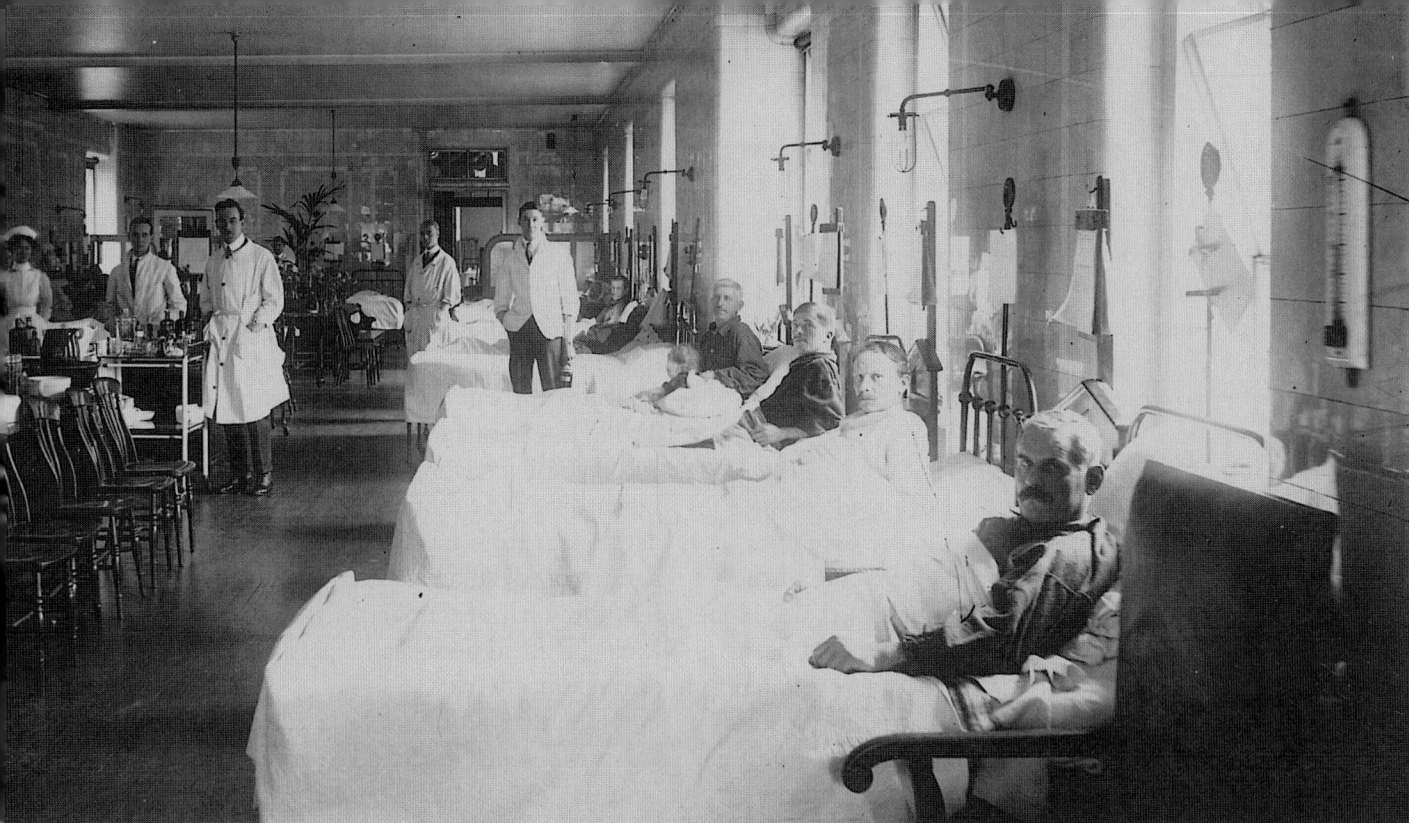

mangled men and the lotions and lint with which I had dressed them. Looking, now, at the pregnant buds, the green veil flung over the trees and the spilt cream of primroses in the bright, wet grass, I realized with a pang of astonishment that the spring had come.

I can look back more readily, I think, upon the War's tragedies—which at least had dignity—than upon those miserable weeks that followed my return from France. From a world in which life or death, victory or defeat, national survival or national extinction, had been the sole issues, I returned to a society where no one discussed anything but the price of butter and the incompetence of the latest "temporary."[17] . . .

Keyed up as I had been by the month-long strain of daily rushing to and fro in attendance on the dying, and nightly waiting for the death which hovered darkly in the sky overhead, I found it <u>excruciating</u> to maintain even an appearance of interest and sympathy. Probably I did not succeed, for the triviality of everything drove me to despair. The old feeling of frustra-

tion that I had known . . . came back a thousand times intensified; while disasters smashed up the world around me I seemed to be marooned in a kind of death-in-life, with the three years' experience that now made me of some use to the Army all thrown away.

. . . Most bitterly of all I resented the constant <u>dissipation</u> of energy on what appeared to me to be nonessentials. My youth and health had mattered so much when the task was that of dragging wounded men back to life; I believed that the vitality which kept me going had helped others who had lost their own to live, and it seemed rather thrown away when it was all exploded upon persuading the grocer to give us a pot of jam. The agony of the last few weeks in France appeared not to interest London in comparison with the struggle to obtain sugar; the latter was discussed incessantly, but no one wanted even to hear about the former. . . .

---

17. **temporary:** a domestic servant hired for a short time.

I was no better reconciled to staying at home when I read in *The Times* a few weeks after my return that the persistent German raiders had at last succeeded in their intention of smashing up the Étaples hospitals, which, with the aid of the prisoner-patients, had so satisfactorily protected the railway line for three years without further trouble or expense to the military authorities.

It was clear from the guarded *communiqué*[18] that this time the bombs had dropped on the hospitals themselves, causing many casualties and far more damage than the breaking of the bridge over the Canche in the first big raid. Hope Milroy, I was thankful to remember, had been moved to Havre[19] a fortnight earlier, but a few days later a letter from Norah filled in the gaps of the official report. The hospital next door, she told me, had suffered the worst, and several Canadian Sisters had been killed. At 24 General one of the death-dealing bombs had fallen on Ward 17, where I had nursed the pneumonias on night duty; it had shattered the hut, together with several patients, and wounded the VAD in charge, who was in hospital with a fractured skull. The Sisters' quarters were no longer safe after dark, she concluded, and they all had to spend their nights in trenches in the woods.

More than ever, as I finished her letter, I felt myself a deserter, a coward, a traitor to my patients and the other nurses.

How could I have played with the idea—as I had, once or twice lately—of returning to Oxford[20] before the end of the War? What did the waste of an immature intellect matter, when such things could happen to one's friends? My comrades of the push had been frightened, hurt, smashed up—and I was not there with them, skulking[21] safely in England. Why, oh why, had I listened to home demands when my job was out there?

A brief note that came just afterwards from Edward seemed an appropriate—and fear-provoking—comment on the news from Étaples.

"*Ma chère,*" he had written just before midnight on May 12th, "*la vie est brève*[22]—usually too short for me to write adequate letters, and likely to be shorter still."

For some time now, my apprehensions for his safety had been lulled by the long <u>quiescence</u> of the Italian front, which had seemed a haven of peace in contrast to our own raging vortex.[23] Repeatedly, during the German offensive, I had thanked God and the Italians who fled at Caporetto[24] that Edward was out of it, and rejoiced that the worst I had to fear from this particular push was the comparatively trivial danger that threatened myself. But now I felt the familiar stirrings of the old tense fear which had been such a persistent companion throughout the War. . . .

On Sunday morning, June 16th, I opened the *Observer,* which appeared to be chiefly concerned with the new offensive—for the moment at a standstill—in the Noyon-Montdidier[25] sector of the Western Front, and instantly saw at the head of a column the paragraph for which I had looked so long and so fearfully:

ITALIAN FRONT ABLAZE
GUN DUELS FROM MOUNTAIN TO SEA
BAD OPENING OF AN OFFENSIVE

. . . There was nothing to do in the midst of one's family but practice that concealment of fear which the long years of war had instilled,

---

18. *communiqué* (kô-mü-nē-kā´) *French:* an official communication.

19. **Havre** (hä´vrə): Le Havre, a French seaport used as an Allied troop and supply base.

20. **Oxford:** Oxford University.

21. **skulking:** hiding out.

22. *Ma chère, . . . la vie est brève* (mä shĕr´ lä vē´ ā brĕv´) *French:* My dear, . . . life is short.

23. **vortex:** whirl of activity.

24. **Caporetto** (kăp´ə-rĕt´ō): a 1917 battle near the Italian–Austro-Hungarian border that resulted in a major Allied defeat. (Edward was stationed in Italy.)

25. **Noyon-Montdidier** (nwä-yôn´ môn-dē-dyā´).

thrusting it inward until one's subconscious became a regular prison house of apprehensions and inhibitions which were later to take their revenge. My mother had arranged to stay with my grandmother at Purley[26] that week in order to get a few days' change from the flat; it was the first time that she had felt well enough since her breakdown to think of going away, and I did not want the news from Italy to make her change her plans. At length, though with instinctive reluctance, she allowed herself to be prevailed upon to go, but a profound depression hung over our parting at Charing Cross.[27]

A day or two later, more details were published of the fighting in Italy, and I learnt that the Sherwood Foresters[28] had been involved in the "show" on the plateau.[29] After that I made no pretense at doing anything but wander restlessly round Kensington or up and down the flat, and, though my father retired glumly to bed every evening at nine o'clock, I gave up writing the semi-fictitious record which I had begun of my life in France. Somehow I couldn't bring myself even to wrap up the *Spectator* and *Saturday Review* that I sent every week to Italy, and they remained in my bedroom, silent yet eloquent witnesses to the dread which my father and I, determinedly conversing on commonplace topics, each refused to put into words.

By the following Saturday we had still heard nothing of Edward. The interval usually allowed for news of casualties after a battle was seldom so long as this, and I began, with an artificial sense of lightness unaccompanied by real conviction, to think that there was perhaps, after all, no news to come. I had just announced to my father, as we sat over tea in the dining room, that I really must do up Edward's papers and take them to the post office before it closed for the weekend, when there came the sudden loud clattering at the front-door knocker that always meant a telegram.

For a moment I thought that my legs would not carry me, but they behaved quite normally as I got up and went to the door. I knew what was in the telegram—I had known for a week—but because the persistent hopefulness of the human heart refuses to allow intuitive certainty to persuade the reason of that which it knows, I opened and read it in a tearing anguish of suspense.

"Regret to inform you Captain E. H. Brittain M.C.[30] killed in action Italy June 15th."

"No answer," I told the boy mechanically, and handed the telegram to my father, who had followed me into the hall. As we went back into the dining room I saw, as though I had never seen them before, the bowl of blue delphiniums on the table; their intense color, vivid, <u>ethereal</u>, seemed too radiant for earthly flowers. Then I remembered that we should have to go down to Purley and tell the news to my mother.

I knew what was in the telegram—I had known for a week—

Late that evening, my uncle brought us all back to an empty flat. Edward's death and our sudden departure had offered the maid—at that time the amateur prostitute—an agreeable opportunity for a few hours' freedom of which she had taken immediate advantage. She had not even finished the household handkerchiefs, which I had washed that morning and intended to iron after tea; when I went into the kitchen I found them still hanging, stiff as boards, over the clotheshorse near the fire where I had left them to dry.

---

26. **Purley:** a town south of London.

27. **Charing Cross:** Charing Cross Station, a railway terminal in central London.

28. **Sherwood Foresters:** the British regiment to which Edward belonged.

29. **"show" on the plateau:** battle on the Asiago Plateau in northeastern Italy.

30. **M.C.:** holder of the Military Cross, a medal of honor.

Long after the family had gone to bed and the world had grown silent, I crept into the dining room to be alone with Edward's portrait. Carefully closing the door, I turned on the light and looked at the pale, pictured face, so dignified, so steadfast, so tragically mature. He had been through so much—far, far more than those beloved friends who had died at an earlier stage of the interminable War, leaving him alone to mourn their loss. Fate might have allowed him the little, sorry compensation of survival, the chance to make his lovely music[31] in honor of their memory. It seemed indeed the last irony that he should have been killed by the countrymen of Fritz Kreisler, the violinist whom of all others he had most greatly admired.

And suddenly, as I remembered all the dear afternoons and evenings when I had followed him on the piano as he played his violin, the sad, searching eyes of the portrait were more than I could bear, and falling on my knees before it I began to cry "Edward! Oh, Edward!" in dazed repetition, as though my persistent crying and calling would somehow bring him back.

The loss of Brittain's fiancé, brother, and friends in the war, as well as the death and suffering she witnessed in the hospitals, shaped the rest of her life. She became a pacifist and worked tirelessly to oppose war and to urge the resolving of differences through rational and peaceful means. Testament of Youth *was published in 1933, the same year Adolf Hitler became the head of government in Germany. Brittain wrote in the foreword to the book that her object was "to challenge that too easy, too comfortable relapse into forgetfulness which is responsible for history's most grievous repetitions." The following paragraph comes near the end of the book and gives her perspective on war several years after the end of World War I.*

. . . In spite of the War, which destroyed so much hope, so much beauty, so much promise, life is still here to be lived; so long as I am in the world, how can I ignore the obligation to be part of it, cope with its problems, suffer claims and interruptions? The surge and swell of its movements, its changes, its tendencies, still mold me and the surviving remnant of my generation whether we wish it or not, and no one now living will ever understand so clearly as ourselves, whose lives have been darkened by the universal breakdown of reason in 1914, how completely the future of civilized humanity depends upon the success of our present halting endeavors to control our political and social passions, and to substitute for our destructive impulses the vitalizing[32] authority of constructive thought. To rescue mankind from that domination by the irrational which leads to war could surely be a more exultant fight than war itself, a fight capable of enlarging the souls of men and women with the same heightened consciousness of living, and uniting them in one dedicated community whose common purpose transcends the individual. Only the purpose itself would be different, for its achievement would mean, not death, but life. ❖

31. **his lovely music:** Edward was an accomplished musician.
32. **vitalizing:** life-giving; invigorating.

. . . In spite of the War, which destroyed so much hope, so much beauty, so much promise, life is still here to be lived.

Connect to the Literature

1. What Do You Think?
What did you think of Vera Brittain when you finished reading?

> **Comprehension Check**
> - What does Brittain's father request in his letter?
> - How does Brittain manage to leave the war?
> - What happens to Edward?

Think Critically

2. What is your opinion of the way Brittain handled her conflicting obligations?

THINK ABOUT
- her responsibilities at the field hospital
- her parents' situation and expectations
- the position of women in society at the time
- what she most wanted for herself

3. **ACTIVE READING** **DISTINGUISHING FACT FROM OPINION** According to the writer Carolyn Heilbrun, Brittain's memoirs are effective because she "understood the terror of the world she lived through." In the light of this statement, review the lists you made in your **READER'S NOTEBOOK**. How do you think the historical facts and the feelings and opinions presented in the memoir support Heilbrun's claim?

4. What do you think was hardest for Brittain to deal with after she returned to England?

5. Reread the last paragraph of the selection. Do you agree with Brittain's ideas about humanity and war? Explain your opinion.

Extend Interpretations

6. What If? What might have happened if Brittain had not returned to England when she did?

7. Different Perspectives If Brittain had been a man, how would her sense of obligation have been different during World War I?

8. Connect to Life Do you think that women today face conflicting obligations similar to those experienced by Brittain? Support your answer with examples.

Literary Analysis

MEMOIR Most **memoirs**—autobiographical writing in which a person recalls significant events in his or her life—share the following characteristics:
- They usually are structured as narratives told by the writers themselves, using the **first-person point of view.**
- They are true accounts of actual events.
- Although basically personal, they may deal with events having a significance beyond the writers' lives.
- Unlike strictly historical accounts, they often include the writers' feelings and opinions about historical events.

Paired Activity At one point, Brittain planned to fictionalize her war experiences in a long novel. With a partner, discuss how the selection's being a memoir rather than a fictionalized account affects its impact. Keep in mind the characteristics of a memoir as you discuss your ideas.

REVIEW **THEME** **Theme** is an idea or message communicated by a work of literature. It is a perception about life or human nature. Some themes are stated directly, and some are implied; but every theme is an expression of the significance of the story being told. Certain works contain more than one theme. With a group of classmates, determine the theme or themes of Brittain's memoir. State each one in a single sentence.

Writing Options

1. Letter to Father If Brittain had decided to remain in France, how might she have explained her decision to her father? Imagine you are Brittain and write a letter to your father, explaining why you are not returning to England.

2. Words of Advice After returning to England, Brittain felt herself to be "a deserter, a coward, a traitor to my patients and the other nurses." Make notes of what you might say to her in response to these feelings.

3. War Poem Create a poem that conveys Brittain's thoughts and emotions about the bombing raids, about the death of her brother, or about war's effects on humanity.

Activities & Explorations

1. Book Jacket Design an eye-catching book jacket for Vera Brittain's *Testament of Youth.* Illustrate a scene from her memoir, and write a brief advertising message that would appeal to people of Brittain's generation. ~ **ART**

2. Class Survey Conduct a class survey to determine how many people think Brittain's decision to return home at her father's request was the right one. Tabulate the results and discuss why people responded as they did.
~ **SPEAKING AND LISTENING**

Inquiry & Research

1. Chemical Warfare Research and report on the development of chemical warfare during World War I. What chemical weapons and other technologies used in World War I were new? How did the technological developments affect the nature of war?

More Online: Research Starter
www.mcdougallittell.com

2. World War I On a map of the world, mark the battlefronts of World War I. Use encyclopedias or books about the war as resources. Be sure to identify the area of France where Vera Brittain served as a nurse and the area of Italy where her brother was killed.

Vocabulary in Action

ACTIVITY: MEANING CLUES On your paper, write the word that is described by each clue below.

1. Recyclers and conservationists oppose this in people's use of nature.

2. A person who wears expensive clothes may be wealthy only in this.

3. It would be foolish to expect to find this in an emergency room or a basketball game.

4. One's clothing might be this after a wrestling match, as might one's emotions after an argument.

5. Dentists use Novocain and other anesthetics to keep their treatments from being this.

6. Most people will quit working on a problem that seems this.

7. This is a harsh misrepresentation of what it copies.

8. Rain during a monsoon, cold at the North Pole, and complaints about taxes can all be said to be this.

9. Certain otherworldly works of art might be called this.

10. This is what a dog demonstrates by barking fiercely at a bigger dog that is safely on the other side of a sturdy fence.

WORDS TO KNOW			
awry	excruciating	semblance	
bravado	incessant	travesty	
dissipation	insoluble		
ethereal	quiescence		

Building Vocabulary
Several Words to Know in this lesson contain prefixes and suffixes. For an in-depth study of word parts, see page 1104.

Vera Brittain
1893–1970

Other Works
Testament of Friendship
Testament of Experience

The Great War Vera Brittain was reared in a comfortable middle-class home in northern England. She grew up, fell in love, and expected to live a rather conventional life—except for attending college, which few women of her time could do—but World War I got in the way of her plans. By the time she entered Oxford University's Somerville College in 1914, the war was already underway in Europe, and in 1915 she decided to postpone her studies to serve in the war like her brother, her fiancé, and her friends. From 1915 to 1919, she worked as a Red Cross nurse in several British army hospitals.

Birth of a Pacifist Brittain lost her fiancé, two friends, and her brother in the war. She also lost her youth. "My work and experiences during the war," she wrote, "turned me from an ordinary patriotic young woman into a convinced pacifist." Yet when Brittain finally returned to college after the war, she found herself serving as an unwelcome reminder of the war that her fellow students longed to forget.

Something of Value Throughout the war years, Brittain had recorded her experiences in a diary. At first, she attempted to fictionalize her experiences, but finding that her efforts rang false, she began writing a personal account of the war in the hope that she could "rescue something that might be of value . . . from the smashing up of my own youth by the war." She also hoped to remind her readers of the great suffering caused by war and to convince them to work for peace. First published in 1933, *Testament of Youth* became an immediate success, with more than 167,000 copies sold in the first year. It was acclaimed as "a moving elegy to a lost generation."

Groundbreaker Brittain continued to write memoirs about her experiences; she also continued to break new ground for women by persisting in her career after marrying. Throughout her life, Brittain was active in peace movements, for she firmly believed that "war, which is man-created, can be man-prevented."

Author Activity

Worker for Peace Brittain was a committed pacifist. Find out more about her long involvement in antiwar movements.

PREPARING to *Read*

from The Speeches, May 19, 1940

Speech by WINSTON CHURCHILL

Connect to Your Life

Moving Words Think about the most memorable speech you have ever heard. It may be one delivered by a classmate or a politician, or it may be one in a play or movie. Jot down words and phrases that describe your most vivid memories of the speech. Your description may touch on powerful statements made by the speaker, details of the speaker's tone of voice and body language, emotions you felt during the speech, or the reaction of the audience. Share your experience with some classmates.

Build Background

World War II World War II began in Europe two years before the United States became involved. Between September 1939 and May 1940, Germany—which had already annexed Austria and most of Czechoslovakia—conquered Poland, Denmark, and Norway. Just nine days before Churchill's speech, Hitler's army invaded Holland and Belgium, sweeping through those countries on its way into France. By May 19, 1940, the British troops that had been fighting in western Europe had been backed up against the ocean, ready to retreat to England.

Winston Churchill, who had just been chosen prime minister, had only three hours to prepare this speech for delivery on a BBC (British Broadcasting Corporation) radio broadcast. Although Churchill had been in politics for years, his wartime speeches made him famous and inspired the British people working on the home front to greater efforts. The spirit and determination of these workers, both male and female, during the darkest moments of the war are reflected in Churchill's speeches.

> WORDS TO KNOW
> **Vocabulary Preview**
>
> animate   indomitable
> dogged   retaliate
> gravity

Focus Your Reading

LITERARY ANALYSIS | **PERSUASION** Churchill made this radio speech at a time when the Germans appeared to be winning World War II. His goal was to persuade the British people not to lose heart. **Persuasion**—the technique of convincing an audience to adopt an opinion, perform an action, or both—generally involves two elements:

- **logical appeals** that put forward reasons and evidence to support opinions
- **emotional appeals** that stir feelings within the audience

As you read Churchill's speech, consider how well he balances these persuasive techniques.

ACTIVE READING | **EVALUATING PERSUASIVE LANGUAGE**
In making emotional appeals to an audience, a speaker or writer may use **loaded language**—words and phrases with strong emotional content. Loaded language may be used legitimately to reinforce arguments, or it may be used inappropriately to mislead by manipulating the feelings of the audience. Be on the lookout for loaded language in persuasive writing and consider its impact.

READER'S NOTEBOOK In a chart like the one shown, note examples of loaded language in the speech. Record the information they convey, the ideas they suggest, and the emotions they inspire.

Loaded Word or Phrase	Information Provided	Ideas Suggested	Emotions Inspired

from

The
SPEECHES
May 19, 1940

UPI/Bettmann.

Winston Churchill

I speak to you for the first time as Prime Minister in a solemn hour for the life of our country, of our Empire, of our Allies, and, above all, of the cause of Freedom. A tremendous battle is raging in France and Flanders.[1] The Germans, by a remarkable combination of air bombing and heavily armored tanks, have broken through the French defenses north of the Maginot Line, and strong columns of their armored vehicles are ravaging the open country, which for the first day or two was without defenders. They have penetrated deeply and spread alarm and confusion in their track. Behind them there are now appearing infantry in lorries,[2] and behind them, again, the large masses are moving forward. The regroupment of the French armies to make head against, and also to strike at, this intruding wedge has been proceeding for several days, largely assisted by the magnificent efforts of the Royal Air Force.

We must not allow ourselves to be intimidated by the presence of these armored vehicles in unexpected places behind our lines. If they are behind our Front, the French are also at many points fighting actively behind theirs. Both sides are therefore in an extremely dangerous position. And if the French Army, and our own Army, are well handled, as I believe they will be; if the French retain that genius for recovery and counterattack for which they have so long been

famous; and if the British Army shows the dogged endurance and solid fighting power of which there have been so many examples in the past—then a sudden transformation of the scene might spring into being.

It would be foolish, however, to disguise the gravity of the hour. It would be still more foolish to lose heart and courage or to suppose that well-trained, well-equipped armies numbering three or four millions of men can be overcome in the space of a few weeks, or even months, by a scoop, or raid of mechanized vehicles, however formidable. We may look with confidence to the stabilization of the Front in France, and to the general engagement of the masses, which will enable the qualities of the French and British soldiers to be matched squarely against those of their adversaries. For myself, I have invincible confidence in the French Army and its leaders. Only a very small part of that splendid army has yet been heavily engaged; and only a very small part of France has yet been invaded. There is good evidence to show that practically the whole of the specialized and mechanized forces of the enemy have been already thrown into the battle; and we know that very heavy losses have been inflicted upon them. No officer or man, no brigade or division, which grapples at close quarters with the enemy, wherever encountered, can fail to make a worthy contribution to the general result. The Armies must cast away the idea of resisting behind concrete lines or natural obstacles, and must realize that mastery can only be regained by furious and unrelenting assault. And this spirit must not only animate the High Command, but must inspire every fighting man.

In the air—often at serious odds—often at odds hitherto thought overwhelming—we have

---

1. **Flanders:** western Belgium.
2. **lorries:** the British term for motor trucks.

WORDS TO KNOW
dogged (dô′gĭd) *adj.* persistent; stubborn
gravity (grăv′ĭ-tē) *n.* seriousness; importance
animate (ăn′ə-māt′) *v.* to encourage; motivate

Our task is not only to win the battle— but to win the War.

Copyright © Hulton Deutsch Collection Limited.

been clawing down three or four to one of our enemies; and the relative balance of the British and German Air Forces is now considerably more favorable to us than at the beginning of the battle. In cutting down the German bombers, we are fighting our own battle as well as that of France. My confidence in our ability to fight it out to the finish with the German Air Force has been strengthened by the fierce encounters which have taken place and are taking place. At the same time, our heavy bombers are striking nightly at the taproot of German mechanized power, and have already inflicted serious damage upon the oil refineries on which the Nazi effort to dominate the world directly depends.

We must expect that as soon as stability is reached on the Western Front, the bulk of that hideous apparatus of aggression which gashed Holland into ruin and slavery in a few days, will be turned upon us. I am sure I speak for all when I say we are ready to face it; to endure it; and to <u>retaliate</u> against it—to any extent that the unwritten laws of war permit. There will be many men, and many women, in this island who when the ordeal comes upon them, as come it will, will feel comfort, and even a pride—that they are sharing the perils of our lads at the Front—soldiers, sailors and airmen, God bless

them—and are drawing away from them a part at least of the onslaught they have to bear. Is not this the appointed time for all to make the utmost exertions in their power? If the battle is to be won, we must provide our men with ever-increasing quantities of the weapons and ammunition they need. We must have, and have quickly, more airplanes, more tanks, more shells, more guns. There is imperious[3] need for these vital munitions. They increase our strength against the powerfully armed enemy. They replace the wastage of the obstinate struggle; and the knowledge that wastage will speedily be replaced enables us to draw more readily upon our reserves and throw them in now that everything counts so much.

Our task is not only to win the battle—but to win the War. After this battle in France abates its force, there will come the battle for our island—for all that Britain is, and all that Britain means. That will be the struggle. In that supreme emergency we shall not hesitate to take every step, even the most drastic, to call forth from our people the last ounce and the last inch of effort of which they are capable. The interests of property, the hours of labor, are nothing compared with the struggle for life and honor, for right and freedom, to which we have vowed ourselves.

I have received from the Chiefs of the French Republic, and in particular from its <u>indomitable</u> Prime Minister, M. Reynaud,[4] the most sacred pledges that whatever happens they will fight to the end, be it bitter or be it glorious. Nay, if we fight to the end, it can only be glorious.

Having received His Majesty's commission, I have found an administration of men and women of every party and of almost every point of view. We have differed and quarreled in the past; but now one bond unites us all—to wage war until victory is won, and never to surrender ourselves to servitude and shame, whatever the cost and the agony may be. This is one of the most awe-striking periods in the long history of France and Britain. It is also beyond doubt the most sublime. Side by side, unaided except by their kith and kin[5] in the great Dominions[6] and by the wide Empires which rest beneath their shield—side by side, the British and French peoples have advanced to rescue not only Europe but mankind from the foulest and most soul-destroying tyranny which has ever darkened and stained the pages of history. Behind them—behind us—behind the armies and fleets of Britain and France—gather a group of shattered States and bludgeoned races: the Czechs, the Poles, the Norwegians, the Danes, the Dutch, the Belgians—upon all of whom the long night of barbarism will descend, unbroken even by a star of hope, unless we conquer, as conquer we must; as conquer we shall.

Today is Trinity Sunday.[7] Centuries ago words were written to be a call and a spur to the faithful servants of Truth and Justice: "Arm yourselves, and be ye men of valor, and be in readiness for the conflict; for it is better for us to perish in battle than to look upon the outrage of our nation and our altar. As the Will of God is in Heaven, even so let it be."[8] ❖

---

3. **imperious** (ĭm-pîr′ē-əs): urgent; pressing.

4. **M. Reynaud:** Paul Reynaud, who had long argued, like Churchill, for firmness toward Germany and for a close British-French alliance. (*M.* is an abbreviation of *Monsieur,* "Mister.")

5. **kith and kin:** friends and relatives.

6. **Dominions:** self-governing nations within the British Commonwealth.

7. **Trinity Sunday:** the eighth Sunday after Easter, dedicated to the Trinity (Father, Son, and Holy Spirit).

8. **"Arm yourselves . . . let it be":** a quotation from 1 Maccabees 3:58–60. This book of the Apocrypha (found in only some versions of the Bible) tells of the heroism of the Maccabees, a Jewish family, in preventing the destruction of Judaism by the Syrians during the second century B.C.

To My
MOTHER

George Barker

Portrait of Mrs. B. (1937),
Edwin Dickinson. The
Baltimore (Maryland)
Museum of Art, Thomas E.
Benesch Memorial Collection
(BMA 1974.5).

Most near, most dear, most loved and most far,
Under the window where I often found her
Sitting as huge as Asia, seismic with laughter,
Gin and chicken helpless in her Irish hand,
5   Irresistible as Rabelais, but most tender for
The lame dogs and hurt birds that surround her,—
She is a procession no one can follow after
But be like a little dog following a brass band.

She will not glance up at the bomber, or condescend
10   To drop her gin and scuttle to a cellar,
But lean on the mahogany table like a mountain
Whom only faith can move, and so I send
O all my faith, and all my love to tell her
That she will move from mourning into morning.

Thinking through the LITERATURE

Connect to the Literature

1. **What Do You Think?**
   If you had been in England at the time of this speech, would Churchill's words have inspired you to help the war effort? Why or why not?

   Comprehension Check
   • What was the situation in France at the time Churchill made the speech?
   • What economic task does Churchill ask the British people to perform?
   • What does Churchill expect to happen after the fighting in France eases up?

Think Critically

2. In your opinion, which parts of the speech are most effective? Support your answer with details from the speech.

3. **ACTIVE READING** **EVALUATING PERSUASIVE LANGUAGE**
   Review the chart and examples you noted in your **READER'S NOTEBOOK**. Does Churchill use **loaded language** to reinforce logical arguments in his speech? Do you think he is justified in his use of loaded language? Explain your answers.

4. How would you describe Churchill's attitudes toward the English, the French, and the Germans? Cite words and phrases that suggest those attitudes.

Extend Interpretations

5. **Comparing Texts** Reread George Barker's poem "To My Mother" on page 1132. How do you think the speaker's mother would react to Churchill's speech?

6. **Writer's Style** Churchill's speech features the use of **parallelism**—the repetition of similar grammatical structures to express related ideas. Find two or three examples of parallelism in the speech. What do they add to the speech's effectiveness?

7. **Connect to Life** If Churchill were to give his speech today, it would be televised. How might he change it? Do you think the speech would be more or less powerful on television? Why?

Literary Analysis

PERSUASION Churchill's speech is considered one of the greatest persuasive speeches of all time because it stirred the British people to hold out against the German assault on their homeland. Effective **persuasion**—the technique of convincing an audience to adopt an opinion, perform an action, or both—appeals to both the intellect and the emotions.
• Appeals to the intellect involve putting forward **reasons** and **evidence** to support opinions.
• Appeals to the emotions involve stirring feelings within the audience.
In most good persuasive writing, emotional appeals are used to add to the impact of logical arguments.

Cooperative Learning Activity
Reread the speech, or have one member of your group read it aloud. Discuss how effectively you think Churchill's speech balances intellectual and emotional appeals. Use a chart like the one shown to organize your thoughts.

Intellectual Appeals	Emotional Appeals

Writing Options

Web Site Page Prepare notes for the first screen of a Web site presentation about World War II or about Churchill's role in the war. Your screen should include an introductory paragraph, an idea for a visual, and the contents of the rest of the presentation. Place the notes in your **Working Portfolio.**

Activities & Explorations

War Debate Churchill ends his speech by quoting a statement that "it is better for us to perish in battle than to look upon the outrage of our nation and our altar." Stage a debate in which you argue for and against this statement. ~ **SPEAKING AND LISTENING**

Inquiry & Research

Western Europe in World War II Find out what happened in western Europe during the six months following Churchill's speech. Write a documentary news report explaining your findings.

 More Online: Research Starter
www.mcdougallittell.com

Vocabulary in Action

EXERCISE: ASSESSMENT PRACTICE For each group of words below, write the letter of the word that is an antonym of the boldfaced word.

1. **animate:** (a) stifle, (b) appreciate, (c) liberate
2. **gravity:** (a) height, (b) clearness, (c) insignificance
3. **dogged:** (a) respectable, (b) nonchalant, (c) friendly
4. **retaliate:** (a) praise, (b) forgive, (c) discourage
5. **indomitable:** (a) angry, (b) strong, (c) vulnerable

Building Vocabulary
For an in-depth study on how to use a thesaurus to find a word's antonyms, see page 574.

Winston Churchill
1874–1965

Other Works
The Gathering Storm
Blood, Sweat, and Tears
Their Finest Hour
History of the English-Speaking Peoples (4 volumes)
The Second World War (6 volumes)

Military Career The son of a noble English father and an American mother, Winston Churchill received a traditional English secondary education. Because his school record was not particularly distinguished, he did not go on to a university, instead entering the Royal Military College at Sandhurst at the age of 18 and then joining the military. There he found his niche, serving both as a war correspondent and as an officer.

A Nation's Leader Churchill entered politics in 1900, and 40 years later he became a compromise prime minister in a deeply divided government. With his public-speaking ability and talent at working with opposing forces, he was able to unite the British people and lead them to victory over the Germans in World War II. Despite his lifetime involvement in politics, Churchill never stopped writing. He was awarded the Nobel Prize in literature in 1953.

Author Activity

Inspiring Words Churchill's radio speeches had a tremendous impact on the British people. Search the Internet or your local library to find an audio recording of Churchill's speeches. Listen to them with your class, and discuss what you think his delivery adds to the speeches' effectiveness.

from **Night**

Autobiography by ELIE WIESEL (vē-zĕl′)

The Effect of the War Across Cultures

Churchill's Speeches and Wiesel's *Night* Winston Churchill's World War II speeches rallied the British in part by reminding them of the dark forces they were fighting. In *Night,* a victim of those dark forces gives a firsthand account of the terror he experienced after his homeland was overrun by Nazi Germany.

Points of Comparison As you read the excerpt from *Night,* think about the evidence it provides to support Churchill's description of Nazi Germany as "the foulest and most soul-destroying tyranny which has ever darkened and stained the pages of history."

Map labels: Ukraine, Slovakia, Moldova, Hungary, Romania, Yugoslavia, Bulgaria, Macedonia, Black Sea

Build Background

Nightmare Years As the leader of the Nazi Party, Adolf Hitler promoted racist nationalism and a policy of military expansion intended to make Germany a world empire. After he became chancellor of Germany in 1933, he began a huge military buildup; he also set up a private army, called the SS, and a secret police force, called the Gestapo, to crack down on opposition of any kind. His launching of an invasion of Poland in 1939 was the beginning of World War II.

In his quest for German supremacy, Hitler was determined to rid his empire of Jews, whom he blamed for every evil in the world. In Germany and all the European nations the Nazis invaded, Jews were rounded up and sent—usually by train—to concentration camps, where many were killed in gas chambers, were shot by firing squads, or died of torture, starvation, and disease. The dead were cremated in huge ovens.

Auschwitz-Birkenau, in Poland, was the largest of these death camps. Its director, Rudolf Hess, later testified that 2 million people were executed there and another half-million starved to death. Among those taken to Auschwitz was a Jewish teenager named Elie Wiesel, who survived the death camps and was eventually able to write about his experiences. It was Wiesel who first used the term *holocaust* to refer to the Nazis' mass slaughter.

Focus Your Reading

LITERARY ANALYSIS **STYLE IN NONFICTION** **Style** is the way in which a work is written—not what is said but how it is said. Elements that contribute to a writer's style include **word choice; sentence length, structure,** and **variety; tone; imagery;** and the use of **dialogue.** As you read, notice how these elements contribute to Wiesel's style, and consider the relationship between Wiesel's style and his subject matter.

ACTIVE READING **USING PRIOR KNOWLEDGE TO INTERPRET TEXTS** Most readers come to Wiesel's account with **prior knowledge** about the Holocaust. For example, though the name of the train's final stop—Auschwitz—is unfamiliar to Wiesel and his fellow prisoners when they arrive there, its significance is almost always known to readers. As you read the excerpt, look for other moments when your knowledge of historical events allows you to understand the wider implications of events described in Wiesel's account.

READER'S NOTEBOOK As you read, take notes about events or details that your prior knowledge makes meaningful to you. Pay special attention to details whose significance is clear to most readers but not to the prisoners on the train.

From NIGHT

ELIE WIESEL

Deportation of Jews from Westerbork transit camp in the Netherlands to a Nazi death camp in Poland

The train stopped at Kaschau, a little town on the
Czechoslovak frontier.[1] We realized then that we were not
going to stay in Hungary. Our eyes were opened, but too late.

The door of the car slid open. A German officer,
accompanied by a Hungarian lieutenant-interpreter, came up
and introduced himself.

"From this moment, you come under the authority of the
German army. Those of you who still have gold, silver, or
watches in your possession must give them up now. Anyone

who is later found to have kept anything will be shot on the spot. Secondly, anyone who feels ill may go to the hospital car. That's all."

The Hungarian lieutenant went among us with a basket and collected the last possessions from those who no longer wished to taste the bitterness of terror. "There are eighty of you in the wagon," added the German officer. "If anyone is missing, you'll all be shot, like dogs . . . ."

They disappeared. The doors were closed. We were caught in a trap, right up to our necks. The doors were nailed up; the way back was finally cut off. The world was a cattle wagon hermetically[2] sealed.

We had a woman with us named Madame Schächter. She was about fifty; her ten-year-old son was with her, crouched in a corner. Her husband and two eldest sons had been deported with the first transport by mistake. The separation had completely broken her.

I knew her well. A quiet woman with tense, burning eyes, she had often been to our house. Her husband, who was a pious man, spent his days and nights in study, and it was she who worked to support the family.

Madame Schächter had gone out of her mind. On the first day of the journey she had already begun to moan and to keep asking why she had been separated from her family. As time went on, her cries grew hysterical. On the third night, while we slept, some of us sitting one against the other and some standing, a piercing cry split the silence:

"Fire! I can see a fire! I can see a fire!"

There was a moment's panic. Who was it who had cried out? It was Madame Schächter. Standing in the middle of the wagon, in the pale light from the windows, she looked like a withered tree in a cornfield. She pointed her arm toward the window, screaming:

"Look! Look at it! Fire! A terrible fire! Mercy! Oh, that fire!"

Some of the men pressed up against the bars. There was nothing there; only the darkness.

The shock of this terrible awakening stayed with us for a long time. We still trembled from it.

With every groan of the wheels on the rail, we felt that an abyss was about to open beneath our bodies. Powerless to still our own anguish, we tried to consol ourselves:

"She's mad, poor soul. . . ."

Someone had put a damp cloth on her brow, to calm her, but still her screams went on:

"Fire! Fire!"

Her little boy was crying, hanging onto her skirt, trying to take hold of her hands. "It's all right, Mummy! There's nothing there . . . Sit down . . . ." This shook me even more than his mother's screams had done.

Some women tried to calm her. "You'll find your husband and your sons again . . . in a few days. . . ."

She continued to scream, breathless, her voice broken by sobs. "Jews, listen to me! I can see a fire! There are huge flames! It is a furnace!"

It was as though she were possessed by an evil spirit which spoke from the depths of her being.

We tried to explain it away, more to calm ourselves and to recover our own breath than to comfort her. "She must be very thirsty, poor thing! That's why she keeps talking about a fire devouring her.

"But it was in vain. Our terror was about to burst the sides of the train. Our nerves were at breaking point. Our flesh was creeping. It was as though madness were taking possession of us all. We could stand it no longer. Some of the young men forced her to sit down, tied her up, and put a gag in her mouth.

Silence again. The little boy sat down by his mother, crying. I had begun to breathe normally again. We could hear the wheels churning out that monotonous rhythm of a train traveling through the night. We could begin to doze, to rest, to dream. . . .

---

1. **Czechoslovak** (chĕk´ə-slō´väk) **frontier:** the border of Czechoslovakia, a former European country occupied by Germany during World War II.

2. **hermetically** (hər-mĕt´ĭ-klē): in an airtight manner; thoroughly.

An hour or two went by like this. Then another scream took our breath away. The woman had broken loose from her bonds and was crying out more loudly than ever:

"Look at the fire! Flames, flames everywhere...."

Once more the young men tied her up and gagged her. They even struck her. People encouraged them:

"Make her be quiet! She's mad! Shut her up! She's not the only one. She can keep her mouth shut. . . ."

They struck her several times on the head—blows that might have killed her. Her little boy clung to her; he did not cry out; he did not say a word. He was not even weeping now.

An endless night. Toward dawn, Madame Schächter calmed down. Crouched in her corner, her bewildered gaze scouring the emptiness, she could no longer see us.

She stayed like that all through the day, dumb, absent, isolated among us. As soon as night fell, she began to scream: "There's a fire over there!"

She would point at a spot in space, always the same one. They were tired of hitting her. The heat, the thirst, the pestilential[3] stench, the suffocating lack of air—these were as nothing compared with these screams which tore us to shreds. A few days more and we should all have started to scream too.

But we had reached a station. Those who were next to the windows told us its name: "Auschwitz."[4]

No one had ever heard that name.

The train did not start up again. The afternoon passed slowly. Then the wagon doors slid open. Two men were allowed to get down to fetch water. When they came back, they told us that, in exchange for a gold watch, they had

---

3. **pestilential** (pĕs′tə-lĕn′shəl): disease-bearing; noxious.

4. **Auschwitz** (oush′vĭts′): a town in southern Poland, near the site of the Auschwitz-Birkenau extermination camp, where between 1 million and 4 million people (mostly Jews from Germany and eastern Europe) were systematically murdered by the Nazis between 1942 and 1945.

View of the Birkenau concentration camp, February 1945

discovered that this was the last stop. We would be getting out here. There was a labor camp. Conditions were good. Families would not be split up. Only the young people would go to work in the factories. The old men and invalids would be kept occupied in the fields.

The barometer of confidence soared. Here was a sudden release from the terrors of the previous nights. We gave thanks to God.

Madame Schächter stayed in her corner, wilted, dumb, indifferent to the general confidence. Her little boy stroked her hand.

As dusk fell, darkness gathered inside the wagon. We started to eat our last provisions. At ten in the evening, everyone was looking for a convenient position in which to sleep for a while, and soon we were all asleep. Suddenly: "The fire! The furnace! Look, over there! . . ."

Waking with a start, we rushed to the window. Yet again we had believed her, even if only for a moment. But there was nothing outside save the darkness of night. With shame in our souls, we went back to our places, gnawed by fear, in spite of ourselves. She continued to scream, they began to hit her again, and it was with the greatest difficulty that they silenced her.

The man in charge of our wagon called a German officer who was walking about on the platform, and asked him if Madame Schächter could be taken to the hospital car.

"You must be patient," the German replied. "She'll be taken there soon."

Jewish captives from the ghetto in Lublin, Poland, being transported to a death camp

Entrance to the concentration camp in Auschwitz. The sign in German above the gate says "Work makes you free."

Toward eleven o'clock, the train began to move. We pressed against the windows. The convoy was moving slowly. A quarter of an hour later, it slowed down again. Through the windows we could see barbed wire; we realized that this must be the camp.

We had forgotten the existence of Madame Schächter. Suddenly, we heard terrible screams:"

"Jews, look! Look through the window! Flames! Look!"

And as the train stopped, we saw this time that flames were gushing out of a tall chimney into the black sky.

Madame Schächter was silent herself. Once more she had become dumb, indifferent, absent, and had gone back to her corner.

We looked at the flames in the darkness. There was an abominable odor floating in the air. Suddenly, our doors opened. Some odd-looking characters, dressed in striped shirts and black trousers leapt into the wagon. They held electric torches[5] and truncheons.[6] They began to strike out to right and left, shouting:

"Everybody get out! Everyone out of the wagon! Quickly!"

We jumped out. I threw a last glance toward Madame Schächter. Her little boy was holding her hand. In front of us flames. In the air that smell of burning flesh. It must have been about midnight. We had arrived—at Birkenau, reception center for Auschwitz. ❖

---

5. **electric torches:** flashlights.

6. **truncheons** (trŭn'chənz): small clubs, like those carried as weapons by police officers.

Thinking through the LITERATURE

Connect to the Literature

1. What Do You Think? What are your thoughts after reading this excerpt?

> **Comprehension Check**
> - What recurring vision frightens Madame Schächter?
> - What do the Jews see when they get off the train?

Think Critically

2. What is your opinion of the way the other prisoners treat Madame Schächter? Why do you think they treat her so harshly?

3. What do you think is the most likely explanation for Madame Schächter's visions?

4. How do you think the **settings** described in this excerpt contribute to its **mood?** Give examples to support your answer.

5. **ACTIVE READING** **USING PRIOR KNOWLEDGE TO INTERPRET TEXTS** Review the notes you jotted down in your **READER'S NOTEBOOK** and discuss any details whose significance you understood because of your **prior knowledge** of relevant historical events. How did your prior knowledge affect your reading of the excerpt?

6. What do you think is the significance of the title *Night?*

> **THINK ABOUT**
> - the physical descriptions of the train and the concentration camp
> - the behavior of the prisoners and their captors
> - the ultimate fate of the Jews
> - what *night* might symbolize

Extend Interpretations

7. Connect to Life Do you think something like the Holocaust could happen today to people of a particular race or religion or to some other group? Why or why not?

8. **Points of Comparison** Consider Winston Churchill's speech of May 19, 1940 (page 1127), in the light of the information that Wiesel provides. How do the details of Wiesel's experience add impact to the reasons Churchill gives for Britain's fight against Nazi Germany?

Literary Analysis

STYLE IN NONFICTION A writer's **style**—the unique way he or she handles elements such as **word choice, sentence length** and **variety, imagery,** and **dialogue**—is influenced in part by the ideas he or she wants to convey. In *Night,* Wiesel employs a style having the following characteristics:

- a reliance on simple words and short sentences
- an occasional use of imagery, as when Madame Schächter is described as looking "like a withered tree in a cornfield"
- a use of dialogue to show how the Jews on the train react to their situation

Cooperative Learning Activity Work with a group of three or four classmates to find passages that illustrate these characteristics of Wiesel's style. Record your findings in a chart like the one shown. How do you think Wiesel's style reinforces the ideas he wants to convey about his subject?

Element of Style	Example
Simple words	
Short sentences	
Imagery	
Dialogue	

REVIEW **TONE** A writer's choice of words and details is in part determined by the **tone,** or attitude toward his or her subject, that the writer wants to convey. A work might, for example, have a sad tone, an angry tone, or a matter-of-fact tone. How would you describe the tone of this excerpt from *Night?* What effect does the tone have on you?

Choices & CHALLENGES

Writing Options

1. Rewritten Version Rewrite this excerpt, narrating the events from Madame Schächter's point of view. Place your rewritten version in your **Working Portfolio.** 📁

2. **Points of Comparison**
Write an essay in which you compare and contrast the effects on you of Churchill's speech and the excerpt from *Night.* In your opinion, which work's portrayal of the evils of Nazism evokes a more powerful reaction? Explain your answer.

Writing Handbook
See page 1367: Compare and Contrast.

Activities & Explorations

1. Holocaust Monument Create a design for a monument memorializing the victims of the Holocaust. ~ **ART**

2. Movie Review Obtain and view a videotape of *Schindler's List,* the Oscar-winning 1993 film about an industrialist who helped more than a thousand Jews to escape the Holocaust.

Discuss the impact of the film in an oral review. ~ **VIEWING AND REPRESENTING**

Inquiry & Research

The Holocaust Investigate and prepare an oral report on the conditions at the Auschwitz-Birkenau concentration camp and on the camp's liberation near the end of the war.

 More Online: Research Starter
www.mcdougallittell.com

Elie Wiesel
1928–

Other Works
The Accident
Dawn
Legends of Our Time
The Oath
One Generation After

A Cut-Off Village Elie Wiesel was born in Sighet (sē′gĕt), a town in the Romanian region of Transylvania (the town was annexed by Hungary during World War II but later returned to Romania). Raised as a devout orthodox Jew, Wiesel was just 15 when, in the spring of 1944, the Nazis ordered the deportation of Sighet's 15,000 Jews, shipping them on a cattle train to Auschwitz in Poland. The Jews of Sighet, cut off by the war from most communication, had no idea where they were going. Although they had been warned of Nazi atrocities by a man passing through the town, who told them to run for their lives, they had taken the man for a madman and refused to believe him.

Into the Night Wiesel's mother and one of his three sisters were murdered at Auschwitz. Separated from the women in the family, Wiesel and his father were eventually sent to the Buchenwald concentration camp in Germany, where Wiesel's father died of starvation and dysentery less than three months before the camp was liberated. When Wiesel was freed, he vowed to remain silent about the Holocaust for ten years, writing nothing about his experiences even though he worked as a journalist and writer. "I didn't want to use the wrong words," he later explained. "I was afraid that words might betray it."

Bearing Witness Wiesel's first attempt at writing about the Holocaust was an 800-page autobiographical account in Yiddish, the language of his childhood. He then wrote a French version of the account, condensed to just over 100 pages, which was published as *La Nuit* in 1958. Two years later, the English version, *Night,* appeared. Since then Wiesel has written numerous histories, novels, and stories bearing witness to the Holocaust. He has also worked tirelessly to call attention to human rights violations around the world, winning the 1986 Nobel Peace Prize for his efforts.

Author Activity

Human Rights Champion Find out more about Wiesel's involvement in battling human rights violations and genocide in Cambodia, Rwanda, Bosnia, and other places around the world.

from

Letters from Westerbork

by **Etty Hillesum**

① 24 August 1943

I have told you often enough that no words and images are adequate to describe nights like these. But still I must try to convey something of it to you. One always has the feeling here of being the ears and eyes of a piece of Jewish history, but there is also the need sometimes to be a still, small voice. We must keep one another in touch with everything that happens in the various outposts of this world, each one contributing his own little piece of stone to the great mosaic that will take shape once the war is over. . . .

③ In the afternoon I did a round of the hospital barracks one more time, going from bed to bed. Which beds would be empty the next day? The transport lists are never published until the very last moment, but some of us know well in advance that our names will be down. A young girl called me. She was sitting bolt upright in her bed, eyes wide open. This girl has thin wrists and a peaky little face. She is partly paralyzed, and has just been learning to walk again, between two nurses, one step at a time. "Have you heard? I have to go." We look at each other for a long moment. It is as if her face has disappeared; she is all eyes. Then she says in a level, gray little voice, "Such a pity, isn't it? That everything you have learned in life goes for nothing." And, "How hard it is to die." Suddenly the unnatural rigidity of her expression gives way and she sobs, "Oh, and the worst of it all is having to leave Holland!" And, "Oh, why wasn't I allowed to die before . . ." Later, during the night, I saw her again, for the last time.

There was a little woman in the washhouse, a basket of dripping clothes on her arm. She grabbed hold of me; she looked deranged. A flood of words poured over me: "That isn't right, how can that be right? I've got to go and I won't even be able to get my washing dry by tomorrow. And my child is sick, he's feverish, can't you fix things so that I don't have to go? And I don't have enough things for the child, the rompers they sent me are too small, I need the bigger size, oh, it's enough to drive you mad. . . ."

Reading for Information

During World War II, more than 100,000 Dutch Jews were sent by the Nazis to the transit camp of Westerbork, from which most were transported to the death camp at Auschwitz in Poland. After being sent to Westerbork in 1943, Etty Hillesum worked in the hospital barracks. She also kept a diary and wrote many letters to friends outside the camp. In this excerpt from one of her letters, Hillesum describes the preparations for transporting prisoners by train to Auschwitz.

ANALYZING PRIMARY SOURCES

Letters are important primary sources because they reveal the feelings and attitudes of real people. As eyewitness accounts of the operations of a concentration camp, Etty Hillesum's letters are especially valuable. When you analyze letters as primary sources, consider when they were written and what they can tell you about life during those times. Use the activities below to analyze this letter.

❶ Recall what you already know about the situation in Europe in August 1943. The unit time line on pages 980–981 can help you.

❷ Notice Hillesum's awareness of her important role in history. How do you think this awareness influenced her choice of what to write about?

❸ When you read a primary source, you need to evaluate the reliability of its writer. In other words, can the writer be trusted

continued on p. 1144

④ You really can't tell who is going and who isn't this time. Almost everyone is up, the sick help each other to get dressed. There are some who have no clothes at all, whose luggage has been lost or hasn't arrived yet. Ladies from the "Welfare" walk about doling out clothes, which may fit or not, it doesn't matter so long as you've covered yourself with something. Some old women look a ridiculous sight. Small bottles of milk are being prepared to take along with the babies, whose pitiful screams punctuate all the frantic activity in the barracks. . . . The little woman with the wet washing is on the point of hysterics. "Can't you hide my child for me? Go on, please, won't you hide him, he's got a high fever, how can I possibly take him along?" She points to a little bundle of misery with blond curls and a burning, bright-red little face. The child tosses about in his rough wooden cot. The nurse wants the mother to put on an extra woolen sweater, tries to pull it over her dress. She refuses. "I'm not going to take anything along, what use would it be? . . . ⑤ my child." And she sobs, "They take the sick children away and you never get them back. . . ."

Slowly but surely six o'clock in the morning has arrived. The train is due to depart at eleven, and they are starting to load it with people and ⑥ luggage. . . . The camp has been cut in two halves since yesterday by the train: a depressing series of bare, unpainted freight cars in the front, and a proper coach for the guards at the back. Some of the cars have paper mattresses on the floor. These are for the sick. . . .

My God, are the doors really being shut now? Yes, they are. Shut on the herded, densely packed mass of people inside. Through small openings at the top we can see heads and hands, hands that will wave to us later when the train leaves. . . .

⑦ The tide of helpers gradually recedes; people go back to their sleeping quarters. So many exhausted, pale, and suffering faces. One more piece of our camp has been amputated. Next week yet another piece will follow. This is what has been happening now for over a year, week in, week out. . . .

Translated by Arnold J. Pomerans

---

to tell the truth, and was he or she in a position to know the truth? Do you think Hillesum is a credible source of information about life in Westerbork? Explain your conclusion.

④ What does this paragraph tell you about life inside the barracks?

⑤ This woman's statement, like Hillesum's earlier statement that some people know that their names are going to appear on a transport list, suggests that not everything in the camp could be kept secret. How do you think information was spread in the camp?

⑥ What does this description tell you about the conditions under which prisoners were transported?

⑦ From Hillesum's statements, what impression do you get about the number of people transported to the death camp? (Etty Hillesum herself was transported to Auschwitz, where she died on November 30, 1943.)

Comparing Texts How does Hillesum's account of the Holocaust compare with Elie Wiesel's account in the excerpt from *Night*?

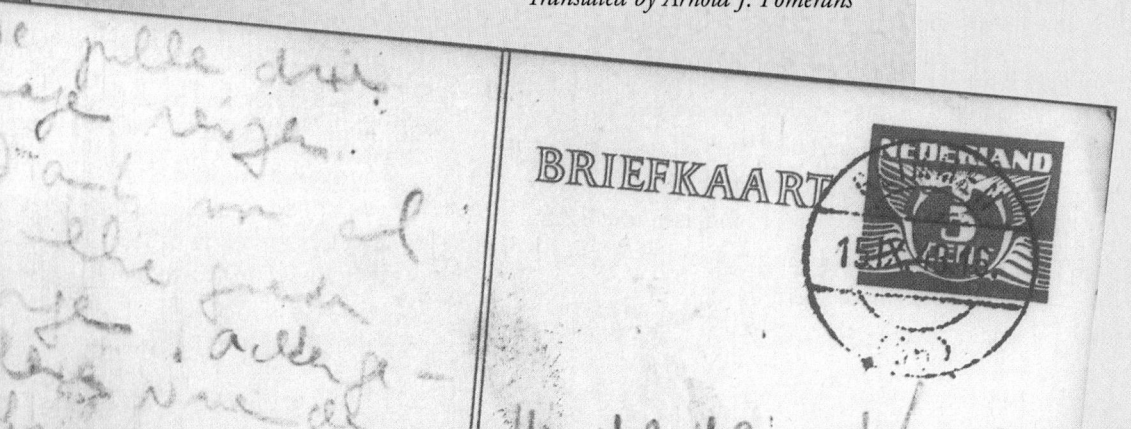

BRIEFKAART

This card, thrown out of the train by Etty on 7 September, was found by farmers outside Westerbork camp and posted by them.

Words and Behavior

Essay by ALDOUS HUXLEY

(**Connect to Your Life**)

Breaking the News Suppose that you accidentally backed the family car into a tree, causing serious damage to the vehicle. How would you break the news to your parents? Would you describe the damage accurately and completely, or would you try to conceal or gloss over the facts? Share your thoughts with classmates.

Build Background

Social and Political Writings Throughout his life, the English novelist Aldous Huxley was concerned with social and political issues. His earliest novels satirize the vanity and foolishness of English society, and his later works reflect his skepticism about the direction in which the world was headed. Today, Huxley is best known for his 1932 novel *Brave New World,* which was viewed as a satiric warning of how dismal the world could become as a result of technology and political manipulation.

In the late 1930s, Huxley became alarmed at the turmoil that seemed to be leading up to a second world war. During the 20th century, most governments at war, or about to enter into a war, have naturally been concerned about the manner in which their activities are reported to the general public. Often, they have formed special bureaus to control the type and amount of information released to the public. The information that has been released has usually been presented in carefully worded language designed to evoke feelings of patriotism and to diminish antiwar sentiment. A few years before the start of World War II, Huxley wrote the essay "Words and Behavior," in which he reflects upon the nature of wartime communication.

WORDS TO KNOW
Vocabulary Preview

ardent	inexorable
balefully	inherently
diabolical	iniquity
embellish	odious
euphemism	vitiate

Focus Your Reading

LITERARY ANALYSIS **DICTION** As you would expect in an essay with this title, Huxley chooses his words very carefully. Most of the **diction,** or choice of words, in this essay is rather formal. As you read, be aware of Huxley's formal diction and the impact it has on the effectiveness of his arguments.

ACTIVE READING **ANALYZING PATTERNS OF ORGANIZATION**

Writers may present logical arguments in two ways:

- A **deductive argument** begins with a generalization, or premise, and then presents facts and evidence that support it and lead to a conclusion.
- An **inductive argument** begins with examples or facts and builds toward a generalization on the basis of them.

To support his main premise about the nature of language, Huxley presents **deductive arguments** about two linguistic areas—the language of war and the language of politics.

READER'S NOTEBOOK As you read Huxley's essay, complete a deductive reasoning frame, like the one shown, to track Huxley's arguments about the language of war and the language of politics. In the first box, summarize Huxley's generalization. In the smaller boxes, list the examples he uses to illustrate the generalization.

Language of War

Generalization:

Example 1:

Example 2:

Example 3:

Words and Behavior

ALDOUS HUXLEY

Words form the thread on which we string our experiences. Without them we should live spasmodically and intermittently. Hatred itself is not so strong that animals will not forget it, if distracted, even in the presence of the enemy. Watch a pair of cats, crouching on the brink of a fight. Balefully the eyes glare; from far down in the throat of each come bursts of a strange, strangled noise of defiance; as though animated by a life of their own, the tails twitch and tremble. With aimed intensity of loathing! Another moment and surely there must be an explosion. But no; all of a sudden one of the two creatures turns away, hoists a hind leg in a more than fascist salute[1] and, with the same fixed and focused attention as it had given a moment before to its enemy, begins to make a lingual toilet.[2] Animal love is as much at the mercy of distractions as animal hatred. The dumb creation lives a life made up of discrete[3] and mutually irrelevant episodes. Such as it is, the consistency of human characters is due to the words upon which all human experiences are strung. We are purposeful because we can describe our feelings in rememberable words, can justify and rationalize our desires in terms of some kind of argument. Faced by an enemy we do not allow an itch to distract us from our emotions; the mere word "enemy" is enough to keep us reminded of our hatred, to convince us that we do well to be angry. Similarly the word "love" bridges for us those chasms of momentary indifference and boredom which gape from time to time between even the most ardent lovers. Feeling and desire provide us with our motive power; words give continuity to what we do and to a considerable extent determine our direction. Inappropriate and badly chosen words vitiate thought and lead to wrong or foolish conduct. Most ignorances are vincible,[4] and in the greater number of cases stupidity is what the Buddha pronounced it to be, a sin. For, consciously, or subconsciously, it is with deliberation

that we do not know or fail to understand—because incomprehension allows us, with a good conscience, to evade unpleasant obligations and responsibilities, because ignorance is the best excuse for going on doing what one likes, but ought not, to do. Our egotisms are incessantly fighting to preserve themselves, not only from external enemies, but also from the assaults of the other and better self with which they are so uncomfortably associated. Ignorance is egotism's most effective defense against that Dr. Jekyll[5] in us who desires perfection; stupidity, its subtlest stratagem. If, as so often happens, we choose to give continuity to our experience by means of words which falsify the facts, this is because the falsification is somehow to our advantage as egotists.

ACTIVE READING

CLARIFY According to Huxley, how do people use ignorance as a defense?

Consider, for example, the case of war. War is enormously discreditable to those who order it to be waged and even to those who merely tolerate its existence. Furthermore, to developed sensibilities the facts of war are revolting and horrifying. To falsify these facts, and by so doing to make war seem less evil than it really is, and our own responsibility in tolerating war less heavy, is doubly to our advantage. By suppressing and distorting the truth, we protect our sensibilities and preserve our self-esteem. Now, language is, among other things, a device which men use for suppressing and distorting the

---

1. **fascist** (făsh′ĭst) **salute:** a salute, used in Nazi Germany, in which the arm is rigidly extended forward, slightly above the horizontal.
2. **make a lingual toilet:** clean itself with its tongue.
3. **discrete:** separate; distinct.
4. **vincible** (vĭn′sə-bəl): capable of being overcome.
5. **Dr. Jekyll:** in Robert Louis Stevenson's novel *The Strange Case of Dr. Jekyll and Mr. Hyde*, an idealistic medical researcher who is transformed by an experimental drug into the murderously evil Mr. Hyde.

WORDS	**balefully** (bāl′fə-lē) *adv.* in a menacing way; wickedly
TO	**ardent** (är′dnt) *adj.* passionate
KNOW	**vitiate** (vĭsh′ē-āt′) *v.* to destroy the quality of; corrupt; debase

truth. Finding the reality of war too unpleasant to contemplate, we create a verbal alternative to that reality, parallel with it, but in quality quite different from it. That which we contemplate thenceforward is not that to which we react emotionally and upon which we pass our moral judgments, is not war as it is in fact, but the fiction of war as it exists in our pleasantly falsifying verbiage. Our stupidity in using inappropriate language turns out, on analysis, to be the most refined cunning.

The most shocking fact about war is that its victims and its instruments are individual human beings, and that these individual human beings are condemned by the monstrous conventions of politics to murder or be murdered in quarrels not their own, to inflict upon the innocent and, innocent themselves of any crime against their enemies, to suffer cruelties of every kind.

The language of strategy and politics is designed, so far as it is possible, to conceal this fact, to make it appear as though wars were not fought by individuals drilled to murder one another in cold blood and without provocation, but either by impersonal and therefore wholly non-moral and impassible forces, or else by personified abstractions.

Here are a few examples of the first kind of falsification. In place of "cavalrymen" or "foot soldiers" military writers like to speak of "sabers" and "rifles." Here is a sentence from a description of the Battle of Marengo:[6] "According to Victor's report, the French retreat was orderly; it is certain, at any rate, that the regiments held together, for the six thousand Austrian sabers found no opportunity to charge home." The battle is between sabers in line and muskets in échelon[7]— a mere clash of ironmongery.[8]

On other occasions there is no question of anything so vulgarly material as ironmongery. The battles are between Platonic ideas,[9] between the abstractions of physics and mathematics. Forces interact; weights are flung into scales; masses are set in motion. Or else it is all a matter of geometry. Lines swing and sweep; are protracted or curved; pivot on a fixed point.

Alternatively the combatants are personal, in the sense that they are personifications. There is "the enemy," in the singular, making "his" plans, striking "his" blows. The attribution of personal characteristics to collectivities,[10] to geographical expressions, to institutions, is a source, as we shall see, of endless confusions in political thought, of innumerable political mistakes and crimes. Personification in politics is an error which we make because it is to our advantage as egotists to be able to feel violently proud of our country and of ourselves as belonging to it, and to believe that all the misfortunes due to our own mistakes are really the work of the Foreigner. It is easier to feel violently toward a person than toward an abstraction; hence our habit of making political personifications. In some cases military personifications are merely special instances of political personifications. A particular collectivity, the army or the warring nation, is given the name and, along with the name, the attributes of a single person, in order that we may be able to love or hate it more intensely than we could do if we thought of it as what it really is: a number of diverse individuals. In other cases personification

---

6. **Battle of Marengo:** a battle fought in 1800, in which French troops led by Napoleon Bonaparte defeated an Austrian army near the town of Marengo in northern Italy.

7. échelon (ĕsh′ə-lŏn′): an arrangement of groups of soldiers in a steplike formation.

8. **ironmongery** (ī′ərn-mŭng′gə-rē): hardware.

9. **Platonic ideas:** in the thought of Plato (a Greek philosopher of the fourth century B.C.), immaterial realities that all actual things are copies of.

10. **collectivities:** groups of people.

Official Photograph, United States Air Force, courtesy of Sam. R. Quincey.

SOMEONE

TALKED !

is used for the purpose of concealing the fundamental absurdity and monstrosity of war. What is absurd and monstrous about war is that men who have no personal quarrel should be trained to murder one another in cold blood. By personifying opposing armies or countries, we are able to think of war as a conflict between individuals. The same result is obtained by writing of war as though it were carried on exclusively by the generals in command and not by the private soldiers in their armies. ("Rennenkampf had pressed back von Schubert.") The implication in both cases is that war is indistinguishable from a bout of fisticuffs[11] in a bar room. Whereas in reality it is profoundly different. A scrap between two individuals is forgivable; mass murder, deliberately organized, is a monstrous iniquity. We still choose to use war as an instrument of policy; and to comprehend the full wickedness and absurdity of war would therefore be inconvenient. For, once we understood, we should have to make some effort to get rid of the abominable thing. Accordingly, when we talk about war, we use a language which conceals or embellishes its reality. Ignoring the facts, so far as we possibly can, we imply that battles are not fought by soldiers, but by things, principles, allegories, personified collectivities, or (at the most human) by opposing commanders, pitched against one another in single combat. For the same reason, when we have to describe the processes and the results of war, we employ a rich variety of euphemisms. Even the most violently patriotic and militaristic are reluctant to call a spade by its own name. To conceal their intentions even from themselves, they make use of picturesque metaphors. We find them, for example, clamoring for war planes numerous and powerful enough to go and "destroy the hornets in

---

11. **fisticuffs** (fĭs′tĭ-kŭfs′): fighting with the fists.

WORDS TO KNOW	**iniquity** (ĭ-nĭk′wĭ-tē) *n.* immorality; wickedness **embellish** (ĕm-bĕl′ĭsh) *v.* to add ornamental or fictitious details to; decorate **euphemism** (yōō′fə-mĭz′əm) *n.* a mild or vague term used in place of a blunt or offensive one

1149

their nests"—in other words, to go and throw thermite,[12] high explosives and vesicants[13] upon the inhabitants of neighboring countries before they have time to come and do the same to us. And how reassuring is the language of historians and strategists! They write admiringly of those military geniuses who know "when to strike at the enemy's line" (a single combatant deranges the geometrical constructions of a personification); when to "turn his flank"; when to "execute an enveloping movement." As though they were engineers discussing the strength of materials and the distribution of stresses, they talk of abstract entities called "man power" and "fire power." They sum up the long-drawn sufferings and atrocities of trench warfare in the phrase, "a war of attrition";[14] the massacre and mangling of human beings is assimilated to the grinding of a lens.[15] A dangerously abstract word, which figures in all discussions about war, is "force." Those who believe in organizing collective security by means of military pacts against a possible aggressor are particularly fond of this word. "You cannot," they say, "have international justice unless you are prepared to impose it by force." "Peace-loving countries must unite to use force against aggressive dictatorships." "Democratic institutions must be protected, if need be, by force." And so on.

Now, the word "force," when used in reference to human relations, has no single, definite meaning. There is the "force" used by parents when, without resort to any kind of physical violence, they compel their children to act or refrain from acting in some particular way. There is the "force" used by attendants in an asylum when they try to prevent a maniac from hurting himself or others. There is the "force" used by the police when they control a crowd, and that

war

ACTIVE READING

CLARIFY How can words conceal the reality of war?

other "force" which they use in a baton charge.[16] And finally there is the "force" used in war. This, of course, varies with the technological devices at the disposal of the belligerents, with the policies they are pursuing, and with the particular circumstances of the war in question. But in general it may be said that, in war, "force" connotes violence and fraud used to the limit of the combatants' capacity.

Variations in quantity, if sufficiently great, produce variations in quality. The "force" that is war, particularly modern war, is very different from the "force" that is police action, and the use of the same abstract word to describe the two dissimilar processes is profoundly misleading. (Still more misleading, of course, is the explicit assimilation of a war, waged by allied League-of-Nations powers against an aggressor, to police action against a criminal. The first is the use of violence and fraud without limit against innocent and guilty alike; the second is the use of strictly limited violence and a minimum of fraud exclusively against the guilty.)

Reality is a succession of concrete and particular situations. When we think about such situations we should use the particular and concrete words which apply to them. If we use abstract words which apply equally well (and equally badly) to other, quite dissimilar situations, it is certain that we shall think incorrectly.

Let us take the sentences quoted above and translate the abstract word "force" into language

---

12. **thermite:** a mixture of chemicals that burns very intensely, used in certain kinds of bombs.

13. **vesicants** (vĕs′ĭ-kənts): chemical agents, such as mustard gas, that cause inflammation and blistering of the skin and internal tissues.

14. **attrition:** a gradual process of wearing down.

15. **assimilated . . . lens:** likened to the process by which glass is ground into lenses.

16. **baton charge:** the beating back of a mob by policemen wielding wooden clubs.

that will render (however inadequately) the concrete and particular realities of contemporary warfare.

"You cannot have international justice, unless you are prepared to impose it by force." Translated, this becomes: "You cannot have international justice unless you are prepared, with a view to imposing a just settlement, to drop thermite, high explosives and vesicants upon the inhabitants of foreign cities and to have thermite, high explosives and vesicants dropped in return upon the inhabitants of your cities." At the end of this proceeding, justice is to be imposed by the victorious party—that is, if there is a victorious party. It should be remarked that justice was to have been imposed by the victorious party at the end of the last war. But, unfortunately, after four years of fighting, the temper of the victors was such that they were quite incapable of making a just settlement. The Allies are reaping in Nazi Germany what they sowed at Versailles.[17] The victors of the next war will have undergone intensive bombardments with thermite, high explosives and vesicants. Will their temper be better than that of the Allies in 1918? Will they be in a fitter state to make a just settlement? The answer, quite obviously, is: No. It is psychologically all but impossible that justice should be secured by the methods of contemporary warfare.

The next two sentences may be taken together. "Peace-loving countries must unite to use force against aggressive dictatorships. Democratic institutions must be protected, if need be, by force." Let us translate. "Peace-loving countries must unite to throw thermite, high explosives and vesicants on the inhabitants of countries ruled by aggressive dictators. They must do this, and of course abide the consequences, in order to preserve peace and democratic institutions." Two questions immediately propound[18] themselves. First, is it likely that peace can be secured by a process calculated to reduce the orderly life of our complicated societies to chaos? And, second, is it likely that democratic institutions will flourish in a state of chaos? Again, the answers are pretty clearly in the negative.

By using the abstract word "force," instead of terms which at least attempt to describe the realities of war as it is today, the preachers of collective security through military collaboration disguise from themselves and from others, not only the contemporary facts, but also the probable consequences of their favorite policy. The attempt to secure justice, peace and democracy by "force" seems reasonable enough until we realize, first, that this noncommittal word stands, in the circumstances of our age, for activities which can hardly fail to result in social chaos; and second, that the

He's Watching You (1942), Glenn Grohe. American World War II poster, The Granger Collection, New York.

17. **The Allies . . . Versailles** (vər-sī′): The peace treaty ending World War I—signed at the Palace of Versailles, near Paris, in 1919—imposed humiliating punishments on Germany, which led to the rise of German nationalism and Nazism in the 1920s and 1930s.

18. **propound:** to put forward for consideration; pose.

consequences of social chaos are injustice, chronic warfare and tyranny. The moment we think in concrete and particular terms of the concrete and particular process called "modern war," we see that a policy which worked (or at least didn't result in complete disaster) in the past has no prospect whatever of working in the immediate future. The attempt to secure justice, peace and democracy by means of a "force," which means, at this particular moment of history, thermite, high explosives and vesicants, is about as reasonable as the attempt to put out a fire with a colorless liquid that happens to be, not water, but petrol.

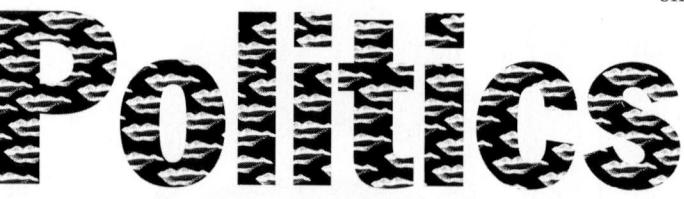

What applies to the "force" that is war applies in large measure to the "force" that is revolution. It seems inherently very unlikely that social justice and social peace can be secured by thermite, high explosives and vesicants. At first, it may be, the parties in a civil war would hesitate to use such instruments on their fellow-countrymen. But there can be little doubt that, if the conflict were prolonged (as it probably would be between the evenly balanced Right and Left of a highly industrialized society), the combatants would end by losing their scruples.

The alternatives confronting us seem to be plain enough. Either we invent and conscientiously employ a new technique for making revolutions and settling international disputes; or else we cling to the old technique and, using "force" (that is to say, thermite, high explosives and vesicants), destroy ourselves. Those who, for whatever motive, disguise the nature of the second alternative under inappropriate language, render the world a grave disservice. They lead us into one of the temptations we find it hardest to resist—the temptation to run away from reality, to pretend that facts are not what they are. Like Shelley (but without Shelley's acute awareness of what he was doing) we are perpetually weaving

> *A shroud of talk to hide us from the sun*
> *Of this familiar life.*

We protect our minds by an elaborate system of abstractions, ambiguities, metaphors and similes from the reality we do not wish to know too clearly; we lie to ourselves, in order that we may still have the excuse of ignorance, the alibi of stupidity and incomprehension, possessing which we can continue with a good conscience to commit and tolerate the most monstrous crimes:

> *The poor wretch who has learned his only prayers*
> *From curses, who knows scarcely words enough*
> *To ask a blessing from his Heavenly Father,*
> *Becomes a fluent phraseman, absolute*
> *And technical in victories and defeats,*
> *And all our dainty terms for fratricide;*[19]
> *Terms which we trundle smoothly o'er our tongues*
> *Like mere abstractions, empty sounds to which*
> *We join no meaning and attach no form!*
> *As if the soldier died without a wound:*
> *As if the fibers of this godlike frame*
> *Were gored without a pang: as if the wretch*
> *Who fell in battle, doing bloody deeds,*
> *Passed off to Heaven translated and not killed;*
> *As though he had no wife to pine for him,*
> *No God to judge him.*

The language we use about war is inappropriate, and its inappropriateness is designed to conceal a reality so odious that we do not wish to know it. The language we use about politics is also inap-

---

19. **fratricide** (frăt′rĭ-sīd′): the killing of one's brother or sister.

propriate; but here our mistake has a different purpose. Our principal aim in this case is to arouse and, having aroused, to rationalize and justify such intrinsically[20] agreeable sentiments as pride and hatred, self-esteem and contempt for others. To achieve this end we speak about the facts of politics in words which more or less completely misrepresent them. . . .

The evil passions are further justified by another linguistic error—the error of speaking about certain categories of persons as though they were mere embodied abstractions. Foreigners and those who disagree with us are not thought of as men and women like ourselves and our fellow-countrymen; they are thought of as representatives and, so to say, symbols of a class. In so far as they have any personality at all, it is the personality we mistakenly attribute to their class—a personality that is, by definition, intrinsically evil. We know that the harming or killing of men and women is wrong, and we are reluctant consciously to do what we know to be wrong. But when particular men and women are thought of merely as representatives of a class, which has previously been defined as evil and personified in the shape of a devil, then the reluctance to hurt or murder disappears. Brown, Jones and Robinson are no longer thought of as Brown, Jones and Robinson, but as heretics, gentiles, Yids, niggers, barbarians, Huns, communists, capitalists, fascists, liberals[21]—whichever the case may be. When they have been called such names and assimilated to the accursed class to which the names apply, Brown, Jones and Robinson cease to be conceived as what they really are—human persons—and become for the users of this fatally inappropriate language mere vermin or, worse, demons whom it is right and proper to destroy as thoroughly and as painfully as possible. Wherever persons are present, questions of morality arise. Rulers of nations and leaders of parties find morality embarrassing. That is why they take such pains to deperson-

The Only Road for an Englishman (1914), Gerald Spencer Pryse. Imperial War Museum, London.

alize their opponents. All propaganda directed against an opposing group has but one aim: to substitute <u>diabolical</u> abstractions for concrete persons. The propagandist's purpose is to make one set of people forget that certain other sets of people are human. By robbing them of their per-

20. **intrinsically** (ĭn-trĭn′zĭk-lē): inherently; essentially.

21. **heretics . . . liberals:** terms used to disparage groups of people. (*Yid* is an offensive term for a Jew, and *Huns* was what some British people called the Germans during World War I.)

WORDS
TO
KNOW   **diabolical** (dī′ə-bŏl′ĭ-kəl) *adj.* extremely wicked or cruel; devilish

sonality, he puts them outside the pale of moral obligation. Mere symbols can have no rights—particularly when that of which they are symbolical is, by definition, evil.

ACTIVE READING

ANALYZE What **argument** does Huxley give for why rulers "depersonalize their opponents"?

Politics can become moral only on one condition: that its problems shall be spoken of and thought about exclusively in terms of concrete reality; that is to say, of persons. To depersonify human beings and to personify abstractions are complementary errors which lead, by an <u>inexorable</u> logic, to war between nations and to idolatrous worship of the State, with consequent governmental oppression. All current political thought is a mixture, in varying proportions, between thought in terms of concrete realities and thought in terms of depersonified symbols and personified abstractions. In the democratic countries the problems of internal politics are thought about mainly in terms of concrete reality; those of external politics, mainly in terms of abstractions and symbols. In dictatorial countries the proportion of concrete to abstract and symbolic thought is lower than in democratic countries. Dictators talk little of persons, much of personified abstractions, such as the Nation, the State, the Party, and much of depersonified symbols, such as Yids, Bolshies,[22] Capitalists. The stupidity of politicians who talk about a world of persons as though it were not a world of persons is due in the main to self-interest. In a fictitious world of symbols and personified abstractions, rulers find that they can rule more effectively, and the ruled, that they can gratify instincts which the conventions of good manners and the

Enjoy Your War Work (1941), unknown artist. London Transport Museum.

imperatives of morality demand that they should repress. To think correctly is the condition of behaving well. It is also in itself a moral act; those who would think correctly must resist considerable temptations. ❖

---

22. **Bolshies:** Communists (after *Bolshevik*, the name of the Russian Communist faction that came to power in the 1917 revolution).

WORDS TO KNOW

inexorable (ĭn-ĕk′sər-ə-bəl) *adj.* unyielding; relentless

Thinking through the LITERATURE

Connect to the Literature

1. **What Do You Think?**
   What is your overall reaction to Huxley's ideas in this essay?

   ....
   Comprehension Check
   - According to Huxley, why do military powers talk about "lines" and "forces" instead of "soldiers"?
   - What does Huxley think people must do in order to behave well?
   ....

Think Critically

2. Adopting the role of Aldous Huxley, explain what you hoped to achieve by writing this **essay.**

3. If Huxley were asked to describe the worst effect of using **euphemisms** and **abstractions** to gloss over the facts of war, what do you think he would say?

   THINK ABOUT
   - the examples of euphemisms and abstractions that he gives
   - the reasons people use euphemisms
   - the dangers of using abstractions

4. **ACTIVE READING** **ANALYZING PATTERNS OF ORGANIZATION**
   Review the deductive reasoning frame you made in your **READER'S NOTEBOOK.** What are Huxley's main points about the language of war and of politics? Which of his examples do you think best illustrate these two main points?

5. Do you think Huxley's arguments are objective and convincing? Explain your answer.

Extend Interpretations

6. **Comparing Texts** How do you think Huxley might have reacted to Winston Churchill's speech of May 19, 1940 (page 1127)? Cite specific passages in your answer.

7. **Connect to Life** If people always spoke as directly as possible and never used euphemisms or abstractions to gloss over facts, what do you think would be the results? Be specific in your answer.

Literary Analysis

DICTION One important element of any writer's style is **diction,** or choice of words. Diction includes both **vocabulary** (individual words) and **syntax** (the order or arrangement of words). A writer's diction may be described as formal or informal, as technical or ordinary, as abstract or concrete. Most of the language in Huxley's essay is formal, as in the sentence beginning "Our egotism are incessantly fighting to preserve themselves . . ." (page 1147).

Activity Rewrite the sentence cited above in informal language. Then find two other examples of formal diction in the essay and rewrite them as well. How do you think the use of less formal diction affects the sentences' impact on the reader?

"Our egotisms are incessantly fighting . . ."

Informal: Our egos are constantly at war . . .

REVIEW **PERSUASION** As you recall, **persuasion**—the technique of convincing an audience to adopt an opinion, perform an action, or both—may use both logical appeals and emotional appeals. Does Huxley use both of these approaches in his essay? Explain your answer.

Writing Options

Analysis of Persuasion Look at the posters that illustrate Huxley's essay. What modes of persuasion—valid and faulty—do you see reflected in the words and images? List examples of logical, deceptive, and faulty modes of persuasion used in the posters.

Activities & Explorations

Debate on the Language of War With a partner, conduct a debate in which the two of you argue for and against the use of euphemisms and abstract language during wartime. Support your position. ~ **SPEAKING AND LISTENING**

Inquiry & Research

Propaganda Find out about the uses of propaganda during the 20th century—for example, in Nazi Germany or during the Cold War. Report your findings to the class, and discuss what insights your research has given you into Huxley's essay.

Vocabulary in Action

EXERCISE: SYNONYMS For each phrase in the first column, write the letter of the synonymous phrase in the second column.

1. **odious** poultry
2. **ardent** protection
3. a fiendish romp
4. **vitiate** the efforts
5. destined to **embellish**
6. direct **balefully**
7. sayin' "powder room"
8. **inherently** harmonious
9. an unrelenting power
10. an evil from the past

a. spoil the toil
b. naturally matchable
c. an **iniquity** from antiquity
d. born to adorn
e. usin' a **euphemism**
f. sickening chicken
g. intense defense
h. administer sinisterly
i. a **diabolical** frolic
j. an **inexorable** force

Building Vocabulary
For an in-depth lesson on how to use a thesaurus to find a word's synonyms, see page 574.

Aldous Huxley
1894–1963

Other Works
Crome Yellow
Point Counter Point
Brave New World
Brave New World Revisited
Island

Changing Paths Aldous Huxley was born in Surrey, England, into a family of gifted intellectuals, including scientists, educators, and writers. As a student at Eton College, a prestigious English prep school, he was pursuing studies in science when he contracted keratitis, an eye disease that resulted in near-blindness. Although he had to abandon any hope of a career in science or medicine, he learned Braille in order to continue his education. He studied English literature at Oxford University, where his sight improved, and he was awarded an honors degree in 1916. During the same year, he published his first book, a collection of poetry.

Literary Rebel After working as a teacher and as a journalist for a literary magazine, Huxley concentrated on his own writing, moving away from poetry to fiction and essays. The witty skepticism of his first two novels, published in the 1920s, established his reputation and also brought him a certain popularity as a rebel. During the 1930s, Huxley's writing focused on political and cultural trends that he felt to be alarming.

Go West Huxley and his wife, Maria, had been traveling extensively since the mid-1920s, and in 1937 they settled in California, where both the climate and new medical treatments improved Huxley's vision. His later work, which reflected his wide range of interests, included film scripts and explorations of mysticism and parapsychology. Huxley endured a painful battle with cancer at the end of his life, but he continued to write, relentless in his attention to the problems facing society.

The Demon Lover

Short Story by ELIZABETH BOWEN

Connect to Your Life

The Unexplained Most people are intrigued by unexplained events—mysterious occurrences or strange coincidences that seem outside the limits of ordinary life. Jot down descriptions of any events of this sort that you have read about, heard about, or experienced yourself. Discuss these events with your classmates.

Build Background

London During World War II
During World War II, German aircraft bombed British cities for more than four years. From September 1940 to May 1941, Germany hit London with a series of nightly air attacks—known as the Blitz—designed to force Britain to surrender. Londoners sought safety in subway tunnels and air-raid shelters during the bombings. Those who could afford to do so left the city and moved to the countryside.

Mrs. Drover, the main character in this story, lived with her family in the wealthy Kensington district of London before moving to the country to escape the Blitz. As the story begins, she is returning to her Kensington home to reclaim some valued personal belongings.

WORDS TO KNOW
Vocabulary Preview

assent	precipitately
emanate	prosaic
impassively	

Focus Your Reading

LITERARY ANALYSIS **SETTING AND SUSPENSE** As the plot develops in "The Demon Lover," Bowen builds **suspense,** making the reader increasingly eager to find out what will happen. One technique she uses to create suspense is her description of **setting,** as in the following example:

> *The room looked over the garden and other gardens: the sun had gone in; as the clouds sharpened and lowered, the trees and rank lawns seemed already to smoke with dark.*

As you read, look for other examples in which description of the time and place of the story's action contributes to the building of suspense.

ACTIVE READING **ANALYZING FLASHBACK** "The Demon Lover" is set during World War II, but the story involves a **flashback** to events 25 years earlier. A flashback is an account of a conversation, an episode, or an event that happened before the main sequence of events in a story. Flashbacks often reveal significant thoughts, experiences, or events in characters' lives, and may contain **foreshadowing,** or hints of what is to come. As you read "The Demon Lover," identify where the flashback begins and ends, and consider what the use of this technique adds to Bowen's story.

READER'S NOTEBOOK In a chart like the one shown, identify important details presented in flashback. Note what significant information you think each detail reveals about Mrs. Drover or her former fiancé. Then jot down possible outcomes that the flashback might foreshadow.

Flashback Detail	Mrs. Drover	Fiancé	Possible Outcomes

E l i z a b e t h B o w e n

THE Demon LOVER

Towards the end of her day in London Mrs. Drover went round to her shut-up house to look for several things she wanted to take away. Some belonged to herself, some to her family, who were by now used to their country life. It was late August; it had been a steamy, showery day: at the moment the trees down the pavement glittered in an escape of humid yellow afternoon sun. Against the next batch of clouds, already piling up ink-dark, broken chimneys and parapets stood out. In her once familiar street, as in any unused channel, an unfamiliar queerness had silted up;[1] a cat wove itself in and out of railings, but no human eye watched Mrs. Drover's return. Shifting some parcels under her arm, she slowly forced round her latchkey in an unwilling lock, then gave the door, which had warped, a push with her knee. Dead air came out to meet her as she went in.

The staircase window having been boarded up, no light came down into the hall. But one door, she could just see, stood ajar, so she went quickly through into the room and unshuttered the big window in there. Now the prosaic woman, looking about her, was more perplexed than she knew by everything that she saw, by traces of her long former habit of life—the yellow smoke stain up the white marble mantelpiece, the ring left by a vase on the top of the escritoire;[2] the bruise in the wallpaper where, on the door being thrown open widely, the china handle had always hit the wall. The piano, having gone away to be stored, had left what looked like claw marks on its part of the parquet.[3] Though not much dust had seeped in, each object wore a film of another kind; and, the only

---

1. **silted up:** piled up, like sediment deposited in a river channel.
2. **escritoire** (ĕs′krĭ-twär′): a writing desk or table.
3. **parquet** (pär-kā′): a wood floor made of small blocks laid in a geometric pattern.

ventilation being the chimney, the whole drawing room smelled of the cold hearth. Mrs. Drover put down her parcels on the escritoire and left the room to proceed upstairs; the things she wanted were in a bedroom chest.

She had been anxious to see how the house was—the part-time caretaker she shared with some neighbors was away this week on his holiday, known to be not yet back. At the best of times he did not look in often, and she was never sure that she trusted him. There were some cracks in the structure, left by the last bombing, on which she was anxious to keep an eye. Not that one could do anything—

A shaft of refracted daylight now lay across the hall. She stopped dead and stared at the hall table—on this lay a letter addressed to her.

She thought first—then the caretaker *must* be back. All the same, who, seeing the house shuttered, would have dropped a letter in at the box? It was not a circular, it was not a bill. And the post office redirected, to the address in the country, everything for her that came through the post. The caretaker (even if he *were* back) did not know she was due in London today— her call here had been planned to be a surprise— so his negligence in the manner of this letter, leaving it to wait in the dusk and the dust, annoyed her. Annoyed, she picked up the letter, which bore no stamp. But it cannot be important, or they would know . . . She took the letter rapidly upstairs with her, without a stop to look at the writing till she reached what had been her bedroom, where she let in light. The room looked over the garden and other gardens: the sun had gone in; as the clouds sharpened and lowered, the trees and rank lawns seemed already to smoke with dark. Her reluctance to look again at the letter came from the fact that she felt intruded upon—and by someone contemptuous of her ways. However, in the tenseness preceding the fall of rain she read it: it was a few lines.

Dear Kathleen: You will not have forgotten that today is our anniversary, and the day we said. The years have gone by at once slowly and fast. In view of the fact that nothing has changed, I shall rely upon you to keep your promise. I was sorry to see you leave London, but was satisfied that you would be back in time. You may expect me, therefore, at the hour arranged. Until then . . .   K.

Mrs. Drover looked for the date: it was today's. She dropped the letter onto the bedsprings, then picked it up to see the writing again—her lips, beneath the remains of lipstick, beginning to go white. She felt so much the change in her own face that she went to the mirror, polished a clear patch in it and looked at once urgently and stealthily in. She was confronted by a woman of forty-four, with eyes starting out under a hat brim that had been rather carelessly pulled down. She had not put on any more powder since she left the shop where she ate her solitary tea. The pearls her husband had given her on their marriage hung loose round her now rather thinner throat, slipping in the V of the pink wool jumper her sister knitted last autumn as they sat round the fire. Mrs. Drover's most normal expression was one of controlled worry, but of <u>assent</u>. Since the birth of the third of her little boys, attended by a quite serious illness, she had had an intermittent muscular flicker to the left of her mouth, but in spite of this she could always sustain a manner that was at once energetic and calm.

Turning from her own face as <u>precipitately</u> as she had gone to meet it, she went to the chest where the things were, unlocked it, threw up the lid and knelt to search. But as rain began to come crashing down she could not keep from looking over her shoulder at the stripped bed on which the letter lay. Behind the blanket of rain the clock of the church that still stood struck six—with rapidly heightening apprehension she counted each of the slow strokes. "The hour

arranged . . . My God," she said, "*what* hour? How should I . . . ? After twenty-five years . . ."

The young girl talking to the soldier in the garden had not ever completely seen his face. It was dark; they were saying goodbye under a tree. Now and then—for it felt, from not seeing him at this intense moment, as though she had never seen him at all—she verified his presence for these few moments longer by putting out a hand, which he each time pressed, without very much kindness, and painfully, onto one of the breast buttons of his uniform. That cut of the button on the palm of her hand was, principally, what she was to carry away. This was so near the end of a leave from France that she could only wish him already gone. It was August 1916. Being not kissed, being drawn away from and looked at, intimidated Kathleen till she imagined spectral[4] glitters in the place of his eyes. Turning away and looking back up the lawn she saw, through branches of trees, the drawing-room window alight: she caught a breath for the moment when she could go running back there into the safe arms of her mother and sister, and cry: "What shall I do, what shall I do? He has gone."

Hearing her catch her breath, her fiancé said, without feeling: "Cold?"

"You're going away such a long way."

"Not so far as you think."

"I don't understand?"

"You don't have to," he said. "You will. You know what we said."

"But that was—suppose you—I mean, suppose."

"I shall be with you," he said, "sooner or later. You won't forget that. You need do nothing but wait."

Only a little more than a minute later she was free to run up the silent lawn. Looking in through the window at her mother and sister, who did not for the moment perceive her, she already felt that unnatural promise drive down between her and the rest of all humankind. No other way of having given herself could have made her feel so apart, lost and foresworn.[5] She could not have plighted a more sinister troth.[6]

Kathleen behaved well when, some months later, her fiancé was reported missing, presumed killed. Her family not only supported her but were able to praise her courage without stint[7] because they could not regret, as a husband for her, the man they knew almost nothing about. They hoped she would, in a year or two, console herself—and had it been only a question of consolation things might have gone much straighter ahead. But her trouble, behind just a little grief, was a complete dislocation from everything. She did not reject other lovers, for these failed to appear: for years she failed to attract men—and with the approach of her thirties she became natural enough to share her family's anxiousness on this score. She began to put herself out, to wonder; and at thirty-two she was very greatly relieved to find herself being courted by William Drover. She married him, and the two of them settled down in this quiet, arboreal[8] part of Kensington:[9] in this house the years piled up, her children were born and they all lived till they were driven out by the bombs of the next war. Her movements as Mrs. Drover were circumscribed,[10] and she dismissed any idea that they were still watched.

As things were—dead or living the letter-writer sent her only a threat. Unable, for some minutes, to go on kneeling with her back exposed to the empty room, Mrs. Drover rose from the chest to sit on an upright chair whose back was firmly against the wall. The desuetude[11] of her former bedroom, her married London home's whole air

---

4. **spectral**: ghostly; phantomlike.

5. **foresworn**: guilty of perjury.

6. **plighted . . . troth**: made a more ominous promise of marriage.

7. **stint**: limitation or restriction.

8. **arboreal** (är-bôr′ē-əl): tree-filled.

9. **Kensington**: a residential section of London.

10. **circumscribed**: restricted; confined.

11. **desuetude** (dĕs′wĭ-tōōd′): disuse.

of being a cracked cup from which memory, with its reassuring power, had either evaporated or leaked away, made a crisis—and at just this crisis the letter-writer had, knowledgeably, struck. The hollowness of the house this evening canceled years on years of voices, habits and steps. Through the shut windows she only heard rain fall on the roofs around. To rally herself, she said she was in a mood—and for two or three seconds shutting her eyes, told herself that she had imagined the letter. But she opened them—there it lay on the bed.

On the supernatural side of the letter's entrance she was not permitting her mind to dwell. Who, in London, knew she meant to call at the house today? Evidently, however, this had been known. The caretaker, *had* he come back, had had no cause to expect her: he would have taken the letter in his pocket, to forward it, at his own time, through the post. There was no other sign that the caretaker had been in—but, if not? Letters dropped in at doors of deserted houses do not fly or walk to tables in halls. They do not sit on the dust of empty tables with the air of certainty that they will be found. There is needed some human hand—but nobody but the caretaker had a key. Under circumstances she did not care to consider, a house can be entered without a key. It was possible that she was not alone now. She might be being waited for, downstairs. Waited for—until when? Until "the hour arranged." At least that was not six o'clock: six has struck.

She rose from the chair and went over and locked the door.

Interior with Seated Woman (1908), Vilhelm Hammershøi. Oil on canvas, 76 cm × 66 cm, Aarhus (Denmark) Kunstmuseum.

The thing was, to get out. To fly? No, not that: she had to catch her train. As a woman whose utter dependability was the keystone of her family life she was not willing to return to the country, to her husband, her little boys and her sister, without the objects she had come up to fetch. Resuming work at the chest she set about making up a number of parcels in a rapid, fumbling-decisive way. These, with her shopping parcels, would be too much to carry; these meant a taxi—at the thought of the taxi her heart went up and her normal breathing resumed. I will ring up the taxi now; the taxi cannot come too soon: I shall hear the taxi out there running its engine, till I walk calmly down to it through the hall. I'll ring up—But no: the telephone is cut off . . . She tugged at a knot she had tied wrong.

The idea of flight . . . He was never kind to me, not really. I don't remember him kind at all. Mother said he never considered me. He was set on me, that was what it was—not love. Not love, not meaning a person well. What did he do, to make me promise like that? I can't remember—But she found that she could.

She remembered with such dreadful acuteness that the twenty-five years since then dissolved like smoke and she instinctively looked for the weal[12] left by the button on the palm of her hand. She remembered not only all that he said and did but the complete suspension of *her* existence during that August week. I was not

myself—they all told me so at the time. She remembered—but with one white burning blank as where acid has dropped on a photograph: *under no conditions* could she remember his face.

So, wherever he may be waiting, I shall not know him. You have no time to run from a face you do not expect.

The thing was to get to the taxi before any clock struck what could be the hour. She would slip down the street and round the side of the square to where the square gave on the main road. She would return in the taxi, safe, to her own door, and bring the solid driver into the house with her to pick up the parcels from room to room. The idea of the taxi driver made her decisive, bold: she unlocked her door, went to the top of the staircase and listened down.

She heard nothing—but while she was hearing nothing the *passé*[13] air of the staircase was disturbed by a draft that traveled up to her face. It <u>emanated</u> from the basement: down there a door or window was being opened by someone who chose this moment to leave the house.

The rain had stopped; the pavements steamily shone as Mrs. Drover let herself out by inches from her own front door into the empty street. The unoccupied houses opposite continued to meet her look with their damaged stare. Making towards the thoroughfare and the taxi, she tried not to keep looking behind. Indeed, the silence was so intense—one of those creeks of London silence exaggerated this summer by the damage of war—that no tread could have gained on hers unheard. Where her street debouched[14] on the square where people went on living, she grew conscious of, and checked, her unnatural pace. Across the open end of the square two buses <u>impassively</u> passed each other: women, a

---

12. **weal:** a mark or ridge raised on the skin.

13. *passé* (pä-sā') *French:* old; stale; past its prime.

14. **debouched** (dĭ-boucht'): emerged.

WORDS TO KNOW

emanate (ĕm'ə-nāt') *v.* to come forth; flow out
impassively (ĭm-păs'ĭv-lē) *adv.* without feeling or emotion

perambulator,[15] cyclists, a man wheeling a barrow signalized, once again, the ordinary flow of life. At the square's most populous corner should be—and was—the short taxi rank. This evening, only one taxi—but this, although it presented its blank rump, appeared already to be alertly waiting for her. Indeed, without looking round the driver started his engine as she panted up from behind and put her hand on the door. As she did so, the clock struck seven. The taxi faced the main road: to make the trip back to her house it would have to turn—she had settled back on the seat and the taxi *had* turned before she, surprised by its knowing movement, recollected that she had not "said where." She leaned forward to scratch at the glass panel that divided the driver's head from her own.

The driver braked to what was almost a stop, turned round and slid the glass panel back: the jolt of this flung Mrs. Drover forward till her face was almost into the glass. Through the aperture[16] driver and passenger, not six inches between them, remained for an eternity eye to eye. Mrs. Drover's mouth hung open for some seconds before she could issue her first scream. After that she continued to scream freely and to beat with her gloved hands on the glass all round as the taxi, accelerating without mercy, made off with her into the hinterland of deserted streets. ❖

---

15. **perambulator:** baby carriage.
16. **aperture** (ăp′ər-chər): opening.

At the square's most populous corner

should be—and was—

the short taxi rank.

Thinking *through the* LITERATURE

Connect to the Literature

1. What Do You Think?
Do you think that Mrs. Drover's former fiancé is still alive? Why or why not?

Comprehension Check
- Why does Mrs. Drover return to the house in London?
- What does she find in the house?
- How does she feel at the prospect of seeing her fiancé?

Think Critically

2. What conclusions can you draw about Mrs. Drover's former fiancé?

THINK ABOUT

- his words and actions during their 1916 farewell meeting
- her reactions to him during their farewell
- her current memories of him

3. How would you describe Mrs. Drover's emotions during the course of the story?

4. ACTIVE READING ANALYZING FLASHBACK Review the chart you made in your 📖 **READER'S NOTEBOOK**. What do you learn about Mrs. Drover and her former fiancé in the **flashback?** In what ways do you think the flashback **foreshadows** the story's outcome?

5. Would the story be as powerful if the events were told in chronological order? Why or why not?

6. How would you describe the **tone** of the story's narrator?

7. Do you think there is a rational explanation for the events in this story?

Extend Interpretations

8. Writer's Style Bowen creates a **mood** of foreboding by choosing words carefully. Such phrases as "no human eye" (page 1158) and "spectral glitters" (page 1160) add to this mood. Look for other examples of words and phrases that have similar effects. How important do you think **word choice** is in making the action of this story convincing?

9. Connect to Life Bowen does not offer an explanation for the events at the end of the story, and the reader may interpret the ending in several ways. In general, what is your opinion of stories that are open to more than one interpretation in this way? Support your answer with examples of stories or movies that you know.

Literary Analysis

SETTING AND SUSPENSE The **setting**—the time and place in which a story's action occurs—may play a significant role in creating **suspense** (the tension readers feel as they are drawn into a story). In "The Demon Lover," the setting of war-torn London and Mrs. Drover's empty house—abandoned because of the Blitz—contributes to building suspense by conveying a sense of uncertainty and fear.

Activity Use a chart like the one shown to record your thoughts about the relationship between setting and suspense in Bowen's story.

Details of Setting	How Details Create Suspense
"Dead air came out to meet her as she went in."	Detail creates atmosphere of apprehension and fear.

SURPRISE ENDING A **surprise ending** is an unexpected twist at the end of a story's **plot.** The surprise may be a sudden turn in the action or a revelation that provides a different perspective on the entire story. The last paragraph of "The Demon Lover" reveals an unexpected turn in the action. Identify the twist in the plot, and explain what contributes to making it a surprise.

Choices & CHALLENGES

Writing Options

1. The Next Scene The story ends with Mrs. Drover screaming and pounding her fists on the windows of a speeding taxi. What do you think happens next? Write a new scene to add to the end of the story.

Writing Handbook
See pages 1365–1366: Narrative Writing.

2. Missing-Person Report Using evidence from the story, write a missing-person report about Mrs. Drover. Describe her appearance, actions, and state of mind before her disappearance.

3. Explanatory Paragraph Explain what you think Bowen's purpose for writing this story might have been. Support your ideas with evidence from the story.

Activities & Explorations

1. Dramatic Performance Work with classmates to select music, create sound effects, and develop lighting for a dramatic reading of the story. Cast different people to read the soldier's letter, the thoughts of Mrs. Drover, and the narration. Rehearse and perform the reading. ~ **PERFORMING**

2. Movie Poster Suppose that a movie version of this story has been made. Draw or paint a poster, depicting the taxi scene, to advertise the movie. ~ **ART**

3. Journalists' Meeting You are the editor in chief of a sensational tabloid newspaper. Choose several classmates to act as reporters and editors, and role-play a staff meeting to discuss how you want to cover Mrs. Drover's disappearance.
~ **SPEAKING AND LISTENING**

Art Connection

Moody Image Do you think the painting *Interior with Seated Woman*, reproduced on page 1161, is a suitable image to accompany this story? Explain your answer, commenting on the mood of the painting.

Inquiry & Research

London During the War Research what life was like in London during World War II. Prepare a report that includes copies of photos of wartime London, as well as quotations from people who experienced the Blitz.

Vocabulary in Action

EXERCISE A: MEANING CLUES Answer the following questions.

1. Would you be most likely to signal **assent** by nodding your head up and down, yawning and stretching, or holding your nose?

2. Would a person who is reacting **impassively** be laughing, gasping, or shrugging?

3. What **emanates** from a bouquet of roses—fragrance, thorns, or roots?

4. Would a **prosaic** lifestyle tend to be full of excitement, routine, or danger?

5. If you needed to act **precipitately,** would you be cautious, quick, or sneaky?

EXERCISE B Work with four classmates to describe a fictional school or social event, using the five vocabulary words. One student should begin the description and keep going until he or she has used one of the words; then another student should continue the description, using a second vocabulary word; and so on until all the words have been used.

Building Vocabulary
For an in-depth study of context clues, see page 938.

WORDS TO KNOW	assent	precipitately
	emanate	prosaic
	impassively	

Elizabeth Bowen
1899–1973

Other Works
The Death of the Heart
The Heat of the Day
Collected Stories

Neither English Nor Irish Born in Dublin, Ireland, of Anglo-Irish parents, Elizabeth Bowen spent her early childhood at Bowen's Court, an estate that had been in the family since the 17th century. Although her early childhood was happy, her later childhood years were difficult. When she was seven, her father suffered a nervous breakdown, and she was sent to England with her mother and a governess. Six years later, her mother died after a three-year battle with cancer. Bowen then attended a boarding school for a few years, increasingly feeling herself part of neither England nor Ireland. During the last year of World War I, she returned to Dublin and nursed soldiers suffering from shell shock.

London Years In 1918 Bowen returned to London, where she began writing stories. She later wrote of that time, "From the moment that my pen touched paper, I thought of nothing but writing, and since then I have thought of practically nothing else. . . . [W]hen I have nothing to write, I feel only half alive." In 1923, she married Alan C. Cameron, an educator, and published her first collection of stories, *Encounters*. Her first novel, *The Hotel*, appeared in 1927, when she also inherited Bowen's Court, becoming the first woman owner of the estate, although she did not move there until 1952.

Bowen's Fiction Bowen had a prolific career, publishing more than 20 novels and volumes of short stories. Her fiction, which deals primarily with the upper middle class, is beautifully crafted, with finely drawn characters and detailed, evocative descriptions of setting. Many of her best works are set in wartime London, a setting she presents with realism and force.

Diverse Career Bowen's career was diversified as well as distinguished. She was a reviewer for the *Tatler* in 1941 and worked for the Ministry of Information during the early years of World War II. In addition to short stories and novels, she published *Bowen's Court* (a history of her family) and nonfiction works dealing with her life and writing. She is considered a major 20th-century British writer.

Author Activity

War Duties During the early years of World War II, Bowen worked for the Ministry of Information. Find out what she did and why her Anglo-Irish background made her particularly suited to the work.

A Hanging

Personal Essay by GEORGE ORWELL

Connect to Your Life

Crime and Punishment Do you believe that some crimes merit the death penalty, or do you oppose any use of capital punishment? With a small group of classmates, discuss your views on capital punishment.

Build Background

British Burma Orwell's essay is set in Burma, a Southeast Asian country now known as Myanmar. In a series of wars in the 19th century, the British gradually gained control of the country, which in 1886 was made a province of British India. The Burmese people deeply resented British rule, under which they endured poverty, a lack of political freedom, and religious restrictions. It was into this atmosphere of discontent that Eric Blair—later to assume the pen name George Orwell—came in 1922.

Born in India but educated in England, Orwell arrived in Burma as an assistant superintendent in the Indian Imperial Police. He and his fellow British officers, many of whom were inexperienced in police work, led a native-born police force 13,000 men strong. Orwell became increasingly disillusioned with his role as a police officer and with British colonialism in general, and he later gave a scathing account of British society in Burma in his novel *Burmese Days.* His classic essays "A Hanging" and "Shooting an Elephant" also focus on his experiences of and reactions to British colonial rule.

WORDS TO KNOW
Vocabulary Preview

anecdote   oscillate
formality   timorously
genially

Focus Your Reading

LITERARY ANALYSIS **PERSONAL ESSAY** **Personal essays** allow writers to express their viewpoints on subjects by reflecting on events or incidents in their own lives. Such essays tend to contain more descriptive details than formal and objective essays do—like this detail in "A Hanging":

> *And once, in spite of the men who gripped him by each shoulder, he [the prisoner] stepped slightly aside to avoid a puddle on the path.*

As you read Orwell's essay, look for other descriptive passages that reveal the writer's observations.

ACTIVE READING **INFERRING THE AUTHOR'S PERSPECTIVE** A writer's view of his or her subject is called the **author's perspective.** A perspective can be a result of a political standpoint or of an attitude, a belief, or a feeling that affects a writer's treatment of a topic. To identify the author's perspective in a personal essay, you have to **infer** it from clues such as the following:

- **details** that the author chose to include
- **opinions,** as when Orwell says that he suddenly realized the "unspeakable wrongness" of the execution
- **language** that reveals the author's emotions about the events he or she describes

READER'S NOTEBOOK Use a cluster diagram like the one shown to keep track of details, opinions, and language that reveal Orwell's perspective.

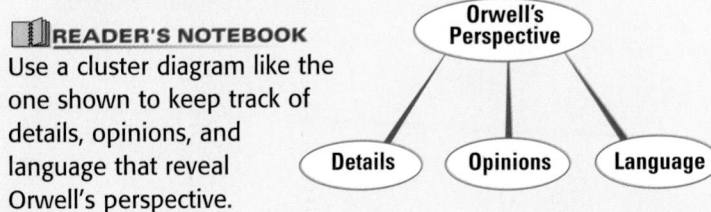

A HANGING   **1167**

A Hanging

George Orwell

IT was in Burma, a sodden morning of the rains. A sickly light, like yellow tinfoil, was slanting over the high walls into the jail yard. We were waiting outside the condemned cells, a row of sheds fronted with double bars, like small animal cages. Each cell measured about ten feet by ten and was quite bare within except for a plank bed and a pot of drinking water. In some of them brown silent men were squatting at the inner bars, with their blankets draped round them. These were the condemned men, due to be hanged within the next week or two.

One prisoner had been brought out of his cell. He was a Hindu, a puny wisp of a man, with a shaven head and vague liquid eyes. He had a thick, sprouting moustache, absurdly too big for his body, rather like the moustache of a comic man on the films. Six tall Indian warders[1] were guarding him and getting him ready for the gallows. Two of them stood by with rifles and fixed bayonets, while the others handcuffed him, passed a chain through his handcuffs and fixed it to their belts, and lashed his arms tight to his sides. They crowded very close about him, with their hands always on him in a careful, caressing grip, as though all the while feeling him to make sure he was there. It was like men handling a fish which is still alive and may jump back into the water. But he stood quite unresisting, yielding his arms limply to the ropes, as though he hardly noticed what was happening.

Eight o'clock struck and a bugle call, desolately thin in the wet air, floated from the distant barracks. The superintendent of the jail, who was standing apart from the rest of us, moodily prodding the gravel with his stick, raised his head at the sound. He was an army doctor, with a grey toothbrush moustache and a gruff voice. "For God's sake hurry up, Francis," he said irritably. "The man ought to have been dead by this time. Aren't you ready yet?"

Francis, the head jailer, a fat Dravidian[2] in a white drill suit and gold spectacles, waved his black hand. "Yes sir, yes sir," he bubbled. "All iss satisfactorily prepared. The hangman iss waiting. We shall proceed."

"Well, quick march, then. The prisoners can't get their breakfast till this job's over."

We set out for the gallows. Two warders marched on either side of the prisoner, with their rifles at the slope; two others marched close against him, gripping him by arm and shoulder, as though at once pushing and supporting him. The rest of us, magistrates and the like, followed behind. Suddenly, when we had gone ten yards, the procession stopped short without any order or warning. A dreadful thing had happened—a dog, come goodness knows whence, had appeared in the yard. It came bounding among us with a loud volley of barks, and leapt round us wagging its whole body, wild with glee at finding so many human beings together. It was a large, wooly dog, half Airedale, half pariah.[3] For a moment it pranced round us, and then, before anyone could stop it, it had made a dash for the prisoner, and jumping up tried to lick his face. Everyone stood aghast, too taken aback even to grab at the dog.

"Who let that bloody brute in here?" said the superintendent angrily. "Catch it, someone!"

A warder, detached from the escort, charged clumsily after the dog, but it danced and gamboled[4] just out of his reach, taking everything as part of the game. A young Eurasian jailer picked up a handful of gravel and tried to stone the dog away, but it dodged the stones and came after us again. Its yaps echoed from the jail walls. The prisoner, in the grasp of the two warders, looked on incuriously, as though this was another formality of the hanging. It was several minutes

---

1. **warders:** prison guards.
2. **Dravidian** (drə-vĭd′ē-ən): a member of a dark-skinned people of southern India.
3. **pariah:** a wild or domesticated mongrel dog.
4. **gamboled** (găm′bəld): jumped about playfully.

before someone managed to catch the dog. Then we put my handkerchief through its collar and moved off once more, with the dog still straining and whimpering.

It was about forty yards to the gallows. I watched the bare brown back of the prisoner marching in front of me. He walked clumsily with his bound arms, but quite steadily, with that bobbing gait of the Indian who never straightens his knees. At each step his muscles slid neatly into place, the lock of hair on his scalp danced up and down, his feet printed themselves on the wet gravel. And once, in spite of the men who gripped him by each shoulder, he stepped slightly aside to avoid a puddle on the path.

It is curious, but till that moment I had never realized what it means to destroy a healthy, conscious man. When I saw the prisoner step aside to avoid the puddle, I saw the mystery, the unspeakable wrongness, of cutting a life short when it is in full tide. This man was not dying, he was alive just as we were alive. All the organs of his body were working—bowels digesting food, skin renewing itself, nails growing, tissues forming—all toiling away in solemn foolery. His nails would still be growing when he stood on the drop, when he was falling through the air with a tenth of a second to live. His eyes saw the yellow gravel and the grey walls, and his brain still remembered, foresaw, reasoned—reasoned even about puddles. He and we were a party of men

walking together, seeing, hearing, feeling, understanding the same world; and in two minutes, with a sudden snap, one of us would be gone—one mind less, one world less.

The gallows stood in a small yard, separate from the main grounds of the prison, and overgrown with tall prickly weeds. It was a brick erection like three sides of a shed, with planking on top, and above that two beams and a cross-bar with the rope dangling. The hangman, a grey-haired convict in the white uniform of the prison, was waiting beside his machine. He greeted us with a servile[5] crouch as we entered.

---

5. **servile:** slavelike; cringing.

George Orwell at the police training school at Mandalay, Burma, in 1922. Photo courtesy of Roger Beadon. Orwell is circled.

At a word from Francis the two warders, gripping the prisoner more closely than ever, half led, half pushed him to the gallows and helped him clumsily up the ladder. Then the hangman climbed up and fixed the rope round the prisoner's neck.

WE stood waiting, five yards away. The warders had formed in a rough circle round the gallows. And then, when the noose was fixed, the prisoner began crying out to his god. It was a high, reiterated cry of "Ram! Ram! Ram! Ram!"[6] not urgent and fearful like a prayer or a cry for help, but steady, rhythmical, almost like the tolling of a bell. The dog answered the sound with a whine. The hangman, still standing on the gallows, produced a small cotton bag like a flour bag and drew it down over the prisoner's face. But the sound, muffled by the cloth, still persisted, over and over again: "Ram! Ram! Ram! Ram! Ram!"

The hangman climbed down and stood ready, holding the lever. Minutes seemed to pass. The

---

6. **Ram** (räm): a form of *Rama*, the name of an incarnation of Vishnu, one of the three main Hindu gods.

steady, muffled crying from the prisoner went on and on, "Ram! Ram! Ram!" never faltering for an instant. The superintendent, his head on his chest, was slowly poking the ground with his stick; perhaps he was counting the cries, allowing the prisoner a fixed number—fifty, perhaps, or a hundred. Everyone had changed color. The Indians had gone grey like bad coffee, and one or two of the bayonets were wavering. We looked at the lashed, hooded man on the drop, and listened to his cries—each cry another second of life; the same thought was in all our minds: oh, kill him quickly, get it over, stop that abominable noise!

Suddenly the superintendent made up his mind. Throwing up his head he made a swift motion with his stick. "Chalo!"[7] he shouted almost fiercely.

There was a clanking noise, and then dead silence. The prisoner had vanished, and the rope was twisting on itself. I let go of the dog, and it galloped immediately to the back of the gallows; but when it got there it stopped short, barked, and then retreated into a corner of the yard, where it stood among the weeds, looking timorously out at us. We went round the gallows to inspect the prisoner's body. He was dangling with his toes pointed straight downwards, very slowly revolving, as dead as a stone.

The superintendent reached out with his stick and poked the bare body; it oscillated, slightly. "*He's* all right," said the superintendent. He backed out from under the gallows, and blew out a deep breath. The moody look had gone out of his face quite suddenly. He glanced at his wristwatch. "Eight minutes past eight. Well, that's all for this morning, thank God."

The warders unfixed bayonets and marched away. The dog, sobered and conscious of having misbehaved itself, slipped after them. We walked out of the gallows yard, past the condemned cells with their waiting prisoners, into the big central yard of the prison. The convicts, under the command of warders armed with lathis,[8] were already receiving their breakfast. They squatted in long rows, each man holding a tin pannikin,[9] while two warders with buckets marched round ladling out rice; it seemed quite a homely, jolly scene, after the hanging. An enormous relief had come upon us now that the job was done. One felt an impulse to sing, to break into a run, to snigger. All at once everyone began chattering gaily.

THE Eurasian boy walking beside me nodded towards the way we had come, with a knowing smile: "Do you know, sir, our friend (he meant the dead man), when he heard his appeal had been dismissed, he pissed on the floor of his cell. From fright.—Kindly take one of my cigarettes, sir. Do you not admire my new silver case, sir? From the boxwallah,[10] two rupees eight annas.[11] Classy European style."

Several people laughed—at what, nobody seemed certain.

Francis was walking by the superintendent, talking garrulously:[12] "Well, sir, all hass passed off with the utmost satisfactoriness. It wass all finished—flick! like that. It iss not always so—oah, no! I have known cases where the doctor

---

7. **Chalo!** (chä′lō) *Hindi:* Go!

8. **lathis** (lä′tēz): heavy bamboo sticks bound with iron, used as weapons by the police in India.

9. **pannikin:** a small pan or shallow cup.

10. **boxwallah:** in India, a peddler.

11. **rupees** (rōō-pēz′) . . . **annas** (ä′nəz): Indian units of money. (Annas, which are no longer used, were coins worth ¹⁄₁₆ of a rupee.)

12. **garrulously** (găr′ə-ləs-lē): in a wordy, long-winded manner.

WORDS TO KNOW

timorously (tĭm′ər-əs-lē) *adv.* in a fearful or apprehensive way; timidly
oscillate (ŏs′ə-lāt′) *v.* to swing back and forth

1172

wass obliged to go beneath the gallows and pull the prisoner's legs to ensure decease. Most disagreeable!"

"Wriggling about, eh? That's bad," said the superintendent.

"Ach, sir, it iss worse when they become refractory![13] One man, I recall, clung to the bars of hiss cage when we went to take him out. You will scarcely credit, sir, that it took six warders to dislodge him, three pulling at each leg. We reasoned with him. 'My dear fellow,' we said, 'think of all the pain and trouble you are causing to us!' But no, he would not listen! Ach, he wass very troublesome!"

I found that I was laughing quite loudly. Everyone was laughing. Even the superintendent grinned in a tolerant way. "You'd better all come out and have a drink," he said quite genially. "I've got a bottle of whisky in the car. We could do with it."

We went through the big double gates of the prison, into the road. "Pulling at his legs!" exclaimed a Burmese magistrate suddenly, and burst into a loud chuckling. We all began laughing again. At that moment Francis's anecdote seemed extraordinarily funny. We all had a drink together, native and European alike, quite amicably.[14] The dead man was a hundred yards away. ❖

---

13. **refractory:** hard to manage; stubborn.
14. **amicably:** in a friendly manner.

WORDS TO KNOW

genially (jēn′yə-lē) *adv.* in a friendly manner
anecdote (ăn′ĭk-dōt′) *n.* a brief account of an interesting or humorous incident

A HANGING   **1173**

Connect to the Literature

1. What Do You Think?
What is your reaction to the events described in "A Hanging"? Discuss your thoughts with a classmate.

> **Comprehension Check**
> - What event disrupts the procession to the gallows?
> - What do the men do after the hanging takes place?

Think Critically

2. How would you account for the men's laughter and chatter after the hanging?

3. How do you think the intrusion of the dog affects the **mood** of this essay?

THINK ABOUT
- the moods of the prisoner and the warders
- the behavior of the dog
- the warders' struggle to catch the dog

4. Orwell does not tell the reader what the condemned man's crime was. Why do you think he chose not to include this information?

5. **ACTIVE READING** | **INFERRING THE AUTHOR'S PERSPECTIVE**
Review the cluster diagram you made in your **READER'S NOTEBOOK.** What can you **infer** about Orwell's **perspective** on the subject of the essay?

Extend Interpretations

6. Different Perspectives How might the essay be different if it were written by one of the Indian warders or by one of the prisoners in the condemned cells?

7. Connect to Life Think back to your discussion of capital punishment for the Connect to Your Life feature on page 1167. Has reading "A Hanging" altered your view on the subject of the death penalty? Share your thoughts with a classmate.

Literary Analysis

PERSONAL ESSAY Whereas a formal essay usually presents carefully structured arguments, a **personal essay** is a brief nonfiction work that expresses a writer's thoughts, feelings, and opinions on a subject in a less systematic way. Frequently, a personal essay is (like "A Hanging") a reflection on an episode in the writer's life.

Most personal essays are written with more than one **purpose** in mind. Identifying the writer's main purpose for writing can help you to determine an essay's **theme**—the message that the writer conveys about the events described.

Paired Activity Bearing in mind your thoughts about Orwell's perspective, answer the following questions:
- What do you think was Orwell's main purpose in writing this essay?
- What do you think is the main theme of the essay?

Jot down your thoughts, and discuss them with a partner. How might Orwell have conveyed the same theme in a formal essay?

REVIEW | **IRONY IN NONFICTION**
As you know, **irony** involves a contrast between what is expected and what actually happens. In works of nonfiction, irony can be used to reveal and reinforce important ideas. What details or statements in "A Hanging" might be considered ironic? What effect do you think Orwell's use of irony has on the **tone** of the essay? How does irony relate to the essay's main **theme?**

Choices & CHALLENGES

Writing Options

Orwell's Diary Imagine you are George Orwell. Write a diary entry describing the day of the hanging. Remember, a diary writer, unlike the writer of a personal essay, is not writing for an audience.

Activities & Explorations

Still Life In "A Hanging," the setting and several events are described in great detail. Draw a picture of a key scene in the work, relying as much as possible on the details Orwell provided. ~ **ART**

Inquiry & Research

End of British Rule Research the final decades of British rule in Burma. Find out about the country's nationalist movement, its fate during World War II, and its gaining of independence in 1948. Present your findings to the class in an oral report.

Vocabulary in Action

EXERCISE: CONTEXT CLUES On your paper, write the Word to Know that best completes each sentence.

1. The condemned man _____ observed the noose.

2. His guards treated him _____, as if they were all on a picnic.

3. The hanging was a strange combination of a ceremonial _____ and a sudden killing.

4. The noose began to _____ in the breeze.

5. After the prisoner was dead, one of the guards told an amusing _____.

Building Vocabulary

For an in-depth lesson on how to expand your vocabulary, see page 1182.

WORDS TO KNOW	anecdote formality genially	oscillate timorously

George Orwell
1903–1950

Other Works
"Shooting an Elephant"
"How the Poor Die"
Animal Farm
Nineteen Eighty-Four

Voluntary Poverty "George Orwell" was the pen name of Eric Arthur Blair, who was born in the Indian province of Bengal, where his father was serving in the Indian civil service. In 1922 Orwell joined the Indian Imperial Police and left for Burma, which was at that time under British rule. When Orwell discovered how much the Burmese disliked British rule, however, he became disenchanted with Britain's imperialist policies. He eventually quit his job and, at the age of 25, decided to live the life of the poor and downtrodden, for whom he had deep, abiding sympathies. Working as a dishwasher and a day laborer, he tramped through the countryside with the homeless. Out of these experiences came his first book, *Down and Out in Paris and London,* published in 1933.

Speaking Out for Justice and Freedom
Throughout his short life, Orwell continued to sympathize with the underdog and to speak out against social and political injustice. Like many other young writers, he left England to fight with the anti-Fascist forces in Spain's civil war. He was wounded in the fighting, but his experiences provided him with the material for his book *Homage to Catalonia.* Near the end of World War II, he completed the first of his famous novels— *Animal Farm,* a satire in which he warned prophetically of the dangers of dictatorships. In 1949 he published *Nineteen Eighty-Four,* focusing on the appalling possibilities of life in a totalitarian state. Orwell completed *Nineteen Eighty-Four* while battling tuberculosis, from which he died at the peak of his career.

Communication Workshop · Web Site

Reaching out through the Web . . .

During World Wars I and II, people around the world tuned in their radios to learn how the war was progressing and to listen to political leaders such as Winston Churchill deliver important speeches. Radio broadcasting revolutionized communication by allowing people to learn about events as they happened. Today, the World Wide Web allows more people to communicate faster than ever before. The Web contains millions of **Web sites** that offer news and information about individuals, companies, and organizations.

For Your Portfolio

PROMPT Create a Web site that gives information about yourself, an area that interests you, or an issue you feel is important.

Purpose: To share information about you and your interests
Audience: The diverse users of the Web

Basics in a Box

Web Site at a Glance

Visual Information
- pictures
- graphics
- colors
- tints

Verbal Information
- paragraphs
- captions
- labels

Web Site

Hypertext Links

Links to supporting documents and other Web sites

GUIDELINES & STANDARDS

A successful Web site should

- clearly show what the site is about
- be designed in a logical manner so that users can easily navigate through the parts of the site
- use graphics to add to or clarify written information
- include well-written text that provides accurate and current information
- provide working links to other reliable Web sites related to the main topics
- offer text, graphics, and links that relate to each other and that work together to create a whole

Analyzing a Model Web Site

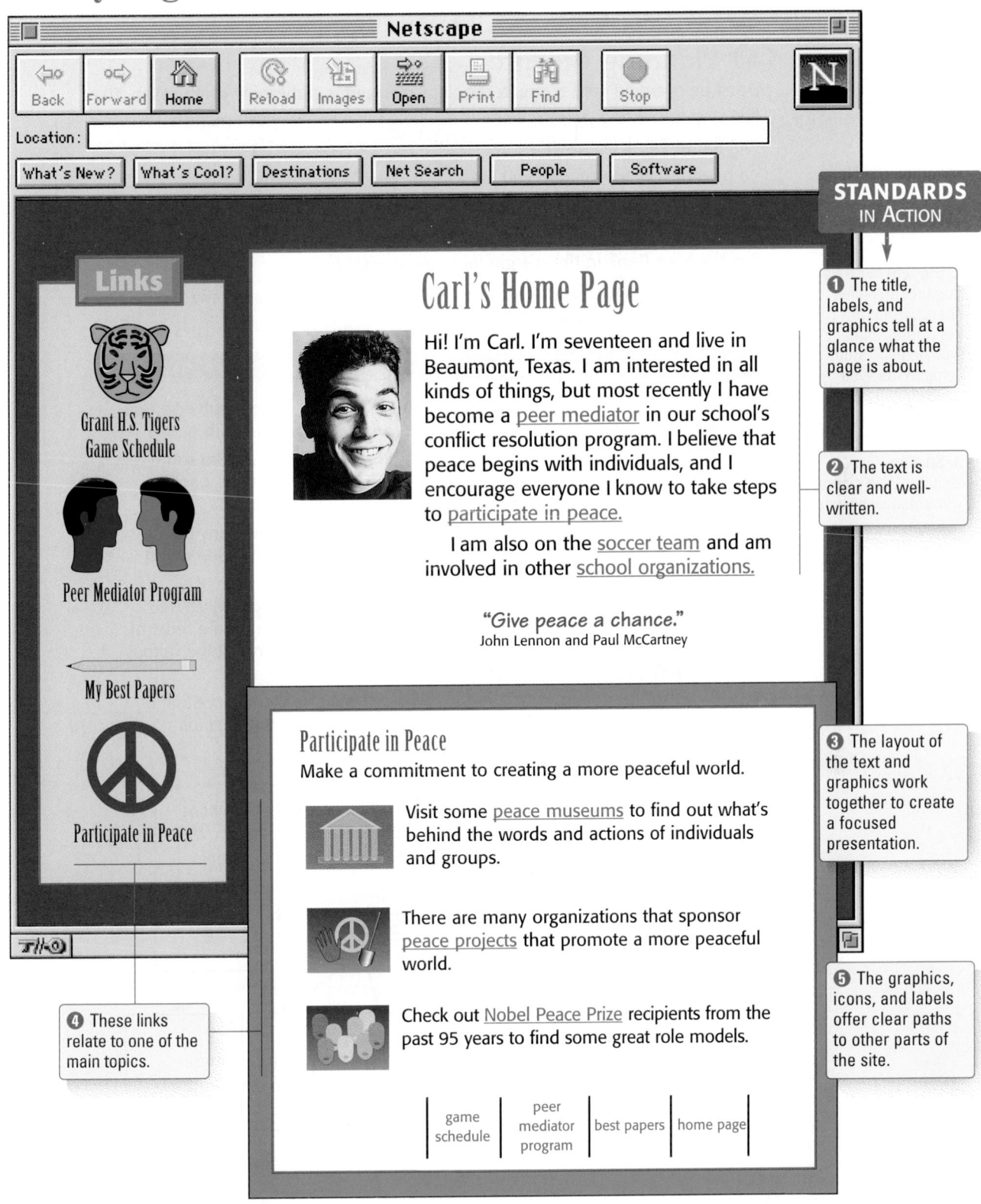

Netscape

Back | Forward | Home | Reload | Images | Open | Print | Find | Stop

Location:

What's New? | What's Cool? | Destinations | Net Search | People | Software

STANDARDS IN ACTION

Links

Grant H.S. Tigers Game Schedule

Peer Mediator Program

My Best Papers

Participate in Peace

Carl's Home Page

Hi! I'm Carl. I'm seventeen and live in Beaumont, Texas. I am interested in all kinds of things, but most recently I have become a peer mediator in our school's conflict resolution program. I believe that peace begins with individuals, and I encourage everyone I know to take steps to participate in peace.

I am also on the soccer team and am involved in other school organizations.

"Give peace a chance."
John Lennon and Paul McCartney

❶ The title, labels, and graphics tell at a glance what the page is about.

❷ The text is clear and well-written.

Participate in Peace
Make a commitment to creating a more peaceful world.

Visit some peace museums to find out what's behind the words and actions of individuals and groups.

There are many organizations that sponsor peace projects that promote a more peaceful world.

Check out Nobel Peace Prize recipients from the past 95 years to find some great role models.

| game schedule | peer mediator program | best papers | home page |

❸ The layout of the text and graphics work together to create a focused presentation.

❹ These links relate to one of the main topics.

❺ The graphics, icons, and labels offer clear paths to other parts of the site.

1. Your Working Portfolio
Build on one of the **Writing Options** you completed earlier in this unit:

• **Multimedia Notes,** p. 1112
• **Web Site Page,** p. 1134

2. Student Web Pages
Conduct an online search using the keywords "student web pages." Study some of the Web pages you find to get ideas for your own Web site.

3. Surfing
Visit our Web site at www.mcdougallittell.com

Creating Your Web Site

❶ Planning the Site

Don't be overwhelmed by the technology involved in publishing on the Web. The first step in creating your Web site is deciding what you want to publish. Your site might include:

• a brief description of who you are
• information about your hobbies, interests, talents, job, or school
• your stories, poems, and school essays

See the **Idea Bank** in the margin for more suggestions.

Your Web site will integrate text, graphics, and Hypertext links to other Web sites. Follow the planning steps below.

Text: Planning the Content

▶ **1. Choose your subject or subjects.** Stick with three or four subjects that you think are interesting and that you would like to share with others.

▶ **2. Develop the subjects or issues that you will include.** Make some notes about all that you already know and all that you might want to include about each subject.

▶ **3. Decide how many pages to include in your site.** How many pages will you need to clearly cover the content? Use the notes you made about your subjects to help you figure this out.

▶ **4. Organize your home page.** How will you set up your page? Most Web sites cluster around various topics. You will need to decide on the order of topics on your first page and how to encourage users to try out the various possibilities you are offering them.

▶ **5. Look for resources.** Books or the Web itself will give you information on planning your Web site. You may find diagrams like this one helpful.

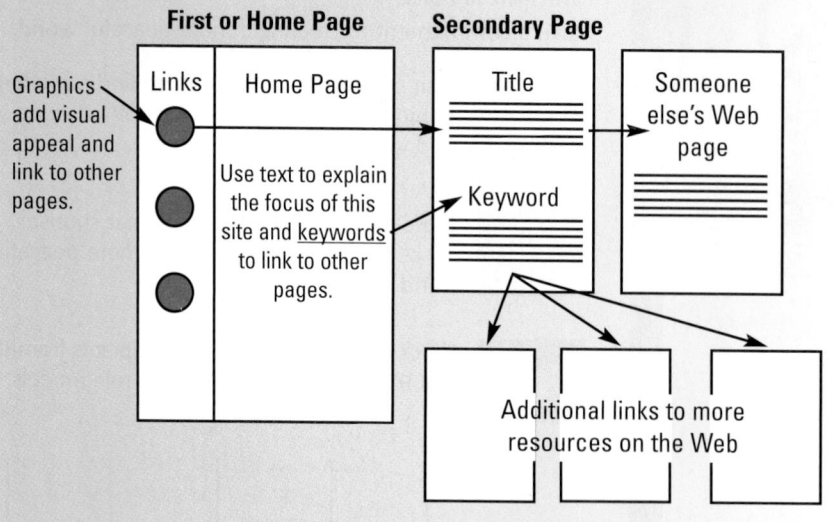

First or Home Page — Links — Home Page — Graphics add visual appeal and link to other pages. — Use text to explain the focus of this site and <u>keywords</u> to link to other pages. — Secondary Page — Title — Keyword — Someone else's Web page — Additional links to more resources on the Web

Graphics: Planning the Design

▶ 1. **Focus on the first page, or home page, of your Web site.** Visitors to your home page should be able to learn quickly what the site is about, who created it, and what links are available.

▶ 2. **Think about the balance of graphics and text.** How many illustrations or visual aids will you provide? How much text will you include? Make several sketches to help you achieve the right balance.

▶ 3. **Keep it simple.** Make sure the elements of your site work together to create a clear presentation. Don't crowd your screen with unnecessary colors or visuals. Also avoid using large or complicated illustrations that take a long time to download. Visitors to your site will be frustrated by this.

▶ 4. **Compile an annotated list of Hypertext links.** Make a list of several other Web sites that offer additional information about your topics. Be sure these other sites contain reliable information. Jot down a brief description of each site. Later, you can decide which ones to link to from your site.

TECH Tutor

The Web is your best source of information on the technical skills required for creating a Web page. Spend some time working through one of the excellent on-line tutorials or workshops that give you step-by-step guidance in creating a Web page. Your teacher may provide the addresses for tutorials or you can find them by doing a search using the keywords "creating web pages."

❷ Developing the Site

Maintain a clear focus on your goals as you develop your content. Follow the steps below.

• First, write the text. This can include short paragraphs that introduce the site and labels or captions for the graphics, as well as other paragraphs that provide more in-depth information on a topic.

• Next, arrange the text and graphics so that the organization of each page in your site is clear. Use your planning sketch as a guide. Remember that space is limited. The more text you use, the smaller the graphics need to be.

• Finally, add your links. Review your annotated planning list of links and select those that are most relevant. Make sure you haven't connected your site to any bad links—links that don't work.

Ask Your Peer Reviewer

• Which parts of the site, if any, were confusing? Why?
• What are the most interesting parts?
• What problems did you have in navigating through my site?

❸ Revising

TARGET SKILL ▶ **ELIMINATING CLUTTER** Visual clutter can make a Web site hard to understand. Delete any text or graphics that seem to distract viewers from the main points of your page.

WEB Shortcuts

A basic template is provided for this lesson on the McDougal Littell Web site. You can avoid much of the HTML coding if you choose to use this template. Access the Web site at this address: www.mcdougallittell.com

Need revising help?

Review the **Guidelines and Standards,** p. 1176

Consider **peer reader** comments

Check **Revision Guidelines,** p. 1355

Make sure that every heading, picture, color, and background contributes to the clarity of the page. Review your site and note any long paragraphs that look hard to read. Can these be shortened? One technique that makes reading on the Web easier is to use bulleted lists to set off the major points in a text.

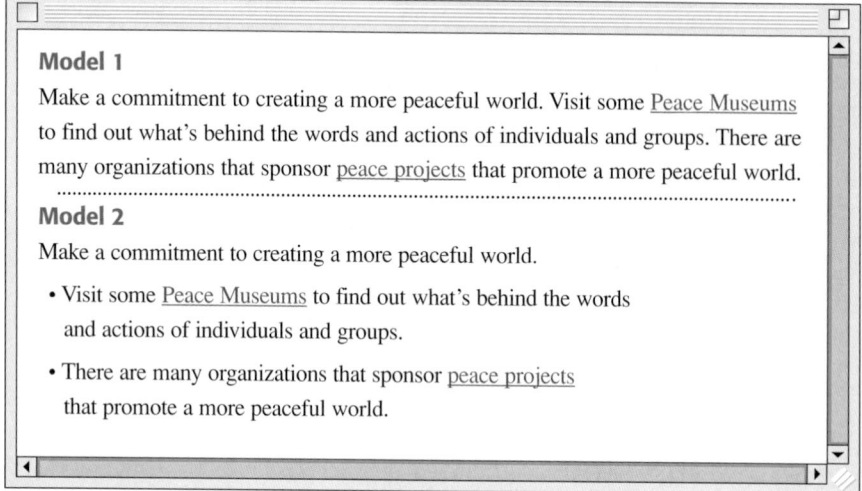

Model 1

Make a commitment to creating a more peaceful world. Visit some Peace Museums to find out what's behind the words and actions of individuals and groups. There are many organizations that sponsor peace projects that promote a more peaceful world.

Model 2

Make a commitment to creating a more peaceful world.

• Visit some Peace Museums to find out what's behind the words and actions of individuals and groups.

• There are many organizations that sponsor peace projects that promote a more peaceful world.

❹ Editing and Proofreading

TARGET SKILL ▶ COMPLETE SENTENCES Your Web site will create a better impression if you take the time to edit your text. Reread captions and paragraphs to check that you have written complete sentences. Be sure that each sentence contains a subject and a predicate. Rewrite any fragments you find. Check for errors in punctuation and capitalization too.

Have a question?

See the **Communications Handbook**

Inquiry and Research, pp. 1381–1383

Viewing and Representing, pp. 1388–1390

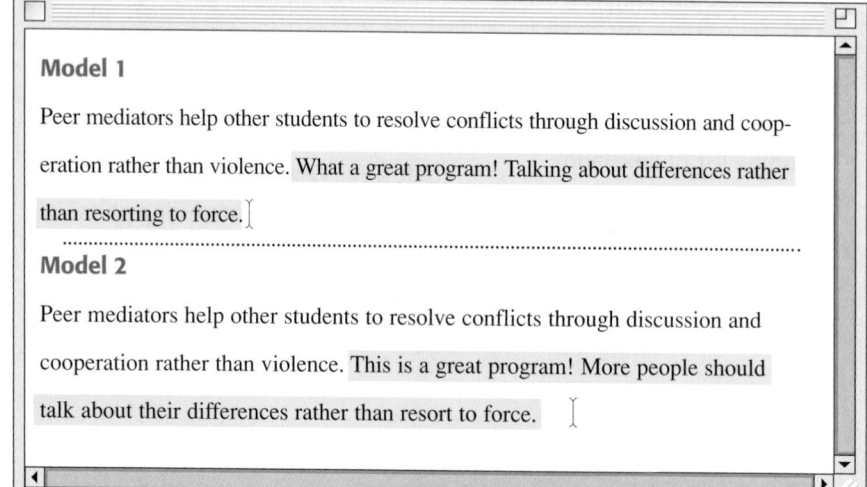

Model 1

Peer mediators help other students to resolve conflicts through discussion and cooperation rather than violence. What a great program! Talking about differences rather than resorting to force.

Model 2

Peer mediators help other students to resolve conflicts through discussion and cooperation rather than violence. This is a great program! More people should talk about their differences rather than resort to force.

❺ Reflecting

FOR YOUR WORKING PORTFOLIO What did you learn about writing for the Web? How is the writing process different in this media? What new skills would you like to develop to help you with future online writing projects? Attach your responses to a print-out of your Web site. Save these in your **Working Portfolio.**

Read this excerpt from a Web page. The underlined sections may include the following kinds of errors:

- **redundant or unnecessary phrases**
- **comma errors**
- **sentence fragments**
- **lack of subject-verb agreement**

For each underlined section, choose the revision that most improves the writing.

> Welcome to *Words of Peace*. On this Web page you will find a selection of my favorite quotations about peace, <u>which I especially like.</u> Together they present an inspiring survey of <u>feelings, and ideas</u> about this important topic. <u>People who have not experienced war. Peace is often taken for granted.</u> Young people today may believe that peace is something hippies talked about in the 1960s. Perhaps <u>some people believes</u> peace is a worn-out idea; maybe they find it embarrassing. <u>At this point in time, these attitudes are</u> dangerous and irresponsible. I hope these quotations will help <u>readers abandons</u> such cynical points of view.
>
> (1)   (2)   (3)   (4)   (5)   (6)

1. **A.** which I like a lot.
   B. that I especially like.
   C. Delete phrase and add period after *peace*.
   D. Correct as is

2. **A.** feelings, and, ideas
   B. feelings and ideas
   C. feelings and, ideas
   D. Correct as is

3. **A.** People who have not experienced war often take peace for granted.
   B. People who have not experienced war they often take peace for granted.
   C. People who have not experienced war, they often take peace for granted.
   D. Correct as is

4. **A.** some peoples believe
   B. some peoples believes
   C. some people believe
   D. Correct as is

5. **A.** At this point in time—these attitudes are
   B. Nowadays these attitudes are
   C. At this point in time. These attitudes are
   D. Correct as is

6. **A.** readers abandoned
   B. readers abandon
   C. reader abandon
   D. Correct as is

Need extra help?

See the **Grammar Handbook**

Correcting fragments, p. 1409

Punctuation chart, pp. 1413–1414

Subject-verb agreement, pp. 1410–1411

Clues to Word Meaning

> From a world in which life or death, victory or defeat, national survival or national extinction, had been the sole issues, I returned [home] to a society where no one discussed anything but the price of butter. . . .
>
> Keyed up as I had been by the month-long strain of daily rushing to and fro in attendance on the dying, and nightly waiting for the death which hovered darkly in the sky overhead, I found it excruciating to maintain even an appearance of interest and sympathy.
>
> —Vera Brittain, *Testament of Youth*

There are many ways of deciphering the unfamiliar words that you encounter when you read. In the excerpt on the left, Vera Brittain describes her sense of alienation upon returning home to England from the battlefields of France. How might you figure out the meaning of *excruciating*, a word whose meaning provides an insight into Brittain's feelings?

Note that Brittain contrasts the "life or death, victory or defeat" concerns of those fighting the war with the trivial, "price of butter" problems of those at home. Then imagine yourself just home from the front-lines, trying to sympathize with civilians who have not experienced the intensity of war. By examining context clues and putting yourself in a character's place, you can make a good guess that Brittain's efforts to cope might be extremely painful—that is, *excruciating*.

Strategies for Building Vocabulary

Using context clues is just one strategy that can be used to decipher the meaning of a word. Other strategies include comparing the unfamiliar word with a known word and noting familiar word parts. The chart on this page demonstrates how those strategies can be applied to the deciphering of meanings.

❶ **Plan Your Attack** Read this excerpt from George Orwell's "A Hanging." Note the word *servile*. Then study the chart.

> The hangman, a grey-haired convict in the white uniform of the prison, was waiting beside his machine. He greeted us with a servile crouch as we entered.
>
> —George Orwell, "A Hanging"

Step	Example
1. Think of Similar Words	*Serve* and *servant* are like *servile*.
2. Compare Roots	All three words are so similar; I think their roots must be the same. They might be part of the same word family.

Step	Example
3. Analyze the Context	The hangman is a prisoner, and he greets the officers in a crouch, as a servant afraid of displeasing his master might.
4. Develop a Meaning	So *servile* has something to do with serving and with fear; it must mean something like "behaving fearfully, like a powerless servant."
5. Check a Dictionary	*Servile* means "slavish in character or attitude," so my definition was good. The word's etymology indicates that it is related to *servant* and *serve*.

❷ **Record and Use the Word** To make the word a part of your permanent vocabulary, write it down and make a point of using it in class discussions or other conversations during the next few days.

EXERCISE Choose five unfamiliar words from the selections in Unit Six, and apply the deciphering strategies outlined above to each word.

Grammar from Literature

Experienced writers sometimes use special structures called sentence openers to begin their sentences. A **sentence opener** is a word or phrase that calls attention to certain details. The main idea in a sentence always comes after the sentence opener. Using sentence openers allows a writer to add concrete detail, to improve sentence variety and rhythm, and to increase readers' interest by building suspense. Look at the examples of sentence openers below.

> single word
> **Annoyed,** she picked up the letter, which bore no stamp.
> —Elizabeth Bowen, "The Demon Lover"
>
> infinitive phrase
> **To conceal their intentions even from themselves,** they make use of picturesque metaphors.
> —Aldous Huxley, "Words and Behavior"
>
> adverb clause
> **Long after the family had gone to bed and the world had grown silent,** I crept into the dining room to be alone with Edward's portrait.
> —Vera Brittain, *Testament of Youth*

A writer may use grammatical structures of more than one kind in an opener.

> infinitive phrase   prepositional phrase
> **To conceal their intentions even from themselves,** they make use of picturesque metaphors.
> —"Words and Behavior"
>
> prepositional phrase   adjective clause
> **In spite of the War, which destroyed so much hope, so much beauty, so much promise,** life is still here to be lived.
> —*Testament of Youth*

Using Sentence Openers in Your Writing Professional writers take advantage of the impact of sentence openers, and so can you. Openers offer not only the opportunity to add detail and improve sentence variety, they also provide a way to hold your reader's attention. By placing detail in the opener, you intentionally delay the main idea. You control your reader's focus. Study the effect of the opener in the example below.

> ORIGINAL
> **The Germans bombed Britain.**
>
> REWRITTEN
> **Almost nightly from August to October 1940, the Germans bombed Britain.**

Usage Tip Avoid dangling modifiers when writing periodic sentences. A **dangling modifier** does not clearly modify any noun or pronoun in the sentence. Make sure the sentence opener clearly modifies a word in the sentence.

> INCORRECT   participial phrase
> **Having contracted blood poisoning early in the war, Rupert Brooke's poems were published posthumously because he died.**
>
> CORRECT   participial phrase
> **Having contracted blood poisoning early in the war, Rupert Brooke died, and his poems were published posthumously.**

In the first example above, although the opener appears to modify *poems,* it does not clearly modify any noun in the sentence. In the second example, the opener clearly modifies *Rupert Brooke.*

WRITING EXERCISE Rewrite each sentence by adding a sentence opener of the type named in parentheses.
1. The young airman spoke of the wastefulness of war. (single word)
2. Winston Churchill gave powerful radio speeches. (infinitive phrase)
3. Patients often found it difficult to sleep at the hospital. (participial phrase)
4. The plane returned to the base in England. (adverb clause)
5. The soldier's mother stared at the photograph of her son. (prepositional phrase)

GRAMMAR EXERCISE Rewrite these sentences, correcting any errors in punctuation and usage. If a sentence is correct, write *Correct.*
1. With a surprise ending, the reader is unprepared for the last paragraph of "The Demon Lover."
2. Wounded several times in combat, World War I affected Siegfried Sassoon for the rest of his life.
3. In "The Demon Lover," Elizabeth Bowen tells the story of Kathleen Drover.
4. Trying to get her packages to the train station, a taxi picks up Drover and takes her on a terrifying ride.
5. Ending with a reference to the dead prisoner who "was a hundred yards away," Orwell underscores the horror of the hanging.

Emerging Modernism

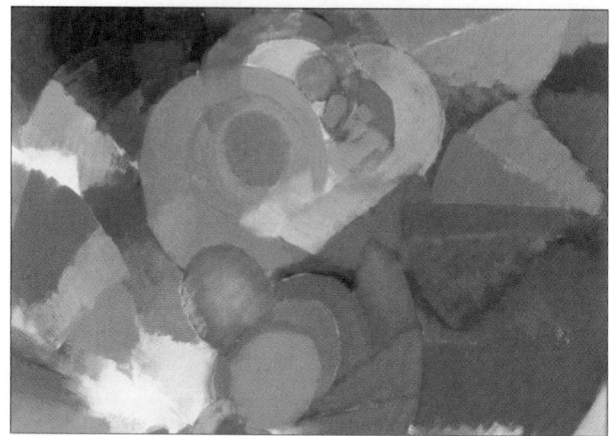

What important issues of the first half of the 20th century can you identify from your reading of the selections in this unit? In what ways do you think your life has been influenced by these issues? To explore these questions, choose one or more options in each of the following sections.

Reflecting on the Unit

OPTION 1

Comparing Perspectives In these works from the first half of the 20th century, the writers approach various aspects of reality—war, love, motivation, truth—from different perspectives. Pick two selections from the unit, in which writers offer differing interpretations of some topic or experience. In a chart, identify the topic or experience, list the important points each writer makes, and summarize the opinion of each. Then comment on which perspective matches your own most closely.

OPTION 2

Tracking Sudden Changes In many selections in this unit, circumstances take unexpected turns, or actions have unforeseen consequences. With a small group of classmates, choose four or five selections in which such shifts occur. How do the speakers or characters react to the new developments? What effect do they have on the speakers' or characters' understanding of the world and other people? Discuss whether you think such sudden changes can lead to important insights into reality.

OPTION 3

Evaluating Public and Private Realities Some of the writers represented in this unit address public issues, and some deal with private concerns. Work with a partner to identify the main focus of each selection as public or private. Then look for relationships between the public and the private: How do the larger issues of public life affect people's private lives? How do people's personal experiences and viewpoints affect their interpretation of public events? Summarize your conclusions and then present them to the class.

Self ASSESSMENT

📖 **READER'S NOTEBOOK**

To explore how your understanding of modern literature has developed over the course of this unit, jot down words and phrases that you associate with literature from the first half of the 20th century. Then get together with a group of classmates and compare and assess your lists. As a group, identify the pieces of literature from this unit that you think most contributed to your impressions.

Reviewing Literary Concepts

OPTION 1

Identifying Irony Irony plays a major role in modern literature. Review the three types of irony identified on pages 1004–1005: verbal irony, situational irony, and dramatic irony. Then look over the selections in this unit and find at least one example of each type of irony. Which type of irony seems to be most prevalent in the literature of this unit?

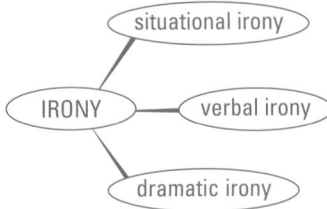

OPTION 2

Analyzing Style Writers convey their ideas and attitudes in part through details of style. From this unit, choose two selections that you think have particularly interesting or forceful styles. List the main characteristics of each style, and then make notes about how the styles work to express the writers' thoughts and feelings.

Building Your Portfolio

- **Writing Options** Of the Writing Options you completed for this unit, choose the one in which you think you displayed the most creativity. Write a brief note explaining your choice, and place it with the piece in your **Presentation Portfolio.**

- **Writing and Communication Workshops** During this unit, you created a Dramatic Scene and explored ways to develop a Web site. Which of these assignments would you like to continue developing? Write up your explanation, and place it in your **Presentation Portfolio.**

- **Additional Activities** Think about the various assignments you completed under **Activities & Explorations** and **Inquiry & Research.** Keep a record in your portfolio of any assignments that you think are representative of your best work.

Pygmalion

BERNARD SHAW

One of the most entertaining and best-loved modern British plays, *Pygmalion* explores human relations and the complex modern social order. Shaw, born in Dublin, moved to London at age 20, where he wrote many brilliant and witty plays, including *Major Barbara, Heartbreak House, Caesar and Cleopatra,* and *Man and Superman,* but *Pygmalion* remains his most popular play.

These thematically related readings are provided along with *Pygmalion*:

The Story of Pygmalion
***from* The Metamorphoses**
BY OVID

***Excerpt from* My Fair Lady**
BY ALAN JAY LERNER

Her First Ball
BY KATHERINE MANSFIELD

The London Language
***from* The Story of English**
BY ROBERT McCRUM, WILLIAM
CRAN, AND ROBERT MacNEIL

Mother Tongue
BY AMY TAN

Two Words
BY ISABEL ALLENDE

The Model
BY BERNARD MALAMUD

Words
BY VERN RUTSALA

And Even *More* . . .

Schindler's List

THOMAS KENEALLY

This book, which won Britain's Booker Prize in 1983, tells the true story of Oskar Schindler, a German war profiteer who came to save more than a thousand Jews from unspeakable deaths during the Holocaust. Steven Spielberg directed a film version of the book, which won Academy Awards for best picture and best director in 1993.

Books

Dubliners

JAMES JOYCE

This collection of related stories, first published in 1914, asks probing questions about Irish history, identity, and culture.

Mrs. Dalloway

VIRGINIA WOOLF

A montage of thoughts and images help paint a day in the life of Clarissa Dalloway, a middle-aged English society woman. This was the first of Woolf's novels to make use of her unique style of stream of consciousness.

1984

George Orwell

In this book, Orwell portrays a fictional future world in which a totalitarian government controls individual thought and even reality itself. A modern classic, *1984* remains timely and continues to stir the imagination while asking important questions about human nature.

These thematically related readings are provided along with *1984*:

What Can They
BY JULIA HARTWIG

End Game
BY J. G. BALLARD

The Spy
BY BERTOLT BRECHT

from **Politics and the English Language**
BY GEORGE ORWELL

No One Died in Tiananmen Square
BY WILLIAM LUTZ

The Invasion of Privacy
BY REED KARAIM

The IWM 1000
BY ALICIA YÁÑZ COSSÍO

Thumbprint
BY EVE MERRIAM

Testament of Youth
VERA BRITTAIN
Brittain's gripping memoir of her experiences during World War I echo with poignancy the realities of this painful chapter of history. It has been called "a moving elegy to a lost generation."

The Guns of August
BARBARA TUCHMAN
Barbara Tuchman has been praised for her ability to make history come alive. This narrative on the outbreak of World War I, published in 1962, won the Pulitzer Prize.

Other Media

The Great War: 1918
PBS Video, 1989. World War I is examined through the letters and diaries of U.S. soldiers.
(VIDEOCASSETTE)

Upstairs, Downstairs
London Weekend Television, 1971; A&E Home Video. This series presents the life and times of the Bellamy household in England in the early years of this century.
(VIDEOCASSETTES)

We Must Never Forget: The Story of the Holocaust
Society for Visual Education, 1994.
(VIDEOCASSETTE)

The Wasteland and Other Poems
Listening Library.
(AUDIOCASSETTE)

UNIT SEVEN

CONTEMPORARY

1950 – PRESENT

VOICES

IT WAS A BRIGHT COLD DAY
IN APRIL, AND THE CLOCKS
WERE STRIKING THIRTEEN.

George Orwell
novelist, essayist,
and critic

Invasion (1987–1988), Carel Weight. Oil on canvas, 48″ × 60″, The Saatchi Collection, London.

CONTEMPORARY
VOICES

EVENTS IN BRITISH LITERATURE

1950   **1960**

1952 Samuel Beckett's play *Waiting for Godot* published

1953 Winston Churchill wins Nobel Prize in literature

1954 William Golding's *Lord of the Flies* published

1956 South African Nadine Gordimer's *Six Feet of the Country and Other Stories* published; poet Ted Hughes and American poet Sylvia Plath marry

1957 Harold Pinter's first one-act play, *The Room*, produced

1962 Anthony Burgess's satirical *A Clockwork Orange* published

1965 Doris Lessing's *African Stories* published

1966 Poet Seamus Heaney publishes first collection, *Death of a Naturalist*

EVENTS IN BRITAIN

1950   **1960**

1952 George VI dies and is succeeded by daughter, Elizabeth II; Britain becomes atomic power

1956 British troops sent to Egypt in Suez crisis

1957 Britain grants independence to Gold Coast (now Ghana), first African colony south of Sahara to achieve such status

1961 South Africa withdraws from British Commonwealth

1963 Britain's attempt to join Common Market rejected

1964 Beatles enjoy huge international popularity in rock music

1969 Violence erupts in Northern Ireland following attempt to grant civil rights to Catholic minority

EVENTS IN THE WORLD

1950   **1960**

1950 Korean War begins (to 1953)

1953 First television broadcasting in color begins in the U.S.

1955 Soviets counter NATO with Warsaw Pact alliance of Eastern European countries

1956 Revolutions against Communist rule in Poland and Hungary crushed

1957 Soviets launch Sputnik, first artificial space satellite; European Economic Community (known as Common Market) forms to provide tariff-free trading

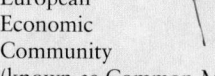

1959 Fidel Castro takes control of Cuba after ouster of dictator

1961 Soviet Yuri Gagarin first human to orbit earth

1962 Cuban missile crisis ends with removal of Soviet missiles from Cuba

1964 U.S. becomes leading outside power in Vietnam War (to 1975)

1967 Israel claims Jerusalem, Golan Heights, and West Bank after Six-Day War with Arab states

1968 Soviets crush Czech uprising

1969 American Neil Armstrong walks on moon

PERIOD PIECES

The Concorde, a supersonic passenger plane

1950s television

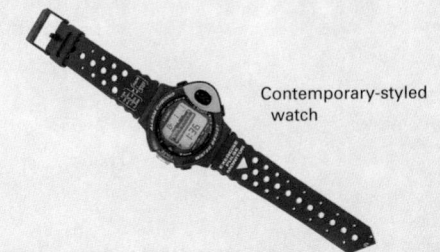

Contemporary-styled watch

1970   **1980**   **1990**

1975 Stevie Smith's illustrated *Collected Poems* published

1977 Penelope Lively, former children's author, publishes first adult fiction

1983 Golding wins Nobel Prize in literature

1984 Ted Hughes named poet laureate

1991 Gordimer wins Nobel Prize in literature

1995 Heaney wins Nobel Prize in literature; Margaret Atwood's first poetry collection in ten years, *Morning in the Burned House*, published

---

1970   **1980**   **1990**

1970 Equal Pay Act ensures that British women's wages will equal those of men with same jobs

1973 Britain and Ireland allowed into Common Market (now European Union or EU)

1979 Margaret Thatcher becomes first female prime minister

1981 Racial tensions and unemployment lead to riots in London; Charles, heir to British throne, marries Lady Diana Spencer

1982 Britain defeats Argentina in Falklands War

1987 Construction begins on 31-mile long "chunnel" joining Britain to France under English Channel (to 1994)

1991 Britain joins with United States and other nations in Persian Gulf War

1997 Britain returns Hong Kong to China after 155 years of colonial rule; Princess Diana dies in Paris auto accident

---

1970   **1980**   **1990**

1972 SALT talks between U. S. and Soviet Union limit missiles

1973 Arab attack surprises Israel but fails

1977 First practical home computer, Apple II, hits market

1978 Camp David accords unite Israel and Egypt in peace

1979 Shah flees Iran, and Muslims take U.S. hostages (to 1981); Soviets invade Afghanistan

1985 Mikhail Gorbachev comes to power in Soviet Union and initiates reforms

1989 Berlin Wall falls, uniting two Germanys; students demonstrating for Chinese democracy killed in Beijing's Tiananmen Square

1991 Soviet Union breaks up into 15 republics; Iraq invades Kuwait, prompting short Persian Gulf War

1993 Oslo Peace agreements signed between Israelis and Palestinians

1994 Nelson Mandela becomes South African president in nation's first all-race election

CONTEMPORARY
VOICES

1950 – PRESENT

In 1953, a year after succeeding her father, George VI, as Britain's monarch, Elizabeth II was crowned in a glorious ceremony in Westminster Abbey. To many, the coronation symbolized a return of hope after the enormous loss and suffering of World War II, yet even though the ceremony recalled Britain's long tradition of greatness, there was no question that Britain was a greatly altered nation. The political power of the working class had been firmly established and the influence of the upper class substantially diminished. The economic instability caused by Britain's huge war debt which affected all classes, had prompted a series of nationwide strikes and other crises. The Labor government's social welfare programs and nationalization of industries, begun just after the war to address the dire economic situation, had continued even when the Conservatives returned to power in the 1950s. The dismantling of the empire was also continuing, with Britain—in response to both economic and nationalistic pressures—relinquishing control of most of its colonies in Asia, Africa, and the West Indies. At the same time, immigration from the former colonies was transforming what had formerly been a homogeneous population, creating racial and ethnic tensions on a scale never before known in Britain.

A SHIFT IN POWER AND LEADERSHIP

During the international political struggle that dominated the postwar decades—the so-called cold war between Western democracies and Communist nations—the United States became the chief champion of the West. Britain, though it became an atomic power and an important member of both the United Nations and the North Atlantic Treaty Organization (NATO), generally followed the lead of its powerful American ally. One

Top: Queen Elizabeth II at her coronation ceremony, 1953. *Center:* Newly built row houses in postwar England. *Above left* and *above:* Increasing religious and ethnic diversity is shown in two London photographs, one of a Hindu temple and the other of spectators watching a cricket match between a team of West Indians and a police team. *Right:* The Beatles, 1966.

exception was the Suez crisis of the mid-1950s, in which Britain joined with France in an unsuccessful military effort to reverse the Egyptian government's nationalization of the Suez Canal. Although the United States criticized the policy, the differences were soon smoothed over, and Britain retained its position as one of the United States' closest allies.

The new international supremacy of the United States extended beyond the political arena. As the world's most powerful nation and richest market, the United States became the center of Western technological development, particularly in the decades preceding the full recovery of the Japanese and German economies. Britain made valuable contributions in such areas as DNA research and fiber optics but clearly had lost the preeminent position in science and technology that it had once enjoyed. During the "brain drain" of the early 1960s, many of Britain's top scientists and engineers immigrated to the United States, lured by greater opportunities and financial resources. Similarly, the worldwide dominance of U.S. popular culture attracted much of Britain's entertainment talent to American shores.

Britain's greatest international success in the sphere of popular culture came in the 1960s, with the "British invasion" of the American rock-music scene. Led by the Beatles and the Rolling Stones, British rock groups not only dominated international pop music but also launched a teenage craze for long hair

Development of the *English Language*

Since the 1960s, the women's movement has left its mark on the English language, promoting existing alternatives and new coinages as replacements for terms perceived as sexist. For example, the title *Ms.* was introduced, and efforts were made to secure acceptance of such gender-neutral terms as *humanity* and *firefighter* in place of *mankind* and *fireman.* Technology, however, has proved the greatest source of vocabulary expansion. From space exploration have come a host of new or rejuvenated terms, including *liftoff, astronaut,* and *A-OK;* the spread of computer technology has given us such terms as *software, floppy disk,* and *user-friendly.*

At the same time, satellite broadcasting, computer modems, fax machines, and other advances in communications have helped turn the world into a "global village" in which English—spread originally by British and more recently by American influence—has become a universal language. If a Greek does business with someone in Japan, or a Norwegian diplomat negotiates with an Israeli, they are likely to communicate in English, a second language common to both. In such former British colonies as India and Malaysia, English bridges the gaps between dozens of native languages and dialects.

LITERARY HISTORY

British writers have responded in several ways to the changes of the contemporary era. During the 1950s, a group of young poets called the Movement—including Ted Hughes, Thom Gunn, Elizabeth Jennings, and Philip Larkin—achieved recognition by rejecting complex styles and producing clear, rational, understated poetry on subjects

and for things British—British TV shows, British slang, and the "mod" fashions of London's Carnaby Street, for example.

Although prominence in the pop-culture scene had its economic rewards, the weaknesses of the British economy required far more extensive remedies. One was provided by the discovery in 1969 of oil beneath the North Sea off the Scottish coast; in the next 12 years, Britain would be transformed from an oil-importing nation to one self-sufficient in energy. Another solution to the nation's economic problems, according to some Britons—particularly members of the Conservative party—lay in joining the European Community (EC), or Common Market, which several Western European nations had established in 1957. Opponents of this view, mainly in the Labor party, felt that EC membership would weaken trade ties within the British Commonwealth, entangle Britain in continental politics, and threaten the nation's sovereignty and agricultural interests. Since the Labor party held sway for most of the 1960s, British efforts to join the Common Market were not vigorously pursued during those years. Soon after the Conservative party returned to power in 1970, however, Britain's application for membership was accepted.

THE THATCHER ERA

In 1975, following defeats in two general elections the year before, the Conservative party elected a new leader who four years later would become Britain's first woman prime minister. The daughter of a small-town grocer, Margaret Thatcher had risen in the ranks of Britain's new "meritocracy," in which success was attained not through birth or wealth but through hard work and talent. Her 11 years as prime minister (1979–1990), known as the Thatcher Era, left their mark on both Britain and the rest of the world. A pragmatist in the fight against communism, Thatcher was the first Western leader to recognize and promote the changes that were occurring in the Soviet Union, and she encouraged President Ronald Reagan to do the same. Under her leadership, Britain successfully waged the Falklands War of 1982 and joined the victorious U.S.-led coalition in the Persian Gulf War of 1991. Meanwhile, on the domestic front, Thatcher was leading her country in a new economic direction. Insisting that Britain become a "wealth-producing" rather than merely a "wealth-redistributing" nation, she began privatizing the previously nationalized industries and instituting other changes to make British industry more

Above: Twiggy, an internationally famous model of the 1960s, poses in front of a life-size poster of herself. *Right:* Margaret Thatcher, Great Britain's first woman prime minister. *Below:* A 1940s bronze sculpture, *Family Group,* by Henry Moore, one of Britain's most renowned sculptors

competitive.

A significant problem faced by Thatcher and her successor, John Major, was the ongoing conflict in Northern Ireland. A decade before Thatcher took office, Northern Ireland's Roman Catholic minority had begun a civil-rights movement, calling for an end to discrimination against Catholics there. When clashes broke out between Catholics and Protestants, the British government sent in troops that the Catholics perceived as favoring the Protestants. Before long, Irish Republican Army (IRA) extremists had gained prominence over the civil-rights moderates among the Catholics, and Protestant extremists had formed militant groups of their own, including the Ulster Defense League (UDL). For over two decades, violence between these factions rocked Northern Ireland and spilled over, in the form of bombings and other terrorist attacks, into other parts of the United Kingdom. A peace effort led by two Northern Irish women, Mairead Corrigan and Betty Williams, earned them the Nobel Peace Prize but failed to end the violence. Finally, in 1994, both the IRA and the UDL agreed to a cease-fire, and British and Irish officials began peace negotiations that seemed more promising than past efforts.

Street scene in Northern Ireland, 1991

drawn from everyday experience. Even more simple in style was the work of Stevie Smith, who—like Dylan Thomas before her—helped popularize the oral reading of poetry for modern audiences.

The 1950s also gave birth to the fiction of the so-called Angry Young Men and to the "kitchen sink" school of drama. Works like John Osborne's play *Look Back in Anger* (1957) and Alan Sillitoe's story collection *The Loneliness of the Long Distance Runner* (1959) expressed the contempt for authority and middle-class values felt by British working-class and student radicals. The social radicalism of these works was matched by the stylistic radicalism of the plays of Samuel Beckett and others associated with the "theater of the absurd," who abandoned realism, plot, and characterization in order to focus on the isolation and absurdity of contemporary life—themes that have also reverberated in the plays of Harold Pinter. Meanwhile, some contemporary dramatists have drawn on British tradition: in *A Man for All Seasons* (1960), for example, Robert Bolt dramatized the life of the Renaissance hero Thomas More, and in *Rosenkrantz and Guildenstern Are Dead* (1967), Tom Stoppard retold Shakespeare's *Hamlet* from the viewpoint of two minor characters.

Another significant contemporary trend is the increasingly favorable reception given to regional and commonwealth writers, broadening the concept of "English" literature. Seamus Heaney (Northern Ireland), Muriel Spark (Scotland), Nadine Gordimer (South Africa), Chinua Achebe (Nigeria), Margaret Atwood (Canada), Judith Wright (Australia), and Derek Walcott (St. Lucia and Trinidad) are just a few of the talented writers who have enriched English letters with their unique perceptions of human experience.

PART 1   Appearance and Reality

In the second half of the 20th century, many writers have explored the disquieting realities and startling insights lying beneath the surface of ordinary life. In a world in which technological development has threatened to depersonalize society, these writers have probed the significance of passing moments in individual experience. As you read the selections in this part of Unit Seven, look for the ways in which hidden realities and meaning emerge from seemingly ordinary times in life.

Point of View in Contemporary Fiction

The Narrative Lens

Like a photographer who switches lenses to vary the view of an object, a writer chooses a method of narration that can reveal, to varying degrees, what is happening within a story. In contemporary fiction of the 20th century, writers have made use of narrators with various **points of view,** or vantage points. The choice of a particular point of view determines *what* is presented to the reader and *how* it is presented. There are three basic types of point of view:

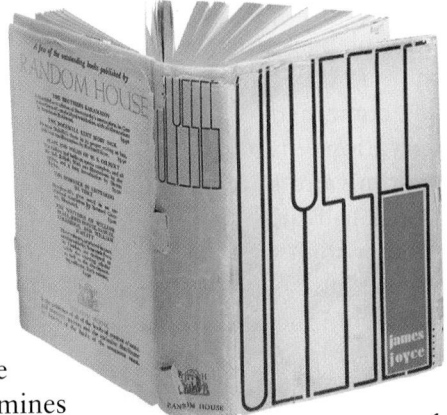

James Joyce's *Ulysses* (published in novel form in 1922) is noted for its stream-of-consciousness technique.

POINTS OF VIEW
First-Person Narrator • Narrator is a major or a minor character who tells the story. • Narrator can be actively involved or merely an observer.
Third-Person Omniscient • Narrator can see into the past and into the future. • Narrator relates characters' thoughts and comments on events. • Writer can make "editorial" comments about the characters and their motivations.
Third-Person Limited • The narrator is not a participant in the story, but relates events from one character's viewpoint. • All the reader knows is what the narrator reveals of that character's thoughts, feelings, observations, and experiences.

Traditional Points of View

The **third-person omniscient** point of view is the most established type of narration, used by Chaucer in the 14th century and by the early novelists of the 18th century. The third-person omniscient narrator allows the writer the freedom to reveal a variety of information about a number of characters or events. In William Trevor's "The Distant Past" (page 1263), for

example, the narrator is able to show the shifting thoughts and feelings of several townspeople during a time of political and religious conflicts.

Traditional **first-person narrators** are popular with authors because they can provide a firsthand account of events, but also appeal to contemporary writers' love of irony. Nadine Gordimer's "Six Feet of the Country" (page 1289), for example, demonstrates how a first-person narrator can tell a story that is ironic insofar as he is not aware of the effect on readers of his own part in the story.

Perhaps the most common use of point of view in contemporary fiction is the **third-person limited** point of view. Its limitations, ironically, are what make it attractive to contemporary writers. For one thing, the writer can focus primarily on the development of one character. Events are related from the perspective of that character, who rarely "editorializes" (or comments) on events. In addition, the restriction of the focus to a single character makes the fiction seem more realistic. The advantages of this point of view are evident in Doris Lessing's "A Sunrise on the Veld" (page 1210), which "looks over the shoulder" of a young South African on a day he is witness to an event that changes his attitude about life.

The Experimenters

In contemporary fiction of the early 20th century, Virginia Woolf, James Joyce, and other "modernist" writers were known for their innovative use of point of view. They experimented with **stream of consciousness,** a technique that departs from literal description

to reveal the flow of a character's thoughts. These experimenters also used multiple narrators.

Woolf's **multiple-narrator** technique was quite inventive. Passages of her writing combined both spoken and unspoken observations of different characters—many of whom were never actually identified. (See "Milestones in British Literature" on page 1058.) Although some readers might find it challenging to figure out who's who, the advantage of this technique lies in the amount of information and insight it allows Woolf to reveal.

Many contemporary British writers have returned to a more traditional style of writing, but that does not mean they have abandoned experimentation altogether. A case in point is Muriel Spark's use of a first-person narrator in "The First Year of My Life" (page 1220). A first-person point of view is, by definition, limited to what can be known by a single character. Spark's first-person narrator, however, is an imaginative departure from ordinary narrators. She creates an unusual first-person narrator who has the omniscience of a third-person narrator.

Cases of Mistaken Identity

Actors and actresses often complain that fans confuse them with the characters they play. In a similar fashion, writers are often confused with the narrators they have invented. This error is probably easiest to make when the story is related by an omniscient, impersonal voice that has no characteristics that set it apart from the writer.

A practiced reader will resist the temptation to assume the narrator really is the writer. After all, the writer is deliberately telling a story. Nonfiction would be the better choice for a writer who wants to convey a direct connection to information he or she presents. In creating a work of fiction, the writer removes him- or herself from the events and puts on a kind of mask in the form of the narrator. As Oscar Wilde noted, "Give a man a mask and he will tell you the truth."

YOUR TURN What characters from books, TV shows, and films have you identified with closely? What do you think the writers did to breathe life into those characters? Discuss your responses with a partner.

Strategies for Reading: Point of View

1. Remember that in the first-person point of view, the narrator's account of events will reflect his or her knowledge and experiences within the story, as well as possible bias.

2. See what insights you gain about a narrator by observing how other characters respond to him or her.

3. Be aware of the possibility that the point of view may shift during the story.

4. Draw conclusions about the narrator. For example, is the narrator always reliable? What personal flaws or ulterior motives might the narrator reveal, even unconsciously?

5. Infer why the writer chose a particular point of view. Challenge yourself to explore how the story might be different if told from another perspective.

6. **Monitor** your reading strategies and modify them when your understanding breaks down. Remember to use your Strategies for Active Reading: **predict, visualize, connect, question, clarify,** and **evaluate.**

PIERELLA LENA

At the Pitt-Rivers

Short Story by PENELOPE LIVELY

Connect to Your Life

Other Lives Recall a time when you became completely engrossed in the conversation or activities of strangers you observed in a park, restaurant, or other public place. What attracted your attention to these people? Did you begin to speculate about their lives or situations? Share your thoughts with classmates.

Build Background

Fact Behind the Fiction "At the Pitt-Rivers" takes place in 20th-century Oxford, a city northwest of London. More specifically, it takes place in the Pitt-Rivers, an actual museum located on the campus of Oxford University. The Pitt-Rivers Museum was established in 1883 when a collection of early weapons, tools, pottery, and other artifacts was donated to the university by an English soldier and archaeologist, Lieutenant-General Pitt-Rivers. He believed that by sharing his treasures with the public, he could give ordinary people a better understanding of their ancestors. The Pitt-Rivers Museum is well-known for its exhibits in anthropology (the study of the origin and development of human beings) and archaeology (the excavation and study of items belonging to ancient cultures). It also contains an extensive collection of musical instruments from around the world.

Penelope Lively, the award-winning author of "At the Pitt-Rivers," has a personal link to the setting of her story, being a graduate of Oxford University, with a degree in modern history. In many of her stories, Lively reveals her preoccupation with history, especially its ability to change one's perspective on life. She frequently relates experiences in which a child matures greatly as a result of a new awareness about history or humanity. In the following story, a teenage boy gains insights into life by observing the relationship of two adults.

WORDS TO KNOW
Vocabulary Preview

benign	explicit
bleak	pretentious
compulsory	

Focus Your Reading

LITERARY ANALYSIS **SETTING** **Setting** is the time and place of the action of a short story or other literary work. In addition to time and place, however, setting may include the social and moral environment that form the background for a narrative. As you read this story, be aware of the way in which the setting of two adjoining museums in Oxford contributes to the plot.

ACTIVE READING **DRAWING CONCLUSIONS ABOUT THE NARRATOR**

When you **draw conclusions** about characters in literature, you form opinions about them on the basis of their actions, speech, and appearance. In addition, you can draw conclusions about the **narrator** of a story on the basis of the thoughts and feelings he or she expresses. The narrator of this story encounters a couple three times on his trips to the museum. On each occasion, as he describes the couple, he reveals something about himself.

READER'S NOTEBOOK In a chart like the one shown, briefly describe what the boy tells about the couple he encounters and what he reveals about himself.

	The Couple	The Boy
1st Visit		
2nd Visit		
3rd Visit		

OXEOSCHISTUS PRONAX

PIERELLA LENA

At the Pitt-Rivers

Penelope Lively

HAETERA PIERA

HELICONIUS NUMATA

They've got this museum in Oxford,[1] called the Pitt-Rivers; I spend a lot of time there. It's a weird place, really weird, stuff from all over the world crammed into glass cases like some kind of mad junk-shop—native things from New Guinea and Mexico and Sumatra and wherever you like to think of. Spears and stone axes and masks and a thousand different kinds of fishhook. And bead jewelry and peculiar musical instruments. And a great totem from Canada. You can learn a lot there about what people get up to: it makes you think. Mostly it's pretty depressing—umpteen different nasty ways of killing each other.

I didn't start going there to learn anything; just because it was a nice quiet place to mooch around and be on my own, Saturdays, or after school. It got to be a kind of habit. There aren't often people there—the odd art student, a few kids gawping at the shrunken heads, one or two serious-looking blokes[2] wandering around. The porter's[3] usually reading the *Sun* or having a snooze; there's not a lot of custom.[4] The Natural History Museum is a bigger draw; you have to go through that to get into the Pitt-Rivers. You'll always get an audience for a dinosaur and a few nasty-looking jellyfish in formalin.[5] Actually I'm partial to the Natural History Museum myself; that makes you think, too. All those fossils, and then in the end you and me. I had a go at reading *The Origin of Species* last term, not that I got very far. There's a room upstairs in the museum where Darwin's friend—Huxley[6]—had this great argument with that bishop and the rest of them. It says so on the door. I like that, it seems kind of respectful. Putting up a plaque to an argument, instead of just JOE SOAP WAS BORN HERE or whatever. It should be done more often.

It was in the Natural History Museum—underneath the central whale—that I first saw her, and since my mind was on natural selection I thought she wasn't all that good an example of it. I remember thinking that it was funny it doesn't seem to operate with girls, so you got them getting prettier and prettier, because good-looking girls have a better deal than bad-looking ones, you've only got to observe a bit to see that. I always notice girls, to see if they're pretty or not, and she wasn't. She wasn't specially ugly; just very ordinary—you wouldn't look at her twice. She was sitting on a bench, watching the entrance.

All the girls I know—at school or round where I live—are either attractive or they're not. If they're attractive they have lots of blokes after them and if they're not they don't. It's as simple as that. If they're attractive just looking at them makes you think of all sorts of things, imagine what it would be like and so forth, and if they're not then it doesn't really occur to you, except in so far as it occurs to you a good deal of the time,

---

1. **Oxford:** a city in England that is the site of Oxford University, the world's oldest English-speaking university.

2. **blokes:** British slang meaning "fellows," "guys."

3. **porter:** a British term for a doorman.

4. **custom:** the customers or patrons of a business or store. (The narrator is saying that there are usually not many visitors in the museum.)

5. **formalin** (for'mə-lĭn): a solution of formaldehyde in water, used as a preservative.

6. **Huxley:** One of the main supporters of Darwin's theory of evolution was Thomas Henry Huxley (1825–1895), a British biologist.

actually. This girl was definitely not attractive. In the first place she was in fact quite old, not far off thirty, I should think, and in the second she hadn't got a nice figure; her legs were kind of dumpy and she didn't have pretty hair or anything like that. I gave her a look, just automatically, to check, and then didn't bother with her.

Until I came alongside, where I could see her face clearly, and then I looked again. And again. She still wasn't pretty, but she had the most beautiful expression I've ever seen in my life. She glowed; that's the only way I can put it. She sat there with her hands in her lap, watching the door, and radiating away so that in a peculiar fashion it made you feel good just to look at her, a bit like you were joining in how she felt. Stupid, I daresay, but that's how it was.

And I thought to myself: oh ho . . . I mean, I've seen films and I've read books and I know a bit about things.

As a matter of fact I've been in love myself twice. The first time was with a girl in my class at school and I suppose it was a bit of a trial run, really, I mean I'm not altogether sure how much I was feeling it but it seemed quite important when it was going on. The second time was last year, when I was fifteen. She came to stay with her married sister who lives round the corner from us and though it's months and months ago now I still feel quite faint and weak when I go past the house.

Oh ho, I thought. I felt kindly—sort of benign—and a bit curious to see what the bloke would be like. I thought he couldn't be much because of her not being pretty. I mean, in films you can always tell who's going to fall for who because they'll be the two good-lookers and while I'm not saying real life's like that there is a way people match each other, isn't there, you've only got to look round at married people. Let me hasten to say that I'm not all that good-looking

. . . she had the most beautiful expression I've ever seen in my life. She glowed; that's the only way I can put it.

myself, only about B+. Not too bad, but not all that marvelous, either.

But he didn't show up and I wanted to get on into the Pitt-Rivers, so I left her there, waiting. What I haven't said is that one of the things I go to the Pitt-Rivers for is to write poetry. I write quite a lot of poetry. I could do it at home—I often do—and it's not that I'm coy or anything, my parents know about it and they're quite interested, but I just like the idea of having a special place to go to. It's quiet there, and a bit odd like I've said, and nobody takes any notice of me.

Sometimes I feel I'm getting somewhere with this poetry, and other times it looks to me pretty awful. I showed a few poems to our English master[7] and he was very helpful: he said what was good and pointed out where I'd used words badly, or not worked out what I was thinking very well, so that was quite encouraging. He's a nice bloke. I like his lessons. He's very good at explaining poetry. I mean, I think poetry's amazingly difficult: sometimes you read a thing again and again and you just can't see what . . . the person's getting at. He reads all sorts of poetry to us, our English master, and you really get the hang of it after a bit—hard stuff like Hopkins and *The Hound of Heaven*,[8] and Donne. He read us some of those Donne poems about love the other day which are all very explicit and I must say first time round I hadn't quite got the point—"License my roving hands . . ."—and so forth—but he wasn't embarrassed or anything, our English master, and when you realize that it's not geography he's talking about, the poet, then as a matter of fact I think that

---

7. **English master:** English teacher.
8. *The Hound of Heaven:* a poem by the English poet Francis Thompson (1859–1907).

WORDS
TO
KNOW

benign (bǐ-nīn′) *adj.* gentle; mild
explicit (ǐk-splǐs′ǐt) *adj.* clear and fully expressed

poem's lovely. I got a bit fed up with the way some of my mates were sniggering about it, being all-knowing; truth to tell I doubt if they know any more than I do, it's all just show. And that's a beautiful poem: I mean, if anything makes it clear that there's nothing wrong about sex, that poem does, they ought to make it compulsory reading for some people.

Anyway, I went on into the Pitt-Rivers and I was up on the first floor, in a favorite corner of mine among the arrow-heads, when I saw her again, and I must say I got quite a shock. Because the man with her was an old bloke: he was older than my father, fiftyish and more, he must have been at least twenty years older than her. So I reckoned I must have made a mistake. Not that at all.

They were talking, though I couldn't hear what they were saying because they were on the far side of the gallery. They stopped in front of a case and I could see their faces quite clearly. They stood there looking at each other, not talking any more, and I realized I hadn't made a mistake after all. Absolutely not. They didn't touch each other, they just stood and looked; it seemed like ages. I don't imagine they knew I was there.

And that time I was shocked. Really shocked. I don't mind telling you, I thought it was disgusting. He was an ordinary-looking person—he might have been a schoolmaster or something, he wore those kind of clothes, old trousers and sweater, and he had greyish hair, a bit long. And there was she, and as I've said she wasn't pretty, not at all, but she had this marvelous look about her, and she was years and years younger.

It was because of him, I realized, that she had that look.

I didn't like it at all. I got up, from where I was sitting, with quite a clatter to make sure they heard me and I went stumping off out of the museum. I wasn't going to write any more poetry that day, I could see. I went off home and truth to tell I didn't really think much more

about them, that man and the girl, mainly because of being rather disgusted, like I said.

A couple of weeks later they were there again. They were on the ground floor, at the back, by the rush matting[9] and ceremonial gear for with-it tribesmen, leaning up against a glass case that they weren't looking into, and talking. At least he was talking, quiet and serious, and she was listening, and nodding from time to time. I was busy with some thinking I wanted to do, and I tried not to take any notice of them; I mean, they were neither here nor there as far as I was concerned, none of my business, though I still thought it was a bit creepy. I couldn't see *why*, frankly. You fancy people your own age, and that's all there is to it, is what I thought. What I'd always thought.

So I ignored them, except that I couldn't quite. I kept sneaking a look, every now and then, and the more I did the more I felt kind of friendly towards them; I liked them. Which was a bit weird considering they didn't know I even existed—they certainly weren't interested in *me*—so it was a pretty one-sided kind of relationship. I thought he seemed like a nice bloke, whatever you thought about him and her and all that. It was something about the way he smiled, and the way he told her things (not that I ever heard a word they said, I wasn't eavesdropping, not ever, let's be quite clear about that) that made her look interested and say things back and so on. I thought it was obvious they liked talking to each other, quite apart from anything else. I thought that was nice.

I only took out that girl I mentioned—the one who came to stay with her sister—once, and

---

9. **rush matting:** mats made from the stems of stiff marsh plants called rushes.

Portrait of Scott (1968), Robert Vickrey. Collection of Remson Scott Vickrey.

as a matter of fact we couldn't find much to talk about. I was still in love with her—no doubt about that—but it was a bit sticky, I don't mind admitting. In fact I was quite glad when it was time to take her back to her sister's. In many ways the best part was just thinking about her.

Every time I looked at the girl—the Pitt-Rivers one, that is—I found myself imagining what it must be like being able to feel that you've made someone look like that. Radiant, like she was. Which is what that bloke must have been able to feel. I found myself putting myself in his place, as it were, and wondering. I've done a lot of wondering about things like that—everybody does, I suppose—but mostly it's been more kind of basic. Now, I began to think I didn't really know anything. Looking at those two—watching them, if you like—was a bit like seeing something go on behind a thick glass window, so it was half removed from you. You could see but not hear, hear but not touch, or whatever. I could see, but I didn't know.

I suppose you could say I was envious, in a funny kind of way. I don't mean jealous in that I fancied the girl, or anything like that. As I've said already, she wasn't pretty, or even attractive. And I wasn't envious like you might be envious of someone for being happier than you are, because I'm not specially unhappy, as it happens. I think I was envious of them for being what they were—as though one fossil creature might be envious of a more evolved kind of fossil creature, which of course is a stupid idea.

When I was in the Pitt-Rivers again I looked for them, quite deliberately, but they weren't there. I was disappointed, though I pretended to myself it really didn't matter. I wondered about why they went there in the first place; I mean, people have to meet each other somewhere but why *there?* It doesn't exactly spring to mind as a romantic spot. I supposed there were reasons they didn't want to meet somewhere obvious and public: maybe he was married, I thought, or

I found myself imagining what it must be like being able to feel that you've made someone look like that.

maybe she was, even. I wondered if that was the only place they met, or did they have others. Once walking through the botanical gardens, I found myself looking for them in the big glasshouses there.

I know the inside of the Pitt-Rivers pretty well by now. Considering it's not anthropology or ethnology[10] or whatever I went there for in the first place, it's quite surprising what a lot I could tell you about the things people believe and do. Primitive people, that is—what the Pitt-Rivers calls primitive people. And I think it's all very sad, actually: sad because it's like children, not understanding how things work and getting it all wrong, and carving each other up because of it a lot of the time. It does actually make you feel things get better—wars and bombs and everything notwithstanding. Nobody wants to go on being a child all their lives.

I was thinking about this—looking at a case full of particularly loony stuff to do with witchcraft—when I saw them again. At least I saw her first, standing by the totem with her hands in her coat pockets, and I didn't have to look at the door to know he'd arrived: her face told you that. He came up to her and gave her a kind of hug—arm round her shoulders and then quickly off again—and they wandered away up the stairs, heads together, talking.

I didn't follow them; it had been nice to see them again, and know they were there, and that was it. I was busy on a poem I'd been writing and unpicking and rewriting for some time. It was a poem about an old man sitting on a bench in a park and getting into conversation with a boy—someone around my age—and they swap opinions and observations (it's all dialogue, this poem, like a long conversation) and it's not till the end you realize they're the same person. It sounds

---

10. **ethnology** (ĕth-nŏl′ə-jē): the branch of anthropology that involves the study and comparison of human cultures.

either corny, or <u>pretentious</u>, I know; and what I could never decide was whether to have it as though the old man's looking back, or the boy's kind of projecting forward—imagining himself, as it were. So I went on fiddling about with this, and didn't really think much about the man and the girl, until I saw it was latish and there was no one else in the museum except me and some feet on the wooden floor of the gallery overhead, walking round and round, round and round. Two pairs of feet. They'd been doing that for ages, I realized; I'd been hearing them without registering.

I saw them go past—just their heads, above the glass cases—and something wasn't right. They weren't talking. She had her arm through his, and she was looking straight in front of her, and when I saw her face I had a nasty kind of twinge in my stomach. Because she was miserable. Once, she looked at him, and they both managed a <u>bleak</u> sort of smile. And then they walked on, round the gallery again, and next time past they still weren't talking, just holding on to each other like that, like people who're ill, or very old. And then the attendant rang the bell, and I heard them come down the stairs, and they came past me and went out into the Natural History Museum.

I don't know what had happened. I never will.

I went after them. I saw them stop—under the central whale, just where I first saw her—and then they did say something to each other. I couldn't see her face; she had her back to me. He went off then, on his own, out through the main entrance, quickly, and she sat down on a bench. For a moment or two she just sat staring at that wretched whale, and then she felt in her bag and got out a comb and did her hair, as though that might help. And then she dropped the comb and didn't seem to have noticed, even, because she just sat; she didn't bother to pick it up or anything. I could see her face then, and I hope I don't ever see anyone look so unhappy again. I truly hope that.

I don't know what had happened. I never will. Somehow, I don't think they were ever going to see each other again, but why . . . well, that's their concern, just like the rest of it was, except that in this peculiar way I'd come to feel it was mine too. I didn't think there was anything disgusting about them any more, or creepy—I hadn't for a long time. I suppose you could say I'd learned something else in the Pitt-Rivers, by accident. I never did go on with that poem. I tore it up, as far as it had got; I wasn't so sure any more about that conversation, that there could even be one, or not like I'd been imagining, anyway. ❖

Connect to the Literature

1. What Do You Think?
Did you like the narrator in this story? Why or why not?

:::: Comprehension Check ::::
- Why is the narrator surprised that the man and woman are a couple?
- What happens to the couple at the end of the story?
::::

Think Critically

2. Why do you think the **narrator** becomes so interested in the woman at the museum?

3. How would you explain the narrator's reaction to the couple the first time he observed them?

4. The narrator says that he "learned something else in the Pitt-Rivers, by accident." What do you think he learned?

5. Why do you think the narrator tore up his poem at the end of the story?

> THINK ABOUT
- how the narrator's opinion of the couple has changed
- how he feels when he sees the woman's unhappy face
- what the narrator means when he says, "I wasn't so sure any more about that conversation"

6. **ACTIVE READING DRAWING CONCLUSIONS ABOUT THE NARRATOR** Based on the information you recorded in the chart in your **READER'S NOTEBOOK**, what conclusions can you draw about the **narrator** and about the couple he encounters? Did your opinion of the couple or of the boy change as you read the story?

Extend Interpretations

7. Critic's Corner Critic John Mellors said of Lively: "She is particularly good at showing how one generation looks at, or ignores, the activities and preoccupations of another." Describe how this comment applies to "At the Pitt-Rivers." Use evidence from the story to support your opinion.

8. Connect to Life Consider the narrator's thoughts, feelings, and interests. In your estimation, is he a believable teenager? In other words, does he seem like a real person, like someone you might know? Why or why not?

Literary Analysis

SETTING Setting is one of the main elements in fiction and often plays an important role in what happens and why. In many stories, the setting, or time and place of the action, is critical to a complete understanding of the plot and characters. In other stories, the setting plays a more subtle role, perhaps supporting or enhancing the theme. In the following passage from "At the Pitt-Rivers," notice how the museum setting reflects the relationship between the couple and the narrator:

A couple of weeks later they were there again. They were on the ground floor, at the back, by the rush matting and ceremonial gear for with-it tribesmen, leaning up against a glass case that they weren't looking into, and talking. . . . I kept sneaking a look, every now and then, and the more I did the more I felt kind of friendly towards them. . . .

Paired Activity Consider both the atmosphere and the function of the Pitt-Rivers Museum. Why do you think Lively chose it as the setting for this story? With a partner, complete a diagram like the one shown. Briefly describe the story's setting, and then note ways in which the setting connects to the plot, characters, and theme of the story.

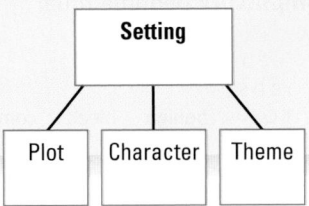

Choices & CHALLENGES

Writing Options

1. Narrator's Poem As the narrator of this story, write a poem expressing your feelings about the couple.

2. Character Sketch Write a character sketch of the narrator based on what he reveals about himself and on your own judgment of his attitudes.

3. Short Story Plot Unravel the mystery of the couple at the Pitt-Rivers Museum. Outline the plot for a short story that focuses on their relationship.

4. Museum Description Write a two-paragraph description of a museum you have enjoyed visiting. Be sure to tell what kind of museum it was, what sorts of exhibits it had, and where it is located. Use the narrator's description of the Pitt-Rivers as a model for your description.

Activities & Explorations

1. Dramatic Conversation With a partner, rehearse and present a dramatization of a conversation the narrator might have had with the woman in the story.
~ PERFORMING

2. Silent Movie Plan and shoot a silent movie that depicts a variety of relationships and conversations between couples of all ages. Stage your film with friends or family members role-playing the different couples. Share your work with the class. ~ **VIEWING AND REPRESENTING**

3. Natural History Museum Imagine that you are in charge of designing and planning a natural history museum for your community. What sorts of exhibitions would you want to present? Draw up a floor plan for your museum and sketch in the sorts of exhibits you would mount. ~ **ART**

Inquiry & Research

Museum Origins Research the origins of a famous museum or a museum in your community. Find out why the museum was founded, who funded it, and what its early collections consisted of. Share your information with the class in an oral report.

Vocabulary in Action

EXERCISE: SYNONYMS

For each phrase in the first column, write the letter of the synonymous phrase from the second column.

1. **pretentious** nonsense
2. **explicit** counsel
3. harmless scheme
4. dreary pinnacle
5. **compulsory** bedtime ritual

a. mandatory story
b. **benign** design
c. phony baloney
d. precise advice
e. **bleak** peak

Building Vocabulary
For an in-depth lesson on how to use a thesaurus to find a word's synonyms, see page 574.

WORDS TO KNOW	benign	bleak	compulsory	explicit	pretentious

Penelope Lively
1933–

Other Works
"Customers"
"Miss Carlton and the Pop Concert"
"A World of Her Own"
"Yellow Trains"
"Black Dogs"

Egyptian Childhood In a memoir of her childhood called *Oleander, Jacaranda,* Penelope Lively describes what it was like growing up in Egypt—a culture that included mosquito netting, water buffalo, pyramids, and annual visits from the snake charmer. Although her parents were English, Lively was born in Egypt, which at that time was a protectorate of the British government. Her father had moved from England as a young man to accept a position with the National Bank of Egypt. Lively's world was vastly different from that of her English contemporaries, but it was a world she would desperately miss when forced to leave Cairo at the age of 12.

School in England While living in Egypt, Lively was educated at home by her governess, who used a program designed for teaching English children living in foreign countries. In 1945, after the divorce of her parents, she was sent to England and enrolled in a boarding school. For a long time, Lively was an unhappy exile, living in an unfamiliar country and attending a school where success was equated with athletic and social skills rather than intellectual ability. It was a family friend who eventually sparked Lively's interest in history, an interest she later pursued at Oxford University.

Writing Career Lively has earned considerable recognition as a versatile author. She has successfully woven her historical knowledge into numerous books for younger readers, including *The Ghost of Thomas Kempe* and *A Stitch in Time*. In the late 1970s, after writing juvenile literature for about ten years, the author turned her energies to adult fiction, writing both novels and short stories.

Author Activity

Growing Up in Egypt Get a copy of *Oleander, Jacaranda* at a library and find out more about Lively's childhood in Egypt. Choose one or two incidents that you find especially interesting and share them with the class.

A Sunrise on the Veld

Short Story by DORIS LESSING

Connect to Your Life

Changing Your Mind Consider how easy or hard it is for you to change your ideas and viewpoints. How do you respond when an experience leads you to new insights? Do you enjoy being challenged to see the world in a new way or to think about your life from a different perspective? Jot down some of your thoughts.

Build Background

Growing Up on the Veld Doris Lessing grew up on a farm in the African country of Southern Rhodesia (rō-dē'zha), today known as Zimbabwe (zĭm-bäb'wē). The farm was situated on the edge of the veld (fĕlt), a vast grassy land having only a few bushes and almost no trees, but a land that teemed with wildife in the years of Lessing's childhood. She spent her youth exploring her surroundings and later claimed that her real education came not from school but from observing nature on the veld. In her nonfiction work *African Laughter,* she wrote about what the veld was like for her and her brother:

> *Lying in our blankets under the trees on the sandveld of Marandellas, or in the house on the farm in Banket, the shrilling, clamoring, exulting of the birds as the sun appeared was so loud the ears seemed to curl up and complain before . . . we leaped up into the early morning, to become part of all that tumult and activity.*

Not surprisingly, the same veld that taught Lessing so much about nature and life became the setting for many of her stories, including "A Sunrise on the Veld."

WORDS TO KNOW
Vocabulary Preview

fastidious	superfluity
incredulously	vigilant
myriad	

Focus Your Reading

LITERARY ANALYSIS KINESTHETIC IMAGERY

In addition to using **imagery** that relates to the five senses—sight, hearing, taste, touch, and smell—Lessing employs **kinesthetic imagery.** Kinesthetic imagery re-creates the tension felt through muscles, tendons, or joints in the body, as in the following description from "A Sunrise on the Veld":

> *As soon as he stepped over the lintel, the flesh of his soles contracted on the chilled earth. . . .*

Look for other examples of kinesthetic imagery.

ACTIVE READING ANALYZING CHARACTER DEVELOPMENT **Characters** frequently change over the course of a narrative. A key event often precipitates this change. Being aware of a character's thoughts and actions can help you figure out what event causes a character to change and how the character develops as a result.

📖 **READER'S NOTEBOOK** As you read "A Sunrise on the Veld," fill out a chart like the one shown, listing the boy's thoughts and actions.

Thoughts	Actions

A Sunrise on the Veld

DORIS LESSING

Every night that winter he said aloud into the dark of the pillow: Half-past four! Half-past four! till he felt his brain had gripped the words and held them fast. Then he fell asleep at once, as if a shutter had fallen; and lay with his face turned to the clock so that he could see it first thing when he woke.

It was half-past four to the minute, every morning. Triumphantly pressing down the alarm-knob of the clock, which the dark half of his mind had outwitted, remaining <u>vigilant</u> all night and counting the hours as he lay relaxed in sleep, he huddled down for a last warm moment under the clothes, playing with the idea of lying abed for this once only. But he played with it for the fun of knowing that it was a weakness he could defeat without effort; just as he set the alarm each night for the delight of the moment when he woke and stretched his limbs, feeling the muscles tighten, and thought: Even my brain—even that! I can control every part of myself.

Luxury of warm rested body, with the arms and legs and fingers waiting like soldiers for a word of command! Joy of knowing that the precious hours were given to sleep voluntarily!—for he had once stayed awake three nights running, to prove that he could, and then worked all day, refusing even to

admit that he was tired; and now sleep seemed to him a servant to be commanded and refused.

The boy stretched his frame full-length, touching the wall at his head with his hands, and the bedfoot with his toes; then he sprung out, like a fish leaping from water. And it was cold, cold.

He always dressed rapidly, so as to try and conserve his night-warmth till the sun rose two hours later; but by the time he had on his clothes his hands were numbed and he could scarcely hold his shoes. These he could not put on for fear of waking his parents, who never came to know how early he rose.

As soon as he stepped over the lintel,[1] the flesh of his soles contracted on the chilled earth, and his legs began to ache with cold. It was night: the stars were glittering, the trees standing black and still. He looked for signs of day, for the greying of the edge of a stone, or a lightening in the sky where the sun would rise, but there was nothing yet. Alert as an animal he crept past the dangerous window, standing poised with his hand on the sill for one proudly <u>fastidious</u> moment, looking in at the stuffy blackness of the room where his parents lay.

Feeling for the grass-edge of the path with his toes, he reached inside another window further along the wall, where his gun had been set in readiness the night before. The steel was icy, and numbed fingers slipped along it, so that he had to hold it in the crook of his arm for safety. Then he tiptoed to the room where the dogs slept, and was fearful that they might have been tempted to go before him; but they were waiting, their haunches crouched in reluctance at the cold, but ears and swinging tails greeting the gun ecstat-

THE AIR SMELLED OF MORNING AND THE STARS WERE DIMMING.

ically. His warning undertone kept them secret and silent till the house was a hundred yards back: then they bolted off into the bush, yelping excitedly. The boy imagined his parents turning in their beds and muttering: Those dogs again! before they were dragged back in sleep; and he smiled scornfully. He always looked back over his shoulder at the house before he passed a wall of trees that shut it from sight. It looked so low and small, crouching there under a tall and brilliant sky. Then he turned his back on it, and on the frowsting[2] sleepers, and forgot them.

He would have to hurry. Before the light grew strong he must be four miles away; and already a tint of green stood in the hollow of a leaf, and the air smelled of morning and the stars were dimming.

He slung the shoes over his shoulder, veld skoen[3] that were crinkled and hard with the dews of a hundred mornings. They would be necessary when the ground became too hot to bear. Now he felt the chilled dust push up between his toes, and he let the muscles of his feet spread and settle into the shapes of the earth; and he thought: I could walk a hundred miles on feet like these! I could walk all day, and never tire!

He was walking swiftly through the dark tunnel of foliage that in day-time was a road. The dogs were invisibly ranging the lower travelways of the bush, and he heard them panting. Sometimes he felt a cold muzzle on his leg before they were off again, scouting for a trail to follow. They were not trained, but free-running companions of the hunt, who often tired of the long stalk before the final shots, and went off on their own pleasure. Soon he could see them, small and wild-looking in a wild

---

1. **lintel:** used here to mean "threshold" (the wood or stone sill at the bottom of a doorway).

2. **frowsting** (frou′stĭng): a British term for lounging about.

3. *skoen* (skσ̄on) *Afrikaans:* shoes.

strange light, now that the bush stood trembling on the verge of color, waiting for the sun to paint earth and grass afresh.

The grass stood to his shoulders; and the trees were showering a faint silvery rain. He was soaked; his whole body was clenched in a steady shiver.

Once he bent to the road that was newly scored with animal trails, and regretfully straightened, reminding himself that the pleasure of tracking must wait till another day.

He began to run along the edge of a field, noting jerkily how it was filmed over with fresh spiderweb, so that the long reaches of great black clods seemed netted in glistening grey. He was using the steady lope he had learned by watching the natives, the run that is a dropping of the weight of the body from one foot to the next in a slow balancing movement that never tires, nor shortens the breath; and he felt the blood pulsing down his legs and along his arms, and the exultation and pride of body mounted in him till he was shutting his teeth hard against a violent desire to shout his triumph.

Soon he had left the cultivated part of the farm. Behind him the bush was low and black. In front was a long vlei,[4] acres of long pale grass that sent back a hollowing gleam of light to a satiny sky. Near him thick swathes of grass were bent with the weight of water, and diamond drops sparkled on each frond.

The first bird woke at his feet and at once a flock of them sprang into the air calling shrilly that day had come; and suddenly, behind him, the bush woke into song, and he could hear the guinea fowl[5] calling far ahead of him. That meant they would now be sailing down from their trees into thick grass, and it was for them he had come: he was too late. But he did not mind. He forgot he had come to shoot. He set his legs wide, and balanced from foot to foot, and swung his gun up and down in both hands horizontally, in a kind of improvised exercise, and let his head sink back till it was pillowed in his neck muscles, and watched how above him small rosy clouds floated in a lake of gold.

Suddenly it all rose in him: it was unbearable. He leapt up into the air, shouting and yelling wild, unrecognizable noises. Then he began to run, not carefully, as he had before, but madly, like a wild thing. He was clean crazy, yelling mad with the joy of living and a superfluity of youth. He rushed down the vlei under a tumult of crimson and gold, while all the birds of the world sang about him. He ran in great leaping strides, and shouted as he ran, feeling his body rise into the crisp rushing air and fall back surely on to sure feet; and thought briefly, not believing that such a thing could happen to him, that he could break his ankle any moment, in this thick tangled grass. He cleared bushes like a duiker,[6] leapt over rocks; and finally came to a dead stop at a place where the ground fell abruptly away below him to the river. It had been a two-mile-long dash through waist-high growth, and he was breathing hoarsely and could no longer sing. But he poised on a rock and looked down at stretches of water that gleamed through stooping trees, and thought suddenly, I am fifteen! Fifteen! The words came new to him; so that he kept repeating them wonderingly, with swelling excitement; and he felt the years of his life with his hands, as if he were counting marbles, each one hard and separate and compact, each one a wonderful shining thing. That was what he was: fifteen years of this rich soil, and this slow-moving water, and air that smelt like a challenge whether it was warm and sultry at noon, or as brisk as cold water, like it was now.

There was nothing he couldn't do, nothing! A vision came to him, as he stood there, like when a child hears the word "eternity" and tries to understand it, and time takes possession of the mind. He felt his life ahead of him as a great and wonderful thing, something that was his; and he

---

4. **vlei** (flā): low, swampy land.

5. **guinea fowl:** pheasantlike birds that have dark gray bodies flecked with white.

6. **duiker** (dī′kər): small African antelope.

1213

Horned Forms (1944), Graham Sutherland. Tate Gallery, London/Art Resource, New York.

And for minutes he stood there, shouting and singing and waiting for the lovely eddying[7] sound of the echo; so that his own new strong thoughts came back and washed round his head, as if someone were answering him and encouraging him; till the gorge was full of soft voices clashing back and forth from rock to rock over the river. And then it seemed as if there was a new voice. He listened, puzzled, for it was not his own. Soon he was leaning forward, all his nerves alert, quite still: somewhere close to him there was a noise that was no joyful bird, nor tinkle of falling water, nor ponderous[8] movement of cattle.

There it was again. In the deep morning hush that held his future and his past, was a sound of pain, and repeated over and over: it was a kind of shortened scream, as if someone, something, had no breath to scream. He came to himself, looked about him, and called for the dogs. They did not appear: they had gone off on their own business, and he was alone. Now he was clean sober, all the madness gone. His heart beating fast, because of that frightened screaming, he stepped carefully off the rock and went towards a belt of trees. He was moving cautiously, for not so long ago he had seen a leopard in just this spot.

said aloud, with the blood rising to his head: all the great men of the world have been as I am now, and there is nothing I can't become, nothing I can't do; there is no country in the world I cannot make part of myself, if I choose. I contain the world. I can make of it what I want. If I choose, I can change everything that is going to happen: it depends on me, and what I decide now.

The urgency, and the truth and the courage of what his voice was saying exulted him so that he began to sing again, at the top of his voice, and the sound went echoing down the river gorge. He stopped for the echo, and sang again: stopped and shouted. That was what he was!—he sang, if he chose; and the world had to answer him.

At the edge of the trees he stopped and peered, holding his gun ready; he advanced, looking steadily about him, his eyes narrowed. Then, all at once, in the middle of a step, he faltered, and his face was puzzled. He shook his head impatiently, as if he doubted his own sight.

There, between two trees, against a background of gaunt black rocks, was a figure from a dream, a strange beast that was horned and drunken-legged, but like something he had never even imagined. It seemed to be ragged. It looked like a small buck

---

7. **eddying** (ĕd′ē-ĭng): moving contrary to the main current; circling.

8. **ponderous**: clumsy because of heaviness and size.

that had black ragged tufts of fur standing up irregularly all over it, with patches of raw flesh beneath . . . but the patches of rawness were disappearing under moving black and came again elsewhere; and all the time the creature screamed, in small gasping screams, and leaped drunkenly from side to side, as if it were blind.

Then the boy understood: it *was* a buck. He ran closer, and again stood still, stopped by a new fear. Around him the grass was whispering and alive. He looked wildly about, and then down. The ground was black with ants, great energetic ants that took no notice of him, but hurried and scurried towards the fighting shape, like glistening black water flowing through the grass.

And, as he drew in his breath and pity and terror seized him, the beast fell and the screaming stopped. Now he could hear nothing but one bird singing, and the sound of the rustling, whispering ants.

He peered over at the writhing blackness that jerked convulsively with the jerking nerves. It grew quieter. There were small twitches from the mass that still looked vaguely like the shape of a small animal.

It came into his mind that he should shoot it and end its pain; and he raised the gun. Then he lowered it again. The buck could no longer feel; its fighting was a mechanical protest of the nerves. But it was not that which made him put down the gun. It was a swelling feeling of rage and misery and protest that expressed itself in the thought: if I had not come it would have died like this: so why should I interfere? All over the bush things like this happen; they happen all the time; this is how life goes on, by living things dying in anguish. He gripped the gun between his knees and felt in his own limbs the myriad swarming pain of the twitching animal that could no longer feel, and set his teeth, and said over and over again under his breath: I can't stop it. I can't stop it. There is nothing I can do.

He was glad that the buck was unconscious and had gone past suffering so that he did not have to make a decision to kill it even when he was feeling with his whole body: this is what happens, this is how things work.

It was right—that was what he was feeling. *It was right and nothing could alter it.*

The knowledge of fatality, of what has to be, had gripped him and for the first time in his life; and he was left unable to make any movement of brain or body, except to say: "Yes, yes. That is what living is." It had entered his flesh and his bones and grown in to the furthest corners of his brain and would never leave him. And at that moment he could not have performed the smallest action of mercy, knowing as he did, having lived on it all his life, the vast unalterable, cruel veld, where at any moment one might stumble over a skull or crush the skeleton of some small creature.

Suffering, sick, and angry, but also grimly satisfied with his new stoicism,[9] he stood there leaning on his rifle, and watched the seething black mound grow smaller. At his feet, now, were ants trickling back with pink fragments in their mouths, and there was a fresh acid smell in his nostrils. He sternly controlled the uselessly convulsing muscles of his empty stomach, and reminded himself: the ants must eat too! At the same time he found that the tears were streaming down his face, and his clothes were soaked with the sweat of that other creature's pain.

The shape had grown small. Now it looked like nothing recognizable. He did not know how long it was before he saw the blackness thin, and bits of white showed through, shining in the sun— yes, there was the sun, just up, glowing over the rocks. Why, the whole thing could not have taken longer than a few minutes.

He began to swear, as if the shortness of the time was in itself unbearable, using the words he had heard his father say. He strode forward, crushing ants with each step, and brushing them

---

9. **stoicism** (stō′ĭ-sĭz′əm): calm acceptance of events as inevitable. This viewpoint is identified with ancient Greek Stoic philosophy.

off his clothes, till he stood above the skeleton, which lay sprawled under a small bush. It was clean-picked. It might have been lying there years, save that on the white bone were pink fragments of gristle. About the bones ants were ebbing away, their pincers full of meat.

The boy looked at them, big black ugly insects. A few were standing and gazing up at him with small glittering eyes.

"Go away!" he said to the ants, very coldly. "I am not for you—not just yet, at any rate. Go away." And he fancied that the ants turned and went away.

He bent over the bones and touched the sockets in the skull; that was where the eyes were, he thought incredulously, remembering the liquid dark eyes of a buck. And then he bent the slim foreleg bone, swinging it horizontally in his palm.

That morning, perhaps an hour ago, this small creature had been stepping proud and free through the bush, feeling the chill on its hide even as he himself had done, exhilarated by it. Proudly stepping the earth, tossing its horns, frisking a pretty white tail, it had sniffed the cold morning air. Walking like kings and conquerors it had moved through this free-held bush, where each blade of grass grew for it alone, and where the river ran pure sparkling water for its slaking.[10]

And then—what had happened? Such a swift surefooted thing could surely not be trapped by a swarm of ants?

The boy bent curiously to the skeleton. Then he saw that the back leg that lay uppermost and strained out in the tension of death, was snapped midway in the thigh, so that broken bones jutted over each other uselessly. So that was it! Limping into the ant-masses it could not escape, once it had sensed the danger. Yes, but how had the leg been broken? Had it fallen, perhaps? Impossible, a buck was too light and graceful. Had some jealous rival horned it?

What could possibly have happened? Perhaps some Africans had thrown stones at it, as they do, trying to kill it for meat, and had broken its leg. Yes, that must be it.

Even as he imagined the crowd of running, shouting natives, and the flying stones, and the leaping buck, another picture came into his mind. He saw himself, on any one of these bright ringing mornings, drunk with excitement, taking a snap shot at some half-seen buck. He saw himself with the gun lowered, wondering whether he had missed or not; and thinking at last that it was late, and he wanted his breakfast, and it was not worth while to track miles after an animal that would very likely get away from him in any case.

For a moment he would not face it. He was a small boy again, kicking sulkily at the skeleton, hanging his head, refusing to accept the responsibility.

Then he straightened up, and looked down at the bones with an odd expression of dismay, all the anger gone out of him. His mind went quite empty: all around him he could see trickles of ants disappearing into the grass. The whispering noise was faint and dry, like the rustling of a cast snakeskin.

At last he picked up his gun and walked homewards. He was telling himself half defiantly that he wanted his breakfast. He was telling himself that it was getting very hot, much too hot to be out roaming the bush.

Really, he was tired. He walked heavily, not looking where he put his feet. When he came within sight of his home he stopped, knitting his brows. There was something he had to think out. The death of that small animal was a thing that concerned him, and he was by no means finished with it. It lay at the back of his mind uncomfortably.

Soon, the very next morning, he would get clear of everybody and go to the bush and think about it. ❖

---

10. **slaking:** quenching of thirst.

Connect to the Literature

1. **What Do You Think?**
   What was your reaction to the events of this story? Share your thoughts with your classmates.

   Comprehension Check
   - Why does the boy exult as he runs through the veld?
   - What sight puts an end to his exultation?

Think Critically

2. Why do you think it is so important to the boy to go out on the veld each morning?

   THINK ABOUT
   - his attitude toward his abilities and powers
   - his attitude toward his parents
   - the scene on the veld at sunrise

3. Why do you think the buck's death upsets the boy so much?

4. **ACTIVE READING** | **ANALYZING CHARACTER DEVELOPMENT**
   Get together with a classmate and compare the charts you made in your ☐ **READER'S NOTEBOOK** of the boy's thoughts and actions. How does the experience with the buck affect the character's view of the world and of himself?

5. Would you have reacted to the buck's death in the same way as the boy in the story? Explain your answer.

Extend Interpretations

6. **Critic's Corner** Critics have noted that Lessing has a remarkable ability to understand **characters** and to interpret their thoughts, feelings, and motivations. Think about the boy in "A Sunrise on the Veld." What are some of the important things you learn about him that make him believable and worth your attention?

7. **Comparing Texts** In both "At the Pitt-Rivers" by Penelope Lively (page 1199) and "A Sunrise on the Veld," the main character is a teenage boy. Compare the attitudes of the two boys. How do they view themselves, others, and the world? Which boy do you think changes the most from the beginning to the end of the story? Explain your answer.

8. **Connect to Life** For what different reasons do people around the world hunt wild animals? Do you think hunting is an acceptable activity? Why or why not?

Literary Analysis

KINESTHETIC IMAGERY Imagery that conveys the tension and movement of muscles, tendons, and joints is called **kinesthetic imagery.** In "A Sunrise on the Veld," Lessing uses this type of imagery to describe the boy, his dogs, and the veld wildlife. Notice the images conveyed by the following examples:

The boy stretched his frame full-length, touching the wall at his head with his hands, and the bedfoot with his toes. . . .

. . . he let the muscles of his feet spread and settle into the shapes of the earth. . . .

. . . he ran, feeling his body rise into the crisp rushing air and fall back surely on to sure feet. . . .

Cooperative Learning Activity With a small group of classmates, find other examples of kinesthetic imagery in the story. Discuss why you think Lessing uses this kind of imagery. Be specific in your answer.

THIRD-PERSON LIMITED POINT OF VIEW

When a writer uses the **third-person limited point of view,** the narrator tells the story from only one character's perspective. In Lessing's story, the reader learns only what the boy thinks, feels, observes, and experiences. The reader sees the boy, his parents, and the veld through the boy's eyes. How does this narrative point of view affect your perception of the boy at the beginning of the story? at the end of the story?

Choices & CHALLENGES

Writing Options

1. Diary Entry Imagine that you are the boy in this story. Write a diary entry describing your thoughts and feelings after witnessing the buck's death. Place the entry in your **Working Portfolio.**

2. Story Sequel Write a short sequel to "A Sunrise on the Veld," describing the boy's thoughts, feelings, and actions the next morning.

3. Nature Log With a partner, take a walk in a nature preserve. Keep a log of things you see, hear, smell, or feel and of your reaction to each. You may want to continue keeping your log over a period of time, recording experiences with nature in other settings, such as your own yard or parks.

Activities & Explorations

1. Veld Collage The boy in the story experiences both the beauty and the cruelty of nature on the veld. Make a collage of pictures that illustrates these two opposing views of life on the veld. ~ **ART**

2. Soundtrack of the Veld Using voice, musical instruments, sound effects, and brief passages from recordings, create a soundtrack expressing your impression of the veld. Record your sound landscape on tape and present it to the class. ~ **MUSIC**

3. Interior Monologue Use what you learn about the boy's thoughts and feelings in the story to create an interior monologue that reveals the inner workings of his mind. Practice the monologue, and present it to the class. ~ **SPEAKING AND LISTENING**

Inquiry & Research

1. Independent Africa Locate two political maps of Africa, one from about 1955 and one from the present. List all the countries that were once colonies and are now independent nations; include their former and current names. What European countries held colonies in Africa? Approximately how much of the continent was colonized? Summarize your information for the class.

 More Online: Research Starter www.mcdougallittell.com

2. Preserving the Balance of Nature With a small group, research the importance of balance within an ecosystem. Explain what an ecosystem is, how the balance of nature is maintained, and what can happen if the balance is upset. Present your findings to the rest of the class.

Art Connection

Setting the Mood Look again at the painting *Horned Forms* on page 1214. Note especially the colors and shapes used. In what ways does the painting convey the **mood** and **themes** of the story?

Vocabulary in Action

EXERCISE: IDIOMS Write the vocabulary word that is suggested by each set of idioms below.

1. over and above; too much of a good thing; the icing on the cake; money to burn

2. countless as the sands of the sea; more than you can count; a thousand and one; everything but the kitchen sink

3. be a fussbudget; cross all *t*'s and dot all *i*'s; be persnickety

4. be on the lookout; stay on one's toes; keep one ear to the ground; look alive

5. have to pinch oneself; that'll be the day; take with a grain of salt

WORDS TO KNOW	fastidious	incredulously	myriad	superfluity	vigilant

Building Vocabulary
For an in-depth study of context clues, see page 938.

Doris Lessing
1919–

Other Works
"The Old Chief Mshlanga"
"No Witchcraft for Sale"
"Through the Tunnel"
"Homage for Isaac Babel"
"A Mild Attack of Locusts"
African Laughter

Getting Started Doris Lessing was born in Persia (now Iran), but when she was 5, her British parents moved to Southern Rhodesia, where her father bought a farm. Lessing was not interested in socializing with other British settlers—a part of life that was important to her mother—and she disliked school intensely, much preferring to wander the lonely veld. Rebelling against her parents' wishes, Lessing left school at the age of 14 and worked for several years as a nursemaid, a typist, and a telephone operator in Salisbury, Southern Rhodesia. During these years, she read a great deal, especially the works of 19th-century novelists, and began to write fiction. When she was in her mid-20s, she quit her job in a lawyer's office to write what turned out to be her first major novel. Lessing was married and divorced twice, and in 1949 she moved to Great Britain with her youngest child, Peter. The publication of her novel *The Grass Is Singing* in the following year marked the beginning of her professional career.

Author and Activist Lessing has been a prolific writer—publishing more than 30 works in several genres—and is considered by many to be one of the most important novelists of the 20th century. Her early fiction was based on her own life and on her intimate knowledge of the culture and people of Southern Rhodesia, especially the problems between blacks and whites. Because of her out-spoken criticism of racism and her radical political sympathies, Lessing was banned for many years from her homeland and from South Africa.

Works in Progress Lessing's fiction has become increasingly more complex and ambitious, ranging from novels of social realism to science fiction. Her most widely read and controversial work is *The Golden Notebook,* a novel exploring women's concerns and experiences that is written in the form of a conventional narrative interwoven with a writer's notebooks. Lessing feels that contemporary society is in the midst of monumental change and crisis and that the writer must speak with integrity, imagination, and a clear sense of moral responsibility. Her work continues to evolve as she develops new formats and addresses the dilemmas of contemporary life.

Author Activity

Coming Home Find out about Doris Lessing's relationship to her homeland since Zimbabwe gained its independence. Has she been allowed to return to her homeland? Does she approve of the country's new government? What does she think of the changes that have taken place in Zimbabwe since 1949?

The First Year of My Life

Short Story by MURIEL SPARK

(Connect to Your Life)

Baby Talk What kind of baby were you, according to your parents and other relatives? Were you happy? cranky? Did you seem interested in the world around you or indifferent to it? Briefly describe yourself at that point in your life. Then, as you read this story, compare yourself with the rather astonishing baby being depicted.

Build Background

World War I The story you are about to read is set in 1918, the final year of World War I. By that time,

the bloodshed and devastation of the Great War, as it was then called, had reached levels never seen in any previous conflict. The use of advanced weaponry and poison gas in the brutal stalemate of trench warfare had resulted in heavy casualties, and many families across Europe suffered the loss of loved ones. The war also left deep political and economic scars on almost every European country—scars that eventually led to the eruption of World War II only two decades later.

In her account of her life as an infant, the narrator of this story provides an unusual perspective on the final year of World War I. Although the premise of the story is pure fantasy, the narrator makes allusions to many individuals who actually lived during the time, including figures famous in history and the arts.

WORDS TO KNOW
Vocabulary Preview

authenticity	omniscient
demented	seditious
discern	

Focus Your Reading

LITERARY ANALYSIS | **POINT OF VIEW** In a story that is told from the **first-person point of view,** the narrator is the "I" who is speaking. In a story that is told from the **third-person omniscient point of view,** the narrator is outside the story and can see into the minds of the characters. As you read this story, be aware of the way in which the writer merges these two points of view in order to provide an unusual perspective on events.

ACTIVE READING | **ANALYZING SATIRE** **Satire** is a literary technique in which criticism is mixed with humor in order to expose the faults of society. The **tone** of a satirical work may be gently witty, mildly abrasive, or even bitterly critical. As you read "The First Year of My Life," look for specific instances of satire and decide what effects are created by the narrator's unusual **point of view.** Note passages in which you think the satire is particularly effective.

READER'S NOTEBOOK List some of the individuals and groups that are satirized in this story. Then identify what fault the narrator finds with each one. Use a chart like the one shown to record their faults.

Individual/Group	Fault

The First Year of My Life

Muriel Spark

I was born on the first day of the second month of the last year of the First World War, a Friday. Testimony abounds that during the first year of my life I never smiled. I was known as the baby whom nothing and no one could make smile. Everyone who knew me then has told me so. They tried very hard, singing and bouncing me up and down, jumping around, pulling faces. Many times I was told this later by my family and their friends; but, anyway, I knew it at the time.

You will shortly be hearing of that new school of psychology, or maybe you have heard of it already, which after long and far-adventuring research and experiment has established that all of the young of the human species are born <u>omniscient</u>. Babies, in their waking hours, know everything that is going on everywhere in the world; they can tune in to any conversation they choose, switch on to any scene. We have all experienced this power. It is only after the first year that it was brainwashed out of us; for it is demanded of us by our immediate environment that we grow to be of use to it in a practical way. Gradually, our know-all brain-cells are blacked out, although traces remain in some individuals in the form of E.S.P., and in the adults of some primitive tribes.

It is not a new theory. Poets and philosophers, as usual, have been there first. But scientific proof is now ready and to hand. Perhaps the final touches are being put to the new manifesto[1] in some cell[2] at Harvard University. Any day now it will be given to the world, and the world will be convinced.

Let me therefore get my word in first, because

---

1. **manifesto:** a declaration of principles.
2. **cell:** a small group forming a unit of a larger organization.

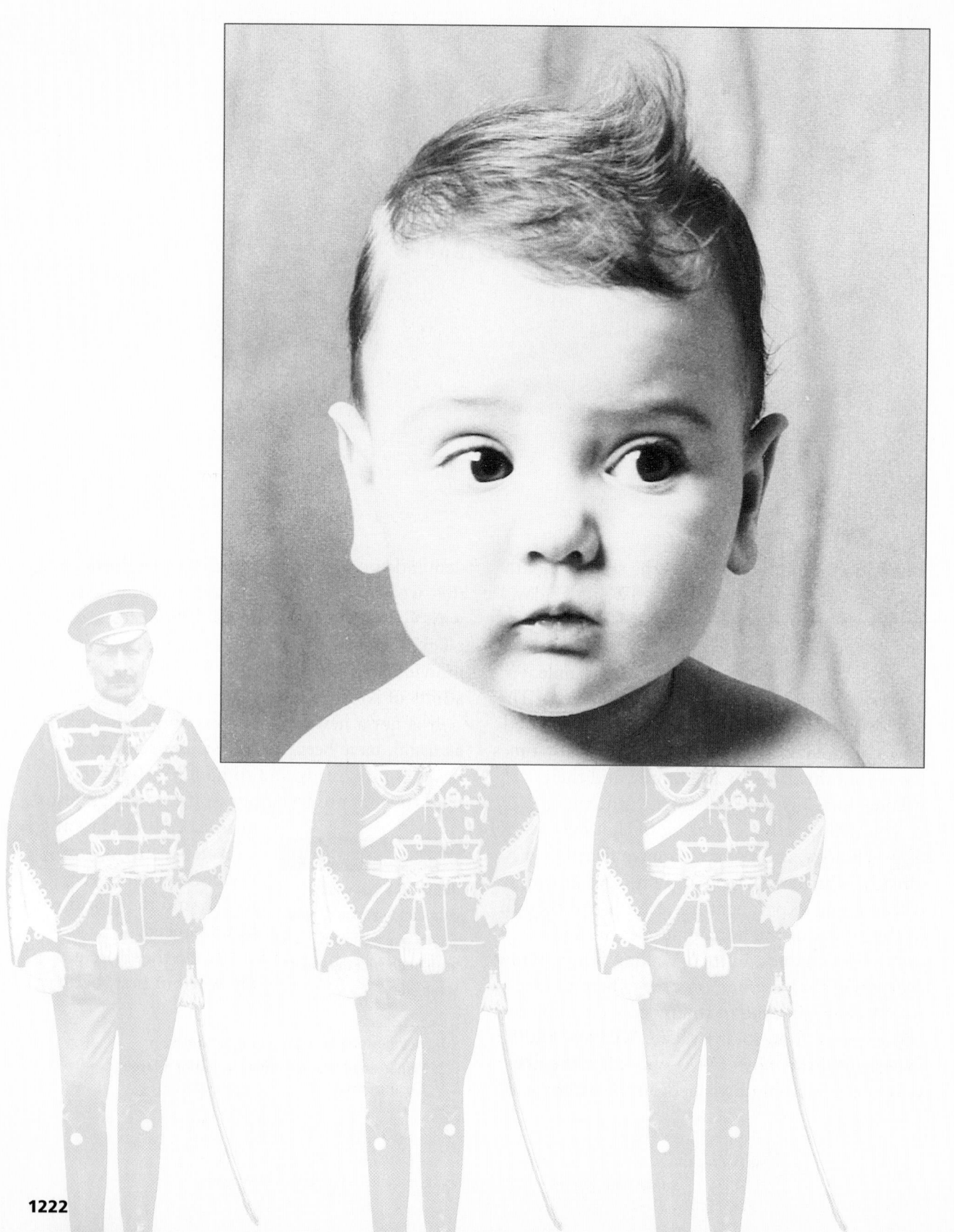

I feel pretty sure, now, about the authenticity of my remembrance of things past. My autobiography, as I very well perceived at the time, started in the very worst year that the world had ever seen so far. Apart from being born bedridden and toothless, unable to raise myself on the pillow or utter anything but farmyard squawks or police-siren wails, my bladder and my bowels totally out of control, I was further depressed by the curious behavior of the two-legged mammals around me. There were those black-dressed people, females of the species to which I appeared to belong, saying they had lost their sons. I slept a great deal. Let them go and find their sons. It was like the special pin for my nappies[3] which my mother or some other hoverer dedicated to my care was always losing. These careless women in black lost their husbands and their brothers. Then they came to visit my mother and clucked and crowed over my cradle. I was not amused.

ACTIVE READING

CLARIFY Why are the women dressed in black?

"Babies never really smile till they're three months old," said my mother. "They're not *supposed* to smile till they're three months old."

My brother, aged six, marched up and down with a toy rifle over his shoulder:

The grand old Duke of York
He had ten thousand men;
He marched them up to the top of the hill
And he marched them down again.

And when they were up, they were up.
And when they were down, they were down.
And when they were neither down nor up
They were neither up nor down.

"Just listen to him!"
"Look at him with his rifle!"

I was about ten days old when Russia stopped fighting. I tuned in to the Czar,[4] a prisoner, with the rest of his family, since evidently the country had put him off his throne and there had been a revolution not long before I was born. Everyone was talking about it. I tuned in to the Czar. "Nothing would ever induce me to sign the treaty of Brest-Litovsk,"[5] he said to his wife. Anyway, nobody had asked him to.

At this point I was sleeping twenty hours a day to get my strength up. And from what I discerned in the other four hours of the day I knew I was going to need it. The Western Front[6] on my frequency was sheer blood, mud, dismembered bodies, blistering crashes, hectic flashes of light in the night skies, explosions, total terror. Since it was plain I had been born into a bad moment in the history of the world, the future bothered me, unable as I was to raise my head from the pillow and as yet only twenty inches long.

ACTIVE READING

ANALYZE What is the main target of the **satire** in the paragraph?

"I truly wish I were a fox or a bird," D. H. Lawrence was writing to somebody. . . .

Red sheets of flame shot across the sky. It was 21st March, the fiftieth day of my life, and the German Spring Offensive[7] had started before my morning feed. Infinite slaughter. I scowled at the scene, and made an effort to kick out. But the

---

3. **nappies:** the British term for diapers.
4. **Czar:** Nicholas II, the last czar of Russia, who was forced from power in the Russian Revolution of 1917.
5. **treaty of Brest-Litovsk:** the treaty—signed on March 3, 1918—by which the new Communist government of Russia made peace with Germany, withdrawing from World War I eight months before its end.
6. **Western Front:** a 450-mile-long battlefront across Belgium and northeastern France, along which the Allies and Germany were locked in bloody trench warfare from 1914 to 1918.
7. **German Spring Offensive:** In late March 1918, after its peace treaty with Russia ended the fighting on the eastern front, Germany began a major push to win the war on the western front.

WORDS
TO
KNOW

authenticity (ô'thĕn-tĭs'ĭ-tē) *n.* genuineness
discern (dĭ-sûrn') *v.* to observe; perceive

attempt was feeble. Furious, and impatient for some strength, I wailed for my feed. After which I stopped wailing but continued to scowl.

> *The grand old Duke of York*
> *He had ten thousand men . . .*

They rocked the cradle. I never heard a sillier song. Over in Berlin and Vienna the people were starving, freezing, striking, rioting and yelling in the streets. In London everyone was bustling to work and muttering that it was time the whole . . . business was over.

The big people around me bared their teeth; that meant a smile, it meant they were pleased or amused. They spoke of ration cards[8] for meat and sugar and butter.

"Where will it all end?"

I went to sleep. I woke and tuned in to Bernard Shaw[9] who was telling someone to shut up. I switched over to Joseph Conrad[10] who, strangely enough, was saying precisely the same thing. I still didn't think it worth a smile, although it was expected of me any day now. I got on to Turkey. Women draped in black huddled and chattered in their harems; yak-yak-yak. This was boring, so I came back to home base.

In and out came and went the women in British black. My mother's brother, dressed in his uniform, came coughing. He had been poison-gassed in the trenches. *"Tout le monde à la bataille!"*[11] declaimed Marshal Foch[12] the old swine. He was now Commander-in-Chief of the Allied Forces. My uncle coughed from deep within his lungs, never to recover but destined to return to the Front. His brass buttons gleamed in the firelight. I weighed twelve pounds by now; I stretched and kicked for exercise, seeing that I had a lifetime before me, coping with this crowd. I took six feeds a day and kept most of them down by the time the *Vindictive* was sunk in Ostend harbor,[13] on which day I kicked with special vigor in my bath.

In France the conscripted[14] soldiers leapfrogged over the dead on the advance and littered the fields with limbs and hands, or drowned in the mud. The strongest men on all fronts were dead before I was born. Now the sentries used bodies for barricades and the fighting men were unhealthy from the start. I checked my toes and fingers, knowing I was going to need them. *The Playboy of the Western World*[15] was playing at the Court Theatre in London, but occasionally I beamed over to the House of Commons[16] which made me drop off gently to sleep. Generally, I preferred the Western Front where one got the true state of affairs. It was essential to know the worst, blood and explosions and all, for one had to be prepared, as the boy scouts said. Virginia Woolf yawned and reached for her diary. Really, I preferred the Western Front.

8. **ration cards:** cards entitling the bearers to limited amounts of certain foods and other goods that were in short supply during the war.

9. **Bernard Shaw:** George Bernard Shaw, an Irish-born British playwright and social critic.

10. **Joseph Conrad:** a Polish-born British novelist.

11. *Tout le monde à la bataille!* (tōō′ lə môN d′ ä lä bä-tī′) *French:* The whole world into the battle!

12. **Marshal Foch** (fôsh): Ferdinand Foch, a French general who in March 1918 became commander of all Allied forces on the western front.

13. *Vindictive . . . Ostend harbor:* In May 1918, a crew of Allied volunteers sunk the ship *Vindictive* to block the entrance of the harbor of Ostend, Belgium, which the Germans had been using as a submarine base.

14. **conscripted:** drafted into military service.

15. *The Playboy of the Western World:* a controversial drama by the Irish playwright John Millington Synge.

16. **House of Commons:** the lower house of the British parliament.

In the fifth month of my life I could raise my head from my pillow and hold it up. I could grasp the objects that were held out to me. Some of these things rattled and squawked. I gnawed on them to get my teeth started. "She hasn't smiled yet?" said the dreary old aunties. My mother, on the defensive, said I was probably one of those late smilers. On my wavelength Pablo Picasso[17] was getting married and early in that month of July the Silver Wedding of King George V and Queen Mary was celebrated in joyous pomp at St. Paul's Cathedral. They drove through the streets of London with their children. Twenty-five years of domestic happiness. A lot of fuss and ceremonial handing over of swords went on at the Guildhall where the King and Queen received a check for £53,000 to dispose of for charity as they thought fit. *Tout le monde à la bataille!* Income tax in England had reached six shillings in the pound. Everyone was talking about the Silver Wedding; yak-yak-yak, and ten days later the Czar and his family, now in Siberia, were invited to descend to a little room in the basement. Crack, crack, went the guns; screams and blood all over the place, and that was the end of the Romanoffs.[18] I flexed my muscles. "A fine healthy baby," said the doctor; which gave me much satisfaction.

Tout le monde à la bataille! That included my gassed uncle. My health had improved to the point where I was able to crawl in my playpen. Bertrand Russell[19] was still cheerily in prison for writing something <u>seditious</u> about pacifism. Tuning in as usual to the Front Lines it looked as if the Germans were winning all the battles yet losing the war. And so it was. The upper-income people were upset about the income tax at six shillings to the pound. But all women over thirty got the vote. "It seems a long time to wait," said one of my drab old aunts, aged twenty-two. The speeches in the House of Commons always sent me to sleep which was why I missed, at the actual time, a certain oration by Mr. Asquith[20] following the armistice on 11th November.[21] Mr. Asquith was a greatly esteemed former prime minister later to be an Earl, and had been ousted by Mr. Lloyd George.[22] I clearly heard Asquith, in private, refer to Lloyd George as "that . . . Welsh goat."

The armistice was signed and I was awake for that. I pulled myself on to my feet with the aid of the bars of my cot. My teeth were coming through very nicely in my opinion, and well worth all the trouble I was put to in bringing them forth. I weighed twenty pounds. On all the world's fighting fronts the men killed in action or dead of wounds numbered 8,538,315 and the warriors wounded and maimed were 21,219,452. With these figures in mind I sat up in my high chair and banged my spoon on the table. One of my mother's black-draped friends recited:

I have a rendezvous with Death
At some disputed barricade,
When spring comes back with rustling shade
And apple blossoms fill the air—
I have a rendezvous with Death.[23]

Most of the poets, they said, had been killed. The poetry made them dab their eyes with clean white handkerchiefs.

---

17. **Pablo Picasso:** a Spanish painter and sculptor.
18. **Romanoffs:** the ruling family of Russia from 1613 to 1917.
19. **Bertrand Russell:** a British philosopher, mathematician, and writer.
20. **Mr. Asquith:** Herbert Henry Asquith, prime minister of Britain from 1908 to 1916.
21. **armistice on 11th November:** the agreement that marked the end of fighting in World War I.
22. **Lloyd George:** David Lloyd George, prime minister of Britain from 1916 to 1922.
23. *I . . . Death:* the beginning of "I Have a Rendezvous with Death" by the American poet Alan Seeger, who was killed in action during World War I. (Another quotation from the poem appears three paragraphs farther on.)

WORDS
TO   **seditious** (sĭ-dĭsh′əs) *adj.* stirring up discontent or rebellion
KNOW

Next February on my first birthday, there was a birthday-cake with one candle. Lots of children and their elders. The war had been over two months and twenty-one days. "Why doesn't she smile?" My brother was to blow out the candle. The elders were talking about the war and the political situation. Lloyd George and Asquith, Asquith and Lloyd George. I remembered recently having switched on to Mr. Asquith at a private party where he had been drinking a lot. He was playing cards and when he came to cut the cards he tried to cut a large box of matches by mistake. On another occasion I had seen him putting his arm around a lady's shoulder in a Daimler[24] motor car, and generally behaving towards her in a very friendly fashion. Strangely enough she said, "If you don't stop this nonsense immediately I'll order the chauffeur to stop and I'll get out." Mr. Asquith replied, "And pray, what reason will you give?" Well anyway it was my feeding time.

The guests arrived for my birthday. It was so sad, said one of the black widows, so sad about Wilfred Owen who was killed so late in the war, and she quoted from a poem of his:

What passing-bells for these who die as cattle?
Only the monstrous anger of the guns.[25]

The children were squealing and toddling around. One was sick and another wet the floor and stood with his legs apart gaping at the puddle. All was mopped up. I banged my spoon on the table of my high chair.

But I've a rendezvous with Death
At midnight in some flaming town;
When spring trips north again this year,
And I to my pledged word am true,
I shall not fail that rendezvous.

More parents and children arrived. One stout man who was warming his behind at the fire, said, "I always think those words of Asquith's after the armistice were so apt . . ."

They brought the cake close to my high chair for me to see, with the candle shining and flickering above the pink icing. "A pity she never smiles."

"She'll smile in time," my mother said, obviously upset.

"What Asquith told the House of Commons just after the war," said that stout gentleman with his backside to the fire, "—so apt, what Asquith said. He said that the war has cleansed and purged the world. . . . I recall his actual words: 'All things have become new. In this great cleansing and purging it has been the privilege of our country to play her part . . .' "

That did it. I broke into a decided smile and everyone noticed it, convinced that it was provoked by the fact that my brother had blown out the candle on the cake. "She smiled!" my mother exclaimed. And everyone was clucking away about how I was smiling. For good measure I crowed like a <u>demented</u> raven. "My baby's smiling!" said my mother.

"It was the candle on her cake," they said.

. . . Since that time I have grown to smile quite naturally, like any other healthy and house-trained person, but when I really mean a smile, deeply felt from the core, then to all intents and purposes it comes in response to the words uttered in the House of Commons after the First World War by the distinguished, the immaculately dressed and the late Mr. Asquith. ❖

---

24. **Daimler** (dīm′lər): a German automobile-manufacturing company.

25. **What . . . guns:** the beginning of Owen's "Anthem for Doomed Youth."

demented (dǐ-mĕn′tǐd) *adj.* insane

Connect to the Literature

1. **What Do You Think?** What is your reaction to the story? Share your thoughts with your classmates.

> **Comprehension Check**
> - Why is the narrator's mother worried about her baby?
> - Why do the relatives think the baby smiles?

Think Critically

2. Why do you think Muriel Spark chose to tell the story from the unusual perspective of a baby?

3. Why do you think the **narrator** finally smiles after hearing Asquith's postwar remarks?

THINK ABOUT
- her opinion of world figures and the people around her
- her reactions to news about the war
- Asquith's reference to the war as "this great cleansing and purging"

4. **ACTIVE READING** **ANALYZING SATIRE** Review the chart that you completed in your **READER'S NOTEBOOK**. What do you think is the main point of the **satire** in this story? How does the unusual **point of view** of the narrator contribute to creating the satire?

Extend Interpretations

5. **Critic's Corner** The critic Michiko Kakutani has remarked that Spark presents a "distinctly dark view of human nature" in her stories. Do you think her comment can be applied to this story?

6. **Comparing Texts** How do you think Vera Brittain, author of the excerpt from *Testament of Youth* (page 1114), would respond to this story? Explain your answer.

7. **Connect to Life** If an author chose to tell a similar story from the perspective of a baby living today, what people and events might the baby "tune in to"?

Literary Analysis

POINT OF VIEW Many stories are told from a **first-person point of view,** by narrators who participate in the stories' action. Another common narrative point of view is the **third-person omniscient** (all-knowing) **point of view,** in which the narrator is outside the story's action but can see into the minds of more than one character. It is unusual, however, for these two narrative techniques to be merged in a **first-person omniscient point of view** like that used in "The First Year of My Life."

Cooperative Learning Activity With a group of three or four classmates, look through the story and choose a passage that you find particularly amusing. Rewrite the passage, telling the events from either a first-person or a third-person limited point of view. What changes do you notice in the **tone** of the passage?

At this point, the baby was sleeping twenty hours a day.

Choices & CHALLENGES

Writing Options

Letter to Asquith As the narrator of this story, write a letter to Mr. Asquith, giving your opinion of his comments to the House of Commons.

Activities & Explorations

Parliament Debate Imagine that you were in the House of Commons when Asquith made his remarks about the results of the war. Role-play a scene in which other members of Parliament take issue with Asquith and dispute his comments. ~ **SPEAKING AND LISTENING**

Vocabulary in Action

EXERCISE: WORD MEANING Answer the following questions.

1. If you called someone **demented,** would you mean that the person was insulting, powerful, or crazy?
2. If you were **omniscient,** would someone find it difficult to see you, to soothe you, or to fool you?
3. What cannot be successful without the involvement of **seditious** people—a contest, a mutiny, or a charity fundraiser?
4. If you questioned the **authenticity** of something, would you be doubting its truth, its safety, or its legality?
5. What do soldiers sometimes use to make it difficult for the enemy to **discern** them—radar, helmets, or camouflage?

Building Vocabulary
Several Words to Know in this lesson contain prefixes and suffixes. For an in-depth study of word parts, see page 1104.

Muriel Spark
1918–

Other Works
"The Twins"
"The Ormolu Clock"
"Miss Pinkerton's Apocalypse"
"You Should Have Seen the Mess"
"The Playhouse Called Remarkable"

Early Adventures Born in Edinburgh, Scotland, Muriel Spark attended James Gillespie's Girls' School in that city, where her literary efforts were encouraged and she was considered the school's "poet and dreamer." In 1937, at the age of 19, she moved to Central Africa, marrying there shortly afterward. Although her African venture provided her with excellent material for some of the stories she would later publish, her marriage was not successful; after a divorce, she returned to Great Britain in 1944. In order to have a closer view of the realities of World War II, which was then raging, she decided to live in London rather than Edinburgh. There she worked for the Intelligence Service's anti-Nazi propaganda department until the war's end.

A Writing Career Spark remained in London for more than a decade after the war, writing poetry, short stories, and biographies and working as an editor. In 1957, she published the first of her many novels, *The Comforters.* A few of her best-known works, including *The Prime of Miss Jean Brodie,* have been made into movies.

A People Watcher Many of the characters in Spark's stories are based on real people who have touched her life. In her autobiography, *Curriculum Vitae,* she states, "I can't remember a time when I was not a person-watcher, a behaviorist." Of her very early years, she remarks, "People were far more important to me than toys or nature."

The Moment

Poetry by MARGARET ATWOOD

Connect to Your Life

Moments of Revelation Think about a moment when you were struck by a new awareness or had an important insight into something you didn't understand or recognize before. What prompted the revelation? What effect, if any, did the insight have on you? Discuss your insight with a classmate.

Build Background

Canadian Literature Since 1867, Canada has functioned as a British Dominion, one of a group of nations allied under the British Crown. Although the reigning English monarch is the official head of state, Canada is self-governing. British influence is seen in the structure of Canada's government, which is modeled after British Parliament, but Canada has developed its own heritage and is a blend of distinctly different cultures, of which English is only one.

Canadian literature did not begin to flourish until the 1960s, when a sense of nationalism spurred efforts to promote Canadian culture. One of the most effective promoters of Canadian literature, and one of its most talented contributors, is Margaret Atwood.

Atwood began her writing career as a poet. She went on to write many successful novels and short stories but, unlike many who have achieved success in fiction, she has continued to write poetry. Atwood's writing in both genres is characterized by her use of vivid images and precise language. Her poem "The Moment" appears in *Morning in the Burned House,* a collection of her poetry published in 1995.

Focus Your Reading

LITERARY ANALYSIS THEME IN CONTEMPORARY POETRY

Themes, or central ideas, in contemporary poetry are usually implied rather than stated and can therefore be difficult to understand. Read "The Moment" slowly, paying attention to the ideas suggested. Then read the poem a second time in order to see what further insights can be gained.

ACTIVE READING ANALYZING STRUCTURE **Structure** in poetry involves the arrangement of words and lines to produce a desired effect and emphasize certain aspects of content. "The Moment" is organized into three free-verse stanzas of six lines each. As you read the poem, notice the structure of each stanza and the relationship between the stanzas.

READER'S NOTEBOOK Using a chart like the one shown, **summarize** each stanza's major idea and then jot down what you notice about the structure of each stanza.

Stanza	Major Idea	Details About Structure

Autumn (1984). Watercolor, 21″ × 291/2″.
Collection of Mr. and Mrs. Andrew Wyeth.
Copyright Andrew Wyeth.

THE Moment
MARGARET ATWOOD

The **moment** when, after many years
of hard work and a long voyage
you stand in the centre of your room,
house, half-acre, square mile, island, country,
5 knowing at last how you got there,
and say, *I own this,*

is the same **moment** the trees unloose
their soft arms from around you,
the birds take back their language,
10 the cliffs fissure and collapse,
the air moves back from you like a wave
and you can't breathe.

No, they whisper. *You own nothing.*
You were a visitor, time after time
15 *climbing the hill, planting the flag, proclaiming.*
We never belonged to you.
You never found us.
It was always the other way round.

10 fissure (fĭsh′ər):
to crack; split apart

Connect to the Literature

1. What Do You Think? What **image** lingers in your mind after reading this poem?

> **Comprehension Check**
> • What has the person being addressed in the poem apparently accomplished?
> • What happens after the person says, "I own this"?

Think Critically

2. What do you think is meant by "the voyage" in line 2?

3. How would you explain the events described in the second stanza?

THINK ABOUT
- the declaration made in line 6
- the description of the person being addressed as "a visitor" in line 14
- the statement made in line 16

4. What do you think the speakers in the last stanza mean when they say, "It was always the other way round"?

THINK ABOUT
- who the speakers are
- who they are addressing
- why they whisper

5. **ACTIVE READING** **ANALYZING STRUCTURE** Look over the summaries and details you wrote down in the chart in your **READER'S NOTEBOOK.** How is the structure in the third stanza different from that of the first two stanzas? What is the effect of this change in structure?

Extend Interpretations

6. Critic's Corner According to critic John Bemrose, "Atwood's hallmark as a poet has always been a combination of startling, razor-sharp images held in tight control." Do you think the images in "The Moment" are "startling" and "razor-sharp"? Why or why not? In what way are they held in "tight control"?

7. Comparing Texts Compare the attitude toward nature expressed in this poem with that in William Wordsworth's "The World Is Too Much with Us" on page 725.

8. Connect to Life In your opinion, are possessiveness and territoriality part of human nature? If so, do you think people should try to curb their desire to own material goods and land?

Literary Analysis

> **THEME IN CONTEMPORARY POETRY**

The **theme** or themes in a contemporary poem can often be conveyed by the sensory experiences created through **imagery.** What senses does this line from "The Moment" appeal to?

the cliffs fissure and collapse

Theme can also be understood by examining the effects created by the **figurative language** in a poem. Atwood uses both **simile** and **personification** to express her ideas. Personification is a type of figurative language in which human qualities are attributed to an object, an animal, or an idea. Think about the effect created by personification in the following lines from the poem:

. . . the trees unloose their soft arms from around you

What ideas and emotions do these examples of imagery and figurative language suggest?

Activity Notice the relationship between theme, imagery, and figurative language in Atwood's poem, paying particular attention to her use of personification. Write down some of the themes in the poem. Beside each theme you identify, list the images and figurative language that are used to develop it. Then answer the following questions: What is the impact of the poem's imagery? Why does Atwood use personification to convey theme?

Writing Options

1. Dialogue Between Opposites
Write a dialogue between the "you" and the "they" in the poem. Have both sides explain and defend their positions.

2. Personal Essay Write a personal essay about the insight you recalled in Connect to Your Life on page 1229. Place the essay in your **Working Portfolio.**

Activities & Explorations

Musical Reading Choose a piece of music to accompany a dramatic reading of "The Moment." The music should evoke the images and convey the mood in the poem. Play the background music while you read the poem to the class.
~ **PERFORMING/MUSIC**

Inquiry & Research

Canadian Literature Find out more about Canadian literature. In addition to Margaret Atwood, who are some of the country's major contemporary writers? What subjects or themes do they deal with in their work? What, if anything, have these writers done to promote Canadian culture? Present your findings in an oral report.

Margaret Atwood

1939–

Other Works
The Circle Game
Wilderness Tips
Alias Grace

Child of the Wilderness During much of her childhood, Margaret Atwood and her family spent six or seven months of every year living in the Canadian bush, the sparsely populated areas of northern Quebec and Ontario. These trips were an important part of her father's job as an entomologist, a scientist who collects and studies insects. For Atwood, the trips provided vast knowledge of the natural world, knowledge that would appear in her writing many years later.

Supportive Family Atwood began writing poems at age 5, and by age 16, she knew that writing was her sole ambition. She has credited her parents for their supportive role in her early pursuits. Although they did not urge her to become a writer, they did expect her to put her intelligence and creative talent to good use. Atwood grew up in a highly educated family of readers and storytellers who believed that girls as well as boys should acquire all the education they could. In this respect, her parents were unlike many of their contemporaries during the 1950s, when society generally pushed young women toward marriage and often discouraged them from other pursuits.

Academic Life In 1961, Atwood graduated with honors in English from Victoria College at the University of Toronto, where she had displayed her creativity not only in writing but also in drama and art. That same year, her first collection of poetry was published. She received a Master of Arts degree in English from Radcliffe College at Harvard University in 1962 and later began working toward a doctorate at Harvard. She has taught English literature and creative writing in universities in Canada, Australia, Germany, and the United States.

Accolades and Adulation By the 1970s, Atwood's writing had gained worldwide attention, and by 1982, her work had been published in 14 different languages. She is especially popular in her native Canada, where she has gained the status usually accorded only to movie stars and musicians. Atwood was honored for her first book of poems and has been receiving awards for both her poetry and her prose ever since. She has twice been the recipient of the Governor General's Award, Canada's most prestigious literary honor.

Digging

Poetry by SEAMUS HEANEY (shā′məs hā′nē)

The Horses

Poetry by TED HUGHES

Comparing Literature of the World

The Poetry of Seamus Heaney, Ted Hughes, and Czeslaw Milosz

This lesson and the one that follows present an opportunity for comparing lyric poems by the Irish poet Seamus Heaney, the English poet Ted Hughes, and the Polish poet Czeslaw Milosz. Specific points of comparison in the Milosz lesson will help you note similarities and differences in the poets' reflections on ordinary experiences and the larger meanings of those experiences.

Connect to Your Life

Lasting Impressions Think about the kinds of experiences that have made lasting impressions on you. Did those experiences involve ordinary events or extraordinary moments? Jot down some of your lasting impressions and your thoughts about them.

Build Background

Two Gifted Poets The Irish poet Seamus Heaney grew up on a farm in Northern Ireland. Although much of Heaney's work is concerned with the political unrest in his native land, there is also a concern with the poet as a craftsman who interacts with the force and mystery of language. Heaney's poems are characterized by themes and images taken from the natural world and rural life. His early poems, in particular, reflect the land and experiences of his childhood. His work shows the influence of both William Wordsworth and Gerard Manley Hopkins. "Digging" was the opening poem in his first book, *Death of a Naturalist,* published in 1966. In describing the poem, Heaney once said, "This was the first place where I felt I had done more than make an arrangement of words: I felt that I had let down a shaft into real life."

As a young man, Heaney was inspired by the writing of a slightly older contemporary, the English poet Ted Hughes. Many of Hughes's poems describe wild natural settings. He frequently focused on the savage, predatory aspects of animals and sometimes used animals to probe the instinctual, nonrational side of human life. Hughes's fascination with nature began during his youth, when he loved to hunt. Gradually, his passion shifted from literal hunting to searching for the essential qualities and energies of animals and writing about his discoveries in poetry. "The Horses," one of Hughes's earliest poems, appeared in his first book, *The Hawk in the Rain,* published in 1957.

Focus Your Reading

LITERARY ANALYSIS **SOUND DEVICES** Poets employ various **sound devices.** These include the following:

- **repetition**—the repeated use of words and phrases
- **alliteration**—the repetition of consonant sounds at the beginning of words
- **consonance**—the repetition of consonant sounds within words
- **assonance**—the repetition of vowel sounds within words

As you read these poems, be aware of the various sound devices used by the two poets.

ACTIVE READING **INTERPRETING IMAGERY**
Read through each poem and look for **imagery** that appeals to one or more of the five senses—sight, hearing, smell, taste, touch. Note how images help the reader to visualize and otherwise bring to mind the characters, settings, or events being described and how they relate to the meaning of the poem.

READER'S NOTEBOOK List the images from each poem. Then indicate which senses each image appeals to.

DIGGING

SEAMUS HEANEY

Between my finger and my thumb
The squat pen rests; snug as a gun.

Under my window, a clean rasping sound
When the spade sinks into gravelly ground:
5   My father, digging. I look down

Till his straining rump among the flowerbeds
Bends low, comes up twenty years away
Stooping in rhythm through potato drills
Where he was digging.

8 drills: furrows for planting
seeds.

10 The coarse boot nestled on the lug, the shaft
    Against the inside knee was levered firmly.
    He rooted out tall tops, buried the bright edge deep
    To scatter new potatoes that we picked
    Loving their cool hardness in our hands.

15 By God, the old man could handle a spade.
    Just like his old man.

    My grandfather cut more turf in a day
    Than any other man on Toner's bog.
    Once I carried him milk in a bottle
20 Corked sloppily with paper. He straightened up
    To drink it, then fell to right away
    Nicking and slicing neatly, heaving sods
    Over his shoulder, going down and down
    For the good turf. Digging.

25 The cold smell of potato mold, the squelch and slap
    Of soggy peat, the curt cuts of an edge
    Through living roots awaken in my head.
    But I've no spade to follow men like them.

    Between my finger and my thumb
30 The squat pen rests.
    I'll dig with it.

10 lug: a widening at the top of a shovel blade to support the foot.

17–18 Turf, or peat—partially decayed vegetable matter found in wet areas called bogs—was cut in blocks, called sods, and used as fuel in Ireland.

Thinking Through the Literature

1. **Comprehension Check** What do the speaker's father and grandfather do for a living?

2. How would you describe the relationship between the **speaker** and his father and grandfather? Be specific in your answer.

3. How important are the lasting impressions of the past to the speaker's understanding of his future?

 THINK ABOUT
- how his father "buried the bright edge deep" (line 12)
- his grandfather "heaving sods" (line 22) and "going down and down" (line 23)
- what kind of digging the speaker plans to do

THE HORSES

TED HUGHES

I climbed through woods in the hour-before-dawn dark.
Evil air, a frost-making stillness,

Not a leaf, not a bird—
A world cast in frost. I came out above the wood

5   Where my breath left tortuous statues in the iron light.
But the valleys were draining the darkness

Till the moorline—blackening dregs of the brightening gray—
Halved the sky ahead. And I saw the horses:

Huge in the dense gray—ten together—
10 Megalith-still. They breathed, making no move,

With draped manes and tilted hind-hooves,
Making no sound.

I passed: not one snorted or jerked its head.
Gray silent fragments

15 Of a gray silent world.

5 tortuous: winding or twisting.

7 moorline: the horizon at the edge of a moor, a large area of high, open land; **dregs:** small amounts left over.

10 megalith: a very large stone of the sort used in various prehistoric formations, such as Stonehenge in England.

I listened in emptiness on the moor-ridge.
The curlew's tear turned its edge on the silence.

Slowly detail leafed from the darkness. Then the sun
Orange, red, red, erupted

20 Silently, and splitting to its core tore and flung cloud,
Shook the gulf open, showed blue,

And the big planets hanging.
I turned,

Stumbling in the fever of a dream, down toward
25 The dark woods, from the kindling tops,

And came to the horses.
                              There, still they stood,
But now steaming and glistening under the flow of light,

Their draped stone manes, their tilted hind-hooves
30 Stirring under a thaw while all around them

The frost showed its fires. But still they made no sound.
Not one snorted or stamped,

Their hung heads patient as the horizons,
High over valleys, in the red leveling rays—

35 In din of the crowded streets, going among the years, the faces,
May I still meet my memory in so lonely a place

Between the streams and the red clouds, hearing curlews,
Hearing the horizons endure.

17 **curlew:** a large, brownish,
long-legged shore bird with a
long, slender, downward-curving
bill.

Thinking through the **LITERATURE**

Connect to the Literature

1. **What Do You Think?**
   Did you find the mood in "The Horses" appealing? Why or why not?

   Comprehension Check
   - Where, and at what time of day, does the scene take place?
   - What are the horses doing?

Think Critically

2. Why do you think the horses made such an impression on the **speaker?**

   THINK ABOUT
   - the phrase "a world cast in frost"
   - his references to darkness and silence
   - his descriptions of the horses after sunrise

3. How would you describe the relationship between the speaker and the horses?

4. **ACTIVE READING** **INTERPRETING IMAGERY** Look at the list of images you made in your **READER'S NOTEBOOK**. What images in each of these two poems do you think are the most forceful? How do these images help convey the ideas and experiences being expressed in each poem?

5. Compare the speakers' experiences as described in "Digging" and "The Horses." Which experience had the stronger effect on you as a reader?

Extend Interpretations

6. **Comparing Texts** Both Dylan Thomas in "Do Not Go Gentle into That Good Night" (page 1087) and Seamus Heaney in "Digging" write about their fathers. What kinds of feelings and attitudes toward the father does each poet express? Compare the impression of the father that each poet leaves with the reader.

7. **Connect to Life** Which of the speakers in "Digging" and "The Horses" seems to deal more with issues and concerns similar to your own? Explain your opinion.

Literary Analysis

SOUND DEVICES Both Heaney and Hughes experiment with **sound devices** such as the **repetition** of words and phrases, **alliteration** (the repetition of consonant sounds at the beginning of words), **consonance** (the repetition of consonant sounds within words), and **assonance** (the repetition of vowel sounds within words). For example, look at the use of **alliteration** (*s* and *gr*) and **consonance** (*n, d,* and *nd*) in these lines from "Digging":

Under my window, a clean
*   rasping sound*

When the spade sinks into a
*   gravelly ground . . .*

Activity Look for at least one example of each technique in each of the poems. Make a list of your examples and discuss them with the class. Explain how each example provides focus or reinforces meaning.

	"Digging"	"The Horses"
Repetition		
Alliteration		
Consonance		
Assonance		

Choices & CHALLENGES

Writing Options

1. Comparison Booklet In "Digging" the speaker implies that, figuratively, he'll use his writing to "dig," just as his father and grandfather dug with a spade. Develop as many comparisons as you can think of that equate writing with other actions. Then, with other students, combine your comparisons in a booklet titled "Writing Is Like . . ."

2. Descriptive Paragraph In a descriptive paragraph, try to capture the images of an experience that made a lasting impression on you. Place the paragraph in your **Working Portfolio.**

Activities & Explorations

Scene Illustrations Create a series of drawings to illustrate three or more scenes from either "Digging" or "The Horses." ~ **ART**

Seamus Heaney
1939–

Other Works
"Blackberry-Picking"
"Follower"
"Personal Helicon"
"A Drink of Water"

Ted Hughes
1930–1998

Other Works
"Thistles"
"Hawk Roosting"
"The Thought-Fox"
"Wind"
"A March Calf"

Youth and First Writing Seamus Heaney was the oldest of nine children. He went to Queen's University in Belfast on a scholarship and, while there, became interested in poets who wrote about their local surroundings. The work of these poets affirmed for Heaney the validity of his own background, and after graduating in 1961, he began to write poetry regularly. His first book was published when he was 27.

Teacher and Poet Heaney took a teaching position at Queen's University and later lectured at other universities in Ireland and at universities in England and the United States. In 1969, violent conflicts erupted in Northern Ireland between the Irish Protestant allies of England and the Irish Republican Army. Shortly thereafter, Heaney, a Catholic, left Queen's and eventually settled near Dublin.

Nobel Prize Winner Today, Heaney divides his time between Dublin and Cambridge, Massachusetts, where he has taught at Harvard since 1982. Although Heaney is not comfortable being viewed as a political poet, he has dealt with the tensions and devastation of the Irish struggles with deep feeling and power. Many consider him to be the most important Irish poet since W. B. Yeats. Heaney won the Nobel Prize in literature in 1995.

Youth and Marriage Ted Hughes grew up in Yorkshire, England, and began writing poetry when he was 15. After serving in the Royal Air Force, he went to Cambridge University, where he first studied English and then anthropology and archaeology. In 1956 he met and married the American poet Sylvia Plath, and for two years they lived in the United States, where Hughes taught at the University of Massachusetts. Hughes's first book of poetry, *The Hawk in the Rain,* was published in 1957 to critical acclaim.

Poet Laureate Hughes and Plath returned to England in late 1959, and his second book, *Lupercal,* was published the next year, establishing his reputation as an important new poet. In 1962 Hughes and Plath separated, and in 1963 Plath committed suicide; for nearly three years, Hughes wrote no poetry at all. When he began writing again, however, he was prolific, producing numerous works for adults and children that included poetry, drama, short stories, and criticism. Hughes received many awards for his literary achievements and in 1984 was named England's poet laureate.

from

Crediting *Poetry*

THE NOBEL LECTURE

Speech by Seamus Heaney

Seamus Heaney won the 1995 Nobel Prize in literature for, in the words of the Nobel committee, "works of lyrical beauty and ethical depth, which exalt everyday miracles and the living past." This is an excerpt from the speech Heaney gave in Stockholm, Sweden, when he accepted the prize.

When I first encountered the name of the city of Stockholm, I little thought that I would ever visit it, never mind end up being welcomed to it as a guest of the Swedish Academy and the Nobel Foundation. At that particular time, such an outcome was not just beyond expectation: it was simply beyond conception. In the nineteen-forties, when I was the eldest child of an ever-growing family in rural County Derry, we crowded together in the three rooms of a traditional thatched farmstead and lived a kind of den life which was more or less emotionally and intellectually proofed against the outside world. It was an intimate, physical, creaturely existence in which the night sounds of the horse in the stable beyond one bedroom wall mingled with the sounds of adult conversation from the kitchen beyond the other. We took in everything that was going on, of course—rain in the trees, mice on the ceiling, a steam train rumbling along the railway line one field back from the house—but we took it in as if we were in the doze of hibernation. Ahistorical, pre-sexual, in suspension between the archaic and the modern, we were as susceptible and impressionable as the drinking water that stood in a bucket in our scullery: every time a passing train made the earth shake, the surface of that water used to ripple delicately, concentrically, and in utter silence.

But it was not only the earth that shook for us: the air around and above us was alive and signaling as well. When a wind stirred in the beeches, it also stirred

Reading for Information

What would you expect to hear in a speech by someone accepting an important prize? Heaney expresses gratitude and discusses poetry and personal experiences.

ANALYZING A SPEECH

A person giving a speech can use tones of voice, body language, and timing to make his or her meaning clear to the audience; but when the audience is a reader, those clues are lost. Nevertheless, in a well-written speech, the following devices can help convey ideas to readers as well as listeners:

- **parallel construction,** a use of like grammatical structures to make connections clear
- **repetition** of words and phrases for emphasis and clarification
- **sound devices,** such as rhythm, alliteration, and onomatopoeia (the use of words whose sound echoes their meaning), which can draw attention to concepts and descriptions
- strong **imagery** that helps the audience visualize scenes
- **figurative language** that illustrates concepts

Use the activities below to analyze this speech.

❶ **Parallelism** Notice the balance created by the parallel phrasing of the two parts of this sentence. Find another sentence in which Heaney achieves a similar balance.

❷ **Figurative Language** In this simile, what features of the bucket of water are likened to characteristics of Heaney's family?

Nobel Medal

❸ Sound Devices What instances of onomatopoeia can you find in this sentence?

❹ Imagery Which of the five senses does the imagery in this speech mainly appeal to? Why do you think that sense is important to Heaney?

❺ Repetition and Parallelism Notice the repetition of the phrase "there was something" in this long sentence. Read the sentence aloud to hear the rhythm of the language. How do repetition and parallelism help to clarify the sentence's meaning?

❸ an aerial wire attached to the topmost branch of the chestnut tree. Down it swept, in through a hole bored in the corner of the kitchen window, right on into the innards of our wireless set, where a little pandemonium of burbles and squeaks would suddenly give way to the voice of a BBC newsreader speaking out of the unexpected like a deus ex machina.[1] And that voice too we could hear in our bedroom, transmitting from beyond and behind the voices of the adults in the kitchen; just as we could often hear, behind and
❹ beyond every voice, the frantic, piercing signaling of Morse code.

We could pick up the names of neighbors being spoken in the local accents of our parents, and in the resonant English tones of the newsreader the names of bombers and of cities bombed, of war fronts and army divisions, the numbers of planes lost and of prisoners taken, of casualties suffered and advances made; and always, of course, we would pick up too those other, solemn, and oddly bracing words "the enemy" and "the allies." But even so, none of the news of these world spasms entered me as terror. If there was something ominous in the newscaster's tones, there was something
❺ torpid[2] about our understanding of what was at stake; and if there was something culpable[3] about such political ignorance in that time and place, there was something positive about the security I inhabited as a result of it.

The wartime, in other words, was pre-reflective time for me. Pre-literate too. Pre-historical in its way. Then as the years went on and my listening became more deliberate, I would climb up on an arm of our big sofa to get my ear closer to the wireless speaker. But it

---

1. **deus ex machina** (dāʹəs ĕks mäʹkə-nə): in ancient Greek and Roman drama, a god suddenly lowered onto the stage to resolve a conflict.
2. **torpid:** sluggish.
3. **culpable:** blameworthy.

was still not the news that interested me; what I was after was the thrill of story, such as a detective serial about a British special agent called Dick Barton or perhaps a radio adaptation of one of Captain W. E. Johns's adventure tales about an RAF flying ace called Biggles. Now that the other children were older and there was so much going on in the kitchen, I had to get close to the actual radio set in order to concentrate my hearing, and in that intent proximity to the dial I grew familiar with the names of foreign stations, with Leipzig and Oslo and Stuttgart and Warsaw and, of course, with Stockholm.

I also got used to hearing short bursts of foreign languages as the dial hand swept round from BBC to Radio Eireann, from the intonations of London to those of Dublin, and even though I did not understand what was being said in those first encounters with the gutturals and sibilants of European speech, I had already begun a journey into the wideness of the world. This in turn became a
6   journey into the wideness of language, a journey where each point of arrival—whether in one's poetry or one's life—turned out to be a stepping-stone rather than a destination, and it is that journey which has brought me now to this honored spot. And yet the platform here feels more like a space station than a stepping-stone, so that is why, for once in my life, I am permitting myself the luxury of walking on air.

I credit poetry for making this space walk possible. I credit it immediately because of a line I wrote fairly recently encouraging myself (and whoever else might be listening) to "walk on air against your better judgement." But I credit it ultimately because poetry can make an order as true to the impact of external reality and as sensitive to the inner laws of the poet's being as the ripples that rippled in and rippled out across the water in that scullery bucket fifty years ago. An order where we can at last grow up to that which we stored up as we grew. An order which satisfies all that is
7   appetitive[4] in the intelligence and prehensile[5] in the affections. I credit poetry, in other words, both for being itself and for being a help, for making possible a fluid and restorative relationship between the mind's center and its circumference, between the child gazing at the word "Stockholm" on the face of the radio dial and the man facing the faces that he meets in Stockholm at this most privileged moment. I credit it because credit is due to it, in our time and in all time, for its truth to life, in every sense of that phrase. . . .

---

4. **appetitive** (ə-pĕt′ĭ-tĭv): desirous.
5. **prehensile** (prē-hĕn′səl): perceptive; insightful.

6   **Repetition** Heaney packs a lot of meaning into the sentence that begins "This in turn . . . ," using repetition to help the audience keep its bearings. Read the sentence aloud, employing pauses, changes in tone of voice, or gestures in a way that would help listeners understand it.

7   In this paragraph, Heaney returns to many of the devices he has used earlier in the speech. Identify some of these devices, and explain how they help him sum up the ideas he has been expressing.

Comparing Texts Reread Heaney's poem "Digging" on page 1234. Now that you have learned more about Heaney by reading this excerpt of his Nobel Prize acceptance speech, what new insights do you have about the poem?

In Music

Poetry by CZESLAW MILOSZ (chě′släv mē′wŏsh′)

Comparing Literature of the World

Poetic Contemplations Across Cultures

"Digging," "The Horses," and "In Music" Contemporary lyric poetry is often reflective, focusing on impressions and moments of experience that yield insights about life. Ted Hughes in England, Seamus Heaney in Ireland, and Czeslaw Milosz in Poland and the United States all have written poems that use a particular event or image as the occasion for contemplating the meaning and significance of certain aspects of life.

Points of Comparison As you read the following poem by Milosz, compare it with those of Heaney and Hughes in terms of the following:

- the experience that each poet is responding to
- how each experience is portrayed
- the insights revealed in each poem

Build Background

Poetry in Exile Like Seamus Heaney and many other contemporary poets, Czeslaw Milosz frequently examines the past and its associations as he searches for insights into life's experiences. Sometimes called the greatest poet in Poland, he has not lived in that country since 1951, the year he defected to the West. Even after moving to the United States in 1960, Milosz continued writing in his native language, but in the 1970s he began translating his own poetry into English with the help of some of his graduate students. When his *Selected Poems* was published in 1973, his readership and his international reputation grew rapidly. In 1980 he was awarded the Nobel Prize in literature.

Focus Your Reading

LITERARY ANALYSIS | **IMAGERY AND MOOD** Milosz makes extensive use of **imagery** in this poem, and the images shape the overall **mood** of the piece. Although many images are visual, some appeal to the sense of smell, hearing, taste, or touch. As you read, look for words and phrases that create vivid sensory experiences. Be aware of the mood that these images help to create.

ACTIVE READING | **ANALYZING STRUCTURE** The **structure** of a poem can reflect important transitions from one thought, perspective, or image to another. These transitions are often quick and subtle, particularly in poetry, where ideas are usually expressed briefly and compactly. The two-part structure of "In Music" reflects a major transition in the poet's development of his impressions and ideas in the poem.

READER'S NOTEBOOK As you read "In Music," look for the transition that occurs between the first and second stanzas. In a chart such as the one shown, note what is described in each of the poem's stanzas.

First Stanza:

Second Stanza:

In Music

Czeslaw Milosz

Wailing of a flute, a little drum.
A small wedding cortege accompanies a couple
Going past clay houses on the street of a village.
In the dress of the bride much white satin.
5   How many pennies put away to sew it, once in a lifetime.
The dress of the groom black, festively stiff.
The flute tells something to the hills, parched, the color of deer.
Hens scratch in dry mounds of manure.

I have not seen it, I summoned it listening to music.
10   The instruments play for themselves, in their own eternity.
Lips glow, agile fingers work, so short a time.
Soon afterwards the pageant sinks into the earth.
But the sound endures, autonomous, triumphant,
For ever visited by, each time returning,
15   The warm touch of cheeks, interiors of houses,
And particular human lives
Of which the chronicles make no mention.

Translated by the poet
and Robert Hass

2 cortege (kôr-tĕzh′): a ceremonial procession, as at a funeral or wedding.

Wedding Procession. Elek Györy. Hungarian National Gallery, Budapest.

Connect to the Literature

1. **What Do You Think?**
   What are your thoughts after reading this poem?

   ┄┄┄┄┄┄┄┄┄┄┄┄┄┄┄
   Comprehension Check
   • Summarize what you think has happened in the poem.
   ┄┄┄┄┄┄┄┄┄┄┄┄┄┄┄

Think Critically

2. What aspects of life seem to concern the **speaker**?

   THINK ABOUT
   - the scene he describes in the first **stanza**
   - the kinds of **details** he notices
   - what he means by "particular human lives / Of which the chronicles make no mention" (lines 16–17)

3. What contrasts does the poet make within each stanza? What ideas are conveyed through these contrasts?

4. **ACTIVE READING** | **ANALYZING STRUCTURE** Review the chart you completed in your ⬛📖**READER'S NOTEBOOK**. What is the transition that occurs between the two stanzas in the poem? Do you think the poem's two-part **structure** conveys this transition clearly? Explain your answer.

Extend Interpretations

5. **Connect to Life** What different effects can music have on its listeners? Base your response on your own experience or observations.

6. **Comparing Texts** Compare "In Music" with Thomas Gray's "Elegy Written in a Country Churchyard" (page 666). Can you find any similarities in the framework of the two poems or in the thoughts expressed about humanity? Cite lines from the poems to help you explain your answer.

7. **Points of Comparison** Compare the poems by Heaney, Hughes, and Milosz. In your opinion, which offers the most meaningful insight into life? Explain your answer.

Literary Analysis

IMAGERY AND MOOD | **Imagery** refers to words and phrases that create vivid sensory experiences for the reader. As you know, imagery may appeal to the senses of sight, smell, hearing, taste, and touch. For example, in Milosz's poem the line "Hens scratch in dry mounds of manure" appeals to the senses of sight, hearing, and smell. The imagery that a writer uses can help set a poem's **mood,** the feeling or atmosphere the work creates for the reader.

Paired Activity With a partner, come up with a word or phrase that seems to capture the mood of the poem. Then make a list of images that contribute to the overall mood. Share your description of mood and list of images with the class.

Mood of poem:

Imagery that contributes to mood:

Choices & CHALLENGES

Writing Options

1. Letter to a Friend In a letter to a friend, explain how a certain song affected you and what thoughts it suggests. Place the letter in your **Working Portfolio.**

2. Points of Comparison In an essay, compare and contrast the sights and sounds that inspire the poems by Heaney, Hughes, and Milosz. How effectively do these sights and sounds contribute to the main ideas of each poem?

Writing Handbook
See page 1367: Compare and Contrast.

Activities & Explorations

1. Association Game With a group of classmates, play an association game in which everyone responds independently to various pictures of people, places, or objects. As each picture is shown to your group, write down your associations. Then discuss your responses with those of other group members. ~ **SPEAKING AND LISTENING**

2. Dramatic Reading Plan and present for your class a dramatic reading of the poem, accompanied by flute and drum music. Students who play in your school band or orchestra could provide live music, or you could play a recording. ~ **PERFORMING**

Czeslaw Milosz
1911–

Other Works
"Song on Porcelain"
"Rivers"
"Incantation"
"Earth"
"Should, Should Not"

Multicultural Beginnings Czeslaw Milosz was born in Lithuania, a country that once existed as a Polish-Lithuanian confederation. Long before Milosz's birth, the confederation collapsed and was taken over by Russia. As a result, the poet, during his early years, was exposed to the language and customs of three different cultures.

The Outbreak of War Milosz attended the Stefan Batory University in Wilno (now called Vilnius), where he studied law and published his first book of poems at the age of 21. At the university, he also became involved with a group of poets called the Catastrophists, who predicted the outbreak of World War II. After the war erupted, Milosz moved to Nazi-occupied Warsaw, where he helped the Polish Resistance movement by contributing anti-Nazi writings and by promoting the cultural activities of the Polish underground. In order to have access to books, he worked as a janitor in a university library that had been closed to the general public.

Ambassador and Refugee When the war ended, Poland's new Communist government rewarded Milosz with a job in the foreign service. He was assigned as a cultural ambassador first to the United States and then to France. Milosz became disillusioned with Poland's totalitarian government, however, and in 1951 he asked the French government for political asylum. That same year he began writing his prose work *The Captive Mind,* an explanation of his reasons for defecting and of the effects of communism on creativity.

American Experience In 1960, Milosz moved to the United States to accept a teaching position at the University of California in Berkeley. Ten years later, he became an American citizen. His poetry and political writings reflect his diverse life experiences, and his recent poetry also probes aspects of American culture.

Author Activity

Milosz's Life Story In *Native Realm,* Milosz wrote an autobiography that covered his life from childhood up to the 1950s. Locate a copy of the book at a library and find out more about Milosz's experiences during World War II. Write a summary of his anti-Nazi activities during the war and present it to the class.

The Frog Prince
Not Waving but Drowning

Poetry by STEVIE SMITH

Connect to Your Life

Can You Believe Your Eyes? Get together with a partner and examine the image on the right. What do you see? Look at it longer. Do you see something different? This type of image is sometimes referred to as an optical illusion; what you see on the surface at first glance becomes something different as you look longer. Literature, too, can have this effect, as you will see in the poems you are about to read.

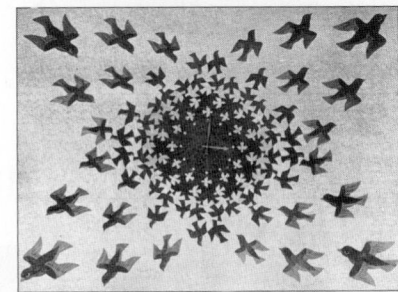

Build Background

Her Own Style During her early years as a writer, Florence Margaret Smith—better known as Stevie Smith—read widely in older works of literature, avoiding the poetic works of her contemporaries for fear that their influence would keep her from developing her own style. She did indeed achieve a distinctive style, and critics have therefore found her work hard to compare with that of other poets. At first glance, her poems appear simple both in subject matter and in their use of conventional rhyme, but closer scrutiny often reveals deep insights in her supposedly "light" verse.

   Although Smith did not consider herself a visual artist, she illustrated many of her poems with drawings—she called them doodles—that she thought helped readers to understand the poetry. The drawing that appears on page 1253 is the one Smith chose to print with "The Frog Prince."

Focus Your Reading

LITERARY ANALYSIS **DICTION IN POETRY** Stevie Smith's style is distinguished by her use of a simple, straightforward **diction,** or choice of words. This simplicity can be deceiving, however. Smith often uses words with multiple meanings to convey her messages. She also depends on a word's **connotation**—the attitudes or feelings associated with the word—to develop meaning. As you read these poems, think about the layers of meaning in the words Smith uses.

ACTIVE READING **SUMMARIZING A POEM'S MAJOR IDEAS** Poetry, even poetry with relatively simple diction, can be hard to understand. As you read Smith's poems, it may be useful to try to **summarize** the major idea in each stanza or selected group of lines.

READER'S NOTEBOOK "The Frog Prince" can be divided into four sections. Use a chart like the one shown to summarize the major idea in each section. Make a similar chart for "Not Waving but Drowning," and summarize the major idea of each stanza.

"The Frog Prince"	
Lines	**Major Idea**
1–9	Speaker identifies himself as prince-turned-frog who is waiting for princess to kiss him and break spell.
10–29	
30–42	
43–48	

The Frog Prince STEVIE SMITH

I am a frog,
I live under a spell,
I live at the bottom
Of a green well.

5   And here I must wait
Until a maiden places me
On her royal pillow,
And kisses me,
In her father's palace.

10   The story is familiar,
Everybody knows it well,
But do other enchanted people feel as nervous
As I do? The stories do not tell,

Ask if they will be happier
15   When the changes come,
As already they are fairly happy
In a frog's doom?

I have been a frog now
For a hundred years
20   And in all this time
I have not shed many tears,

I am happy, I like the life,
Can swim for many a mile
(When I have hopped to the river)
25   And am for ever agile.

And the quietness,
Yes, I like to be quiet
I am habituated
To a quiet life,

30 But always when I think these thoughts
As I sit in my well
Another thought comes to me and says:
It is part of the spell

To be happy
35 To work up contentment
To make much of being a frog
To fear disenchantment

Says, It will be *heavenly*
To be set free,
40 Cries, *Heavenly* the girl who disenchants
And the royal times, *heavenly,*
And I think it will be.

Come, then, royal girl and royal times,
Come quickly,
45 I can be happy until you come
But I cannot be heavenly,
Only disenchanted people
Can be heavenly.

Thinking Through the Literature

1. **Comprehension Check** What is the frog in the poem waiting for?

2. What is your opinion of this poem? Explain your answer.

3. Why do you think the frog prince is nervous?

   THINK ABOUT { • what his life is like now
   • what changes he anticipates

4. What do you think is the underlying **theme** of this poem?

Not Waving but Drowning

Stevie Smith

Nobody heard him, the dead man,
But still he lay moaning:
I was much further out than you thought
And not waving but drowning.

5   Poor chap, he always loved larking
And now he's dead
It must have been too cold for him his heart gave way,
They said.

Oh, no no no, it was too cold always
10   (Still the dead one lay moaning)
I was much too far out all my life
And not waving but drowning.

Connect to the Literature

1. **What Do You Think?**
   What emotions did "Not Waving but Drowning" evoke in you?

   Comprehension Check
   • Why did the man die?
   • Why didn't anyone try to rescue him?

Think Critically

2. What different voices, or **speakers,** do you hear in the poem?

3. Although the poem has more than one speaker, it has a single overall **tone.** How would you describe the tone?

THINK ABOUT
   • the attitude of the first speaker
   • the fact that a dead man speaks
   • what the dead man says
   • the fact that the dead man is heard by no one

4. What do you think the speaker means in the last stanza?

5. **ACTIVE READING** | **SUMMARIZING A POEM'S MAJOR IDEAS**
   Get together in a small group and discuss the summary charts you created in your **READER'S NOTEBOOK.** Identify specific lines in each poem where the ideas progress from simple to complex. Taking these complex ideas into account, how would you **summarize** each poem's major idea?

Extend Interpretations

6. **Critic's Corner** Muriel Spark once wrote that Smith's "style is comic and her vision melancholy but dry-eyed." Do you think Smith displays both a comic style and a melancholy vision in "The Frog Prince" and "Not Waving but Drowning"? Support your opinion with details from the two poems.

7. **Connect to Life** Smith once called the time period in which she was living and writing an "age of unrest." Do you think her poetry also speaks to your generation? Explain your opinion.

Literary Analysis

DICTION IN POETRY | **Diction** is a writer's choice of words. The diction in Stevie Smith's poetry is deceptively simple. The poet relies on **wordplay**—a clever use of the multiple meanings of words—to express ambiguities. In "The Frog Prince," for instance, she plays with the different meanings of *disenchantment* and *heavenly* to give added depth to the poem and its message. In "Not Waving but Drowning," Smith uses the different meanings of such words as *far out* and *cold* to create an image of the speaker as misunderstood and alone. The connotations of words in Smith's poems also influence meaning. For example, you may find as you read "The Frog Prince" that your reaction to words like *frog* and *spell* has changed.

Paired Activity With a partner, discuss your ideas for adding your own lines to one of Smith's poems. For example, in "The Frog Prince," you might tell what happens when the princess finally kisses the frog. In "Not Waving but Drowning," you might explain in what way the speaker was "much too far out" all his life. Be sure to maintain Smith's simple diction, but at the same time try to use wordplay and the connotations of words to express deeper meaning and insights.

Choices & CHALLENGES

Writing Options

1. **Fairy Tale Poem** Following the style of "The Frog Prince," write your own poem based on a famous fairy tale or nursery rhyme. Try to give the original story a humorous twist while at the same time conveying an insight about life. Place the poem in your **Working Portfolio.**

2. **Diary Entry** As the man in "Not Waving but Drowning," write a diary entry in which you explain why it's been "too cold always" and you've been "not waving but drowning."

Activities & Explorations

Drawings of the Frog Prince With a partner, create a series of drawings depicting the frog prince as he sits in his well. Be sure to convey his various thoughts about his impending "disenchantment." Add your drawings to a class display, and discuss any similarities and differences between them and Stevie Smith's frog "doodle" shown here.
~ **ART**

Inquiry & Research

Artistic Mind Games The image next to Connect to Your Life on page 1248 is by M. C. Escher, a 20th-century Dutch graphic artist. Find other examples of Escher's work. Then get together with a small group of classmates to share what you've found.

Stevie Smith
1902–1971

Other Works
"There Is an Old Man"
"Tender Only to One"
"The New Age"
"Pretty"
"Is It Wise?"

New Name Florence Margaret Smith acquired her nickname in the early 1930s, while horseback riding. Alluding to a well-known jockey named Steve Donaghue, some boys jokingly called her Steve; her friends picked up the name, changing it to "Stevie." Smith loved the nickname and continued to use it the rest of her life.

Restricted Family Circle For most of her life, Smith lived in a house in Palmers Green, a northern suburb of London, having moved there at the age of three with her mother, her sister, and a favorite aunt (whom she affectionately called the Lion Aunt) shortly after her father deserted the family. After her mother died and her sister left home, Smith and her best friend, the Lion Aunt, continued to live together until the older woman died at the age of 96.

Filling in Free Time In grammar school and high school, Smith was an average student. Instead of going on to college, she entered a secretarial school and then worked for the next 30 years as secretary to a magazine publisher. She found the job boring, but it did afford her ample free time to write stories and poems. Her first published work was a novel she wrote on the yellow paper used in her office, to which she gave the title *Novel on Yellow Paper.*

Recognition and Achievement Although she first gained recognition as a novelist, Smith is known primarily for her achievements as a poet. She was awarded the Cholmondeley Poetry Award in 1966, and in 1969 Queen Elizabeth II personally presented Smith with the Queen's Gold Medal for Poetry. She undoubtedly would have received many more honors for her unique work, but she died in 1971, at the height of her popularity. A few years later, her life and literary achievements became the subject of a stage play and a movie, both entitled *Stevie.*

Author Activity

Life on Film View a video recording of *Stevie,* the movie about Stevie Smith's life. Share several anecdotes or interesting scenes from the film with your classmates.

That's All

Drama by HAROLD PINTER

(Connect to Your Life)

Small Talk What kinds of conversations do people engage in most of the time? Do you think people typically talk about important issues, or do most conversations consist of small talk about everyday routines and events? Discuss your responses to these questions with your classmates.

Build Background

Distinctive Style Harold Pinter began writing plays in the late 1950s, when various new styles were emerging in British drama. Some critics saw similarities between Pinter's style of writing and that of the "kitchen sink" school of realists, with its focus on the language and lifestyle of the working class. Others likened his plays to those of the "theater of the absurd," in which disjointed, seemingly meaningless dialogue was used to convey the absurdity of many of life's circumstances.

Pinter, however, has never belonged to a single school. Instead, he has drawn from various dramatic styles to create his own distinctive approach—a style sometimes referred to as Pinteresque. Typically, a Pinter play involves just one setting, only two or three characters, and a minimal amount of action. The dialogue tends to be very simple—sometimes even ordinary and conversational—but it usually conveys a level of meaning beyond the literal meanings of the words that are spoken. According to Pinter, "The speech we hear is an indication of that which we don't hear."

That's All, written in 1959, is one of Pinter's early works. It is a short dramatic sketch intended to be performed either as one segment of a variety show or as a short radio skit.

Focus Your Reading

LITERARY ANALYSIS | DIALOGUE IN A PLAY In drama, **dialogue** is the main means of characterization and the main vehicle for conveying events and **themes.** One characteristic of Pinter's dialogue is repetition; another is the use of pauses, always indicated by **stage directions.** As you read the play, note Pinter's use of repetition and pauses.

ACTIVE READING | READING UNCONVENTIONAL WORKS The play you are about to read is unconventional both in subject matter and in the style of the dialogue. As you read it, try to abandon your expectations of typical dramatic works so that you can experience Pinter's unique brand of humor.

📖 READER'S NOTEBOOK Jot down your reactions to the play while you are reading. Make a note if something strikes you as funny, sad, confusing, or annoying. Also write down any questions or comments triggered by the play.

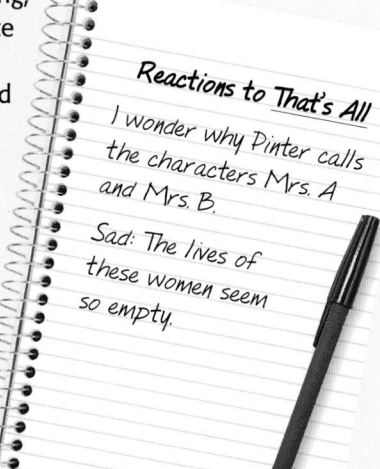

Reactions to That's All

I wonder why Pinter calls the characters Mrs. A and Mrs. B.

Sad: The lives of these women seem so empty.

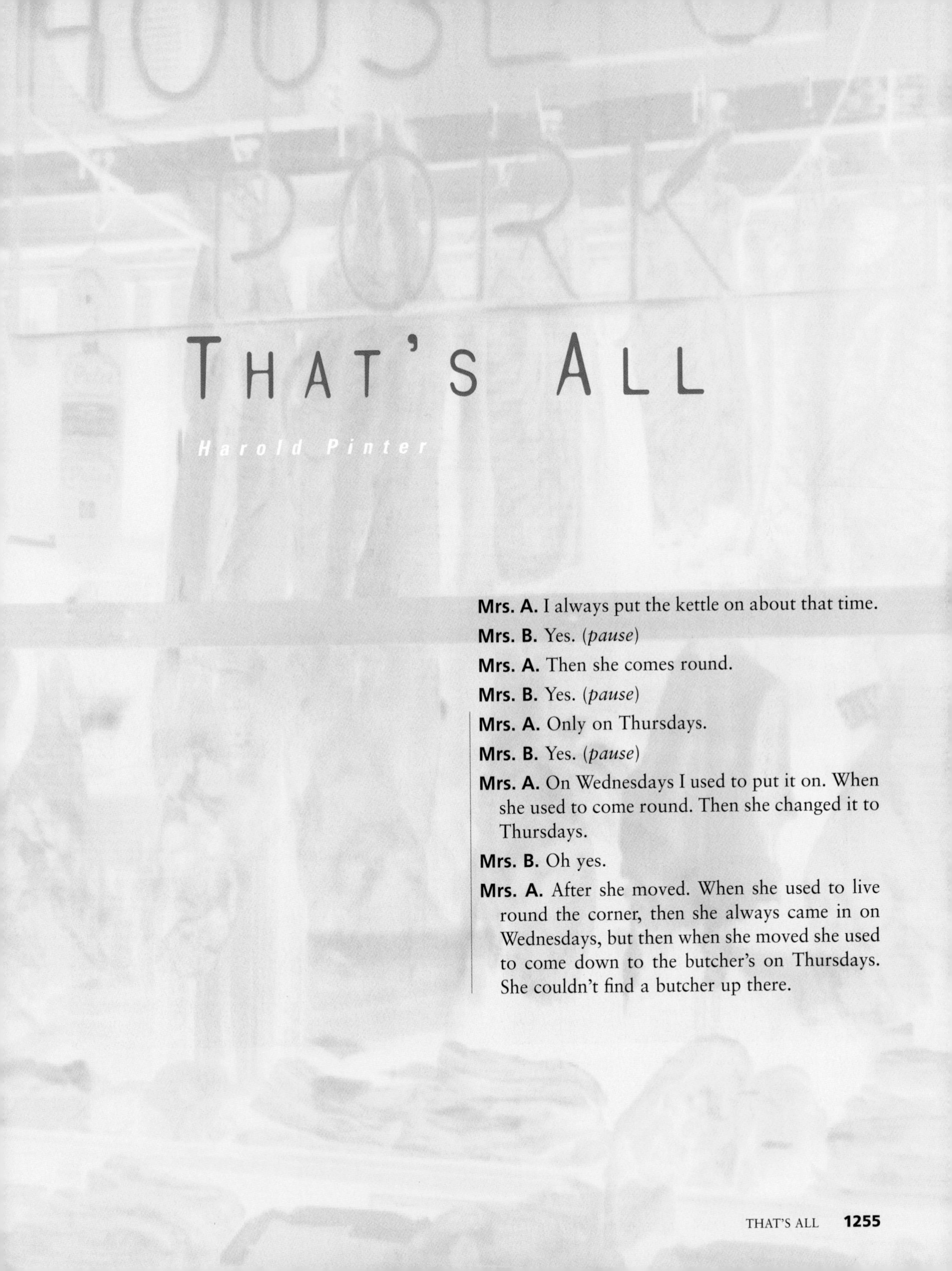

THAT'S ALL

Harold Pinter

Mrs. A. I always put the kettle on about that time.

Mrs. B. Yes. (*pause*)

Mrs. A. Then she comes round.

Mrs. B. Yes. (*pause*)

Mrs. A. Only on Thursdays.

Mrs. B. Yes. (*pause*)

Mrs. A. On Wednesdays I used to put it on. When she used to come round. Then she changed it to Thursdays.

Mrs. B. Oh yes.

Mrs. A. After she moved. When she used to live round the corner, then she always came in on Wednesdays, but then when she moved she used to come down to the butcher's on Thursdays. She couldn't find a butcher up there.

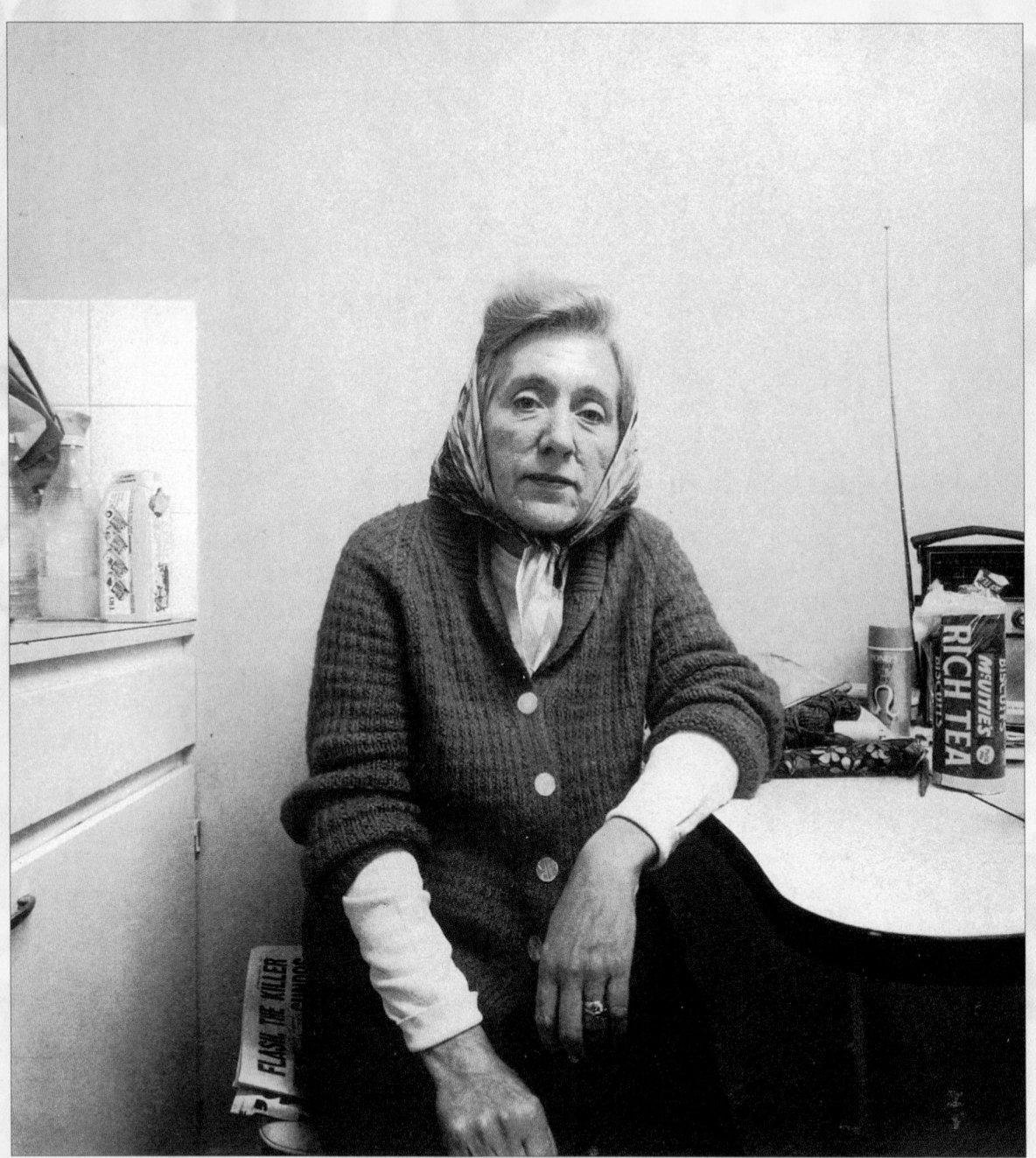

May Shield (1974), Nancy Hellebrand. Copyright © 1974 Nancy Hellebrand.

Mrs. B. No.

Mrs. A. Anyway, she decided she'd stick to her own butcher. Well, I thought, if she can't find a butcher, that's the best thing.

Mrs. B. Yes. (*pause*)

Mrs. A. So she started to come down on Thursdays. I didn't know she was coming down on Thursdays until one day I met her in the butcher.

Mrs. B. Oh yes.

Mrs. A. It wasn't my day for the butcher, I don't go to the butcher on Thursdays.

Mrs. B. No, I know. (*pause*)

Mrs. A. I go on Friday.

Mrs. B. Yes. (*pause*)

Mrs. A. That's where I see you.

Mrs. B. Yes. (*pause*)

Mrs. A. You're always in there on Fridays.

Mrs. B. Oh yes. (*pause*)

Mrs. A. But I happened to go in for a bit of meat, it turned out to be a Thursday. I wasn't going in for my usual weekly on Friday. I just slipped in, the day before.

Mrs. B. Yes.

Mrs. A. That was the first time I found out she couldn't find a butcher up there, so she decided to come back here, once a week, to her own butcher.

Mrs. B. Yes.

Mrs. A. She came on Thursday so she'd be able to get meat for the weekend. Lasted her till Monday, then from Monday to Thursday they'd have fish. She can always buy cold meat, if they want a change.

Mrs. B. Oh yes. (*pause*)

Mrs. A. So I told her to come in when she came down after she'd been to the butcher's and I'd put a kettle on. So she did. (*pause*)

Mrs. B. Yes. (*pause*)

Mrs. A. It was funny because she always used to come in Wednesdays. (*pause*) Still, it made a break. (*long pause*)

Mrs. B. She doesn't come in no more, does she? (*pause*)

Mrs. A. She comes in. She doesn't come in so much, but she comes in. (*pause*)

Mrs. B. I thought she didn't come in. (*pause*)

Mrs. A. She comes in. (*pause*) She just doesn't come in so much. That's all.

Connect to the Literature

1. **What Do You Think?** What word best describes your impression of this play? Compare it with the words suggested by your classmates.

   Comprehension Check
   - What do the two women in the play talk about?
   - What misunderstanding does Mrs. A clear up at the end of the play?

Think Critically

2. How does *That's All* differ from other dramas or skits you have encountered? Cite details in your answer.

3. What emotions do you think lie beneath the women's mundane **dialogue**?

   THINK ABOUT {
   - the subject matter of the characters' conversation
   - the way the characters interact

4. **ACTIVE READING** **READING UNCONVENTIONAL WORKS** With a group of classmates, share the reactions, questions, and comments you recorded in your **READER'S NOTEBOOK**. What do you think was Pinter's **purpose** in writing this play?

5. Why do you think Pinter chose to use Mrs. A's last remark, "That's all," as the **title** of his play?

Extend Interpretations

6. **Critic's Corner** The critic Alrene Sykes has written that Pinter tends to establish a "lack of communication between his characters" at the beginning of each of his plays. Do you see any evidence of this in *That's All?* Support your answer.

7. **Connect to Life** Do you think the conversation in this play is typical of small talk between friends? Why or why not?

Literary Analysis

DIALOGUE IN A PLAY In *That's All,* Pinter communicates his message by using **dialogue** filled with repetition and frequent pauses, as seen in the following lines from the play:

Mrs. B. *She doesn't come in no more, does she?* (pause)

Mrs. A. *She comes in. She doesn't come in so much, but she comes in.* (pause)

Mrs. B. *I thought she didn't come in.* (pause)

Mrs. A. *She comes in.* (pause) *She just doesn't come in so much.*

What effect do you think Pinter creates by having his characters repeat certain words and phrases? What effects does he achieve with pauses?

Cooperative Learning Activity How dialogue is read or performed will determine to a great extent the reactions of the reader or audience to the play. Work with a small group of classmates to give several dramatic readings of the play, taking turns in the roles of Mrs. A and Mrs. B and experimenting with inflections, facial expressions, and ways of observing the pauses. Then discuss how different ways of reading the play can affect its meaning.

Writing Options

1. Second Scene Dialogue Compose dialogue and stage directions for a second scene in the encounter between Mrs. A and Mrs. B. Then, with a partner, perform your scene for your classmates.

2. Drama Review Write a review of *That's All,* stating your overall opinion of the play and pointing out its strengths and weaknesses. Place the review in your **Working Portfolio.**

Activities & Explorations

1. Set Design Create a three-dimensional model of the set design you would use for a production of *That's All.* ~ **ART**

2. Mood Music Select several pieces of music that you think reflect the characters and mood in *That's All.* Bring in the recordings and play two or three for the class. Explain your selections. ~ **MUSIC**

Inquiry & Research

Real Versus Absurd Find out more about the "kitchen sink" school of realists and the theater of the absurd. Which playwrights lead or belong to these movements? Which plays are representative of each one?

Harold Pinter

1930–

Other Works
Last to Go
Trouble in the Works
The Black and White
The Birthday Party
The Dumb Waiter
The Caretaker

Early Memories Harold Pinter was born and educated in a working-class neighborhood of London's East End. Though he was a child during World War II, he vividly recalls the German bombing raids that took him away from his parents for a year, when he was evacuated to the country along with other London children. A son of Jewish parents, he also recalls the anti-Jewish sentiment that was widespread in some sectors of British society during and after the war. On many occasions, he found himself involved in fistfights as a result of attacks by unruly neighborhood thugs.

Acting Days As a teenager, Pinter acted in plays and wrote poetry for a school magazine, but he also showed his proficiency in sports. He played soccer, broke a school record in sprinting, and received an award for his accomplishments in cricket, a sport that he continued to play into adulthood. At the age of 18, he received a grant to study at London's Royal Academy of Dramatic Art, but he left the school after only a few months. Later, he studied acting with more success at the Central School of Speech and Drama, and he spent his early and middle 20s acting in various productions and repertory theaters throughout England.

Prolific Playwright During his years as an actor, Pinter continued to write, but all his early works were poetry and fiction. In 1957, he composed his first play—a one-act drama called *The Room,* which he wrote in four days. In explaining how he started writing plays, Pinter has stated, "I went into a room one day and saw a couple of people in it. . . . I started off with this picture of the two people and let them carry on from there. . . . It was quite a natural movement." Pinter has since written scripts for television and movies as well as for the theater and has won numerous literary prizes, including a Tony Award.

Author Activity

Pinter's Roles Research Pinter's acting career. Find out what roles he played and whether his efforts were reviewed favorably.

PART 2   Culture and Conflict

ngland has had complex relationships with other countries—especially the other parts of the United Kingdom and the countries that were once British colonies, some of which still belong to the British Commonwealth. Political conflicts have ravaged Northern Ireland, and citizens of former colonies find themselves caught in transition within their own countries and faced with the tensions of culture clash when they immigrate to England. Some of the writers represented in this part of Unit Seven describe struggles for peace and justice in their homelands, whereas others detail the prejudice many immigrants experience in England. As you read the selections, think about how you would react in similar situations.

Literature as Social Criticism

When Life Is Unfair

If you've ever been critical of the way things are—something as small as roadside littering, for example, or as large as race discrimination—then you've probably engaged in social criticism. **Social criticism** is also a term used to distinguish literature that addresses specific political, social, and sometimes religious and economic issues. Jonathan Swift's fantasy *Gulliver's Travels* can be classified as social criticism because it broadly satirizes, or pokes fun at, ideas and practices that Swift felt were either wrong or downright ridiculous.

In Northern Ireland, a place suffering from decades of turmoil, a mother carries her child past a peace sign.

Throughout the history of English literature, writers have focused on social and political issues. In the 19th century, for example, the novelist Charles Dickens addressed the darker side of England's industrial development, while in the early 20th century, English poet Siegfried Sassoon graphically depicted the horrors of World War I. Since World War II, social criticism has achieved widespread exposure in the literature of writers throughout the world.

Writer's Purposes

Unlike journalists or political writers, most fiction writers don't set out to write social criticism; their primary purpose is to tell a story, express a feeling, or create an impression. South African writer Nadine Gordimer has written about the reality and the evils of apartheid, the rigid system of racial segregation that governed her country until the 1990s. In her words, "What else can an honest writer do but draw on the life around him?"

Typically, the writers who include social criticism in their works hope to do more than merely entertain readers. Although their reasons for addressing political and social problems may vary, most writers feel a responsibility to make readers aware of certain facts. Sometimes a writer's motives may be personal, based on direct experiences; in other instances, the writer may simply be presenting thoughts on a problem that has bothered his or her conscience.

In her essay "Writing As an Act of Hope" (page 1302), Chilean writer Isabel Allende expresses the goal to change "the conscience of some readers." This goal separates the literature of social criticism from other forms of social criticism, such as propaganda, which aims to stir people to direct action.

The Active Ingredients

Fiction writers differ in the way they introduce social criticism into their work. One or many of the following elements may be evident in a single work of social criticism.

TREATMENT OF ISSUE In some stories, a political or social issue may dominate the entire plot and become the central theme around which all actions revolve. In other stories, the social criticism is less direct, and the political or social issue serves as a backdrop for another situation.

USE OF TONE Other writers convey their views through the use of tone. Nadine Gordimer, in her story "Six Feet of the Country" (page 1289), sharpens her social criticism with irony and casts a critical eye on her main character.

INVOLVEMENT OF READERS Like George Orwell, most writers of social criticism ask their readers to bear witness to the wrongs they expose.

FOCUS ON INDIVIDUALS Typically, writers cast their characters as ordinary individuals caught up in the context of larger world issues. The reader then observes how the larger issues affect the motives, behaviors, and destinies of real people. Both William Trevor's "The Distant Past" (page 1263) and Chinua Achebe's "Civil Peace" (page 1274) portray the lingering effects of civil war on neighbors. Some writers simply dramatize a demeaning personal experience in order to shed light on a larger social problem—such as Wole Soyinka in his poem "Telephone Conversation" (page 1281), which portrays a man trying to rent an apartment.

Often the best examples of social criticism in fiction are those in which writers present the truth about situations without injecting their personal beliefs, thereby allowing readers to form their own opinions. In "The Distant Past" (on page 1263), William Trevor captures how a large problem—the growing hostility between Protestants and Catholics in Northern Ireland—affects people's daily lives.

Regardless of their methods, however, all writers appeal to the readers' sense of humanity. The communion between writer and reader lasts only as long as the act of reading; then it is up to the reader to live with what he or she has learned.

Social Critics Speak

George Orwell   TARGETS TOTALITARIANISM

VIEWPOINT *"When I saw the prisoner step aside to avoid the puddle, I saw the mystery, the unspeakable wrongness, of cutting a life short when it is in full tide."*

from "A Hanging"

Nadine Gordimer   TARGETS APARTHEID

VIEWPOINT *"I am not a preacher or a politician. It is simply not the purpose of a novelist. I am totally opposed to apartheid and all the cruel and ugly things it stands for, and have been so all my life. But my writing does not deal with my personal convictions; it deals with the society I live and write in . . ."*

Isabel Allende   TARGETS POLITICAL TURMOIL

VIEWPOINT *"I feel that writing is an act of hope, a sort of communion with our fellow men. The writer of good will carries a lamp to illuminate the dark corners. Only that, nothing more—a tiny beam of light to show some hidden aspect of reality, to help decipher and understand it and thus to initiate, if possible, a change in the conscience of some readers."*

from "Writing as an Act of Hope"

YOUR TURN On the basis of these statements, which of these social critics would you like to explore further? Discuss your choice with a classmate.

Strategies for Reading: Social Criticism

1. Consider the context of the work. If necessary, refer to the Build Background section accompanying each selection.
2. Pay attention to how great historical, political, and social forces affect people's everyday lives.
3. Evaluate what you read. Don't hesitate to judge characters.
4. Be aware of how writers use irony and figurative language to uncover truths.
5. Draw conclusions about themes, which tend to be unstated in works of social criticism.
6. **Monitor** your reading strategies and modify them when your understanding breaks down. Remember to use your Strategies for Active Reading: **predict, visualize, connect, question, clarify,** and **evaluate.**

The Distant Past

Short Story by WILLIAM TREVOR

Connect to Your Life

Living in the Past Do you know someone who seems to live in the past—who likes to think and talk about events that happened long ago? What do you think might make such a person dwell on past experiences? Share your thoughts with classmates.

Build Background

A Divided Ireland Conflicts between the English and the Irish extend back to the 12th century, when England first succeeded in gaining control of part of Ireland. Later, when the English tried to establish Protestantism as the sole religion in the predominantly Roman Catholic land, they naturally met with resistance and considerable anti-English sentiment. In the late 1800s, Irish Catholics began demanding self-rule, but the mostly Protestant settlements in northern Ireland opposed the plan.

In 1920, Britain divided Ireland into two countries with some powers of self-government. Northern Ireland, with its Protestant majority, readily accepted the decision. The Catholics in the rest of Ireland, however, wanted complete independence. In 1921 southern Ireland agreed to become a self-governing dominion called the Irish Free State. By 1949, the nation had severed all ties with Great Britain, becoming the independent Republic of Ireland. Meanwhile, dissension between Protestants and Catholics in Northern Ireland continued, and in the late 1960s the Irish Republican Army (IRA), an outlawed group of Catholic militants, began a series of terrorist attacks aimed at removing the British from that country as well.

The author William Trevor was born in 1928 to a Protestant family living in the Irish Free State. Many of Trevor's stories are set in Ireland, and his characters are often forced to confront the realities of a long history of violence and hatred.

WORDS TO KNOW **Vocabulary Preview**

adversity   convivial   regime
anachronism   perversity

Focus Your Reading

LITERARY ANALYSIS   **CONFLICT**

Many contemporary short stories revolve around a character's **internal conflicts**—the inner struggles a character wrestles with. In other stories, however, the **plot** and **themes** develop primarily out of **external conflicts,** which involve outside forces. As you read, be aware of the conflicts in this story, and note whether they are internal or external.

ACTIVE READING   **INFERRING CAUSE AND EFFECT**

During the course of this story, the events that the narrator describes affect the characters, causing changes in their attitudes about themselves, others, and important events in their lives.

📖 **READER'S NOTEBOOK** Make two columns, one labeled **Causes** and one labeled **Effects.** As you read, list events from the story in the first column. Then, in the second column, list the effects of each event on the attitudes and relationships of the Middletons and the townspeople.

The Distant Past

William Trevor

In the town and beyond it they were regarded as harmlessly peculiar. Odd, people said, and in time this reference took on a burnish[1] of affection.

They had always been thin, silent with one another, and similar in appearance: a brother and sister who shared a family face. It was a bony countenance, with pale blue eyes and a sharp, well-shaped nose and high cheek-bones. Their father had had it too, but unlike them their father had been an irresponsible and careless man, with red flecks in his cheeks that they didn't have at all. The Middletons of Carraveagh the family had once been known as, but now the brother and sister were just the Middletons, for Carraveagh didn't count any more, except to them.

They owned four Herefords,[2] a number of hens, and the house itself, three miles outside the town. It was a large house, built in the reign of George II,[3] a monument that reflected in its glory and later decay the fortunes of a family. As the brother and sister aged, its roof increasingly ceased to afford protection, rust ate at its gutters, grass thrived in two thick channels all along its avenue. Their father had mortgaged his inherited estate, so local rumor claimed, in order to keep a Catholic Dublin woman in brandy and jewels. When he died, in 1924, his two children discovered that they possessed only a dozen acres. It was locally said also that this <u>adversity</u> hardened their will and that because of it they came to love the remains of Carraveagh more than they could ever have loved a husband or a wife. They blamed for their ill-fortune the Catholic Dublin woman whom they'd never met and they blamed as well the new national <u>regime</u>, contriving in their eccentric way to relate the two. In the days of the Union Jack[4] such women would have known their place: wasn't it all part and parcel?

Twice a week, on Fridays and Sundays, the Middletons journeyed into the town, first of all in a trap[5] and later in a Ford Anglia car. In the shops and elsewhere they made, quite gently, no secret of their continuing loyalty to the past. They attended on Sundays St. Patrick's Protestant Church, a place that matched their mood, for prayers were still said there for the King whose sovereignty[6] their country had denied. The revolutionary regime would not last, they quietly informed the Reverend Packham: what sense was there in green-painted pillar-boxes and a language that nobody understood?[7]

On Fridays, when they took seven or eight dozen eggs to the town, they dressed in pressed tweeds and were accompanied over the years by a series of red setters, the breed there had always been at Carraveagh. They sold the eggs in Keogh's grocery and then had a drink with Mrs. Keogh in the part of her shop that was devoted to the consumption of refreshment. Mr. Middleton had whisky and his sister Tio Pepe.[8] They enjoyed the occasion, for they liked Mrs. Keogh and were liked by her in return. Afterwards they shopped, chatting to the shopkeepers about whatever news there was, and then they went to Healy's Hotel for a few more drinks before driving home.

Drink was their pleasure and it was through it that they built up, in spite of their loyalty to the past, such <u>convivial</u> relationships with the people of the town. Fat Driscoll, who kept the butcher's shop, used even to joke about the past when he

---

1. **burnish:** a smooth, polished finish.
2. **Herefords** (hûr′fərdz): cattle of a breed raised for beef.
3. **George II:** king of Great Britain, 1727–1760.
4. **Union Jack:** the flag of Great Britain.
5. **trap:** a light two-wheeled carriage.
6. **sovereignty:** royal authority.
7. **green-painted . . . understood:** mailboxes painted Irish green (instead of red British mailboxes) and Gaelic—also known as Irish—the traditional language of Ireland's Celtic inhabitants and one of the official languages of the Republic of Ireland.
8. **Tio Pepe:** a brand of Spanish sherry.

WORDS TO KNOW **adversity** (ăd-vûr′sĭ-tē) *n.* hardship; misfortune
regime (rā-zhēm′) *n.* a government in power
convivial (kən-vĭv′ē-əl) *adj.* characterized by friendly companionship; sociable

stood with them in Healy's Hotel or stood behind his own counter cutting their slender chops or thinly slicing their liver. "Will you ever forget it, Mr. Middleton? I'd ha' run like a rabbit if you'd lifted a finger at me." Fat Driscoll would laugh then, rocking back on his heels with a glass of stout in his hand or banging their meat on to his weighing-scales. Mr. Middleton would smile. "There was alarm in your eyes, Mr. Driscoll," Miss Middleton would murmur, smiling also at the memory of the distant occasion.

Fat Driscoll, with a farmer called Maguire and another called Breen, had stood in the hall of Carraveagh, each of them in charge of a shot-gun. The Middletons, children then, had been locked with their mother and father and an aunt into an upstairs room. Nothing else had happened: the expected British soldiers had not, after all, arrived and the men in the hall had eventually relaxed their vigil. "A massacre they wanted," the Middletons' father said after they'd gone. "Damn bloody ruffians."

The Second World War took place. Two Germans, a man and his wife called Winkelmann who ran a glove factory in the town, were suspected by the Middletons of being spies for the Third Reich.[9] People laughed, for they knew the Winkelmanns well and could lend no credence to the Middletons' latest fantasy: typical of them, they explained to the Winkelmanns, who had been worried. Soon after the War the Reverend Packham died and was replaced by the Reverend Bradshaw, a younger man who laughed also and regarded the Middletons as an <u>anachronism</u>. They protested when prayers were no longer said for the Royal Family in St. Patrick's, but the Reverend Bradshaw considered that their protests were as absurd as the prayers themselves had been. Why pray for the monarchy of a neighboring island when their own island had its chosen

President now? The Middletons didn't reply to that argument. In the Reverend Bradshaw's presence they rose to their feet when the BBC[10] played "God Save the King," and on the day of the coronation of Queen Elizabeth II[11] they drove into the town with a small Union Jack propped up in the back window of their Ford Anglia. "Bedad, you're a holy terror, Mr. Middleton!" Fat Driscoll laughingly exclaimed, noticing the flag as he lifted a tray of pork-steaks from his display shelf. The Middletons smiled. It was a great day for the Commonwealth of Nations, they replied, a remark which further amused Fat Driscoll and which he later repeated in Phelan's public house. "Her Britannic Majesty," guffawed[12] his friend Mr. Breen.

Situated in a valley that was noted for its beauty and with convenient access to rich rivers and bogs over which game-birds flew, the town benefited from post-war tourism. Healy's Hotel changed its title and became, overnight, the New Ormonde. Shopkeepers had their shop-fronts painted and Mr. Healy organized an annual Salmon Festival. Even Canon[13] Kelly, who had at first commented severely on the habits of the tourists, and in particular on the summertime dress of the women, was in the end obliged to confess that the morals of his flock remained unaffected. "God and good sense," he proclaimed, meaning God and his own teaching. In time he even derived pride from the fact that people with other values came briefly to the town and that the values esteemed by his parishioners were in no way diminished.

---

9. **Third Reich** (rīk): Nazi-controlled Germany.
10. **BBC:** British Broadcasting Corporation.
11. **the day . . . Queen Elizabeth II:** June 2, 1953—more than four years after Ireland withdrew from the British Commonwealth of Nations, severing all official ties with England.
12. **guffawed:** laughed loudly.
13. **Canon:** the title of certain Roman Catholic priests.

WORDS TO KNOW
anachronism (ə-năk′rə-nĭz′əm) *n.* something out of keeping with a specified time; especially, something proper to a former age but not to the present

A Self-Portrait (about 1965), William Leech. National Gallery of Ireland, Dublin.

The town's grocers now stocked foreign cheeses, brie and camembert and Port Salut, and wines were available to go with them. The plush Cocktail Room of the New Ormonde set a standard: the wife of a solicitor, a Mrs. O'Brien, began to give six o'clock parties once or twice a year, obliging her husband to mix gin and Martini in glass jugs and herself handing round a selection of nuts and small Japanese crackers. Canon Kelly looked in as a rule and satisfied himself that all was above board. He rejected, though, the mixture in the jugs, retaining his taste for a glass of John Jameson.[14]

From the windows of their convent the Loretto nuns[15] observed the long, sleek cars with G.B. plates; English and American accents drifted on the breeze to them. Mothers cleaned up their children and sent them to the Golf Club to seek employment as caddies. Sweet shops sold holiday mementoes. The brown, soda and currant breads of Murphy-Flood's bakery were declared to be delicious. Mr. Healy doubled the number of local girls who served as waitresses in his dining-room, and in the winter of 1961 he had the builders in again, working on an extension for which the Munster and Leinster Bank had lent him twenty-two thousand pounds.

---

14. **John Jameson:** a brand of Irish whiskey.
15. **Loretto nuns:** members of a Roman Catholic religious order founded near Dublin in 1822.

But as the town increased its prosperity Carraveagh continued its decline. The Middletons were in their middle-sixties now and were reconciled to a life that became more uncomfortable with every passing year. Together they roved the vast lofts of their house, placing old paint tins and flowerpot saucers beneath the drips from the roof. At night they sat over their thin chops in a dining-room that had once been gracious and which in a way was gracious still, except for the faded appearance of furniture that was dry from lack of polish and of a wallpaper that time had rendered colorless. In the hall their father gazed down at them, framed in ebony and gilt, in the uniform of the Irish Guards. He had conversed with Queen Victoria, and even in their middle-sixties they could still hear him saying that God and Empire and Queen formed a trinity unique in any worthy soldier's heart. In the hall hung the family crest, and on ancient Irish linen the Cross of St. George.[16]

The dog that accompanied the Middletons now was called Turloch, an animal whose death they dreaded for they felt they couldn't manage the antics of another pup. Turloch, being thirteen, moved slowly and was blind and a little deaf. He was a reminder to them of their own advancing years and of the effort it had become to tend the Herefords and collect the weekly eggs. More and more they looked forward to Fridays, to the warm companionship of Mrs. Keogh and Mr. Healy's chatter in the hotel. They stayed longer now with Mrs. Keogh and in the hotel, and idled longer in the shops, and drove home more slowly. Dimly, but with no less loyalty, they still recalled the distant past and were listened to without ill-feeling when they spoke of it and of Carraveagh as it had been, and of the Queen whose company their careless father had known.

The visitors who came to the town heard about the Middletons and were impressed. It was a pleasant wonder, more than one of them remarked, that old wounds could heal so completely, that the Middletons continued in their loyalty to the past and that, in spite of it, they were respected in the town. When Miss Middleton had been ill with a form of pneumonia in 1958 Canon Kelly had driven out to Carraveagh twice a week with pullets and young ducks that his housekeeper had dressed. "An upright couple," was the Canon's public opinion of the Middletons, and he had been known to add that eccentric views would hurt you less than malice. "We can disagree without guns in this town," Mr. Healy pronounced in his Cocktail Room, and his visitors usually replied that as far as they could see that was the result of living in a Christian country. That the Middletons bought their meat from a man who had once locked them into an upstairs room and had then waited to shoot soldiers in their hall was a fact that amazed the seasonal visitors. You lived and learned, they remarked to Mr. Healy.

The Middletons, privately, often considered that they led a strange life. Alone in their two beds at night they now and again wondered why they hadn't just sold Carraveagh forty-eight years ago when their father had died: why had the tie been so strong and why had they in <u>perversity</u> encouraged it? They didn't fully know, nor did they attempt to discuss the matter in any way. Instinctively they had remained at Carraveagh, instinctively feeling that it would have been cowardly to go. Yet often it seemed to them now to be no more than a game they played, this worship of the distant past. And at other times it seemed as real and as important as the remaining acres of land, and the house itself.

---

16. **Cross of St. George:** horizontal and vertical red bars crossing on a white background—an ancient flag of England.

WORDS TO KNOW

perversity (pər-vûr′sĭ-tē) *n.* a stubborn determination to act in an inappropriate or unexpected way

Au Cinquième [On the fifth floor]: *A Portrait of the Artist's Wife* (about 1940), William Leech. Oil on canvas, 74 cm × 60 cm, National Gallery of Ireland, Dublin.

"Isn't that shocking?" Mr. Healy said one day in 1967. "Did you hear about that, Mr. Middleton, blowing up them post offices in Belfast?"[17]

Mr. Healy, red-faced and short-haired, spoke casually in his Cocktail Room, making midday conversation. He had commented in much the same way at breakfast-time, looking up from the *Irish Independent*. Everyone in the town had said it too: that the blowing up of sub–post offices in Belfast was a shocking matter.

"A bad business," Fat Driscoll remarked, wrapping the Middletons' meat. "We don't want that old stuff all over again."

"We didn't want it in the first place," Miss Middleton reminded him. He laughed, and she laughed, and so did her brother. Yes, it was a game, she thought: how could any of it be as real or as important as the afflictions and problems of the old butcher himself, his rheumatism and his reluctance to retire? Did her brother, she wondered, privately think so too?

"Come on, old Turloch," he said, stroking the flank of the red setter with the point of his shoe, and she reflected that you could never tell what he was thinking. Certainly it wasn't the kind of thing you wanted to talk about.

"I've put him in a bit of mince," Fat Driscoll said, which was something he often did these

---

17. **blowing up . . . in Belfast:** In Northern Ireland, Belfast (the capital) and the town of Londonderry were sites of terrorist attacks by members of the IRA.

days, pretending the mince would otherwise be thrown away. There'd been a red setter about the place that night when he waited in the hall for the soldiers: Breen and Maguire had pushed it down into a cellar, frightened of it.

"There's a heart of gold in you, Mr. Driscoll," Miss Middleton murmured, nodding and smiling at him. He was the same age as she was, sixty-six: he should have shut up shop years ago. He would have, he'd once told them, if there'd been a son to leave the business to. As it was, he'd have to sell it and when it came to the point he found it hard to make the necessary arrangements. "Like us and Carraveagh," she'd said, even though on the face of it it didn't seem the same at all.

Every evening they sat in the big old kitchen, hearing the news. It was only in Belfast and Derry,[18] the wireless[19] said; outside Belfast and Derry you wouldn't know anything was happening at all. On Fridays they listened to the talk in Mrs. Keogh's bar and in the hotel. "Well, thank God it has nothing to do with the South," Mr. Healy said often, usually repeating the statement.

The first British soldiers landed in the North of Ireland, and soon people didn't so often say that outside Belfast and Derry you wouldn't know anything was happening. There were incidents in Fermanagh and Armagh, in Border villages and towns. One Prime Minister resigned and then another one. The troops were unpopular, the newspapers said; internment[20] became part of the machinery of government. In the town, in St. Patrick's Protestant Church and in the Church of the Holy Assumption, prayers for peace were offered, but no peace came.

"We're hit, Mr. Middleton," Mr. Healy said one Friday morning. "If there's a dozen visitors this summer it'll be God's own stroke of luck for us."

"Luck?"

"Sure, who wants to come to a country with

all that malarkey[21] in it?"

"But it's only in the North."

"Tell that to your tourists, Mr. Middleton."

The town's prosperity ebbed. The Border was more than sixty miles away, but over that distance had spread some wisps of the fog of war. As anger rose in the town at the loss of fortune so there rose also the kind of talk there had been in the distant past. There was talk of atrocities and counter-atrocities, and of guns and gelignite[22] and the rights of people. There was bitterness suddenly in Mrs. Keogh's bar because of the lack of trade, and in the empty hotel there was bitterness also.

On Fridays, only sometimes at first, there was a silence when the Middletons appeared. It was as though, going back nearly twenty years, people remembered the Union Jack in the window of their car and saw it now in a different light. It wasn't something to laugh at any more, nor were certain words that the Middletons had gently spoken, nor were they themselves just an old, peculiar couple. Slowly the change crept about, all around them in the town, until Fat Driscoll didn't wish it to be remembered that he had ever given them mince for their dog. He had stood with a gun in the enemy's house, waiting for soldiers so that soldiers might be killed: it was better that people should remember that.

One day Canon Kelly looked the other way when he saw the Middletons' car coming and

---

18. **Derry:** another name for Londonderry.
19. **wireless:** radio.
20. **internment:** confinement or imprisonment, especially in wartime.
21. **malarkey:** foolishness.
22. **gelignite** (jĕl′ĭg-nīt′): a powerful explosive.

they noticed this movement of his head, although he hadn't wished them to. And on another day Mrs. O'Brien, who had always been keen to talk to them in the hotel, didn't reply when they addressed her.

The Middletons naturally didn't discuss these rebuffs but they each of them privately knew that there was no conversation they could have at this time with the people of the town. The stand they had taken and kept to for so many years no longer seemed ridiculous in the town. Had they driven with a Union Jack now they would, astoundingly, have been shot.

"It will never cease." He spoke disconsolately one night, standing by the dresser where the wireless was.

She washed the dishes they'd eaten from, and the cutlery. "Not in our time," she said.

"It is worse than before."

"Yes, it is worse than before."

They took from the walls of the hall the portrait of their father in the uniform of the Irish Guards because it seemed wrong to them that at this time it should hang there. They took down also the crest of their family and the Cross of St. George, and from a vase on the drawing-room mantelpiece they removed the small Union Jack that had been there since the Coronation of Queen Elizabeth II. They did not remove these articles in fear but in mourning for the *modus vivendi*[23] that had existed for so long between them and the people of the town. They had given their custom[24] to a butcher who had planned to shoot down soldiers in their hall and he, in turn,

had given them mince for their dog. For fifty years they had experienced, after suspicion had seeped away, a tolerance that never again in the years that were left to them would they know.

One November night their dog died and he said to her after he had buried it that they must not be depressed by all that was happening. They would die themselves and the house would become a ruin because there was no one to inherit it, and the distant past would be set to rest. But she disagreed: the *modus vivendi* had been easy for them, she pointed out, because they hadn't really minded the dwindling of their fortunes while the town prospered. It had given them a life, and a kind of dignity: you could take a pride out of living in peace.

He did not say anything and then, because of the emotion that both of them felt over the death of their dog, he said in a rushing way that they could no longer at their age hope to make a living out of the remains of Carraveagh. They must sell the hens and the four Herefords. As he spoke, he watched her nodding, agreeing with the sense of it. Now and again, he thought, he would drive slowly into the town, to buy groceries and meat with the money they had saved, and to face the silence that would sourly thicken as their own two deaths came closer and death increased in another part of their island. She felt him thinking that and she knew that he was right. Because of the distant past they would die friendless. It was worse than being murdered in their beds. ❖

---

23. *modus vivendi* (mō′dəs vĭ-věn′dē) *Latin:* way of life.
24. **custom:** business; trade.

Thinking through the LITERATURE

Connect to the Literature

1. **What Do You Think?** What parts of the story did you find most thought-provoking? Share your reactions with a partner.

   Comprehension Check
   - Who is Fat Driscoll?
   - What is the relationship between the Middletons?

Think Critically

2. How would you describe the relationship between the Middletons and the people of the town?

   THINK ABOUT

   - how the townspeople felt about the Middletons' parents
   - the Middletons' behavior
   - the changing feelings of all involved
   - the political loyalties of all involved

3. **ACTIVE READING** | **INFERRING CAUSE AND EFFECT** What events do you think have the most significant effect on the relationship between the Middletons and the townspeople? Review the lists you created in your **READER'S NOTEBOOK** to help you answer this question.

4. Do you think the townspeople are justified in their behavior? Why or why not?

5. How would you describe the Middletons' feelings about the past, and how do these feelings change at the end of the story?

Extend Interpretations

6. **Writer's Style** Throughout the story, Trevor repeats the word *past* and the phrase "the distant past." How does this **repetition** reinforce the **themes** in the story?

7. **Comparing Texts** Compare the characters in "The Distant Past" with those in Lady Gregory's *The Rising of the Moon* (page 994). What conflicts do they share? Are those conflicts resolved in either selection?

8. **Connect to Life** Do you think that a situation similar to the one depicted in "The Distant Past" could occur in your own community? Defend your position.

Literary Analysis

CONFLICT As you know, a **conflict** is a struggle between opposing forces that moves a plot forward. The conflict provides the interest or suspense in a short story. Conflict may be **external,** with a character being pitted against some outside force—another person, a physical obstacle, nature, or society. Conflict may also be **internal,** occurring within a character. In "The Distant Past," the Middletons experience internal conflicts, primarily in their relationship to the values of the past. However, most of the conflicts in the story are external. Some of them are between individual characters, while others involve factions in the society at large.

Paired Activity With a partner, list the conflicts between characters and the conflicts in the larger society. How are the two kinds of conflicts related? Are any of the conflicts resolved? Could any of the conflicts have been avoided? Discuss your conclusions with other classmates.

Conflicts Between Characters	Conflicts in Society

REVIEW **SETTING** **Setting** can refer not only to the time and place of a story but also to the social and moral environment that forms the background of a narrative. All of these aspects of setting contribute to the development of the **plot, characters,** and **themes.** Think about the setting of "The Distant Past." Briefly describe how it relates to the plot, characters, and themes in the story.

Writing Options

Paragraph Critique In a paragraph, discuss the effectiveness of the last sentence of the story: "It was worse than being murdered in their beds." Consider such questions as the following: What responses does the sentence draw from the reader? How does the statement relate to the lives of the Middletons? to the political climate of the times? Why do you think Trevor ended the story with this comment? Place the paragraph in your **Working Portfolio**.

Activities & Explorations

Role-Play Conversations With a partner, role-play two different conversations between Fat Driscoll and Mrs. Keogh, one during the 1950s and one in the late 1960s, after the British soldiers land in Northern Ireland. ~ **SPEAKING AND LISTENING**

Vocabulary in Action

EXERCISE: WORD MEANINGS Write the word suggested by each of the following descriptions.

1. An example of this might be a Neanderthal man in modern Berlin or a helicopter hovering over King Arthur and his Round Table.

2. More exasperating than mere misbehavior and harder to deal with than simple stubbornness, this is a trait found in real brats and people we call ornery.

3. This may or may not change when there's a national election, but it does change when there's a successful revolution.

4. This word describes the guests we are happiest to entertain and most likely to invite again.

5. If you retire to a bed of thorns after having a hard row to hoe, your life has a good deal of this in it.

WORDS TO KNOW	adversity	convivial	regime
	anachronism	perversity	

Building Vocabulary
For an in-depth lesson on how to expand your vocabulary, see page 1182.

William Trevor
1928–

Other Works
"Mrs. Silly"
"Autumn Sunshine"
"The Tennis Court"
Mrs. Acland's Ghosts

An Irregular Education William Trevor was born William Trevor Cox in County Cork, Ireland. During his childhood, his family relocated often, moving from town to town throughout southern Ireland as his father pursued a career in banking. As a result, Trevor's education was somewhat irregular; he went to 13 different grammar schools and, at times, no school at all. Later, he attended St. Columba's College and Trinity College in Dublin. Immediately after receiving a degree from Trinity, he accepted a position as a history teacher in Northern Ireland. In 1952, he moved to England, where he taught art and began a career as a sculptor.

A Late Bloomer As a youth, Trevor never entertained thoughts of a writing career. In fact, he always assumed that he would someday enter the business world, perhaps working in a store or a bank. He did not publish his first novel until 1958, and not until he was in his mid-30s did he abandon art in order to write full-time. The numerous novels, plays, and short stories he has published since then have been commended for their restrained style, subtle humor, and compassionate characterization. Although his writing often deals with the people, culture, and history of his native Ireland, he has continued to reside and work in England.

Author Activity

Trinity College, Dublin William Trevor was educated at Trinity College, also called the University of Dublin. It is the oldest university in Ireland, having been founded by Queen Elizabeth I in 1591. Many famous writers have attended this university. Do some research and draw up a list of names of writers who have graduated from Dublin's Trinity College.

Civil Peace

Short Story by CHINUA ACHEBE (chĭn'wä ä-chā'bā)

Connect to Your Life

Life After War Think about articles or books you have read that describe the aftermath of war. What is life typically like for ordinary civilians after a war has been fought on their land? Share your knowledge with classmates.

Build Background

War and Independence Chinua Achebe often writes about the conflicts and transitions in his native Nigeria, a former British colony on the western coast of Africa. After more than 100 years of British influence, Nigeria finally gained its independence in 1960. Although English is the country's official language, over 250 ethnic groups, each with its own language and customs, live there. The three largest of these are the Hausa, the Yoruba, and the Ibo.

Throughout the 1960s, various ethnic groups struggled, often violently, for control of Nigeria's government. The principal opponents were the Ibo and the Hausa. In 1967, the Ibo in the eastern part of the country seceded from Nigeria and formed their own republic, called Biafra. A period of civil war followed, lasting until 1970 and causing massive hardship and devastation—especially in Biafra, which suffered from a lack of supplies. It is estimated that over 1.5 million Biafrans starved to death before their leaders surrendered. Chinua Achebe was a tireless spokesperson for the Biafran cause, but in the war's aftermath he just as diligently joined in the long process of unifying and rebuilding the country.

Focus Your Reading

LITERARY ANALYSIS **DIALECT** A **dialect** is a form of a language that is spoken in one place by a certain group of people. Here are some examples of words from one dialect of English found in "Civil Peace," along with the meanings of the words:

na ("is" or "it is") soja ("soldiers")
commot ("leave") am ("it")
wetin ("what") katakata ("trouble")

As you read the story, try to decipher the meanings of other words in dialect.

ACTIVE READING **MAKING JUDGMENTS ABOUT CHARACTERS** When you read a narrative, you make judgments about characters based on their speech, thoughts, feelings, and reactions to events. In "Civil Peace," the narrator says that Jonathan Iwegbu considers himself very lucky. As you read the story, think about whether you agree with this assessment.

READER'S NOTEBOOK To assess Jonathan's luck, make a chart like the one shown here and record what you consider to be his losses and blessings.

Jonathan's Luck	
Losses	Blessings

CIVIL PEACE

Chinua Achebe

Jonathan Iwegbu counted himself extraordinarily lucky. "Happy survival!" meant so much more to him than just a current fashion of greeting old friends in the first hazy days of peace. It went deep to his heart. He had come out of the war with five inestimable blessings—his head, his wife Maria's head and the heads of three out of their four children. As a bonus he also had his old bicycle— a miracle too but naturally not to be compared to the safety of five human heads.

The bicycle had a little history of its own. One day at the height of the war it was commandeered "for urgent military action." Hard as its loss would have been to him he would still have let it go without a thought had he not had some doubts about the genuineness of the officer. It wasn't his disreputable rags, nor the toes peeping out of one blue and one brown canvas shoes, nor yet the two stars of his rank done obviously in a hurry in biro,[1] that troubled Jonathan; many good and heroic soldiers looked the same or worse. It was rather a certain lack of grip and firmness in his manner. So Jonathan, suspecting he might be amenable to influence, rummaged in his raffia[2] bag and produced the two pounds with which he had been going to buy firewood which his wife, Maria, retailed to camp officials for extra stock- fish and corn meal, and got his bicycle back. That night he buried it in the little clearing in the bush where the dead of the camp, including his own youngest son, were buried. When he dug it up again a year later after the surrender all it needed was a little palm-oil greasing. "Nothing puzzles God," he said in wonder.

He put it to immediate use as a taxi and accumulated a small pile of Biafran money ferrying camp officials and their families across the four-mile stretch to the nearest tarred road.

His standard charge per trip was six pounds and those who had the money were only glad to be rid of some of it in this way. At the end of a fortnight he had made a small fortune of one hundred and fifteen pounds.

Then he made the journey to Enugu[3] and found another miracle waiting for him. It was unbelievable. He rubbed his eyes and looked again and it was still standing there before him. But, needless to say, even that monumental blessing must be accounted also totally inferior to the five heads in the family. This newest miracle was his little house in Ogui Overside. Indeed nothing puzzles God! Only two houses away a huge concrete edifice some wealthy contractor had put up just before the war was a mountain of rubble. And here was Jonathan's little zinc house[4] of no regrets built with mud blocks quite intact! Of course the doors and windows were missing and five sheets off the roof. But what was that? And anyhow he had returned to Enugu early enough to pick up bits of old zinc and wood and soggy sheets of card- board lying around the neighborhood before thousands more came out of their forest holes looking for the same things. He got a destitute carpenter with one old hammer, a blunt plane and a few bent and rusty nails in his tool bag to turn this assortment of wood, paper and metal into door and window shutters for five Nigerian shillings or fifty Biafran pounds. He paid the

---

1. **biro** (bîr′ō) a British term for a ballpoint pen. (The officer's insignia, that is, had been drawn in ink.)

2. **raffia:** a palm fiber used for weaving such items as mats, baskets, and hats.

3. **Enugu** (ā-n$\overline{oo}$′g$\overline{oo}$): a city in southeastern Nigeria.

4. **zinc house:** a house roofed with sheets of galvanized metal.

Copyright © Chester Higgins Jr.

pounds, and moved in with his overjoyed family carrying five heads on their shoulders.

His children picked mangoes near the military cemetery and sold them to soldiers' wives for a few pennies—real pennies this time—and his wife started making breakfast akara[5] balls for neighbors in a hurry to start life again. With his family earnings he took his bicycle to the villages around

---

5. **akara** (ä-kä′rä) **balls:** bean cakes.

and bought fresh palm-wine which he mixed generously in his rooms with the water which had recently started running again in the public tap down the road, and opened up a bar for soldiers and other lucky people with good money.

At first he went daily, then every other day and finally once a week, to the offices of the Coal Corporation where he used to be a miner, to find out what was what. The only thing he did find out in the end was that that little house of his was even a greater blessing than he had thought. Some of his fellow examiners who had nowhere to return at the end of the day's waiting just slept outside the doors of the offices and cooked what meal they could scrounge together in Bournvita tins. As the weeks lengthened and still nobody could say what was what Jonathan discontinued his weekly visits altogether and faced his palm-wine bar.

But nothing puzzles God. Came the day of the windfall when after five days of endless scuffles in queues[6] and counter-queues in the sun outside the Treasury he had twenty pounds counted into his palms as ex-gratia[7] award for the rebel money he had turned in. It was like Christmas for him and for many others like him when the payments began. They called it (since few could manage its proper official name) *egg-rasher.*

As soon as the pound notes were placed in his palm Jonathan simply closed it tight over them and buried fist and money inside his trouser pocket. He had to be extra careful because he had seen a man a couple of days earlier collapse into near-madness in an instant before that oceanic crowd because no sooner had he got his twenty pounds than some heartless ruffian picked it off him. Though it was not right that a man in such an extremity of agony should be blamed yet many in the queues that day were able to remark quietly on the victim's carelessness, especially after he pulled out the innards of his pocket and revealed a hole in it big enough to pass a thief's head. But of course he had insisted that the money had been in the other pocket, pulling it out too to show its comparative wholeness. So one had to be careful.

Jonathan soon transferred the money to his left hand and pocket so as to leave his right free for shaking hands should the need arise, though by fixing his gaze at such an elevation as to miss all approaching human faces he made sure that the need did not arise, until he got home.

He was normally a heavy sleeper but that night he heard all the neighborhood noises die down one after another. Even the night watchman who knocked the hour on some metal somewhere in the distance had fallen silent after knocking one o'clock. That must have been the last thought in Jonathan's mind before he was finally carried away himself. He couldn't have been gone for long, though, when he was violently awakened again.

"Who is knocking?" whispered his wife lying beside him on the floor.

"I don't know," he whispered back breathlessly.

The second time the knocking came it was so loud and imperious that the rickety old door could have fallen down.

"Who is knocking?" he asked then, his voice parched and trembling.

"Na tief-man and him people," came the cool reply. "Make you hopen de door." This was followed by the heaviest knocking of all.

Maria was the first to raise the alarm, then he followed and all their children.

"Police-o! Thieves-o! Neighbors-o! Police-o! We are lost! We are dead! Neighbors, are you asleep? Wake up! Police-o!"

This went on for a long time and then stopped suddenly. Perhaps they had scared the thief away. There was total silence. But only for a short while.

"You done finish?" asked the voice outside. "Make we help you small. Oya, everybody!"

"Police-o! Tief-man-o! Neighbors-o! we done loss-o! Police-o! . . ."

---

6. **queues** (kyo͞oz): lines of waiting people.

7. **ex-gratia** (ĕks′grā′shə): given as a favor rather than as a legal obligation.

There were at least five other voices besides the leader's.

Jonathan and his family were now completely paralyzed by terror. Maria and the children sobbed inaudibly like lost souls. Jonathan groaned continuously.

The silence that followed the thieves' alarm vibrated horribly. Jonathan all but begged their leader to speak again and be done with it.

"My frien," said he at long last, "we don try our best for call dem but I tink say dem all done sleep-o. . . . So wetin we go do now? Sometaim you wan call soja? Or you wan make we call dem for you? Soja better pass police. No be so?"

"Na so!" replied his men. Jonathan thought he heard even more voices now than before and groaned heavily. His legs were sagging under him and his throat felt like sandpaper.

"My frien, why you no de talk again. I de ask you say you wan make we call soja?"

"No."

"Awrighto. Now make we talk business. We no be bad tief. We no like for make trouble. Trouble done finish. War done finish and all the katakata wey de for inside.[8] No Civil War again. This time na Civil Peace. No be so?"

"Na so!" answered the horrible chorus.

"What do you want from me? I am a poor man. Everything I had went with this war. Why do you come to me? You know people who have money. We . . ."

"Awright! We know say you no get plenty money. But we sef no get even anini.[9] So derefore make you open dis window and give us one hundred pound and we go commot. Orderwise we de come for inside now to show you guitar-boy like dis . . ."

A volley of automatic fire rang through the sky. Maria and the children began to weep aloud again.

"Ah, missisi de cry again. No need for dat. We done talk say we na good tief. We just take our small money and go nwayorly. No molest. Abi we de molest?"

"At all!" sang the chorus.

"My friends," began Jonathan hoarsely. "I hear what you say and I thank you. If I had one hundred pounds . . ."

"Lookia my frien, no be play we come play for your house. If we make mistake and step for inside you no go like am-o. So derefore . . ."

"To God who made me; if you come inside and find one hundred pounds, take it and shoot me and shoot my wife and children. I swear to God. The only money I have in this life is this twenty-pounds *egg-rasher* they gave me today . . ."

"OK. Time de go. Make you open dis window and bring the twenty pound. We go manage am like dat."

There were now loud murmurs of dissent among the chorus: "Na lie de man de lie; e get plenty money. . . . Make we go inside and search properly well. . . . Wetin be twenty pound? . . ."

"Shurrup!" rang the leader's voice like a lone shot in the sky and silenced the murmuring at once. "Are you dere? Bring the money quick!"

"I am coming," said Jonathan fumbling in the darkness with the key of the small wooden box he kept by his side on the mat.

At the first sign of light as neighbors and others assembled to commiserate with him he was already strapping his five-gallon demijohn[10] to his bicycle carrier and his wife, sweating in the open fire, was turning over akara balls in a wide clay bowl of boiling oil. In the corner his eldest son was rinsing out dregs of yesterday's palm wine from old beer bottles.

"I count it as nothing," he told his sympathizers, his eyes on the rope he was tying. "What is *egg-rasher*? Did I depend on it last week? Or is it greater than other things that went with the war? I say, let *egg-rasher* perish in the flames! Let it go where everything else has gone. Nothing puzzles God." ❖

---

8. **wey de for inside:** Nigerian dialect for "that went with it."

9. **anini** (ä-nē′nē): a small coin worth less than a penny.

10. **demijohn** (dĕm′ē-jŏn′): a large bottle with a narrow neck, usually encased in wicker.

Thinking *through the* LITERATURE

Connect to the Literature

1. What Do You Think? How did you react to the events in this story? Discuss your reaction with several classmates.

> **Comprehension Check**
> • How does Jonathan and his family make money after the war?
> • What happens to the ex-gratia award money Jonathan receives?

Think Critically

2. How would you describe Jonathan's approach to life?

> **THINK ABOUT**
> • the value he places on "the safety of five human heads"
> • his ways of earning money
> • his reaction to the thieves
> • what he means when he says "Nothing puzzles God"

3. What **ironies** did you find in this story?

4. **ACTIVE READING** | **MAKING JUDGMENTS ABOUT CHARACTERS**
With a partner, look at the charts you created in your **READER'S NOTEBOOK** to assess Jonathan's luck. Based on what you identified as losses and blessings, do you agree with Jonathan's view of himself as lucky? Why or why not?

5. What ideas about the aftermath of war do you think the story conveys?

Extend Interpretations

6. Comparing Texts Compare Jonathan in "Civil Peace" with Miss Middleton in "The Distant Past" (page 1263). What similarities and differences can you find in their attitudes toward life? Which character is more prepared to cope with hardship?

7. What If? Suppose the thieves had robbed one of Jonathan's neighbors. Do you think Jonathan would have ignored his neighbor's cry for help, or do you think he would have done something to stop the robbery? Support your opinion.

8. Critic's Corner The student reviewer Carrie Mitchell indicated that the **suspense** in "Civil Peace" kept her attention and that she "couldn't read fast enough" to discover the outcome of Jonathan's encounter with the thieves. Did you experience a similar feeling during your reading? Explain your answer.

9. Connect to Life Do you think Jonathan's attitude in the wake of the war's destruction and tragedy is common among the survivors of wars? Give reasons for your opinion.

Literary Analysis

DIALECT **Dialect** reflects the pronunciations, vocabulary, and grammatical rules that are typical of a region. In "Civil Peace," Chinua Achebe actually uses two dialects of English, the Nigerian dialect of the thieves and the near-standard dialect of Jonathan and his family. The Nigerian dialect is first used when Jonathan asks who is knocking on his door and the thief answers as follows:

"Na tief-man and him people," *came the cool reply. "Make you* *hopen de door."*

Jonathan's own dialect is evident in this passage, when he and his family raise the alarm about the thieves:

"Police-o! Thieves-o! Neighbors-o! *Police-o! We are lost! We are dead!* *Neighbors, are you asleep? Wake* *up! Police-o!"*

Cooperative Learning Activity Get together in small groups and read other passages that contain dialect. Discuss any words or phrases you have trouble understanding. Then answer these questions: What does the use of dialect add to the story? Why do you think Achebe chose to include both dialects?

REVIEW **CONFLICT** **Conflict,** a struggle between opposing forces, provides the interest or suspense in a literary work. Are the conflicts in "Civil Peace" primarily **external** or **internal?** What is the main conflict in the story? How does Jonathan deal with it?

Choices & CHALLENGES

Writing Options

1. Job Recommendation Write a job recommendation for Jonathan, telling a prospective employer what you consider to be his strengths and weaknesses.

2. Front-Page News With a group of classmates, plan and write the front page of a newspaper for the residents of Jonathan's town. Include a report of the robbery and other articles based on newsworthy details in the story. If a desktop-publishing program is available to you, use it to design your page. Make copies of your work to share with classmates.

Activities & Explorations

1. Oral Reading With a small group of classmates, practice and perform an oral reading of the robbery scene. Use appropriate tones of voice to convey the characters' emotions, and try to reproduce the thieves' dialect. **~ SPEAKING AND LISTENING**

2. Book-Jacket Design Imagine that "Civil Peace" is to be published as a small book. Design a book jacket that might entice people to read the story. Display your work in the classroom. **~ ART**

3. CARE Package Using pictures or real objects, put together a package of items that you might send Jonathan and his family to help them adjust to life after the war. **~ INTERPRETING**

Inquiry & Research

Nigeria's Past and Present Find out more about Nigeria's history. What economic, political, and social progress has Nigeria made since 1970? What problems still beset the nation?

 More Online: Research Starter www.mcdougallittell.com

Chinua Achebe

1930–

Other Works
"Marriage Is a Private Affair"
"Vengeful Creditor"
"The Sacrificial Egg"
"Dead Men's Path"
Things Fall Apart

Educational Achievements A son of Ibo missionaries in eastern Nigeria, Chinua Achebe was raised a Christian and attended British-run schools, studying first in the Ibo language and later in English. A gifted student, Achebe became one of the few 14-year-olds chosen to attend Government College, one of the best high schools in Nigeria. At the age of 18, he left high school with a scholarship to study medicine at the University of Ibadan in western Nigeria. Achebe quickly changed his course of study, however, and it was in English literature that he received his degree in 1953.

Impact of War After teaching for a year, Achebe went to work for the Nigerian Broadcasting Corporation in Lagos, where he eventually became the director of external broadcasting. In 1966, amidst the often violent strife between the Ibo and other

ethnic groups, Achebe felt that he and his family were no longer safe in Lagos. He quit his job and returned to eastern Nigeria, where he became an outspoken advocate of—and fundraiser for—the Biafran cause. He also started a publishing company with the poet Christopher Okigbo, who was later killed in the war.

Writer and Lecturer In addition to short stories, Achebe has written novels, essays, poems, and children's books. His first novel, *Things Fall Apart* (1958), focuses on the effects of European colonialism in Nigeria. Many of his other works focus on problems associated with Nigeria's emergence as a modern nation. Throughout his literary career, Achebe has taught and lectured at universities in both Nigeria and the United States.

Author Activity

Rulers and Ruled Read excerpts from *Things Fall Apart*. Note how the European colonialists are portrayed and how native Nigerians react to European rule. What poem does Achebe quote in the book's title?

Telephone Conversation

Poetry by WOLE SOYINKA (wō'lĕ shô-yĭng'kə)

from Midsummer

Poetry by DEREK WALCOTT

Connect to Your Life

Prejudice Recall a time when you read about or witnessed an obvious display of prejudice against someone because of his or her race, gender, nationality, or religion. What was your reaction? Do you think any form of prejudice exists in your school or community? Share your thoughts with classmates.

Build Background

Two Nobel Prize Winners A native of Nigeria, on the west coast of Africa, Wole Soyinka was awarded the 1986 Nobel Prize in literature, becoming the first African to receive that honor. In 1992, Derek Walcott—born on St. Lucia, a small island in the West Indies—became the first native Caribbean author to receive the Nobel literature prize. For many years, the now-independent countries of Nigeria and St. Lucia were British colonies, and both Soyinka's and Walcott's works draw upon the often antagonistic African and English cultures that have played such a significant role in their lives.

Both authors include social criticism—on racial prejudice and other issues—in their writing, undoubtedly in an attempt to enlighten their readers and encourage change. According to Soyinka, writers must become "a part of that machinery that will actually shape events." He often speaks out against political corruption and violations of human rights and is frequently at odds with government leaders in his own country. Walcott, while appreciating the literary traditions of England, often voices opposition to the neglect of West Indian culture by the islands' British colonizers and by present-day tourists. Acknowledging his own diverse cultural background, Walcott from time to time contemplates his own identity and role as a poet. In his Nobel Prize acceptance speech, he stated that "the process of poetry is one of excavation and of self-discovery."

LaserLinks: Background for Reading
Historical Connection
Visual Vocabulary

Focus Your Reading

LITERARY ANALYSIS **TONE IN SATIRE** **Tone** is a writer's attitude toward a subject. Tone plays an important part in **satire,** writing that combines criticism with wit and humor for the purpose of improving some aspect of society. Tone in satiric works can range from light and humorous to bitter and harsh. "Telephone Conversation" and the excerpt from *Midsummer* are both satires. As you read, try to identify the tone in each.

ACTIVE READING **COMPARING AND CONTRASTING POEMS** Wole Soyinka and Derek Walcott are each writing about racial prejudice. However, they use very different **speakers,** situations, language, and **imagery** in their poems to express their ideas. Comparing and contrasting the ways the poets use these four elements can help you understand the ideas in each poem.

READER'S NOTEBOOK Make a Venn diagram like the one shown for each of the four elements listed above. As you read, note the similarities and differences for each element in each poem.

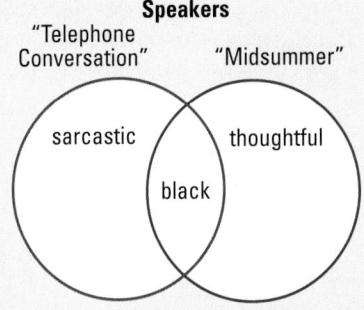

Speakers
"Telephone Conversation" — "Midsummer"
sarcastic — black — thoughtful

TELEPHONE CONVERSATION

WOLE SOYINKA

The price seemed reasonable, location
Indifferent. The landlady swore she lived
Off premises. Nothing remained
But self-confession. "Madam," I warned,
5 "I hate a wasted journey—I am African."
Silence. Silenced transmission of
Pressurized good-breeding. Voice, when it came,
Lipstick-coated, long gold-rolled
Cigarette-holder pipped. Caught I was, foully.

10 "HOW DARK?" . . . I had not misheard . . . "ARE YOU LIGHT
"OR VERY DARK?" Button B. Button A. Stench
Of rancid breath of public hide-and-speak.
Red booth. Red pillar-box. Red double-tiered
Omnibus squelching tar. It *was* real! Shamed
15 By ill-mannered silence, surrender
Pushed dumbfoundment to beg simplification.
Considerate she was, varying the emphasis—

12 rancid (răn′sĭd): smelling of decay; rotten.

13 pillar-box: a pillar-shaped mailbox.

Second Bus (1962), Allen Jones. Oil on canvas, collection of Granada Television, Manchester, England, reproduced by courtesy of the artist.

"ARE YOU DARK? OR VERY LIGHT?" Revelation came.
"You mean—like plain or milk chocolate?"
20 Her assent was clinical, crushing in its light
Impersonality. Rapidly, wave-length adjusted,
I chose, "West African sepia"—and as an afterthought,
"Down in my passport." Silence for spectroscopic
Flight of fancy, till truthfulness clanged her accent
25 Hard on the mouthpiece "WHAT'S THAT?", conceding,
"DON'T KNOW WHAT THAT IS." "Like brunette."

"THAT'S DARK, ISN'T IT?" "Not altogether.
"Facially, I am brunette, but madam, you should see
"The rest of me. Palm of my hand, soles of my feet
30 "Are a peroxide blonde. Friction, caused—
"Foolishly, madam—by sitting down, has turned
"My bottom raven black.—One moment madam!"—sensing
Her receiver rearing on the thunder clap
About my ears—"Madam," I pleaded, "wouldn't you rather
35 "See for yourself?"

22 sepia (sē′pē-ə): a dark yellow brown or olive brown.

23 spectroscopic: here, pertaining to the analysis of colors. (A spectroscope is an instrument that separates light into its various wavelengths—colors—for scientific study.)

Thinking Through the Literature

1. **Comprehension Check** Why does the landlady hesitate to rent the speaker an apartment?

2. What is your impression of the landlady?

3. How and why does the **speaker's** attitude change as the poem progresses? Cite evidence to support your answer.

4. How would you describe the **tone** of this poem?

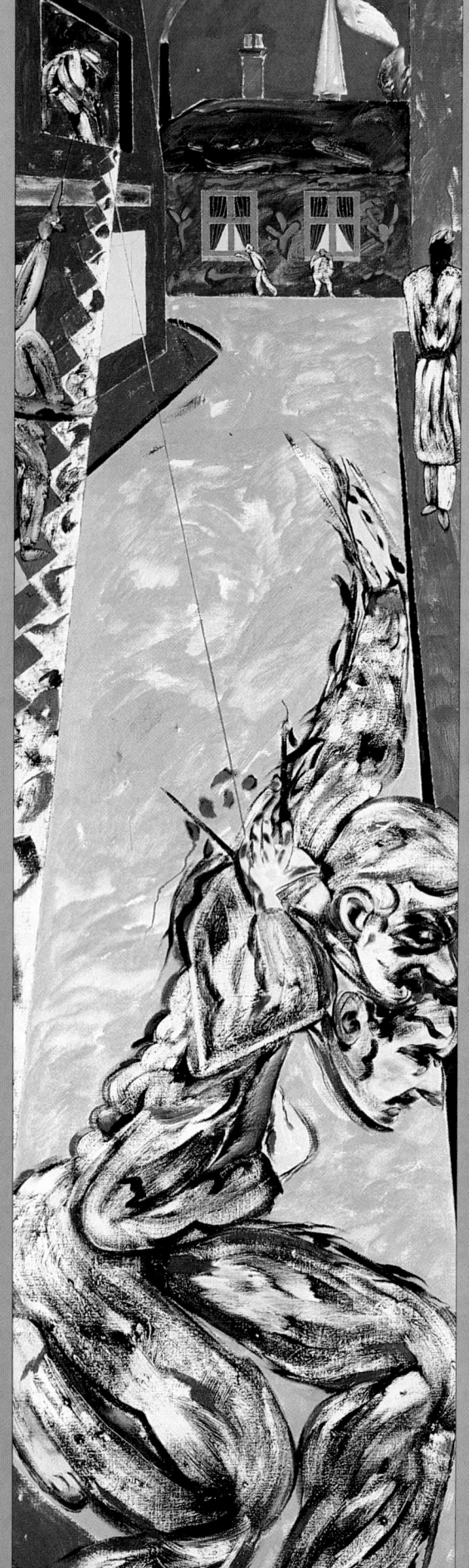

1284

The Sniper (1987), R. B. Kitaj. Oil on canvas, 120″ × 36″. The Saatchi Collection, London.

from Midsummer

Derek Walcott

With the stampeding hiss and scurry of green lemmings,
midsummer's leaves race to extinction like the roar
of a Brixton riot tunneled by water hoses;
they seethe toward autumn's fire—it is in their nature,
5 being men as well as leaves, to die for the sun.
The leaf stems tug at their chains, the branches bending
like Boer cattle under Tory whips that drag every wagon
nearer to apartheid. And, for me, that closes
the child's fairy tale of an antic England—fairy rings,
10 thatched cottages fenced with dog roses,
a green gale lifting the hair of Warwickshire.
I was there to add some color to the British theater.
"But the blacks can't do Shakespeare, they have no experience."
This was true. Their thick skulls bled with rancor
15 when the riot police and the skinheads exchanged quips
you could trace to the Sonnets, or the Moor's eclipse.
Praise had bled my lines white of any more anger,
and snow had inducted me into white fellowships,
while Calibans howled down the barred streets of an empire
20 that began with Caedmon's raceless dew, and is ending
in the alleys of Brixton, burning like Turner's ships.

1 lemmings: small rodents whose migrations in northern Europe sometimes end in mass drownings.

3 Brixton: an area in London.

7 Boer (bōr): belonging to South Africans of Dutch ancestry.

8 apartheid (ə-pärt′hīt′): the official policy of racial segregation formerly practiced in South Africa.

11 Warwickshire (wär′ĭk-shîr′): the English county where Shakespeare was born.

14 rancor (răng′kər): bitter resentment; ill will.

15 skinheads: young British working-class hoodlums—typically having hair cut very short—who are known for their use of violence against members of minority groups.

16 Sonnets: Shakespeare's 154 sonnets; **Moor's eclipse:** a reference to the downfall of the black hero of Shakespeare's *Othello.*

19 Calibans: beastlike human beings (from the name of a grotesque slave in Shakespeare's *The Tempest).*

20 Caedmon (kăd′mən): a seventh-century Anglo-Saxon poet.

21 Turner's ships: burning ships in paintings by the 19th-century British artist J. M. W. Turner.

Connect to the Literature

1. **What Do You Think?** What **image** in the excerpt from *Midsummer* made the greatest impression on you?

Think Critically

2. With what specific social issues does the **speaker** of this poem seem to be most concerned?

THINK ABOUT

- his comparison of leaves to human beings
- his references to historical events and works of art
- the quotation about blacks in the theater

3. What message about the English, or about European culture in general, do you think the speaker is trying to convey?

4. How does the speaker appear to feel about his own role in society? Cite evidence from the poem to support your answer.

5. **ACTIVE READING** | **COMPARING AND CONTRASTING POEMS** |
In what ways are these poems most alike? most different? How would you summarize what each poem conveys about the realities and consequences of racial prejudice? Look back at the Venn diagrams you created in your **READER'S NOTEBOOK** to help you answer these questions.

Extend Interpretations

6. **Critic's Corner** The critic Sven Birkerts has written that in Walcott's *Midsummer* "sharply etched **descriptions** give way to dark surges." What do you think he meant by this statement? Support your answer with examples from the excerpt in this book.

7. **Comparing Texts** Do you think either of these poems share any **themes** about humanity with W. H. Auden's "The Unknown Citizen" (page 1076)? Explain your opinion.

8. **Connect to Life** Do you think there will ever be a time when the majority of the world's people accept cultural and racial differences? Why or why not?

Literary Analysis

TONE IN SATIRE The **tone** of a work is established in part by the writer's choice of words and details. In a satiric work, the tone is also influenced by what the writer is satirizing—the fault or foible that is being exposed for criticism and correction. If, for example, the object of the **satire** is a minor annoyance, such as the tendency of some people to dominate a conversation, the tone might be humorous and playful. On the other hand, if—as in "Telephone Conversation" and the excerpt from *Midsummer*—the object of the satire is a serious human failing, the tone is likely to be much more biting and harsh.

Cooperative Learning Activity Both of these poems satirize racist attitudes and behavior, but they do not use an identical tone. With three or four classmates, decide what the tone of each poem is and list all the aspects of the poem that contribute to creating it. Then take turns reading each poem aloud, paying particular attention to conveying the tone. Do you gain any more insights into the tone of each poem as you read it aloud or listen to it being read?

Choices & CHALLENGES

Writing Options

1. Critical Review In an essay, evaluate how effectively you think each poem satirizes the effects of racial prejudice in a society. Cite evidence from the poems to support your conclusions. Place the paper in your **Working Portfolio.**

2. Advice Column With a partner, create an advice column, writing letters in which the speakers of these poems seek help in dealing with the issues presented in the poems. Then write responses to each letter.

3. Guest Editorial Write a guest editorial for your school paper, expressing your concerns about a specific violation of human rights that you have either read about or witnessed.

Activities & Explorations

1. T-Shirt Design Create a design for a T-shirt that promotes what one or both of the speakers might consider an ideal society. Display your work in the classroom. **~ ART**

2. Mock Trial With a group of classmates, prepare a mock trial in which the speaker of "Telephone Conversation" accuses the landlady of discrimination. With different members of the group taking on the roles of prosecutor, defense attorney, plaintiff, defendant, and judge, prepare questions and arguments for both sides of the case. Then conduct your trial while the rest of the class acts as the jury. **~ SPEAKING AND LISTENING**

3. Scrapbook of Social Issues Create a scrapbook of photographs, political cartoons, news articles, and other items that you think reflect the social issues dealt with in these poems. **~ SOCIAL STUDIES**

Inquiry & Research

Civil Rights Laws Investigate the history of civil rights legislation in the United States since 1950. What civil rights laws have been enacted? What events led to their enactment? How have the laws affected race relations?

More Online:
Research Starter
www.mcdougallittell.com

Art Connection

Summer and Shadow Look again at the painting *The Sniper* on page 1284. What thoughts come to mind when you look at the scene? How do these thoughts relate to the social issues raised in the excerpt from *Midsummer*? Discuss your ideas with your classmates.

Wole Soyinka
1934–

Other Works
"After the Deluge"
"Your Logic Frightens Me, Mandela"
"Massacre, October 66"
"Civilian and Soldier"

Derek Walcott
1930–

Other Works
"A Far Cry from Africa"
"A Sea Change"
"The Liberator"
"Port of Spain"
"Hurucan"

Between England and Nigeria Though his travels extend far beyond Nigeria, Wole Soyinka's main interest is in promoting his native Yoruba culture. Like his Nigerian contemporary Chinua Achebe, Soyinka attended high school at Government College and then entered the University of Ibadan. Later, he studied at the University of Leeds in England, graduating with honors in English. His early jobs included work as a bricklayer and a nightclub bouncer, but a job as play reader for London's Royal Court Theatre proved more suitable to his temperament. In 1960, he returned to Nigeria and launched his own theater company, called The 1960 Masks.

Playwright Soyinka is probably best known as a playwright. His first major play, *A Dance of the Forests,* was commissioned as a salute to Nigeria's independence in 1960. Since then, his works have been presented in cities throughout the world. In addition, he has produced, directed, and acted in plays and films—both in English and in his native Yoruba language—has organized theater groups at various schools in Nigeria, and has lectured at universities in Britain and the United States.

Politics and Poetry Like Achebe, Soyinka was actively involved in the Nigerian civil war of the late 1960s. Accused of helping the Biafrans secede, he was arrested by the Nigerian government and imprisoned for over two years. His confinement did not stifle his writing voice, however; in 1969, while he was still incarcerated, his volume *Poems from Prison* was published.

A Cultural Spokesman Derek Walcott's interest in the arts was inspired by his parents. His mother was a teacher on St. Lucia and acted in a local theater group, and his father, who died when Walcott was just a baby, was an aspiring painter and poet. Walcott once said, "I have felt from my boyhood that I had one function and that was somehow to articulate, not my own experience, but what I saw around me." While hoping to preserve his own culture through his writing, the witty and outgoing writer also relishes cultural diversity. His closest friends include two other Nobel Prize winners featured in this book—the Irish poet Seamus Heaney and the Polish poet, essayist, and novelist Czeslaw Milosz.

The Young Writer Walcott's literary talent developed early. He recalls that as a child he rejected sports for reading, writing, and playing with puppets. At the age of 18, he borrowed $200 from his mother to publish his first book of poems and then sold copies on the street to pay back the loan. At the age of 20, he and his twin brother organized a theater group in St. Lucia and staged a play that Walcott had written. While still a student at the University of the West Indies in Jamaica, he published several works, among them a play.

Teaching Career After studying drama in New York for a year, Walcott moved to Trinidad, where he recruited and trained the first professional West Indian acting troupe. Since 1970, he has taught at various schools in the United States—including Yale, Columbia, and Boston University—in recent years dividing his time between homes in Boston, Trinidad, and St. Lucia.

Six Feet of the Country

Short Story by NADINE GORDIMER

Comparing Literature of the World

Six Feet of the Country and *from* Writing as an Act of Hope

This lesson and the one that follows present an opportunity for comparing Nadine Gordimer's examination of the effects of South African apartheid with Isabel Allende's observations on the political unrest and economic hardship in Chile. Specific points of comparison in the Allende lesson will help you contrast the two writers' portrayals of the people and conditions in their homeland.

Connect to Your Life

Lip Service Have you ever encountered a situation in which a person claimed to understand and respect another race or culture but really showed little understanding or respect? Discuss your experiences and insights with your classmates.

Build Background

Separate but Unequal Nadine Gordimer writes about the people of her South African homeland and reveals how the system of apartheid has affected their lives. The term *apartheid*—which means "separateness" in Afrikaans, the language of the Dutch settlers of South Africa—refers to an official system of racial separation enforced by the South African government from 1948 to 1991. During the first 20 years of that period, laws were enacted that segregated education and housing, restricted the movement and voting rights of nonwhites, and gave the government far-reaching police powers to ensure compliance with apartheid. In 1961, South Africa withdrew from the United Nations after other member nations severely criticized its racial policies.

In the 1970s and 1980s, the government of South Africa, responding to years of national and international protest, began to repeal some apartheid laws and to open public facilities and transportation systems to all races. Many apartheid regulations remained, however, as did segregation of schools and neighborhoods. Finally, in 1991, the government granted full rights to nonwhites, repealing the last of the discriminatory laws that had formed the basis of apartheid. Although apartheid has now been officially dismantled, its economic and social effects are likely to linger for some time.

From the first days of apartheid, many white South Africans opposed the system for its inhumanity and lack of respect for people of other cultures. A few, like Nadine Gordimer, openly expressed their disapproval of the system. In "Six Feet of the Country," first published in the 1950s, she examines the experiences and attitudes of a white British couple—a businessman and a former actress—who have moved to the South African countryside.

WORDS TO KNOW **Vocabulary Preview**	
attenuated	inane
enamor	laconic
expostulate	stint
extraneous	submissive
imbue	untainted

Focus Your Reading

LITERARY ANALYSIS **POINT OF VIEW**

As you know, the term *point of view* refers to the narrative method used in a literary work. "Six Feet of the Country" is told from the **first-person point of view** of a narrator who is also the story's **main character.** As you read, keep in mind that the events and other characters in the story are described from the main character's personal perspective.

ACTIVE READING **PREDICTING**

When you make a **prediction,** you try to figure out what will happen next. Historical knowledge about a narrative's subject and even the story's title can help you make predictions. Use the information provided in the Build Background and the title "Six Feet of the Country" to predict what the story will be about.

READER'S NOTEBOOK Write your prediction about the story in your notebook. Then, at key moments in the story, continue to jot down your predictions about what will happen next.

Six Feet of the Country

Nadine Gordimer

My wife and I are not real farmers—not even Lerice, really. We bought our place, ten miles out of Johannesburg on one of the main roads, to change something in ourselves, I suppose; you seem to rattle about so much within a marriage like ours. You long to hear nothing but a deep, satisfying silence when you sound a marriage. The farm hasn't managed that for us, of course, but it has done other things, unexpected, illogical. Lerice, who I thought would retire there in Chekhovian sadness for a month or two, and then leave the place to the servants while she tried yet again to get a part she wanted and become the actress she would like to be, has sunk into the business of running the farm with all the serious intensity with which she once <u>imbued</u> the shadows in a playwright's mind. I should have given it up long ago if it had not been for her. Her hands, once small and plain and well-kept—she was not the sort of actress who wears red paint and diamond rings—are hard as a dog's pads.

WORDS
TO
KNOW

imbue (ĭm-byōō′) *v.* to fill with a quality; saturate

I, of course, am there only in the evenings and at week-ends. I am a partner in a luxury-travel agency, which is flourishing—needs to be, as I tell Lerice, in order to carry on the farm. Still, though I know we can't afford it, and though the sweetish smell of the fowls Lerice breeds sickens me, so that I avoid going past their runs, the farm is beautiful in a way I had almost forgotten—especially on a Sunday morning when I get up and go out into the paddock and see not the palm trees and fish pond and imitation-stone bird-bath of the suburbs but white ducks on the dam, the lucerne[1] field brilliant as window-dresser's grass, and the little, stocky, mean-eyed bull, lustful but bored, having his face tenderly licked by one of his ladies. Lerice comes out with her hair uncombed, in her hand a stick dripping with cattle-dip. She will stand and look dreamily for a moment, the way she would pretend to look sometimes in those plays. "They'll mate tomorrow," she will say. "This is their second day. Look how she loves him, my little Napoleon." So that when people come out to see us on Sunday afternoon, I am likely to hear myself saying, as I pour out the drinks, "When I drive back home from the city every day, past those rows of suburban houses, I wonder how the devil we ever did stand it. . . . Would you care to look around?" And there I am, taking some pretty girl and her young husband stumbling down to our river-bank, the girl catching her stockings on the mealie-stooks[2] and stepping over cow-turds humming with jewel-green flies while she says, ". . . the *tensions* of the damned city. And you're near enough to get into town to a show, too! I think it's wonderful. Why, you've got it both ways!"

And for a moment I accept the triumph as if I *had* managed it—the impossibility that I've been trying for all my life—just as if the truth was that you could get it "both ways," instead of finding yourself with not even one way or the other but a third, one you had not provided for at all.

But even in our saner moments, when I find Lerice's earthy enthusiasms just as irritating as I once found her histrionical[3] ones, and she finds what she calls my "jealousy" of her capacity for enthusiasm as big a proof of my inadequacy for her as a mate as ever it was, we do believe that we have at least honestly escaped those tensions peculiar to the city about which our visitors speak. When Johannesburg people speak of "tension" they don't mean hurrying people in crowded streets, the struggle for money, or the general competitive character of city life. They mean the guns under the white men's pillows and the burglar bars on the white men's windows. They mean those strange moments on city pavements when a black man won't stand aside for a white man.

Out in the country, even ten miles out, life is better than that. In the country, there is a lingering remnant of the pretransitional stage; our relationship with the blacks is almost feudal.[4] Wrong, I suppose, obsolete, but more comfortable all round. We have no burglar bars, no gun. Lerice's farm-boys have their wives and their piccanins[5] living with them on the land. They brew their sour beer without the fear of police raids. In fact, we've always rather prided ourselves that the poor devils have nothing much to fear, being with us; Lerice even keeps an eye on their children, with all the competence of a woman who has never had a child of her own, and she certainly doctors

---

1. **lucerne** (loo-sûrn′): a British term for alfalfa.
2. **mealie-stooks**: a South African term for cornstalks.
3. **histrionical**: theatrical; dramatic.
4. **feudal** (fyood′l): characteristic of feudalism—the medieval European economic, political, and social system in which the serfs who worked the land were protected by, and owed allegiance to, their overlords.
5. **piccanins** (pĭk′ə-nĭnz′): in South Africa, a term (usually considered derogatory) for native African children.

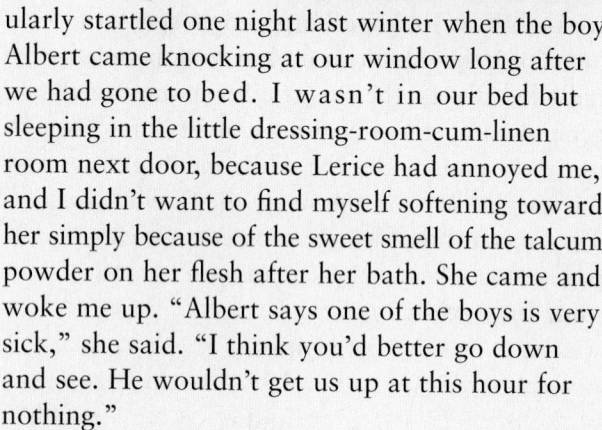

them all—children and adults—like babies whenever they happen to be sick.

It was because of this that we were not particularly startled one night last winter when the boy Albert came knocking at our window long after we had gone to bed. I wasn't in our bed but sleeping in the little dressing-room-cum-linen room next door, because Lerice had annoyed me, and I didn't want to find myself softening toward her simply because of the sweet smell of the talcum powder on her flesh after her bath. She came and woke me up. "Albert says one of the boys is very sick," she said. "I think you'd better go down and see. He wouldn't get us up at this hour for nothing."

"What time is it?"

"What does it matter?" Lerice is maddeningly logical.

I got up awkwardly as she watched me—how is it I always feel a fool when I have deserted her bed? After all, I know from the way she never looks at me when she talks to me at breakfast the next day that she is hurt and humiliated at my not wanting her—and I went out, clumsy with sleep.

"Which of the boys is it?" I asked Albert as we followed the dance of my torch.

"He's too sick. Very sick, *Baas*,"[6] he said.

"But who? Franz?" I remembered Franz had had a bad cough for the past week.

Albert did not answer; he had given me the path, and was walking along beside me in the tall dead grass. When the light of the torch caught his face, I saw that he looked acutely embarrassed. "What's this all about?" I said.

He lowered his head under the glance of the light. "It's not me, *Baas*. I don't know. Petrus he send me."

Irritated, I hurried him along to the huts. And there, on Petrus's iron bedstead, with its brick stilts, was a young man, dead. On his forehead there was still a light, cold sweat; his body was warm. The boys stood around as they do in the kitchen when it is discovered that someone has broken a dish—uncooperative, silent. Somebody's wife hung about in the shadows, her hands wrung together under her apron.

ACTIVE READING

PREDICT Who do you think the dead man is?

I had not seen a dead man since the war. This was very different. I felt like the others—<u>extraneous</u>, useless.

"What was the matter?" I asked.

The woman patted at her chest and shook her head to indicate the painful impossibility of breathing.

He must have died of pneumonia.

I turned to Petrus. "Who was this boy? What was he doing here?" The light of a candle on the floor showed that Petrus was weeping. He followed me out the door.

When we were outside, in the dark, I waited for him to speak. But he didn't. "Now come on, Petrus, you must tell me who this boy was. Was he a friend of yours?"

"He's my brother, *Baas*. He come from Rhodesia to look for work."

The story startled Lerice and me a little. The young boy had walked down from Rhodesia to look for work in Johannesburg, had caught a chill from sleeping out along the way, and had lain ill in his brother Petrus's hut since his arrival three days before. Our boys had been

6. *baas* (bäs) *Afrikaans:* master; boss (formerly used as a term of address by black South Africans when speaking to a white man).

WORDS
TO
KNOW

extraneous (ĭk-strā'nē-əs) *adj.* not relevant; inessential

frightened to ask us for help for him because we had not been intended ever to know of his presence. Rhodesian natives are barred from entering the Union[7] unless they have a permit; the young man was an illegal immigrant. No doubt our boys had managed the whole thing successfully several times before; a number of relatives must have walked the seven or eight hundred miles from poverty to the paradise of zoot suits,[8] police raids, and black slum townships that is their *Egoli*,[9] City of Gold—the Bantu name for Johannesburg. It was merely a matter of getting such a man to lie low on our farm until a job could be found with someone who would be glad to take the risk of prosecution for employing an illegal immigrant in exchange for the services of someone as yet <u>untainted</u> by the city.

Well, this was one who would never get up again.

"You would think they would have felt they could tell *us*," said Lerice next morning. "Once the man was ill. You would have thought at least—" When she is getting intense over something, she has a way of standing in the middle of a room as people do when they are shortly to leave on a journey, looking searchingly about her at the most familiar objects as if she had never seen them before. I had noticed that in Petrus's presence in the kitchen, earlier, she had the air of being almost offended with him, almost hurt.

In any case, I really haven't the time or inclination any more to go into everything in our life that I know Lerice, from those alarmed and pressing eyes of hers, would like us to go into. She is the kind of woman who doesn't mind if she looks plain, or odd; I don't suppose she would even care if she knew how strange she looks when her whole face is out of proportion with urgent uncertainty. I said, "Now, I'm the one who'll have to do all the dirty work, I suppose."

She was still staring at me, trying me out with those eyes—wasting her time, if she only knew.

"I'll have to notify the health authorities," I said calmly. "They can't just cart him off and bury him. After all, we don't really know what he died of."

She simply stood there, as if she had given up—simply ceased to see me at all.

I don't know when I've been so irritated. "It might have been something contagious," I said. "God knows?" There was no answer.

I am not <u>enamored</u> of holding conversations with myself. I went out to shout to one of the boys to open the garage and get the car ready for my morning drive to town.

As I had expected, it turned out to be quite a business. I had to notify the police as well as the health authorities, and answer a lot of tedious questions: How was it I was ignorant of the boy's presence? If I did not supervise my native quarters, how did I know that that sort of thing didn't go on all the time? Et cetera, et cetera. And when I flared up and told them that so long as my natives did their work, I didn't think it my right or concern to poke my nose into their private lives, I got from the coarse, dull-witted police sergeant one of those looks that come not from any thinking process going on in the brain but from that faculty common to all who are possessed by the master-race theory—a look of insanely <u>inane</u> certainty. He grinned at me with a mixture of scorn and delight at my stupidity.

Then I had to explain to Petrus why the health authorities had to take away the body

---

7. **Union:** Union of South Africa—the South African state preceding the formation of the Republic of South Africa in 1961.

8. **zoot suits:** flashy men's suits with broad padded shoulders and baggy trousers.

9. *Egoli* (ā-gō′lē).

WORDS   **untainted** (ŭn-tān′tĭd) *adj.* not contaminated; unspoiled
TO   **enamor** (ĭ-năm′ər) *v.* to inspire with love; fascinate
KNOW   **inane** (ĭn-ān′) *adj.* foolish; senseless

for a post-mortem[10]—and, in fact, what a post-mortem was. When I telephoned the health department some days later to find out the result, I was told the cause of death was, as we had thought, pneumonia, and that the body had been suitably disposed of. I went out to where Petrus was mixing a mash for the fowls and told him that it was all right, there would be no trouble; his brother had died from that pain in his chest. Petrus put down the paraffin tin and said, "When can we go to fetch him, *Baas?*"

"To fetch him?"

"Will the *Baas* please ask them when we must come?"

I went back inside and called Lerice, all over the house. She came down the stairs from the spare bedrooms, and I said, "*Now* what am I going to do? When I told Petrus, he just asked calmly when they could go and fetch the body. They think they're going to bury him themselves."

"Well, go back and tell him," said Lerice. "You must tell him. Why didn't you tell him then?"

When I found Petrus again, he looked up politely. "Look, Petrus," I said. "You can't go to fetch your brother. They've done it already—they've *buried* him, you understand?"

"Where?" he said, slowly, dully, as if he thought that perhaps he was getting this wrong.

"You see, he was a stranger. They knew he wasn't from here, and they didn't know he had some of his people here, so they thought they must bury him." It was difficult to make a pauper's grave sound like a privilege.

"Please, *Baas*, the *Baas* must ask them?" But he did not mean that he wanted to know the burial-place. He simply ignored the incomprehensible machinery I told him had set to work on his dead brother; he wanted the brother back.

"But Petrus," I said, "how can I? Your brother is buried already. I can't ask them now."

"Oh *Baas!*" he said. He stood with his bran-smeared hands uncurled at his sides, one corner of his mouth twitching.

"Good God, Petrus, they won't listen to me! They can't, anyway. I'm sorry, but I can't do it. You understand?"

He just kept on looking at me, out of his knowledge that white men have everything, can do anything; if they don't, it is because they won't.

And then, at dinner Lerice started. "You could at least phone," she said.

"*Christ*, what d'you think I am? Am I supposed to bring the dead back to life?"

But I could not exaggerate my way out of this ridiculous responsibility that had been thrust on me. "Phone them up," she went on. "And at least you'll be able to tell him you've done it and they've explained that it's impossible."

She disappeared somewhere into the kitchen quarters after coffee. A little later she came back to tell me, "The old father's coming down from Rhodesia to be at the funeral. He's got a permit and he's already on his way."

Unfortunately, it was not impossible to get the body back. The authorities said that it was somewhat irregular, but that since the hygiene conditions had been fulfilled, they could not refuse permission for exhumation.[11] I found out that, with the undertaker's charges, it would cost twenty pounds. Ah, I thought, that settles it. On five pounds a month, Petrus won't have twenty pounds—and just as well, since it couldn't do the dead any good. Certainly I should not offer it to him myself. Twenty pounds—or anything else within reason, for that matter—I would have spent without grudging it on doctors or medicines that might have helped the boy when he was alive. Once he was dead, I had no intention of encouraging Petrus to throw away, on a gesture, more than he spent to clothe his whole family in a year.

When I told him, in the kitchen that night, he said, "Twenty pounds?"

---

10. **post-mortem:** an examination of a corpse to determine the cause of death.

11. **exhumation** (ĕg′zyo͞o-mā′shən): the removal of a corpse from a grave.

I said, "Yes, that's right, twenty pounds."

For a moment, I had the feeling, from the look on his face, that he was calculating. But when he spoke again I thought I must have imagined it. "We must pay twenty pounds!" he said in the far-away voice in which a person speaks of something so unattainable that it does not bear thinking about.

"All right, Petrus," I said in dismissal, and went back to the living-room.

The next morning before I went to town, Petrus asked to see me. "Please *Baas*," he said, awkwardly handing me a bundle of notes. They're so seldom on the giving rather than the receiving side, poor devils, that they don't really know how to hand money to a white man. There it was, the twenty pounds, in ones and halves, some creased and folded until they were soft as dirty rags, others smooth and fairly new—Franz's money, I suppose, and Albert's, and Dora the cook's, and Jacob the gardener's, and God knows who else's besides, from all the farms and small holdings round about. I took it in irritation more than in astonishment, really—irritation at the waste, the uselessness of this sacrifice by people so poor. Just like the poor everywhere, I thought, who <u>stint</u> themselves the decencies of life in order to insure themselves the decencies of death. So incomprehensible to people like Lerice and me, who regard life as something to be spent extravagantly and, if we think about death at all, regard it as the final bankruptcy.

ACTIVE READING

CLARIFY Why is the narrator so surprised by the farm hands' efforts?

The servants don't work on Saturday afternoon anyway, so it was a good day for the funeral. Petrus and his father had borrowed our donkey-cart to fetch the coffin from the city, where, Petrus told Lerice on their return, everything was "nice"—the coffin waiting for them, already sealed up to save them from what must have been a rather unpleasant sight after two weeks' interment. (It had taken all that time for the authorities and the undertaker to make

the final arrangements for moving the body.) All morning, the coffin lay in Petrus's hut, awaiting the trip to the little old burial-ground, just outside the eastern boundary of our farm, that was a relic of the days when this was a real farming district rather than a fashionable rural estate. It was pure chance that I happened to be down there near the fence when the procession came past; once again Lerice had forgotten her promise to me and had made the house uninhabitable on a Saturday afternoon. I had come home and been infuriated to find her in a pair of filthy old slacks and with her hair uncombed since the night before, having all the varnish scraped off the living-room floor, if you

WORDS
TO   **stint** (stĭnt) *v.* to limit to a small amount; give sparingly
KNOW

please. So I had taken my No. 8 iron and gone off to practice my approach shots. In my annoyance I had forgotten about the funeral, and was reminded only when I saw the procession coming up the path along the outside of the fence toward me; from where I was standing, you can see the graves quite clearly, and that day the sun glinted on bits of broken pottery, a lopsided homemade cross, and jam-jars brown with rain-water and dead flowers.

I felt a little awkward, and did not know whether to go on hitting my golf ball or stop at least until the whole gathering was decently past. The donkey-cart creaks and screeches with every revolution of the wheels and it came along in a slow, halting fashion somehow peculiarly suited to the two donkeys who drew it, their little potbellies rubbed and rough, their heads sunk between the shafts, and their ears flattened back with an air

Funeral Procession (1940), Ellis Wilson. Armistad Research Center, Tulane University, New Orleans, Louisiana.

submissive and down-cast; peculiarly suited, too, to the group of men and women who came along slowly behind. The patient ass. Watching, I thought, you can see now why the creature became a Biblical symbol. Then the procession drew level with me and stopped, so I had to put down my club. The coffin was taken down off the cart—it was a shiny, yellow-varnished wood, like cheap furniture—and the donkeys twitched their ears against the flies. Petrus, Franz, Albert and the old father from Rhodesia hoisted it on

ACTIVE READING

QUESTION Why does the narrator feel awkward as the funeral passes?

their shoulders and the procession moved on, on foot. It was really a very awkward moment. I stood there rather foolishly at the fence, quite still, and slowly they filed past, not looking up, the four men bent beneath the shiny wooden box, and the straggling troop of mourners. All of them were servants or neighbors' servants whom I knew as casual, easygoing gossipers about our lands or kitchen. I heard the old man's breathing.

I had just bent to pick up my club again when there was a sort of jar in the flowing solemnity of their processional mood; I felt it at once, like a wave of heat along the air, or one of those sudden currents of cold catching at your legs in a placid stream. The old man's voice was muttering

something, and they bumped into one another, some pressing to go on, others hissing at them to be still. I could see that they were embarrassed, but they could not ignore the voice; it was much the way that the mumblings of a prophet, though not clear at first, arrest the mind. The corner of the coffin the old man carried was sagging at an angle; he seemed to be trying to get out from under the weight of it. Now Petrus expostulated with him.

The little boy who had been left to watch the donkeys dropped the reins and ran to see. I don't know why—unless it was for the same reason people crowd round someone who has fainted in a cinema—but I parted the wires of the fence and went through, after him.

Petrus lifted his eyes to me—to anybody—with distress and horror. The old man from Rhodesia had let go of the coffin entirely, and the three others, unable to support it on their own, had laid it on the ground, in the pathway. Already there was a film of dust lightly wavering up its shiny sides. I did not understand what the old man was saying; I hesitated to interfere. But now the whole seething group turned on my silence. The old man himself came over to me, with his hands outspread and shaking, and spoke directly to me, saying something that I could tell from the tone, without understanding the words, was shocking and extraordinary.

"What is it, Petrus? What's wrong?" I appealed.

Petrus threw up his hands, bowed his head in a series of hysterical shakes, then thrust his face up at me suddenly.

"He says, 'My son was not so heavy.'"

Silence. I could hear the old man breathing; he kept his mouth a little open as old people do.

"My son was young and thin," he said, at last, in English.

Again silence. Then babble broke out. The old man thundered against everybody; his teeth were yellowed and few, and he had one of those fine, grizzled, sweeping moustaches that one doesn't

often see nowadays, which must have been grown in emulation of early Empire builders.[12] It seemed to frame all his utterances with a special validity, perhaps merely because it was the symbol of the traditional wisdom of age—an idea so fearfully rooted that it carries still something awesome beyond reason. He shocked them; they thought he was mad, but they had to listen to him. With his own hands he began to prise the lid off the coffin and three of the men came forward to help him. Then he sat down on the ground; very old, very weak, and unable to speak, he merely lifted a trembling hand toward what was there. He abdicated, he handed it over to them; he was no good any more.

They crowded round to look (and so did I), and now they forgot the nature of this surprise and the occasion of grief to which it belonged, and for a few minutes were carried up in the astonishment of the surprise itself. They gasped and flared noisily with excitement. I even noticed the little boy who had held the donkeys jumping up and down, almost weeping with rage because the backs of the grown-ups crowded him out of his view.

In the coffin was someone no one had ever seen before: a heavily built, rather light-skinned native with a neatly stitched scar on his forehead—perhaps from a blow in a brawl that had also dealt him some other, slower-working injury which had killed him.

I wrangled with the authorities for a week over that body. I had the feeling that they were shocked, in a laconic fashion, by their own mistake, but that in the confusion of their anonymous dead they were helpless to put it right. They said to me, "We are trying to find out," and "We are still making enquiries." It was as if at any moment they might conduct me into their mortuary and say, "There! Lift up the sheets; look for him—your poultry boy's brother. There are so many black faces—surely one will do?"

---

12. **Empire builders:** British colonizers.

WORDS TO KNOW   **expostulate** (ĭk-spŏs′chə-lāt′) *v.* to reason earnestly in an effort to correct or dissuade
laconic (lə-kŏn′ĭk) *adj.* making use of few words

And every evening when I got home Petrus was waiting in the kitchen. "Well, they're trying. They're still looking. The *Baas* is seeing to it for you, Petrus," I would tell him. "God, half the time I should be in the office I'm driving around the back end of town chasing after this affair," I added aside, to Lerice, one night.

She and Petrus both kept their eyes turned on me as I spoke, and, oddly, for those moments they looked exactly alike, though it sounds impossible: my wife, with her high, white forehead and her <u>attenuated</u> Englishwoman's body, and the poultry boy, with his horny bare feet below khaki trousers tied at the knee with string and the peculiar rankness of his nervous sweat coming from his skin.

ACTIVE READING

QUESTION Why do Lerice and Petrus look alike to the narrator at this point?

"What makes you so indignant, so determined about this now?" said Lerice suddenly.

I stared at her. "It's a matter of principle. Why should they get away with a swindle? It's time these officials had a jolt from someone who'll bother to take the trouble."

She said, "Oh." And as Petrus slowly opened the kitchen door to leave, sensing that the talk had gone beyond him, she turned away too.

I continued to pass on assurances to Petrus every evening, but although what I said was the same, and the voice in which I said it was the same, every evening it sounded weaker. At last, it became clear that we would never get Petrus's brother back, because nobody really knew where he was. Somewhere in a graveyard as uniform as a housing scheme, somewhere under a number that didn't belong to him, or in the medical school, perhaps, laboriously reduced to layers of muscles and strings of nerves? Goodness knows. He had no identity in this world anyway.

It was only then, and in a voice of shame, that Petrus asked me to try and get the money back.

"From the way he asks, you'd think he was robbing his dead brother," I said to Lerice later. But as I've said, Lerice had got so intense about this business that she couldn't even appreciate a little ironic smile.

I tried to get the money; Lerice tried. We both telephoned and wrote and argued, but nothing came of it. It appeared that the main expense had been the undertaker, and, after all, he had done his job. So the whole thing was a complete waste, even more of a waste for the poor devils than I had thought it would be.

The old man from Rhodesia was about Lerice's father's size, so she gave him one of her father's old suits and he went back home rather better off, for the winter, than he had come. ❖

WORDS TO KNOW   **attenuated** (ə-tĕn′yōō-ā′tĭd) *adj.* slender; thin **attenuate** *v.*

Connect to the Literature

1. What Do You Think? How did you react to the ending of this story? Share your impressions with your classmates.

> **Comprehension Check**
> - What happens to Petrus's brother?
> - What does Petrus ask the narrator to do for him?
> - How does Petrus's father know that the wrong body is in the coffin?

Think Critically

2. **ACTIVE READING** **PREDICTING** Get together with a class-mate and compare the **predictions** you each wrote down in your **READER'S NOTEBOOK** with what actually happens in the story. How accurate were your predictions? With your partner, discuss the clues and information you used to make your predictions. What helped you the most?

3. Could the **narrator** have done anything differently in dealing with the mix-up of the corpses?

4. How would you describe the relationship between the narrator and Lerice?

> **THINK ABOUT**
> - how he describes their marriage
> - each **character's** values and interests
> - the effect of this incident on their relationship

5. What do you consider the most powerful **conflict** in this story? Give reasons for your opinion.

6. What do you think of the narrator's comment, in the last sentence of the story, that the old man "went back home rather better off . . . than he had come"?

Extend Interpretations

7. Different Perspectives Think about the events in the story from Petrus's perspective. How do you think he feels when he discovers that his brother's body is not in the coffin? How do you think he views the narrator? Support your answers with details from the story.

8. Connect to Life Despite poverty and extreme hardship, Petrus and his neighbors are resourceful, strong, and supportive to one another. Do you think it is possible to form such a close-knit group in contemporary American society? Why or why not?

Literary Analysis

POINT OF VIEW "Six Feet of the Country" is narrated from the **point of view** of the main character. All we know about the characters and the story's events is based on his observations and thoughts, which may be colored or distorted by his personal perspective. Notice the narrator's attitude toward nonwhites in the following observation:

They're so seldom on the giving rather than the receiving side, poor devils, that they don't really know how to hand money to a white man.

The comment reveals the narrator's narrow view of the world. He doesn't seem to realize that people like Petrus receive very little and are constantly "giving."

Cooperative Learning Activity With a small group of classmates, choose a passage that has a particularly strong effect on you. Then rewrite the passage, telling the events from a **third-person point of view.** Discuss the two versions. Why do you think Gordimer chose to use the **first-person point of view?**

REVIEW **IMAGERY** **Imagery** refers to the words and phrases that create vivid sensory experiences for the reader. Notice how the following description appeals to several senses:

And there I am, taking some pretty girl and her young husband stumbling down to our river-bank, the girl catching her stockings on the mealie-stooks and stepping over cow-turds humming with jewel-green flies. . . .

How does the imagery in the story affect your impressions of the characters and events?

Writing Options

1. Story Review Nadine Gordimer has been praised for her ability to convey the importance of respecting other cultures. Write a critical review of "Six Feet of the Country" in which you explain how the story demonstrates this idea. Place the review in your **Working Portfolio.**

2. Memo for the Teacher Compose a memo to a history teacher, recommending that Gordimer's story be required reading for a unit on South Africa.

3. Letter to the Authorities Write a letter to the South African health authorities, demanding that the body of Petrus's brother be found.

Activities & Explorations

1. Monument Design Create a design for a monument to Petrus's brother, symbolizing the plight of his family and others like them. **~ ART**

2. Improvised Dialogue With a classmate, improvise a dialogue in which the narrator and Lerice, after the old man's departure, talk over the events of the story. Try to convey the nature of their marital relationship, as well as the reactions of each to the events. **~ SPEAKING AND LISTENING**

3. Character Portrait Choose one of the main characters of the story—the narrator, Lerice, Petrus, or Petrus's father—and draw a portrait of the character. **~ ART**

Inquiry & Research

1. New Leader As a result of the April 1994 election in South Africa, in which blacks were permitted to vote for the first time, Nelson Mandela became the leader of the nation. Use the *Readers' Guide to Periodical Literature* to locate recent articles on Mandela and events in South Africa. Summarize the articles and share the information with the class.

More Online:
Research Starter
www.mcdougallittell.com

2. On the Map Using a reliable atlas as a resource, draw a map of South Africa, outlining its four provinces and highlighting the one in which this story is set. Be sure to indicate the main cities and physical features of each province.

Art Connection

Mood in Art What mood is conveyed by *Funeral Procession,* the painting on page 1296? How does the mood in the painting compare with that created by the procession described in the story—both before and after the terrible discovery?

Vocabulary in Action

EXERCISE A: SYNONYMOUS PHRASES For each phrase in the first column, write the letter of the synonymous phrase in the second column.

1. **laconic** account
2. idiotic chorus
3. manageable sibling
4. infatuated faltering
5. pure pigment
6. **stint** the stallion
7. **expostulate** on the way
8. permeate with sadness
9. **attenuated** agent
10. variety of unnecessary things

a. dispute en route
b. **untainted** paint
c. short report
d. **inane** refrain
e. delicate delegate
f. **enamored** stammering
g. **submissive** sister
h. **imbue** with the blues
i. **extraneous** miscellany
j. underfeed the steed

EXERCISE B Work with a partner to come up with an appropriate phrase—such as "**extraneous** details" or "**inane** chatter"—for each vocabulary word. Then challenge another pair of students to compete with each other to guess one of the phrases, allowing them to suggest letters one by one (as in the game hangman or the TV show *Wheel of Fortune).* When one has guessed the phrase, compete with your partner to guess a phrase that they have written.

WORDS TO KNOW			
	attenuated	imbue	submissive
	enamor	inane	untainted
	expostulate	laconic	
	extraneous	stint	

Building Vocabulary
For an in-depth lesson on how to use a thesaurus to find a word's synonyms, see page 574.

Nadine Gordimer
1923–

Other Works
Burger's Daughter
July's People
Jump and Other Stories

Solitary Writer Nadine Gordimer is known for her beautifully crafted novels and short stories dealing with themes of exile, alienation, and life's missed opportunities. Born into a white middle-class family in the Transvaal province of South Africa, she spent much of her childhood in solitude, which she relieved by visiting her local library. She began to write while still a child, publishing her first short story at the age of 15.

Reflections on Society At first Gordimer concentrated on writing short stories, but as her subject matter grew increasingly complex, she turned to the novel. Almost from the beginning, critics noted her precise ear for spoken language, her sensitivity to the rhythm of the spoken word, her keen sense of social satire, and the strong moral purpose of her work. Since much of her writing is set in South Africa, her characters have inevitably been shaped by the political situation there; yet even as she has used her talents and influence to oppose apartheid, she has refused to let her writing become propaganda. Instead, she has said, she strives simply to portray the society in which she lives: "I thrust my hand as deep as it will go, deep into the life around me, and I write about what comes up."

Accolades and Achievements In 1974, Gordimer won the Booker Prize for her novel *The Conservationist,* and in 1991, she received the Nobel Prize in literature. She has been called "one of the most gifted practitioners of the short story anywhere in English."

Author Activity

Building Character Read a short story by Nadine Gordimer that takes place after the abolition of apartheid laws. Compare the characters in the story with those in "Six Feet of the Country." In what ways has the relationship between whites and blacks changed in the more recent story? What, if anything, has not changed?

from **Writing as an Act of Hope**

Essay by ISABEL ALLENDE (ä-yĕn'dä)

Peru
Bolivia
Paraguay
South Pacific Ocean
Argentina
Chile
South Atlantic Ocean

Comparing Literature of the World

Politics and Literature Across Cultures

"Six Feet of the Country" and *from* "Writing as an Act of Hope" Both Gordimer and Allende write about the social, political, and economic inequalities in their homeland. In "Six Feet of the Country," Gordimer uses a white man's biased perspective to reveal the injustices perpetuated by apartheid in South Africa. In the excerpt from "Writing as an Act of Hope," Allende examines what she calls the "contrasts" and violence in Latin America.

Points of Comparison As you read Allende's essay, compare her observations of the people and conditions in Latin America with those shown in Gordimer's story.

Build Background

A Woman's Voice Like South African literature, the literature of Latin America—where political unrest and economic hardship have been facts of life during much of the past century—is characterized by a good deal of social commentary. Since the 19th century, many Latin American writers, even those living in exile elsewhere, have had a strong reason for writing—to speak out about the social and political problems of their homelands. Until recently, however, the handling of such issues was the exclusive domain of male writers. In the region's male-dominated culture, female writers were discouraged from engaging in political or intellectual commentary, even in fiction. It was the Chilean author Isabel Allende who, in the 1980s, became the first Latin American female to produce a widely read novel that focuses on the effects of social and political turmoil.

Allende's writing is inspired principally by her Chilean roots and her family's experiences. In all of her novels, she skillfully interweaves **realism** and **fantasy**—so much so that she herself claims to find it difficult to distinguish reality from the inventions of her mind in her writing.

WORDS TO KNOW
Vocabulary Preview

cataclysm	narcissistic
exorcising	pathological
hyperbole	pretension
illusory	rancor
imperialist	repression

Focus Your Reading

LITERARY ANALYSIS **ESSAY** An **essay** is a brief work of nonfiction that offers an opinion on a subject. The writer of an essay may seek to express ideas and feelings, to analyze, to inform, to entertain, or to persuade. In an **informative essay,** the writer's purpose is to reveal information on a subject about which he or she is particularly knowledgeable or concerned. In a **persuasive essay,** the writer's intent is to persuade readers to adopt a particular opinion or to perform a certain action. As you read Allende's essay, try to determine whether it is informative or persuasive.

ACTIVE READING **DETERMINING MAIN IDEAS AND SUPPORTING DETAILS** At the beginning of her essay, Allende states the two questions she will try to answer: "Why do I write?" and "Who do I write for?" The answers to these questions can help you determine the essay's **main ideas** and identify the **supporting details** for each idea.

READER'S NOTEBOOK As you read the excerpt from Allende's essay, write down all the answers you can find for each question.

FROM

Writing as an Act of Hope

ISABEL ALLENDE

IN EVERY INTERVIEW DURING THE LAST FEW YEARS I ENCOUNTERED TWO QUESTIONS THAT FORCED ME TO DEFINE MYSELF AS A WRITER AND AS A HUMAN BEING: WHY DO I WRITE? AND WHO DO I WRITE FOR? TONIGHT I WILL TRY TO ANSWER THOSE QUESTIONS. IN 1981, IN CARACAS, I PUT A SHEET OF PAPER IN MY TYPEWRITER AND WROTE THE FIRST SENTENCE OF *THE HOUSE OF THE SPIRITS*: "BARABBAS CAME TO US BY SEA." AT THAT MOMENT I DIDN'T KNOW WHY I WAS DOING IT, OR FOR WHOM.

In fact, I assumed that no one would ever read it except my mother, who reads everything I write. I was not even conscious that I was writing a novel. I thought I was writing a letter—a spiritual letter to my grandfather, a formidable old patriarch,[1] whom I loved dearly. He had reached almost one hundred years of age and decided that he was too tired to go on living, so he sat in his armchair and refused to drink or eat, calling for Death, who was kind enough to take him very soon.

I wanted to bid him farewell, but I couldn't go back to Chile, and I knew that calling him on the telephone was useless, so I began this letter. I wanted to tell him that he could go in peace because all his memories were with me. I had forgotten nothing. I had all his anecdotes, all the characters of the family, and to prove it I began writing the story of Rose, the fiancée my grandfather had had, who is called Rose the Beautiful in the book. She really existed; she's not a copy from García Márquez,[2] as some people have said.

For a year I wrote every night with no hesitation or plan. Words came out like a violent torrent. I had thousands of untold words stuck in my chest, threatening to choke me. The long silence of exile was turning me to stone; I needed to open a valve and let the river of secret words find a way out. At the end of that year there were five hundred pages on my table; it didn't look like a letter anymore. On the other hand, my grandfather had died long before, so the spiritual message had already reached him. So I thought, "Well, maybe in this way I can tell some other people about him, and about my country, and about my family and myself." So I just organized it a little bit, tied the manuscript with a pink ribbon for luck, and took it to some publishers.

The spirit of my grandmother was protecting the book from the very beginning, so it was refused everywhere in Venezuela. Nobody wanted it—it was too long; I was a woman; nobody knew me. So I sent it by mail to Spain, and the book was published there. It had reviews, and it was translated and distributed in other countries.

In the process of writing the anecdotes of the past, and recalling the emotions and pains of my fate, and telling part of the history of my country, I found that life became more comprehensible and the world more tolerable. I felt that my roots had been recovered and that during that patient exercise of daily writing I had also recovered my own soul. I felt at that time that writing was unavoidable—that I couldn't keep away from it. Writing is such a pleasure; it is always a private orgy, creating and recreating the world according to my own laws, fulfilling in those pages all my dreams and <u>exorcising</u> some of my demons.

But that is a rather simple explanation. There are other reasons for writing.

Six years and three books have passed since *The House of the Spirits*. Many things have changed for me in that time. I can no longer pretend to be naïve, or elude questions, or find refuge in irony. Now I am constantly confronted

---

1. **patriarch** (pā′trē-ärk′): a respected old man, especially one who is head of a family, clan, or tribe.
2. **García Márquez** (gär-sē′ə mär′kĕs): Gabriel García Márquez (1928–), a Colombian novelist and short story writer.

WORDS
TO
KNOW

exorcising (ĕk′sôr-sī′zĭng) *adj.* driving out (an evil spirit) by prayer, ceremony, or command **exorcise** *v.*

Sin título [Untitled] (1985), Rocío Maldonado. Acrylic with collaged elements on canvas with painted frame, 69″ × 85″ × 6″, courtesy of Gallery OMR, Mexico City.

by my readers, and they can be very tough. It's not enough to write in a state of trance, overwhelmed by the desire to tell a story. One has to be responsible for each word, each idea. Be very careful: the written word cannot be erased. . . .

Maybe the most important reason for writing is to prevent the erosion of time, so that memories will not be blown away by the wind. Write to register history, and name each thing. Write what should not be forgotten. But then, why write novels? Probably because I come from Latin America, a land of crazy, illuminated people, of geological and political cataclysms— a land so large and profound, so beautiful and frightening, that only novels can describe its fascinating complexity.

A novel is like a window, open to an infinite landscape. In a novel we can put all the interrogations, we can register the most extravagant, evil, obscene, incredible or magnificent facts— which, in Latin America, are not hyperbole, because that is the dimension of our reality. In a novel we can give an illusory order to chaos. We can find the key to the labyrinth of history. We can make excursions into the past, to try to understand the present and dream the future. In a novel we can use everything: testimony, chronicle, essay, fantasy, legend, poetry and other devices that might help us to decode the mysteries of our world and discover our true identity.

For a writer who nourishes himself or herself on images and passions, to be born in a fabulous continent is a privilege. In Latin America we don't have to stretch our imaginations. Critics in Europe and the United States often stare in disbelief at Latin American books, asking how the authors dare to invent those incredible lies of young women who fly to heaven wrapped in linen sheets; of black emperors who build fortresses with cement and the blood of emasculated bulls; of outlaws who die of hunger in the Amazon with bags full of emeralds on their backs; of ancient tyrants who order their mothers to be flogged naked in front of the troops and modern tyrants who order children to be tortured in front of their parents; of hurricanes and earthquakes that turn the world upside down; of revolutions made with machetes, bullets, poems and kisses; of hallucinating landscapes where reason is lost.

It is very hard to explain to critics that these things are not a product of our pathological imaginations. They are written in our history; we can find them every day in our newspapers. We hear them in the streets; we suffer them frequently in our own lives. It is impossible to speak of Latin America without mentioning violence. We inhabit a land of terrible contrasts and we have to survive in times of great violence.

Contrast and violence, two excellent ingredients for literature, although for us, citizens of that reality, life is always suspended from a very fragile thread.

The first, the most naked and visible form of violence, is the extreme poverty of the majority, in contrast with the extreme wealth of the very few. In my continent two opposite realities coexist. One is a legal face, more or less comprehensible and with a certain pretension to dignity and civilization. The other is a dark and tragic face, which we do not like to show but which is always threatening us. There is an apparent

WORDS TO KNOW	**cataclysm** (kăt′ə-klĭz′əm) *n.* a violent change or sudden upheaval
	hyperbole (hī-pûr′bə-lē) *n.* an exaggeration used for emphasis or effect
	illusory (ĭ-lōō′sə-rē) *adj.* unreal; deceptive
	pathological (păth′ə-lŏj′ĭ-kəl) *adj.* diseased; unhealthy
	pretension (prĭ-tĕn′shən) *n.* a claim or aspiration

world and a real world—nice neighborhoods where blond children play on their bicycles and servants walk elegant dogs, and other neighborhoods, of slums and garbage, where dark children play naked with hungry mutts. There are offices of marble and steel where young executives discuss the stock market, and forgotten villages where people still live and die as they did in the Middle Ages. There is a world of fiction created by the official discourse, and another world of blood and pain and love, where we have struggled for centuries.

In Latin America we all survive on the borderline of those two realities. Our fragile democracies exist as long as they don't interfere with imperialist interests. Most of our republics are dependent on submissiveness. Our institutions and laws are inefficient. Our armed forces often act as mercenaries[3] for a privileged social group that pays tribute to transnational enterprises. We are living in the worst economic, political and social crisis since the conquest of America by the Spaniards. There are hardly two or three leaders in the whole continent. Social inequality is greater every day, and to avoid an outburst of public rancor, repression also rises day by day. Crime, drugs, misery and ignorance are present in every Latin American country, and the military is an immediate threat to society and civil governments. We try to keep straight faces while our feet are stuck in a swamp of violence,

exploitation, corruption, the terror of the state and the terrorism of those who take arms against the status quo.

But Latin America is also a land of hope and friendship and love. Writers navigate in these agitated waters. They don't live in ivory towers; they cannot remove themselves from this brutal reality. In such circumstances there is no time and no wish for narcissistic literature. Very few of our writers contemplate their navel in self-centered monologue. The majority want desperately to communicate.

I feel that writing is an act of hope, a sort of communion with our fellow men. The writer of good will carries a lamp to illuminate the dark corners. Only that, nothing more—a tiny beam of light to show some hidden aspect of reality, to help decipher and understand it and thus to initiate, if possible, a change in the conscience of some readers. This kind of writer is not seduced by the mermaid's voice of celebrity or tempted by exclusive literary circles. He has both feet planted firmly on the ground and walks hand in hand with the people in the streets. He knows that the lamp is very small and the shadows are immense. This makes him humble. ❖

---

3. **mercenaries** (mûr′sə-nĕr′ēz): soldiers who will do anything for money.

Thinking *through the* LITERATURE

Connect to the Literature

1. What Do You Think? Discuss your response to this excerpt from "Writing as an Act of Hope" with your classmates.

> **Comprehension Check**
> - Why did Allende write her first novel?
> - What words does she use to describe Latin America?
> - What role does she see for Latin American writers?

Think Critically

2. **ACTIVE READING** **DETERMINING MAIN IDEAS AND SUPPORTING DETAILS** With a partner, discuss the answers you wrote down in your **READER'S NOTEBOOK**. Based on these answers, what do you think are the **main ideas** of Allende's essay? What **details** does the writer use to support her ideas?

3. On the basis of this **essay,** how would you describe Allende?

THINK ABOUT
- her reasons for writing
- her relationship with her family
- her feelings of responsibility to her readers

4. What qualities do you think Allende most admires in other writers? Cite evidence to support your answer.

5. Do you think Allende feels that it is important for a writer to be able to answer the questions "Why do I write?" and "Whom do I write for?" Give reasons to support your answer.

6. Does reading this essay make you want to read Allende's fiction? Why or why not?

Extend Interpretations

7. Connect to Life What "hidden aspect of reality" do you think should be exposed in American society? Which writers have tried to shed some light on the problem?

8. **Points of Comparison** Compare Allende's description of the contrast between rich and poor in Latin America with Gordimer's depiction of the narrator and Petrus in "Six Feet of the Country." What connections do you see between the realities in Latin America and South Africa?

Literary Analysis

ESSAY An **essay**—whether intended to inform, to persuade, or to entertain—serves to express the opinions of its writer. Allende's essay contains aspects of both an **informative** and a **persuasive essay.** In the following passage from the essay, the author tells the reader that violence is a fact of life in Latin America:

The first, the most naked and visible form of violence, is the extreme poverty of the majority, in contrast with the extreme wealth of the very few.

In this next passage, Allende tries to convince the reader that a writer should try to "illuminate the dark corners":

Only that, nothing more—a tiny beam of light to show some hidden aspect of reality, to help decipher and understand it and thus to initiate, if possible, a change in the conscience of some readers.

Notice that throughout her essay, Allende uses facts, reasons, and examples that support her opinions.

Cooperative Learning Activity
Get together with a small group of classmates to discuss the following question: Would you describe Allende's essay as primarily informative or as primarily persuasive? Back up your opinion with reasons. Then decide what details would need to be added to make the essay more informative or more persuasive.

Choices & CHALLENGES

Writing Options

1. Explanatory Paragraph In a paragraph, identify your favorite passage in this selection, giving reasons for your choice.

2. Letter to Allende Write a letter to Isabel Allende, in which you evaluate the ideas expressed in her essay. Tell Allende whether or not you agree with her views on the role of a writer as a social critic. Place the letter in your **Working Portfolio**.

3. Anecdote About a Memory Write an anecdote—either fictional or nonfictional—in which you capture an important memory involving a parent or grandparent. Write a brief introduction, addressed to the older person, telling the person what you are trying to do.

4. **Points of Comparison** Write an essay explaining which selection—"Writing as an Act of Hope" or "Six Feet of the Country"—you think presents the social, political, and economic inequalities of the writer's homeland more forcefully and convincingly. Cite evidence from the selections to support your opinions.

Activities & Explorations

1. Nomination Speech Deliver a speech in which you nominate Allende for an award on the basis of her ideas about writing. ~ **SPEAKING AND LISTENING**

2. Collage of Contrasts Create a collage of pictures to illustrate some of the contrasts that, according to Allende's essay, exist in Latin America. ~ **ART**

3. Poster Promoting Speech "Writing as an Act of Hope" originated as a lecture that Allende gave at the New York Public Library—part of a series of lectures by writers on particular aspects of the craft of writing. Allende was one of a group of writers who were asked why they wrote political novels. Design a poster advertising Allende's speech, being sure to include all pertinent information and to make the poster interesting and eye-catching. ~ **ART**

Inquiry & Research

Allende's Home Work with a group of classmates to prepare an oral report on Chile, Allende's native country. Individual group members can investigate different aspects of Chile's culture and history—for example, its geography, its early history, the military coup of 1973, and the current political and social conditions in the country. Where appropriate, use slides, pictures, maps, charts, and graphs in presenting your report to the class.

More Online: Research Starter
www.mcdougallittell.com

Art Connection

Illustrated Ideas Look at the painting on page 1305. What ideas or details in the essay does the painting help illustrate?

Choices & CHALLENGES

Vocabulary in Action

EXERCISE A: CONTEXT CLUES Write the word that best completes each sentence.

1. "The pen is mightier than the sword" is not a _____; it is quite true.

2. Thomas Paine's widely read pamphlet *Common Sense* spoke so harshly against British _____ of the American colonists that it helped to inspire the American Revolution.

3. The novel *Uncle Tom's Cabin,* written by an abolitionist, created so much antislavery _____ that it is considered one of the causes of the Civil War.

4. Not every change that a book or article may help to bring about is a _____; some are more gradual and subtle alterations of people's perceptions of reality.

5. Rudyard Kipling's writings, which made the British presence in India look both appealing and righteous, were influential in perpetuating Great Britain's _____ attitude toward its colonies.

EXERCISE B: ASSESSMENT PRACTICE Write the letter of the word that is a synonym of each boldfaced word.

1. **exorcise:** (a) maneuver, (b) expel, (c) glorify

2. **pretension:** (a) claim, (b) ability, (c) decision

3. **illusory:** (a) imaginary, (b) evasive, (c) flexible

4. **pathological:** (a) skillful, (b) lasting, (c) sick

5. **narcissistic:** (a) numb, (b) addictive, (c) self-centered

WORDS TO KNOW				
cataclysm	hyperbole	imperialist	pathological	rancor
exorcising	illusory	narcissistic	pretension	repression

Building Vocabulary
For an in-depth study of context clues, see page 938.

Isabel Allende
1942–

Other Works
The House of the Spirits
Of Love and Shadows
Eva Luna
The Stories of Eva Luna

Family Ties Isabel Allende traveled extensively as a child. Born in Peru, she moved to Chile with her mother after her parents' divorce. Although she lost contact with her father, she remained close to his family—especially to her uncle, a prominent politician. After her mother remarried, the family moved again, first to Bolivia, then to Europe and the Middle East, and finally, when Allende was 15, back to Chile. Allende's mother nurtured her creativity by encouraging her to record all her thoughts in a notebook and to draw anything she wanted on a bedroom wall.

Upheaval and Exile A rebellious teenager, Allende quit school early, married, and eventually found a job as a journalist, writing and reporting for television and magazines. By the time she was 30, she felt settled and expected to spend the rest of her life in Chile, but a military coup in 1973 changed her plans dramatically. The Chilean government was overthrown, and Allende's uncle, who was then president, was assassinated. In spite of the widespread violence in Chile, she remained there for a time, secretly helping those who opposed the new regime. After her own life was threatened, however, she fled to Venezuela, where she lived in exile for 13 years before coming to the United States. She currently resides near San Francisco.

Body of Work Allende was in her late 30s before she started writing fiction. After gaining worldwide attention with her first novel, *The House of the Spirits,* she has continued to write in Spanish, but her work has been translated into 27 languages, including English. In 1994, she published an autobiography, entitled *Paula* in memory of her daughter who had died a year earlier.

Writing Workshop

Evaluating a literary work . . .

From Reading to Writing How do you decide what movies to see, what books to read, or what concerts to attend? You might read a **critical review,** an essay in which a writer expresses a personal opinion of a literary or artistic work by referring to some of the elements of that work. The word *critical* does not mean that the writer must find fault; it means that the writer evaluates a work based on certain criteria.

For Your Portfolio

WRITING PROMPT Write a critical review of a literary work based on criteria you establish.

Purpose: To interpret and evaluate
Audience: Persons interested in the work you are reviewing

Basics in a Box

Literary Interpretation at a Glance

Introduction
Introduces the literary work and provides a focused interpretation

Body
Supports the interpretation with evidence from the literary work

Explanation

Proof

Proof

Proof

Conclusion
Summarizes the interpretation

RUBRIC Standards for Writing

A successful critical review should

- identify the work you are reviewing
- briefly tell what the work is about
- state your opinions clearly
- state the criteria by which you judged the work
- use enough details from the work to support your review
- summarize your opinion

Analyzing a Student Model

Ali Nagib
New Trier High School

"Six Feet of the Country"

    "Six Feet of the Country" is a politically and personally based short story written by Nadine Gordimer. In the story, the author draws on her experience as a white woman during the time of apartheid in South Africa to examine the many flaws and injustices inherent in that system. Gordimer wrote this story before apartheid was ever significantly challenged. Because her society's racial attitudes are at the forefront of her story, the story must be judged on how effectively she illustrates them. Her story succeeds because, while bringing the problems of her society to light, she gives her characters very human dimensions. They are neither totally good nor totally evil but mixtures of good intentions, blindness to injustice, and petty concerns. Had Gordimer preached about the injustice of apartheid, people probably would have been turned off by her message. Instead, she uses subtlety and ambiguity in creating both white and black characters. She presents an engaging story—not a sermon.

    The main character, the narrator, is a man living with his wife on an isolated farmstead outside of Johannesburg during the 1950s. His wife manages the farm with the help of several black farmhands. The narrator commutes to Johannesburg and is home evenings and weekends. In the narrator, Gordimer has created a character with whom any white South African of the time could identify. Through him, Gordimer shows the attitudes of many white South Africans.

    The narrator is by no means an oppressor. He is not a slave-owner, nor is he a cruel master. In fact, Gordimer shows that the scenario in South Africa was not treacherous, only unjust. Nonetheless, the narrator's true feelings are ambiguous. He treats his workers well, and he helps them in many ways, as does his wife. From his perspective, however, they are more like children than adults:

> [The workers] brew their sour beer without the fear of police raids. In fact, we've always rather prided ourselves that the poor devils have nothing much to fear, being with us; Lerice even keeps an eye on their children, with all the competence of a woman who has never had a child of her own, and she certainly doctors them all—children and adults—like babies whenever they happen to be sick.

RUBRIC
IN ACTION

❶ Identifies the work being reviewed

❷ States the criteria

❸ States a general opinion of the work based on the criteria

❹ This writer begins to tell what the work is about.
Another Option:
· Give a complete summary of the work.

❺ Uses short quotes to support the statements about the narrator's view of the workers

He acts within the system of apartheid and believes in its values. In response to dealing with the dead body of Petrus's brother, the narrator laments, "Now, I'm the one who'll have to do all the dirty work, I suppose." He is obviously annoyed with the system, but he accepts its injustice and makes no attempt to change it. By highlighting this attitude, Gordimer is clearly trying to inspire change.

While creating a sympathetic narrator with whom readers can identify, the author also shows him the white South Africans' misguided belief that what they were doing was perfectly all right, and even moral. They treated the blacks as lower-class citizens and never questioned the inequity they perpetuated. In Gordimer's story, it is hard to tell if a white South African is a bigot or a well-meaning, ignorant person. "There are so many black faces—surely one will do?" asks the health official when the narrator tries to retrieve the real body of Petrus's brother. Is this a complete lack of respect bred of hatred, or a pathetic ignorance arising from a long-standing cultural bias? By showing the racial attitudes without comments, Gordimer effectively leads readers to see the injustice for themselves.

Another issue that Gordimer brings out is how the blacks' fear and distrust due to oppression have made them seemingly accept their status. She portrays the main black character, Petrus, as a simple-minded worker who has lived under oppression for so long that he feels he can do nothing to change it. Gordimer illustrates the blacks' mistrustful attitude when the workers won't ask their employers for help even to save a man's life. "You would think they would have felt they could tell *us,*" exclaims Lerice in response to the workers' fear. Gordimer shows how neither group understands the other.

In "Six Feet of the Country," Gordimer successfully creates interesting, realistic characters. She also effectively illustrates the injustice of apartheid. Finally, she expresses a larger theme relevant to all readers: It is easy to accept the status quo, even a harmful or unjust one. But it can be detrimental to individuals and society to do so.

❻ Uses details from the work to support the review

❼ Provides evidence that the author effectively illustrates the society's racial attitudes

❽ Uses a quote to support a statement about the work

❾ Restates the writer's original opinion that Gordimer's writing is successful

Another Option:
· Summarize the points of the review.

1. Your Working Portfolio 📁
Build on one of the **Writing Options** you completed earlier in this unit:

• **Paragraph Critique,** p. 1273

• **Critical Review,** p. 1287

• **Story Review,** p. 1300

• **Letter to Allende,** p. 1309

2. Your Preferences
What types of literature do you enjoy most? Science fiction? Stories with a foreign setting? Plays? Poetry? Choose from a type of literature that you like to read.

3. Critics' Conference
Discuss the work you chose with a small group of classmates. Find out how others reacted to it and why.

Writing Your Critical Review

The critic should describe, and not prescribe.
Eugène Ionesco

❶ Prewriting

Begin by choosing a literary work about which you have a strong opinion. You might choose a work you like or one you strongly dislike. See the **Idea Bank** in the margin for more suggestions. After you choose a work to review, follow the steps below.

Planning Your Critical Review

▶ **1. Identify key elements of your subject.** Consider the theme, characters, plot, and setting of a story you plan to review. If you choose a poem or a drama, you will want to examine such elements as the rhythm and language of a poem or the dialogue and actions of a drama.

▶ **2. Establish criteria for evaluation.** How do you decide what makes an element especially strong or weak? By stating that you believe the theme is expressed clearly through the actions of the characters, for example, you are establishing criteria.

▶ **3. Analyze each element of your subject.** Now examine each element and make some notes about the way the literary work handled that element. As you make your notes, be sure to list specific things in the work that support your opinion. You might make a chart like this one.

Element	Critique	Support
plot		
character		

▶ **4. Choose a focus.** Your review doesn't need to evaluate every element in the work. After you have examined most elements, you can choose to focus on one or two. Look for strengths and weaknesses in each area you choose.

❷ Drafting

Begin writing even if you haven't worked out all the details of your opinion about the work. Some of your ideas will become clearer as you draft. Just keep going. You can add details and refine your ideas as you revise.

Start out by identifying the title, author, and type of work, and state a general **opinion** of it. Once you are comfortable with your ideas, begin reworking your material into a more formal review format.

In the body of the review, let your subject guide your **organization.** For a story, you might **summarize** the plot and then state the **criteria** by which you measured the work. Then **evaluate** the various elements of the work that fit your criteria. For a poem, you could **describe the work as a whole,** state the criteria for evaluation, and then address those specific elements in turn. Always **support your opinions** with specific details or examples. End by summing up your opinion.

Ask Your Peer Reader

- How would you summarize my opinions about this work?

- What elements of this work did I analyze? Should I have analyzed any other elements?

- Which supporting example is most convincing?

❸ Revising

TARGET SKILL ▶ USING APPOSITIVES You can use appositive phrases in your review to include important details without being wordy. An appositive phrase renames a noun by clarifying it or giving additional information about the noun.

> The main character ~~is~~ the narrator, ~~He~~ is a man living with his wife
>
> on an isolated farmstead outside of Johannesburg during the 1950s.

❹ Editing and Proofreading

TARGET SKILL ▶ MODIFIER PLACEMENT Modifiers can help make your review specific and interesting. Some modifiers function as adjectives and some function as adverbs. Be sure to place each modifier, whether it is a word or a phrase, close to the word it modifies. Beware of dangling modifiers, which do not clearly modify anything in a sentence or appear to modify words that they cannot sensibly modify.

> By showing the racial attitudes without comments, *Gordimer leads to* readers see the
>
> injustice for themselves ~~effectively.~~
>
> Another issue that Gordimer brings out is how the blacks' fear
>
> and distrust have made them seemingly *accept* ~~except~~ their status
>
> ~~due to oppression.~~ She offers a mirror to the black south africans
>
> of the system and tries to convince them to change it.

Mystified by modifier placement?

See the **Grammar Handbook**

Using Modifiers Correctly, pp. 1399–1400

Publishing IDEAS

- Meet with classmates who wrote reviews of the same work. Compare your class-mates' reviews to your own reactions.

- Submit your review to an online Web site about the author or to the school newspaper or literary magazine.

More Online: Publishing Options www.mcdougallittell.com

❺ Reflecting

FOR YOUR WORKING PORTFOLIO Would you recommend the story you reviewed? How would your audience affect your recommendation? Attach your answers to your finished work. Save your critical review in your **Working Portfolio.**

Read this paragraph from the first draft of a critical review. The underlined sections may include the following kinds of errors:

- **comma errors**
- **misplaced modifiers**
- **capitalization errors**
- **incorrect possessive forms**

For each underlined section, choose the revision that most improves the writing.

The painting *Caesar Asks for Fries with His Hot Dog* is representative of the work by the <u>Irish-born british artist Francis Kelly.</u> <u>Kelly a retired history teacher often</u> depicts historical figures in modern situations. In *Caesar*, Kelly depicts the Roman emperor in line at a fast-food restaurant. As in many of <u>Kelly's</u> paintings, humor and pathos are essential elements. <u>In this painting, Caesar appears undecided as he addresses the cashier wearing a toga and sandals.</u> <u>The cashier, a teenaged girl seems</u> bored to tears as she waits. The <u>paintings</u> humor makes it impossible to look at the image without smiling.
(1) ... (2) ... (3) ... (4) ... (5) ... (6)

---

1. A. Irish-Born British Artist Francis Kelly
B. Irish-born British Artist Francis Kelly
C. Irish-born British artist Francis Kelly
D. Correct as is

2. A. Kelly, a retired history teacher often
B. Kelly a retired history teacher, often
C. Kelly, a retired history teacher, often
D. Correct as is

3. A. Kellys
B. Kellie's
C. Kellys'
D. Correct as is

4. A. In this painting, Caesar, wearing a toga and sandals, appears undecided as he addresses the cashier.
B. In this painting, wearing a toga and sandals, Caesar appears undecided as he addresses the cashier.
C. In this painting, Caesar appears undecided, wearing a toga and sandals, as he addresses the cashier.
D. Correct as is

5. A. The cashier a teenaged girl seems
B. The cashier, a teenaged girl, seems
C. The cashier a teenaged girl, seems
D. Correct as is

6. A. painting's
B. paintings'
C. painting
D. Correct as is

Need extra help?

See the **Grammar Handbook**

Capitalization Chart, p. 1415

Possessive Nouns, p. 1392

Punctuation Chart, pp. 1413–1414

Using Modifiers Correctly, pp. 1399–1400

The Logic of Words

Good writers are always drawing our attention to connections that we may not have noticed between things, people, and experiences. One way they do so is by making comparisons, or **analogies.** In the following excerpt from the poem "Digging," for example, Seamus Heaney draws an analogy between the work and tools of a turf cutter and the work and tools of a poet. The speaker says that the poet's pen is analogous, or similar, to the turf cutter's spade.

> The cold smell of potato mold, the
>   squelch and slap
> Of soggy peat, the curt cuts of an edge
> Through living roots awaken in my head.
> But I've no spade to follow men like them.
>
> Between my finger and my thumb
> The squat pen rests.
> I'll dig with it.
>
> —Seamus Heaney, "Digging"

Strategies for Building Vocabulary

A word analogy states that the relationship between one pair of words or things is similar to the relationship between another pair. Word analogies are often stated as formulas. Here is the formula for Heaney's analogy:

PEN : POET :: spade : turf cutter

This analogy is based on the relationship of tools to the workers who use them. To read the formula, you would say, "A pen *is to* a poet *as* a spade *is to* a turf cutter."

❶ **Solve Test Analogies** Word analogies often appear in standardized tests. One type of test analogy consists of a formula in which one word is missing, as in this example:

THERMOMETER : TEMPERATURE :: odometer :

_____
(a) heat, (b) automobile, (c) distance,
(d) numerals

To solve such an analogy, first identify the relationship between the first pair of words. In this example, the relationship is one of measure, since a thermometer measures temperature. Then ask yourself, What does an odometer measure? The answer is (c) *distance.*

In another type of test analogy, you must select a pair of words to complete the analogy:

EXHIBIT : MUSEUM ::
(a) marsupial : mammal, (b) enthrall : captivate,
(c) clean : immaculate, (d) merchandise : store

To solve an analogy of this type, identify the

relationship between the first two words, and then find the corresponding relationship among the answer choices. In this case, an exhibit is found in a museum; so the relationship is one of location. Which pair of words also shows a location relationship? The answer is (d) because merchandise is found in a store.

❷ **Distinguish Among Types of Analogies** The chart below identifies some other relationships you might encounter in test analogies.

Common Relationships in Analogies		
Type	**Example**	**Relationships**
Cause to Effect	DROUGHT : FAMINE	is the cause of
Part to Whole	KNOB : DOOR	is a part of
Antonyms	OVERT : COVERT	is opposite in meaning to
Degree of Intensity	JOY : EXULTATION	is less (or more) intense
Manner	WORK : ASSIDUOUSLY	how
Characteristic to Object (or Person)	STINGINESS : MISER	is a quality of
Classification	LATIN : LANGUAGE	is a type of
Location	DESK : OFFICE	is found in

EXERCISE Complete each analogy, identifying the relationship between the words in each pair.

1. SUBMISSIVE : SERVANT :: rebellious : _____
2. POSITIVE : NEGATIVE :: laconic : _____
3. NILE : AFRICA :: Mississippi : _____
4. TRANSPARENCY : GLASS :: fluidity : _____
5. GRANITE : STONE :: cedar : _____

Grammar from Literature

Sentences can be expanded in a number of ways. Writers sometimes add words between the subject and the verb. The inserted structure is called an interrupter, and it creates what is known as a subject-verb split. Writers use subject-verb splits to add detail, explain relationships, and create sentence variety and rhythm. The examples below from William Trevor's "The Distant Past" illustrate the variety of structures that may be used in subject-verb splits.

> adverb
> **The Middletons, naturally, didn't discuss these rebuffs.**
>
> prepositional phrase
> **The brown, soda and currant breads of Murphy-Flood's bakery were declared to be delicious.**
>
> appositive
> **The Middletons, children then, had been locked with their mother and father and an aunt into an upstairs room.**
>
> participial phrase
> **Mr. Healy, red-faced and short-haired, spoke casually in his Cocktail Room, making midday conversation.**
>
> adjective clause
> **The visitors who came to town heard about the Middletons and were impressed.**

Using Subject-Verb Splits in Your Writing Look for opportunities in your own writing to vary sentence structure and add detail by inserting information as a subject-verb split. Sometimes, you can streamline wording by combining sentences, inserting information from one sentence as a subject-verb split into an another sentence.

> ORIGINAL
> **Often writers hope to do more than entertain. This is true of those who comment on social issues.**
>
> REVISED
> **Often writers who comment on social issues hope to do more than entertain.**

Usage Tip When using a subject-verb split, make sure that the verb agrees with the subject in number. Nouns in an interrupter do not affect subject-verb agreement.

> INCORRECT   subject   noun
> **The pro-British stand of the Middletons**
> verb
> **were often unpopular in the community.**
>
> CORRECT   subject   noun
> **The pro-British stand of the Middletons**
> verb
> **was often unpopular in the community.**

The subject, *stand,* is singular, so *was* is the correct verb.

Punctuation Tip Nonessential interrupters should be set off with commas; essential interrupters should not. A nonessential interrupter adds extra detail to a sentence in which the meaning is already complete. An essential interrupter is part of the main idea of a sentence.

> nonessential
> **Fat Driscoll, the town butcher, was the man who liked to joke around with the Middletons.**
>
> essential
> **The man who liked to joke around with the Middletons was Fat Driscoll.**

WRITING EXERCISE Combine each pair of sentences. Add the information in the second sentence to the first as a subject-verb split of the type indicated in parentheses. Eliminate words as necessary.

1. "The Distant Past" deals with conflict in Ireland. It is a story by William Trevor. (appositive)
2. The story is set in an area not far from Northern Ireland. The story covers a period of about 40 years. (adjective clause)
3. The Middletons become unpopular with their neighbors. The Middletons remain loyal to Britain. (participial phrase)
4. "The First Year of My Life" is a humorous example of satire. The story is written from an infant's viewpoint. (adjective clause)
5. Muriel Spark goes on to make fun of politicians. First, she makes some sarcastic comments about war. (adverb phrase)

GRAMMAR EXERCISE Rewrite the sentences below, correcting any errors in punctuation and usage.

1. Ireland, the birthplace of many famous writers, have had a history of conflicts with Great Britain.
2. These conflicts at the cost of many lives have had an important influence on Irish literature.
3. In the 1920s an Irish writer, named Sean O'Casey, wrote powerful plays about civil war in Ireland.
4. Modern British writers, including Muriel Spark, inspires readers with moving stories about war.

Contemporary Voices

The selections in this unit depict contemporary conflicts, characters, and speakers who gain insights into life by observing the world. How did you respond to the perspectives presented? Which of the selections caused you to think more about particular problems or to change your own attitudes? Choose one or more of the options in each of the following sections to help you answer these questions and further analyze your reactions as a reader.

Reflecting on the Unit

OPTION 1

Analyzing Appearance and Reality Get together with a group of classmates and discuss how the Part 1 title "Appearance and Reality" applies to each selection in this part. Compare your conclusions with those of other groups.

OPTION 2

Comparing and Contrasting The selections in Part 2 of this unit focus on social and political issues, revealing how individuals are affected by conflict. Select two of these individuals that you find most memorable. With a partner, role-play a conversation in which the two reflect on their experiences with conflict. You may also want to have them comment on each other's words and actions, as depicted in the selections.

OPTION 3

Applying a Quotation Think about the quotation from George Orwell's novel *1984* that introduces this unit: "It was a bright cold day in April, and the clocks were striking thirteen." Which selection in the unit do you think best reflects the tone and mood of Orwell's sentence? Write a paragraph explaining your opinion.

Self ASSESSMENT

📖 **READER'S NOTEBOOK**

Recall the thoughts and impressions that the selections in this unit conveyed to you. Then, working with a small group of classmates, create a cluster diagram for each part of the unit—"Appearance and Reality"and "Culture and Conflict." In each diagram, record the messages, ideas, and insights you and your group members received from the selections.

Reviewing Literary Concepts

OPTION 1

Examining Point of View With a group, review the fictional works in this unit and list the point of view used in each. Why do you think each writer chose that particular point of view? If the point of view were changed in each story, how would this alter its effectiveness? Discuss these questions with your group members.

OPTION 2

Analyzing Style A writer's style is an expression of his or her individuality. Although writers may have similar styles, there are usually certain characteristics that distinguish each writer's work from the work of others. With a small group of classmates, review the selections in this unit, choosing from each a passage that you think exemplifies the writer's style. Then quiz other groups by reading each a passage and asking them to identify the writer and the selection. Allow groups to glance over the Table of Contents if they need help recalling the names of the writers and selections.

Self ASSESSMENT

READER'S NOTEBOOK

Copy the following list of literary terms covered in this unit. Put a question mark next to each term that you do not fully understand. Then consult the **Glossary of Literary Terms** (page 1328) to clarify meanings of the terms you've marked.

setting	consonance
kinesthetic imagery	assonance
	imagery
point of view	mood
theme	diction
repetition	dialogue
alliteration	

🗁 Building Your Portfolio

• **Writing Options** Some of the Writing Options in this unit asked you to reflect on experiences and people's reactions to them—either your own or those of characters or speakers in the selections. Look over your responses and select one or two pieces that you think give the best accounts of experiences and reactions. Write a short note explaining why you think those pieces are successful. Add the pieces and the note to your **Presentation Portfolio.** 🗁

• **Writing Workshop** In this unit, you wrote a Critical Review in response to a piece of literature. Reread your review and assess the quality of your writing. What do you see as the strengths of the review? the weaknesses? Attach a note indicating your evaluation, and place the writing in your **Presentation Portfolio.** 🗁

• **Additional Activities** Reflect on any assignments you completed under **Activities & Explorations** and **Inquiry & Research.** Keep a record in your portfolio of any assignments that you think are worth expanding into a more comprehensive project.

Self ASSESSMENT

READER'S NOTEBOOK

At this stage, the contents of your portfolio should represent the work of an entire year. Review the pieces in your portfolio and choose three of your best works—one done in the fall, one in the winter, and one in the spring. Write a note explaining what these works reveal about your progress and abilities as a writer.

Setting GOALS

Reflect on all the goals that you set for yourself during the course of the year. Which goals did you reach? Which goals seem nearly within your reach? Which goals seem as far away as ever? Write an evaluation of your progress this year, and identify three goals for the future.

Nervous Conditions

TSITSI DANGAREMBGA

A young girl must choose between her own African heritage and the education provided by the British in Zimbabwe in the 1960s. The oldest daughter of a native Shona family living in the British colony of Rhodesia (now Zimbabwe), Tambudzai is intent on getting an education and developing her independence. To do so, she must overcome the autocratic authority exercised by the men in her family and the racism and patriarchy of the colonial culture.

These thematically related readings are provided along with *Nervous Conditions*:

Professions for Women
BY VIRGINIA WOOLF

Back to School
BY ANDREA LEE

from **Hunger of Memory**
BY RICHARD RODRIGUEZ

Losing a Language
BY W. S. MERWIN

Points of View
BY LUCINDA ROY

The Old Chief Mshlanga
BY DORIS LESSING

Young Africa's Plea
BY DENNIS OSADEBAY

And Even *More* . . .

When Rain Clouds Gather

BESSIE HEAD

In this novel from Botswana, the characters' personal feelings of love, bitterness, and hope reveal themselves in the midst of a village's efforts to survive and prosper. This book is also part of the *Literature Connections* series published by McDougal Littell.

Books
July's People
NADINE GORDIMER
This novella is set in an unspecified future time when, in an ironic reversal, white people are servants of black people.

African Laughter: Four Visits to Zimbabwe
DORIS LESSING
In this book, the author recounts her observations and experiences during four visits to Zimbabwe between 1982 and 1992.

LITERATURE CONNECTIONS
Things Fall Apart

CHINUA ACHEBE

Set in an Ibo village in Nigeria at the turn of the century, the story of Okonkwo unfolds like a Greek tragedy, as traditional Ibo customs are challenged by new European ways. When Okonkwo, through a series of incidents, finds himself alienated from his clansmen, he is plunged into despair. The novel is a profound meditation on the psychological disintegration that occurs as the ties of kinship unravel in a traditional society.

These thematically related readings are provided along with *Things Fall Apart:*

The Second Coming
BY WILLIAM BUTLER YEATS

Genesis 22: 1–19 The Sacrifice of Isaac
THE BIBLE

Mother Was a Great Man
BY CATHERINE OBIANUJU ACHOLONU

Prayer to Masks
BY LEOPOLD SEDAR SENGHOR

Shooting an Elephant
BY GEORGE ORWELL

The Significance of a Veteran's Day
BY SIMON ORTIZ

Able, Baker, Charlie, Dog
BY STEPHANIE VAUGHN

Exiles
BY MARK STRAND

And Even *More* . . .

Books
The Caretaker
HAROLD PINTER
This classic play combines absurdity and reality to reveal the tensions and struggles of its characters.

Death of a Naturalist
SEAMUS HEANEY
In this volume of Heaney's early poems, the poet celebrates different aspects of rustic life and reveals his strong tie to the farmlands of his youth.

Other Media
Doris Lessing Reads Her Short Stories
Jeffrey Norton Publishers.
(AUDIOCASSETTE)

The Poetry and Voice of Ted Hughes
Caedmon.
(AUDIOCASSETTE)

A World of Ideas
PBS Video, 1988. Bill Moyers interviews Chinua Achebe.
(VIDEOCASSETTE)

The House of the Spirits
Live Home Video, 1993. Film adaptation of Isabel Allende's novel.
(VIDEOCASSETTE)

Student *Resource Bank*

Reading for Different Purposes

You read for many different reasons. In a single day, you might read a short story for fun, a textbook for information to help you pass a test, and a weather map to find out if it will rain. For every type of reading, there are specific strategies that can help you understand and remember the material. This handbook will help you become a better reader in school, at home, and on the job.

Reading Literature

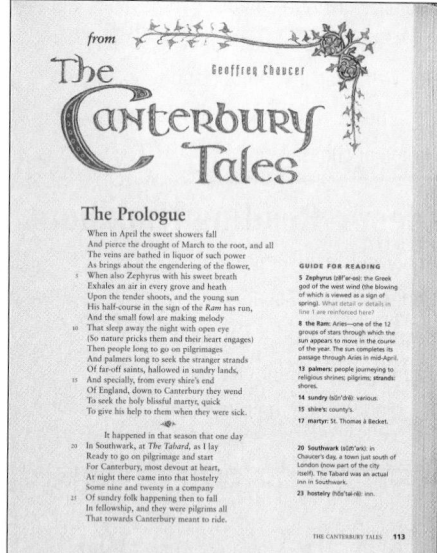

Before Reading

- Set a **purpose** for reading. Are you reading as part of an assignment or for fun? What do you want to learn? Establishing a purpose will help you focus.
- **Preview** the work by looking at the title and any images and captions. Try to **predict** what the work will be about.
- Ask yourself if you can **connect** the subject matter with what you already know.

During Reading

- **Check your understanding** of what you read. Can you restate the plot in your own words?
- Try to **connect** what you're reading to your own life. Have you experienced similar events or emotions?

- **Question** what's happening. You may wonder about events and characters' feelings.
- **Visualize** or create a mental picture of what the author describes.
- **Pause** from time to time to predict what will happen next.

After Reading

- **Review** your predictions. Were they correct?
- Try to **summarize** the work, expressing the **main idea** or the basic plot.
- **Reflect on** and evaluate what you have read. Did the reading fulfill your purpose?
- To **clarify** your understanding, write down opinions or thoughts about the work, or discuss it with someone.

Reading for Information

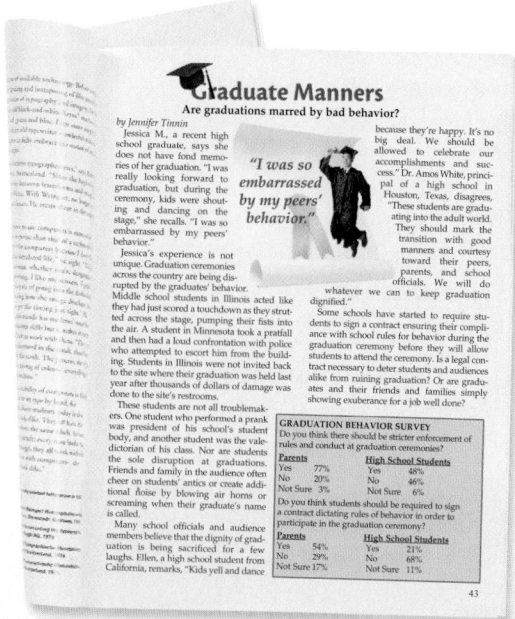

Set a Purpose for Reading

- Decide why you are reading the material—to study for a test, to do research, or to find out more about a topic that interests you.
- Use your **purpose** to determine how detailed your **notes** will be.

Look at Design Features

- Look at the **title** and **subheads** and at **boldfaced words** or phrases, **boxed text,** and any other text that is highlighted in some way.
- Use these **text organizers** for help in previewing the text and identifying the main ideas.
- Study **photographs, maps, charts,** and **captions.**

Notice Text Structures and Patterns

- Does the text make **comparisons?** Does it describe **causes and effects?** Is there a **sequence** of events?
- Look for **signal words** such as *same, different, because, first,* and *then.* They can reveal the material's organizational pattern.

Read Slowly and Carefully

- **Take notes** on the main ideas. State the information in your own words.
- Map the information by using a word web or another **graphic organizer.**
- Notice **unfamiliar words.** These are sometimes defined in the text.
- If there are **questions** accompanying the text, be sure that you can answer them.

Evaluate the Information

- Think about what you have read. Does the text make sense? Is it complete?
- **Summarize** the information—state the main points in just a few words.

Functional Reading

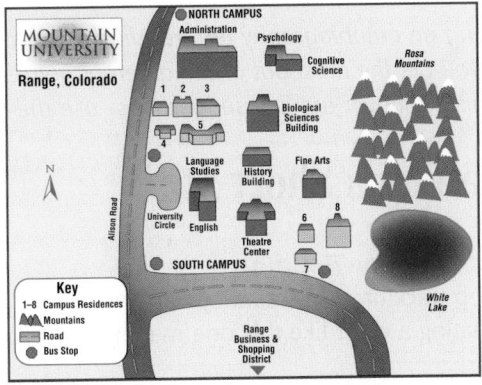

Identify the Audience, Source, and Purpose

- Look for clues that tell you for whom the document is intended. Is there an **address** or a **title?** Does the information in the document affect you?
- Look for clues that tell you who created the document. Is the **source** likely to be **reliable?**
- Think about the **purpose** of the document. Is it to show you how to do something? to warn you about something? to tell you about community events?

Read Carefully

- Notice **headings** or **rules** that separate one section from another.
- Look for numbers or letters that signal steps in a **sequence.** If you are reading directions, read them all the way through at least once before performing the steps.
- Examine any charts, photographs, or other **visuals** and their captions.
- **Reread** complex instructions if necessary.

Evaluate the Information

- Think about whether you have found the information you need.
- Look for telephone numbers, street addresses, or e-mail addresses of places where you could find more information.

Reading Different Genres

Reading an autobiography and reading a poem require different skills. Here are some tips to help you get the most out of the different genres, or types, of literature you read. The graphic organizers shown are just suggestions—use the note-taking method that works best for you.

Reading a Short Story

Strategies for Reading

- Keep track of events as they happen. Creating a chart like this one may help you.

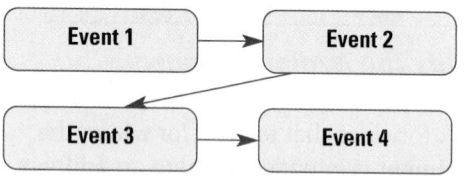

- From the details the writer provides, **visualize** the characters. **Predict** what they might do next.

- Look for specific adjectives that help you visualize the **setting**—the time and place in which events occur.

Reading a Poem

Strategies for Reading

- Notice the **form** of the poem, or the number of its lines and their shape on the page.

- Read the poem aloud a few times. Listen for **rhymes** and **rhythms.**

- Visualize the **images** and **comparisons.**

- Connect with the poem by asking yourself what **message** the poet is trying to send.

- Create a word web or other graphic organizer to record your reactions and questions.

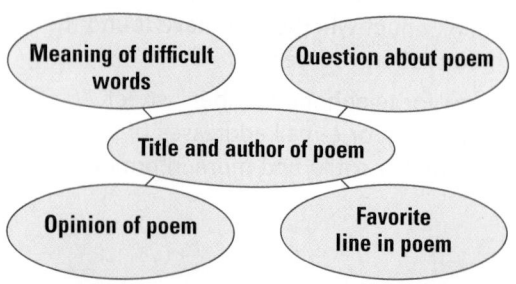

Reading an Epic

Strategies for Reading

- Since an epic is a long narrative poem that celebrates a hero's deeds, it's important to identify the **hero.** What virtues and flaws does this person have?

- Notice **rhythms** and **repetitions.** Most epics were memorized and then told or even sung aloud.

- Try to **visualize** the actions described in the epic. Which passages might make the audience cheer, boo, or gasp in surprise?

- Think about the **values** and **themes** of the epic. Which quality is valued over all others? courage? virtue? true love? Does the epic describe a battle between good and evil?

Reading Nonfiction

Strategies for Reading

- If you are reading a biography or autobiography, keep track of the people who are mentioned. You may want to sketch a family tree or a word web.

- When reading an essay, **evaluate** the writer's ideas and reasoning. Does the writer support opinions with facts?

- When reading an article or interview, **skim** it first to learn what its subject is. Look at any **headings** or **captions.** Then read slowly, looking for the **main idea.** Use a chart like this one to help you.

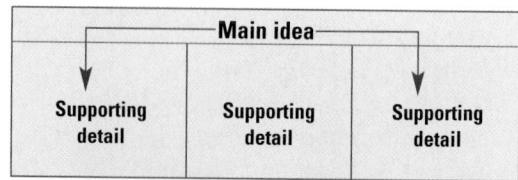

Reading Different Formats

These strategies will help you when you need to do research, learn about current events, or just find out more about a topic that interests you.

Reading Online Text

Strategies for Reading

- Notice the page's **Web address,** sometimes called a URL. You may want to make a note of it if you will need to return to that page. Most Web addresses begin with the coding http://www.

- Read the **title** of the page to get a general idea of what topics the page covers.

- Notice **links** to related pages. Links are often "buttons" or underlined words. Clicking on a link will take you to a different page—one that may or may not have been created by the same person or organization.

- Look for a **menu bar** along the top, bottom, or side of the page. This gives you links to other parts of the Web site.

- Notice any **source citations.** Some sites tell you where their information is from, enabling you to judge its reliability.

- Write down **important ideas and details.** Try to restate the text in your own words. Then decide whether you need to check other sources.

Reading a Newspaper or Magazine Article

Strategies for Reading

- Read the **headline** and any **subheads** to learn what the article is about and how it is organized.

- Notice any photographs, charts, graphs, or other **visuals.** Read their **captions.** Be sure you understand how the visuals and the main text are related.

- Notice any **quotations.** Think about whether the people who are quoted are likely to be reliable authorities on the topic.

Reading an Encyclopedia Article

Strategies for Reading

- Read the **headline** and any **subheads** to make sure that the article covers the topic of interest to you.

- Look at **visuals** and read their **captions.** Some online or CD-ROM encyclopedias also include sound files, animated maps, or short movies.

- Pay attention to how the article is organized. You may want to **skim** the article, or read it quickly, as you look for **key words** related to your topic. Once you find the information you need, read slowly and carefully.

- Watch for a **"see also"** or **"related articles"** section, or—if the encyclopedia is online—for highlighted links. These features direct you to additional articles that include information on your subject.

Enriching Your Vocabulary

Context Clues

One way to figure out the meaning of a word you don't know is by using context clues. The context of a word consists of the punctuation marks, other words, sentences, and paragraphs that surround the word.

General Context Sometimes you need to read all the information in the sentence or paragraph in order to infer the meaning of an unfamiliar word. The underlined words below give clues to the meaning of the word in boldface type.

> Since <u>he has received perfect scores on all of the tests</u>, I'd say his **forte** is definitely history.

Definition Clues Often a difficult word will be followed by its definition. Commas, dashes, or other punctuation marks may signal a definition.

> **Tuberculosis**—<u>a type of lung disease</u>— was once one of the most common causes of death in the world.

Restatement Clues Sometimes a writer restates a word or term in easier language. Commas, dashes, or other punctuation may signal restatement clues, as may expressions such as *that is, in other words,* and *or.*

> Ellen **scrutinized** the bracelet before she bought it; <u>that is, she looked at it closely from every possible angle</u>.

Example Clues Sometimes writers suggest the meaning of a word with one or two examples.

> During the 1500s, ships from the Americas introduced many important **commodities** to the rest of the world, including <u>potatoes, tobacco, corn, gold, and silver</u>.

Comparison Clues Sometimes a word's meaning is suggested by a comparison. *Like* and *as* are words that signal comparison clues.

> We snorkeled in water that was as **translucent** <u>as a window</u>.

Contrast Clues Sometimes writers point out differences between things or ideas. Contrast clues are often signaled by such words as *although, but, however, unlike,* and *in contrast to.*

> Edward is usually very focused during rehearsals, <u>but</u> today he seemed **preoccupied.**

Idioms and Slang An idiom is an expression whose overall meaning is different from the meaning of the individual words. Slang is informal language that comprises both made-up words and ordinary words that carry different meanings than in formal English. Use context clues to figure out the meaning of idioms and slang.

> With only seconds left before the bell, Alison made it to class **by the skin of her teeth.** (idiom)

> We both thought the movie was really **cool.** (slang)

TIP One way to clarify your understanding of a word is to write a sentence using that word. Even better, use one of the context-clue strategies in your sentence. For example, include a restatement or definition clue.

For more about context clues, see page 938.

Word Parts

If you know base words, roots, and affixes—that is, prefixes and suffixes—you can figure out the meanings of many new words.

Base Words A **base word** is a word that can stand alone. Other words or word parts can be added to base words to form new words.

Roots Many English words contain roots that come from older languages, such as Greek, Latin, and Old English. A **root** is a word part to which a prefix, a suffix, and/or another root must be added. Knowing the meaning of a word's root or roots can help you figure out the word's meaning.

Root	Meaning	Examples
aristo (Greek)	best	aristocracy, aristocrat
micro (Greek)	small	microphone, microscope
cont (Latin)	to join, unite	continent, continue
dur (Latin)	to harden, hold out	durable, duration
ped (Latin)	foot	pedal, pedestrian
hus (Old English)	house	husband, husbandry
lor(e)n (Old English)	lost	forlorn, lovelorn

Prefixes A **prefix** is a word part that appears at the beginning of a base word or another word part. Attaching a prefix to an existing word usually changes the meaning of that word. Familiarizing yourself with the meanings of common prefixes can help you be prepared to figure out the meanings of unfamiliar words.

Prefix	Meaning	Examples
de-	from, away, off	decaffeinated, deconstruct
hemi-	half	hemicycle, hemisphere
mal-	bad, ill	maladjusted, malnutrition
multi-	many, much	multicolored, multiracial
pre-	before	predispose, preview
sub-	under, below	submarine, substandard

Suffixes A **suffix** is a word part attached to the end of a base word or another word part. Attaching a suffix to an existing word may alter the word's meaning. However, a suffix does not change a word's meaning when it is added as follows:

- to a noun to change the number
- to a verb to change the tense
- to an adjective to change the degree of comparison
- to an adverb to show how

Suffix	Purpose	Examples
-s, -es	to change the number of a noun	application + s, applications
-ed, -ing	to change verb tense	breach + ed, breached breach + ing, breaching
-er, -est	to change the degree of comparison in modifiers	tall + er, taller tall + est, tallest
-ly	to show how	quick + ly, quickly

Other suffixes are added to a root or base word to change the word's meaning. These suffixes can also be used to change the word's part of speech.

Suffix	Meaning	Examples
-or	person or thing that	dictator, elevator
-able	capable of being	curable, understandable
-ize	to make	dramatize, energize

To infer the meaning of an unfamiliar word from its parts, follow these steps:

- Divide the word into parts. Think of other words you know that share the same root(s) or base word.
- Ask, Do these words have the same or similar meanings?
- Consider the meanings of any prefixes or suffixes in the unfamiliar word.
- From the meanings of the word's parts, predict what the word means.
- Check the context of the sentence and consult a dictionary or glossary to find out whether your prediction is correct.

For more about root words, see page 432; for more about prefixes and suffixes, see page 1104.

Word Origins

When you study a word's origin and history, you find out when, where, and how the word came to be. A complete dictionary entry includes each word's history.

dra•ma (drä′mə) *n.* 1. A work that is meant to be performed by actors. 2. Theatrical works of a certain type or period in history. [Late Latin *drāma, drāmat-,* from Greek *drān,* to do or perform.]

This entry shows you that the earliest form of the word *drama* was the Greek word *drān.*

Word Families Words that have the same root have related meanings. Such words make up a word family. The charts below show common Greek and Latin roots. Notice how the meanings of the English words are related to the meanings of their roots.

Greek Root: *soph,* wise

> **English: philosophy** "love of wisdom"; the study of logic and basic truths
>
> **sophisticated** worldly, refined, or complex
>
> **sophomore** "wise fool"; a student in the second year of high school or college

Latin Root: *struct,* to build

> **English: construct** to build
>
> **destructive** wanting to ruin or eliminate something
>
> **structure** a building

Latin Root: *vac,* empty

> **English: evacuate** to empty or remove the contents of
>
> **vacant** containing nothing; empty
>
> **vacuum** a space empty of matter

TIP Once you recognize a root in one English word, you will notice the same root in other words—members of the same word family. Because these words developed from the same root, they are similar in meaning.

Foreign Words Some foreign words that enter the English language keep their original form.

Algonquian (family of Native American languages)	Dutch	Gaelic (language of Ireland and Scotland)	Spanish
Massachusetts	dock	bog	alligator
moccasins	grab	clan	canyon
moose	lottery	glamour	cargo
raccoon	rant	pet	patio
skunk	skate	smithereens	stampede
tomahawk	waffle	trousers	vanilla

For more about word families and researching word origins, see page 206.

Synonyms and Antonyms

When you read, pay attention to the precise words a writer uses.

Synonyms A **synonym** is a word that has the same or almost the same meaning as another word. Read each set of synonyms listed below:

> awe/wonder
> extra/surplus
> generate/produce
> laugh/chuckle
> possible/likely
> rug/carpet
> scared/frightened
> yell/shout

TIP You can find synonyms in a thesaurus or dictionary. In a dictionary, synonyms are often given following the definition of a word.

Antonyms An **antonym** is a word with a meaning opposite that of another word. Read each set of antonyms listed below:

> bland/tasty
> create/destroy
> ferocious/gentle
> friend/enemy
> graceful/clumsy
> temporary/permanent
> unique/common
> whisper/scream

Some antonyms are formed by adding one of the negative prefixes *anti-, in-,* and *un-* to a word, as in the chart below.

Word	Prefix	Antonym
freeze	anti-	antifreeze
social	anti-	antisocial
appropriate	in-	inappropriate
capacity	in-	incapacity
limited	un-	unlimited
professional	un-	unprofessional

TIP You can find antonyms in dictionaries of synonyms and antonyms, as well as in some thesauruses.

TIP Some dictionaries contain notes that discuss synonyms and antonyms. These notes often include sentences that illustrate the relationships among the words.

Denotative and Connotative Meaning

Good writers choose just the right word to communicate a specific meaning.

Denotative Meaning A word's dictionary meaning is called its **denotation.** The denotation of the word *casual,* for example, is "for everyday use; informal."

Connotative Meaning The images or feelings you connect to a word are called **connotations.** Connotative meaning stretches beyond a word's dictionary definition. Writers rely on connotations of words to communicate shades of meaning, as well as positive or negative feelings. For example, each of these sentences has a slightly different connotation.

> For her first day on the job, Marta wore *relaxed* clothing.
>
> For her first day on the job, Marta wore *casual* clothing.
>
> For her first day on the job, Marta wore *sloppy* clothing.

Examples of similar words with different connotations are listed below:

Positive Connotations	Negative Connotations
cheer	scream
collect	hoard
debate	argue
easygoing	lazy
wildflower	weed
inquisitive	nosy
interest	obsession
reserved	prudish
sound	noise
straightforward	blunt

TIP Some dictionaries contain notes that discuss connotative meanings of the entry word and other related words.

For more information about denotative and connotative meanings, see page 645.

Homonyms, Multiple-Meaning Words, and Homophones

Homonyms, multiple-meaning words, and homophones can be confusing to readers and can plague writers.

Homonyms Words that have the same spelling and pronunciation but different meanings and origins are called **homonyms**. Consider this example:

> I had to **stoop** to see the snake my brother found under the front **stoop**.

Stoop can mean "to bend forward and down," but it can also mean "a small porch, platform, or staircase leading to the entrance of a house or building."

Words with Multiple Meanings Multiple-meaning words are words that have over time acquired additional meanings based on the original meaning. Consider these examples:

> During the **fall,** my town often has festivals, concerts, and contests.

> The leaves will **fall** from the trees soon.

Fall clearly has multiple meanings, but all of the additional meanings have developed from the original meaning. You will find all the meanings for *fall* under one entry in the dictionary.

Homophones Words that sound alike but have different meanings and spellings are called **homophones.** Consider these examples:

> We were so busy at work that I managed to take only a five-minute **break.**

> Greg had to **brake** quickly when the dog ran into the street.

Many common words with Anglo-Saxon origins have homophones (*there, their; write, right*). Check your writing to make sure you have used the right word and not its homophone.

For more about homonyms and homophones, see page 816; for more about multiple-meaning words, see page 266.

Analogies

Analogy An **analogy** is a comparison between two things that are similar in some way. Analogies often appear on tests, usually in a format like this:

> SOCK : CLOTHING :: A) cotton : shirt
> B) denim : fabric
> C) stain : wash
> D) wash : clean
> E) shirt : skirt

To determine the correct answer, follow these steps:

- Read the part in capital letters as *"Sock is to clothing as…"*
- Read the answer choices as *"cotton is to shirt," "denim is to fabric," "stain is to wash,"* and so on.
- Ask yourself how the first two words, *sock* and *clothing*, are related. (A sock is a type of clothing. So *sock* is an item in the larger category of *clothing*.)
- Then look for the answer that best shows the same relationship. (Of these possible answers, only item B shows the relationship of an item to a category.)

Here are some relationships that are often expressed in analogies:

Relationship	Example
Part to Whole	IRIS : EYE
Word to Synonym	SMART : INTELLIGENT
Word to Antonym	SUNNY : CLOUDY
Degree of Intensity	DIFFICULT : IMPOSSIBLE
Item to Category	JUPITER : PLANET
Characteristics to Object	ROUNDNESS : BASEBALL

For more about analogies, see page 1317.

Specialized Vocabulary

Professionals who work in fields such as law, science, and sports use their own technical or specialized vocabulary. Use these strategies to help you figure out the meanings of specialized vocabulary.

Use Context Clues Often the surrounding text gives clues that help you infer the meaning of an unfamiliar term.

> Professional golfers need to avoid **bogeys** if they want to win tournaments.

Use Reference Tools Textbooks often define a special term when it is first introduced. Look for definitions or restatements in parentheses. You may also find definitions in footnotes, a glossary, or a dictionary. If you need more information, refer to a specialized reference, such as one of the following:

- an encyclopedia
- a field guide
- an atlas
- a user's manual
- a technical dictionary

Decoding Multisyllabic Words

Many words that are familiar to you when you speak them or hear them may be unfamiliar to you when you see them in print. When you come across a word that is unfamiliar in print, first try to pronounce it to see if you might recognize it. The following syllabication generalizations can help you figure out a word's pronunciation.

Generalization 1: VCCV

When there are two consonants between two vowels, divide between the two consonants, unless they are a blend or a digraph.

    sur/round   se/cret   slen/der

Generalization 2: VCCCV

When there are three consonants between two vowels, divide between the blend or the digraph and the other consonant.

    ex/claim   in/stead   hand/some

Generalization 3: VCCV

When there are two consonants between two vowels, divide between the consonants, unless they are a blend or a digraph, the first syllable is a closed syllable, and the vowel is short.

    gasp/ing   zip/per   bud/get

Generalization 4: Common Vowel Clusters

Do not split common vowel clusters, such as long vowel digraphs, r-controlled vowels, and vowel diphthongs.

    par/ted   rea/son   dai/sy

Generalization 5: VCV

When you see a VCV pattern in the middle of a word, divide the word either before or after the consonant. If you divide the word after the consonant, pronounce the first vowel sound as short. If you divide the word before the consonant, pronounce the first vowel sound as long.

    mod/el   mo/tel   la/zy

Generalization 6: Compound Words

Divide compound words between the individual words.

    whirl/wind   hard/ship

Generalization 7: Affixes

When a word includes an affix, divide between the base word and the affix.

    joy/ous   harm/less

Reading for Information

Reading informational materials—such as textbooks, magazines, newspapers, and Web pages—requires the use of special strategies. For example, you need to study text organizers, such as headings and special type, to learn the main ideas, facts, terms, and names that are of importance. You also need to identify patterns of organization in the text. Using such strategies will help you to read informational materials with ease and quickly gain a clear understanding of their contents.

Reading a Textbook

Reading a math textbook requires different strategies from those needed when reading other kinds of textbooks. Since most of the text will be explaining a concept rather than telling a story, you should pay careful attention to all of the features on the page.

Strategies for Reading

A First, look at the **title** and any **subheads.** These will tell you what concepts are covered.

B Notice any **key terms** in the text. Key terms are often boldfaced or underlined when they first appear in the text. Be sure that you understand what they mean.

C Some math textbooks will have a **checklist** or a list of **objectives** at the beginning of each lesson. Keeping these in mind as you read will help you identify the most important facts and details.

D Many math textbooks have an **activity box** that supplements each lesson. These activities will give you more practice and will help you further understand each concept.

---

110 Chapter 1 ▶ Functions and Their Graphs

1.2 Linear Equations in Two Variables **A**

▶ **What you should learn**

C
- How to use slope to graph linear equations in two variables
- How to find slopes of lines
- How to write linear equations in two variables
- How to use slope to identify parallel and perpendicular lines
- How to use linear equations in two variables to model and solve real-life problems

▶ **Why you should learn it**

Linear equations in two variables can be used to model and solve real-life problems. For instance, Exercise 112 on page 123 shows how to use a linear equation to model the average annual salaries of major league baseball players from 1988 to 1998.

Walter Schmid/The Stock Market

A computer simulation of this concept appears in the *Interactive* CD-ROM and *Internet* versions of this text.

Using Slope

The simplest mathematical model for relating two variables is the **linear** **in two variables** $y = mx + b$. The equation is called *linear* because its line. (In mathematics, the term *line* means *straight line*.) By letting $x = 0$ see that the line crosses the y-axis at $y = b$, as shown in Figure 1.14 words, the y-intercept is $(0, b)$. The steepness or slope of the line is m.

$$y = mx + b$$

Slope ↑ ↑ y-Intercept

B The **slope** of a nonvertical line is the number of units the line rises vertically for each unit of horizontal change from left to right, as Figure 1.14.

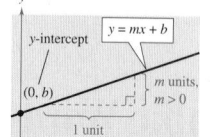

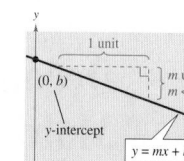

Positive slope, line rises.
FIGURE 1.14

Negative slope, line falls.

A linear equation that is written in the form $y = mx + b$ is sa written in **slope-intercept form.**

The Slope-Intercept Form of the Equation of a Line

The graph of the equation

$$y = mx + b$$

is a line whose slope is m and whose y-intercept is $(0, b)$.

D ◆ **Exploration** ◆

Use a graphing utility to compare the slopes of the lines $y = mx$ where $m = 0.5, 1, 2,$ and 4. Which line rises most quickly? Now, let $m = -0$ $-1, -2,$ and -4. Which line falls most quickly? Use a square setting obtain a true geometric perspective. What can you conclude about the s and the "rate" at which the line rises or falls?

E Be sure to notice any **examples** in a math lesson that will give you a step-by-step overview of how to use the concept. Look closely at any **diagrams** or **graphs,** and study the text referring to them.

More Strategies for Reading Textbooks

- Read slowly and carefully. If you see an unfamiliar word and can't find a definition in the text or in a marginal note, check the **glossary** or a dictionary.
- You may want to keep a **notebook** of important **equations, terms,** or **concepts.** Doing this will help you keep important information organized and easily accessible.
- Be sure to follow all **directions.** Many math concepts are taught in a step-by-step format. Missing one of the steps may cause you to misunderstand the concept.

Section 1.2 ▶ Linear Equations in Two Variables **111**

Once you have determined the slope and the y-intercept of a line, it is a relatively simple matter to sketch its graph. In the following example, note that none of the lines is vertical. A vertical line has an equation of the form

$x = a.$ Vertical line

The equation of a vertical line cannot be written in the form $y = mx + b$ because the slope of a vertical line is undefined, as indicated in Figure 1.15.

E **Example 1** ▶ **Graphing a Linear Equation**

Sketch the graph of each linear equation.

a. $y = 2x + 1$

b. $y = 2$

c. $x + y = 2$

Solution

a. Because $b = 1$, the y-intercept is $(0, 1)$. Moreover, because the slope is $m = 2$, the line *rises* 2 units for each unit the line moves to the right, as shown in Figure 1.16(a).

b. By writing this equation in the form $y = (0)x + 2$, you can see that the y-intercept is $(0, 2)$ and the slope is zero. A zero slope implies that the line is horizontal—that is, it doesn't rise *or* fall, as shown in Figure 1.16(b).

c. By writing this equation in slope-intercept form

$$x + y = 2 \qquad \text{Write original equation.}$$
$$y = -x + 2 \qquad \text{Subtract } x \text{ from each side.}$$
$$y = (-1)x + 2 \qquad \text{Write in slope-intercept form.}$$

you can see that the y-intercept is $(0, 2)$. Moreover, because the slope is $m = -1$, the line *falls* 1 unit for each unit the line moves to the right, as shown in Figure 1.16(c).

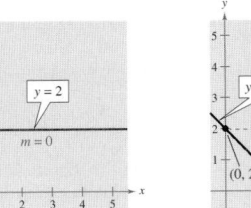

(b) When m is 0, the line is horizontal.

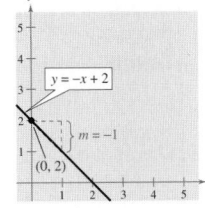

(c) When m is negative, the line falls.

(3, 5)

$x = 3$

(3, 1)

1 2   4 5 x

RE 1.15   *Slope is undefined.*

mon Error

y students confuse the line $x = a$ the point $x = a$ on the real number or the line $y = b$ with the point b. Point out to students that they to be aware of the context in h $x = a$ or $y = b$ is presented to w whether it refers to the line in the e or the point on the number line.

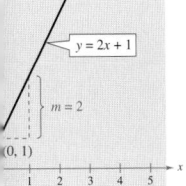

$y = 2x + 1$

$m = 2$

(0, 1)

1 2 3 4 5 x

When m is positive, the line rises.

RE 1.16

Reading a Magazine Article

Strategies for Reading

A Read the **title** and any other **headings** to get an idea of what the article is about and how it is organized.

B As you read the main text, notice any **quotations.** Who is quoted? Is the person a reliable authority on the subject?

C Notice text that is set off in some way, such as a passage in a **different typeface.** A quotation or statistic that sums up the article is sometimes presented in this way.

D Study **visuals,** such as photographs, graphs, charts, and maps. Read their **captions** and make sure you know how they relate to the main text.

Graduate Manners **A**

Are graduations marred by bad behavior?

by Jennifer Tinnin

Jessica M., a recent high school graduate, says she does not have fond memories of her graduation. "I was really looking forward to graduation, but during the ceremony, kids were shouting and dancing on the stage," she recalls. "I was so embarrassed by my peers' behavior."

Jessica's experience is not unique. Graduation cermonies across the country are being disrupted by the graduates' behavior. Middle school students in Illinois acted like they had just scored a touchdown as they strutted across the stage, pumping their fists into the air. A student in Minnesota took a pratfall and then had a loud confrontation with police who attempted to escort him from the building. Students in Illinois were not invited back to the site where their graduation was held last year after thousands of dollars of damage was done to the site's restrooms.

These students are not all troublemakers. One student who performed a prank was president of his school's student body, and another student was the valedictorian of his class. Nor are students the sole disruption at graduations. Friends and family in the audience often cheer on students' antics or create additional noise by blowing air horns or screaming when their graduate's name is called.

Many school officials and audience members believe that the dignity of graduation is being sacrificed for a few laughs. Ellen, a high school student from California, remarks, "Kids yell and dance

C *"I was so embarrassed by my peers' behavior."*

because they're happy. It's no big deal. We should be allowed to celebrate our accomplishments and success." Dr. Amos White, principal of a high school in Houston, Texas, disagrees, "These students are graduating into the adult world. They should mark the transition with good manners and courtesy toward their peers, parents, and school officials. We will do whatever we can to keep graduation dignified."

Some schools have started to require students to sign a contract ensuring their compliance with school rules for behavior during the graduation ceremony before they will allow students to attend the ceremony. Is a legal contract necessary to deter students and audiences alike from ruining graduation? Or are graduates and their friends and families simply showing exuberance for a job well done?

GRADUATION BEHAVIOR SURVEY **D**

Do you think there should be stricter enforcement of rules and conduct at graduation ceremonies?

Parents		High School Students	
Yes	77%	Yes	48%
No	20%	No	46%
Not Sure	3%	Not Sure	6%

Do you think students should be required to sign a contract dictating rules of behavior in order to participate in the graduation ceremony?

Parents		High School Students	
Yes	54%	Yes	21%
No	29%	No	68%
Not Sure	17%	Not Sure	11%

43

Reading a Web Page

Strategies for Reading

A Look for the page's **Web address,** sometimes called a URL. If you think you will return to the page, write down the address.

B Read the **title** of the page to find out what topics the page covers.

C Look for a **menu bar** along the top, bottom, or side of the page. This tells you about other parts of the site.

D Notice any **links** to related pages. Links are often "buttons" or underlined words.

E Look for text that tells you when the Web page was last **updated.** There might also be a link to send e-mail to the **Webmaster** or to staff of the organization.

Patterns of Organization

Reading any type of writing is easier if you understand how it is organized. A writer organizes ideas in a structure, or pattern, that helps the reader see how the ideas are related. The following are five important structures:

- main idea and supporting details
- chronological order
- comparison and contrast
- cause and effect
- problem-solution

This page contains an overview of the five structures, which you will learn about in more detail on pages 1339–1343. Each type has been represented graphically to help you see how the ideas are organized in it.

Main Idea and Supporting Details

The main idea of a paragraph or a longer piece of writing is its most important point. Supporting details give more information about the main idea.

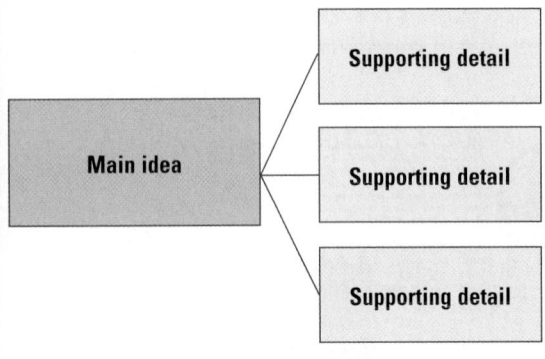

Chronological Order

Writing that is organized in chronological order presents events in the order in which they occur.

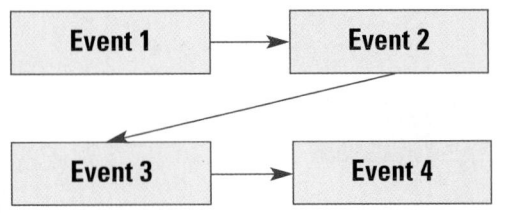

Comparison and Contrast

Comparison-and-contrast writing explains how two or more subjects are similar and how they are different.

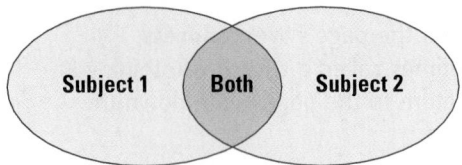

Cause and Effect

Cause-and-effect writing explains the relationship between events. A cause is an event that gives rise to another event or a condition, called an effect. A cause may have more than one effect, and an effect may have more than one cause.

Single Cause with Multiple Effects

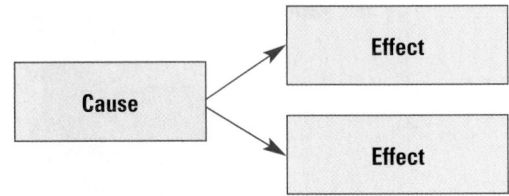

Multiple Causes with Single Effect

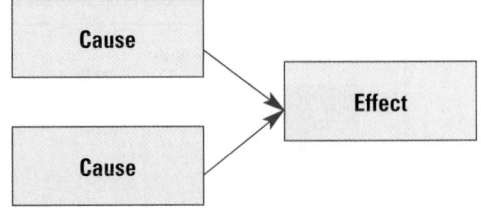

Problem-Solution

This type of writing describes a difficult issue and suggests at least one way to deal with it. The writer provides reasons to support his or her suggestion.

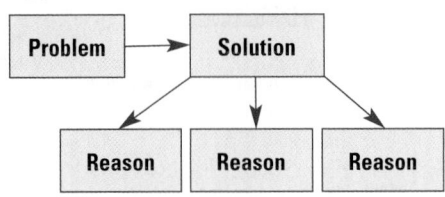

Main Idea and Supporting Details

The **main idea** of a paragraph is the basic point the writer is making in that paragraph. The **supporting details** give you additional information about the main idea. A main idea may be stated directly or it may be implied. If it is stated, it may appear anywhere in the paragraph. Often it appears in the first or the last sentence. An implied main idea is suggested through the details that are provided.

Strategies for Reading

- To find the **main idea**, ask, What is this paragraph about?
- To find **supporting details**, ask, What else do I learn about the main idea?

MODEL

Main Idea in the First Sentence

Main idea

King James I of England inherited the unsettled issues of Queen Elizabeth I's reign. Elizabeth left a huge debt. This debt, combined with James's foreign wars and expensive court, caused constant struggles between the king and Parliament about money. Another issue was how much power Parliament should have. James I also clashed with the Puritans over remaining Catholic practices in the Church of England.

Supporting details

MODEL

Main Idea in the Last Sentence

Supporting details

Queen Elizabeth I of England had frequent conflicts with Parliament. Many of the arguments were over money. By the time Elizabeth died in 1603, she left a huge debt for her successor to deal with. **Parliament's financial power was one obstacle to English rulers becoming absolute monarchs.**

Main idea

MODEL

Implied Main Idea

Implied main idea: Charles I waged ongoing battles with Parliament about money.

In 1625, James I died. Charles I, his son, took the throne. Charles always needed money—in part because he was at war with both Spain and France. Several times when Parliament refused to give him funds, he shut Parliament down. By 1628, Charles was forced to call Parliament again. This time it refused to grant him any money until he signed a document that reduced some of his power.

PRACTICE AND APPLY

MODEL

In 1659, Parliament voted to ask the older son of Charles I to rule England. When Prince Charles entered London in 1660, crowds shouted joyfully and bells rang. On this note of celebration, the reign of Charles II began. Because Charles II restored the monarchy, his rule is called the Restoration. He also restored many aspects of English cultural and political life. Charles restored the theater, sporting events, and dancing, all of which the Puritans had banned. Theater, especially comedy, and other arts flourished during the Restoration.

Read the model above and then do the following activities:

1. Identify the main idea of the paragraph. Is it stated or implied?
2. List three details that support the main idea.

Chronological Order

Events discussed in **chronological order,** also called time order, are presented in the order they happen. Historical events are usually recounted in chronological order. The steps of a process may also be recorded this way.

Strategies for Reading

- Look for the **individual events** or **steps in the sequence.**

- Look for words or phrases that identify **time,** such as *in a year, three hours earlier, in 1667,* and *a century ago.*

- Look for words that signal **order,** such as *first, afterward, then, before, finally,* and *next.*

MODEL

Event	**Born in 1491, Henry VIII was crowned king of England** when he was 18 years old. He was a devout Catholic, but his politics soon clashed with his religion.
Time phrases	
Order words	**Henry's father had become king after a long civil war.** Henry was afraid that a similar war might start if he died without a son to take over the throne. The history of England during his reign became the bloody story of his need for a son.

Henry and his wife, Catherine of Aragon, had one living child—a daughter, Mary, born in 1516. However, a woman had never successfully claimed the English throne. By 1529, Catherine was 42 and Henry was convinced that she would have no more children. He wanted to divorce her and marry a younger woman, but Church law did not permit divorce. Henry asked the pope to annul his marriage—in other words, declare that it had never existed. The pope refused.

Henry then decided to take matters into his own hands. Later in 1529, he asked Parliament to pass laws to end the pope's power in England. Four years later, he secretly married Anne Boleyn and Parliament voted to make his divorce from his first wife legal. But Henry was not satisfied and wanted to break completely with the pope. In 1534, Parliament passed the Act of Supremacy, which made the king the official head of the Church of England.

Although Henry had turned the country inside out in his attempt to have a son, Anne Boleyn gave birth to a daughter. Following the birth, Henry had her imprisoned in the Tower of London. In 1536, he had her beheaded.

Henry did not get his wish for a son until his third wife, Jane Seymour, gave birth to Edward. Jane died in childbirth. In 1540, Henry married his fourth wife but quickly divorced her to marry his fifth wife, Catherine Howard. However, the king soon found out that Catherine had had affairs before their marriage and had her beheaded in 1543. Henry's sixth wife survived her husband, who died in 1547 at the age of 56.

PRACTICE AND APPLY

Reread the model and then do the following activities:

1. List six of the order and time words used in the model. Do not include those that have been identified for you.

2. Draw a time line beginning with Henry's birth in 1491 and ending with his death in 1547. Include each event mentioned in the model.

Comparison and Contrast

Comparison-and-contrast writing explains how subjects are alike and different. This type of writing is usually organized by subject or by feature. In **subject organization,** the writer discusses one subject, then discusses the other. In **feature organization,** the writer compares a feature of one subject with the same feature of the other, then compares another feature of both, and so on.

Strategies for Reading

- Look for words and phrases that signal **comparisons,** such as *like, similarly, both,* and *in the same way.*

- Look for words and phrases that signal **contrasts,** such as *unlike, differences, in contrast, opposite,* and *differ.*

MODEL

During the Renaissance, many poets expressed their thoughts and feelings in a type of poem called a pastoral. Pastorals paint a romantic picture of shepherds and their lives in the country. Many pastorals are about love.

Subject → One pastoral written by Christopher Marlowe, "The Passionate Shepherd to His Love," (see page 290) became very famous in sixteenth-century England. In fact, it became so famous that many poets wrote responses to it. One of these responses was Sir Walter Raleigh's pastoral, "The Nymph's Reply to the *Comparison words* → Shepherd (see page 292)." These two poems have both similarities and differences.

Contrast words → Both poems are pastorals. They are set in the country and deal with love. They also have similar structures. Each has six stanzas with four lines. In each stanza, lines one and two rhyme and lines three and four rhyme. The poems even repeat the same rhyming words—*move* and *love.*

However, the two poems evoke very different moods. "The

Passionate Shepherd to His Love" creates a very romantic scene. The shepherd talks about the beauty of nature—lush valleys, tumbling waterfalls, and singing birds. He offers his love colorful, sweet-smelling flowers, soft wool dresses, and jewels—everything her heart might desire. It's almost too good to be true.

On the other hand, the mood of "The Nymph's Reply to the Shepherd" is practical and not at all romantic. The nymph doesn't focus on the beauty of the world, but rather on the passage of time, which destroys that beauty. She points out that "flowers do fade" and "rocks grow cold," and that love "is fancy's spring, but sorrow's fall." She mocks the love-struck attitude of the shepherd in Marlowe's poem and concludes that love is more or less a silly waste of time.

It's interesting that two poems written at about the same time and using the same form and structure can convey such opposite messages. However, that is what creativity is all about.

PRACTICE AND APPLY

Reread the model and then do the following activities:

1. Identify whether the model is organized by subject or by feature.

2. List the features of the two poems that the writer compares and contrasts.

3. Create a Venn diagram showing the similarities and differences between the poems. For an example of a Venn diagram, see page 1338.

Reading Handbook

Cause and Effect

Cause-and-effect writing explains the relationship between events. A **cause** is an event that brings about another event or a condition. An **effect** is something that happens as a result of a cause or causes. Cause-and-effect writing is usually organized in one of three ways:

1. as a description of the cause(s) followed by an explanation of the effect(s)

2. as a description of the effect(s) followed by an explanation of the cause(s)

3. as a chain of causes and effects

Strategies for Reading

- To find the **effect(s),** ask, What happened?
- To find the **cause(s),** ask, Why did it happen?
- Look for **words and phrases that signal relationships between events,** such as *because, as a result, for that reason, so, consequently,* and *since.*

MODEL

At the peak of the last Ice Age, about 20,000 years ago, herds of giant animals—megafauna— lumbered through the forests and plains of North America. There were beavers the size of modern bears, hairy mastodons and mammoths with massive, curved tusks, and bison with horns measuring six feet across. These awesome animals were hunted by jaguars, saber-toothed tigers, and bears that weighed twice as much as today's grizzlies. But by about 13,000 years ago—not long after the first

Effect humans appeared on the scene— almost all of these huge beasts had disappeared.

No one knows for sure what caused this mass extinction, but there are several competing theories. One

Cause possible cause might have been a change in climate. Increasing

Signal words temperatures resulted in a retreat of the glaciers that had covered the land during the Ice Age. Consequently, the forests and grasslands that thrived in the cold climate and provided food

for the animals grew smaller. Without a source of food, the animals eventually died off.

According to another theory, the disappearance of the giant animals was caused by an epidemic outbreak of disease. Some scientists think that prehistoric humans may have brought disease-causing organisms with them when they crossed the land bridge connecting Asia and North America. Since the animals living in North America had no immunity to these diseases, great numbers of them may have died.

A third theory points a finger straight at human hunters. This doesn't mean that people killed every single animal in the prehistoric world. If hunters had killed only a few more animals than were born each year, the populations of megafauna would have decreased steadily. As a result, nearly all the species could have become extinct within a thousand years or so.

Scientists are now using new techniques to learn whether the disappearance of the giant animals was caused by climate changes, disease, or overhunting by humans. They are looking at fossils and rocks for evidence, analyzing frozen tissues and bone marrow from mammoths, and using new ways of dating ancient remains. Scientists hope to solve this mystery soon.

PRACTICE AND APPLY

Reread the model and then do the following activities:

1. Identify three possible causes for the extinction of the megafauna.

2. Use a flow chart or other graphic organizer to show how a climate change may have caused the megafauna to become extinct. For examples of graphic organizers, see page 1338.

Problem-Solution

Problem-solution writing clearly presents various aspects of a problem and offers a solution for it. It presents logical arguments to convince readers that the proposed solution will solve the problem.

Strategies for Reading

- To find the **problem,** ask, What is this writing about?
- To find the **solution,** ask, What suggestion does the writer offer to remedy the problem?
- Look for the **reasons** the writer gives to support the solution. Is the thinking behind them logical? Is the evidence presented strong and convincing?

MODEL

Energy supplies are decreasing, and the cost of electricity in the western United States has been extremely high in the past few years. Blackouts and brownouts have forced residents of California to come face to face with the energy problem. **If new sources of energy aren't found soon, we may be headed for a new Dark Age.**

Problem

The good news is that the earth has an abundant source of energy just waiting to be tapped. This energy is called geothermal energy, and it is stored in the rocks and water of the earth's crust. **Geothermal energy can be used to power turbines to generate electricity and to heat homes and businesses reliably and inexpensively.**

Solution

Geothermal means "earth heat," and the Northwest—especially Nevada, Utah, California, and Oregon—lies on top of a real hotbed. This heat is caused by underground streams of molten rock, or magma. The average temperature in many areas is more than 212 degrees Fahrenheit, the boiling point of water. **Some scientists believe that harnessing the geothermal energy in Oregon alone would produce as much electricity as two nuclear power plants.**

Reason

To put the earth's heat to work, scientists must first locate underground pools of superheated water. Then they must drill wells to bring it to the surface. At the surface, the hot water is allowed to turn into steam and is piped into a turbine, where it turns the blades. These blades power a generator, which produces electricity. Excess steam from the turbine is then turned back into water and recycled into the underground reservoir.

Building a geothermal plant is expensive, but once it is running, it can operate day and night for 30 or more years at little additional cost.

Geothermal energy is also inexpensive to use. Because geothermal heat pumps in homes use electricity only to move heat, not to generate it, they can reduce electricity costs by as much as 75 percent.

Geothermal energy is not just a fantasy. Sixty-two countries are already using geothermal energy, including the Philippines, which gets 21 percent of its energy from the earth.

Geothermal energy is reliable, clean, and ecologically responsible. It has no effect on wildlife and is not affected by changes in climate. What are we waiting for?

PRACTICE AND APPLY

Reread the model and then do the following activities:

1. List the reasons the writer gives for developing sources of geothermal energy.

2. Write down at least three questions you might want to ask the writer about the proposed solution to the problem.

Functional Reading

Functional reading is reading to discover such information as instructions on how to do something. When you read a map, a memo, or a product manual, you are engaged in functional reading. These guidelines show how you can improve your functional-reading skills.

Guide to Colleges

Strategies for Reading

A Look at the **head** on the page to find out what state the university is located in.

B Notice the **name** of the university and the university's **contact information.** If you have any questions, you can use this information to contact the school.

C Notice any **icons** that appear on the page. These icons give basic information about the university such as cost or location. A key to these icons will appear in the college guide's introduction.

D Study the **feature list** to find important information about the university. This list highlights aspects of the university that you may want to compare with those of other universities.

E Study any **subheads** and the **text** that follows them. This text will give more in-depth information about the university.

PRACTICE AND APPLY

Reread the college profile below and then answer the following questions:

1. Where is Mountain University located?

2. How expensive is Mountain University?

3. How many women attend Mountain University?

4. What types of on-campus housing does Mountain University offer?

A **COLORADO**

 **MOUNTAIN UNIVERSITY** **B**

Contact: 511 University Circle
Range, CO 80695
(303) 555-8179
www.mountainu.edu

 **$$** **C**

Mountain University Features & Facts **D**

- Public, four-year university
- 4,232 undergraduates
- 2,196 women, 2,036 men

- 70% of applicants admitted
- Mid 50% SAT 1050; Mid 50% ACT 23
- Financial aid available

E *Student Life:* 67% of undergraduates are from Colorado. Others are from 34 states and 19 foreign countries. The average age of freshmen is 18 and the average age of all undergraduates is 20. 8% do not continue beyond their first year.

Housing: 60% of students can be accommodated in on-campus housing, which includes single-sex and coed dormitories. On-campus housing is guaranteed for all 4 years. 45% of students live on campus. All students may keep cars.

Key to symbols

	e-application available	🏠	suburban campus
$	inexpensive	🏙	urban campus
$$	moderately expensive	⌂	rural campus
$$$	very expensive		

Campus Map

Strategies for Reading

(A) Read the **title** to find out what area the map shows.

(B) Study the building **labels.** Notice if one building contains more than one department.

(C) Look at the **pointer,** or **compass rose,** to figure out directions.

(D) Study the **key,** or **legend,** to learn what the symbols and colors on the map mean.

(E) Look for other **arrows** that tell you what is not visible on the map, but nearby.

PRACTICE AND APPLY

Reread the map below and then answer the following questions:

1. What are the numbered buildings?

2. Are the north or south campus residences closer to the business and shopping district?

3. Which department shares a building with the English department?

4. If you study biology, would it be more convenient to live on north campus or south campus?

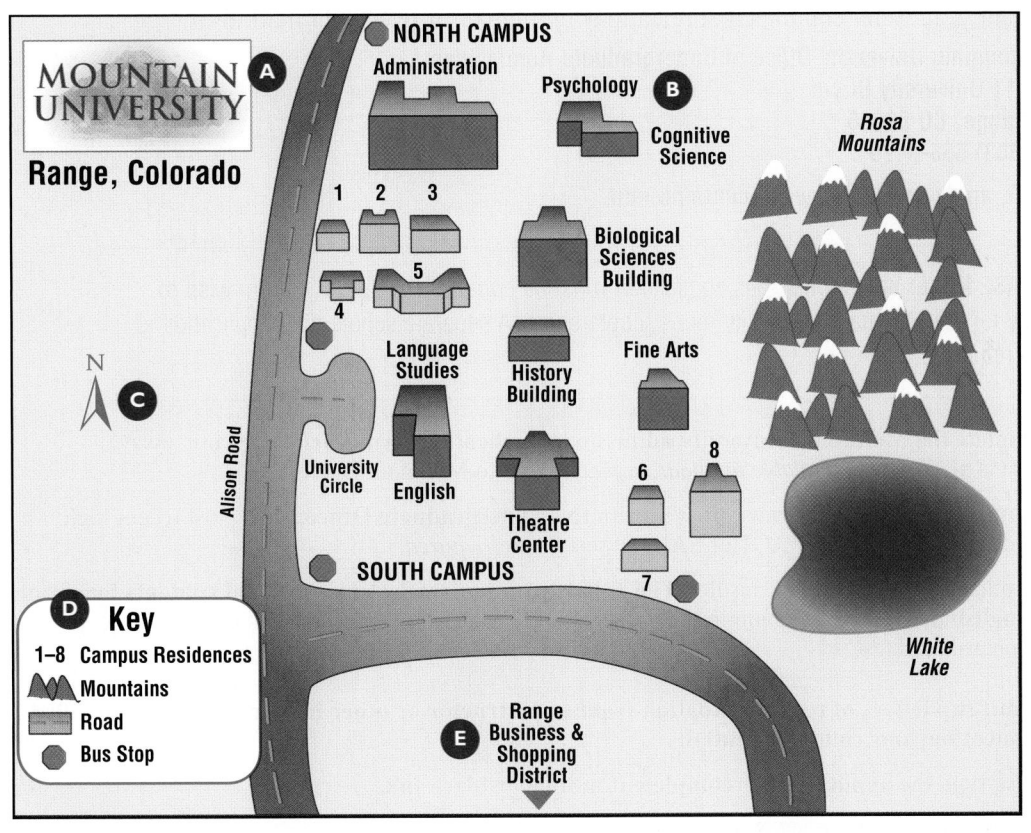

MOUNTAIN UNIVERSITY

Range, Colorado

(A)

NORTH CAMPUS

Administration

Psychology

(B)

Cognitive Science

Rosa Mountains

1 2 3

Biological Sciences Building

5

4

Language Studies

History Building

Fine Arts

(C) N

Alison Road

University Circle

English

Theatre Center

6

8

7

SOUTH CAMPUS

White Lake

(D) Key

1–8 Campus Residences
Mountains
Road
Bus Stop

(E) Range Business & Shopping District

College Application

Strategies for Reading

A Read the **title** of the form to make sure it is the one you need.

B Look for **boldfaced, italicized,** and **underlined** words. These may signal important information such as due dates, required materials, or fees.

C Make sure you fill in any **charts** accurately and completely.

D All college applications will include a set of **terms** and a place for you to **sign,** usually at the end of the application. In order for your application to be valid and complete, you will have to agree to the terms the university gives.

MOUNTAIN UNIVERSITY

A APPLICATION FOR UNDERGRADUATE ADMISSION

APPLICATION INSTRUCTIONS

B This application is for students who will enter Mountain University in <u>the fall of the current year</u>. Send completed applications by regular or overnight mail to:

Mountain University Office of Undergraduate Admissions
511 University Circle
Range, CO 80695
(303) 555-8179

Or, apply online at www.mountainu.edu.

B **PLEASE NOTE:** Your admissions application *must be completed by April 1* if you wish to apply for the Mountain University merit scholarships. A separate scholarship application is also required.

Complete the Mountain University admissions application form (including your essay). There is a *$25 non-refundable application fee* payable to Mountain University.

Arrange to have official transcripts sent to the Undergraduate Office. Your most recent high school transcript and your ACT or SAT test results are *required*.

If applicable, submit TOEFL results. **The TOEFL is required for international students for proof of English proficiency.** The minimum score required is 550 on the written test or 213 on the computer-based test.

Submit two letters of recommendation from an instructor or other individual who is qualified to comment on your college potential.

Please type the application or complete it in blue or black ink.

Autobiographical Information

Social Security Number _____-_____-_____

Last name _____   First name _____

Mailing Address _____

City _____ State _____ Zip _____

Phone Number (_____) _____

Date of Birth: Month _____ Day _____ Year _____

If you are not a U.S. citizen, please complete the following (check one):

❏ Immigrant   ❏ Visa

Type of Visa (e.g., F-1 Student, J-2 Dependent, etc.): _____

❏ Permanent Resident in the U.S.

I plan to enter Mountain University as a

❏ full-time student (12 credit hours or more)   ❏ part-time student

Residency Information (answer both questions)

❏ Yes   ❏ No   I will have lived in Colorado one full year before becoming a student at Mountain.

❏ Yes   ❏ No   I will be claimed as a tax dependent by at least one parent who resides in Colorado.

C Please provide the name of the high school from which you will graduate:

High School	City, State	GPA	(Expected) Graduation Date

Intended Major

_____

PERSONAL STATEMENT

Please submit an original personal statement of 1500 words or less describing what your goals are in the coming year, the next five years, and the next ten years.

D Attach a separate sheet of paper.

I understand that providing false information may make me ineligible for admission to Mountain University. I agree to abide by the regulations of Mountain as set forth in its current catalog and other official publications. I attest that all information I have supplied in this application and accompanying documentation is true and valid.

Applicant's Signature _____

Date Submitted _____

PRACTICE AND APPLY

Reread the application and then answer the following questions:

1. Can a student who is planning to enter Mountain University in the spring term use this form? Why or why not?

2. What other materials are required besides the application?

3. Name at least three items of personal information the application requests.

4. How many credit hours do you need to take to be a full-time student?

5. According to the application, what will make you ineligible for admission to Mountain University?

Online Job Search

Strategies for Reading

A Take note of the page's **Web address,** or **URL,** in case you need to return to the site. If you like the site, you can **bookmark** it or save it as a **"favorite site."**

B Look for **links** on the page. Links can appear as underlined words or as "buttons."

C When doing a **search,** you will need to enter criteria that are relevant to what you are looking for. For a job search, these might include keywords or a specific city.

D Look for any **pull-down menus** that appear on the search page. These menus require you to select from a list of options by scrolling down the list.

E If the search did not result in any matches, some sites let you do a **subsearch** using more specific keywords.

F An **entry** in a list of job search results will usually include the date the job was posted, the location, the job title, and the company name. See more detailed information by clicking on the link in the entry.

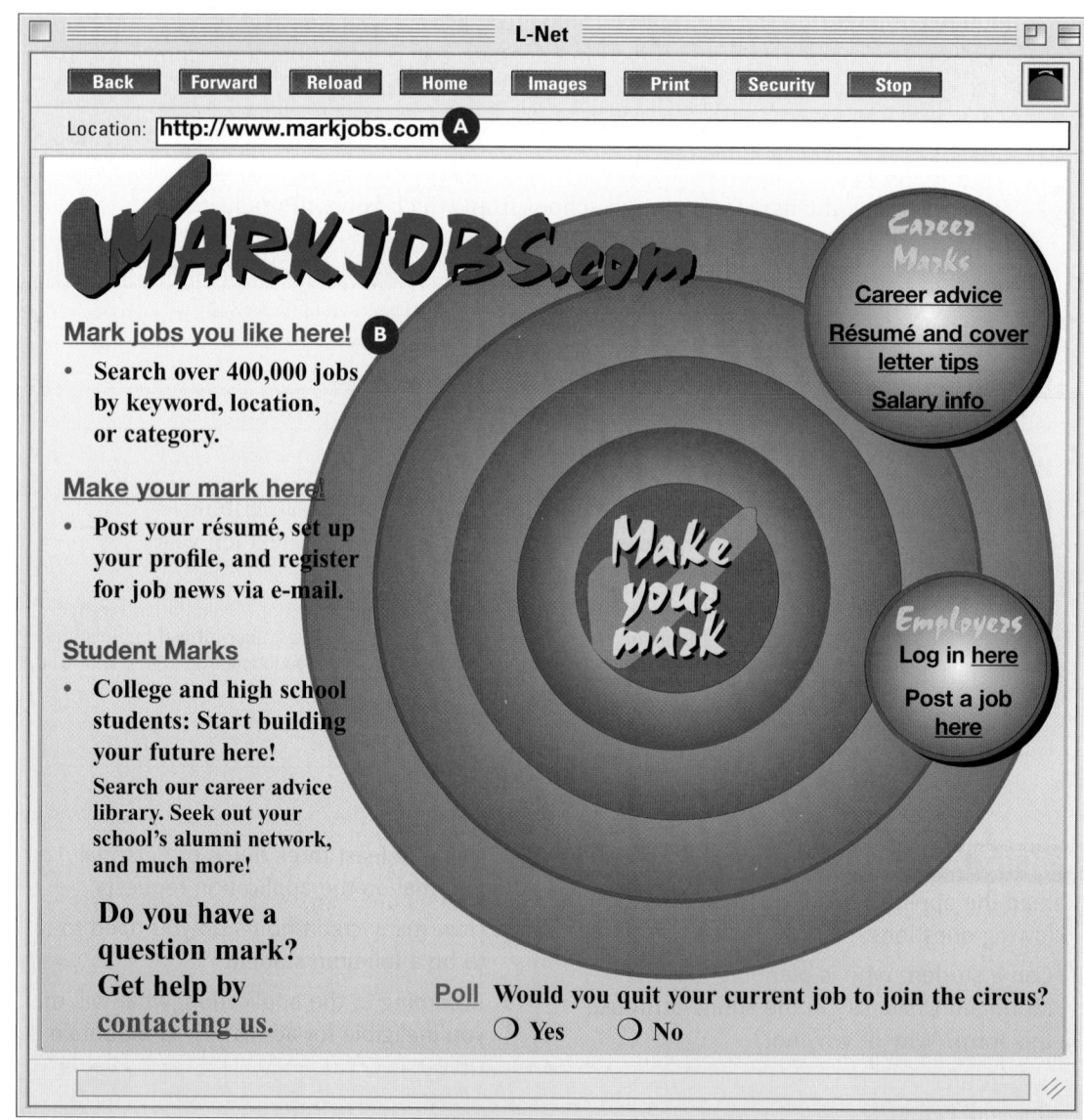

L-Net

Back | Forward | Reload | Home | Images | Print | Security | Stop

Location: http://www.markjobs.com **A**

MARKJOBS.com

Mark jobs you like here! **B**

* Search over 400,000 jobs by keyword, location, or category.

Make your mark here!

* Post your résumé, set up your profile, and register for job news via e-mail.

Student Marks

* College and high school students: Start building your future here!

  Search our career advice library. Seek out your school's alumni network, and much more!

Do you have a question mark? Get help by contacting us.

Career Marks
Career advice
Résumé and cover letter tips
Salary info

Make your mark

Employers
Log in here
Post a job here

Poll Would you quit your current job to join the circus?
◯ Yes   ◯ No

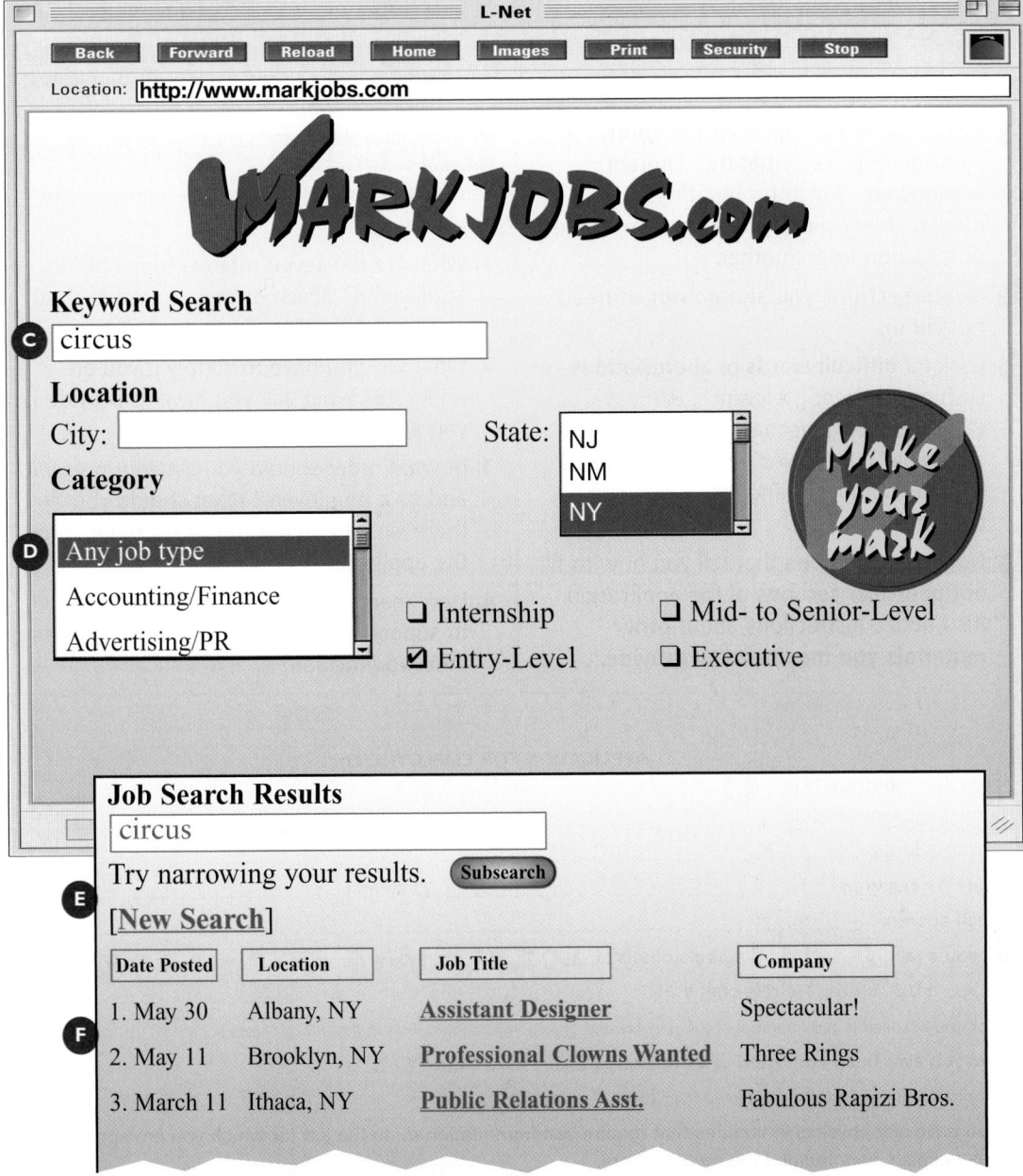

L-Net

Back Forward Reload Home Images Print Security Stop

Location: **http://www.markjobs.com**

MARKJOBS.com

Keyword Search

C circus

Location

City: State: NJ / NM / NY

Category

D Any job type
Accounting/Finance
Advertising/PR

☐ Internship   ☐ Mid- to Senior-Level
☑ Entry-Level   ☐ Executive

Make your mark

Job Search Results

circus

Try narrowing your results. (Subsearch)

E [**New Search**]

Date Posted	Location	Job Title	Company
1. May 30	Albany, NY	**Assistant Designer**	Spectacular!
2. May 11	Brooklyn, NY	**Professional Clowns Wanted**	Three Rings
3. March 11	Ithaca, NY	**Public Relations Asst.**	Fabulous Rapizi Bros.

F

PRACTICE AND APPLY

Reread the Web pages and then answer the following questions:

1. On which link would you click to post your résumé?

2. Which search option would you use to find all of the jobs in a specific field?

3. What words might you use to narrow the results of the search shown to jobs relating to training circus animals?

4. What is the name of the company that posted a job on March 11?

Job Application

Strategies for Reading

(A) Beginning at the top, scan the entire application to see what the different sections are. Watch for **headings** that identify the sections and **lines** that divide one section from another.

(B) Notice **sections you should not or need not fill in.**

(C) Look for **difficult words** or **abbreviations**—such as *pertinent* ("relevant"), *B/P* ("business" or "personal"), *N/A* ("not applicable"), *Y/N* ("yes" or "no"), and *ph. #* ("phone number")—and determine what they mean.

(D) Notice **instructions** that tell you how to fill out particular sections of the application. Also notice instructions about **other materials you may need to provide.**

(E) Pay special attention to any part of the application that calls for your **signature.** Be sure to read all statements carefully before signing your name to them.

PRACTICE AND APPLY

Reread the application and then answer the questions.

1. What are the seven main sections of this application? Which of these sections should you leave blank?

2. What will you have to supply if you are under 18? What will you have to provide if you are not a U.S. citizen?

3. In what order should you list your present and past employers? What should you do if there isn't enough room to list them all on the application?

4. How many business references do you need to supply? How many personal references must you include?

Fruit Junction
APPLICATION FOR EMPLOYMENT

PERSONAL INFORMATION (A)
Name (Last, First, Middle) _____

Current Address _____

Phone #   Daytime ( ) _____ Evening ( ) _____

E-mail address _____

Are you over 16 years of age? (circle one) Y / N (If you are under 18, you will need to have a work permit.) **(D)**

Are you a U.S. citizen? (circle one) Y / N

(If not, you will need to provide proof of your identity and of your legal right to work in the United States.)

Have you ever been convicted of a criminal offense? (circle one) Y / N

(Minor traffic offenses are not considered "criminal.")

(B) If you have any physical limitations that require accommodation to do the job for which you are applying, please explain accommodation requirements. _____

_____

EDUCATION

Name of School	Location	Years Completed	Did You Graduate?
		1 2 3 4	Y / N
		1 2 3 4	Y / N
		1 2 3 4	Y / N

Please provide an accurate and complete full-time and part-time employment record. (D)
List employers chronologically, starting with your present or most recent employer. Attach additional pages, if needed.

EMPLOYMENT HISTORY

Employer	Job(s) Held	Time Worked	Reason for Leaving
Name _____ Address _____ _____ Supervisor _____ Phone # _____		Start date _____ End date* _____ (circle one) full / part time	_____ *If you are currently employed, may we contact your present employer? (Y / N)
Name _____ Address _____ _____ Supervisor _____ Phone # _____		Start date _____ End date* _____ (circle one) full / part time	

C REFERENCES: **Please provide at least two business (B) and two personal (P) references we can contact.**

B / P	Name	Phone #	Relationship	Years Known

ADDITIONAL INFORMATION

Please fill in the hours you are available to work each week.

	Mon.	Tues.	Wed.	Thurs.	Fri.	Sat.	Sun.
Starting at							
Ending at							

How long do you hope to be part of the team at Fruit Junction? _____

What else should we know about you that might be pertinent to considering you for this job? _____

_____

APPLICANT'S STATEMENT

I certify that the information provided in this employment application (and accompanying documentation, if any) is true, valid, and complete to the best of my knowledge. I understand that if I am employed, any falsified statements or documents or misleading information given in my application or interview may be considered sufficient grounds for termination. I also agree by my signature to allow the company to verify the information I provide and to release from legal liability any person, school, current employer, past employer, or organization named in this application for statements given with regard to my qualifications.

E **Applicant's Signature** _____ **Date** _____

B INFORMATION TO BE SUPPLIED BY INTERVIEWER

Job applied for: _____   **Interviewed by:** _____

(Check all that apply)

_____ offer extended and accepted   _____ offer extended but rejected

_____ hold for future opening   _____ no openings at this time

_____ could not locate   _____ not qualified

Comments: _____

Workplace Document

Whether you work as a lifeguard or a library aide, part-time or full, you need to fill out and return Form W-4 before you can get a paycheck. This form helps your employer calculate the correct portion of your pay to withhold, or set aside, for payment of your Federal income tax.

To complete Form W-4, you will need to understand the following terms:

dependent: someone who relies on another person for financial support; you are considered a dependent if someone else supports you and claims you as a dependent on his or her income tax return

exempt: freed or excused from being taxed; if you are exempt, you don't have to have any money withheld from your paycheck for taxes

unearned income: interest, dividends, or other profits; if you have money in a savings account gaining interest, the interest is considered unearned income

withholding allowance: a number that is equal to or less than the one you calculate by completing the Personal Allowances Worksheet; the number an employer uses to determine how much money to take out of your paycheck for payment of income tax

The following Strategies for Reading may also be helpful. If you need additional help to complete Form W-4, ask your employer or a parent or guardian for assistance.

Strategies for Reading

A Notice the **headings** or **lines** that separate one section from another. Skim the whole form before you go back to read each instruction. If the form is printed on a single sheet of paper, be sure to check both sides.

B Read the **headings** to learn what each section covers and which section(s) you need to fill out.

C Read the introductory information carefully, paying particular attention to **subheads** that are especially useful to you. When you come across **references** to charts or other sections in the form, refer to those charts or sections as you read the related information.

D Within each section, look for **numbers** or **letters** that signal **steps in a sequence.** Read all the steps in a sequence before you follow any of them.

E Look for **numbered and/or lettered write-on lines.** Write your answers to each numbered or lettered step on the line with the same number or letter.

Form W-4 (2001)

Form W-4 (2001) **A**

Purpose. Complete Form W-4 so your employer can withhold the correct Federal income tax from your pay. Because your tax situation may change, you may want to refigure your withholding each year.

Exemption from withholding. If you are exempt, complete only lines 1, 2, 3, 4, and 7, and sign the form to validate it. Your exemption for 2001 expires February 18, 2002.

Note: You cannot claim exemption from withholding if (1) your income exceeds $750 and includes more than $250 of unearned income (e.g., interest and dividends) and (2) another person can claim you as a dependent on their tax return.

C **Basic instructions.** If you are not exempt, complete the **Personal Allowances Worksheet** below. The worksheets on page 2 adjust your withholding allowances based on itemized deductions, certain credits, adjustments to

income, or two-earner/two-job situations. Complete all worksheets that apply. They will help you figure the number of withholding allowances you are entitled to claim. **However, you may claim fewer (or zero) allowances.**

Head of household. Generally, you may claim head of household filing status on your tax return only if you are unmarried and pay more than 50% of the costs of keeping up a home for yourself and your dependent(s) or other qualifying individuals. See line **E** below.

Tax credits. You can take projected tax credits into account in figuring your allowable number of withholding allowances. Credits for child or dependent care expenses and the child tax credit may be claimed using the **Personal Allowances Worksheet.** See **Pub. 919,** How Do I Adjust My Tax Withholding? for information on converting your other credits into withholding allowances.

Nonwage income. If you have a large amount of nonwage income, such as interest or dividends,

consider making estimated tax payments using **Form 1040-ES,** Estimated Tax for Individuals. Otherwise, you may owe additional tax.

Two earners/two jobs. If you have a working spouse or more than one job, figure the total number of allowances you are entitled to claim on all jobs using worksheets from only one Form W-4. Your withholding usually will be most accurate when all allowances are claimed on the Form W-4 for the highest paying job and zero allowances are claimed on the others.

Check your withholding. After your Form W-4 takes effect, use Pub. 919 to see how the dollar amount you are having withheld compares to your projected total tax for 2001. Get Pub. 919 especially if you used the **Two-Earner/Two-Job Worksheet** on page 2 and your earnings exceed $150,000 (Single) or $200,000 (Married).

Recent name change? If your name on line 1 differs from that shown on your social security card, call 1-800-772-1213 for a new social security card.

Ⓑ **Personal Allowances Worksheet** (Keep for your records.)

A Enter "1" for **yourself** if no one else can claim you as a dependent . . . .   **A** _____

B Enter "1" if: {
- You are single and have only one job; or
- You are married, have only one job, and your spouse does not work; or
- Your wages from a second job or your spouse's wages (or the total of both) are $1,000 or less.
 } . .   **B** _____ Ⓔ

C Enter "1" for your **spouse.** But, you may choose to enter -0- if you are married and have either a working spouse or more than one job. (Entering -0- may help you avoid having too little tax withheld.) . . . .   **C** _____

D Enter number of **dependents** (other than your spouse or yourself) you will claim on your tax return . . . .   **D** _____

E Enter "1" if you will file as **head of household** on your tax return (see conditions under **Head of household** above)   **E** _____

F Enter "1" if you have at least $1,500 of **child or dependent care expenses** for which you plan to claim a credit .   **F** _____
  (**Note:** *Do* **not** *include child support payments. See* **Pub. 503,** *Child and Dependent Care Expenses, for details.*)

G **Child Tax Credit** (including additional child tax credit):
- If your total income will be between $18,000 and $50,000 ($23,000 and $63,000 if married), enter "1" for each eligible child.
- If your total income will be between $50,000 and $80,000 ($63,000 and $115,000 if married), enter "1" if you have two eligible children, enter "2" if you have three or four eligible children, or enter "3" if you have five or more eligible children.   **G** _____

H Add lines A through G and enter total here. (**Note:** *This may be different from the number of exemptions you claim on your tax return.*) ▶   **H** _____

For accuracy, complete all worksheets that apply. {
- If you plan to **itemize or claim adjustments to income** and want to reduce your withholding, see the **Deductions and Adjustments Worksheet** on page 2.
- If you are **single,** have **more than one job** and your combined earnings from all jobs exceed $35,000, **or** if you are **married** and have a **working spouse or more than one job** and the combined earnings from all jobs exceed $60,000, see the **Two-Earner/Two-Job Worksheet** on page 2 to avoid having too little tax withheld.
- If **neither** of the above situations applies, **stop here** and enter the number from line H on line 5 of Form W-4 below.

- - - - - - - - - - - - - - - - - - Cut here and give Form W-4 to your employer. Keep the top part for your records. - - - - - - - - - - - -

Form **W-4**
Department of the Treasury
Internal Revenue Service

Employee's Withholding Allowance Certificate

▶ **For Privacy Act and Paperwork Reduction Act Notice, see page 2.**

OMB No. 1545-0010

2001

| 1 | Type or print your first name and middle initial | Last name | 2 | Your social security number |

| Home address (number and street or rural route) | 3 | ☐ Single ☐ Married ☐ Married, but withhold at higher Single rate. |
| | **Note:** *If married, but legally separated, or spouse is a nonresident alien, check the Single box.* |

| City or town, state, and ZIP code | 4 | If your last name differs from that on your social security card, check here. You must call 1-800-772-1213 for a new card. ▶ ☐ |

Ⓓ
5   Total number of allowances you are claiming (from line **H** above **or** from the applicable worksheet on page 2)   **5** _____

6   Additional amount, if any, you want withheld from each paycheck . . . .   **6** $ _____

7   I claim exemption from withholding for 2001, and I certify that I meet **both** of the following conditions for exemption:
- Last year I had a right to a refund of **all** Federal income tax withheld because I had **no** tax liability **and**
- This year I expect a refund of **all** Federal income tax withheld because I expect to have **no** tax liability.

If you meet both conditions, write "Exempt" here . . . . ▶ **7** _____ Ⓔ

Under penalties of perjury, I certify that I am entitled to the number of withholding allowances claimed on this certificate, or I am entitled to claim exempt status.

Employee's signature
(Form is not valid
unless you sign it.) ▶   Date ▶

| 8 | Employer's name and address (Employer: Complete lines 8 and 10 only if sending to the IRS.) | 9 | Office code (optional) | 10 | Employer identification number |

Cat. No. 10220Q

PRACTICE AND APPLY

Reread the introductory information on Form W-4 and review the Employee's Withholding Allowance Certificate. Then answer the following questions:

1. Which part of Form W-4 is the Employee's Withholding Allowance Certificate? What are you supposed to do with this part of the form?

2. If you are exempt from withholding, which numbered lines do you need to complete? What else must you do to make this form valid?

3. If you are not writing "Exempt" on line 7, which worksheet on this page do you need to complete? What will completing this worksheet help you to do?

4. According to the document, if your last name differs from that on your social security card, what must you do?

5. After your Form W-4 takes effect, what publication can you use to see if enough money is being withheld from your paychecks to cover the total tax you're likely to owe for the year?

① The Writing Process

Different writers use different processes. Try out different strategies and figure out what works best for you. For some assignments, it is best to start by figuring out what you need to end up with, make a plan or outline, and stick to it. Other writing assignments may be more successful if you start by writing everything you know about the topic, allow things to get messy, and then reshape and revise the writing so it fits the assignment. Try both approaches and get to know yourself as a writer.

Also consider whether the assignment is high-stakes or low-stakes writing. When the success of the piece is very important, such as in a test, you might choose to focus on meeting the requirements or criteria of the assignment. When the purpose of the writing is to develop your ideas, there is more opportunity to experiment and take risks. Take into account the time factor as well. In a timed writing test, you may not have time to explore and revise.

Correct grammar and spelling are very important in your final product. You don't need to focus on these as you shape your ideas and draft your piece, but be sure you allow time for a careful edit before turning in your final piece.

ⓘ Prewriting

In the prewriting stage, you explore your ideas and discover what you want to write about.

Finding Ideas for Writing

Try one or more of the following techniques to help you find a writing topic.

> **Personal Techniques**
>
> - Practice imaging, or trying to remember mainly sensory details about a subject—its look, sound, feel, taste, and smell.
>
> - Complete a knowledge inventory to discover what you already know about a subject.
>
> - Browse through magazines, newspapers, and on-line bulletin boards for ideas.
>
> - Start a clip file of articles that you want to save for future reference. Be sure to label each clip with source information.

> **Sharing Techniques**
>
> - With a group, brainstorm a topic by trying to come up with as many ideas as you can without stopping to critique or examine them.
>
> - Interview someone who knows a great deal about your topic.

> **Writing Techniques**
>
> - After freewriting on a topic, try looping, or choosing your best idea for more freewriting. Repeat the loop at least once.
>
> - Make a list to help you organize ideas, examine them, or identify areas for further research.

> **Graphic Techniques**
>
> - Create a pro-and-con chart to compare the positive and negative aspects of an idea or a course of action.
>
> - Use a cluster map or tree diagram to explore subordinate ideas that relate to your general topic or central idea.

Determining Your Purpose

Your purpose for writing may be to express yourself, to entertain, to describe, to explain, to analyze, or to persuade. To clarify it, ask questions like these:

- Why did I choose to write about my topic?

- What aspects of the topic mean the most to me?

- What do I want others to think or feel after they read my writing?

LINK TO LITERATURE One purpose for writing is to clarify a subject. For example, the Nigerian writer

Chinua Achebe, author of "Civil Peace," page 1274, wrote to correct the errors and misunderstandings about Africans in European literature and to show the value of African cultures.

Identifying Your Audience

Knowing who will read your writing can help you focus your topic and choose relevant details. As you think about your readers, ask yourself questions like these:

- What does my audience already know about my topic?
- What will they be most interested in?
- What language is most appropriate for this audience?

 **Drafting**

In the drafting stage, you put your ideas on paper and allow them to develop and change as you write.

Two broad approaches in this stage are discovery drafting and planned drafting.

Discovery drafting is a good approach when you are not quite sure what you think about your subject. You just plunge into your draft and let your feelings and ideas lead you where they will. After finishing a discovery draft, you may decide to start another draft, do more prewriting, or revise your first draft.

Planned drafting may work better for research reports, critical reviews, and other kinds of formal writing. Try making a writing plan or a scratch outline before you begin drafting. Then, as you write, you can fill in the details.

LINK TO LITERATURE Sometimes the creative process is accelerated out of necessity. Harold Pinter, author of *That's All,* page 1254, wrote his first play, *The Room,* in just four afternoons while he was working as an actor. Spending mornings in rehearsal and evenings in performance, he wrote the play for a group of college drama students.

 Revising, Editing, and Proofreading

The changes you make in your writing during this stage usually fall into three categories: revising for content, revising for structure, and proofreading to correct mistakes in mechanics.

Use the questions that follow to assess problems and determine what changes would improve your work.

Revising for Content

- Does my writing have a main idea or central focus? Is my thesis clear?
- Have I incorporated adequate detail? Where might I include a telling detail, revealing statistic, or vivid example?
- Is any material unnecessary, irrelevant, or confusing?

WRITING TIP Be sure to consider the needs of your audience as you answer the questions under Revising for Content and Revising for Structure. For example, before you can determine whether any of your material is unnecessary or irrelevant, you need to identify what your audience already knows.

Revising for Structure

- Is my writing unified? Do all ideas and supporting details pertain to my main idea or advance my thesis?
- Is my writing clear and coherent? Is the flow of sentences and paragraphs smooth and logical?
- Do I need to add transitional words, phrases, or sentences to make the relationships among ideas clearer?
- Are my sentences well constructed? What sentences might I combine to improve the grace and rhythm of my writing?

Proofreading to Correct Mistakes in Grammar, Usage, and Mechanics

When you are satisfied with your revision, proofread your paper, looking for mistakes in grammar, usage, and mechanics. You may want

to do this several times, looking for different types of mistakes each time. The following checklist may help.

Sentence Structure and Agreement
- Are there any run-on sentences or sentence fragments?
- Do all verbs agree with their subjects?
- Do all pronouns agree with their antecedents?
- Are verb tenses correct and consistent?

Forms of Words
- Do adverbs and adjectives modify the appropriate words?
- Are all forms of *be* and other irregular verbs used correctly?
- Are pronouns used correctly?
- Are comparative and superlative forms of adjectives correct?

Capitalization, Punctuation, and Spelling
- Is any punctuation mark missing or not needed?
- Are all words spelled correctly?
- Are all proper nouns and all proper adjectives capitalized?

WRITING TIP For help identifying and correcting problems that are listed in the Proofreading Checklist, see the Grammar Handbook, pages 1391–1420.

You might wish to mark changes on your paper by using the proofreading symbols shown in the chart below.

Proofreading Symbols

∧	Add letters or words.	/	Make a capital letter lowercase.
⊙	Add a period.	¶	Begin a new paragraph.
≡	Capitalize a letter.	⌒	Delete letters or words.
⌒	Close up space.	∿	Switch the positions of letters or words.
∧	Add a comma.		

1.4 Publishing and Reflecting

Always consider sharing your finished writing with a wider audience. Reflecting on your writing is another good way to bring closure to a project.

Creative Publishing Ideas
Following are some ideas for publishing and sharing your writing.
- Post your writing on an electronic bulletin board or send it to others via e-mail.
- Create a multimedia presentation and share it with classmates.
- Publish your writing in a school newspaper or literary magazine.
- Present your work orally in a report, a speech, a reading, or a dramatic performance.
- Submit your writing to a local newspaper or a magazine that publishes student writing.
- Form a writing exchange group with other students.

WRITING TIP You might work with other students to publish an anthology of class writing. Then exchange your anthology with another class or another school. Reading the work of other student writers will help you get ideas for new writing projects and find ways to improve your work.

Reflecting on Your Writing
Think about your writing process and whether you would like to add what you have written to your portfolio. You might attach a note in which you answer questions like these:
- What did I learn about myself and my subject through this writing project?
- Which parts of the writing process did I most and least enjoy?
- As I wrote, what was my biggest problem? How did I solve it?
- What did I learn that I can use the next time I write?

1.5 Using Peer Response

Peer response consists of the suggestions and comments your peers or classmates make about your writing.

You can ask a peer reader for help at any point in the writing process. For example, your peers can help you develop a topic, narrow your focus, discover confusing passages, or organize your writing.

Questions for Your Peer Readers

You can help your peer readers provide you with the most useful kinds of feedback by following these guidelines:

- Tell readers where you are in the writing process. Are you still trying out ideas, or have you completed a draft?

- Ask questions that will help you get specific information about your writing. Open-ended questions that require more than yes-or-no answers are more likely to give you information you can use as you revise.

- Give your readers plenty of time to respond thoughtfully to your writing.

- Encourage your readers to be honest when they respond to your work. It's OK if you don't agree with them—you always get to decide which changes to make.

Tips for Being a Peer Reader

Follow these guidelines when you respond to someone else's work:

- Respect the writer's feelings.

- Make sure you understand what kind of feedback the writer is looking for, and then respond accordingly.

- Use "I" statements, such as "I like . . . ," "I think . . . ," or "It would help me if . . . ." Remember that your impressions and opinions may not be the same as someone else's.

WRITING TIP Writers are better able to absorb criticism of their work if they first receive positive feedback. When you act as a peer reader, try to start your review by telling something you like about the piece.

The chart below explains different peer-response techniques to use when you are ready to share your work.

Peer-Response Techniques

Sharing Use this when you are just exploring ideas or when you want to celebrate the completion of a piece of writing.

- *Will you please read or listen to my writing without criticizing or making suggestions afterward?*

Summarizing Use this when you want to know if your main idea or goals are clear.

- *What do you think I'm saying? What's my main idea or message?*

Replying Use this strategy when you want to make your writing richer by adding new ideas.

- *What are your ideas about my topic? What do you think about what I have said in my piece?*

Responding to Specific Features Use this when you want a quick overview of the strengths and weaknesses of your writing.

- *Are the ideas supported with enough examples? Did I persuade you? Is the organization clear enough for you to follow the ideas?*

Telling Use this to find out which parts of your writing are affecting readers the way you want and which parts are confusing.

- *What did you think or feel as you read my words? Would you show me which passage you were reading when you had that response?*

---

2 Building Blocks of Good Writing

Whatever your purpose in writing, you need to capture your readers' interest, organize your ideas well, and present your thoughts clearly. Giving special attention to some particular parts of a story or an essay can make your writing more enjoyable and more effective.

2.1 Introductions

When you flip through a magazine trying to decide which articles to read, the opening paragraph is often critical. If it does not grab your attention, you are likely to turn the page.

Kinds of Introductions

Here are some introduction techniques that can capture a reader's interest.

- Make a surprising statement
- Provide a description
- Pose a question
- Relate an anecdote
- Address the reader directly
- Begin with a thesis statement

Make a Surprising Statement Beginning with a startling statement or an interesting fact can capture your reader's curiosity about the subject, as in the model below.

> MODEL
> Since it was first published in 1883, Robert Louis Stevenson's *Treasure Island* has never been out of print, and it has been translated into languages as diverse as Welsh, Zulu, and Ukrainian. This unusual success attests to the universal appeal of Stevenson's storytelling skills.

Provide a Description A vivid description sets a mood and brings a scene to life for your reader. Here, details about visitors at Ellis Island set the tone for an essay about immigration to the United States.

> MODEL
> The visitors to the museum at Ellis Island wander almost reverently through rooms filled with photos and memorabilia. The walls seem to reverberate with countless stories—many long since forgotten—of immigrants who passed through this island.

Pose a Question Beginning with a question can make your reader want to read on to find out the answer. The following introduction asks a significant question about the careers of two women writers.

> MODEL
> George Eliot and George Sand were both successful writers in the 19th century; both were also women. At this time in history, why did they need to use male pen names?

Relate an Anecdote Beginning with a brief anecdote, or story, can hook readers and help you make a point in a dramatic way. The anecdote below introduces an essay about gangsters in the 1920s.

> MODEL
> The man, in an immaculate suit with broad lapels, narrowed his eyes against the sun as he stepped from the shadowy doorway. Pulling his hat down, he tossed a dime to the dazed, grubby boy standing before him. "Go get me a coupla Cokes, willya?—and step on it, kid!" So it was that my grandfather met Al Capone.

Address the Reader Directly Speaking directly to readers establishes a friendly, informal tone and involves them in your topic.

> MODEL
> If you are concerned about the appearance of our community, you should learn how you can participate in the Adopt-a-Street program that begins this April.

Begin with a Thesis Statement A thesis statement expressing a paper's main idea may be woven into both the beginning and the end of nonfiction writing. The following is a thesis statement that introduces a literary analysis.

> MODEL
> In "Words and Behavior," Aldous Huxley argues that language must be used carefully. He shows that its misuse can establish and perpetuate great evil.

WRITING TIP In order to write the best introduction for your paper, you may want to try more than one of the methods and then decide which is the most effective for your purpose and audience.

2.2 Paragraphs

A paragraph is made up of sentences that work together to develop an idea or accomplish a purpose. Whether or not it contains a topic sentence stating the main idea, a good paragraph must have unity and coherence.

Unity

A paragraph has unity when all the sentences support and develop one stated or implied idea. Use the following techniques to create unity in your paragraphs.

Write a Topic Sentence A topic sentence states the main ideas of the paragraph; all other sentences in the paragraph provide supporting details. A topic sentence is often the first sentence in a paragraph. However, it may also appear later in the paragraph or at the end, to summarize or reinforce the main idea, as shown in the model that follows.

> MODEL
> Magnesium is a mineral found in food sources such as beans, nuts, meats, and dairy products. This mineral is necessary for the breakdown of nutrients in cells and is important to the stimulation of muscles and nerves. A healthy body effectively conserves magnesium. Insufficient amounts of the mineral, however, are related to various health problems. Dietary magnesium is clearly vital to human health.

Relate All Sentences to an Implied Main Idea A paragraph can be unified without a topic sentence as long as every sentence supports the implied, or unstated, main idea. In the model below, all the sentences work together to create a unified impression of an impending storm.

> MODEL
> All morning the wind had gently rustled the branches of trees and tossed back curtains from open windows. By early afternoon, however, it had picked up a force that tore green leaves from the trees and pushed thick and menacing clouds across the sky.

Coherence

A paragraph is coherent when all its sentences are related to one another and flow logically from one to the next. The following techniques will help you achieve coherence in paragraphs.

- Present your ideas in the most logical order.
- Use pronouns, synonyms, and repeated words to connect ideas.
- Use transitional devices to show the relationships among ideas.

In the model below, the writer used some of these techniques to create a unified paragraph.

> MODEL
> Most people know that the gravitational pull of the moon causes tides in the ocean. Are you aware, though, that the moon exerts the same pull on the solid part of the earth? Unlike ocean tides, however, earth tides are deformations of as much as a foot in the earth's surface. The extent to which its surface bulges is greatest during full moon and new moon because the gravitational pull of the moon combines with that of the sun.

2.3 Transitions

Transitions are words and phrases that show the connections between details. Clear transitions help show how your ideas relate to each other.

Kinds of Transitions

Transitions can help readers understand several kinds of relationships:

- Time or sequence
- Spatial relationships
- Degree of importance
- Compare and contrast
- Cause and effect

Time or Sequence Some transitions help to clarify the sequence of events over time. When you are telling a story or describing a process, you can connect ideas with such transitional words as *first, second, always, then, next, later, soon, before, finally, after, earlier, afterward,* and *tomorrow.*

> MODEL
> **Before a blood donation can be used, it must be processed carefully. First, a sample is tested for infectious diseases and identified by blood type. Next, preservatives are added. Finally, a blood cell separator breaks up the blood into its parts, such as red blood cells, platelets, and plasma.**

Spatial Relationships Transitional words and phrases, such as *in front, behind, next to, along, nearest, lowest, above, below, underneath, on the left,* and *in the middle,* can help readers visualize a scene.

> MODEL
> **A theater-in-the-round stage is constructed in the middle of the theater space, with the audience sitting around the entire stage. To create a more intimate setting, the seats nearest the stage are often only a few feet away.**

Degree of Importance Transitional words such as *mainly, strongest, weakest, first, second, most important, least important, worst,* and *best* may be used to rank ideas or to show degree of importance.

> MODEL
> **Cory made several New Year's resolutions. Most important, he decided to cut back on watching TV.**

Compare and Contrast Words and phrases such as *similarly, likewise, also, like, as, neither . . . nor,* and *either . . . or* show similarity between details. *However, by contrast, yet, but, unlike, instead, whereas,* and *while* show difference. Note the use of both types of transitions in the model below.

> MODEL
> **Like running and bicycling, swimming helps you maintain aerobic fitness; however, swimming has the added benefit of exercising muscles throughout your body.**

WRITING TIP Both *but* and *however* may be used to join two independent clauses. When *but* is used as a coordinating conjunction, it is preceded by a comma. When *however* is used as a conjunctive adverb, it is preceded by a semicolon and followed by a comma.

Cause and Effect When you are writing about a cause-and-effect relationship, use transitional words and phrases, such as *since, because, thus, therefore, so, due to, for this reason,* and *as a result,* to help clarify that relationship and to make your writing coherent.

> MODEL
> **Because the temperature dropped to 28 degrees after it rained for five hours, car door locks froze.**

(2.4) Conclusions

A conclusion should leave readers with a strong final impression. Try any of these approaches.

Kinds of Conclusions

Here are some effective methods for bringing your writing to a conclusion:

- Restate your thesis
- Ask a question
- Make a recommendation
- Make a prediction
- Summarize your information

Restate Your Thesis A good way to conclude an essay is by restating your thesis, or main idea, in different words. The conclusion below restates the thesis introduced on page 1359.

> MODEL
> Aldous Huxley's "Words and Behavior" clearly warns of the danger of misusing language to manipulate and control. Unless we begin using concrete words and plain language, he maintains, we may ultimately destroy our civilization.

Ask a Question Try asking a question that sums up what you have said and gives readers something new to think about. The question below concludes an appeal to halt funding for space exploration.

> MODEL
> Given all the evidence, can you imagine that continued investment in the space program will benefit future generations more than the same investment in the basic needs of those living now?

Make a Recommendation When you are persuading your audience to take a position on an issue, you can conclude by recommending a specific course of action.

> MODEL
> Voting is a vital way to influence your world. Add voter registration to your birthday plans.

Make a Prediction Readers are concerned about matters that may affect them and therefore are moved by a conclusion that predicts the future.

> MODEL
> If we continue to overuse antibiotics, we will speed the development of infections that resist treatment. Such infections will kill millions despite the best medical science.

Summarize Your Information Summarizing reinforces the writer's main ideas, leaving a strong, lasting impression. The model below concludes with a statement that summarizes a review of a book.

> MODEL
> James Gurney's book *Dinotopia* appeals to adult readers, as well as to children, with its imaginative adventures, its fascinating drawings of dinosaurs, and its timeless theme of cooperation in a diverse community.

(2.5) Elaboration

Elaboration is the process of developing a writing idea by providing specific supporting details that are relevant and appropriate to the purpose and form of your writing.

- **Facts and Statistics** A fact is a statement that can be verified, while a statistic is a fact stated in numbers. Make sure the facts and statistics you supply are from a reliable, up-to-date source. As in the model below, the facts and statistics you use should strongly support the statements you make.

> MODEL
> The decade from 1900 to 1910 saw 8,795,000 immigrants come to the United States. Then Congress passed the Emergency Quota Act of 1921. Between 1921 and 1930, only 4,107,000 immigrants entered the United States. The law had cut immigration by more than half.

- **Sensory Details** Details that show how something looks, sounds, tastes, smells, or feels can enliven a description, making readers feel they are actually experiencing what you are describing. Which senses does the writer appeal to in this paragraph?

MODEL

Gina wasn't sure she enjoyed her first hayride. As the wagon bumped along the furrows, she clumsily bounced between Marty and Deanna. She tried to imagine she was having fun as she shivered under the scratchy wool blankets that smelled of straw and dust.

- **Incidents** From our earliest years, we are interested in hearing "stories." One way to illustrate a point powerfully is to relate an incident or tell a story, as shown in the example below.

MODEL

Reforms often do not happen until a significant tragedy brings a problem to public attention. The deaths of 146 women workers in a fire at New York City's Triangle Shirtwaist factory in 1911 led to tougher protective labor laws in New York State and a national awareness of unsafe management practices.

- **Examples** An example can help make an abstract or a complex idea concrete or can provide evidence to clarify a point for readers.

MODEL

There was a time when many of the foods eaten around the world today were found only in North, Central, and South America. For example, tomatoes, potatoes, beans, and corn all originated in the Americas.

- **Quotations** Choose quotations that clearly support your points and be sure that you copy each quotation word for word. Remember always to credit the source.

MODEL

Technological advances in the design of tennis rackets have changed the nature of the sport, but many players lament the passing of the wood racket. In his article "The Feel of Wood," Marshall Fisher states that after he switched to an aluminum racket in college competition, he concluded that the unavoidable "march of technology had degraded tennis."

2.6 Using Language Effectively

Effective use of language can help readers to recognize the significance of an issue, to visualize a scene, or to understand a character. The specific words and phrases that you use have everything to do with how effectively you communicate meaning. This is true of all kinds of writing, from novels to office memos. Keep these particular points in mind.

- **Specific Nouns** Nouns are specific when they refer to individual or particular things. If you refer to a *city*, you are being general. If you refer to *London*, you are being specific. Specific nouns help readers identify the *who, what,* and *where* of your message.

- **Specific Verbs** Verbs are the most powerful words in sentences. They convey the action, the movement, and sometimes the drama of thoughts and observations. Verbs such as *trudged, skipped,* and *sauntered* provide a more vivid picture of the action than the verb *walked.*

- **Specific Modifiers** Use modifiers sparingly, but when you use them, make them count. Is the building *big* or *towering*? Are your poodle's paws *small* or *petite*? Once again, it is the more specific word that carries the greater impact.

③ Descriptive Writing

Descriptive writing allows you to paint word pictures about anything and everything in the world, from events of global importance to the most personal feelings. It is an essential part of almost every piece of writing, including essays, poems, letters, field notes, newspaper reports, and videos.

RUBRIC **Standards for Writing**

A successful description should

- have a clear focus and sense of purpose.
- use sensory details and precise words to create a vivid image, establish a mood, or express emotion.
- present details in a logical order.

③.1 Key Techniques

Consider Your Goals What do you want to accomplish in writing your description? Do you want to show why something is important to you? Do you want to make a person or scene more memorable? Do you want to explain an event?

Identify Your Audience Who will read your description? How familiar are they with your subject? What background information will they need? Which details will they find most interesting?

Think Figuratively What figures of speech might help make your description vivid and interesting? What simile or metaphor comes to mind? What imaginative comparisons can you make? What living thing does an inanimate object remind you of?

MODEL

Her laughter was a powerful potion that soothed the hurt feelings and damaged egos of the dinner guests. She was the antidote to her husband's rude and dismissive behavior, and she knew it.

Gather Sensory Details Which sights, smells, tastes, sounds, and textures make your subject come alive? Which details stick in your mind when you observe or recall your subject? Which senses does it most strongly affect?

MODEL

The stowaways were wedged between the rough-hewn crates deep in the bowels of the creaking ship. Through the blackness of the dank and putrid air, a thin shaft of light was their only measure of day and night.

You might want to use a chart like the one shown here to collect sensory details about your subject.

Sights	Sounds	Textures	Smells	Tastes

Create a Mood What feelings do you want to evoke in your readers? Do you want to soothe them with comforting images? Do you want to build tension with ominous details? Do you want to evoke sadness or joy?

MODEL

The heavy gray sky hung above the vast expanse of empty plains. The families, exhausted from too much travel and precious little rest, trudged beside their tattered wagons containing those few but cherished treasures from their former lives. They lived in the present. Remembering life before this journey was too painful. The uncertainty of life after this journey was too frightening.

3.2 Options for Organization

Spatial Order Choose one of these options to show the spatial order of a scene.

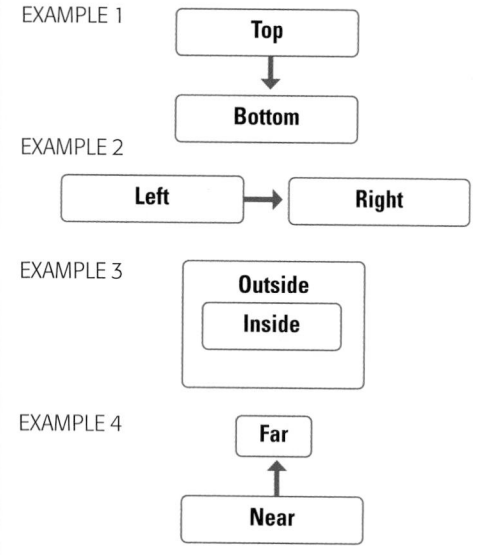

EXAMPLE 1
Top → Bottom

EXAMPLE 2
Left → Right

EXAMPLE 3
Outside / Inside

EXAMPLE 4
Far ← Near

MODEL

Detective Malloy surveyed the scene. Just inside the ruined door, a torn letter lay on the floor. In the middle of the room stood a large oak desk, neatly organized except for a lamp that hung off the edge. Behind the desk, a chair lay against the far wall.

WRITING TIP Use transitions that help the reader picture the relationship among the objects you describe. Some useful transitions for showing spatial relationships are *behind, below, here, in the distance, on the left, over,* and *on top.*

Order of Impression Order of impression is how you notice details.

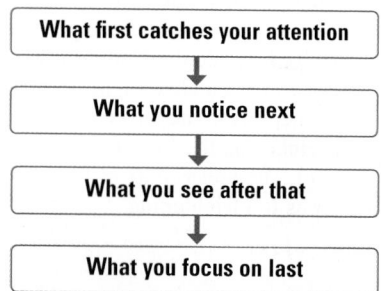

What first catches your attention
↓
What you notice next
↓
What you see after that
↓
What you focus on last

MODEL

First, we heard the screech of a car braking before our house. Next came the slam of a car door and then the staccato clicking of a woman's high heels as she ran up the cobblestone walk. It was already late in the evening, and we couldn't imagine who it could be.

WRITING TIP Use transitions that help readers understand the order of the impressions you are describing. Some useful transitions are *after, next, during, first, before, finally,* and *then.*

Order of Importance You might want to use order of importance as the organizing structure for your description.

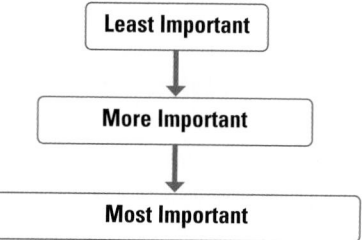

Least Important
↓
More Important
↓
Most Important

MODEL

All the Thanksgiving fixings were there: the perfectly browned, steaming turkey, the cranberry sauce glistening like rubies in the candlelight, the mounds of mashed potatoes like fluffy snowdrifts. The dining room resounded with chatter and laughter, but an emptiness clung to the corners and a silence cut through the conversation. Grandma wasn't with us.

WRITING TIP Use transitions that help the reader understand the order of importance that you attach to the elements of your description. Some useful transitions are *first, second, mainly, more important, less important,* and *least important.*

4 Narrative Writing

Narrative writing tells a story. If you write a story from your imagination, it is a fictional narrative. A true story about actual events is a nonfictional narrative. Narrative writing can be found in short stories, novels, news articles, and biographies.

RUBRIC Standards for Writing

A successful narrative should

- include descriptive details and dialogue to develop the characters, setting, and plot.
- have a clear beginning, middle, and end.
- have a logical organization with clues and transitions to help the reader understand the order of events.
- maintain a consistent tone and point of view.
- use language that is appropriate for the audience.
- demonstrate the significance of events or ideas.

4.1 Key Techniques

Identify the Main Events What are the most important events in your narrative? Is each event part of the chain of events needed to tell the story? In a fictional narrative, this series of events is the story's plot.

> MODEL
>
> Event 1   The morning after my grandfather's funeral, I go to the cemetery.
>
> Event 2   I stare at his grave and become angry and frustrated.
>
> Event 3   A cool rain reminds me of my grandfather's love of nature.
>
> Event 4   At the beach, I sit on the piece of driftwood near where my grandfather and I used to walk.

Describe the Setting When do the events occur? Where do they take place? How can you use setting to create mood and to set the stage for the characters and their actions?

> MODEL
>
> The morning after the funeral, my grandfather's grave is covered with flowers and wreaths that are just starting to wilt from the cold.

Depict Characters Vividly What do your characters look like? What do they think and say? How do they act? What vivid details can show readers what the characters are like?

> MODEL
>
> I stand shivering in my black sweatshirt before my grandfather's grave. My cold stare and stony face mask the anger and frustration that is welling up inside me. A muffled cry escapes, and the question "Why?" echoes in the emptiness of the cemetery.

WRITING TIP Dialogue is an effective way of developing characters in a narrative. As you write dialogue, choose words that express your characters' personalities and show how they feel about one another and about the events in the plot.

> MODEL
>
> I could just hear my grandfather say, "Boy, smell that salty wind. You just can't get a whiff of boiling nature like that any old where!"
>
> I'd look at him and say, "Yeah, I know." But I might be thinking that I'd like a whiff of juicy hot dogs and even bus fumes back in the city.
>
> Then he'd pull me into his world—our world—with something like "You and I, Boy. We're just alike. We love the water and the wind."

4.2 Options for Organization

Option 1: Chronological Order One way to organize a piece of narrative writing is to arrange the events in chronological order, as shown below.

Introduction characters and setting	MODEL
	The morning after my grandfather's funeral, I wake up early and walk to the cemetery.
Event 1	I stand by his grave and become angry and frustrated.
Event 2	I want to find some place where I can remember my grandfather and all the good times we had together.
End *perhaps show the significance of the events*	On the beach, I sit on the huge piece of driftwood where my grandfather and I used to sit. The cool lake wind and the noise of the waves bring back my favorite memories of him.

Option 2: Flashback It is also possible in narrative writing to arrange the order of events by starting with an event that happened before the beginning of the story.

> **Flashback**
> Begin with a key event that happened before the time in which the story takes place.
>
> ↓
>
> Introduce characters and setting.
>
> ↓
>
> Describe the events leading up to the conflict.

Option 3: Focus on Conflict When the telling of a fictional narrative focuses on a central conflict, the story's plot may follow the model shown below.

MODEL

Describe the main characters and setting	The brothers arrive at the school gym long before the rest of the basketball team. Although the twins are physically identical, their personalities couldn't be more different. Mark is outgoing and impulsive, while Matt is thoughtful and shy.
Present the conflict	Matt realizes his brother is missing shots on purpose and believes they will lose the championship.
Relate the events that make the conflict complex and cause the characters to change	• Matt has a chance at a basketball scholarship if they win the championship. • Mark needs money to buy a car. • Matt and Mark have stood by each other no matter what.
Present the resolution or outcome of the conflict	Matt retells a family story in which their grandfather chose honor and integrity over easy money. Mark plays to win.

Explanatory Writing

Explanatory writing informs and explains. For example, you can use it to evaluate the effects of a new law, to compare two movies, to analyze a piece of literature, or to examine the problem of greenhouse gases in the atmosphere.

5.1 Types of Explanatory Writing

There are many types of explanatory writing. Think about your topic and select the type that presents the information most clearly.

Compare and Contrast How are two or more subjects alike? How are they different?

> MODEL
> **King Arthur and Sir Launcelot share similar qualities that lead to their friendship, but they also share weaknesses that ensure their deaths.**

Cause and Effect How does one event cause something else to happen? Why do certain conditions exist? What are the results of an action or a condition?

> MODEL
> **King Arthur dies in battle with Sir Modred because he adheres too closely to the honor of knighthood and believes too much in the knights of his court.**

Analysis How does something work? How can it be defined? What are its parts?

> MODEL
> **Legends, such as the story of King Arthur, change over time as they are retold and take on new interpretations.**

Problem-Solution How can you identify and state a problem? How would you analyze the problem and its causes? How can it be solved?

> MODEL
> **Arthur has to choose between honor and friendship—two values that are equally desirable until they conflict.**

5.2 Compare and Contrast

Compare-and-contrast writing examines the similarities and differences between two or more subjects. You might, for example, compare and contrast two short stories, the main characters in a novel, or two movies.

> **RUBRIC** **Standards for Writing**
>
> **Successful compare-and-contrast writing should**
> - clearly identify the subjects that are being compared and contrasted.
> - include specific, relevant details.
> - follow a clear plan of organization dealing with the same features of both subjects under discussion.
> - use language and details appropriate to the audience.
> - use transitional words and phrases to clarify similarities and differences.

Options for Organization
Compare-and-contrast writing can be organized in different ways. The examples that follow demonstrate feature-by-feature organization and subject-by-subject organization.

Option 1: Feature-by-Feature Organization

MODEL

Feature 1

I. Noble qualities

Subject A. Arthur: admires Launcelot as great knight, so is reluctant to fight him

Subject B. Launcelot: respects Arthur as his liege, so is reluctant to fight him

Feature 2

II. Weaknesses

Subject A. Arthur: trusts his knights' judgment over his own

Subject B. Launcelot: love for Arthur's wife stronger than respect for Arthur

Option 2: Subject-by-Subject Organization

MODEL

Subject A

I. Arthur:

Feature 1. Noble quality: admires Launcelot as great knight, so is reluctant to fight him

Feature 2. Weakness: trusts his knights' judgment over his own

Subject B

II. Launcelot:

Feature 1. Noble Quality: respects Arthur as his liege, so is reluctant to fight him

Feature 2. Weakness: love for Arthur's wife stronger than respect for Arthur

WRITING TIP Remember your purpose for comparing and contrasting your subjects, and support your purpose with expressive language and specific details.

5.3 Cause and Effect

Cause-and-effect writing explains why something happened, why certain conditions exist, or what resulted from an action or a condition. You might use cause-and-effect writing to explain a character's actions, the progress of a disease, or the outcome of a war.

RUBRIC Standards for Writing

Successful cause-and-effect writing should

- clearly state the cause-and-effect relationship.
- show clear connections between causes and effects.
- present causes and effects in a logical order and use transitions effectively.
- use facts, examples, and other details to illustrate each cause and effect.
- use language and details appropriate to the audience.

Options for Organization

Your organization will depend on your topic and purpose for writing.

- If you want to explain the causes of an event such as the closing of a factory, you might first state the effect and then examine its causes.

Option 1: Effect to Cause Organization

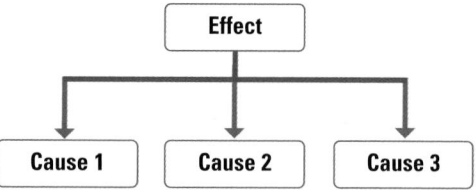

- If your focus is on explaining the effects of an event, such as the passage of a law, you might first state the cause and then explain the effects.

Option 2: Cause to Effect Organization

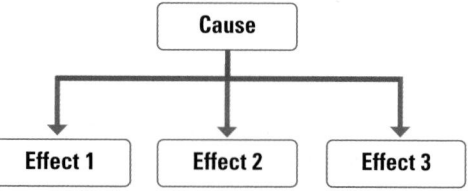

- Sometimes you'll want to describe a chain of cause-and-effect relationships to explore a topic such as the disappearance of tropical rain forests or the development of home computers.

Option 3: Cause-and-Effect Chain Organization

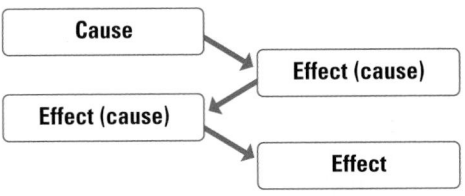

WRITING TIP Don't assume that a cause-and-effect relationship exists just because one event follows another. Look for evidence that the later event could not have happened if the first event had not caused it.

5.4 Problem-Solution

Problem-solution writing clearly states a problem, analyzes the problem, and proposes a solution to the problem. It can be used to identify and solve a conflict between characters, analyze a chemistry experiment, or explain why the home team keeps losing.

RUBRIC Standards for Writing

Successful problem-solution writing should

- identify the problem and help the reader understand the issues involved.
- analyze the causes and effects of the problem.
- integrate quotations, facts, and statistics into the text.
- explore possible solutions to the problem and recommend the best one(s).
- use language, tone, and details appropriate to the audience.

Options for Organization

Your organization will depend on the goal of your problem-solution piece, your intended audience, and the specific problem you choose to address. The organizational methods that follow are effective for different kinds of problem-solution writing.

Option 1: Simple Problem-Solution

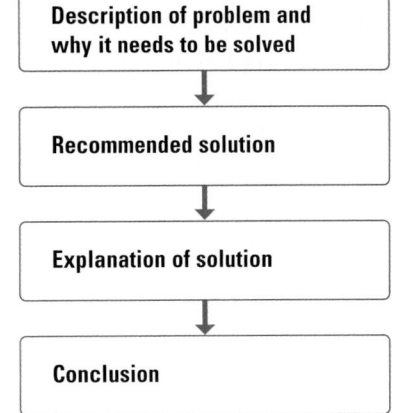

Option 2: Deciding Between Solutions

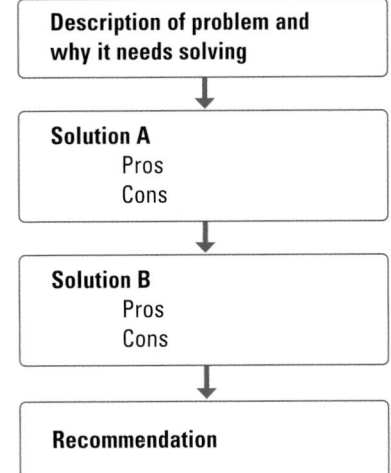

WRITING TIP Have a classmate read and respond to your problem-solution writing. Ask your peer reader: Is the problem clearly stated? Is the organization easy to follow? Do the proposed solutions seem logical?

5.5 Analysis

In writing an analysis, you explain how something works, how it is defined, or what its parts are. The details you include will depend upon the kind of analysis you write.

Process Analysis What are the major steps or stages in a process? What background information does the reader need to know—such as definitions of terms or a list of needed

equipment—to understand the analysis? You might use process analysis to explain how to program a VCR or prepare for a test.

Definition What are the most important characteristics of a subject? You might use definition analysis to explain a quality, such as honor or loyalty, the characteristics of a sonnet, or the skills of a physicist.

Parts Analysis What are the parts, groups, or types that make up a subject? Parts analysis could be used to explain the makeup of King Arthur's army or the parts of the brain.

RUBRIC Standards for Writing

A successful analysis should

- hook the readers' attention with a strong introduction.
- clearly state the subject and its parts.
- use a specific organizing structure to provide a logical flow of information.
- show connections among facts and ideas through subordinate clauses and transitional words and phrases.
- use language and details appropriate for the audience.

Options for Organization

Organize your details in a logical order appropriate for the kind of analysis you're writing.

Option 1: Process Analysis A process analysis is usually organized chronologically, with steps or stages in the order they occur.

MODEL

Introduction	**Arthurian legends reinterpreted**
Background	**British ruler in 500s**
Explain Steps	**Step 1: Around 1469, *Le Morte d'Arthur* is compiled.**
	Step 2: Between 1842 and 1885, *Idylls of the King* is published.
	Step 3: In 1960, the musical *Camelot* opens.

Option 2: Definition Analysis You can organize the details in a definition or parts analysis in order of importance or impression.

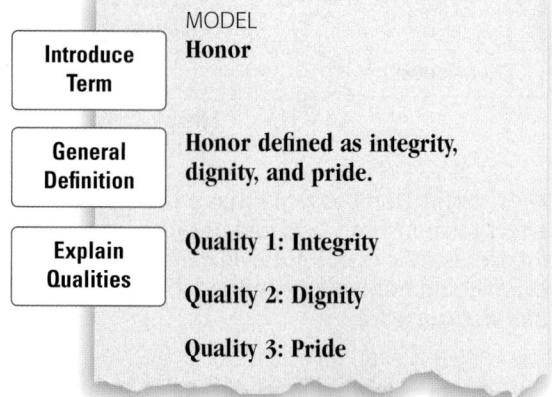

MODEL

Introduce Term	**Honor**
General Definition	**Honor defined as integrity, dignity, and pride.**
Explain Qualities	**Quality 1: Integrity**
	Quality 2: Dignity
	Quality 3: Pride

Option 3: Parts Analysis The following parts analysis explores three elements of a medieval knight's code of chivalry.

MODEL

Introduce Subject	**Code of chivalry**
Explain Parts	**Part 1: Devoted to Christianity**
	Part 2: Protect the defenseless
	Part 3: Fight injustices, never surrender

WRITING TIP Try to capture your readers' interest in your introduction. You might begin with a vivid description or an interesting fact, detail, or quotation. For example, an exciting excerpt from the narrative could open the process analysis.

An effective way to conclude an analysis is to return to your thesis and restate it in different words.

6 Persuasive Writing

Persuasive writing allows you to use the power of language to inform and influence others. It can take many forms, including speeches, newspaper editorials, billboards, advertisements, and critical reviews.

RUBRIC · Standards for Writing

Successful persuasion should

- state the issue and the writer's position.
- give opinions and support them with facts or reasons.
- have a reasonable and respectful tone.
- answer opposing views.
- use sound logic and effective language.
- conclude by summing up reasons or calling for action.

6.1 Key Techniques

Clarify Your Position What do you believe about the issue? How can you express your opinion most clearly?

> MODEL
> **We must find ways to depend less on the use of paper communication in order to save the forests.**

Know Your Audience Who will read your writing? What do they already know and believe about the issue? What objections to your position might they have? What additional information might they need? What tone and approach would be most effective?

> MODEL
> **We must take responsibility for using fewer of the products that come from trees. Meanwhile, we need to take a hard look at the chip mill practices which wipe out whole sections of forests.**

Support Your Opinion Why do you feel the way you do about the issue? What facts, statistics, examples, quotations, anecdotes, or opinions of authorities support your view? What reasons will convince your readers? What evidence can answer their objections?

> MODEL
> **Each mill can cause the clear-cutting of 10,000 acres of forest land in one year. The *St. Louis Post-Dispatch* quotes a member of the Department of Natural Resources that the clear-cutting of the Ozark forests has "had a well-documented, widespread, and devastating effect."**

Ways to Support Your Argument	
Statistics	Facts that are stated in numbers
Examples	Specific instances that explain your point
Observations	Events or situations you yourself have seen
Anecdotes	Brief stories that illustrate your point
Quotations	Direct statements from authorities

Begin and End with a Bang How can you hook your readers and make a lasting impression? What memorable quotation, anecdote, or statistic will catch their attention at the beginning or stick in their minds at the end? What strong summary or call to action can you conclude with?

> BEGINNING
> **Our forests are being cut down. The chip mill industry, which supplies the raw material for making so-called "high quality" paper, has tripled in the southwest United States in the last decade.**

> CONCLUSION
> **It's time to stop the rapid devastation of the forests. If it means less slick paper for magazines and computer printouts, so be it. Write the Conservation Department, the Forest Service, and especially your state's members of Congress.**

(6.2) Options for Organization

In a two-sided persuasive essay, you want to show the weaknesses of other opinions as you explain the strengths of your own.

The example below demonstrates one method of organizing your persuasive essay to convince your audience.

Option 1: Reasons for Your Opinion

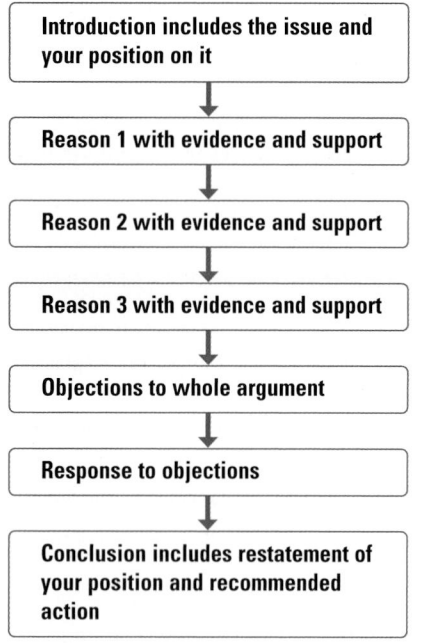

Introduction includes the issue and your position on it

↓

Reason 1 with evidence and support

↓

Reason 2 with evidence and support

↓

Reason 3 with evidence and support

↓

Objections to whole argument

↓

Response to objections

↓

Conclusion includes restatement of your position and recommended action

Option 2: Point-by-Point Basis

In the organization that follows, each reason and its objections are examined on a point-by-point basis.

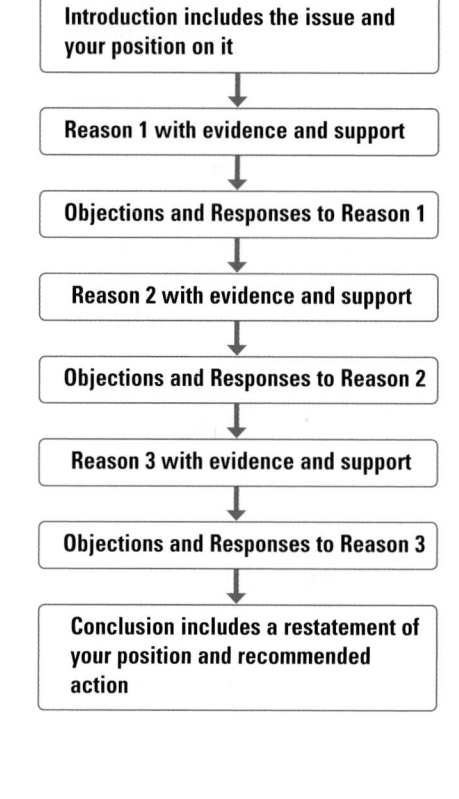

Introduction includes the issue and your position on it

↓

Reason 1 with evidence and support

↓

Objections and Responses to Reason 1

↓

Reason 2 with evidence and support

↓

Objections and Responses to Reason 2

↓

Reason 3 with evidence and support

↓

Objections and Responses to Reason 3

↓

Conclusion includes a restatement of your position and recommended action

Beware of Illogical Arguments Be careful about using illogical arguments. Opponents can easily attack your argument if you present illogical material.

Circular reasoning—trying to prove a statement by just repeating it in different words

> The forests are disappearing because the trees are being cut down.

Over-generalization—making a statement that is too broad to prove

> The chip-mill companies don't care about trees.

Either-or fallacy—stating that there are only two alternatives when they are many

> Either we quit using slick paper for magazines, or the forests will die.

Cause-and-effect fallacy—falsely assuming that because one event follows another the first event caused the second

> Chip mills are needed because we read so many magazines.

7 Research Report Writing

A research report explores a topic in depth, incorporating information from a variety of sources.

> **RUBRIC**   Standards for Writing
>
> **An effective research report should**
> - clearly state the purpose of the report in a thesis statement.
> - use evidence and details from a variety of sources to support the thesis.
> - contain only accurate and relevant information.
> - document sources correctly.
> - develop the topic logically and include appropriate transitions.
> - include a properly formatted Works Cited list.

7.1 Key Techniques

Develop Relevant, Interesting, and Researchable Questions Asking thoughtful questions is an ongoing part of research. Begin with a list of basic questions that are relevant to your topic. Focus on getting basic facts that answer the *who, what, where, when,* and *why* of your topic. If you were researching the social context of Dickens's novels, you might develop a set of questions like these.

> MODEL
> **What were living conditions like in London during the 1800s?**
> **What happened to orphans?**

As you become more familiar with your topic, think of questions that might provide an interesting perspective that makes readers think.

> MODEL
> **How did the legal system reflect society's values?**

Check that your questions are researchable. Ask questions that will uncover facts, statistics, case studies, and other documentable evidence.

Clarify Your Thesis A thesis statement is one or two sentences clearly stating the main idea that you will develop in your report. A thesis may also indicate the organizational pattern you will follow and reflect your tone and point of view.

> MODEL
> **In *Oliver Twist*, instead of drawing clear lines between the dark underworld of London and the light of the more civilized world, Charles Dickens blurs the distinction, making good and evil in society difficult to define.**

Document Your Sources You need to document, or credit, the sources where you find your evidence. In the example below, the writer uses and documents a quotation from the novel.

> MODEL
> **In *Oliver Twist*, Dickens shows the intertwining of good and evil in the world. The narrator states, "Men who look on nature . . . and cry that all is dark and gloomy, are in the right; but the somber colours are reflections from their own jaundiced eyes and hearts. The real hues . . . need a clearer vision." (Pool 256–257)**

Support Your Ideas You should support your ideas with relevant evidence—facts, anecdotes, and statistics—from reliable sources. In the example below, the writer includes a fact about the conditions of workhouses.

> MODEL
> **Oliver is condemned to a workhouse. The living conditions in workhouses were deliberately worse than in prisons in order to discourage the poor from depending on the publicly funded institutions. (Pool 245)**

7.2 Gathering Information: Sources

You will use a range of sources to collect the information you need to develop your research paper. These will include both print and electronic resources.

General Reference Works To clarify your thesis and begin your research, consult reference works that give quick, general overviews on a subject. General reference works include encyclopedias, almanacs and yearbooks, atlases, and dictionaries.

Specialized Reference Works Once you have a good idea of your specific topic, you are ready to look for detailed information in specialized reference works. In the library's reference section, specialized dictionaries and encyclopedias can be found for almost any field. For example, in the field of literature, you will find specialized reference sources such as *Contemporary Authors* and *Twentieth-Century Literary Criticism.*

Periodicals Journals and periodicals are a good source for detailed, up-to-date information. Periodical indexes, found in print and on-line catalogs in the library, will help you find articles on a topic. The *Readers' Guide to Periodical Literature* indexes many popular magazines. More specialized indexes include the *Humanities Index* and the *Social Sciences Index.*

Electronic Resources **Commercial information services** offer access to reference works such as dictionaries and encyclopedias, databases, and periodicals.

The **Internet** is a vast network of computer networks. News services, libraries, universities, researchers, organizations, and government agencies use the Internet to communicate and to distribute information. The Internet gives you access to the World Wide Web, which provides information on particular topics and links you to related topics and resources.

A **CD-ROM** is a research aid that stores information on a compact disk. Reference works on CD-ROMs may include text, sound, images, and video.

Databases are large collections of related information stored electronically. You can scan the information or search for specific facts.

RESEARCH TIP To find books on a specific topic, check the library's on-line catalog. Be sure to copy the correct call numbers of books that sound promising. Also look at books shelved nearby. They may relate to your topic.

7.3 Gathering Information: Validity of Sources

When you find source material, you must determine whether it is useful and accurate.

Credibility of Authorship Check whether an author has written several books or articles on the subject and has published in a well-respected newspaper or journal.

Objectivity Decide whether the information is fact, opinion, or propaganda. Reputable sources credit other sources of information.

Currency Check the publication date of the source to see whether the information is current.

Credibility of Publisher Seek information from a respected newspaper or journal, not from a tabloid newspaper or popular-interest magazine.

WEB TIP Be especially skeptical of information you locate on the Internet since virtually anyone can post anything there. Read the URL, or Internet address. Sites sponsored by a government agency (*.gov*) or an educational institution (*.edu*) are generally more reliable.

7.4 Taking Notes

As you find useful information, record the bibliographic information of each source on a separate index card. Then you are ready to take notes on your sources. You will probably use these three methods of note-taking.

Paraphrase, or restate in your own words, the main ideas and supporting details of the passage.

Summarize, or rephrase in fewer words, the original materials, trying to capture the key ideas.

Quote, or copy word for word, the original text, if you think the author's own words best clarify a particular point. Use quotation marks to signal the beginning and the end of the quotation.

For more details on making source cards and taking notes, see the Research Report Workshop on pages 423–430.

7.5 Options for Organization

Begin by reading over your note cards and sorting them into groups. The main-idea headings may help you find connections among the notes. Then arrange the groups of related note cards so that the ideas flow logically from one group to the next.

Option 1: Topic Outline

The Two Worlds of Oliver Twist
Introduction Dickens blurs the distinction between good and evil
I. The underworld of London
    A. The criminal characters
        1. Sikes and Monks
        2. Fagin
    B. The good characters
II. The civilized world of London

Like other forms of writing, research reports can be organized in several different ways. Some subjects may fit in chronological order. For other subjects, you may want to compare and contrast two topics. Other possibilities are a cause-and-effect organization or least-important to most-important evidence. If your material does not lend itself to any of the above organizations, try a general-to-specific approach.

Whatever your organizational pattern, making an outline can help guide the drafting process. The subtopics that you located in sorting your note cards will be the major topics of your outline, preceded by Roman numerals. Make sure that items of the same importance are parallel in form. For example, in the Option 1 Topic Outline below, topics I and II are both phrases. So are subtopics A and B.

A second kind of outline, shown below in Option 2, uses complete sentences instead of phrases for topics and subtopics.

Option 2: Sentence Outline

The Two Worlds of Oliver Twist
Introduction Dickens blurs the distinction between good and evil.

I. Dickens depicts the underworld of London by showing both evil criminal characters and those who commit crimes due to poverty or misfortune.
    A. The criminal characters are cruel and brutal.
        1. Sikes and Monks are characterized as men who will do anything to get what they want.
        2. Fagin's amorality is shown in his manipulating children into committing crimes.
    B. The good characters have believable human weaknesses and failings.
II. The civilized world of London is populated with people who are far from perfect.

7.6 Documenting Sources

When you quote, paraphrase, or summarize information from a source, you need to credit that source. Parenthetical documentation is the accepted method for crediting sources. You may choose to name the author in parentheses following the information along with the page number on which the information is found.

> **MODEL**
> Workhouses were purposely made "as grim and forbidding as possible" (Pool 245).

In parenthetical documentation, you may also use the author's name in the sentence along with the information. If so, enclose, in parentheses after the sentence, only the page number on which the information is found.

> **MODEL**
> According to Pool, many poor children like Oliver Twist populated London in the 1800s (31).

In either case, your reader can find out more about the source by turning to your Works Cited page, which lists complete bibliographical information for each source.

PUNCTUATION TIP When only the author and page number appear in parentheses, there is no punctuation between the two items. Also notice that the parenthetical citation comes after the closing quotation marks of a quotation, if there is one, and before the end punctuation of the sentence.

The examples above show citations for books with one author. The list that follows shows the correct way to write parenthetical citations for several kinds of sources.

Guidelines for Parenthetical Documentation

Work by One Author
Put the author's last name and the page reference in parentheses: (Pool 191).

If you mention the author's name in the sentence, put only the page reference in parentheses: (191).

Work by Two or Three Authors
Put the authors' last names and the page reference in parentheses:
(Mitchell and Deane 42).

Work by More Than Three Authors
Give the first author's last name followed by *et al.* and the page reference: (Bentley et al. 122).

Work with No Author Given
Give the title or a shortened version and (if appropriate) the page reference:
("Hurried Trials" 742).

One of Two or More Works by Same Author
Give the author's last name, the title or a shortened version, and the page reference:
(Dunn, "But We Grow" 54).

Selection from a Book of Collected Essays
Give the name of the author of the essay and the page reference: (Bayley 54).

Dictionary Definition
Give the entry title in quotation marks:
("Workhouse").

Unsigned Article in an Encyclopedia
Give the article title in quotation marks followed by a shortened source title:
("English Literature," World Book).

WRITING TIP Presenting someone else's writing or ideas as your own is plagiarism. To avoid plagiarism, you need to credit sources. However, if a piece of information is common knowledge—information available in several sources—you do not need to credit a source.

7.7 Following MLA Manuscript Guidelines

The final copy of your report should follow the Modern Language Association (MLA) guidelines for manuscript preparation.

- The heading in the upper left-hand corner of the first page should include your name, your teacher's name, the course name, and the date, each on a separate line.

- Below the heading, center the title on the page.

- Number all the pages consecutively in the upper right-hand corner, one-half inch from the top. Also, include your last name before the page number.

- Double-space the entire paper.

- Except for the margins above the page numbers, leave one-inch margins on all sides of every page.

The Works Cited page at the end of your report is an alphabetized list of the sources you have used and documented. In each entry all lines after the first are indented an additional one-half inch.

WRITING TIP When your report includes a quotation that is longer than four lines, set if off from the rest of the text by indenting the entire quotation one inch from the left margin. In this case, you should not use quotation marks.

Works Cited

Works Cited
Models for Works Cited entries

Works Cited

Bayley, John. "Oliver Twist: 'Things as They Really Are.'" Dickens and the Twentieth Century. Ed. John Gross and Gabriel Pearson. London: Routledge, 1962. 49–64.

1 Selection from a book of collected essays; note that publishers' names are shortened.

Bentley, Nicholas, et al. The Dickens Index. Oxford: Oxford UP, 1988.

2 Book with more than three authors

Collins, Philip. "Dickens, Charles." Encyclopaedia Britannica Online. Online. 9 March 1999.

3 Article in online encyclopedia

---, ed. Sikes and Nancy: A Facsimile. London: Dickens, 1982.

4 Second work by same individual; book with editor but no author

Dickens, Charles. Oliver Twist. New York: Bantam, 1981.

5 Book with one author

Dunn, Richard J. "'But We Grow Affecting: Let Us Proceed.'" Dickensian 62 (1966): 53–55.

6 Article in scholarly journal

Mitchell, B. R., and Phyllis Deane. Abstract of British Historical Statistics. Cambridge: Cambridge UP, 1962.

7 Work with two authors

7.8 MLA Documentation: Electronic Sources

As with print sources, information from electronic sources such as CD-ROMs or the Internet must be documented on your Works Cited page. You may find a reference to a source on the Internet and then use the print version of the article. If so, document it as you do other printed works. However, if you read or print out an article directly off the Internet, document it as shown below for an electronic source. Although electronic sources are shown separately below, they should be included on the Works Cited page with print sources.

Internet Sources Works Cited entries for Internet sources include the same kind of information as those for print sources. They also include the date you accessed the information and the electronic address of the source. Some of the information about the source may be unavailable. Include as much as you can. For more information on how to write Works Cited entries for Internet sources, see the MLA guidelines posted on the Internet or access this document through the McDougal Littell website.

More Online: Style Guidelines
www.mcdougallittell.com

CD-ROMs Entries for CD-ROMs include the publication medium (CD-ROM), the distributor, and the date of publication. Some of the information shown may not be always available. Include as much as you can.

Works Cited

Works Cited

Models for Works Cited entries for electronic sources

Works Cited

"Charles Dickens." <u>Britannica Online</u>. Vers. 98.2. Apr. 1998. Encyclopaedia Britannica. 17 Sept. 1998 <http://www.eb.com:180>

❶ Encyclopedia entry from online version

Dickens, Charles. <u>Oliver Twist</u>. London: Chapman & Hall. 1897. University of Virginia Library Electronic Text Center. 14 June 1998. <http://etext.lib.virginia.edu/etcbin/browse-mixed-new?id=DicOliv&tag=public&images=images/modeng&data=/texts/english/modeng/parsed>

❷ The complete text of the novel, available on the Internet; includes access date

<u>The Dickens Page</u>. Nagoya U. 14 June 1998 <http://lang.nagoya-u.ac.jp/~matsuoka/ Dickens.html>

❸ Scholarly site; shows date you accessed it

Rosenberg, Brian. "Character and Contradiction in Dickens." <u>Nineteenth Century Literature—Electronic Edition</u> 47.2 (1992): 18 pp. 15 June 1998 <http://www-ucpress.berkeley.edu:8080/scan/ncl-e/472/articles/rosenberg. art472.html>

❹ Article in a scholarly journal available on the Internet; includes number of pages and access date

"Workhouse." <u>Oxford English Dictionary</u>. 2nd ed. CD-ROM. Oxford: Oxford UP, 1992.

❺ Dictionary entry from CD-ROM version

Business Writing

⑧ Business Writing

The ability to write clearly and succinctly is an essential skill in the business world. As you prepare to enter the job market, you will need to know how to create letters, memos, and resumes.

Writing Handbook (side)

RUBRIC
Standards for Writing
Successful business writing should
- have a tone and language geared to the appropriate audience.
- state the purpose clearly in the opening sentences or paragraph.
- use precise words and avoid jargon.
- present only essential information.
- present details in a logical order.
- conclude with a summary of important points.

8.1 Key Techniques

Think About Your Purpose Why are you doing this writing? Do you want to "sell" yourself to a college admissions committee or a job interviewer? Do you want to order or complain about a product? Do you want to set up a meeting or respond to someone's ideas?

Identify Your Audience Who will read your writing? What background information will they need? What questions might they have? What tone or language is appropriate?

Support Your Points What specific details clarify your ideas? What reasons do you have for your statements? What points most strongly support them?

Finish Strongly How can you best sum up your statements? What is your main point? What action do you want others to take?

8.2 Options

Model 1: Letter

223 Harvest Way
Austin, TX 78712
May 2, 20__

Heading *Where the letter comes from and when*

Inside Address *To whom the letter is being sent*

Ms. Anne Shields, Department Head
Theater Department
Parker State University
Tulsa, OK 74133

Salutation *Greeting*

Dear Ms. Shields:

Body *Text of the message*

I am a high school senior. I am considering attending Parker State University and majoring in theater. I attended a performance of *Our Town* last fall and was very impressed with your production.

Could you please send me any available information about your department, including requirements for a major and a list of the year's productions?

Thank you very much.

Sincerely yours,
Jason Woemack

Closing

WRITING HANDBOOK **1379**

Model 2: Memo

Heading *Whom the memo is to and from, what it's about, and when it's being sent*	To: Mark From: Anne Shields Re: Student Request Date: 5/12/__
Body	Mark, I'm attaching a copy of a letter from a high school student. Please send him a department bulletin and a performance calendar. Also put him on our mailing list of prospective students.

Model 3: Resume A well-written resume is invaluable when you apply for a part-time or full-time job or for college. It should highlight your skills, accomplishments, and experience. Proofread your resume carefully to make sure it is clear and accurate and free of errors in grammar and spelling. It is a good idea to save a copy of your resume on your computer or on a disk so that you can easily update it.

State your purpose. *This resume is for a job application. A modified style can be used for a college application.*

List your previous employment experience *in reverse chronological order.*

Extracurricular activities and hobbies *can give a fuller picture of you and point out special job-related skills.*

MARY LLANOS
6642 W. Water Street, Denver, CO 80201
(303)555-8842

Objective A part-time position as a teacher's assistant

Qualifications Talent and interest in working with children
Skills in arts and crafts activities
Ability to cooperate with others

Work Experience *Summers 1999–Present: Handicamp, Denver, CO*
Was counselor for 9- and 10-year-olds at camp for handicapped children; planned arts and crafts activities for all age groups
1999–Present: Learn with Llanos, Denver, CO
Tutored a total of twelve children in English and math

Education *Lakeland High School, Class of 2000*
• Honor Roll
• Three years of Art
• One semester of Children's Literature

Extracurricular Activities • Treasurer, Future Teachers of America
• Vice President, Art Club
• Soccer Team

Hobbies Reading, arts and crafts, gardening

References Available upon request

① Inquiry and Research

In this age of seemingly unlimited information, the ability to locate and evaluate resources efficiently can spell the difference between success and failure—in both the academic and the business worlds. Make use of print and nonprint information sources.

ⓘ Finding Sources

Good research involves using the wealth of resources available to answer your questions and raise new questions. Knowing where to go and how to access information can lead you to interesting and valuable sources.

Reference Works

Reference works are print and nonprint sources of information that provide quick access to both general overviews and specific facts about a subject. These include

Dictionaries—word definitions, pronunciations, and origins

Thesauruses—lists of synonyms and antonyms for each entry

Glossaries—collections of specialized terms, such as those pertaining to literature, with definitions

Encyclopedias—detailed information on nearly every subject, arranged alphabetically (*Encyclopaedia Britannica*). Specialized encyclopedias deal with specific subjects, such as music, economics, and science (*Encyclopedia of Economics*).

Almanacs and Yearbooks—current facts and statistics (*World Almanac, Statistical Abstract of the United States*)

Atlases—maps and information about weather, agricultural and industrial production, and other geographical topics (*National Geographic Atlas of the World*)

Specialized Reference Works—biographical data (*Who's Who, Current Biography*), literary information (*Contemporary Authors, Book Review Digest, Cyclopedia of Literary Characters, The Oxford Companion to English Literature*), and quotations (*Bartlett's Familiar Quotations*)

Electronic Sources—Many of these reference works and databases are available on CD-ROMs, which may include text, sound, photographs, and video. CD-ROMs can be used on a home or library computer. You can subscribe to services that offer access to these sources on-line.

Periodicals and Indexes

One kind of specialized reference is a periodical.

- Some periodicals, such as *Atlantic Monthly* and *Psychology Today,* are intended for a general audience. They are indexed in the *Readers' Guide to Periodical Literature.*

- Many other periodicals, or journals, are intended for specialized or academic audiences. These include titles and subject matter as diverse as *American Psychologist* and *Studies in Short Fiction.* These are indexed in the *Humanities Index* and the *Social Sciences Index.* In addition, most fields have their own indexes. For example, articles on literature are indexed in the *MLA International Bibliography.*

- Many indexes are available in print, CD-ROM, and on-line forms.

Internet

The Internet is a vast network of computers. News services, libraries, universities, researchers, organizations, and government agencies use the Internet to distribute information and to communicate. The Internet can provide links to library catalogs, newspapers, government sources, and many of the reference sources described above. The Internet includes two key features:

World Wide Web—source of information on specific subjects and links to related topics

Electronic mail (e-mail)—communications link to other e-mail users worldwide

Other Resources

In addition to reference works found in the library and over the Internet, you can get information from the following sources: corporate publications, lectures, correspondence, and media such as films, television programs, and recordings. You can also observe directly, conduct your own interviews, and collect data from polls or questionnaires that you create yourself.

Evaluating Sources

Not all information is equal. You need to be a discriminating consumer of information and evaluate the credibility of the source, the reliability of the specific information included, and its value in answering your research needs.

Credibility of Sources

You must determine the credibility and appropriateness of each source in order to write an effective report or speech. Ask yourself the following questions:

Is the writer an authority? A writer who has written several books on a subject or whose name is included in many bibliographies may be considered an authoritative source.

Is the source reliable and unbiased? What is the author's motivation? For example, a defense of an industry in which the author has a financial interest may be biased. A profile of a writer or scientist written by a close relative may also be biased.

WEB TIP Be especially skeptical of information you locate on the Internet, since virtually anyone can post anything there. Read the URL, or Internet address. Sites sponsored by a government agency (*.gov*) or an educational institution (*.edu*) are generally more reliable.

Is the source up-to-date? It is important to consult the most recent material, especially in fields, such as medicine and technology, that undergo constant research and development. Some authoritative sources have withstood the test of time, however, and should not be overlooked.

Is the source appropriate? What audience is the material written for? In general, look for information directed at the educated reader. Material geared to experts or to popular audiences may be too technical or too simplified and therefore not appropriate for most research projects.

Distinguishing Fact from Opinion

As you gather information, it is important to recognize facts and opinions. A **fact** can be proven to be true or false. You could verify the statement "Congress rejected the bill" by checking newspapers, magazines, or the *Congressional Record.* An **opinion** is a judgment based on facts. The statement "Congress should not have rejected the bill" is an opinion. To evaluate an opinion, check for evidence presented logically and validly to support it.

Recognizing Bias

A writer may have a particular bias. This does not automatically make his or her point of view unreliable. However, recognizing an author's bias can help you evaluate a source. Recognizing that the author of an article about immigration is a Chinese immigrant will help you understand that author's bias. On the other hand, an author may have a hidden agenda that makes him or her less than objective about a topic. To avoid relying on information that may be biased, check an author's background and gather a variety of viewpoints.

Collecting Information

People use a variety of techniques to collect information during the research process. Try out several of those suggested below and decide which ones work best for you.

Paraphrasing and Summarizing

You can adapt material from other sources by quoting it directly or by paraphrasing or summarizing it. A paraphrase involves restating the information in your own words. It is often a simpler version but not necessarily a shorter

version. A summary involves extracting the main ideas and supporting details and writing a shorter version of the information.

Remember to credit the source when you paraphrase or summarize. See the Writing Handbook—Research Report, pp. 1373–1378.

Strategies for Paraphrasing
1. Select the portion of the article you want to record.
2. Read it carefully and think about those ideas you find most interesting and useful to your research. Often these will be the main ideas.
3. Retell the information in your own words.

Strategies for Summarizing
1. Read the article carefully. Determine the main ideas.
2. In your own words, write a shortened version of these main ideas.

Avoiding Plagiarism

Plagiarism is copying someone else's ideas or words and using them as if they were your own. This can happen inadvertently if you are sloppy about collecting information and documenting your sources. Plagiarism is intellectual stealing and can have serious consequences.

How to Avoid Plagiarism

1. When you paraphrase or summarize, be sure to change entirely the wording of the original by using your own words.

2. Both in notes and on your final report, enclose in quotation marks any material copied directly from other sources.

3. Indicate in your final report the sources of any ideas that are not general knowledge—including those in the visuals—that you have paraphrased or summarized.

4. Include a list of Works Cited with your finished report. See the Writing Handbook—Research Report Writing, pp. 1373–1378.

② Study Skills and Strategies

As you read an assignment for the first time, review material for a test, or search for information for a research report, you use different methods of reading and studying.

2.1 Skimming

When you run your eyes quickly over a text, paying attention to overviews, headings, topic sentences, highlighted words, and graphic features, you are skimming.

Skimming is a good technique for previewing material in a textbook or other source that you must read for an assignment. It is also useful when you are researching a self-selected topic. Skimming a source helps you determine whether it has pertinent information. For example, suppose you are writing a research report on three protagonists of Charles Dickens: Pip, Oliver Twist, and David Copperfield. Skimming an essay or a book on Dickens can help you quickly determine whether any part of it deals with your topic.

2.2 Scanning

To find a specific piece of information in a text, use scanning. To scan, place a card under the first line of a page and move it down slowly. Look for key words and phrases that signal the information you are looking for.

Scanning is useful in reviewing for a test or in finding a specific piece of information for a paper. Suppose you are looking for a discussion of Pip's relationship with Estella for your research report. You can scan a book chapter or an essay, looking for the key names *Pip* and *Estella*.

2.3 In-Depth Reading

When you must thoroughly understand the material in a text, you use in-depth reading.

In-depth reading involves asking questions, taking notes, looking for main ideas, and drawing conclusions as you read slowly and carefully. For example, in researching your report on Dickens's characters, you may find an essay on how Pip's relationship with Estella affects his life. Since this is closely related to your topic, you will read it in depth and take notes. You also should use in-depth reading for reading textbooks and literary works.

2.4 Outlining

Outlining is an efficient way of organizing ideas and is useful in taking notes.

Outlining helps you retain information as you read in depth. For example, you might outline a chapter in a history textbook, listing the main subtopics and the ideas or details that support them. An outline can also be useful for taking notes for a research report or in reading a piece of literature. The following is an example of a topic outline, which uses short phrases, that summarizes part of a chapter.

MAIN IDEA: **Oliver Twist is compared to Pip and David Copperfield.**
I. Pip and David Copperfield
    A. Independent
    B. Have growing self-awareness
    C. Tell own stories
II. Oliver Twist
    A. Dependent on outside forces
    B. Described by third-person narrator

2.5 Identifying Main Ideas

To understand and remember any material you read, identify its main idea.

In informative material, the main idea is often stated. The thesis statement of an essay or article and the topic sentence of each paragraph often state the main idea. In other material, especially literary works, the main idea is implied. After reading the piece carefully, analyze the important parts, such as characters and plot. Then try to sum up in one sentence the general point that the story makes.

2.6 Taking Notes

As you listen or read in depth, take notes to help you understand the material. Look and listen for key words that point to main ideas.

One way to help you summarize the main idea and supporting details is to take notes in modified outline form. In using a modified outline form, you do not need to use numerals and letters. Unlike a formal outline, a modified outline does not require two or more points under each heading, and headings do not need to be grammatically parallel. Yet, like a formal outline, a modified outline organizes a text's main ideas and related details. The following modified outline describes social classes in nineteenth-century England.

House of Lords
Peerage
- **Dukes**
- **Barons**
- **Viscounts**
- **Earls**
- **Marquises**

Church of England clergy
- **Bishops**
- **Archbishops**

"Gentry"
- **upper middle class**
- **Baronets**
- **Knights**

Use abbreviations and symbols to make note taking more efficient. Following are some commonly used abbreviations for note taking.

w/	with	re	regarding
w/o	without	=	is, equals
#	number	*	important
&, +	and	def	definition
>	more than	Amer	America
<	less than	tho	although

③ Critical Thinking

Critical thinking includes the ability to analyze, evaluate, and synthesize ideas and information. Critical thinking goes beyond simply understanding something. It involves making informed judgments based on sound reasoning skills.

3.1 Avoiding Faulty Reasoning

When you write or speak for a persuasive purpose, you must make sure your logic is valid. Avoid these mistakes in reasoning, called **logical fallacies.**

Overgeneralization
Conclusions reached on the basis of too little evidence result in the fallacy called overgeneralization. A person who saw three cyclists riding bicycles without helmets might conclude, "Nobody wears bicycle helmets." That conclusion would be an overgeneralization.

Circular Reasoning
When you support an opinion by simply repeating it in different terms, you are using circular reasoning. For example, "Sport utility vehicles are popular because more people buy them than any other category of new cars." This is an illogical statement because the second part of the sentence simply uses different words to restate the first part of the sentence.

Either-Or Fallacy
Assuming that a complex question has only two possible answers is called the either-or fallacy. "Either we raise the legal driving age or accidents caused by teenage drivers will continue to increase" is an example of the either-or fallacy. The statement ignores other ways of decreasing the automobile accident rate of teenagers.

Cause-and-Effect Fallacy
The cause-and-effect fallacy occurs when you say that event B was caused by event A just because event B occurred after event A. A person might conclude that, because a city's air quality worsened two months after a new factory began operation, that new factory caused the air pollution. However, this cause-and-effect relationship would have to be supported by more specific evidence.

3.2 Identifying Modes of Persuasion

Understanding persuasive techniques can help you evaluate information, make informed decisions, and avoid persuasive techniques intended to deceive you. Some modes of persuasion appeal to your various emotions.

Loaded Language
Loaded language is words or phrases chosen to appeal to the emotions. It is often used in place of facts to shape opinion or to evoke a positive or negative reaction. For example, you might feel positive about a politician who has a *plan.* You might, however, feel negative about a politician who has a *scheme.*

Bandwagon
Bandwagon taps into the human desire to belong. This technique suggests that "everybody" is doing it, or buying it, or believing it. Phrases such as "Don't be the only one . . ." and "Everybody is . . ." signal the bandwagon appeal.

Testimonials
Testimonials offer well-known people or satisfied customers to promote and endorse a product or idea. This technique taps into the appeal of celebrities or into people's need to identify with others just like themselves.

3.3 Logical Thinking

Persuasive writing and speaking require good reasoning skills. Two ways of creating logical arguments are deductive reasoning and inductive reasoning.

Deductive Arguments

A deductive argument begins with a generalization, or premise, and then advances with facts and evidence that lead to a conclusion. The conclusion is the logical outcome of the premise. A false premise leads to a false conclusion; a valid premise leads to a valid conclusion provided that the specific facts are correct and the reasoning is correct.

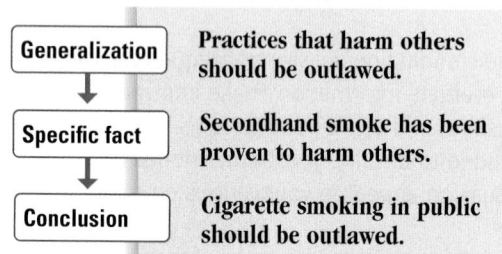

Generalization	Practices that harm others should be outlawed.
Specific fact	Secondhand smoke has been proven to harm others.
Conclusion	Cigarette smoking in public should be outlawed.

You may use deductive reasoning when writing a persuasive paper or speech. Your conclusion is the thesis of your paper. Facts in your paper supporting your premise should lead logically to that conclusion.

Inductive Arguments

An inductive argument begins with specific evidence that leads to a general conclusion.

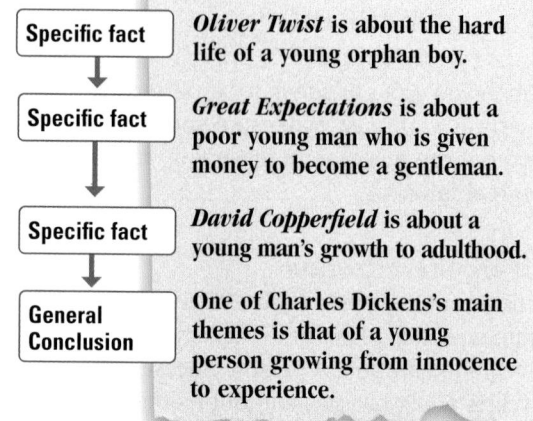

Specific fact	*Oliver Twist* is about the hard life of a young orphan boy.
Specific fact	*Great Expectations* is about a poor young man who is given money to become a gentleman.
Specific fact	*David Copperfield* is about a young man's growth to adulthood.
General Conclusion	One of Charles Dickens's main themes is that of a young person growing from innocence to experience.

The conclusion of an inductive argument often includes a qualifying term such as *some, often,* or *most.* This usage helps to avoid the fallacy of overgeneralization.

4 Speaking and Listening

Good speakers and listeners do more than just talk and hear. They use specific techniques to present their ideas effectively, and they are attentive and critical listeners.

4.1 Giving a Speech

In school, in business, and in community life, giving a speech is one of the most effective ways of communicating. Whether to persuade, to inform, or to entertain, you may often speak before an audience.

Analyzing Audience and Purpose

In order to speak effectively, you need to know to whom you are speaking and why you are speaking. When preparing a speech, think about how much knowledge and interest your audience has in your subject. A speech has one of two main purposes: to inform or to persuade. A third purpose, to entertain, is often considered closely related to these two purposes.

A speech **to inform** gives the audience new information, provides a better understanding of information, or enables people to use information in a new way. An informative speech is presented in an objective way.

In a speech **to persuade,** a speaker tries to change the actions or beliefs of an audience.

Preparing and Delivering a Speech

There are four main methods of preparing and delivering a speech:

Manuscript When you speak from **manuscript,** you prepare a complete script of your speech in advance and use it to deliver your speech.

Memory When you speak from **memory,** you prepare a written text in advance and then memorize it so you can deliver it word for word.

Impromptu When you speak **impromptu,** you speak on the spur of the moment without any special preparation.

Extemporaneous When you give an **extemporaneous** speech, you research and prepare your speech and then deliver it with the help of notes.

Points for Effective Speech Delivery
• Avoid speaking either too fast or too slow. Vary your **speaking rate** depending on your material. Slow down for difficult concepts. Speed up to convince your audience that you are knowledgeable about your subject.
• Speak loud enough to be heard clearly, but not so loud that your voice is overwhelming.
• Use a **conversational tone.**
• Use a change of **pitch,** or inflection, to help make your tone and meaning clear.
• Let your **facial expression** reflect your message.
• Make **eye contact** with as many audience members as possible.
• Use **gestures** to emphasize your words. Don't make your gestures too small to be seen. On the other hand, don't gesture too frequently or wildly.
• Use **good posture**—not too relaxed and not too rigid. Avoid nervous mannerisms.

4.2 Analyzing, Evaluating and Critiquing a Speech

Evaluating speeches helps you make informed judgments about the ideas presented in a speech. It also helps you learn what makes an effective speech and delivery. Use these criteria to help you analyze, evaluate, and critique speeches.

CRITERIA	How to Evaluate a Persuasive Speech

- Did the speaker have a clear goal or argument?
- Did the speaker take the audience's biases into account?
- Did the speaker support the argument with convincing facts?
- Did the speaker use sound logic in developing the argument?
- Did the speaker use voice, facial expression, gestures, and posture effectively?
- Did the speaker hold the audience's interest?

CRITERIA	How to Evaluate an Informative Speech

- Did the speaker have a specific, clearly focused topic?
- Did the speaker take the audience's previous knowledge into consideration?
- Did the speaker cite sources for the information?
- Did the speaker communicate the information objectively?
- Did the speaker present the information in an organized manner?
- Did the speaker use visual aids effectively?
- Did the speaker use voice, facial expression, gestures, and posture effectively?

4.3 Using Active Listening Strategies

Listeners play an active part in the communication process. A listener has a responsibility just as a speaker does. Listening, unlike hearing, is a learned skill.

As you listen to a public speaker, use the following active listening strategies:

- Determine the **speaker's purpose.**
- Listen for the **main idea** of the message and not simply the individual details.
- **Anticipate the points** that will be made based on the speaker's purpose and main idea.
- Listen with an open mind, but **identify faulty logic, unsupported facts,** and **emotional appeals.**

4.4 Conducting Interviews

Conducting a personal interview can be an effective way to get information.

Preparing for the Interview
- Read any articles by or about the person you will interview. This background information will help you get to the point during the interview.
- Prepare a list of questions. Think of more questions than you will need. Include some yes/no questions and some open-ended questions. Order your questions from most important to least important.

Participating in the Interview
- Listen interactively. Be prepared to follow up on a response you find interesting.
- Avoid arguments. Be tactful and polite.

Following Up on the Interview
- Summarize your notes while they are still fresh in your mind.
- Send a thank-you note to the interviewee.

5 Viewing and Representing

In our media-saturated world, we are immersed in visual messages that convey ideas, information, and attitudes. To understand and use visual representations effectively, you need to be aware of the techniques and the range of visuals that are commonly used.

5.1 Understanding Visual Messages

Information is communicated not only with words but with graphic devices. A **graphic device** is a visual representation of data and ideas and the relations among them.

Reading Charts and Graphs
A chart organizes information by arranging it in rows and columns. It is helpful in showing complex information clearly. When interpreting a chart, first read the title. Then analyze how the information is presented. Charts can take many different forms. The following chart compares two English literary eras.

A Comparison of Neoclassicism and Romanticism	
Neoclassicism	**Romanticism**
Focus on society	Focus on individual
Emphasis on intellect	Emphasis on emotions
Emphasis on science	Emphasis on humanity
Reflected mainstream views	Reflected radical protest against society
Formal style	Personal, natural style

There are several different types of **graphs,** visual aids that are often used to display numerical information.

- A **circle graph** shows proportions of the whole. The following circle graph shows the kinds of plays Shakespeare wrote.

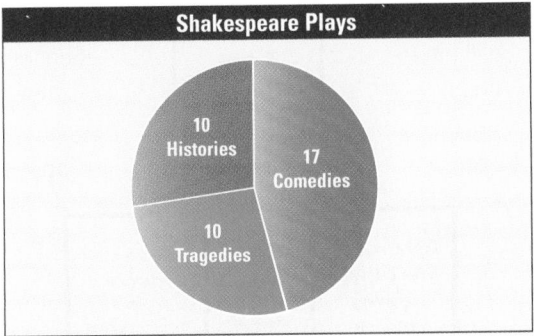

- A **line graph** shows the change in data over a period of time.
- A **bar graph** compares amounts. The following bar graph shows how many plays Shakespeare wrote in each period of his artistic development.

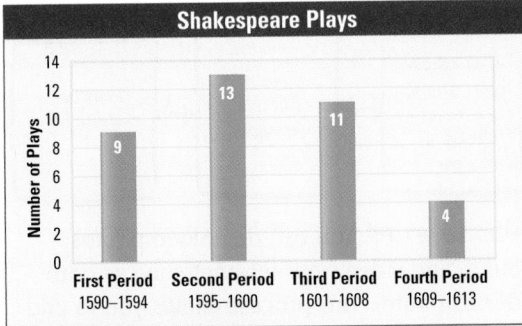

Interpreting Images

Speakers and writers often use visual aids to inform or persuade their audiences. These aids can be invaluable in helping you understand the information being communicated. However, you must interpret visual aids critically, as you do written material.

- **Examine photographs critically.** Does the camera angle or the background in the photo intentionally evoke a positive or negative response? Has the image been altered or manipulated?
- **Evaluate carefully the data presented in charts and graphs.** Some charts and graphs

may exaggerate the facts. For example, a circle graph representing a sample of only ten people may be misleading if the speaker suggests that this data represents a trend.

 Evaluating Visual Messages

When you view images, whether they are cartoons, advertising art, photographs, or paintings, there are certain elements to look for.

CRITERIA   How to Analyze Images

- Is color used realistically? Is it used to emphasize certain objects? To evoke a specific response?
- What tone is created by color and by light and dark in the picture?
- Do the background images intentionally evoke a positive or negative response?
- What is noticeable about the picture's composition, that is, the arrangement of lines, colors, and forms? Does the composition emphasize certain objects or elements in the picture?
- For graphs and charts, does the visual accurately represent the data?

 Using Visual Representations

Tables, graphs, diagrams, pictures, and animations often communicate information more effectively than words alone do.

Use visuals with written reports to illustrate complex concepts and processes or to make a page look more interesting. Computer programs, CD-ROMs, and on-line services can help you generate

- **graphs** that present numerical information;
- **charts** and **tables** that allow easy comparison of information;
- **logos** and **graphic devices** that highlight important information;
- **borders** and **tints** that signal different kinds of information;

- **clip art** that adds useful pictures;
- **interactive animations** that illustrate difficult concepts.

You might want to explore ways of displaying data in more than one visual format before deciding which will work best for you.

Making Multimedia Presentations

A multimedia presentation is an electronically prepared combination of text, sound, and visuals such as photographs, videos, and animation. Your audience reads, hears, and sees your presentation at a computer, following different "paths" you create to lead the user through the information you have gathered.

Planning Presentations

To create a multimedia presentation, first choose your topic and decide what you want to include. Then plan how you want your user to move through your presentation. For a multimedia presentation on the changing faces of heroes through the ages, you might include the following items:

- text defining *hero* and discussing heroic qualities
- taped reading from *Beowulf*
- taped reading from Malory's Arthurian tales
- chart comparing heroic qualities of Arthur and a modern superhero
- video interview with a scholar on the mythic origins of modern heroes
- video from *Batman* or Bond film
- photo of real-life modern hero

You can choose one of the following ways to organize your presentation:

step by step, with only one path, or order, in which the user can see and hear the information

a branching path that allows users to make some choices about what they will see and hear, and in what order

A flow chart can help you figure out the paths a user can take through your presentation. Each box in the flow chart that follows represents something about heroes for the user to read, see, or hear. The arrows on the flow chart show the possible paths the user can follow.

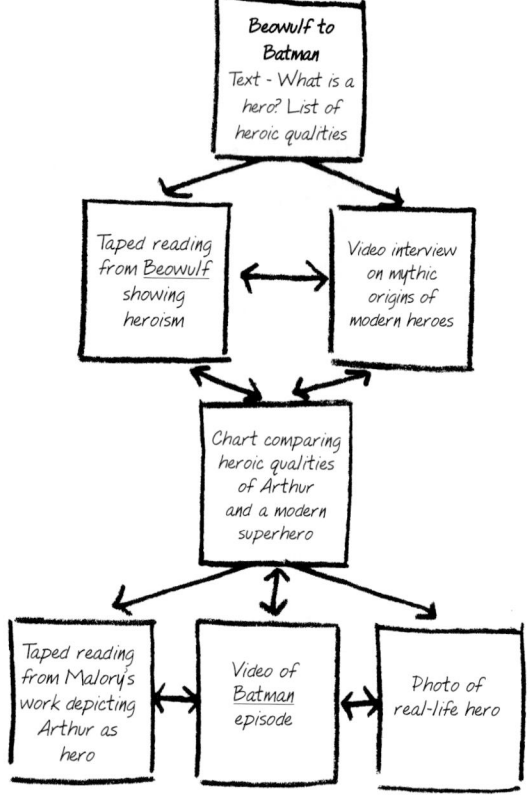

TECHNOLOGY TIP You can download photos, sound, and video from Internet sources onto your computer. This process allows you to add to your multimedia presentation various elements that would usually require complex editing equipment.

Guiding Your User

Your user will need directions to follow the path you have planned for your multimedia presentation.

Most multimedia authoring programs allow you to create screens that include text or audio directions that guide the user from one part of your presentation to the next.

If you need help creating your multimedia presentation, ask your school's technology adviser. You may also be able to get help from your classmates or your software manual.

Grammar Handbook

❶ Quick Reference: Parts of Speech

Part of Speech	Definition	Examples
Noun	Names a person, place, thing, idea, quality, or action.	Beowulf, England, boxes, liberty, kindness, hiking
Pronoun	Takes the place of a noun or another pronoun.	
Personal	Refers to the one speaking, spoken to, or spoken about.	I, me, my, mine, we, us, our, ours, you, your, yours, she, he, it, her, him, hers, his, its, they, them, their, theirs
Reflexive	Follows a verb or preposition and refers to a preceding noun or pronoun.	myself, yourself, herself, himself, itself, ourselves, yourselves, themselves
Intensive	Emphasizes a noun or another pronoun.	(Same as reflexives)
Demonstrative	Points to specific persons or things.	this, that, these, those
Indefinite	Refers to person(s) or thing(s) not specifically mentioned.	both, all, most, many, anyone, everybody, several, none, some
Interrogative	Signals questions.	who, whom, whose, which, what
Relative	Introduces subordinate clauses and relates them to words in the main clause.	who, whom, whose, which, that
Verb	Expresses action, condition, or state of being.	
Action	Tells what the subject does or did, physically or mentally.	run, reaches, listened, consider, decides, dreamt
Linking	Connects subjects to that which identifies or describes them.	am, is, are, was, were, sound, taste, appear, feel, become, remain, seem
Auxiliary	Precedes and introduces main verbs.	be, have, do, can, could, will, would, may, might
Adjective	Modifies nouns or pronouns.	**strong** women, **two** epics, **enough** time
Adverb	Modifies verbs, adjectives, or other adverbs.	walked **out**, **really** funny, **far** away
Preposition	Relates one word to another (following) word.	at, by, for, from, in, of, on, to, with
Conjunction(s)	Joins words or word groups.	
Coordinating	Joins words or word groups used the same way.	and, but, or, for, so, yet, nor
Correlative	Join words or word groups used the same way and are used in pairs.	both . . . and, either . . . or, neither . . . nor
Subordinating	Joins word groups not used the same way.	although, after, as, before, because, when, if, unless
Interjection	Expresses emotion.	wow, ouch, hurrah

2 Nouns

A noun is a word used to name a person, place, thing, idea, quality, or action. Nouns can be classified in several ways. All nouns can be placed in at least two classifications. They are either common or proper. All are also either abstract or concrete. Some nouns can be classified as compound, collective, and possessive as well.

2.1 **Common Nouns** are general names, common to an entire group.

> EXAMPLES: *author, poem, valor, battle*

2.2 **Proper Nouns** name specific, one-of-a-kind things. (See Capitalization, page 1415.)

> EXAMPLES: *Denmark, Beowulf, Viking*

2.3 **Concrete Nouns** name things that can be perceived by the senses.

> EXAMPLES: *bird, scream, Troy, Homer*

2.4 **Abstract Nouns** name things that cannot be observed by the senses.

> EXAMPLES: *intelligence, fear, joy, loneliness*

	Common	Proper
Abstract	bravery	Middle Ages
Concrete	monster	Denmark

2.5 **Compound Nouns** are formed from two or more words but express a single idea. They are written as single words, as separate words, or with hyphens. Use a dictionary to check the correct spelling of a compound noun.

> EXAMPLES: *kingmaker, mead hall, ring-giver*

2.6 **Collective Nouns** are singular nouns that refer to groups of people or things. (See Subject-Verb Agreement, page 1410.)

> EXAMPLES: *army, flock, class, species*

2.7 **Possessive Nouns** show who or what owns something. Consult the chart below for the proper use of the possessive apostrophe.

Category	Possessive Nouns Rule	Examples
All singular nouns	Add apostrophe plus -*s*	Beowulf's witness's, city's father-in-law's
Plural nouns not ending in -*s*	Add apostrophe plus -*s*	children's women's people's
Plural nouns ending in -*s*	Add apostrophe only	witnesses' churches' males' Johnsons'

GRAMMAR PRACTICE

A. For each underlined noun, first tell whether it is common or proper. Then tell whether it is concrete or abstract.

1. The story of Beowulf is a great epic.
2. Warriors praised his heroism.
3. Grendel was a powerful force.
4. The roof boards swayed, and the Danes shook with terror.
5. Their footprints were bloody.
6. The group had high hopes of victory.
7. Beowulf killed the fire dragon.
8. In doing so, he defeated evil.
9. Heroism is a common theme of great literature.
10. Is there any similarity to today's society?

B. 11–15. From the sentences above, write three compound nouns and two collective nouns.

C. Write the possessive forms of the following nouns.

16. Hrothgar
17. Danes
18. heroism
19. family
20. darkness
21. oceans
22. army
23. warrior
24. scop
25. companions

③ Pronouns

A pronoun is a word that is used in place of a noun or another pronoun. The word or word group to which the pronoun refers is called its antecedent.

3.1 **Personal Pronouns** are pronouns that change their form to express person, number, gender, and case. The forms of these pronouns are shown in the chart that follows.

	Nominative	Objective	Possessive
Singular			
First Person	I	me	my, mine
Second Person	you	you	your, yours
Third Person	she, he, it	her, him, it	her, hers, his, its
Plural			
First Person	we	us	our, ours
Second Person	you	you	your, yours
Third Person	they	them	their, theirs

3.2 **Pronoun Agreement** Pronouns should agree with their antecedents in number and person. Singular pronouns are used to replace singular nouns. Plural pronouns are used to replace plural nouns. Pronouns must also match the gender (masculine, feminine, or neuter) of the nouns they replace.

3.3 **Pronoun Case** Personal pronouns change form to show how they function in a sentence. This change of form is called *case.* The three cases are **nominative, objective,** and **possessive.**

A nominative pronoun is used as the subject or the predicate nominative of a sentence.

An objective pronoun is used as the direct or indirect object of a sentence or as the object of a preposition.

> SUBJECT   OBJECT
>
> *He will lead them to us.*
>
> OBJECT OF PREPOSITION

A possessive pronoun shows ownership. The pronouns *mine, yours, hers, his, its, ours,* and *theirs* can be used in place of nouns.

> EXAMPLE: *This horse is mine.*

The pronouns *my, your, her, his, its, our,* and *their* are used before nouns.

> EXAMPLE: *This is my horse.*

USAGE TIP To decide which pronoun to use in a comparison, such as *He tells better tales than (I* or *me),* fill in the missing words: *He tells better tales than I tell.*

WATCH OUT! Many spelling errors can be avoided if you watch out for *its* and *their.* Don't confuse the possessive pronoun *its* with the contraction *it's,* meaning *it is* or *it has.* The homonyms *they're* (contraction for *they are*) and *there* (a place or an expletive) are often mistakenly used for *their.*

3.4 **Reflexive and Intensive Pronouns** These pronouns are formed by adding *-self* or *-selves* to certain personal pronouns. Their forms are the same, and they differ only in how they are used.

Reflexive pronouns follow verbs or prepositions and reflect back on an earlier noun or pronoun.

> EXAMPLES: *He likes himself too much. She is now herself again.*

Intensive pronouns intensify or emphasize the nouns or pronouns to which they refer.

> EXAMPLES: *They themselves will educate their children. You did it yourselves.*

Singular	
First Person	myself
Second Person	yourself
Third Person	herself, himself, itself

Plural	
First Person	ourselves
Second Person	yourselves
Third Person	themselves

WATCH OUT! Avoid using *hisself* or *theirselves.* Standard English does not include these forms.

> **NONSTANDARD:** *John enjoyed hisself at the play.*
> **STANDARD:** *John enjoyed himself at the play.*

USAGE TIP Reflexive and intensive pronouns should never be used without antecedents.

> **INCORRECT:** *Read a tale to my brother and myself.*
> **CORRECT:** *Read a tale to my brother and me.*

3.5 Demonstrative Pronouns point out things and persons near and far.

	Singular	Plural
Near	this	these
Far	that	those

WATCH OUT! Avoid using the objective pronoun *them* in place of the demonstrative *those.*

> **INCORRECT:** *Let's dramatize one of them tales.*
> **CORRECT:** *Let's dramatize one of those tales.*

3.6 Indefinite Pronouns do not refer to specific persons or things and usually have no antecedents. The chart shows some commonly used indefinite pronouns:

Singular	Plural	Singular or Plural	
each	both	all	half
either	few	any	plenty
neither	many	more	none
another	several	most	some

Here is another set of indefinite pronouns, all of which are singular. Notice that, with one exception, they are spelled as one word:

anyone	everyone	no one	someone
anybody	everybody	nobody	somebody
anything	everything	nothing	something

USAGE TIP Since all these are singular, pronouns referring to them should be singular.

> **INCORRECT:** *Did everybody play their part well?*
> **CORRECT:** *Did everybody play his or her part well?*

If the antecedent of the pronoun is both male and female, *his or her* may be used as an alternative, or the sentence may be recast:

> **EXAMPLES:** *Did everybody play his or her part well?*
> *Did all the students play their parts well?*

GRAMMAR PRACTICE

Write the correct form of all incorrect pronouns in the sentences below.

1. Chaucer hisself appears as a pilgrim in one tale.
2. Each student selected one of them tales to read aloud.
3. Did everybody have their turn?
4. My best friend and myself read "The Pardoner's Tale."
5. After the performance, the students treated theirselves to a medieval supper.

3.7 Interrogative Pronouns tell a reader or listener that a question is coming. The interrogative pronouns are *who, whom, whose, which,* and *what.*

> **EXAMPLES:** *Who is going to rehearse with you? From whom did you receive the script?*

USAGE TIP *Who* is used for subjects, *whom* for objects. To find out which pronoun you need to use in a question, change the question to a statement:

> **QUESTION:** *(Who/Whom?) did you meet there?*
> **STATEMENT:** *You met (?) there.*

Since the verb has a subject *(you)*, the needed word must be the object form, *whom.*

> **EXAMPLE:** *Whom did you meet there?*

WATCH OUT! A special problem arises when you use an interrupter such as *do you think* within a sentence:

>   **EXAMPLE:** *(Who/Whom) do you think will win?*

If you eliminate the interrupter, it is clear that the word you need is *who.*

3.8 *Relative Pronouns* relate, or connect, clauses to the words they modify in sentences. The noun or pronoun that the clause modifies is the antecedent of the relative pronoun. Here are the relative pronouns and their uses:

Replacing:	Subject	Object	Possessive
Persons	who	whom	whose
Things	which	which	whose
Things/Persons*	that	that	whose

> * *That* generally will not replace specific names, such as *Geoffrey Chaucer.*

Often short sentences with related ideas can be combined using relative pronouns to create a more effective sentence.

>   **SHORT SENTENCE:** *Chaucer was the father of English poetry.*
>   **RELATED SENTENCE:** *Chaucer wrote* The Canterbury Tales.
>   **COMBINED SENTENCE:** *Chaucer, who wrote* The Canterbury Tales, *was the father of English poetry.*

GRAMMAR PRACTICE

Choose the appropriate interrogative or relative pronoun from the words in parentheses.

1. Can you name most of the characters (who, whom) Chaucer portrayed?

2. The pilgrims, (who/whom) were traveling to Canterbury, told tales to one another.

3. The Pardoner, (which/ whose) greed is exceptional, is not a sympathetic character.

4. (Who/Whom) do you think is the most sympathetic character?

5. Chaucer portrays himself as a somewhat foolish man (who/whom) others might overlook.

 4 **Verbs**

A verb is a word that expresses an action, a condition, or a state of being. There are two main kinds of verbs: action and linking. Other verbs, called auxiliary verbs, are sometimes used with action verbs and linking verbs.

4.1 *Action Verbs* tell what action someone or something is performing, physically or mentally.

>   **PHYSICAL ACTION:** *You hit the target.*
>   **MENTAL ACTION:** *She dreamed of me.*

4.2 *Linking Verbs* do not express action. Linking verbs link subjects to complements that identify or describe them. Linking verbs may be divided into two groups:

>   **FORMS OF** *TO BE*: *She is our queen.*
>   **VERBS THAT EXPRESS CONDITION**: *The writer looked thoughtful.*

4.3 *Auxiliary Verbs,* sometimes called helping verbs, precede action or linking verbs and modify their meanings in special ways. The most commonly used auxiliary verbs are parts of the verbs *be, have,* and *do.*

>   **Be:** *am, is, are, was, were, be, being, been*
>   **Have:** *have, has, had*
>   **Do:** *do, does, did*

Other common auxiliary verbs are *can, could, will, would, shall, should, may, might,* and *must.*

>   **EXAMPLES:** *I always have admired her.*
>   *You must listen to me.*

4.4 *Transitive and Intransitive Verbs*
Action verbs can be either transitive or intransitive. A transitive verb directs the action toward someone or something. The transitive verb has an object. An intransitive verb does not direct the action toward someone or something. It does not have an object. Since linking verbs convey no action, they are always intransitive.

>   **Transitive:** *The storm sank the ship.*
>   **Intransitive:** *The ship sank.*

4.5 *Principal Parts* Action and linking verbs typically have four principal parts, which are used to form verb tenses. The principal parts are the *present*, the *present participle*, the *past*, and the *past participle*.

If the verb is a regular verb, the past and past participle are formed by adding the ending *-d* or *-ed* to the present part. Here is a chart showing four regular verbs:

Present	Present Participle	Past	Past Participle
risk	(is) risking	risked	(have) risked
solve	(is) solving	solved	(have) solved
drop	(is) dropping	dropped	(have) dropped
carry	(is) carrying	carried	(have) carried

Note that the present participle and past participle forms are preceded by a form of *be* or *have*. These forms cannot be used alone as main verbs and always need an auxiliary verb.

> **EXAMPLES**: *The rescuers were risking their lives. The doctor has solved the problem.*

The past and past participle of irregular verbs are not formed by adding *-d* or *-ed* to the present; they are formed in irregular ways.

Present	Present Participle	Past	Past Participle
begin	(is) beginning	began	(have) begun
break	(is) breaking	broke	(have) broken
bring	(is) bringing	brought	(have) brought
choose	(is) choosing	chose	(have) chosen
go	(is) going	went	(have) gone
lose	(is) losing	lost	(have) lost
see	(is) seeing	saw	(have) seen
swim	(is) swimming	swam	(have) swum
write	(is) writing	wrote	(have) written

4.6 *Verb Tense* The tense of a verb tells the time of the action or the state of being. An action or state of being can occur in the present, the past, or the future. There are six tenses, each expressing a different range of time.

Present tense expresses an action that is happening at the present time, occurs regularly, or is constant or generally true. Use the present part.

> **EXAMPLES**
> **NOW**: *That ballad sounds great.*
> **REGULAR**: *I read every day.*
> **GENERAL**: *The sun rises in the east.*

Past tense expresses an action that began and ended in the past. Use the past part.

> **EXAMPLE**: *The storyteller finished his tale.*

Future tense expresses an action (or state of being) that will occur. Use *shall* or *will* with the present part.

> **EXAMPLE**: *They will attend the next festival.*

Present perfect tense expresses action (1) that was completed at an indefinite time in the past or (2) that began in the past and continues into the present. Use *have* or *has* with the past participle.

> **EXAMPLE**: *Poetry has inspired readers throughout the ages.*

Past perfect tense shows an action in the past that came before another action in the past. Use *had* before the past participle.

> **EXAMPLE**: *The messenger had traveled for days before he delivered his knight's response.*

Future perfect tense shows an action in the future that will be completed before another action in the future. Use *shall have* or *will have* before the past participle.

> **EXAMPLE**: *They will have finished the novel before seeing the movie version of the tale.*

4.7 *Progressive Forms* The progressive forms of the six tenses show ongoing action. Use a form of *be* with the present participle of a verb.

> **PRESENT PROGRESSIVE**: *She is rehearsing her lines.*
> **PAST PROGRESSIVE**: *She was rehearsing her lines.*
> **FUTURE PROGRESSIVE**: *She will be rehearsing her lines.*

PRESENT PERFECT PROGRESSIVE: *She has been rehearsing her lines.*
PAST PERFECT PROGRESSIVE: *She had been rehearsing her lines.*
FUTURE PERFECT PROGRESSIVE: *She will have been rehearsing her lines.*

WATCH OUT! Do not shift tense needlessly. Watch out for these special cases.

- In most compound sentences and in sentences with compound predicates, keep the tenses the same.

  INCORRECT: *We work hard, and they paid us well.*
  CORRECT: *We work hard, and they pay us well.*

- If one past action happens before another, do shift tenses—from the past to the past perfect:

  INCORRECT: *They wished they started earlier.*
  CORRECT: *They wished they had started earlier.*

GRAMMAR PRACTICE

Identify the tense of the verb(s) in each of the following sentences. If you find an unnecessary tense shift, correct it.

1. Many consider *Le Morte d' Arthur* one of the greatest legends in Western culture.
2. King Arthur himself led his knights into battle.
3. While King Arthur is fighting in France, Sir Modred usurped his throne.
4. After Launcelot had defeated the French army, he settled in France.
5. A terrible struggle began, and each knight wounds the other.

4.8 *Active and Passive Voice* The voice of a verb tells whether the subject of a sentence performs or receives the action expressed by the verb. When the subject performs the action, the verb is in the active voice. When the subject is the receiver of the action, the verb is in the passive voice.

Compare these two sentences:

ACTIVE: *Launcelot beat Gawain in the battle.*
PASSIVE: *Gawain was beaten by Launcelot in the battle.*

To form the passive voice use a form of *be* with the past participle of the main verb.

WATCH OUT! Use the passive voice sparingly. It tends to make writing less forceful and less direct. It can also make the writing awkward.

AWKWARD: *An oath of allegiance was sworn by the knights.*
CORRECT: *The knights swore an oath of allegiance.*

There are occasions when you will choose to use the passive voice because

- you want to emphasize the receiver: *The king was shot.*

- the doer is unknown: *My books were stolen.*

- the doer is unimportant: *French is spoken here.*

4.9 *Mood* The mood identifies the manner in which the verb expresses an idea. There are three moods.

The indicative mood states a fact or asks a question. You use this mood most often.

EXAMPLE: *His trust was shattered by the betrayal.*

The imperative mood is used to give a command or make a request.

EXAMPLE: *Be there by eight o'clock sharp.*

The subjunctive mood is used to express a wish or a condition that is contrary to fact.

EXAMPLE: *If I were you, I wouldn't get my hopes up.*

GRAMMAR PRACTICE

Identify the verbs as active or passive.

1. *Le Morte d'Arthur* has influenced many other Arthurian stories.
2. It was written by Sir Thomas Malory, the son of a gentleman.
3. Malory did not live a settled life.
4. He was put in prison for his various offenses.
5. Malory was buried near Newgate, in a chapel at the Grey Friars.

For the following items, identify the boldfaced verb as indicative or subjunctive in mood.

6. If Malory **were** alive today, he'd probably be writing romance fiction.

7. Scholars **have praised** the style of *Le Morte d'Arthur* very highly.

8. The stories **were printed** by William Caxton in 1485.

9. Malory's knights **were** chivalrous.

10. If there **were** female knights then, would they have slain dragons?

❺ Modifiers

Modifiers are words or groups of words that change or limit the meanings of other words. The two kinds of modifiers are adjectives and adverbs.

5.1 *Adjectives* An adjective is a word that modifies a noun or pronoun by telling *which one, what kind, how many,* or *how much.*

WHICH ONE: *this, that, these, those*
EXAMPLE: *Those shoes need new soles.*

WHAT KIND: *small, ugly, brave, black*
EXAMPLE: *The brave knight won the battle.*

HOW MANY: *some, few, thirty, none, both, each*
EXAMPLE: *Each village paid a tax for protection.*

HOW MUCH: *more, less, enough, scarce*
EXAMPLE: *Food was scarce.*

The **articles** *a, an*, and *the* are usually classified as adjectives. These are the most common adjectives that you will use.

EXAMPLES: *The bridge was burned before the attack.*
A group of peasants led the procession in the town.

5.2 *Predicate Adjectives* Most adjectives come before the nouns they modify, as in the examples above. Predicate adjectives, however, follow linking verbs and describe the subject.

EXAMPLE: *My friends are very intelligent.*

Be especially careful to use adjectives (not adverbs) after such linking verbs as *look, feel, grow, taste,* and *smell.*

EXAMPLE: *The weather grows cold.*

5.3 *Adverbs* modify verbs, adjectives, or other adverbs by telling *where, when, how,* or *to what extent.*

WHERE: *The children played outside.*
WHEN: *The author spoke yesterday.*
HOW: *We walked slowly behind the leader.*
TO WHAT EXTENT: *He worked very hard.*

Unlike adjectives, adverbs tend to be mobile words; they may occur in many places in sentences.

EXAMPLES: *Suddenly the wind shifted. The wind suddenly shifted. The wind shifted suddenly.*

Changing the position of adverbs within sentences can vary the rhythm in your writing.

5.4 *Adjective or Adverb* Many adverbs are formed by adding *-ly* to adjectives.

EXAMPLES: *sweet, sweetly; gentle, gently*

However, *-ly* added to a noun will usually yield an adjective.

EXAMPLES: *friend, friendly; woman, womanly*

5.5 *Comparison of Modifiers* The form of an adjective or adverb indicates the degree of comparison that the modifier expresses. Both adjectives and adverbs have three forms, or degrees: the positive, comparative, and superlative.

The positive form is used to describe individual things, groups, or actions.

EXAMPLES: *Arthur's jousting team is strong. The new weapons are useful.*

The comparative form is used to compare two things, groups, or actions.

EXAMPLES: *Arthur's jousting team is stronger than theirs. The new weapons are more useful than Stone Age clubs.*

The superlative form is used to compare more than two things, groups, or actions.

> **EXAMPLES**: *Arthur's jousting team is the strongest in the land. The new weapons are the most useful they have ever had.*

5.6 Regular Comparisons One-syllable and some two-syllable adjectives and adverbs form their comparative and superlative forms by adding *-er* or *-est.* All three-syllable and most two-syllable modifiers form their comparative and superlative by using *more* or *most.*

Positive	Comparative	Superlative
small	smaller	smallest
thin	thinner	thinnest
sleepy	sleepier	sleepiest
useless	more useless	most useless
precisely	more precisely	most precisely

WATCH OUT! Note that spelling changes must sometimes be made to form the comparative and superlative of modifiers.

> **EXAMPLES**: *friendly, friendlier* (change *y* to *i* and add the ending)
> *sad, sadder* (double the final consonant and add the ending)

5.7 Irregular Comparisons Some commonly used modifiers have irregular comparative and superlative forms. You may wish to memorize them.

Positive	Comparative	Superlative
good	better	best
bad	worse	worst
far	farther or further	farthest or furthest
little	less or lesser	least
many	more	most
well	better	best
much	more	most

5.8 Using Modifiers Correctly Study the tips that follow to avoid common mistakes.

Farther and Further *Farther* is used for distances; use *further* for everything else.

Avoiding double comparisons You make a comparison by using *-er/-est* or by using *more/most.* Using *-er* with *more* or using *-est* with *most* is incorrect.

> **INCORRECT**: *I like her more better than she likes me.*
> **CORRECT**: *I like her better than she likes me.*

Avoiding illogical comparisons An illogical or confusing comparison results if two unrelated things are compared or if something is compared with itself. The word *other* or the word *else* should be used in a comparison of an individual member with the rest of the group.

> **ILLOGICAL**: *Sir Walter Raleigh was as interesting as any English explorer.* (Was Raleigh an English explorer?)
> **LOGICAL**: *Sir Walter Raleigh was as interesting as any other English explorer.*

Bad vs. Badly *Bad,* always an adjective, is used before nouns or after linking verbs to describe the subject. *Badly,* always an adverb, never modifies a noun. Be sure to use the right form after a linking verb.

> **INCORRECT**: *Ed felt badly after his team lost.*
> **CORRECT**: *Ed felt bad after his team lost.*

Good vs. Well *Good* is always an adjective. It is used before nouns or after a linking verb to modify the subject. *Well* is often an adverb meaning "expertly" or "properly." *Well* can also be used as an adjective after a linking verb, when it means "in good health."

> **INCORRECT**: *Helen writes very good.*
> **CORRECT**: *Helen writes very well.*
> **CORRECT**: *Yesterday I felt bad; today I feel well.*

Double negatives If you add a negative word to a sentence that is already negative, the result will be an error known as a double negative. When using *not* or *-n't* with a verb, use "any-" words, such as *anybody* or *anything,* rather than "*no-*" words, such as *nobody* or *nothing,* later in the sentence.

> INCORRECT: *I don't have no money.*
> CORRECT: *I don't have any money.*
>
> INCORRECT: *We haven't seen nobody.*
> CORRECT: *We haven't seen anybody.*

Using *hardly, barely,* or *scarcely* after a negative word is also incorrect.

> INCORRECT: *They couldn't barely see two feet ahead.*
> CORRECT: *They could barely see two feet ahead.*

Misplaced modifiers A misplaced modifier is one placed so far away from the word it modifies that the intended meaning of the sentence is unclear. Place modifiers as close as possible to the words they modify.

> MISPLACED: *We found the child in the park who was missing.* (The child was missing, not the park.)
>
> CLEARER: *We found the child who was missing in the park.*

GRAMMAR PRACTICE

Rewrite these sentences, correcting mistakes in modifiers.

1. The author of "Female Orations" enjoyed the most freedom than almost any other Englishwoman of her time.

2. Her education and position allowed her to travel further than many men.

3. Many feel that women of the 17th century had the most hardest lives.

4. The life of a farmer's wife was particularly difficult, especially when important crops failed bad.

5. Farmers forced to leave their land didn't have nowhere to go.

6. It is hard to tell whether a farmer's wife or an aristocratic lady had the most interesting life.

7. Although Cavendish wrote good on a number of subjects, some people thought she was mad.

6 Prepositions, Conjunctions, and Interjections

6.1 *Prepositions* A preposition is a word used to show the relationship between a noun or a pronoun and another word in the sentence.

Commonly Used Prepositions			
above	down	near	through
at	for	of	to
before	from	on	up
below	in	out	with
by	into	over	without

The preposition is always followed by a word or group of words which serve as its object. The preposition, its object, and modifiers of the object are called the **prepositional phrase.** In each example below, the prepositional phrase is underlined and the object of the preposition is in boldface type.

> EXAMPLES:
> *The future of the entire **kingdom** is uncertain.*
> *We searched through the deepest **woods.***

Prepositional phrases may be used as adjectives or as adverbs. The phrase in the first example is used as an adjective modifying the noun *future.* In the second example, the phrase is used as an adverb modifying the verb *searched.*

WATCH OUT! Prepositional phrases must be as close as possible to the word they modify.

> MISPLACED: *We have clothes for leisure wear of many colors.*
> CLEARER: *We have clothes of many colors for leisure wear.*

6.2 *Conjunctions* A conjunction is a word used to connect words, phrases, or sentences. There are three kinds of conjunctions: **coordinating conjunctions, correlative conjunctions,** and **subordinating conjunctions.**

Coordinating conjunctions connect words or word groups that have the same function in a sentence. These include *and, but, or, for, so, yet,* and *nor.*

Coordinating conjunctions can join nouns, pronouns, verbs, adjectives, adverbs, prepositional phrases, and clauses in a sentence.

These examples show coordinating conjunctions joining words of the same function:

> **EXAMPLES:**
>
> *I have many friends but few enemies.* (two noun objects)
>
> *We ran out the door and into the street.* (two prepositional phrases)
>
> *They are pleasant yet seem aloof.* (two predicates)
>
> *We have to go now, or we will be late.* (two clauses)

Correlative conjunctions are similar to coordinating conjunctions. However, correlative conjunctions are always used in pairs.

Correlative Conjunctions		
both . . . and	neither . . . nor	whether . . . or
either . . . or	not only . . . but also	

Subordinating conjunctions introduce subordinate clauses—clauses that cannot stand by themselves as complete sentences. The subordinating conjunction shows how the subordinate clause relates to the rest of the sentence. The relationships include time, manner, place, cause, comparison, condition, and purpose.

SUBORDINATING CONJUNCTIONS	
TIME	*after, as, as long as, as soon as, before, since, until, when, whenever, while*
MANNER	*as, as if*
PLACE	*where, wherever*
CAUSE	*because, since*
COMPARISON	*as, as much as, than*
CONDITION	*although, as long as, even if, even though, if, provided that, though, unless, while*
PURPOSE	*in order that, so that, that*

In the example below, the boldface word is the conjunction, and the underlined words are called a subordinate clause:

> **EXAMPLE:** *I whistle a happy tune* **whenever** *I feel afraid.*

I whistle a happy tune is an independent clause because it can stand alone as a complete sentence. *Whenever I feel afraid* cannot stand alone as a complete sentence; it is a subordinate clause.

Conjunctive adverbs are used to connect clauses that can stand by themselves as sentences. Conjunctive adverbs include *also, besides, finally, however, moreover, nevertheless, otherwise,* and *then.*

> **EXAMPLE:** *She loved the fall; however, she also enjoyed winter.*

6.3 *Interjections* are words used to show strong emotion, such as *wow* and *cool.* Often followed by an exclamation point, they have no grammatical relationship to the rest of a sentence.

> **EXAMPLE:** *Whew! It's really hot outside.*

GRAMMAR PRACTICE

Label each of the boldface words as a preposition, conjunction, or interjection.

1. Fanny Burney went to the party **because** she wished to hear the great tenor sing.

2. **After** Burney arrived, she greeted her hosts **and** listened to the singer perform.

3. **Because of** the great heat in the crowded room, the singer decided to move **into** another one.

4. Lady Say and Sele accosted Burney **before** the writer could escape.

5. **"Oh!"** cried Lady S. and S. "'Tis the authoress of *Evelina.*"

⑦ Quick Reference: The Sentence and Its Parts

The diagrams that follow will give you a brief review of the essentials of the sentence—subjects and predicates—and of some of its parts.

The Pilgrims' **ship** | **reached** North America.

The **complete subject** includes all the words that identify the person, place, thing, or idea that the sentence is about.

The **complete predicate** includes all the words that tell or ask something about the subject.

ship

reached

The **simple subject** tells exactly whom or what the sentence is about. It may be one word or a group of words, but it does not include modifiers.

The **simple predicate**, or **verb**, tells what the subject does or is. It may be one word or several, but it does not include modifiers.

During the harsh winter, | Native Americans | **had given** the starving | **Pilgrims food.**

A **prepositional phrase** consists of a preposition, its object, and any modifiers of the object. In this phrase, *during* is the preposition and *winter* is its object.

subject

An **indirect object** is a word or a group of words that tells *to whom* or *for whom* or *to what* or *for what* about the verb. A sentence can have an indirect object only if it has a direct object. The indirect object always comes before the direct object in a sentence.

Verbs often have more than one part. They may be made up of a **main verb**, like *given,* and one or more **auxiliary**, or **helping, verbs,** like *had.*

A **direct object** is a word or group of words that tells who or what receives the action of the verb in the sentence.

8 The Sentence and Its Parts

A sentence is a group of words used to express a complete thought. A complete sentence has a subject and predicate.

8.1 Kinds of Sentences

Sentences make statements, ask questions, give commands, and show feelings. There are four basic types of sentences.

Type	Definition	Example
Declarative	states a fact, wish, intent, or feeling	I read Malory's poem recently.
Interrogative	asks a question	Did you read his poem?
Imperative	gives a command, request, or direction	Read the poem or else.
Exclamatory	expresses strong feeling or excitement	This writer is good!

WRITING TIP One way to vary your writing is to employ a variety of different types of sentences. In the first example below, each sentence is declarative. Notice how much more interesting the revised paragraph is.

SAMPLE PARAGRAPH: *You have to see Niagara Falls in person. You can truly appreciate their awesome power in no other way. You should visit them on your next vacation. They are a spectacular sight.*

REVISED PARAGRAPH: *Have you ever seen Niagara Falls in person? You can truly appreciate their awesome power in no other way. Visit them on your next vacation. What a spectacular sight they are!*

WATCH OUT! Conversation frequently includes parts of sentences, or **fragments.** In formal writing, however, you need to be sure that every sentence is a complete thought and includes a subject and predicate. (See Correcting Fragments, page 1409.)

8.2 Complete Subjects and Predicates

A sentence has two parts: a subject and a predicate. The complete subject includes all the words that identify the person, place, thing, or idea that the sentence is about. The complete predicate includes all the words that tell what the subject did or what happened to the subject.

Complete Subject	Complete Predicate
The poets of the time	wrote about nature.
This new approach	was extraordinary.

8.3 Simple Subjects and Predicates

The simple subject is the key word in the complete subject. The simple predicate is the key word in the complete predicate. In the examples that follow they are underlined.

Simple Subject	Simple Predicate
The poets of the time	wrote about nature.
This new approach	was extraordinary.

8.4 Compound Subjects and Predicates

A compound subject consists of two or more subjects that share the same verb. They are typically joined by the coordinating conjunction *and* or *or.*

EXAMPLE: *The knight and his horse rode into the forest.*

A compound predicate consists of two or more predicates that share the same subject. They, too, are usually joined by the coordinating conjunction *and, but,* or *or.*

EXAMPLE: *Sir Gawain beheaded the Green Knight but did not kill him.*

8.5 Subjects and Predicates in Questions

In many interrogative sentences, the subject may appear after the verb or between parts of a verb phrase.

INTERROGATIVE: *Was Gawain living by the code of chivalry?*
INTERROGATIVE: *Why is this story very popular?*

8.6 Subjects and Predicates in Imperative Sentences

Imperative sentences give commands, requests, or directions. The subject of an imperative sentence is the person spoken to, or *you*. While it is not stated, it is understood to be *you*.

> EXAMPLE: *(You) Please tell me what you're thinking.*

8.7 Subjects in Sentences That Begin with There and Here

When a sentence begins with *there* or *here*, the subject usually follows the verb. Remember that *there* and *here* are never the subjects of a sentence. The simple subjects in the example sentences are underlined.

> EXAMPLES
>
> *Here is the solution to the mystery.*
>
> *There is no time to waste now.*
>
> *There were too many passengers on the boat.*

GRAMMAR PRACTICE

Copy each of the following sentences. Then draw one line under the complete subject and two lines under the complete predicate.

1. The Old English alliterative tradition emerged about 1350.
2. There were four texts in the manuscript.
3. None of the four texts originally had a title.
4. The last of the four texts was *Sir Gawain and the Green Knight*.
5. It may well be the greatest Arthurian romance in English.
6. Twelve rough illustrations accompanied the original texts.
7. The Pearl Poet evidently was not an artist.
8. Think about the way that the Green Knight tests Gawain's virtues.
9. Why has the code of chivalry disappeared?
10. The knights of King Arthur's court have all become legendary figures.

8.8 Complements

A complement is a word or group of words that completes the meaning of the sentence. Some sentences contain only a subject and a verb. Most sentences, however, require additional words placed after the verb to complete the meaning of the sentence. There are three kinds of complements: **direct objects, indirect objects,** and **subject complements.**

Direct objects are words or word groups that receive the action of action verbs. A direct object answers the question *what?* or *whom?* In the examples that follow the direct objects are underlined.

> EXAMPLES
>
> *The students asked many questions.*
> (asked what?)
>
> *The teacher quickly answered them.*
> (answered what?)
>
> *The school accepted <u>girls and boys</u>.*
> (accepted whom?)

Indirect objects tell *to* or *for whom* or *what* the action of the verb is performed. Indirect objects come before direct objects. In the examples that follow the indirect objects are underlined.

> EXAMPLES
>
> *My sister usually gave her friends good advice.* (gave to whom?)
>
> *Her brother sent the post office a heavy package.* (sent to what?)
>
> *His kind grandfather mailed him a new tie.*
> (mailed to whom?)

Subject complements come after linking verbs and identify or describe the subject. Subject complements that name or identify the subject of the sentence are called **predicate nominatives.** These include **predicate nouns** and **predicate pronouns.** In the examples that follow the subject complements are underlined.

> EXAMPLES
>
> *My friends are very hard workers.*
>
> *The best writer in the class is she.*

Other subject complements describe the subject of the sentence. These are called **predicate adjectives.**

EXAMPLE: *The pianist appeared very energetic.*

Write all of the complements in the following sentences and label them as direct objects, indirect objects, predicate nouns, predicate pronouns, or predicate adjectives.

1. William Wordsworth inaugurated the English Romantic period.
2. With Samuel Taylor Coleridge, he published *Lyrical Ballads* in 1798.
3. That volume quickly became immensely popular.
4. The last poem in *Lyrical Ballads* was "Lines Composed a Few Miles Above Tintern Abbey."
5. Wordsworth wrote the poem after a walking tour in June 1798.
6. In 1800, while living at Dove Cottage near Grasmere, Wordsworth and his friend enlarged their famous collection.
7. In that edition, Wordsworth gave the world his famous "Preface."
8. He stated his convictions and intentions about poetry.
9. He would draw his material from nature and everyday events.
10. Wordsworth offered readers a radical new philosophy.

9 Phrases

A phrase is a group of related words that does not have a subject and predicate and functions in a sentence as a single part of speech.

9.1 **Prepositional Phrases** A prepositional phrase is a phrase that consists of a preposition, its object, and any modifiers of the object. Prepositional phrases that modify nouns or pronouns are called **adjective phrases.** Prepositional phrases that modify a verb, an adjective, or another adverb are **adverb phrases.**

ADJECTIVE PHRASE: *The central character of the story is a wicked villain.*

ADVERB PHRASE: *He reveals his nature in the first scene.*

9.2 **Appositives and Appositive Phrases** An appositive is a noun or pronoun that usually comes directly after another noun or pronoun and identifies or provides further information about that word. An appositive phrase includes the appositive and all its modifiers. In the following examples, the appositive phrases are underlined.

EXAMPLES

We were discussing Mary Shelley, my hero.

Mary Wollstonecraft, the famous feminist, was considered a radical.

Occasionally, an appositive phrase may precede the noun it tells about.

EXAMPLE: *A great feminist, Mary Wollstonecraft wrote many essays.*

10 Verbals and Verbal Phrases

A verbal is a verb form that is used as a noun, an adjective, or an adverb. A verbal phrase consists of a verbal, all its modifiers, and all its complements. There are three kinds of verbals: infinitives, participles, and gerunds.

10.1 **Infinitives and Infinitive Phrases** An infinitive is a verb form that usually begins with *to* and functions as a noun, adjective, or adverb. The infinitive and its modifiers constitute an infinitive phrase. The examples that follow show several uses of infinitives and infinitive phrases. Each infinitive phrase is underlined.

NOUN: *To know her is my only desire.* (subject)

She wrote to voice her opinions. (direct object)

Her goal was to promote women's rights. (predicate nominative)

ADJECTIVE: *We saw his need to be loved.*
(adjective modifying *need*)
ADVERB: *I'm planning to walk with you.*
(adverb modifying *planning*)

Like verbs themselves, infinitives can take objects (*her* in the first noun example), be made passive (*to be loved* in the adjective example), and take modifiers (*with you* in the adverb example).

Because *to*, the sign of the infinitive, precedes infinitives, it is usually easy to recognize them. However, sometimes *to* may be omitted.

EXAMPLE: *Let no one dare [to] enter this shrine.*

10.2 Participles and Participial Phrases

A participle is a verb form that functions as an adjective. Like adjectives, participles modify nouns and pronouns. Most participles use the present participle form, ending in *-ing*, or the past participle form, ending in *-ed* or *-en*. In the examples below the participles are underlined.

MODIFYING A NOUN: *The dying man had a smile on his face.*
MODIFYING A PRONOUN: *Frustrated, everyone abandoned the cause.*

Participial phrases are participles with all their modifiers and complements.

MODIFYING A NOUN: *The dogs searching for survivors are well trained.*
MODIFYING A PRONOUN: *Having approved your proposal, we are ready to act.*

10.3 Dangling and Misplaced Participles

A participle or participial phrase should be placed as close as possible to the word that it modifies. Otherwise the meaning of the sentence may not be clear.

MISPLACED: *The boys were looking for squirrels searching the trees.*
CLEARER: *The boys searching the trees were looking for squirrels.*

A participle or participial phrase that does not clearly modify anything in a sentence is called a **dangling participle.** A dangling participle causes confusion because it appears to modify a word that it cannot sensibly modify.

Correct a dangling participle by providing a word for the participle to modify.

CONFUSING: *Running like the wind, my hat fell off.* (The hat wasn't running.)
CLEARER: *Running like the wind, I lost my hat.*

10.4 Gerunds and Gerund Phrases

A gerund is a verb form ending in *-ing* that functions as a noun. Gerunds may perform any function nouns perform.

SUBJECT: *Running is my favorite pastime.*
DIRECT OBJECT: *I truly love running.*
SUBJECT COMPLEMENT: *My deepest passion is running.*
OBJECT OF PREPOSITION: *Her love of running keeps her strong.*

Gerund phrases are gerunds with all their modifiers and complements. The gerund phrases are underlined in the following examples.

SUBJECT: *Wishing on a star never got me far.*
OBJECT OF PREPOSITION: *I will finish before leaving the office.*
APPOSITIVE: *Her avocation, flying airplanes, finally led to full-time employment.*

GRAMMAR PRACTICE

Identify the underlined phrases as appositive phrases, infinitive phrases, participial phrases, or gerund phrases.

1. Concerned about the injustices in Ireland, Swift wrote his satiric essay "A Modest Proposal."

2. Irony, a contrast between expectations and reality, can be an effective literary device.

3. Swift's modest proposal to prevent the children of Ireland from becoming a burden is ironic.

4. Referring to people as a commodity is a strong insult.

5. Was Swift a misanthrope, someone who mistrusts mankind?

6. What can be done to change the abhorrent conditions of the Irish poor?

7. *Gulliver's Travels,* an English satire, has many admiring readers.

11 Clauses

A clause is a group of words that contains a subject and a verb. There are two kinds of clauses: independent clauses and subordinate clauses.

11.1 Independent and Subordinate Clauses

An independent clause can stand alone as a sentence, as the word *independent* suggests.

INDEPENDENT CLAUSE: *The English are noted for their independence.*

A sentence may contain more than one independent clause.

EXAMPLE: *The English are noted for their independence, and they are proud of their history of leadership in the Western world.*

In the example above the coordinating conjunction *and* joins the two independent clauses.

A subordinate clause cannot stand alone as a sentence. It is subordinate to, or dependent on, the main clause.

EXAMPLE: *The English are known for their independence, although they are also very willing to work with others.*

Although they are also very willing to work with others cannot stand by itself.

11.2 Adjective Clauses

An adjective clause is a subordinate clause used as an adjective. It usually follows the noun or pronoun it modifies.

EXAMPLE: *William Wordsworth is someone whom millions have read.*

Adjective clauses are typically introduced by the relative pronouns *who, whom, whose, which,* and *that* (see Relative Pronouns, page 1395). In the examples that follow, the adjective clauses are underlined.

EXAMPLES

A person who wants friends should be a friend.

Mary Ann Evans, whose pen name was George Eliot, wrote several great novels.

I read novels that let me escape from daily life.

WATCH OUT! The relative pronouns *whom, which,* and *that* may sometimes be omitted when they are objects of their own clauses.

EXAMPLE: *William Wordsworth is someone [whom] millions admire.*

11.3 Adverb Clauses

An adverb clause is a subordinate clause that is used as an adverb to modify a verb, an adjective, or another adverb. It is introduced by a subordinating conjunction (see Subordinating Conjunctions, page 1401).

Adverb clauses typically occur at the beginning or end of sentences. The clauses are underlined in these examples.

MODIFYING A VERB: *When we need you, we will call.*

MODIFYING AN ADVERB: *I'll stay here where there is shelter from the rain.*

MODIFYING AN ADJECTIVE: *Roman felt good when he finished his essay.*

11.4 Noun Clauses

A noun clause is a subordinate clause that is used in a sentence as a noun. A noun clause may be used as a subject, a direct object, an indirect object, a predicate nominative, or an object of a preposition. Noun clauses are often introduced by pronouns such as *that, what, who, whoever, which,* and *whose,* and by subordinating conjunctions, such as *how, when, where, why,* and *whether.* (See Subordinating Conjunctions, page 1401.)

USAGE TIP Because the same words may introduce adjective and noun clauses, you need to consider how the clause functions within its sentence.

To determine if a clause is a noun clause, try substituting *something* or *someone* for the clause. If you can do it, it is probably a noun clause.

EXAMPLES: *I know whose woods these are.* ("I know something." The clause is a noun clause, direct object of the verb know.)

Give a copy to whoever wants one. ("Give a copy to someone." The clause is a noun clause, object of the preposition *to.*)

Identify each underlined clause as an adjective clause, an adverb clause, or a noun clause.

1. Some people think that John Keats is the best Romantic poet.
2. When I read the last line of "Ode on a Grecian Urn," I cried.
3. Did Keats, who wrote "When I Have Fears That I May Cease to Be," have a premonition of his own early death?
4. At first, Keats could not decide whether he wanted to be a poet or a surgeon.
5. He made the fateful decision, which the world welcomed, at about the age of 21.

🔟2 The Structure of Sentences

When classified by their structure, there are four kinds of sentences: simple, compound, complex, and compound-complex.

12.1 *Simple Sentences* A simple sentence is a sentence that has one independent clause and no subordinate clauses. The fact that they are called "simple" does not mean that such sentences are uncomplicated. Various parts of simple sentences may be compound, and they may contain grammatical structures such as appositives and verbals.

EXAMPLES

Lord Byron, a symbol of romanticism, has influenced poets, composers, and artists. (appositive and compound direct object)

Percy Bysshe Shelley, best known for writing poetry, was also an essayist. (participial and gerund phrases)

12.2 *Compound Sentences* A compound sentence has two or more independent clauses. The clauses are joined together with a comma and a coordinating conjunction (*and, but, or, nor, yet, for, so*), a semicolon, or a conjunctive adverb with a semicolon. Like simple sentences, compound sentences do not contain any dependent clauses.

EXAMPLES

I love Shelley's poem "Ozymandias," yet I don't admire Ozymandias himself.

Jane Austen lived a relatively quiet life; however, that did not prevent her from writing great novels.

WATCH OUT! Do not confuse compound sentences with simple sentences that have compound parts.

EXAMPLE: *A subcommittee drafted a document and immediately presented it to the entire group.* (here *and* signals a compound predicate, not a compound sentence)

12.3 *Complex Sentences* A complex sentence has one independent clause and one or more subordinate clauses. Each subordinate clause can be used as a noun or as a modifier. If it is used as a modifier, a subordinate clause usually modifies a word in the main clause, and the main clause can stand alone. However, when a subordinate clause is a noun clause, it is a part of the independent clause; the two cannot be separated.

MODIFIER: *One should not complain, unless she or he has a better solution.*

NOUN CLAUSE: *We sketched pictures of whomever we wished.* (noun clause is the object of the preposition *of* and cannot be separated from the rest of the sentence)

12.4 *Compound-Complex Sentences* A compound-complex sentence has two or more independent clauses and one or more subordinate clauses. Compound-complex sentences are, simply, both compound and complex. If you start with a compound sentence, all you need to do to form a compound-complex sentence is add a subordinate clause.

COMPOUND: *All the students knew the answer, yet they were too shy to volunteer.*

COMPOUND-COMPLEX: *All the students knew the answer that their teacher expected, yet they were too shy to volunteer.*

GRAMMAR PRACTICE

Tell whether each sentence is a simple sentence, a compound sentence, a complex sentence, or a compound-complex sentence.

1. Keats is my favorite romantic poet.

2. His life was tragically short, but he produced a remarkable body of work.

3. Although he became engaged to Fanny Brawne, poverty and poor health prevented him from marrying her.

4. Despite his illness, he produced many great works.

5. As his illness progressed, Keats moved to the milder climate of Italy, but he died six months later.

⑬ Writing Complete Sentences

A sentence is a group of words that expresses a complete thought. In writing that you wish to share with a reader, try to avoid both sentence fragments and run-on sentences.

13.1 **Correcting Fragments** A sentence fragment is a group of words that is only part of a sentence. It does not express a complete thought and may be confusing to the reader or the listener. A sentence fragment may be lacking a subject, a predicate, or both.

> **FRAGMENT**: *waited for the boat to arrive* (no subject)
> **CORRECTED**: *We waited for the boat to arrive.*
> **FRAGMENT**: *people of various races, ages, and creeds* (no predicate)
> **CORRECTED**: *People of various races, ages, and creeds gathered together.*
> **FRAGMENT**: *near the old cottage* (neither subject nor predicate)
> **CORRECTED**: *The burial ground is near the old cottage.*

In your own writing, fragments are usually the result of haste or incorrect punctuation. Sometimes fixing a fragment will be a matter of attaching it to a preceding or following sentence.

> **FRAGMENT**: *We saw the two girls. Waiting for the bus to arrive.*
> **CORRECTED**: *We saw the two girls waiting for the bus to arrive.*
> **FRAGMENT**: *Newspapers appeal to a wide audience. Including people of various races, ages, and creeds.*
> **CORRECTED**: *Newspapers appeal to a wide audience, including people of various races, ages, and creeds.*

13.2 **Correcting Run-on Sentences**
A run-on sentence is made up of two or more sentences written as though they were one. Some run-ons have no punctuation within them. Others may use only a comma where a conjunction or stronger punctuation is necessary. Use your judgment in correcting run-on sentences, as you have choices. You can make two sentences if the thoughts are not closely connected. If the thoughts are closely related, you can keep the run-on as one sentence by adding a semicolon or a conjunction.

> **RUN-ON**: *We found a place by a small pond for the picnic it is three miles from the village.*
> **MAKE TWO SENTENCES**: *We found a place by a small pond for the picnic. It is three miles from the village.*
> **RUN-ON**: *We found a place by a small pond for the picnic it was perfect.*
> **USE A SEMICOLON**: *We found a place by a small pond for the picnic; it was perfect.*
> **ADD A CONJUNCTION**: *We found a place by a small pond for the picnic, and it was perfect.*

WATCH OUT! When you add a conjunction, make sure you use appropriate punctuation before it: a comma for a coordinating conjunction, a semicolon for a conjunctive adverb. (See Conjunctions, page 1401.) A very common mistake is to use a comma instead of a conjunction or an end mark. This error is called a **comma splice**.

> **INCORRECT**: *He finished the apprenticeship, then he left the village.*
> **CORRECT**: *He finished the apprenticeship, and then he left the village.*

Rewrite the following paragraph, correcting all fragments and run-ons.

Rudyard Kipling was born in India. Where his father was a teacher at the University of Bombay. When he was only six years old. He was sent to school in England. There, at an early age, he wrote verses, some of them were very good. He turned many of his earlier experiences to literary use. In such works as *The Light That Failed.*

14 Subject-Verb Agreement

The subject and verb of a sentence must agree in number. Agreement means that when the subject is singular, the verb must be singular; when the subject is plural, the verb must be plural.

14.1 Basic Agreement Fortunately, agreement between subject and verb in English is simple. Most verbs show the difference between singular and plural only in the third person present tense. The present tense of the third person singular ends in *-s*.

Present Tense Verb Forms	
Singular	**Plural**
I sleep	we sleep
you sleep	you sleep
she, he, it sleeps	they sleep

14.2 Agreement with Be The verb *be* presents special problems in agreement because this verb does not follow the usual verb patterns.

Forms of *Be*			
Present Tense		**Past Tense**	
Singular	**Plural**	**Singular**	**Plural**
I am	we are	I was	we were
you are	you are	you were	you were
she, he, it is	they are	she, he, it was	they were

14.3 Words Between Subject and Verb
A verb agrees only with its subject. When words come between a subject and its verb, ignore them when considering proper agreement. Identify the subject and make sure the verb agrees with it.

EXAMPLES

A story in the newspapers tells about the 1890s.

Dad as well as Mom reads the paper daily.

14.4 Agreement with Compound Subjects Use a plural verb with most compound subjects joined by the word *and*.

EXAMPLE: *My father and his friends (they) read the paper daily.*

You could substitute the plural pronoun *they* for *my father and his friends*. This shows that you need a plural verb.

If the compound subject is thought of as a unit, you use the singular verb. Test this by substituting the singular pronoun *it*.

EXAMPLE: *Peanut butter and jelly [it] is my brother's favorite sandwich.*

Use a singular verb with a compound subject that is preceded by *each, every,* or *many a*.

EXAMPLE: *Each novel and short story seems grounded in personal experience.*

With *or, nor*, and the correlative conjunctions *either . . . or* and *neither . . . nor*, make the verb agree with the noun or pronoun nearest the verb.

EXAMPLES

Cookies or ice cream is my favorite dessert.

Either Cheryl or her friends are being invited.

Neither ice storms nor snow is predicted today.

14.5 Personal Pronouns as Subjects
When using a personal pronoun as a subject, make sure to match it with the correct form of the verb *be*. (See the chart in 14.2.) Note especially that the pronoun *you* takes the verbs *are* and *were*, regardless of whether it is referring to the singular *you* or to the plural *you*.

WATCH OUT! *You is* and *you was* are nonstandard forms and should be avoided in writing and speaking. *We was* and *they was* are also forms to be avoided.

INCORRECT: *You was my best friend. They was going away.*

CORRECT: *You were my best friend. They were going away.*

14.6 Indefinite Pronouns as Subjects

Some indefinite pronouns are always singular; some are always plural. Others may be either singular or plural.

Singular Indefinite Pronouns			
another	either	neither	other
anybody	everybody	nobody	somebody
anyone	everyone	no one	someone
anything	everything	nothing	something
each	much	one	

EXAMPLES
Each of the writers was given an award.
Somebody in the room upstairs is sleeping.

The indefinite pronouns that are always plural include *both, few, many*, and *several*. These take plural verbs.

EXAMPLES
Many of the books in our library are not in circulation.

Few have been returned recently.

Still other indefinite pronouns may be either singular or plural.

Singular or Plural Indefinite Pronouns			
all	enough	most	plenty
any	more	none	some

The number of the indefinite pronouns *any* and *none* depends on the intended meaning.

EXAMPLES
Any of these topics has potential for a good article. (any singular topic)

Any of these topics have potential for a good article. (any of the many topics)

The indefinite pronouns *all, some, more, most,* and *none* are singular when they refer to a quantity or part of something. They are plural when they refer to a number of individual things. Context will usually give a clue.

EXAMPLES
All of the flour is gone. (referring to a quantity)

All of the flowers are gone. (referring to individual items)

14.7 Inverted Sentences

Problems in agreement often occur in inverted sentences beginning with *here* or *there*; in questions beginning with *why, where*, and *what*; and in inverted sentences beginning with a phrase. Identify the subject—wherever it is—before deciding on the verb.

EXAMPLES
There clearly are far too many cooks in this kitchen.

What is the correct ingredient for this stew?

Far from the embroiled cooks stands the master chef.

GRAMMAR PRACTICE

Locate the subject of each sentence. Then choose the correct verb.

1. Many writers have been controversial, but few (is/are) as controversial as D. H. Lawrence.

2. Neither his novels nor that shocking short story (is/are) censored today, however.

3. Nearly everybody who has read him either (love/loves) him or (hate/hates) him.

4. There (is/are) no opinions in between.

5. He and his wife Frieda searched for new ways to relate to people; they (was/were) a remarkable couple.

14.8 Sentences with Predicate Nominatives

When a predicate nominative serves as a complement in a sentence, use a verb that agrees with the subject, not the complement.

EXAMPLES

The novels of Dickens are a milestone in British literature. (*Novels* is the subject, not *milestone,* and it takes the plural verb *are.*)

A milestone in British literature is the novels of Dickens. (The subject is the singular noun *milestone.*)

14.9 Don't *and* Doesn't *as Auxiliary Verbs*

The auxiliary verb *doesn't* is used with singular subjects and with the personal pronouns *she, he,* and *it.* The auxiliary verb *don't* is used with plural subjects and with the personal pronouns *I, we, you*, and *they.*

SINGULAR

He doesn't know Elizabeth Barrett Browning's famous "Sonnet 43."
Doesn't the young man read very much?

PLURAL

I don't know what time it is now.
Novelists don't necessarily write short stories.

14.10 Collective Nouns as Subjects

Collective nouns are singular nouns that name a group of persons or things. *Team,* for example, is the collective name of a group of individuals. A collective noun takes a singular verb when the group acts as a single unit. It takes a plural verb when the members of the group act separately.

EXAMPLES

Our team usually wins. (the team as a whole wins)

Our team vote differently on most issues. (the individual members vote)

14.11 Relative Pronouns as Subjects

When a relative pronoun is used as a subject of its clause—*who, which,* and *that* can serve as subjects—the verb of the clause must agree in number with the antecedent of the pronoun.

SINGULAR: *I didn't read the book on trees that was given to me, but I did leaf through it.*

The antecedent of the relative pronoun *that* is the singular *book*; therefore, *that* is singular and must take the singular verb *was.*

PLURAL: *D. H. Lawrence and James Joyce, who were very different from each other, are both outstanding novelists.*

The antecedent of the relative pronoun *who* is the plural compound subject *D. H. Lawrence and James Joyce.* Therefore, *who* is plural, and it takes the plural verb *were.*

GRAMMAR PRACTICE

Choose the correct verb for each of the following sentences.

1. "The Rocking-Horse Winner" (don't/doesn't) end happily.
2. Nevertheless, it is a story that (entertain/entertains) most readers.
3. Even a collection of toys (hear/hears) the secret whisper.
4. The boy asked why some people (attract, attracts) luck.
5. Paul (are/is) partners with the older men.
6. What do you think the voices in the house that (were/was) speaking to Paul symbolize?
7. Why is it that Paul's horse (don't/doesn't) have a name?
8. Our class (vote/votes) on each story we read.
9. Lawrence's story about Paul's family, which (were/was) read last week, was a big winner in our poll.
10. A group of students (have/has) decided to dramatize it.

Quick Reference: Punctuation

Punctuation	Function	Examples
End Marks period, question mark, exclamation point	to end sentences	It was the best time of my life. Was it the best time for you? What an architect Inigo Jones was!
	initials and other abbreviations	Dr. Robert Boyle, I. M. Pei, McDougal Littell Inc., A.M., B.C., yds., ft., Ave., St.

	items in outlines	I. Volcanoes
		    A. Central-vent
		        1. Shield

	exception: P.O. states	NE (Nebraska), NV (Nevada)
Commas	before conjunction in compound sentence	I have never disliked poetry, but now I really love it.
	items in a series	She is brave, loyal, and kind. The slow, easy route is best.
	words of address	"Bright star, would I were steadfast . . . ." We need to solve this problem, men.
	parenthetical expressions	Well, just suppose that we can't? Hard workers, as you know, don't quit. I'm not a quitter, believe me.
	introductory phrases and clauses	In the beginning of the day, I feel fresh. While she was out, I was here. Having finished my chores, I went out.
	nonessential phrases and clauses	Ed Pawn, captain of the chess team, won. Ed Pawn, who is the captain, won. The two leading runners, sprinting toward the finish line, ended in a tie.
	in dates and addresses	Send it by June 20, 1998, to Maple Industry, 22 Spring Street, York, PA
	in letter parts	Dear Jim, Sincerely yours,
	for clarity, or to avoid confusion	By noon, time had run out. What the minister does, does matter. While cooking, Jim burned his hand.
Semicolons	in compound sentences that are not joined by coordinators *and,* etc.	The last shall be first; the first shall be last. I read the Bible; however, I have not memorized it.
	with items in series that contain commas	We invited my sister, Jan; her friend, Don; my uncle Jack; and Mary Dodd.
	in compound sentences that contain commas	After I ran out of money, I called my parents; but only my sister was home, unfortunately.

Grammar Handbook

Punctuation	Function	Examples
Colons	to introduce lists	**Correct:** Those we wrote were the following: Dana, John, and Will. **Incorrect:** Those we wrote were: Dana, John, and Will.
	before a long quotation	Winston Churchill wrote: "It would be foolish, however, to disguise the gravity of the hour. It would be still more foolish to lose heart."
	after the salutation of a business letter	To Whom It May Concern: Dear Prime Minister:
	with certain numbers	1:28 P.M., Genesis: 2–5
Dashes	to indicate an abrupt break in thought	I was thinking of my mother—who is arriving tomorrow—just as you walked in.
Parentheses	to enclose less important material	Like Dave (but without his English accent), Fran told many funny stories. Big Ben (Have you ever seen it?) is really big!
Hyphens	with a compound adjective before nouns	I come from a line of big-boned Englishmen.
	in compounds with *all-, ex-, self-, -elect*	She's an ex-MP but all-British. Our senator-elect is too self-important.
	in compound numbers (to *ninety-nine*)	Today, I turn twenty-one.
	in fractions used as adjectives	My cup is one-third full.
	between prefixes and words beginning with capital letters	Who was the best pre-Elizabethan poet? The weather was good in mid-May.
	when dividing words at the end of a line	Churchill won the Nobel Prize in litera-ture in 1953.
Apostrophes	to form possessives of nouns and indefinite pronouns	my friend's book, my friends' book, anyone's guess, somebody else's problem
	for omitted letters in numbers/contractions	don't (omitted **o**); he'd (omitted **woul**) the class of '99 (omitted **19**)
	to form plurals of letters and numbers	I had two A's and no 2's on my report card.
Quotation Marks	to set off a speaker's exact words	Sara said, "I'm finally ready." "I'm ready," Sara said, "finally." Did Sara say, "I'm ready"? Sara said, "I'm ready!"
	for titles of stories, short poems, essays, songs, book chapters	I liked Joyce's "Araby," Brooke's "The Soldier," and Orwell's "A Hanging." My favorite is the Beatles' "Yesterday."
Ellipses	for material omitted from a quotation	"It would be foolish . . . to disguise the gravity of the hour. . . ."
Italics	for titles of books, plays, magazines, long poems, operas, films, names of ships	*Pride and Prejudice, Macbeth, Time, The Rime of the Ancient Mariner, Carmen, Titanic,* HMS *Queen Elizabeth II*

Quick Reference: Capitalization

Category/Rule	Examples
People and Titles	
Names and initials of people	Isabel Allende, A. E. Housman
Titles with names or in place of them	Professor Holmes, Senator Long, The Senator has arrived.
Deities and members of religious groups	Jesus, Allah, the Buddha, Zeus, Baptists, Roman Catholics
Names of ethnic and national groups	Hispanics, Jews, African Americans
Geographical Names	
Cities, states, countries, continents	London, Avon, Ireland, Australia
Regions, bodies of water, mountains	the Far West, Loch Lomond, Mount Ida
Geographic features, parks	Great Plains, Kensington Gardens
Streets and roads, planets	55 West Third Avenue, Green Lane, Mars, Saturn
Organizations and Events	
Companies, organizations, teams	Maxwell Industries, the Masons
Buildings, bridges, monuments	Blarney Castle, Westminster Bridge, Vietnam War Memorial
Documents, awards	Magna Carta, Distinguished Flying Cross
Special named events	Super Bowl, World Series
Governmental bodies, historical periods and events	the House of Lords, Parliament, the Elizabethan Age, World War I
Days and months, holidays	Friday, May, Easter, Guy Fawkes Day
Specific cars, boats, trains, planes	MG, *Titanic*, *Orient Express*
Proper Adjectives	
Adjectives formed from proper nouns	Socratic method, Irish cooking, Chaucerian age, Atlantic coast
First Words and the Pronoun *I*	
The first word in a sentence or quote	This is it. He said, "Let's go."
Complete sentence in parentheses	(Consult the previous chapter.)
Salutation and closing of letters	Dear Madam, Very truly yours,
First lines of most poetry The personal pronoun, I	Then am I A happy fly If I live Or if I die.
First, last, and all important words in titles	*A Tale of Two Cities*, "The World Is Too Much with Us"

Little Rules That Make A Big Difference

Sentences

Avoid sentence fragments. Make sure all your sentences express complete thoughts.

A sentence fragment is a group of words that does not express a grammatically complete thought. It may lack a subject, a predicate, or both. Fragments may be corrected by adding the missing element(s) or by changing the punctuation to make the fragment part of another sentence.

> **FRAGMENT**: *We admire George Eliot. A woman who prevailed over many prejudices of her time.*
>
> **COMPLETE**: *We admire George Eliot. She was a woman who prevailed over many prejudices of her time.* (adding a subject and a predicate)
>
> **COMPLETE**: *We admire George Eliot, a woman who prevailed over many prejudices of her time.* (changing the punctuation)

Avoid run-on sentences. Make sure all clauses in a sentence have the proper punctuation and/or conjunctions between them.

A run-on sentence consists of two or more sentences written as though they were one or separated only by a comma. Correct run-ons by making two separate sentences, using a semicolon, adding a conjunction, or rewriting the sentence.

> **RUN-ON**: *James Galway is a great musician, he plays the flute.*
>
> **CORRECT**: *James Galway is a great musician. He plays the flute.*
>
> **CORRECT**: *James Galway is a great musician; he plays the flute.*
>
> **CORRECT**: *James Galway, who plays the flute, is a great musician.*

Use end marks correctly. Use a period, not a question mark, at the end of an indirect question.

An indirect question is a question that does not use the exact words of the original speaker. Note the difference between the following sentences, and observe that the second sentence ends in a period, not a question mark.

> **DIRECT**: *Lou asked, "What is that?"*
>
> **INDIRECT**: *Lou asked what it was.*

Do not use quotation marks with indirect quotations within a sentence.

A direct quotation uses the speaker's exact words. An indirect quotation puts the speaker's words in other words. Compare these sentences:

> **DIRECT**: *Jean said, "I'm going to be up all night writing my essay."* (quotation marks appropriate)
>
> **INDIRECT**: *Jean said that she was going to be up all night writing her essay.* (no quotation marks)

Phrases

Place participial and prepositional phrases as close as possible to the words they modify. Participial and prepositional phrases are modifiers; that is, they tell about some other word in a sentence. To avoid confusion, they should be placed as close as possible to the word that they modify.

> **INCORRECT**: *Tiny microphones are planted by agents called bugs.*
>
> **CORRECT**: *Tiny microphones called bugs are planted by agents.*

Avoid dangling participles. Make sure a participial phrase does modify a word in the sentence.

> **INCORRECT**: *Disappointed in love, a hermit's life seemed attractive.* (Who was disappointed?)
>
> **CORRECT**: *Disappointed in love, the man became a hermit.*

Clauses

Use commas to set off nonessential adjective clauses.

Do you need the clause in order to indicate precisely who or what is meant? If not, it is nonessential and should be set off by commas.

USE COMMAS: *Nadine Gordimer, who is a great role model for young writers, received the 1991 Nobel Prize in literature.*

NO COMMAS: *A writer who is a great role model for young writers received the 1991 Nobel Prize in literature.*

Verbs

Don't use past tense forms with an auxiliary verb or past participle forms without an auxiliary verb. (See Auxiliary Verbs, page 1395.)

INCORRECT: *I have saw her somewhere before.* (*saw* is past tense and shouldn't be used with *have*)

CORRECT: *I have seen her somewhere before.*

INCORRECT: *I seen her somewhere before.* (*seen* is a past participle and shouldn't be used without an auxiliary)

Shift tense only when necessary.

Usually, when you are writing in present tense, stay in present tense; when you are writing in past tense, stay in past tense.

INCORRECT: *When my grandmother tells stories, everybody listened.*

CORRECT: *When my grandmother told stories, everybody listened.*

Sometimes a shift in tense is necessary to show a logical sequence of actions or the relationship of one action to another.

CORRECT: *After he had told his story, everybody went to sleep.*

Subject-Verb Agreement

Make sure subjects and verbs agree in number.

INCORRECT: *The Brontë sisters of England was great writers.*

CORRECT: *The Brontë sisters of England were great writers.*

INCORRECT: *Charlotte, as well as her sisters, were reserved.*

CORRECT: *Charlotte, as well as her sisters, was reserved.*

INCORRECT: *Emily and Anne was dead before 1850.*

CORRECT: *Emily and Anne were dead before 1850.*

Use a singular verb with nouns that look plural but have singular meaning.

Some nouns that end in *-s* are singular, even though they look plural. Examples are *measles, news, Wales,* and the names ending in *-ics* when they refer to a school subject, science, or general practice.

EXAMPLES: *Measles is a serious disease. Politics was the bane of Daniel Defoe.*

Use a singular verb with titles.

EXAMPLE: Scenes of Clerical Life *was published in 1858.* "At the Pitt-Rivers" *was written by Penelope Lively.*

Rule: Use a singular verb with words of weight, time, and measure.

EXAMPLES: *Seven years is the length of time Joyce took to write* Ulysses. *Fifty pounds was a great deal of money in the 1800s.*

Pronouns

Use personal pronouns correctly in compounds.

Don't be confused about case when *and* joins a noun and a personal pronoun; the case of the pronoun still depends upon its function.

INCORRECT: *Him and his friends went to a Renaissance festival.*

CORRECT: *He and his friends went to a Renaissance festival.*

INCORRECT: *The teacher recommended John Donne's poetry to Lisa and I.*

CORRECT: *The teacher recommended John Donne's poetry to Lisa and me.*

INCORRECT: *Give Mary and they some flowers.*

CORRECT: *Give Mary and them some flowers.*

Usually, if you remove the noun and *and,* the correct pronoun will be obvious.

Use *we* and *us* correctly with nouns.

When a noun directly follows *we* or *us,* the case of the pronoun depends upon its function.

INCORRECT: *Us readers enjoy romantic poetry.*

CORRECT: *We readers enjoy romantic poetry.* (*we* is the subject)

INCORRECT: *The teacher read Kipling's "If" to we students.*

CORRECT: *The teacher read Kipling's "If" to us students.* (*us* is the object of *to*)

Avoid unclear pronoun reference.

The reference of a pronoun is ambiguous when the reader cannot tell which of two preceding nouns is its antecedent. The reference is indefinite when the idea to which the pronoun refers is only weakly or vaguely expressed.

AMBIGUOUS: *Homer, not Hesiod, wrote the* Iliad, *and he* [who?] *wrote the* Odyssey *too.*

CLEARER: *Homer, not Hesiod, wrote the* Iliad, *and Homer wrote the* Odyssey *too.*

INDEFINITE: *The Nobel Prize was won by Seamus Heaney in 1995, which is given to the greatest writers.*

CLEARER: *The Nobel Prize, which is given to the greatest writers, was won by Seamus Heaney in 1995.*

Avoid change of person.

If you are writing in third person—using pronouns such as *she, he, it, they, them, his, her, its*—do not shift to second person—*you.*

INCORRECT: *The feudal laborer had to obey his lord, and you needed to obey the king as well.*

CORRECT: *The feudal laborer had to obey his lord, and he needed to obey the king as well.*

Use correct pronouns in elliptical comparisons.

An elliptical comparison is a comparison from which words have been omitted. In order to choose the proper pronoun, fill in the missing words. Note the difference below:

EXAMPLES: *I know my math teacher better than* (I know) *him. I know my math teacher better than he* (knows my math teacher).

Don't confuse pronouns and contractions.

Personal pronouns are made possessive without the use of an apostrophe, as is the relative pronoun *whose.* Whenever you are unsure whether to write *it's* or *its, who's* or *whose,* ask if you mean *it is/has* or *who is/has.* If you do, write the contraction. Do the same for *you're* and *your, they're* and *their,* except that the contraction in this case is for the verb *are.*

> ### Modifiers

Avoid double comparisons.

A double comparison is a comparison made twice. In general, if you use *-er* or *-est* on the end of a modifier, you would not also use *more* or *most* in front of it.

INCORRECT: *I like Shakespeare more better since I've read* Macbeth.

CORRECT: *I like Shakespeare better since I've read* Macbeth.

INCORRECT: *He's the most greatest playwright in the world.*

CORRECT: *He's the greatest playwright in the world.*

Avoid illogical comparisons.

Can you tell what is wrong with the following sentence?

Plays are more entertaining than any kind of performance art.

This sentence is difficult to understand. To avoid such illogical comparisons, use *other* when comparing an individual member with the rest of the group.

Plays are more entertaining than any other kind of performance art.

To avoid another kind of illogical comparison, use *than* or *as* after the first member in a compound comparison.

> **ILLOGICAL**: *Josh baked as many tasty pies if not more than Marsha.* (Did he bake as many pies or as many tasty pies?)

> **CLEARER**: *Josh baked as many tasty pies as Marsha, if not more.*

Avoid misplacing modifiers.

Modifiers of all kinds must be placed as close as possible to the words they modify. If you place them elsewhere, you risk being misunderstood.

> **MISPLACED**: *The Parson is "a holy man of good renown" in Chaucer's* Canterbury Tales.

> **CLEARER**: *The Parson in Chaucer's* Canterbury Tales *is "a holy man of good renown."*

It is the particular parson in Chaucer's poem who is "a holy man of good renown."

Words Not to Capitalize

Do not capitalize *north, south, east,* and *west* when they are used to tell direction.

> **EXAMPLES**: *London is east and south of Oxford.*

> *Leeds is located in West Yorkshire.* (West Yorkshire is the name of a county in the United Kingdom.)

Do not capitalize *sun* and *moon,* and capitalize *earth* only when it is used with the names of other planets.

> **EXAMPLES**: *The sun and the moon are heavenly bodies in a solar system that includes Mars, Jupiter, and the Earth.*

> *We now live on the earth, not in heaven.*

Do not capitalize the names of seasons.

> **EXAMPLE**: *One of Gerard Manley Hopkins's best poems alludes to the seasons of spring and fall.*

Do not capitalize the names of most school subjects.

School subjects are capitalized only when they name a specific course, such as World History I. Otherwise, they are not capitalized.

> **EXAMPLE**: *I'm taking physics, social studies, and a foreign language this year.*

Note: English and the names of other languages are always capitalized.

> **EXAMPLE**: *Everybody takes English and either Spanish or French.*

GRAMMAR PRACTICE

Rewrite each sentence correctly.

1. The professor, a renowned authority on Shakespeare.
2. A modern version of *King Lear* is *A Thousand Acres* by Jane Smiley, an award-winning novel.
3. The tragedies of Shakespeare is more popular than his histories.
4. When *Macbeth* was performed, the tickets are impossible to get.
5. Make sure to reserve tickets for Mark and I.
6. Several productions of *A Midsummer Night's Dream* are performed on warm Summer nights in Central Park.
7. Having written both plays and sonnets, millions of readers admire the work of Shakespeare.
8. I like *West Side Story* more better than *Romeo and Juliet.*
9. The cast held a workshop for we students.
10. Founded in 1599, people still enjoy performances of Shakespeare's plays in the Globe Theatre.

Commonly Confused Words

accept/except	The verb *accept* means "to receive or believe"; *except* is usually a preposition meaning "excluding."	The ticket office accepted all forms of payment except personal checks.
advice/advise	*Advise* is a verb; *advice* is a noun naming that which an *adviser* gives.	How did the witches advise Macbeth? Did they give him good advice?
affect/effect	As a verb *affect* means "to influence." *Effect* as a verb means "to cause." If you want a noun, you will almost always want *effect*.	Did the passionate shepherd's plea affect his beloved? It may effect a change in her attitude. Its effect is unknown.
all ready/already	*All ready* is an adjective meaning "fully ready." *Already* is an adverb meaning "before or by this time."	Two hours later, they were all ready to leave. I had already read Sonnets 116 and 130.
allusion/illusion	An *allusion* is an indirect reference to something. An *illusion* is a false picture or idea.	T. S. Eliot makes many allusions to the literary works of others. It's an illusion to believe you are always right.
among/between	*Between* is used when you are speaking of only two things. *Among* is used for three or more.	I had to choose between chocolate and vanilla. The "Rubáiyát" is among my favorite poems.
bring/take	*Bring* is used to denote motion toward a speaker or place. *Take* is used to denote motion away from such a person or place.	Bring the books over here, and I will take them to the library.
fewer/less	*Fewer* refers to the number of separate, countable units. *Less* refers to bulk quantity.	We have less literature and fewer selections in this year's curriculum.
leave/let	*Leave* means "to allow something to remain behind." *Let* means "to permit."	The librarian will leave some books on display but will not let us borrow any.
lie/lay	To *lie* is "to rest or recline." It does not take an object. To *lay* always takes an object.	Dogs love to lie in the sun. We always lay some bones next to him.
loose/lose	*Loose* (loos) means "free, not restrained"; *lose* (looz) means "to misplace or fail to find."	Who turned the horses loose? I hope we won't lose any of them.
precede/proceed	*Precede* means "to go or come before." Use *proceed* for other meanings.	The Anglo-Saxon period precedes Middle English. The teacher proceeded to read to the class.
than/then	Use *than* in making comparisons; use *then* on all other occasions.	Marlowe is better than Raleigh; We read one, and then the other.
two/too/to	*Two* is the number. *Too* is an adverb meaning "also" or "very." Use *to* before a verb or as a preposition.	Meg had to go to town, too. We had too much reading to do. Two chapters is too much.

Grammar Glossary

This glossary contains various terms you need to understand when you use the Grammar Handbook. Used as a reference source, this glossary will help you explore grammar concepts and the ways they relate to one another.

Abbreviation An abbreviation is a shortened form of a word or word group; it is often made up of initials. (B.C., A.M., *Maj.*)

Active voice. *See* **Voice.**

Adjective An adjective modifies, or describes, a noun or pronoun. (*happy* camper, she is *small*)

A *predicate adjective* follows a linking verb and describes the subject. (The day seemed *long.*)

A *proper adjective* is formed from a proper noun. (*Jewish* temple, *Alaskan* husky)

The *comparative* form of an adjective compares two things. (*more alert, thicker*)

The *superlative* form of an adjective compares more than two things. (*most abundant, weakest*)

What Adjectives Tell	Examples
How many	*some* writers *much* joy
What kind	*grand* plans *wider* streets
Which one(s)	*these* flowers *that* star

Adjective phrase. *See* **Phrase.**

Adverb An adverb modifies a verb, an adjective, or another adverb. (Clare sang *loudly.*)

The *comparative* form of an adverb compares two actions. (*more generously, faster*)

The *superlative* form of an adverb compares more than two actions. (*most sharply, closest*)

What Adverbs Tell	Examples
How	climb *carefully* chuckle *merrily*
When	arrived *late* left *early*
Where	climbed *up* moved *away*
To what extent	*extremely* upset *hardly* visible

Adverb, conjunctive. *See* **Conjunctive adverb.**

Adverb phrase. *See* **Phrase.**

Agreement Sentence parts that correspond with one another are said to be in agreement.

In *pronoun-antecedent agreement,* a pronoun and the word it refers to are the same in number, gender, and person. (*Bill* mailed *his* application. The *students* ate *their* lunches.)

In *subject-verb agreement,* the subject and verb in a sentence are the same in number. (A *child cries* for help. *They cry* aloud.)

Ambiguous reference An ambiguous reference occurs when a pronoun may refer to more than one word. (Bud asked his brother if *he* had any mail.)

Antecedent An antecedent is the noun or pronoun to which a pronoun refers. (If *Adam* forgets *his* raincoat, *he* will be late for school. *She* learned *her* lesson.)

Appositive An appositive is a noun or phrase that explains one or more words in a sentence. (Cary Grant, an *Englishman,* spent most of his adult life in America.)

An *essential appositive* is needed to make the sense of a sentence complete. (A comic strip inspired the musical *Annie.*)

A *nonessential appositive* is one that adds information to a sentence but is not necessary to its sense. (O. Henry, a *short story writer,* spent time in prison.)

Article Articles are the special adjectives *a, an,* and *the.* (*the* day, *a* fly)

The *definite article* (the word *the*) refers to a particular thing. (*the* cabin)

An *indefinite article* is used with a noun that is not unique but refers to one of many of its kind. (*a* dish, *an* otter)

Auxiliary verb. *See* **Verb.**

Clause A clause is a group of words that contains a verb and its subject. (*they slept*)

An *adjective clause* is a subordinate clause that modifies a noun or pronoun. (Hugh bought the sweater *that he had admired.*)

An *adverb clause* is a subordinate clause used to modify a verb, an adjective, or an adverb. (Ring the bell *when it is time for class to begin.*)

A **noun clause** is a subordinate clause that is used as a noun. (*Whatever you say* interests me.)

An **elliptical clause** is a clause from which a word or words have been omitted. (We are not as lucky as *they*.)

A **main (independent) clause** can stand by itself as a sentence. (the *flashlight flickered*)

A **subordinate (dependent) clause** does not express a complete thought and cannot stand by itself. (*while the nation watched*)

Clause	Example
Main (independent)	The hurricane struck
Subordinate (dependent)	while we were preparing to leave.

Collective noun. *See* **Noun.**

Comma splice A comma splice is an error caused when two sentences are separated with a comma instead of a correct end mark. (*The band played a medley of show tunes, everyone enjoyed the show.*)

Common noun. *See* **Noun.**

Comparative. *See* **Adjective; Adverb.**

Complement A complement is a word or group of words that completes the meaning of a verb. (The kitten finished the *milk*.) *See also* **Direct object; Indirect object.**

An **objective complement** is a word or a group of words that follows a direct object and renames or describes that object. (The parents of the rescued child declared Gus a *hero*.)

A **subject complement** follows a linking verb and renames or describes the subject. (The coach seemed *anxious*.) *See also* **Noun (predicate noun); Adjective (predicate adjective).**

Complete predicate The complete predicate of a sentence consists of the main verb plus any words that modify or complete the verb's meaning. (The student *produces work of high caliber*.)

Complete subject The complete subject of a sentence consists of the simple subject plus any words that modify or describe the simple subject. (*Students of history* believe that wars can be avoided.)

Sentence Part	Example
Complete subject	The man in the ten-gallon hat
Complete predicate	wore a pair of silver spurs.

Compound sentence part A sentence element that consists of two or more subjects, verbs, objects, or other parts is compound. (*Lou* and *Jay* helped. Laura *makes* and *models* scarves. Jill sings *opera* and *popular music*.)

Conjunction A conjunction is a word that links other words or groups of words.

A **coordinating conjunction** connects related words, groups of words, or sentences. (*and, but, or*)

A **correlative conjunction** is one of a pair of conjunctions that work together to connect sentence parts. (*either . . . or, neither . . . nor, not only . . . but also, whether . . . or, both . . . and*)

A **subordinating conjunction** introduces a subordinate clause. (*after, although, as, as if, as long as, as though, because, before, if, in order that, since, so that, than, though, till, unless, until, whatever, when, where, while*)

Conjunctive adverb A conjunctive adverb joins the clauses of a compound sentence. (*however, therefore, yet*)

Contraction A contraction is formed by joining two words and substituting an apostrophe for a letter or letters left out of one of the words. (*didn't, we've*)

Coordinating conjunction. *See* **Conjunction.**

Correlative conjunction. *See* **Conjunction.**

 D

Dangling modifier A dangling modifier is one that does not clearly modify any word in the sentence. (*Dashing for the train, the barriers got in the way.*)

Demonstrative pronoun. *See* **Pronoun.**

Dependent clause. *See* **Clause.**

Direct object A direct object receives the action of a verb. Direct objects follow transitive verbs. (Jude planned the *party*.)

Direct quotation. *See* **Quotation.**

Divided quotation. *See* **Quotation.**

Double negative A double negative is the incorrect use of two negative words when only one is needed. (*Nobody didn't care.*)

 E

End mark An end mark is one of several punctuation marks that can end a sentence. See the punctuation chart on page 1413.

Fragment. *See* **Sentence fragment.**

Future tense. *See* **Verb tense.**

Gender The gender of a personal pronoun indicates whether the person or thing referred to is male, female, or neuter. (My cousin plays the tuba; *he* often performs in school concerts.)

Gerund A gerund is a verbal that ends in *-ing* and functions as a noun. (*Making* pottery takes patience.)

Helping verb. *See* **Verb (auxiliary verb).**

Illogical comparison An illogical comparison is a comparison that does not make sense because words are missing or illogical. (My computer is *newer than Kay.*)

Indefinite pronoun. *See* **Pronoun.**

Indefinite reference Indefinite reference occurs when a pronoun is used without a clear antecedent. (My aunt hugged me in front of my friends, and *it* was embarrassing.)

Independent clause. *See* **Clause.**

Indirect object An indirect object tells to whom or for whom (sometimes to what or for what) something is done. (Arthur wrote *Kerry* a letter.)

Indirect question An indirect question tells what someone asked without using the person's exact words. (*My friend asked me if I could go with her to the dentist.*)

Indirect quotation. *See* **Quotation.**

Infinitive An infinitive is a verbal beginning with *to* that functions as a noun, an adjective, or an adverb. (He wanted *to go* to the play.)

Intensive pronoun. *See* **Pronoun.**

Interjection An interjection is a word or phrase used to express strong feeling. (*Wow! Good grief!*)

Interrogative pronoun. *See* **Pronoun.**

Intransitive verb. *See* **Verb.**

Inverted sentence An inverted sentence is one in which the subject comes after the verb. (*How was the movie? Here come the clowns.*)

Irregular verb. *See* **Verb.**

Linking verb. *See* **Verb.**

Main clause. *See* **Clause.**

Main verb. *See* **Verb.**

Modifier A modifier makes another word more precise. Modifiers most often are adjectives or adverbs; they may also be phrases, verbals, or clauses that function as adjectives or adverbs. (*small* box, smiled *broadly*, house *by the sea*, dog *barking loudly*)

An *essential modifier* is one that is necessary to the meaning of a sentence. (Everybody *who has a free pass* should enter now. None *of the passengers* got on the train.)

A *nonessential modifier* is one that merely adds more information to a sentence that is clear without the addition. (We will use the new dishes, *which are stored in the closet.*)

Noun A noun names a person, a place, a thing, or an idea. (*auditor, shelf, book, goodness*)

An *abstract noun* names an idea, a quality, or a feeling. (*joy*)

A *collective noun* names a group of things. (*bevy*)

A *common noun* is a general name of a person, a place, a thing, or an idea. (*valet, hill, bread, amazement*)

A *compound noun* contains two or more words. (*hometown, pay-as-you-go, screen test*)

A *noun of direct address* is the name of a person being directly spoken to. (*Lee,* do you have the package? No, *Suki,* your letter did not arrive.)

A *possessive noun* shows who or what owns or is associated with something. (*Lil's* ring, a *day's* pay)

A *predicate noun* follows a linking verb and renames the subject. (Karen is a *writer.*)

A *proper noun* names a particular person, place, or thing. (*John Smith, Ohio, Sears Tower, Congress*)

Number A word is **singular** in number if it refers to just one person, place, thing, idea, or action, and **plural** in number if it refers to more than one person, place, thing, idea, or action. (The words *he, waiter,* and *is* are singular. The words *they, waiters,* and *are* are plural.)

Object of a preposition The object of a preposition is the noun or pronoun that follows a preposition. (The athletes cycled along the *route.* Jane baked a cake for *her.*)

Object of a verb The object of a verb receives the action of the verb. (Sid told *stories.*)

Participle A participle is often used as part of a verb phrase. (had *written*) It can also be used as a verbal that functions as an adjective. (the *leaping* deer, the medicine *taken* for a fever)

The **present participle** is formed by adding *-ing* to the present form of a verb. (*Walking* rapidly, we reached the general store.)

The **past participle** of a regular verb is formed by adding *-d* or *-ed* to the present form. The past participles of irregular verbs do not follow this pattern. (*Startled,* they ran from the house. *Spun* glass is delicate. A *broken* cup lay there.)

Passive voice. *See* **Voice.**

Past tense. *See* **Verb tense.**

Perfect tenses. *See* **Verb tense.**

Person Person is a means of classifying pronouns.

A **first-person** pronoun refers to the person speaking. (*We* came.)

A **second-person** pronoun refers to the person spoken to. (*You* ask.)

A **third-person** pronoun refers to some other person(s) or thing(s) being spoken of. (*They* played.)

Personal pronoun. *See* **Pronoun.**

Phrase A phrase is a group of related words that does not contain a verb and its subject. (*noticing everything, under a chair*)

An **adjective phrase** modifies a noun or a pronoun. (The label *on the bottle* has faded.)

An **adverb phrase** modifies a verb, an adjective, or an adverb. (Come *to the fair.*)

An **appositive phrase** explains one or more words in a sentence. (Mary, *a champion gymnast,* won gold medals at the Olympics.)

A **gerund phrase** consists of a gerund and its modifiers and complements. (*Fixing the leak* will take only a few minutes.)

An **infinitive phrase** consists of an infinitive, its modifiers, and its complements. (*To prepare for a test,* study in a quiet place.)

A **participial phrase** consists of a participle and its modifiers and complements. (*Straggling to the finish line,* the last runners arrived.)

A **prepositional phrase** consists of a preposition, its object, and the object's modifiers. (The Saint Bernard does rescue work *in the Swiss Alps.*)

A **verb phrase** consists of a main verb and one or more helping verbs. (*might have ordered*)

Possessive A noun or pronoun that is possessive shows ownership or relationship. (*Dan's* story, *my* doctor)

Possessive noun. *See* **Noun.**

Possessive pronoun. *See* **Pronoun.**

Predicate The predicate of a sentence tells what the subject is or does. (The van *runs well even in winter.* The job *seems too complicated.*) See also **Complete predicate; Simple predicate.**

Predicate adjective. *See* **Adjective.**

Predicate nominative A predicate nominative is a noun or pronoun that follows a linking verb and renames or explains the subject. (Joan is a computer *operator.* The winner of the prize was *he.*)

Predicate pronoun. *See* **Pronoun.**

Preposition A preposition is a word that relates its object to another part of the sentence or to the sentence as a whole. (Alfredo leaped *onto* the stage.)

Prepositional phrase. *See* **Phrase.**

Present tense. *See* **Verb tense.**

Pronoun A pronoun replaces a noun or another pronoun. Some pronouns allow a writer or speaker to avoid repeating a proper noun. Other pronouns let a writer refer to an unknown or unidentified person or thing.

A **demonstrative pronoun** singles out one or more persons or things. (*This* is the letter.)

An **indefinite pronoun** refers to an unidentified person or thing. (*Everyone* stayed home. Will you hire *anybody?*)

An **intensive pronoun** emphasizes a noun or pronoun. (The teacher *himself* sold tickets.)

An **interrogative pronoun** asks a question. (*What* happened to you?)

A **personal pronoun** shows a distinction of person. (*I* came. *You* see. *He* knows.)

A **possessive pronoun** shows ownership. (*My* spaghetti is always good. Are *your* parents coming to the play?)

A **predicate pronoun** follows a linking verb and renames the subject. (The owners of the store were *they*.)

A **reflexive pronoun** reflects an action back on the subject of the sentence. (Joe helped *himself*.)

A **relative pronoun** relates a subordinate clause to the word it modifies. (The draperies, *which* had been made by hand, were ruined in the fire.)

Pronoun-antecedent agreement. *See* **Agreement.**

Pronoun forms

The **subject form** of a pronoun is used when the pronoun is the subject of a sentence or follows a linking verb as a predicate pronoun. (*She* fell. The star was *she*.)

The **object form** of a pronoun is used when the pronoun is the direct or indirect object of a verb or verbal or the object of a preposition. (We sent *him* the bill. We ordered food for *them*.)

Proper adjective. *See* **Adjective.**

Proper noun. *See* **Noun.**

Punctuation Punctuation clarifies the structure of sentences. See the punctuation chart below.

Quotation A quotation consists of words from another speaker or writer.

A **direct quotation** is the exact words of a speaker or writer. (Martin said, "*The homecoming game has been postponed.*")

A **divided quotation** is a quotation separated by words that identify the speaker. ("*The homecoming game,*" said Martin, "*has been postponed.*")

An **indirect quotation** reports what a person said without giving the exact words. (Martin said that the homecoming game had been postponed.)

Reflexive pronoun. *See* **Pronoun.**

Regular verb. *See* **Verb.**

Relative pronoun. *See* **Pronoun.**

Run-on sentence A run-on sentence consists of two or more sentences written incorrectly as one. (*The sunset was beautiful its brilliant colors lasted only a short time.*)

Sentence A sentence expresses a complete thought. The chart at the top of the next page shows the four kinds of sentences.

A **complex sentence** contains one main clause and one or more subordinate clauses. (*Open the windows before you go to bed. If she falls, I'll help her up.*)

Punctuation	Uses	Examples
Apostrophe (')	Shows possession	Lou's garage Alva's script
	Indicates a contraction	I'll help you. The baby's tired.
Colon (:)	Introduces a list or quotation	three colors: red, green, and yellow
	Divides some compound sentences	This was the problem: we had to find our own way home.
Comma (,)	Separates ideas	The glass broke, and the juice spilled all over.
	Separates modifiers	The lively, talented cheerleaders energized the team.
	Separates items in series	We visited London, Rome, and Paris.
Exclamation point (!)	Ends an exclamatory sentence	Have a wonderful time!
Hyphen (-)	Joins parts of some compound words	daughter-in-law, great-grandson
Period (.)	Ends a declarative sentence	Swallows return to Capistrano in spring.
	Indicates most abbreviations	min. qt. Blvd. Gen. Jan.
Question mark (?)	Ends an interrogative sentence	Where are you going?
Semicolon (;)	Divides some compound sentences	Marie is an expert dancer; she teaches a class in tap.
	Separates items in series that contain commas	Jerry visited Syracuse, New York; Athens, Georgia; and Tampa, Florida.

A ***compound sentence*** is made up of two or more independent clauses joined by a conjunction, a colon, or a semicolon. (*The ship finally docked, and the passengers quickly left.*)

A ***simple sentence*** consists of only one main clause. (*My friend volunteers at a nursing home.*)

Kind of Sentence	Example
Declarative (statement)	Our team won.
Exclamatory (strong feeling)	I had a great time!
Imperative (request, command)	Take the next exit.
Interrogative (question)	Who owns the car?

Sentence fragment A sentence fragment is a group of words that is only part of a sentence. (*When he arrived. Merrily yodeling.*)

Simple predicate A simple predicate is the verb in the predicate. (John *collects* foreign stamps.)

Simple subject A simple subject is the key noun or pronoun in the subject. (The new *house* is empty.)

Split infinitive A split infinitive occurs when a modifier is placed between the word *to* and the verb in an infinitive. (*to quickly speak*)

Subject The subject is the part of a sentence that tells whom or what the sentence is about. (*Lou* swam.) *See also* **Complete subject; Simple subject.**

Subject-verb agreement. *See* **Agreement.**

Subordinate clause. *See* **Clause.**

Subordinating conjunction. *See* **Conjunction.**

Superlative. *See* **Adjective; Adverb.**

Transitive verb. *See* **Verb.**

Unidentified reference An unidentified reference usually occurs when the word *it, they, this, which,* or *that* is used. (In California *they* have good weather most of the time.)

Verb A verb expresses an action, a condition, or a state of being.

An ***action verb*** tells what the subject does, has done, or will do. The action may be physical or mental. (Susan *trains* guide dogs.)

An ***auxiliary verb*** is added to a main verb to express tense, add emphasis, or otherwise affect the meaning of the verb. Together the auxiliary and main verb make up a verb phrase. (*will* intend, *could have* gone)

A ***linking verb*** expresses a state of being or connects the subject with a word or words that describe the subject. (The ice *feels* cold.) Linking verbs include *appear, be (am, are, is, was, were, been, being), become, feel, grow, look, remain, seem, smell, sound,* and *taste.*

A ***main verb*** expresses action or state of being; it appears with one or more auxiliary verbs. (will be *staying*)

The ***progressive form*** of a verb shows continuing action. (She *is knitting.*)

The past tense and past participle of a ***regular verb*** are formed by adding *-d* or *-ed.* (*open, opened*) An ***irregular verb*** does not follow this pattern. (*throw, threw, thrown; shrink, shrank, shrunk*)

The action of a ***transitive verb*** is directed toward someone or something, called the object of a verb. (Leo *washed* the windows.) An ***intransitive verb*** has no object. (The leaves *scattered.*)

Verb phrase. *See* **Phrase.**

Verb tense Verb tense shows the time of an action or the time of a state of being.

The ***present tense*** places an action or condition in the present. (Jan *takes* piano lessons.)

The ***past tense*** places an action or condition in the past. (We *came* to the party.)

The ***future tense*** places an action or condition in the future. (You *will understand.*)

The ***present perfect tense*** describes an action in an indefinite past time or an action that began in the past and continues in the present. (*has called, have known*)

The ***past perfect tense*** describes one action that happened before another action in the past. (*had scattered, had mentioned*)

The ***future perfect tense*** describes an event that will be finished before another future action begins. (*will have taught, shall have appeared*)

Verbal A verbal is formed from a verb and acts as another part of speech, such as a noun, an adjective, or an adverb.

Verbal	Example
Gerund (used as a noun)	Lamont enjoys *swimming.*
Infinitive (used as an adjective, an adverb, or a noun)	Everyone wants *to help.*
Participle (used as an adjective)	The leaves *covering the drive* made it slippery.

Voice The voice of a verb depends on whether the subject performs or receives the action of the verb.

In the ***active voice*** the subject of the sentence performs the verb's action. (We *knew* the answer.)

In the ***passive voice*** the subject of the sentence receives the action of the verb. (The team *has been eliminated.*)

Analyzing Text Features

Reading a Magazine Article

A **magazine article** is designed to catch and hold your interest. Learning how to recognize the items on a magazine page will help you read even the most complicated articles. Look at the sample magazine article as you read each strategy below.

Strategies for Reading

A Read the **title** and any other **headings** to get an idea of what the article is about. Frequently, the title presents the article's main topic. Smaller headings may introduce subtopics related to the main topic.

B Note text that is set off in some way, such as an **indented paragraph** or a passage in a **different typeface**. This text often summarizes the article.

C Study **visuals**—photos, pictures, or maps. Read their captions and make sure you know how they relate to the main text.

D Look for **special features**, such as charts, tables, or graphs, that provide more detailed information on the topic or on a subtopic.

PRACTICE AND APPLY

Use the sample magazine page at right and the tips above to help you answer the following questions.

1. What is the article's main topic?
2. Which sentence states the main idea of the article?
3. Do you think the use of a contract will ensure student compliance with school rules for behavior? Why or why not?
4. How does the visual help you understand the article?
5. What information appears in the box?

Graduation Manners

Are graduations marred by bad behavior?

by Jennifer Tinnin

Jessica M., a recent high school graduate, says she does not have fond memories of her graduation. "I was really looking forward to graduation, but during the ceremony, kids were shouting and dancing on the stage," she recalls. "I was so embarrassed by my peers' behavior."

Jessica's experience is not unique. Graduation ceremonies across the country are being disrupted by the graduates' behavior. Middle school students in Illinois acted like they had just scored a touchdown as they strutted across the stage, pumping their fists into the air. A student in Minnesota took a pratfall and then had a loud confrontation with police who attempted to escort him from the building. Students in Illinois were not invited back to the site where their graduation was held last year after thousands of dollars of damage was done to the site's restrooms.

These students are not all troublemakers. One student who performed a prank was president of his school's student body, and another student was the valedictorian of his class. Nor are students the sole disruption at graduations. Friends and family in the audience often cheer on students' antics or create additional noise by blowing air horns or screaming when their graduate's name is called.

Many school officials and audience members believe that the dignity of graduation is being sacrificed for a few

"I was so embarrassed by my peers' behavior."

laughs. Ellen, a high school student from California, remarks, "Kids yell and dance because they're happy. It's no big deal. We should be allowed to celebrate our accomplishments and success." Dr. Amos White, principal of a high school in Houston, Texas, disagrees: "These students are graduating into the adult world. They should mark the transition with good manners and courtesy toward their peers, parents, and school officials. We will do whatever we can to keep graduation dignified."

Some schools have started to require students to sign a contract ensuring their compliance with school rules for behavior during the graduation ceremony before they will allow students to attend the ceremony. Is a legal contract necessary to deter students and audiences alike from ruining graduation? Or are graduates and their friends and families simply showing exuberance for a job well done?

GRADUATION BEHAVIOR SURVEY

Do you think there should be stricter enforcement of rules and conduct at graduation ceremonies?

Parents		High School Students	
Yes	77%	Yes	48%
No	20%	No	46%
Not Sure	3%	Not Sure	6%

Do you think students should be required to sign a contract dictating rules of behavior in order to participate in the graduation ceremony?

Parents		High School Students	
Yes	54%	Yes	21%
No	29%	No	68%
Not Sure	17%	Not Sure	11%

Reading a Textbook

The first page of a **textbook** lesson introduces you to a particular topic. The page also provides important information that will guide you through the rest of the lesson. Look at the sample textbook page as you read each strategy below.

Strategies for Reading

A Preview the **title** and other **headings** to find out the lesson's main topic and related subtopics.

B Look for a list of terms or **vocabulary words**. These words will be identified and defined throughout the lesson. They are often set in special type, such as **italics** or **boldface**.

C Read the **main idea**, **objectives**, **or focus**. These items summarize the lesson and establish a purpose for your reading.

D Many mathematics textbooks have an **activity box** that supplements each lesson. These activities will give you more practice and help you further understand each concept.

E Examine **visuals**, such as graphs, photos, and drawings, and their captions. Visuals can help the topic come alive.

PRACTICE AND APPLY

Use the sample textbook page and the tips above to help you answer the following questions.

1. What does this lesson focus on?
2. List the vocabulary terms defined in the lesson.
3. What does Figure 1.14 illustrate?
4. Where is the activity box in this lesson?
5. Give an example of how graphing linear equations in two variables can be used to solve a real-life problem.

1.2   Linear Equations in Two Variables

▶ **What you should learn**
- How to use slope to graph linear equations in two variables
- How to find slopes of lines
- How to write linear equations in two variables
- How to use slope to identify parallel and perpendicular lines
- How to use linear equations in two variables to model and solve real-life problems

▶ **Why you should learn it**

Linear equations in two variables can be used to model and solve real-life problems. For instance, Exercise 112 on page 123 shows how to use a linear equation to model the average annual salaries of major league baseball players from 1988 to 1998.

Walter Schmid/The Stock Market

A computer simulation of this concept appears in the *Interactive* CD-ROM and *Internet* versions of this text.

Using Slope

The simplest mathematical model for relating two variables is the **linear equation in two variables** $y = mx + b$. The equation is called *linear* because its graph is a line. (In mathematics, the term *line* means *straight line*.) By letting $x = 0$, you can see that the line crosses the y-axis at $y = b$, as shown in Figure 1.14. In other words, the y-intercept is $(0, b)$. The steepness or slope of the line is m.

$$y = mx + b$$

Slope ⟋   ⟍ y-Intercept

The **slope** of a nonvertical line is the number of units the line rises (or falls) vertically for each unit of horizontal change from left to right, as shown in Figure 1.14.

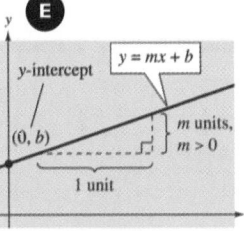

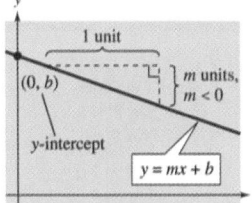

Positive slope, line rises.   *Negative slope, line falls.*

FIGURE 1.14

A linear equation that is written in the form $y = mx + b$ is said to be written in **slope-intercept form.**

The Slope-Intercept Form of the Equation of a Line

The graph of the equation

$$y = mx + b$$

is a line whose slope is m and whose y-intercept is $(0, b)$.

◀ Exploration ▶

Use a graphing utility to compare the slopes of the lines $y = mx$ where $m = 0.5, 1, 2,$ and 4. Which line rises most quickly? Now, let $m = -0.5, -1, -2,$ and -4. Which line falls most quickly? Use a square setting to obtain a true geometric perspective. What can you conclude about the slope and the "rate" at which the line rises or falls?

Understanding Visuals

Reading a Graph

Graphs arrange data so that you can see the relationships among numbers at a glance. Line graphs connect each point on a graph, which makes it easy to see trends over time. Use these strategies to read the line graph below.

Strategies for Reading

A Read the **title** to find out what the graph illustrates.

B Read the **labels** for each line on the graph to find out what is being compared.

C Look at the **relationship** among different elements on the graph. Try to express it in a sentence. For example, this graph shows how levels of pollutants released into the air from 1970 to 1998 compare to pollutant levels in 1970.

D Look at the **heading** of each row and column. To find specific information, find the place where a row and column intersect.

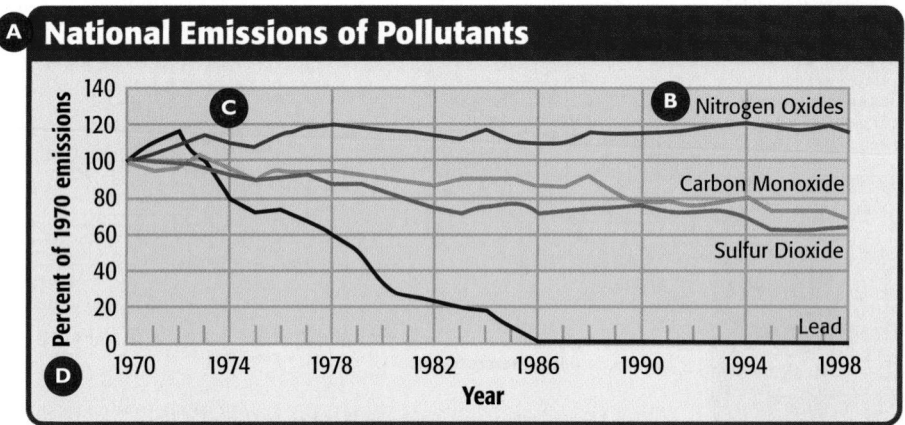

A **National Emissions of Pollutants**

PRACTICE AND APPLY

Answer the following questions using the graph of pollutant emissions.

1. What are emissions levels after 1970 being compared to?

2. What period of time is covered by the graph?

3. Which pollutant was emitted at higher levels in 1994 than it was in 1970?

4. What conclusion(s) can you draw from the direction of the lines on the graph?

Reading a Diagram

Diagrams combine pictures with a few words to provide a lot of information. Look at the example on the opposite page as you read each of the following strategies.

Strategies for Reading

A Look at the **title** to get a sense of what the diagram is about.

B Carefully examine the **images** to understand each part of the diagram.

C Read the **captions** written beneath the pictures.

D Study the **labels** to understand what different parts are named.

E Look for **arrows** or other markers that show relationships between different parts of the diagram.

PRACTICE AND APPLY

Study the diagram on the next page, then answer the following questions using the strategies above.

1. What is this diagram about?

2. Explain the process of fission.

3. According to the diagram, what are two substances needed to produce electricity by means of nuclear power?

4. Why is fission an important part of the process?

A

Nuclear Power

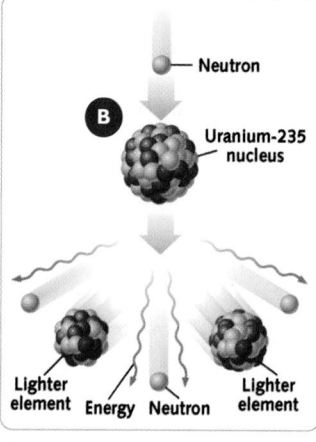

Neutron

B Uranium-235 nucleus

Lighter element — Energy — Neutron — Lighter element

C

1 Fission occurs when the nucleus of a uranium isotope absorbs a neutron. Lighter elements form and much energy is released.

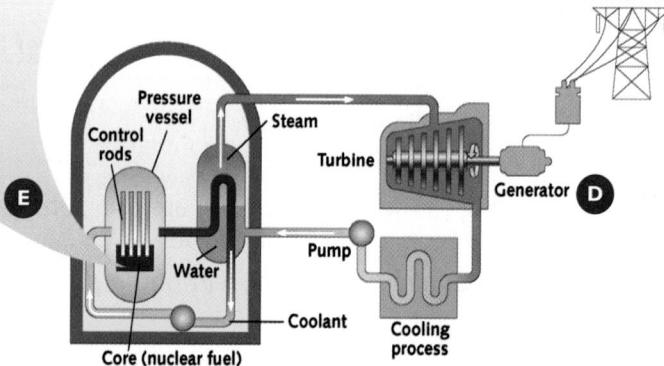

Power lines

Pressure vessel

Control rods

Steam

Turbine

Generator **D**

E

Water

Pump

Coolant

Cooling process

Core (nuclear fuel)

2 The energy produced by fission heats the nuclear reactor's coolant.

3 The hot coolant converts water to steam. The steam is used to generate electricity.

Recognizing Text Structures

Main Idea and Supporting Details

The **main idea** in a paragraph is its most important point. **Details** in the paragraph support the main idea. Identifying the main idea will help you focus on the main message the writer wants to communicate. Use the following strategies to help you identify a paragraph's main idea and supporting details.

Strategies for Reading

- Look for the **main idea**, which is often the first or last sentence in a paragraph.
- Use the main idea to help you **summarize** what the paragraph is about.
- Identify specific **details**, including facts and examples, that **support** the main idea.

Problems Faced by James I

Main Idea — King James I of England inherited the unsettled issues of Queen Elizabeth's reign.

Details — Elizabeth left a huge debt. This debt, combined with James's foreign wars and expensive court, caused constant struggles between the king and Parliament about money. Another issue was how much power Parliament should have. James I also clashed with the Puritans over remaining Catholic practices in the Church of England.

PRACTICE AND APPLY

Read the following paragraph. List the main idea and three supporting details.

   The Restoration, which began in 1660 when Charles II assumed the throne, is known as a period when the arts thrived. Charles II restored many aspects of English cultural and political life. Charles restored the theater, sporting events, and dancing, all of which the Puritans had banned. Theater, especially comedy, and other arts flourished during the Restoration.

Problem and Solution

Does the proposed **solution** to a **problem** make sense? In order to decide, you need to look at each part of the text. Use the following strategies to read the text below.

Strategies for Reading

- Look at the beginning or middle of a paragraph to find the **statement of the problem**.
- Find **details** that explain the problem and tell why it is important.
- Look for the **proposed solution**.
- Identify the **supporting details** for the proposed solution.
- Think about whether the solution is a good one.

An Untapped Resource *by Iris Goldfarb*

Statement of problem

Energy supplies are decreasing, and the cost of electricity in the western United States has been extremely high in the past few years. Blackouts and brownouts have forced residents of California to come face-to-face with the energy problem. If new sources of energy aren't found soon, we may be headed for a new Dark Age.

The good news is that the earth has an abundant source of energy just waiting to be tapped: geothermal energy, or "earth heat." This energy, stored in the rocks and water of the earth's crust, can be used to generate electricity and provide heat.

Explanation of solution

Underground streams of magma, or molten rock, are found throughout the Northwest. Some scientists believe that the geothermal energy in Oregon alone could produce as much electricity as two nuclear power plants. Geothermal heat pumps installed in homes could reduce electricity costs by as much as 75 percent.

What are we waiting for?

PRACTICE AND APPLY

Read the text above. Then answer these questions.

1. What is the proposed solution?
2. List at least one detail that supports the solution.
3. Do you think the solution is a good one? Explain why or why not.

Sequence

It's important to understand the **sequence**, or order of events, in what you read. It helps you know what happens and why. Read the tips below to make sure a sequence is clear to you. Then look at the example on the opposite page.

Strategies for Reading

- Read through the passage and think about what its **main steps**, or stages, are.
- Look for **words and phrases that signal time**, such as *in a year, three hours earlier, 202 B.C.,* or *later.*
- Look for **words and phrases that signal order**, such as *first, second, now, after that,* or *finally.*

PRACTICE AND APPLY

Read the article on the next page, which describes Henry VIII 's efforts to secure a male heir to the English throne. Use the information from the article and the tips above to answer the questions.

1. List any words or phrases that signal time.

2. List any phrases in the article that signal order.

3. A timeline can help you understand a sequence of events. Use the information from the article to copy and complete this timeline.

Events in the Life of Henry VIII

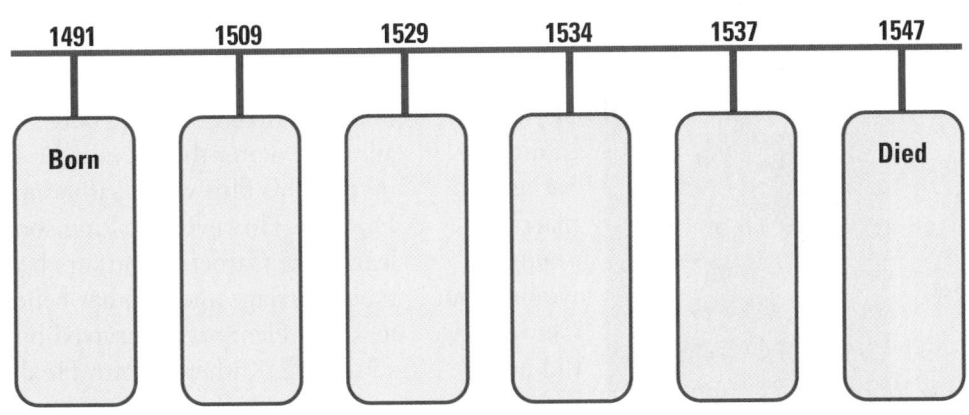

1491	1509	1529	1534	1537	1547
Born					**Died**

Henry VIII and His Six Wives

Born in 1491, Henry VIII was crowned king of England when he was 18 years old. He was a devout Catholic, but his politics soon clashed with his religion.

Henry's father had become king after a long civil war. Henry was afraid that a similar war might start if he died without a son to take over the throne. The history of England during his reign became the bloody story of his need for a son.

Henry and his wife, Catherine of Aragon, had one living child— a daughter, Mary, born in 1516. However, a woman had never successfully claimed the English throne. By 1529, Catherine was 42 years

old, and Henry was convinced that she would have no more children. He wanted to divorce her and marry a younger woman, but Church law did not permit divorce. Henry asked the pope to annul the marriage—in other words, declare that it had never existed. The pope refused.

Henry then decided to take matters into his own hands. Later in 1529, he asked Parliament to pass laws to end the pope's power in England. Four years later, he secretly married Anne Boleyn, and Parliament voted to make his divorce from his first wife legal. But Henry was not satisfied and wanted to break completely with the pope. In 1534, Parliament passed the Act of Supremacy, which made the king the official head of the Church of England.

Although Henry had turned the country inside out in his attempt to have a son, Anne Boleyn gave birth to a daughter. Following the birth, Henry had her imprisoned in the Tower of London. In 1536, he had her beheaded.

Henry did not get his wish for a son until his third wife, Jane Seymour, gave birth to Edward in 1537. Jane died in childbirth. In 1540, Henry married Anne of Cleves, but the marriage was quickly annulled. Later that same year, he married his fifth wife, Catherine Howard. However, the king soon learned of Catherine's affairs before their marriage and had her beheaded in 1543. Henry was survived by his sixth wife, Katherine Parr. He died in 1547 at the age of 56.

Cause and Effect

A **cause** is an event that brings about another event. An **effect** is something that happens as a result of the first event. Identifying causes and effects helps you understand how events are related. The tips below can help you find causes and effects in any reading.

Strategies for Reading

- Look for an action or event that answers the question "What happened?" This is the **effect**.
- Look for an action or event that answers the question "Why did it happen?" This is the **cause**.
- Identify words or phrases that **signal** causes and effects, such as *because, as a result, therefore, thus, consequently, since,* and *led to.*

PRACTICE AND APPLY

Read the cause-and-effect passage on the next page. Then answer the following questions. Notice that the first cause and effect in the passage are highlighted.

1. Identify the main effect the writer describes.
2. List any words in the passage that signal causes and effects. The first one is highlighted for you.
3. Sometimes an effect has more than one cause. Use information from the article to copy and complete the following diagram.

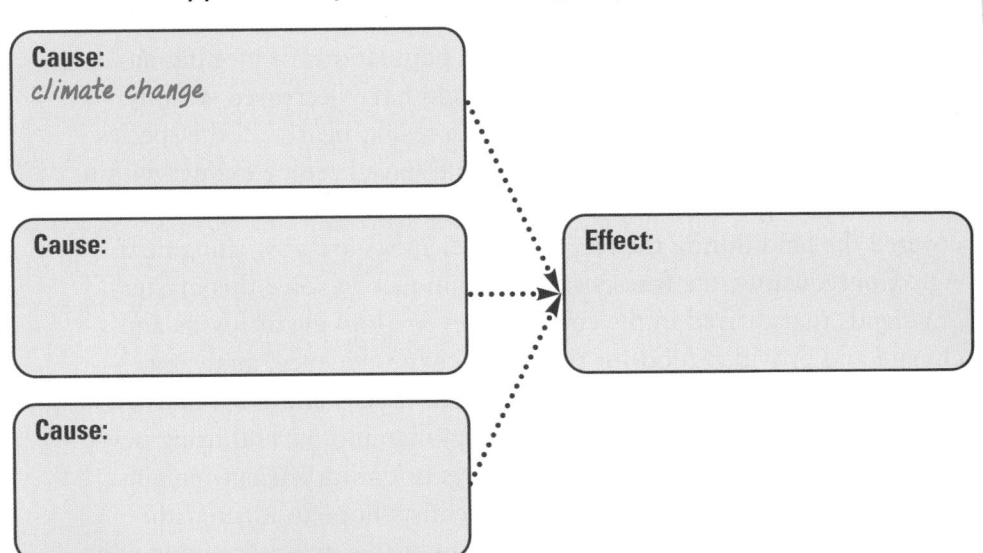

Cause:
climate change

Cause:

Cause:

Effect:

Mass Extinction: A Scientific Mystery

At the peak of the last Ice Age, about 20,000 years ago, herds of giant animals—megafauna—lumbered through the forests and plains of North America. There were beavers the size of modern bears, hairy mastodons and mammoths with massive curved tusks, and bison with horns measuring six feet across. These awesome animals were hunted by jaguars, saber-toothed tigers, and bears that weighed twice as much as today's grizzlies. **[Effect]** But by about 13,000 years ago—not long after the first humans appeared on the scene—almost all of these huge beasts had disappeared.

No one knows for sure what caused this mass extinction, but there are several competing theories. **[Cause]** One possible cause might have been a change in climate. Increasing temperatures resulted in a retreat of the glaciers that had covered the land during the Ice Age. **[Signal word]** Consequently, the forests and grasslands that thrived in the cold climate and provided food for the animals grew smaller. Without a source of food, the animals eventually died off.

According to another theory, the disappearance of the giant animals was caused by an epidemic outbreak of disease. Some scientists think that prehistoric humans may have brought disease-causing organisms with them when they crossed the land bridge connecting Asia and North America. Since the animals living in North America had no immunity to these diseases, great numbers of them may have died.

A third theory points a finger straight at human hunters. If hunters had killed only a few more animals than were born each year, the populations of megafauna would have decreased steadily. As a result, nearly all the species could have become extinct within a thousand years or so.

Scientists are now using new techniques to solve this mystery. They are looking at fossils and rocks for evidence, analyzing frozen tissues and bone marrow from mammoths, and using new ways of dating ancient remains. Scientists hope to identify the cause of this mass extinction soon.

Comparison and Contrast

Comparing two things means showing how they are the same. **Contrasting** two things means showing how they are different. Comparisons and contrasts are often used in science and history books to make a subject clearer. Use these tips to help you understand comparison and contrast in reading assignments, such as the article on the opposite page.

Strategies for Reading

- Look for **direct statements** of comparison and contrast: "These things are similar because . . . " or "One major difference is. . . ."
- Pay attention to **words and phrases that signal comparisons**, such as *also, both, is the same as,* and *in the same way.*
- Notice **words and phrases that signal contrasts**. Some of these are *however, still, but,* and *on the other hand.*

PRACTICE AND APPLY

Read the essay on the opposite page. Then use the information from the article and the tips above to answer the questions.

1. List any words and phrases that signal comparisons. A sample has been highlighted for you.

2. List any words and phrases that signal contrasts. A sample has been highlighted for you.

3. A Venn diagram shows how two subjects are similar and how they are different. Copy this diagram, which uses information from the essay to compare and contrast jazz music with classical music. Add at least one similarity to the middle part of the diagram. Add at least one difference to each outer circle.

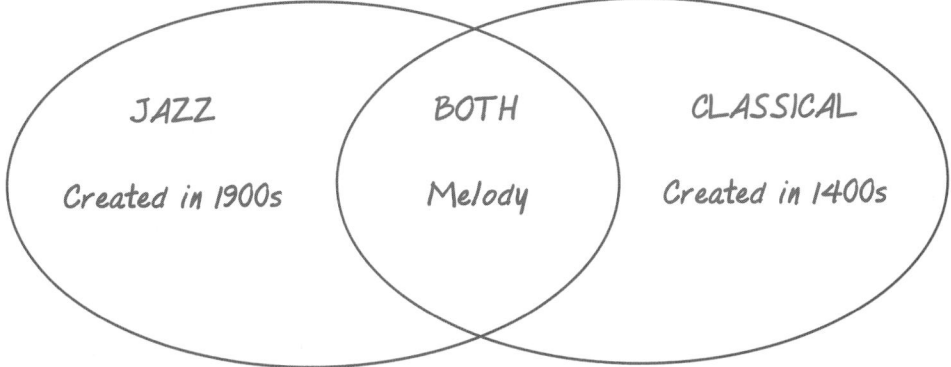

JAZZ

Created in 1900s

BOTH

Melody

CLASSICAL

Created in 1400s

Jazz: Music in Motion

As the piano player's hands bounce off the keys, the bassist slaps his strings, the drummer drives the beat forward, and the trumpet player splits the air with rapid-fire notes. At this moment, jazz is created.

For a newcomer to this music, jazz is perhaps easiest to understand when it is compared with the music of the Western classical tradition. The melody and harmony in traditional classical music are based on the seven-note major scale that most of us have sung in school— do-re-mi-fa-sol-la-ti-do (*do* is repeated at a higher pitch). European in origin, classical music developed in the 1400s during the Renaissance. Until the twentieth century, the rhythms used in classical music were very regularly accented on the beat. Also, the classical composer strictly controls a musical performance by writing exactly what each musician will play. The written music is followed closely.

Contrast In contrast, jazz is still in its infancy, having originated in the southern United States in the early 1900s. Both the European and African traditions contributed to **Comparison** its development. Like classical music, jazz is composed of melody, harmony, and rhythm.

However, because jazz is a direct descendent of the blues, the melody and harmony are based on the blues scale, which has a flatted third and a flatted seventh scale note. Also, jazz rhythms are syncopated. This means that the accents come on the off-beats. The rhythms produce a bouncing or swinging feeling.

What most distinguishes jazz from classical music is the art of improvisation. The word *improvise* means "to compose without preparation." A jazz trumpeter, for example, improvises when he or she replaces the melody of a song with a new melody played over the chords, or the harmony of the song. The improviser composes in the moment while the band provides rhythmic and harmonic support. As a result, new musical ideas are expressed each time a jazz musician takes a solo. Louis Armstrong summed it up when he said, "Jazz is music that's never played the same way once."

Argument

An **argument** is an opinion backed up with reasons and facts. Examining an opinion and the reasons and facts that back it up will help you decide if the opinion makes sense. Look at the argument on the right as you read each of these tips.

Strategies for Reading

- Look for words that **signal an opinion**: *I believe; I think; in my view; they claim, argue,* or *disagree.*
- Look for reasons, facts, or expert opinions that **support** the argument.
- Ask yourself if the argument and reasons **make sense**.
- Look for overgeneralizations or other **errors in reasoning** that might affect the argument.

PRACTICE AND APPLY

Read the argument on the next page, and then answer the questions below.

1. List any words that signal an opinion.

2. List any words or phrases that give the writer's opinion.

3. The writer presents both sides of the argument. Copy and complete the chart below to show the two sides. One example has been provided for you.

Reasons to Ban Soft Drinks	Reasons Not to Ban Soft Drinks
1. lack of nutritional value	

Should Soft Drinks Be Banned from Schools?

by J. T. Fox

A new substance has joined the list of those banned on school grounds: soft drinks. As the number of obese teenagers rises, a movement to limit the empty calories available in school vending machines is growing. Los Angeles has banned the sale of soft drinks on the district's high school and elementary campuses. Other districts are debating whether to implement similar policies. Activists who favor the soda ban say schools must make a choice between student health and vending machine revenues.

Advocates of banning sodas point out that a typical can of soda has at least 10 teaspoons of sugar. Its 140 calories contain no vitamins, minerals, fiber, or other nutritional value. Poor eating habits contribute to teenage obesity. Dr. Jonathan E. Fielding, director of Public Health for Los Angeles County, describes obesity as a fast-growing, chronic disease that is "entirely preventable."

However, not everyone agrees that carbonated soft drinks are a hazard to students' health. A Georgetown University study found no link between 12- to 16-year-olds' soda consumption and obesity.

Surgeon General David Hatcher, while concerned about unhealthy eating habits, considers lack of physical activity another important cause of excess weight.

Some schools are responding to the problem by expanding instead of restricting students' choices. A pilot program that offered Metro Detroit students a choice of pop or flavored milk was so successful that the district installed 80 more milk machines. In Hemingford, Nebraska, students organized an effort to purchase a machine that sells seven flavors of milk. Other schools offer students a selection of juice-based drinks.

Stakes on both sides of the question are high: student health versus the $750 million students put into school vending machines each year. The evidence currently available does not prove that having soda pop available in school vending machines causes obesity. Until that evidence is provided, I believe banning pop is an extreme solution. Instead, schools should keep both students and the budget healthy by offering both soft drinks and healthier alternatives.

Reading in the Content Areas

Social Studies

Social studies class becomes easier when you understand how your textbook's words, pictures, and maps work together to give you information. Following these tips can make you a better reader of social studies lessons. As you read the tips, look at the sample lesson on the right-hand page.

Strategies for Reading

A First, look at any **headlines** or **subheads** on the page. These give you an idea of what each section covers.

B Make sure you know the meaning of any boldfaced or underlined **vocabulary terms**. These terms often appear on tests.

C Carefully read the text and think about **ways the information is organized**. Social studies books are full of sequence, comparison and contrast, and organization by geographic location.

D Look closely at **graphics**, such as tables, maps, and illustrations. Think about how the graphic and the text are related.

E Read any **study tips** in the margins or at the bottom of the page. These let you check your understanding as you read.

PRACTICE AND APPLY

Carefully read the textbook page at right. Use the information from the page and from the tips above to answer these questions.

1. What is the main subject covered on this page?

2. What secondary subject is covered?

3. Summarize the background information about what will be presented in the chapter.

4. What role did Zhou Enlai play in Chinese politics?

5. What is the relationship between the table of "Mao's Attempts to Change China" and the subject of this chapter?

A 5

China Follows Its Own Path

TERMS & NAMES
- Zhou Enlai
- Deng Xiaoping
- Four Modernizations
- Tiananmen Square
- Hong Kong

MAIN IDEA	WHY IT MATTERS NOW
In recent years, China's government has experimented with capitalism but has rejected calls for democracy.	After the 1997 death of Chinese leader Deng Xiaoping, President Jiang Zemin seemed to be continuing those policies.

SETTING THE STAGE The trend toward democracy around the world also affected China to a limited degree. A political reform movement arose in the late 1980s. It built on economic reforms begun earlier in the decade. China's Communist government clamped down on the reformers, however, and maintained a firm grip on power.

Mao's Unexpected Legacy

After the Communists came to power in China in 1949, Mao Zedong set out to transform China. Mao believed that peasant equality, revolutionary spirit, and hard work were all that was needed to improve the Chinese economy. For example, intensive labor could make up for the lack of tractors on the huge agricultural cooperatives that the government had created.

However, lack of modern technology damaged Chinese efforts to increase agricultural and industrial output. In addition, Mao's policies stifled economic growth. He eliminated incentives for higher production. He tried to replace family life with life in the communes. These policies took away the peasants' motive to work for the good of themselves and their families.

Facing economic disaster, some Chinese Communists talked of modernizing the economy. Accusing them of "taking the capitalist road," Mao began the Cultural Revolution to cleanse China of anti-revolutionary influences. The movement proved so destructive, however, that it caused many Chinese to distrust party leadership. Instead of saving radical communism, the Cultural Revolution turned many people against it. In the early 1970s, China entered another moderate period under **Zhou Enlai** (joh ehn·ly). Zhou had been premiere since 1949. During the Cultural Revolution, he had tried to restrain the radicals.

Mao's Attempts to Change China

Mao's Programs	Program's Results
First Five-Year Plan 1953–1957	• Industry grew 15 percent a year. • Agricultural output grew very slowly.
Great Leap Forward 1958–1962	• China suffered economic disaster—industrial declines and food shortages. • Mao lost influence.
Cultural Revolution 1966–1976	• Mao regained influence by backing radicals. • Purges and conflicts among leaders created economic, social, and political chaos. • Moderates increasingly opposed radicals in Communist Party.

SKILLBUILDER: Interpreting Charts
1. Which had more successful results, the first five-year plan or the Great Leap Forward? Explain.
2. Did conditions improve or grow worse during the Cultural Revolution? Explain.

E

THINK THROUGH HISTORY
A. Recognizing Effects What was the ultimate result of Mao's radical Communist policies? Why?

China and the West

Throughout the Cultural Revolution, China played almost no role in world affairs. In the early 1960s, China had split with the Soviet Union over the leadership of world communism. In addition, China displayed hostility toward the United States because of U.S. support for the government on Taiwan and memories of the Korean War.

China Opened Its Doors China's isolation worried Zhou. He began to send out signals that he was willing to form ties to the West. In 1971, Zhou startled the world by

Science

Reading a **science** textbook becomes easier when you understand how the explanations, drawings, and special terms work together. Use the strategies below to help you better understand your science textbook. Look at the examples on the opposite page as you read each strategy in this list.

Strategies for Reading

A Preview the **title** and **headings** on the page to see what scientific concepts will be covered.

B Read the **key idea**, **objectives**, or **focus**. These items summarize the lesson and establish a purpose for your reading.

C Look for **boldfaced** and **italicized** words that appear in the text and for **definitions** of those words.

D Carefully examine any **pictures** or **diagrams**. Read the **captions** and evaluate how the graphics help to illustrate and explain the text.

E Many science textbooks discuss **scientific concepts** in terms of **everyday events** or **experiences**. Look for these places and consider how they improve your understanding.

PRACTICE AND APPLY

Use the sample science page and the tips above to help you answer the following questions.

1. What is the objective of this lesson?

2. Define the key term *energy.*

3. What are the two types of energy?

4. What law states that the energy of the universe is constant?

5. What does Figure 10.1 illustrate?

E nergy is the essence of our very existence as individuals and as a society. The food that we eat furnishes the energy to live, work, and play, just as the coal and oil consumed by manufacturing and transportation systems power our modern industrialized civilization.

Huge quantities of carbon-based fossil fuels have been available for the taking. This abundance of fuels has led to a world society with a voracious appetite for energy, consuming millions of barrels of petroleum every day. We are now dangerously dependent on the dwindling supplies of oil, and this dependence is an important source of tension among nations in today's world. In an incredibly short time we have moved from a period of ample and cheap supplies of petroleum to one of high prices and uncertain supplies. If our present standard of living is to be maintained, we must find alternatives to petroleum. To do this, we need to know the relationship between chemistry and energy, which we explore in this chapter.

10.1 The Nature of Energy

Objective: *To understand the general properties of energy.*

A lthough energy is a familiar concept, it is difficult to define precisely. For our purposes we will define **energy** as *the ability to do work or produce heat.* We will define these terms below.

Energy can be classified as either potential or kinetic energy. **Potential energy** is energy due to position or composition. For example, water behind a dam has potential energy that can be converted to work when the water flows down through turbines, thereby creating electricity. Attractive and repulsive forces also lead to potential energy. The energy released when gasoline is burned results from differences in attractive forces between the nuclei and electrons in the reactants and products. The **kinetic energy** of an object is energy due to the motion of the object and depends on the mass of the object m and its velocity v: $KE = \frac{1}{2}mv^2$.

One of the most important characteristics of energy is that it is conserved. The **law of conservation of energy** states *that energy can be converted from one form to another but can be neither created nor destroyed.* That is, the energy of the universe is constant.

Although the energy of the universe is constant, it can be converted from one form to another. Consider the two balls in **Figure 10.1a.** Ball A, because of its initially higher position, has more potential energy than ball B.

When ball A is released, it moves down the hill and strikes ball B. Eventually, the arrangement shown in **Figure 10.1b** is achieved. What has happened in going from the initial to the final arrangement? The potential energy of A has decreased because its position was lowered. However, this energy cannot disappear. Where is the energy lost by A?

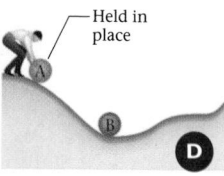

— Held in place

(a) Initial

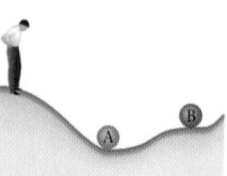

(b) Final

Figure 10.1
(a) In the initial positions, ball A has a higher potential energy than ball B. (b) After A has rolled down the hill, the potential energy lost by A has been converted to random motions of the components of the hill (frictional heating) and to an increase in the potential energy of B.

Mathematics

Reading in **mathematics** is different from reading in history, literature, or science. Use the strategies below to help you better understand your mathematics textbook. Look at the example on the opposite page as you read each strategy in the list.

Strategies for Reading

A Preview the **title** and **headings** on the page to see what math concepts will be covered.

B Find and read the **goals** or **objectives** for the lesson. These will tell you the most important points to know.

C Read **explanations** carefully. Sometimes a concept is explained in more than one way to make sure you understand it.

D Look for **special features**, such as study or vocabulary tips. They provide more help or information.

E Study any **worked-out solutions** to sample problems. These are the key to understanding how to do the homework assignment.

PRACTICE AND APPLY

Use the sample mathematics page and the strategies above to help you answer the following questions.

1. What is the learning goal for this lesson?
2. What is the definition of the vocabulary word *intersection?*
3. What do the illustrations under the heading "Modeling Intersections" demonstrate?
4. How would you sketch the intersection in part a under Example 4?
5. Why should you use dashes in part b of Example 4?

 **GOAL 2** **SKETCHING INTERSECTIONS OF LINES AND PLANES**

Two or more geometric figures **intersect** if they have one or more points in common. The **intersection** of the figures is the set of points the figures have in common.

> **◐ ACTIVITY**
>
> **Developing Concepts**
>
> ## Modeling Intersections
>
> Use two index cards. Label them as shown and cut slots halfway along each card.
>
>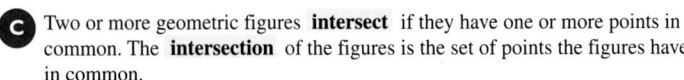
>
> **1.** What is the intersection of $\overline{AB}$ and $\overline{CD}$? of $\overline{AB}$ and $\overline{EF}$?
>
> **2.** Slide the cards together. What is the intersection of $\overline{CD}$ and $\overline{EF}$?
>
> **3.** What is the intersection of planes M and N?
>
> **4.** Are $\overleftrightarrow{CD}$ and $\overleftrightarrow{EF}$ coplanar? Explain.

EXAMPLE 4 *Sketching Intersections*

Sketch the figure described.

a. a line that intersects a plane in one point

b. two planes that intersect in a line

STUDENT HELP

▸ **HOMEWORK HELP**
Visit our Web site
www.mcdougallittell.com
for extra examples.

SOLUTION

a.

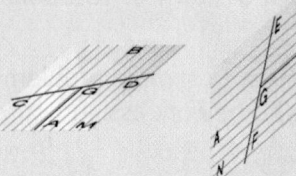

b.

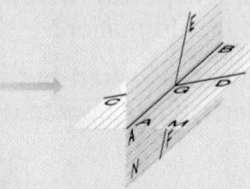

Draw a plane and a line.

Emphasize the point where they meet.

Dashes indicate where the line is hidden by the plane.

Draw two planes.

Emphasize the line where they meet.

Dashes indicate where one plane is hidden by the other plane.

Reading Beyond the Classroom

Reading a Public Notice

Public notices can tell you about events in your community and give you valuable information about safety. When you read a public notice, follow these tips. Each tip relates to a specific part of the notice on the opposite page.

Strategies for Reading

A Read the notice's **title**, if it has one. The title often gives the main idea or purpose of the notice.

B See if there is a logo, credit, or other way of telling **who created the notice**.

C Ask yourself, **"Who should read this notice?"** If the information in it might be important to you or someone you know, then you should pay attention to it.

D Look for **instructions**—things the notice is asking or telling you to do.

E See if there are details that tell you how you can **find out more** about the topic.

PRACTICE AND APPLY

The notice on the opposite page is from a town government's bylaws. Read it carefully and answer the questions below.

1. Who is the notice from?

2. Who is the notice for?

3. What is the purpose of the notice?

4. How much must the owner pay each day that a dog is in the custody of the animal control officer?

5. Where can people get more information?

6. According to the notice, for what would a dog owner pay a fine of $75.00?

PUBLIC NOTICE

B Arlan Heights Town Bylaws: Title VIII

A *PUBLIC HEALTH AND SAFETY:*
ARTICLE 2: CANINE CONTROL

Section 1. Dogs

No person shall own or keep any dog which by biting, barking, howling, or in any other manner disturbs the peace and quiet of any neighborhood, or endangers the safety of any person.

Section 2. Leashing of Dogs

C A. **Leash Required** No person owning or keeping a dog in the Town of Arlan Heights shall permit such dog to be at large in the Town of Arlan Heights elsewhere than on the premises of the owner or keeper, except if it be on the premises of another person with the knowledge and permission of such other person. Such owner or keeper of a dog in the Town of Arlan Heights, which is not on the premises of the owner or upon the premises of another person with the knowledge and permission of such person, shall restrain such dog by a chain or leash not exceeding six feet in length.

D B. **Enforcement** Any dog found to be at large in violation of this Bylaw shall be caught and confined by the dog officer who shall notify forthwith the licensed owner or keeper of said dog, giving the owner or keeper a period of ten days within which to recover the dog. The dog officer shall enter and prosecute a complaint against the owner or keeper of any dog taken into his custody under this section. A dog officer having custody of a dog confined under this Bylaw shall be allowed the sum of five dollars per day for each day of confinement for the care of such dog, payable by the owner or keeper thereof.

C. **Fines** Violations of Sections 2 of this Article shall be punishable as follows:
First offense: Warning
Second offense: By a fine of $50.00
Third offense: By a fine of $75.00
Fourth and each subsequent offense: By a fine of $100.00

E D. **Reporting Offenses** Residents who wish to report problems with a dog, or who have questions about this ordinance, can contact Animal Control at 321-3380.

Reading a Web Page

If you need information for a report, project, or hobby, the World Wide Web can probably help you. The tips below will help you understand the **Web pages** you read. As you look at the tips, notice where they match up to the sample Web page on the right.

Strategies for Reading

A Notice the page's **Web address**, or URL. You may want to write it down in case you need to access the same page at another time.

B Look for **menu bars** along the top, bottom, or side of the page. These guide you to other parts of the site that may be useful.

C Look for **links** to other parts of the site or to related pages. Links are often shown as underlined words.

D Use a **search** feature to quickly find out whether information about a specific topic can be found anywhere on the site.

E Many sites have a link that allows you to **contact** the creators with questions or feedback.

PRACTICE AND APPLY

Read the Web page on the next page. Then use the information from the page and the tips above to answer the questions.

1. What is the Web address?

2. Read the description of the link "Traveling Exhibits." What would you expect to find if you clicked on this link?

3. What link would take you to the schedule of events?

4. If you wanted to know about internship opportunities at the Natural History Museum, what link would allow you to communicate your interest to museum personnel?

5. What makes the Natural History Museum's *Triceratops* exhibit different from other prehistoric exhibits you might find at other museums?

L-Net

Back | Forward | Reload | Home | Images | Print | Security | Stop

L

Location: http://www.nhmmuseum.com **A**

NATURAL HISTORY MUSEUM

C Information Desk
Calendar of Events
Exhibits
Educational Resources

D What's New?
Research & Collections
Search the NHM Web

Natural History Highlight

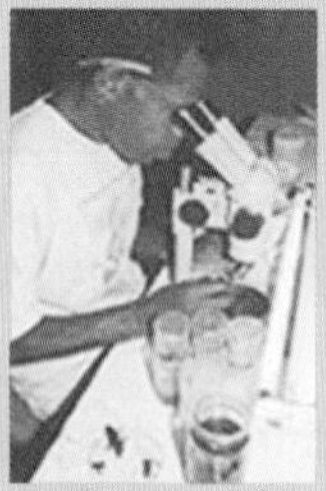

Parataxonomy

NHM scientist are part of a growing trend – training of and reliance upon parataxonomists.

INSECT SAFARI

The Natural History Museum is dedicated to understanding the natural world and our place in it.

New Exhibits

Triceratops A new mount of Triceratops has been unveiled. Also, as the first digital dinosaur, it can be shared with researchers as easily as e-mail. This new approach will tell us many more things about how this three-horned dinosaur lived and moved over 65 million years ago.

African Voices examines the diversity dynamism and global influence of Africa's peoples and cultures over time in the realms of family, work, community, and the natural environment.

Traveling Exhibits

Vikings: The North Atlantic Sags - Opening July 13, 2006 at the Museum of Natural History.

B Home   What's New?   Search the NHM Site   Research & Collections   Contact **E**

Reading Technical Directions

Reading **technical directions** will help you understand how to use the products you buy. Use the following tips to help you read a variety of technical directions.

Strategies for Reading

A Look carefully at any **diagrams** or **other images** of the product.

B **Read all the directions** carefully at least once before using the product.

C Notice **headings** or **rules** that separate one section from another.

D Watch for **warnings** or **notes** with more information.

PRACTICE AND APPLY

Use the tips above and the technical directions on the next page to help you answer the following questions.

1. What does this page explain how to do?

2. Which control would you use to increase or decrease the amount of bass you hear?

3. According to the instructions, how do you reduce tape hiss?

4. Under what heading would you find directions about how to adjust the left and right output levels?

5. Where is the balance control found on this system?

Adjusting the Sound

B When playing CDs, tapes, or radio programs, use the MEGA BASS/GRAPHIC EQUALIZER controls to equalize the reproduced sound. You can also adjust the balance of the left and right output levels.

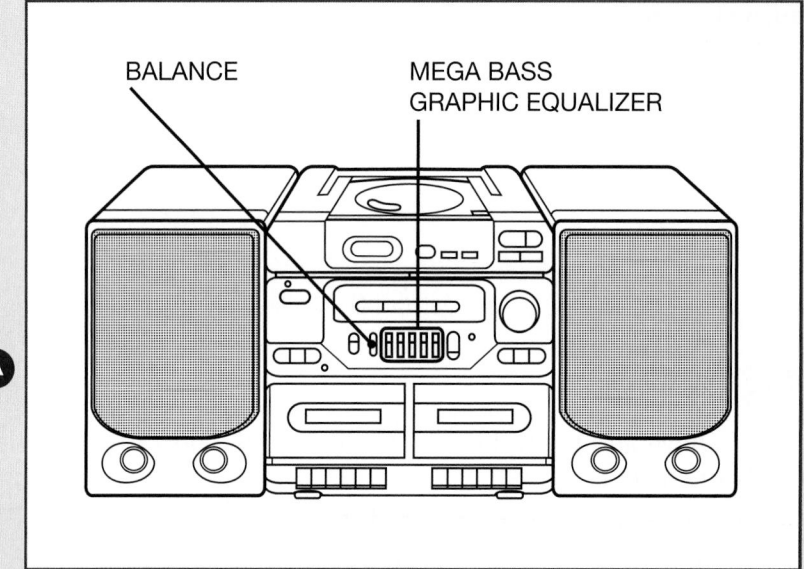

BALANCE MEGA BASS GRAPHIC EQUALIZER

C **To equalize the reproduced sound** Adjust the MEGA BASS/GRAPHIC EQUALIZER controls

Frequency coverage	Slide the control toward +10	Slide the control toward -10
MEGA BASS 100 Hz	**D** to increase heavy bass sounds	**D** to decrease heavy bass sounds
400 Hz	to emphasize speaking voice, middle frequencies of instrumental music	to de-emphasize speaking voice, middle frequencies of instrumental music
1 kHz	to provide more presence of vocals	to provide less presence of vocals
4 kHz	to heighten overall brightness of sound	to lessen overall brightness of sound
10 kHz	to increase high treble sounds	to decrease high treble sounds or reduce high frequencey noise/tape hiss

Product Information: Safety Guidelines

Safety guidelines are facts and recommendations provided by government agencies or product manufacturers offering instructions and warnings about safe use of these products. Look at the sample guidelines as you read each strategy below.

Strategies for Reading

A The **title** identifies what product the safety guidelines focus on.

B This section lists **recommendations** that product owners and users should follow in order to ensure safe usage of the product.

C This section lists the **hazards** associated with the product.

D This section includes a phone number and e-mail address where dangerous products or product-related injuries can be reported.

A Proper Child Safety Seat Use Chart

	Infants	Toddlers	Young Children
Weight	Birth to 1 year At least 20–22 lbs.	Over 1 year and Over 20–40 lbs.	Over 40 lbs. Ages 4–8, unless 4' 9"
Type of Seat	Infant only or rear-facing convertible	Convertible/Forward-facing	Belt-positioning booster seat
Seat Position	Rear-facing only	Forward-facing	Forward-facing
Always Make Sure: B C	Children to one year and at least 20 lbs. are in rear-facing seats. Harness straps are at or below shoulder level (to avoid abdominal injury).	Harness straps are at or above shoulders. Most seats require top slot for forward-facing seats.	Belt-positioning booster seats are used with both lap and shoulder belt. The shoulder belt crosses the chest and shoulder (to avoid abdominal injury).
Warning	All children age 12 and under should ride in the back seat.	All children age 12 and under should ride in the back seat.	All children age 12 and under should ride in the back seat.

D For more information, contact the National Highway Traffic Safety Administration at 1-888-327-4236 or send e-mail to webmaster@nhtsa.dot.gov.

PRACTICE AND APPLY

Read the safety guidelines to help you answer these questions.

1. Which way should safety seats for infants face?
2. What are the two types of seats that can be used with toddlers?
3. What e-mail address can you use to contact the agency that issued these guidelines?
4. Who are these safety guidelines from?

Reading a Bus Schedule

Knowing how to read a **transportation schedule** accurately will help you figure out how to get where you want to go. Look at the example as you read each strategy on this list.

Strategies for Reading

A Scan the **title** to know what the schedule covers.

B Look for **labels** or **explanations** that explain what **dates** or **days of the week** the service is available.

C Look for **expressions of time** to know what hours or minutes are listed on the schedule.

D Study the **labels** identifying the different stops on the schedule.

E Look for changes or **exceptions** to the regular schedule.

A **SCHEDULE** **SPRING/SUMMER 2002**

		TO YOSEMITE	FROM YOSEMITE
Mammoth Lakes	Mammoth Mountain Inn	7:00AM	8:50PM
	Juniper Springs Summit	7:08AM	8:42PM
	Old Mammoth Road	7:13AM	8:37PM
	Highway 203- Shilo Inn	7:15AM	8:35PM
	Highway 203- Mammoth Mountain RV Park	7:17AM	8:33PM
June Lake	Scenic Byway Kiosk	7:30AM	8:20PM
	June Mountain Ski Area Parking Lot	7:40AM	8:10PM
	Silver Lake Parking Lot	7:55AM	7:55PM
Lee Vining	Best Western Motel	8:10AM	7:40PM
	Forest Svc Visitor Center	8:13AM	7:37PM
	Tioga Mobil Gas Mart	8:18AM	7:32PM
Tuolumne Meadows	Tuolumne Meadows Store	9:00AM	6:50PM
	Tuolumne Meadows Visitors' Center	9:05AM	6:45PM
	Cathedral Trailhead	9:10AM	6:40PM
	White Wolf Lodge	9:50AM	6:00PM
	Crane Flat Gas Station	10:20AM	5:30PM
	Yosemite Visitor Center	10:50AM	5:00PM

B Spring/Summer 2002 service runs on Saturday and Sunday only through June. Starting July 1, runs are available daily through September 2. Starting on September 7, weekend-only service returns running Saturday and Sunday until September 29.

Service is available on the following holidays: May 27, July 4 and September 2.

E Service dates are based upon the assumption that Tioga Pass will be open. Service dates will change if the status of the pass differs.

Multi-passenger vans may be used on this run. Those riders with children requiring a car child seat or those riders with bikes or large backpacks should inquire about availability when calling for tickets.

CONNECTIONS

Runs connect to/from many tours in the Park, including the Valley Tour starting as early as Noon. **For information on tours call Yosemite Concession Services at (209) 372-1240.**

PRACTICE AND APPLY

Answer the following questions using the bus schedule.

1. What time span is covered by this schedule?

2. Do the buses run on July 4?

3. What is the latest time you could catch a bus from Yosemite Visitor Center?

4. In Mammoth Lakes, where can you catch the bus?

Glossary of Literary Terms

Allegory An allegory is a story in verse or prose in which characters are used to personify abstract qualities. Like a fable or parable, an allegory is often used to express generalizations about human existence and teach religious or moral lessons.

Example: The best-known allegory in the English language is John Bunyan's *Pilgrim's Progress.* Christian, the hero of Bunyan's work, represents all people. Other allegorical characters include Mr. Worldly Wiseman, Faithful, and Hopeful. The allegory traces Christian's efforts to achieve a godly life.

Alliteration Alliteration is the repetition of consonant sounds at the beginning of words.

> Out from the marsh, from the foot of misty
> Hills and bogs, bearing God's hatred,
> Grendel came,
> —from *Beowulf*

Writers use alliteration to emphasize certain words, to heighten mood, to establish a musical effect, to unify a passage, and to help create meaning. Often alliteration is reinforced by repeating the same consonant sound within and at the end of other words. Look for examples of alliteration in the following lines:

> In Xanadu did Kubla Khan
> A stately pleasure dome decree:
> Where Alph, the sacred river, ran
> Through caverns measureless to man
>   Down to a sunless sea.
> —Samuel Taylor Coleridge, from "Kubla Khan"

See pages 63, 96, 300, 744, 806, 950, 1239.
See also **Assonance; Consonance.**

Allusion An allusion is a reference to a historical or fictional person, place, or event with which the reader is assumed to be familiar. Understanding the allusions in a work can give the reader a better understanding of it.

Examples: In Thomas Gray's "Elegy Written in a Country Churchyard," the speaker alludes to

Milton, the famous English poet, and Cromwell, the leader of the Puritan revolt in the 17th century. These allusions to two of the most well-known figures in English life emphasize the poet's ideas about what the lives of the obscure people buried in the churchyard might have been like had they had different opportunities. In the excerpt from Derek Walcott's poem *Midsummer,* allusions contribute to the satiric tone of the poem.

See pages 479, 945.

Analogy An analogy is a comparison between two dissimilar things made to clarify a point or create an image.

Example: In his essay "On Spring," Samuel Johnson compares animals that can blend in with their surroundings to people who are able to appreciate and be inspired by the objects around them.

Anglo-Saxon Poetry Anglo-Saxon poetry, which was written between the 7th and 12th centuries, is characterized by a strong rhythm, or cadence, that makes it easily chanted or sung. It was originally recited by **scops,** poet-singers who traveled from place to place. Lines of Anglo-Saxon poetry are unified through alliteration and through use of the same number of accented syllables in each line. Typically, a line is divided by a **caesura,** or pause, into two parts, with each part having two accented syllables. Usually, one or both of the accented syllables in the first part alliterate with an accented syllable in the second part. This passage illustrates some of these characteristics:

> Hĕ *to*ók whăt hĕ wántĕd, // alĺ thĕ
>   *tre*ásurĕs
> Thăt *pl*eásĕd hiš eyĕ, // heávў *pl*átĕs
> Ănd *g*óldĕn cúps // ănd thĕ *gl*óriŏuš
>   bánnĕr,
> Loádĕd hiš *ar*ms // with *a*lĺ thĕy coŭld
>   hóld.
> —from *Beowulf*

Another characteristic of Anglo-Saxon poetry is the use of **kennings,** metaphorical compound words or phrases substituted for simple nouns.

Examples: Kennings from "The Seafarer" include "whales' home" for the sea and "givers of gold" for rulers or emperors. Examples from *Beowulf* include "shepherd of evil" for Grendel, and "folk-king" for Beowulf.

See page 96.

Antagonist The antagonist of a novel, short story, drama, or narrative poem is the character or force against which the main character, or **protagonist,** is pitted. The antagonist may be another character, some aspect of society or nature, or an internal force within the protagonist.

Examples: In *Sir Gawain and the Green Knight,* the antagonist is the Green Knight, who challenges Sir Gawain. In Doris Lessing's "A Sunrise on the Veld," the antagonist is the natural world, which confronts the boy with his limits.

See also **Conflict; Protagonist.**

Antithesis Antithesis is a figure of speech in which sharply contrasting words, phrases, clauses, or sentences are juxtaposed to emphasize a point. In a true antithesis, both the ideas and the grammatical structures are balanced. An example is the second line of the following couplet:

> Regard not then if wit be old or new,
> But blame the false, and value still the true.
> —Alexander Pope, from *An Essay on Criticism*

See page 741.

Aphorism An aphorism is a brief statement that expresses a general observation about life in a witty, pointed way. Unlike proverbs, which may stem from oral folk tradition, aphorisms originate with specific authors. "A blighted spring makes a barren year," from Samuel Johnson's essay "On Spring," is an example of an aphorism.

See page 656.

Apostrophe Apostrophe is a figure of speech in which an object, an abstract quality, or an absent or imaginary person is addressed directly, as if present and able to understand. Writers use apostrophe to express powerful emotions, as in this apostrophe to the ocean:

> Roll on, thou deep and dark blue Ocean, roll!
> Ten thousand fleets sweep over thee in vain;
> Man marks the earth with ruin, his control
> Stops with the shore; upon the watery plain
> The wrecks are all thy deed, nor doth remain
> A shadow of man's ravage, save his own,
> When, for a moment, like a drop of rain,
> He sinks into thy depths with bubbling groan,
> Without a grave, unknell'd, uncoffin'd, and unknown. . . .
> —George Gordon, Lord Byron,
> from *Childe Harold's Pilgrimage*

See page 779.

Argumentation Argumentation is speech or writing intended to convince an audience that a proposal should be adopted or rejected. Most argumentation begins with a statement of an idea or opinion, which is then supported with logical evidence. Another technique of argumentation is the anticipation and rebuttal of opposing views.

Examples: One example of argumentation is the excerpt from *A Vindication of the Rights of Woman,* in which Mary Wollstonecraft argues for the rights of women and argues against views that would subjugate women. Another example is Margaret Cavendish's "Female Orations," in which seven women present their arguments for and against women's rights.

See pages 500, 637.

Aside In drama, an aside is a remark spoken in an undertone by a character, either to the audience or to another character. A traditional dramatic convention, the aside is heard by the audience but supposedly not by the other characters on stage. Asides can be used to express characters' feelings, opinions, and reactions, so they function as a method of characterization.

> Macbeth. [*Aside*] If chance will have me King,
> why, chance may crown me,
> Without my stir.
> —William Shakespeare, from *Macbeth*

See page 346.
See also **Drama.**

Assonance Assonance is the repetition of a vowel sound in two or more stressed syllables that do not end with the same consonant. Poets use assonance to emphasize certain words, to impart a musical quality, to create a mood, or to unify a passage. An example of assonance is the repetition of the long *e* sound in the following lines. Note that the repeated sounds are not always spelled the same.

> When I have f**ea**rs that I may c**ea**se to b**e**
> Before my pen has gl**ea**n'd my t**ee**ming brain
> —John Keats, from "When I Have
> Fears That I May Cease to Be"

See pages 806, 1092, 1239.
See also **Alliteration; Consonance; Rhyme.**

Author's Purpose An author's purpose may be to entertain, to inform, to express opinions, or to persuade. Although a writer can fulfill more than one of these purposes in a work, one is usually the most important. The purposes of the excerpt from the Venerable Bede's *A History of the English Church and People* are to inform and to persuade.

See pages 866, 929.

Autobiography An autobiography is a writer's account of his or her own life. Autobiographies often convey profound insights as writers recount past events from the perspective of greater understanding and distance. A formal autobiography involves a sustained, lengthy narrative of a person's history, but other autobiographical narratives may be less formal and briefer. Under the general category of autobiography fall such writings as diaries, journals, memoirs, and letters. Both formal and informal autobiographies provide revealing insights into the writer's character, attitudes, and motivations, as well as some understanding of the society in which the writer lived. *The Book of Margery Kempe* is an autobiography.

See page 256.
See also **Diary; Memoir.**

Ballad A ballad is a narrative poem that was originally intended to be sung. Traditional folk ballads, written by unknown authors and handed down orally, usually depict ordinary people in the midst of tragic events and adventures of love and bravery. They tend to begin abruptly, focus on a single incident, use dialogue and repetition, and suggest more than they actually state. They often contain supernatural elements.

Typically, a ballad consists of four-line stanzas, or quatrains, with the second and fourth lines of each stanza rhyming. Each stanza has a strong rhythmic pattern, usually with four stressed syllables in the first and third lines and three stressed syllables in the second and fourth lines. The rhyme scheme is usually *abcb* or *aabb.* "Barbara Allan," "Sir Patrick Spens," and "Get Up and Bar the Door" are ballads. Notice the rhythmic pattern in the following stanza:

> Ŏ slówlў, slówlў raíse shĕ úp,   *a*
> Tŏ thĕ pláce whĕre hé wăs lýiň',   *b*
> Aňd whén shĕ dréw thĕ cúrtaiň bý: *c*
> "Yŏuňg mán, Ĭ thiňk you're dýiň'."   *b*
> —from "Barbara Allan"

A **literary ballad** is a ballad with a single author. Modeled on the early English and Scottish folk ballads, literary ballads became popular during the romantic period. Samuel Taylor Coleridge's "The Rime of the Ancient Mariner" is a romantic literary ballad.

See pages 198, 766.
See also **Narrative Poem; Quatrain.**

Biography A biography is an account of a person's life written by another person. In a good biography, the presentation of the subject's life is comprehensive, unified, and accurate. The skilled biographer synthesizes information from sources such as letters, journals, interviews, and documents and strives for a balanced portrayal through detailed anecdotes, reconstructed dialogue, description,

quotations, and interpretive passages. An outstanding example of a biography is James Boswell's *The Life of Samuel Johnson.*

Although full-length biographies cover the life history of a person from birth to death, less extensive writings also may be considered biographical. These include the anecdote, which relates a revealing incident in a person's life, and the character sketch, a brief descriptive essay that highlights certain qualities of the subject.

See page 664.

Blank Verse   Blank verse is unrhymed poetry written in iambic pentameter. Because iambic pentameter resembles the natural rhythm of spoken English, it has been considered the most suitable meter for dramatic verse in English. Shakespeare's plays are written largely in blank verse, as is Milton's epic *Paradise Lost.* Blank verse has also been used frequently for long poems, as in the following:

> And now, with gleams of half-
>   extinguished thought
> With many recognitions dim and
>   faint,
> And somewhat of a sad perplexity,
> The picture of the mind revives
>   again;
>   —William Wordsworth, from "Lines
> Composed a Few Miles Above Tintern Abbey"

See pages 362, 491, 852.
See also **Iambic Pentameter; Meter.**

Caesura   *See* **Anglo-Saxon Poetry.**

Character   Characters are the people who participate in the action of a work. The most important characters are the **main characters.** Less prominent characters are known as **minor characters.** In Katherine Mansfield's "A Cup of Tea," Rosemary and the girl are main characters, and the shopman is a minor character.

Whereas some characters are two-dimensional, with only one or two dominant traits, a fully developed character possesses many traits, mirroring the psychological complexity of a real person. In longer works of fiction, main characters often undergo change as the plot unfolds. Such

characters are called **dynamic characters,** as opposed to **static characters,** who remain the same. In D. H. Lawrence's story "The Rocking-Horse Winner," Paul is a dynamic character because he becomes increasingly absorbed by his obsession to get money for his mother. Uncle Oscar is a static character who primarily observes and responds to Paul's actions.

See also **Characterization.**

Characterization   Characterization refers to the techniques that writers use to develop characters. There are four basic methods of characterization:

1. A writer may describe the physical appearance of a character. In William Trevor's "The Distant Past," the narrator describes the Middletons: "They had always been thin, silent with one another, and similar in appearance: a brother and sister who shared a family face. It was a bony countenance, with pale blue eyes and a sharp, well-shaped nose and high cheek-bones."

2. A character's nature may be revealed through his or her own speech, thoughts, feelings, or actions. In Trevor's story, the reader learns about the kind of life the Middletons lead: "Together they roved the vast lofts of their house, placing old paint tins and flowerpot saucers beneath the drips from the roof. At night they sat over their thin chops in a dining-room that had once been gracious . . ."

3. The speech, thoughts, feelings, and actions of other characters can be used to develop a character. The attitudes of the townspeople to the Middletons help the reader understand the old couple better: "'An upright couple,' was the Canon's public opinion of the Middletons, and he had been known to add that eccentric views would hurt you less than malice."

4. The narrator can make direct comments about the character's nature. The narrator in Trevor's story comments, "The Middletons were in their middle-sixties now and were reconciled to a life that became more uncomfortable with every passing year."

See pages 111, 237.
See also **Character.**

Climax See **Plot**.

Comedy A comedy is a dramatic work that is light and often humorous in tone, usually ending happily with a peaceful resolution of the main conflict. A comedy differs from a farce by having a more believable plot, more realistic characters, and less boisterous behavior. Shakespeare's *A Midsummer Night's Dream* is a comedy.

See also **Drama; Farce**.

Comic Relief Comic relief is a humorous scene, incident, or speech that is included in a serious drama to provide respite from emotional intensity. Because it breaks the tension, comic relief allows an audience to internalize preceding plot events and to prepare emotionally for events to come. The sharp contrasts afforded by comic relief may intensify the themes of a literary work.

Example: In many of Shakespeare's plays, a scene involving a fool or humorous interplay among common folks provides comic relief. Comic relief in *Macbeth* is provided by Macbeth's garrulous, vulgar porter at the beginning of Act II, Scene 3, just after Duncan's murder. This scene is needed to relax the tension built up in the preceding scenes.

Conceit See **Extended Metaphor**.

Conflict A conflict is a struggle between opposing forces that moves a plot forward. The conflict provides the interest or suspense in a short story, drama, novel, narrative poem, or nonfiction narrative. Conflict may be **external,** with a character being pitted against some outside force—another person, a physical obstacle, nature, or society. Conflict may also be **internal,** occurring within a character.

Examples: In Elizabeth Gaskell's "Christmas Storms and Sunshine," Mrs. Hodgson is in a running conflict with Mrs. Jenkins. The sergeant in Lady Gregory's *The Rising of the Moon* faces an external conflict with the escaped prisoner and an internal conflict involving his double loyalties.

See pages 190, 883, 1272.
See also **Plot**.

Connotation *Connotation* refers to the attitudes and feelings associated with a word, in contrast to **denotation,** which is the literal or dictionary meaning of a word. The connotation of a word may be positive or negative. For example, *enthusiastic* has positive associations, but *rowdy* has negative ones. Connotations of words can have an important influence on style and meaning and are particularly important in poetry.

Example: In W. B. Yeats's poem "Sailing to Byzantium," the connotations of the words *paltry* and *tattered* in the lines "An aged man is but a paltry thing, / A tattered coat upon a stick, . . ." help to create the image of a thin, ragged scarecrow.

See page 1252.

Consonance Consonance is the repetition of consonant sounds within and at the ends of words, as in "lonely afternoon." Consonance is unlike rhyme in that the vowels preceding or following the repeated consonant sounds differ. Sometimes the repeated sounds have different spellings, as in *hours* and *squeeze*. Consonance is often used together with alliteration, assonance, and rhyme to create a musical quality, to emphasize certain words, or to unify a poem. The repetition of the *l* sound in the following lines reinforces the meaning of *leisurely* and helps create a slow pace:

In Breughel's *Icarus*, for instance: how
  everything turns away
Quite leisurely from the disaster; the
  ploughman may
Have heard the splash, the forsaken cry,
But for him it was not an important failure; . . .
—W. H. Auden, from "Musée des Beaux Arts"

See pages 806, 1092, 1239.
See also **Assonance**.

Contrast Contrast is a stylistic device in which one element is put into opposition with another. The opposing elements might be contrasting structures, such as sentences of varying lengths or stanzas of different configurations. They could also be contrasting ideas or images juxtaposed within phrases, sentences, paragraphs, stanzas, or sections of a

longer work of literature. Writers use contrast to clarify or emphasize ideas and to elicit emotional responses from the reader.

Example: Part of the force of Siegfried Sassoon's poem "Dreamers" lies in the contrast between images of war, such as "death's gray land," and images of ordinary life, such as "firelit homes."

See page 534.

Controlling Image *See* **Extended Metaphor; Imagery.**

Couplet A couplet is a rhymed pair of lines. A simple couplet may be written in any rhythmic pattern. The following couplet is written in iambic tetrameter (lines of four iambs):

> Hăd wé bŭt wórld ĕnoúgh, ănd tíme,
> Thĭs cóyness, lády, wére nŏ críme.
> —Andrew Marvell, from "To His Coy Mistress"

A **heroic couplet** consists of two rhyming lines written in iambic pentameter. The term *heroic* comes from the fact that English poems having heroic themes and elevated style have often been written in iambic pentameter. Alexander Pope's masterful use of the heroic couplet made it a popular verse form during the neoclassical period. The following lines are one of many possible examples from his work:

> Ăvoíd extrémes; ănd shún thĕ faúlt
>   ŏf súch,
> Whŏ stíll ăre pleásed tŏo líttlĕ ŏr
>   tŏo múch.
> —Alexander Pope, from *An Essay on Criticism*

See page 538.

Denotation *See* **Connotation.**

Denouement *See* **Plot.**

Description Description is writing that helps a reader to picture scenes, events, and characters. It helps the reader understand exactly what someone or something is like. To create description, writers often use sensory images—words and phrases that enable the reader to see, hear, smell, taste, or feel the subject described—and figurative language. Effective description also relies on precise nouns, verbs, adjectives, and adverbs, as well as carefully selected details. The following passage contains clear details and images:

> Air, musty from having been long enclosed, hung in all the rooms, and the waste room behind the kitchen was littered with old useless papers. Among these I found a few paper-covered books, the pages of which were curled and damp. . . . The wild garden behind the house contained a central apple-tree and a few straggling bushes under one of which I found the late tenant's rusty bicycle-pump.
> —James Joyce, from "Araby"

See page 690.

Dialect Dialect is a particular variety of language spoken in one place by a distinct group of people. A dialect reflects the colloquialisms, grammatical constructions, distinctive vocabulary, and pronunciations that are typical of a region. At times writers use dialect to establish or emphasize settings, as well as to develop characters.

Example: The thieves in Chinua Achebe's story "Civil Peace" speak in a Nigerian dialect of English, which highlights the contrast between the thieves and Jonathan Iwegbu.

See page 1279.

Dialogue Written conversation between two or more people, in either fiction or nonfiction, is called dialogue. Writers use dialogue to bring characters to life and to give readers insights into the characters' qualities, personality traits, and reactions to other people. Realistic, well-paced dialogue also advances the plot of a narrative.

Dialogue in drama is critical to an understanding of the playwright's story or message. How the dialogue is read or performed will determine to a great extent the reactions of the reader or audience to the play. Dramatists use **stage directions** to indicate how they intend the dialogue to be interpreted by the actors. In Lady Gregory's play *The Rising of the Moon,* the words *gasps* and *furious* are stage directions

used to indicate how the Sergeant is supposed to react and speak at two different times. In Harold Pinter's play *That's All,* the frequent pauses and breaks in conversation are indicated by stage directions.

Although dialogue is most common in novels, short stories, and dramas, it is also used in other forms of prose as well as in poetry. Fanny Burney's account of the party in the excerpt from *The Diary and Letters of Madame d'Arblay* makes effective use of dialogue.

See pages 679, 1258.
See also **Characterization; Drama.**

Diary A diary is a writer's personal day-to-day account of his or her experiences and impressions. Most diaries are private and not intended to be shared. Some, however, have been published because they are well written and provide useful perspectives on historical events or on the everyday life of particular eras. The excerpt from *The Diary of Samuel Pepys* is an example of a well-written diary of great historical interest.

See page 532.
See also **Autobiography.**

Diction Diction is a writer's choice of words, a significant component of style. Diction encompasses both vocabulary (individual words) and syntax (the order or arrangement of words). Diction can be described with terms such as *formal* or *informal, technical* or *common, abstract* or *concrete.*

Examples: Much of the diction in Aldous Huxley's essay "Words and Behavior" is formal, which is appropriate to the seriousness of his subject. The lofty, elevated diction in John Milton's *Paradise Lost* befits the poem's exalted subject and themes. By contrast, the blandness of the diction in W. H. Auden's "The Unknown Citizen"—for example, the words *employers, advertisements, advantages,* and *population—*helps establish the detached, ironic tone of the poem.

See pages 491, 1155, 1252.
See also **Connotation; Style.**

Drama Drama is literature that develops plot and character through dialogue and action; in other words, drama is literature in play form. Dramas are meant to be performed by actors who appear on a stage, before radio microphones, or in front of television or movie cameras.

Unlike other forms of literature, such as fiction and poetry, a drama requires the collaboration of many people in order to come to life. In an important sense, a drama in printed form is an incomplete work of art. It is a skeleton that must be fleshed out by a director, actors, set designers, and others who interpret the work and stage a performance. When the members of an audience become caught up in a drama and forget to a degree the artificiality of the play, the process is called the "suspension of disbelief."

Most plays are divided into acts, with each act having an emotional peak, or climax, of its own. The acts sometimes are divided into scenes; each scene is limited to a single time and place. Shakespeare's plays have five acts. Contemporary plays usually have two or three acts, although some, such as Lady Gregory's *The Rising of the Moon* and Harold Pinter's *That's All,* have only one.

All plays have **stage directions,** instructions included in the script to help performers and directors put on the play or to help readers visualize the action. Stage directions can describe setting, lighting, sound effects, the movement of actors, or the way in which dialogue is spoken.

See page 325.
See also **Aside; Dialogue; Plot; Soliloquy.**

Dramatic Irony *See* **Irony.**

Dramatic Monologue A dramatic monologue is a lyric poem in which a speaker addresses a silent or absent listener in a moment of high intensity or deep emotion, as if engaged in private conversation. The speaker proceeds without interruption or argument, and the effect on the reader is that of hearing just one side of a conversation. This technique allows the poet to focus on the feelings, personality, and motivations of the speaker—in a sense, taking the reader

inside the speaker's mind. Robert Browning's poems "Porphyria's Lover" and "My Last Duchess" are both dramatic monologues.

See page 859.

Elegy An elegy is an extended meditative poem in which the speaker reflects upon death—often in tribute to a person who has died recently—or on an equally serious subject. Most elegies are written in formal, dignified language and are serious in tone. Alfred, Lord Tennyson's *In Memoriam,* written in memory of his friend Arthur Henry Hallam, is a famous elegy.

Elizabethan (Shakespearean) Sonnet *See* **Sonnet.**

End Rhyme *See* **Rhyme.**

English (Shakespearean) Sonnet *See* **Sonnet.**

Epic An epic is a long narrative poem on a serious subject, presented in an elevated or formal style. It traces the adventures of a great hero. Most epics share some or all of the following characteristics:

1. The hero is a figure of high social status and often of great historical or legendary importance.

2. The actions of the hero often determine the fate of a nation or group of people.

3. The hero performs exceedingly courageous, sometimes even superhuman, deeds that reflect the ideas and values of the era.

4. The plot is complicated by supernatural beings and events.

5. The setting is large in scale, involving more than one nation and often a long and dangerous journey through foreign lands.

6. Long formal speeches are often given by the main character.

7. The poem treats universal ideas, such as good and evil, life and death.

Beowulf, the *Iliad,* the *Ramayana,* and *Paradise Lost* are all epics.

See pages 28, 81, 250.

Epic Simile *See* **Simile.**

Epigram The epigram is a literary form that originated in ancient Greece. It developed from simple inscriptions on monuments into a literary genre—short poems or sayings characterized by conciseness, balance, clarity, and wit. A classic epigram is written in two parts, the first establishing the occasion or setting the tone and the second stating the main point. A few lines taken from a longer poem can also be an epigram. Epigrams are used for many purposes, including the expression of friendship, grief, criticism, praise, and philosophy. Many passages in Pope's *An Essay on Criticism* constitute epigrams, as in the following example:

> Good nature and good sense must ever join;
> To err is human, to forgive, divine.
> —Alexander Pope, from *An Essay on Criticism*

Epitaph An epitaph is an inscription on a tomb or monument to honor the memory of a deceased person. The term *epitaph* is also used to describe any verse commemorating someone who has died. Although a few humorous epitaphs have been composed, most are serious in tone. Ben Jonson's "On My First Son" is sometimes called an epitaph.

See page 461.

Epithet An epithet is a brief phrase that points out traits associated with a particular person or thing. Homer's *Iliad* contains many examples of epithets, such as the references to Achilles as "the great runner" (line 34) and to Hector as "killer of men" (line 328).

Essay An essay is a brief work of nonfiction that offers an opinion on a subject. The purpose of an essay may be to express ideas and feelings, to analyze, to inform, to entertain, or to persuade. In a **persuasive essay,** a writer attempts to convince readers to adopt a particular opinion or to perform a certain action. Most persuasive essays present a series of facts, reasons, or examples in support of an opinion or proposal. Sir Francis Bacon's "Of Studies" and "Of Marriage and Single Life" are good examples of the persuasive essay.

Essays can be formal or informal. A **formal essay** examines a topic in a thorough, serious, and highly organized manner. An **informal essay** presents an opinion on a subject, but not in a completely serious or formal tone. Characteristics of this type of essay include humor, a personal or confidential approach, a loose and sometimes rambling style, and often a surprising or unconventional topic. Daniel Defoe's essay "An Academy for Women" is a formal essay, meant to analyze and persuade. Joseph Addison's essays from *The Spectator* are informal, meant to express observations, ideas, and feelings and to entertain with gentle humor and wit.

A **personal essay** is a type of informal essay. Personal essays allow writers to express their viewpoints on subjects by reflecting on events or incidents in their own lives. George Orwell's "A Hanging" is an example of a personal essay.

See pages 447, 552, 582, 1174, 1308.

Exaggeration *See* **Hyperbole**.

Exposition *See* **Plot**.

Extended Metaphor Like any metaphor, an extended metaphor is a comparison between two essentially unlike things that nevertheless have something in common. It does not contain the word *like* or *as.* In an extended metaphor, two things are compared at length and in various ways—perhaps throughout a stanza, a paragraph, or even an entire work. The likening of God to a shepherd in Psalm 23 is an example of an extended metaphor.

Like an extended metaphor, a **conceit** parallels two essentially dissimilar things on several points. A conceit, though, is a more elaborate, formal, and ingenious comparison than the ordinary extended metaphor. Sometimes a conceit forms the framework of an entire poem, as in John Donne's "A Valediction: Forbidding Mourning," in which the poet describes his own and his lover's souls as the two legs of a mathematician's compass.

See pages 456, 945.
See also **Figurative Language; Metaphor; Simile**.

External Conflict *See* **Conflict**.

Fable A fable is a brief tale, in either prose or verse, told to illustrate a moral or teach a lesson. Often, the moral of a fable appears in a distinct and memorable statement near the tale's beginning or end. Jean de La Fontaine's "The Acorn and the Pumpkin" and "The Value of Knowledge" are both fables.

See page 544.

Falling Action *See* **Plot**.

Fantasy *Fantasy* is a term applied to works of fiction that display a disregard for the restraints of reality. The aim of a fantasy may be purely to delight or may be to make a serious comment. Some fantasies include extreme or grotesque characters. Others portray realistic characters in a realistic world who only marginally overstep the bounds of reality.

Examples: In *Gulliver's Travels,* Jonathan Swift creates imaginary worlds to present his satire of 18th-century England. Mary Coleridge uses fantasy to underscore the situational irony in her short story "The King Is Dead, Long Live the King." In Muriel Spark's "The First Year of My Life," the presentation of events from the perspective of an infant is an element of fantasy.

See page 607.

Farce A farce is a type of exaggerated comedy that features an absurd plot, ridiculous situations, and humorous dialogue. The main purpose of a farce is to keep an audience laughing. The characters are usually stereotypes, or simplified examples of different traits or qualities. They may seem reasonable at the start but soon become far-fetched. Comic devices typically used in farces include mistaken identity, deception, wordplay—such as puns and double meanings—and exaggeration.

See also **Stereotype**.

Fiction *Fiction* refers to imaginative works of prose, primarily the novel and the short story. Although fiction sometimes draws on actual events and real people, it springs mainly from the imagination of the writer. The purpose of fiction is to entertain, but it also enlightens by providing a deeper understanding of the human

condition. The basic elements of fiction are plot, character, setting, and theme.

See page 868.
See also **Character; Fable; Fantasy; Novel; Plot; Setting; Short Story; Theme.**

Figurative Language Language that communicates meanings beyond the literal meanings of the words is called figurative language. A figurative expression is not literally true, but rather creates an impression in the reader's mind. Writers use figurative language to create effects, to emphasize ideas, and to evoke emotions. Figurative language is used in both prose and poetry, as well as in oral expression. Special types of figurative language, called figures of speech, include simile, metaphor, personification, hyperbole, and apostrophe.

Examples: In his poem "Preludes," T. S. Eliot uses four kinds of figurative language: (1) simile—"The worlds revolve like ancient women / Gathering fuel in vacant lots"; (2) metaphor—"The burnt-out ends of smoky days"; (3) personification—"The morning comes to consciousness"; (4) hyperbole—"The thousand sordid images." An example of apostrophe is in Milton's *Paradise Lost,* line 6, "Sing, Heavenly Muse . . ."

See pages 306, 1054.
See also **Apostrophe; Hyperbole; Metaphor; Personification; Simile.**

First-Person Point of View *See* **Point of View.**

Flashback A flashback is an account of a conversation, an episode, or an event that happened before the beginning of a story. By revealing significant thoughts, experiences, or events in a character's life, a flashback can help readers understand a character's present situation. Flashbacks may take the form of reminiscences, dream sequences, or descriptions by third-person narrators; they usually interrupt the chronological flow of a story. Flashbacks may contain foreshadowing or other clues to the outcome of a story.

Examples: The use of flashback in Virginia Woolf's "The Duchess and the Jeweller" helps to reveal the conflicting emotions and motivations of the jeweller. The use of flashback in William Trevor's "The Distant Past" provides important background for understanding the relationship of the Middletons to the townspeople.

See page 1157.

Foil A foil is a character who provides a striking contrast to another character. By using a foil, a writer can call attention to certain traits possessed by a main character or simply enhance a character by contrast.

Folk Ballad *See* **Ballad.**

Folk Tale A folk tale is a story that is handed down, usually by word of mouth, from generation to generation. Folk tales reflect the unique characteristics of the regions they come from, showing how the inhabitants live and what their values are. Many involve supernatural events, and most suggest morals. Often, things happen in threes in folk tales. Leo Tolstoy's "What Men Live By" is a version of a Russian folk tale.

See page 929.

Foreshadowing Foreshadowing is a writer's use of hints or clues that suggest what events will occur later in a narrative. The use of foreshadowing creates suspense while preparing readers for what is to come.

Example: In "The Rocking-Horse Winner," the strange mad frenzy with which Paul rides his rocking horse early in the story foreshadows the tragedy of his final ride.

See pages 399, 1019.

Form When applied to poetry, the term *form* refers to all the principles of arrangement in a poem—the ways in which the words and images are organized and patterned to produce a pleasing whole, including the length and placement of lines and the grouping of lines into stanzas. Elements of form—such as the sound devices of rhythm, rhyme, alliteration, consonance, and assonance—work together with elements such as figurative language and imagery to shape a poem, convey meaning, and create a total experience for the reader. The term *form* can also refer to a type of poetry,

such as the sonnet or the dramatic monologue. William Wordsworth's "The World Is Too Much with Us," "It Is a Beauteous Evening," and "I Wandered Lonely As a Cloud" all provide good examples of the poet's artful use of form.

See page 771.
See also **Structure.**

Frame Story A frame story exists when a story is told within a narrative setting or frame—hence creating a story within a story.

Examples: The collection of tales in Chaucer's *The Canterbury Tales,* including "The Pardoner's Tale" and "The Wife of Bath's Tale," are set within a frame story. The frame is introduced in "The Prologue," in which 30 characters on a pilgrimage to Canterbury agree to tell stories to pass the time. "Federigo's Falcon" and the other tales in Boccaccio's *Decameron* are set within a similar framework. The frame, or outer story, is about ten characters fleeing plague-ravaged Florence, Italy, who decide to amuse themselves by telling stories.

See page 154.

Free Verse Free verse is verse that does not contain regular patterns of rhythm and rhyme. The lines in free verse often flow more naturally than do rhymed, metrical lines and thus achieve a rhythm more like that of everyday speech. Although free verse lacks conventional meter, it may contain various rhythmic and sound effects, such as repetitions of syllables or words. Free verse can also contain rhyme, although the rhyme will not follow predictable patterns. Much 20th-century poetry, such as Stephen Spender's "What I Expected" and T. S. Eliot's "The Hollow Men," is written in free verse.

See pages 1073, 1085.

Haiku Haiku is a form of Japanese poetry that embodies three qualities greatly valued in Japanese art: precision, economy, and delicacy. Nature is a particularly important source of inspiration for Japanese haiku poets, and details from nature are often the subject of their poems. The rules of haiku are strict—in only 17 syllables, arranged in 3 lines of 5, 7, and 5 syllables, the poet must create a clear picture

that will evoke a strong emotional response in the reader. The poems of Matsuo Bashō and Kobayashi Issa are examples of haiku.

See page 720.

Hero A hero, or **protagonist,** is a central character in a work of fiction, drama, or epic poetry. A traditional hero possesses good qualities that enable him or her to triumph over an antagonist who is bad or evil in some way.

The term *tragic hero,* first used by the Greek philosopher Aristotle, refers to a central character in a drama who is dignified or noble. According to Aristotle, a tragic hero possesses a defect, or tragic flaw, that brings about or contributes to his or her downfall. This flaw may be poor judgment, pride, weakness, or an excess of an admirable quality. The tragic hero, Aristotle noted, recognizes his or her flaw and its consequences, but only after it is too late to change the course of events. The characters Macbeth and Hamlet in Shakespeare's tragedies are tragic heroes.

A **cultural hero** is a hero who represents the values of his or her culture. Such a hero ranks somewhere between ordinary human beings and the gods. The role of a cultural hero is to provide a noble image that will inspire and guide the actions of mortals. Beowulf is a cultural hero.

In more recent literature, heroes do not necessarily command the attention and admiration of an entire culture. They tend to be individuals whose actions and decisions reflect personal courage. The conflicts they face are not on an epic scale but instead involve moral dilemmas presented in the course of living. Such heroes are often in a struggle with established authority because their actions challenge accepted beliefs. The sergeant in Lady Gregory's play *The Rising of the Moon* might be viewed as such a hero.

See also **Epic; Protagonist; Tragedy.**

Heroic Couplet *See* **Couplet.**

Historical Writing Historical writing is the systematic telling, often in narrative form, of the past of a nation or group of people. Historical writing generally has the following

characteristics: (1) it is concerned with real events; (2) it uses chronological order; and (3) it is usually an objective retelling of facts rather than a personal interpretation. The Venerable Bede's *A History of the English Church and People* is an example of historical writing.

See page 104.

Humor In literature there are three basic types of humor, all of which may involve exaggeration or irony. **Humor of situation** is derived from the plot of a work. It usually involves exaggerated events or situational irony, which occurs when something happens that is different from what was expected. **Humor of character** is often based on exaggerated personalities or on characters who fail to recognize their own flaws, a form of dramatic irony. **Humor of language** may include sarcasm, exaggeration, puns, or verbal irony, which occurs when what is said is not what is meant. In *Candide,* Voltaire uses all three kinds of humor, including absurd situations, ridiculous characters, and ironic descriptions.

See page 629.

Hyperbole Hyperbole is a figure of speech in which the truth is exaggerated for emphasis or for humorous effect. Notice the jarring effect created by this hyperbole:

> "Through the aperture driver and passenger, not six inches between them, remained for an eternity eye to eye."
> —Elizabeth Bowen, from "The Demon Lover"

The following example of hyperbole has a humorous effect:

> "A court-martial sat upon him, and he was asked which he liked best, either to run the gauntlet six and thirty times through the whole regiment, or to have his brains blown out with a dozen musket balls."
> —Voltaire, from *Candide*

See page 468.
See also **Figurative Language.**

Iambic Pentameter Iambic pentameter is a metrical line of five feet, or units, each of which is made up of two syllables, the first unstressed and the second stressed. Iambic pentameter is the most common form of meter used in English poetry; it is the meter used in blank verse, the heroic couplet, and the sonnet. The following line is an example of iambic pentameter:

> Hŏw sóon hăth Tíme, thĕ súbtlĕ thíef
> ŏf yóuth
> —John Milton, from "How Soon Hath Time"

Iambic pentameter is also the meter Milton used in his epic *Paradise Lost.*

See page 790.
See also **Blank Verse; Couplet; Meter; Sonnet.**

Imagery The term *imagery* refers to words and phrases that create vivid sensory experiences for the reader. The majority of images are visual, but imagery may also appeal to the senses of smell, hearing, taste, and touch. In addition, images may re-create sensations of heat (thermal), movement (kinetic), and bodily tension (kinesthetic). Effective writers of both prose and poetry frequently use imagery that appeals to more than one sense simultaneously. For example, in John Keats's ode "To Autumn," the image "Thy hair soft-lifted by the winnowing wind," appeals to two senses—sight and touch.

When an image describes one sensation in terms of another, the technique is called **synesthesia.** For example, the phrase "cold smell of potato mold" from Seamus Heaney's poem "Digging" is an image appealing to smell described in terms of touch (temperature).

A poet may use a **controlling image** to convey thoughts or feelings. A controlling image is a single image or comparison that extends throughout a literary work and shapes its meaning. A controlling image sometimes is an **extended metaphor.** The image of the Greek vase in Keats's "Ode on a Grecian Urn" and the image of digging in Heaney's poem "Digging" are controlling images.

See pages 738, 945, 992, 1085, 1246, 1299.
See also **Kinesthetic Imagery.**

Informal Essay *See* **Essay.**

Interior Monologue *See* **Stream of Consciousness.**

Internal Conflict *See* **Conflict.**

Internal Rhyme *See* **Rhyme.**

Irony Irony is a contrast between expectation and reality. This incongruity often has the effect of surprising the reader or viewer. The techniques of irony include hyperbole, understatement, and sarcasm. Irony is often subtle and easily overlooked or misinterpreted.

There are three main types of irony. **Situational irony** occurs when a character or the reader expects one thing to happen but something else actually happens. In Mary Coleridge's story "The King Is Dead, Long Live the King," the king's—and the reader's—expectations are repeatedly overturned. In Thomas Hardy's poem "Ah, Are You Digging on My Grave?" the speaker questions who is digging on her grave and why. The responses to her questions and the final revelation shock the speaker and create a shattering irony in the poem.

Verbal irony occurs when a writer or character says one thing but means another. An example of verbal irony is the title of Jonathan Swift's essay "A Modest Proposal." The reader soon discovers that the narrator's proposal is outrageous rather than modest and unassuming.

Dramatic irony occurs when the reader or viewer knows something that a character does not know. In Muriel Spark's story "The First Year of My Life," the characters in the final scene think that the baby smiles because her brother blows out the candle on her birthday cake. The reader knows, however, that she smiles in response to hearing someone quote a prominent politician.

See pages 381, 620, 896, 961, 1004, 1019, 1081, 1174.

Italian (Petrarchan) Sonnet *See* **Sonnet.**

Kenning *See* **Anglo-Saxon Poetry.**

Kinesthetic Imagery Kinesthetic imagery re-creates the tension felt through muscles, tendons, or joints in the body.

Example: An example of kinesthetic imagery is the following description from Doris Lessing's "A Sunrise on the Veld": "he felt the chilled dust push up between his toes."

See page 1217.
See also **Imagery.**

Letters *Letters* refers to the written correspondence exchanged between acquaintances, friends, or family members. Most such letters are private and not designed for publication.

Examples: *The Paston Letters,* the correspondence of a family in Norfolk, England, is a famous collection of letters. Other well-known letter writers include Lord Chesterfield, Lady Mary Wortley Montagu, Fanny Burney, and John Keats. Letters provide an invaluable source of information about the social, historical, and political conditions of the period in which they were written.

See page 180.

Literary Ballad *See* **Ballad.**

Lyric A lyric is a short poem in which a single speaker expresses personal thoughts and feelings. Most poems other than dramatic and narrative poems are lyrics. In ancient Greece, lyrics were meant to be sung—the word *lyric* comes from the word *lyre,* the name of a musical instrument that was used to accompany songs. Modern lyrics are not usually intended for singing, but they are characterized by strong, melodic rhythms. Lyrics can be in a variety of forms and cover many subjects, from love and death to everyday experiences. They are marked by imagination and create for the reader a strong, unified impression.

Examples: "The Wife's Lament," Shakespeare's sonnets, Keats's odes, and Margaret Atwood's "The Moment" are all lyrics. Sir Thomas Wyatt's "My Lute, Awake!" is an example of a lyric that was written to be set to music.

See also **Poetry.**

Major Character *See* **Character.**

Memoir A memoir is a form of auto-biographical writing in which a person recalls significant events in his or her life. Most memoirs share the following characteristics: (1) they usually are structured as narratives told by the writers themselves, using the first-person point of view; (2) though some names may be changed to protect privacy, memoirs are true accounts of actual events; (3) although basically personal, memoirs may deal with newsworthy events having a significance beyond the confines of the writers' lives; (4) unlike strictly historical accounts, memoirs often include the writers' feelings and opinions about historical events, giving the reader insight into the impact of history on people's lives. Vera Brittain's *Testament of Youth* is a memoir from the period of World War I.

See page 1124.
See also **Autobiography.**

Metaphor A metaphor is a figure of speech that makes a comparison between two things that are basically unlike but have something in common. Unlike a simile, a metaphor does not contain the word *like* or *as.* In the following poem, the phrase "Time's wingéd chariot" is a metaphor in which the swift passage of time is compared to a speeding chariot:

> But at my back I always hear
> Time's wingéd chariot hurrying near
> —Andrew Marvell, from "To His Coy Mistress"

See pages 306, 468, 474.
See also **Extended Metaphor; Figurative Language; Simile.**

Metaphysical Poetry Metaphysical poetry is a style of poetry written by a group of 17th-century poets, of whom John Donne was the first. The metaphysical poets rejected the conventions of Elizabethan love poetry, with its musical quality and themes of courtly love. Instead, they approached subjects such as religion, death, and even love by analyzing them logically and philosophically. The metaphysical poets were intellectuals who, like the ideal Renaissance man, were well-read in a broad spectrum of subjects. The characteristics of

metaphysical poetry include more than just an intellectual approach to subject matter, however. Instead of the lyrical style of most Elizabethan poetry, metaphysical poets used a more colloquial, or conversational, style. In spite of the simplicity of the words, the ideas may seem obscure or confusing at first, because metaphysical poets loved to play with language. Donne's writing is filled with surprising twists: unexpected images and comparisons, as well as the use of **paradox,** seemingly contradictory statements that in fact reveal some element of truth. Donne's poem "A Valediction: Forbidding Mourning" contains many characteristics of metaphysical poetry.

See page 449.
See also **Paradox.**

Meter Meter is the repetition of a regular rhythmic unit in poetry. The meter of a poem emphasizes the musical quality of the language. Each unit of meter is known as a **foot,** consisting of one stressed syllable and one or two unstressed syllables. In representations of meter, a stressed syllable is often indicated by the symbol ´, an unstressed syllable by the symbol ˘. The four basic types of metrical feet are the **iamb,** an unstressed syllable followed by a stressed syllable (˘ ´); the **trochee,** a stressed syllable followed by an unstressed syllable (´ ˘); the **anapest,** two unstressed syllables followed by a stressed syllable (˘ ˘ ´); and the **dactyl,** a stressed syllable followed by two unstressed syllables (´ ˘ ˘).

Two words are used to identify the meter of a line of poetry. The first word describes the predominant type of metrical foot in the line. The second word describes the number of feet in the line: dimeter (two feet), trimeter (three feet), tetrameter (four feet), pentameter (five feet), hexameter (six feet), and so forth. The meter in this poem is iambic tetrameter:

> Ĭ hóld ĭt trúe, whătĕ'ér bĕfáll;
>   Ĭ féel ĭt, whén Ĭ sórrŏw móst;
>   'Tĭs béttĕr tó hăve lovéd ănd lóst
> Thăn névĕr tó hăve lovéd ăt áll.
> —Alfred, Lord Tennyson, from *In Memoriam*

Poets use variations within a regular metrical pattern—adding an extra syllable or reversing the stressed and unstressed syllables in a foot—to create the effects they want and to reinforce meaning. In his poem "Still to Be Neat," Ben Jonson also uses iambic tetrameter, but he frequently changes iambs to trochees to achieve emphasis and to create interesting rhythmic effects:

> Stíll tŏ bĕ néat, stíll tŏ bĕ dréssed,
> Aš yóu wĕre góing tŏ ă féast;
> Stíll tŏ bĕ pówdeřed, stíll pĕrfúmĕd;
> Lády̆, it iš tŏ bé prĕsúmĕd,
> Thŏugh árt's hid cáusĕs aře nŏt fóund,
> Áll iš nŏt swéet, all iš nŏt sóund.
> —Ben Jonson, from "Still to Be Neat"

See page 790.
See also **Free Verse; Iambic Pentameter; Rhythm.**

Minor Character *See* **Character.**

Miracle Play *See* **Mystery Play.**

Monologue *See* **Dramatic Monologue; Soliloquy.**

Mood Mood is the feeling, or atmosphere, that a writer creates for the reader. The use of connotation, details, dialogue, imagery, figurative language, foreshadowing, setting, and rhythm can help set the mood.

Example: The mood of Rudyard Kipling's "The Miracle of Purun Bhagat" is one of peace and reflection, created in part by the descriptions of the main character and his relationships with other people, the land, and the animals.

See pages 796, 1246.
See also **Tone.**

Morality Play *See* **Mystery Play.**

Motif A motif is a recurring word, phrase, image, object, idea, or action in a work of literature. Motifs function as unifying devices and often relate directly to one or more major themes. Motifs in "The Prologue" to *The Canterbury Tales,* for example, include images of earthly love along with images of spiritual devotion. In *Macbeth,* references to blood, sleep, and water form motifs in the play.

Mystery Play A mystery play is a drama, written in the Middle Ages, that portrays a biblical story. Mystery plays were first performed in churches but were later staged outdoors. Closely related to mystery plays were **miracle plays**, which dramatized saints' lives, and **morality plays**, which dramatized moral conflicts through allegory; the characters in morality plays were allegorical figures, such as Vice, Mercy, Death, and Good Deeds. These types of plays became increasingly elaborate and popular, and some were performed well into the Renaissance period.

Narration *See* **Narrative; Narrator; Point of View.**

Narrative A narrative is any type of writing that is primarily concerned with relating an event or a series of events. A narrative can be imaginary, like a short story or a novel, or it can be factual, like a newspaper account or a work of history. *Memoirs of Madame Vigée-Lebrun* and Penelope Lively's story "At the Pitt-Rivers" are both narratives.

Narrative Poem A narrative poem tells a story. Like a short story or a novel, a narrative poem has the following elements: characters, setting, plot, and point of view, all of which combine to develop a theme.

Examples: Epics, such as *Beowulf* and the *Iliad,* are narrative poems, as are ballads. Samuel Taylor Coleridge's *The Rime of the Ancient Mariner* is also a narrative poem.

See page 745.

Narrator The narrator of a literary work is the person or voice that tells the story. The narrator can be a character in the story or a voice outside the action.

Examples: In Nadine Gordimer's "Six Feet of the Country," the narrator participates in the incidents he recounts. The narrator of Elizabeth Gaskell's "Christmas Storms and Sunshine," is, on the other hand, observant but detached.

See page 167.

Naturalism An extreme form of realism, naturalism in fiction involves the depiction of

life objectively and precisely, without idealizing. Like the realist, the naturalist accurately portrays the world. However, the naturalist creates characters who are victims of environmental forces and internal drives beyond their comprehension and control. Naturalistic fiction conveys the belief that everything that exists is part of the scheme of nature, explainable entirely by natural and physical causes.

Example: Doris Lessing's "A Sunrise on the Veld," which depicts a boy who encounters death and brutality in nature, has naturalistic aspects.

See also **Realism.**

Neoclassicism *Neoclassicism* refers to the attitudes toward life and art that dominated English literature during the Restoration and the 18th century. Neoclassicists respected order, reason, and rules and viewed humans as limited and imperfect. To them, the intellect was more important than emotions, and society was more important than the individual. Imitating classical literature, neoclassical writers developed a style that was characterized by strict form, logic, symmetry, grace, good taste, restraint, clarity, and conciseness. Their works were meant not only to delight readers but also to instruct them in moral virtues and correct social behavior. Among the literary forms that flourished during the neoclassical period were the essay, the literary letter, and the epigram. The heroic couplet was the dominant verse form, and satire and parody prevailed in both prose and poetry. For examples of neoclassical works, see the selections by Alexander Pope, Jonathan Swift, and Samuel Johnson.

See also **Romanticism.**

Nonfiction Nonfiction is prose writing that is about real people, places, and events. Unlike fiction, nonfiction is largely concerned with factual information, although the writer selects and interprets the information according to his or her purpose and viewpoint. Although the subject matter of nonfiction is not imaginative, the writer's style may be individualistic and innovative. Types of nonfiction include autobiographies, biographies, letters, essays, diaries, journals, memoirs, and speeches.

Examples include *The Paston Letters* and Winston Churchill's speeches.

See page 546.
See also **Autobiography; Biography; Diary; Essay; Letters; Memoir.**

Novel A novel is an extended work of fiction. Like a short story, a novel is essentially the product of a writer's imagination. The most obvious difference between a novel and a short story is length. Because the novel is considerably longer, a novelist can develop a wider range of characters and a more complex plot.

Octave *See* **Sonnet.**

Ode An ode is an exalted, complex lyric that develops a serious and dignified theme. Odes appeal to both the imagination and the intellect, and many commemorate events or praise people or elements of nature. Examples of odes that celebrate an element of nature are Percy Bysshe Shelley's "Ode to the West Wind" and "To a Skylark."

Off Rhyme *See* **Rhyme.**

Omniscient Point of View *See* **Point of View.**

Onomatopoeia Onomatopoeia is the use of words whose sounds echo their meanings, such as *buzz, whisper, gargle,* and *murmur.* Onomatopoeia as a literary technique goes beyond the use of simple echoic words, however. Skilled writers, especially poets, choose words whose sounds in combination suggest meaning. In the following lines, the poet uses onomatopoeia to help convey the images and meanings he wants to express:

> Whatever is fickle, freckled (who knows how?)
> With swift, slow; sweet, sour; adazzle, dim
> —Gerard Manley Hopkins, from "Pied Beauty"

See page 744.

Oxymoron *See* **Paradox.**

Parable A parable is a brief story that is meant to teach a lesson or illustrate a moral truth. A parable is more than a simple story,

however. Each detail of the parable corresponds to some aspect of the problem or moral dilemma to which it is directed. The story of the prodigal son in the Bible is a classic parable.

Paradox A paradox is a statement that seems to contradict itself but, in fact, reveals some element of truth. Paradox is found frequently in the poetry of the 16th and 17th centuries. The first line of the following couplet contains two examples of paradox:

> I am and not, I freeze and yet am burned,
> Since from myself another self I turned.
> —Elizabeth I, from "On Monsieur's Departure"

A special kind of concise paradox is the **oxymoron,** which brings together two contradictory terms. Examples are "cruel kindness" and "brave fear."

See pages 451, 1096.
See also **Metaphysical Poetry.**

Parallelism Parallelism is the use of similar grammatical constructions to express ideas that are related or equal in importance. The parallel elements may be words, phrases, sentences, or paragraphs. In Lady Mary Montagu's letters, the writer frequently uses parallelism to reflect the relationship between ideas:

> It seemed your business to learn how to live in the world, as it is hers to know how to be easy out of it.
> —Lady Mary Wortley Montagu, from "Letter to Her Daughter"

See page 564.
See also **Repetition.**

Parody A parody imitates or mocks another work or type of literature. Like caricature in art, parody in literature mimics a subject or a style. The purpose of a parody may be to ridicule through broad humor. On the other hand, a parody may broaden understanding of or add insight to the original work. Some parodies are even written in tribute to a work of literature.

Example: Shakespeare's "Sonnet 130" is in part a parody of love poetry of other Renaissance

poets. The sonnet mocks some of the characteristics of the traditional beautiful woman praised in the earlier poems.

Pastoral A pastoral is a poem presenting shepherds in rural settings, usually in an idealized manner. The language and form of pastorals are artificial. The supposedly simple, rustic characters tend to use formal, courtly speech, and the meters and rhyme schemes are characteristic of formal poetry. Renaissance poets were drawn to the pastoral as a means of conveying their own emotions and ideas, particularly about love. Christopher Marlowe's "The Passionate Shepherd to His Love" is a pastoral.

See page 293.

Personal Essay *See* **Essay.**

Personification Personification is a figure of speech in which human qualities are attributed to an object, animal, or idea. Writers use personification to communicate feelings and images in a concise, concrete way. In line 117 of Thomas Gray's "Elegy Written in a Country Churchyard," for example, the earth is personified: "Here rests his head upon the lap of Earth." In these lines, time is personified:

> Love's not Time's fool, though rosy lips and cheeks
> Within his bending sickle's compass come,
> —William Shakespeare, from "Sonnet 116"

See pages 672, 796.
See also **Figurative Language; Metaphor; Simile.**

Persuasion Persuasion is a technique used by speakers and writers to convince an audience to adopt a particular opinion, perform an action, or both. Effective persuasion appeals to both the intellect and the emotions. The most common form of persuasion is the oration, or speech, as in Winston's Churchill's speech of May 19, 1940.

See pages 1133, 1155.
See also **Essay.**

Persuasive Essay *See* **Essay; Persuasion.**

Persuasive Speech *See* **Persuasion.**

Petrarchan (Italian) Sonnet See **Sonnet.**

Plot Plot is the sequence of actions and events in a narrative. Usually, the events of a plot progress because of a conflict, or struggle between opposing forces. Most plots include the following stages:

1. The **exposition** lays the groundwork for the plot and provides the reader with essential background information. Characters are introduced, the setting is described, and the major conflict is identified. Although the exposition generally appears at the opening of a work, it may also occur later in the narrative.

2. In the **rising action,** complications usually arise, causing difficulties for the main characters and making the conflict more difficult to resolve. As the characters struggle to find solutions to the conflict, suspense builds.

3. The **climax** is the turning point of the action, the moment when interest and intensity reach their peak. The climax of a work usually involves an important event, decision, or discovery that affects the final outcome.

4. The **falling action** consists of the events that occur after the climax. Often, the conflict is resolved, and the intensity of the action subsides. Sometimes this phase of the plot is called the **resolution** or the **denouement** (dā′nōō-män′). *Denouement* is from a French word that means "untying"—in this stage the tangles of the plot are untied and mysteries are solved.

See pages 177, 883, 896.
See also **Conflict.**

Poetry Poetry is an arrangement of lines on the page in which form and content fuse to suggest meanings beyond the literal meanings of the words. Like other forms of literature, poetry attempts to re-create emotions and experiences. Poetry, however, is usually more compressed and suggestive than prose. Because poetry frequently does not include the kind of explanation common in the short story or the novel, it tends to leave more to the reader's imagination.

Many poems are divided into stanzas. The stanzas of a poem may contain the same number of lines, or they may vary in length. Some poems have definite patterns of meter and rhyme. Others, especially poems of the 20th century, rely more on the sounds of words and less on fixed rhythms and rhyme schemes. Characteristic of poetry is the use of imagery, language that appeals to the senses. Poetry is also rich in connotative words and figurative language.

See also **Figurative Language; Form; Free Verse; Imagery; Meter; Repetition; Rhyme; Rhythm; Stanza.**

Point of View *Point of view* refers to the method of narrating a short story, novel, narrative poem, or work of nonfiction. The three most common points of view are first-person, third-person omniscient, and third-person limited. The point of view that a writer employs determines to a great degree the reader's view of the action and the characters; manipulation of point of view creates many striking effects in fiction.

In **first-person point of view,** the narrator is a character in the work, narrating the action as he or she perceives and understands it. First-person narration imparts an immediacy to the narrative and usually leads to involvement with the narrating character. Two short stories using first-person narration are "Araby" by James Joyce and "At the Pitt-Rivers" by Penelope Lively. Almost all autobiographies have first-person narration.

In **third-person point of view,** events and characters are described by a narrator outside the action. In **third-person omniscient point of view,** the narrator is omniscient, or all-knowing, and can see into the mind of more than one character. The use of a third-person omniscient narrator gives the writer great flexibility and provides the reader with access to all the characters' motivations and responses and to events that may be occurring simultaneously. In D. H. Lawrence's "The Rocking-Horse Winner," the use of a third-person omniscient narrator allows for psychological complexity and depth that would not be possible with a first-person narrator.

When a writer uses **third-person limited point of view,** the narrator tells the story from the perspective of only one of the characters. The reader learns only what that character thinks, feels, observes, and experiences. Doris Lessing's "A Sunrise on the Veld" is told from a

third-person limited point of view. Lessing's use of this point of view allows the reader to see how the boy's character changes as the story develops.

See pages 883, 1029, 1197, 1217, 1227, 1299.
See also **Narrator.**

Primary Source A primary source is a book, document, or person that provides original, firsthand information about a topic. Primary sources for an event or period of history might include letters, wills, diaries, tape recordings, and government records. A person can be a primary source for events that he or she has experienced or witnessed. Etty Hillesum's letters are a primary source for information about the Holocaust.

Prop The word *prop,* an abbreviation of *property,* refers to any physical object that is used in a stage production. In Lady Gregory's *The Rising of the Moon,* the props include placards and a hat and wig.

See also **Drama.**

Prose Generally, *prose* refers to all forms of written or spoken expression that are organized and that lack regular rhythmic patterns. Prose is characterized by logical order, continuity of thought, and individual style. Prose style varies from one writer to another, depending on such elements as word choice, sentence length and structure, use of figurative language, and tone.

Examples: Examples of the variety of prose styles can be seen in John Donne's religious meditations from the 17th century, Samuel Johnson's essays from the 18th century, Elizabeth Gaskell's fiction from the 19th century, and Katherine Mansfield's fiction from the 20th century.

See also **Poetry.**

Protagonist The central character in a story, novel, or play is called the protagonist. The protagonist is always involved in the main conflict of the plot and often changes during the course of the work. The force or person who opposes the protagonist is the **antagonist.**

Examples: In Boccaccio's story "Federigo's Falcon," the protagonist is Federigo, who

considers himself opposed by Fortune. In 20th-century fiction and drama, the conflict may be subtle, and the protagonist is not always opposed by an antagonist. In Penelope Lively's story "At the Pitt-Rivers," for example, the main character changes in his perceptions as the story develops, but he is not opposed by another character or by an outside force.

See also **Antagonist; Hero.**

Quatrain A quatrain is a four-line stanza, or unit, of poetry. The most common stanza in English poetry, the quatrain can display a variety of meters and rhyme schemes. The following quatrain follows a typical *abab* rhyme scheme:

> Gather ye rosebuds while ye may, *a*
> Old time is still a-flying; *b*
> And this same flower that smiles today *a*
> Tomorrow will be dying. *b*
> —Robert Herrick, from
> "To the Virgins, to Make Much of Time"

See also **Ballad; Form; Sonnet; Stanza.**

Realism As a general term, *realism* refers to any effort to offer an accurate and detailed portrayal of actual life. In this sense, realism has been a significant element in almost every school of writing in human history. Thus, critics praise Geoffrey Chaucer's realistic descriptions of people from all social classes and analyze Shakespeare's realistic portrayals of character.

Realism also refers to a literary method developed in the 19th century. The 19th-century realists based their writing on careful observations of ordinary life, often focusing on the middle or lower classes. They attempted to present life objectively and honestly, without the sentimentality or idealism that had characterized earlier literature, particularly fiction. Typically, the realists developed settings in great detail in an effort to re-create specific times and places for the reader. Modern realists focus on characterization and avoid contrived plot structures.

Examples: Elements of realism can be found in the novels of Jane Austen and Charles Dickens, but it is not fully developed until the fiction of George Eliot. James Joyce's story "Araby" and

Nadine Gordimer's "Six Feet of the Country" are examples of 20th-century realistic fiction.

See page 1042.
See also **Naturalism.**

Repetition Repetition is a technique in which a sound, word, phrase, or line is repeated for emphasis or unity. The use of repetition often helps to reinforce meaning and to create an appealing rhythm. *Repetition* is a general term that includes specific devices associated with both prose and poetry, such as alliteration and parallelism. Examples of effective repetition can be found in William Blake's "The Lamb" and "The Tyger" and in Elizabeth Barrett Browning's "Sonnet 43."

See pages 440, 461, 1239.
See also **Alliteration; Assonance; Consonance; Parallelism; Rhyme; Rhyme Scheme.**

Resolution *See* **Plot.**

Rhyme Words rhyme when the sounds of their accented vowels and all succeeding sounds are identical, as in *amuse* and *confuse.* For true rhyme, the consonants that precede the vowels must be different. Rhyme that occurs at the end of lines of poetry is called **end rhyme,** as in Thomas Hardy's rhyming of *face* and *place* in "The Man He Killed." End rhymes that are not exact but approximate are called **off rhyme,** or **slant rhyme,** as in the words *come* and *doom* in Stevie Smith's "The Frog Prince." Rhyme that occurs within a single line is called **internal rhyme:**

> Give cr<u>ow</u>ns and p<u>ou</u>nds and guineas
> —A. E. Housman, from
> "When I Was One-and-Twenty"

Rhyme Scheme A rhyme scheme is the pattern of end rhyme in a poem. A rhyme scheme is charted by assigning a letter of the alphabet, beginning with *a,* to each line. Lines that rhyme are given the same letter—in the following poem, for example, the rhyme scheme of each stanza is *aabab:*

> Vengeance shall fall on thy disdain   *a*
> That makest but game on earnest pain.   *a*
> Think not alone under the sun   *b*
> Unquit to cause thy lovers plain,   *a*
> Although my lute and I have done.   *b*
> —Sir Thomas Wyatt, from "My Lute, Awake!"

See page 287.
See also **Ballad; Couplet; Quatrain; Rhyme; Sonnet; Spenserian Stanza; Villanelle.**

Rhythm Rhythm is a pattern of stressed and unstressed syllables in a line of poetry. Poets use rhythm to bring out the musical quality of language, to emphasize ideas, to create mood, to unify a work, and to heighten emotional response. Devices such as alliteration, rhyme, assonance, consonance, and parallelism often contribute to creating rhythm. The slow rhythms of the following lines help to convey the mysterious mood of the poem:

> Ĭ lĭstĕnĕd ĭn ĕmptĭnĕss ŏn thĕ
> mŏor-ridge.
> Thĕ cŭrlĕw's tĕar turnĕd ĭts edge ŏn
> thĕ sĭlĕnce.
> —Ted Hughes, from "The Horses"

See page 790.
See also **Anglo-Saxon Poetry; Ballad; Meter; Spenserian Stanza; Sprung Rhythm.**

Rising Action *See* **Plot.**

Romance The romance has been a popular narrative form since the Middle Ages. Generally, the term *romance* refers to any imaginative adventure concerned with noble heroes, gallant love, a chivalric code of honor, daring deeds, and supernatural events. Romances usually have faraway settings, depict events unlike those of ordinary life, and idealize their heroes as well as the eras in which the heroes lived. Medieval romances are often lighthearted in tone, usually consist of a number of episodes, and often involve one or more characters in a quest.

Example: Thomas Malory's *Le Morte d'Arthur* is an example of a medieval romance. Its stories of kings, knights, and ladies relate many

adventures, tales of love, superhuman feats, and quests for honor and virtue.

See pages 222, 237.

Romanticism *Romanticism* refers to a literary movement that flourished in Britain and Europe throughout much of the 19th century. Romantic writers looked to nature for their inspiration, idealized the distant past, and celebrated the individual. In reaction against neoclassicism, their treatment of subjects was emotional rather than rational, imaginative rather than analytical. The romantic period in English literature is generally viewed as beginning with the publication of *Lyrical Ballads,* poems by William Wordsworth and Samuel Taylor Coleridge.

See page 707.
See also **Neoclassicism.**

Sarcasm *Sarcasm* refers to a type of verbal irony in which a remark's literal meaning is complimentary but the actual meaning is critical. One such contemptuous remark is this one:

> You have clearly proved that ignorance, idleness, and vice are the proper ingredients for qualifying a legislator.
> —Jonathan Swift, from *Gulliver's Travels*

See also **Irony.**

Satire Satire is a literary technique in which ideas, customs, behaviors, or institutions are ridiculed for the purpose of improving society. Satire may be gently witty, mildly abrasive, or bitterly critical, and it often uses exaggeration to force readers to see something in a more critical light. Often, a satirist will distance himself or herself from a subject by creating a fictional speaker—usually a calm, and often a naive, observer—who can address the topic without revealing the true emotions of the writer. The title character of Voltaire's *Candide* is an example of such an observer. Whether the object of a satiric work is an individual person or a group of people, the force of the satire will almost always cast light on foibles and failings that are universal to human experience.

There are two main types of satire, named for the Roman satirists Horace and Juvenal; they

differ chiefly in tone. **Horatian satire** is playfully amusing and seeks to correct vice or foolishness with gentle laughter and sympathetic understanding. Joseph Addison's essays are examples of Horatian satire. **Juvenalian satire** provokes a darker kind of laughter. It is biting and criticizes corruption or incompetence with scorn and outrage. Jonathan Swift's "A Modest Proposal" is an example of Juvenalian satire.

See pages 584, 607, 961, 1286.
See also **Irony.**

Scripture Scripture is literature that is considered sacred—that is, it is used in religious rituals of worship, initiation, celebration, and mourning. Such literature is usually preserved in what are considered holy books. The hymns, chants, prayers, myths, and other forms passed down through generations and combined as a body of scripture express the core beliefs of a group of people. The excerpts from the King James Bible are examples of scripture gathered from the Jewish and Christian traditions.

Sestet *See* **Sonnet.**

Setting *Setting* is usually defined as "the time and place of the action of a short story, novel, play, narrative poem, or nonfiction narrative." In addition to time and place, however, setting may include the social and moral environment that form the background for a narrative. Setting is one of the main elements in fiction and often plays an important role in what happens and why. Sometimes it serves as a source of conflict, as in Doris Lessing's story "A Sunrise on the Veld."

See pages 912, 929, 1029, 1164, 1207.
See also **Fiction.**

Shakespearean (English) Sonnet *See* **Sonnet.**

Short Story A short story is a work of fiction that can be read in one sitting. Generally, a short story develops one major conflict. The basic elements of a short story are setting, character, plot, and theme.

A short story must be unified; all the elements must work together to produce a total effect. This unity of effect is reinforced through

an appropriate title and through the use of symbolism, irony, and other literary devices.

See also **Fiction.**

Simile A simile is a figure of speech that compares two things that are basically unlike yet have something in common. Unlike a metaphor, which implies or suggests a comparison, a simile states it by means of the word *like* or *as.* Both poets and prose writers use similes to intensify emotional response, stimulate vibrant images, provide imaginative delight, and concentrate the expression of ideas. In her story "The Duchess and the Jeweller," Virginia Woolf uses similes to describe the duchess as she sits down:

> As a parasol with many flounces, as a peacock with many feathers, shuts its flounces, folds its feathers, so she subsided and shut herself as she sank down in the leather armchair.
> —Virginia Woolf, from "The Duchess and the Jeweller"

An **epic simile** is a long comparison that often continues for a number of lines. It does not always contain the word *like* or *as.* Here is an example of an epic simile:

> Conspicuous as the evening star that comes, amid the first in heaven, at fall of night, and stands most lovely in the west, so shone in sunlight the fine-pointed spear Achilles poised in his right hand. . . .
> —Homer, from the *Iliad*

See pages 81, 306, 738, 766.
See also **Figurative Language; Metaphor.**

Situational Irony *See* **Irony.**

Slant Rhyme *See* **Rhyme.**

Soliloquy A soliloquy is a speech in a dramatic work in which a character speaks his or her thoughts aloud. Usually the character is on the stage alone, not speaking to other characters and perhaps not even consciously addressing the audience. (If there are other characters on stage, they are ignored temporarily.) The purpose of a soliloquy is to reveal a character's inner thoughts, feelings, and plans to the audience. Soliloquies are characteristic of Elizabethan drama; *Macbeth* has several soliloquies. Following is part of Macbeth's most famous soliloquy.

> Life's but a walking shadow, a poor player,
> That struts and frets his hour upon the stage
> And then is heard no more. It is a tale
> Told by an idiot, full of sound and fury,
> Signifying nothing.
> —William Shakespeare, from *Macbeth*

See page 346.

Sonnet A sonnet is a lyric poem of 14 lines, commonly written in **iambic pentameter.** For centuries the sonnet has been a popular form because it is long enough to permit development of a complex idea yet short and structured enough to challenge any poet's skills. Sonnets written in English usually follow one of two forms.

The **Petrarchan,** or **Italian, sonnet,** introduced into English by Sir Thomas Wyatt, is named after Petrarch, the 14th-century Italian poet. This type of sonnet consists of two parts, called the **octave** (the first eight lines) and the **sestet** (the last six lines). The usual rhyme scheme for the octave is *abbaabba.* The rhyme scheme for the sestet may be *cdecde, cdccdc,* or a similar variation. The octave generally presents a problem or raises a question, and the sestet resolves or comments on the problem. John Milton's sonnets are written in the Petrarchan form.

The **Shakespearean,** or **English, sonnet** is sometimes called the **Elizabethan sonnet.** It consists of three quatrains, or four-line units, and a final couplet. The typical rhyme scheme is *abab cdcd efef gg.* In the English sonnet, the rhymed couplet at the end of the sonnet provides a final commentary on the subject developed in the three quatrains. Shakespeare's sonnets are the finest examples of this type of sonnet.

A variation of the Shakespearean sonnet is the **Spenserian sonnet,** which has the same structure but uses the interlocking rhyme scheme *abab bcbc cdcd ee.* Spenser's "Sonnet 30" is an example.

Some poets have written a series of related sonnets that have the same subject. These are

called **sonnet sequences,** or **sonnet cycles.** Toward the end of the 16th century, writing sonnet sequences became fashionable, with a common subject being love for a beautiful but unattainable woman. Francesco Petrarch, Edmund Spenser, and Elizabeth Barrett Browning wrote sonnet sequences.

See pages 295, 300, 306, 311, 479.

See also **Iambic Pentameter; Lyric; Meter; Quatrain.**

Sound Devices *See* **Alliteration; Assonance; Consonance; Meter; Onomatopoeia; Repetition; Rhyme; Rhyme Scheme; Rhythm.**

Speaker The speaker in a poem is the voice that "talks" to the reader, like the narrator in fiction. The speaker is sometimes a distant observer and at other times intimately involved with the experiences and ideas being expressed in the poem. The speaker and poet are not necessarily identical. Often a poet creates a speaker with a distinct identity in order to achieve a particular effect.

Examples: The speaker of Alfred, Lord Tennyson's poem "The Lady of Shalott" is neutral and objective, as though merely recording observations. The speaker in Tennyson's "Ulysses," on the other hand, is passionately involved in the ideas and feelings he is expressing.

See pages 852, 1111.

Spenserian Stanza The Spenserian stanza (named for Edmund Spenser, who invented it for his romance *The Faerie Queene*) consists of nine iambic lines rhyming in the pattern *ababbcbcc.* Each of the first eight lines contains five feet, and the ninth contains six. The rhyming pattern helps to create unity, and the six-foot line, called an **alexandrine,** slows down the stanza and so gives dignity and allows for reflection on the ideas in the stanza. Byron used the Spenserian stanza in *Childe Harold's Pilgrimage.*

See also **Stanza.**

Sprung Rhythm In order to approximate the rhythms of natural speech in poetry, the poet Gerard Manley Hopkins developed what he called sprung rhythm. The lines of a poem written in sprung rhythm have fixed numbers of stressed syllables but varying numbers of unstressed syllables. A line may contain several consecutive stressed syllables, or a stressed syllable may be followed by one, two, or even three unstressed syllables. The following lines are written in sprung rhythm:

> Landscape plottĕd and piécĕd—fold,
>   fallŏw, and plouǵh;
> And all trádes, theĭr geár and tácklĕ
>   and trím.
> —Gerard Manley Hopkins, from "Pied Beauty"

See page 950.

Stage Directions *See* **Drama.**

Stanza A stanza is a group of lines that form a unit in a poem. The stanza is roughly comparable to the paragraph in prose. In traditional poems, the stanzas usually have the same number of lines and often have the same rhyme scheme and meter. In the 20th century, poets have experimented more freely with stanza form, sometimes writing poems that have no stanza breaks at all.

Examples: The quatrains in Richard Lovelace's "To Lucasta, Going to the Wars," are a traditional stanza form. The two stanzas of W. B. Yeats's "The Second Coming," one 8 lines long and the other 14 lines long, are an example of an unconventional stanza form.

See page 967.

See also **Quatrain; Spenserian Stanza; Villanelle.**

Stereotype In literature, simplified or stock characters who conform to a fixed pattern or are defined by a single trait are called stereotypes. Such characters do not usually demonstrate the complexities of real people.

Examples: Familiar stereotypes in popular literature include the absent-minded professor, the busybody, and the merciless villain. The figure of the rejected lover in many ballads is another example of a stereotype.

Stream of Consciousness *Stream of consciousness* refers to a style of fiction that takes as its subject the flow of thoughts,

responses, and sensations of one or more characters. A stream-of-consciousness narrative is not structured as a coherent, logical presentation of ideas. Rather, the connections between ideas are associative, with one idea suggesting another.

A character's stream of consciousness is often expressed as an interior monologue, a record of the total workings of the character's mind and emotions. An interior monologue may reveal the inner experience of the character on many levels of consciousness, often represented through a sequence of images and impressions. Virginia Woolf and James Joyce make extensive use of stream of consciousness in their fiction.

See also **Characterization; Point of View; Style.**

Structure Structure is the way in which the parts of a work of literature are put together. Paragraphs are a basic unit in prose, as are chapters in novels, acts and scenes in plays, and stanzas and lines in poems. A prose selection can be structured by idea or incident, like most essays, short stories, narrative poems, and one-act plays. Structure in poetry involves the arrangement of words and lines to produce a desired effect; a poem's structure takes into account the sounds in the poem as well as the ideas.

The structure of a poem, short story, novel, play, or work of nonfiction usually emphasizes certain important aspects of content. For example, the division of T. S. Eliot's poem "Preludes" into sections enables him to shift between different times of day and between the interior of a room and the street outside. The structure of each stanza in Margaret Atwood's poem "The Moment" and the relationship between the stanzas help convey the theme that nature cannot be possessed.

Structure is also a means through which a writer adds layers of psychological complexity to characters. Katherine Mansfield's story "A Cup of Tea" begins and ends with questions about whether Rosemary is pretty. This framework suggests the element in Rosemary's character— her vanity—that proves to be the crux of the story.

See pages 741, 1229.
See also **Form.**

Style Style is the particular way in which a piece of literature is written. Style is not what is said but how it is said. It is the writer's uniquely individual way of communicating ideas. Many elements contribute to style, including word choice, sentence length, tone, figurative language, use of dialogue, and point of view. A literary style may be described in a variety of ways, such as *formal, conversational, journalistic, wordy, ornate, poetic,* or *dynamic.*

Examples: The interior monologue and detailed, evocative imagery in Virginia Woolf's "The Duchess and the Jeweller" are important elements of the style of the story. In the excerpt from Elie Wiesel's *Night,* the author uses simple words, short sentences, imagery, and dialogue to convey his horrifying experiences.

See pages 1054, 1141.

Supernatural Elements *See* **Supernatural Tale.**

Supernatural Tale A supernatural tale is a story that goes beyond the bounds of reality, usually by involving **supernatural elements**— beings, powers, or events that are unexplainable by known forces or laws of nature. In Valmiki's Indian epic *Ramayana,* Ravana's brother Kumbakarna is a supernatural being. In Sir Thomas Malory's romance *Le Morte d'Arthur,* Sir Launcelot uses supernatural powers in his battles against Sir Gawain.

In many supernatural tales, **foreshadowing**— hints or clues that point to later events—is used to encourage readers to anticipate the unthinkable. Sometimes readers are left wondering whether a supernatural event has really taken place or is the product of a character's imagination. In an effective supernatural tale, the writer manipulates readers' feelings of curiosity and fear to produce a mounting sense of excitement. Elizabeth Bowen's "The Demon Lover" is a supernatural tale.

See page 250.

Surprise Ending A surprise ending is an unexpected twist in the plot at the end of a story. The surprise may be a sudden turn in the action or a revelation that gives a different perspective to the entire story.

Example: The final paragraph of "The Demon Lover," which sets off a new direction in the plot instead of bringing it to its expected conclusion, is an example of a surprise ending.

See page 1164.
See also **Plot.**

Suspense Suspense is the tension or excitement readers feel as they are drawn into a story and become increasingly eager to learn the outcome of the plot. Suspense is created when a writer purposely leaves readers uncertain or apprehensive about what will happen.

Example: In *The Rising of the Moon,* Lady Gregory uses suspense-building techniques when she describes the sounds the sergeant hears in the dark.

See pages 1002, 1164.

Symbol A symbol is a person, place, object, or activity that stands for something beyond itself. Certain symbols are commonly used in literature, such as a journey to represent life or night to represent death. Other symbols, however, acquire their meanings within the contexts of the works in which they occur.

Examples: In Boccaccio's story "Federigo's Falcon," the falcon comes to symbolize the passionate and consuming love of Federigo for Monna Giovanna. In Tennyson's "The Lady of Shalott," the lady symbolizes the poet. Sometimes a literary symbol has more than one possible meaning. For example, the rose in Blake's poem "The Sick Rose" might symbolize goodness, innocence, or all of humanity.

See pages 715, 992.

Synecdoche Synecdoche is a figure of speech in which the name of a part is used to refer to a whole—for example, the use of *wheels* to mean "automobile."

Example: T. S. Eliot uses synecdoche in his poem "Preludes" when he uses words for body parts to refer to people, as in line 17, where "muddy feet" refers to early-morning crowds of people going to work.

Synesthesia *See* **Imagery.**

Theme A theme is a central idea or message in a work of literature. Theme should not be confused with subject, or what the work is about. Rather, theme is a perception about life or human nature shared with the reader. Sometimes the theme is directly stated within a work; at other times it is implied, and the reader must infer the theme. There may be more than one theme in a work. In *Macbeth,* for example, the themes include the corrupting effect of unbridled ambition, the corrosiveness of guilt, the lure and power of inscrutable supernatural forces, and the tragedy of psychological disintegration. The theme of Coleridge's "The Rime of the Ancient Mariner" has been interpreted as the transformation of the human personality through a loss of innocence and youth; another interpretation of the theme concerns the effects of sin and spiritual redemption.

One way to discover the theme of a literary work is to think about what happens to the central characters. The importance of those events, stated in terms that apply to all human beings, is the theme. In poetry, imagery and figurative language also help convey theme. In Chaucer's "The Pardoner's Tale," what happens to the three young men illustrates the theme "The love of money is the root of all evil."

See pages 420, 468, 474, 1124, 1232.

Third-Person Point of View *See* **Point of View.**

Title The title of a literary work introduces readers to the piece and usually reveals something about its subject or theme. Although works are occasionally untitled or, in the case of some poems, merely identified by their first line, most literary works have been deliberately and carefully named. Some titles are straightforward, stating exactly what the reader can expect to discover in the work. Others suggest possibilities, perhaps hinting at the subject and forcing the reader to search for interpretations.

Examples: "1996," the title of a poem by Rabindranath Tagore, gives the reader a direct clue about the subject of the poem, as does "Writing," the title of a poem by Octavio Paz. On the other hand, "Dover Beach," the title of a

poem by Matthew Arnold, is open to interpretation, and the reader has to work through the significance of the title in relation to the poem.

See page 972.

Tone Tone is an expression of a writer's attitude toward a subject. Unlike mood, which is intended to shape the reader's emotional response, tone reflects the feelings of the writer. The writer's choice of words and details helps establish the tone, which might be serious, humorous, sarcastic, playful, ironic, bitter, or objective. To identify the tone of a work, you might find it helpful to read the work aloud. The emotions you convey in reading should give you clues to the tone of the work.

Examples: The tone of Jonathan Swift's "A Modest Proposal" is searingly ironic; the tone of Katherine Mansfield's "A Cup of Tea" is amused and ironic. In "The Prologue" from *The Canterbury Tales,* Chaucer's restrained, detached tone accounts for much of the work's humor.

See pages 137, 190, 1042, 1141, 1286.
See also **Mood.**

Tragedy A tragedy is a dramatic work that presents the downfall of a dignified character who is involved in historically or socially significant events. The main character, or **tragic hero,** has a **tragic flaw,** a quality that leads to his or her destruction. The events in a tragic plot are set in motion by a decision that is often an error in judgment caused by the tragic flaw. Succeeding events are linked in a cause-and-effect relationship and lead inevitably to a disastrous conclusion, usually death. A tragic hero evokes both pity and fear in readers or viewers: pity because readers or viewers feel sorry for the character, and fear because they realize that the problems and struggles faced by the character are perhaps a necessary part of human life. At the end of a tragedy, a reader or viewer generally feels a sense of waste, because humans who were in some way superior have been destroyed. Shakespeare's plays *Macbeth, Hamlet, Othello,* and *King Lear* are famous examples of tragedies.

See page 321.

Tragic Flaw *See* **Hero; Tragedy.**

Tragic Hero *See* **Hero; Tragedy.**

Understatement Understatement is a technique of creating emphasis by saying less than is actually or literally true. Understatement is the opposite of hyperbole, or exaggeration. One of the primary devices of irony, understatement can be used to develop a humorous effect, to create biting satire, or to achieve a restrained tone. Understatement is an important element in the dramas of Harold Pinter, as in his one-act play *That's All.*

Verbal Irony *See* **Irony.**

Villanelle The villanelle is an intricately patterned French verse form, planned to give the impression of simplicity. A villanelle has 19 lines, composed of 5 tercets, or 3-line stanzas, followed by a quatrain. The first line is repeated as a refrain at the end of the second and fourth stanzas. The last line of the first stanza is repeated at the end of the third and fifth stanzas. Both lines reappear as the final two lines of the poem. The rhyme scheme of a villanelle is *aba* for each tercet and then *abaa* for the quatrain. Dylan Thomas's "Do Not Go Gentle into That Good Night" is an example of a villanelle.

See page 1092.
See also **Quatrain; Stanza.**

Wordplay Wordplay is the intentional use of more than one meaning of a word to express ambiguities, multiple interpretations, and irony.

Examples: In the excerpt from Derek Walcott's poem *Midsummer,* the poet achieves some of his irony through the use of wordplay—for example, through his use of the words *color* and *white.* In Stevie Smith's poem "Not Waving but Drowning," the poet plays with the different meanings of *far out* and *cold* to give added meaning to her poem.

See page 1252.

Glossary of Words to Know

In English and Spanish

A

abominably (ə-bŏm′ə-nə-blē) *adv.* unpleasantly; terribly
abominablemente *adv.* de modo desagradable; terriblemente

abstain (ăb-stān′) *v.* to hold oneself back deliberately
abstenerse *v.* contenerse a propósito

accrue (ə-krōō′) *v.* to come as gain; accumulate
aumentar *v.* obtener una ganancia; acumular

acquiesce (ăk′wē-ĕs′) *v.* to agree or give in without protest
conformarse *v.* aceptar o consentir sin protestar

adversary (ăd′vər-sĕr′ē) *n.* an enemy; opponent
adversario *s.* enemigo; opositor

adversity (ăd-vûr′sĭ-tē) *n.* hardship; misfortune
adversidad *s.* calamidad; infortunio

affectation (ăf′ĕk-tā′shən) *n.* unnatural behavior; conduct intended to give a false impression
afectación *s.* comportamientoque no es natural; conducta que busca dar una falsa impresión

affliction (ə-flĭk′shən) *n.* a cause of pain or distress
aflicción *s.* causa de dolor o angustia

affronted (ə-frŭn′tĭd) *adj.* offended **affront** *v.*
afrentado *adj.* ofendido **afrentar** *v.*

aghast (ə-găst′) *adj.* struck with terror or amazement; shocked
horrorizado *adj.* aterrorizado; espantado

agility (ə-jĭl′ĭ-tē) *n.* an ability to move quickly and easily; nimbleness
agilidad *s.* capacidad para moverse rápida y fácilmente; ligereza

allude (ə-lōōd′) *v.* to make an indirect reference
aludir *v.* hacer una referencia indirecta

amended (ə-mĕn′dĭd) *adj.* corrected **amend** *v.*
enmendado *adj.* corregido **enmendar** *v.*

amiability (ā′mē-ə-bĭl′ĭ-tē) *n.* good nature; friendliness
amabilidad *s.* buen carácter; afabilidad

anachronism (ə-năk′rə-nĭz′əm) *n.* something out of keeping with a specified time; especially, something proper to a former age but not to the present
anacronismo *s.* lo que no corresponde al tiempo que se le atribuye; en especial, algo que pertenece a una época anterior pero no al presente

anecdote (ăn′ĭk-dōt′) *n.* a brief account of an interesting or humorous incident
anécdota *s.* recuento breve de un incidente interesante o chistoso

anguish (ăng′gwĭsh) *n.* agony
angustia *s.* agonía

animate (ăn′ə-māt′) *v.* to encourage; motivate
animar *v.* alentar; motivar

animosity (ăn′ə-mŏs′ĭ-tē) *n.* hostility; hatred
animosidad *s.* hostilidad; odio

ardent (är′dnt) *adj.* passionate
ardiente *adj.* apasionado

arrogance (ăr′ə-gəns) *n.* overbearing pride; exaggerated self-importance
arrogancia *s.* orgullo exagerado; superioridad

ascribed (ə-skrībd′) *adj.* assigned; referred to as a source **ascribe** *v.*
atribuido *adj.* asignado; que se refiere a una fuente **atribuir** *v.*

aspire (ə-spīr′) *v.* to strive to attain
aspirar *v.* luchar por obtener

assail (ə-sāl′) *v.* to attack, either with blows or with words
acometer *v.* atacar con golpes o palabras

assent (ə-sĕnt′) *n.* agreement; acceptance
asentimiento *s.* acuerdo; aceptación

assiduous (ə-sĭj′ōō-əs) *adj.* steadily and carefully attentive
asiduo *adj.* frecuente, puntual y perseverante

astute (ə-stōōt′) *adj.* clever; shrewd
astuto *adj.* sagaz; agudo

attenuated (ə-tĕn′yōō-ā′tĭd) *adj.* slender; thin **attenuate** *v.*
disminuido *adj.* delgado; flaco **disminuir** *v.*

authenticity (ô′thĕn-tĭs′ĭ-tē) *n.* genuineness
autenticidad *s.* calidad de genuino

avarice (ăv′ə-rĭs) *n.* an excessive desire for wealth; greed
avaricia *s.* deseo excesivo de riqueza; codicia

awry (ə-rī′) *adj.* twisted; faulty; disordered
sesgado *adj.* torcido; con fallas; desordenado

B

balefully (bāl′fə-lē) *adv.* in a menacing way; wickedly
malsanamente *adv.* en forma amenazadora; maléficamente

benign (bĭ-nīn′) *adj.* gentle; mild
benigno *adj.* gentil; suave

bequeath (bĭ-kwēth′) *v.* to leave in a will; give as an inheritance
legar *v.* dejar en un testamento; heredar

bleak (blēk) *adj.* gloomy; hopeless
desolado *adj.* triste; sin esperanza

bravado (brə-vä′dō) *n.* a reckless or false show of courage
bravata *s.* muestra falsa o temeraria de valentía

C

career (kə-rîr′) *v.* to move at full speed; rush
correr *v.* moverse a toda velocidad; precipitarse

castigate (kăs′tĭ-gāt′) *v.* to criticize harshly
condenar *v.* criticar duramente

cataclysm (kăt′ə-klĭz′əm) *n.* a violent change or sudden upheaval
cataclismo *s.* cambio violento o trastorno súbito

censure (sĕn′shər) *n.* criticism; blame
censura *s.* crítica; culpa

chagrin (shə-grĭn′) *n.* a feeling of embarrassment caused by humiliation or failure
mortificación *s.* vergüenza causada por humillación o fracaso

civility (sĭ-vĭl′ĭ-tē) *n.* politeness; courtesy
urbanidad *s.* amabilidad; cortesía

clamor (klăm′ər) *n.* a loud, confused noise or outcry
clamor *s.* ruido fuerte y confuso; alboroto

clemency (klĕm′ən-sē) *n.* mildness
clemencia *s.* bondad

cloister (kloi′stər) *v.* to confine or seclude, as in a convent
enclaustrar *v.* confinar o encerraren un convento o un sitio aislado

commend (kə-mĕnd′) *v.* to express approval of; praise
felicitar *v.* expresar aprobación; halagar

compel (kəm-pĕl′) *v.* to urge irresistibly; constrain
obligar *v.* instar de manera irresistible; constreñir

complacently (kəm-plā′sənt-lē) *adv.* in a contented, self-satisfied way; smugly
suficientemente *adv.* de modo satisfecho; presuntuosamente

compulsory (kəm-pŭl′sə-rē) *adj.* required; mandatory
obligatorio *adj.* requerido; forzoso

concede (kən-sēd′) *v.* to grant or acknowledge, often unwillingly
conceder *v.* dar o reconocer, a menudo contra la voluntad

concurring (kən-kûr′ĭng) *adj.* occurring at the same time; acting together **concur** *v.*
concurrente *adj.* que ocurre al mismo tiempo; que actúa en forma conjunta **concurrir** *v.*

condescend (kŏn′dĭ-sĕnd′) *v.* to do something considered to be beneath one's dignity
condescender *v.* hacer algo considerado por debajo de la dignidad propia

conjecture (kən-jĕk′chər) *v.* to guess or infer
conjeturar *v.* adivinar o inferir

consternation (kŏn′stər-nā′shən) *n.* a sudden fear or amazement that makes one feel helpless; dismay
consternación *s.* miedo o sorpresa que hace sentirse inútil; desaliento

contemptuous (kən-tĕmp′choo-əs) *adj.* scornful; openly disrespectful
desdeñoso *adj.* burlón; abiertamente irrespetuoso

contrive (kən-trīv′) *v.* to plan cleverly; devise
maquinar *v.* planear astutamente; inventar

controverted (kŏn′trə-vûr′tĭd) *adj.* disputed; denied **controvert** *v.*
controvertido *adj.* disputado; rebatido **controvertir** *v.*

convivial (kən-vĭv′ē-əl) *adj.* characterized by friendly companionship; sociable
jovial *adj.* caracterizado por su agradable compañía; sociable

corporal (kôr′pər-əl) *adj.* bodily; physical
corporal *adj.* del cuerpo; físico

cosset (kŏs′ĭt) *v.* to treat like a pet; pamper
mimar *v.* tratar como a una mascota; acariciar

courtliness (kôrt′lē-nĭs) *n.* refined behavior; elegance
cortesía *s.* conducta refinada; elegancia

covetousness (kŭv′ĭ-təs-nĭs) *n.* an excessive desire for wealth or possessions
codicia *s.* deseo excesivo de riqueza o posesiones

cowering (kou′ə-rĭng) *adj.* cringing in fear **cower** *v.*
agazapado *adj.* contraído por el miedo **agazapar** *v.*

crone (krōn) *n.* an ugly old woman; hag
bruja *s.* vieja fea; fea

D

daunt (dônt) *v.* to destroy the courage of; dismay
atemorizar *v.* destruir la valentía; desalentar

defer (dĭ-fûr′) *v.* to postpone
diferir *v.* posponer

deference (dĕf′ər-əns) *n.* courteous regard or respect
deferencia *s.* respeto cortés

deferential (dĕf′ə-rĕn′shəl) *adj.* showing courteous respect
deferente *adj.* que muestra respeto cortés

defile (dĭ-fīl′) *v.* to make filthy; violate the honor of
profanar *v.* ensuciar; violar el honor

degenerate (dĭ-jĕn′ə-rāt′) *v.* to sink to a lower condition; deteriorate
degenerar *v.* caer en una condición más baja; deteriorar

deign (dān) *v.* to consider worthy of one's dignity; condescend
dignarse *v.* tener la bondad de hacer algo; condescender

dejected (dĭ-jĕk′tĭd) *adj.* sad; depressed
  abatido *adj.* triste; deprimido

demeanor (dĭ-mē′nər) *n.* a way of behaving; manner
  porte *s.* forma de conducta; manera

demented (dĭ-mĕn′tĭd) *adj.* insane
  demente *adj.* desvariado

deplorable (dĭ-plôr′ə-bəl) *adj.* miserable; woeful
  deplorable *adj.* miserable; lamentable

depredation (dĕp′rĭ-dā′shən) *n.* destruction caused by robbery or looting
  depredación *s.* destrucción causada por robo o saqueo

desecrate (dĕs′ĭ-krāt′) *v.* to violate the sacredness of
  profanar *v.* violar lo sagrado

destitute (dĕs′tĭ-tōot′) *adj.* lacking in resources; bereft
  indigente *adj.* carente de recursos; necesitado

devout (dĭ-vout′) *adj.* showing religious devotion and piety
  devoto *adj.* que muestra devoción y piedad religiosa

dexterity (dĕk-stĕr′ĭ-tē) *n.* skill and quickness of bodily movement
  destreza *s.* agilidad y rapidez en los movimientos

diabolical (dī′ə-bŏl′ĭ-kəl) *adj.* extremely wicked or cruel; devilish
  diabólico *adj.* sumamente malo o cruel; endemoniado

diligent (dĭl′ə-jənt) *adj.* painstaking; hard-working
  diligente *adj.* esforzado; trabajador

diminutive (dĭ-mĭn′yə-tĭv) *adj.* tiny
  diminutivo *adj.* pequeño

discern (dĭ-sûrn′) *v.* to observe; perceive
  discernir *v.* observar; percibir

discernment (dĭ-sûrn′mənt) *n.* goodjudgment
  discernimiento *s.* buen juicio

disconsolate (dĭs-kŏn′sə-lĭt) *adj.* unable to be comforted; cheerless and gloomy
  desconsolado *adj.* imposible de ser consolado; triste y deprimido

discourse (dĭs′kôrs′) *n.* a discussion of a subject in speech or writing
  discurso *s.* discusión hablada o por escrito de un tema

discretion (dĭ-skrĕsh′ən) *n.* a sense of carefulness and restraint in one's actions or words
  discreción *s.* control y cuidado en las acciones o palabras

disdain (dĭs-dān′) *n.* a show of contempt; scorn
  desdén *s.* desprecio; menosprecio

dispatch (dĭ-spăch′) *n.* promptness; efficiency
  prontitud *s.* puntualidad; eficiencia

disposition (dĭs′pə-zĭsh′ən) *n.* temperament
  disposición *s.* temperamento

dissipation (dĭs′ə-pā′shən) *n.* a wasteful expenditure of resources
  disipación *s.* gasto innecesario de recursos

dissuade (dĭ-swād′) *v.* to divert from a course of action by persuasion
  disuadir *v.* desviar de un curso de acción por medio de persuasión

diverting (dĭ-vûr′tĭng) *n.* entertaining; amusing
  divert *v.*
  diversión *s.* entretenimiento **divertir** *v.*

doctrine (dŏk′trĭn) *n.* the ideas taught by an authority
  doctrina *s.* ideas enseñadas por una autoridad

dogged (dô′gĭd) *adj.* persistent; stubborn
  necio *adj.* persistente; testarudo

dwindle (dwĭn′dl) *v.* to become steadily less
  menguar *v.* disminuir gradualmente

E

ecstasy (ĕk′stə-sē) *n.* intense joy or delight; bliss
éxtasis *s.* júbilo o alegría intensa; dicha

edifice (ĕd′ə-fĭs) *n.* a building, especially a large and impressive one
edificio *s.* construcción, especialmente grande e impresionante

effectual (ĭ-fĕk′chōō-əl) *adj.* able to produce a desired effect
efectivo *adj.* capaz de producir el efecto deseado

efficacious (ĕf′ĭ-kā′shəs) *adj.* effective
eficaz *adj.* efectivo

eloquently (ĕl′ə-kwənt-lē) *adv.* with powerful and persuasive words
elocuentemente *adv.* con palabras fuertes y persuasivas

elude (ĭ-lōōd′) *v.* to avoid or escape
eludir *v.* evadir o escapar

emanate (ĕm′ə-nāt′) *v.* to come forth; flow out
emanar *v.* brotar; fluir

embellish (ĕm-bĕl′ĭsh) *v.* to add ornamental or fictitious details to; decorate
embellecer *v.* añadir detalles ornamentales o ficticios; decorar

eminent (ĕm′ə-nənt) *adj.* standing out above others; high-ranking; prominent
eminente *adj.* que sobresale por encima de otros; de alto rango; prominente

emulation (ĕm′yə-lā′shən) *n.* an effort to equal or outdo another person; rivalry
emulación *s.* esfuerzo por igualar o superar a otro; rivalidad

enamor (ĭ-năm′ər) *v.* to inspire with love; fascinate
enamorar *v.* inspirar amor; fascinar

encumbrance (ĕn-kŭm′brəns) *n.* a burden
impedimento *s.* carga

ensue (ĕn-sōō′) *v.* to occur as a result; follow
sobrevenir *v.* ocurrir como resultado; seguir

enticing (ĕn-tī′sĭng) *adj.* tempting **entice** *v.*
tentador *adj.* que atrae con maña **tentar** *v.*

entreaty (ĕn-trē′tē) *n.* an earnest request; plea
súplica *s.* petición urgente; ruego

esoteric (ĕs′ə-tĕr′ĭk) *adj.* understood only by a chosen few
esotérico *adj.* entendido sólo por unos cuantos elegidos

ethereal (ĭ-thîr′ē-əl) *adj.* delicate; heavenly
etéreo *adj.* delicado; celestial

euphemism (yōō′fə-mĭz′əm) *n.* a mild or vague term used in place of a blunt or offensive one
eufemismo *s.* término suave o vago usado en lugar de una palabra franca u ofensiva

evade (ĭ-vād′) *v.* to escape by cleverness or deception
evadir *v.* escapar por medio de ingenio o engaño

evocation (ĕv′ə-kā′shən) *n.* a bringing to mind
evocación *s.* recuerdo

excruciating (ĭk-skrōō′shē-ā′tĭng) *adj.* intensely painful; agonizing
atroz *adj.* intensamente doloroso; penosísimo

execrable (ĕk′sĭ-krə-bəl) *adj.* detestable; hateful
execrable *adj.* detestable; odioso

exorcising (ĕk′sôr-sī′zĭng) *adj.* driving out (an evil spirit) by prayer, ceremony or command **exorcise** *v.*
exorcizador *adj.* que expulsa un espíritu maligno con oraciones, ceremonias u órdenes **exorcisar** *v.*

expedient (ĭk-spē′dē-ənt) *n.* a means to an end
expediente *s.* medio para un fin

explicit (ĭk-splĭs′ĭt) *adj.* clear and fully expressed
explícito *adj.* claro y plenamente expresado

expostulate (ĭk-spŏs'chə-lāt') *v.* to reason earnestly in an effort to correct or dissuade
objetar *v.* razonar en contra con el fin de corregir o disuadir

extraneous (ĭk-strā'nē-əs) *adj.* not relevant; inessential
ajeno *adj.* que no viene al caso; que no es esencial

exult (ĭg-zŭlt') *v.* to feel great joy, especially in conquest or triumph
exultar *v.* regocijarse, especialmente en la conquista o el triunfo

F

fastidious (fă-stĭd'ē-əs) *adj.* displaying meticulous attention to detail
exigente *adj.* que pone atención meticulosa a los detalles

feign (fān) *v.* to give a false appearance of; simulate or counterfeit
fingir *v.* dar falsa apariencia; simular o falsificar

fetter (fĕt'ər) *n.* a shackle or chain; restraint
grillete *s.* grillo o cadena; traba

flinch (flĭnch) *v.* to pull back from something unpleasant or surprising
recular *v.* echarse atrás ante algo desagradable o sorprendente

flouting (flout'ĭng) *adj.* disregarding in a contemptuous way; scorning **flout** *v.*
irrespetuoso *adj.* desconsiderado; altanero; desdeñoso **irrespetar** *v.*

foible (foi'bəl) *n.* a minor weakness or character flaw
punto débil *s.* debilidad menor o falla de carácter

forbearance (fôr-bâr'əns) *n.* self-control; patient restraint
paciencia *s.* autocontrol; dominio de sí mismo

forge (fôrj) *v.* to form, shape, or produce
forjar *v.* formar, moldear o producir

formality (fôr-măl'ĭ-tē) *n.* a procedure that is required or customary in performing a particular activity
formalidad *s.* procedimiento requerido o acostumbrado para hacer una actividad específica

formidable (fôr'mĭ-də-bəl) *adj.* hard to handle or overcome
formidable *adj.* difícil de manejar o de superar

fortitude (fôr'tĭ-tōōd') *n.* the strength to bear misfortune or pain calmly and patiently; firm courage
fortaleza *s.* valor para soportar la desgracia o el dolor con calma y paciencia; fuerza y vigor

frugal (frōō'gəl) *adj.* careful with money; thrifty
frugal *s.* cuidadoso con el dinero; ahorrativo

G

garrulous (găr'ə-ləs) *adj.* rambling in speech; tiresomely talkative
parlanchín *adj.* que divaga al hablar; que habla demasiado

gauntlet (gônt'lĭt) *n.* a punishment in which a person is forced to run between two lines of people who beat the person as he or she passes
baqueta *s.* castigo que obliga a una persona a correr entre dos filas de personas que la golpean al pasar

genially (jēn'yə-lē) *adv.* in a friendly manner
cordialmente *adv.* de manera amistosa

gorge (gôrj) *v.* to stuff with food
atiborrar *v.* llenar de comida

gravity (grăv'ĭ-tē) *n.* seriousness; importance
gravedad *s.* seriedad; importancia

grovel (grŏv'əl) *v.* to behave with exaggerated submission or humility
arrastrarse *v.* comportarse con exagerada sumisión o humildad

guile (gīl) *n.* clever trickery; deceit
maña *s.* truco ingenioso; engaño

H

havoc (hăv′ək) *n.* widespread destruction
  devastación *s.* destrucción extensa

heft (hĕft) *v.* to lift up; hoist
  levantar *v.* alzar; sopesar

hyperbole (hī-pûr′bə-lē) *n.* an exaggeration used for emphasis or effect
  hipérbole *s.* exageración para dar énfasis

I

ignoble (ĭg-nō′bəl) *adj.* not noble; degrading; contemptible
  innoble *adj.* degradante; despreciable

illusory (ĭ-lōō′sə-rē) *adj.* unreal; deceptive
  ilusorio *adj.* irreal; engañoso

imbue (ĭm-byōō′) *v.* to fill with a quality; saturate
  imbuir *v.* llenar de una cualidad; saturar

impassively (ĭm-păs′ĭv-lē) *adv.* without feeling or emotion
  imperturbablemente *adv.* sin emoción

imperialist (ĭm-pîr′ē-ə-lĭst′) *adj.* pertaining to a government's domination of the economic or political affairs of a weaker nation
  imperialista *adj.* dícese de un gobierno que domina los asuntos económicos o políticos de una nación más débil

imperturbable (ĭm′pər-tûr′bə-bəl) *adj.* not easily disturbed; calm
  imperturbable *adj.* que no se altera fácilmente; calmado

impervious (ĭm-pûr′vē-əs) *adj.* incapable of being penetrated; unaffected
  impermeable *adj.* que no se puede penetrar; imperturbable

implacable (ĭm-plăk′ə-bəl) *adj.* impossible to appease; unforgiving
  implacable *adj.* imposible de apaciguar; que no perdona

implicitly (ĭm-plĭs′ĭt-lē) *adv.* without question or doubt
  implícitamente *adv.* sin duda ni cuestionamiento

implore (ĭm-plôr′) *v.* to plead; beg
  implorar *v.* rogar; pedir

imprecation (ĭm′prĭ-kā′shən) *n.* a curse
  imprecación *s.* maldición

impunity (ĭm-pyōō′nĭ-tē) *n.* freedom from punishment or penalty
  impunidad *s.* falta de castigo, penalidad o daño

inane (ĭn-ān′) *adj.* foolish; senseless
  necio *adj.* tonto; sonso

incantation (ĭn′kăn-tā′shən) *n.* a chant intended to bring forth supernatural powers; magic spell
  conjuro *s.* canto para atraer poderes sobrenaturales; hechizo

incarnation (ĭn′kär-nā′shən) *n.* a bodily form taken on by a spirit
  encarnación *s.* forma corporal que adopta un espíritu

incessant (ĭn-sĕs′ənt) *adj.* never ceasing; constant
  incesante *adj.* que no cesa; constante

inconsiderable (ĭn′kən-sĭd′ər-ə-bəl) *adj.* not worth consideration; insignificant
  insignificante *adj.* que no merece consideración

incredulously (ĭn-krĕj′ə-ləs-lē) *adv.* in a manner showing disbelief
  incrédulamente *adv.* con incredulidad

incumbent (ĭn-kŭm′bənt) *adj.* required as a duty or obligation
  obligatorio *adj.* que se impone como deber u obligación

indomitable (ĭn-dŏm′ĭ-tə-bəl) *adj.* not easily discouraged or defeated; unconquerable
  indómito *adj.* que no es fácil de desalentar o vencer; inconquistable

inducement (ĭn-dōōs′mənt) *n.* a motive for action; incentive
  aliciente *s.* estímulo; incentivo

indulge (ĭn-dŭlj′) *v.* to yield to; devote oneself to
  satisfacer *v.* complacer; dedicarse

inexorable (ĭn-ĕk'sər-ə-bəl) *adj.* unyielding; relentless
inexorable *adj.* que no cede; implacable

infallibly (ĭn-făl'ə-blē) *adv.* without fail; certainly
infaliblemente *adv.* sin falla; con seguridad

infamous (ĭn'fə-məs) *adj.* having a bad reputation; notorious
infame *adj.* de mala reputación; notorio

ingeniously (ĭn-jēn'yəs-lē) *adv.* in a way marked by skill and imagination; cleverly
ingeniosamente *adv.* con talento e imaginación; hábilmente

inherently (ĭn-hîr'ənt-lē) *adv.* essentially; naturally
inherentemente *adv.* esencialmente; naturalmente

iniquity (ĭ-nĭk'wĭ-tē) *n.* immorality; wickedness
iniquidad *s.* inmoralidad; maldad

insoluble (ĭn-sŏl'yə-bəl) *adj.* incapable of being solved
insoluble *adj.* imposible de solucionar

inveterate (ĭn-vĕt'ər-ĭt) *adj.* firmly established and deep-rooted
arraigado *adj.* firmemente establecido y enraizado

invincibility (ĭn-vĭn'sə-bĭl'ĭ-tē) *n.* a state of being unbeatable
invencibilidad *s.* calidad de invencible

inviolably (ĭn-vī'ə-lə-blē) *adv.* with absolute security
inviolablemente *adv.* con absoluta seguridad

L

laconic (lə-kŏn'ĭk) *adj.* making use of few words
lacónico *adj.* de pocas palabras

lament (lə-mĕnt') *n.* an audible expression of grief; wail
lamento *s.* expresión audible de dolor; gemido

languid (lăng'gwĭd) *adj.* sluggish; weak
lánguido *adj.* sin fuerza; débil

languish (lăng'gwĭsh) *v.* to be weak or depressed
languidecer *v.* debilitarse o deprimirse

laudable (lô'də-bəl) *adj.* praiseworthy
loable *adj.* digno de admiración

legitimate (lə-jĭt'ə-mĭt) *adj.* born of parents who are legally married to each other
legítimo *adj.* nacido de padres casados legalmente

lissome (lĭs'əm) *adj.* easy and graceful in movement
ágil *adj.* de movimiento fácil y ligero

litany (lĭt'n-ē) *n.* a repetitive chant or recital
letanía *s.* canto o recitación repetitiva

livid (lĭv'ĭd) *adj.* discolored; black and blue
lívido *adj.* pálido; amoratado

loathsome (lōth'səm) *adj.* disgusting; hateful
odioso *adj.* repulsivo; despreciable

loquacious (lō-kwā'shəs) *adj.* very talkative
locuaz *adj.* que habla mucho

lugubrious (lŏŏ-gōō'brē-əs) *adj.* dismal or gloomy to an exaggerated degree
lúgubre *adj.* deprimido o triste a un grado exagerado

luxuriate (lŭg-zhŏŏr'ē-āt') *v.* to take great delight
deleitarse *v.* disfrutar

M

maim (mām) *v.* to disable or permanently wound
lisiar *v.* dejar impedido o herido de por vida

malady (măl'ə-dē) *n.* a disease or disorder; ailment
mal *s.* padecimiento o trastorno; enfermedad

malevolence (mə-lĕv'ə-ləns) *n.* wickedness; ill will
malevolencia *s.* maldad; mala voluntad

malicious (mə-lǐsh′əs) *adj.* spiteful; nasty
  malévolo *adj.* rencoroso; malicioso

malignant (mə-lǐg′nənt) *adj.* extremely harmful
  maligno *adj.* extremadamente dañino

manifest (măn′ə-fěst′) *adj.* obvious; clear
  manifiesto *adj.* obvio; claro

meagerly (mē′gər-lē) *adv.* poorly; scantily
  escasamente *adv.* pobremente

mien (mēn) *n.* the manner in which one carries and conducts oneself; demeanor
  porte *s.* forma en que uno se mueve y se comporta; conducta

mode (mōd) *n.* a current fashion or style
  moda *s.* estilo del momento

morose (mə-rōs′) *adj.* gloomy
  taciturno *adj.* malhumorado; hosco

mortal (môr′tl) *adj.* intense or severe
  mortal *adj.* intenso o severo

mortification (môr′tə-fǐ-kā′shən) *n.* extreme embarrassment; humiliation
  mortificación *s.* vergüenza extrema; humillación

murky (mur′kē) *adj.* cloudy; gloomy
  turbio *adj.* oscuro; lóbrego

myriad (mǐr′ē-əd) *adj.* made up of many different elements or parts
  miriada *adj.* hecho de muchos elementos o piezas

N

narcissistic (när′sǐ-sǐs′tǐk) *adj.* characterized by excessive self-love or self-involvement
  narcisista *adj.* caracterizado por amor propio excesivo o por interés sólo en sí

O

oblige (ə-blīj′) *v.* to make it one's duty to act
  cumplir *v.* actuar por deber

obscure (ŏb-skyŏŏr′) *adj.* not well-known; undistinguished
  oscuro *adj.* desconocido; sin distinción

obsequiously (ŏb-sē′kwē-əs-lē) *adj.* in a subservient or fawning manner
  obsequiosamente *adj.* de manera servil o sumisa

obviate (ŏb′vē-āt′) *v.* to prevent; avert
  obviar *v.* evitar; desviar

odious (ō′dē-əs) *adj.* disgusting; hateful
  odioso *adj.* repugnante; repulsivo

omniscient (ŏm-nǐsh′ənt) *adj.* having complete knowledge; all-knowing
  omnisciente *adj.* con conocimiento completo; que lo sabe todo

oscillate (ŏs′ə-lāt′) *v.* to swing back and forth
  oscilar *v.* moverse de un lado a otro

ostentation (ŏs′tĕn-tā′shən) *n.* a showy display, especially of wealth or knowledge; boastful showiness
  ostentación *s.* despliegue presuntuoso, especialmente de riqueza o de conocimiento; alarde

P

pallor (pǎl′ər) *n.* a lack of color; extreme paleness
  palidez *s.* falta de color; palidez extrema

panegyric (pǎn′ə-jǐr′ǐk) *n.* a public speech of praise
  panegírico *s.* discurso de elogio público

paradox (pǎr′ə-dŏks′) *n.* a statement that appears to be self-contradictory or contrary to common sense but may nevertheless be true
  paradoja *s.* declaración que parece contradictoria pero que es verdadera

parley (pär′lē) *n.* a discussion or conference
  parlamento *s.* discusión o conferencia

parry (pǎr′ē) *v.* to respond by turning aside or evading (a question or argument)
  evadir *v.* responder haciéndose a un lado o evitando una pregunta o discusión

parrying (păr′ē-ĭng) *n.* warding off or turning aside **parry** *v.*
evasión *s.* acto de esquivar o hacerse a un lado **evadir** *v.*

pathological (păth′ə-lŏj′ĭ-kəl) *adj.* diseased; unhealthy
patológico *adj.* enfermo; insalubre

perfidiousness (pər-fĭd′ē-əs-nĭs) *n.* treachery; betrayal
perfidia *s.* deslealtad; traición

pernicious (pər-nĭsh′əs) *adj.* destructive; wicked
pernicioso *adj.* destructivo; malvado

perpetual (pər-pĕch′ōō-əl) *adj.* everlasting; continual
perpetuo *adj.* perenne; continuo

personable (pûr′sə-nə-bəl) *adj.* pleasing in behavior and appearance
atractivo *adj.* de conducta y apariencia agradable

pervade (pər-vād′) *v.* to spread throughout; completely fill
penetrar *v.* saturar por completo; llenar completamente

perversity (pər-vûr′sĭ-tē) *n.* a stubborn determination to act in an inappropriate or unexpected way
perversidad *s.* determinación terca de actuar en forma inadecuada o inesperada

pilgrimage (pĭl′grə-mĭj) *n.* a journey to a sacred place or with a lofty purpose
peregrinación *s.* viaje a un lugar sagrado o con propósito elevado

pivot (pĭv′ət) *adj.* acting as a center around which something turns
central *s.* que está en el centro y a cuyo alrededor gira lo demás

pompous (pŏm′pəs) *adj.* characterized by excessive pride or exaggerated dignity
pomposo *adj.* caracterizado por orgullo excesivo o dignidad exagerada

ponderous (pŏn′dər-əs) *adj.* very heavy
voluminoso *adj.* muy pesado

precept (prē′sĕpt′) *n.* a rule or principle of conduct
precepto *s.* regla o principio de conducta

precipitately (prĭ-sĭp′ĭ-tĭt-lē) *adv.* hurriedly; suddenly
precipitadamente *adv.* apresuradamente; repentinamente

prepossess (prē′pə-zĕs′) *v.* to influence beforehand; prejudice
predisponer *v.* influenciar previamente; prejuiciar

presently (prĕz′ənt-lē) *adv.* in a short time; soon
prontamente *adv.* en poco tiempo; pronto

presumption (prĭ-zŭmp′shən) *n.* bold or outrageous behavior
presunción *s.* atrevimiento

pretension (prĭ-tĕn′shən) *n.* a claim or aspiration
pretensión *s.* reclamo o aspiración

pretentious (prĭ-tĕn′shəs) *adj.* marked by an artificial display intended to impress others
pretencioso *adj.* presumido; ostentoso

primordial (prī-môr′dē-əl) *adj.* first existing; original
primordial *adj.* primero en existir; original

procure (prō-kyŏŏr′) *v.* to obtain; acquire
obtener *v.* adquirir; lograr; gestionar

prodigious (prə-dĭj′əs) *adj.* enormous
prodigioso *adj.* enorme

profess (prə-fĕs′) *v.* to claim belief in or allegiance to
profesar *v.* afirmar una creencia; manifestar lealtad

proficiency (prə-fĭsh′ən-sē) *n.* competence; expertise
pericia *s.* competencia; experiencia

propensity (prə-pĕn′sĭ-tē) *n.* an inclination or tendency
propensión *s.* inclinación o tendencia

propitious (prə-pĭsh′əs) *adj.* favorable; advantageous
propicio *adj.* favorable; ventajoso

prosaic (prō-zā′ĭk) *adj.* commonplace; ordinary; dull
prosaico *adj.* ordinario; tedioso

prostrating (prŏs′trā′tĭng) *adj.* kneeling or bowing down **prostrate** *v.*
postrado *adj.* arrodillado o inclinado **postrarse** *v.*

prowess (prou′ĭs) *n.* superior skill; great ability
destreza *s.* capacidad superior; gran habilidad

prudent (prōōd′nt) *adj.* showing wisdom or good judgment
prudente *adj.* que muestra sabiduría o buen juicio

purge (pûrj) *v.* to cleanse or purify
purgar *v.* limpiar o purificar

Q

quell (kwĕl) *v.* to quiet; suppress
sofocar *v.* aquietar; reprimir

quiescence (kwē-ĕs′əns) *n.* a state of quiet, stillness, or rest; inactivity
quietud *s.* estado de silencio, calmao descanso; inactividad

R

rampart (răm′pärt′) *n.* an embankment or wall for defense against attack
terraplén *s.* parapeto o muralla de defensa

rancor (răng′kər) *n.* bitter resentment; ill will
rencor *s.* resentimiento; inquina

ravage (răv′ĭj) *v.* to cause great damage to; devastate
destruir *v.* causar gran daño; devastar

rebuke (rĭ-byōōk′) *v.* to criticize
reprender *v.* criticar

recapitulate (rē′kə-pĭch′ə-lāt′) *v.* to repeat in concise form; summarize
recapitular *v.* repetir en forma concisa; resumir

redress (rĭ-drĕs′) *n.* repayment for a wrong or injury
reparación *s.* compensación por un mal o herida

reeling (rē′lĭng) *adj.* falling back **reel** *v.*
tambaleante *adj.* que se mueve sin estabilidad; vacilante **tambalearse** *v.*

regime (rā-zhēm′) *n.* a government in power
régimen *s.* gobierno en el poder

relish (rĕl′ĭsh) *v.* to enjoy keenly
gustar *v.* disfrutar profundamente

remonstrate (rĭ-mŏn′strāt′) *v.* to protest or object
protestar *v.* reconvenir u objetar; corregir o disuadir

render (rĕn′dər) *v.* to express in another language or form
vertir *v.* expresar en otro idioma o forma

renounce (rĭ-nouns′) *v.* to give up or reject
renunciar *v.* ceder o rechazar

renown (rĭ-noun′) *n.* fame
renombre *s.* fama

repine (rĭ-pīn′) *v.* to complain; fret
lamentarse *v.* quejarse; afligirse

repression (rĭ-prĕsh′ən) *n.* the act of subduing or keeping down by force
represión *s.* acto de someter o de aplacar por la fuerza

reprieve (rĭ-prēv′) *v.* to cancel a punishment
indultar *v.* cancelar un castigo

reproach (rĭ-prōch′) *v.* to express disapproval of or disappointment in
reprochar *v.* expresar desaprobación o desilusión

reprobate (rĕp′rə-bāt′) *n.* an immoral person; one without principles
réprobo *s.* persona inmoral; alguien sin principios

reproof (rĭ-pr<del>oo</del>f′) *n.* an expression of disapproval; criticism
reprobación *s.* desaprobación; crítica

repugnance (rĭ-pŭg′nəns) *n.* an extreme dislike or distaste
repugnancia *s.* extrema aversión o asco

respite (rĕs′pĭt) *n.* a period of rest or delay
respiro *s.* período de descanso; aplazamiento

retaliate (rĭ-tăl′ē-āt) *v.* to take revenge; pay back in kind
vengarse *v.* tomar revancha; pagar con la misma moneda

retentive (rĭ-tĕn′tĭv) *adj.* able to retain knowledge or information easily
retentivo *adj.* capaz de retener conocimiento o información fácilmente

retinue (rĕt′n-<del>oo</del>′) *n.* a group of people accompanying an important person
comitiva *s.* grupo de personas que acompaña a una persona importante

rudiment (r<del>oo</del>′də-mənt) *n.* a basic principle or skill
rudimento *s.* principio o destreza básica

S

saunter (sôn′tər) *v.* to walk in a slow and leisurely manner; stroll
pasearse *v.* caminar lenta y tranquilamente

schism (sĭz′əm) *n.* a split or division, especially one within a religious group
cisma *s.* división, especialmente de un grupo religioso

scourge (skûrj) *n.* a source of great suffering or destruction
azote *s.* causa de gran sufrimiento o destrucción

scruple (skr<del>oo</del>′pəl) *n.* an uneasiness about the rightness of an action
escrúpulo *s.* inquietud por la corrección de un acto

scrupulous (skr<del>oo</del>′pyə-ləs) *adj.* showing great strictness and care, especially in matters of right and wrong
escrupuloso *adj.* estricto y cuidadoso, especialmente en asuntos del bien y el mal

secular (sĕk′yə-lər) *adj.* unrelated to religion
secular *adj.* seglar; que no está relacionado con la religión

sedately (sĭ-dāt′lē) *adv.* in a composed, dignified manner; calmly
serenamente *adv.* con calma y dignidad; sosegadamente

seditious (sĭ-dĭsh′əs) *adj.* stirring up discontent or rebellion
sedicioso *adj.* que incita descontento o rebelión

semblance (sĕm′bləns) *n.* an outward appearance
apariencia *s.* aspecto

sentiment (sĕn′tə-mənt) *n.* tender or nostalgic feeling
sentimiento *s.* emoción tierna o nostálgica

solace (sŏl′ĭs) *v.* to console; comfort
aliviar *v.* consolar; confortar

solicitation (sə-lĭs′ĭ-tā′shən) *n.* a plea or request
solicitación *s.* ruego o pedido

solicitude (sə-lĭs′ĭ-t<del>oo</del>d′) *n.* care or concern
solicitud *s.* cuidado o preocupación

specious (spē′shəs) *adj.* attractive in a deceptive or insincere way
engañoso *adj.* atractivo de manera insincera o falsa

speculation (spĕk′yə-lā′shən) *n.* a consideration of a subject
especulación *s.* consideración de un tema

statute (stăch′<del>oo</del>t) *n.* a law
estatuto *s.* ley

stint (stĭnt) *v.* to limit to a small amount; give sparingly
escatimar *v.* limitar a una cantidad pequeña; cicatear

submissive (səb-mĭs′ĭv) *adj.* yielding to the control of another
sumiso *adj.* que cede al control de otro

subordinate (sə-bôr′dn-ĭt) *adj.* less important; lower in rank
subordinado *adj.* menos importante; de rango menor

subsistence (səb-sĭs′təns) *n.* the obtaining of the necessities of life; livelihood
subsistencia *s.* obtención de lo necesario para vivir; sustento

succor (sŭk′ər) *n.* aid in a time of need; relief
socorro *s.* ayuda en momento de necesidad; alivio

suffer (sŭf′ər) *v.* to allow; permit
permitir *v.* autorizar; tolerar

superficial (sōō′pər-fĭsh′əl) *adj.* showing little attention to detail; shallow
superficial *adj.* que muestra poca atención al detalle; hueco

superfluity (sōō′pər-flōō′ĭ-tē) *n.* excess; overabundance; oversupply
superfluidad *s.* exceso; demasía; superabundancia

T

talon (tăl′ən) *n.* a claw
garra *s.* zarpa

taut (tôt) *adj.* pulled tight
tirante *adj.* estirado

temper (tĕm′pər) *v.* to make less intense; moderate
atemperar *v.* bajar de intensidad; moderar

temperate (tĕm′pər-ĭt) *adj.* moderate; restrained
templado *adj.* moderado

temporal (tĕm′pər-əl) *adj.* of the material world; not eternal
temporal *adj.* del mundo material; no eterno

timorously (tĭm′ər-əs-lē) *adv.* in a fearful or apprehensive way; timidly
tímidamente *adv.* en forma miedosa o aprensiva

transcend (trăn-sĕnd′) *v.* to go beyond; surpass
trascender *s.* ir más allá; sobrepasar

transport (trăns′pôrt′) *n.* a state of being carried away by emotion; a state of bliss
éxtasis *s.* arrobo; embeleso; estado de dicha

travesty (trăv′ĭ-stē) *n.* a distorted, bizarre imitation
parodia *s.* imitación distorsionada y extraña

tribulation (trĭb′yə-lā′shən) *n.* suffering; great distress
tribulación *s.* sufrimiento; gran dolor

U

uncanny (ŭn-kăn′ē) *adj.* frighteningly unnatural or supernatural; mysterious
extraordinario *adj.* sobrenatural o antinatural; misterioso

unconscionable (ŭn-kŏn′shə-nə-bəl) *adj.* showing no conscience; shockingly unreasonable or unjust
desmedido *adj.* inconsciente; irrazonable o injusto

untainted (ŭn-tān′tĭd) *adj.* not contaminated; unspoiled
inmaculado *adj.* sin contaminación; intacto

unwieldy (ŭn-wēl′dē) *adj.* so large, heavy, or oddly shaped as to be difficult to hold or use
abultado *adj.* tan grande, pesado o raro que es difícil de sostener o usar

usurp (yōō-sûrp′) *v.* to seize unlawfully by force
usurpar *v.* tomar ilegalmente por la fuerza

V

vehement (vē′ə-mənt) *adj.* forceful in expression or feeling; intense
vehemente *adj.* de expresión o sentimiento fuerte; intenso

vermin (vûr′mĭn) *n.* small animals that are destructive or carriers of disease
sabandijas *s.* animales pequeños destructivos o portadores de enfermedades

vie (vī) *v.* to compete
contender *v.* competir

vitiate (vĭsh′ē-āt′) *v.* to destroy the quality of; corrupt; debase
viciar *v.* dañar o corromper física o moralmente

vivacity (vĭ-văs′ĭ-tē) *n.* liveliness
vivacidad *s.* viveza

vulnerable (vŭl′nər-ə-bəl) *adj.* open to attack; easily hurt
vulnerable *adj.* abierto al ataque; fácil de lastimar

W

wary (wâr′ē) *adj.* cautious; on one's guard
precavido *adj.* cauto; en guardia

whetted (hwĕt′ĭd) *adj.* sharpened **whet** *v.*
afilado *adj.* de bordes cortantes **afilar** *v.*

wield (wēld) *v.* to handle skillfully
manejar *v.* realizar con destreza

wince (wĭns) *v.* to spring back involuntarily, as in pain
estremecerse *v.* contraerse involuntariamente por un dolor

writhing (rī′thĭng) *adj.* twisting and turning in pain **writhe** *v.*
retorcido *adj.* contraído por el dolor **retorcer** *v.*

Z

zealous (zĕl′əs) *adj.* filled with enthusiasm; eager
fervoroso *adj.* lleno de entusiasmo; dispuesto

Pronunciation Key

Symbol	Examples	Symbol	Examples	Symbol	Examples
ă	at, gas	m	man, seem	v	van, save
ā	ape, day	n	night, mitten	w	web, twice
ä	father, barn	ng	sing, anger	y	yard, lawyer
âr	fair, dare	ŏ	odd, not	z	zoo, reason
b	bell, table	ō	open, road, grow	zh	treasure, garage
ch	chin, lunch	ô	awful, bought, horse	ə	awake, even, pencil,
d	dig, bored	oi	coin, boy		pilot, focus
ĕ	egg, ten	o͝o	look, full	ər	perform, letter
ē	evil, see, meal	o͞o	root, glue, through		
f	fall, laugh, phrase	ou	out, cow		**Sounds in Foreign Words**
g	gold, big	p	pig, cap	KH	*German* ich, auch;
h	hit, inhale	r	rose, star		*Scottish* loch
hw	white, everywhere	s	sit, face	N	*French* entre, bon, fin
ĭ	inch, fit	sh	she, mash	œ	*French* feu, cœur;
ī	idle, my, tried	t	tap, hopped		*German* schön
îr	dear, here	th	thing, with	ü	*French* utile, rue;
j	jar, gem, badge	*th*	then, other		*German* grün
k	keep, cat, luck	ŭ	up, nut		
l	load, rattle	ûr	fur, earn, bird, worm		

Stress Marks

′ This mark indicates that the preceding syllable receives the primary stress. For example, in the word *language,* the first syllable is stressed: lăng′gwĭj.

′ This mark is used only in words in which more than one syllable is stressed. It indicates that the preceding syllable is stressed, but somewhat more weakly than the syllable receiving the primary stress. In the word *literature,* for example, the first syllable receives the primary stress, and the last syllable receives a weaker stress: lĭt′ər-ə-cho͝or′.

Adapted from *The American Heritage Dictionary of the English Language, Third Edition;* Copyright © 1992 by Houghton Mifflin Company. Used with the permission of Houghton Mifflin Company.

Index of Fine Art

Index of Skills

Literary Concepts

Alexandrine, 1450

Allegory, 502–503, 1428

Alliteration. *See* Poetic elements.

Allusion, 476, 479, 480, 945, 1428

Analogy, 1428

Anapest, 1441. *See also* Meter.

Antagonist, 322, 1429

Antithesis, 741, 1429

Aphorism, 648, 656, 1429

Apostrophe. *See* Figurative language.

Argumentation, 493, 500, 631, 637, 1429

Aside, 324, 346, 505, 1429

Assonance. *See* Poetic elements.

Author's attitude. *See* Tone. *See also* Tone, recognizing *under* Reading and Critical Thinking Skills.

Author's perspective, 659, 1167. *See also* Author's perspective *under* Reading and Critical Thinking Skills.

Author's purpose (motivation), 98, 104, 306, 548, 552, 798, 861, 866, 929, 972, 1002, 1096, 1174, 1261–1262, 1430. *See also* Author's purpose (motivation) *under* Reading and Critical Thinking Skills.

Autobiography, 252, 256, 1430

Ballad, 192, 198, 1430

    folk, 745, 766, 1430

    literary, 745, 766, 1430

Biography, 547, 659, 664, 1430

Blank verse. *See* Poetic elements.

Book review, 1071

Caesura, 31, 1428

Catastrophe, 322

Character(s), 29, 66, 81, 93, 111, 152, 209, 222, 240, 250, 380, 381, 399, 420, 599, 629, 745, 883, 888, 950, 953, 961, 1029, 1046, 1210, 1217, 1272, 1299, 1431

Characterization, 111, 225, 237, 346, 1042, 1431

Character traits, 63, 525

Chorus, 321

Climax, 177, 897, 1034, 1042, 1445. *See also* Plot.

Comedy, 321, 1432

    Restoration, 521

Comic relief, 321, 1432

Conceit, metaphysical, 449, 450, 451, 456, 1436

Conflict, 171, 177, 180, 190, 222, 309, 420, 745, 766, 883, 1263, 1272, 1279, 1299

    external and internal, 180, 190, 222, 1263, 1272, 1279, 1432

Connotation, 658, 744, 1248, 1432

Consonance. *See* Poetic elements.

Contrast, 554, 1432

Controlling image. *See* Poetic elements.

Couplet. *See* Poetic elements.

Cultural hero, 1438

Dactyl, 1441. *See also* Meter.

Denotation, 658, 744, 1432

Denouement, 1445. *See also* Plot.

Description, 263, 681, 690, 1433, 1358

Details, 84, 96, 263

Dialect, 192, 1274, 1279, 1433

Dialogue, 198, 263, 325, 674, 679, 953, 994, 1135, 1141, 1254, 1258, 1433

Diary, 525, 532, 547, 674, 1434

Diction, 29, 450, 480, 491, 739, 1073, 1145, 1155, 1248, 1252, 1434

Drama, 325, 1433, 1434. *See also* Play.

Dramatic monologue. *See* Poetic elements.

Dynamic character, 1431. *See also* Character.

Elegy, 672, 1455

End rhyme, 1447. *See also* Poetic elements; Rhyme scheme.

Epic, 19, 28–29, 31, 63, 81, 240, 250, 1435

    characteristics of, 28–29, 30, 1435

Epic simile. *See* Poetic elements.

Epigram, 534, 538, 1435

Epiphany, 1022

Epitaph, 199, 458, 461, 1435

Epithet, 28, 82, 1435

Essay, 442, 447, 546, 631, 1155, 1302, 1308, 1435–1436

    formal, 547, 1436

    humorous, 417

    informal, 547, 548, 552, 656, 693, 1436

    informative, 1302, 1308

    personal, 1167, 1174, 1436

    persuasive, 447, 577, 582, 693, 1302, 1308, 1435

Exposition, 177, 896, 1034, 1445. *See also* Plot.

Extended metaphor. *See* Figurative language.

Fable, 540, 544, 1436

Falling action, 177, 896, 1034, 1445. *See also* Plot.

Fantasy, 590, 607, 1302, 1436

Farce, 1436

Fiction, 868, 869, 1436–1437

Figurative language, 306, 362, 505, 738, 793, 1054, 1241, 1437

    apostrophe, 773, 779, 1429

    extended metaphor, 449, 451, 456, 852, 945, 961, 1436, 1439

    hyperbole, 463, 468, 793, 1439

    metaphor, 84, 306, 449, 451, 456, 468, 471, 474, 793, 852, 945, 961, 1054, 1436, 1439, 1441

    personification, 153, 666, 672, 796, 1444

    simile, 66, 81, 104, 306, 738, 766, 793, 1054, 1449

    synecdoche, 1452

Flashback, 1157, 1164, 1437, 1366

Foil, 1437

Folk ballad, 745, 766, 1430

Folk tale, 914, 929, 1437

Reading and Critical Thinking Skills

main idea and supporting details, 1338, 1339
problem-solution, 1338, 1343
Peer discussion, 76, 82, 96, 167, 177, 191, 199, 203, 222, 250, 263, 288, 421, 429, 448, 571, 642, 716, 720, 785, 798, 884, 935, 993, 1054, 1112, 1142, 1167
Performance reviews, 61–62
Personal experiences. *See* Connections to personal experiences.
Personal response, 63, 81, 93, 96, 104, 137, 152, 167, 177, 190, 198, 222, 237, 250, 256, 285, 287, 293, 298, 303, 309, 436, 437, 440, 444, 453, 459, 464, 466, 474, 477, 535, 541, 544, 558, 607, 652, 674, 711, 733, 737, 774, 785, 802, 845, 852, 859, 862, 912, 941, 943, 945, 948, 950, 957, 961, 964, 967, 972, 989, 992, 1002, 1019, 1029, 1042, 1054, 1069, 1073, 1078, 1085, 1089, 1092, 1096, 1111, 1124, 1133, 1141, 1155, 1164, 1174, 1207, 1210, 1217, 1227, 1239, 1246, 1248, 1252, 1258, 1272, 1279, 1286, 1299, 1308
Persuasion, modes of
deceptive, 1372, 1385
faulty, 1385
logical, 631, 637, 793, 1386
Persuasive techniques
evaluating, 1127, 1133, 1385
identifying, 793, 1385
Plot, analyzing, 1034, 1042
Prior knowledge, activating, 30, 63, 81, 84, 96, 98, 104, 111, 137, 140, 141, 152, 154, 167, 177, 180, 190, 192, 198, 209, 222, 225, 237, 250, 252, 256, 283, 287, 289, 293, 297, 300, 302, 306, 311, 381, 399, 419, 420, 435, 440, 442, 447, 451, 456, 458, 461, 463, 468, 474, 476, 479, 480, 491, 493, 500, 525, 532, 534, 538, 548, 552, 554, 564, 577, 582, 590, 607, 611, 629, 631, 637, 648, 656, 659, 664, 666, 672, 674, 679, 690, 709, 715, 720, 725, 738, 741, 744, 745, 766, 773, 779, 781, 782, 790, 796, 798, 806, 839, 852, 854, 859, 861, 866, 872, 883, 888, 896, 900, 929, 941, 945, 947, 950, 953, 961, 963, 967, 972, 988, 992, 994, 1002, 1006, 1019, 1022, 1029, 1034, 1042, 1046, 1054, 1064, 1073, 1076, 1081, 1083, 1085, 1087, 1096, 1107, 1111, 1114, 1124, 1127, 1133, 1135, 1141, 1145, 1155, 1157, 1164, 1167, 1174, 1199, 1207, 1210, 1220, 1227, 1229, 1234, 1239, 1246, 1252, 1263, 1272, 1274, 1279, 1281, 1286, 1289, 1299, 1308, 1324
Problem-solution, 1338, 1343
Purposes for reading, 1324–1325. *See also* Prior knowledge, activating.
Reader's experiences. *See* Connections to personal experiences.
Reading for information, 1334–1337
magazine article, 1336
textbook, 1334–1335
web page, 1337
Reasoning, faulty
cause-and-effect fallacy, 1385
circular reasoning, 1385
either-or fallacy, 1385
overgeneralization, 1385

Satire, analyzing, 1220, 1227
Sensory language, analyzing, 302, 306, 766
Silent reading (reinforced throughout)
Sources, evaluating, 180, 190, 427, 1143, 1241, 1374, 1382
Speaker(s)
analyzing, 839, 852, 1241
comparing, 773, 779
Strategies for reading. *See also* Connections; Monitoring.
clarifying, 6–7, 9, 10, 11, 29, 81, 89, 93, 96, 137, 167, 190, 256, 283, 287, 309, 311, 346, 362, 381, 399, 447, 456, 468, 474, 476, 479, 480, 491, 500, 532, 582, 607, 610, 629, 664, 690, 720, 744, 766, 775, 779, 785, 790, 796, 802, 806, 845, 850, 883, 943, 950, 955, 961, 964, 967, 972, 988, 992, 1002, 1019, 1029, 1054, 1085, 1092, 1096, 1108, 1111, 1133, 1141, 1164, 1207, 1217, 1227, 1236, 1246, 1250, 1252, 1279, 1286, 1324
connecting, 6–7, 9, 10, 1324
evaluating, 6–7, 9, 10, 11, 29, 51, 63, 81, 89, 93, 96, 104, 152, 157, 177, 198, 222, 237, 250, 256, 287, 291, 293, 300, 304, 306, 322, 346, 362, 381, 420, 436, 440, 442, 447, 454, 468, 474, 532, 552, 564, 584, 620, 679, 711, 733, 859, 862, 896, 912, 967, 989, 1057, 1069, 1207, 1262, 1325, 1326
predicting, 6–7, 9, 10, 11, 29, 141, 152, 296, 322, 399, 450, 508, 547, 585, 629, 869, 888, 896, 1004, 1005, 1262, 1289, 1299, 1324, 1326
previewing, 1324
questioning, 6–7, 9, 29, 51, 89, 104, 137, 152, 198, 222, 237, 285, 287, 291, 293, 346, 437, 444, 453, 491, 508, 532, 598, 610, 629, 779, 844, 852, 945, 964, 1042, 1109, 1324
summarizing, 1324
visualizing, 6–7, 9, 29, 63, 81, 84, 89, 590, 607, 1087, 1092, 1324, 1326
Strategies for functional reading
campus maps, 1345
college applications, 1346–1347
guide to colleges, 1344
job application, 1350–1351
online job search, 1348–1349
workplace document, 1352–1353
Strategies for reading types of literature
autobiography, 252, 256
ballads, 192, 198
drama, 325, 399, 420
encyclopedia article, 1327
epic poetry, 29, 1326
irony in modern literature, 1005
magazine aricle, 1327, 1336
memoir, 1114
metaphysical poetry, 450
modern poetry, 1064, 1073
narrative poetry, 209, 222, 745, 766
newspaper, 1327
nonfiction, 547, 1326

online text, 1327, 1337
poetry, 794, 796, 1326
satire, 585, 693
Shakespeare, 325
short story, 1326
social criticism, 1262
sonnet form, 296
test selection, 508, 822
Victorian fiction, 869
Structure, analyzing, 154, 167, 493, 741, 969, 972, 1229, 1244, 1246
Study strategies
   in-depth reading, 63, 81, 137, 177, 198, 209, 250, 283, 346, 435, 471, 564, 611, 717, 745, 781, 866, 938, 945, 988, 1064, 1074, 1092, 1133, 1135, 1167, 1182, 1184, 1197, 1217, 1234, 1246, 1252, 1258, 1272, 1279, 1286, 1299, 1308, 1384
   outlining, 82, 138, 312, 428, 501, 897, 914, 1101, 1208, 1384
   scanning, 63, 81, 137, 190, 198, 237, 346, 440, 461, 474, 552, 620, 672, 738, 806, 883, 950, 1042, 1054, 1383
   skimming, 325, 508, 510, 822, 945, 993, 1383
   study guide questions, 44, 51, 89, 93, 140, 285, 291, 298, 303, 304, 309, 380, 436, 437, 444, 453, 454, 464, 466, 477, 535, 541, 558, 599, 610, 652, 711, 731, 733, 737, 775, 782, 785, 800, 802, 845, 847, 850, 856, 862, 943, 948, 955, 957, 964, 989, 1069, 1078, 1089, 1108, 1109, 1236, 1250, 1283
   taking notes, 4, 5, 64, 98, 111, 180, 192, 209, 252, 289, 324, 427, 463, 493, 648, 709, 745, 781, 791, 798, 822, 854, 866, 869, 872, 888, 900, 941, 947, 953, 963, 988, 992, 994, 1002, 1006, 1020, 1022, 1046, 1076, 1087, 1112, 1114, 1127, 1134, 1157, 1184, 1199, 1220, 1244, 1248, 1254, 1314, 1384
Style, analyzing, 104, 168, 421, 621, 664, 739, 744, 766, 779, 796, 972, 992, 1074, 1133, 1185, 1272, 1320
Summarizing, 29, 297, 300, 308, 381, 435, 540, 547, 866, 914, 929, 1324, 1375, 1382
Text organizers, using, 104
Text structures
   cause and effect, 1325, 1360, 1368
   chronological, 1366
   compare and contrast, 493, 1325, 1360, 1368
   frame story, 154, 167, 1438
   main idea and supporting details, 1229
   problem and solution, 493, 1367
   spatial, 1360, 1364
   thesis, antithesis, and synthesis, 741
Tone. *See also* Tone *under* Literary Concepts.
   analyzing, 839, 852, 1078, 1081, 1109, 1164, 1282
   recognizing, 471, 474, 715
   word choice and, 674, 679
Unconventional works, reading, 1254, 1258
Vocabulary. *See* Vocabulary Skills.

Writer's motivation, stance, position. *See* Author's perspective; Author's purpose; Credibility.

Vocabulary Skills

Analogies, 224, 852, 945, 1054, 1317, 1332
Antonyms, 105, 138, 170, 178, 574, 583, 608, 623, 645, 657, 1134, 1330–1331
Archaic language, 658, 701
Base words, 1104, 1329
Building vocabulary, 53, 65, 83, 105, 138, 153, 170, 178, 206, 224, 238, 251, 266, 432, 501, 553, 565, 574, 583, 608, 623, 630, 638, 645, 657, 665, 680, 691, 816, 867, 884, 897, 938, 1020, 1031, 1055, 1104, 1125, 1134, 1156, 1165, 1172, 1182, 1208, 1218, 1228, 1273, 1301, 1310, 1317
Coined words, 833, 947, 950, 983, 1193
Connotation, 645, 1331
Context clues
   comparison, 938, 1328
   contrast, 1328
   definition or restatement, 938, 1328
   example, 1328
   general context, 1328
   idioms and slang, 1328
   inference, 65, 138, 153, 238, 251, 266, 501, 608, 630, 657, 665, 691, 884, 938, 1175, 1310, 1333
Decoding multisyllabic words, 1333
Denotation, 645, 1228, 1273, 1331
Dialect, 23, 701, 994
Etymology. *See* Word origins.
Euphemism, 833
Figurative language. *See* Figurative language *under* Literary Concepts; Figurative language, using, *under* Writing Skills, Modes, and Formats.
History of English, 19, 23, 26, 277, 519, 701, 833, 983, 1193
Homographs, 816
Homonyms, 816, 1332
Homophones, 816, 1332
Idioms, 565, 680, 1218
Meaning clues, 553, 565, 638, 867, 897, 1031, 1055, 1124, 1165, 1182. *See also* Context clues.
Multiple-meaning words, 266, 1332
Obsolete inflections, 277, 441
Prefixes, 153, 206, 565, 680, 1104, 1329
Reference materials, using
   dictionaries, 206, 266, 432, 574, 1374
   thesauruses, 574, 583, 623, 657, 1134, 1156
Roots, 432, 1104, 1329
Slang, 701, 833, 983
Specialized vocabulary, 1333
Suffixes, 153, 565, 680, 1104, 1228, 1329
   derivational, 1104
   inflectional, 1104
Synonyms, 83, 105, 138, 170, 178, 553, 574, 608, 623, 645, 1156, 1208, 1330
   phrases, 1301
Technical language, 833, 983, 1193

Grammar, Usage, and Mechanics

Writing Skills, Modes, and Formats

Inquiry and Research

Assessment

Index of Titles and Authors

Acknowledgments *(continued)*

Doubleday: Excerpts from *The Iliad* by Homer, translated by Robert Fitzgerald. Copyright © 1974 by Robert Fitzgerald. Used by permission of Doubleday, a division of Bantam Doubleday Dell Publishing Group, Inc.

Yale University Press: "The Seafarer" and "The Wanderer," from *Poems and Prose from the Old English*, translated by Burton Raffel. Copyright © 1997 by Yale University Press. Used by permission of Yale University Press.

Rosanna White Norton: "The Wife's Lament," from *The Women Poets in English*, edited by Ann Stanford. Reprinted by permission of Rosanna White Norton, trustee.

Penguin Books Ltd: Excerpts from *A History of the English Church and People* by Bede, translated by Leo Sherley-Price, revised translation by R. E. Latham (Penguin Classics 1955, revised edition 1968); Copyright © 1955, 1968 by Leo Sherley-Price. Excerpts from "The Prologue," "The Pardoner's Prologue," "The Pardoner's Tale," "The Wife of Bath's Prologue," and "The Wife of Bath's Tale," from *The Canterbury Tales* by Geoffrey Chaucer, translated by Nevill Coghill. (Penguin Classics 1951, fourth revised edition 1977). Copyright © 1951, 1958, 1960, 1975, 1977 by Nevill Coghill. Excerpts from Chapter 1 from *The Book of Margery Kempe*, translated by B. A. Windeatt (Penguin Classics, 1985); Copyright © 1985 B. A. Windeatt. Reproduced by permission of Penguin Books Ltd.

The Folio Society: Excerpts from *The Pastons: A Family in the Wars of the Roses*, edited by Richard Barber (The Folio Society 1981; Boydell Press [Woodbridge, U.K., and Rochester, NY] 1993). Reprinted by permission of The Folio Society.

Jennifer Yu: "Her Three-Inch Feet," from the Niskayuna High School (NY) Web Page, by Jennifer Yu. Reprinted with the permission of Jennifer Yu.

University of Chicago Press: Excerpts from *Sir Gawain and the Green Knight*, translated by John Gardner. Copyright © 1965 by The University of Chicago. Reprinted by permission of The University of Chicago Press.

Northwestern University Press: From the preface by William Caxton from *Le Morte d'Arthur*, parts seven and eight by Sir Thomas Malory, edited by D. S. Brewer. Copyright © 1968 by D. S. Brewer. Reprinted by permission.

Viking Penguin: "The Siege of Lanka" and "Rama and Ravana in Battle," from *The Ramayana*, translated by R. K. Narayan. Copyright © 1972 by R. K. Narayan. Used by permission of Viking Penguin, a division of Penguin Putnam Inc.

Mustang Publishing: "Whomp!" from *Essays That Worked: 50 Essays from Successful Applications to the Nation's Top Colleges*, edited by Boykin Curry & Brian Kasbar. Copyright © 1986. Reprinted by permission of Mustang Publishing.

Unit Two

University of Alabama Press: Sonnet 169 and Sonnet 292 from *Petrarch: Selected Poems*, English translation by Anthony Mortimer, Copyright © 1977 by The University of Alabama Press. Used by permission of The University of Alabama Press.

Barbara Hogenson Agency: "The Macbeth Murder Mystery" by James Thurber, from *My World—And Welcome to It*. Copyright © 1942 by James Thurber. Copyright © renewed 1970 by Helen Thurber and Rosemary A. Thurber. Reprinted by arrangement with Rosemary A. Thurber and the Barbara Hogenson Agency.

The New York Times: "Network Helps Children Cope with Serious Illness" by Catherine Greenman, from *The New York Times*, May, 28, 1998. Copyright © 1998 by *The New York Times*. Reprinted by permission.

Unit Three

University of California Press: Excerpts from *Diary of Samuel Pepys*, edited by Robert Latham and William Matthews. Copyright © 1972–1986 by The Master, Fellows and Scholars of Magdalen College, Cambridge, Robert Latham, and the

Executors of William Matthews. Reprinted by permission of the University of California Press, Berkeley, California.

University of Illinois Press: "The Acorn and the Pumpkin" and "The Value of Knowledge," from *The Fables of La Fontaine*, translated by Norman R. Shapiro. Copyright © 1985, 1988 by Norman R. Shapiro. Used with the permission of the author and of the University of Illinois Press.

The Washington Post: "A New Modest Proposal" by Ellen Goodman, from *The Boston Globe*, August, 1996. Copyright © 1996, *The Washington Post*. Reprinted with permission of The Washington Post Writers Group.

Unit Four

Lucien Stryk: Selected haiku from *Penguin Book of Zen Poetry*, edited and translated by Lucien Stryk and Takashi Ikemoto. London: Penguin Books Ltd., 1977. Reprinted by permission of the author.

Harcourt Brace & Company: "The Lotus-Blossom Cowers," from *Heinrich Heine: Paradox and Poet, The Poems* by Louis Untermeyer, copyright 1937 by Harcourt Brace & Company and renewed 1965 by Louis Untermeyer, reprinted by permission of the publisher.

Random House, Inc.: "Why Leaves Turn Color in the Fall," from *A Natural History of the Senses* by Diane Ackerman. Copyright © 1990 by Diane Ackerman. Reprinted by permission of Random House, Inc.

Unit Five

L. A. Wilson: "No One Stops to Say 'Thank You' Anymore" by L. A. Wilson, from *The Humanist*, November/December 1997. Copyright © 1997 by L. A. Wilson. Reprinted with the permission of the author.

Henry Holt and Company, Inc., and The Society of Authors: "To an Athlete Dying Young" and "When I Was One-and-Twenty," from *The Collected Poems of A. E. Housman* by A. E. Housman. Copyright 1939, 1940 by Henry Holt & Co., Inc. Copyright © 1967 by Robert E. Symons. Reprinted by permission of Henry Holt and Company, Inc., and The Society of Authors as the literary representative of the Estates of A. E. Housman.

Unit Six

Simon & Schuster, Inc.: "Sailing to Byzantium" by William Butler Yeats, Copyright 1928 by Macmillan Publishing Company, renewed 1956 by Georgie Yeats, and "The Second Coming" by William Butler Yeats, Copyright 1924 by Macmillan Publishing Company, renewed 1952 by Bertha Georgie Yeats, from *The Poems of W. B. Yeats: A New Edition*, edited by Richard J. Finneran. Reprinted with the permission of Simon & Schuster, Inc.

Viking Penguin and Laurence Pollinger Ltd.: "The Rocking-Horse Winner" by D. H. Lawrence; Copyright 1933 by the Estate of D. H. Lawrence, renewed © 1961 by Angelo Ravagli and C. M. Weekley, Executors of the Estate of Frieda Lawrence Ravagli. From *Complete Short Stories of D. H. Lawrence* by D. H. Lawrence. Used by permission of Viking Penguin, a division of Penguin Putnam Inc., and Laurence Pollinger Ltd.

Alfred A. Knopf, Inc. and The Society of Authors: "A Cup of Tea," from *The Short Stories of Katherine Mansfield* by Katherine Mansfield. Copyright 1923 by Alfred A. Knopf, Inc., and renewed 1951 by John Middleton Murry. Reprinted by permission of the publisher and The Society of Authors.

Harcourt Brace & Company and The Hogarth Press: "The Duchess and the Jeweller," from *A Haunted House and Other Short Stories* by Virginia Woolf; Copyright 1944 and renewed 1972 by Harcourt Brace & Company, reprinted by permission of the publisher and the Hogarth Press.

Cambridge University Press: Excerpt from *Virginia Woolf* by E. M. Forster. Reprinted with the permission of Cambridge University Press.

University of the South: "A Personal Memoir" by Robert Giroux, from *The Oxford Book of Literary Anecdotes*. First published in *The Sewanee Review*, vol. 74, no. 1, Winter 1966. Copyright © 1966 by the University of the South. Reprinted with the permission of the editor.

Harcourt Brace & Company and Faber and Faber Limited: "Preludes," from *Collected Poems 1909–1962* by T. S. Eliot, copyright 1936 by Harcourt Brace & Company, copyright © 1963, 1964 by T. S. Eliot, reprinted by permission of the publisher and Faber and Faber Limited. "The Hollow Men" by T. S. Eliot, from *Collected Poems 1909–1962*. Copyright 1936 by Harcourt Brace & Company, copyright © 1964, 1963 by T. S. Eliot. "The Naming of Cats" by T. S. Eliot, from *Old Possum's Book of Practical Cats*. Copyright 1939 by T. S. Eliot and renewed 1967 by Esme Valerie Eliot. Reprinted by permission of Harcourt Brace & Company and Faber and Faber Limited.

Random House, Inc.: "Musée des Beaux Arts" and "The Unknown Citizen," from *W. H. Auden: Collected Poems* by W. H. Auden, edited by Edward Mendelson. Copyright © 1940 and renewed 1968 by W. H. Auden. Reprinted by permission of Random House, Inc.

Random House, Inc., and Faber and Faber Ltd.: "What I Expected," from *Selected Poems* by Stephen Spender. Copyright © 1934 and renewed 1962 by Stephen Spender. Reprinted by permission of Random House, Inc., and Faber and Faber Ltd.

New Directions Publishing Corporation and David Higham Associates: "Do Not Go Gentle into That Good Night" and "In My Craft or Sullen Art," from *The Poems of Dylan Thomas* by Dylan Thomas. Copyright 1946 by New Directions Publishing Corporation, Copyright 1952 by Dylan Thomas. Reprinted by permission of New Directions Publishing Corporation and David Higham Associates.

Indiana University Press and Fondo de Cultura Económica: "Writing/Escritura," from *Selected Poems of Octavio Paz*, edited and translated by Muriel Rukeyser. Copyright © 1963 by Octavio Paz and Muriel Rukeyser. Reprinted by permission of Indiana University Press and Fondo de Cultura Económica, Mexico.

Penguin Putnam Inc. and G. T. Sassoon: "Dreamers," from *Collected Poems of Siegfried Sassoon* by Siegfried Sassoon. Copyright 1918, 1920 by E. P. Dutton. Copyright 1936, 1946, 1947, 1948 by Siegfried Sassoon. Used by permission of Viking Penguin, a division of Penguin Putnam Inc., and George Sassoon.

Paul Berry, Literary Executor, and Virago Press, London: Excerpts from *Testament of Youth* by Vera Brittain are included with the permission of Paul Berry, literary executor for Vera Brittain, Victor Gollanez and The Virago Press, London.

Curtis Brown Ltd.: "Be Ye Men of Valour," from *Blood, Toil, Tears and Sweat* by Winston Churchill. Reproduced with permission of Curtis Brown Ltd., London, on behalf of the Estate of Sir Winston S. Churchill. Copyright © the Estate of Sir Winston S. Churchill. "The Demon Lover," from *The Collected Stories of Elizabeth Bowen* by Elizabeth Bowen. Copyright © 1941 by Elizabeth Bowen. Reproduced by permission of Curtis Brown Ltd., London.

Faber and Faber Limited: "To My Mother," from *Collected Poems* by George Barker. Copyright © 1987 by George Barker. Reprinted by permission of Faber and Faber Ltd.

Hill and Wang: Excerpt from *Night* by Elie Wiesel. Copyright © 1960 by MacGibbon & Kee. Copyright © 1988 by The Collins Publishing Group. Reprinted by permission of Hill and Wang, a division of Farrar, Straus & Giroux, Inc.

Pantheon Books: Excerpts from *Letters from Westerbork* by Etty Hillesum, translated by Arnold J. Pomerans. Translation copyright © 1986 by Random House, Inc. Reprinted by permission of Pantheon Books, a division of Random House, Inc.

Reece Halsey Agency: Excerpt from "Words and Behavior," from *Collected Essays* by Aldous Huxley. Reprinted by permission of Dorris Halsey, as agent for the Aldous Huxley Literary Estate.

Harcourt Brace & Company: "A Hanging," from *Shooting an Elephant and Other Essays* by George Orwell, copyright 1950 by Sonia Brownell Orwell and renewed 1978 by Sonia Pitt-Rivers. Reprinted by permission of Harcourt Brace & Company.

Unit Seven

Grove/Atlantic, Inc., and Murray Pollinger: "At the Pitt-Rivers," from *Pack of Cards and Other Stories* by Penelope Lively. Copyright © 1986 by Penelope Lively. Used by permission of Grove/Atlantic, Inc., and Murray Pollinger, Literary Agent.

Simon & Schuster and Jonathan Clowes Ltd.: "A Sunrise on the Veld," from *African Stories* by Doris Lessing. Copyright © 1965 by Doris Lessing; Copyright renewed © 1993 by Doris Lessing. Reprinted by permission of Simon & Schuster, Inc., and of Jonathan Clowes Limited, London, on behalf of Doris Lessing.

Georges Borchardt, Inc.: "The First Year of My Life," from *The Stories of Muriel Spark* by Muriel Spark. (New York: E. P. Dutton, 1985) Copyright © 1985 by Copyright Administration. Reprinted by permission of Georges Borchardt, Inc. and David Higham Associates on behalf of Muriel Spark. This story originally appeared in *The New Yorker.*

Houghton Mifflin Company and McClelland & Stewart, Inc.: "The Moment," from *Morning in the Burned House* by Margaret Atwood. Copyright © 1995 by Margaret Atwood. Reprinted by permission of Houghton Mifflin Company and McClelland & Stewart, Inc., the Canadian Publishers. All rights reserved.

Farrar, Straus & Giroux, Inc., and Faber and Faber Ltd.: "Digging," from *Poems 1965–1975* by Seamus Heaney. Copyright © 1980 by Seamus Heaney. Used by arrangement with Farrar, Straus & Giroux, Inc., and Faber and Faber Ltd. All rights reserved.

Faber and Faber Ltd.: "The Horses," from *The Hawk in the Rain* by Ted Hughes. Reprinted by permission of Faber and Faber Ltd.

Farrar, Straus & Giroux, Inc.: Excerpt from *Crediting Poetry: The Nobel Lecture* by Seamus Heaney. Copyright © 1995 by The Nobel Foundation. Reprinted by permission of Farrar, Straus & Giroux, Inc.

The Ecco Press: "In Music," from *Provinces* by Czeslaw Milosz. Copyright © 1991 by Czeslaw Milosz Royalties Inc. First printed by The Ecco Press in 1991. Reprinted by permission of The Ecco Press.

New Directions Publishing Corp.: "The Frog Prince" and "Not Waving but Drowning," from *Collected Poems* by Stevie Smith. Copyright © 1972 by New Directions Publishing Corp. Reprinted by permission of New Directions Publishing Corp.

Grove/Atlantic, Inc., and Faber and Faber Ltd.: "That's All," from *Revue Sketches* by Harold Pinter. Copyright © 1966 by H. Pinter Ltd. Used by permission of Grove/Atlantic, Inc., and Faber and Faber Ltd.

Viking Penguin: "The Distant Past," from *Angels at the Ritz and Other Stories* by William Trevor. Copyright © 1975 by William Trevor. Used by permission of Viking Penguin, a division of Penguin Putnam Inc.

Doubleday and Harold Ober Associates: "Civil Peace," from *Girls at War and Other Stories* by Chinua Achebe. Copyright © 1972, 1973 by Chinua Achebe. Used by permission of Doubleday, a division of Bantam Doubleday Dell Publishing Group, Inc., and Harold Ober Associates Incorporated.

Wole Soyinka: "Telephone Conversation" by Wole Soyinka, first published in *Reflections: Nigerian Prose and Verse,* edited by Frances Ademola. Copyright © Wole Soyinka. Reprinted by permission of Wole Soyinka.

Farrar, Straus & Giroux, Inc.: "XXIII," from *Midsummer* by Derek Walcott. Copyright © 1984 by Derek Walcott. Used by arrangement with Farrar, Straus & Giroux, Inc. All rights reserved.

Russell & Volkening, Inc.: "Six Feet of the Country," from *Six Feet of the Country and Other Stories* by Nadine Gordimer. Copyright © 1956 by Nadine Gordimer, Copyright © renewed 1984 by Nadine Gordimer. Reprinted by permission of Russell & Volkening as agents for the author.

Agencia Literaria Carmen Balcells, S.A.: Excerpts from "Writing as an Act of Hope" by Isabel Allende in *Paths of Resistance,* edited by William Zinsser. Copyright © 1989 by Isabel Allende. Reprinted by permission of the author's agent.

Reading Handbook

Houghton Mifflin Company: "Linear Equations in Two Variables," from *Precalculus, Fifth Edition* by Ron Larson and Robert P. Hostetler. Copyright © 2001 by Houghton Mifflin Company. All rights reserved. Used by permission.

The editors have made every effort to trace the ownership of all copyrighted material found in this book and to make full acknowledgment for its use. Omissions brought to our attention will be corrected in a subsequent edition.

Art Credits

Cover, Frontispiece

Illustration copyright © 1997 David Bowers.

Front Matter

x *left* Detail of the Bayeux Tapestry (late 11th–early 12th century). Musée de la Tapisserie, Bayeux, France. Giraudon/Art Resource, New York; *right* The Granger Collection, New York; **xi** Stock Montage/SuperStock; xii Photograph from *Angkor* by Michael Freedman and Roger Warner, edited and designed by David Larkin. Photographs copyright © 1990 by Michael Freedman. Reprinted by permission of Houghton Mifflin Company. All rights reserved; **xiii** *left* Ashburnham watch (mid-7th century). Courtesy of the Bickersteth family, Ashburnham, England; *right* Detail of the altarpiece of the Virgin of the Navigators (16th century), unknown artist. Reales Alcázares, Seville, Spain; **xiv** *top* The Granger Collection, New York; *bottom* Photofest; **xv** Detail of nativity of Christ. Stained glass. Abbey Ste. Foy, Conques, France. Giraudon/Art Resource, New York; **xvi** *left* Carved day bed (1695). Private collection. Bridgeman/Art Resource, New York; *right, Spring Gardens, Ranelagh,* Thomas Rowlandson. Victoria & Albert Museum, London/SuperStock; **xvii** The Granger Collection, New York; **xviii** Pocket watch (about 1700), M. Marcou. Musée des Arts Décoratifs, Paris; **xix** *left* Victoria & Albert Museum, London/Art Resource, New York; *right, The Lake, Petworth: Sunset, Fighting Bucks* (about 1828), Joseph Mallord William Turner. Clore Collection, Tate Gallery, London/Art Resource, New York; **xx** *top* The Granger Collection, New York; *bottom* Copyright © British Museum; **xxii** *left* Photo by Peter Roberts; *right, The Stone Pickers* (1887), George Clausen. Oil on canvas, 42″ × 31″. Tyne and Wear Museums, Newcastle upon Tyne, England; **xxiv** *Abstraction on Spectrum (Organization, 5)* (about 1914–1917), Stanton MacDonald-Wright. Oil on canvas, 30⅛″ × 24³⁄₁₆″. Des Moines (Iowa) Art Center, Nathan Emory Coffin Collection, purchased with funds from the Coffin Fine Arts Trust (1962.21); **xxv** Detail of *Portrait of T. S. Eliot,* Sir Gerald Kelly. Oil on canvas, 45⅛″ × 37″. National Portrait Gallery, Smithsonian Institution/Art Resource, New York; **xxvii** *top, Invasion* (1987–1988), Carel Weight. Oil on canvas, 48″ × 60″. The Saatchi Collection, London; *bottom* Copyright © 1971 John Dommers/Photo Researchers, Inc.; **xxviii** *Funeral*

Procession (1940), Ellis Wilson. Amistad Research Center, Tulane University, New Orleans, Louisiana; **2** *right* Photofest; **3** *left* Photofest; *right, L'Ange du Destin,* Odilon Redon. Private collection. Bridgeman Art Library, London/New York; **6–7** Photofest.

Unit One
16 *Hadrian's Wall* Nawrocki Stock Photo, Inc.; *helmet* The Granger Collection, New York; **17** *sandals* Museum of London; *candlestick* Photo copyright © British Museum; *sundial* R. Krubner/H. Armstrong Roberts; *Prioress* Ellesmere manuscript of *The Canterbury Tales* (1410), The Huntington Library, San Marino, California; *Battle of Crécy* Bibliothèque Nationale, Paris. Giraudon/Art Resource, New York; **18** *top left* Excavation site at Sutton Hoo (seventh century). The Granger Collection, New York; *bottom left* Gundestrup cauldron (Celtic, about 100 B.C.), detail from inner plate depicting the god Teutates accepting human sacrifice from warriors. Embossed silver, gilded, probably from Gaul. National Museum, Copenhagen, Denmark. Erich Lessing/Art Resource, New York; *right* Illustration by John Sandford; **19** *left* M. Berman/H. Armstrong Roberts; *right* Silver groat of King Henry VI of England. Ancient Art and Architecture Collection, London; **20** *background* Illustration by John Sandford; *center* Portrait of St. John with the tools of a scribe, from the Book of Kells, fol. 291v. Trinity College Library, by permission of the Board of Trinity College, Dublin; *bottom* Beginning of the Gospel of St. Luke, from the Lindisfarne Gospels (about A.D. 698), MS Cott. Nero D.IV, fol. 139. British Library, London. Bridgeman/Art Resource, New York; **21** *background* Knudsens-Giraudon/Art Resource, New York; *bottom left* Alfred the Great in majesty, late-9th-century jewel worked in cloisonné enamel. The Granger Collection, New York; **22** *left* By permission of The British Library, London; *right* John Bethell Photography; **23** MS Douce 383, fol. 16. The Bodleian Library, Oxford, U.K.; **24** *bottom left, top right, bottom right* Bibliothèque Nationale, Paris; *top center* Suit of armor for George IV of Puchheim (about 1515). Kunsthistorisches Museum, Vienna, Austria. Erich Lessing/Art Resource, New York; *center right* The Magna Carta of Liberties (1215). Department of the Environment, London. Bridgeman/Art Resource, New York; **25** The Bettmann Archive, New York; **26** *top* Edimedia, Paris; *bottom* Illustration from the Mary Evans Picture Library, London; **28** The Granger Collection, New York; **29** Photofest; **32–33** Illustration by Stephen Johnson; **34** Knudsens-Giraudon/Art Resource, New York; **37** Courtesy Museet ved Trelleborg, Denmark. Photo by Georg Hemmingsen; **40** The Granger Collection, New York; **45, 46** Illustration by Stephen Johnson; **47** Copyright © Statens Historiska Museum, Stockholm, Sweden; **49** Courtesy of the Royal Ontario Museum, Toronto, Canada; **50** Copyright © British Museum; **52** *top* Illustration by Rebecca McClellan; *center* The Granger Collection, New York; **53, 54–55** Illustration by Rebecca McClellan; **56, 57** The Granger Collection, New York; **59** Giraudon/Art Resource, New York; **60** By permission of the British Museum. Photograph copyright © Michael Holford, showing a previous restoration, recently reconstructed by the experts of the museum. See *The Sutton Hoo Ship Burial* by Angela Evans (1974); **61, 62** Copyright © Stephanie Berger. All rights reserved; **64** Copyright © British Museum; **65** MS Cott. Vitellius A.XV, fol. 132. By permission of the British Library; **67** Ancient Art and Architecture Collection, London; **73** Copyright © George Hunter/H. Armstrong Roberts; **77** Scala/Art Resource, New York; **82** *right* Copyright © SuperStock; **83** The Bettmann Archive, New York; **85** *top, center left* Copyright © Mapfile/Westlight; **85** *bottom right,* **86** Details of the Whale, MS Ashmole 1511, fol. 86v. The Bodleian Library, Oxford, U.K.; **94** The Pierpont Morgan Library/Art Resource, New York; **97** *left* Reproduced by kind permission of *The Times*, London. Copyright; *right* Copyright © Sonia Halliday Photographs; **98**

Erich Lessing/Art Resource, New York; **99** Trinity College MS R.17.1, fol. 283v. The Master and Fellows of Trinity College, Cambridge, U.K.; **107–111** *border* Photo by Sharon Hoogstraten; **107** *signature* The Granger Collection, New York; *portrait* Stock Montage/SuperStock; **108** *left* National Portrait Gallery, London/SuperStock; *bottom right,* upper Nicolò Orsi Battaglini/Art Resource, New York; *bottom right, lower* Copyright © Sonia Halliday & Laura Lushington; **109** The Granger Collection, New York; **110** *top* Charles Duke of Orleans, Tower of London, MS Royal 16.F.11, fol. 73. By permission of The British Library; *bottom* Copyright © Museum of London; **113–136, 142–151, 155–166** Calligraphy by Sharon D. Siegel; **115, 116, 117, 119, 122, 123, 129, 130** From the 1911 facsimile edition of the Ellesmere manuscript. Bridgeman Art Library, London; **139** Detail of *Visscher's View of London.* By permission of the Folger Shakespeare Library; **141, 142** Detail of the Pardoner. From the Ellesmere manuscript of Chaucer's *Canterbury Tales,* EL 26.C.9, fol. 138r. The Huntington Library, San Marino, California; **144** Nawrocki Stock Photo; **147** Detail from the *Psalter and Prayer Book of Bonne of Luxembourg, Duchess of Normandy* (French, Paris, 14th century), fol. 321v. Grisaille, color, gilt, and brown ink on vellum, $4^{15}/_{16}'' \times 3^{3}/_{16}''$. The Metropolitan Museum of Art, New York, The Cloisters Collection (69.86). Photograph copyright © 1991 The Metropolitan Museum of Art; **150** The Metropolitan Museum of Art, New York, The Cloisters Collection (69.86). Photograph copyright © 1991 The Metropolitan Museum of Art; **155** From the 1911 facsimile edition of the Ellesmere manuscript. Bridgeman Art Library, London; **159** Detail from *Le roman de Lancelot du lac* (early 14th century), MS M. 805, fol. 48. The Pierpont Morgan Library, New York/Art Resource, New York; **160** MS Douce 195, fol. 105r. The Bodleian Library, Oxford, U.K.; **162** Duomo, Florence, Italy. Scala/Art Resource, New York; **166** MS Douce 195, fol. 155r; The Bodleian Library, Oxford, U.K.; **167–170** *border* Photo by Sharon Hoogstraten; **168** Stock Montage/SuperStock; **169** *top* Christie's Images, London; *bottom* Copyright © David H. Endersbee/Tony Stone Worldwide; **170** *Chaucer portrait* The Granger Collection, New York; **178** Miniature from Codex Manesse (about 1300), unknown artist. Universitätsbibliothek Heidelberg, Germany. Photo by Lossen Foto; **179** The Granger Collection, New York; **180** July sheep shearing, from a book of hours by Simon Benninck. British Library. Bridgeman/Art Resource, New York; **182** *background* With permission of the Trustees of the British Library; *foreground left* Detail of women defending a castle with bow and crossbow (about 1326–1327). Manuscript illumination from *De nobilitatibus, sapientiis, et prudentiis regum* by Walter de Milemete, MS CH.CH.92, fol. 4r. By permission of the Governing Body of Christ Church, Oxford, U.K.; *foreground right,* The Governing Body of Christ Church, Oxford, U.K.; **183, 184, 185** *left,* **186** The Governing Body of Christ Church, Oxford, U.K.; **187** Letter from Richard Calle to Margery Paston, MS Add. 34889, fol. 78v–79v. By permission of The British Library; **188** *left background* With permission of the Trustees of the British Library; *right* The Governing Body of Christ Church, Oxford, U.K.; **189** The Governing Body of Christ Church, Oxford, U.K.; **191** *right* Gaia Caecilia, from MS Royal 16.G.V, fol. 56 Det. By permission of the British Library; **194** Illustration by Gordon Grant; **199** Copyright © Paul Merideth/Tony Stone Worldwide; **200–204** Photos by Sharon Hoogstraten; **209, 210, 215, 216, 218** *shield device* Illustration by Rebecca McClellan; **210–211, 216–217, 218–219, 221** Illustrations by Lorraine Silvestri; **210, 211, 215, 216, 217, 218** Calligraphy by Sharon D. Siegel; **223** *right* Armor (16th century), anonymous, attributed to Chevalier Bayard. Musée de l'Armée, Paris. Giraudon/Art Resource, New York; **235** MS Add. 10294, fol. 94 Det. By permission of the British Library; **241, 242, 243, 244, 246, 248, 249** Photograph from *Angkor* by Michael Freedman and Roger Warner, edited and designed by David Larkin. Photographs copyright © 1990 by Michael Freedman. Reprinted by permission of Houghton Mifflin Co. All rights reserved; **252** Victoria & Albert Museum, London/Art Resource, New York; **253, 254**

Woman tending fire and reading, from the Bruges illuminated manuscript, Royal 15.D.1, fol. 18. By permission of the British Library; **258** *top left* By permission of the Folger Shakespeare Library, Washington, D.C.; *top right* Illustration from *Romance of Alexander* (Flemish, about 1340). The Granger Collection, New York; **259** *bottom* By permission of the British Library; **260–264** Photos by Sharon Hoogstraten; **268** Detail of the Bayeux Tapestry (late 11th–early 12th century). Musée de la Tapisserie, Bayeux, France. Giraudon/Art Resource, New York.

Unit Two

274 *map of Utopia* The Granger Collection, New York; *Henry VIII* (1518), unknown artist. The Granger Collection, New York; *Queen Elizabeth* (about 1588), attributed to George Cower. The Granger Collection, New York; **275** *household items* Two basting spoons, an Elizabeth I apostle spoon (1561), and a William III spoon (late 17th century). Christie's Images, London; *microscope* (about 1675) used by Robert Hooke. Science & Society Picture Library, London; *floral clock* Ashburnham watch (mid-17th century). Courtesy of the Bickersteth family, Ashburnham, England; **276** *top, Portrait of Henry VIII* (about 1540), Hans Holbein the Younger. Galleria Nazionale d'Arte Antica, Rome. Scala/Art Resource, New York; *bottom* Self-portrait, number 15741, Leonardo da Vinci. Biblioteca Reale, Turin, Italy. Scala/Art Resource, New York; **277** *top* Derrick E. Witty/The National Trust Photographic Library, London; *bottom* The Granger Collection, New York; **278** *top, Edward VI as a Child* (about 1538), Hans Holbein the Younger. Oil on panel, 22⅜″ × 17⅜″. National Gallery of Art, Washington, D.C., Andrew W. Mellon Collection. Photo by Richard Carafelli; *center, Queen Mary I of England* (1544), Master John. The Granger Collection, New York; *bottom* Gold medal of Queen Elizabeth I, commemorating defeat of the Spanish Armada in 1588. The Granger Collection, New York; **279** Map of the English Channel from *The Mariner's Mirrour*. By permission of the Folger Shakespeare Library, Washington, D.C.; **280** *top* Portrait of James I. The Royal Collection, copyright © Her Majesty Queen Elizabeth II; *bottom, Charles I on Horseback* (1637), Anthony Van Dyck. Canvas, 367 cm × 292.1 cm. National Gallery, London; **281** *left, Sailing of the Pilgrims from Plymouth, England* (1941), Charles Shimmin. Woolaroc Museum, Bartlesville, Oklahoma; *right* The Granger Collection, New York; **283** *The Huguenot* (1893), Sir John Everett Millais. Christie's, London. Bridgeman/Art Resource, New York; **286** Queen Elizabeth I of England as a princess (about 1542–1547), unknown artist. The Granger Collection, New York; **288** *left* The Granger Collection, New York; *right* North Wind Picture Archives; **289, 291, 292** Details of *The Hireling Shepherd* (1851), William Holman Hunt. Manchester (U.K.) City Art Gallery. A.K.G., Berlin/SuperStock; **294** *left* The Granger Collection, New York; *right* North Wind Picture Archives; **295** *Henry Percy, Ninth Earl of Northumberland* (about 1595), Nicholas Hilliard. Bodycolor on vellum stuck to a playing card. Fitzwilliam Museum, University of Cambridge, U.K./Bridgeman Art Library, London; **299** Copyright © Dave Bjorn/Tony Stone Worldwide; **301** North Wind Picture Archives; **303, 304–305** *chain* Photo by Sharon Hoogstraten; **307** *top, Anne of Gonzaga*, Nathaniel Hatch. Victoria & Albert Museum, London/Art Resource, New York; *bottom, Catherine Howard*, John Hoskins. Victoria & Albert Museum, London/Art Resource, New York; **312** Copyright © Culver Pictures; **314–325** *border* Photo by Sharon Hoogstraten; **314** *Shakespeare signature and portrait* The Granger Collection, New York; *bottom, upper* Camerique/H. Armstrong Roberts; *bottom, lower* The Granger Collection, New York; **315** Special Collections Department, Colgate University; **316** *left, right* The Granger Collection, New York; **317** North Wind Picture Archives; **318** Mansell Collection, Time/Life Syndication; **319** *right* By permission of the Folger Shakespeare Library; **320** AP/Wide World

Photos/ROTA; *inset* Copyright © Jacqueline Arzt/AP/Wide World Photos; **321** Photofest; **322** *left* National Museum, Athens; *right* Copyright © 1996 20th Century Fox. Photo by Merrick Morton; **323** *top left* Shakespeare Centre Library, Stratford-upon-Avon, U.K., photo copyright © Angus McBean; **326** Licensed by the Estate of Orson Welles. All rights reserved. Represented by Thomas A. White, Beverly Hills, California. The Kobal Collection; **328** Photofest; **332** *top* British Film Institute; *bottom* Photofest; **342** Photofest; **344** Licensed by the Estate of Orson Welles. All rights reserved. Represented by Thomas A. White, Beverly Hills, California. Photofest; **347** *clockwise from top left* Copyright © Hulton Getty Picture Collection/Tony Stone Images; Shakespeare Centre Library, Stratford-upon-Avon, U.K., photo copyright © Angus McBean; British Film Institute; Photofest; **349** Photofest; **351** *top* Copyright © Donald Cooper/Photostage; *bottom* Deutsches Institut für Filmkunde, Frankfurt am Main, Germany; **354** Copyright © Culver Pictures; **366** Photofest; **369** *top* Copyright © Shooting Star; *bottom* Shakespeare Centre Library, Stratford-upon-Avon, U.K., photo copyright © Angus McBean; **373** Licensed by the Estate of Orson Welles. All rights reserved. Represented by Thomas A. White, Beverly Hills, California. The Kobal Collection; **382** Erich Lessing/Art Resource, New York; **385** The Kobal Collection; **389** Licensed by the Estate of Orson Welles. All rights reserved. Represented by Thomas A. White, Beverly Hills, California. Archive Photos; **400** *clockwise from top* Photofest; Photofest; Tate Gallery, London/Art Resource, New York; Photofest; **402** *top* Copyright © Reg Wilson; *bottom* Photofest; **406** Licensed by the Estate of Orson Welles. All rights reserved. Represented by Thomas A. White, Beverly Hills, California. The Kobal Collection; **411** Photofest; **413** *top, bottom* Copyright © Shooting Star; **419** Reprinted by arrangement with Rosemary A. Thurber and the Barbara Hogenson Agency; **420–422** *border* Photo by Sharon Hoogstraten; **421, 422** Shakespeare portrait North Wind Picture Archives; **423–430** Photos by Sharon Hoogstraten; **441** Detail of *Return of the Prodigal Son* (1667–1668), Rembrandt van Rijn. The Hermitage Museum, St. Petersburg, Russia. Bridgeman Art Library, London/SuperStock; **442, 445** *center* Copyright © Shoji Yoshida/The Image Bank; **448, 449** The Granger Collection, New York; **455** *top left* Camerique/H. Armstrong Roberts; *top right* H. Abernathy/H. Armstrong Roberts; **457** Copyright © Culver Pictures; **458** Portrait said to be of Ben Jonson and Shakespeare playing chess (1603), Karel van Mander. Courtesy of Frank de Heyman, Brooklyn, New York; **459** *background* Copyright © Arnulf Husmo/Tony Stone Worldwide; **462** Copyright © Culver Pictures; **464–465** *background,* **466** *The Genus Rosa,* Ellen Willmott. Royal Horticultural Society, Lindley Library; **467** *background* Erich Lessing/Art Resource, New York; **469** Detail of *The Proposal* (1872), Adolphe William Bouguereau. Oil on canvas, 64⅜″ × 44″. The Metropolitan Museum of Art, New York, gift of Mrs. Elliot L. Kamen in memory of her father, Bernard R. Armour, 1960 (60.122); **470** *left* North Wind Picture Archives; *right* The Granger Collection, New York; **472–73** *top background* Copyright © Suzanne and Nick Geary/Tony Stone Worldwide; **475** *top* Courtesy of the Trustees of the British Museum; *bottom* Copyright © Culver Pictures; **476** The Granger Collection, New York; **477** Copyright © 1989 Barry Seidman/The Stock Market; **480** *The Expulsion from Paradise,* Masaccio (before restoration). Brancacci Chapel, S. Maria del Carmine, Florence, Italy. Scala/Art Resource, New York; **482, 488** Copyright © Stock Montage; **492** Copyright © Culver Pictures; **499** *Detail of Adam Tempted by Eve* (1517), Hans Holbein the Younger. Öffentliche Kunstsammlung Basel, Switzerland (313); **501** The Granger Collection, New York; **502** *top, bottom* The Granger Collection, New York; **503** *top* Copyright © The Frick Collection, New York; *bottom* The Granger Collection, New York; **504** Detail of the altarpiece of the Virgin of the Navigators (16th century), unknown artist. Reales Alcázares, Seville, Spain; **508–510** Photos by Sharon Hoogstraten.

Unit Three

516 *James II* (1684), Sir Godfrey Kneller. Courtesy of the National Portrait Gallery, London; *Anne, England's Last Stuart Monarch* (about 1694), unknown artist. Courtesy of the National Portrait Gallery, London; **517** *washstand* Cooper-Bridgeman Library; *carved day bed* (1695). Private collection. Bridgeman/Art Resource, New York; *painted watch* Copyright © British Museum; *British coin commemorating capture of Quebec* Copyright © Hulton Deutsch Collection Ltd.; **518** *left* Perspective view of the garden and chateau, Versailles, France, by Pierre Patel. Giraudon/Art Resource, New York; *center* Museum of London; *top right, Charles II*, John M. Wright. The Royal Collection, copyright © Her Majesty Queen Elizabeth II; *bottom right* Copyright © R. Korh/H. Armstrong Roberts; **519** *top, William III* (1677), unknown artist, after Sir Peter Lely. The Granger Collection, New York; *bottom, Queen Mary II, Wife of William III,* William Wissing. National Portrait Gallery, Edinburgh, U.K. Bridgeman/Art Resource New York; **520** *top, King George I of England* (1716), Sir Godfrey Kneller. Oil on canvas. The Granger Collection, New York; *frame* Photo by Sharon Hoogstraten; *bottom, George III, Queen Charlotte and Their Six Eldest Children,* Johann Zoffany. The Royal Collection, copyright © Her Majesty Queen Elizabeth II; **521** *The Boston Massacre, March 5, 1770,* Paul Revere, after a drawing by Henry Pelham. The Granger Collection, New York; **522** *top, Sir Isaac Newton* (about 1726), John Vanderbank. The Granger Collection, New York; *center, The Ladies Waldegrave,* Sir Joshua Reynolds. National Gallery of Scotland; *bottom, Mr. Healey's Sheep,* W. H. Davis. Lincoln (U.K.) Museum and Art Galleries/E.T. Archive, London; **533** The Granger Collection, New York; **538** Detail of *The Sense of Touch* (around 1615–1616), Jusepe de Ribera. Oil on canvas, 45⅝″ × 34¾″. The Norton Simon Foundation, Pasadena, California; **539** The Granger Collection, New York; **541** J. Nettis/H. Armstrong Roberts; **545** The Granger Collection, New York; **546** *bottom left* The printer's workshop, from a woodcut by Jost Amman in Hartmann Schopper's *Panoplia* (Frankfurt am Main, 1568). Ann Ronan Picture Library; **553** The Granger Collection, New York; **554** *Lady Mary Wortley Montagu* (about 1725), Jonathan Richardson. Private collection. Courtesy of the Earl of Harrowby; **565** *left, right* The Granger Collection, New York; **566** *top, Daniel Defoe* (1706), unknown artist, after Michiel van der Gucht. Colored engraving. The Granger Collection, New York; *bottom, Rio de Janeiro Bay* (1864), Martin Johnson Heade. Canvas, 17⅞″ × 35⅞″. National Gallery of Art, Washington, D.C., gift of the Avalon Foundation; **567** *top right* Illustration from *A Field Guide to Eastern Birds,* copyright © 1980 by Roger Tory Peterson. Reprinted by permission of Houghton Mifflin Company. All rights reserved; **568–572** Photos by Sharon Hoogstraten; **582** Detail of *Portrait of a Young Woman, Called Mademoiselle Charlotte du Val d'Ognes* (about 1800), unknown French artist. Oil on canvas, 63½″ × 50⅝″. The Metropolitan Museum of Art, bequest of Isaac D. Fletcher, 1917, Mr. and Mrs. Isaac D. Fletcher Collection (17.120.204). Copyright © 1989 The Metropolitan Museum of Art; **583** The Granger Collection, New York; **584** The Granger Collection, New York; **585** Copyright © 1977 Charles E. Martin/The New Yorker Collection, from cartoonbank.com. All rights reserved; **586–590** *border* Photo by Sharon Hoogstraten; **586** *signature, top, bottom* The Granger Collection, New York; *portrait frame* Photo by Sharon Hoogstraten; **587** The Granger Collection, New York; **588** *top* The Granger Collection, New York; *bottom* North Wind Picture Archives; **589** *top* British Museum, London/E.T. Archive, London; *bottom* H. Sutton/H. Armstrong Roberts; **591, 600** The Granger Collection, New York; **601** Victoria & Albert Museum, London/E.T. Archive, London; **605** The Granger Collection, New York; **607–608** *border* Photo by Sharon Hoogstraten; **609** North Wind Picture Archives; **611** *border* Photo by Sharon Hoogstraten; **614, 618** Details of *Industry and Idleness: The Idle*

'Prentice Executed at Tyburn (1747), William Hogarth. The Granger Collection, New York; **620–623** border Photo by Sharon Hoogstraten; **621** top The Granger Collection, New York; frame Photo by Sharon Hoogstraten; **622** National Gallery of Ireland; **623** Swift portrait The Granger Collection, New York; **626** Erich Lessing/Art Resource, New York; **628** Mansell Collection; **630** Copyright © Culver Pictures; **631, 632, 633, 634–635** Copyright © Hulton Deutsch Collection Ltd.; **638** The Granger Collection, New York; **639–643** Photos by Sharon Hoogstraten; **648** Detail of Sandleford Priory (1744), Edward Haytley. Oil on canvas. The Leger Galleries Ltd., London; **649** Solanum macrocarpum, G. van Spa'ndonck. Courtesy of the Natural History Museum, London; **657** The Granger Collection, New York; **665** The Granger Collection, New York; **667–671** background Photo by Allan I. Ludwig; **673** The Granger Collection, New York; **675–678** Copyright © Phil Brodatz. Reproduction and publication rights reserved; **675, 678** Details of The Porten Family, Gawen Hamilton. Museum of Fine Arts, Springfield, Massachusetts, James Philip Gray Collection; **680** The Granger Collection, New York; **682** foreground Copyright © Editions d'Art Lys, Versailles, France; background Department of Rare Books and Special Collections, University of Rochester Library; **685, 686, 687, 689** Copyright © Editions d'Art Lys, Versailles, France; **691** The Granger Collection, New York; **692** Detail of Spring Gardens, Ranelagh, Thomas Rowlandson. Victoria & Albert Museum, London/SuperStock; **695** top From Robinson Crusoe (jacket cover) by Daniel Defoe. Copyright. Used by permission of Bantam Books, a division of Bantam Doubleday Dell Publishing Group, Inc.; bottom, Gulliver's Travels by Jonathan Swift, Penguin Books Ltd. Published in Penguin English Library 1967, reprinted in Penguin Classics 1985.

Unit Four

698 William Wordsworth (1818), Benjamin Robert Haydon. Courtesy of the National Portrait Gallery, London; **699** night lamp (about 1820). Victoria & Albert Museum, London/Art Resource, New York; early-19th-century iron From Everyday Life Through the Ages, copyright © 1992 Reader's Digest; twelve-month equation clock (1830), Charles Edward Viner. Collection of L. A. Mayer Memorial Institute for Islamic Art, Jerusalem, Israel; Mary Shelley (1841), Richard Rothwell. The Granger Collection, New York; **702** bottom The Granger Collection, New York; **704** top Courtesy Barnaby's Picture Library; bottom Manchester heroes, September 1819. E.T. Archive, London; **705** The Circulating Library, Issac Cruikshank. Pen, ink, watercolor, and wash on woven paper, 6⅞″ × 8⁷⁄₁₆″. Yale Center for British Art, Paul Mellon Collection (B1975.4.867); **707** Sleeping Shepherd—Morning (about 1857), Samuel Palmer. Watercolor. Fitzwilliam Museum, University of Cambridge, U.K. Bridgeman Art Library, London/New York; **709** The Granger Collection, New York; **710–711** background Copyright © Linda Dufurrena/Grant Heilman Photography, Inc.; **712** Tiger in Africa. Mark Newman/Adventure Photo & Film; **714** Photo by Sharon Hoogstraten; **715** top, bottom The Granger Collection, New York; **716** Copyright © Culver Pictures; **718–719** Illustrations by Rebecca McClellan; **721** left, Portrait of Bashō, Suzuki Manrei. New Orleans (Louisiana) Museum of Art, anonymous donor; right Heibonsha Ltd., Tokyo; **722–725** border Photo by Sharon Hoogstraten; **722** signature, top, bottom The Granger Collection, New York; **723** Photo by Soalhat/Sipa Press, New York; **724** top Copyright © David Ball/Tony Stone Images; bottom left, bottom right The Granger Collection, New York; **725** Detail of Mortlake Terrace (1827), Joseph Mallord William Turner. Oil on canvas, 36¼″ × 48⅛″. National Gallery of Art, Washington, D.C., Andrew W. Mellon Collection. Photo by Richard Carafelli; **736** Silhouette of Dorothy Wordsworth, unknown artist. The Wordsworth Trust; **737** Photo by Sharon Hoogstraten; **738–740** border Photo by Sharon Hoogstraten; **739, 740** Wordsworth portrait Copyright © Culver Pictures; **741** Detail of In a Harem Garden (about 1765), attributed to Faiz Allah of Faizabad (Mughal empire). Opaque watercolor on paper.

The David Collection, Copenhagen, Denmark; **745, 746, 748, 749, 750, 754, 756, 758, 760, 762, 765** Copyright © Stock Montage; **767** Copyright © Culver Pictures; **768** *top, Jane Austen* (about 1810), Cassandra Austen. Pencil and watercolor. The Granger Collection, New York; **769** *bottom* From *The Repository of Arts, Literature, Commerce, Manufacture, Fashions and Politics,* published by R. Ackerman (London, 1809–1828); **771** *The Sick Rose,* from *Songs of Experience* by William Blake. Library of Congress, Washington, D.C. Bridgeman Art Library, London/New York; **773** Detail of *Comus, Disguised as a Rustic, Addresses the Lady in the Wood* (1801–1802), William Blake. Henry E. Huntington Library and Art Gallery, San Marino, California; **775** *Lone Tree in the Snow,* D. Petku/H. Armstrong Roberts; **780** The Granger Collection, New York; **782** *top center* Abu Simbel, Egypt. R. Benson/ H. Armstrong Roberts; *left border* Calendar of Elephantine, with Egyptian hieroglyphs. Musée du Louvre, Paris. Giraudon/Art Resource, New York; *background* Original manuscript of Shelley's "Ozymandias." The Bodleian Library, Oxford, U.K. (MS Shelley e.4, fol. 85r); **791, 793** The Granger Collection, New York; **795** *background* Copyright © William Thompson/Tony Stone Images; **797** German Information Center, New York; **798** Detail of *John Keats* (1821), Joseph Severn. Oil on canvas. The Granger Collection, New York; **799** *background* Copyright © Jerry Schad/Science Source/Photo Researchers; **801** *background* Illustration by Rebecca McClellan; *signature* The Granger Collection, New York; **802** Illustration by Rebecca McClellan; **803** *signature,* **804** *signature,* **807** The Granger Collection, New York; **808** *top* The Granger Collection, New York; *background* Copyright © SuperStock; **810–814** Photos by Sharon Hoogstraten; **818** Detail of *The Lake, Petworth: Sunset, Fighting Bucks* (about 1828), Joseph Mallord William Turner. Clore Collection, Tate Gallery, London/Art Resource, New York; **821** *top, L'Ange du Destin,* Odilon Redon. Private collection. Bridgeman Art Library, London/New York; *bottom,* John Keats (1819), Joseph Severn. Courtesy of the National Portrait Gallery, London; **822–824** Photos by Sharon Hoogstraten.

Unit Five

828 Detail of *The Stone Pickers* (1887), George Clausen. Oil on canvas, 42″ × 31″. Tyne and Wear Museums, Newcastle upon Tyne, England; **830** *Prince Albert* (1867), F. X. Winterhalter. Oil on canvas. The Granger Collection, New York; **831** *Benz Viktoria* Photo by Peter Roberts; *mangle* Copyright © Marshall Cavendish; *Big Ben* Copyright © Geoffrey C. Garner/SuperStock; *Treasure Island illustration, Israel Hands* (1911), N. C. Wyeth. Oil on canvas, 47¼″ × 38½″. New Britain (Connecticut) Museum of American Art, Harriet Russell Stanley Fund. Photo by Michael Agee; **832** *top, Queen Victoria* (1840), Aaron Edwin Penley. By courtesy of the National Portrait Gallery, London; *bottom, Great Exhibition, 1851: Waiting for the Queen at Coalbrookdale Gates,* Joseph Nash. Lithograph. Guildhall Library, London. Bridgeman/Art Resource, New York; *background* Floral patterns. Victoria and Albert Museum, London/Art Resource, New York; **833** From *The Illustrated London News,* xiii, 1848; **834** *top left* Detail of Benjamin Disraeli, Sir John Everett Millais. The Granger Collection, New York; *top right, William E. Gladstone* (1879), Sir John Everett Millais. Oil on canvas. The Granger Collection, New York; *center, Sketch of a Ward at the Hospital at Scutari,* Joseph-Austin Benwell. Greater London Council, London. Bridgeman/Art Resource, New York; *bottom, Florence Nightingale,* Sir William Blake Richmond (1842–1921). Claydon House, U.K. Bridgeman/Art Resource, New York; **836** *top* Copyright © Hulton Deutsch Collection Ltd.; *bottom, Charles Darwin* (1894), John Collier. Oil on canvas. The Granger Collection, New York; *bottom inset* By permission of the Syndics of Cambridge (U.K.) University Library; **837** *bottom left* Copyright © Hulton Deutsch Collection Ltd.; **839** Detail of *May Day* (1960), Andrew Wyeth. Watercolor.

Copyright © 1995 Andrew Wyeth; **840** Detail of *The Lady of Shalott*, John William Waterhouse. Tate Gallery, London/Art Resource, New York; **853** Stock Montage; **854** Detail of *Vespertina Quies* (1893), Sir Edward Burne-Jones. Oil on canvas, 120.6 cm × 62.2 cm. Tate Gallery, London, bequeathed by Miss Maud Beddington, 1940. Art Resource, New York; **860** The Granger Collection, New York; **861, 862** Copyright © 1995 G. Heck/Panoramic Images, Chicago; **863** Photo by Sharon Hoogstraten; **867** *left* Courtesy of Armstrong Browning Library, Baylor University, Waco, Texas; *right* The Granger Collection, New York; **868** *top* Library of Congress; *bottom* The Granger Collection, New York; **869** *top to bottom* Stock Montage; Copyright © Culver Pictures; Stock Montage; Copyright © Culver Pictures; Stock Montage; **870** *top, Portrait of Charles Dickens* (1859), William Powell Frith. Victoria and Albert Museum, London. Bridgeman/Art Resource, New York; *bottom* Sam Weller's first appearance in Dickens's *The Pickwick Papers*. Illustration by Phiz; **871** *top* Photofest; *center* Mansell Collection; *bottom* Copyright © Hulton Deutsch Collection Ltd.; **872, 874, 877, 881** Illustrations by John Leach; **884** Detail of *Newgate* (late 1800s), Frank Holl. Royal Holloway and Bedford Collection, New College, Egham, Surrey, U.K. Bridgeman/Art Resource, New York; **885** The Granger Collection, New York; **886** *top left* Detail of *Charlotte Brontë* (1850), G. Richmond. Chalk drawing. The Granger Collection, New York; *top right, Emily Brontë* (about 1833), Patrick Branwell Brontë. Oil on canvas. The Granger Collection, New York; *bottom left* Copyright © Simon Warner; *bottom right* Copyright © The Brontë Society; **887** *top, The First Meeting of Jane Eyre and Mr. Rochester*, Thomas Davidson. Copyright © The Brontë Society; *bottom, Merlin Hawk*, Emily Brontë. Watercolor. Copyright © The Brontë Society; **898** The Granger Collection, New York; **899** *center* Photofest; *bottom* From the Castle Howard Archives, by kind permission of the Honorable Simon Howard and Mr. Jonathan Ouvry; **901** *background*, **903, 910, 911** Roloff Beny/National Archives of Canada/1986-009; **913** The Granger Collection, New York; **915** Copyright © Greg Heck/Montresor; **916–928** *border* Photo by Sharon Hoogstraten; **930** Detail of *Nightfall at Hradčany* (1909–1913), Jakub Schikaneder. Oil on canvas, 33.7″ × 41.9″. National Gallery, Prague, Czech Republic; **931** The Granger Collection, New York; **932–934** Photos by Sharon Hoogstraten; **941** Detail of *Am Meer* [By the sea] (1875), Anselm Feuerbach. Kunstmuseum Düsseldorf im Ehrenhof, Germany; **942** Copyright © Masao Ota/Photonica; **946** The Granger Collection, New York; **947, 948** Copyright © Ross Hamilton/Tony Stone Images; **948** *background* Copyright © E. Cooper/H. Armstrong Roberts; **951** The Granger Collection, New York; **953** Copyright © H. Abernathy/H. Armstrong Roberts; **954** Copyright © Hulton Deutsch Collection Ltd.; **956–957** Copyright © H. Abernathy/H. Armstrong Roberts; **958–959** The Granger Collection, New York; **960** *Sunken Titanic*, Ken Marschall. By permission of Madison Press Ltd.; **962** The Granger Collection, New York; **964** H. Armstrong Roberts. Photo by Sharon Hoogstraten; **965, 966** The Bettmann Archive; **968** The Granger Collection, New York; **973** The Bettmann Archive; **974** *The Stone Pickers* (1887), George Clausen. Oil on canvas, 42″ × 31″. Tyne and Wear Museums, Newcastle upon Tyne, England.

Unit Six
978 Illustration by Rebecca McClellan; **980** Underwood Collection/The Bettmann Archive, New York; **981** *California Clipper* Pan American Airways/H. Armstrong Roberts; *woman on telephone* H. Armstrong Roberts; *art deco clock* From *Pastime* by Phillip Collins. Copyright © 1993, published by Chronicle Books; *1984* by George Orwell. Copyright © 1949 by Harcourt Brace Jovanovich. Used by permission of Harcourt Brace & Company; **982** *left, bottom right* Copyright © Hulton Deutsch Collection Ltd.; *top right* The Bettmann Archive; *center right, background* Imperial War Museum, London; **983** *left* Imperial War Museum, London; *right* Copyright © Hulton Deutsch Collection Ltd.; **984** *top, center, bottom left* Copyright © Hulton

Deutsch Collection Ltd.; *bottom right* Imperial War Museum, London; **985** *top left* Copyright © Hulton Deutsch Collection Ltd.; *top right* The Granger Collection, New York; *bottom left, David Herbert Lawrence* (1920), Jan Juta. By courtesy of the National Portrait Gallery, London; *bottom right* The Granger Collection, New York; **986** *top left, Portrait of Dylan Thomas*, Augustus John. National Museum of Wales, Cardiff, U.K. Bridgeman/Art Resource, New York; *bottom left* Copyright © Hulton Deutsch Collection Ltd.; *right, Gandhi* (1946), Margaret Bourke-White. *Life* magazine. Copyright © Time Inc.; **988** Detail of Saint Mark arriving in Venice, Byzantine mosaic from San Marco, Venice, Italy (about A.D. 800–1000). Scala/Art Resource, New York; **989** Copyright © M. Thonig/H. Armstrong Roberts; **993** Copyright © Hulton Deutsch Collection Ltd.; **994, 995** H. Armstrong Roberts; **1003** The Bettmann Archive; **1004** Copyright © Geraldine Prentice/Tony Stone Worldwide; **1005** *left, right* The Granger Collection, New York; **1006** Detail of *The Races at Longchamp* (1866), Édouard Manet. Oil on canvas, 43.9 cm × 84.5 cm. The Art Institute of Chicago, Mr. and Mrs. Potter Palmer Collection (1922.424). Photo Copyright © 1994 The Art Institute of Chicago, all rights reserved; **1018** *left* Copyright © William S. Nawrocki, all rights reserved; *right* Photo by Sharon Hoogstraten; **1020** Photo by Sharon Hoogstraten; **1021** The Granger Collection, New York; **1022, 1023** *St. Patrick's Close, Dublin* (1887), Walter Frederick Osborne. Oil on canvas, 27¼″ × 20″. National Gallery of Ireland, Dublin; **1024, 1025, 1030** *top* Details of *St. Patrick's Close, Dublin* (1887), Walter Frederick Osborne. Oil on canvas, 27¼″ × 20″. National Gallery of Ireland, Dublin; **1026, 1027, 1030** *bottom* Copyright © Evelyn Hofer, courtesy of The Witkin Gallery, Inc., New York; **1031** UPI/Bettmann; **1032** *top, Portrait of James Joyce* (1935), Sean O'Sullivan. Red chalk and charcoal with white highlights on gray paper, 21⁷⁄₁₆″ × 15″. National Gallery of Ireland, Dublin; *bottom left* O'Connell Bridge and Sackville Street, Dublin. National Library of Ireland; *bottom center* The Slide File; *bottom right* Trinity College Library, Dublin; **1033** *left* From the collections of the Library of Congress; **1034** Photo by Sharon Hoogstraten; **1035** Copyright © 1994 Photonica; **1036, 1039, 1041** Photos by Sharon Hoogstraten; **1043** The Granger Collection, New York; **1044** *Greene portrait* The Bettmann Archive; **1044–1045** *background,* **1045** *top right* Photo of Freetown, Sierra Leone, by Islay Lyons; *bottom right* Graham Greene in Cuba. Peter Stackpole, *Life* magazine. Copyright © Time Inc.; **1046, 1047, 1049, 1051, 1052–1053** Copyright © 1994 Rita Maas/The Image Bank; **1056** Copyright © Archive Photos; **1057** Copyright © Mrs. Vinogradoff; **1058–1059** *background* Copyright © SuperStock; **1058** *top left* Virginia Woolf. Photo by Man Ray. Copyright © 1996 Artists Rights Society (ARS), New York/ADAGP/Man Ray Trust, Paris; **1059** *center* Leonard Woolf and Virginia Woolf at Asheham House. By permission of Mrs. Angelica Garnett; *bottom* Cover of *Mrs. Dalloway* by Virginia Woolf, a Harvest Book, copyright © 1990 Harcourt Brace & Company. By permission of Harcourt Brace & Company; **1060–1064** *border* Photo by Sharon Hoogstraten; **1060** *signature* The Granger Collection, New York; *top, Portrait of T. S. Eliot*, Sir Gerald Kelly. Oil on canvas, 45⅛″ × 37″. National Portrait Gallery, Smithsonian Institution/Art Resource, New York; *bottom* By permission of the Houghton Library, Harvard University; **1061** The Granger Collection, New York; **1062** *top* The Granger Collection, New York; *bottom* Woodfin Camp & Associates; **1063** *left* Photofest; **1064** Musée de la Publicité, Paris; **1071** Copyright © Hulton Getty Collection/Tony Stone Images; **1072** By permission of the Houghton Library, Harvard University (AC9.E1464.Zzx Box 2, env. 6); **1073–1075** *border* Photo by Sharon Hoogstraten; **1074** The Granger Collection, New York; **1075** *Eliot portrait* By permission of the Houghton Library, Harvard University (AC9.E1464.Zzx Box 2, env. 6); **1076** *La grande guerre* [The great war] (1964), René Magritte. Private collection. Giraudon/Art Resource, New York. Copyright © 1996 Herscovici/Artists Rights Society (ARS), New York; **1078** Detail

of *Landscape with the Fall of Icarus* (about 1560), Pieter Brueghel the Elder. Musée Royaux des Beaux Arts de Belgique, Brussels, Belgium/SuperStock; **1081** *Landscape with the Fall of Icarus* (about 1560), Pieter Brueghel the Elder. Musée Royaux des Beaux Arts de Belgique, Brussels, Belgium/SuperStock; **1082** Copyright © Hulton Deutsch Collection Ltd.; **1086** *top* The Granger Collection, New York; *bottom* Detail of *1933 (St. Rémy-Provence)* (1933), Ben Nicholson. Copyright © 1995 Mrs. Angela Verren-Taunt/Licensed by VAGA, New York/DACS, London; **1093** The Granger Collection, New York; **1097** Copyright © Globe Photos; **1098–1102** Photos by Sharon Hoogstraten; **1110** *top left* Roger-Viollet, Paris; *top right* Copyright © Robert Tardio/Graphistock; *center* Courtesy Martin Middlebrook, author of *The First Day on the Somme; bottom left* Troops of the Canadian Fourth Division, 1917. Imperial War Museum, London; *bottom right* UPI/Bettmann **1112** Copyright © Culver Pictures; **1113** *left, right* The Granger Collection, New York; **1115** National Archives; **1118, 1118–1119** Copyright © Hulton Deutsch Collection Ltd.; **1123** Photo by Sharon Hoogstraten; **1125** West Point Museum; **1126** Copyright © Hulton Deutsch Collection Ltd.; **1130–1131** *background* UPI/Bettmann; **1134** Woodfin Camp & Associates; **1136** State Institute for War Documentation, Netherlands; **1138–1139** Sovfoto/Eastfoto; **1139** Zydowski Instytut Historyczny Instytut Naukowo-Badawczy, courtesy of USHMM Photo Archives; **1140** Main Commission for the Investigation of Nazi War Crimes in Poland, courtesy of USHMM Photo Archives; **1142** Magnum Photos; **1143** *background,* **1144** Collection Jewish Historical Museum, Amsterdam, Netherlands; **1146** Official photograph, United States Air Force, courtesy of Sam R. Quincey; **1156** The Granger Collection, New York; **1157, 1158** Copyright © 1994 Alain Choisnet/The Image Bank; **1161** *top* Courtesy Martin Middlebrook, author of *The First Day on the Somme;* **1162** Copyright © 1992 Color Box/FPG International; **1163** Copyright © 1994 Masaru Suzuki/Photonica; **1165** Detail of *Interior with Seated Woman* (1908), Vihelm Hammersh¿i. Oil on canvas, 76 cm × 66 cm. Aarhus (Denmark) Kunstmuseum; **1166** Copyright © Elliott Erwitt/Camera Press/Globe Photos; **1167** George Orwell at the police training school at Mandalay, Burma, in 1922. Photo courtesy of Roger Beadon; **1168, 1173** Photo by Sharon Hoogstraten; **1175** Copyright © Globe Photos; **1176** Photo by Sharon Hoogstraten; **1177** Photo copyright © Ron Krisel/Tony Stone Images; **1184** Detail of *Abstraction on Spectrum (Organization, 5)* (about 1914–1917), Stanton MacDonald-Wright. Oil on canvas, 30⅛″ × 24³⁄₁₆″. Des Moines (Iowa) Art Center, Nathan Emory Coffin Collection, purchased with funds from the Coffin Fine Arts Trust (1962.21).

Unit Seven
1190 *Queen Elizabeth II* Hulton Getty/Gamma-Liaison Agency; *Sputnik 1* Tass/Sovfoto; **1191** *Concorde, television* Copyright © H. Armstrong Roberts; *watch* Casio Pulse Monitor Watch by Casio, Inc.; *Ted Hughes* Copyright © Michael Blackman/Camera Press London/Globe Photos; *Nelson Mandela* Copyright © 1994 John Harrington/Black Star; **1192** *top* Copyright © R. B. Goodman/National Geographic Society Image Collection; *center left* Alistair Berg FSP/Gamma Liaison; *center right, bottom* Copyright © Hulton Deutsch Collection Ltd.; **1193** Copyright © Hulton Deutsch Collection Ltd.; *background* Photo by Sharon Hoogstraten; **1194** *top* Copyright © Hulton Deutsch Collection Ltd.; *center* Copyright © Peter Jordan/Gamma Liaison; *bottom, Family Group* (1945–1949), Henry Moore. Bronze (cast 1950), 59¼″ × 46½″ x 29⅞″. The Museum of Modern Art, New York, A. Conger Goodyear Fund. Photo copyright © 1996 The Museum of Modern Art, New York; **1195** Copyright © 1991 Peter Stone/Black Star; **1197** Photo by permission of Chronicle Books. *Ulysses* cover by permission of Random House; **1199, 1200** Photos by Sharon Hoogstraten; **1208** Copyright © The British Museum; **1209** Copyright © Jane Brown/Camera Press/Globe Photos; **1218** Detail of *Horned Forms* (1944), Graham Sutherland. Tate

Multicultural Advisory Board (continued)

Janna Rigby, Clovis High School, Clovis, California

Noreen M. Rodriguez, Trainer for Hillsborough County School District's Staff Development Division, independent consultant, Gaither High School, Tampa, Florida

Olga Y. Sanmaniego, English Department Chairperson, Burges High School, El Paso, Texas

Liz Sawyer-Cunningham, Los Angeles Senior High School, Los Angeles, California

Michelle Dixon Thompson, Seabreeze High School, Daytona Beach, Florida

Teacher Review Panels (continued)

CALIFORNIA *(continued)*

Steve Bass, 8th Grade Team Leader, Meadowbrook Middle School, Ponway Unified School District

Cynthia Brickey, 8th Grade Academic Block Teacher, Kastner Intermediate School, Clovis Unified School District

Karen Buxton, English Department Chairperson, Winston Churchill Middle School, San Juan School District

Bonnie Garrett, Davis Middle School, Compton School District

Sally Jackson, Madrona Middle School, Torrance Unified School District

Sharon Kerson, Los Angeles Center for Enriched Studies, Los Angeles Unified School District

Gail Kidd, Center Middle School, Azusa School District

Corey Lay, ESL Department Chairperson, Chester Nimitz Middle School, Los Angeles Unified School District

Myra LeBendig, Forshay Learning Center, Los Angeles Unified School District

Dan Manske, Elmhurst Middle School, Oakland Unified School District

Joe Olague, Language Arts Department Chairperson, Alder Middle School, Fontana School District

Pat Salo, 6th Grade Village Leader, Hidden Valley Middle School, Escondido Elementary School District

FLORIDA

Judith H. Briant, English Department Chairperson, Armwood High School, Hillsborough County School District

Beth Johnson, Polk County English Supervisor, Polk County School District

Sharon Johnston, Learning Resource Specialist, Evans High School, Orange County School District

Eileen Jones, English Department Chairperson, Spanish River High School, Palm Beach County School District

Jan McClure, Winter Park High School, Orange County School District

Wanza Murray, English Department Chairperson (retired), Vero Beach Senior High School, Indian River City School District

Shirley Nichols, Language Arts Curriculum Specialist Supervisor, Marion County School District

Debbie Nostro, Ocoee Middle School, Orange County School District

Barbara Quinaz, Assistant Principal, Horace Mann Middle School, Dade County School District

OHIO

Glyndon Butler, English Department Chairperson, Glenville High School, Cleveland City School District

Ellen Geisler, English/Language Arts Department Chairperson, Mentor Senior High School, Mentor School District

Dr. Paulette Goll, English Department Chairperson, Lincoln West High School, Cleveland City School District

Loraine Hammack, Executive Teacher of the English Department, Beachwood High School, Beachwood City School District

Marguerite Joyce, English Department Chairperson, Woodridge High School, Woodridge Local School District

Sue Nelson, Shaw High School, East Cleveland School District

Dee Phillips, Hudson High School, Hudson Local School District

Carol Steiner, English Department Chairperson, Buchtel High School, Akron City School District

Nancy Strauch, English Department Chairperson, Nordonia High School, Nordonia Hills City School Dictrict

Ruth Vukovich, Hubbard High School, Hubbard Exempted Village School District

TEXAS

Dana Davis, English Department Chairperson, Irving High School, Irving Independent School District

Susan Fratcher, Cypress Creek High School, Cypress Fairbanks School District

Yolanda Garcia, Abilene High School, Abilene Independent School District

Patricia Helm, Lee Freshman High School, Midland Independent School District

Joanna Huckabee, Moody High School, Corpus Christi Independent School District

Josie Kinard, English Department Chairperson, Del Valle High School, Ysleta Independent School District

Mary McFarland, Amarillo High School, Amarillo Independent School District

Gwen Rutledge, English Department Chairperson, Scarborough High School, Houston Independent School District

Bunny Schmaltz, Assistant Principal, Ozen High School, Beaumont Independent School District

Michael Urick, A. N. McCallum High School, Austin Independent School District

Manuscript Reviewers *(continued)*

Jacqueline Anderson, James A. Foshay Learning Center, Los Angeles, California

Kathleen M. Anderson-Knight, United Township High School, East Moline, Illinois

Anita Arnold, Thomas Jefferson High School, San Antonio, Texas

Cassandra L. Asberry, Dean of Instruction, Carter High School, Dallas, Texas

Jolene Auderer, Pine Tree High School, Longview, Texas

Don Baker, English Department Chairperson, Peoria High School, Peoria, Illinois

Beverly Ann Barge, Wasilla High School, Wasilla, Alaska

Louann Bohman, Wilbur Cross High School, New Haven, Connecticut

Rose Mary Bolden, J. F. Kimball High School, Dallas, Texas

Lydia C. Bowden, Boca Ciega High School, St. Petersburg, Florida

Angela Boyd, Andrews High School, Andrews, Texas

Judith H. Briant, Armwood High School, Seffner, Florida

Hugh Delle Broadway, McCullough High School, The Woodlands, Texas

Stephan P. Clarke, Spencerport High School, Spencerport, New York

Kathleen D. Crapo, South Fremont High School, St. Anthony, Idaho

Dr. Shawn Eric DeNight, Miami Edison Senior High School, Miami, Florida

JoAnna R. Exacoustas, La Serna High School, Whittier, California

Linda Ferguson, English Department Head, Tyee High School, Seattle, Washington

Ellen Geisler, Mentor Senior High School, Mentor, Ohio

Ricardo Godoy, English Department Chairman, Moody High School, Corpus Christi, Texas

Meredith Gunn, Secondary Language Arts Instructional Specialist, Katy, Texas

Judy Hammack, English Department Chairperson, Milton High School, Alpharetta, Georgia

Robert Henderson, West Muskingum High School, Zanesville, Ohio

Martha Watt Hosenfeld, English Department Chairperson, Churchville-Chili High School, Churchville, New York

Janice M. Johnson, Assistant Principal, Union High School, Grand Rapids, Michigan

Eileen S. Jones, English Department Chair, Spanish River Community High School, Boca Raton, Florida

Paula S. L'Homme, West Orange High School, Winter Garden, Florida

Bonnie J. Mansell, Downey Adult School, Downey, California

Linda Maxwell, MacArthur High School, Houston, Texas

Ruth McClain, Paint Valley High School, Bainbridge, Ohio

Rebecca Miller, Taft High School, San Antonio, Texas

Deborah Lynn Moeller, Western High School, Fort Lauderdale, Florida

Bobbi Darrell Montgomery, Batavia High School, Batavia, Ohio

Bettie Moody, Leesburg High School, Leesburg, Florida

Margaret L. Mortenson, English Department Chairperson, Timpanogos High School, Orem, Utah

Marjorie M. Nolan, Language Arts Department Head, William M. Raines Sr. High School, Jacksonville, Florida

Julia Pferdehirt, freelance writer, former Special Education teacher, Middleton, Wisconsin